THE OILY GRAIL

A STORY OF THE
INDY 500

THE OILY GRAIL

A STORY OF THE

INDY 500

By
JACK
ALBINSON

Publishers
T. S. DENISON & COMPANY, INC.
Minneapolis, Minnesota

T. S. DENISON & COMPANY, INC.

All rights reserved, including the right to reproduce this book, or portions thereof, except that permission is hereby granted to reviewers to quote brief passages in a review to be printed in magazines and newspapers, or for radio and television reviews.

Standard Book Number: 513-01322-9
Library of Congress Card Number: 73-87667
Printed in the United States of America
by The Brings Press
Copyright © MCMLXXIV by T. S. Denison & Co., Inc.
Minneapolis, Minn. 55437

To Mel Larson

The race was nearly perfect.

His secrets were patience and purpose.

He was beautiful in the Son.

Contents

Introduction 9

Chapter One
Harry Hartz Front Drive—1930 15

Chapter Two
Cloudy Skies—1931-1932 20

Chapter Three
A New Dimension—1933 26

Chapter Four
"Slow 'Em Down"—1934 30

Chapter Five
Front Drive—1934 33

Chapter Six
The Beautiful Blue Crowns 37

Chapter Seven
Chitwood and Shaw 40

Chapter Eight
The Belt 45

Chapter Nine
Vukie, the Fresno Flash 49

Chapter Ten
Le Mans—1955 54

Chapter Eleven
Special Entry Le Mans—Update 1972 59

Chapter Twelve
Help! Turn Three 60

Chapter Thirteen
The Flimsy Cars 66

Chapter Fourteen
Cry Peace 75

Chapter Fifteen
Fire and Water 82

Chapter Sixteen
Robes and Palms 89

Chapter Seventeen
The Belt 91

Chapter Eighteen
The Roll Bar 93

Chapter Nineteen
Fire Control 95

Chapter Twenty
Helmet to Helmet 97

Introduction

The World's Greatest Racecourse

Carl G. Fisher incorporated the Indianapolis Motor Speedway in February, 1909. Capitalization was $250,000, which works out to just about a dollar for each spectator at a modern Memorial Day Classic. The two-and-one-half-mile rectangle was initially finished with gravel topping. In the opening series of race meets in the late summer of 1909, the surface disintegrated under the pounding of heavy wheels. Five people were killed and the whole operation was scored a disaster. Carl Fisher went back to the drawing board.

Three million, two hundred thousand bricks were laid over the gravel by 1911 and a five-hundred-mile race planned. The total purse would be $35,000.

Ray Harroun won the race with an average speed of 74.59 mph. His car was a single seat Marmon "Wasp" with the first known rear-view mirror. In 1972, driver Sam Posey drove 198 of the possible 200 laps before being flagged off the course. His average speed for the 495 miles completed was 165.721 mph. Race officials awarded him fifth place and paid $37,410.89 for the effort . . . $2,410.89 more than the entire field received in 1911.

Today the same bricks that carried Ray Harroun are in place under an immaculate asphalt surface. Rear-engined racers, shaped like hammerhead sharks, rocket at over 195 mph in quest of over $1,000,000. Mark Donohue, winner in 1972, received more than six times the total purse of 1911. His precision work required just three hours and four minutes.

The configuration of the speedway has remained nearly constant through the years. The men trying to solve its secret, to find the faster way around . . . have paid dearly in every dimension human beings can. If Carl Fisher could have looked back from where we stand in time, he might have elected to build "flats" or grow cabbages on West 16th Street.

The two-and-one-half miles of Indianapolis Motor Speedway . . . conceived in 1909. The turn closest to you in the picture is the southwest turn. This area is called the "'first turn" because it is just down track from the start/finish line. The "start/finish" line and pits are behind the Goodyear blimp seen in the picture. In the extreme right of the picture you see the "south short-stretch" and "southeast turn" (turn No. 2). You drive 200 mph up the "backstretch" to the "northeast turn" (turn No. 3) at the top of the picture. Get through the "north short chute" and you are in the "northwest turn" (turn No. 4) and the "front stretch" lies just ahead. Crossing the "start/finish line," you prepare for turn No. 1. Less than one minute has gone by and you have traveled more than two-and-one-half miles. More than 200,000 people on location have watched you.

World Champion Jackie Stewart is a serious threat at Indy any time he enters. Mechanical failure has cost him several victories at the old Speedway. The million dollar purse of today draws all of the best. There is nothing like it in the world.

Physically, the track is very simple. It has four straight passes and four turns.[1] A good driver in a powerful modern passenger car should average 90 mph on the course. The turns have shallow banking, not unlike that found on a modern freeway. The black paved surface is velvet smooth.

---

[1]The track has two 3,301-foot straights and two 660-foot straight portions. The four turns are 1,320 feet. Each turn has a distinct personality.

Ray Harroun and the Marmon "Wasp" . . . winner of the first Indy 500 at 74.59 mph. Ray attached the first rear-view mirror on record, to watch the opposition.

In May, 1911, the surface was not smooth and clean. It was dusty, slippery and brutally rough. For the "record" the corner banking from the beginning was 16° 40″. The ten feet of brick surface closest to the wall in the corners pitched up to 36° 40″. The designers' thinking was that the high banking at the top could be used by drivers to salvage a bad job and see them through. The builder's intentions were good . . . his product—lethal. The concrete "retaining wall" at the top of the track was vertical to the fields of Indiana, but where it linked to the brick racing surface . . . a launch platform for desperate men in runaway machines was struck. The angle of intersect for track and wall was not 90° and a real "stopper," but 54°.

THE OILY GRAIL

During the administration of Capt. Eddie Rickenbacker in the 1930s, the banking in the turns was cut down to 9° 12″ all the way to the wall. A true retaining wall was created with the advantage of know-how from bitter experience.

The original brick surface has, in stages, been blacktopped by men who are artists with their material. The place is universally called the "Brick Yard" in spite of the fact that since the early 1960s only one yard of bricks has been exposed. These old red blocks are more than a nod to history. They are in the mind of every man who runs the course. They are his point of departure; they alone confirm his work is done. Officially they are called THE FINISH LINE.

Improvements are introduced by the score for each new running. However, walls that forgive a little are still in the future. If progress is the end product of a great series of mistakes, the Indianapolis Motor Speedway is one of man's great shrines to progress. A tiny portion of the story follows.

Eddie Rickenbacker . . . Race driver, war hero, builder of empires and great American. Capt. Eddie owned and managed the Speedway through the lean years of depression and war (1928-1946). Without him the track would not exist.

The Greatest Moment in Sport

The swelling tension of a quarter million people marking time,
Hush to the rich sounds of *Back Home Again in Indiana*.
Aerial bombs and bright balloons spanning clear sky,
The scream of high performance engines rising to strength,
Uniformed crews with hands raised,
Goggles in place, a last handshake . . .
    To those who listen well, there is the unmistakable awareness of
        a host,
    Men who with strong quick steps mounted racing machines
        another day,
    Squinted in the sunlight through clean goggles and . . .
    Never stepped to earth again.
They are in some way here and the cry of the engines gives them
    voice,
Ours is to wonder, to ask them in the impatient shriek, "The price
    you paid . . .
"Did it really mean anything? Did anyone really care?"
The high whine drops to a steady throb. No answers now.
Today's warriors are underway.
    Like Moby Dick in the depths, a scarred old wall glides with
        them.
    An odyssey is muffled by layers of white paint.
    To those who elect to make the run, the wall is a silent Goliath.
    Their slings are great engines,
    Smooth stones are their cars.
        Lord keep them straight as they fly their charted way.

CHAPTER ONE

Harry Hartz Front Drive 1930

It was the winter of national despair. The stock market had crumbled and thousands of banks were closing with the passing of the "Roaring 20s." Captain Eddie Rickenbacker was pondering bankruptcy of the Rickenbacker Automobile Works and the potential collapse of his Indianapolis Motor Speedway.

To buy the track, $700,000 had been raised in bonds at 6½% interest. That was before the roof fell in on the nation's economy. Buying was easy . . . keeping it . . . an uphill struggle.

Battle was familiar to Rickenbacker. He had fought lots of them in the air over France, on the nation's speedways and in the world of business, but this was like fighting fog with an ax. How could he weather "The Crash" and this unreal obligation?

Close friends of a lifetime, who raced automobiles as a way of life, were looking to him as the one man who could take them through. If the rewards from the world's greatest and richest motor race should be denied them, they were finished.

Rick would try to keep the program going, make those interest payments, and find a formula for racing cars that would keep old friends in business. He would have to attract new entrants to fill the ranks of those who had already fallen out. He would do it somehow, because he had to.

The new cars could be modified stock production cars. Why not? He would involve the major auto manufacturers. Detail work would need long and expert consideration by the best minds on the AAA Contest Board. The finest engineering minds would be needed immediately.

Months later, Harry Hartz stood in the middle of his garage in southern California in serious calculation. He was one of the first to receive the technical committee's new specifications for championship cars of 1930. He had determined to build himself a brand-new and radical racer to win the Indianapolis 500. Considering the state of the nation's economy, unemployment and all, he was in pretty good shape. He had some cash reserve and the resolve to commit whatever would be necessary to see this project through. Everybody in auto racing was strong on resolve; precious few could do anything for lack of funds. Many were improvising from day to day for basic personal needs.

A hard-pressed group from the Midwest had towed down to Florida in the hopes of making something from several February race programs. Actually these were the only dates on the national racing calendar. The meets were all on weekends so the task was simply keeping body and soul together through the week. A wild reserve area, far off the beaten path, was selected as a base of operations. Unattended orange trees were the key to the choice. The men could sleep on the ground or in their tow rigs and live off the oranges without bothering anyone.

The area was not truly vacant, however. The world's largest rattlesnakes were cautiously watching and so was the owner, who could have passed for Robinson Crusoe or John the Baptist. The huge, strange owner in full black beard elected to present himself. He came, in fact, with an offer to sell the whole tract for next to nothing to the startled racing men. Having nothing, they were forced to decline. This was a real pity! The property eventually became the Cape Kennedy Space Center!

During training for one of the Indy 500's, a promising young driver made no issue of the fact that he couldn't afford a place to stay. He had discovered a nearby courthouse lawn that was soft and deep. Rain-free nights gave excellent sleep. Race day morning he and his partner could not find a suitable breakfast for the 50c they could amass together. A hungry, sizzling five-hundred-mile drive over oily bricks changed their prospects for a late lunch. The young man found himself in Victory Lane, many thousands of dollars to the "good" ... 50c still in his pocket.

As racing fortunes could go in 1930, Harry Hartz was certainly "on top of the heap." Genius race car and engine builder Harry Miller had been hired on the project which keyed off from a radical front-drive principle.[1]

Jean Marcenac was on the building team, too. The tiny master mechanic had come from France with a factory team that flopped miserably in the 500. Jean elected to stay in America and have another "crack at it." He probably would have laughed heartily if told then that he would spend forty-five years of his life with the cars and quests of Indianapolis Motor Speedway.

The specifications laid down by Captain Eddie Rickenbacker for the 1930 Indy 500 allowed for rugged nonsupercharged stock engines of up to 366 cubic inches to replace the terribly expensive "jewel-like" 91½ cubic-inch thoroughbreds that had sprinted so dramatically across the 1920s.

The end of the era for the screaming little supercharged "91s" was a real strain to people like Hartz. Special "know-how" in pampering these cars came the hard way. A harder lump still, was the word that the new cars would have to carry two men! This was an out-and-out overture to American car manufacturers to modify a little sheet metal and come join the fun. "Why," Hartz muttered, "those wouldn't be race cars ... they'd be boxes! You could go down to the corner and watch 'em pass by the thousands in the street!"

Rumor had it that Studebakers, Fords, Chryslers, Hudsons, Marmons and others were being prepared ... to the absolute horror of most manufacturing executives. Major car builders judged that failure could only cause embarrassment. Success would be most unlikely and at best a "mixed blessing." The era of race cars with cigar lighters was just around the corner.

Native Californian Spider Matlock was brought into the project by Harry Hartz as a riding mechanic. There were good reasons. Matlock had blind faith to sit helpless in the position of riding mechanic and optimism enough to contract for pay only if the project made money.

Spring brought the long trek east to Indianapolis and Gasoline Alley. From the first shake-down runs and timed practice periods, two important facts became increasingly clear. Harry Hartz, weakened and out of form, was not the powerful sprinter he had been before his hideous crash at Salem, New Hampshire in 1927. Car-mate Matlock sensed it and discussed it in confidence with Hartz. The two agreed that the car was fantastic ... beyond their hopes. Concern about Harry Hartz' ability to go the distance was no reflection

---
[1] Power applied to the road surface from the front wheels instead of the rear wheels had been the norm. 1922 Indy 500 winner Jimmy Murphy was credited with pioneering the idea. Several General Motors passenger cars still offer the principle.

NATIONAL HEADQUARTERS

OFFICERS
Dr. Tom Hanna, President
William Klein, V. P.
Herman Winkler, V. P.
Howard Wilcox, Treasurer
Robert Laycock, Exec. Sec.
George M. Ober, Gen. Counsel
C. James Smith, Director of Publicity

BOARD OF DIRECTORS
Harry McQuinn, Hon. Chairman
Karl Kizer, Chairman
William Klein
Al Bloemker
Lou Meyer
Tom Carnegie
Paul Butler
Harlan Fengler
Walter Myers
Harry Hartz
Herman Winkler
Lee Oldfield
Dr. Tom Hanna
Howard Wilcox
John Berry
Robert Laycock
Clarence Cagle
Frank Bain

INDIANAPOLIS '500' OLDTIMERS CLUB, INC.

P. O. Box 24404
Speedway, Indiana 46224

June 20, 1973

Jack Albinson
115 Mender Road
Golden Valley, Minnesota 55422

Dear Jack,

It was a great thrill for me to receive your beautiful and most complimentary letter. I don't believe I have ever received a nicer letter.

The models are excellent and I am very pleased for Julia and Paul that they have had real success in gravity racing.

I appreciate your generous offer for one of the models, however, as much as I would appreciate the compliment, I'm sure the youngsters will continue to get additional pleasure from these as time goes on.

In addition to the safety features or survival gear you have already mentioned, to name a few are, Disc Brakes, Telescope Steering Columns, Rubber Fuel Cells, and Shoulder Harness.

I think one big step by the industry as standard equipment are better tires. The Steel Belted Tires are definitely an important safety feature.

Sincerely yours,

Harry Hartz

HH/ce
ENCL:

on the man. He had proved his greatness. Three second-place finishes here at Indianapolis had established him with the finest. The driving title of the entire nation had been claimed in 1926. That summer day of 1927, on a treacherous eastern board track, racing had demanded everything but life itself from him. Nearly three years of painful recuperation might not have been enough. In any case, there was no shame, and . . . he just might fool them.

A happy, sturdy boy made a point of stopping by the Hartz Miller Garage every day to ogle the car and tell anyone who would listen what he could do if he were its driver.

Harry Hartz pressed on in the determined belief that the lost strength would return to him with practice. The first day of qualification runs for the race, he struggled over the bricks for speed. The totally impersonal tale of a stopwatch is the key to one of the most amazing twists of fortune in the history of sport. His lap times were good enough to earn a front row starting position, but his crew waved him off the run with less than a quarter of a mile of straightaway to complete. Harry stepped from the car without questioning the judgment that had been made. Today he chuckles when he says, "You know, those old time tapes still show that I would have started in the front row!"

While the determined Miller Team huddled around their beautiful gray car, the optimistic youngster stood by the pit wall with a cloth helmet and gloves in hand. In one of those moments where great careers end and others begin, Harry Hartz turned to Billy Arnold and said, "Billy, I want you to take it out."

Arnold was behind the wheel in an instant. On the race track, he and Matlock were at speed in a frightening few laps. The "ride" was his!

HARRY HARTZ — PERMANENT WINNER
THE WHEELER-SCHEBLER TROPHY
INDIANAPOLIS MOTOR SPEEDWAY
1930-1931-1932

The second time the car was presented to the line for qualification, lightning struck in Indianapolis. Billy Arnold throttle-stomped the beautiful gray Miller over the two-and-one-half-mile track at 113.263 mph. Their nearest contender was almost eight miles per hour behind.

Memorial Day, a magnificent Cord Roadster paced the field to a beautiful flying start. Former winner Lou Meyer outgunned Billy Arnold into the first turn. Two times around the course Meyer's white number 1 held off Arnold's gray number 4. Lou Meyer sensed the pressure from Arnold every inch of the way and by lap three he could hold no longer. Billy Arnold led the race as the bunched cars streaked over the start/finish line. Leader . . . Lap 3 . . . Car No. 4 . . . Arnold.

Arnold and Spider Matlock simply ran away and hid from the field. They won by

18

The terrible trio of the early thirties . . . Driver, Billy Arnold; mechanic, "Spider" Matlock; car, the Harry Hartz Miller Front Drive. This remarkable car was in the action at Indy seventeen years after this victory photo was taken in 1930.

more than seven minutes and could, it seemed, have shaved, showered and done a commercial or two by the time second-place finisher "Shorty" Cantlon took the finish flag. Billy Arnold was credited with the lead for an unprecedented one ninety-eight of two hundred laps.

On the leader's 23rd lap, seven cars crumpled together in the northeast turn. Young Lou Moore was moving in contention when caught in the mayhem and smashed! Moore stood by his wrecked Miller and watched Arnold's front drive make a shambles of the race. Lou made a vow against this background of broken hopes and machinery that would surface in the form of a race team in the mid-1940s, a race team that would annihilate all competition. The cars Lou Moore would create would give the "front-drive school" its most glorious hour.

Ten minutes after Moore and associates had crunched on this day in May, 1930, Cy Marshall got into the mess and oil they had strewn on the bricks. Cy couldn't get straightened out, and, in fighting the problem, got over the wall. Rescue personnel found driver Marshall injured under his green Duesenberg, and the riding mechanic, his kid brother Paul, beyond help. Promising young Paul Marshall was dead in the car.

The death of a youngster in Indiana and an experiment halfway around the world in the running of the Monte Carlo Grand Prix stirred the imagination of racing men. The experiment in Monte Carlo involved a crash helmet that French driving-ace Louis Chiron had made for himself. Chiron wore the helmet for half the race, then threw it from his graceful blue Bugatti because it was too hot and too heavy.

The helmet did not return to use in racing in Europe for twenty years, but alert American racing men had taken careful note and a new thrust was irrevocably in motion. Armor of a radical new kind would be created that would give men of the racing wheel . . . life!

CHAPTER TWO

Cloudy Skies 1931-1932

The annual migration to the garages of Indianapolis came as expected with the spring of 1931. The multi-colored machines and the men who made them tick appeared in force. The front-drive Hartz Miller that had "racked 'em up" with apparent ease in the 1930 running arrived flawlessly prepared. Groans were audible everywhere in Gasoline Alley as the car was carefully rolled off its van and into a garage. The machine was No. 1 in every way. In it Billy Arnold would not only defend his Indianapolis 500 championship but his 1930 AAA National Driving Title.

Through practice and a blistering qualification run at nearly 119 mph, Billy Arnold and Spider Matlock seemed to practically own the place. Russ Snowberger was the closest thing to a challenge and his official timed run was 112.796 mph.

The technical committee shocked Billy Arnold and the Hartz Team with the announcement that the car had failed to meet safety standards. A brake rod had been disconnected. The car would have to be brought up to standards and requalified.

The second weekend of qualification Arnold gunned to a 116.080 and "dialed in," but had to settle for the eighteenth starting position. His personal wrath was hard to conceal. His circle of "good ol' racing buddies" was shrinking. The rules stated that the whole group qualified the first weekend will start in front of all who come in the last weekend. Arnold would start behind Dave Evans in a diesel car qualified at an electrifying 96.871 mph.[1]

Threatening race-day skies set the tone for a violent 1931 Five Hundred Mile Classic. In seven dizzy laps, Arnold and Matlock charged from eighteenth place to slam past Wild Bill Cummings for the lead. Records started to fall like card houses. The pair was on the way again!

On lap six an orange car got airborne after mixing with a white Duesenberg. Details back at race control on the front stretch were sketchy, but it seemed apparent that Harry Butcher and mechanic had ridden their Buick up and over the wall on the northwest turn. Joe Russo was also involved but was still racing.

In the pits a native Hoosier barely more than five feet tall was bouncing up and down in anticipation. Rookie Wilbur Shaw was due to replace Phil Pardee in a team Duesenberg. The sign was up for Pardee to come in. Behind the wheel of the giant orange Duesenberg, Shaw started driving like a madman! There was no way little Wilbur could look normally over the top of the cowling, so he poked his head out the left side and mashed on the accelerator.

Moving in heavy traffic up the backstretch, he tried to pass one too many before dipping down into the third turn. The car started spin-

---

[1]While burning about $2 worth of kerosene fuel, driver Evans would go nonstop in the diesel while eager pitman Jimmy Doolittle waited in vain to service the car. A decade later General Jimmy Doolittle would get all the action a man could ever ask while leading a carrier-launched bombing raid on Tokyo to start things rolling our way in World War II. Dave Evans averaged a modest 86.1 mph in the race for 13th position.

20

Wilbur Shaw in epic flight over northeast wall in 1931 race. The heavy Duesenberg flew more than forty feet. Freddy Winnai, second from right in photo, followed Shaw in flight over the wall. Drivers and mechanics involved needed only minor first aid.

ning wildly on oil-coated bricks. Shaw and his mechanic lunged for the floor of the 2,400 pound brute as it thudded loudly into the wall . . . and took flight in an epic that could be compared to the Wright brothers' efforts. Distance was in excess of forty feet and height a minimum twenty-five feet! The original *Chitty Chitty Bang Bang* was a long lethal orange "Duesy."[2]

[2]The colloquial expression "It's a Duesy!" comes from the term Duesenberg.

Back on earth, Shorty Cantlon and Ralph Hepburn slid wildly through the mayhem left by Shaw.

Fred Winnai didn't. Watching Shaw's aerobatics, things got all out of hand. Matters were beyond recovery when full attention returned to driving his big "Bowes Miller," and over the wall he went! Ambulance crews bounced out into the rough below the track and found, miraculously, both drivers and both mechanics in working order. Antiseptic and bandages were enough for a mass of contusions. A practical shortcut would have been to dip each in a tub of iodine.

With just thirty laps to go and a gaping twelve-and-one-half-mile lead over second place, Billy Arnold would not slow his torrid pace. Team chief Harry Hartz used every gesture, every sign, and every means short of a shotgun to make Arnold slow down, conserve the car and assure the victory.

He would not!

Lightning had to strike him and it did . . . in the northwest turn. The rear axle snapped, the car whirled like a spent bullet.

A blue racer speared Arnold's car in an unreal flaming shunt. Luther Johnson's car sent the leader flaming down into the inside wall.

Mechanic Matlock flew out with a broken shoulder. Arnold crawled out of the exploding wreckage with cuts, burns and a broken pelvis.

A wheel from the Hartz Miller sailed high into the air, out of the racetrack and a quarter of a mile overland where . . . it struck and killed an eleven-year-old boy. Wilbur Brink was at play in his own front yard when the heavy wheel found him.

Lou Schneider hung on to inherit victory while, in the last forty laps, four cars holding positions from the lead to sixth place were eliminated by a crash or breakdown. Schneider and his Bowes Seal Fast sponsors reveled in the hour without any notion that TB was consuming the winner's life.

"High flight artist" Wilbur Shaw returned half skinned from the field hospital to drive relief for Jimmy Gleason in a team Duesenberg. To his dying day Wilbur Shaw relished describing the face of his riding mechanic when in the same northeast corner . . . he came in too high and too hard, and lost it again. The car got all out of shape until the "Song of Firestone" underneath them reached high "C." I don't really believe that Shaw had time to get a reading on the boy's expression or that his new partner had been anywhere in the area to see the original "high flight," but the story was a winner for twenty years and who would knock that. Wilbur threaded the needle at the top of the track and powered on totally uninhibited for all the experience. The name of the wild-eyed mechanic never appears in the records again. Some say the last recall of him around the Speedway . . . he was looking for a parachute.

A point must be made concerning the configuration on the wall. It was poured concrete that was, in fact, vertical to the earth. The surface of the racetrack was banked (16-36° in the turns) so that the juncture of wall and track was far from a right angle. Rising up the banking, a speeding car would often find the wall a launch pad and not a retainer. Cars flying over became somewhat routine. To anyone present or involved, the word routine could hardly apply. Capt. Eddie Rickenbacker corrected this with a true retaining wall late in his administration.

In all the crunching and flying, not every team got through. A practice incident took the lives of driver Joe Caccia and riding mechanic Clarence Grove. Their Jones and Maley Duesenberg powered into and over the southwest wall.

The car was judged repairable. Hard work over many months restored it, and it rolled onto the track for practice and qualification a year later. Benny Benifield, a strong "rookie," was at the wheel and Harry Cox was in the mechanic's seat. In a senseless way . . . tragedy compounded. This cruel Duesenberg carried its new crew to death over the same portion of wall in an accident that was similar to the point of being mysterious.

Milt Jones was justifiably proud to be both the owner and driver of a wonderfully

Gus Schrader could well have been the greatest race driver ever on a clay surface. Probably his only try on pavement was at Indianapolis in 1932. He crashed hard before the fans were even in their seats... and took a very advanced four-wheel-drive machine out before its potential was in any way displayed.

Fred Frame won the 500 in 1932 in a "sister car" to Billy Arnold's 1930 winner. Some evidence would point to a win by Howdy Wilcox, II. Both men were silent to the grave on the matter.

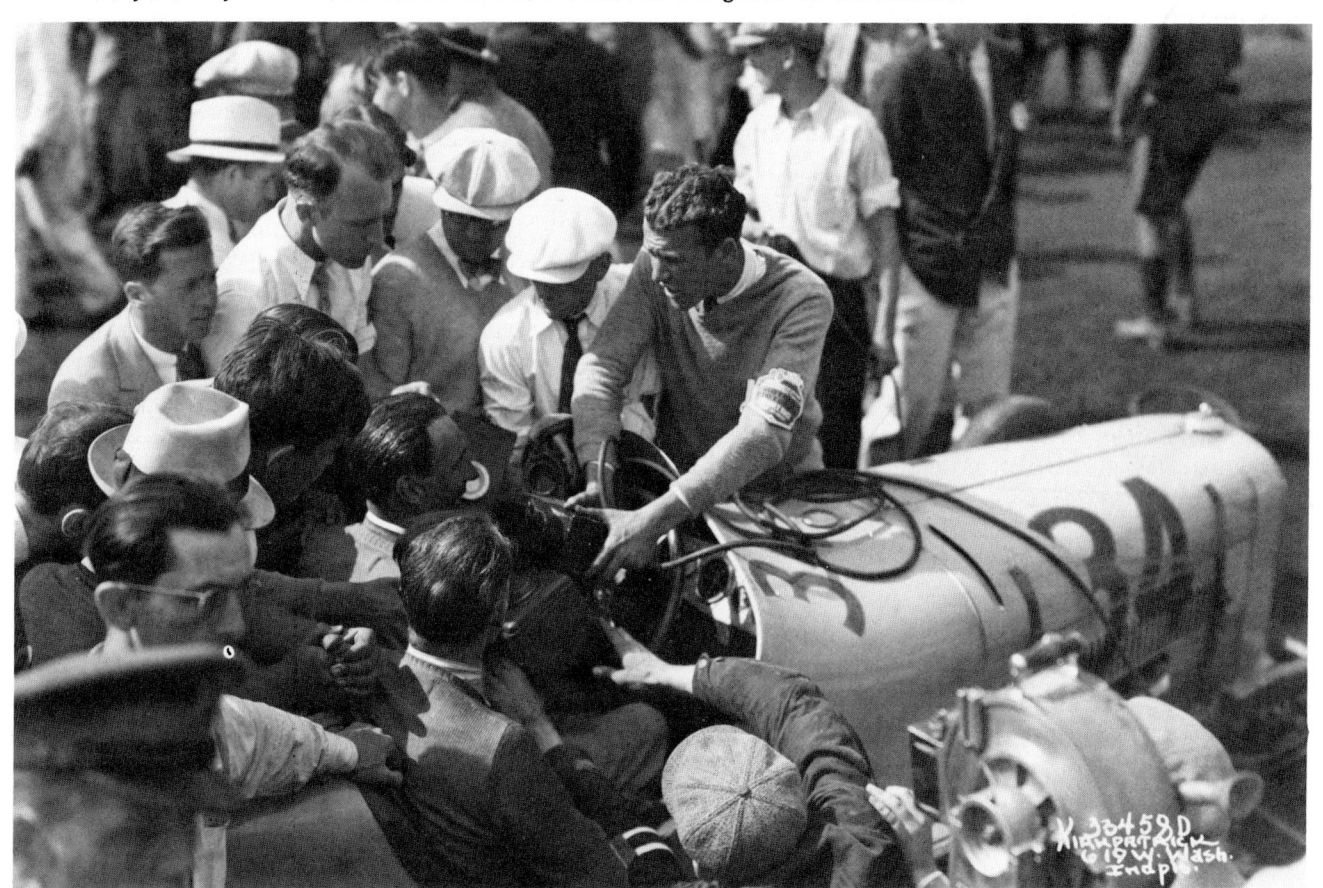

prepared Miller. He felt that a great opportunity was in hand. It wasn't. His "pride and joy" turned on him in a practice lap and took his life. Three men were dead. The starting field for the 1932 running was yet to be qualified.

The race-day charge of Billy Arnold and Spider Matlock had a lethal familiar ring. Their gray and blue Hartz Miller pushed out to a commanding lead . . . and right through the "EZ" (slow down) signs of Harry Hartz. With a lead counted in laps more than seconds, Arnold roared into the northeast turn. Impatience took command for a brief moment. There just wasn't room as he attempted a mid-turn pass on a slower car. Oily bricks and the unbending laws of physics combined to draw the car to the wall and high into the air beyond it.

Safely in the track hospital the irony of "racing luck" was confirmed. Arnold and Matlock had simply exchanged injuries from the year before. Driver Arnold had broken his shoulder and Matlock his pelvis.

Probably the finest dirt track driver of all time came from the dusty state fair tracks of the International Motor Contest Association to drive the bricks of Indianapolis. Gus Schrader was assigned to drive a brand-new sixteen-cylinder creation of Harry Miller that incorporated four-wheel drive (power applied to the track through all four wheels). The car, in principle, was about thirty-five years ahead of its time, but never really got a chance. While Schrader was the greatest in deep clay, you wouldn't want him to take your soap box derby chug out on pavement. Driving a passenger car on a public highway was a real task for him.

To make a painful story short . . . Gus drove the car into the wall on lap three and wrecked it. The course of automotive history pivoted on moments like this.

Justice was, in a sense, served to Harry Hartz at the finish line. Fred Frame "claimed" a narrow victory over Howdy Wilcox at 104.144 mph. Frame's car was a team copy of Arnold's Hartz Miller right down to light gray and blue paint. A solid stake in the $70,000 purse was salvaged. The story is widely told by those who were involved in the affairs of Indianapolis during these days that a mistake was made in scoring the race. A check of the total lap record showed the actual winner to be Howdy Wilcox II. The Speedway management faced the error and paid a double first prize. Howdy Wilcox was a gentleman and a professional. The more than $20,000 received took the sting out of being overlooked in the ledger of race winners. His lovely wife lives in central Florida today and is a delight to know. Perhaps she alone knows the real story.

Frustration, injury, and thoughts of a little boy at play were possibly part of what combined to silence the challenge of one of the greatest "Chargers" to ever go out in a race car. Billy Arnold would heal and quit racing. He would pursue the life of a real estate executive, and with the call of World War II, rise to the rank of Colonel.

Optimistic riding mechanic Spider Matlock would go to California and die with popular driver Al Gordon at Ascot Speedway. Their deaths in 1935 would all but halt racing in that state for several years.

The ill-fated Al Gordon would later be noted as "Crash Gordon" in the Indianapolis Press. His record at the Speedway showed: 1932, crash on lap three; 1933, over the wall on lap seventeen; 1934, crash into the wall on lap sixty-six.

Important note must be made that a small man with giant courage had worn a crash helmet all through practice, qualification, and the 1932 race. He had stood up to a great deal of laughter while the lone helmet stayed fast on his head. The press had called the helmet "thundermug" because of its shape and finish. Early speed king Barney Oldfield presented the helmet to Wilbur in California. It had been worn by Major Seagrave of England in a land speed record try.

In the race, axle failure stopped Shaw on his one hundred fifty-seventh round. The most exciting character ever to take the American racing scene was still waiting in frustration for the "right ride." Wilbur Shaw had the vision and good sense to wait—in a good solid HELMET.

CHAPTER THREE

A New Dimension 1933

It was the year 1933 that gave the Indianapolis 500 a new dimension . . . sheer horror. Everything seemed to be out of joint. The nation's favorite song was *Buddy Can You Spare a Dime?* The depths of national depression threatened the race itself. The purse was down $29,000 from 1932. The lap prize total was under $4,000. Entrants were struggling to pay their way. Car builders thought a new rule that limited the amount of oil available to six gallons per car an impossible handicap. True race engines were known to require twice that amount in five hundred miles. They had been designed to use "a little" and were set up "loose." Fuel tanks carrying forty gallons had been allowed a year ago, but nasty little fifteen-gallon tanks would be the rule for this trip.

The technical committee thought these changes would take some of the oily skim off already treacherous bricks and bring cars into the pits more often. Frequent stops, it was judged, would catch worn tires, faulty pieces, etc. and stop tragedy which might happen.

The drivers were at odds with racing management over the disqualification of popular driver Howdy Wilcox for a diabetic condition. Newsmen had been mixed up in their releases and reported that Wilcox was an epileptic. Legal action by Howdy was, understandably, immediate.

Trying to find that "something extra" during the desperate moments of qualification, driver Bill Denver and mechanic Hugh Hurst rode their Studebaker racer over the wall in the northeast corner. There was nothing skilled rescue men could do for them when their crumpled car was righted.

The morning of the race, Memorial Day 1933, a threatened driver boycott of the entire program came to a showdown. Less than thirty minutes before the cars were to fall into formation behind the handsome Chrysler convertible pace car, Capt. Eddie Rickenbacker, Speedway President, stood before the assembled drivers. He had to answer their threat which held that if Howdy Wilcox did not start in the position he had qualified, to the last man, they would not go. Rickenbacker, hero of World War I, founder of Eastern Airlines, auto racing great and owner of the Speedway, declared that he honored their loyalty to Wilcox. He restated the medical judgments that had been made, and confirmed that they must stand. Drivers and mechanics were told to get to their cars immediately or the race would be called and all money refunded to spectators.

Nobody moved!

Eddie Rickenbacker believed in the Speedway—in what racing had given automobile development in brakes, shock absorbers, suspension concepts. Racing had led the way in tire development. This crucible of speed was vitally important. The fifteen-minute warning bomb went off and Rickenbacker's face hardened. This was it!

"Get to your cars and start your engines! Otherwise, I'll cancel the race and close the speedway forever!"

The drivers straggled toward their cars. Problematically it would have been better if

THE OILY GRAIL

they had held their ground. Promising young "rookie" Mauri Rose was assigned to the red and silver Miller of Howdy Wilcox. Unfortunately for Rose, it was pushed from a front-row starting place to the fourteenth row and forty-second starting position. The car had qualified at 117.619 miles per hour, but was moved in behind Ralph Hepburn who was in at 110.001. Mauri Rose was so far back at the start of the race that the front end of the field appeared to him to be over the horizon.

The pace car finally brought the field around for a flying start and "Wild Bill" Cummings pushed his white Boyle Miller into the lead. Fred Frame in a familiar gray and blue Hartz Miller gave challenge. One could almost imagine it was Billy Arnold behind that wheel preparing to make his move.

Young Mauri Rose charged from last to fourth position before timing gears failed and took him out. In forty-eight laps he had dueled and beaten thirty-eight cars, each for an important position. In time he would know the exhilaration of three great victories here. Fans would thrill to his abandon for nearly two more decades.

On the seventy-ninth lap, car No. 64, the Kemp Manix Special, came into the first turn out of shape. The car skidded, whirled around and straddled the unyielding white barrier. Elmer Lombard was thrown like a rag doll more than fifty feet outside the wall where he was found painfully lacerated and injured. His predicament was mild compared to the agony of driver Mark Billman. Billman was pinned against the wall by the left front wheel of his giant red and white Duesenberg. His left arm was torn off and his legs broken. Massive internal injuries demanded immediate care. Blood transfusions were readied in the hospital. During the twenty minutes required to wrench him free, the veterans managed to look away while sliding by time after time.

Rookie Lester Spangler and his riding mechanic, G. S. Jordan, couldn't resist watching the tragedy unfold up by the wall. The yellow caution flag gave way to the green and the field sped away again on a clear racing surface. Driver Spangler's thoughts locked onto his battle for sixth position. He had come "east" for his first 500, but was no rookie to the racing business. He was 1931 runnerup in the brilliant series at Ascot Speedway in Los Angeles. These meets had made his name a table word in the racing fraternity. Right now he was a "Rookie" with a magnificent Hartz Miller car—lying solid in the first ten. Why . . . some of the established "greats" had never had an opportunity in a car like this!

Three hundred thirty miles of the race were behind him. He charged hard down the front straight and toward the first turn. He was still in a striking position to win it all . . . but had just sixty-eight laps to work.

In the southeast turn a powerful front-drive car bolted, the driver lifted and fought a wild slide.

Close behind, Malcom Fox in a blue and black Studebaker steered violently out to his right to clear the lurching "front drive"!

The correction carried him into the "fast car groove!" Lester Spangler, at great speed, was committed to that line. With the lane totally blocked, Lester could perhaps only scream some unheard word to mechanic Jordan. The cry may have been for the rushing natural forces to turn for one life-giving moment.

They didn't. There was an awareness of impact, flight and eternity. Their car had gone over the Fox car, flipped in mid-air and landed on the white wall in such a way that it was impossible immediately to tell which man had been which.

The car rolled back on its wheels and carried backwards down the banking to the

27

The ill-fated Miller Hartz Special in 1933. Driver Lester Spangler and mechanic G. S. Jordan died instantly in a violent wall crash on lap 132. Practice, qualification and the 500-mile race would cost the lives of five men.

track's inside wall. The two lifeless men were deposited by it in mid-track. The once beautiful machine squatted cold and empty against the inner barrier. The injured Fox and his mechanic could only stare in hazy unbelief at what lay beside them on the track. Groping more than twenty-seven miles behind Spangler and Jordan, they had been party to this destruction.

Lou Meyer, in an anti-climax, drove to the victor's flag with more than five minutes in hand over "position 2."

A strange black car made of stock "Whippet" and other nondescript parts took the second dip of the checkered flag. Driver Wilbur Shaw savored, for the first time, the rewards of finishing near the front and in the money. The helmet he wore would never again be the center of laughter to the men who, in the comparative solitude of their garages, could shrink at the full accounting.

Driver Mark Billman was dead at the hospital. Five good men from their small and unique fraternity had come to Indiana this May full of optimism and never left . . . alive!

In spite of wise technical moves to make the 1933 race a safe one, things had become worse. Limiting oil consumption had not made a safer and cleaner race. Smaller fuel tanks had not seemed to make safer cars or turn any tide from disaster. The national press was up in arms, in the name of humanity, to stop these tragedies. Officials from every phase of racing were baffled. Sponsors could wonder if association with the sport generated more evil than good for their hard-earned dollars.

In the long view, a seed that would grow into safer racing was now showing leaf. Safety equipment for men who brave the racing road was on its way. The first key fruit . . . THE CRASH HELMET.

CHAPTER FOUR

"Slow 'Em Down" 1934

The motto for the world's greatest motor race, May 1934, could have been "Slow 'Em Down!" The six-and-one-half-gallon oil limitation of 1933 carried over, with an awesome new limitation on fuel added. Forty-five gallons would be allowed for the 500-mile drive.

Race teams couldn't imagine how they could coax more than eleven miles per gallon out of their fine-tuned but thirsty breed. Charles Tramison couldn't make the program in the "Economy Gas Special." He used too much gas in his qualification run!

They did find a way, and the eventual winner, Bill Cummings, stretched thirteen and nine-tenths miles per gallon in a record run. He averaged a mighty 104.865 miles per hour.

Mauri Rose finished twenty-seven seconds behind the victor in a bitter contest.

Handsome "Wild Bill" Cummings was a very popular race winner. He was an Indiana native and had a business in Indianapolis. His personal qualifications made him very successful in his "racing hobby" and business was seldom allowed to get in the way. He lived long enough to be National Champion in 1934 and drive Indianapolis once more. Cummings loved life, racing and fun.

His sense of good humor was lost on Mauri Rose. Rose argued long that Bill had cheated him by violating the speed limitations of the caution flag. The "stewing" only added to the twinkle in Cummings' eye. The finish was the closest in track history . . . to that time.

In the early going, Wilbur Shaw burst into the lead on lap fourteen. He shouted angrily over the roar of his engine to his mechanic about some "oil puker" who was really greasing up the track.

Someone was!

George Bailey got skating in it and crunched over the northeast wall. Young Chet Miller went the same way in the southwest turn in his gold Bohnalite Ford. No one was seriously hurt.

As leader Shaw powered into lap fifteen, his anger with the people dropping all the oil on the track suddenly softened. His mechanic was desperately pointing at their oil gauge. It read . . . zero!

The oil plug on their machine had fallen out on lap fourteen as they swept to the lead. Six gallons of oil had instantly pumped down on the bricks. Shaw reached for the kill switch, shuddered and turned to his partner, "It's us!"

The little giant, who always wore a helmet, had not gone far—but he had gone fast. He was certainly not alone in the use of a solid crash helmet. The 1934 field was generously spotted with helmets, and before the year was out, championship racing drivers of the United States would wear them by RULE.

Important improvements at the track for the 1935 running deserve mention. Caution lights were installed around the course to alert drivers of accident or danger. The large yellow lenses were directed toward oncoming drivers so that when turned on . . . they were seen in the brightest sunlight. The rac-

30

Wild Bill Cummings sends a good-humored message to Mauri Rose across the years. Cummings won the 1934 running of the 500 in a very close match with Mauri Rose. Rose felt Cummings violated the rules to win.

ers' response was to slow down and form a single line. The light normally meant men would be walking on the course for some reason. The message was that the surface is not safe and track or medical people need cooperation and protection. There were no exceptions, too much was at stake. Today, great beams send either a green signal for all clear or yellow for caution.

Driver's tests were initiated for the 1935 running as another great step forward. A minimum of experience in championship events was required before a driver was allowed on the track. Once on the track, the would-be "chauffeur" was watched in his every motion while driving a series of tests. His speed was worked up in increments and very little tolerance was given. Through the years the tests have gotten tougher but remain pretty much the same. The fundamental difference is that today a would-be "hot shoe" has to test at nearly twice the speed his racing uncle turned in 1935.

31

A wonderful study of the surface of the Speedway and the construction of a Ford-powered car in 1935. The machines were dangerous little masterpieces of fabrication. Note detail work around the hood . . . the coachwork is unbelievable.

Mel Kenyon in the "Sprite Special" represents Indianapolis Motor Speedway at its best. On or off the track, Mel is a champion and a Christian gentleman. He has something to say in this book.
(Speedway Photo)

The greatest moment in the world of sport . . . The pace car is clear and safe, the green flag is waving and thirty-three magnificent racers thunder toward Turn No. 1!
(Speedway Photo)

The Golden Anniversary 500 is ready to roll. The year is 1961. Eddie Sachs commands the pole position, Don Branson is in the middle and the great Jim Hurtubise in the Demler No. 99 moves from the outside.
(Albinson Photo)

The immortal Tony Bettenhausen turns the track at 142 mph in the graceful Hoover Motor Special. Tony carried No. 1 as national champion during 1959.
(Albinson Photo)

Very possibly the greatest of them all—A. J. Foyt—winning his first 500. The car is a Bowes Seal Fast Special. His race average in 1961 was 139.130 mph. (Albinson Photo)

The field is away for the 1960 Classic. Every man in the picture is a legend. Eddie Sachs waves from the pole in the Dean Van No. 6. Winner Jim Rathmann drives in the "sandwich" while Rodger Ward salutes from his No. 1 Leader Card Special. (Albinson Photo)

A classic Indy concept that goes back to the 1930s and today still rules the USAC Championship Dirt Circuit . . . The Front Engine, Straight-Up Champ Car. Al Unser drifts this one in the "Hoosier 100."

(John R. Mahoney Photo)

The revolutionary "Fuel Injection Special" with Bill Vukovich at the wheel! The year was 1954 and Bill made it two 500s in a row in this beautiful little roadster. His better lap times were 138-plus mph.

(Albinson Photo)

Jack Brabham came from the Grand Prix tracks of Europe to stun Indy into the "rear engine revolution" in 1961. His tiny car with a little 167.6-cubic-inch engine would point "The only way to go!"

(Albinson Photo)

The STP Oil Treatment turbine was the greatest piece of engineering ever to roll out on track at Indianapolis. The silent red rocket was probably the safest, most spellbinding entry as well. Parnelli Jones was its complete master. The year was 1967.

(Speedway Photo)

The driver's route to a chance at Indianapolis is always tough. Larry Cannon survived this scene at Winchester, Indiana, and presses toward Indy. (Beetle Bailey Photo)

Mario Andretti gets a winner's kiss from car owner Andy Granatelli during a near riot of celebration in Victory Lane, 1969. Mario's face bears evidence of burns from a terrible flaming crash a few days before. STP products have made a lot of people happy. (STP Photo)

Eddie Sachs had victory in hand in 1961. His right rear tire sent him a message that changed the course of his whole life. (Albinson Photo)

1971 and the pace car is out of control! The mistake was easy to understand, but the fact was small comfort to dozens who were injured. God was merciful to a stand full of photographers. (STP Photo)

National champion Joe Leonard pits for fuel and tires in his Parnelli Offenhauser. Every man has a job. Failure by just one can dash all hope of victory. The tools for many must come from S-K. These perfectionists insist on it.

(S-K Tools Photo)

CHAPTER FIVE

Front Drive 1934

A violent event during training for the 1934 "500" served as a type of things yet to come. The problems inherent in a principle would surface and destroy again and again. Peter Kreis and mechanic Bob Hahn were on the track turning a routine practice run. Down the front stretch they took a signal from their pit, set up for the southwest turn, and drove in. Their gray and blue Harry Hartz Miller seemed to be in perfect control.

Heads along pit row snapped up as a sudden roar came from the corner. Traction gone, the car was out of control in the middle of the turn and headed straight for the wall. Striking the wall, it rose into the air and in mid-flight was severed by a tree. Death to the men aboard was probably instantaneous. People who watched the incident and experts who tried to reconstruct and explain it were totally baffled. It appeared that the car simply broke out and shot over the wall.

The natural destructive tendencies of the front-drive racer (power translated to the racetrack through the front or steering wheels) were not fully appreciated at the time. Any mistake by the driver or mechanical malfunction that would upset normal pulling could cause the car to charge straight ahead without the slightest hope of recovery. The surface would take on the quality of polished ice.

Cars with power translated through the rear wheels, by contrast, in a crisis had a tendency to spin . . . turn about in a tight circle. The spin was often the life saving "out" of the immediate problem.

Ralph Hepburn puzzled with the rest at the track on the day of tragedy for Kreis and Hahn. Thankfully he couldn't see into his own future. He would drive fifteen 500s before a brutish eight-cylinder Novi Special front-drive racer would wrestle control from him and crush his life. He was working, at the time, to improve on his own then unbelievable lap record of 134.4 mph. No other driver had ever come within five mph of his mark. The most powerful racing car of its time would, for reasons unknown, fly out of the low groove in the northeast turn and bury itself into the wall. That date for Ralph would be Sunday, May 16, 1948.

Chet Miller was there that fateful day for Kreis and Hahn, May 1934. He pondered the matter carefully, too. Miller had no way of knowing that he would live five more years, lacking one day, than Ralph Hepburn, before that same Novi Front Drive would turn on him in a re-creation of the Hepburn tragedy. His life, too, would be taken instantly. Like Ralph Hepburn, he was trying to improve on his own track record, 139.034 mph, when the car turned killer. Chet drove in sixteen 500s.

William "Shorty" Cantlon was another at the track, in 1934, who wondered about Pete Kreis and why? He had watched that Hartz Miller for years. He made his first start at Indy the same year the car was created. He had chased Billy Arnold in it toward the victor's flag, race day 1930 . . . and lost. In thirteen tries this second-place finish would stand as his best.

Ralph Hepburn gave his life on a sunny day in May, 1948. His front-drive V8 Novi was the most powerful racer of its day. Five years later an identical car would kill the great Chet Miller in an identical accident.

Duke Nalon had lapped all but teammate Rex Mays in the 1949 race when an overstressed rear axle let go. He threw himself over the outside wall and healed to race another day. Mauri Rose is ducking and driving for the infield grass. The bravest of the brave tried to drive the infamous "Novis."

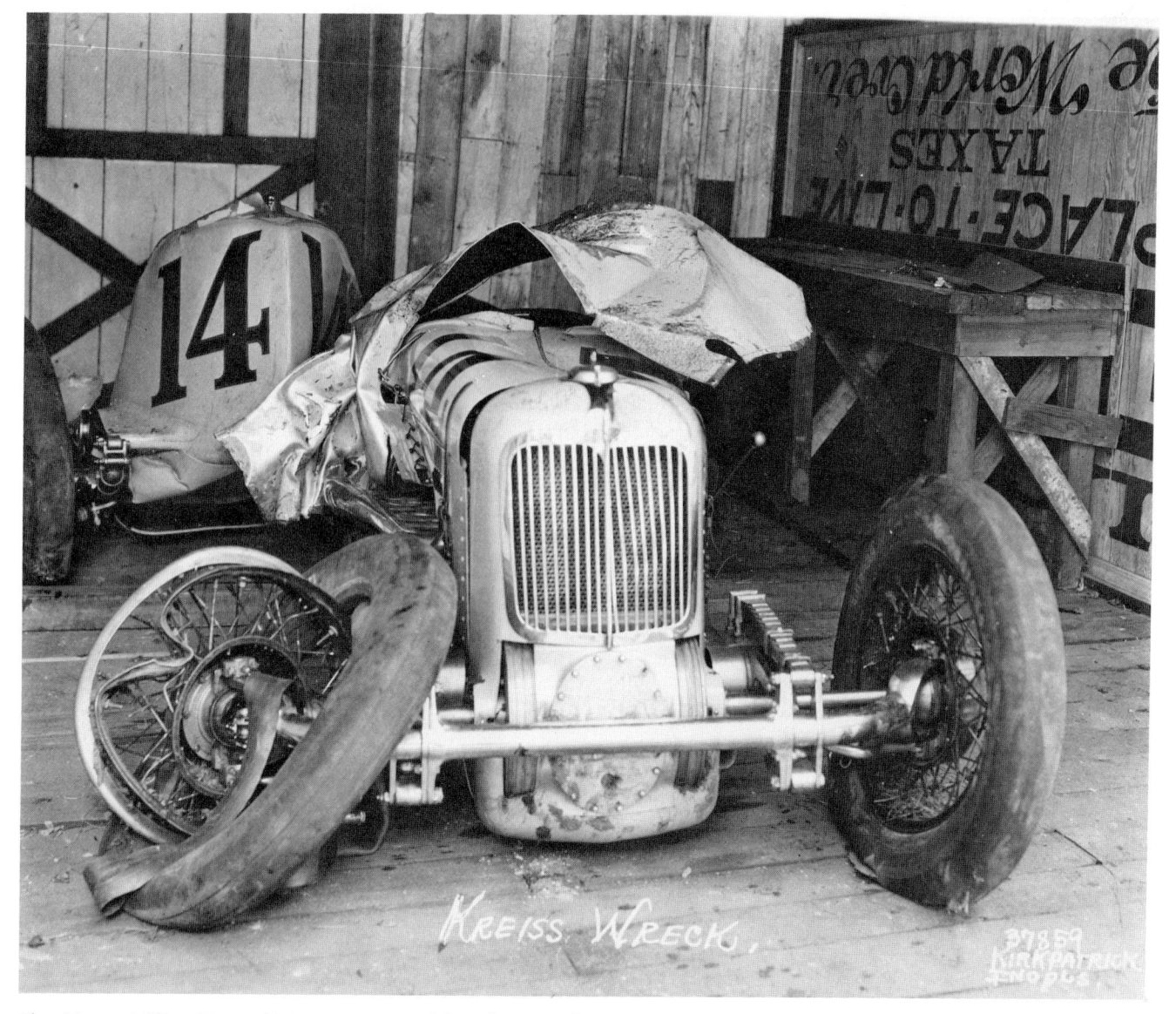

The Hartz Miller Front Drive was capable of more than winning. Driver Peter Kreis and mechanic Bob Hahn died in this practice-run disaster. The year was 1934. The machine was severed by a tree.

The end would come for Shorty Cantlon on Memorial Day 1947. Bill Holland's front-drive Blue Crown Spark Plug Special would break away, get sideways in the infield grass, come violently back up on the track and force Cantlon into the wall.

The car Harry Hartz brought to the Speedway in 1930 would take its final start this day with Shorty Cantlon. Seventeen incredible years and the end would be a spin-out on the eighty-seventh lap. Roland Free, its last pilot, would be awarded seventeenth place.

It was appropriate that mystery man Roland Free should be the last man to drive the Harry Hartz Miller. He was an extremely well-groomed man who was at the same time gracious and aloof. He had, like Billy Arnold, risen to high rank in World War II. His name was more commonly linked with motorcycle land speed records than racing cars. Everything about him said "businessman." He made two drives at Indianapolis. He raced the year the Harry Hartz Miller car was created, and that was 1930. Seventeen years would pass and he would come to race again. The refresher driving test he turned in was a masterpiece. His second and last effort at Indy would be in the veteran of all-time veteran machines. It would almost appear that he had measured his time for seventeen long years until the chance would come to drive the car of his dreams. He chose to pass on the updated Offenhauser engine of 1947. An authentic and original Miller power plant was installed. He must have enjoyed great personal satisfaction in doing the impossible in a machine altogether out of another time.

Today the car stands tall in a museum, as a jewel of auto racing history. It had been a fountain that poured both sweet and bitter. It had given victory and turned and killed. In the seventeen years, greats like Billy Arnold, Fred Frame, Ted Horn, Herb Ardinger, Mel Hansen, Tony Bettenhausen and ... Peter Kreis would all have had a turn at the wheel.

CHAPTER SIX

The Beautiful Blue Crowns

The strongest and most consistent front-drive racers to appear on the world's greatest racecourse were the creations of Lou Moore. He had come to Indy as a driver in 1928 and qualified for every running through 1936. His official record showed one second and two third-place finishes. He believed in the pulling principle of the front-drive car, meticulous building, and a detailed race plan. His bullet-shaped, low-slung Blue Crown Spark Plug Specials appeared as a two-car team for the first time in 1947. Four-cylinder Offenhauser engines were wrapped in spotless baby-blue sheet metal. Trimming was red and white.

Tough old veteran Mauri Rose was assigned one of the cars and young Bill Holland the other. The required ten-mile qualification run indicated that Holland's was clearly the faster of the two, with 128.756 mph average against 124.040 for Rose.

During this period of American racing it was not uncommon for a team director like Moore to determine an average speed that he felt would win the race and hold his driver to it without regard for other cars that could, by straining, move out to a sizable lead. Then judgments were made on the basis of what tires, engines and men could stand for the long pull.

Race Day 1947, the Moore "Blue Crowns" moved out and into a commanding lead on schedule. Bill Holland survived the violent gyrations of his car that took the life of Shorty Cantlon, and maintained a lead over Mauri Rose with apparent ease.

The two cars raced and pitted with perfect discipline. Both drivers clearly understood that in the late stages no "flat-out-all-the-way" tactic ala Billy Arnold would be tolerated. Moore had been driving in those days when Arnold had lost race after race for no justifiable reason. Blinding speed for speed's sake was out!

In the late laps of the race, owner Moore put out the "EZ" sign to both his men. This clearly meant that they were to slow down; the victory was assured. Bill Holland was driving under the impression that he had at least a lap on mate Mauri Rose. Crafty old Rose smelled the faint perfume of victory and poured on speed. The pit sign remained constant "EZ." Rose sailed by Holland on the 193rd lap and received a big wave and smile from the youngster. Bill believed that owner Moore simply wanted to have Rose on the same lap with him when he took the victor's flag.

Seven laps later the checkered flag was taken by Holland with an elated salute. A routine precaution lap was carefully driven and a swing down to "Victory Lane" started. It never was completed. Mauri Rose was already inside and a wall of excited humanity had closed in behind him. When Rose slipped by on the 193rd lap, he already was on the same lap. Young Holland was furious and confused. He never was given an explanation by Lou Moore.

Capable and tough are words that describe three-time winner, Mauri Rose. He won the last race before W. W. II (1941), and in the "Blue Crown Special" in 1947 and 1948. These cars gave the "front-drive theorists" their finest hour. Mauri holds an important position at General Motors Corp. today.

Mauri Rose raced and beat Bill Holland all the way in 1948 for another one-two finish.

Holland won for Lou Moore in the 1949 Classic. In the late stages, Mauri Rose was making another run at the now watchful Bill Holland when a magneto strap broke. A ball of fire rolled out the tail, and the rear of the car bounced off the track. In desperation Rose leaped from the crippled car and tried to push it toward victory . . . physically.

The records would show for Lou Moore and the Blue Crown Spark Plug Special team a mark of three wins and three second-place finishes from 1947 through 1950. Their efforts would, for practical purposes, mark the end of the front-drive racing car.

Jim Hurtubise · 1963 · Indianapolis Motor Speedway

The last of the brutish "Novis" were not supercharged front-drive machines like those that took Ralph Hepburn and Chet Miller. They were supercharged and super powerful—but drew their power from rear wheels. Jim Hurtubise was one of the few men who would keep them between the walls.

CHAPTER SEVEN

Chitwood and Shaw

A twenty-seven-year-old Indian boy from Texas came to drive the 500 in May of 1941. Joie Chitwood had raced sprint cars on the dirt tracks of the nation with a cool precision that inspired sports writers to say that he was completely free from fear. He alone was said to have absolute confidence in his own ability. His unshakable composure and velvet driving style just naturally gave rise to the notion. Chitwood was a brilliant driver and still is. His driving was featured in 1971 in some excellent television commercials. Response to this author's question about being above fear was thoughtful, "Every normal person knows fear."

Peering over the cowling of his 1941 Indy ride, Chitwood wondered if it was worth it all. He had earned fifteenth place here the year before, but this was an "all new ball game."

The brick surface of the old speedway bounced him until his teeth rattled. The atmosphere of the whole place was cold and strictly business. He felt very much alone. The era of the two-man cars had ended with the 1937 running, so thankfully all the drivers raced alone. A helpless riding mechanic was no longer present to compound the hazards. The cars were still giants powered by potent Miller engines (now called Offenhauser).

The single-seat racers had suited tiny Wilbur Shaw very nicely. He, in fact, had become a three-time 500 winner. Adolph Hitler seemed invincible as his troopers stomped about Europe. Wilbur Shaw was about as convincing as he stormed around the great speedway in a sparkling maroon Maserati purchased for him in Italy.

Little Wilbur had craned his neck and pressed hard with his right foot in the last event for the two-man racers in 1937. His margin in victory was a breathtaking 2.16 seconds over his close friend Ralph Hepburn. Hepburn actually led for an instant on the last straightaway. In Victory Lane, Shaw's tires were found completely spent and oil reserve burned. One more lap could have been his undoing.

Shaw misjudged the potential of driver Floyd Roberts in a Miller-powered single-seater in 1938. Lou Moore had prepared and entered the car for Floyd and it was a masterpiece.

In the race, Shaw believed the pace Roberts established would certainly end in tragedy or breakdown. Wilbur held tenaciously to his race plan with a speed ceiling far off Floyd's average. He was unflinching . . . but wrong!

Driver Roberts did not spill or break, and had a "field day" with a record run at 117.200 mph. The nearly perfect effort would stand as the target and record for ten long years.

May, 1939, Shaw unveiled an incredibly beautiful eight-cylinder Maserati import from Italy. The car stands today as the crown jewel of the Speedway Museum. Maserati had shown very badly against the "Silver Arrows" of Mercedes Benz and the rear-engined Auto Unions in world road racing. The German teams didn't come to Mid-America in 1939 and it was a glorious day for Shaw and the

Joie Chitwood drove his first 500 in 1940. He is credited with installing and using the first seat belt in a racing car. The belt grew out of need for stability in a terribly "rough-handling car" in 1941.

The end of a perfect run for Floyd Roberts in 1938. His record run at 117.200 miles per hour would stand for ten years. He had 364 days and 22 hours to bask in glory.

THE OILY GRAIL

Maserati brothers. Lap one hundred and seven . . . a chain of events robbed the day of any immediate personal joy.

A red and white car carrying No. 25 went out of control starting up the backstretch. A red and black racer hit it hard and flipped it. The red and black one caromed and shot violently over the outside retaining wall. Fuel from the overturned car on the track exploded. A driver lay crumpled near spreading oily flame.

Driver Chet Miller powered off the corner and into the scene. He jerked his wheel hard left to miss the unconscious figure and

Wilbur Shaw won the Indianapolis 500 three times. After World War II he did a superhuman job of rebuilding the Classic while serving as president of the Speedway. Two of his victories came in this magnificent little Maserati from Italy.

rolled viciously on the track apron. Car No. 25 was being driven by Ralph Hepburn, but that wasn't Hepburn laying on the track. It was Bob Swanson who had just taken over in relief. The car over the wall was painted red and black and it carried silver No. 1s. Defending Indianapolis and National Champion Floyd Roberts was at the wheel.

Drivers Swanson and Miller were injured but would recover. Floyd Roberts was dead. The recorded cause . . . neck injuries. The chubby, happy man from California was done driving with the pressures of being "No. 1." For the first time, the old Speedway had claimed the life of its own defending champion.

Racing goes on, and Wilbur Shaw's average was 115.035 mph. One hundred miles of running under the caution light modified the average performances a great deal.

Two laps from the finish, Lou Meyer pushed a little too hard in a desperate dash to catch Wilbur Shaw. Spinning at 100 mph, his right front wheel caught the inner hub fence. His body rocketed out of the cockpit as the car snapped violently around.

Before the spectators could accept what their eyes had registered as fact, Meyer was on his feet. Apparently uninjured, he was moving about on the infield grass several yards behind the broken fencing. His unspoken response to these incredible events was immediate and poignant, "I quit!"

His attention turned to building race engines, once called Miller, later Offenhauser, today Meyer and Drake. They still win races at Indianapolis and across the U.S. Today's price tags start from about $22,000 for Championship power.

The now retired Lou Meyer was at trackside when things started rolling at Indy in early May of 1941. He was interested in all the rookie drivers and quick to offer help to anybody with a problem. He stared in unbelief as a youngster slipped past the pit area in Joe Lencki's big blue and white Blue Crown Spark Plug Special. Some kind of strap had been worked around the frame that passed over the driver's thighs and . . . tied him in the car!! In alarm, Meyer conferred with Wilbur Shaw. When the car rolled to a stop in the pits, the worst was confirmed.

Driver Joe Chitwood explained that he had worked out the "seat belt" because he had a problem. The big Lencki chassis had bounced him about so violently in the seat that he was convinced that sooner or later he would wind up flat on his back in the middle of the track. He had asked the Blue Crown crew to change the shock absorbers and suspension to take some of the "buck" out, but nothing was done. The crew chief advised Chitwood that if he wasn't man enough to hang in there . . . they would get someone who could.

Joie wanted the ride—in the car—all the way. The bricks wouldn't get any smoother. Something else would have to be done. In a moment of inspiration, he went to the trunk of his passenger car and got a strap. Threaded under frame members, it was solid. Cinched up tight, his foot was firm on the throttle, hand steady on the wheel.

Lou Meyer and Wilbur Shaw reasoned earnestly with him about the danger of his belt. Their rationale was that in accident or fire he would be trapped . . . in the seat. Joie could only answer that safety, or lack of it, was not his problem. Without the belt his foot was like a "jackhammer" on the accelerator, seat airborne most of the time and the car all over the track. With his belt, he was solid! He stayed with his strap and today laughs about being the first to race the 500 with a safety belt.

43

THE OILY GRAIL

Seven 500 races, including a near win in 1950, and he would abandon the speedways. His word for the time was "frustrating." Full attention to his great auto thrill show would establish him as one of the nation's foremost showmen. Fine young sons, Joe Jr. and Tim, now keep the million-dollar program in front of throngs all across the nation. A strong Chevrolet dealership in Zephyrhills, Florida, has been added to the family operation.

The creativeness of Chitwood and his belt would be lost for a pitifully long time. Dozens of men would perish in race cars for lack of a belt. The seat belt would not be unconditionally required in racing until 1955. Tragic as the loss of racing men may have been, it pales beside the loss of multiplied thousands of people who would have survived in their passenger cars with a proper belt. Transference from racing to passenger vehicle is virtually absolute. Laws concerning belts in American passenger autos did follow in the 1960s. In European racing and passenger cars, tragically, the issue is not resolved.

Joe Chitwood is best known for his Auto Thrill Show. He is a Texas-born American Indian, and one of the most fearless race drivers of all time. In 1951, to file a protest on the posted order of finish for the Indianapolis 500, he and his car owner were able to raise $100,000.00 cash in less than thirty minutes from friends standing in a parking lot.

CHAPTER EIGHT

The Belt

Quick-release belts from World War II fighter planes started to appear in a few cars in the late 1940s. Most veteran Indianapolis caliber drivers wouldn't touch them. Just two drivers accounted for all the National Big Car titles from 1940 to 1948. Both were opposed to the use of seat belts.

Ted Horn, champion from '46-'48, didn't speak much on the subject, but never used them. He was one of the most consistent race drivers ever, with a mark at Indianapolis of fourth place or better in eight straight classics. His influence was immense on drivers everywhere.

Rex Mays carried the reputation of a living legend. At Indianapolis his record was impressive enough. He was fastest qualifier a record four times. He never won the 500, but was second twice. Mays was sometimes vocal against the belts. Ted Horn and Rex Mays both made a point that belts could be a fatal trap if they bound a man in a stricken machine, but could not protect his head and upper body. They frowned on the possibilities of "wearing the car."

The legend of Rex Mays had a broad base in fact. It really crystallized the weekend after Mauri Rose won the 1948 Indy 500. The schedule called for the racers to move from the garages of Indianapolis to Milwaukee for a 100-mile event. The long State Fair track was, at that time, one of the fastest dirt tracks in the country.

Exploding out of the dust, the leaders at the end of one lap of racing were young Johnny Mantz, colorful Duke Dinsmore, Rex Mays and Ted Horn. The field thundered into the second lap in a collective controlled slide. Mays was applying pressure to Dinsmore for "Pos. 2" as they churned over the start/finish line for the third time. Dinsmore made a mistake, slid wide and hooked a rut. The car flipped violently in the approach to the first turn. The driver flew out of the cockpit and landed unconscious in the middle of the dusty surface.

Rex Mays had to make an instant decision. He could plunge over Dinsmore, dead ahead in the dust, or turn straight into the wall on his right. Mays turned hard right—full power into the wall. In an instant Mays was out of his smashed car and on the track over the body of Dinsmore. Ted Horn had somehow seen and driven under the unconscious Duke, but . . . the rest of the field was pouring in, virtually blinded by swirling dust. Mays waved cars at point blank range to left and right. Miraculously, all got by!

This had to be one of the bravest acts ever certified by thousands of viewers. Today a plaque in the wall at Milwaukee records the day, place and the man. The Milwaukee Race still follows the Indy 500 on the Championship Calendar. The event is called the "Rex Mays Memorial."

Four months passed and the men of the AAA Big Car Series gathered at DuQuoin, Illinois. Ted Horn, who had clinched the driving championship, was in the qualified field and favored to win. On the second lap of the

INDIANAPOLIS MOTOR SPEEDWAY CORPORATION
MAINTAINING THE GREATEST RACE COURSE IN THE WORLD
SPEEDWAY, INDIANA
46224

July 13, 1971

Mr. Jack Albinson
115 Meander Road
Minneapolis, Minnesota 55422

Dear Mr. Albinson:

Although we have nothing in the way of prepared material to send you concerning racing's contribution to passenger car safety, I feel certain that you can put together an interesting article on that subject by describing such racing innovations as Ray Harroun's first rear view mirror in 1911, plus the emphasis of safety belts, shoulder harness and helmets.

Four-wheel brakes, low pressure tires and improved shock absorbers also were developed to a great extent by the racing fraternity, but I don't have any specific information to send you.

Cordially,

Al Bloemker
Director of Public Relations.

AB:bw

Indianapolis cars in action on the Milwaukee Fair Grounds track. Rex Mays clinched a place with the all-time greats of racing on this surface in June of 1948. He covered the body of injured Duke Dinsmore with his own body in swirling dust like this.

one-hundred-mile event, the right front spindle of the Horn car snapped. The right corner of his blue and white "Beauty" dug in, flipped into the air and cast him down next to the wall. His white uniform was carefully lettered, "Ted Horn, National Champion 1946-1947." Only eulogies and record books would add . . . 1948 National Champion. Horn lay dead where the car had thrown him.

Rex Mays, without a word to anyone, trailered his car and left the grounds. He must have, in the months left to him, done a great deal of serious thinking about racing in machinery that could protect a man. It would come. The "first principle" of staying in via the seat belt escaped him.

Late summer of 1949, the men of Indianapolis were locked in battle at Del Mar, California. They were just underway and the surface was drying and tearing badly. Above the ruts and dust, a racer loomed high in the air. The driver flew free of the machine and fell back into the dust. His race car plunged to the apron of the track where it stopped on all four wheels. On-coming pilots could see

Fuel at your neck, against your back and under your legs . . . the hazards were great in the Indianapolis and Championship cars of the 1940s and 1950s. Study the fabrication carefully and ask yourself if you could drive at 170-plus miles per hour in heavy traffic.

the car down inside, but couldn't possibly see its driver crawling stunned down the track. One, two, three cars missed him . . . then bunched traffic and sudden death. The mighty Rex Mays was dead of massive head injuries. His bolt upright driving style, incredible charge and natural charisma were gone forever. It was too much!! Something had to be done about it. A seat belt probably would have meant survival for him, and men of auto racing took careful note. Seat belts were mounted for the vast majority overnight.

CHAPTER NINE

Vukie, the Fresno Flash

An impetuous little man came from Fresno, California, to completely scramble all 1952 projections at Indianapolis Speedway. Bill Vukovich was his name. His parents were immigrant Czechoslovakian vine keepers. Basic training for the Speedway had been taken on the fiery midget ovals of California.

Since World War II most Indy drivers have had a wealth of experience in the "Midgets." These tricky little monsters sort out the "great" and the "not so great" in short order. Nobody injured in this indoor upset at Ft. Wayne, Indiana.

His thundering, relentless style would cause writers to forget Billy Arnold and all others like him. They tabbed him "Vukie" for short. Before he was done at Indianapolis he would open a new era—some would call him THE ORIGINAL CHARGER.

His approach to race driving was radical and professional. Anything really original is often misunderstood. Example: Long hours spent standing hatless and alone at remote points around the tracks earned him the title of "The Mad Russian." Those lonely hours in the sun can best be understood today when compared to the countless hours successful football coaches and players spend pouring over game films. From dozens of vantage points, Vukie made a complete mental record of the moves of his competition.

Behind the wheel or at work on his car, his concentration was not to be broken. He applied the principle that what you do in practice, you will do in the game. Yawning race projections like "131.5 mph should get the job done," ended forever with Vukovich. He came to show what 100% every inch of the way could generate.

He was impatient with the working press to the point of being crude. He would do almost anything to avoid engaging people. Conversely, on a racetrack "backing off" for anybody was out of the question. He was not to be distracted! He was not to be entangled!

To his wife Esther, children and a few close friends, he was devoted and kind.

He never bothered to straighten out that "Mad Russian" business. Vukie really didn't care. A typical response to probing writers would be, "Write whatever you want. You don't need me!" What he had to say could wait until race day and then the message would come in the sharp report of a cracked throttle.

When "High Noon" came, he sped away from a classy, talent-laden field. In the best racing parlance, "He blew their doors off." It was no contest!

THE OILY GRAIL

Sweeping along with grace and ease in lap 191, it looked like a ten-minute Sunday drive to the flag. VIPs and officials were already migrating down to Victory Lane. Spectators on the front stretch cheered as Esther Vukovich was escorted from her seat. Vukie had this one! He had thundered through their tunnel of ponderous stands for hours with consistency that made one think he could go on forever. Then he was overdo . . . seconds . . . a minute . . . two minutes. HE WAS OUT OF IT!

Beyond the view of all but a very few, his roadster had knifed into the wall in the northeast turn. A steering pin had failed.

He climbed out unhurt and stood on the wall while twenty-two-year-old Troy Ruttman wound by to claim *his* day.

Vukovich glowered in stoic silence. His bitter word to young Troy Ruttman took the form of a one-sentence blast over world radio facilities, "He'll never win an easier one!"

Vukie was the re-creation of Billy Arnold and total dominance of Indianapolis the fol-

Bill Vukovich, the Fresno Flash, with Wilbur Shaw (man with field glasses on left) in Victory Lane. Vukie has just won the "hottest 500" ever. Terribly high temperature took the life of driver Carl Scarborough, and tormented all. The wear on the man tells the tale.

The one and only Bill Vukovich in the Fuel Injection Special. Vukovich came as close as any man ever to winning three 500s in a row.

lowing May. He blitzed the competition in the same way Arnold had twenty-three years before. Qualification at 138.393 mph gave him the pole position and a track record. He led all but five laps of the 1953 race, on a day so incredibly hot for the drivers that some confused it with the day of judgment. The temperature on track for their desperate work was above 130°.

Carl Scarborough stopped at his pits on lap seventy in obvious agony from the heat. Bodily lifted from his car, he was dead in less than an hour in the infield hospital.

Victory Lane did little to change or sweeten Bill Vukovich. Those unfortunate enough to try for radio interviews keyed off the effect of the heat on the new champion. Vukie snapped, "Think this was hot? Drive a tractor in Fresno in July!"

Bill had elected to use a seat belt and even experimented with various forms of shoulder harness.

Mechanical problems made May of 1954 a near nightmare for the defending champion. He was not helped in his chain of mechanical setbacks by the corps of writers and photographers that dogged his every move, even to the restrooms. The parades in there were unreal. On the third of four possible days of qualification, he earned nineteenth starting position. Buried deep in the seventh row of starters . . . things looked terribly black.

Memorial Day dawned a thing of beauty for a motor race. The first two hundred miles were wide open and everything suggested that Victory Lane would open to a new face. It might well be a powerhouse cowboy from Phoenix named Jimmy Bryan. Jim was running like the wind against craggy veteran driver and mechanic Jack McGrath. The 250,000 spectators were getting a great show.

51

THE OILY GRAIL

Through heavy traffic, a flat gray racer trimmed in red and yellow was methodically moving up in the standings. It was "Vukie out picking grapes." His hours in the sun were bearing fruit. Through mid-race doldrums, necessary pitting for tires and fuel, Bill Vukovich lurked in a position of contention. One hundred twenty-five miles from the finish he struck past Jimmy Bryan and stroked away to win by a full lap.

Checks earned in two Indy outings totaled $164,431 . . . enough to take some of the "Mad" out of any Russian or even a Czechoslovakian. His driving, in a wonderfully contested race, was more crafty than bruising.

He could, some said, turn into a genuine public relations man for somebody . . . a steel wool company, maybe? He passed on all the dollar potential of endorsements and personal appearances. He wisely chose Fresno, family, and home.

Shortly after the world's greatest racecourse opened in the spring of 1955, Bill Vukovich dispatched any rumors about a new outgoing image. He reported to the track on May 6 and found his tormentors from the press ready and waiting. To a torrent of questions he grumped, "I haven't come here for my health."

Practice and qualification went well for the impetuous little man. He seemed very pleased with a second row starting position. In any case, this year he would be able to see the early leaders. Jack McGrath, poised on the outside of the front row, had driven brilliantly in practice and was judged by the experts "the man to beat."

Race day was a disappointment to those who anticipated the greatest race ever. Dark clouds rolled and tumbled. It was bitter cold. Singer Dinah Shore was paraded around the track with dozens of Latin American diplomats in pre-race activities. Chevrolet put on a great show with beautiful little red and white convertibles. Hundreds of decorative flags around the course stood straight out in high winds.

Fans conjectured about the signs of rain, the effects of the high winds on the race cars if it didn't rain, and where to huddle to beat the chill until 11 a.m.

The cars were rolled out to starting positions while the Purdue University Band did its part in the ritual. Moments before track owner Antone Hulman gave the command, "Gentlemen, start your engines!" Bill Vukovich appeared at carside in a spotless white tee shirt. The cold meant nothing to him, his total being was set for battle.

In the thunder of a beautiful three-abreast flying start, Jack McGrath moved his cream-colored "Hinkle Special" to the front. He claimed laps one, two and three. Vukie moved right up on his tail. Down the bricks to the starting line on lap four and it was the blue and orange "Hopkins Special!" Vukovich led! Ten laps passed with McGrath lurking inches behind the Fresno Flash. Lap fifteen fell to McGrath. Vukie roared back on sixteen. The greatest speed duel of all time was unfolding. Spectators didn't feel cold or anything. They were totally captivated. Jack McGrath led laps twenty-five and twenty-six. Vukie got by to claim the twenty-seventh by less than a car length. One hundred thirty-five miles, fifty-four laps, and the dice was suddenly ended. A temperamental magneto let go on Jack McGrath and he was coasting toward his pit. On the fifty-third lap the average of the two front runners was exactly the same, 136.091 mph. The time was a perfect tie and a record. The struggle at razor's edge was over, or was it?

Vukovich received messages from his pit for three passes. The first told that McGrath had come in. The others told that Jack was finished. It was over and Vukie had won. He

THE OILY GRAIL

never gave any acknowledgment and held the pace.

As the leader powered through the short stretch at the south end of the track, beyond his view around the turn ahead terrible things were shaping. The wind caught Rodger Ward and sent his car spinning into a bridge barrier on the inside of the track. A wheel tore off as the car skidded to a stop broadside. Drivers Al Keller and Johnny Boyd came on Ward while running side by side. Keller tried to go under the wrecked Ward car, but lost it and slid across the track into Johnny Boyd. Keller's black roadster flipped over Boyd and tore off all four wheels. Boyd's car was shoved violently toward the outer wall where Bill Vukovich was trying to accelerate around the holocaust. Vukie struck Boyd and flew over the wall. The car soared more than twenty-five feet in the air before landing nose first, bounced and landed on three parked cars and then into a power pole. The machine burst into dirty orange flames. Vukie was sealed in the cockpit underneath.

A column of oily smoke blowing up from the backstretch suddenly left everybody cold and miserable again. It started with a whisper and rose to a shout! Vukovich was missing. Other cars came by two . . . three . . . four times. Vukie didn't! They could only pray, shiver and hope for all the men involved.

Ed Elisian, driving immediately behind Vukovich, put his car into an intentional spin. Before the car stopped in the infield grass, he was out of it. He rushed first to Al Keller and then to the overturned and burning Hopkins Special. He tried so desperately to help his friend and hero Bill Vukovich that a sedative had to be given to quiet him. Elisian was never properly honored for his efforts. We will speak more of him.

In California, young Bill Vukovich Jr. huddled with his grandpa by the radio and waited for a word. It came. "We regret to report that Bill Vukovich has met with a fatal accident . . ."

In the months that followed, it became fashionable for minor politicians and second-rate magazines to drum for closing the track. Unfortunately, cooler and more capable heads didn't call for anything. Protective steel caging and fuel cells would come. Bolder minds and hands would shape them for a much later day. Bill Vukovich Jr. would have to grow up and come to the Speedway himself with the first four-point roll cage. Wynns Corp. would sponsor his efforts at the turn of the 1970s.

Vukie's finest antagonist, Jack McGrath, had reached for the "Oily Grail" for the last time, too. He died at the racing wheel in the fall of 1955.

Handsome and gracious Bob Sweikert won the 500 this day of disenchantment. Sweikert went on to be 1955 National Big Car Champion. He got to carry "No. 1" on a gold roadster in one Indianapolis Classic. His legend in the making was cut short in violence on an Indiana sprint track.

Some builders and entrants could well be haunted in the night by the clean, strong faces and clear eyes of men who came to prominence through great skill and dedication and then were destroyed before their rewards could even be savored.

All forms of racing sagged in the summer of 1955. A number of major supporters dropped out. To this day, corporations with much to gain from participation in racing choose only to point back to the life and death of Vukie.

Strange that after nearly twenty years a man so totally different from the executives with whom he *had* to do still translates personal greatness in such a powerful way.

He was "SOMETHING ELSE" . . . that Vukie!

CHAPTER TEN

Le Mans 1955

Less than two weeks after the death of Bill Vukovich, a tragedy in France gave a near-fatal blow to organized automobile racing. June 11, 1955, more than two hundred thousand people gathered to watch the Twenty-Four Hours of Le Mans.

The race seriously pitted the racing green Jaguars of England against the silver and red Mercedes of Germany. Many constructors from across the world were in the race, running for class prizes.

Just about 6:30 p.m., a Jaguar driven by Grand Prix ace Mike Hawthorne slammed past an Austin Healey driven by fellow Englishman, Lance Macklin. The pass was completed in the narrow neck of the track leading to the pits. Hawthorne jumped hard on his giant disc brakes and steered hard for the Jaguar pit counters.

Immediately behind, the Austin Healey had no braking potential to match the lethal Jag. Driver Macklin found himself in a desperate, losing battle. Avoiding the finned green tail just ahead, he spun out!

Behind Macklin a howling silver Mercedes, closing at more than 125 mph, was trapped. The Mercedes launched over the tail of the Austin and hit the track wall in mid-air. The Mercedes broke in two. Like something flaming up from Hell, the severed portions cut shoulder high through an enclosure of standing spectators. Nearly seventy were dead instantly. It was impossible to tell. An ambulance from this author's military organization took the first group to the hospital and not one was alive on arrival. The final total on those killed was probably one hundred.

The race was, wisely, allowed to go on. Roads remained open for emergency vehicles. Stopping the running would have choked every conceivable lane in and out. The majority of spectators knew nothing of the accident for almost six hours. Ironically, the man who triggered the tragedy was declared its winner. Mike Hawthorne, teamed with Ivor Bueb, drove a total of 2,586.1 miles in twenty-four hours to win the over-all prize.

Mercifully, the driver of the fatal Mercedes never knew what happened. The car, No. 20, was in the hands of Frenchman Pierre Levegh. This man believed in the "Glory of France" and French machinery. Levegh had personally paid for a French Talbot racer in

1952, paid the crew that prepared and serviced it from personal funds . . . and drove himself. To say that he drove himself is a massive understatement. He raced the car without relief for twenty-three and one-half hours. Through complete exhaustion, vertigo, throwing up, he drove to a twenty-five-mile lead over a factory German Mercedes. Well back of the lone Mercedes, the balance of the field droned on.

In late pit stops, Pierre could neither speak nor hear. He was only clear in the knowledge that the weight of his own pride and the honor of his France rested squarely on him. Tragic that he didn't comprehend that for the last half-hour of racing he could have dropped his 100 mph lap times in half and won comfortably. In a moment of delirium, traveling at full bore . . . he mal-shifted . . . the drive train snapped and the car coasted to a stop. When lifted from his stricken Talbot, Levegh was too weak to even weep.

His personal agony didn't end when the race car broke. It went on with rejection of what he had done by the people of France. It was judged that his stubbornness in refusing relief had cost a great victory.

Only God knows the personal struggle that brought him to sign with the Germans he hated so much for the 1955 running. Only a true racing man could know anything about his immense hunger for victory.

In the United States, the American Automobile Association (AAA) had "had it" for racing. The AAA Contest Board had been the guiding hand for major league speedway racing for fifty years. They had run things with an "iron fist!" Veteran driver Duane Carter was asked to come from behind the wheel to head a new sanctioning body called the United States Auto Club (USAC). The problems of pulling an organization into being were overshadowed by the need to guarantee that a

Driver Duane Carter came from behind the steering wheel in 1955 to lead the newly formed United States Auto Club when the American Automobile Association dropped racing. The death of Bill Vukovich in the 500 and the death of about 100 in a racing accident in France prompted the AAA to quit.

catastrophe like that in France would not repeat. Cars and tracks would have to be made safer. Spectators would have to be sealed off from the wheeled missiles.

The enclosed letter from USAC historian Donald Davidson speaks of the manner in which records were *not* passed down.

Pete DePaolo in the first racer to run the 500 at more than 100 mph average. Twenty-five years after this Duesenberg appeared, the cars were structurally very little better for a driver. He sat just as high and loose in the cockpit.

Compare Andy Linden's 1952 Indianapolis entry with Pete DePaolo's 1925 winner.

Strides toward driver survival were plateaued on the matter of the waist belt.

Times of relative quiet for the new United States Auto Club must be predated 1958. The USAC, like AAA before it, saw the assignment as supervising and scoring racing. Technical judgments had to do most often with rubber tires, metal alloys and engine oils. Great good came to the American motorist from their work. The men who crawled behind the steering wheels were very little better off than their elder brothers who raced before the balloon tire and automatic starter.

There was nothing in the *INSTRUCTIONS FOR DRIVERS* for the 1953 running of the Indianapolis 500 that spoke about the matter of seat belts. Drivers were "urged" to use fire-repellent fluid on outside clothes. Crews were encouraged to do the same. The "fluid" was of very limited value.

INSTRUCTIONS FOR DRIVERS:

1. All new drivers must pass a physical examination before driving. Contact Mr. Frank Bain at Chief Steward's Office regarding time and place.
2. All other drivers must pass a physical examination before attempting to qualify a car. Physical examinations for such drivers will be held at the SPEEDWAY HOSPITAL, WEDNESDAY, May 13th at 1:00 p.m. If you are unable to be present at that time, contact Mr. Frank Bain.
3. Crash helmets must be worn when driving.
4. Colored goggles, if worn, must be checked by chief observer or medical staff member.
5. Removable bridgework and dentures must be removed before driving.

PLEASE
NOTE:

6. It is urged that all drivers, garage and pit crew members, use fire repellent fluid on their clothes at all times, particularly the outside garments. This material is available in the First-Aid Station in the garage area. Immerse the clothing in the solution and permit it to dry. No harm will result to clothing or skin.
7. Any driver in an accident on the track on any pre-race day must be examined by a member of the Medical Staff before he can drive again.
8. Any driver involved in a minor accident on Race Day will please report to the hospital. This is the quickest way to get the news to your friends and relatives that you are uninjured.
9. A First-Aid Station and ambulance will be available in the pit area after May 1st.
10. Doctors will be on duty at the Speedway Hospital all night preceding the Race.
11. This Medical Staff has been hired to help you. Use it.

C. B. Bohner, M.D.
Medical Director
Indianapolis Motor Speedway

United States Auto Club
4910 West 16th Street, Speedway, Indiana 46224

Cable USAC Indianapolis

Phone (317) 244-7637

October 4, 1971

Mr. Jack Albinson
115 Meander Rd.
Minneapolis, Minnesota 55422

Dear Jack,

The helmet was first used in this country in 1932 and had become mandatory in AAA as of 1935. It was not mandatory in Europe until 1952. I do not have any specific details on seat belts except that crude forms of seat belts were used well before the war. They were optional at least as late as 1949 when Rex Mays' choice not to wear one cost him his life in November of that year. I don't know when they became mandatory other than I am reasonably certain they were required by the time USAC took over in January, 1956. The roll bar was made mandatory January 1, 1959 and the fire retardant uniform, recommended for a number of years, became mandatory January 1, 1960. Rather crudely, uniforms were made fire retardant by soaking them in a barrel containing water mixed with a powder solution. Fuel cells, of course, were made mandatory January 1, 1965. At the moment, there are no legal requirements concerning foot wear, however, fire retardant socks are strongly recommended. A fire retardant shoe is being developed and I would anticipate a mandatory ruling very soon.

I read your book only seconds during the long drive to Pocono and was able to discuss Ramo Stott's mobile home with him that night. By the way, if you have never been to Pocono, it makes Brainerd seem like a metropolitan city.

Please find enclosed, your dollar.

Sincerely,

Donald C. Davidson
Statistician

DCD/jh

Enc.

CHAPTER ELEVEN

Special Entry Le Mans Update 1972

The terrible hours of darkness were past. In the golden first light of dawn over the sprawling grounds of Le Mans, Swedish driver Jo Bonnier prepared to enter the fast left-hand turn called "Indianapolis!" He moved his racing Lola under a Ferrari piloted by Swiss, Florian Velich. At approximately 180 mph, Bonnier appeared to tap the tail of the Ferrari, which was holding its right-of-way on the course. The Lola skidded, vaulted a barrier and flew more than fifteen feet in the air. The car shattered on impact in a growth of trees.

Driver Bonnier was found five hundred feet from the accident. Death had been instantaneous. The last of the great "polo shirt and tennis shoe drivers" was gone. A few days before his death he had pronounced the Le Mans Course, "Very, very safe!" His judgment meant something because Jo had founded the G.P.D.A. (Gran Prix Drivers Assn.) in 1959 and had been the group's only president. Wider, safer and better racecourses around the world are testimony to his efforts.

It is certainly tragic that 42-year-old Joakim Bonnier never saw his way to leading a crusade for seat belts and harnesses.

French builders won their first Le Mans in twenty-two years. A Matra Simca took the win with 2,915 miles in 24 hours. There wasn't much flag waving. Like 1955, 1972 had been very expensive.

CHAPTER TWELVE

Help!! Turn Three

Car builder George Salih was the man with the combination to watch as the forces of racing gathered at The Speedway in 1958. His bright yellow creations presented the lowest profile ever seen at the old raceway. Salih had mastered the intricate lubricating problems encountered in laying a potent Offenhauser engine on its side and winding it full out.

Brilliant old campaigner Sam Hanks had steered his first "layover" creation to victory the year before. Hanks, eyes filled with tears, had announced his retirement from the seat of the car in Victory Lane.

The big cowboy out of Arizona, Jim Bryan, was under contract to drive this 500. Bryan was defending National Champion. On paper, "Big Jim" in the super low, super quick Salih car seemed a sure thing. Like Barney Oldfield in the early days, Jim chomped on a great big unlit cigar as he raced. When the going was rough the cigar wound up half eaten. Two men of Jim's caliber, Pat O'Connor and Tony Bettenhausen, were not to be taken lightly either.

Practice and qualification produced the unexpected. The three drivers who set the pace had not shown this kind of potential before. Dick Rathmann, Ed Elisian and Jimmy Reece were all veterans, but were not men taken seriously to contend or win. Dick Rathmann had a record qualification run of 145.974 mph. He would command the field from the inside front row. Ed Elisian earned the middle of the front row with a qualification run that included a lap of 146.508 mph, a track record. Rathmann and Elisian were not on good terms and had punched and counter-punched lap speeds during the month like a couple of champion middleweight boxers. One would post a blistering lap time and the other would roll out and "shoot it down" before the news was out. Ed Elisian was, increasingly, talked of as a "menace." Much had been said and written about the personal problems that might have motivated him to desperation. Most of the "scuttlebutt" dealt with his gambling debts, traffic violations and terrific personal problems.

Let it be noted here that if debt were a reason for racing drivers to act irresponsibly and generate tragedy, the number who would have survived in fifty years could be counted on one hand. Large personal debts are as much a part of auto racing as motor oil.

The point must be made that Ed Elisian, the unsung hero of the 1955 Indianapolis 500, finally had a car with which he could contend. Dick Rathmann and Jimmy Reece had more car than they had known before, too. Young A. J. Watson of Oklahoma had built for all three men.

Favorite Jimmy Bryan was pushed back to seventh starting position. His big cigars were grinding in his teeth and his eyes were narrowed to slits. Battle lines were drawn. The morning of the race, popular Pat O'Connor told the waiting throng that he had slept well, enjoyed a steak for breakfast and believed all would be well after the first couple of laps.

Cigar-chomping Jimmy Bryan won in this super-low "layover car." The engine was flat on its side, and Bryan flat on the throttle in a close 1958 Classic. Bryan was the first to use a protective roll bar in conjunction with shoulder harness.

It is a merciful thing that driver Ed Elisian couldn't see what was just ahead for him when this picture was taken in 1958. He would be party to two disasters in a little over a year's time. The last would take his life.

Dick Rathmann was on the "pole," and paced the field at the start in 1958. Before the race was thirty seconds old . . . Pat O'Connor was dead and a dozen cars wrecked.

The multicolored cars were pushed into starting positions under warm clear skies.

The parade and pace laps went anything but well. In a fouled-up new starting arrangement, Dick Rathmann thought he got the signal to move slowly down the track. Elisian was standing by his car when Rathmann pulled away. Vaulting in, he charged after the fading Rathmann, Jimmy Reece right on his tail. The Oldsmobile pace car, in a novel arrangement, came next and then more racers in ten rows of three.

The pace car controlled thirty racers for two laps, waiting for the confused front row, half a lap away, to catch up. They didn't and thirty cars came down to a picture start led by the pace car. The green flag was shown. The front row (qualified fourth, fifth and sixth fastest) included veterans Bob Veith, Pat O'Connor and Johnny Parsons.

In the first turn . . . the yellow light blinked on! The field slowed down and reformed. Race director Sam Hanks started to go on the track in the pace car to get control when—down the front straight the field came, with the tardy front row in process of slamming past the tightly bunched formation. All were *roughly* in position at the starting line and the green flag came out the second time. Sam Hanks, on track in the pace car, had to drive for his very life!

Pole-sitter Dick Rathmann led through turns one and two, Elisian on his tail. Both had vowed to lead the first lap. It is impossible to imagine their state of mind, with all the natural problems of the most dangerous moment in sport, compounded with the "Hair Breadth Hairy" they had just gone through.

Flying up the back straight, Elisian would not be denied the lead. He entered the third turn too fast. Official observers judged, or guessed, up to forty miles per hour too fast. He spun around, hit Dick Rathmann, and the two cars went to the outer wall together. The front third of Rathmann's car was severed.

Jim Reece, in third place, hit his brakes in a fatal mistake. He was struck by Bob Veith. The front end of Veith's car was demolished. Reece was shoved down into the course of Pat O'Connor who tripped over him broadside. O'Connor landed upside down and died instantly of head injuries. His worst fears for the start were now grim fact.

Several rows got through and another key and unnecessary spin opened the flood gates again. Jerry Unser flew over the wall off the tail of former motorcycle champion Paul Goldsmith, and went end for end in high bounces outside the wall. Unser survived with shoulder injuries.

Eight racers were reduced to scrap. More than a dozen were damaged, but rolling. Mechanics worked like men on a battlefield to keep shattered equipment moving. Their most important tool had to be the metal shears. Crunched sections were simply cut away. Tar gouged from the surface of pit row, rags, wire and even great globs of chewing gum were used to plug holes and close seams. Great bent pieces, time and time again, fell to the track as the cars staggered on. This author will never forget watching Ed Elisian walking back to the pits to "face the music!" Those who write of his being found wandering, blank, in the huge infield simply were not there or are not interested in the truth.

All the cars from the third row, Jim Bryan, Johnny Boyd and Tony Bettenhausen, joined by little George Amick who survived in the ninth row, put on one of the best races ever. All four had a great shot at victory right down to the flag. Jim Bryan won and George Amick was second. Jimmy Reece, from the maligned front row, was able to keep going after being run into by Veith and over by Pat O'Connor. He actually drove five hundred miles on track faster than any man up to that time. Extensive time in the pits to have his wreckage attended kept him back in sixth place. He would die racing before another Memorial Day, as would starters, George Amick, Jerry Unser, Marshall Teague and Art Bisch.

Little George Amick showed 'em how to qualify on a "super speedway" in the spring of 1959. The 144-pound ace averaged 176.887 mph on the two-and-a-half-mile Daytona International Speedway. Before the start of the first and last race for Indy Cars on a giant highbank, he laughed and said, "If you lose it here . . . your rump's a grape!"

He lost it, got airborne and flipped ten times. His gleaming Bowes Special was literally ground down in a sea of sparks that

Typical flying start of the roadster era. **The moment** was both beautiful and terrible. The leaders have crossed the Start/Finish line . . . gone past the pits into the southwest turn (No. 1).

showed every color in the rainbow. The little Finnish boy from northern Wisconsin never knew what happened. Jim Rathmann, brother of Dick, won the race at 170.261 miles an hour—a new world's record.

Thirteen of the thirty-three drivers who started in 1958 at Indy have given their lives in racing. Some who were in the field are still active in major competition.

Ed Elisian would find opportunity to drive a few more times. He would not appear at Indy again. August of 1959, he would qualify for a championship race at Milwaukee. Death would find him, hanging upside down, uninjured in a virtually unscarred roadster. Spilling fuel ignited and Ed was consumed in nearly invisible alcohol flame. The book on Ed Elisian closed. Fire, the wicked enemy that took him, would be dealt with years later.

The protective roll bar was seen for the first time at Indianapolis in 1958, on winner Jim Bryan's car. The rugged chrome-molly bar was mounted behind the driver's head and conformed to his head and shoulders. In the event of a rollover or a blow from top or side . . . the bar was designed to serve as a shield. Jim Bryan employed a shoulder harness to keep himself firm in the car and aligned with his chrome armor. The pointless death of Pat O'Connor, shown on TV and in photos to the world, was the key to requiring the bar by rule. Every car had one for the 1959 "Race of Races." Jim Bryan and George Salih started something really wonderful for the racing driver.

Jim Bryan determined to race only Indy after his 500 victory in 1958. For some unexplained reason, he traveled to Langhorne,

THE OILY GRAIL

Penn., in the summer of 1960 to race Rodger Ward's "dirt track car." In the heavy traffic of the first lap, the car lost traction. Bryan fought for control. The machine caught a rut in a part of the course called "Puke Hollow" and started to tumble end for end. The equipment in which he had believed and for which he was partially responsible... was not properly employed. Hanging from the car, hands straight over head, he never had a chance. At thirty-three years of age, one of racing's truly great men was dead.

The well-known gulch that started the tragedy was the product of washout around a culvert. For years a stomach-rending lurch was always part of passing this way.

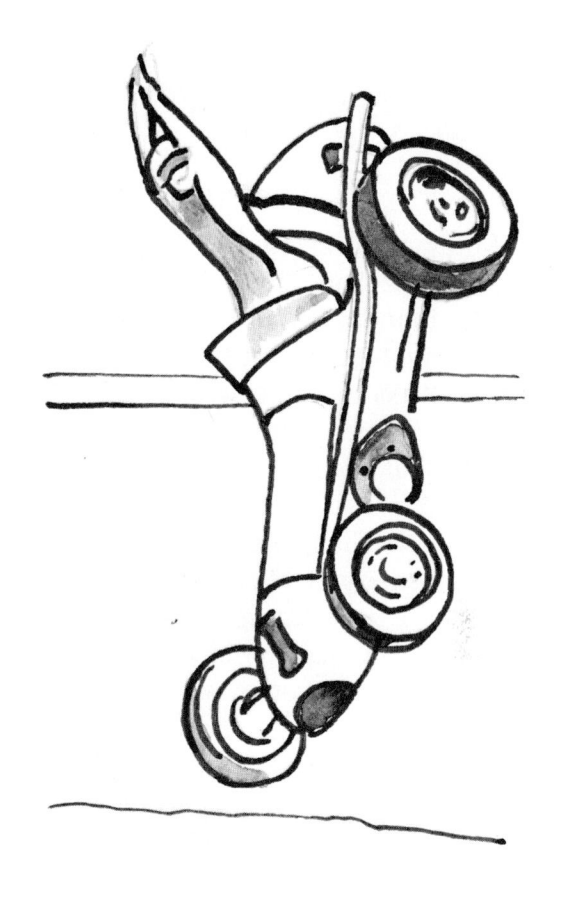

Jim Bryan surely would have lived with a cage like those saving lives daily in USAC sprint racing. Indy cars out of USAC still do not have to have the cages.

Bill Vukovich died in a situation less violent than the one Larry Cannon found himself in at Winchester, Indiana. Cannon was injured, but today is one of the great young stars of open-cockpit racing.

CHAPTER THIRTEEN

The Flimsy Cars

A full-blown invasion from the road courses of Europe had given Indianapolis a shaking to its foundation by 1964. Jim Clark, world road-racing champion, led a delegation from England that threatened to totally outclass American men and machines. The Europeans had come with radical, super-light, rear engine cars that gave USAC technical men nightmares. The major European constructors' philosophy was, "Build light and strengthen where necessary." The established American approach had been, "Build solid and lighten with better engineering and materials."

The dilemma of what to allow truly compromised the Indianapolis Speedway. Poorly engineered and constructed cars were everywhere. Flimsy was the word for steering and suspension. Fuel tank design and placement was truly an offense to sound technical judgment. Drivers described their position as that of a man on his back in a tub of gasoline. Some machines carried fuel in "saddle tanks" that placed cells over a driver's thighs. Eddie Sachs advertised, "I call my car a rolling gas tank!" It surely proved to be one.

The Japanese had rented the Speedway for testing Formula I cars. The machines rolled out of "Gasoline Alley" toward the track pits without any kind of seat belts and no provision to install them. American driver Ronnie Bucknum shrugged his shoulders and climbed in while Speedway Officials swallowed hard. Bucknum suggested that after a few laps he didn't even think about it.

The most curious entries were Mickey Thompson creations on tiny fifteen-inch tires. They were actually Ford-powered 200 mph "Go Karts," radical enough to be banned temporarily in response to protest from veteran owners and drivers. At best they were unpredictable. *Car and Driver Magazine* wrote at the time, "Hopefully we have seen the last of Mickey Thompson at Indianapolis. His machines were ill-conceived and ill-prepared. They were ugly, which is not important. What is important is that they were totally un-aerodynamic, even with their 1937 spaceship styling."

A prominent British tire company came with great confidence and no real knowledge of the problems at hand. Their tires broke up so badly at Indianapolis speeds that chunks could be found lying on the ground two blocks from the track. In the race, their failure pounded the suspension of a leading car to collapse. A team car was called in and retired for safety reasons . . . a decision and announcement that required real character.

This year Parnelli Jones, A. J. Foyt, Bobby Marshman and Eddie Sachs represented America's best hopes. Parnelli Jones elected to race in a heavy, traditional, front-engine roadster like the one that carried him to victory in 1963. A. J. Foyt, 1961 winner, went roadster. Bobby Marshman cast his lot in a lightweight British rear-engine Lotus. The car would trap him in flames during a tire test in late season and demand his life. His

The late Mexican ace, Pedro Rodriguez, in a car at Indianapolis that was a "duke's mixture" of a number of European builders. It could have been entered under the title . . . "You Name It!!!"

Parnelli Jones was able to overcome a serious oil leak and Jim Clark in a rear-engine Lotus, to win the 1963 "500." Those who didn't win the race felt that Parnelli should have been removed from the racecourse through use of the black flag (signaling disqualification). The race and the argument were both excellent.

Eddie Sachs was one of the brightest stars to ever come to Indianapolis. Everything about him had a touch of the spectacular. His death by fire in the 1964 running of the 500 is still deeply felt.

Jim Clark came as World Champion to the great Speedway in 1963. The little Scotchman in his radical, rear-engined Lotus started a revolution in design and driving concepts that hasn't settled yet.

widow would sue for gross negligence. Ad copy said, "Eddie Sachs is the man to keep your eye on." Eddie elected to go rear-engine in a creation that people in the stands thought might go all the way nonstop. The racer was set up to run on gasoline which, in an accident, could act like dynamite. Gasoline could, at the same time, stretch his mileage drastically over machines using alcohol blends . . . the choice could blow sky high or open the way to Victory Lane.

Sachs hungered for victory and had promised his wife Nancy that with it he would unconditionally retire. It had been in his grasp three years before. While Nancy was being ushered to meet him in Victory Lane, a tire flashed a built-in warning strip. He was a few moments from victory and leading by more than a mile. The message from the tire was answered by his brain and not his heavy right foot . . . and victory fell to A. J. Foyt.

Controversy over his decision to stop, against trying to make it on the spent tire, still goes on. Sachs never allowed himself to live in the realm of the past or the "If Onlys." His immediate response was, "Better second than hanging out there on the wall!" He seemed to approach everything in life with the joy and zeal of a small child choosing his first bike. There was something about him that sparkled. He possessed an impish smile and responded to most things with a happy, "Oh, Boy!!" He was a brilliant public speaker, maybe the best ever from the realm of sport, and could do more through appearances and television for a race promoter in three days than an ad company could do in a year. He thought nothing of weeping openly. He loved to go out and walk in the crowds rather than avoid them. He loved people, and contact with them gave him refreshment.

The Indianapolis Speedway, he declared, was the fulfillment of all his dreams. Over the long pull, racing had broken and abused him terribly, as it must anyone who follows it all the way. In a serious moment he said, "When I look at Nancy and my little baby boy—it makes all the hell I've been through worthwhile." There weren't very many serious moments. If he could fall in and lead a marching band with an imaginary baton or do a funny bit . . . he was always "On."

The start of the Indianapolis 500 and the command, "Gentlemen . . . start your engines!" so flooded his eyes with tears that he jokingly declared that it took two laps before he could really see. Eddie Sachs loved race enthusiasts in any form. They were "his people." Race fans from every corner of the nation loved Eddie Sachs just the way he was.

Jim Clark and Jack Brabham had been World Champions on the road circuits across Europe. They had hundreds of hours of driving time in the rear-engine creations so totally strange and new to veterans of the 500. They didn't go walking in the crowds and there wasn't a funny bone in their bodies. They didn't like Indianapolis, but they did like the dollars offered for coming.

There were drivers from American amateur and professional road racing who had never been part of anything like the brutal flying start at Indy. Walt Hansgen and Dave McDonald were sharp American sport car drivers who, on the basis of long experience with rear-engine machinery, qualified very well. The wealth of the world's driving talent was here. With the "salt," a serious number of untried men waited for "race day." The cars were loaded with unknowns. The total situation was so tense you could "hear it tick."

Race day dawned dark and cold. Thankfully, the wind was not a factor. The crowd seemed charged because of the overtone of international pride involved. I remember a tough old character, with credentials to be

Jim Clark jumps pole-position winner A. J. Foyt, to lead in the first turn of the 1965 Indy race. The field of cars is already strung out. Wheel-to-wheel racing went out with the end of the front-engine roadster cars.

in Gasoline Alley, leaning into the garage of Scotchman Jim Clark and barking, "I hope you crash!" Clark thanked him cordially.

Aerial bombs, the release of thousands of colorful balloons, the formal moments of preparation and finally the roar of thirty-three engines . . . the prima moment in sport was here. A "stack fire" in the engine of pole-sitter Jim Clark sent a chill through those near the starting line. The "omen fire" in the green and yellow Lotus was quickly extinguished. The field moved slowly ahead. Clark led a beautiful parade lap and used the gear box of his road racer like a violin to establish

a narrow lead over a screaming Parnelli Jones . . . followed closely by Bobby Marshman and Rodger Ward. Jones fell back and lap one was scored—Clark, Marshman and Ward. Dan Gurney started to move on the leaders from his fourth-row starting place. Lap two fell to Clark and . . . it wasn't important anymore!

Off from turn four, at the head of the straightaway, Dave McDonald had lost control of his red Mickey Thompson "roller skate." He was spinning at 150 mph toward the inside wall. Dust kicked into the air an instant before impact, and then a great geyser of fire rolled toward heaven. Driver Bob Veith sped by on the outside as the engulfed McDonald car caromed back on the racetrack.

Eddie Sachs, brimming with gasoline, tried to move out around McDonald's sliding pyre, but the space closed. Eddie hit McDonald and a second unbelievable gas explosion tore the air. People in nearby grandstands were flash burned and jostled in momentary panic. Drivers coming at more than 140 mph plunged blindly into the smoke and fire. Bobby Unser applied full power in his 800 h.p. Novi in the belief that he would have to bulldoze out to live. Young Johnny Rutherford made the same judgment. In the midst of the inferno, Rutherford vaulted clean over the thundering Unser car. Ronnie Duman was struck by one of the chargers in the "eye of the fire" and pushed out toward the inner wall. Cars emerging from the firestorm were all in flame. Rutherford and Unser tried to blow out their fires by acceleration. They came together and stopped safely along the outer wall. Duman was still in his car which was burning furiously. A photographer rushed to his side and wrenched him free.

Chuck Stevenson led several others through without hitting anything. Norm Hall elected to spin to the inner wall rather than enter the death cloud. Others locked their brakes and ground their tires to a stop. The track was totally blocked.

For the first time in history, the race was stopped for an accident. Eddie Sachs was dead in his wreckage. Dave McDonald was dying of burns. Ronnie Duman was seriously burned. The raging battle on the track was now against fire and not a stopwatch. The crowd was totally stunned. Beautiful little wives of men involved were led stumbling to the field hospital. Thousands left for home, sickened by the unannounced but obvious tragedy on track.

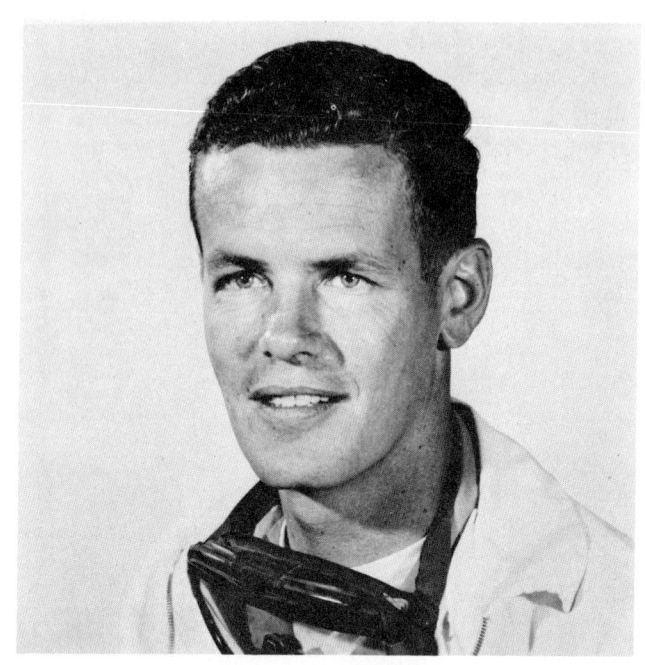

Driver Bobby Unser was in three 500s before he completed one lap of competition. In 1963 he crashed a Novi in the first thirty seconds. In 1964 he had to drive through the ball of fire that took two lives on the first lap. Times changed. He won the race in 1968. He will probably win it again. Young brother, Al Unser, won in 1970 and again in 1971.

Johnny Rutherford has survived terrible injuries to be a great racing driver. In 1964 he had no choice but to drive into the inferno that took Eddie Sachs and Dave McDonald. He got through.

Parnelli Jones vaulted from his burning Bowes Seal Fast Special as it rumbled down pit row toward the southwest turn. The full fuel tank exploded when the filler cap was slammed shut in the last second of a pit stop. Parnelli blasted out of his pit without knowledge of the fire. A static spark was blamed.

One hour and forty minutes passed before the surface was clear and the engines restarted. The race that followed was filled with more pathos. A white cloud of fire-extinguisher dust blinded drivers a second time at the accident scene. In the tight traffic of re-start all somehow got through.

Later, race leader Parnelli Jones jumped from his flaming car as it roared down pit row, a victim of a freak static spark while taking on fuel.

Jim Clark held on while the rear end of his tiny Lotus folded down on the track in a sea of sparks. The Indianapolis Motor Speedway would never be the same again.

Brave winner A. J. Foyt said, "You got to carry on in racin'. I don't have any close friends in racing anymore . . . you can't let anybody get too close."

Fuel tanks containing fuel cells to control fire were made mandatory for all cars on January 1, 1965. Since then, tank placement and capacity has been strictly controlled. Rigid rules concerning fueling during pit stops have been worked out. Fire-retardant uniforms had been required since January 1, 1960. The intention was good, the armor was weak. Uniforms were dipped in a naphtha solution buying a precious few seconds in fire. Technology came through with a better

Jim Clark at speed in his Ford-powered Lotus racer. The car was designed for road racing in Europe, but adapted to Indianapolis and sustained speed very well. Fuel is carried in front of and beside the driver . . . who lays on his back. The engine throbs immediately behind the driver's head.

way in the late 1960s. The *fireproof* wonder material Nomex is required for all uniforms today. An underwear-coverall combination of the material leaves only a modern driver's eyeballs uncovered. Odds are very strong for surviving the worst flames.

Good and bad, joy and sorrow have come to the Speedway since 1964. The "jet turbines" had a couple of glorious seasons. The day-glow red, whisper-quiet creations of Andy Granatelli caught the attention of the world. Eliminated by legislation, they will return.

The prize for the race today is one million dollars. The best drivers from across the entire world vie in cars that look like hammerhead sharks. Graduates of Ivy League Colleges qualify for front row positions. A realistic target is the 200 mph lap. Jim Hurtubise, Mario Andretti and others have survived incredible crashes because of belts, helmets, roll bars, proper fabrication, scientific fuel tanks and fireproof clothing. The concern has been in every way to assure survival. In 1966, eleven cars were shattered before the field of thirty-three got into the first turn. God was good and the cars were excellent. Only A. J. Foyt needed treatment for a cut finger. He got that on wire fencing while trying to jump from the disaster area to the safety of the seats. The worst injury came to a spectator in those seats who sat on a paring knife while trying to duck a flying wheel.

Foyt went through a multi-car last lap crash to win in 1967. Nobody was hurt. Six men have died in track action since 1964. Greater and greater speed will always increase the elements of danger. Come what may, it is expected that the men who qualify to race at Indianapolis will survive.

A. J. Foyt of Houston, Texas, is doubtless the best of American drivers in the modern era. He has won wherever men have raced automobiles, in whatever form the cars have taken. He has three 500 wins to his credit and even won the 24 Hours of Le Mans in France.

CHAPTER FOURTEEN

Cry Peace

The 1971 500 held all the elements of crisis experienced since 1930. A ragged start settled into a velvet-smooth race...for fifteen minutes. Mark Donohue led with ease in a dart-shaped blue and gold "Sunoco McLaren." In the northeast turn on lap sixteen, a group of tightly packed racers re-created the events of thirteen years before and the abortive start of Memorial Day, 1958, that took the life of Pat O'Connor. This day, all the men would run to safety.

The green racer of Mel Kenyon was cut in two by the car of Gordon Johncock. Johncock's orange racer got airborne, hit the wall and was shattered on rebound by Mario Andretti's red STP McNamara Special. The cars involved were junk. Fires flared instantly, but this time the men and machines were prepared. The drivers escaped without burns, and highly trained crews contained the fires with ease.

With the race half gone, a wheel tore free from white No. 4, driven by Hoosier Mike Mosley. The car started a sickening slide just where Dave McDonald had lost control in 1964. Bobby Unser in a dark blue, evil-looking Eagle Racer came out of turn four looking for the leader (his brother Al Unser in No. 1) and victory. He speared Mosley, and like 1964 a great geyser of flame shot into the sky. Gary Bettenhausen, who followed Unser through the turn, braked hard and jumped from his rolling racer to aid striken Mike Mosley. One's mind flashed back to 1955 and Ed Elisian coming to aid Bill Vukovich. This time there was life. One mighty flash of fire and the control bladders took over. Fireproof clothing stood the test. Mosley was injured, but helmet, belts and proper construction had seen him through the impossible. He had been run through by a dart nose at 160 mph and survived to race again the same season.

Bobby Unser was able to stand tall beside his wrecked Eagle and wave his younger brother Al to victory in "Vels-Parnelli Jones Johnny Lightning Topper Toys 500 Special." The car's name was longer than the race. He streaked to victory on his thirty-second birthday at 157.735 mph, a new record. The Speedway's special delivery birthday package was $240,000.

Every man that started this contest got a prize of sorts...the benefit of knowledge and equipment purchased in human heartbreak, suffering and death at the Indianapolis Motor Speedway in over half a century.

The aura of well-being on West 16th Street lasted about ten months. "Men cried peace ...but the Unsers were already in the field!" April of 1972 brought Bobby Unser, winner in 1968, to the track for tire testing in a radical new, white Eagle Racer. A huge wing on the tail seemed to glue mysterious Goodyear tires to the surface. When the signal came to "put your leg in it" Bobby responded with speed that seemed to stop time. Stopwatch figures showed Unser at lap speeds better than 190 mph. Impossible! The news spread like wildfire to the racing world and was

Steve Krisiloff spins in oil at the midpoint of turn three. The stage is set for the entry of Mel Kenyon, Gordon Johncock and STP teammate Mario Andretti. (1971)

Miracle of 1971 Indy 500 . . . Gordon Johncock runs through car of Mel Kenyon and leaves tire print on Mel's helmet. Mario Andretti (lower right) charges toward Johncock. Contact came the next instant. There were no serious injuries.

Gordon Johncock has run over Mel Kenyon. Mario Andretti enters the scene to spear him while still airborne. Johncock, Andretti and Krisiloff escaped without injury. Mel Kenyon ran from his machine with only a leg laceration. Kenyon's escape has to be one of the most incredible of all Speedway history. (Note track observers fleeing positions outside the fence.)

Al Unser has two Indianapolis 500 wins to his credit. He took the "Johnny Lightning 500 Special" home in 1970 and 1971. Sixty years before, the average speed was 74.59 mph. Al averaged 157.735. Compare the tires, car and track surface with the thin tires, cars and bricks of the early days.

My Firestone tires certainly played a major role in this outstanding victory! They performed great!
Al Unser

judged either a joke or a tactical ploy by Goodyear.

Jim Malloy, "the Colorado Comet," made record laps of 180.5 and 181.415 within seconds of the signal for official open practice the first Monday in May. The lid was indeed off!

Handsome and talented Jim Malloy . . . had every reason to smile as he anticipated the 1972 Indy 500. He was a serious contender to win it all.

In spite of days of rain, Bobby Unser, with the countenance of the "Ancient Mariner" worked up to 196.678 mph. (Picture yourself driving two and one-half miles on a flat curved road in 45.76 seconds.)

The wonderful record efforts of Peter Revson in 1971 went down by nearly 17 mph. Historically an increase of three miles per hour in one year had been considered phenomenal.

The men who drive Indy were moving in a dimension they knew almost nothing about. At 180 mph, the sharp, flat turns were full of terror. Jimmy Malloy led many practice sessions and spoke fluently through TV and press about his life as a driver. He projected himself as a nice guy with clear goals and plenty of real fear. He was a natural for the media people. In a Sunday practice session, Jim was on a 185 mph lap when deep in turn three the car inclined to an inside spin. Instantly Jim initiated correction . . . steering into the slide: For reasons totally unexplained, the car snapped 90° to the right and plunged straight into the wall.

Unbelief . . . terrible noise . . . searing fire . . . destruction!! The car had rolled up on Jim's legs.

A powerful new rescue tool was brought in, and opened what was left of the machine in ten minutes.

A dying young man was lifted out. It would appear that helmets, belts, structures, fire materials . . . in any combination couldn't have done a thing for Malloy. The last faint spark of life oozed out of him the following Thursday.

Scotsman Jackie Stewart spoke for European drivers of world stature, confirming their judgment that matters at Indy were out of hand. Percentages for surviving crisis at speeds being generated were not good enough.

Activity at the track had to go on. The slowest of the sober young men to be qualified for the race was a Southerner, Cale Yarborough, who dialed in at 178.864 mph. Peter Revson, fastest man just the year before, had driven the ten miles at 178.696.

Race-day morning, the call from track owner Antone Hulman, "Gentlemen . . . Start your engines!!!" moved the race from the

These one-of-a-kind photos by John Mahoney catch the end for Jim Malloy. The tracks indicate the impossible line the car took as it rocketed into the third turn retaining wall. The car explodes like a bomb against the wall.

The right front corner of the car is doubled back on itself, causing it to return to the wall for a second impact.

Great chunks of what is left of the car fly away as it moves at terrible speed down the "North Short Chute" and finally toward the infield grass. Driver Jim Malloy is trapped and beyond help.

realm of speculation by experts and "doom sayers" to the strong hands of the men at the wheel.

The engine of three-time winner A. J. Foyt didn't cooperate and he all but ate his red driving gloves while his crew struggled at the rear of his cold and temperamental Ford. It would not fire! Surely the field would wait for one of the great champions of all time. Thirty-two racers came out of turn four behind him and swept toward the starting line. Tony Hulman, in the pace car at the head of the field, held one arm high in the air signaling one more parade turn around the course. At the starting line, flagman Pat Vidan held an arm high in the air with the same message. Straight ahead down the track the caution light flashed yellow.

At the last possible instant, Astronaut Pete Conrad received communication in the pace car to get off the track . . . it would be a START!! Pace-car driver Jim Rathmann, winner 1960, steered hard left for the pit entry. Front-row driver Bobby Unser held back and watched in wide-eyed dismay as the pace car swerved within inches of the nose of his precious car.

On the starter's stand, Pat Vidan showed the green flag. Course lights continued to show yellow—their amber message was clear *DON'T RACE!!*

Some drivers paused and waited to reform, some read the flag and boomed up to speed. The thirty-two-car field and the pace car nibbled an instant with the possibilities of reduction to fiery scrap. In God's mercy the "Greatest Moment In Sports" was only ragged—not violent.

Bobby Unser swallowed the lump in his throat and joined the program with a passion. He led with ease until a minor part failed and took him out. Peter Revson inherited the lead and appeared to be on the way until mechanical woes left him cold in the pits.

Mike Mosley took command from Gary Bettenhausen on lap No. 56 as Gary steered his blue "McLaren" toward the pits. Charging out of the fourth turn, the new leader found himself a helpless passenger in his four-year-old Eagle Racer. The car shuddered . . . Mosley braced as the left-front wheel tore free! The white machine slashed the wall and burst into flames—ricocheted away and started a sickening arc to the right as 185 mph traffic closed in. A second bash into the wall at more than 100 mph found Mosley standing in the seat. Feet burning, he threw himself to the pavement.

While rescue and fire personnel rushed to his side, he rose on his tortured feet and stumbled toward the nearest man with an extinguisher.

Ironic as it seems, Mosley made contact on the wall less than five hundred feet from where he crashed just the year before . . . after having a wheel tear away.

One's mind boggles at the notion of lying in the compressed cockpit of a tiny race car and looking straight ahead at a white concrete wall or solid object with full knowledge that you are going to hit at the better part of 200 mph. The armor that is part of your machine and that you wear on your body will be meaningful only if you can go in at a shallow angle. That's it!!!! If you are going to glance it, prepare for fire and where you are going to run. If you are going straight in, anticipate the presence of God.

The race did come to a conclusion in about the time it takes to play a baseball game. A terribly shy young graduate engineer from Brown University, Mark Donohue, took the checkered flag after leading just 13 laps. Some compared his victory to the Schulz

THE OILY GRAIL

Winner of pole position for 1971 Indianapolis 500 ... Brown University graduate in Engineering, Mark Donohue.

The bewildered Jerry Grant.

character "Charlie Brown" winning a world series ball game.

The way officials handled the race from the divided start to post-race penalties for conduct during pit stops will be disputed as long as the meet is recounted.

For 1972, the management reached back to "Rickenbacker Tradition" of the 1930s and limited total fuel consumption for the running of the race. Limitations didn't appear to be too harsh! The racers were required to average a mile and one-half on each gallon of their exotic fuel blends.[1] Believe it or not ... some, including Mario Andretti, couldn't stretch it and didn't get home. Some obvious alternatives to running dry were tried, but didn't prove to be very fruitful. Driver Jerry Grant borrowed a little from a teammate's supply and had to forfeit $72,000 hard-earned prize dollars. Unfortunately for Grant and owner Dan Gurney, nothing absolute concerning a penalty for dipping into another's fuel was registered in entry forms or written race instructions.[2]

Ahhhhh, but in a business like this, what's $72,000!!!!!!

JUDGE THE STUFF IN THE BOYS BY THE COST OF THEIR TOYS!

---

[1] 500-Mile Race Supplementary Reg. 23 read, "The maximum fuel supply other than that carried in the car shall be 250 gallons stored in one cylindrical container."

[2] A USAC Review Panel said, "The rules do not state specifically that a driver can't use fuel from a teammate's pit."

CHAPTER FIFTEEN

Fire and Water

One could confuse the times of Noah with the early days of May in Indianapolis 1973. It rained . . . and it rained. Those trying to work up to projected 200 mph speeds should have had hydroplane speed boats. Everybody and everything at the track fell days behind schedule, and qualification runs were now a few days away.

Rains lifted by mid-week going down to "Big Saturday," but then terrible winds hindered speed runs and kept the fastest in the low 190 range.

The final hours before qualification day, Art Pollard (super grandpa) posted the day's quick time with a 193.9 lap in his copper and blue colored "Cobre Tire" Eagle. Young Swede Savage was close behind at 193.6. Pollard's age and experience would prevail this bellwether day. Indy's elder statesman had celebrated 46 years of life just the week before. This gracious man from Oregon was what a racing driver should be . . . kind and patient. He was a special hero to children confined in hospitals. No matter how hectic the schedule, they got plenty of his time and he was always working on something special for them. He knew the heaviness of days and weeks in a hospital bed. In a race car, Art Pollard was powerful and fast. He drove for good builders and when the boss said, "Let's try a quick one, Art" . . . Pollard drew on every fiber in the car. He always ran to win. Like any charger he crashed a lot. He should have won the 500 in 1967.

This year he had a pace-setting car and a plan. When the checker came down on race day, he might just put a little bounce in the step of every forty-year-old in the country.

Dangerous winds swept the course as fans poured into the seats for this very special "Hoosier Saturday." When the track closed at 6 p.m. today, the racing world could know what to expect for this million dollar 500. Just thirty-seven minutes into the official warming period, course lights flashed yellow. There was a mighty rush of equipment and attention toward turn No. 1. A car had, without warning, turned straight into the first turn wall, exploded against it, slammed back toward the infield grass, flipped four or five times and come to rest upside down over 1400 feet from impact. A wing torn free bore No. 64. Art Pollard carried No. 64 and it was Art under that burning wreckage.

Like Captain Ahab of Melville's "Moby Dick" he had in the course of the brutal flips seemed to beckon anyone behind to follow. Mythical Captain Ahab, lashed to the great killer whale by harpoon lines, waved his shipmates to follow. The real Art Pollard, unconscious and dying, waved an ominous message. He was rushed to Methodist Hospital where he was pronounced dead. Bulletins said he lasted 63 minutes.

Maybe Art was trying to say, "Come away!" But how could the men who mourned him understand? How could they know that Indy's darkest hours lay just ahead?

If the surging crowds of race day had forgotten Art Pollard in the soggy days between qualification and the running, it appeared the heavens had not.

Periods of driving rain gave pause to a tight schedule of tradition, bands and flurry.

This day great drops seemed to say "We miss you Old Timer and all the others like you from across the long years . . . we'll let 'em eat soggy chicken and just wait."

Rains lifted and the call to start the engines came after more than four hours of delay. A 3 p.m. start seemed unreal . . . and so it was.

The highlight of the race has always been the cool control shown by the thirty-three men at the wheel as they flawlessly harness into eleven rows of three, and thunder down to the starter's flag. This time the old discipline disappeared! Eager chargers at the rear, seeking unfair advantage, telescoped the field. Groping men in machines found themselves four abreast. Escape was impossible. In the middle of the sixth row, young "Salt" Walther (curiously enough a boat racer) caught the beckon to death from "Old Ahab." His car was scuffed and turned toward veteran Jerry Grant on his right. He made contact with Grant's left front wheel and was launched into the screen that separated the track from solid humanity. The joy of children in front row seats was instantly turned to agony as flaming fuel spewed into their faces. Walther's car was shredded on the fence like cheese on a huge grater. For one instant the web fencing sagged and split. Death for hundreds was an eyelash away.

God's hand was bared and the car reversed its outward surge to fall back on the race surface. It whirled like a great flame-throwing pinwheel across the track, driver Walther underneath. Eleven racers crashed together and when the awful noise was spent, Walther lay with his feet out the front of his capsized machine. It was a nightmare . . . his legs extending from what could have been the mouth of a great dead fish. At the same time it was miracle upon miracle. The car had not gone into the people and "Salt" was alive. His injuries were terrible but, he was alive.

The heavens wept again and racing for this day was at an end. Eighteen were injured. For the 300,000 plus fans, the race had lasted seven seconds.

It was announced that the restart would involve a full "500" the next morning.

The second day, Tuesday, rains lifted only long enough to tantalize another great crowd with one parade lap. A whole new world of problems entered the picture. Key men in pit crews were returning to jobs and homes across the country. T.V. film crews and track personnel were bailing out from this soggy inland sea. Tension was growing between track officials and racing teams. A meeting Wednesday morning of all directly involved, turned into a wild shouting match.

While a sad percentage of those people holding tickets enjoyed once-in-a-lifetime elbow room (less than 50,000), an early afternoon decision was made to "send 'em out." Rains had lifted in late morning and the track was dry. This was It!

Repairs had been made on cars involved Monday so that thirty-two were presented to the line. Without any of the traditional pomp, the men fell in behind the Cadillac pace car and produced an excellent start. Bobby Unser's "Eagle" sped away from '72 winner Mark Donohue and pole winner Johnny Rutherford to command the early laps with apparent ease. Several minor spins and a host of blown engines in the early going made it look like this could be the race nobody wanted to win. Wrenching five hundred miles from engines turbocharging nearly one thousand horsepower could just be asking too much. Reasons most often given were broken pistons or connecting rods.

One hundred miles into the action Swede Savage, in an Eagle, locked in battle with two time winner Al Unser, in a Parnelli Offy, and Roger McCluskey, in a McLaren. Their crafty dueling at 185+ mph was a thing of

TASMAN TERROR—Graham McRae, international star of the STP racing team, who has won three straight Tasman Cup championships in Australia and New Zealand, shown after he went faster than any other foreign driver in the history of Indianapolis Motor Speedway. After only 10 laps in his red STP racer, McRae averaged 192.031 mph for four laps, to qualify in 13th position for the big Memorial Day racing event.

beauty. Seldom since the early 1960s had men engaged like this. Billy Vukovich Jr. and Bobby Unser lurked close behind the battle.

Swede Savage struggled on the oily surface toward turn No. 4. McCluskey's car had disappeared from his mirrors, but that wasn't important. Race leader Al Unser charged dead ahead. The huge wing on the tail of his orange STP Eagle started to fall back and instantly its downthrust of more than 1500 pounds was gone. The car's sticking power at nearly 180 mph evaporated. Swede sat in helpless horror as the car turned toward the inside track wall. The impact and fire storm created can only be likened to a direct hit by an artillery shell. The car flew into thousands of pieces and these pieces, small and great, caromed back on the racecourse. Observers on location thought several cars had disintegrated.

Bobby Unser was next on the scene and found himself in the same position Eddie Sachs had known in 1964. Instinctively, Unser feathered his brakes and then as wreckage drifted in on him from his left, decided to gamble. He would try to accelerate away from destruction. Blower pressure was good and he cleared by inches at nearly 200 mph.

The red flag was out instantly and rescue people started a frantic dash toward the scene. Nobody in his right mind held any hope for Swede Savage. Everything had rolled into

85

Legendary crew chief George Bignotti, always a favorite to win the "500."

The handsome and dedicated Swede Savage.

"Swede" Savage was talking and struggling to free himself when rescue people first reached him. He was twisted into what was left of the "tub" of the racer. This portion lay near the outer wall. The engine and rear end of the car were at mid track. The wing was near the inner wall while fire was everywhere. "Swede" hung onto life until the first Monday of July, 1973.

"Salt" Walther's legs projected out the front end of his McLaren like those of a man in the jaws of a great dead fish. He survived terrible burns and injury.

STP team driver Graham McRae.

"500" winner Gordon Johncock.

huge balls of flaming "tinfoil." A garbled radio transmission came from inside a large chunk lying close to the outer wall. Swede's helmet radio was working and the message was ". . . what a mess!!" Swede was burned and shattered, but alive. It was a miracle. Another miracle!!! Joy was turned to sorrow thirty days later. Swede died in Indianapolis Methodist Hospital.

An STP crewman running toward the scene never dreamed a fire truck would be rushing the wrong direction up pit row. The truck was real and Armando Teran, 22 years, never knew what hit him. The big board showed 59 laps for the leaders. The race was fifty-four minutes old.

An hour of frantic work put the track in order once more. A single file start set the stage for more mechanical heartbreak. Both Unser brothers and Mark Donohue were soon out of it.

From the soggy grass inside turn three, photographer John Mahoney watched rolling dark clouds and the scoreboard. When the board turned over 101 laps he thanked the Lord with a shout. The next cloudburst would mean it was over. The rules say, anything beyond halfway can be called "A Race."

The yellow flag slowed the field to a crawl on lap No. 129. The track was drenched. The end came at suppertime, 5:33 p.m., on lap 133. There was no checkered flag ever given the winner. Only the red flag established a finish. The winner, 35-year-old Gordon Johncock, was in the throes of bankruptcy so that any personal gain from his portion of the $236-022.82 first prize was in great doubt. Several months after the race a small portion was

87

awarded to Gordon personally by the courts. There was no formal award banquet to honor him. He had driven STP car No. 20 at an average 159.014 mph. His teammate in STP car No. 40 had been Swede Savage. Armando Teran had been with him on the STP team. In victory he spoke of seeing his teammate go up in flames, "I felt like quitting right there and then! I surely hate to see the race have to end this way."

Billy Vukovich Jr. was a strong second. Craggy old Roger McCluskey was third, and a gracious gentleman named Mel Kenyon a solid fourth.

Controversy whirls around the proud old track today as never before. "Change the Start!" "Get rid of those big wings!" "Cut back the horsepower!"

The solid white walls just stand tall and wait. They have a language all their own.

* * *

What was intended to be a great theater for automobiles has become a range for ballistic missiles. Helmets, belts, protective cockpits, fireproof clothing and all the things we have considered from their beginnings seem meaningless. What good are they if whole cars can disappear in mushroom clouds of fire? A final look at the fate of men who came to race Indianapolis in 1973 reveals that Art Pollard lost his life because the car had no provision to absorb punishment given the bottom of the "tub" or driver's compartment. Salt Walther survived, but not through human means.

If firm hands can gain control of Big Car Racing and cut through meaningless tampering with fuel loads, tires, wings, etc., to meet head on the absolute need to slow the cars way down, there is still time. Speeds will only be realistic again when available horsepower is dropped off dramatically. When this day comes, the soundness of the "Driver's Whole Armor" will be confirmed again.

Bobby Unser in a streaking white Eagle duels with Steve Krisiloff in Turn No. 3. (John R. Mahoney Photo)

Jerry Grant pits his Eagle racer during the 1972 running. The holocaust that blew up from his last stop for fuel this day will always be fuse material to start a good argument. It seems he may have borrowed something from a friend.
(S-K Tool Photo)

The four modern schools of Indianapolis for your comparison. Parnelli Jones is the big backer of the men of "Super Team." Mario Andretti, Al Unser and Joe Leonard wheel these Offy-powered creations.

Bobby Unser is stopped cold by the camera of John Mahoney in his Dan Gurney "Eagle" racer.

A. J. Foyt makes everything happen for the cars he calls "Coyote-Foyt."

Offy-powered McLaren racers had their origins in England. Mark Donohue at the wheel and Roger Penske in control of operations make a fantastic team.

(All John R. Mahoney Photos)

Bobby Allison drove McLaren Offy No. 12 in 1973. Bobby is a super driver in any kind of race car. He is best known in Southern stock car circles. He speaks boldly of his faith in The Living God.

(Sears Die-Hard Photo)

Close-up of Mark Donohue's 1973 ride. The Sunoco-backed car is an Eagle Offenhauser that qualified at 197.412 mph.

(Sears Die-Hard Photo)

Mark Donohue is a graduate engineer from Brown University who won it all at Indy in 1972. He has to be one of the all-time greats of America. Mark goes with Sears Die-Hard products all the way. (Sears Die-Hard Photo)

The perfect combination of man and machine—Donohue and Eagle racer. (Sears Die-Hard Photo)

The beautiful Thermo King Air Conditioning Offy arrives in Gasoline Alley, May 1973. Quality is typical of Thermo King!
(Thermo King Air Conditioning Photo)

The car glides from the famous "Alley" toward the pit area. It's shakedown time for a year of careful work.
(Thermo King Photo)

"Rookie Driver of the Year 1972" Mike Hiss pauses beside the car. Note the base of the race control tower behind him.
(Thermo King Photo)

The cockpit is specifically designed for the trim young driver. The flawless skin of the monocoque is .063 aluminum. The car weighs about 1600 pounds.
(Thermo King Photo)

Seventy-five-gallon fuel cells surround the driver. Fire control bladders are installed inside the tanks.
(Thermo King Photo)

The four-cylinder DOHC Offenhauser engine can turn out between 800 and 1000 horsepower. A turbocharger in concert with a 60,000-volt magneto and fuel injection make this kind of unreal power possible.
(Thermo King Photo)

CHAPTER SIXTEEN

Robes and Palms

A veteran fighter pilot from the bamboo and canvas planes of W.W.I. told me of being invited to Indianapolis and the 500 in 1931. He described a restlessness, a charge in the atmosphere that was "other worldly." "People seemed to sense terrible things were going to happen. It was like they didn't want to be there, but the power of curiosity bound them." The Captain got caught up in the mood himself and returned twice.

In 1933 the terrible events at the south end of the racetrack developed right in front of him. "I could never go back there again," he said. "I've never told anyone what I really saw."

Today, the obscure, sinewy men who raced those meets are all but forgotten. The things they worked so hard for seem so puny. The personal price they paid mocks the rewards offered them. They were an expression of a mystery that engages every normal mind at some point. What is it in some men that will make them sacrifice, discipline, break, bleed and even die, just to be part of something they judge worthwhile?

To many, such men are quickly dismissed as complete idiots. To others they are heroes. In a far-out sense they represent mankind at its best.

The thought is not original with me, it comes from the Holy Bible, and from a portion prepared nearly 2000 years ago concerning events yet to happen.

In the very last chapters of Revelation, a man called John is being shown in a vision how God will end human history and deal with men and angels of all the ages. This simple ex-fisherman who traveled with the Lord Jesus writes about alignments of world powers, conditions in the earth, and even natural disasters of the last days. Things we are experiencing today are told with such accuracy that a careful reader has to wince . . . but this is not the point.

Some people are seen beyond the dimension of measured time. They are in the glory of God's presence forever and "are clothed in white robes and palms in their hands." Rev. 7:9. God is telling us something through John about eternity's "Big Winners" and He is using the figure of a *racer* to do it. Those unnumbered millions who rise to praise Him are clearly dressed as victorious drivers from an ancient circus race for chariots. In traditional ceremony a winner got a palm branch in his hand (not on his head as a foot runner) and clean white robes to carry on his lap of honor.

Incredible and delightful!!!

The Lord of lords lifts that figure of the driver for good and obvious reasons.

The guts (called steadfastness) the racer has to display takes into account the possibility that he may have to seal his dedication with his blood. What he gives himself to, he gives totally. There is no mistaking the breed, whether in the Roman Palaestra or the Indianapolis Motor Speedway.

But make no mistake, God is not endorsing racing as a ticket to His presence. What He is saying is that the abandon shown by a racer in moving toward his goal is good, the sort of stuff that pleases Him when the goal is right.

The Father has shown Himself beautifully in His Son, Jesus. A person has to try hard to miss knowing what pleases God if contact has been made with the Son.

His own record puts it, "For it is Christ that worketh in you, giving you the will and the power to do His good pleasure."

The use of racing in God's record doesn't end here. Time and again God moved the hand of a man called Paul in the use of the theme. What he had to say in drawing on the helmet, the belt, the shield, and body covering, prompted the work that filtered down into this book.

The parallels of what Wilbur Shaw, Joie Chitwood, Jimmy Bryan, and Mike Mosley found were laid down a generation after Jesus. God's word says that we should look at the pieces and learn from them. The Speedway put them in a living, moving context that anyone familiar with both can't possibly miss.

* * *

AUTHOR'S NOTE: At the Speedway the helmet came first, and is still the most important piece of safety gear.

God's word treats the helmet as the most significant item, too. In the following breakdown, we have elected to hold it until last. Why not? What came first in time is usually small matter to a God who is from everlasting to everlasting.

CHAPTER SEVENTEEN

The Belt

The safety belt came to the Speedway in 1941 in the form of a chance happening. Innovator Joie Chitwood was thought to be working on his own destruction.

In 30 plus years, the belt has come a long way. This news release of August 2, 1972 in *The Minneapolis Star* gives a pretty good indication of where we stand:

DRIVERS WOULD BUCKLE UP
OR KNUCKLE DOWN TO LAW

WASHINGTON, D.C. (AP)—Motorists would be required by law to fasten their seat belts or possibly risk a jail sentence under national-highway-safety standards proposed by the Transportation Department.

The proposal announced yesterday would require states to enforce the new standards or lose millions of dollars in federal highway funds.

The penalty for driving with an unbuckled seat belt usually would be no more than a reprimand or fine, although in cases where death or injury resulted, a jail sentence might be imposed.

Calling the plan an effort to eliminate the state-to-state variations in safety regulations, the transportation department invited public comment during the next 90 days. The department said it intends to implement the plan next April.

The rules, somewhat tougher than the department's first standardization effort in mid-1967, would:

Follow through on the current regulation requiring all new cars to carry seat belts by also requiring motorists and passengers to buckle them.

Prohibit modification of safety-related equipment on cars, including a ban on disconnecting buzzers which sound if seat belts are left unfastened.

* * *

In Europe and in Japan, a few voices relating to racing still reject safety belts.

Mrs. Rudolf Caracciola wrote me personally after the 1971 death of Swiss Grand Prix Ace, Joe Siffert, "I am not for seat belts in racing cars. Better to be thrown out than burned!"

Paul, God's spokesman, wrote about them in the year 62 A.D., and advised, "Take the *belt* of *truth*." God's word to us through Paul has to do with one of our biggest hang-ups. We have disobeyed God by choice and we all know it. We have run all over His love and violated Him in every way. A vicious little three-letter word is applied to our condition. We are in SIN. The official word from a Holy God is: "All have sinned and fallen short of God's glory" Rom. 3:23. "The wages of sin is death" Rom. 6:23.

So where does the belt come in? How can a "belt of truth" help us? The Lord Jesus says, "Come unto me, you who are weighed down."

If we simply come to God in the name of Jesus and honestly talk about the problems of our sins and our hang-ups . . . God's Spirit will lock in on our minds and things will really open up. Everything we are must be

91

"Wild Bill" Anderson died a few weeks after this picture was taken . . . in this car. When the car pitched over, he never had a chance. Note the belts that tied Bill in.

open to His moving, and everything He points up, called by its right name.

We have taken the "belt of truth"!

God really hears you (maybe for the first time). He forgives you, erasing the record against you. The Father seals you with the Spirit of the Lord Jesus in a kind of a belt arrangement that beats anything in this world.

Now we are on the way to something!

Indy star Red Amick believed in good belts, roll bars and the best of helmets. The impact of headgear worn by modern fighter pilots is obvious.

CHAPTER EIGHTEEN

Roll Bar

Protective roll bars, shields of tube steel, came to the Speedway in 1958. They have stayed! Some of racing's hard-nosed "Old Guard" still elect to liken them to training wheels on a child's bike. They reason that "a real pro" ought to be willing to take his chances if he runs in the major leagues. The fact that hundreds of men are alive because of them doesn't seem to phase them very much.

God's love letter to all men says, "Take the shield of faith." This may not seem to say much to you because the meaning of the word faith has been so abused. In briefest terms, faith is giving yourself to something.

This roll bar, called "The USAC Type," was modest. It was an excellent beginning.

THE OILY GRAIL

Racing involves giving everything to a test.

Love involves giving yourself to a person.

Everything we attempt in some way involves giving or spending what we are. Racing is a sure-fire way of being a big spender.

To take hold of God's shield of faith, the Bible says, "With eyes wide open to the mercies of God, I beg you give Him your bodies as a living sacrifice." Rom. 12:1. Everything is on the line for this one. This giving involves obedience to the Spirit of Jesus. Control is in His hands, but don't mistake this for a "tiptoe through the tulips." The Lord says, "The one who conserves (guards) his life will lose it. The one who loses it for my sake wins."

Compare this with God's use of the figure of the ancient chariot driver from Revelation 7:9.

Jerry Hansen's Lola illustrates what a real cage should be. Deep in the cockpit, he works under a real shield.

CHAPTER NINETEEN

Fire Control

The cockpit of a racer can get terribly hot. Men have been known to lose ten pounds in a drive. Modern flameproof driving suits look like equipment for the Arctic, but an intelligent driver will never compromise a single item. If fuel should spill and things really get hot, any sweat will have been well worth it.

The Bible compares protective body covering to the powerful presence of the Lord Jesus.

Paul wrote, "You will need the body covering of God's approval." This approval by God has nothing to do with being outstanding in human terms. The Savior just wants simple obedience to His guidance on a day-to-day basis; the sort of response you hope for from a small child. He says, "Everyone who hears my words and puts them into practice is like a sensible man."

An illustration might help here. A few race drivers seem to be indwelt with a special gift. Parnelli Jones or A. J. Foyt can step into any kind of car on any course, from punishing desert to super-smooth speedway, and you can plan on their running for the lead. They possess an inner voice that never seems to fail and a fine-tuned body that always responds. They work constantly at their business.

The risen Lord Jesus actually lives within those who ask him. "I will come into him," He says. Revelation 3:20. His presence is a practical reality.

We've been working on a bridge across 2000 years. Can we possibly go any further with it. Absolutely! The equipment of the 70s

Joe Frasson was thankful for a new, fire-retardant uniform. His racer went up in a ball of fire. The suit was ruined. The man in it was fine.

has been there all the way. God points toward protective footwear and says; "Take it."

Life can get hot.

Life can break you.

The command is: "Take on your feet the gospel of peace." The Gospel or Bible can literally be translated, Good News. It is a living miracle that can be as vital to you each day as food.[1]

There is no substitute for study of God's Word with others and with the help of good teaching. Once in it, you will be amazed at your new understanding, your boldness, and ability to love.

Our Heavenly Father introduced THE RACER'S EDGE a long time ago. Take some time with it today.

THE RACER'S EDGE

As for us, we have this large crowd of witnesses around us. Let us rid ourselves of everything that gets in the way, and the sin which holds on so tightly, and run with determination the race that lies before us. Let us keep our eyes fixed on Jesus, on whom our faith depends from beginning to end.

—Letter to Hebrew Christians at Rome 67 A.D.

---

[1] Get a good readable Bible translated for today. Meet the Lord Jesus in the books of John and Mark. From there go to Paul's letter to Romans.

CHAPTER TWENTY

Helmet to Helmet

Merle Bettenhausen, son of the late racing great Tony Bettenhausen, had an experience best described as missing the mark. Bettenhausen was less than five minutes into his very first drive in Indianapolis type cars. The scene was a Championship Race in Michigan. He tells it . . . "At the start of the race, with a full fuel load, the car just didn't feel or handle right. So I backed way off and was almost at the rear of the field. As I went into the second turn, it started to get away so I corrected it and then the rear end stuck and I hit the wall.

"I hit it hard and somehow, the visor of my helmet ripped off. I felt it go and when I looked up there was this big orange ball so I knew there was fire. So I closed my eyes and threw my left hand up in front of them to protect 'em. It was getting pretty hot in there and I thought about getting out.

"I put my hands up on the side of the car and started lifting because I didn't think I was going to hit the wall again. Then I said to myself. 'You're going too fast,' so I started to get back down and then I felt this tug on my right arm. Finally, the car stopped and I knew it was on fire so I started to get out again. I couldn't figure out why I couldn't lift myself and I looked over to the right and there was no arm. I said, 'Oh, my God; Oh, my God.'"

Bettenhausen's cry to God in this scene was more than poetry or profanity. He was calling to God! What he may have thought about God before didn't matter now. The issue was, WHAT DOES GOD THINK OF ME?

The unbreakable Word of God declares that every human being is shrouded by sin in almost the same way Merle was in fire. Sin, by definition, is missing the mark or falling short of God's design. "For all have sinned and come short of the Glory of God." Romans 3:23. A Holy God projects the outcome of all human calamity in a brutal handful of words, "The wages of sin is death." It would appear that doom is inherited as a real part of our natural birthright.

But wait!!! This is not the complete statement God has given. The complete sentence from the Bible reads, "The wages of sin is death; but the gift of God is eternal life through Jesus Christ our Lord." Romans 6:23.

A great expression of the best news ever comes in a song little children sing. "Jesus loves me, this I know . . . for the Bible tells me so."

As always, the Bible teaches in terms that are practical and simple. To our delight this *high impact message* is developed on the theme of the helmet. God's love letter to us speaks of the change the Lord Jesus brings into a human life as, "Taking the helmet of salvation." Ephesians 6.

Wilbur Shaw in his thunder mug was smarter than he ever dreamed.

Let me share a personal experience from France and the middle 1950s. The force of the love and care God's Son brings rings out with life-changing power. It did for me anyhow . . . and from a deep hole in the earth.

Military assignment directed travel from Frankfurt, Germany, to eastern France. We

The evolution of the helmet is clearly seen from the turn-around bill cap of the pioneers of auto racing ... to the exacting helmets of today.

1931 winner Lou Schneider at the wheel of his Bowes Seal Fast Miller. He survived the rugged wars of speed on tracks all across the nation and died of tuberculosis. Study the tires carefully and imagine sustained drives at more than 100 miles per hour.

were in search for evidence of an American P47 "Thunderbolt" fighter plane. The aircraft had disappeared thirteen years before. The pilot had, according to our records, taken a direct hit on his canopy. The plane had powered in. The earth had swallowed everything.

Probing turned up aluminum scraps four and one-half meters in the earth. Major league excavation at five meters (16 feet) produced pieces up to a foot in diameter. It was our "Thunderbolt!"

A rolled sheet of aluminum held a small book . . . a G.I. Gideon Bible. The man we were looking for had signed and dated it just two weeks before being listed with the missing. The condition of the book was, in my judgment, akin to a miracle. It was like handling a live electric wire!

In the 1940s and 50s, good-looking helmets of excellent quality became the standard.

The whole armor of racing . . . World Champion Denny Hulme, in modern helmet, belts and flameproof clothing. A good roll bar (shield) towers over his helmet.

the Greatest Race

The greatest race is life, and we're all participants. But where are we going? Will we arrive safely? Problems and pressures surround everyone, and few have real peace and satisfaction. How about you? Are you content with your showing in life's race?

Mel Kenyon has found that Jesus Christ speaks directly concerning today's needs. Jesus said that man's troubles all stem from the fact he is separated from God and needs to be brought back together with Him. But we can't bring ourselves closer to God by loving our neighbors or going to church or any other attempt to "get straight."

The reason we can't get straight with God is that each of us has a selfish, greedy streak within. When we express this by cheating on our income tax, running around with another man or woman, shoplifting, thinking evil thoughts, or by being selfish, we pollute ourselves and make ourselves unfit for God.

You see, the race of life has rules just like a car race. We can't do anything we want and expect to get away with it. When we break God's laws He is displeased. Neither can we make ourselves fit for God. What we can do is to establish a personal relationship with God like Mel Kenyon has by accepting Jesus Christ as our Savior.

God proved His love for us by sending Jesus Christ to die and take the penalty we deserved for breaking God's laws. Now all we have to do is believe this and commit ourselves to Jesus Christ. God will declare us "not guilty" of offending Him if we will just trust in Jesus Christ. All we have to do is admit we need His help and personally accept Christ. You can do this by praying: "God, I am guilty of breaking your laws but now I accept Jesus Christ as my Savior. I want Him to take away my wickedness and make me fit for heaven."

THE OILY GRAIL

The pilot had signed it to claim the love and life of the Lord Jesus as his own. He had taken a "helmet" that sealed him right into the very presence of God. The fact that his human body was reduced to droplets didn't change a thing.

On a small piece of notebook paper folded near the back of his book he had written a long-hand note to himself.

> I claim this:
> "Behold I stand at the door,
> and knock: if any man hear
> my voice, and open the door,
> I will come into him."
> Revelation
> three, twenty
> I am in the Lord Jesus in life or death. It is enough that I know—I am in His love.

The "helmet of salvation" (Ephesians 6:17) was well in hand!

The crash helmet of today has come at great price to good men. View it as a type of the protective seal of God. No combination of men could secure this; only the sacrifice of God's perfect Son.

A number of the elite Indy drivers of today will tell anyone who will listen that they run a two-helmet system. They use the best in hard hats, but really bank on the promises of God as found in Christ Jesus. His mind and life inside them has created a whole new dimension . . . Their Helmet of Salvation!

Mel Kenyon

Indy driving star, Mel Kenyon, has "The Whole Armor of God" and a brand new lease on life! He sat down with the men of Literature Crusades, Prospect Heights, Illinois, and worked out a pamphlet. Hundreds of thousands of copies are out. Take a look at pages 6 and 7 of "The Greatest Race Ever!"

Jan Opperman was the "winningest" driver on the American race scene in 1972, with more than 40 feature victories.

Jan recently wrote this author, "It is really great to have the Holy Spirit running my affairs. Praise the Lord! Life is so much nicer when one finally climbs into the back seat and lets Jesus do the driving. This way we will sure wind up in victory lane and a-praising our Lord!!!"

At Tampa, Florida, in February of 1973, Jan tests the whole armor of the race driver. He is a powerful public speaker and a dedicated follower of Jesus. His real delight is in possessing the "Whole Armor of God."

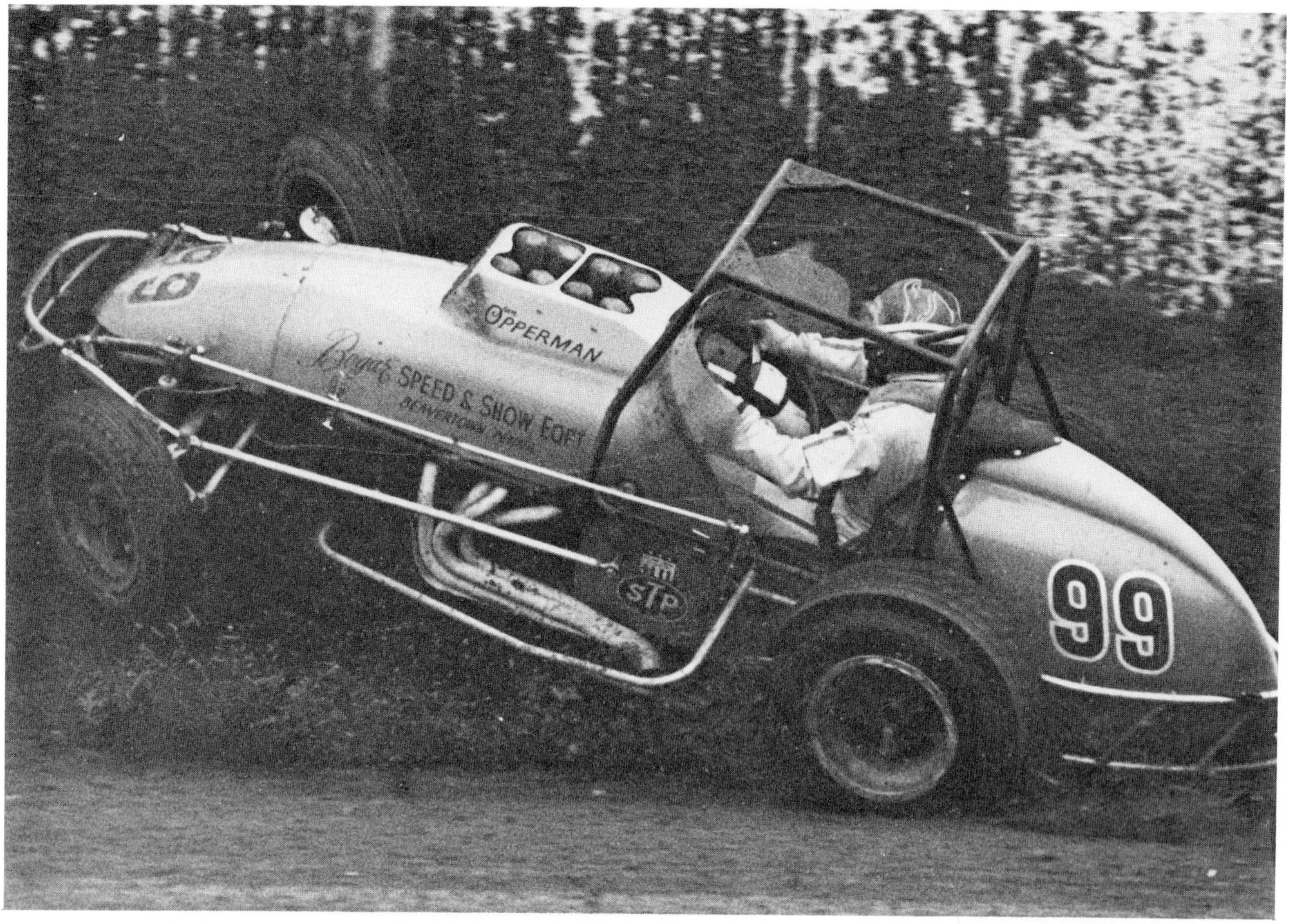
OPPERMAN
SPEED & SNOW EQPT
STP
99

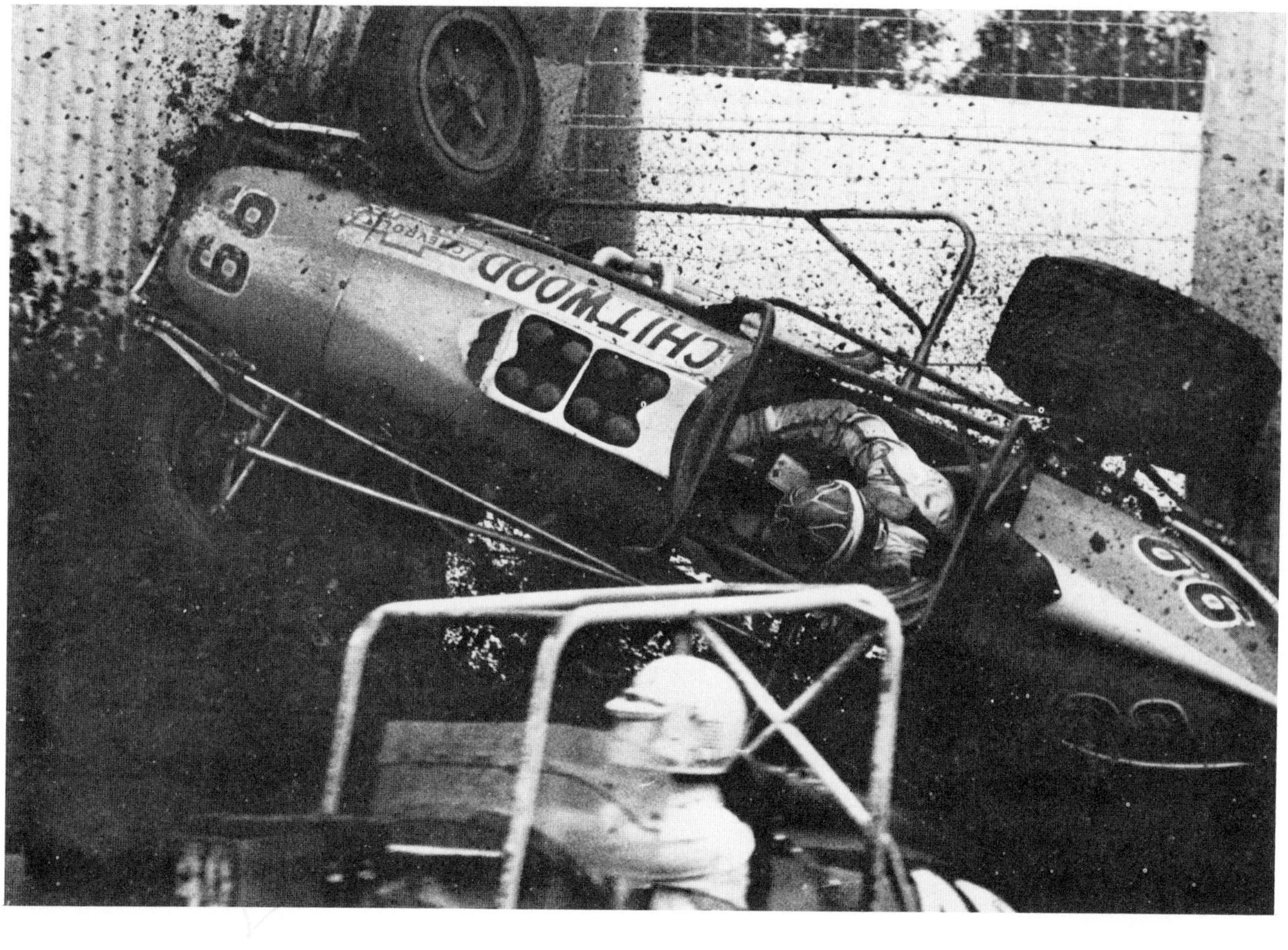
CHITWOOD
99

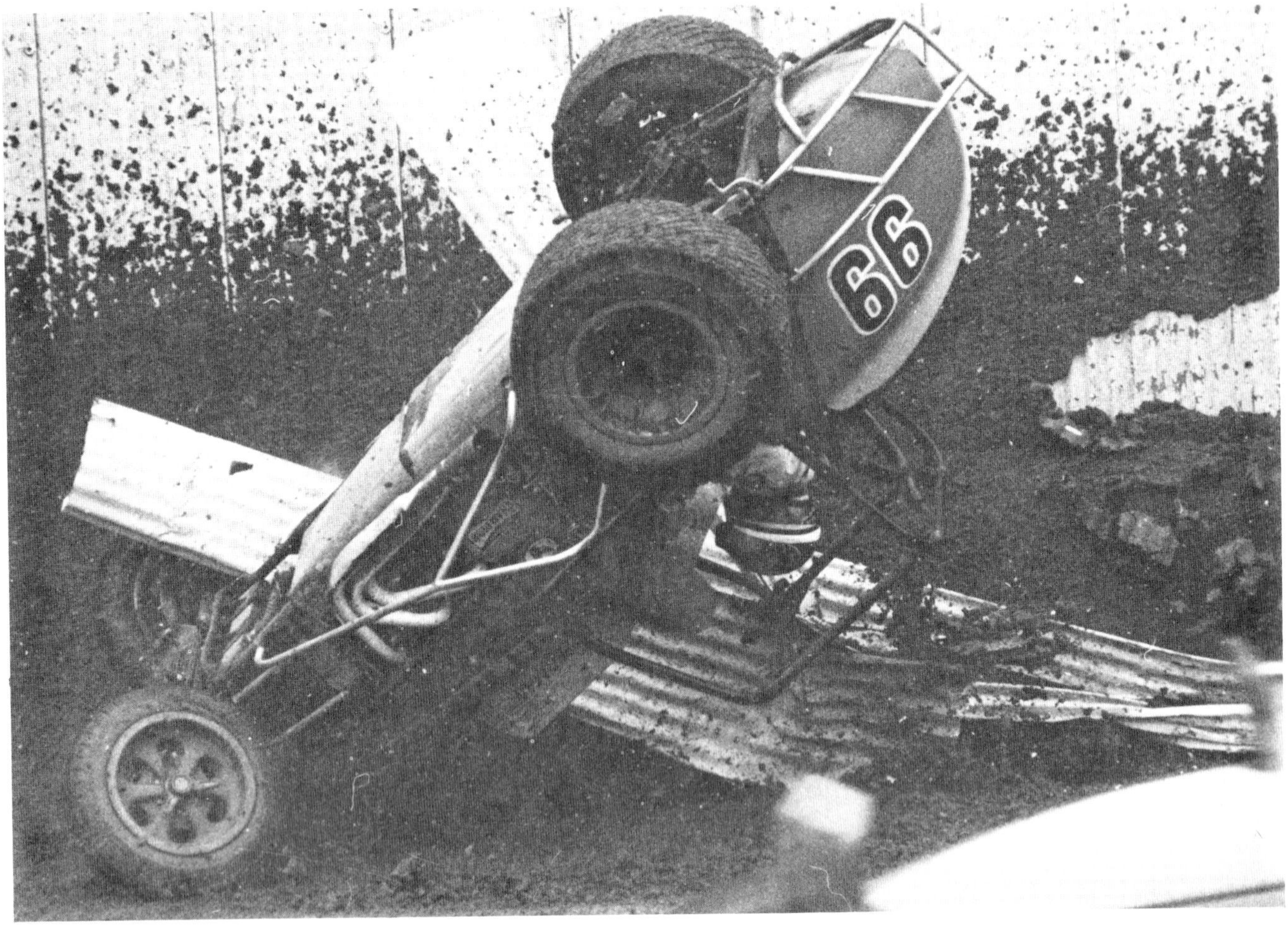
66

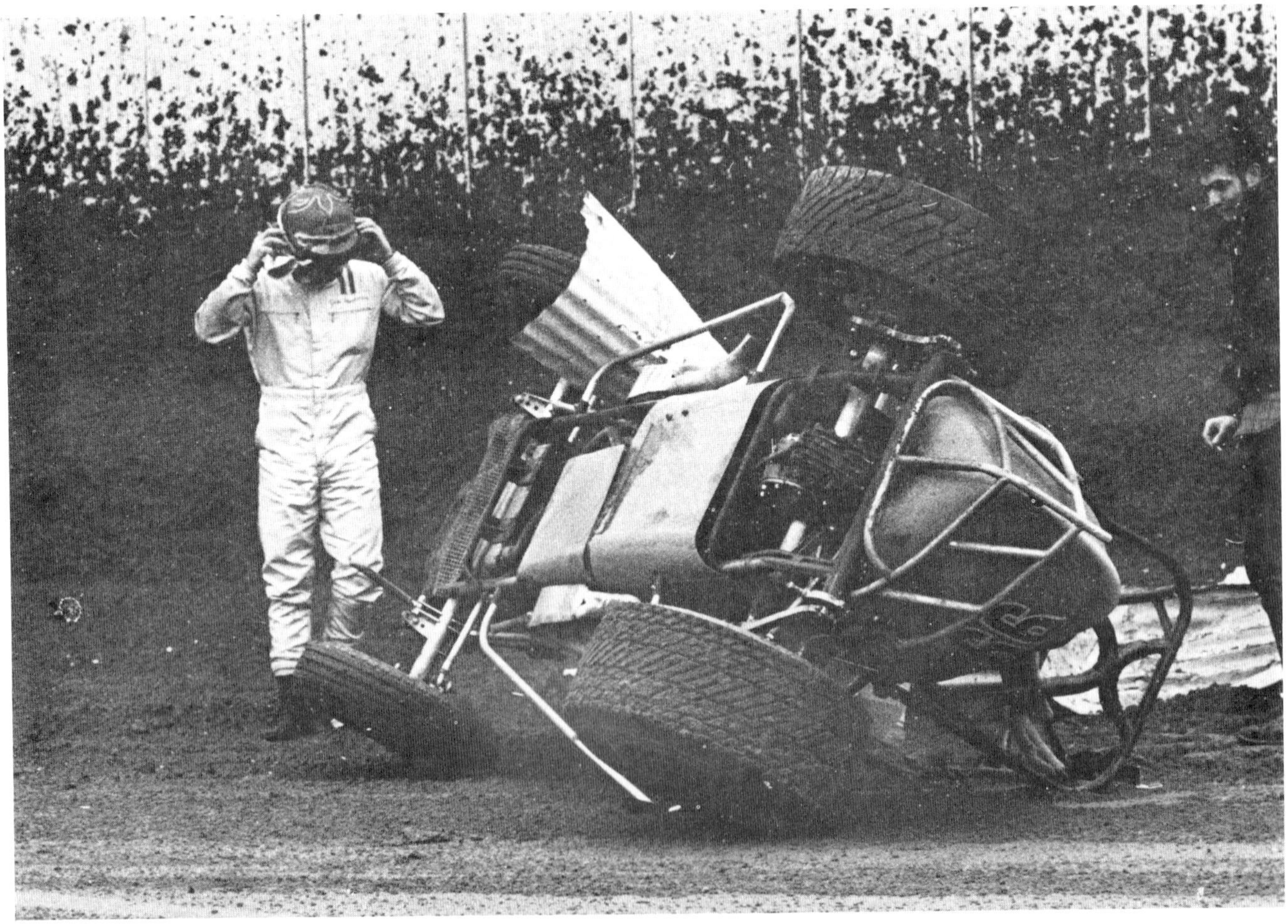

COURSE TECHNOLOGY
CENGAGE Learning

New Perspectives on Adobe Flash CS4 Professional—Comprehensive
Luis A. Lopez, Robin M. Romer

Executive Editor: Marie L. Lee
Senior Product Manager: Kathy Finnegan
Product Manager: Katherine C. Russillo
Associate Acquisitions Editor: Brandi Henson
Associate Product Manager: Leigh Robbins
Editorial Assistant: Julia Leroux-Lindsey
Director of Marketing: Cheryl Costantini
Marketing Manager: Ryan DeGrote
Marketing Specialist: Jennifer Hankin
Developmental Editor: Robin M. Romer
Manuscript Quality Assurance Supervisor: Christian Kunciw
Content Project Manager: Heather Furrow
Composition: GEX Publishing Services
Text Designer: Steve Deschene
Art Director: Marissa Falco
Cover Designer: Elizabeth Paquin
Cover Art: Bill Brown
Copyeditor: Camille Kiolbasa
Proofreader: Christine Clark
Indexer: Rich Carlson

© 2010 Course Technology, Cengage Learning

ALL RIGHTS RESERVED. No part of this work covered by the copyright herein may be reproduced, transmitted, stored or used in any form or by any means graphic, electronic, or mechanical, including but not limited to photocopying, recording, scanning, digitizing, taping, Web distribution, information networks, or information storage and retrieval systems, except as permitted under Section 107 or 108 of the 1976 United States Copyright Act, without the prior written permission of the publisher.

> For product information and technology assistance, contact us at
> **Cengage Learning Customer & Sales Support, 1-800-354-9706**
> For permission to use material from this text or product, submit all requests online at **cengage.com/permissions**
> Further permissions questions can be emailed to
> **permissionrequest@cengage.com**

ISBN-13: 978-0-324-82989-1
ISBN-10: 0-324-82989-2

Course Technology
20 Channel Center Street
Boston, Massachusetts 02210
USA

Cengage Learning is a leading provider of customized learning solutions with office locations around the globe, including Singapore, the United Kingdom, Australia, Mexico, Brazil, and Japan. Locate your local office at:
international.cengage.com/region

Cengage Learning products are represented in Canada by Nelson Education, Ltd.

To learn more about Course Technology, visit **www.cengage.com/coursetechnology**

To learn more about Cengage Learning, visit **www.cengage.com**

Purchase any of our products at your local college store or at our preferred online store **www.ichapters.com**

Some of the product names and company names used in this book have been used for identification purposes only and may be trademarks or registered trademarks of their respective manufacturers and sellers.

Adobe, the Adobe logos, Authorware, ColdFusion, Director, Dreamweaver, Flash, Fireworks, FreeHand, JRun, Photoshop, and Shockwave are either registered trademarks or trademarks of Adobe Systems Incorporated in the United States and/or other countries. All other names used herein are for identification purposes only and are trademarks of their respective owners.

Disclaimer: Any fictional data related to persons or companies or URLs used throughout this book is intended for instructional purposes only. At the time this book was printed, any such data was fictional and not belonging to any real persons or companies.

Printed in Canada
1 2 3 4 5 6 7 15 14 13 12 11 10 09

New Perspectives on

Adobe® Flash® CS4 Professional

Comprehensive

Luis A. Lopez

Robin M. Romer

COURSE TECHNOLOGY
CENGAGE Learning

Australia • Brazil • Japan • Korea • Mexico • Singapore • Spain • United Kingdom • United States

Preface

The New Perspectives Series' critical-thinking, problem-solving approach is the ideal way to prepare students to transcend point-and-click skills and take advantage of all that Adobe Flash CS4 Professional has to offer.

Our goal in developing the New Perspectives Series was to create books that give students the software concepts and practical skills they need to succeed beyond the classroom. This new edition updates our proven case-based pedagogy with more practical content to make learning skills more meaningful to students. With the New Perspectives Series, students understand *why* they are learning *what* they are learning, and are fully prepared to apply their skills to real-life situations.

About This Book

This book offers a case-based, problem-solving approach to learning Adobe Flash CS4 Professional. Using Flash, students learn how to create rich interactive experiences for the Web, ranging from banners and interactive menus to a complete Web site.

- Covers the newest features of Flash CS4, including the new interface, added tools, object-based tween animation process, motion presets, inverse kinematics, 3D transformations, and new Sounds library.
- Follows the New Perspectives Series case-based, problem-solving approach to help students understand the how and the why behind software skills.
- Provides coverage of both ActionScript 2.0 and ActionScript 3.0 programming.
- Incorporates the use of ActionScript, preloaders, components, and video as students create a Flash Web site.
- Includes an overview of the Adobe Certified Associate credential for Flash CS4. The appendix covers the objectives assessed with the Adobe Rich Media Communication Using Flash CS4 Exam.
- *Guide to Using Adobe Flash CS4 on the Macintosh* is available in the Student Downloads and Instructor Downloads sections at: *www.cengage.com/coursetechnology*.

New for This Edition

- New case scenarios and data files for two of the running Case Problems in the end-of-tutorial reinforcement material.
- Coverage of the newest features of Flash CS4, including the added Library features, blends and filters, new object-based tween animations, motion presets, Motion Editor, Bone tool (inverse kinematics), 3D transformations, Sounds library, Accessibility panel, and the Adobe Media Encoder CS4.
- New four-color interior design throughout the text.
- New topics include a discussion of accessibility issues and creating content for mobile devices using Adobe Device Central CS4.

"This text is filled with excellent explanations and activities. My students vary in their abilities, and this text covers exactly what they need in a logical, incremental fashion. It's a great reference book that students will find useful for years."

—Kenneth Wade
Champlain College

"Students enjoy the tutorial approach and learn by doing. For the first time, my students are saying Flash is fun."

—James A. Innis
North Central Texas College

www.cengage.com/ct/newperspectives

System Requirements

This book assumes that students have a default installation of Adobe Flash CS4 Professional, Adobe Flash Player 10, Adobe Media Encoder CS4 with the Xvid codec installed (free download is available from www.xvid.org), Adobe Device Central CS4, and a current Web browser.

The screen shots in this book were produced on a computer running Windows Vista Ultimate with Aero turned off and, for a browser, Internet Explorer 7. If students use a different operating system or browser, their screens might differ from those in the book.

The New Perspectives Approach

Context
Each tutorial begins with a problem presented in a "real-world" case that is meaningful to students. The case sets the scene to help students understand what they will do in the tutorial.

Hands-on Approach
Each tutorial is divided into manageable sessions that combine reading and hands-on, step-by-step work. Colorful screenshots help guide students through the steps. **Trouble?** tips anticipate common mistakes or problems to help students stay on track and continue with the tutorial.

InSight Boxes
InSight boxes offer expert advice and best practices to help students better understand how to work with Adobe Flash CS4 Professional and create interactive graphics, animations, and Web sites. With the information provided in the InSight boxes, students achieve a deeper understanding of the concepts behind the features and skills presented.

Margin Tips
Margin Tips provide helpful hints and shortcuts for more efficient use of Adobe Flash CS4 Professional. The Tips appear in the margin at key points throughout each tutorial, giving students extra information when and where they need it.

Reality Check
Comprehensive, open-ended Reality Check exercises give students the opportunity to practice skills by completing practical, real-world tasks involved in planning and creating a personal Flash Web site.

Review
In New Perspectives, retention is a key component to learning. At the end of each session, a series of Quick Check questions helps students test their understanding of the concepts before moving on. Each tutorial also contains an end-of-tutorial summary and a list of key terms for further reinforcement.

Assessment
Engaging and challenging Review Assignments and Case Problems have always been a hallmark feature of the New Perspectives Series. Icons and brief descriptions accompany the exercises, making it easy to understand, at a glance, both the goal and level of challenge a particular assignment holds.

"The New Perspectives Series approach, which combines definition and real-world application of content, makes it an easy choice for me when selecting textbooks. I am able to teach concepts that students can immediately apply."

—Brian Morgan
Marshall University

www.cengage.com/ct/newperspectives

Reference Window

Task Reference

Reference

While contextual learning is excellent for retention, there are times when students will want a high-level understanding of how to accomplish a task. Within each tutorial, Reference Windows appear before a set of steps to provide a succinct summary and preview of how to perform a task. In addition, a complete Task Reference at the back of the book provides quick access to information on how to carry out common tasks. Finally, each book includes a combination Glossary/Index to promote easy reference of material.

Our Complete System of Instruction

Coverage To Meet Your Needs

Whether you're looking for just a small amount of coverage or enough to fill a semester-long class, we can provide you with a textbook that meets your needs.

- Brief books typically cover the essential skills in just 2 to 4 tutorials.
- Introductory books build and expand on those skills and contain an average of 5 to 8 tutorials.
- Comprehensive books are great for a full-semester class, and contain 9 to 12+ tutorials.

So if the book you're holding does not provide the right amount of coverage for you, there's probably another offering available. Visit our Web site or contact your Course Technology sales representative to find out what else we offer.

CourseCasts – Learning on the Go. Always available…always relevant.

Want to keep up with the latest technology trends relevant to you? Visit our site to find a library of podcasts, CourseCasts, featuring a "CourseCast of the Week," and download them to your mp3 player at http://coursecasts.course.com.

Ken Baldauf, host of CourseCasts, is a faculty member of the Florida State University Computer Science Department where he is responsible for teaching technology classes to thousands of FSU students each year. Ken is an expert in the latest technology trends; he gathers and sorts through the most pertinent news and information for CourseCasts so your students can spend their time enjoying technology, rather than trying to figure it out. Open or close your lecture with a discussion based on the latest CourseCast.

Visit us at http://coursecasts.course.com to learn on the go!

Instructor Resources

We offer more than just a book. We have all the tools you need to enhance your lectures, check students' work, and generate exams in a new, easier-to-use and completely revised package. This book's Instructor's Manual, ExamView test bank, PowerPoint presentations, data files, solution files, figure files, and a sample syllabus are all available on a single CD-ROM or for downloading at www.cengage.com/coursetechnology.

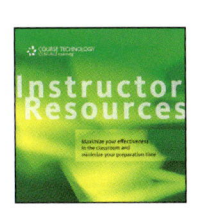

www.cengage.com/ct/newperspectives

Online Content

Blackboard is the leading distance learning solution provider and class-management platform today. Course Technology has partnered with Blackboard to bring you premium online content. Content for use with *New Perspectives on Adobe Flash CS4 Professional, Comprehensive* is available in a Blackboard Course Cartridge and may include topic reviews, case projects, review questions, test banks, practice tests, custom syllabi, and more. Course Technology also has solutions for several other learning management systems. Please visit www.cengage.com/coursetechnology today to see what's available for this title.

www.cengage.com/ct/newperspectives

Acknowledgments

I want to extend my gratitude to all of the members of the New Perspectives Team who made this book possible, especially Kate Russillo, Product Manager, for her patience and guidance of this project. Thanks also to Heather Furrow, Content Project Manager; Lorri Zdunko, GEX Publishing Services; and Christian Kunciw, Manuscript Quality Assurance Supervisor, and the MQA team for this edition, John Freitas, Serge Palladino, Danielle Shaw, and Susan Whalen.

Special thanks to Robin M. Romer, co-author and Developmental Editor, for her guidance, encouragement and dedication to this project. Her writing, editorial, and organizational skills and her great insights and attention to detail helped make this project a success.

And, finally, special thanks to my wife, Gloria, and daughter, Alyssandra, whose love, patience, and support made working on this book possible. This book is dedicated to them.

— Luis A. Lopez

Academic Reviewers

Reviewers who helped provide valuable feedback for this edition:
Cherie Aukland, Thomas Nelson Community College
Dr. Joseph Defazio, IUPUI, School of Informatics
James A. Innis, North Central Texas College
Victor Williams, Argosy University

www.cengage.com/ct/newperspectives

Brief Contents

Flash CS4

Flash—Level I Tutorials

Tutorial 1 Introducing Adobe Flash CS4 Professional . . . . FL 1
Exploring the Basic Features of Flash

Tutorial 2 Drawing Shapes, Adding Text, and Creating Symbols . . . . FL 55
Creating and Exporting a Banner

Tutorial 3 Creating Animations. . . . . FL 115
Developing Tween and Frame-by-Frame Animations

Tutorial 4 Creating Complex Animations . . . . FL 167
Animating with Masks, Text Blocks, Onion Skinning, 3D Rotations, and Inverse Kinematics

Tutorial 5 Making a Document Interactive. . . . . FL 225
Adding Buttons, Actions, and Sounds

Tutorial 6 Creating Special Effects with Graphics and Gradients . . . . FL 267
Working with Bitmaps and Gradients, and Publishing Flash Files

Tutorial 7 Planning and Creating a Flash Web Site . . . . FL 315
Building a Site with a Template, a Navigation Bar, and ActionScript

Tutorial 8 Programming with ActionScript 3.0 . . . . FL 375
Adding Interactive Elements to a Flash Web Site

Tutorial 9 Using Components and Video, and Creating Content for
Printing and Mobile Devices . . . . FL 429
Adding Web Links, Photos, and Video to a Flash Web Site and Creating Content for a Mobile Device

Additional Case 1 Creating an Interactive Banner for a Web Site . . . . ADD 1

Additional Case 2 Creating a Web Site with a Banner, a Payment
Calculator, a Photos Page and a Video Page . . . . ADD 5

Appendix A Becoming an Adobe Certified Associate . . . . FL A1

Using Adobe Flash CS4 on a Macintosh. . . . . Online
This guide is available for download on the book product page at www.cengage.com/coursetechnology.

Glossary/Index   REF 1

Task Reference   REF 9

Table of Contents

Preface v

Flash Level 1 Tutorials

Tutorial 1 Introducing Adobe Flash CS4 Professional
Exploring the Basic Features of Flash .... FL 1

Session 1.1 .... FL 2

Reviewing Types of Web Media .... FL 2

    Bitmap and Vector Graphics .... FL 2

    Bitmap and Vector Animation .... FL 3

Developing Web Media in Flash .... FL 3

    Viewing Flash SWF Files .... FL 5

Starting Flash .... FL 6

    Previewing Documents .... FL 9

Session 1.1 Quick Check .... FL 12

Session 1.2 .... FL 12

Exploring the Workspace Components .... FL 12

    Stage .... FL 12

    Pasteboard .... FL 13

    Timeline .... FL 13

    Tools Panel .... FL 15

    Panels .... FL 17

    Property Inspector .... FL 21

Changing the View of the Stage .... FL 24

    Magnifying and Moving the Stage .... FL 24

    Displaying the Grid, Rulers, and Guides .... FL 27

    Changing the Document Properties .... FL 30

Session 1.2 Quick Check .... FL 32

Session 1.3 .... FL 32

Working with Objects in Flash .... FL 32

    Creating Strokes and Fills .... FL 32

    Drawing and Grouping Objects .... FL 33

    Using the Color Controls and the Color Panel .. FL 35

Selecting Objects .... FL 37

    Selection Tool .... FL 37

    Subselection Tool .... FL 40

    Lasso Tool .... FL 42

Getting Help in Flash .... FL 44

Closing a Document and Exiting Flash .... FL 47

Session 1.3 Quick Check .... FL 48

Tutorial Summary .... FL 48

Key Terms .... FL 48

Review Assignments .... FL 49

Case Problems .... FL 50

Quick Check Answers .... FL 53

Tutorial 2 Drawing Shapes, Adding Text, and Creating Symbols
Creating and Exporting a Banner .... FL 55

Session 2.1 .... FL 56

Drawing Lines and Shapes .... FL 56

    Using the Oval, Rectangle, and PolyStar Tools . FL 58

    Using the Pencil Tool .... FL 68

Changing Strokes and Fills .... FL 71

    Using the Paint Bucket Tool .... FL 71

    Using the Eyedropper Tool .... FL 72

    Using Primitive Tools .... FL 73

    Using the Free Transform Tool .... FL 78

Session 2.1 Quick Check .... FL 82

Session 2.2 .... FL 83
Adding Text .... FL 83
    Using the Text Tool .... FL 83
Checking the Spelling of Text .... FL 85
Exporting a Graphic for Use on the Web .... FL 88
Using the History Panel .... FL 90
    Replaying Steps .... FL 91
    Undoing Steps .... FL 93
Session 2.2 Quick Check .... FL 94

Session 2.3 .... FL 94
Creating and Editing Symbols .... FL 94
    Comparing Symbol Behavior Types .... FL 95
    Creating Symbols .... FL 95
    Using the Library .... FL 96
    Editing a Symbol .... FL 99
    Creating and Editing Instances of Symbols ..... FL 100
    Applying Filters .... FL 101
Session 2.3 Quick Check .... FL 104
Tutorial Summary .... FL 105
Key Terms .... FL 105
Review Assignments .... FL 106
Case Problems .... FL 107
Quick Check Answers .... FL 112

Tutorial 3 Creating Animations
Developing Tween and Frame-by-Frame Animations .... FL 115

Session 3.1 .... FL 116
Elements of Animation .... FL 116
The Timeline .... FL 116
    Layers .... FL 116
    Frames .... FL 116

Working with the Timeline .... FL 117
    Changing the View of the Timeline .... FL 119
    Organizing Layers Using the Timeline .... FL 121
    Adding Layer Folders .... FL 121
    Selecting, Copying, and Moving Frames .... FL 123
Using Scenes and Multiple Timelines .... FL 124
    Using the Scene Panel .... FL 125
    Adding a Duplicate Scene .... FL 127
Session 3.1 Quick Check .... FL 129

Session 3.2 .... FL 129
Creating Animation .... FL 129
Creating a Motion Tween .... FL 129
    Modifying a Motion Tween .... FL 134
Using Motion Presets .... FL 136
    Applying a Motion Preset Animation .... FL 137
    Testing an Animation .... FL 141
Session 3.2 Quick Check .... FL 141

Session 3.3 .... FL 142
Creating a Classic Tween .... FL 142
    Creating a Classic Tween Animation .... FL 142
Using Graphic Symbols in Animations .... FL 148
Creating Frame-by-Frame Animations .... FL 150
    Creating a Shape Tween .... FL 155
Session 3.3 Quick Check .... FL 155
Tutorial Summary .... FL 156
Key Terms .... FL 156
Review Assignments .... FL 157
Case Problems .... FL 158
Quick Check Answers .... FL 165

Tutorial 4 Creating Complex Animations
Animating with Masks, Text Blocks, Onion Skinning, 3D Rotations, and Inverse Kinematics . . . . .FL 167

Session 4.1 . . . . .FL 168

Modifying Motion Tweens . . . . .FL 168

    Modifying a Motion Path . . . . .FL 168

    Modifying a Tween's Motion Path . . . . .FL 169

Using the Motion Editor . . . . .FL 172

    Using a Mask Layer in an Animation . . . . .FL 177

    Creating an Animation Using a Mask Layer . . . . .FL 180

    Session 4.1 Quick Check . . . . .FL 183

Session 4.2 . . . . .FL 183

Animating Text Blocks . . . . .FL 183

    Adding Animated Text . . . . .FL 184

Animating Individual Letters . . . . .FL 191

    Creating a Complex Text Animation . . . . .FL 192

    Distributing Objects to Individual Layers . . . . .FL 194

Creating 3D Graphic Effects . . . . .FL 196

Session 4.2 Quick Check . . . . .FL 198

Session 4.3 . . . . .FL 198

Creating Complex Animation with Nested Symbols . . . . .FL 198

    Creating a Nested Movie Clip . . . . .FL 199

Creating and Testing Animations Using Onion Skinning . . . . . .FL 200

Using Inverse Kinematics . . . . .FL 205

Using the Movie Explorer . . . . .FL 208

Session 4.3 Quick Check . . . . .FL 212

Tutorial Summary . . . . .FL 212

Key Terms . . . . .FL 212

Review Assignments . . . . .FL 213

Case Problems . . . . .FL 214

Quick Check Answers . . . . .FL 222

Tutorial 5 Making a Document Interactive
Adding Buttons, Actions, and Sounds . . . . .FL 225

Session 5.1 . . . . .FL 226

Exploring the Different Button States . . . . .FL 226

Adding a Button from the Buttons Library . . . . .FL 227

    Editing a Button Instance . . . . .FL 229

Creating a Custom Button . . . . .FL 232

    Copying and Editing a Custom Button . . . . .FL 237

Aligning Objects on the Stage . . . . .FL 240

Session 5.1 Quick Check . . . . .FL 242

Session 5.2 . . . . .FL 242

Understanding Actions . . . . .FL 242

Adding Actions Using the Actions Panel . . . . .FL 243

    Adding Actions to Buttons . . . . .FL 244

    Adding Actions to Frames . . . . .FL 245

Session 5.2 Quick Check . . . . .FL 250

Session 5.3 . . . . .FL 250

Using Sounds in a Flash Animation . . . . .FL 250

    Finding Sounds for Animations .FL 250

Adding Sounds to a Document .FL 251

    Adding Sound to a Button . . . . .FL 253

    Adding a Background Sound . . . . .FL 255

    Changing the Sound Sync Settings . . . . .FL 256

    Adding Sound Effects . . . . .FL 257

Session 5.3 Quick Check ....FL 259

Tutorial Summary ....FL 259

Key Terms ....FL 259

Review Assignments ....FL 260

Case Problems ....FL 260

Quick Check Answers ....FL 265

Tutorial 6 Creating Special Effects with Graphics and Gradients
Working with Bitmaps and Gradients, and Publishing Flash Files ....FL 267

Session 6.1 ....FL 268

Working with Bitmaps ....FL 268

    Importing Bitmaps ....FL 268

    Setting a Bitmap's Properties ....FL 270

Animating Bitmaps ....FL 272

Converting a Bitmap to a Vector Graphic ....FL 281

Session 6.1 Quick Check ....FL 286

Session 6.2 ....FL 286

Using Gradients ....FL 286

    Creating and Saving a Custom Gradient ....FL 287

Applying a Gradient Fill ....FL 289

    Filling Text with a Gradient ....FL 291

Transforming Gradient Fills ....FL 292

Session 6.2 Quick Check ....FL 294

Session 6.3 ....FL 294

Comparing Publishing Options ....FL 294

    Selecting a Document's Publish Settings ....FL 295

Exporting a Flash Document as an Image ....FL 300

Adding Flash Graphics to a Web Page ....FL 301

Session 6.3 Quick Check ....FL 304

Tutorial Summary ....FL 304

Key Terms ....FL 304

Review Assignments ....FL 305

Case Problems ....FL 306

Quick Check Answers ....FL 312

Tutorial 7 Planning and Creating a Flash Web Site
Building a Site with a Template, a Navigation Bar, and ActionScript ....FL 315

Session 7.1 ....FL 316

Understanding the Structure of a Flash Web Site ......FL 316

    Creating a Navigation System ....FL 318

    Exploring a Sample Flash Web Site ....FL 319

Planning a Flash Web Site ....FL 320

    Identifying the Site Goals and Objectives ....FL 320

    Determining the Target Audience ....FL 321

    Making a Web Site Accessible ....FL 322

    Developing the Web Site Content ....FL 322

    Developing a Storyboard and Designing the Navigation System and Site Pages ....FL 323

    Session 7.1 Quick Check ....FL 324

Session 7.2 ....FL 325

Creating a Web Site's Contents ....FL 325

    Creating the Main Document ....FL 325

Using a Flash Template to Create Additional Web Pages .....FL 331

Using External Libraries ....FL 334

Creating a Navigation Bar ....FL 340

    Adding an Animation to a Button Frame ....FL 341

Session 7.2 Quick Check ....FL 346

Session 7.3	FL 346
Using ActionScript	FL 346
Using the loadMovieNum Action	FL 346
Using the Actions Panel	FL 347
Loading External Image Files	FL 352
Using the loadMovie Action	FL 353
Using the Behaviors Panel	FL 356
Session 7.3 Quick Check	FL 358
Tutorial Summary	FL 359
Key Terms	FL 359
Review Assignments	FL 360
Case Problems	FL 361
Quick Check Answers	FL 372

Tutorial 8 Programming with ActionScript 3.0
Adding Interactive Elements to a Flash Web Site . . . . FL 375

Session 8.1	FL 376
Programming with ActionScript 3.0	FL 376
Comparing ActionScript 3.0 and ActionScript 2.0	FL 376
Working with Objects and Properties	FL 376
Using Actions, Methods, and Functions	FL 380
Writing ActionScript Code	FL 381
Adding Events and Event Handling	FL 384
Creating an Event Listener	FL 384
Adding Comments	FL 386
Session 8.1 Quick Check	FL 388

Session 8.2	FL 388
Creating Links to Web Sites	FL 388
Using the URLRequest Class	FL 391
Using a Flash Preloader	FL 394
Creating the Preloader	FL 395
Creating the Preloader Animation	FL 396
Completing the Preloader Code	FL 398
Session 8.2 Quick Check	FL 401
Session 8.3	FL 401
Creating an Input Form	FL 401
Using Dynamic and Input Text	FL 401
Writing ActionScript Code to Do a Calculation	FL 405
Using Expressions and Operators	FL 406
Adding Numeric Feedback to the Preloader	FL 410
Session 8.3 Quick Check	FL 413
Tutorial Summary	FL 413
Key Terms	FL 413
Review Assignments	FL 414
Case Problems	FL 417
Quick Check Answers	FL 427

Tutorial 9 Using Components and Video, and Creating Content for Printing and Mobile Devices
Adding Web Links, Photos, and Video to a Flash Web Site and Creating Mobile Content . . . . FL 429

Session 9.1	FL 430
Using Flash Components	FL 430
Using the ComboBox Component	FL 430
Using the UILoader Component to Display Photos	FL 436

Using the ProgressBar Component . . . . .FL 439

Session 9.1 Quick Check . . . . .FL 442

Session 9.2 . . . . **FL 443**

Adding Video to a Flash Document . . . . .FL 443

    Selecting the Frame Rate and Frame Size . . . . .FL 443

    Using Compression and Decompression . . . . .FL 444

    Using Adobe Media Encoder . . . . .FL 444

    Delivering Video . . . . .FL 447

    Using the Import Video Wizard . . . . .FL 448

Session 9.2 Quick Check . . . . .FL 456

Session 9.3 . . . . **FL 456**

Creating Printable Content . . . . .FL 456

    Creating Content for Printing . . . . .FL 457

    Using the PrintJob Class to Control Printing . . . . .FL 459

Creating Mobile Content . . . . .FL 463

    Creating Content for the Flash Lite Player . . . . .FL 463

Session 9.3 Quick Check . . . . .FL 471

Tutorial Summary . . . . .FL 472

Key Terms . . . . .FL 472

Review Assignments . . . . .FL 473

Case Problems . . . . .FL 476

Quick Check Answers . . . . .FL 488

Reality Check . . . . .FL 490

Additional Case 1

Creating an Interactive Banner for a Web Site . . . . .ADD 1

Additional Case 2

Creating a Web Site with a Banner, a Payment Calculator,
a Photos Page and a Video Page . . . . .ADD 5

Appendix A

Becoming an Adobe Certified Associate . . . . .FL A1

Using Adobe Flash CS4 on a Macintosh . . . . **Online**

This guide is available for download on the book product page at
www.cengage.com/coursetechnology.

Glossary/Index . . . . .REF 1

Task Reference . . . . .REF 9

Flash | FL 1

Tutorial 1

Objectives

Session 1.1
- Discover the types of Web media created in Flash
- Compare vector graphics and bitmap graphics
- Learn how Flash graphics are displayed in a Web page
- Start Flash and explore its main workspace components

Session 1.2
- Display grid lines, guides, and rulers
- Set a document's properties

Session 1.3
- Learn about strokes, fills, and colors
- Select and modify objects
- Use Flash Help

Introducing Adobe Flash CS4 Professional

Exploring the Basic Features of Flash

Case | Admiral Web Design

Admiral Web Design, founded in 2001, is a fast-growing Web site design and development company that specializes in building Web sites for small- to medium-sized businesses and organizations. This innovative Web design company has a growing list of clients from various industries, including a national sports equipment company and a local seafood restaurant. The company's rapid growth and success have largely been due to its energetic and creative staff.

Admiral Web Design is owned by Gloria Adamson and Jim Torres, both graduates of a Web design and multimedia program at a local college. The other full-time employees are Aly Garcia, Chris Johnson, and Raj Sharma. Gloria handles the bulk of the business decisions and oversees the Web site design and development projects. Jim is responsible for marketing and manages the company's finances. Aly is the graphic designer, and Chris and Raj are the site designers responsible for developing the content for the clients' Web sites.

Aly uses **Adobe Flash CS4 Professional (Flash)** to create visually exciting and interactive components, such as animated logos and online interactive advertising, to enhance the clients' Web sites. Flash was originally designed to create small, fast-loading animations that could be used in Web pages. Over the years, Flash has evolved into an advanced authoring tool for creating interactive Web media that range from animated logos to Web site navigational controls and interactive Web sites. Flash can also be used to develop engaging content for mobile devices. You will help Aly develop Flash graphics and animations.

Starting Data Files

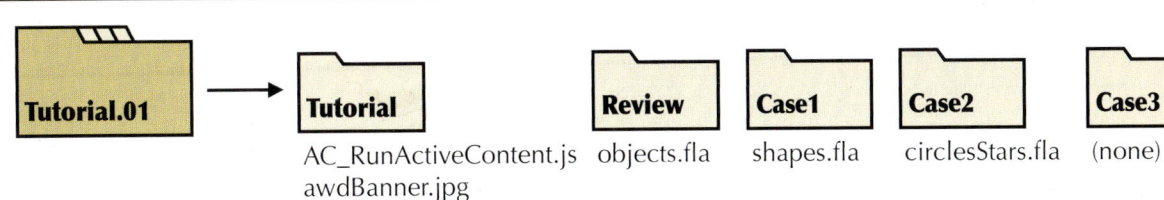

Tutorial.01 →

Tutorial
AC_RunActiveContent.js
awdBanner.jpg
awdFlash.htm
flashAd1.swf
flashAd2.swf
flashAd3.swf
flashAd4.swf
sample.fla
spacewalk.fla

Review
objects.fla

Case1
shapes.fla

Case2
circlesStars.fla

Case3
(none)

Case4
(none)

Session 1.1

Reviewing Types of Web Media

Web pages are made up of text, graphics, animations, sounds, and videos. These elements are referred to as **Web media**. The different types of Web media are created by a variety of programs, and then pulled together to work as a cohesive whole on a Web page through **XHTML**, the underlying code used in creating Web pages. The most common types of Web media besides text are graphics and animations, which can be created in Flash.

Bitmap and Vector Graphics

Graphics fall into essentially two types: bitmap and vector. Each has advantages, disadvantages, and appropriate uses in Web page design.

A **bitmap graphic** is a row-by-row list of every pixel in the graphic, along with each pixel's color. A **pixel** is the smallest picture element on the monitor screen that can be controlled by the computer. A 100×100-pixel bitmap graphic is simply a grid containing 10,000 colored pixels. As a result, resizing a bitmap graphic creates unattractive side effects. If you enlarge a bitmap graphic, for example, the edges become ragged as the pixels are redistributed to fit the larger grid. You cannot easily take a bitmap graphic apart to modify only one portion of the image. Bitmap graphics, however, provide blending and subtle variations in colors and textures. A common bitmap graphic is a digital photograph. You can also create bitmap graphics using imaging software such as Adobe Fireworks or Adobe Photoshop. The two most common file formats for bitmap graphics used in Web pages are JPEG (Joint Photographic Experts Group) and GIF (Graphic Interchange Format).

A **vector graphic** is a set of mathematical instructions that describes the color, outline, and position of all the shapes of the image. Each shape is defined by numbers that represent the shape's position in the window in which it is being displayed. Other numbers represent the points that establish the shape's outline. As a result, vector graphics scale well, which means you can resize a vector image proportionally and the quality remains the same. Vector graphics also appear uniform regardless of the size or resolution of the monitor on which they are displayed. Individual shapes within a vector graphic can be modified independently of the rest. Vector graphics excel at sharp lines, smooth colors, and precise detail. Vector graphic files are generally smaller than bitmap graphic files and take less time to download. Common examples of vector graphics are images created in drawing programs such as Adobe Illustrator as well as images created in Flash.

> **Tip**
>
> Bitmap graphic files in the JPEG format have the file extension .jpg. Bitmap graphic files in the GIF format have the file extension .gif.

InSight | Combining Bitmap and Vector Graphics

Designers often import bitmap graphics into Flash and combine them with vector graphics. For example, bitmap images such as photographs often appear as the background to Flash vector graphics and animations. They tend to soften the overall effect and add a little realism to Flash graphics. Using a bitmap graphic in a Flash document is best when you are developing an advertisement or banner for a business's or professional organization's Web site. You should also edit the bitmap graphic in an image-editing program such as Adobe Photoshop to reduce its size to match the size of the Flash document. Using large bitmap graphics will cause the resulting Flash graphic to download very slowly.

Figure 1-1 shows an image of a basketball as a bitmap graphic (left) and as a vector graphic (right). The bitmap graphic becomes distorted when enlarged, whereas the vector graphic retains its quality.

Figure 1-1 — Bitmap graphic compared to vector graphic

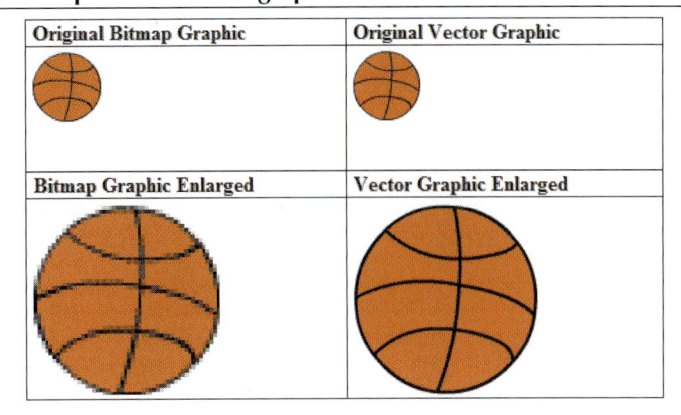

Original Bitmap Graphic	Original Vector Graphic
(small basketball)	(small basketball)
Bitmap Graphic Enlarged	**Vector Graphic Enlarged**
(enlarged pixelated basketball)	(enlarged smooth basketball)

Bitmap and Vector Animation

Animation is a series of still images displayed in sequence to give the illusion of motion. Animation can be accomplished with both bitmap and vector images.

Bitmap animation is created by putting a sequence of bitmap images into one file and playing back the sequence. The playback of the bitmap images produces a perception of motion. Each change the viewer sees requires changing the colors of pixels in the frame. A lot of information is required to keep track of all of the pixel changes even for small images of short duration. The amount of information that must be stored increases dramatically for larger display sizes, longer sequences, or smoother motion. Because of the importance of rapid transmission over the Internet, bitmap motion graphics are usually limited to small display sizes and short sequences.

Vector animation lists shapes and their transformations that are played back in sequence to provide the perception of motion. The information required to describe the modification of shapes in a vector animation is usually less than the information required to describe the pixel changes in a bitmap animation. Also, because vector graphics are resolution-independent, which means that they always appear with the optimum on-screen quality regardless of image size or the screen resolution, increasing the display size of the shapes in a vector animation has no effect on the file size.

Developing Web Media in Flash

Flash allows developers to create media-rich elements that integrate with Web pages and that download quickly. Flash graphics also have streaming capability, which allows animations to start playing even before they download completely. Web media created in Flash are called **documents** and can include text, static images, sound, and video as well as animations. Flash animations are created from a series of graphic objects such as lines, shapes, and text that are then sequenced. The graphics created in Flash are primarily vector graphics but can include bitmap graphics. Flash also supports many import formats so that developers can include media from a broad range of sources including Photoshop and Illustrator files.

| InSight | **Using Media in Flash Documents** |

A completed Flash document can include anything from silent, still imagery to motion graphics with sound and interactivity, as well as elements that incorporate video. Flash enables you to add sound—as sound effects, voiceovers, or music—to any element within a document. You can choose to have sound play all the time, be activated by a mouse click, be turned on and off by the user, or be synchronized with events in your document. You can also incorporate video into a Web page as part of a graphic or animation and add controls to the video elements to enable the viewer to manage the video playback.

Like other media files, a Flash file must be referenced in an XHTML file to be viewed in a Web page. You can publish the XHTML files and references automatically from within the Flash program. If you are experienced with XHTML, you can insert the reference manually or create your own XHTML file to reference and control the Flash file.

While developing content using Flash, you work with a Flash authoring document, referred to as an **FLA file**, which has the .fla file extension. When you're ready to deliver that content for viewing by end users, you publish the Flash document as an **SWF file** (often pronounced "swiff file"), which has the .swf file extension and can be displayed in a Web page. For example, if the Flash document in which you create and develop an animation for the Admiral Web Design Web site is named awdBanner.fla, the published file with the finished animation would be named awdBanner.swf. An SWF file is also called a **Flash movie**.

The SWF file plays in an XHTML file in a Web browser using the **Flash Player plug-in**. All current versions of the major Web browsers come with the Flash Player plug-in installed. Besides allowing Flash documents to be viewed in your browser, the Flash Player plug-in provides controls for zooming in and out of the document, changing the document's quality, printing the document, and other functions. The controls are accessed by right-clicking the animation to open the context menu shown in Figure 1-2.

Tip

The free Flash Player plug-in is available at *www.adobe.com/downloads*.

| Figure 1-2 | Flash Player plug-in context menu |

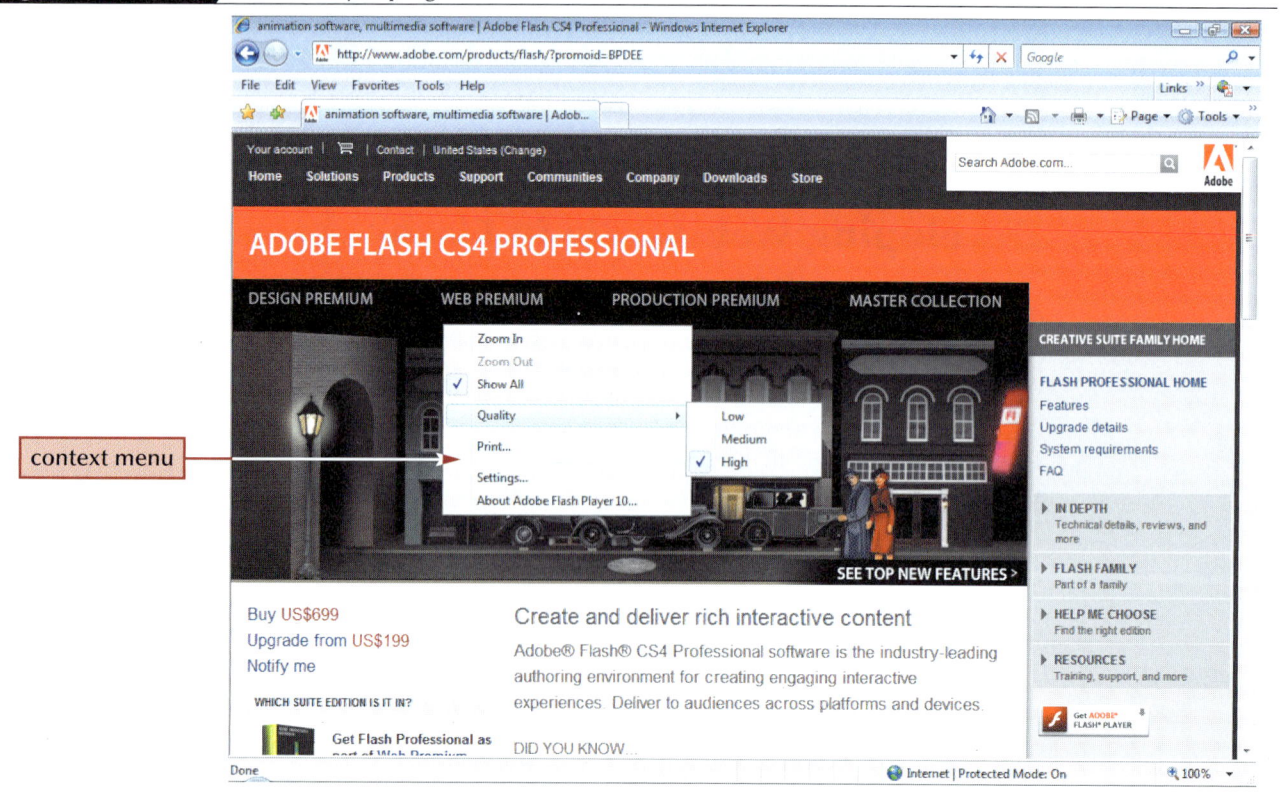

context menu

Another element of Flash is ActionScript, a scripting programming language that enables you to add interactivity to buttons and other Web media that users can click or select to control the Flash graphics or animation they are viewing. You will learn more about ActionScript in later tutorials.

Viewing Flash SWF Files

Aly wants you to look at several examples of Flash SWF files she has created and placed on the Admiral Web Design Web site. You open a Flash Web page in a Web browser the same way you open any other page. If the Flash Player plug-in is installed, the streaming capability of a Flash file allows the player to begin playing the animation as soon as enough of the file has been downloaded. If the Flash Player plug-in is not installed, you can easily install it by downloading the plug-in from the Adobe download Web site.

To view examples of Flash SWF files in your browser:

1. On the taskbar, click the **Start** button, and then click **Internet Explorer**. The Web browser opens, displaying the default home page.

   Trouble? If you don't see Internet Explorer on the Start menu, type Internet Explorer in the Start Search box, and then click Internet Explorer. If you still don't see Internet Explorer, press the Esc key until the Start menu closes, and then ask your instructor or technical support person for assistance.

   Trouble? If you are using Mozilla Firefox or a different Web browser, open that browser, and then modify any Web browser steps in these tutorials as needed.

2. If the Internet Explorer menu bar is not displayed, click the **Tools** button, and then click **Menu Bar**.

3. On the menu bar, click **File**, and then click **Open**. The Open dialog box opens.

4. Click the **Browse** button, navigate to the **Tutorial.01\Tutorial** folder included with your Data Files, click **awdFlash.htm**, click the **Open** button, and then click the **OK** button. The Admiral Web Design sample page appears in the browser window. This page contains several examples of Flash SWF files that are available for Admiral's clients to review.

   Trouble? If you don't have the starting Data Files, you need to get them before you can proceed. Your instructor will either give you the Data Files or ask you to obtain them from a specified location (such as a network drive). In either case, make a backup copy of the Data Files before you start so that you have the original files available in case you need to start over. If you have any questions about the Data Files, see your instructor or technical support person for assistance.

   Trouble? If a dialog box opens stating that Internet Explorer needs to open a new window to display the Web page, click the OK button.

   Trouble? If the Information Bar indicates that your Internet Security settings block the active content in the Admiral Web Design sample page, you need to allow blocked content in this instance and whenever you open an XHTML page in these tutorials. Click the Information Bar, click Allow Blocked Content, and then click the Yes button in the Security Warning dialog box.

5. Right-click one of the animations on the page. The context menu with the controls for the Flash file opens.

6. On the context menu, point to **Quality**. The submenu opens. See Figure 1-3.

Figure 1-3 | **Sample Flash SWF files**

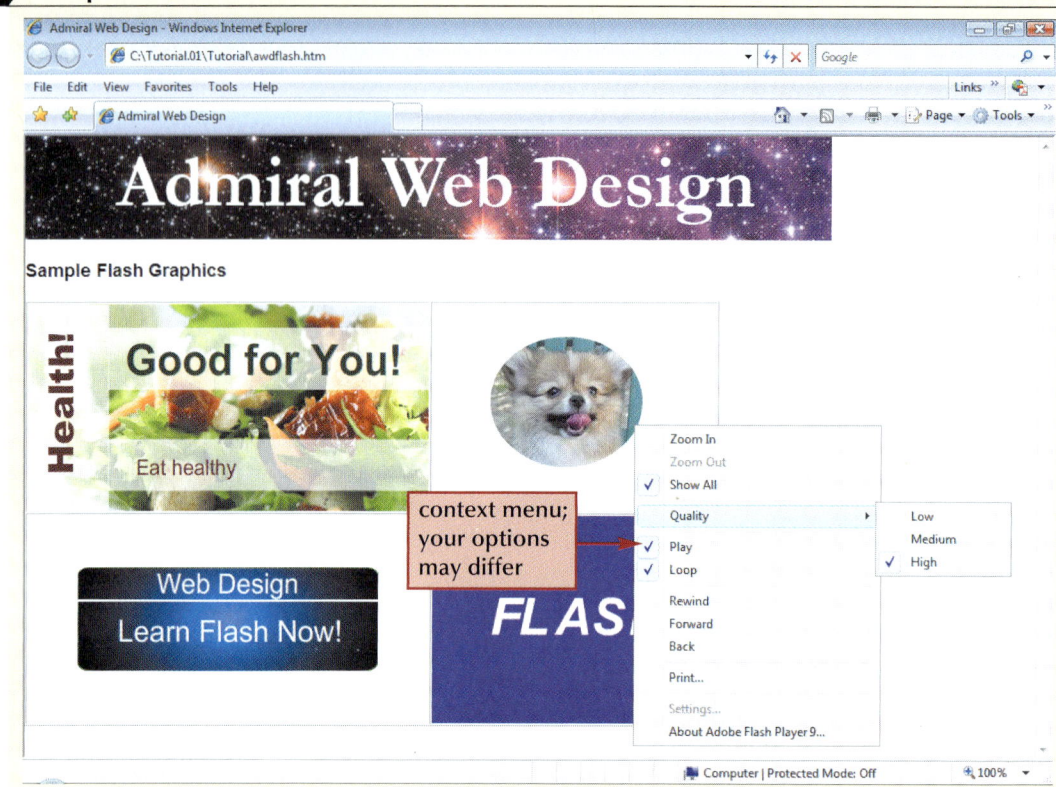

context menu; your options may differ

Trouble? If the text or graphics appear in different locations on your screen, you're probably using a different Web browser. The page layout can differ slightly when viewed with different Web browsers.

▸ 7. On the context menu, click **Play** to remove the check mark. The command is deselected and the animation stops.

▸ 8. Right-click an animation, and then, on the context menu, click **Zoom In**. The graphic's magnification level increases.

▸ 9. Use the context menu controls to rewind, zoom out, and step forward and back through the animation.

▸ 10. On the browser title bar, click the **Close** button . The browser window closes.

Trouble? If a dialog box opens, prompting you to close all of the tabs, click the Close Tabs button.

Tip
When an SWF graphic is magnified, the pointer changes to a hand and you can drag the graphic to see different areas.

Starting Flash

When you first start Flash, or when the program is running but no documents are opened, the Welcome screen appears. The Welcome screen provides access to the most commonly used actions such as opening a recently used file, creating a new Flash document, or creating a document using a template. After you open a document or create a new one, the Flash program window, called the **workspace**, appears. The workspace contains components, such as toolbars and panels, that you can organize to suit your work style and needs.

Aly wants you to set the workspace to its default layout.

To start Flash and open a new Flash file:

▶ 1. Click the **Start** button on the taskbar, click **All Programs**, and then click **Adobe Flash CS4 Professional**. The Flash program window opens and displays the Welcome screen.

   Trouble? If you do not see Adobe Flash CS4 on the All Programs menu, look for and click an Adobe folder, and then click Adobe Flash CS4. If you can't find Adobe Flash CS4 in an Adobe folder, press the Esc key twice to close the Start menu, and then double-click the Adobe Flash CS4 program icon on your desktop. If you still can't find Adobe Flash CS4, ask your instructor or technical support person for help.

   Trouble? If the Adobe Product Activation dialog box opens, this is probably the first time Flash was started on this computer. Click the appropriate option button, click the Continue button, enter the information requested, and then click the Register button. If you do not know your serial number or need further assistance, ask your instructor or technical support person.

▶ 2. If necessary, on the Application bar, click the **Maximize** button ☐ to maximize the Flash program window.

▶ 3. In the Create New section of the Welcome screen, click **Flash File (ActionScript 3.0)**. An untitled Flash file window opens.

   Trouble? If the Welcome screen is hidden, on the Application bar, click File, click New to open the New Document dialog box, click Flash File (ActionScript 3.0) in the Type box on the General tab of the New Document dialog box, and then click the OK button.

The Flash workspace can be customized, which means you can easily change the way different components are arranged. The figures in these tutorials show the Flash workspace in the Essentials layout. You'll reset the workspace to the Essentials layout.

To set the workspace to the default Essentials layout:

▶ 1. On the Application bar, click **Window**, point to **Workspace**, and then click **Reset 'Essentials'**. The panels in the Flash workspace reset to their default Essentials layout.

▶ 2. On the Application bar, click **Window**, and then point to **Toolbars**. The menu of available toolbars opens.

▶ 3. Verify that **Main** and **Controller** do not have check marks next to them and that **Edit Bar** has a check mark next to it. If necessary, click a command to add or remove the check mark; otherwise, press the Esc key twice to close the menu. See Figure 1-4.

> **Tip**
> You can also use the workspace switcher button on the Application bar to select or reset the workspace layout.

| Figure 1-4 | Default Essentials layout |

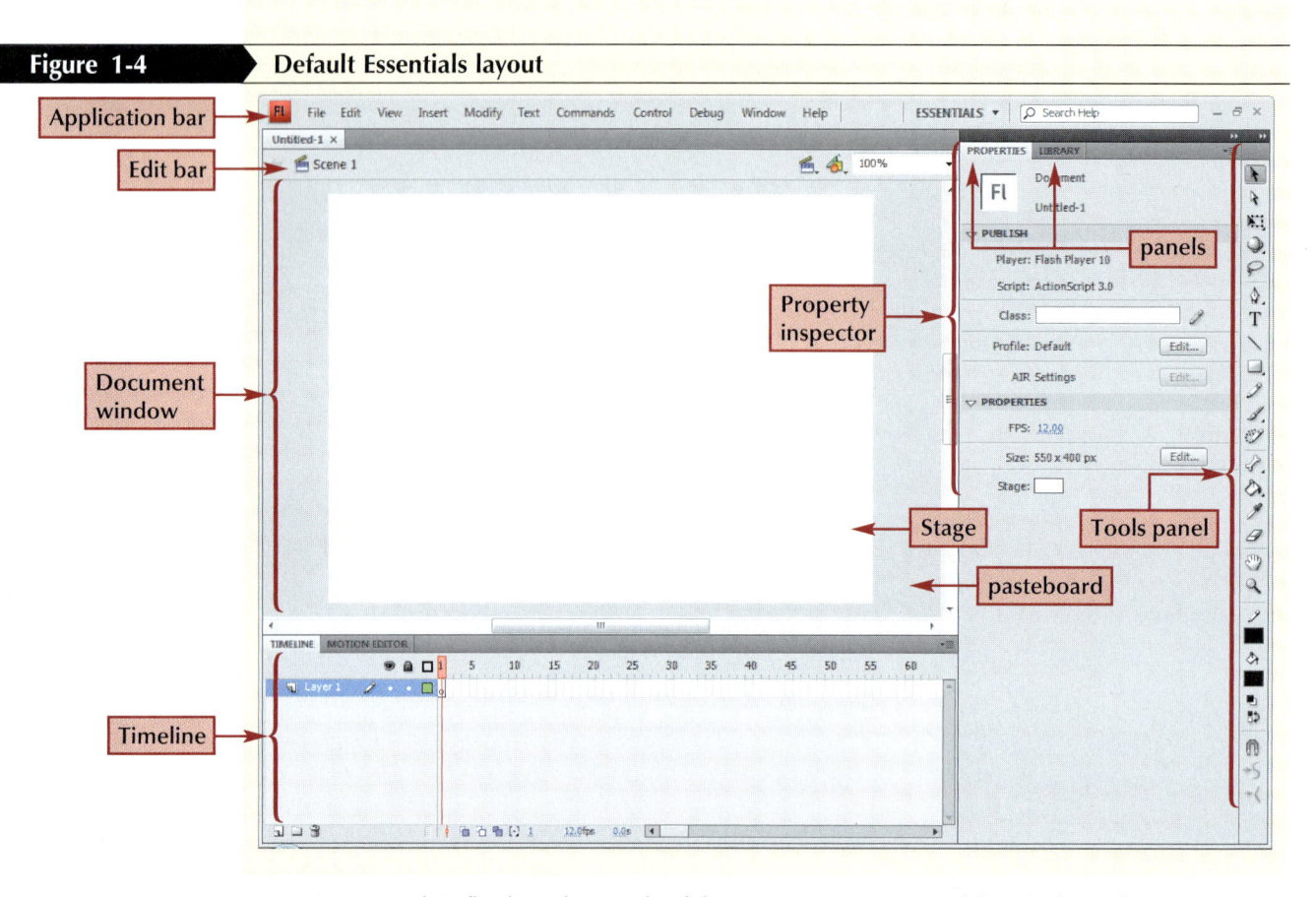

Figure 1-5 briefly describes each of the main components of the Flash workspace.

| Figure 1-5 | Main components of the Flash workspace |

Component	Description
Application bar	Lists the menu categories such as File, Edit, View, Insert, and Help, which include commands to access most of the Flash program features; also includes the workspace switcher and the Search Help box
Document window	The main workspace that consists of the pasteboard and the Stage
Edit bar	Displays the current scene number, the Edit Scene button, the Edit Symbols button, and the Zoom control
Panels	Contain controls for viewing and changing the properties of objects
Pasteboard	Located in the Document window; holds objects that are not part of the viewable Stage and that move onto or off the Stage as part of an animation
Property inspector	Provides easy access to the most common attributes of the currently selected tool or object
Stage	Located in the Document window; the rectangular area where you assemble and position all of the viewable objects that are part of a Flash document
Timeline	Displays and controls the layers and frames that make up an animation and organizes the objects that are part of the document
Tools panel	Contains the Flash tools, such as the tools for drawing and painting lines and shapes, selecting objects, changing the view of the Stage, and choosing colors

The five most commonly used components of the Flash workspace are the Stage, pasteboard, Timeline, Tools panel, and panels. You'll learn more about these components in the next session.

Previewing Documents

As you develop a Flash document, you often need to preview it to check the results of your changes. You can preview your work in Flash in several ways. You can preview or play the document's animation within the Flash workspace, publish the file to play in a separate Flash Player window, or publish it to play in a Web page in your default Web browser. Previewing the document in the Flash workspace is the quickest method, although some animation effects and interactive functions only work in the published format.

You will view Aly's document from the Flash workspace. The spacewalk.fla file is a Flash document consisting of a simple animation.

To preview the spacewalk.fla document in the Flash workspace:

1. On the Application bar, click **File**, and then click **Close**. If a dialog box prompts you to save changes, click the **No** button. The document closes and the Welcome screen appears.

2. On the Application bar, click **File**, and then click **Open**. The Open dialog box opens.

3. Navigate to the location where you store your Data Files, open the **Tutorial.01\Tutorial** folder, click **spacewalk.fla** in the file list, and then click the **Open** button. The spacewalk document opens on the Stage, and its name appears in the page tab.

   Trouble? If the spacewalk.fla file does not include the .fla extension in its filename, your computer's operating system is not configured to display file extensions. Just click spacewalk in the file list.

4. On the Application bar, click **File**, and then click **Save As**. The Save As dialog box opens.

5. Navigate to the **Tutorial.01\Tutorial** folder included with your Data Files if necessary, type **spacewalkNew** in the File name text box, and then click the **Save** button. The document is saved with the new name, which appears in the page tab.

6. On the Application bar, click **View**, point to **Magnification**, and then click **Show All**. The workspace changes to show the entire document. See Figure 1-6.

FL 10 Flash | Tutorial 1 Introducing Adobe Flash CS4 Professional

Figure 1-6 spacewalkNew.fla document

new filename appears in the page tab

entire document displayed in the workspace

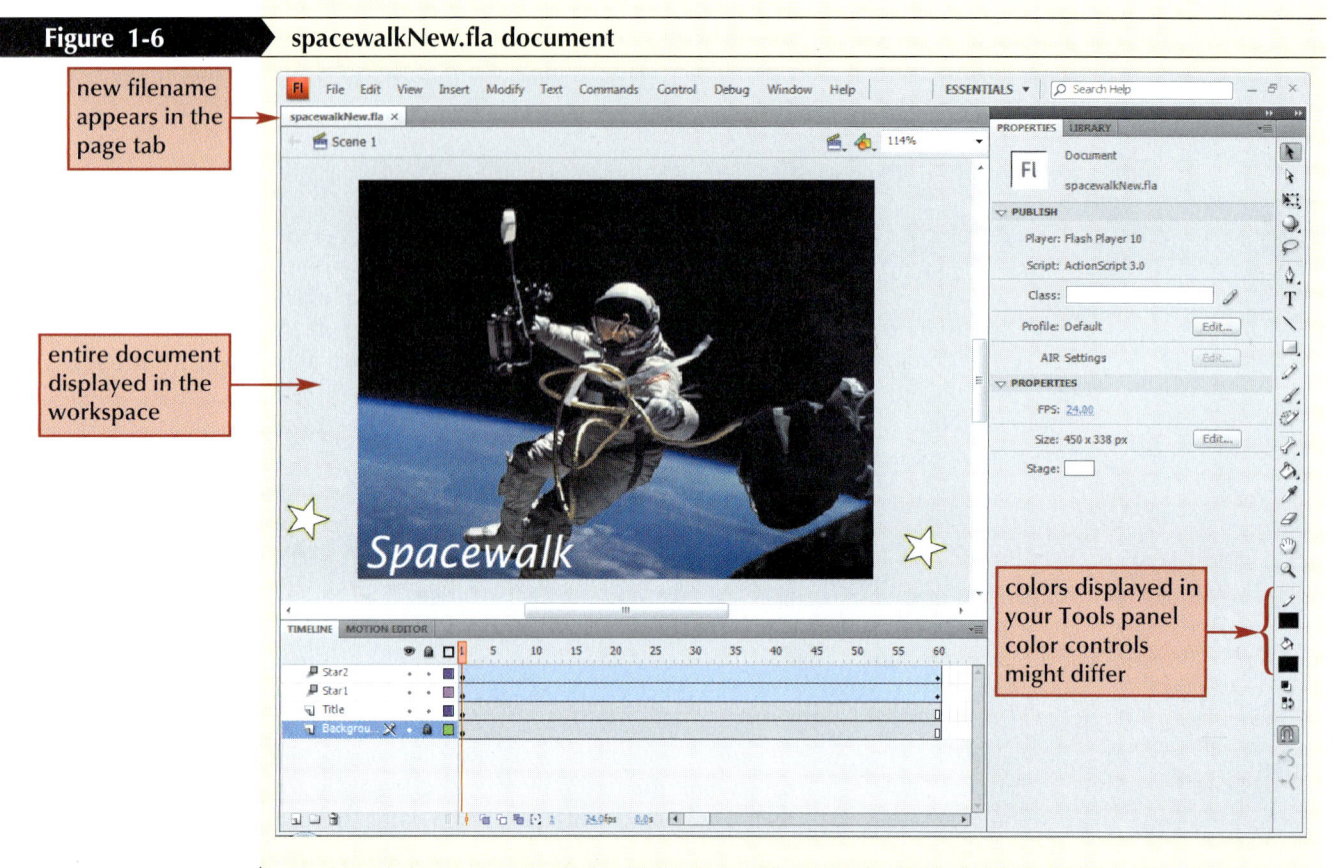

colors displayed in your Tools panel color controls might differ

▸ 7. On the Application bar, click **Control**, and then click **Play**. As the animation plays, notice that the Timeline tracks the animation's progress. You will learn more about the elements in the Timeline later in the next session.

You can also preview the published file in a separate Flash Player window or in a browser window.

To preview the published file in a separate Flash Player window and in a browser:

Tip

You can also test the movie by pressing the Ctrl+Enter keys.

▸ 1. On the Application bar, click **Control**, and then click **Test Movie**. Flash creates a file in the SWF format, opens it in a separate window, and then plays it with the Flash Player. See Figure 1-7.

| Figure 1-7 | spacewalkNew.swf document playing in Flash Player window |

▶ 2. On the Flash Player window title bar, click the **Close** button [X]. Flash Player closes and you to return to the Flash document.

   Trouble? If the Flash program closes, you probably clicked the Close button on the Flash program Application bar. Restart Flash, and then open the spacewalkNew.fla document again.

   Next, you will preview the Flash file in a Web page.

▶ 3. On the Application bar, click **File**, point to **Publish Preview**, and then click **HTML**. The default browser on your computer opens and the SWF file plays in the browser window. See Figure 1-8.

| Figure 1-8 | spacewalkNew.swf file playing in a Web browser |

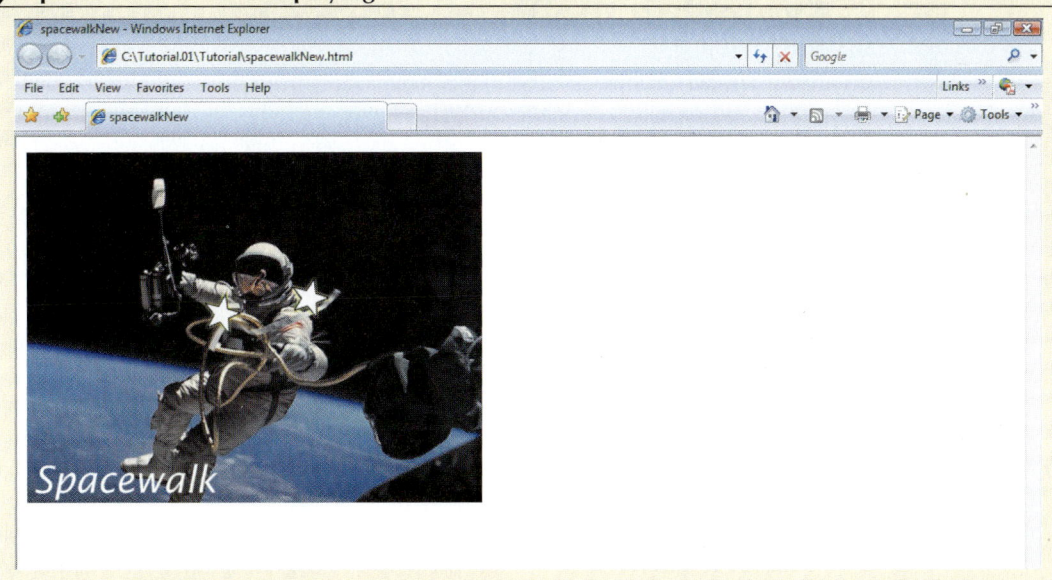

Trouble? If your Web browser window does not appear, it might be minimized. Click the taskbar button for the Web browser.

> **Trouble?** If the animation does not play in your browser window, you may need to allow blocked content. If the animation still doesn't play, start your Web browser, and then open the spacewalkNew.html file located in the Tutorial.01\Tutorial folder included with your Data Files.
>
> ▶ 4. On the browser title bar, click the **Close** button to close the browser window and return to Flash.

So far, you have learned about Web media and viewed sample Flash documents. In the next session, you will learn about the main components of the Flash workspace and how to change a document's settings.

Review | Session 1.1 Quick Check

1. Flash creates _____ -based graphics.
2. What file extension does a Flash document have after it has been published for Web delivery?
3. List three things you might find in a Flash document.
4. True or False? Flash allows you to synchronize sound with events in your document.
5. Bitmap graphics store information as a grid of _____ .
6. How does a vector graphic store image data?
7. Does the term "resolution-independent" apply to bitmap graphics, vector graphics, or both?
8. What are two common results of enlarging a bitmap image?

Session 1.2

Exploring the Workspace Components

The main components of the Flash workspace are the Stage, pasteboard, Timeline, Tools panel, and panels. The Stage and the pasteboard make up the Document window.

Stage

The **Stage** is where you create, import, and assemble all of the graphic objects for a document. The Stage is the central area of the Document window. Any graphic object must be on the Stage to appear in the final document, whether that object is static or animated. The Stage shows only the objects that are visible at a particular point in an animation. In fact, the Stage in Flash is just like the stage in a dramatic production. As the production progresses, actors appear and disappear, and move around from place to place on the Stage.

Because Flash is used to create animations, you expect different objects to be visible at different times during playback. While you are working on a project, the Stage displays only those objects that are associated with the currently selected frame. Flash documents are divided into frames, which represent units of time, and each frame might contain different images or different states of the same image. If you select another frame, objects might appear or disappear, change position or change appearance.

Pasteboard

Surrounding the Stage is a gray area called the **pasteboard**. When you complete a Flash document and publish it to view it on a Web page, only the objects and portions of objects on the Stage appear. Objects and portions of objects in the pasteboard are not shown. You can also place a graphic in the pasteboard and then animate it to move onto the Stage.

InSight	**Using the Pasteboard**

Designers often place instructions or comments in the pasteboard for reference as they work with a Flash document. These instructions or comments are not visible when the document is published, but are only visible to the designer and help guide the designer in the development of the Flash document. The pasteboard is also a convenient place to store graphic objects until you are ready to add them to the Stage. So, you can use the pasteboard as a notes or storage area as you develop Flash documents.

Timeline

The **Timeline**, shown in Figure 1-9, controls and coordinates the layers and frames that make up a Flash document. Layers are used to organize the images, animations, and other objects that are part of a document. As mentioned earlier, a frame represents a unit of time. Another key element of the Timeline is the **playhead**, a marker that indicates which frame is currently selected in the Timeline.

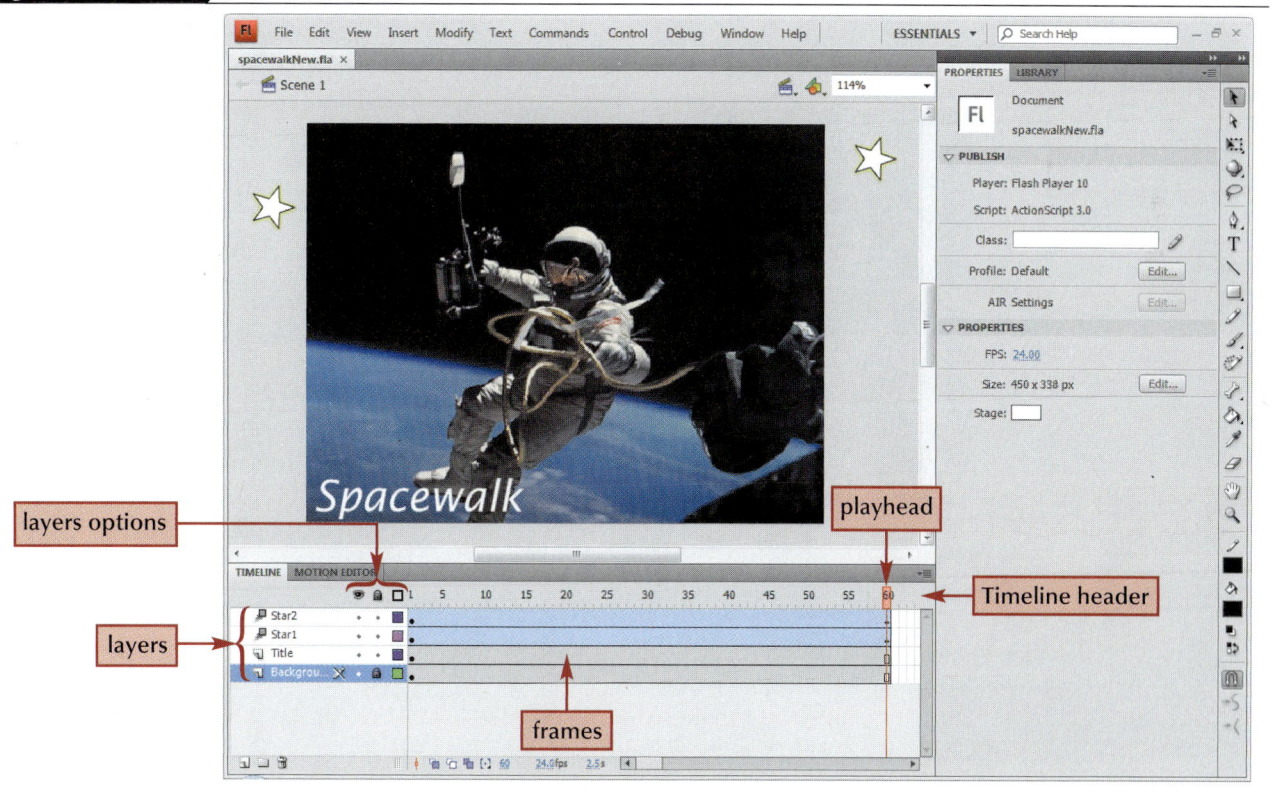

Figure 1-9   Flash Timeline

Flash documents are divided into frames similar to a motion picture film. The Timeline is used to coordinate and control the timing of the animation by determining how and when these frames are displayed. Each frame can contain different images or different states of the same image. As the document's animation is played over time, the playhead

FL 14 Flash | Tutorial 1 Introducing Adobe Flash CS4 Professional

moves from frame to frame and the contents of each frame appear in succession, achieving the perception of motion. You can play an animation using the commands on the Control menu. You can also play the animation manually by **scrubbing**, or dragging the playhead back and forth through the frames. Scrubbing is useful when testing an animation during development. A new document in Flash contains one frame. You add more frames as you build an animation.

The Timeline also controls layers. The layers are listed in a column on the left side of the Timeline. Each row represents one layer. The frames for that layer are shown to the right of the layer name. A new Flash document starts with one layer. For each layer you add, another row is inserted into the Timeline. You can place different objects on the different layers. When you draw or change something on a layer, only the contents of the active layer are changed. The objects on the other layers are not affected.

> **Tip**
> To resize the layer name column of the Timeline, drag the bar separating the layer name column and the frames section left or right.

To explore frames, layers, and the playhead in the Timeline:

1. If you took a break after the previous session, make sure the spacewalkNew.fla document is open, the workspace is reset to the Essentials layout, and the Stage magnification is set to Show All.

2. Scrub the playhead by dragging it back and forth along the Timeline header. As you scrub, the animation on the Stage changes based on the content of the different frames.

3. In the Timeline header, click **Frame 35**. Frame 35 is the current frame, and its contents appear on the Stage. See Figure 1-10.

Figure 1-10   Frame selected in the Timeline header

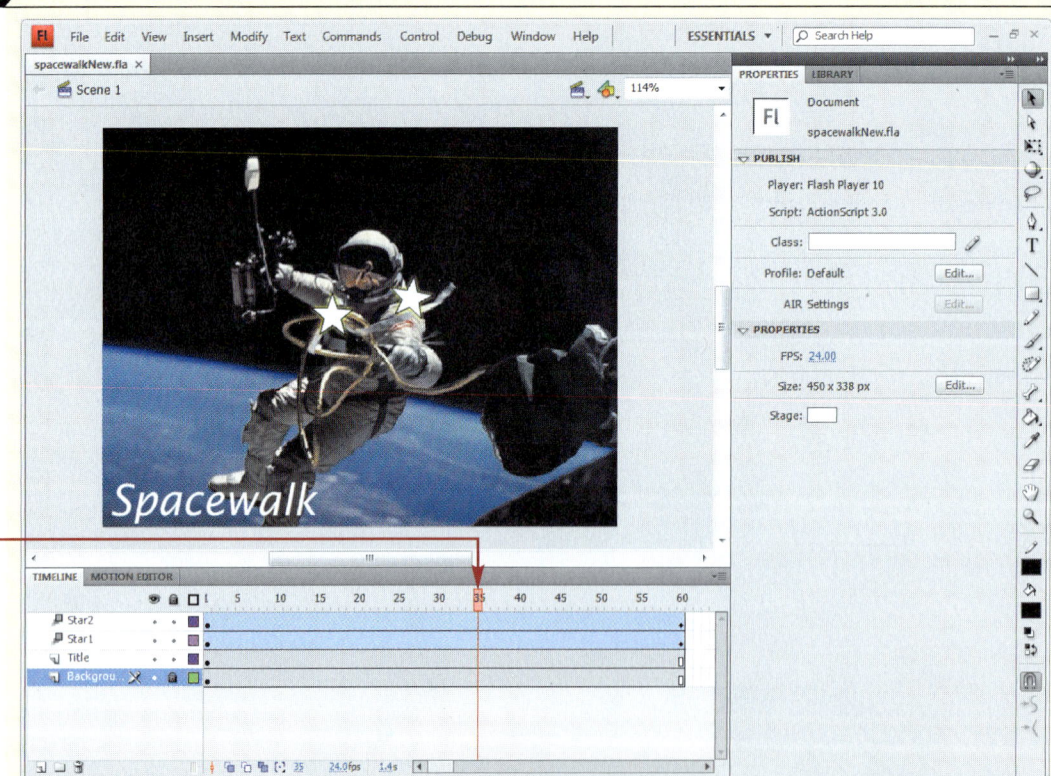

click Frame 35 in the Timeline header

4. In the Title layer under the Show or Hide All Layers column of the Timeline, click the dot. The dot changes to a Hidden Layer icon ❌ and the contents of the Title layer are hidden.

5. In the Title layer, click the **Hidden Layer** icon ❌. The contents of the Title layer are displayed.

Tools Panel

The **Tools panel**, located on the right side of the Flash workspace, contains the tools that you use to draw, paint, select, and modify Flash graphics. The Tools panel also contains tools to change the magnification level of the Stage and to select colors.

You select a tool in the Tools panel by clicking the tool's button or pressing the tool's keyboard shortcut. A small arrow in the lower-right corner of a tool's button indicates that other tools are hidden behind the button. To access the hidden tools, click and hold the tool button to open a pop-up menu, and then click a tool on the pop-up menu to select it. The function of the default tools and their corresponding button and shortcut are described in Figure 1-11.

Figure 1-11   Tools panel tools and their functions

Tool Name	Button	Shortcut Key	Function
Selection		V	Selects objects in the Document window; you must select an object to modify it
Subselection		A	Modifies specific anchor points in a line or curve
Free Transform		Q	Moves, scales, rotates, skews, or distorts objects
3D Rotation		W	Rotates movie clips in three-dimensional space
Lasso		L	Selects individual objects or a group of objects
Pen		P	Draws lines or curves by creating anchor points that connect them; clicking draws points for straight lines; clicking and dragging draws points for smooth, curved lines
Text		T	Creates and edits text
Line		N	Draws straight lines (strokes) of varying lengths, widths, and colors
Rectangle		R	Draws rectangles of different sizes and colors
Pencil		Y	Draws lines and shapes in a free-form mode
Brush		B	Paints fills with brush strokes
Deco		U	Applies a pattern, such as a grid or vine fill, to an area or fill
Bone		X	Links objects so that animations applied to one object also affect the linked objects
Paint Bucket		K	Fills enclosed areas of a drawing with color
Eyedropper		I	Picks up styles of existing lines, fills, and text and applies them to other objects
Eraser		E	Erases lines and fills
Hand		H	Moves the view of the Stage and pasteboard
Zoom		M	Increases or reduces the view of the Stage and pasteboard
Stroke Color control			Sets the stroke color from the color palette
Fill Color control			Sets the fill color from the color palette
Black and white button			Sets the stroke color to black and the fill color to white
Swap colors button			Swaps the current stroke and fill colors

The first area of the Tools panel contains tools to select and modify graphic images in a Flash document. The Selection tool, Subselection tool, and Lasso tool are used to select one or more objects or to select part of an object by dragging a marquee around them. A **marquee** is an outline that encloses an area to be selected. The Selection and Subselection tools create rectangular marquees. The Lasso tool creates a free-form marquee. The Free Transform tool is used to rotate, skew, scale, or distort selected objects. The 3D Rotation tool rotates movie clips to create a three-dimensional effect.

The second area of the Tools panel contains tools that are used to create and modify the lines, shapes, and text that make up the graphic images of a Flash document. For example, you can draw rectangles and ovals, you can draw lines and curves, you can draw patterns, and you can create and edit text.

The third area of the Tools panel contains tools used to fill in shapes with color, to copy color from one object to another, and to erase parts of an object.

The fourth area of the Tools panel contains the Hand tool and the Zoom tool. The Hand tool converts the pointer to a hand that can be dragged to move the view of the Stage. This is especially useful when you want to see a different area of a document that has been magnified. The Zoom tool changes the view of the Stage by reducing or enlarging it. Neither of these tools affects the way the Flash graphic is displayed to the end user.

Some tools have modifiers that change the way a specific tool functions. The modifiers appear at the bottom of the Tools panel when the tool is selected. For example, when you select the Zoom tool, the Enlarge and Reduce modifier buttons appear so you can choose whether the Zoom tool magnifies or shrinks the view of the Stage.

> **Tip**
> To collapse the tools to icons, click the double-arrow icon at the top of the Tools panel.

InSight | Using the Tools Panel Effectively

As you create documents in Flash, you most often will use the tools in the Tools panel. Always look carefully at which tool is selected before you click an object on the Stage. The pointer changes to reflect the function of the tool that is currently selected. For example, when the Zoom tool is selected, the pointer appears as a magnifying glass. Double-check which tool is selected to ensure you make the changes you intended.

You'll use some of the tools in the Tools panel to modify the spacewalkNew.fla document.

To use tools in the Tools panel to modify the spacewalkNew.fla document:

▶ 1. On the Application bar, click **Control**, and then click **Rewind**. Frame 1 of the document becomes the current frame.

▶ 2. In the Tools panel, click the **Selection** tool to select it, if necessary. The pointer changes to .

▶ 3. In the pasteboard to the lower-left of the Stage, click the **star**. A light blue box surrounds the star to indicate that it is selected and a pink dotted line appears across the Stage to indicate the path of the star's animation. See Figure 1-12.

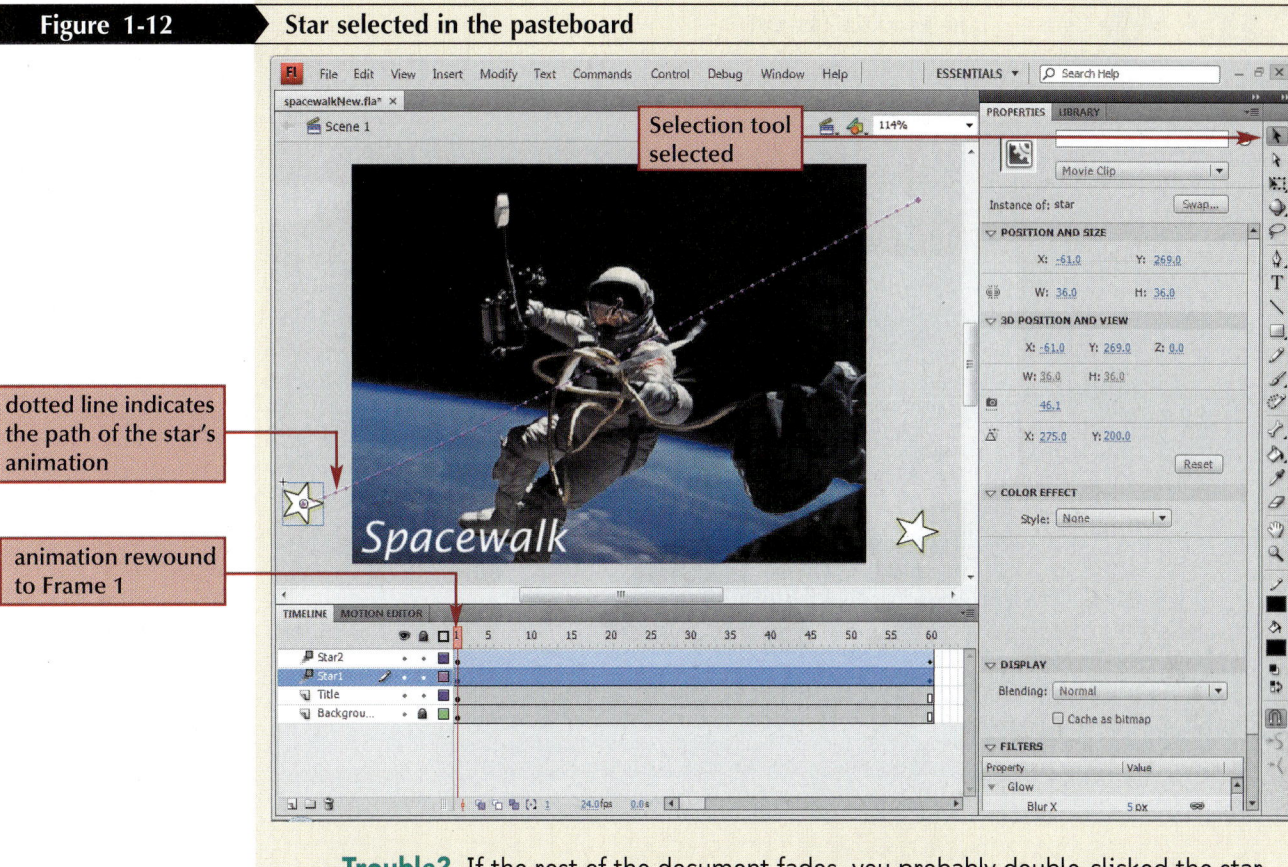

Tutorial 1 Introducing Adobe Flash CS4 Professional | Flash | **FL 17**

Figure 1-12   **Star selected in the pasteboard**

[Screenshot callouts: "Selection tool selected"; "dotted line indicates the path of the star's animation"; "animation rewound to Frame 1"]

Trouble? If the rest of the document fades, you probably double-clicked the star and entered a different editing mode. On the Edit bar, click the Scene 1 link.

4. Drag the selected star up toward the top of the pasteboard just to the left of the Stage. This becomes the new starting point for the star animation. The star's animation path is modified based on the animation's starting point.

   You'll preview the animation to see how moving the star changed its path.

5. On the Application bar, click **Control**, and then click **Play**. The animation changed based on the different starting point of the star.

Panels

Flash puts most of the controls you need into panels that are available as you work. A **panel** contains controls for viewing and changing the properties of objects such as vector and bitmap graphics. Flash includes panels for aligning objects, transforming objects, and mixing and selecting colors. The Window menu lists all of the available panels. Any panel with a check mark next to its name appears in the workspace. Each displayed panel lists its name in a tab. Panel menus are accessible from the panel menu button located in the upper-right corner of the panel. Two or more panels displayed together form a **panel group**. A **dock** is a collection of individual panels or panel groups. Figure 1-13 shows the panels in the Essentials layout.

Figure 1-13 | Panels in the Essentials layout

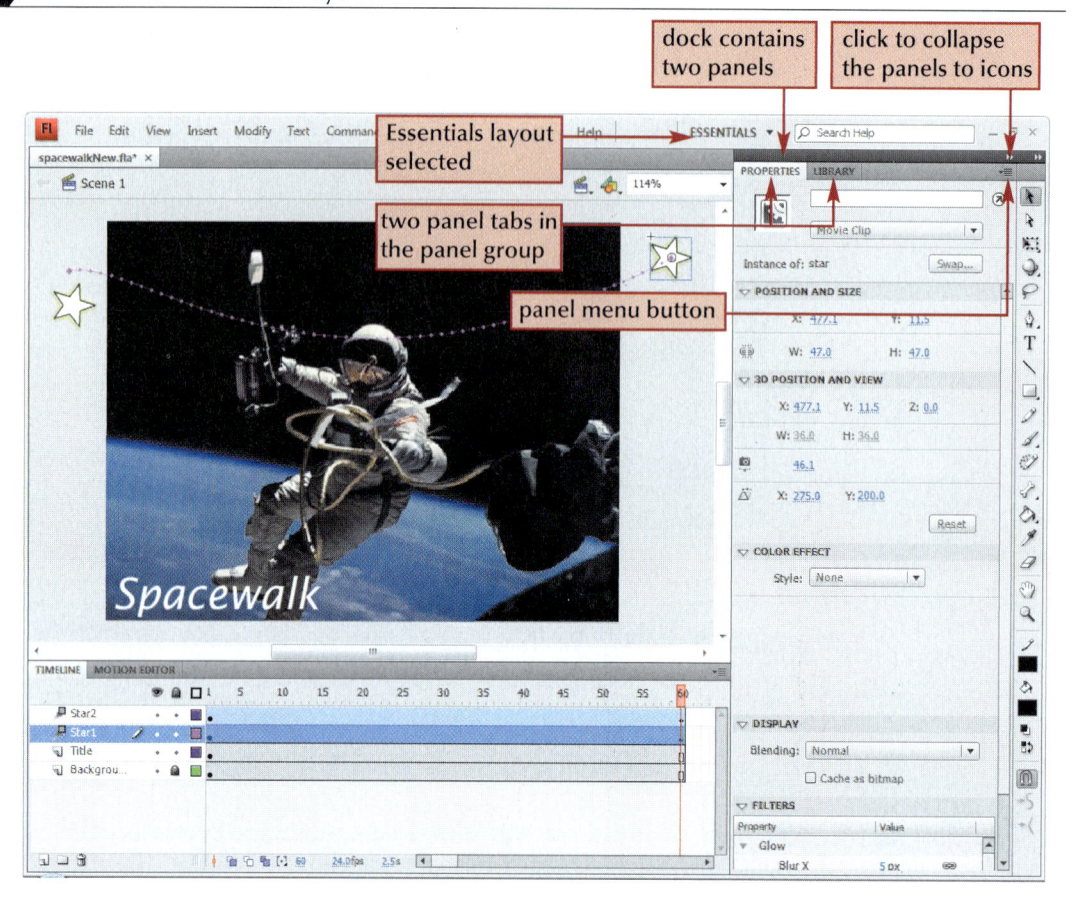

You can organize the panels according to your preference. You can close a panel you don't use often, reposition panels to better fit how you work, and minimize or collapse panels to icons to minimize the space they occupy in the workspace. You can also move a panel into another dock or panel group or create a free-floating panel by moving it onto the workspace.

You can work with panel groups in much the same way. You can close, reposition, minimize, or collapse a panel group. You can move a panel group to a new location in a dock or create a free-floating panel group. You can also stack free-floating panels as one unit. A minimized panel group has only its panel tabs visible. In a collapsed panel group, each panel appears as a button in the dock, as shown in Figure 1-14. You click a panel's button to expand or collapse that panel.

Figure 1-14 | Panels collapsed to icons

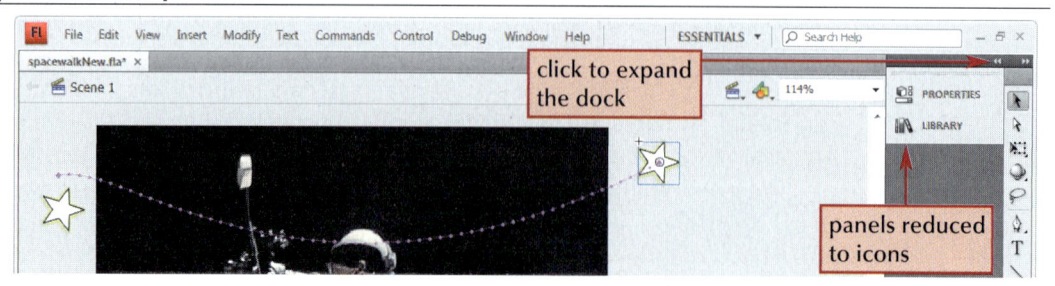

Flash contains several preset arrangements of the workspace which are easily accessible using the workspace switcher on the Application bar. Each preset workspace, such as Designer, Developer, and Essentials, reflects a different way of working with Flash based on the type of project you are creating or your preferred panel and document window arrangement.

Reference Window | Organizing Panels and Panel Groups

- To display or hide a panel, on the Application bar, click Window, and then click the panel name.
- To move a panel, drag and drop its tab into another dock or panel group or the workspace.
- To collapse or expand a panel group, click its title bar.
- To move a panel group, drag its title bar to another location in a dock or in the workspace.
- To minimize or maximize a dock, click the Collapse to Icons button or Expand Panels button in the upper-right corner of the dock.
- To select a preset panel arrangement, on the Application bar, click the workspace switcher, and then click a preset workspace.

After you customize the panel arrangement, you can save the layout. The next time you start Flash, you can select the saved panel layout to quickly rearrange the panels to that layout.

To collapse, expand, and reposition panels:

▶ 1. Click the **LIBRARY** panel tab. The Library panel moves to the front of the panel group. See Figure 1-15.

Figure 1-15 — Library panel

▶ 2. On the Application bar, click **Window**, and then click **Movie Explorer**. The Movie Explorer panel opens as a free-floating panel.

You can combine two or more panels together as a free-floating panel group.

▶ 3. Drag the **LIBRARY** panel tab to the Movie Explorer panel title bar and drop the panel when the blue highlighted line appears around the Movie Explorer panel. The Movie Explorer panel and the Library panel are now grouped as a free-floating panel group. See Figure 1-16.

Figure 1-16 Free-floating panel group

Library panel moved into the panel group

Panels collapsed to icons minimize the amount of occupied space.

4. In the upper-right corner of the dock above the Tools panel, click the **Collapse to Icons** button. The Tools panel collapses to icons.

5. In the dock, click the **Tools** button. The Tools panel expands. See Figure 1-17.

Figure 1-17 Tools panel expanded

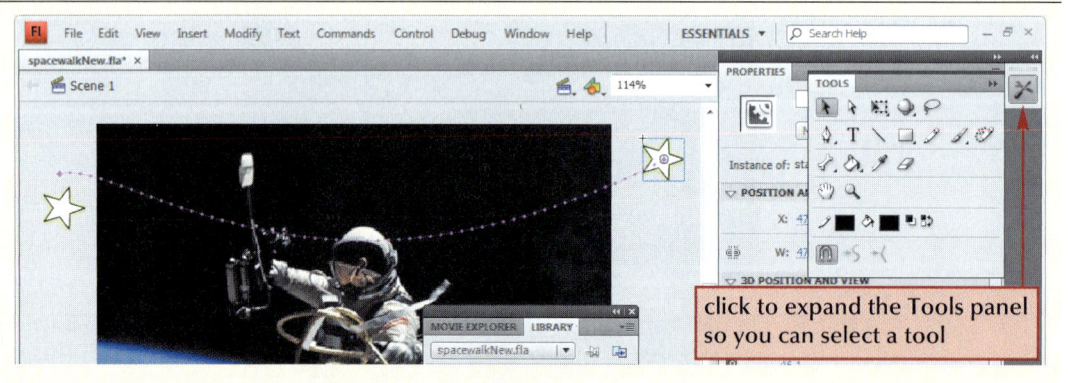

click to expand the Tools panel so you can select a tool

6. In the dock, click the **Tools** button again. The panel collapses to an icon.

   The workspace switcher on the Application bar contains options for quickly changing the layout of the panels.

7. On the Application bar, click the **Workspace Switcher** button (labeled ESSENTIALS), and then click **Designer**. The panels are docked along the right and left sides of the workspace with the Timeline and Document window at the center. See Figure 1-18.

Tutorial 1 Introducing Adobe Flash CS4 Professional | Flash FL 21

| Figure 1-18 | Workspace in the Designer layout |

(Screenshot showing Flash workspace in Designer layout with labels: Tools panel, Document window, Property inspector, Timeline, click to select a workspace layout, panels)

8. On the Application bar, click the **Workspace Switcher** button (labeled DESIGNER), and then click **Essentials**. The panels return to their previous layout.

9. On the Application bar, click the **Workspace Switcher** button (labeled ESSENTIALS), and then click **Reset 'Essentials'**. The panels are arranged in the default Essentials layout.

Property Inspector

The **Property inspector**, which is located at the right side of the Flash workspace and labeled Properties, is a special panel that provides easy access to the most common attributes of the currently selected tool or object. The contents of the Property inspector change to reflect the selected tool. For example, if you click the Selection tool in the Tools panel, the Property inspector displays information about the document such as its Publish settings, the background color, or the frame rate. If you select an object on the Stage, such as the star, the Property inspector displays properties specific to the object, such as the object's name, its X and Y coordinates (location on the Stage), and its width and height.

You'll use the Property inspector to change the star's properties.

To use the Property inspector to change the star's locations and dimensions:

1. On the Application bar, click **Control**, and then click **Rewind**. Frame 1 is the current frame.

2. In the Tools panel, click the **Selection** tool, if necessary. The Property inspector displays information about the spacewalkNew.fla document. See Figure 1-19.

FL 22 Flash | Tutorial 1 Introducing Adobe Flash CS4 Professional

Figure 1-19 | **Property Inspector for the Selection tool**

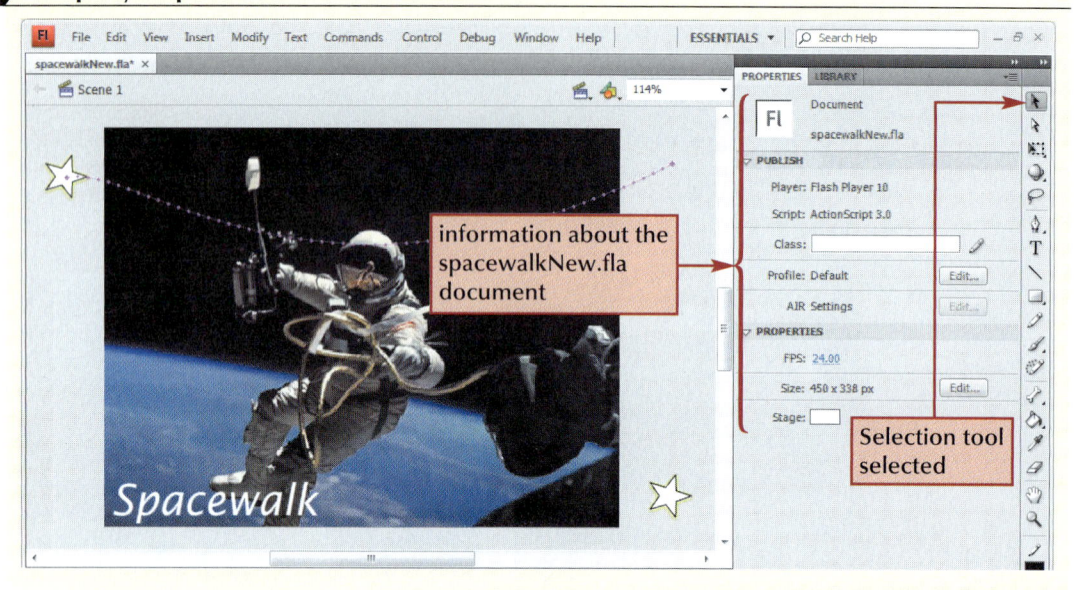

information about the spacewalkNew.fla document

Selection tool selected

Trouble? If only the section names are visible in the Property inspector, you need to expand the sections. Click the section name to expand a collapsed section or collapse an expanded section.

▶ 3. In the pasteboard, click the **star** located to the left of the Stage. The star is selected, and information about the star appears in the Property inspector.

To reposition the star, you will change its X and Y coordinates. These values represent the horizontal (X) and vertical (Y) positions of the star relative to the upper-left corner of the Stage.

▶ 4. In the Position and Size section of the Property inspector, click the X value to select it, type **50**, and then press the **Enter** key. The star is repositioned horizontally.

▶ 5. In the Position and Size section of the Property inspector, click the Y value to select it, type **200**, and then press the **Enter** key. The star is repositioned vertically. See Figure 1-20.

Figure 1-20   **Star repositioned in the pasteboard**

selected star in its new position

information about the selected star

new X and Y coordinates

You can also change the coordinate and size values in the Property inspector by pointing to the value and then dragging the pointer left or right to reduce or increase the value, respectively, as shown in Figure 1-21. The pointer changes to a hand with arrows indicating you can adjust the value.

Figure 1-21   **Hand pointer used to set object's position**

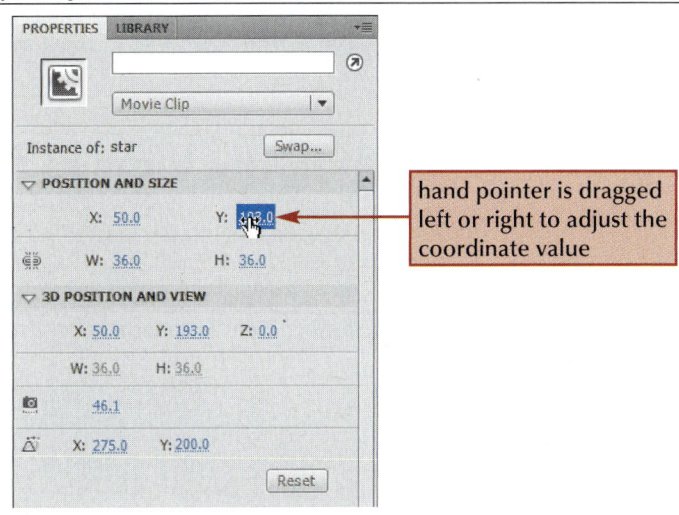

hand pointer is dragged left or right to adjust the coordinate value

You can change the star's dimensions by adjusting the values for the width (W) and the height (H).

To use the Property inspector to change the star's location and dimensions:

▶ 1. In the Position and Size section of the Property inspector, click the **Lock width and height values together** icon, if necessary, to change it to locked.

▶ 2. In the Position and Size section of the Property inspector, point to the W value, and then drag the hand pointer to the left to change the value to **15.0**. The height (H) value adjusts proportionally to the new width value and the star gets smaller.

▶ 3. On the Application bar, click **Control**, and then click **Go To End**. Frame 60 is the current frame. Click the **star** located to the right of the Stage to select it.

▶ 4. In the Position and Size section of the Property inspector, point to the W value, and then drag the hand pointer to the right to change the value to **60**. The height (H) value adjusts proportionally to the new width value and the star gets bigger.

Trouble? If the Position and Size section of the Property inspector is not shown, you might have selected the animation's path instead of the star. Click the star again to select it and repeat Step 4.

You will play the animation to see the effect of the changes you made to the star's properties.

▶ 5. On the Application bar, click **Control**, and then click **Play**. The star starts in its new position and moves to its end position as before. The star gradually changes dimensions. Because you changed the dimensions of the star only in Frame 1 and Frame 60, Flash adjusted the rest of the frames to change the star to its larger dimensions in the last frame.

You are done with the spacewalkNew.fla file. You'll save and then close it.

To save and close the spacewalkNew.fla file:

▶ 1. On the Application bar, click **File**, and then click **Save**. The changes you made to the spacewalkNew.fla file are saved.

▶ 2. On the Application bar, click **File**, and then click **Close**. The file closes and the Welcome screen appears.

Changing the View of the Stage

As you develop graphics on the Stage, you will need to change the view of the Stage. You can adjust the magnification level and move different parts of the Stage into view. You can also display the grid, rulers, and guides to assist you as you draw or align graphics, and you can change a document's properties.

Magnifying and Moving the Stage

You can change the view of the Stage by using the Zoom tool to adjust the magnification level. The Zoom tool includes the Enlarge and Reduce modifiers at the bottom of the Tools panel. The Enlarge modifier, selected by default, sets the Zoom tool to increase the magnification level. To reduce the magnification level of the Stage, you click the Reduce modifier. Then, you click the Zoom tool on the part of the Stage you want to enlarge or reduce. You can also select an area to enlarge by dragging the pointer over an area of the Stage to draw a marquee around it.

Another way to adjust the magnification level is with the View menu. The Zoom In and Zoom Out commands enlarge and reduce the view of the Stage, respectively. The Magnification command has a submenu of percentage levels that you can apply to the view of the Stage. The submenu also includes the Fit in Window, Show Frame, and Show All commands. The Fit in Window command adjusts the Stage to fit completely within the Document window. The Show All command changes the view of the Stage to display all the contents of the current frame, including objects in the pasteboard. The Show Frame command changes the magnification level to make the entire Stage visible. A quick way to access the Magnification submenu commands is by clicking the Zoom control on the Edit bar.

| Reference Window | **Changing the View of the Stage** |

- In the Tools panel, click the Zoom tool.
- In the Tools panel, click the Enlarge or Reduce modifier.
- Click a part of the Stage (or drag the pointer to draw a marquee around the part of the Stage to enlarge or reduce).

or

- On the Application bar, click View, and then click the appropriate command (or on the Edit bar, click the Zoom control, and then click the appropriate command).

or

- In the Tools panel, double-click the Hand tool.

You'll try various ways to change the view of the Stage. You will use a document that contains objects Aly has drawn in Flash.

To open the sample document and change the view of the Stage:

1. On the Application bar, click **File**, and then click **Open**. The Open dialog box opens.

    Tip
    You can also click the Open button on the Welcome screen to open the Open dialog box.

2. Navigate to the **Tutorial.01\Tutorial** folder included with your Data Files if necessary, click **sample.fla** in the file list, and then click the **Open** button. The sample document opens in the workspace.

3. On the Application bar, click **File**, and then click **Save As**. The Save As dialog box opens.

4. Navigate to the **Tutorial.01\Tutorial** folder included with your Data Files, type **mySample** in the File name box, and then click the **Save** button. The document is saved with the new name. You do not need to type the .fla extension when saving a document; Flash enters the file extension for you.

    You'll close the Timeline panel group because you will not use it in this tutorial. Closing the Timeline panel group provides more room for the Stage and pasteboard.

5. On the Timeline's title bar, click the **panel menu** button, and then click **Close Group**. The Timeline panel group closes and the pasteboard expands to fill the space.

6. On the Edit bar, click the **Zoom control arrow**, and then click **50%**. The view of the Stage changes.

    Next, you'll use the Zoom tool to magnify the fish graphic.

7. In the Tools panel, click the **Zoom** tool, and then, if necessary, click the **Enlarge** modifier button. The pointer changes to.

▶ **8.** On the Stage, click the middle of the **fish** object twice. The magnification level increases each time you click. The fish is centered in the Document window each time you click it. See Figure 1-22.

Figure 1-22 | Magnified fish shape

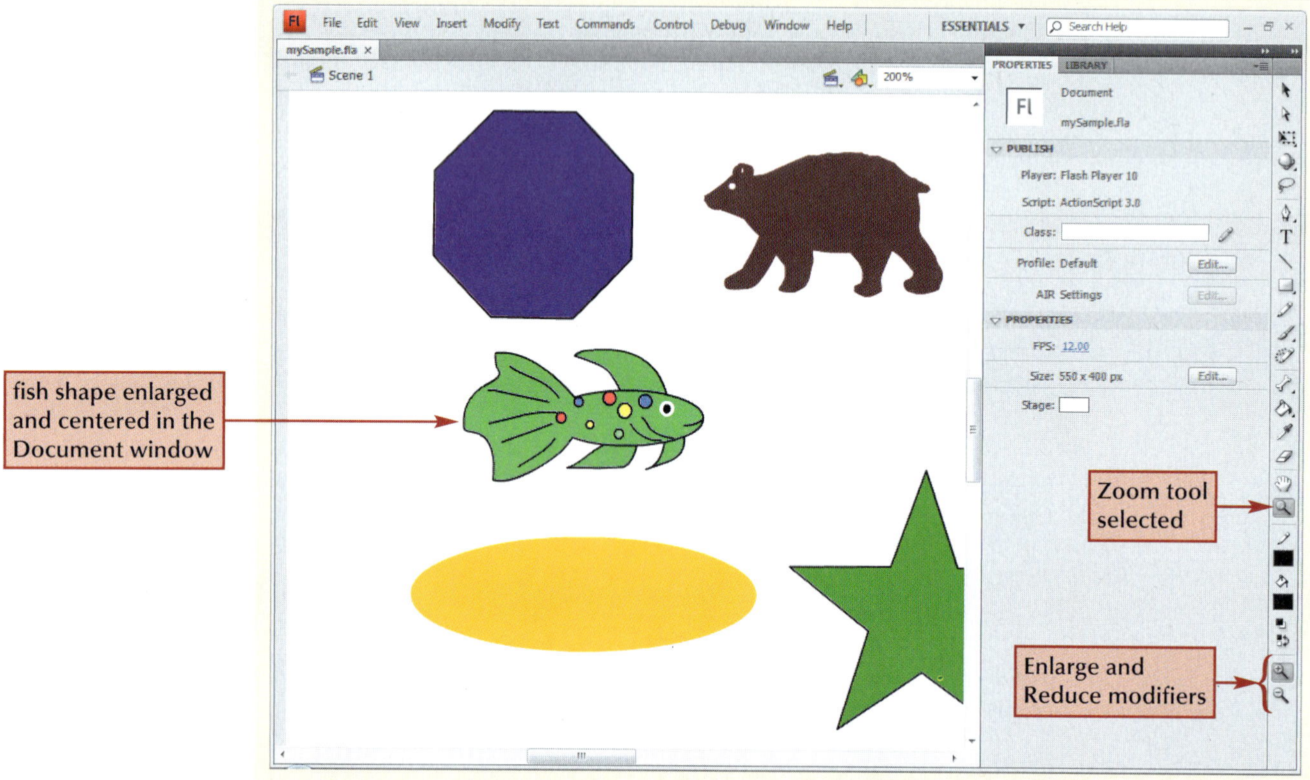

fish shape enlarged and centered in the Document window

Zoom tool selected

Enlarge and Reduce modifiers

After you magnify the view of the Stage, some graphic objects shift out of sight. You can move the Stage without changing the magnification level by using the Hand tool to drag the part of the Stage you want to see into view. You'll shift the beach ball graphic into view.

To use the Hand tool to view the beach ball graphic on the Stage:

▶ **1.** In the Tools panel, click the **Hand** tool. The pointer changes to as you move it over the Stage.

▶ **2.** Drag the Stage to the left until you see the beach ball in the middle of the Document window. See Figure 1-23.

Figure 1-23 | **Stage view shifted**

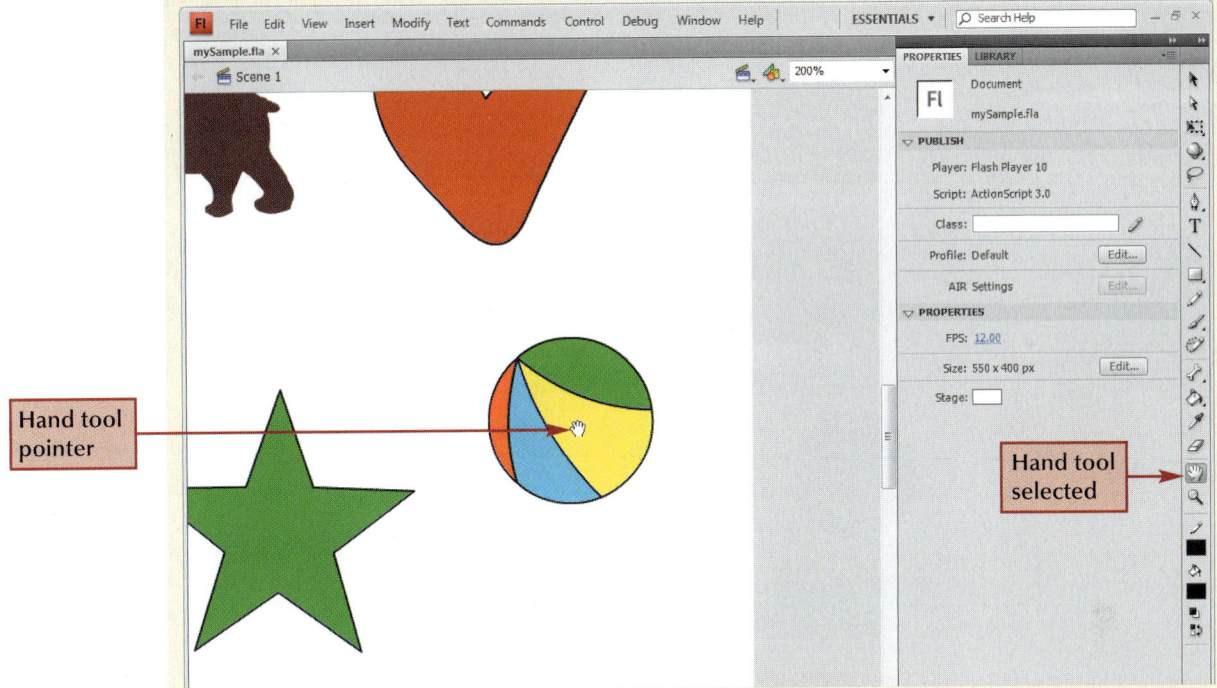

[Screenshot of Flash CS4 interface showing Stage with a bear, heart shape, green star, and beach ball. Callouts indicate "Hand tool pointer" on the beach ball and "Hand tool selected" in the Tools panel.]

Next, you'll reduce the magnification of the Stage.

3. In the Tools panel, click the **Zoom** tool, and then click the **Reduce** modifier button. The pointer changes to .

4. Click the center of the **beach ball**, and then click the center of the **bear**. The magnification level of the Stage reduces each time you click.

5. In the Tools panel, double-click the **Hand** tool. The magnification level of the Stage is enlarged to show all of its contents centered in the Document window.

Displaying the Grid, Rulers, and Guides

The Stage includes grids, rulers, and guides, which help position objects as you create documents. You can lay out objects on the Stage more precisely if you display the grid. The **grid** appears as a set of lines on the Stage behind all of the objects you place or draw on the Stage. The grid lines are not part of the document. They are only visible as you develop the document. The Grid submenu, located on the View menu, offers commands for controlling the grid. The Show Grid command displays the grid on the Stage. The Edit Grid command opens the Grid dialog box so you can customize the grid. For example, you can select a color for the grid lines that is different from the document's background color to make the grid lines easier to see, and you can change the spacing between the lines. You can also select the Snap to grid option to make objects attach to the grid lines as you move or draw them on the Stage. Snapping enables you to more accurately align objects vertically or horizontally. Changes you make to the grid are saved with the currently active document.

You will display the grid in the mySample.fla document.

To display and edit the grid for the mySample.fla document:

▶ 1. On the Application bar, click **View**, point to **Grid**, and then click **Show Grid**. A check mark appears next to the command and the grid lines are displayed on the Stage. See Figure 1-24.

Figure 1-24 | Grid displayed on the Stage

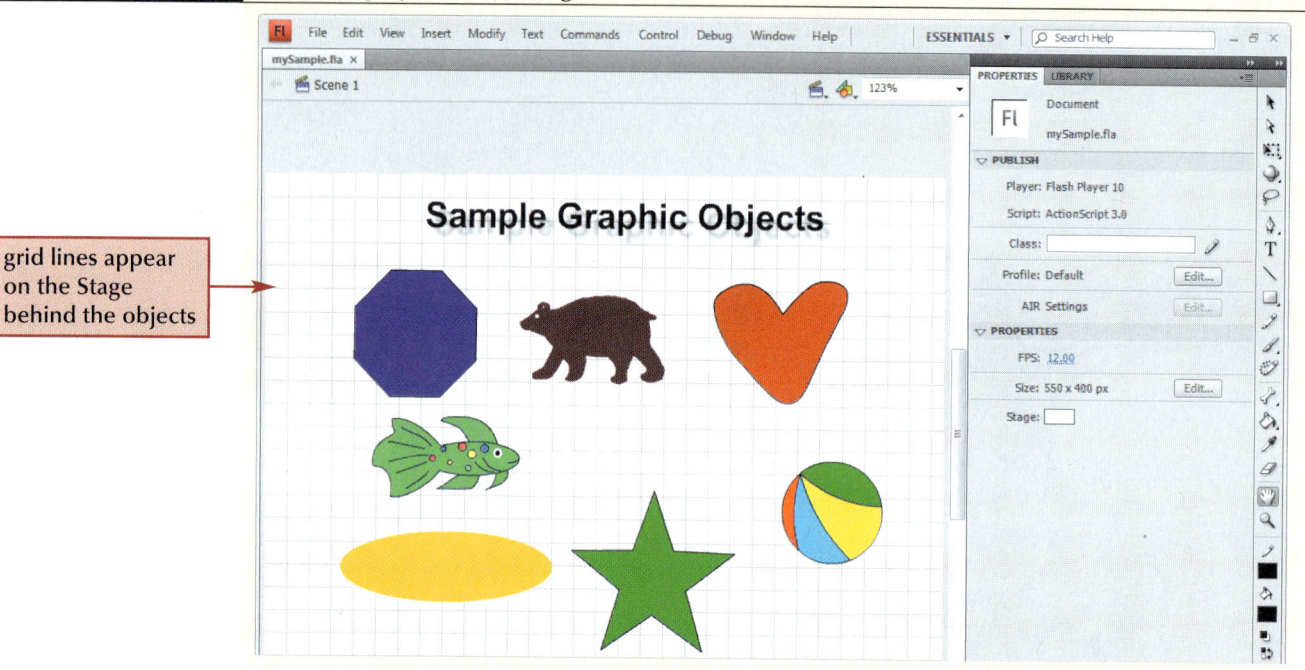

grid lines appear on the Stage behind the objects

You'll use the Grid dialog box to modify how the grid appears on the Stage. You'll change the grid line color and turn on the Snap to grid option.

▶ 2. On the Application bar, click **View**, point to **Grid**, and then click **Edit Grid**. The Grid dialog box opens. See Figure 1-25.

Figure 1-25 | Grid dialog box

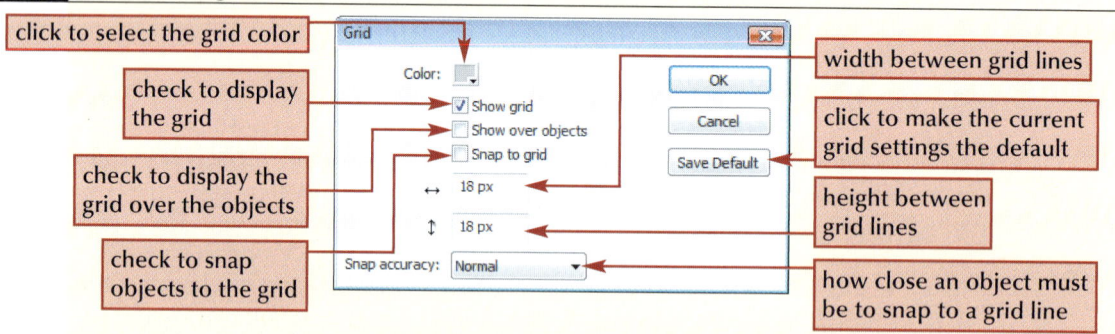

- click to select the grid color
- check to display the grid
- check to display the grid over the objects
- check to snap objects to the grid
- width between grid lines
- click to make the current grid settings the default
- height between grid lines
- how close an object must be to snap to a grid line

▶ 3. Click the **Color** control. The color palette opens and the pointer changes to 🖋.

▶ 4. Click the **black** color swatch in the first column, first row of the color palette. The grid lines change to black.

▶ 5. Click the **Snap to grid** check box to insert a check mark. With this option selected, objects will snap to, or align with, the nearest grid line when you move or draw them.

> 6. Click the **OK** button. The Grid dialog box closes, and the grid lines reflect the settings you selected.

InSight | Measuring in Pixels

You can use various units of measurement in Flash, including inches, points, and centimeters. Because most elements in Web pages are measured in pixels, you should also use pixels to express the width and height values of Web graphics. A pixel, short for picture element, is the Flash default unit of measurement. Pixels represent the smallest picture element on the monitor that can be controlled by the computer. Each pixel is composed of three colors, red, green, and blue.

As you develop graphics, you might want to display rulers. **Rulers** display the selected unit of measurement on the left and top edges of the Document window. The unit of measurement, such as pixels, is specified in the Document Properties dialog box. Rulers are helpful in placing objects on the Stage according to specific coordinates.

When the rulers are displayed, you can create vertical or horizontal guides. A **guide** is a straight line used to align objects that you move to a specific part of the Stage using the rulers as reference. To create a guide, click a ruler and drag a line onto the Stage. If you drag from the top ruler, a horizontal guide is created. If you drag from the left ruler, a vertical guide is created. You can edit the guides to change their color to make them easier to see against the background, snap objects to them, and lock them into place. Guides, like grid lines, do not become part of a document. They are visible only while you are working with the document. Guides can be created whether or not the grid is displayed.

Aly wants you to create guides in the mySample.fla document. You'll need to display the rulers first.

To display the rulers and create guides in the mySample.fla document:

> 1. On the Application bar, click **View**, and then click **Rulers**. The rulers appear along the left and top sides of the pasteboard.
> 2. In the Tools panel, click the **Selection** tool to select it.
> 3. At the top of the pasteboard, click the **horizontal ruler**. The pointer changes to .
> 4. Click the horizontal ruler and drag the pointer down to approximately **105** pixels on the vertical ruler. The horizontal guide you created snaps to the closest grid line. See Figure 1-26.

| Figure 1-26 | Horizontal guide |

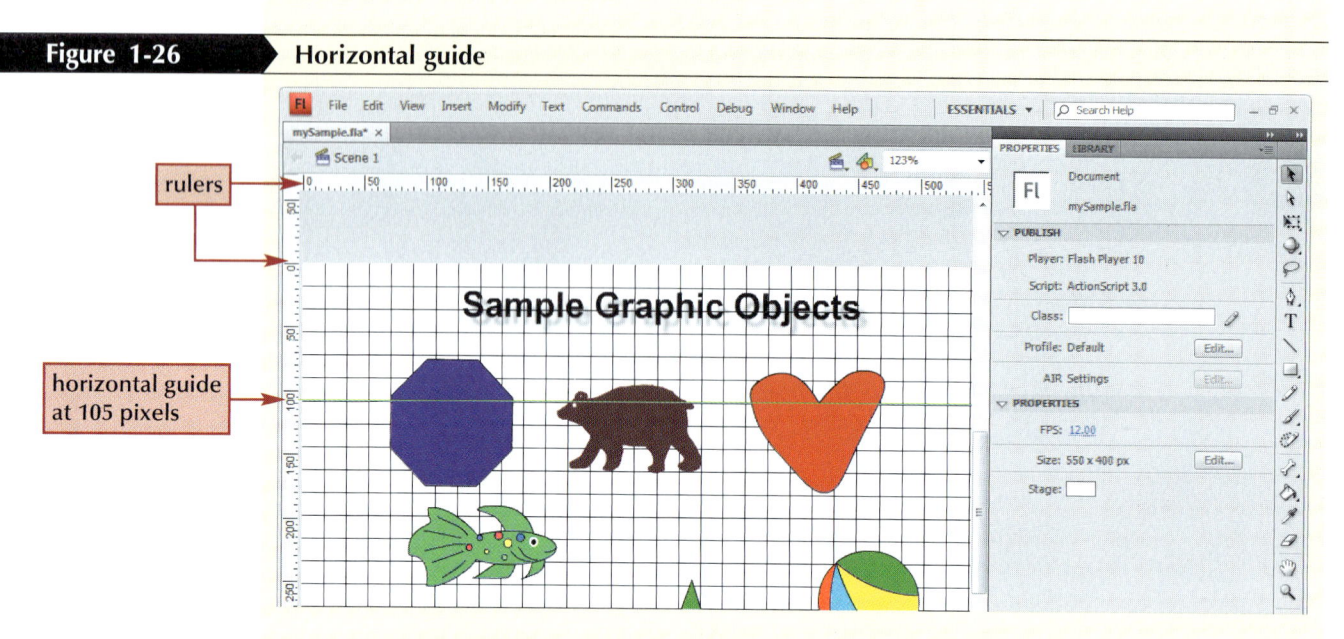

rulers

horizontal guide at 105 pixels

Next, you will create a vertical guide.

▸ 5. Click the vertical ruler and drag the pointer to the right to approximately **105** pixels on the horizontal ruler. The vertical guide you created snaps to the closest grid line.

▸ 6. On the Application bar, click **View**, point to **Guides**, and then click **Edit Guides**. The Guides dialog box opens. See Figure 1-27.

| Figure 1-27 | Guides dialog box |

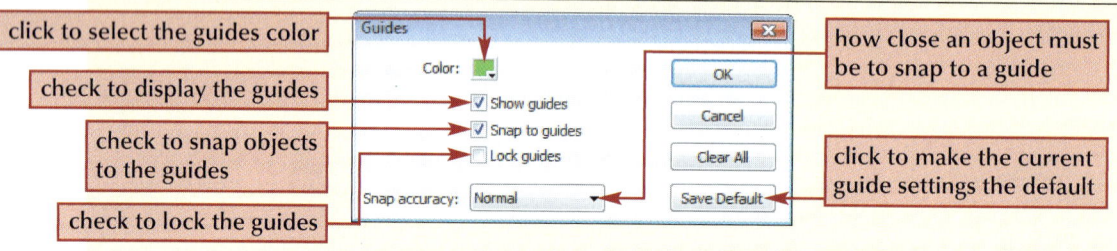

click to select the guides color
check to display the guides
check to snap objects to the guides
check to lock the guides
how close an object must be to snap to a guide
click to make the current guide settings the default

You'll change the color of the guides.

▸ 7. Click the **Color** control. The color palette opens and the pointer changes to 🖋.

▸ 8. Click the **red** color swatch located in the first column, seventh row of the color palette. The guides change to red.

▸ 9. Click the **OK** button. The Guides dialog box closes.

Changing the Document Properties

Every document in Flash has certain properties such as title, description, Stage size, background color, frame rate, and ruler unit. Title and description are embedded within the SWF file and can be used by search engines to categorize Flash content on the Web.

The other document properties are set at default values when you open a new document. For example, the default Stage size is 550 pixels wide by 400 pixels high. In addition, the Stage background color is set to white, the frame rate is set to 12 frames per second, and the ruler units are set to pixels. (The frame rate specifies how many frames in an animation are displayed in one second.) You change a document's default properties in the Document Properties dialog box. Changes you make in the dialog box are reflected on the Stage.

Aly wants you to modify the mySample.fla document's properties by changing its background color.

To change the mySample.fla document's background color:

▶ 1. On the Application bar, click **Modify**, and then click **Document**. The Document Properties dialog box opens. See Figure 1-28.

Figure 1-28 | **Document Properties dialog box**

- set the document width and height
- match the dimensions to the printer page size, the current contents, or the default document size
- select a document background color
- 12 is the default frame rate
- click to make the current document properties the default
- pixels is the default ruler units

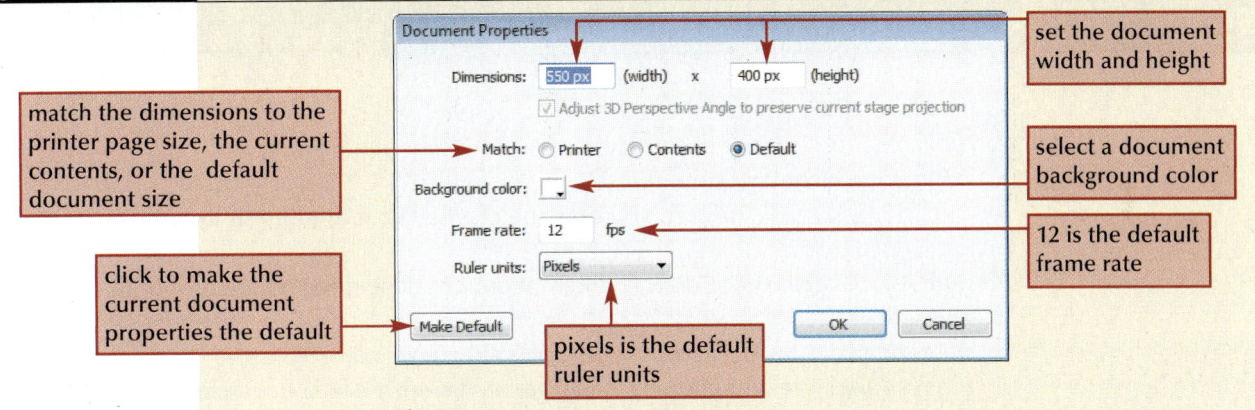

You can use the options in this dialog box to change the background color of the document. The dimensions, frame rate, and ruler units are fine with the defaults.

▶ 2. Click the **Background color** control. The color palette opens and the pointer changes to 🖋.

▶ 3. Click the **gray** color swatch located in the first swatches column, third row of the color palette.

▶ 4. Click the **OK** button. The dialog box closes, and the Stage has a gray background color.

▶ 5. Click the pasteboard, if necessary, to display the document properties in the Property inspector. You can also change the document's background color in the Property inspector.

▶ 6. In the Property inspector, click the **Stage Background color** control, and then click the **white** color swatch located in the first column, sixth row of the color palette. The Stage returns to a white background.

▶ 7. On the Application bar, click **File**, and then click **Save**. The changes you made to the document are saved.

> **Tip**
> You can also open the Document Properties dialog box by clicking the Edit button in the Property inspector.

You no longer need the rulers, grid, or guides. You'll hide them for now. Hiding the guides removes them from view but they will appear in the same place when you show the guides again. Clearing the guides deletes any guides that are on the Stage.

To hide the rulers, grid, and guides:

▶ 1. On the Application bar, click **View**, and then click **Rulers** to hide the rulers.

▶ 2. On the Application bar, click **View**, point to **Grid**, and then click **Show Grid** to hide the grid.

▶ 3. On the Application bar, click **View**, point to **Guides**, and then click **Show Guides** to hide the guides.

In this session, you learned about the basic components of the Flash workspace. You learned how to open and reposition the panels, how to change the display of the Stage, how to modify the document settings, and how to use the tools in the Tools panel. In the next session, you will learn how graphic objects drawn in Flash interact with each other and how to select and group objects.

Review | Session 1.2 Quick Check

1. In what area do you position the objects that will appear in the document?
2. What area displays the document's frame and layer information?
3. What is the Hand tool used for?
4. _____ is when you drag the playhead back and forth in the Timeline to test a document.
5. Which panel changes to display different options depending on the tool or object selected?
6. Describe two ways to change the magnification levels of the Stage.
7. True or False? The grid lines on the Stage become part of the document.
8. How do you create a horizontal guide?

Session 1.3

Working with Objects in Flash

The drawing and painting tools available in the Tools panel include the Line, Pen, Pencil, Oval, Rectangle, Brush, and Deco. These tools allow you to create the lines, shapes, and patterns that make up the images in a Flash document. Before using these tools, it's important to understand how the objects you draw behave and how you can change their basic characteristics, such as their color. In particular, you need to be aware of how shapes or lines you draw interact with existing shapes or lines.

Creating Strokes and Fills

When drawing objects in Flash, you create strokes and fills. **Strokes** are the lines that make up a Flash graphic. These lines can be straight or curved. They can be individual line segments or they can be connected together to form shapes. The Flash drawing tools provide a great deal of flexibility so you can draw almost any type of line you need. **Fills** are the areas in a Flash graphic that you paint with color. These areas can be enclosed by strokes.

Before you draw a shape, such as an oval or a rectangle, you can specify whether you want the shape to have a stroke, a fill, or both, as shown in Figure 1-29. For example, you can draw a circle that has both a fill and a stroke. You can draw a circle that has a fill but has no stroke. Or, you can draw a circle with a stroke but no fill.

Tip

You can also add a stroke or fill after you draw an object, and you can always modify its stroke or fill properties.

| Figure 1-29 | Sample shapes with fills and strokes |

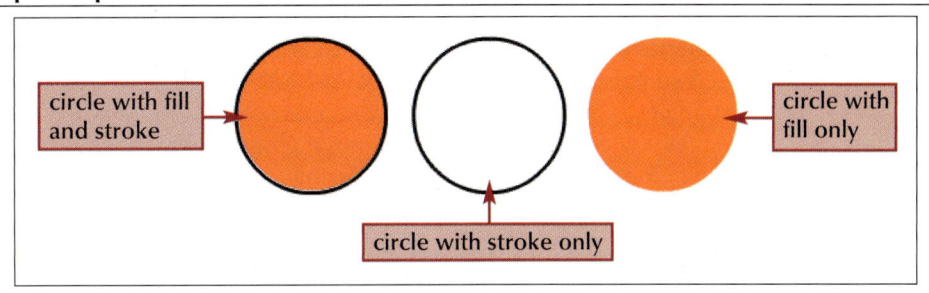

circle with fill and stroke

circle with stroke only

circle with fill only

Drawing and Grouping Objects

Flash provides two modes for how objects created with the drawing tools such as the Pencil, Line, Oval, and Rectangle tools interact: the Merge Drawing mode and the Object Drawing mode. By default, Flash uses the Merge Drawing mode. The drawing mode you use depends on how you want the objects to interact.

With the **Merge Drawing mode**, objects drawn or moved on top of other objects merge with or segment the existing objects. (Objects on the same layer are not considered to be on top of or below one another.) For example, when you draw a line through an existing shape such as a circle, the line is split into line segments at the points where it intersects the circle. The circle is also split into separate shapes. These line segments and split shapes can be moved individually. If you draw or move a fill on top of another fill of the same color, the two fills merge and become one shape. If you draw a fill of one color on top of another fill of a different color, the new fill cuts away the existing fill.

With the **Object Drawing mode**, the drawn shapes are treated as separate objects and do not merge with or alter other objects on the same layer. When you draw an object using the Object Drawing mode, a blue outline appears around the object on the Stage. Figure 1-30 shows how drawn objects interact in each mode.

| Figure 1-30 | Comparison of the drawing modes |

in Merge Drawing mode, a line drawn to intersect a circle splits the line and the circle into separate elements that can then be moved independently

in the Merge Drawing mode, a rectangle drawn on top of a circle cuts away the circle when moved

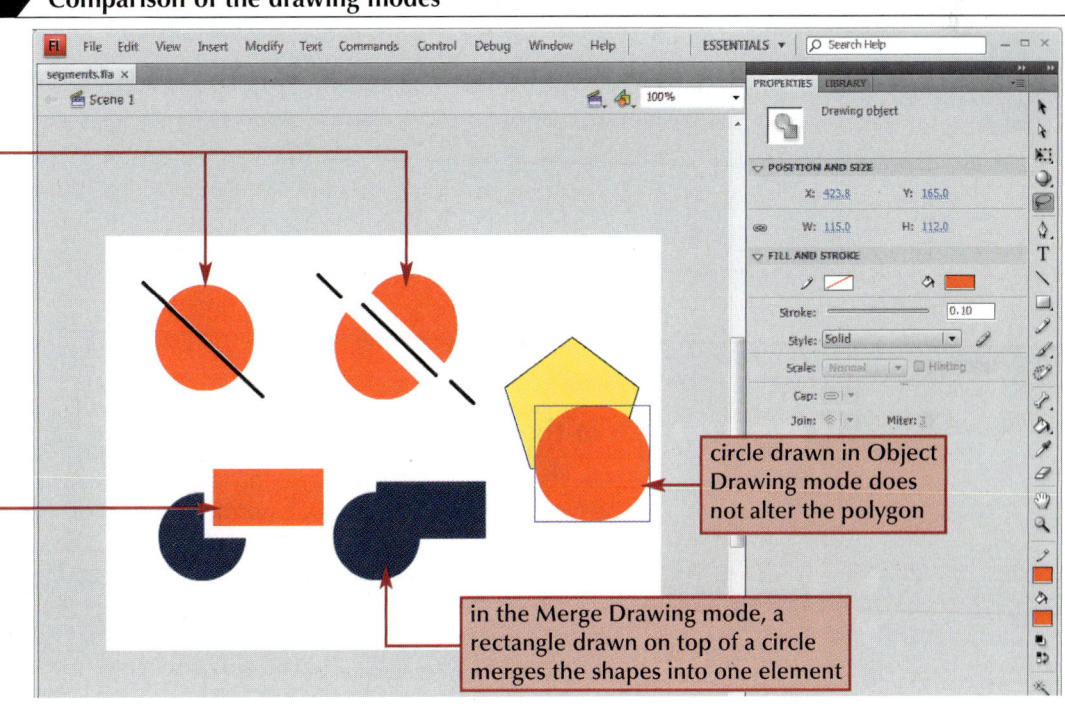

circle drawn in Object Drawing mode does not alter the polygon

in the Merge Drawing mode, a rectangle drawn on top of a circle merges the shapes into one element

FL 34 Flash | Tutorial 1 Introducing Adobe Flash CS4 Professional

To prevent objects from impacting each other, you can **group** them, which treats two or more objects such as a stroke and a fill as one entity. A thin blue rectangle outlines the grouped object when it is selected. Grouped objects are on top of non-grouped objects so they do not alter or merge with other objects. To modify a grouped object, you must enter group-editing mode. You can then edit the individual objects within the group. When editing the objects within a group, the rest of the objects on the Stage are dimmed, indicating they are not accessible, as shown in Figure 1-31. After you finish modifying the individual objects, you exit group-editing mode.

Figure 1-31 Grouped object in group-editing mode

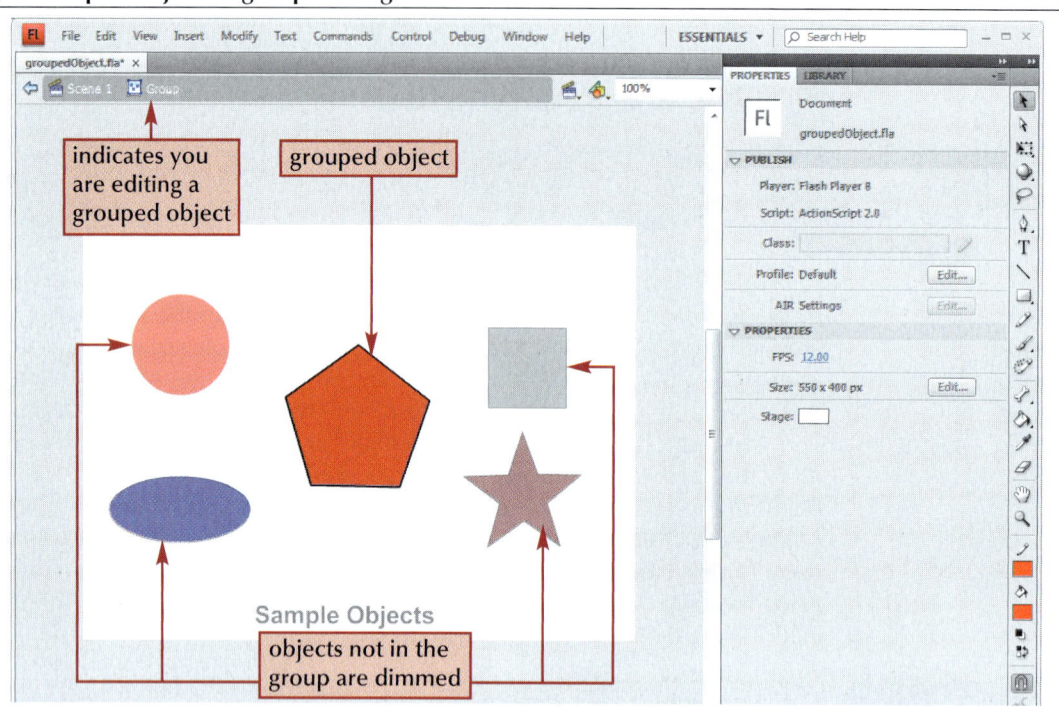

InSight | Grouping Fills and Strokes

When you create a complex object made up of multiple strokes and fills, group the strokes and fills together. This prevents you from accidentally changing one part of the object. It also makes it easier to resize or move the complex object at one time without having to modify or select the strokes and fills within the object individually.

You'll group the objects that make up the fish in the mySample.fla document.

To group the fish in the mySample.fla document:

1. If you took a break after the previous session, make sure the mySample.fla document is open, the workspace is reset to the Essentials layout, the Timeline panels group is closed, and the Stage magnification is set to Show All.

2. In the Tools panel, click the **Selection** tool , if necessary.

3. Draw a marquee around the fish graphic. The graphic is selected and a dotted pattern appears on the fish.

Tutorial 1 Introducing Adobe Flash CS4 Professional | Flash **FL 35**

You will group the selected fills and strokes.

▶ 4. On the Application bar, click **Modify**, and then click **Group**. A blue rectangular outline appears around the fish, indicating it is a grouped object. See Figure 1-32.

| Figure 1-32 | Strokes and fills of fish graphic are grouped |

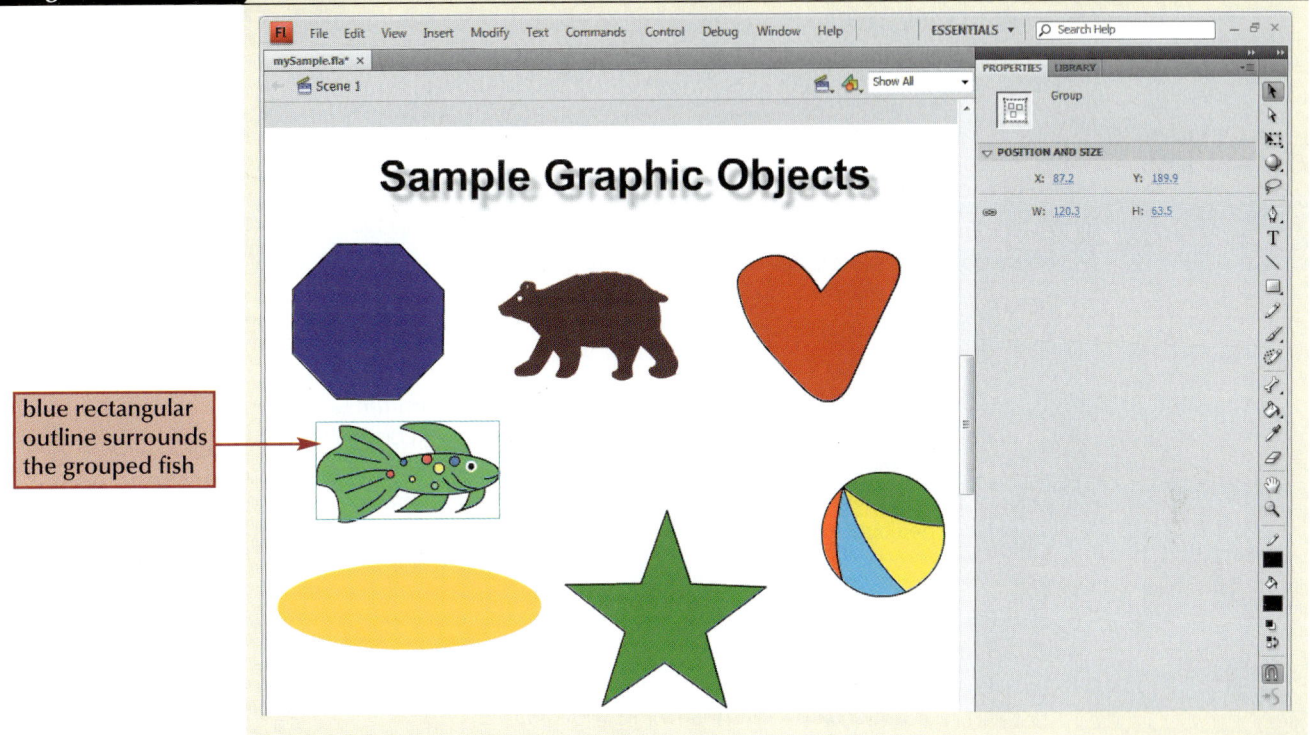

blue rectangular outline surrounds the grouped fish

Using the Color Controls and the Color Panel

All strokes and fills can be drawn with different colors. You can specify the colors before you draw strokes and fills or you can change the colors of existing strokes and fills. The simplest way to change the color of a stroke or fill is by using the Stroke color or Fill color control in the Tools panel. Each of these controls opens a color palette from which you can select a particular color. Figure 1-33 shows the color palette for the Fill color control in the Tools panel.

| Figure 1-33 | Color palette for the Fill color control in the Tools panel |

color's hexadecimal value
click to select no color
color preview
click to open the color picker
color swatches
gradients

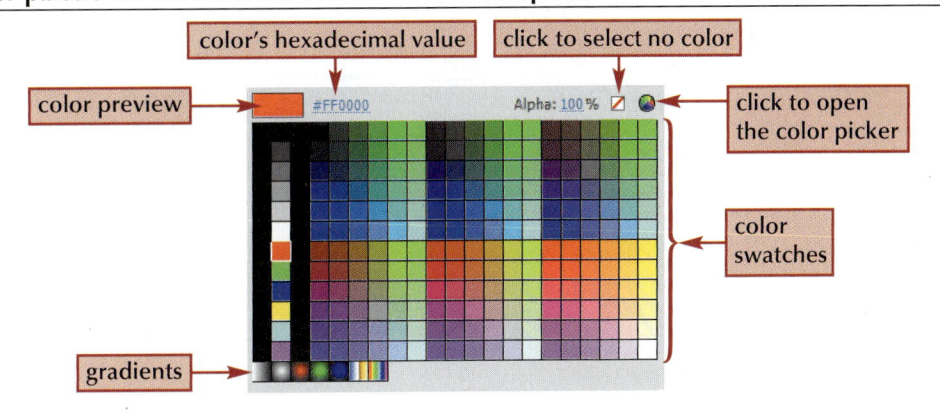

A color square in the palette is referred to as a **swatch**. By default, the color swatches in the color palette are the 216 **Web-safe colors**. These colors were developed to display the same on both Internet Explorer and Netscape Navigator browsers, as well as on both Windows and Macintosh operating systems. Today's computer monitors can display many more than the 216 Web-safe colors, so most graphic programs still use the Web-safe colors but aren't limited to only those 216 colors. The Fill color palette also includes a set of preset gradients. A gradient is a blend of two or more colors. A linear gradient blends the colors from one point to another in a straight line. A radial gradient blends the colors in a circular pattern. Also, you can click the color picker button to open the Color dialog box and create custom colors.

InSight | Using Hexadecimal Codes

All colors can be represented using **hexadecimal codes**. A color's hexadecimal value (such as #00FF00 for green) is based on the three basic colors used on computer monitors: red, green, and blue, referred to as RGB. The first two hexadecimal digits represent the amount of red, the next two digits represent the amount of green, and the last two digits represent the amount of blue. Values for each two-digit pair range from 00 to FF, which are numbers based on the hexadecimal numbering system. These three color values combine to form the desired color. You can enter a color's hexadecimal value into the box above the color swatches in the color palette.

You can also select colors using the Property inspector. When a stroke or fill tool is selected in the Tools panel or an existing stroke or fill is selected on the Stage, its color controls appear in the Property inspector. These controls work the same way as the Stroke color and Fill color controls in the Tools panel.

Finally, you can select colors using the Color panel shown in Figure 1-34. Using this panel, you can select colors in one of several ways. You can use the panel's color controls to open the color palette, you can enter a color's hexadecimal value, or you can create custom colors.

Figure 1-34 Color panel

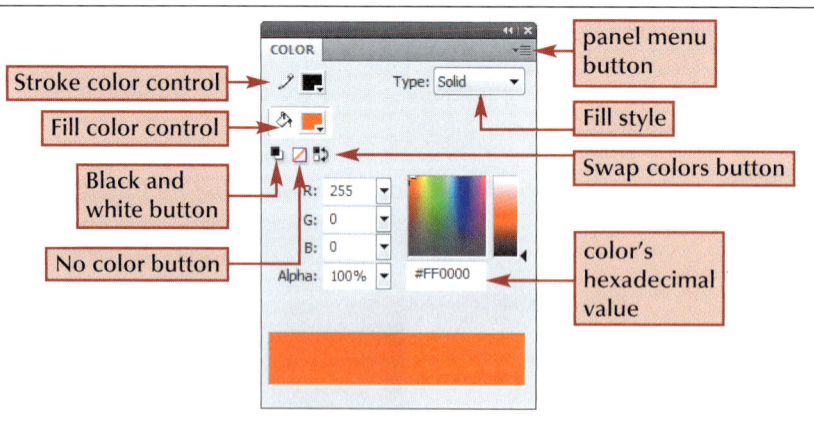

You'll change the color of the strokes in the fish.

Tutorial 1 Introducing Adobe Flash CS4 Professional | Flash | FL 37

To change the stroke color for the grouped fish object:

Tip
To edit a grouped object, you can also select it and click Edit Selected on the Edit menu. To exit group-editing mode, you can also double-click a blank area of the Stage or click Edit All on the Edit menu.

1. Double-click the **fish** graphic. The contents on the Stage are dimmed except for the fish, indicating you are in group-editing mode.

2. Draw a marquee around the fish graphic to select it, if necessary. The strokes and fills of the fish are selected.

3. In the Property inspector, click the **Stroke color** control to open the color palette, and then click the **red** swatch located in the first column, seventh row of the color palette. The strokes on the fish are red. See Figure 1-35.

Figure 1-35 — Fish stroke color changed

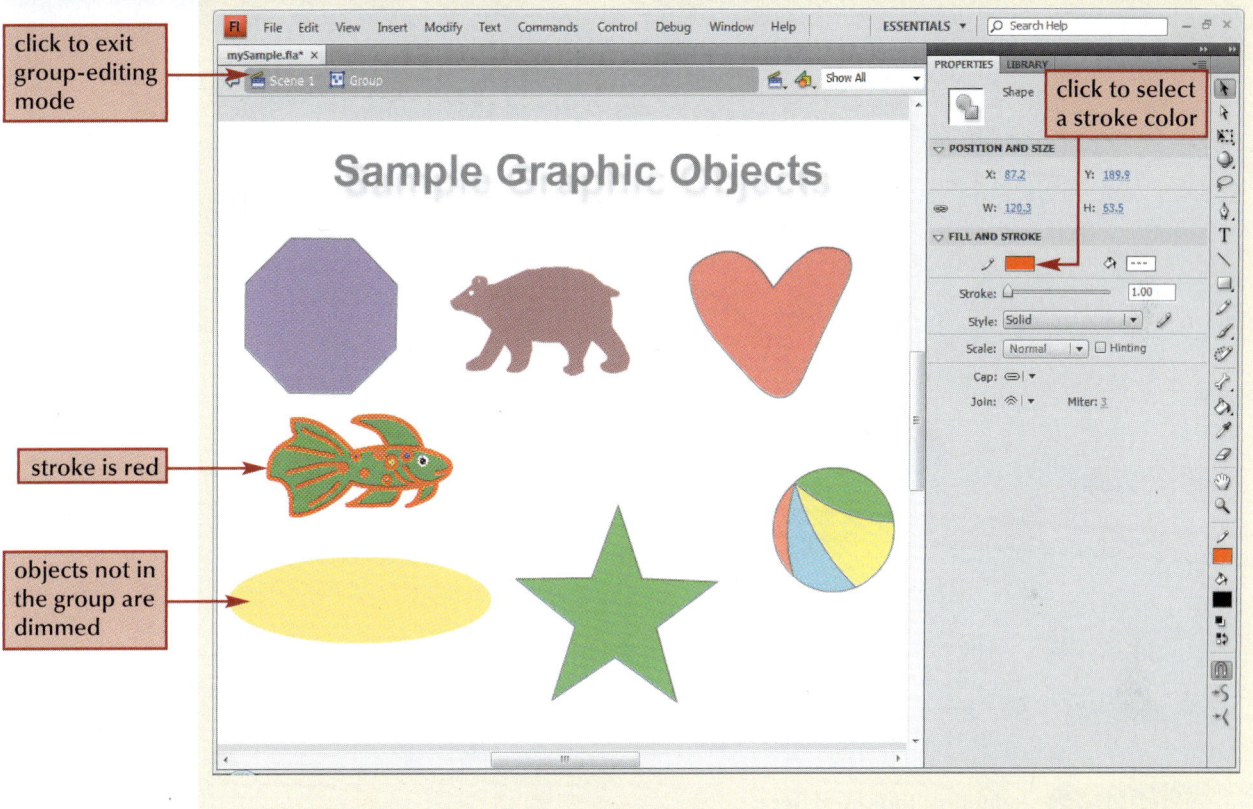

- click to exit group-editing mode
- click to select a stroke color
- stroke is red
- objects not in the group are dimmed

You'll exit group-editing mode.

4. On the Edit bar, click the **Scene 1** link. The contents on the Stage are no longer dimmed.

Selecting Objects

Before you can change the characteristics of a graphic object on the Stage, you must select the object. You can use the Selection, Subselection, and Lasso tools in the Tools panel to select part of an object, the entire object, or several objects at one time. You'll use these tools, especially the Selection tool, frequently as you create graphics.

Selection Tool

The **Selection tool** is used to select strokes or fills as well as a group of objects. You can also use the Selection tool to move selected objects on the Stage or in the pasteboard and to modify objects. You select objects by clicking them or by dragging the pointer to draw a marquee around the object, which is useful for selecting more than one object at a time. When you select a graphic object, a dot pattern covers it to indicate the object is selected. Some selected objects, such as text blocks, have a rectangular outline instead of a dot pattern. You can move a selected object to a new position by dragging it with the Selection tool. To change an object's shape with the Selection tool, deselect the object, move the pointer to one of the object's edges or corners, and then drag to reshape the object. The pointer changes based on the object you are modifying. If you move the pointer to a corner of a star shape, for example, the pointer changes to , as shown in Figure 1-36.

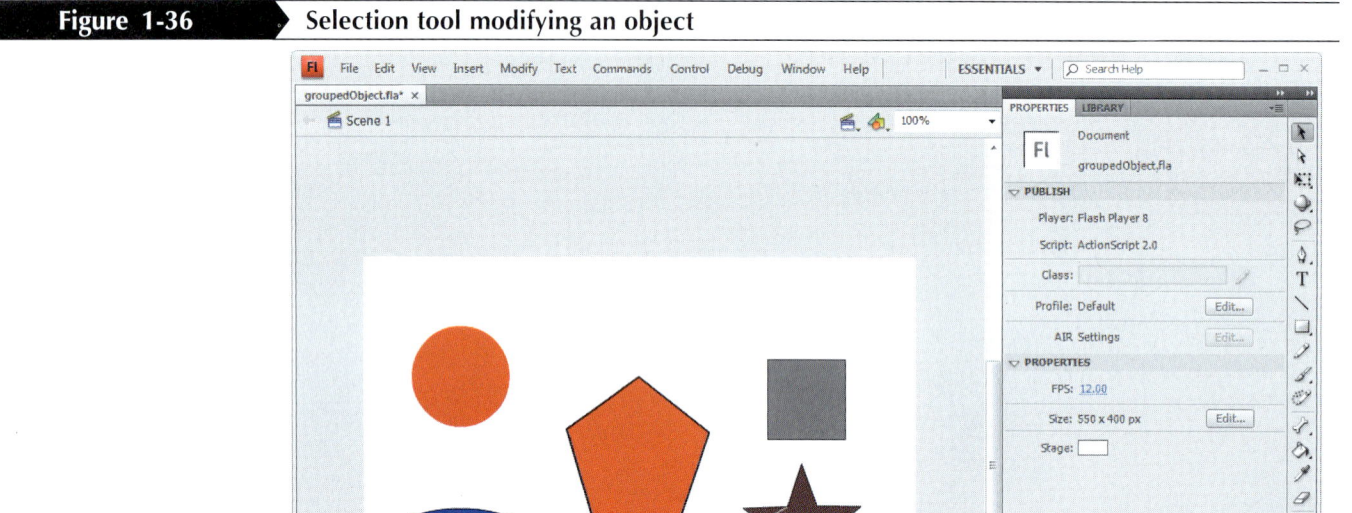

Figure 1-36 Selection tool modifying an object

corner pointer

The Selection tool, like many of the tools in the Tools panel, has modifiers that change the way it works. The Selection tool includes the Snap to Objects, Smooth, and Straighten modifiers, which are shown in Figure 1-37.

Figure 1-37 Selection tool modifiers

Modifier Icon	Modifier	Description
	Snap to Objects	Snaps selected objects to other objects when they are moved close together
	Smooth	Smoothes the selected line or shape outline
	Straighten	Straightens the selected line or shape outline

Aly wants you to use the Selection tool to select and modify the graphics in her sample document.

To select and modify objects with the Selection tool:

1. In the Tools panel, click the **Zoom** tool and then click the **Enlarge** modifier button.

2. Click the purple **octagon**. The octagon is enlarged and centered in the Stage window.

Tutorial 1 Introducing Adobe Flash CS4 Professional | Flash | FL 39

3. In the Tools panel, click the **Selection** tool. The pointer changes to .

4. Click the center of the purple **octagon** and drag it to the right just before the bear. The octagon's fill is separated from its stroke and the dot pattern indicates the fill is selected. See Figure 1-38.

Figure 1-38 | Octagon's fill and stroke separated

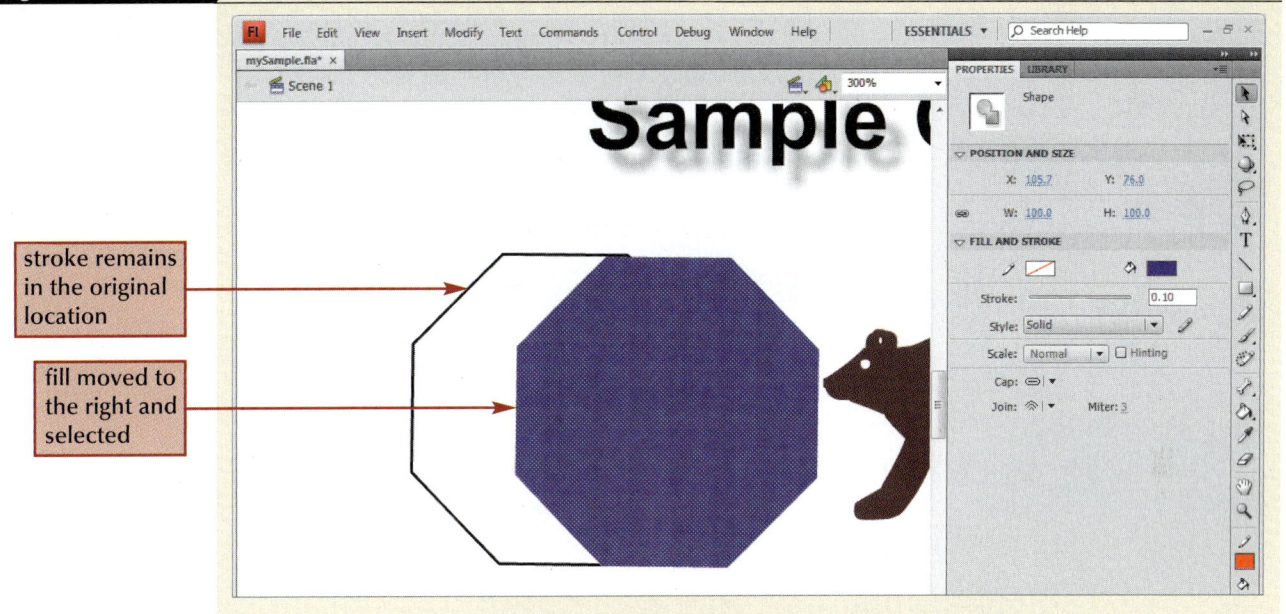

stroke remains in the original location

fill moved to the right and selected

You'll undo this change.

5. On the Application bar, click **Edit**, and then click **Undo Move**. The octagon's fill moves back to its original location.

6. Click a blank area of the Stage to deselect the octagon's fill.

You can use the Selection tool to select both the fill and the stroke of the circle simultaneously.

7. Double-click the purple **octagon**. Both the fill and stroke of the octagon are selected.

8. Drag the selected octagon to the right. The stroke and the fill move together.

9. Click a blank area of the Stage to deselect the octagon.

Next, you'll use the Selection tool to change the shape of the octagon.

10. Move the pointer over the top stroke of the octagon until the pointer changes to .

11. Drag the stroke of the octagon away from the center of the octagon to change its shape (but do not release the mouse button). See Figure 1-39.

Tip

You can also undo a change by pressing the Ctrl+Z keys.

| Figure 1-39 | Octagon's shape being changed |

line shows the new shape being created

curve pointer

▶ 12. Release the mouse button. The fill expands to the new shape.

Subselection Tool

The **Subselection tool** is used to display and modify points, referred to as **anchor points**, on strokes and on the outlines of fills that have no stroke. The strokes and fills can then be modified by adjusting these points. If you click and drag an anchor point on a straight line segment, you can change the angle or the length of the line. If you click an anchor point on a curved line, **tangent handles** appear next to the selected point, as shown in Figure 1-40. You can change the curve by dragging the tangent handles.

| Figure 1-40 | Curve's anchor points and tangent handles |

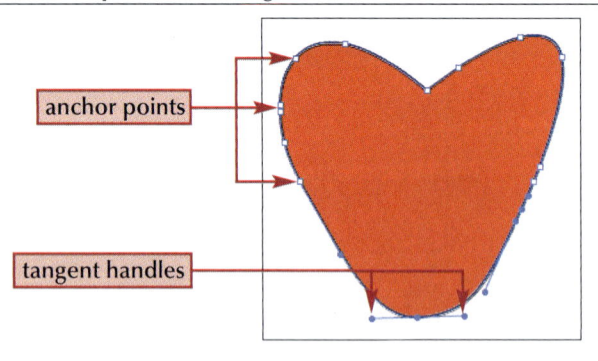

anchor points

tangent handles

Reference Window | Using the Subselection Tool

- In the Tools panel, click the Subselection tool.
- Click an object's stroke or its fill outline to display its anchor points.
- Drag the anchor points or tangent handles to modify the stroke or fill outline.

You'll use the Subselection tool to select and modify objects in the mySample.fla document.

Tutorial 1 Introducing Adobe Flash CS4 Professional | Flash | FL 41

To use the Subselection tool to modify the green star and yellow oval:

1. In the Tools panel, click the **Hand** tool to change the pointer to , and then drag the view of the Stage until the green star is in the middle of the Document window.

2. In the Tools panel, click the **Subselection** tool . The pointer changes to . You'll use this tool to display the star's stroke anchor points.

3. Click the stroke of the green star. A thin blue outline surrounds the star, and square anchor points appear on the star's corners and points.

   You'll drag an anchor point to modify the star's stroke.

4. Drag the anchor point in the star's top point away from the center of the star (but do not release the mouse button). See Figure 1-41.

Figure 1-41	Star's shape being changed

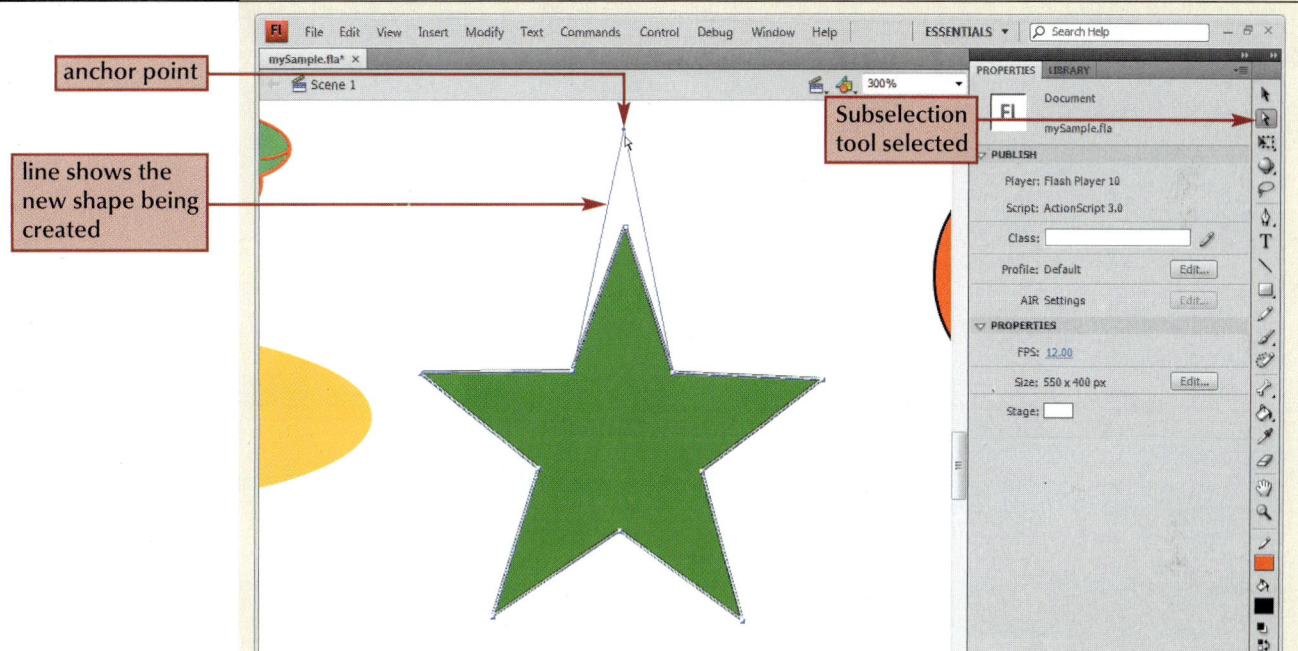

anchor point

line shows the new shape being created

Subselection tool selected

5. Release the mouse button. The star's fill expands to fill the new shape.

   Next, you will use the Subselection tool to modify the yellow oval.

6. In the Tools panel, click the **Hand** tool to change the pointer to , and then drag the view of the Stage until the yellow oval is in the middle of the Document window.

7. In the Tools panel, click the **Subselection** tool , and then click the yellow oval's outline. Anchor points appear along the oval's outline.

8. Click the anchor point at the bottom of the oval's outline. Because this is a curved outline, tangent handles appear. You use a tangent handle to modify the oval.

9. Drag the left tangent handle of the bottom anchor point down to change the oval's shape. The fill expands to fit the new shape. See Figure 1-42.

Figure 1-42　Modified oval with tangent handles

tangent handles

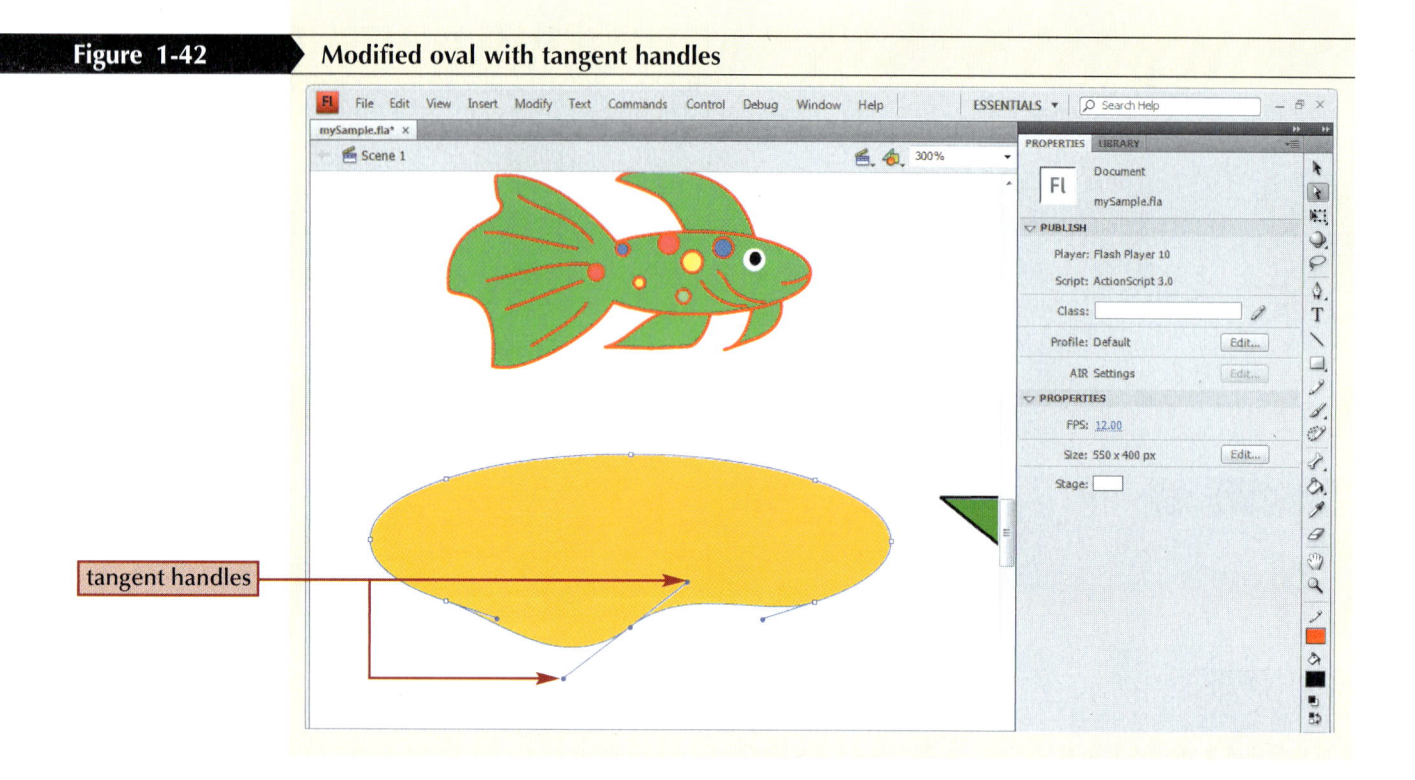

Lasso Tool

If you need to select part of a fill or a stroke, which you cannot do with the Selection or Subselection tools, you can use the Lasso tool. The **Lasso tool** is used to select an object, to select several objects at one time, or to select an irregularly shaped area of an object by drawing a free-form marquee. You can move the selection or apply other effects to it such as changing the color of all the selected fills at one time.

You will use the Lasso tool with the objects in the mySample.fla document.

To select objects in the mySample.fla document with the Lasso tool:

1. In the Tools panel, double-click the **Hand** tool. The entire Stage becomes visible.

2. In the Tools panel, click the **Lasso** tool. The pointer changes to when moved over the Stage. You use this tool to select multiple objects at once.

3. Drag the pointer to create a free-form marquee that includes part of the modified green star, part of the beach ball, part of the red heart, and part of the bear (but do not release the mouse button). See Figure 1-43.

Figure 1-43   Free-form marquee

marquee includes part of four objects

Lasso tool selected

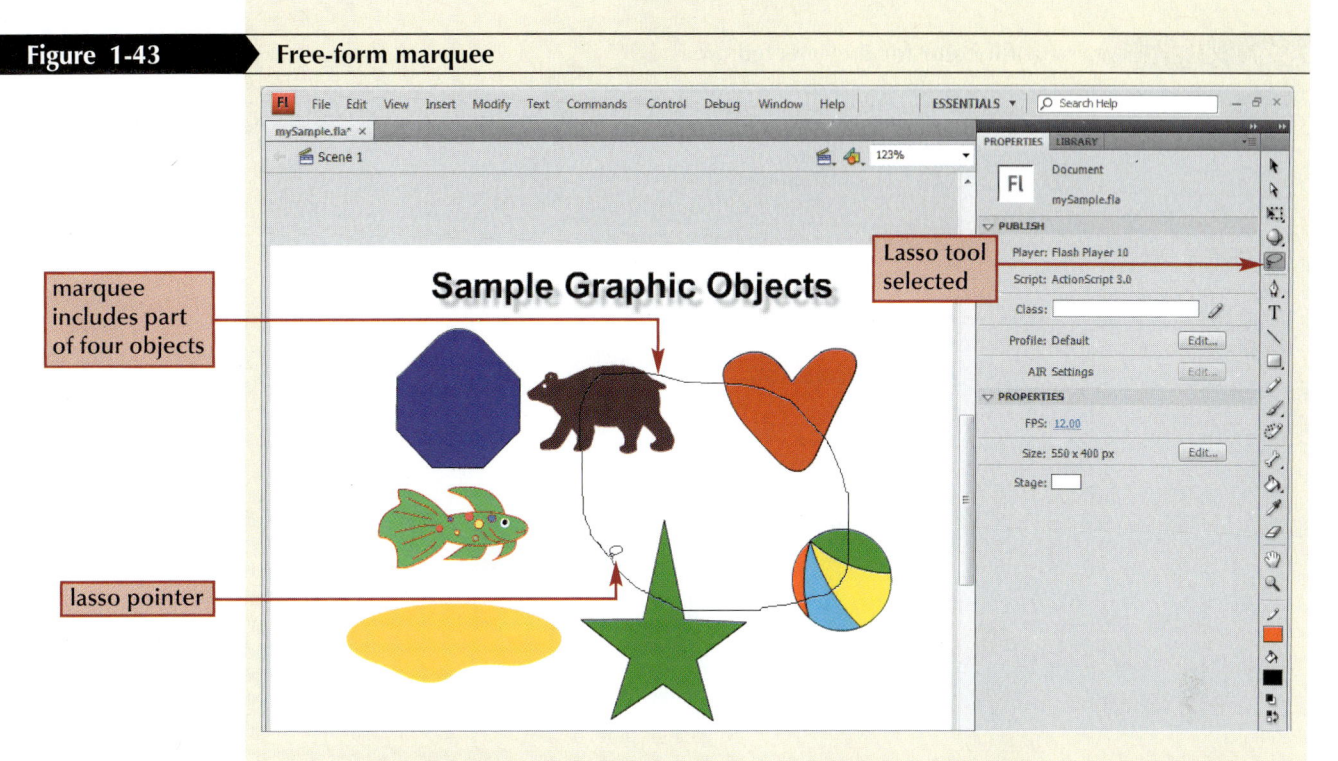

lasso pointer

Trouble? If you cannot create a free-form marquee, the Polygon Mode modifier is probably selected in the Tools panel. Click the Polygon Mode modifier button in the Tools panel to deselect it, and then repeat Step 3.

▶ 4. Release the mouse button. All of the selected areas appear with a dot pattern.

You will change the fill color for the selected area.

▶ 5. In the Tools panel, click the **Fill color** control to open the color palette, and then click the **yellow** color swatch in the first column, tenth row of the color palette. The fill color of the selected areas in the star, beach ball, heart, and bear change to yellow. The strokes are not affected because they are not fills. See Figure 1-44.

Figure 1-44   New fill color for the selected areas

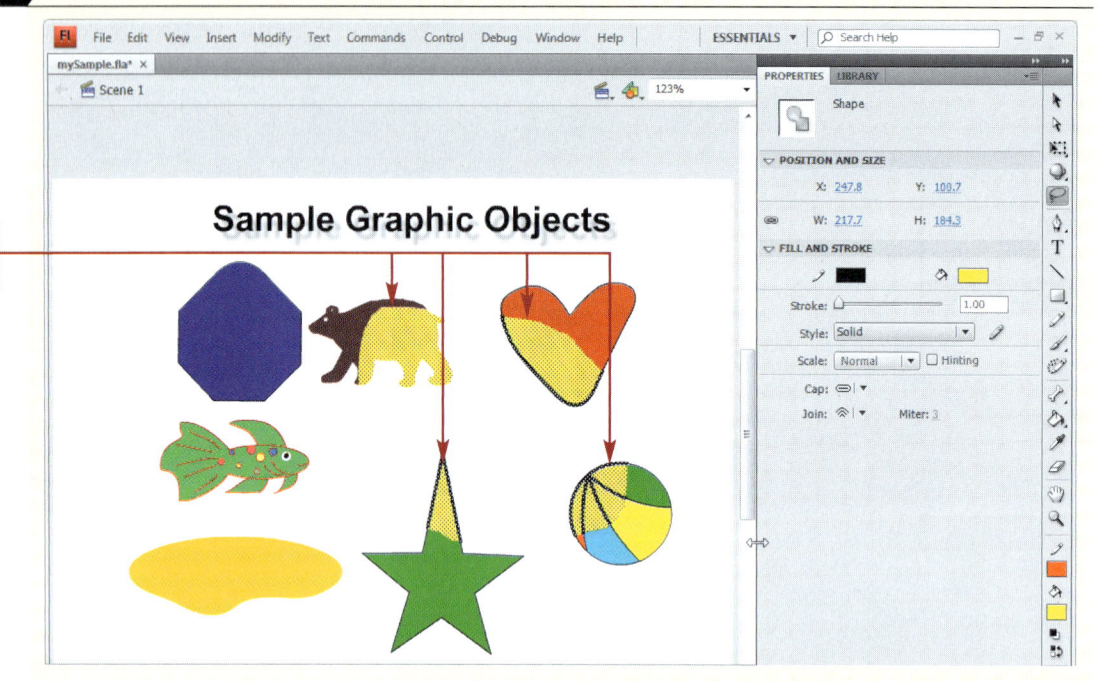

yellow color on the selected fills

▸ **6.** On the Application bar, click **File**, and then click **Save**. The mySample.fla document is saved with all the changes.

Getting Help in Flash

The Flash Help system is useful for finding information about features in Flash as you work with a document. The Help system appears in your default Web browser and is organized topically.

The left column of the Help system's initial Web page shows the list of available categories. The first category is Using Flash, which contains the Help information for most of the features of Flash. The rest of the categories contain information about more advanced features. Clicking one of these initial categories displays subcategories in the right column of the page, which when clicked, display additional Help categories in the left column. When a category in the left column is clicked, a list of topics is displayed. Each topic can be clicked to display a table of contents for the topic, as well as its associated help information.

You can navigate the Help system by clicking any of the categories or topics. You can also use the Previous and Next buttons to navigate between topics.

A Search feature is available on the Help page. You can search by a keyword or phrase to display a list of related topics. The search can be limited to the Flash Help system or can include other resources from the Adobe Web site.

Tip

To expand a category's list of topics, click the plus symbol to the left of the category name. To collapse the list, click the minus symbol to the left of the category name.

Tutorial 1 Introducing Adobe Flash CS4 Professional | Flash | FL 45

Reference Window | Using the Flash Help System

- On the Application bar, click Help, and then click Flash Help (or click a panel menu button, and then click Help).
- Click a main topic category, and then click a subcategory to display.
- In the left column, click a category to display its associated topics, and then click the desired topic.
- In the right column, read the topic information.
- Close the Web browser window to close the Help system.

You'll use the Flash Help system to obtain more information about the Property inspector.

To use get more information about the Property inspector:

1. On the Application bar, click **Help**, and then click **Flash Help**. The Help system opens in a Web browser window.

2. If necessary, on the browser title bar, click the **Maximize** button to maximize the browser window.

3. In the left column, click the **Using Flash** category, if necessary, to display a list of subcategories. See Figure 1-45.

Figure 1-45 | Flash Help system

click a category in the left column

subcategories appear in the right column

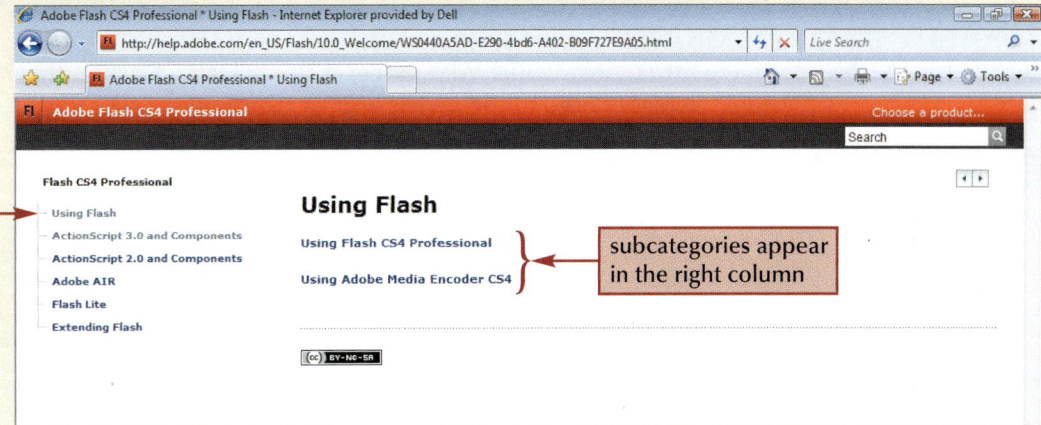

4. Click the **Using Flash CS4 Professional** subcategory, if necessary, to display another list of categories in the left column.

5. In the left column, click **Workspace** to display a list of topics. See Figure 1-46.

Figure 1-46 — Flash Help topics

click a subcategory in the left column

topics appear in the right column

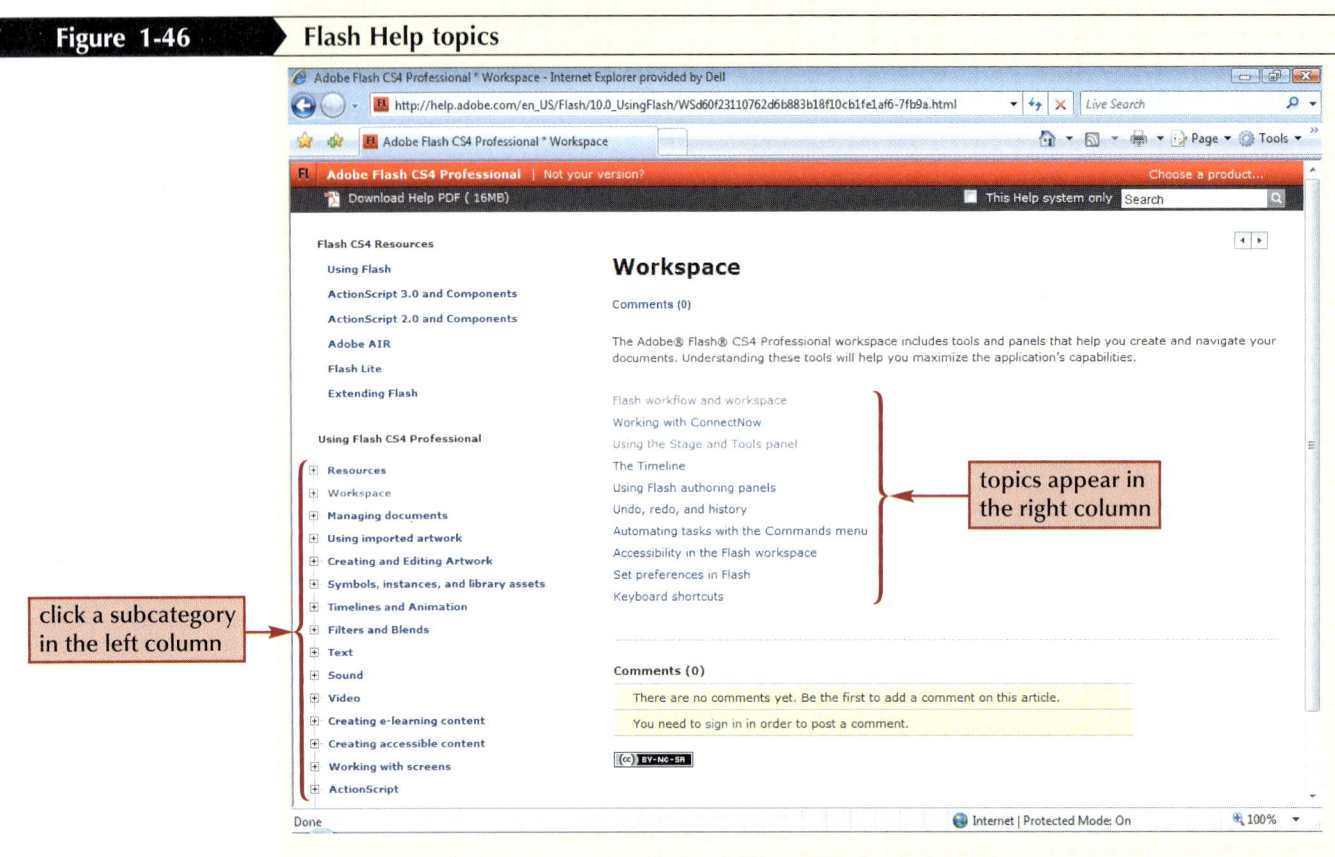

6. In the list of topics under Workspace, click the **Using Flash authoring panels** topic. Topics related to the panels appear. See Figure 1-47.

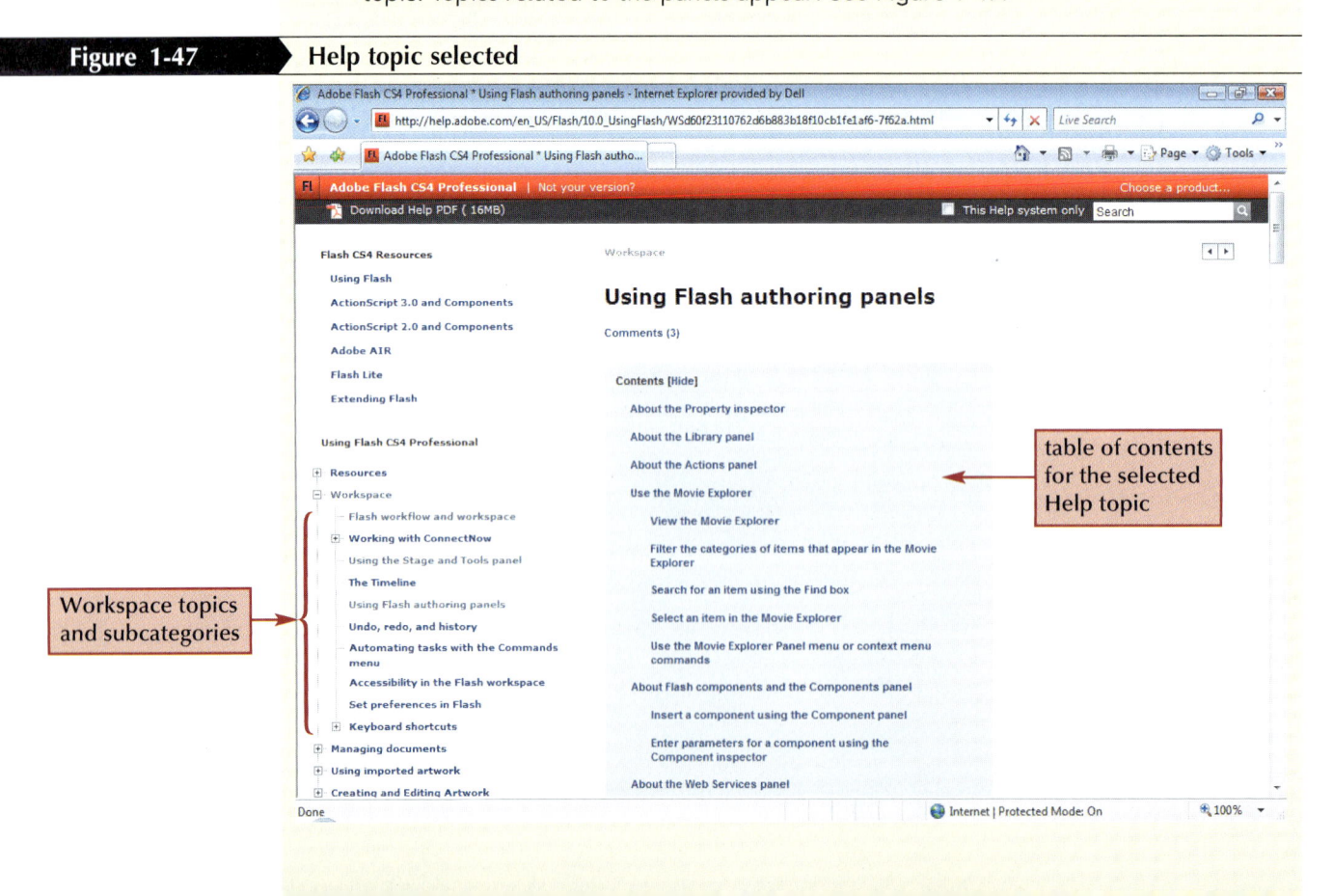

Figure 1-47 — Help topic selected

Workspace topics and subcategories

table of contents for the selected Help topic

Tutorial 1 Introducing Adobe Flash CS4 Professional | Flash | FL 47

▶ **7.** Click the **About the Property inspector** topic. The help information for this topic appears in the right column. See Figure 1-48.

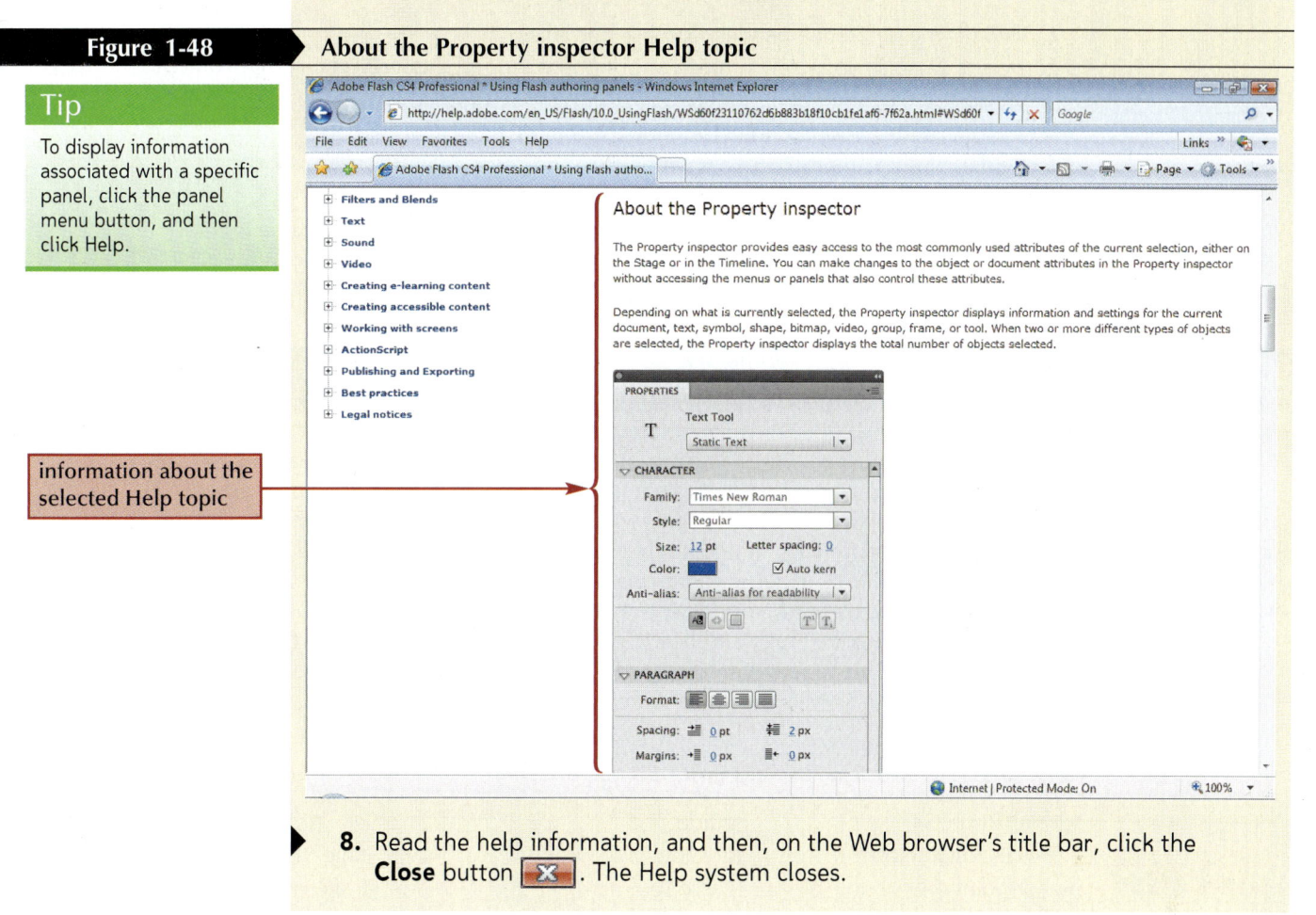

Figure 1-48 | About the Property inspector Help topic

Tip
To display information associated with a specific panel, click the panel menu button, and then click Help.

information about the selected Help topic

▶ **8.** Read the help information, and then, on the Web browser's title bar, click the **Close** button. The Help system closes.

Closing a Document and Exiting Flash

After you finish working with a document in Flash, you should close it. If you haven't already saved the document before you try to close it, Flash prompts you to save the file.

To close the mySample.fla document and exit Flash:

Tip
You can also close a document by clicking the Close button in the page tab and exit Flash by clicking the Close button in title bar.

▶ **1.** On the Application bar, click **File**, and then click **Close**. The mySample.fla document closes and the Welcome screen appears.

Trouble? If you are prompted to save the file, you might have inadvertently made changes since the last time you saved. Click the No button.

▶ **2.** On the Application bar, click **File**, and then click **Exit**. The Flash program exits.

In this session, you learned how objects interact when they are drawn or moved over each other on the Stage. You selected and grouped objects, and you worked with the strokes, fills, and colors of objects. You also used the Help system.

Review | Session 1.3 Quick Check

1. What is the difference between strokes and fills?
2. True or False? If you draw a blue oval on top of an ungrouped red rectangle drawn in Merge Drawing mode, the rectangle will not be modified.
3. True or False? Grouped objects cannot be edited.
4. By default, how many colors are shown on the color palette?
5. What are the three basic colors used on computer monitors?
6. What are two ways to select the stroke and the fill of an oval at the same time?
7. How can you select several objects at the same time using the Lasso tool?
8. How can you find topics containing an exact phrase in the Help system?

Review | Tutorial Summary

In this tutorial, you reviewed the Flash program and the types of Web media you can create using Flash. You previewed a document with a simple animation and you learned about the differences between bitmap and vector graphics. You became familiar with the Flash workspace components, including the Stage, the Tools panel, and the panels. You selected tools in the Tools panel, customized the arrangement of the panels, changed the Stage settings, and changed the document properties. You also learned how objects interact with each other on the Stage and how Flash treats objects drawn using the Merge Drawing mode and the Object Drawing mode. You selected objects and worked with strokes, fills, and colors. Finally, you used the Flash Help system.

Key Terms

Adobe Flash CS4 Professional (Flash)
anchor point
animation
bitmap animation
bitmap graphic
dock
document
fill
FLA file
Flash movie
Flash Player plug-in
grid
group
guide
hexadecimal code
Lasso tool
marquee
Merge Drawing mode
Object Drawing mode
panel
panel group
pasteboard
pixel
playhead
Property inspector
rulers
scrub
Selection tool
Stage
stroke
Subselection tool
swatch
SWF file
tangent handle
Timeline
Tools panel
vector animation
vector graphic
Web media
Web-safe colors
workspace

Practice | Review Assignments

Practice the skills you learned in the tutorial.

Data File needed for the Review Assignments: objects.fla

Aly wants you to work with some of the tools in Flash and to change the document settings by modifying the objects document. You will use these skills to develop graphics for Admiral Web Design's clients.

1. Open the **objects.fla** file located in the Tutorial.01\Review folder included with your Data Files and then save the document as **objectsNew.fla** in the same folder. Set the workspace layout to Essentials. Hide the Timeline and change the magnification level to Show Frame.
2. Display the rulers and the grid.
3. In the Tools panel, click the Selection tool. Double-click the red circle to select both its fill and stroke, and then move the red circle to the lower-right corner of the Stage so that it is approximately 450 pixels from the left of the Stage and 325 pixels from the top of the Stage.
4. In the Tools panel, click the Lasso tool. Drag around the beach ball and the green oval to select both shapes. Make sure no other shapes are selected. Click the Fill color control in the Property inspector, and then click a light pink color in the color palette. The fills in the beach ball and the oval change to light pink.
5. With the Lasso tool, draw a marquee around the tree to select both its leaves and its trunk. Group the tree's strokes and fills.
6. In the Tools panel, click the Zoom tool and, if necessary, click the Enlarge modifier button. Click the kite twice to increase the magnification level.
7. In the Tools panel, click the Selection tool, and then click the stroke representing the kite's tail to select it. Click the Stroke color control on the Property inspector, and then click the red color in the color palette. The kite's tail color changes to red.
8. Change the magnification level of the Stage to Show Frame.
9. Move the pointer to the top stroke of the blue rectangle. Use the curve pointer to drag the stroke slightly down toward the center of the rectangle to create a curved edge. Repeat to curve each of the other three sides of the rectangle toward its center.
10. Click the vertical ruler and drag the pointer to the right to approximately 150 pixels on the horizontal ruler to create a vertical guide. Click the pink oval to select it and then move it so that its left edge aligns with the vertical guide.
11. In the Tools panel, click the Subselection tool, and then click the heart shape's stroke to display its anchor points. Drag any anchor points to reshape the heart. Click an empty area of the Stage to deselect the modified shape.
12. In the Property inspector, click the Background color control, and then click a light yellow color in the color palette to change the background color of the Stage.
13. Save and close the document. Submit the finished document to your instructor.

Apply | Case Problem 1

Use the skills you learned to modify a Flash document for a pet resort.

Data File needed for this Case Problem: shapes.fla

Katie's Pet Resort Katie Summers is the owner of Katie's Pet Resort, a full-service boarding facility for cats and dogs. The resort's services include a pet grooming salon, boarding facilities for cats and dogs, an animal hospital, and a gift shop. The resort also hosts training classes to teach customers how to train their pets. To help promote the pet resort, Katie hired John Rossini to develop a Web site. The site will include graphics and animation in addition to text. John wants to use Flash to develop the elements for the site. John asks you to explore a sample Flash document to become more familiar with the program.

1. Open the **shapes.fla** file located in the Tutorial.01\Case1 folder included with your Data Files, and then save the document as **shapesRevised.fla** in the same folder. Reset the workspace to the default Essentials layout and set the Stage magnification to Show All.
2. Display the rulers and the grid. Drag a horizontal guide from the top ruler to the grid line about 200 pixels from the top of the Stage.
3. Use the Selection tool to move both the fill and stroke of the triangle to the left side of the Stage. The bottom side of the triangle should rest on the guide.
4. Select all of the baseball, group its strokes and fills and move the grouped baseball to the right of the triangle. The baseball's bottom edge should rest on the guide.
5. Move the cube to the right of the baseball and place it so that its center is on the guide.
6. Select all of the basketball, group its strokes and fills, and then move the grouped basketball to the right of the cube. The basketball's top edge should rest below the guide.
7. Select the red pentagon shape (both its fill and stroke), and then move the pentagon to the right of the basketball so that its bottom side rests on the guide.
8. With the pentagon still selected, use the Stroke color control in the Property inspector to change the pentagon's stroke color to green.
9. Use the Selection pointer to curve the top sides of the pentagon toward its center.
10. Change the triangle's fill color to brown and its stroke color to red.
11. Change the baseball's fill color to yellow and its stroke color to gray. (*Hint*: Edit the baseball in group-editing mode.)
12. Change the basketball's fill color to pink.
13. Save and close the document. Submit the finished document to your instructor.

Apply | Case Problem 2

Use the skills you learned to modify a Flash document for a local zoo.

Data File needed for this Case Problem: circleStars.fla

Alamo City Zoo The Alamo City Zoo, established in 1965, provides animal exhibits for San Antonio and the surrounding area. The zoo is opened year-round and has special exhibits throughout the year. Alamo City Zoo staff also work with local schools to arrange field trips and guided tours for students. Janet Meyers, zoo director, commissioned Alex Smith to develop Flash graphics for the Alamo City Zoo Web site. Alex asks you to explore how objects interact with each other in Flash.

1. Open the **circlesStars.fla** file located in the Tutorial.01\Case2 folder included with your Data Files, and then save the document as **circlesStarsNew.fla** in the same folder. Reset the workspace to the default Essentials layout and set the Stage magnification to Show All.

2. Using the Selection tool, drag the red circle on the lower-left side of the Stage to overlay the left side of the blue circle. Click a blank area of the Stage to deselect the circle. Select the red circle again, and then move the circle back to the lower-left side of the Stage. Part of the blue circle has been cut away.
3. Drag the red circle on the upper-left side of the Stage and place it on the green circle. Click a blank area of the Stage to deselect the circle. The red circle is behind the green circle. Move the red circle back to the upper-left side, and then deselect it. The green circle does not change.
4. Point to the bottom of the red circle on the upper-left side of the Stage, and then use the curve pointer to drag the line up slightly to curve it. Repeat this step to modify the bottom of the green circle. Both objects are modified in the same manner with the Selection tool.
5. Select the fill of the star on the upper-right side of the Stage. Then select the star on the lower-right side of the Stage. Each star's selection is displayed differently.
6. Deselect the star, point to the left point of the star on the lower-right side of the Stage, and then use the corner pointer to drag the star's point to the left slightly. Repeat this step to move the left point of the star on the upper-right side of the Stage. Both objects are modified in the same manner with the Selection tool.
7. Record what you think are the differences and similarities between the two star objects. Also record why you think the circle shapes interact differently with each other.
8. Save and close the document. Submit your answers from Step 7 and the finished document to your instructor.

Challenge | Case Problem 3

Customize the Flash workspace for a gardening store.

There are no Data Files needed for this Case Problem.

Westcreek Nursery Alice Washington is the owner of Westcreek Nursery, a specialty store providing a variety of trees, plants, flowers, and gardening accessories. Alice has been in business for 10 years and has gradually expanded her store and services. Alice attributes her success to her focus on customer service. Customers are able to look through the nursery's inventory in a relaxing and inviting environment. A friendly and knowledgeable staff provide expert advice and answers to customers' gardening questions.

Alice contracted Amanda Lester to update the store's Web site. As other local nurseries have developed Web sites, Alice wants to make sure her store's Web site stays current and remains an effective marketing tool. You'll help Amanda develop Flash graphics for the Web site. She wants you to customize the Flash workspace and arrange the panels you will use regularly. You will also look for information in the Flash Help system.

1. Create a new Flash document, and then reset the panels to the Essentials default layout.
2. On the Application bar, click Window, and then click Behaviors to open the Behaviors panel as a free-floating window. Move this window slightly to the left by dragging the panel's tab or title bar. Open the Movie Explorer panel and the Align panel.

EXPLORE

3. Group the Movie Explorer and Behaviors panels into one window. (*Hint*: Drag the Movie Explorer panel from its window and into the Behaviors panel's window.)
4. Drag the Align panel into the window with the Behaviors and Movie Explorer panels. All three panels are grouped.

EXPLORE   5. Click the Collapse to Icons button above the Property inspector and Library panel. Drag the left edge of the panel dock to the right to reduce the width of the dock and display the panels as icons only.

EXPLORE   6. On the Application bar, click the Workspace Switcher button, and then click New Workspace. Type **myLayout** in the Name box, and then click the OK button.

7. Return the workspace to the previous Essentials layout, and then reset the workspace to the default Essentials layout.

8. On the Application bar, click the Workspace Switcher button, and then click myLayout, which appears in the list of panel layouts. The panel arrangement reflects the changes you made.

9. Close the free-floating panel group with the three panels.

EXPLORE   10. Delete the saved layout. On the Application bar, click the Workspace Switcher button, and then click Manage Workspaces. In the Manage Workspaces dialog box, click myLayout, and then click the Delete button. Click the Yes button to confirm you want to delete the workspace layout, and then click the OK button.

11. Find out more about the Align panel. Open the Flash Help system, click Using Flash, and then click Using Flash CS4 Professional.

12. In the list of help categories in the left column, click the plus sign next to Creating and Editing Artwork to expand its list of subcategories. Click the plus sign next to Moving, arranging, and deleting artwork to expand its list of topics.

13. Click Arranging objects to display its help contents. In the contents list, click Align objects to display the help information about using the Align panel to align objects. Read the information for aligning objects. Record the basic steps for aligning objects. Close the browser window.

14. Submit your answers to your instructor.

Apply | Case Problem 4

Explore drawing in Flash and Web Media for a nonprofit organization.

There are no Data Files needed for this Case Problem.

Missions Support Association   Brittany Hill is the current president of the Missions Support Association, a nonprofit organization of citizens in the San Antonio and south Texas area. The association is an advocate for the San Antonio Missions National Historical Park, which preserves the Spanish missions that were established in the eighteenth century. The association provides a forum for its members to volunteer time in support of the park and to meet and learn about the history of the missions.

Brittany hired Anissa Ellison to improve and maintain the association's Web site. She wants to add new graphics and animation to the site to improve its appeal to the association members. Anissa plans to use Flash to develop the new elements for the site. She wants you to review information about drawing shapes and some of the tools used to draw graphics and then view examples of Web media.

1. In the Flash Help system, click Using Flash, and then click Using Flash CS4 Professional to display a list of help categories.

2. Click the Creating and Editing Artwork category, click the Drawing subcategory, and then click the About drawing topic to display its contents.

3. In the About drawing contents list, click Vector and bitmap graphics. Read the information in the right column about vector graphics and bitmap graphics. Record the definitions found in the Help topics for vector graphics and for bitmap graphics.

4. Scroll to the top of the page and click the Next button in the upper-right corner of the page to display the Drawing modes and graphic objects topic. In the contents list, click Merge Drawing mode. Read the information about the Merge Drawing mode and the Object Drawing mode.

5. Scroll to the bottom of the page to the Overlapping shapes topic. Read the information about overlapping shapes.

6. Scroll to the top of the page and in the left column, click the Draw simple lines and shapes topic. In the contents list, click the Draw with the Pencil tool topic and read its associated information.

7. Scroll to the top of the page and in the left column and click the plus sign next to Reshaping objects to expand its list of topics. Click Reshape lines and shapes, and in its contents list, click the Reshape a line or shape topic. Read the information displayed. Note the difference between reshaping an end point and a corner. Close the Help system window.

EXPLORE

8. On the Application bar, click Help, and then click Flash Support Center. Your default browser opens and displays the Flash Help and Support Web site. To view a video, tutorial, or sample, click its link. View, listen, or read the information provided and for the samples, experiment with any interactive components, if available. To return to the center's home page, use the browser's Back button. As you navigate to some of the samples, study and compare the animation effects you see. Listen for sound effects, music, and voiceovers. See if you can distinguish between bitmap and vector graphics.

9. In your browser, open the home page for the Flash Kit site at *www.flashkit.com*. Review the various examples of Flash graphics and animations displayed on the home page. Look for a list of hyperlinks, usually located at the top of page. In this list of hyperlinks, explore several of the categories such as Movies, Tutorials, and Gallery. Note how the various examples make use of animation, colors, sound, and pictures.

10. Close any open files without saving. Submit your answers to your instructor.

Review | Quick Check Answers

Session 1.1

1. vector
2. .swf
3. any three of the following: still imagery, sound, animation, hyperlinks, buttons, text, scripted programming
4. True
5. pixels
6. as a set of mathematical instructions that describe the color, outline, and position of all the shapes of the image
7. vector graphics
8. The enlarged bitmap looks jagged or blurred.

Session 1.2

1. the Stage
2. the Timeline
3. moving the view of the Stage and pasteboard

4. Scrubbing
5. the Property inspector
6. (1) On the Application bar, click View, point to Magnification, and then click a magnification level. (2) On the Edit bar, click the Zoom control arrow, and then click a magnification level.
7. False; the grid lines do not become part of the document.
8. Drag the pointer from the horizontal ruler down to the Stage window.

Session 1.3

1. Strokes are lines and outlines; fills are the areas enclosed by lines and outlines.
2. False; the blue oval cuts away at the ungrouped red rectangle.
3. False; grouped objects can be edited in group-editing mode.
4. the 216 Web-safe colors
5. red, green, and blue
6. (1) Double-click the stroke or fill. (2) Draw a marquee around the oval with the Selection tool.
7. Draw a marquee around the objects to select.
8. Type the phrase enclosed in quotation marks in the Search box, and then click the Search button.

Ending Data Files

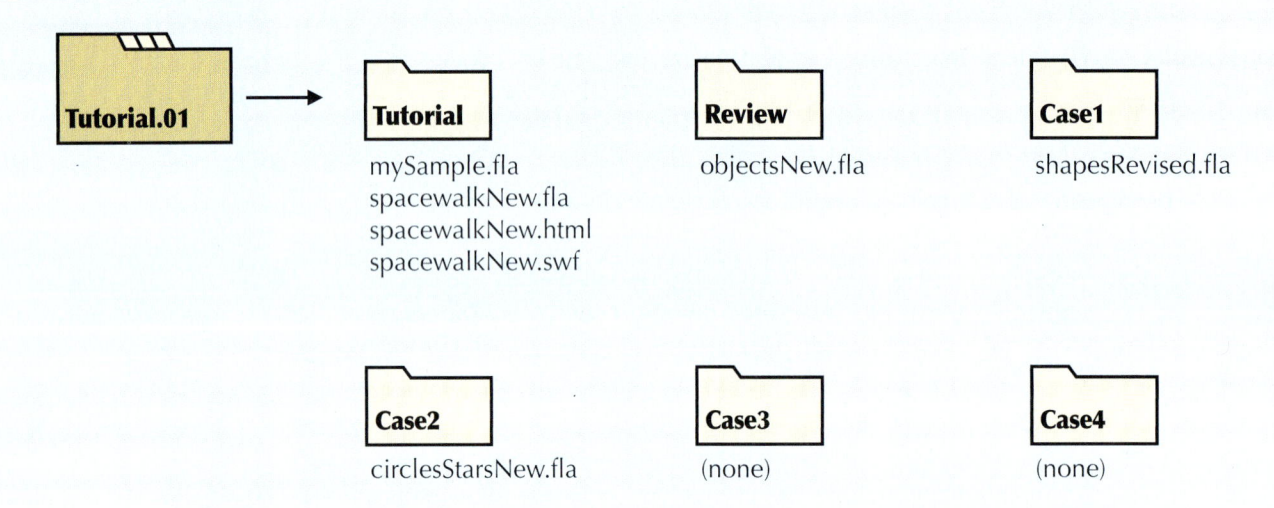

Tutorial.01 →

Tutorial
mySample.fla
spacewalkNew.fla
spacewalkNew.html
spacewalkNew.swf

Review
objectsNew.fla

Case1
shapesRevised.fla

Case2
circlesStarsNew.fla

Case3
(none)

Case4
(none)

Tutorial 2

Objectives

Session 2.1
- Draw lines, curves, ovals, and rectangles
- Apply stroke and fill colors

Session 2.2
- Modify strokes and fills
- Transform graphic objects using the Free Transform tool
- Create text blocks
- Use the History panel

Session 2.3
- Export a graphic for use in a Web site
- Create symbols and instances of symbols
- Organize symbols in the Library panel
- Apply filters to symbol instances and text

Drawing Shapes, Adding Text, and Creating Symbols

Creating and Exporting a Banner

Case | Admiral Web Design

Admiral Web Design focuses on designing easy-to-use, informative, and effective Web sites that meet the specific needs of its clients. One client is Jenny's Oyster Hut, a seafood restaurant that has won numerous local and national awards for its special dishes, customer satisfaction, and contributions to the community during its 10 years of operation. Owner Jenny Emerson wants Admiral Web Design to develop a new banner for the restaurant's Web site for a special promotion celebrating the restaurant's tenth anniversary. You will work on this banner with Aly and Chris.

During the planning meeting, Jenny said that she wants a colorful banner with graphic images depicting a scene related to the sea. Aly suggested that the banner include graphics of a beach scene with sand, the ocean, some fish, and several lines of text. Chris agreed that this banner will blend well with the current design of the restaurant's home page. Jenny liked the idea and approved Aly's final sketch of the new banner. You will use Flash to create the banner according to Aly's sketch.

As you create the banner for Jenny's Oyster Hut in Flash, you will use the drawing tools, text tools, and tools for modifying graphic objects. You will select and apply colors. You will modify existing graphics, create new graphics, and then export the banner for use on the restaurant's Web site.

Starting Data Files

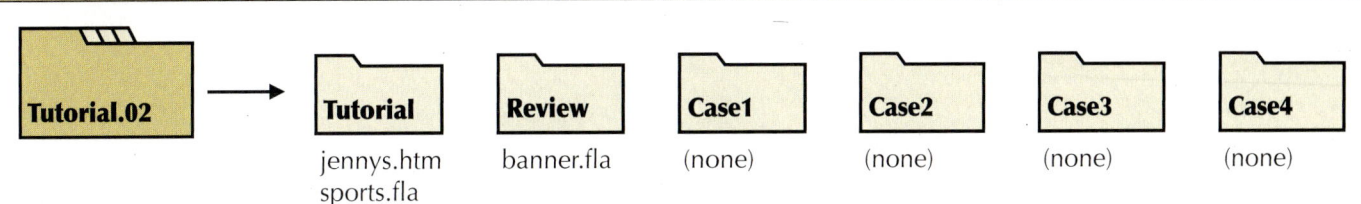

Tutorial.02 →

- **Tutorial**
  jennys.htm
  sports.fla
- **Review**
  banner.fla
- **Case1**
  (none)
- **Case2**
  (none)
- **Case3**
  (none)
- **Case4**
  (none)

Session 2.1

Drawing Lines and Shapes

When working with Flash, you will often create graphic images from scratch. You draw lines and curves with the Line, Pen, and Pencil tools. If you create an enclosed shape, the enclosed area is filled with the fill color selected in the Fill color control in the Tools panel. You draw shapes with the Oval, Rectangle, PolyStar, Brush, Rectangle Primitive, and Oval Primitive tools. These tools allow you to create shapes of various sizes and colors. Ovals, rectangles, and polygons can include strokes as well as fills, or only a stroke or only a fill. The primitive tools create rectangles with modifiable corners and ovals that can be changed into pie shapes or semicircles.

Figure 2-1 shows Aly's sketch of the banner you will create for Jenny's Oyster Hut. You will use the Oval, Pencil, Paint Bucket, and Eyedropper tools to create the fish and background graphics. You will use the Rectangle tool to create a frame around the banner, the Primitive Oval tool to create the umbrella, and the Selection tool to modify the shapes. You will display the guides, which will be useful as you draw and align objects on the Stage. You will also apply a drop shadow effect to some of the graphic objects and text.

Figure 2-1 Sketch of the banner for Jenny's Oyster Hut Web site

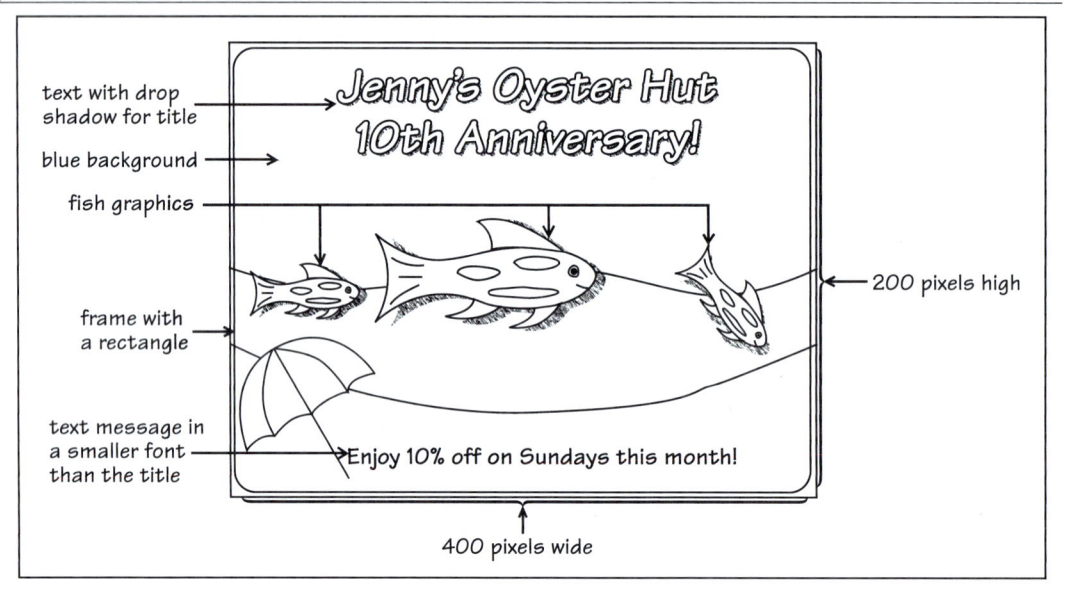

You are ready to begin creating the banner. You will set the document properties, display the rulers, and then save the banner file.

To set the document properties, show the rulers, and save the document:

▶ 1. On the Application bar, click **File**, and then click **New**. The New Document dialog box opens with the General tab active.

▶ 2. Click **Flash File (ActionScript 3.0)**, if necessary, and then click the **OK** button. The new document opens.

Tutorial 2 Drawing Shapes, Adding Text, and Creating Symbols | Flash FL 57

Tip

You can also click Window on the Application bar, point to Workspace, and then click Reset 'Essentials' to reset the workspace.

3. On the Application bar, click the **Workspace Switcher** button, and then click **Reset 'Essentials'**. The workspace returns to the default Essentials layout.

4. On the Application bar, click **Window**, and then click **Timeline**. The Timeline closes.

5. On the Application bar, click **Modify**, and then click **Document**. The Document Properties dialog box opens.

6. In the width box, type **400**, press the **Tab** key to select the value in the height box, and then type **300**. The document dimensions are set according to the banner sketch.

7. Click the **Background color** control to open the color palette, and then click the **light blue** color swatch (#66CCFF) in the second column from the right, sixth row of the color palette. The background color is set to light blue as shown in the sketch.

   You'll leave the frame rate at 12 frames per second and the ruler units at pixels.

8. Click the **OK** button. The dialog box closes and the document changes to match the document settings.

9. On the Edit bar, click the **Zoom control arrow**, and then click **Fit in Window**. The document enlarges to fill the pasteboard.

10. On the Application bar, click **View**, and then click **Rulers**. The rulers appear along the top and left of the pasteboard. See Figure 2-2.

Figure 2-2   Document window showing rulers and new document properties

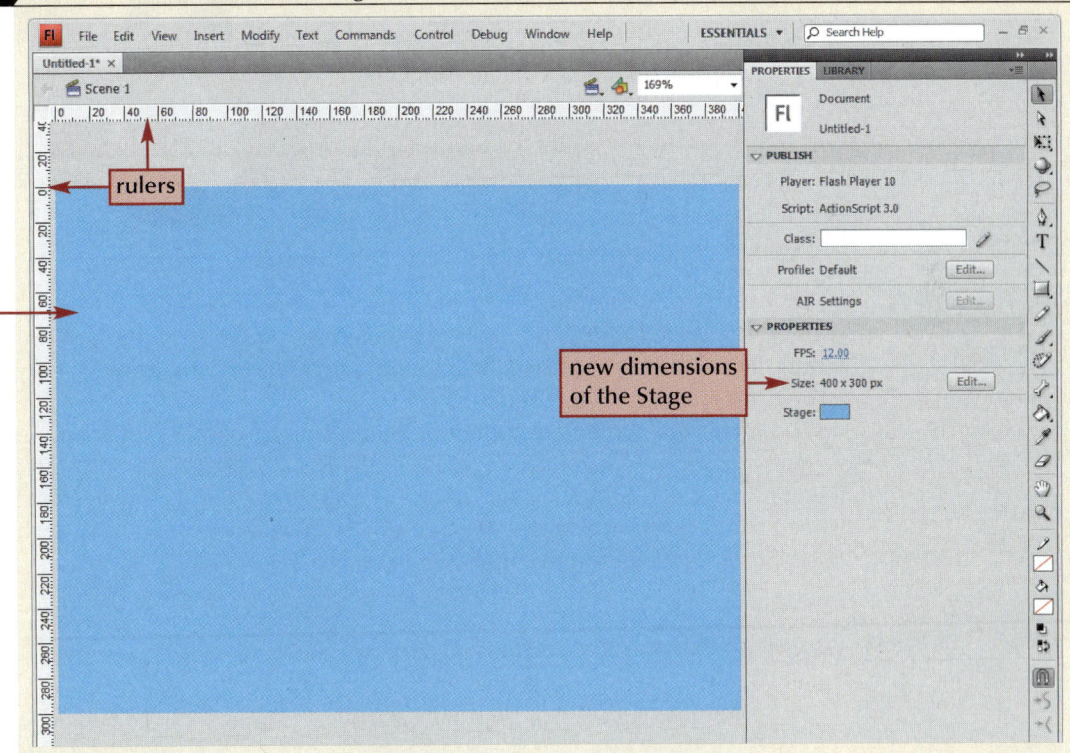

[Screenshot of Flash document window with callouts: "rulers", "blue background and smaller Stage", "new dimensions of the Stage"]

11. Save the document as **johBanner.fla** in the Tutorial.02\Tutorial folder included with your Data Files.

Using the Oval, Rectangle, and PolyStar Tools

Drawing simple shapes is easy with the Oval, Rectangle, and PolyStar tools. These tools all work in a similar manner. As you drag the pointer for the selected tool on the Stage, the size of the drawn shape changes until you release the mouse button. When you use the PolyStar tool, you choose whether to draw a polygon or a star shape. You can also indicate the number of sides the shape will have, which can range from 3 to 32. For star shapes, you can also specify the value of the star point size, which can range from 0 to 1. A number closer to 0 results in narrower star points, and a number closer to 1 results in wider star points, as shown in Figure 2-3.

Figure 2-3 Star shapes with different point sizes

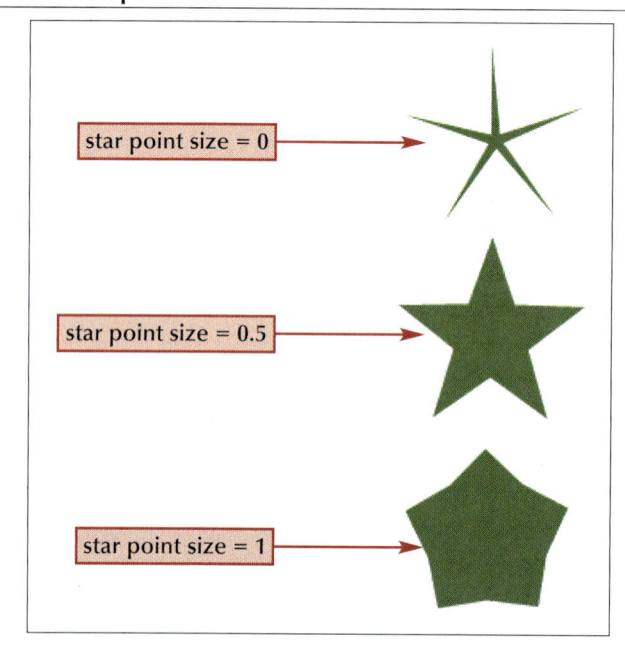

You can use the Oval and Rectangle tools to draw a perfect circle or a perfect square when the Snap to Objects modifier is selected. As you draw with the Oval or Rectangle tool, a small solid ring appears next to the pointer to let you know when you have drawn a perfect circle or a perfect square.

When you select the Rectangle tool, the Rectangle corner radius option appears in the Property inspector. The value you enter in the Rectangle corner radius box represents the number of pixels by which to round the corners of the rectangle shape. A negative value creates inward corners, a 0 value results in square corners, and higher values produce more rounded corners, as shown in Figure 2-4.

> **Tip**
>
> To create a rectangle with specific dimensions and corner radius, press the Alt key as you click the Rectangle tool pointer on the Stage, enter values in the Rectangle Settings dialog box, and then click the OK button.

Tutorial 2 Drawing Shapes, Adding Text, and Creating Symbols | Flash | FL 59

Figure 2-4 — Rectangles with different corner radii

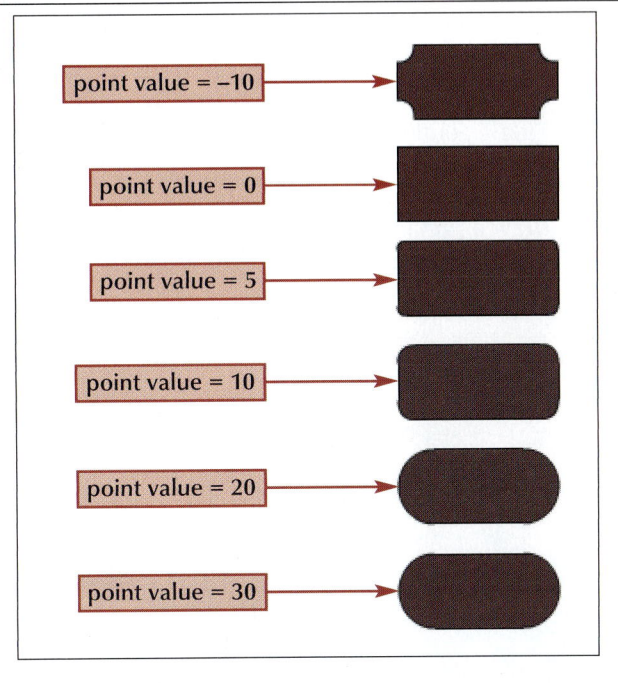

- point value = –10
- point value = 0
- point value = 5
- point value = 10
- point value = 20
- point value = 30

InSight | Using the Drawing Modes to Create Graphics

Before you start creating graphics in Flash, carefully plan how you want the graphic objects to interact with each other. If you want to create graphic shapes that combine to form one shape, draw them using the Merge Drawing mode. If you want to keep the shapes you draw separate from each other, use the Object Drawing mode. You can also switch between drawing modes as you draw the graphics.

You will draw rectangle shapes for the beach and ocean in the banner's background. You will draw another rectangle around the banner to frame all the graphic elements. As indicated in Aly's sketch, the frame rectangle will have a stroke, no fill, and rounded corners. You will draw the background graphics using the Object Drawing mode so that they won't merge with the fish you will create.

To draw the ocean rectangle using the Rectangle tool and guides:

1. Drag a horizontal guide from the horizontal ruler to approximately 150 pixels from the top of the Stage, and then drag another horizontal guide from the horizontal ruler to approximately 200 pixels from the top of the Stage.

2. In the Tools panel, click the **Rectangle** tool, and then click the **Object Drawing** button, if necessary, to select it. The rectangles you draw will not merge with other shapes.

3. In the Rectangle Options section of the Property inspector, click the **Reset** button to set the Rectangle corner radius values to 0, if necessary. The rectangle you draw will have square corners.

4. In the Property inspector, click the **Fill color** control to open the color palette, and then click the **blue** color swatch (#0000FF) in the first swatches column, ninth row. The rectangle you draw will be blue.

▸ 5. In the Property inspector, click the **Fill color** control to open the color palette, click the **Alpha** value and drag to the left until the Alpha value is 50. The reduced Alpha value of the fill color will make the rectangle partially transparent.

▸ 6. In the Property inspector, click the **Stroke color** control to open the color palette, and then click the **No Color** button. The rectangles you draw will not have an outline.

You are ready to draw the rectangle for the ocean.

▸ 7. Draw a rectangle from the left side of the Stage at the top guide to the lower-right corner of the Stage. A partially transparent, blue rectangle without an outline fills the lower part of the Stage. See Figure 2-5.

Figure 2-5   Rectangle for the ocean

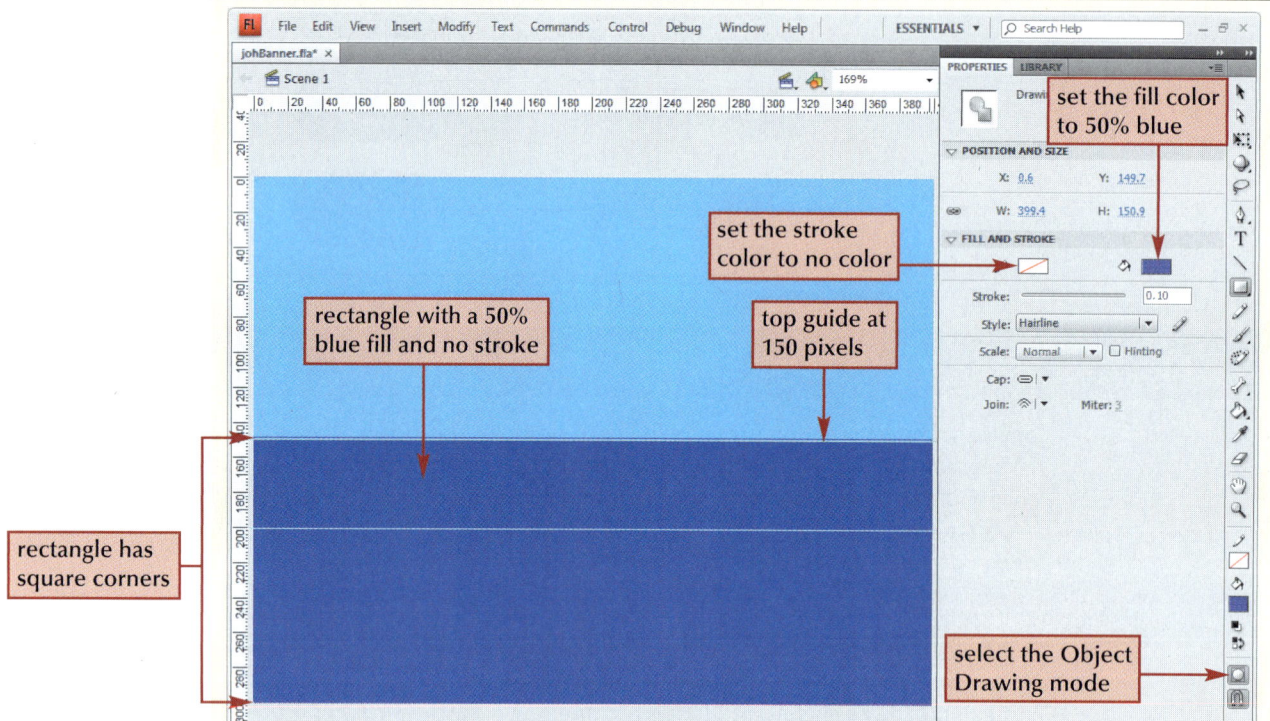

The second rectangle you draw will represent the beach. You need to deselect the ocean rectangle, and then change the fill color in the Color panel.

To draw the beach rectangle using the Rectangle tool and guides:

▸ 1. In the Tools panel, click the **Selection** tool, and then click in another area of the Stage to deselect the blue rectangle.

▸ 2. In the Tools panel, click the **Rectangle** tool to select it.

▸ 3. In the Property inspector, click the **Fill color** control to open the color palette, and then click the **light yellow** color swatch (#FFFFCD) in the last column, second row from the bottom of the color palette. The yellow fill is for the sand.

▸ 4. In the Property inspector, click the **Fill color** control to open the color palette, change the Alpha value to **100%**, and make sure the stroke color is set to no color. The beach rectangle will not have a stroke.

Tutorial 2 Drawing Shapes, Adding Text, and Creating Symbols | Flash | FL 61

5. Draw a rectangle from the left side of the Stage at the lower guide to the lower-right corner of the Stage. An opaque light yellow rectangle with no stroke covers the lower portion of the Stage. See Figure 2-6.

Figure 2-6 **Rectangle for the beach**

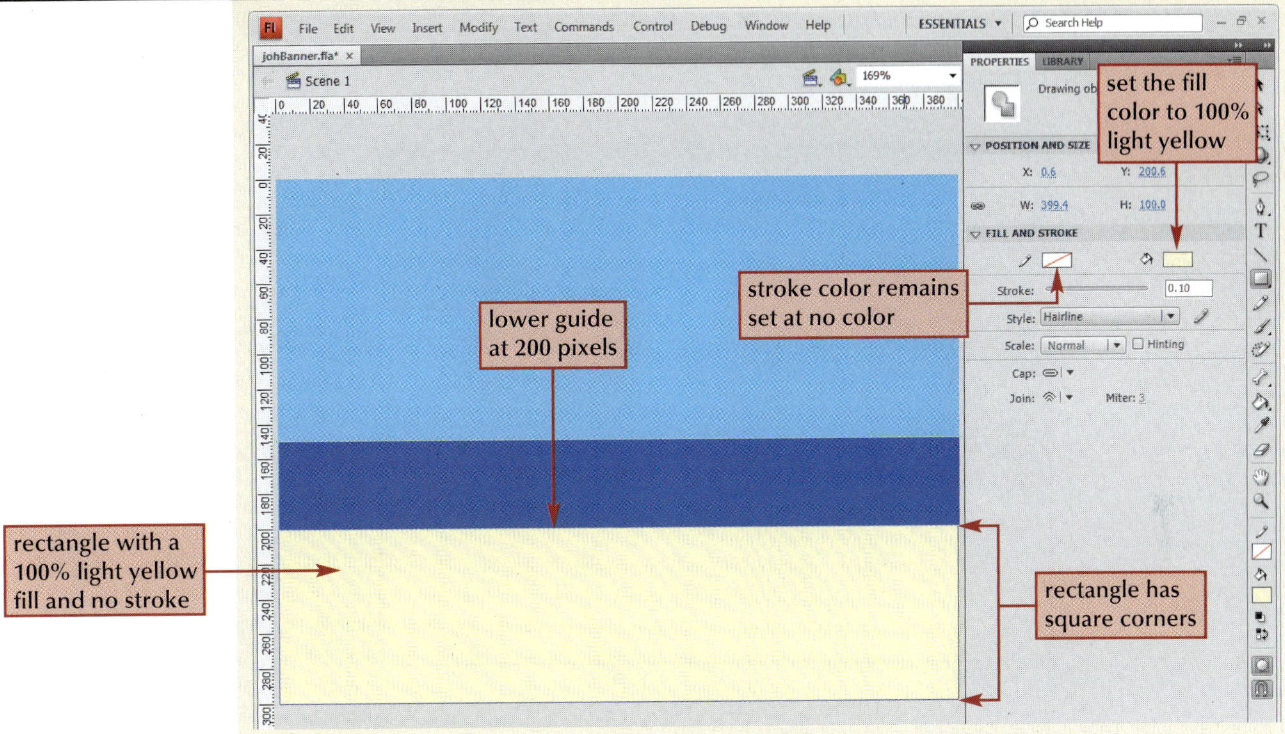

[Figure 2-6: Screenshot of Flash workspace showing a rectangle drawn for the beach. Callouts indicate: "set the fill color to 100% light yellow", "stroke color remains set at no color", "lower guide at 200 pixels", "rectangle with a 100% light yellow fill and no stroke", "rectangle has square corners".]

You will draw another rectangle to frame the banner. This rectangle will have a black stroke color and no fill color. It will also have rounded corners and a stroke height of 2.

To draw the frame rectangle using the Rectangle tool and guides:

1. In the Tools panel, click the **Selection** tool, and then click an empty area of the Stage to deselect the beach rectangle.

2. In the Tools panel, click the **Rectangle** tool, and then, in the Property inspector, click the **Stroke color** control to open the color palette and click the **black** color swatch (#000000) in the first swatches column, first row of the color palette. The rectangle will have a black stroke.

3. In the Property inspector, click the **Fill color** control to open the color palette, and then click the **No Color** button. The rectangle will not have a fill color.

4. In the Property inspector, make sure the stroke style is set to **Solid**, double-click the value in the **Stroke height** box, type **2**, and then press the **Enter** key. The stroke size is set to 2.

5. In the Rectangle Options section of the Property inspector, if necessary, click the **unlock** icon for the Rectangle corner radius to change it to a lock icon.

6. In the Rectangle Options section of the Property inspector, double-click the upper-left **Rectangle corner radius** value to select it, type **10**, and then press the **Enter** key. The value for each corner is set to 10.

7. In the Tools panel, click the **Snap to Objects** modifier button to deselect it, if necessary, so the rectangle won't snap to the edges of the Stage.

▶ 8. Draw a rectangle from just inside the upper-left corner of the Stage to just inside the lower-right corner of the Stage. See Figure 2-7.

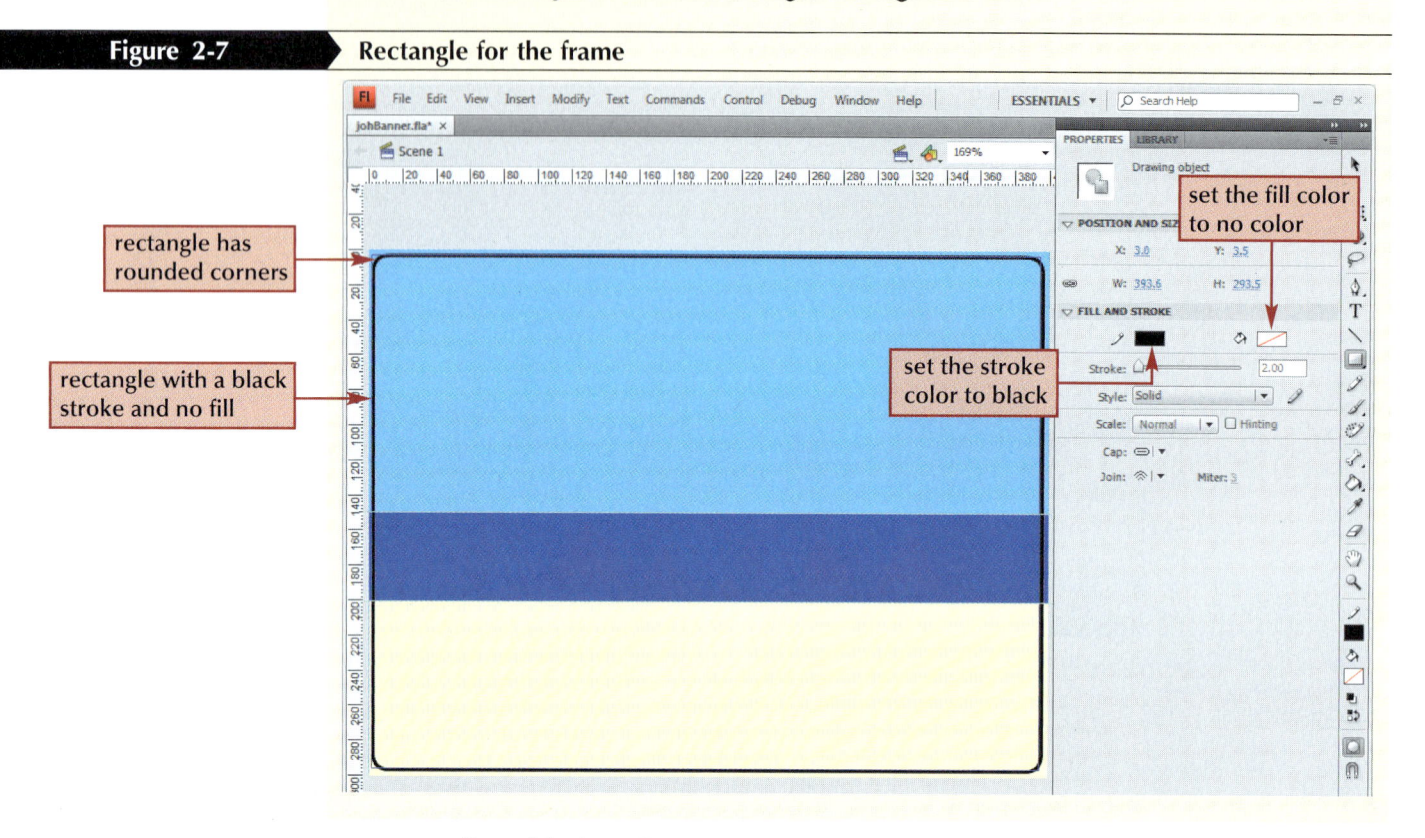

Figure 2-7   **Rectangle for the frame**

rectangle has rounded corners

rectangle with a black stroke and no fill

set the fill color to no color

set the stroke color to black

You will modify the yellow rectangle to more closely resemble the beach graphic that Aly sketched. You will do this by curving the top side of the rectangle using the Selection tool. You will hide the guides because you will not be using them.

To hide the guides and modify the yellow rectangle shape:

▶ 1. On the Application bar, click **View**, point to **Guides**, and then click **Show Guides**. The guides disappear.

▶ 2. In the Tools panel, click the **Selection** tool, and then click an empty area of the Stage to deselect the frame rectangle. You will modify the light yellow rectangle using the Selection tool.

▶ 3. Move the pointer to the upper-middle side of the light yellow rectangle until the pointer changes to ↳, and then drag the top of the rectangle down about 45 pixels to curve it, but do not release the mouse button. See Figure 2-8.

Tutorial 2 Drawing Shapes, Adding Text, and Creating Symbols | Flash **FL 63**

| Figure 2-8 | **Curved rectangle created using the Selection tool** |

line shows the new curved top of the rectangle

curve pointer

▶ **4.** Release the mouse button.

Next, you will create the fish in the center of the banner that Aly sketched. You'll draw a large oval for the body of the fish and a rectangle that you will modify to become the fish's tail. You will use the Merge Drawing mode so that the two shapes combine into one. Guides will help you draw these shapes.

To draw the fish using the Oval and Rectangle tools and guides:

▶ **1.** On the Application bar, click **View**, point to **Guides**, and then click **Show Guides**. The guides appear on the Stage.

▶ **2.** Drag the top guide up to approximately 50 pixels from the top of the Stage, and then drag the bottom guide up to approximately 90 pixels from the top of the Stage.

▶ **3.** Drag a vertical guide from the vertical ruler to approximately 150 pixels from the left of the Stage, and then drag another vertical guide from the vertical ruler to approximately 250 pixels from the left of the Stage. See Figure 2-9.

Figure 2-9   **Guides for creating the fish**

place horizontal guides at 50 and 90 pixels

draw the fish here

place vertical guides at 150 and 250 pixels

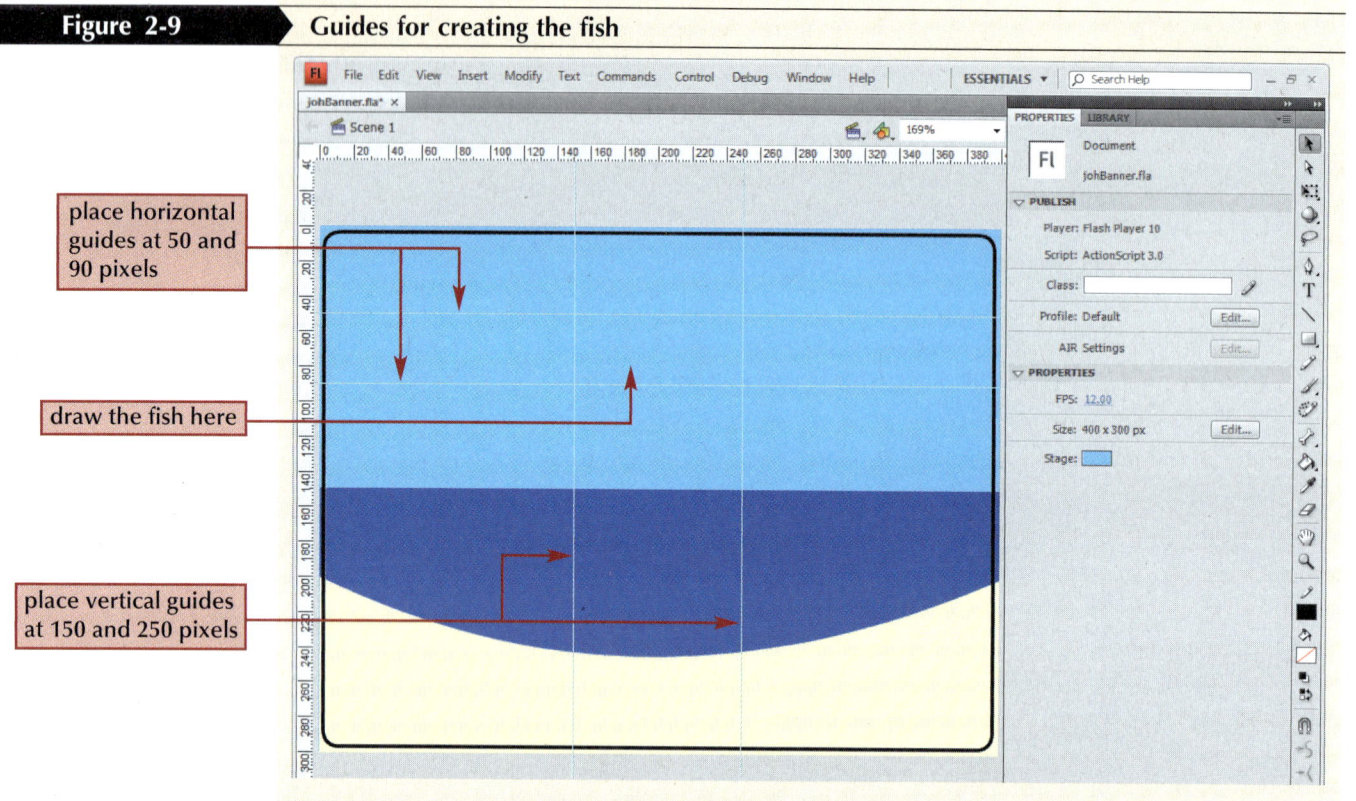

- 4. In the Tools panel, click and hold the **Rectangle** tool to open the pop-up menu, and then click the **Oval** tool. The pointer changes to +.

- 5. In the Tools panel, click the **Object Drawing** button to deselect it. The Merge Drawing mode is now in effect.

- 6. In the Property inspector, if necessary, click the **Stroke color** control to open the color palette, and then click the **black** color swatch (#000000) in the first swatches column, first row of the color palette.

- 7. In the Property inspector, enter **1** in the Stroke height box, and then make sure the Stroke style is set to **Solid**.

- 8. In the Property inspector, click the **Fill color** control to open the color palette, and then click the **orange** color swatch (#FF9900) in the seventh row, third column from the right. The fish body you draw will be orange with a black stroke.

- 9. Draw an oval from the upper-left corner of the rectangular area formed by the guides to the lower-right corner of the rectangular area formed by the guides. See Figure 2-10.

Tutorial 2 Drawing Shapes, Adding Text, and Creating Symbols | Flash FL 65

| Figure 2-10 | Oval for the fish body |

set the fill color to orange

set the stroke color to a 1 pixel, solid black line

draw the oval to fit within the guides

- 10. In the Tools panel, click and hold the **Oval** tool to open the pop-up menu, and then click the **Rectangle** tool. The Rectangle tool is selected.

- 11. In the Rectangle Options section of the Property inspector, click the **Reset** button to set the value in the Rectangle corner radius boxes to 0.

- 12. Draw a rectangle starting approximately **40** pixels from the top of the Stage and **100** pixels from the left of the Stage and ending approximately **100** pixels from the top of the Stage and **170** pixels from the left of the Stage. See Figure 2-11.

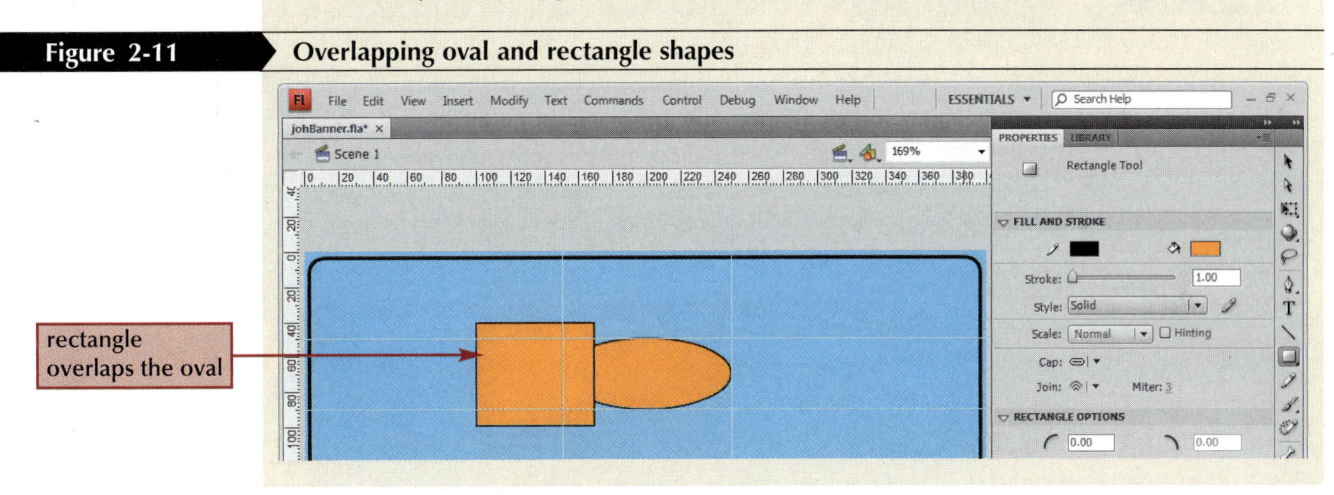

| Figure 2-11 | Overlapping oval and rectangle shapes |

rectangle overlaps the oval

You will use the Selection tool to modify the two shapes so that they more closely resemble the fish Aly sketched. The right corners of the rectangle will be modified to connect to the oval and the sides of the rectangle will be curved. You will clear the guides because you don't need them anymore.

To modify the oval and rectangle shapes using the Selection tool:

- 1. On the Application bar, click **View**, point to **Guides**, and then click **Clear Guides**. The guides are removed from the Stage.

- 2. In the Tools panel, click the **Snap to Objects** modifier button to select it.

- 3. In the Tools panel, click the **Selection** tool, drag the upper-right corner of the rectangle down until it snaps to the top edge of the oval, and then drag the lower-right corner of the rectangle up until it snaps to the lower edge of the oval. See Figure 2-12.

Figure 2-12 | **Modified rectangle**

upper and lower edges of the rectangle snapped to the oval

▶ 4. Move the pointer to the stroke on the left side of the modified rectangle shape until the pointer changes to , and then drag the line slightly to the right.

▶ 5. Drag the top line down slightly to curve it; drag the bottom line up slightly to curve it.

▶ 6. Click the right side of the modified rectangle to select it, and then press the **Delete** key. The unneeded stroke is removed. See Figure 2-13.

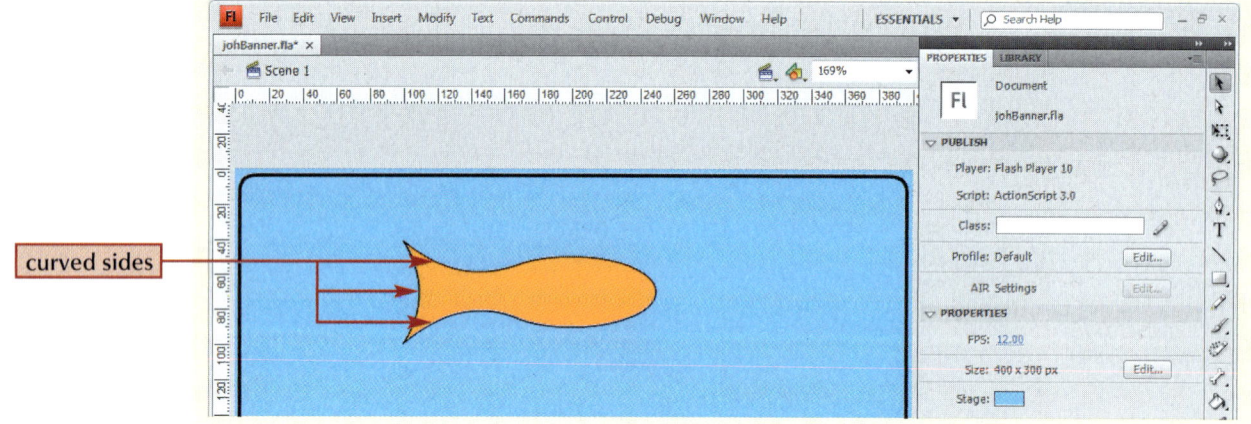

Figure 2-13 | **Sides of the rectangle modified**

curved sides

The modified rectangle and oval resemble a fish shape. You are ready to draw the eye for the fish. You'll also draw several oval spots on the fish. You can use the Oval tool for this.

To use the Oval tool to draw the eye and oval spots on the fish:

▶ 1. In the Tools panel, click the **Zoom** tool , make sure the **Enlarge** modifier button is selected, and then click the right side of the fish shape once to zoom in.

▶ 2. In the Tools panel, click and hold the **Rectangle** tool to open the pop-up menu, and then click the **Oval** tool . The pointer changes to +.

▶ 3. In the Property inspector, click the **Stroke color** control to open the color palette, click the **No Color** button , click the **Fill color** control to open the color palette, and then click the **white** color swatch (#FFFFFF) in the first swatches column, sixth row of the color palette.

Tutorial 2 Drawing Shapes, Adding Text, and Creating Symbols | Flash **FL 67**

▶ **4.** Draw a small circle on the upper-right end of the fish shape for the fish eye, and then draw three ovals of different sizes on the fish body. You will change the color of the ovals later in this session. See Figure 2-14.

Figure 2-14 | **Fish eye and spots drawn**

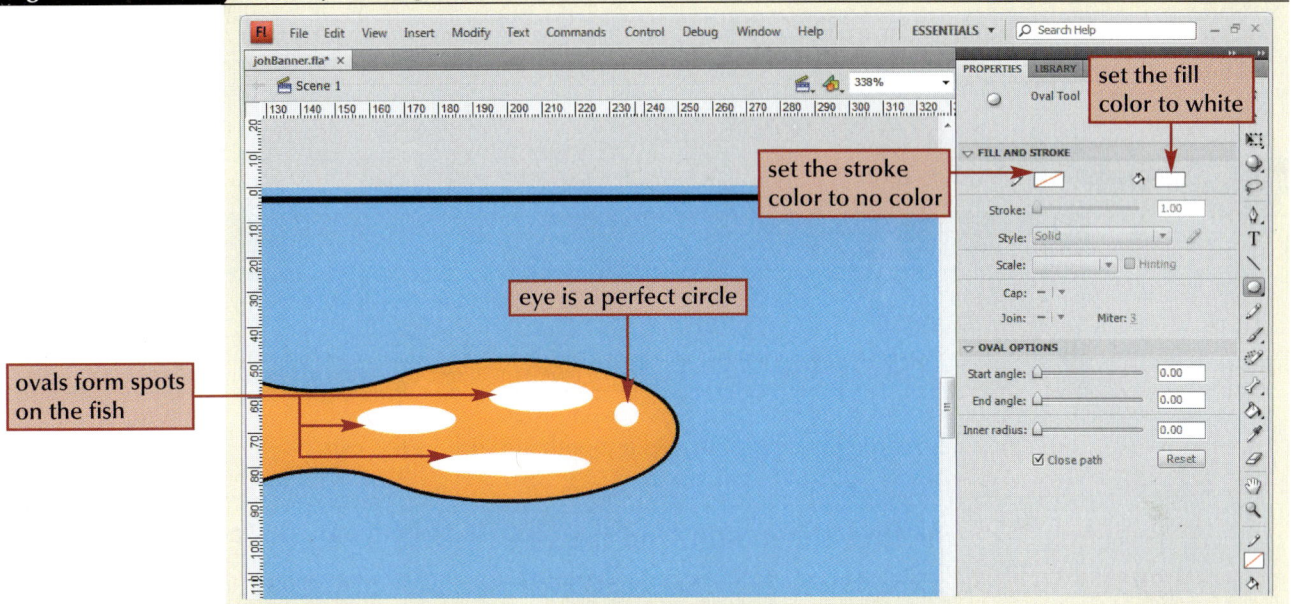

▶ **5.** In the Tools panel, click the **Snap to Objects** modifier button to deselect it. Having the modifier off will make it easier to draw a small circle for the pupil of the fish eye.

▶ **6.** In the Property inspector, click the **Fill color** control to open the color palette, and then click the **black** color swatch (#000000) in the first swatches column, first row of the color palette.

▶ **7.** Draw a smaller circle inside the eye to represent the pupil. See Figure 2-15.

Figure 2-15 | **Pupil for the fish eye**

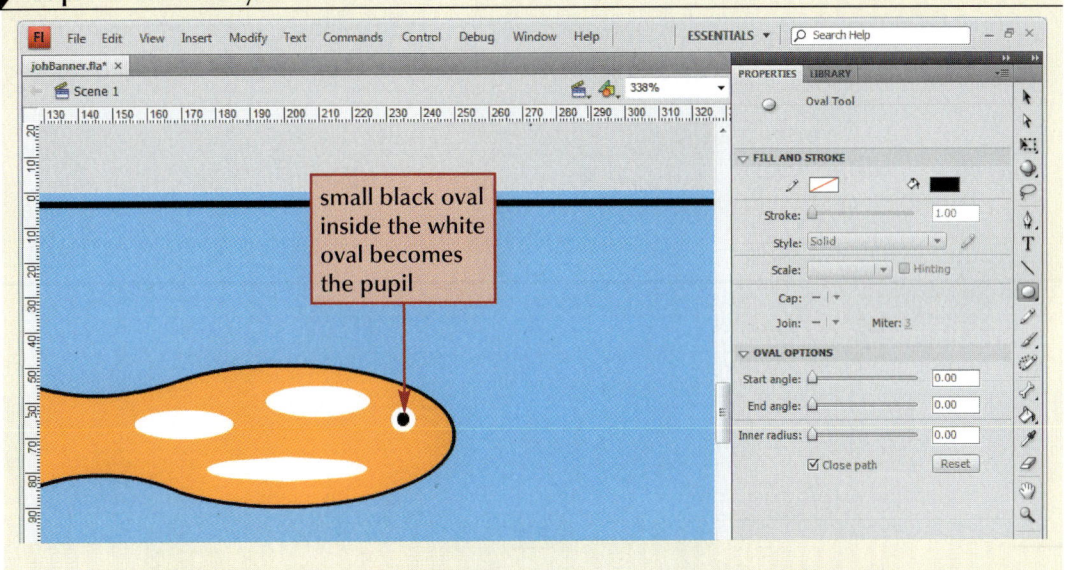

Trouble? If you make a mistake and draw over the orange fill of the fish, click Edit on the Application bar, click Undo Oval, and then repeat Step 7 to redraw the circle for the pupil of the fish eye.

Using the Pencil Tool

The Pencil tool works in a similar way to the Line tool, but it doesn't limit you to drawing straight lines. The **Pencil tool** is used to draw lines and shapes in a free-form manner as if you were using an actual pencil to draw on paper. As is the case with the Line tool, you can select a color, height, and style for the lines drawn with the Pencil tool. The Pencil Mode modifier in the Tools panel lets you control the way lines appear as you draw them. Figure 2-16 summarizes the options for this modifier.

Figure 2-16   Pencil Mode modifier options

Modifier Button	Option	Description
↳	Straighten	Helps straighten the lines you draw
S	Smooth	Smoothes the lines and curves you draw
✎	Ink	Provides minimal assistance as you draw

You will use the Pencil tool to add a mouth and fins to the fish.

To add the fins, the mouth, and lines to the fish using the Pencil tool:

▶ 1. In the Tools panel, click the **Snap to Objects** modifier button 🔘 to select it. Having the modifier on will make it easier to draw lines attached to existing strokes.

▶ 2. In the Tools panel, click the **Pencil** tool ✎ to select it.

▶ 3. In the Tools panel, click the **Pencil Mode** modifier button ↳ to open the menu of options, and then click **Smooth**. The Smooth option for the Pencil Mode modifier ensures that the lines you draw are smooth.

▶ 4. In the Property inspector, make sure the stroke color is **black** (#000000), the stroke height is **1**, and the stroke style is **Solid**. The stroke color, height, and style are set for drawing lines for the fins, mouth, and curves.

▶ 5. Draw a fin on the top side of the fish and two fins on the bottom side. See Figure 2-17.

Tutorial 2 Drawing Shapes, Adding Text, and Creating Symbols | Flash | FL 69

Figure 2-17 Fins drawn on the fish

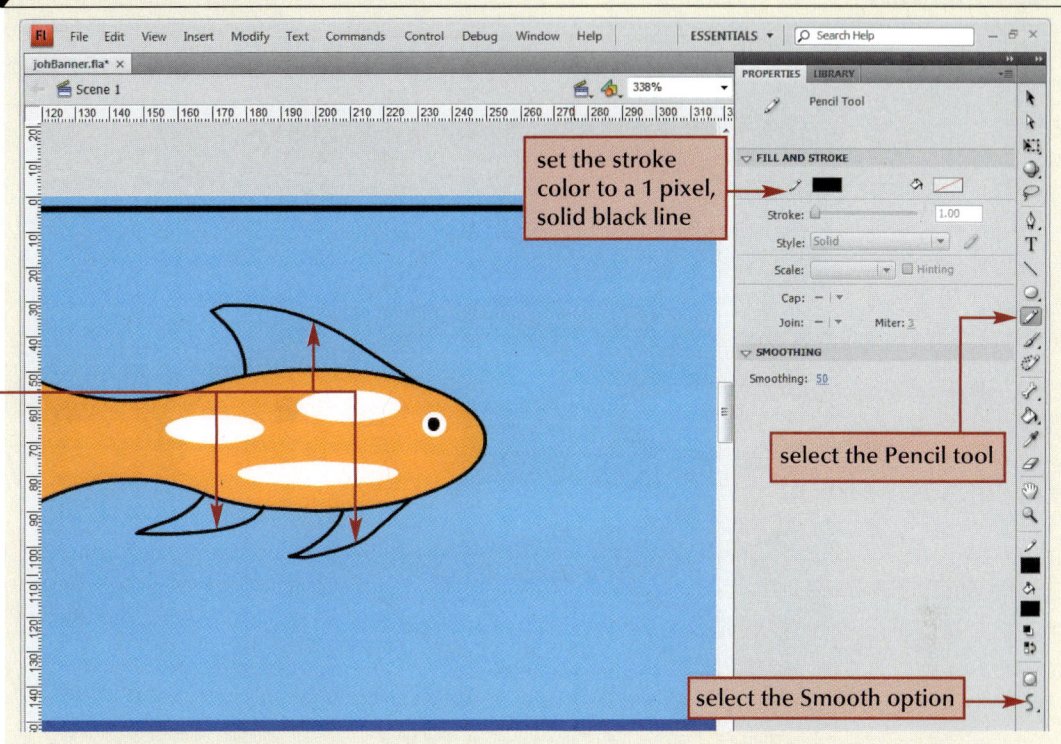

[Screenshot callouts: "draw the fins with the Pencil tool"; "set the stroke color to a 1 pixel, solid black line"; "select the Pencil tool"; "select the Smooth option"]

▸ 6. In the Tools panel, click the **Zoom** tool, make sure the **Enlarge** modifier button is selected, and then click the center of the fish shape once to zoom in.

▸ 7. In the Tools panel, click the **Selection** tool, move the pointer to the left endpoint of the lower-right fin stroke until the pointer changes to, and then drag the endpoint so that it snaps to the stroke representing the body of the fish. See Figure 2-18.

Figure 2-18   Connecting the endpoints of the fins to the fish's body

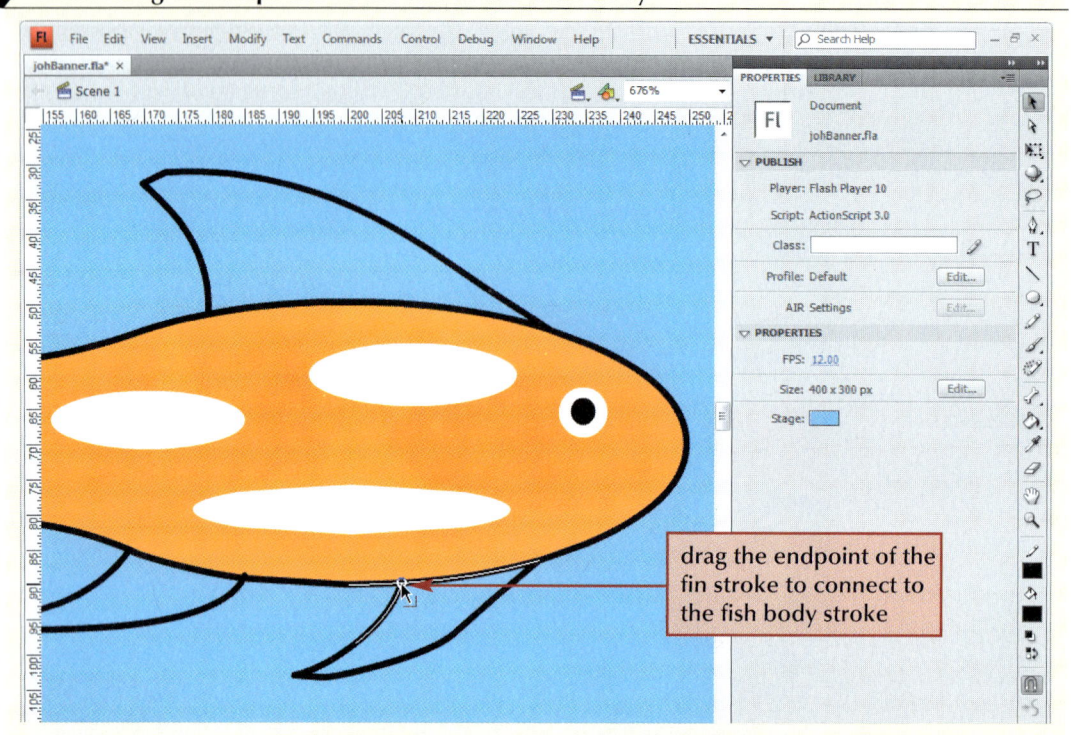

drag the endpoint of the fin stroke to connect to the fish body stroke

- 8. Repeat Step 7 to connect the endpoints of the other fins to the fish's body.
- 9. In the Tools panel, click the **Pencil** tool to select it, make sure the Smooth option is selected in the Pencil Mode modifier, and make sure the stroke is set to 1 pixel, solid black line.
- 10. Draw a small curved line for the fish's mouth from right below the eye to the stroke in the lower-right side of the fish, and then draw three short lines in the tail section of the fish. See Figure 2-19.

Figure 2-19   Fins, mouth, and lines on the fish

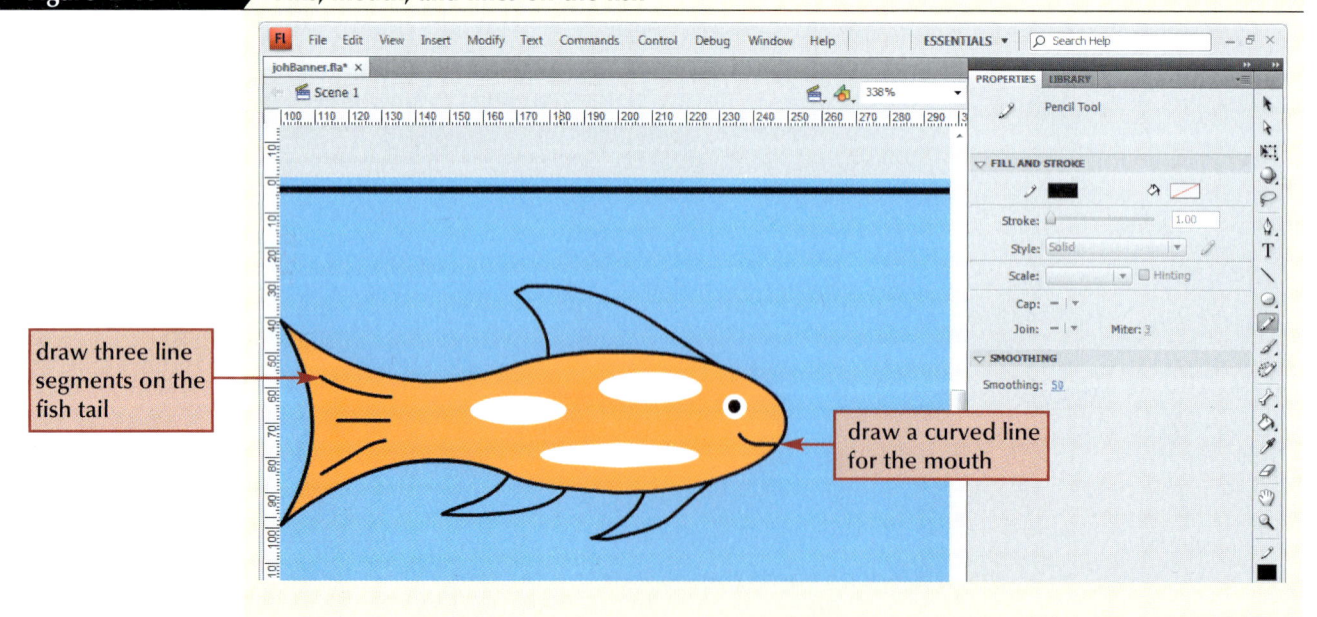

draw three line segments on the fish tail

draw a curved line for the mouth

▶ **11.** In the Tools panel, click the **Zoom** tool, click the **Reduce** modifier button, and then click the center of the fish to zoom out.

Changing Strokes and Fills

After you draw an object, you can still change its stroke and fill. You can change the stroke's color, height, or style, and you can change a fill's color. You can even add a fill or a stroke to an object that does not have one or the other. Based on Aly's sketch of the banner, the oval shapes and the fins on the fish should be areas of color.

To keep the various parts of the fish together, you will group them. This way, you can easily modify the fish graphic as a whole or create copies of the fish graphic. You can still modify individual elements of a grouped object in group-editing mode.

To group the fish graphic:

▶ **1.** On the Edit bar, click the **Zoom control arrow**, and then click **Show Frame** to view all the contents of the Stage.

▶ **2.** In the Tools panel, click the **Selection** tool, and then draw a marquee around the entire fish to select all of its parts.

Tip
You can also press the Ctrl+G keys to group selected elements.

▶ **3.** On the Application bar, click **Modify**, and then click **Group**. The graphic elements are grouped. A thin rectangular line surrounds the grouped object to show it is selected. See Figure 2-20.

Figure 2-20   Grouped fish graphic

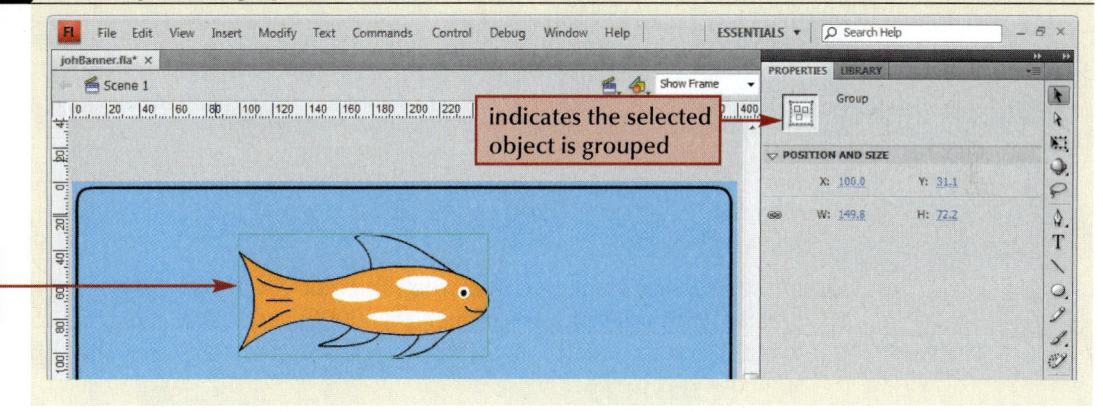

outline indicates a grouped object

indicates the selected object is grouped

Using the Paint Bucket Tool

The **Paint Bucket tool** changes the color of an existing fill or adds a fill to an enclosed area that does not have a fill. The fill color is selected with the Fill color control in the Tools panel, the Property inspector, or the Color panel. The Paint Bucket tool also has a Gap Size modifier and a Lock Fill modifier. The Gap Size modifiers—Don't Close Gaps, Close Small Gaps, Close Medium Gaps, and Close Large Gaps—determine how the tool will paint areas that are not completely enclosed. The Lock Fill modifier extends gradient and bitmap fills across multiple objects.

Tip
The **Ink Bottle tool** changes the attributes or properties of a stroke or applies a stroke to an object that has no stroke.

You will use the Paint Bucket tool to fill the spots on the fish with bright colors.

To apply fills to the fish with the Paint Bucket tool:

▶ 1. Double-click the grouped fish graphic to enter group-editing mode, and then click another area of the Stage to deselect the fish. In group-editing mode, you can modify each part of the fish independently.

▶ 2. In the Tools panel, click the **Paint Bucket** tool. The pointer changes to.

▶ 3. In the Tools panel, click the **Gap Size** modifier button to open the pop-up menu, and then click **Close Medium Gaps**. With this Gap Size modifier, you can use the Paint Bucket tool to paint areas that are not completely enclosed.

▶ 4. In the Property inspector, click the **Fill color** control to open the color palette, and then click the **light green** color swatch (#65FF00) in the last column, first row of the color palette.

▶ 5. Click inside the white oval at the bottom of the fish body to apply the fill color. The fish has a light green spot. See Figure 2-21.

Figure 2-21 Fill color applied with the Paint Bucket tool

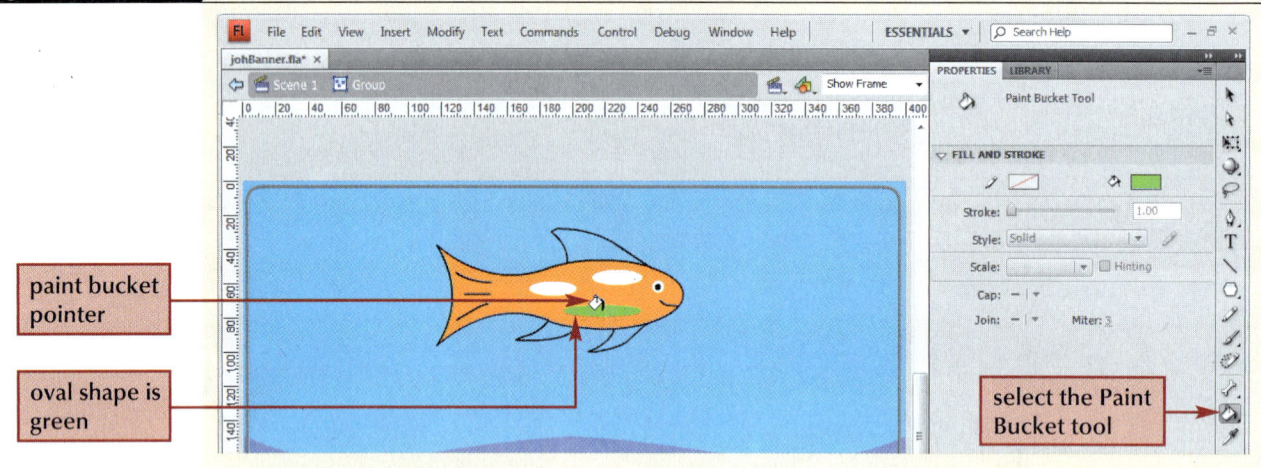

- paint bucket pointer
- oval shape is green
- select the Paint Bucket tool

Trouble? If a padlock icon appears next to the paint bucket pointer, the Lock Fill modifier is selected. This does not affect the way the Paint Bucket tool works. Continue with Step 6.

▶ 6. In the Property inspector, click the **Fill color** control to open the color palette, click the **red** color swatch (#FF0000) in the first swatches column, seventh row of the color palette, and then click the left white oval on the fish body. The spot changes to red.

▶ 7. Repeat Step 6 to apply the **yellow** color (#FFFF00) in the first swatches column, tenth row of the color palette to the top white oval on the fish body. The spot changes to yellow.

Using the Eyedropper Tool

The **Eyedropper tool** copies the properties of a fill or stroke from one object and applies them to the fill or stroke of another object. You can also use the Eyedropper tool to copy the properties of a text block and apply them to another text block. When you select the Eyedropper tool, the pointer changes to. If you move the eyedropper over a stroke, the pointer changes to to indicate that you are about to copy the stroke's attributes. After you click the stroke, the pointer changes to, which indicates that you can apply the copied stroke attributes to another object. If you move the eyedropper over a fill, the pointer changes to to indicate that you are about to copy the fill's attributes. After you

Tutorial 2 Drawing Shapes, Adding Text, and Creating Symbols | Flash   FL 73

click the fill, the pointer changes to 🪣 and you can click another object to apply the copied fill attributes. The pointer includes a padlock 🔒🪣 when the Lock Fill modifier is selected.

| Reference Window | **Using the Eyedropper Tool** |

- In the Tools panel, click the Eyedropper tool.
- Click the stroke or fill whose attributes you want to copy.
- Click the stroke or fill to which you want to apply the copied attributes.

Based on to Aly's sketch, the fins of the fish need to be the same color as the bottom oval spot on the fish. You will use the Eyedropper tool to copy the fill color of the spot to the fins.

To copy the color from the bottom spot to the fins using the Eyedropper tool:

1. In the Tools panel, click the **Eyedropper** tool 🖉. The pointer changes to 🖉.

2. Click the green fill color in the bottom spot of the fish. The pointer changes to 🪣 or 🔒🪣 (depending on whether the Lock Fill modifier is selected) to indicate that you can apply the green color to another part of the fish.

3. Click the blank area enclosed by the top fin. The top fin now has the same color as the bottom spot of the fish. See Figure 2-22.

| Figure 2-22 | **Fill color copied from the green oval to the top fin** |

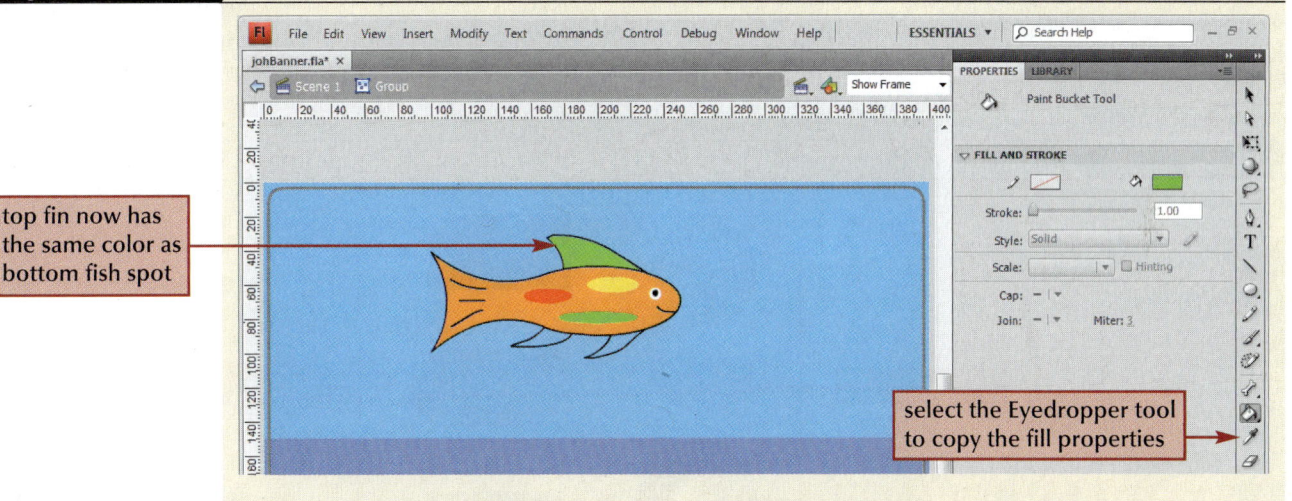

top fin now has the same color as bottom fish spot

select the Eyedropper tool to copy the fill properties

4. Click in the bottom fins. The green fill color is applied to them.

5. On the Edit bar, click the **Scene 1** link to exit group-editing mode.

Using Primitive Tools

The **Rectangle Primitive** and **Oval Primitive tools** create rectangles and ovals that are treated as separate objects whose characteristics you can modify using the Property inspector without having to redraw the shapes from scratch. For example, after you draw a rectangle with the Rectangle tool, you cannot change the roundness of the rectangle's corners. However, if you create a rectangle with the Rectangle Primitive tool, you can easily modify the rectangle's corners by changing the values in the Rectangle corner radius boxes in the Property inspector. Similarly, after you draw an oval with the Oval

Primitive tool, the Property inspector provides several controls for modifying the oval, as shown in Figure 2-23.

Figure 2-23   **Oval Primitive controls in the Property inspector**

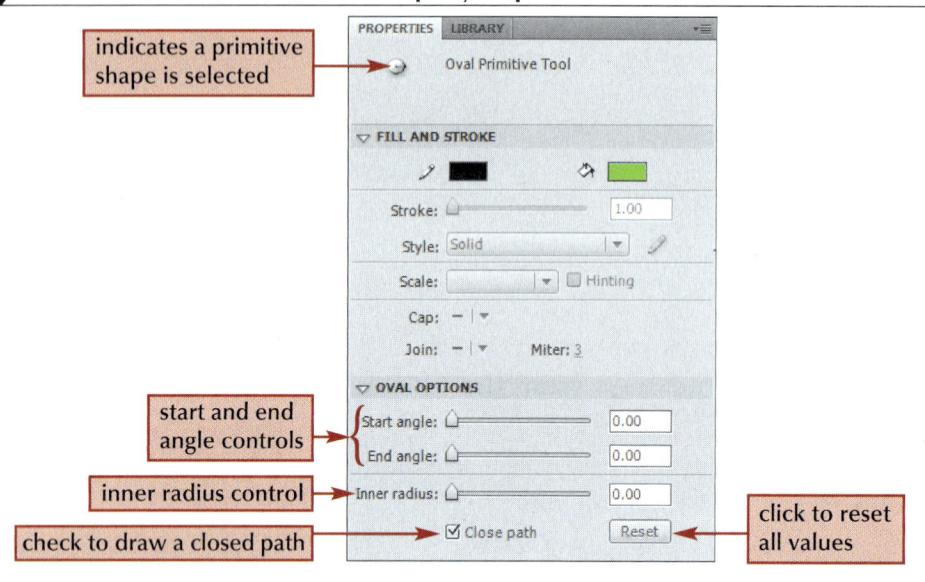

- indicates a primitive shape is selected
- start and end angle controls
- inner radius control
- check to draw a closed path
- click to reset all values

The Start angle and End angle values specify the angles of the starting and ending points of the oval. This can be used to create a pie or semicircle shape. The Inner radius value specifies the percentage of the oval's fill that is removed. For example, you can change the Inner radius value to create a doughnut shape. The Close path option determines whether the path of the oval is closed or open. An open path results in an oval shape with no fill when the start and end angles are not set to zero. Reset returns the oval shape on the Stage to its original size and shape. Figure 2-24 shows shapes drawn with the Rectangle Primitive and Oval Primitive tools.

Figure 2-24   **Sample shapes drawn with the primitive tools**

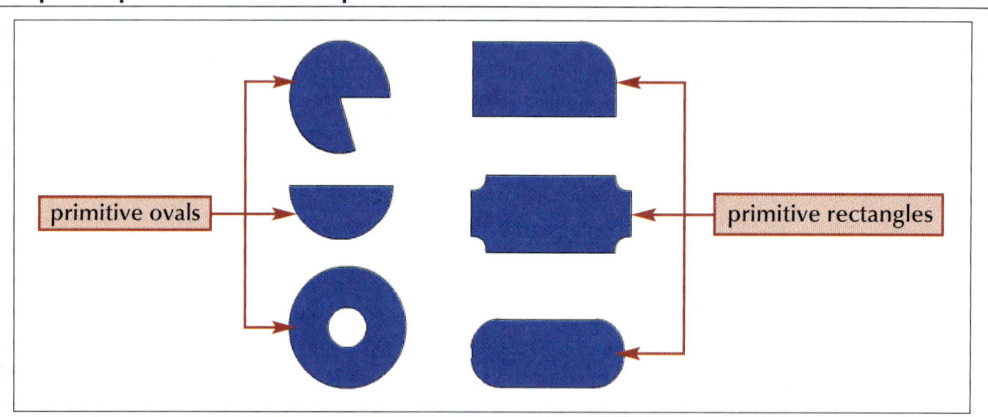

- primitive ovals
- primitive rectangles

You can convert a shape created with a primitive tool to a drawing object to further modify the shape just as if you had drawn the shape using the Object Drawing mode. If you convert a primitive shape into a drawing object, the object is no longer a primitive shape and the primitive tool controls are not available in the Property inspector.

According to Aly's sketch, the umbrella is still needed for the banner. You will use the Oval Primitive tool to draw the semicircle that will form the umbrella.

Tutorial 2 Drawing Shapes, Adding Text, and Creating Symbols | Flash FL 75

To create the umbrella with the Oval Primitive tool:

1. In the Tools panel, click the **Selection** tool, and then drag horizontal guides to about 150 pixels and 250 pixels from the top of the Stage.

2. Drag vertical guides to about 50 pixels and 150 pixels from the left of the Stage. You'll use the guides as you create the umbrella.

3. In the Tools panel, click and hold the **Oval** tool to open the pop-up menu, and then click the **Oval Primitive** tool. The Oval Primitive tool is selected.

4. In the Property inspector, set the stroke color to **black** (#000000), if necessary, and set the fill color to **red** (#FF0000). The stroke and fill colors are set.

5. In the Property inspector, make sure the stroke height is **1** and stroke style is **Solid**.

6. In the Oval Options section of the Property inspector, click the **Reset** button to reset the oval options.

7. Drag + inside the square formed by the guides to create an oval. See Figure 2-25.

Figure 2-25   Primitive oval shape

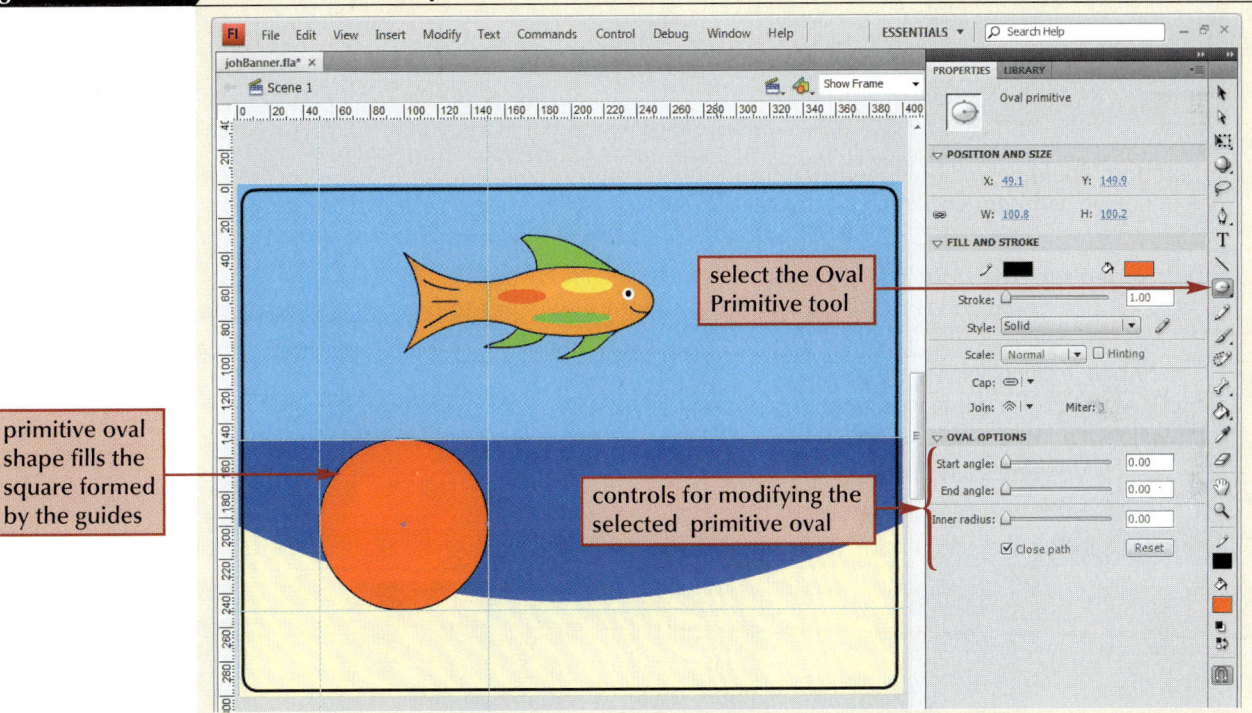

select the Oval Primitive tool

primitive oval shape fills the square formed by the guides

controls for modifying the selected primitive oval

8. In the Oval Options section of the Property inspector, drag the Start angle slider to the right until the Start angle value is **180**. The oval changes to a semicircle. See Figure 2-26.

Flash | Tutorial 2 Drawing Shapes, Adding Text, and Creating Symbols

Figure 2-26 Primitive oval changed to a semicircle shape

oval changed to a semicircle

drag the slider to set the Start angle value

So that the semicircle more closely resembles an umbrella, you'll use the Line tool to draw lines on the umbrella and the pole.

To draw lines on the umbrella with the Line tool:

1. In the Tools panel, click the **Selection** tool, and then double-click the semicircle shape. The Edit Object dialog box opens, informing you that Flash must convert the shape to a drawing object.

   Trouble? If the Edit Object dialog box doesn't open, the warning was disabled for your installation, and the program switches to Drawing Object mode. Continue with Step 3.

2. Click the **OK** button. The program switches to Drawing Object mode.

3. In the Tools panel, click the **Line** tool, and then make sure the stroke color is **black** (#000000), the stroke height is **1**, and the stroke style is **Solid**.

4. In the Tools panel, click the **Snap to Objects** button to select it, if necessary.

5. Draw three lines on the semicircle, as shown in Figure 2-27, for the umbrella frame.

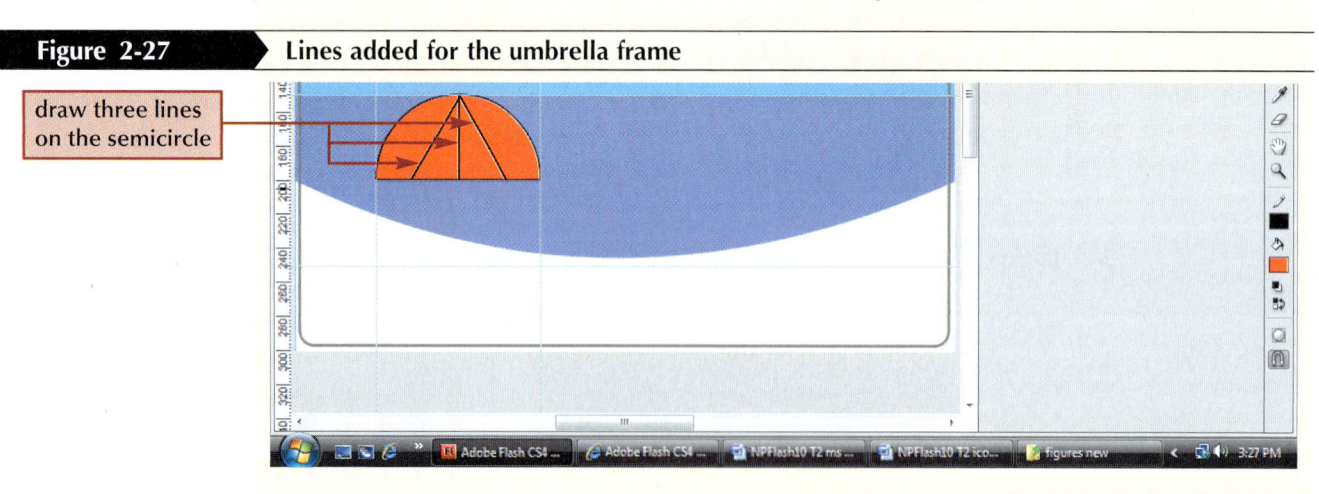

Figure 2-27 Lines added for the umbrella frame

draw three lines on the semicircle

Tip

To draw a straight line, hold the Shift key as you draw with the Line tool.

6. Draw a vertical line from the midpoint at the bottom edge of the semicircle to the bottom guide. See Figure 2-28.

Tutorial 2 Drawing Shapes, Adding Text, and Creating Symbols | Flash | **FL 77**

Figure 2-28 — Line added for the umbrella pole

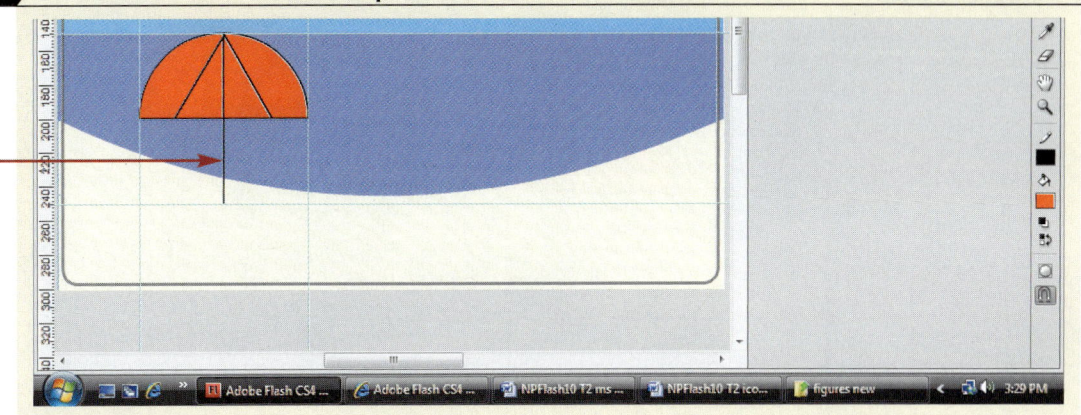

draw a straight line for the pole

Based on Aly's sketch, two of the lines that make up the umbrella frame should be curved, and the bottom edge of the umbrella should be curved. You will use the Selection tool to modify these lines.

To modify the lines on the umbrella using the Selection tool:

1. In the Tools panel, click the **Selection** tool.
2. Using the **Selection** pointer, point to the line on the left side of the umbrella until the pointer changes to, and then drag the left line slightly to the left to curve it.
3. Drag the line on the right side of the umbrella slightly to the right to curve it. See Figure 2-29.

Figure 2-29 — Lines modified with the Selection tool

curved lines on the left and right sides of the umbrella

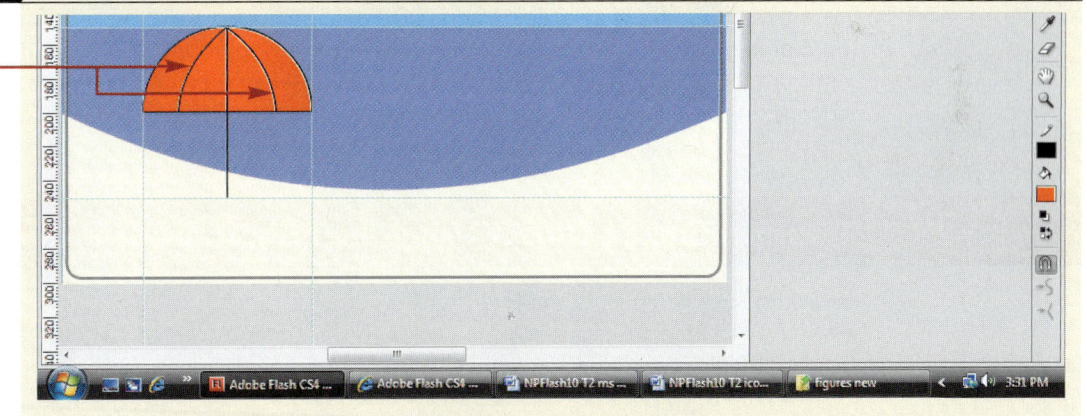

4. In the Tools panel, click the **Zoom** tool, make sure the **Enlarge** modifier button is selected, and then click the umbrella once to zoom in and center the umbrella on the Stage. The increased magnification makes it simpler to modify the bottom edge of the umbrella.
5. In the Tools panel, click the **Selection** tool, point to the first line segment on the left side of the bottom edge of the umbrella to change the pointer to, and then drag the line slightly up to curve it.
6. Repeat Step 5 to drag each of the other three line segments at the bottom edge of the umbrella to curve them. See Figure 2-30.

Figure 2-30 | **Modified line segments**

curved line segments at the bottom of the umbrella

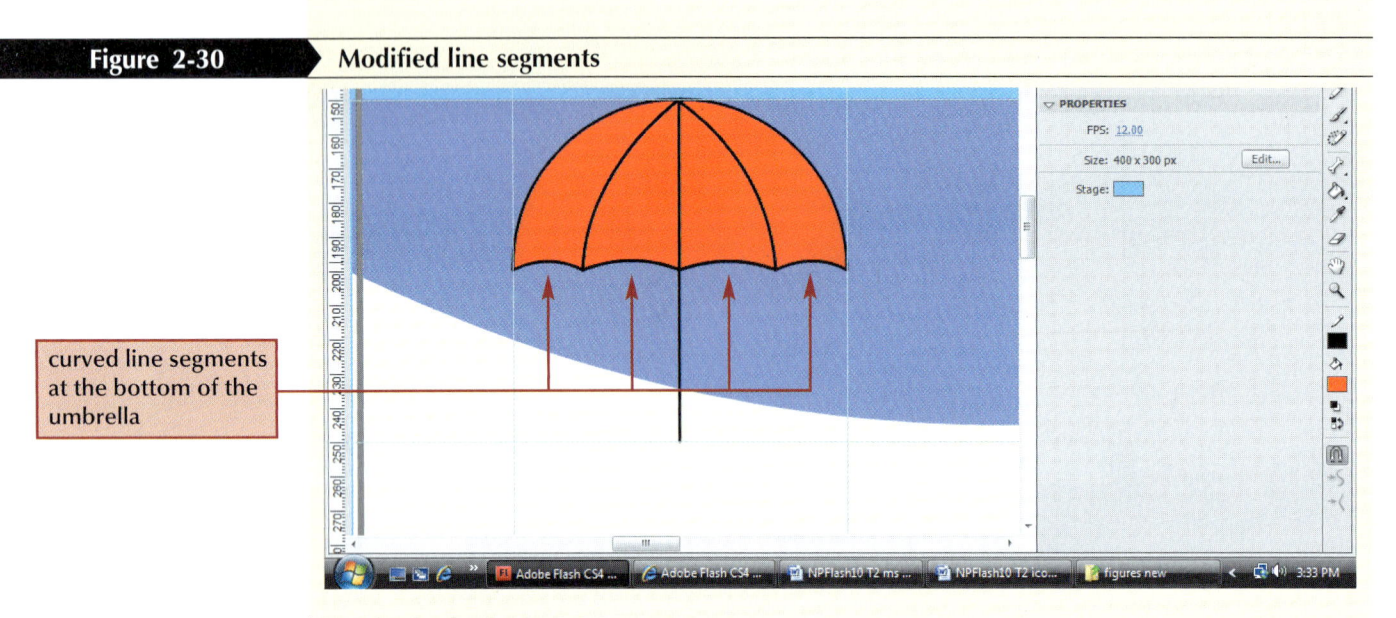

▶ 7. On the Application bar, click **View**, point to **Guides** and click **Clear Guides**. The guides are removed from the Stage.

▶ 8. On the Edit bar, click the **Scene 1** link to exit Object Drawing mode.

Using the Free Transform Tool

You can modify the strokes and fills of objects you draw in ways other than just changing their colors. The **Free Transform tool** allows you to move, rotate, scale, skew, and even distort objects. You can transform a particular stroke or fill of an object, or you can transform the entire object at once. When you select an object with the Free Transform tool, a bounding box with transformation handles surrounds the object. These handles are different from the anchor points you used with the Subselection tool. The anchor points modify curves, lines, or specific shapes. The transformation handles on the bounding box affect the whole object at one time.

Reference Window | Transforming an Object Using the Free Transform Tool

- In the Tools panel, click the Free Transform tool.
- Select the object to transform.
- In the Tools panel, click a modifier.
- Drag the transformation handles on the bounding box to modify the object.

As you move the pointer near a bounding box handle, the pointer changes to indicate how the object will be modified when you drag that handle. For example, when you point just outside a corner handle, the pointer changes to ↻, indicating that you can rotate the object by dragging the corner. The Free Transform tool also has several modifiers in the Tools panel, which are described in Figure 2-31.

Figure 2-31 Free Transform tool modifiers

Button	Modifier	Description
	Rotate and Skew	Freely rotates an object by dragging a corner handle or skews it to a different angle by dragging an edge handle
	Scale	Changes the size of an object by dragging a corner or edge handle
	Distort	Repositions the corner or edge of an object by dragging its handle
	Envelope	Displays a bounding box with points and tangent handles that you can adjust to warp or distort the object

Aly's sketch shows the umbrella angled in the sand and a wavy line for the top of the blue rectangle that represents the ocean. You will use the Free Transform tool to reposition the umbrella and modify the blue rectangle.

To reposition the umbrella and modify the blue rectangle using the Free Transform tool:

1. On the Edit bar, click the **Zoom control arrow**, and then click **Show Frame** to set the magnification level so you can see all of the Stage.

2. Click the umbrella to select it.

3. In the Tools panel, click the **Free Transform** tool, and then click the **Rotate and Skew** modifier button. The bounding box and transformation handles appear around the umbrella.

4. Drag a corner handle counterclockwise to tilt the umbrella to the left, and then drag the umbrella to position it in the lower-left corner of the banner.

5. On the Stage, click the blue rectangle. The ocean rectangle is selected and transformation handles appear around the edge of the rectangle.

6. In the Tools panel, click the **Envelope** modifier button. Tangent handles appear on the bounding box.

   Trouble? If the Envelope modifier button is not visible, click the Collapse to Icons button above the Tools panel, click the Tools button, and then click the Envelope modifier button. Click the Expand Panels button to expand the Tools panel.

7. On the top of the rectangle, drag the leftmost tangent handle slightly down to create a curve. See Figure 2-32.

> **Tip**
> Transformation handles are squares and tangent handles are circles.

FL 80 Flash | Tutorial 2 Drawing Shapes, Adding Text, and Creating Symbols

Figure 2-32 — Curve created by dragging a tangent handle

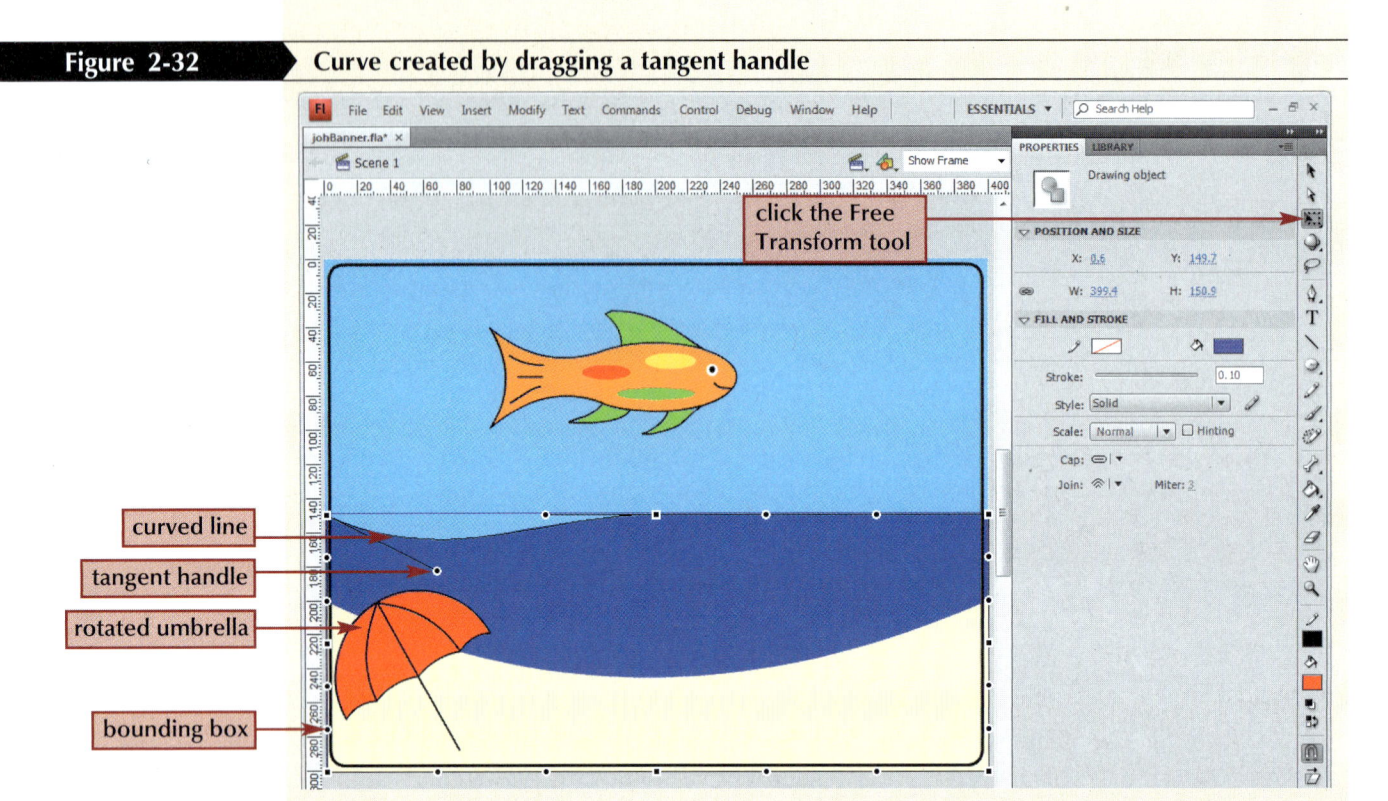

Labels: click the Free Transform tool; curved line; tangent handle; rotated umbrella; bounding box

8. On the top of the rectangle, drag the rightmost tangent handle slightly down to create a curve. See Figure 2-33.

Figure 2-33 — Second curve created by dragging a second tangent handle

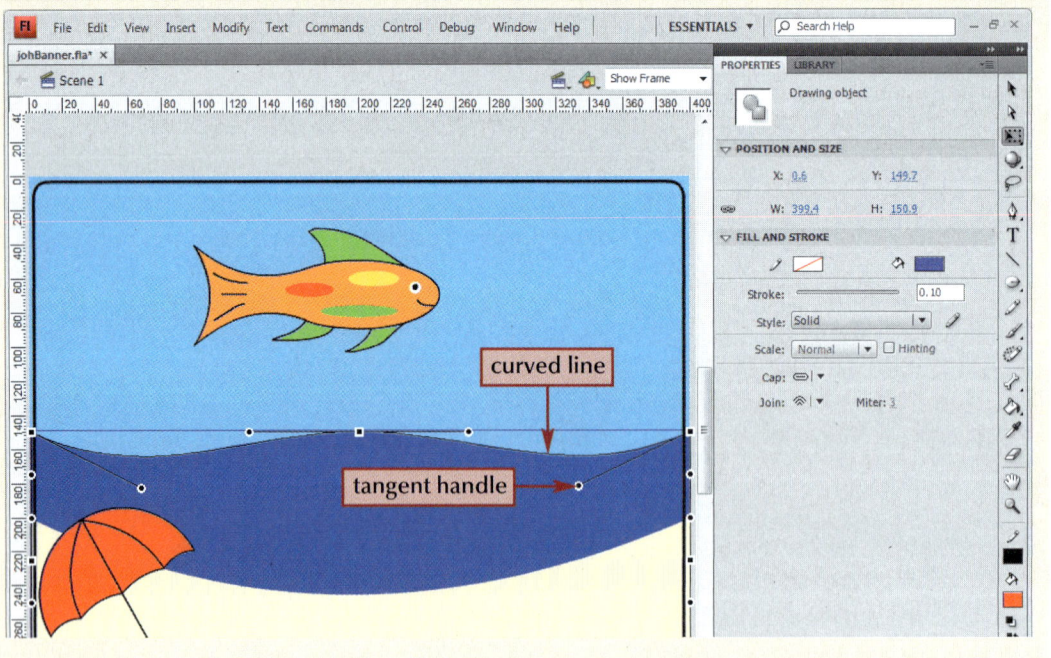

Labels: curved line; tangent handle

Aly's sketch also shows a smaller fish swimming to the right of the larger fish you already drew. Instead of drawing a smaller fish from scratch, you'll copy the existing fish, and then use the Free Transform tool to resize and rotate the copied fish. You will also reposition the first fish.

Tutorial 2 Drawing Shapes, Adding Text, and Creating Symbols | Flash **FL 81**

To copy, reposition, resize, and rotate the fish:

▸ 1. In the Tools panel, click the **Selection** tool, and then click the fish. The grouped fish is selected.

▸ 2. On the Application bar, click **Edit**, and then click **Copy**. The fish is copied to the Windows Clipboard.

▸ 3. On the Application bar, click **Edit**, and then click **Paste in Center**. A copy of the fish appears in the center of the Stage.

▸ 4. Drag the copy of the fish to the right side of the Stage so that half of it is below the ocean line, and then drag the first fish down toward the ocean. See Figure 2-34.

Figure 2-34 ▸ **Repositioned fish**

original fish
copy of the fish

▸ 5. In the Tools panel, click the **Free Transform** tool, and then click the copied fish. A bounding box with transformation handles appears around the selected fish. You want to reduce the size of the copied fish.

▸ 6. In the Tools panel, click the **Scale** modifier button. When you drag a corner handle, the fish will be resized.

▸ 7. Drag a corner handle to reduce the size of the fish to about half its original size.

▸ 8. In the Tools panel, click the **Rotate and Skew** modifier button, and then move the pointer near a corner handle. The pointer changes to ↻.

▸ 9. Drag the corner handle clockwise to rotate the fish so that it appears to be swimming downward. See Figure 2-35.

Figure 2-35 Scaled and rotated fish

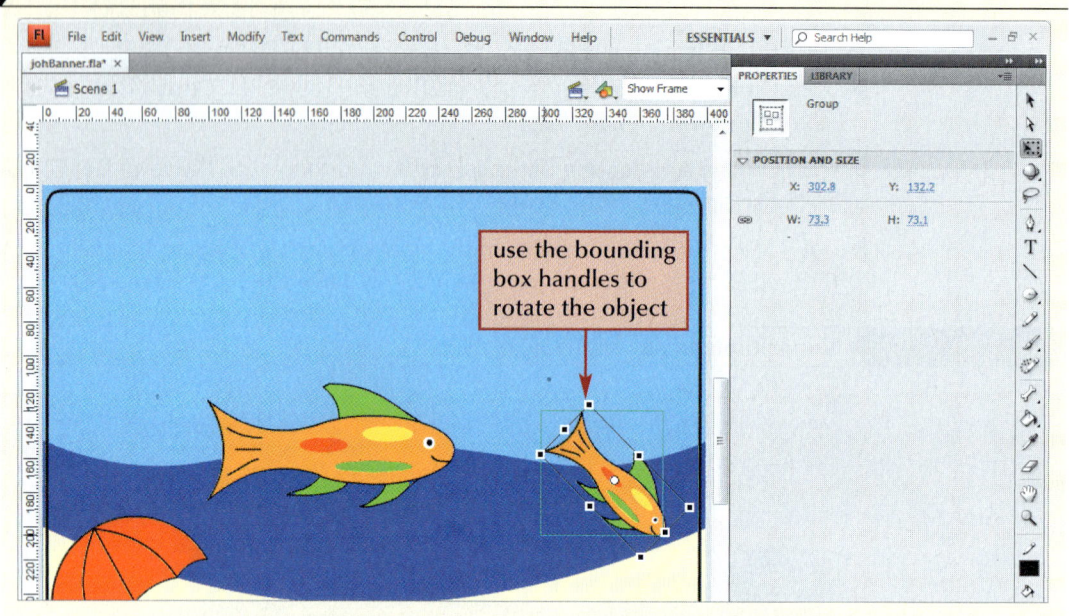

use the bounding box handles to rotate the object

Trouble? If the fish in your banner are in a different location than shown in Figure 2-35, you need to reposition them. Drag the fish as needed to match the locations shown.

▶ 10. Save the banner.

InSight | Transforming Objects Precisely

When you want to make very specific transformations to an object, the Transform panel provides more precise control over how you transform the object. In the Transform panel, you can enter specific values in pixels to resize an object. You can also enter values in degrees to rotate an object or skew an object horizontally or vertically. Another option in the Transform panel is to make a copy of an object and then apply a transformation to the copied object. This lets you try different transformations without affecting the original object.

In this session, you used the drawing tools to create and modify the graphics on the banner, including the fish, the umbrella, and the background. You modified fill colors and stroke colors, heights, and styles. You also scaled and rotated the fish and umbrella. Aly is pleased with the fish, the umbrella, and the background graphics. In the next session, you will add the text to the banner.

Review | Session 2.1 Quick Check

1. True or False? When drawing a shape with the Oval tool, you can draw a perfect circle when the Snap to Grid modifier is selected.
2. How can you draw a rectangle with rounded corners?
3. The _____ tool can be used to draw pie shapes and half circles.
4. The _____ modifier helps straighten lines you draw with the Pencil tool.
5. Describe how to use the Eyedropper tool to copy a stroke's attributes to another object.

6. Which tool can you use to add a fill to an enclosed area that has no fill?
7. Which modifier can be used with the Free Transform tool to resize a selected object?
8. True or False? The Free Transform tool is used to modify an object's gradient fill.

Session 2.2

Adding Text

Graphic images do not always communicate the message you are trying to convey. Many images and animations you create will also need to include text. In Flash, you can easily create text blocks in a variety of colors, sizes, and fonts.

You use the Text tool to add static text blocks to a document. A **static text block** is an object that contains text that is entered when you create the document but does not change after you publish the document. You can also create dynamic text fields or input text fields. A **dynamic text field** is an advanced feature where the text is updated as a result of programming instructions within the SWF file or with information from a Web server when the document is published and displayed in a Web browser. A **field** is a unit of data such as a person's age or phone number. An example of a dynamic text field is one that displays up-to-the-minute sports scores retrieved from a Web server. Dynamic text fields can also display the results of a calculation based on values entered into input text fields. An **input text field** allows the user to enter text in forms or surveys. You will work with static text blocks in this tutorial.

Using the Text Tool

The **Text tool** is used to create text blocks for documents. Text can be created in a **fixed-width text block** that doesn't change as you type, or in a **single-line text block** that extends as you type. If the width of the text block is fixed, the text wraps to create new lines as needed. To create a fixed-width text block, you click the Text tool in the Tools panel, and then drag the text pointer on the Stage. The text block has a square handle in its upper-right corner, indicating that the width of the text block will remain fixed. As you type, the words wrap to the next line when you reach the right margin of the block. To create a single-line text block, click the Stage with the text pointer where you want the text to appear and begin typing. The text block has a round handle on the upper-right corner which indicates that the width of the text block extends as you type.

You can change a fixed-width text block to a single-line text block by double-clicking its square handle. The text block changes to one line and its handle becomes round. Similarly, if you drag the round handle of a single-line text block to adjust the width of the block, the handle becomes square, indicating that the width of the block is now fixed.

After you create a text block, you can move it on the Stage using the Selection tool. You can also resize, rotate, and skew the text block using the Free Transform tool. The font, font size, text fill color, text styles, alignment, and other text properties are specified in the Property inspector. You can set these properties before you type the text, or you can select existing text and then change the properties.

InSight | Anti-aliasing text

To improve readability, Flash uses a rendering engine that provides high-quality, clear text in Flash documents. **Anti-aliasing**, which is part of the rendering process, smoothes the edges of text displayed on the computer screen. Anti-aliasing is especially effective when using small font sizes. When text is selected on the Stage, the Font rendering method drop-list is displayed in the Property inspector. Two of the methods available are Anti-alias for animation and Anti-alias for readability. Select Anti-alias for animation when the text will be animated to create a smoother animation. If the text will not be animated, select Anti-alias for readability, which improves the legibility of the text.

You will use the Text tool to add two text blocks to the banner—one at the top of the banner and one at the bottom. You will set the Property inspector options before you create each text block.

To add a single-line text block to the top of the banner:

▶ 1. If you took a break after the previous session, make sure the johBanner.fla document is open, the workspace is reset to the Essentials layout, the Timeline is closed, and the Stage magnification is set to Show Frame.

▶ 2. In the Tools panel, click the **Text** tool [T]. The pointer changes to ✣. Before you type the banner text, you'll set the text properties.

▶ 3. In the Character section of the Property inspector, set the Family to **Arial**, set the Style to **Bold Italic**, click to the Size value and drag to the right to change the point size to **28**, set the Color to **white** (#FFFFFF), and make sure the font rendering method is **Anti-alias for readability**.

▶ 4. In the Property inspector, click **PARAGRAPH** to expand the paragraph properties, and then click the **Align center** button [≡] to apply the center style.

▶ 5. Click in the top area of the Stage to create a single-line text block, type **Jenny's Oyster Hut**, press the **Enter** key to move the insertion point to the next line, and then type **10th Anniversary!**.

▶ 6. In the Tools panel, click the **Selection** tool [▶], and then, if necessary, drag the text block to center it at the top of the Stage. See Figure 2-36.

Tip

You can also click the Size value, type the desired point size in the box, and then press the Enter key to change the Size value.

Tutorial 2 Drawing Shapes, Adding Text, and Creating Symbols | Flash FL 85

Figure 2-36   Text block for the top of the banner

[Screenshot of Flash interface showing banner with "Jenny's Oyster Hut 10th Anniversary!" text block, with labels: single-line text block, text type, font family, font style, text (fill) color, text alignments]

▸ 7. Click an empty area of the Stage to deselect the text block.

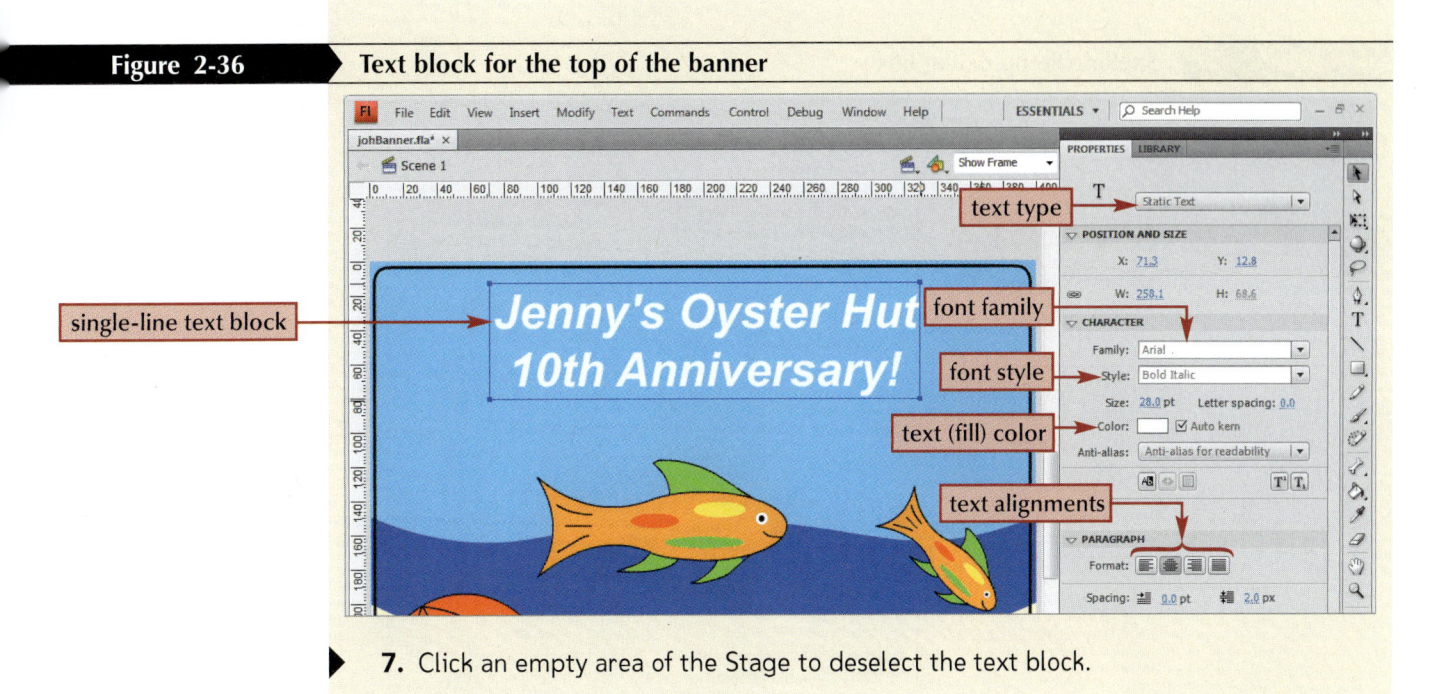

You will create a second text block at the bottom of the banner. Before you create the second text block, you'll change the text properties in the Property inspector.

To add a single-line text block to the bottom of the banner:

▸ 1. In the Tools panel, click the **Text** tool [T].

▸ 2. In the Character section of the Property inspector, set the font family to **Times New Roman**, set the font style to **Bold**, set the size to **16**, and the text fill color to **maroon** (#660000) in the sixth column from the right, first row of the color palette. Center alignment remains in place from the previous settings.

▸ 3. Click the bottom of the Stage in the light yellow beach area to create a single-line text block, and then type **Enjoy 10% off on Sundays this month!** in the text block.

▸ 4. In the Tools panel, click the **Selection** tool [arrow], and then drag the text block to the right of the umbrella's pole.

▸ 5. Click the pasteboard to deselect the text block, and then save the banner.

Tip

You can also press the V key to select the Selection tool in the Tools panel.

Checking the Spelling of Text

Flash can check the spelling of text you add to a document. The Check Spelling command verifies the spelling in each text block in the document. It can also check the spelling of text in other parts of the document, such as symbol names and layer names. Symbols are covered in the next session and layers are covered in Tutorial 3. Before you use the Check Spelling command, you can specify options in the Spelling Setup dialog box, shown in Figure 2-37.

Figure 2-37 Spelling Setup dialog box

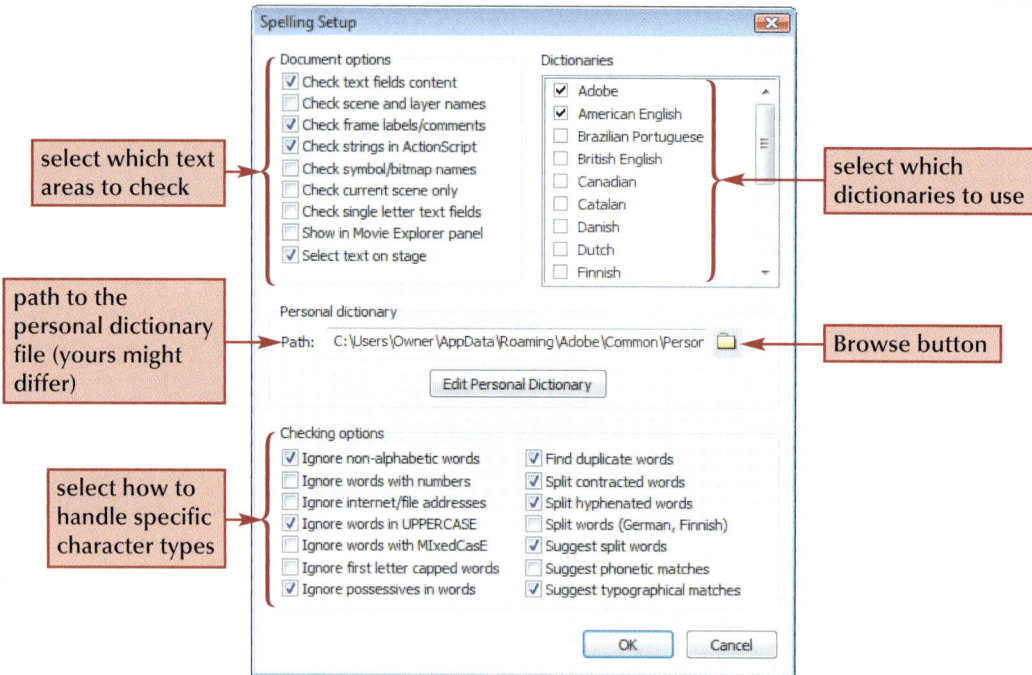

- select which text areas to check
- select which dictionaries to use
- path to the personal dictionary file (yours might differ)
- Browse button
- select how to handle specific character types

Under Document options, you specify which text areas to check, such as the content of text fields and the names of layers. You also select which built-in dictionaries to use, such as the Adobe terms dictionary and a language dictionary such as American English. The personal dictionary is a file that Flash creates on your hard drive to which you add words that are not in the Adobe or language dictionaries but are spelled correctly, such as a company name. You can also edit your personal dictionary after it is created. In the Checking options, you specify whether Flash ignores or finds specific character types such as words with numbers or words with all uppercase letters. You can also select options such as Suggest phonetic matches to have Flash provide a list of suggestions when it encounters a misspelled word. You can then choose one of the suggested words to replace the misspelled word.

Reference Window | Setting Options for the Spelling Checker

- On the Application bar, click Text, and then click Spelling Setup.
- In the Spelling Setup dialog box, select the desired options.
- Click the OK button.

When you check the spelling in a document, the Check Spelling dialog box opens if Flash finds a word that is misspelled or is not in its dictionaries. Depending on the options you selected in the Spelling Setup dialog box, the Check Spelling dialog box might offer suggestions for replacing the word. You can choose to add the word to your personal dictionary, ignore the word, change it, or delete it. The Check Spelling dialog box also shows in what element of the document the word not found is located, such as in a text field, a scene name, or a layer name.

Tutorial 2 Drawing Shapes, Adding Text, and Creating Symbols | Flash **FL 87**

> **InSight** | **The Importance of Correct Spelling**
>
> You should always check the spelling of the text in your documents. Having a misspelled word in a Flash movie can detract from the message or idea you are trying to promote. Keep in mind that the spelling checker only compares words in the document with words in the selected dictionaries. If a word is incorrect in context but is spelled correctly, the spelling checker will not detect it. As a final check, it's a good idea to ask someone who isn't working on the document to proofread the text.

You will set the spelling checker options, and then check the spelling of the text in the banner.

To set the spelling checker options and check spelling in the banner:

1. On the Application bar, click **Text**, and then click **Spelling Setup**. The Spelling Setup dialog box opens.

2. In the Document options, click the **Check text fields content** check box to check it, if necessary.

3. In the Dictionaries box, click the **American English** check box to check it, if necessary.

4. In the Checking options, make sure that the **Ignore possessives in words** check box is checked.

5. Click the **OK** button. The Spelling Setup dialog box closes.

6. On the Application bar, click **Text**, and click **Check Spelling**. The Check Spelling dialog box opens, indicating the first word not found in the selected dictionaries. The word not found in the Check Spelling dialog box is 10th. See Figure 2-38.

Figure 2-38 | **Check Spelling dialog box**

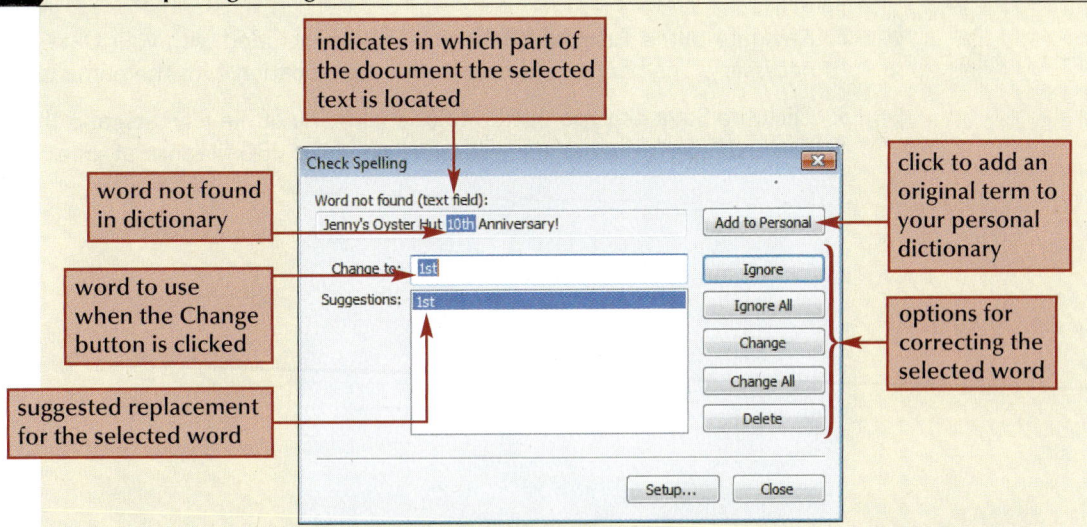

Trouble? If another word is found, you might have another word spelled incorrectly. If the word is spelled correctly, click the Ignore button. If the word is not spelled correctly, click the correct spelling in the Suggestions box or type the correct spelling in the Change to box, and then click the Change button. Repeat until 10th is the word not found.

7. Click the **Ignore** button. A dialog box opens, indicating that the spelling check is complete.

> **Trouble?** If other words are not found, they are not in your selected dictionaries. Click the Ignore button to ignore the suggestion and leave the original spelling. Click the correct spelling in the Suggestions box or type the correct spelling in the Change to box, and then click the Change button to replace the word not found.
>
> ▶ 8. Click the **OK** button.

Exporting a Graphic for Use on the Web

A document you create in Flash is saved in the FLA format. This format contains all of the different elements you create in Flash. To revise the document, you open the FLA file. To place the image in a Web page, however, it needs to be published or exported.

Publishing a document will be covered in more detail in Tutorial 3 when you add animations to documents. A published document is in the SWF file format and is called a Flash movie. It requires the Flash Player plug-in to play in a Web browser.

When you create a document such as Jenny's Oyster Hut banner that doesn't have animation, you can export it instead of publishing it. **Exporting** means that the program converts the document into another file format, such as GIF or JPG (which does not require a plug-in to display in a Web page). Exporting also combines all the individual elements of a document into one graphic. You cannot edit the individual elements of the image in an exported file. To edit the image's elements, you must go back to the corresponding FLA file. After you export a document into a GIF or JPG file format, it can be placed in a Web page.

You'll export the banner into the JPG file format so it can be used on the restaurant's Web site.

To export the banner to the JPG file format:

▶ 1. On the Application bar, click **File**, point to **Export**, and then click **Export Image**. The Export Image dialog box opens.

▶ 2. Navigate to the **Tutorial.02\Tutorial** folder included with your Data Files, if necessary. The banner will be saved in that location with the name johBanner.jpg.

▶ 3. Click the **Save as type** button to open a menu of file formats, and then click **JPEG Image (*.jpg)**. The banner will be saved in the JPG file format. See Figure 2-39.

Tutorial 2 Drawing Shapes, Adding Text, and Creating Symbols | Flash | FL 89

Figure 2-39 | Export Image dialog box

[Export Image dialog box screenshot with callouts: "folder where the file will be saved" pointing to Save in: Tutorial; "filename for the exported file" pointing to johBanner.jpg; "file format for the exported file" pointing to JPEG Image (.jpg)]*

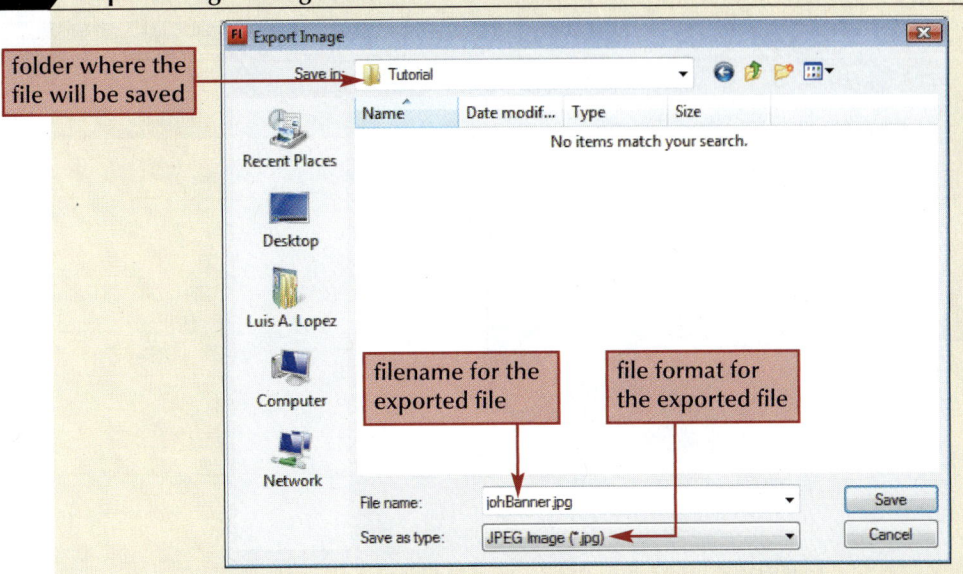

▶ 4. Click the **Save** button. The Export JPEG dialog box opens with additional options and settings, including the document's dimensions and resolution.

▶ 5. Click the **Include** button, and then click **Full Document Size**, if necessary. This option makes the exported JPG image the same size as the Flash document. The Minimum Image Area option might reduce the size of the exported JPG image based on the content on the Stage.

▶ 6. In the Quality box, enter **80** for the quality of the exported image. You'll accept the rest of the default settings.

▶ 7. Click the **OK** button. The banner is exported as a JPG file.

▶ 8. Save the banner.

Chris placed the GIF file with the exported banner in a Web page with the HTML needed to display the johBanner.jpg image. You will preview this Web page in a Web browser.

To preview the johBanner.jpg file in a Web browser:

▶ 1. Start **Internet Explorer** or another Web browser. (If you are using a different Web browser, modify Steps 2 through 4 as needed.)

▶ 2. On the Internet Explorer menu bar, click **File**, and then click **Open**. The Open dialog box opens.

Trouble? If the menu bar is not visible, you need to display it. Click the Tools button, click Menu Bar, and then repeat Step 2.

▶ 3. Click the **Browse** button, navigate to the **Tutorial.02\Tutorial** folder included with your Data Files, click the **jennys.htm** file, and then click the **Open** button.

▶ 4. Click the **OK** button. The Web page opens in the browser and the johBanner.jpg file appears as part of the page. See Figure 2-40.

Figure 2-40   Web page with the exported banner image

exported johBanner.jpg file displayed in the Web page (your banner image might differ slghtly)

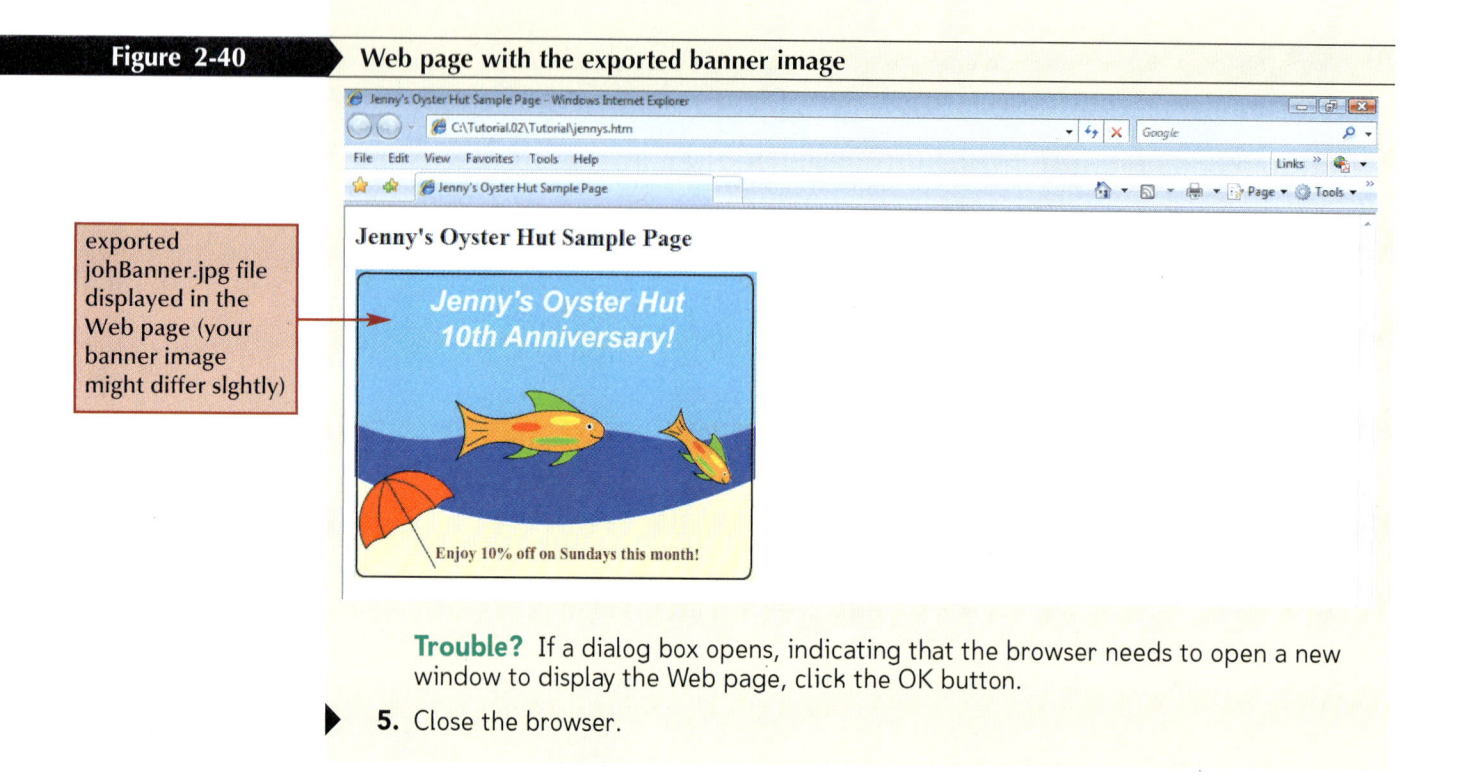

Trouble? If a dialog box opens, indicating that the browser needs to open a new window to display the Web page, click the OK button.

▶ 5. Close the browser.

Using the History Panel

The **History panel** is a record of the steps performed in the current document. After you open or create a document, each step is recorded and displayed in the History panel with an icon that reflects the particular step. The History panel displays only the steps for the current document. If you switch to another document, the History panel shows the steps taken in creating or editing that document. A document's history is maintained until you close the document or clear its history. You can also save selected steps by creating a command based on those steps. The command can then be used in the same document or in another document, and is available each time you use Flash. From the History panel, you can replay, undo, and save the recorded steps.

You will use the History panel as you work with a document Aly created for another Admiral Web Design client, Jackson's Sports.

To use the History panel with the sports.fla document:

▶ 1. In the Application bar, click **File**, and then click **Open**. The Open dialog box opens.

▶ 2. Navigate to the **Tutorial.02\Tutorial** folder included with your Data Files, and then double-click the **sports.fla** file. The Jackson's Sports banner opens.

▶ 3. On the Application bar, click **Window**, point to **Other Panels**, and then click **History**. The History panel opens.

▶ 4. If the History panel appears on top of the document, drag the History panel by its title bar to the right side of the screen.

Before you can work with the document, you need to unlock the layers in the document. You do this using the Timeline.

▶ 5. On the Application bar, click **Window**, and then click **Timeline**. The Timeline appears.

Tip

You can also press the Ctrl+F10 keys to open and close the History panel.

▶ 6. In the Timeline, click the **Lock or Unlock All Layers** icon to unlock all the layers. A step labeled Lock Layers appears in the History panel.

▶ 7. In the Tools panel, click the **Selection** tool, and then click the **Jackson's Sports** text block to select it. The step appears in the History panel.

▶ 8. In the Property inspector, change the Text (fill) color to click **blue** (#0000FF) in the first swatches column, ninth row of the color palette. The letters in the text block change color and this step appears in the History panel. See Figure 2-41.

Figure 2-41 | History panel with the current session's steps

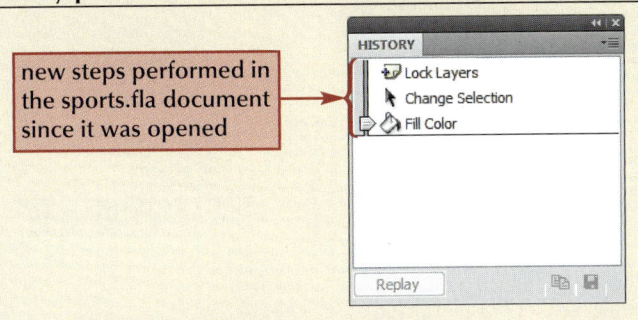

new steps performed in the sports.fla document since it was opened →

HISTORY
- Lock Layers
- Change Selection
- Fill Color

Replay

▶ 9. In the Tools panel, click the **Free Transform** tool, and then click the **Scale** modifier button to select it.

▶ 10. Drag the lower-right corner handle on the text block to make the text block slightly larger. The step appears in the History panel.

Replaying Steps

You can replay one or more selected steps in the History panel. For example, after you create a shape, you can select the steps in the History panel that you took to create the shape, and then replay the steps to create a duplicate of the shape. If you select steps in the History panel that you used to format an object on the Stage, you can replay the steps to apply the same formatting to another object on the Stage. The steps you select in the History panel are applied to the selected object in the order shown in the panel. The replayed steps can be consecutive or nonconsecutive. Steps displayed with an icon that includes a small, red x cannot be replayed.

One or more steps taken in one document can also be selected and copied using the Copy selected steps to the Clipboard button. The copied commands can then be applied using the Paste in Center command in another document.

You will replay the steps you performed previously from the History panel to further modify the sports document.

To replay steps from the History panel:

▶ 1. In the History panel, drag to select the **Fill Color** and **Scale** steps. The two consecutive steps are selected. See Figure 2-42.

Figure 2-42   **Steps selected in the History panel**

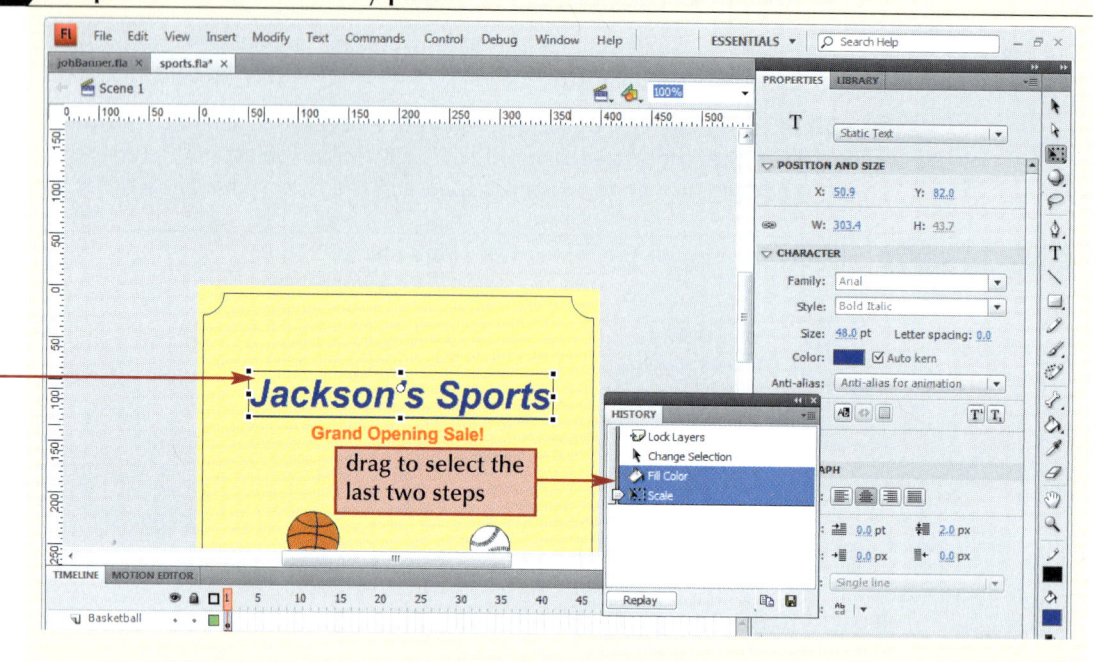

selected text block with the blue fill color and enlarged

drag to select the last two steps

Trouble? If the last steps performed are undone, you probably dragged the slider on the left side of the History panel instead of the actual steps. Drag the slider down to the last step you performed, and then repeat Step 1, being careful to select the steps in the History panel and not the slider.

2. In the center of the Stage, click the **Grand Opening Sale!** text block to select it. The new step is added at the end of the History panel.

3. In the History panel, click the **Replay** button. The two selected steps are replayed: The Grand Opening Sale! text block increases in size and its text color changes to blue. The History panel records the Replay Steps step.

4. In the Tools panel, click the **Selection** tool, and then drag the basketball to the upper-left corner of the Stage. The basketball is repositioned and the Change Selection and Move steps appear in the History panel.

5. Press and hold the **Ctrl** key, and then, in the History panel, click the **Move** step to select it, click the **Fill Color** step to deselect it, and then release the **Ctrl** key. The nonconsecutive Scale and Move steps are selected in the History panel.

6. On the Stage, click the baseball to select it, and then, in the History panel, click the **Replay** button. The nonconsecutive steps are replayed, and the baseball becomes slightly larger and moves to the top of the Stage. The History panel shows the last two steps you performed. See Figure 2-43.

Figure 2-43 Steps replayed and applied to baseball

- baseball is moved and enlarged
- steps selected in the History panel
- click to replay the selected steps

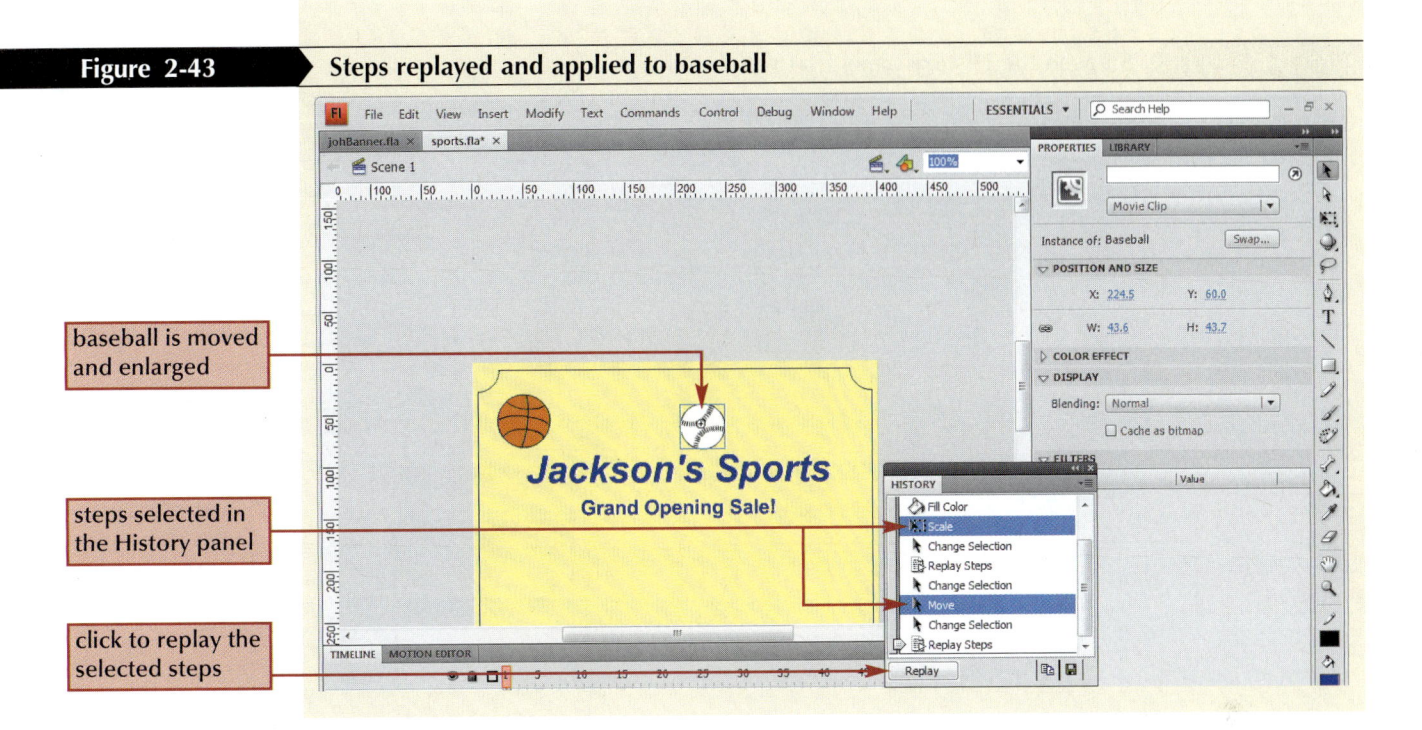

Undoing Steps

As you create and modify graphic images in Flash, you will often want to undo one or more steps within a document. This might occur if you make a mistake and you want to return to the previous step. You can undo one step or, by default, up to 100 steps. This lets you backtrack though a series of steps until the document returns to the particular state at which you want to start over. You can change the default maximum number of steps that can be undone in the Preferences dialog box.

Flash provides two types of undo. In **document-level undo**, the steps you undo affect the entire document. In **object-level undo**, you can undo steps performed on individual objects without affecting the steps performed on other objects. You change from one type of undo to another in the Preferences dialog box. When you change the type of undo, the steps currently recorded in the History panel are deleted. In this tutorial, you work with the default mode, document-level undo.

You can use the History panel to change the document back to how it was before you performed a series of steps. The slider in the History panel initially points to the last step performed. As you drag the slider to a previous step, any subsequent step is undone and is reflected in the document on the Stage. Undone steps appear dimmed in the History panel.

You will use the History panel to undo some of the steps you have performed.

To undo steps in the sports.fla document from the History panel:

1. In the History panel, drag the **slider** up to the Scale step. The steps below the Scale step are dimmed, indicating that they have been undone. The objects on the Stage also change to reflect that the steps were undone. See Figure 2-44.

Tip

You can also undo one step at a time by pressing the Ctrl+Z keys.

Figure 2-44 — Steps in the History panel that were undone

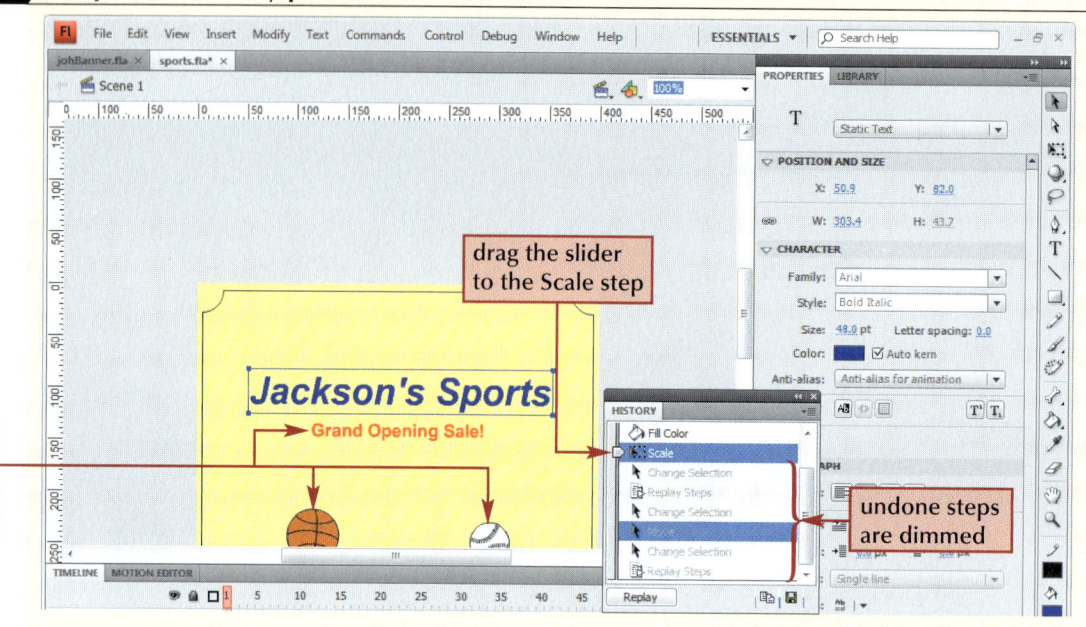

▶ 2. Close the History panel, and then close the sports.fla document without saving changes.

In this session, you added text blocks to the banner for Jenny's Oyster Hut, set the properties for the text, and checked for spelling errors. Then, you exported the banner as a JPG file, and previewed it in a Web page. Finally, you used the History panel to review, undo, and replay steps. In the next session, you will add symbols to the banner.

Review | Session 2.2 Quick Check

1. What is the difference between a static text block and a dynamic text field?
2. How do you create a fixed-width text block?
3. Which panel is used to set text attributes such as the font and size?
4. How can you change a single-line text block into a fixed-width text block?
5. If a text block has a square handle in its upper-right corner, what type of text block is it?
6. What is the purpose of the personal dictionary in the Spelling Setup dialog box?
7. What does the History panel record?
8. How can you undo a series of steps using the History panel?

Session 2.3

Creating and Editing Symbols

A **symbol** is an element such as a graphic or button that can be used more than once in a document. You can create a symbol from an existing object or you can create a new symbol. You can also use symbols from other Flash documents in the current document.

Tutorial 2 Drawing Shapes, Adding Text, and Creating Symbols | Flash | FL 95

Comparing Symbol Behavior Types

Symbols can have one of three types of behavior. The default behavior, **movie clip**, contains its own Timeline and operates independently of the Timeline of the movie in which it appears. For example, a movie clip used in a document contains an animation sequence that spans 10 frames within its own Timeline. The movie clip occupies only one frame within the document's Timeline, yet it still plays its own 10-frame animation. Most of the symbols you create will be movie clips. A **graphic symbol** is a static image or an animated image that operates in sync with the Timeline of the movie in which it appears. For example, a graphic symbol with a 10-frame animation sequence occupies 10 frames in the document's Timeline. A **button symbol** has its own four-frame Timeline, which you use to make a symbol into an interactive button. You will learn more about buttons in Tutorial 5. You can easily change a symbol's type at any time.

Creating Symbols

To create a symbol, you can either convert an existing graphic into a symbol or create a new symbol. For each symbol you create, you specify its name and its type. When converting an existing graphic into a symbol, you can also specify its registration point, which can be used to control how the symbol is animated.

Reference Window | Creating a Symbol

- Select an existing graphic, click Modify on the Application bar, and then click Convert to Symbol.
- Type a symbol name in the Name box, click the Type button and select a symbol type, and then click the OK button.

or

- On the Application bar, click Insert, and then click New Symbol.
- Type a symbol name in the Name box, click the Type button and select a symbol type, and then click the OK button.
- In symbol-editing mode, create the graphic(s) for the symbol.
- On the Application bar, click Insert, and then click Edit Document.

Aly wants you to convert the fish graphic you created for the banner for Jenny's Oyster Hut Web site into a symbol.

To create a symbol from the fish in the banner:

1. If you took a break after the previous session, make sure the johBanner.fla document is open, that the workspace is reset to the Essentials layout, the Timeline is closed, and the magnification is set to Show Frame.

2. In the Tools panel, click the **Selection** tool , if necessary, and then click the larger fish on the center of the Stage. The larger fish graphic is selected. You will ungroup the graphic before converting it to a symbol.

   Trouble? If the ocean graphic is selected instead of the fish graphic, you probably didn't click the fish graphic. Click the top part of the fish again to select the fish.

3. On the Application bar, click **Modify**, and then click **Ungroup**. The fish is no longer grouped, but all of its parts are still selected.

4. On the Application bar, click **Modify**, and then click **Convert to Symbol**. The Convert to Symbol dialog box opens. In this dialog box, you can specify a name for the symbol and select a behavior type.

Tip

You can also ungroup a grouped object by pressing the Ctrl+Shift+G keys.

▶ 5. In the Name box, type **bigFish**, and then, if necessary, click the **Type** button, and click **Movie Clip**. See Figure 2-45.

Figure 2-45   Convert to Symbol dialog box

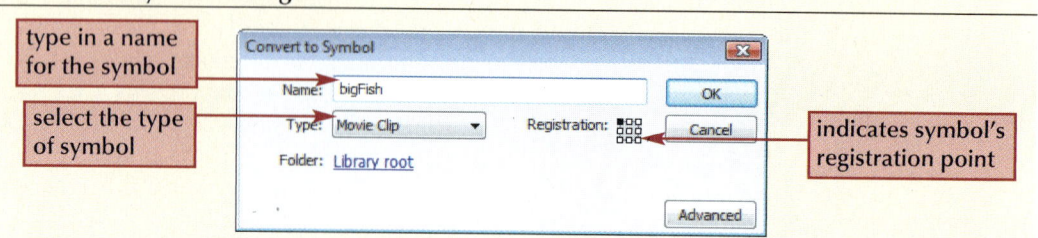

- type in a name for the symbol → Name: bigFish
- select the type of symbol → Type: Movie Clip
- Folder: Library root
- Registration: ← indicates symbol's registration point
- OK / Cancel / Advanced

▶ 6. Click the **OK** button. The dialog box closes. The symbol is created and added to the library for this document.

InSight | Assigning Meaningful Names to Symbols

Assign meaningful names to symbols you create, especially if you plan to have many symbols in a document. Meaningful names make it easier to find the symbol you want in the document's Library panel without having to preview each symbol. If the number of symbols is small, you can use simpler names such as Fish1 and Fish2.

Using the Library

Symbols you create for a document are stored in the **library**. You view, organize, and edit symbols stored in the library from the Library panel. When you create a symbol for a document, you assign a name to it, and then specify its properties. These properties are stored with the symbol in the library. Symbols created within a document are saved with that document. However, you can share symbols with other documents by making them part of a shared library. You can modify a symbol's properties using the Library panel. The Library panel, shown in Figure 2-46, displays a list with the names of all the symbols in the library for a document. Each symbol in the Library panel has an icon to the left of its name to show what type of symbol it is.

Tutorial 2 Drawing Shapes, Adding Text, and Creating Symbols | Flash | FL 97

Figure 2-46 | Library panel

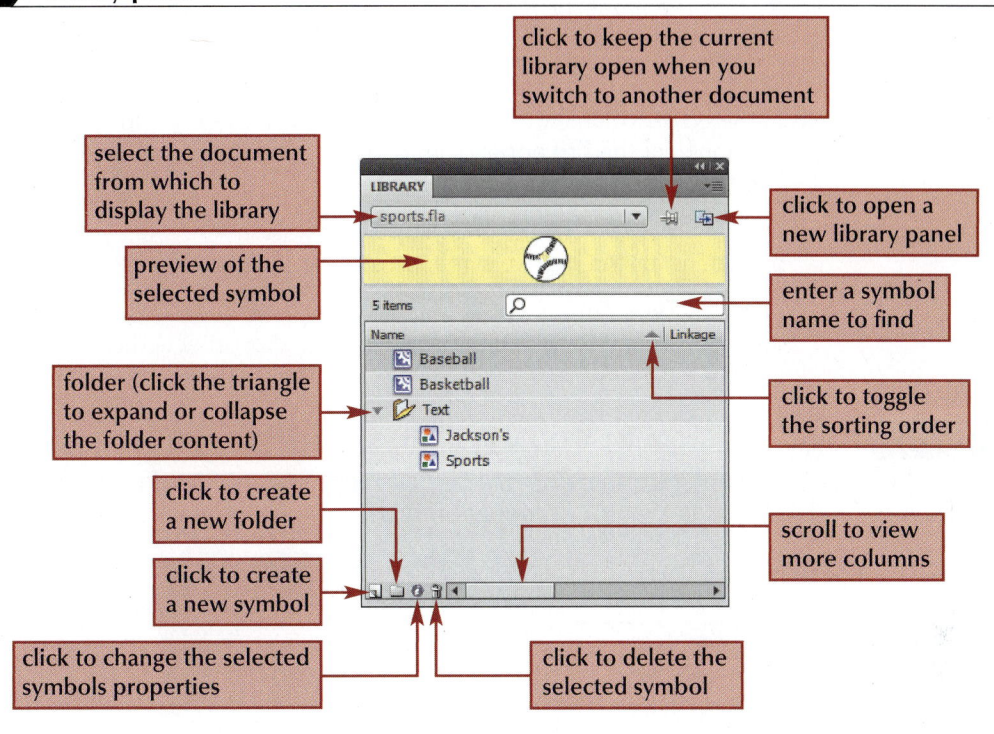

- click to keep the current library open when you switch to another document
- select the document from which to display the library
- click to open a new library panel
- preview of the selected symbol
- enter a symbol name to find
- folder (click the triangle to expand or collapse the folder content)
- click to toggle the sorting order
- click to create a new folder
- scroll to view more columns
- click to create a new symbol
- click to change the selected symbols properties
- click to delete the selected symbol

You can use the horizontal scroll bar at the bottom of the Library panel to show several columns of information about each symbol, including whether the symbol is shared with other documents (Linkage column), the number of times the symbol is used in the document (Use Count column), the date it was last modified (Date Modified column), and the symbol's type (Type column). You can sort the symbols according to a column by clicking the column's header. For example, to sort the symbols by date, click the Date Modified header. The dates range from most recent to oldest. This order can be reversed by clicking the Toggle Sorting Order button.

Additional Library panel options can be accessed using the Library panel's menu. This menu includes options to create new symbols, rename, edit, or delete symbols, as well as to create duplicates of a symbol.

You will explore the johBanner.fla document's library to see how symbols are stored.

InSight | Organizing Symbols in the Library

As you work with a document, you will often create many symbols. Some symbols may be related to a particular graphic in the document. For example, you might have multiple symbols that make up a button on the Stage. As the document gets more complex, the number of symbols in the library can increase significantly and become unmanageable. To make it easier to manage and organize the symbols in the Library panel, you can create folders to group and hold related symbols. By default, the Library panel contains a **root folder** that contains all the document's symbols. All new folders are created within the root folder. Any symbols inside a folder are indented under the folder name.

Enter a symbol's name in the Library panel's search box to quickly display the symbol in the panel.

To explore the johBanner.fla document's library:

> **Tip**
> You can also press the Ctrl+L keys to open and close the Library panel.

1. Next to the Property inspector, click the **LIBRARY** tab to bring the Library panel to the front of the panel group. The Library panel displays the symbols for this document.

2. In the Name column of the Library panel, click the **bigFish** symbol, if necessary. A thumbnail of the fish appears in the preview box at the top of the Library panel. The symbol's icon indicates the symbol is a movie clip.

3. In the Library panel, click the **Properties** button. The Symbol Properties dialog box opens for the bigFish symbol. You'll change this symbol's type.

4. Click the **Type** button, click **Graphic**, and then click the **OK** button. The Properties dialog box closes, and the bigFish symbol's icon reflects the new type. See Figure 2-47.

Figure 2-47   Changed symbol in the Library panel

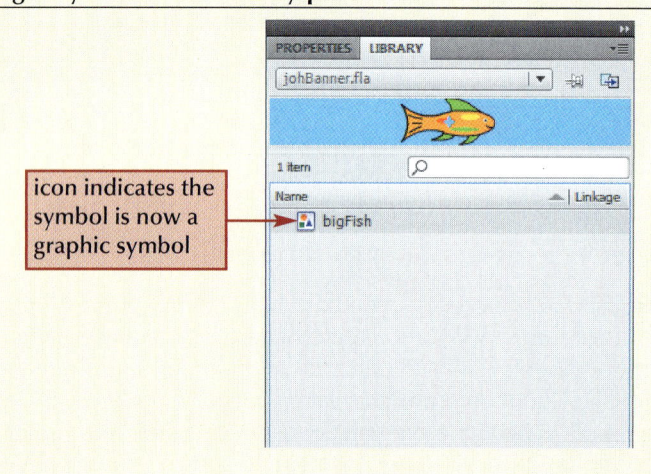

icon indicates the symbol is now a graphic symbol

5. In the bottom of the Library panel, drag the scroll bar to the right to see the rest of the symbol's properties, including Graphic in the Type column, and then drag the scroll bar to the left to display the Name column.

6. In the Library panel, click the **Properties** button, click the **Type** button, click **Movie Clip**, and then click the **OK** button. The symbol's icon and type change to reflect the movie clip type.

After a symbol is added to a document's library, you can create a duplicate of it. The duplicate symbol must have a different name. You will create a duplicate symbol of the bigFish symbol that you can then edit to create a second, different fish symbol.

To create a duplicate of the bigFish symbol:

> **Tip**
> You can also right-click the symbol's name in the Library panel, and then click Duplicate on the context menu to open the Duplicate Symbol dialog box.

1. In the Library panel, click the **panel menu** button to open the panel menu, and then click **Duplicate**. The Duplicate Symbol dialog box opens.

2. In the Name box, type **smallFish**. This is the name for the duplicated movie clip symbol. The movie clip type is already selected.

3. Click the **OK** button. The smallFish symbol is added to the library.

Editing a Symbol

You can modify a symbol by placing it in symbol-editing mode. A symbol can be edited by itself in symbol-editing mode or it can be edited in place with the rest of the graphics on the Stage dimmed. When a symbol is in symbol-editing mode, the name of the symbol appears on the Edit bar next to the scene name. Flash documents can be divided into multiple scenes, but every document has at least one scene.

Reference Window | Editing a Symbol

- Select a symbol instance on the Stage, click Edit on the Application bar, and then click Edit Symbols, Edit Selected, or Edit in Place (or double-click a symbol instance on the Stage or select the symbol in the Library panel, click the Library panel menu button, and then click Edit).
- Modify the symbol in symbol-editing mode.
- On the Edit bar, click the Scene 1 link (or double-click an empty area of the Stage or on the Application bar, click Edit, and then click Edit Document).

Aly wants you to edit the smallFish symbol in the document's library so that it's unique from the bigFish symbol. You will change the fish's body color to pink and make the fish graphic smaller.

To edit the smallFish symbol:

1. In the Library panel, click the **smallFish** symbol to select it, if necessary.
2. In the Library panel, click the **panel menu** button , and then click **Edit**. The symbol opens in symbol-editing mode, and smallFish appears on the Edit bar.
3. Click an empty area of the Stage to deselect the fish.
4. In the Tools panel, click the **Paint Bucket** tool to select it, click the **Fill color** control , and then click the **pink** swatch (#FF99FF) in the third column from the right, bottom row of the color palette.
5. On the Stage, click the orange body of the fish to change it to pink.
6. On the Application bar, click **Edit**, and then click **Select All**. All of the fish is selected.

   Tip
   You can also press the Ctrl+A keys to select all of the objects on the Stage at one time.

7. On the Application bar, click **Window**, and then click **Transform**. The Transform panel opens.
8. In the Transform panel, click the **Constrain** icon to change it to , if necessary. Constrain keeps the width and height proportional when either one is changed.
9. In the Transform panel, drag the Scale Width value to the left to change the value to **50**. The height value also changes to 50%, and the fish becomes smaller.
10. Close the Transform panel, and then, on the Edit bar, click the **Scene 1** link to exit symbol-editing mode. The banner appears on the Stage.

Creating and Editing Instances of Symbols

Every symbol you create is automatically stored in the document's library. To use the symbols in the document, you create instances. An **instance** is a copy of a symbol. Each time you drag a symbol from the Library panel onto the Stage, you create an instance of the symbol in the document. No matter how many instances of a symbol you create, the symbol is stored in the document only once.

InSight | Using Instances of Symbols

If you want to use a graphic multiple times in a document, convert it into a symbol. Then insert instances of the symbol wherever that graphic is needed in the document instead of creating the same graphic multiple times. Using instances of a symbol also makes it easier to modify all instances at the same time by just modifying the symbol. In addition, any graphic you convert into a symbol can be copied from one document's library to another. Finally, using instances of a symbol minimizes the document's size, which in turn reduces the download time of the published SWF file.

Each instance in a document can be edited without changing the symbol in the document's library. For example, consider a document that includes several instances of the same symbol. You can make one instance smaller than the others. You can rotate each instance to a different angle. Any changes you make to one instance do not affect the other instances or the symbol. If you modify the symbol, however, all the instances of that symbol are also changed.

You will place an instance of the smallFish symbol on the banner, and then convert the rightmost fish to a movie clip symbol.

To create a smallFish symbol instance and convert a graphic to a symbol:

1. In the Tools panel, click the **Selection** tool.
2. Drag the **smallFish** symbol from the Library panel to the Stage to create an instance of the symbol.
3. On the Stage, place the **smallFish** instance on the water to the left side of the bigFish instance. See Figure 2-48.

Tutorial 2 Drawing Shapes, Adding Text, and Creating Symbols | Flash | FL 101

Figure 2-48   Instance of the smallFish symbol added to the Stage

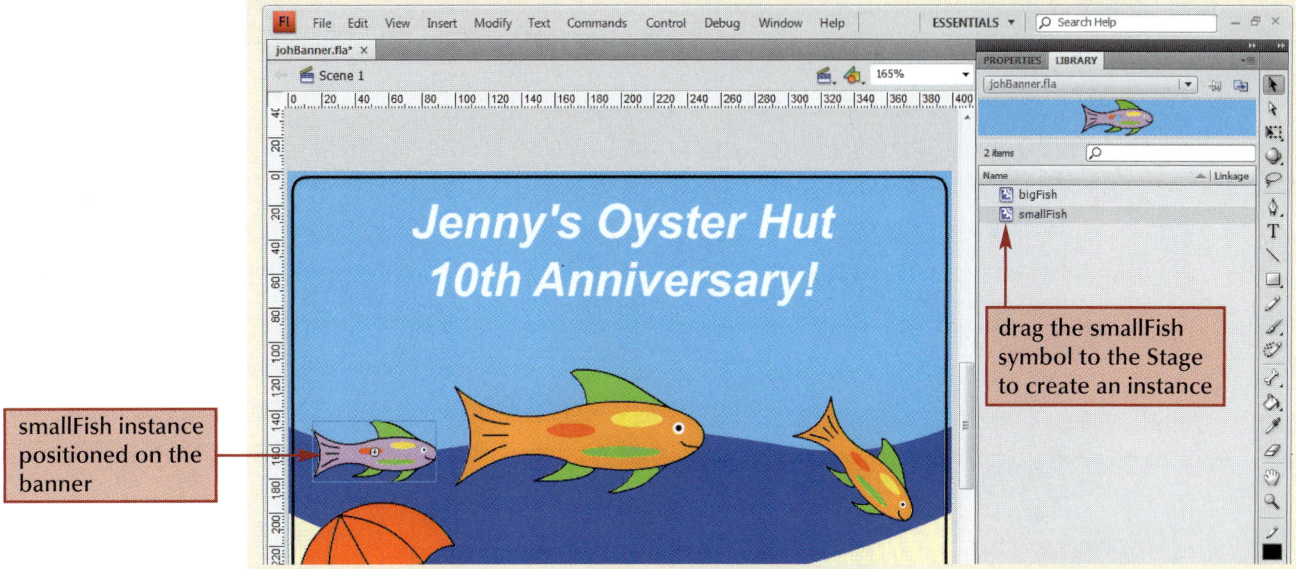

smallFish instance positioned on the banner

drag the smallFish symbol to the Stage to create an instance

▶ 4. Click the grouped fish graphic on the right side of the Stage to select it.

▶ 5. On the Application bar, click **Modify**, and then click **Convert to Symbol**. The Convert to Symbol dialog box opens.

▶ 6. Type **mediumFish** in the Name box, make sure the type is **Movie Clip**, and then click the **OK** button. The grouped fish graphic is converted to a symbol.

Applying Filters

A **filter** is a special graphic effect, such as a drop shadow, you can apply to movie clips, buttons, and text. Filters are applied using the Filters section of the Property inspector, which includes preset filters such as drop shadow, blur, glow, and bevel. Multiple filters can be applied to one object, and each filter has properties you can set to adjust the filter's effect on the object. In the Property inspector, you can enable or disable a filter, reset a filter's properties, and delete a filter. You can also copy the filters and properties that have been applied to one object and apply them to another object. Or, you can save a set of filters and properties as a new preset filter, and then apply the saved preset filter to objects in other Flash documents.

You will apply a drop shadow effect to the movie clip symbols and text on the banner.

To apply a filter to objects in the banner:

▶ 1. Next to the Library panel, click the **PROPERTIES** tab to bring the Property inspector to the front of the panel group.

▶ 2. In the Filters section of the Property inspector, click the **Add filter** button to open a menu of preset filters. See Figure 2-49.

FL 102 Flash | Tutorial 2 Drawing Shapes, Adding Text, and Creating Symbols

Figure 2-49 Menu of preset filters

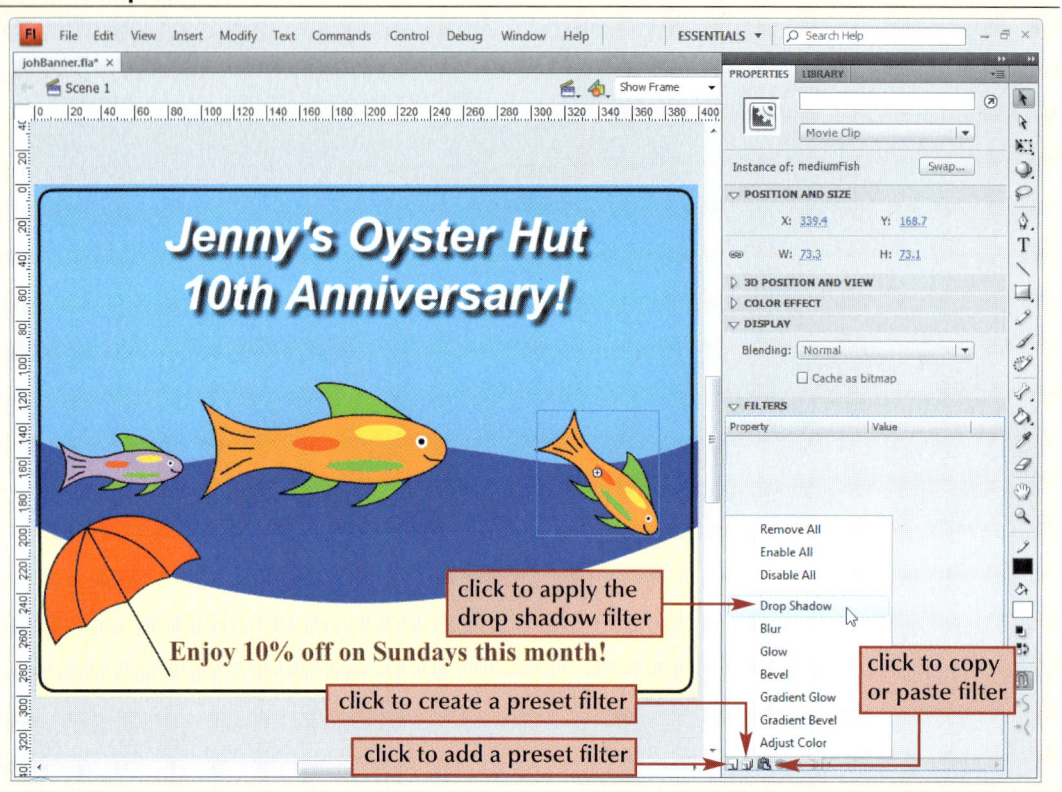

▸ 3. Click **Drop Shadow**. A drop shadow effect is applied to the mediumFish instance on the Stage.

▸ 4. In the Filters section of the Property inspector, drag the **Strength** value to the left to set the filter strength to **80%**, and then drag the **Distance** value to the right to increase the filter distance to **10px**. The drop shadow strength is reduced and its distance from the instance increased. See Figure 2-50.

Figure 2-50   Drop shadow applied to a fish graphic instance

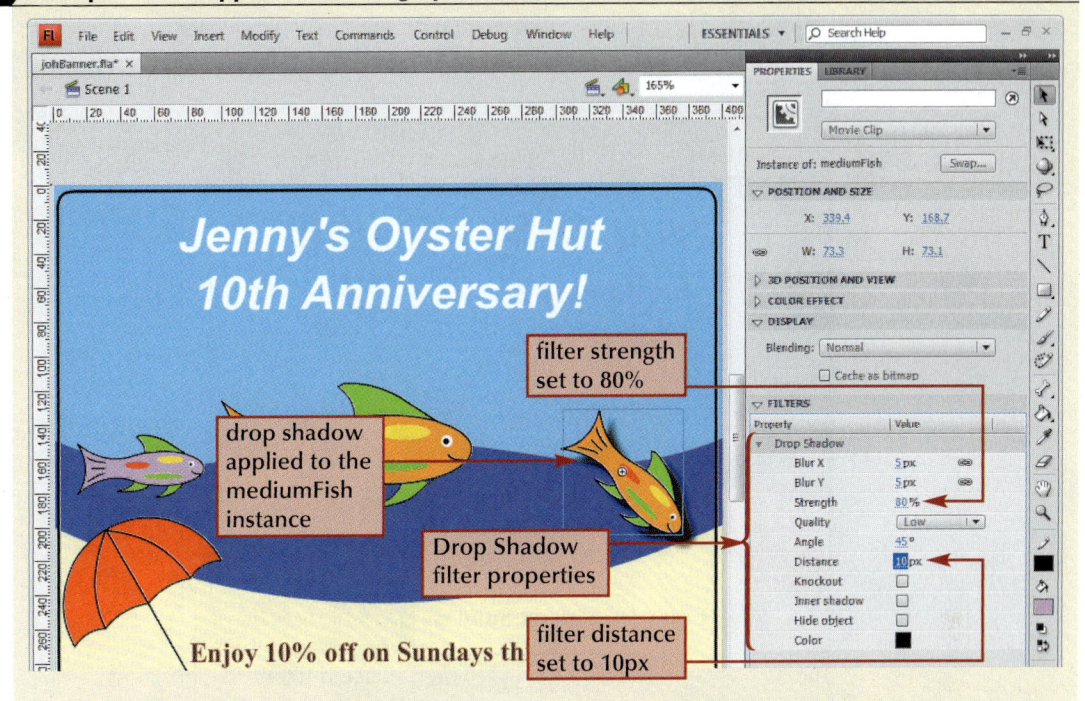

[Screenshot of Flash interface showing the johBanner.fla file with "Jenny's Oyster Hut 10th Anniversary!" banner. Callouts indicate: drop shadow applied to the mediumFish instance, filter strength set to 80%, Drop Shadow filter properties, and filter distance set to 10px.]

You will apply the same filter and properties to the other two fish instances on the Stage.

▶ 5. In the Filters section of the Property inspector, click the **Clipboard** button, and then click **Copy All**. The filter effects are stored in the computer's temporary memory.

▶ 6. On the Stage, click the **smallFish** instance to select it, and then, in the Property inspector, click the **Clipboard** button and click **Paste**. The drop shadow effect is applied to the smallFish instance.

▶ 7. On the Stage, click the **bigFish** instance to select it, and then, in the Property inspector, click the **Clipboard** button and click **Paste**. The drop shadow effect is applied to the bigFish instance.

You will apply a drop shadow filter to the banner's text.

▶ 8. Click the text block at the top of the Stage to select it, and then, in the Property inspector, click the **Clipboard** button and click **Paste**. The drop shadow effect is applied to the text.

You'll collapse the Paragraph section of the Property inspector so you can more easily access the Filters section and reset the filter's properties.

▶ 9. In the Property inspector, click **PARAGRAPH** to collapse the Paragraph section.

▶ 10. In the Filters section of the Property inspector, click **Drop Shadow** in the Property column, and then click the **Reset Filter** button. The filter's properties return to their default values. See Figure 2-51.

Figure 2-51 | Drop shadow effect applied to text

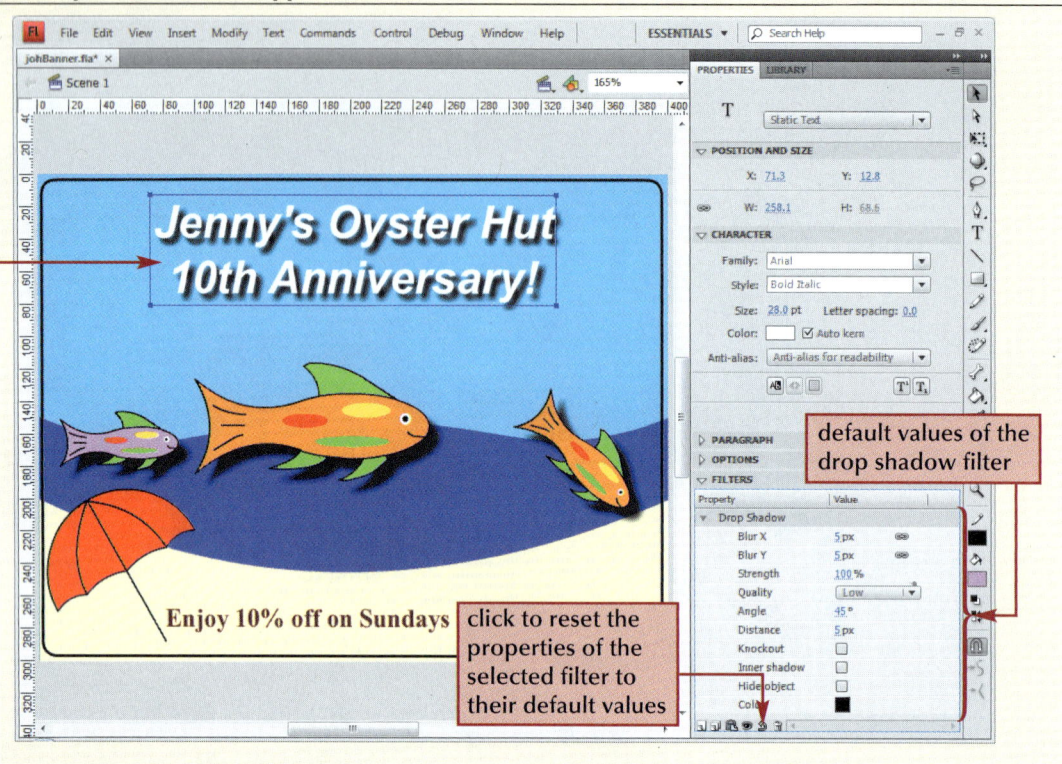

Drop Shadow filter applied to the text block

default values of the drop shadow filter

click to reset the properties of the selected filter to their default values

Tip

You can quickly close a document by pressing the Ctrl+W keys.

11. Save the document, and then close it.

In this session, you learned to use the Library panel to work with symbols in the johBanner.fla document's library. You also applied special graphic effects to movie clips and text. In the next tutorial, you will learn how to create animations with the symbols in Jenny's Oyster Hut banner.

Review | Session 2.3 Quick Check

1. What are the three behavior types for symbols?
2. What is the purpose of the Library panel?
3. Why should you convert a graphic you want to use multiple times in a document into a symbol?
4. What is the difference between a symbol and an instance of a symbol?
5. True or False? When you modify a symbol, the instances created from that symbol are not affected.
6. What is a filter?
7. True or False? You can apply multiple filters to one object.

Review | Tutorial Summary

In this tutorial, you learned how to use the main drawing tools in Flash. You drew lines, curves, ovals, and rectangles to create graphic elements, and then you applied and changed the colors of strokes and fills, and applied the properties of one object to another object. You used the Text tool to create different types of text boxes. Then you exported a document as an image for use in a Web page. You used the History panel to review the steps performed in a document, and then to undo and replay the steps. You created and edited symbols and instances of symbols. Finally, you viewed parts of a document's library and applied a drop shadow filter to symbols and text.

Key Terms

anti-aliasing	Free Transform tool	Oval Primitive tool
button symbol	graphic symbol	Paint Bucket tool
document-level undo	History panel	Pencil tool
dynamic text field	Ink Bottle tool	Rectangle Primitive tool
export	input text field	root folder
Eyedropper tool	instance	single-line text block
field	library	static text block
filter	movie clip	symbol
fixed-width text block	object-level undo	Text tool

Practice | Review Assignments

Practice the skills you learned in the tutorial.

Data File needed for the Review Assignments: banner.fla

Aly is pleased with the banner you created for Jenny's Oyster Hut Web site. She asks you to modify another version of the banner by changing the color of the umbrella, adding a second umbrella, finishing a fish graphic, adding an instance of the fish to the banner, and adding a text block. She also wants you to change the color and style of the rectangle, add drop shadow effects to the fish, and draw lines as underlines for text.

1. Open the **banner.fla** file located in the Tutorial.02\Review folder, save the document as **newBanner.fla** in the same folder, reset the workspace to the Essentials layout, and then close the Timeline.
2. Edit the umbrella symbol in the Library panel by opening it in symbol-editing mode. Use the Paint Bucket tool to change the color of the two maroon panels in the umbrella to red (#FF0000) so that the panels alternate between yellow and red. Use the Transform panel to decrease the width and height of the symbol to 75%. Exit symbol-editing mode.
3. Place one instance of the umbrella symbol in the lower-left corner of the banner, and then rotate it so that the umbrella leans to the left. Place another instance of the umbrella symbol in the lower-right corner of the banner and lean it to the right.
4. Edit the fish symbol in the Library panel. Use the Oval tool to draw a circle that has a white (#FFFFFF) fill color and no stroke color for the fish's eye on the right part of the fish graphic.
5. Change the fill color to black (#000000) and draw a small circle inside the white circle to represent the eye's pupil.
6. Use the Pencil tool to draw a small line that has a black (#000000) stroke color and a stroke height of 1 below the eye to represent the fish's mouth. Draw three short horizontal line segments on the tail of the fish.
7. Create a color band on the fish by drawing a vertical line inside the fish body starting at the top stroke of the fish near the top fin and ending at the bottom stroke of the fish near the bottom fin. Draw another vertical line to the left of the first line on the fish from the top stroke to the bottom stroke of the fish. Make sure the vertical lines connect to the strokes representing the fish's body.
8. Use the Paint Bucket tool to apply a peach color (#FFCC99) to the middle band on the fish created by the vertical lines and to apply a green color (#00FF00) to the areas inside the top and bottom fins. Exit symbol-editing mode.
9. Place an instance of the fish symbol on the water in the center of the banner.
10. Place another instance of the fish symbol to the right of the first instance, and then rotate the second instance so that it appears to be swimming in the water in a downward direction.
11. Apply a drop shadow filter effect to each fish instance on the Stage. Use a filter distance of 7 px and a filter strength of 90%.
12. Add a new single-line text block that reads **Free Drink with a Dinner Entree!**. Use Verdana for the font family, 16pt for the point size, and brown (#663300) for the text color. Center the new text block on the beach at the bottom of the banner.
13. Use the Line tool to draw horizontal lines under each of the two lines of text on the top of the banner. The lines should be blue (#0000FF), have a height of 2, a stroke style of solid, and appear as underlines for the text.
14. Add a drop shadow effect to the text block. Use default settings for the drop shadow, and change its color to gray (#999999).

15. Edit the rectangle that is framing the banner. Change its color to maroon (#660000), set the stroke height to 3, and choose a stroke style other than Solid.
16. Export the image to the Tutorial.02\Review folder with the name **newBanner.jpg** and in the JPG file format, using the default settings in the Export JPEG dialog box.
17. Submit the finished files to your instructor.

| Apply | **Case Problem 1** |

Create a grand opening banner for a store using shapes, text, and symbols.

There are no Data Files needed for this Case Problem.

Katie's Pet Resort Katie's Pet Resort is preparing for its grand opening celebration and sale. Katie meets with John to discuss the development of the store's Web site. John suggests that a banner be developed first that will set the tone for the rest of the Web site. Katie asks John to develop the banner. She wants the banner to help promote the grand opening celebration and sale by including graphics that depict a celebration and text about the grand opening. You will create the banner shown in Figure 2-52.

Figure 2-52

1. Create a new document. Change the document properties so that the width is 500 pixels and the height is 250 pixels. Change the background color to light yellow (#FFFF99).
2. Save the document as **petBanner.fla** in the Tutorial.02\Case1 folder included with your Data Files.
3. Create a square with sides of about 45 pixels in length. Use light orange (#FFCC32) for the fill color and a solid black stroke of 1 pixel in height. Place the square near the upper-left side of the stage.
4. Add a text block inside the square with the uppercase letter **K**. Use a font family such as Comic Sans MS, a point size of 32, bold style, and black text.
5. Group the square and the text, being sure to select both the fill and the stroke for the square.
6. Make a copy of the group and edit the copy to change the letter to **A** and the fill color of the square. Move the copy to the right of the square with the letter K.
7. Repeat Step 6 to make four more copies of the group. Change the letters in the copies to **T, I, E,** and **'S**, respectively and use a different color for each square's fill. Move the copies so that the text blocks and squares spell KATIE'S.
8. Use the Free Transform tool to rotate and position each letter block, as shown in Figure 2-52.

9. Convert each of the letter blocks into a movie clip symbol, naming each symbol according to the letter in the text block: **K**, **A**, **T**, **I**, **E**, and **S**, respectively. Apply a drop shadow filter effect to each of the letter block instances on the Stage. Use the default settings for the filter.
10. Add a text block in the center of the Stage. Use the same font family as in Step 4 with a point size of 50, dark blue (#000066) text, center align the text and use bold style. Type **Pet Resort** in the text block.
11. Add a second text block with a point size of 18, black text, and center alignment. Type **Grand Opening this Saturday!**, and then on a separate line in the same text block type **Bring your pets for a tour!**.
12. Draw two balloons on the left side of the Stage using the Oval tool with different colors for each balloon. Do not include a stroke for the balloons. Draw a string for each balloon using the Pencil tool with a light gray (#999999) color for the stroke.
13. Repeat Step 11 to draw two more balloons on the right side of the Stage with different colors.
14. Use the Brush tool to draw multicolored confetti on the Stage. Select a small brush size from the Brush Size modifier in the Tools panel. Select a brush color of your choice using the Fill color control in the Tools panel, and then click dots with the tool on the banner to create the confetti. Repeat to create different colored dots throughout the Stage using at least three different colors.
15. Create a rectangle as a border around all of the objects on the Stage. The rectangle should have slightly rounded corners, a maroon (#660000) stroke, no fill, a stroke height of 3, and a solid style. Draw the rectangle so that it is just inside the edges of the Stage.
16. Export the image to the Tutorial.02\Case1 folder with the name **petBanner.jpg** and in the JPG file format, using Full Document Size and the rest of the default settings in the Export JPEG dialog box.
17. Submit the finished files to your instructor.

Apply | Case Problem 2

Create a banner advertising a zoo with text, shapes, and symbols.

There are no Data Files needed for this Case Problem.

Alamo City Zoo Janet asks Alex to develop a new banner for the Alamo City Zoo's Web site. The new banner will advertise an open house celebration event promoting a new bear exhibit. The banner will contain text with the zoo's name and event information as well as graphic elements depicting bear paws. You'll create the banner shown in Figure 2-53.

Figure 2-53

1. Create a new document. Change the document properties so that the width is 300 pixels and the height is 200 pixels. Change the background color to light green (#99CC66).
2. Save the document as **zooBanner.fla** in the Tutorial.02\Case2 folder included with your Data Files.
3. Create a single-line text block on the top part of the Stage for the name of the zoo. Use Times New Roman or a font family of your choice, a point size of 36, black text color, center aligned, and bold italic style. Type **Alamo City Zoo** in the text block.
4. Create a fixed-width text block of about 200 pixels wide on the lower part of the Stage. Use the Arial font family, a point size of 22, black text color, bold style, and center alignment. Type **Come Visit the New BEAR Exhibit!** in the text block.
5. Create a single-line text block on the center of the Stage. Use the Arial font family, a point size of 18, light yellow text color (#FFFF99), regular style, and center aligned. Type **Special Open House!** in the text block.
6. Use the Free Transform tool to rotate the text block so that it is in a vertical position on the left side of the Stage, as shown in Figure 2-53.
7. Create a new movie clip symbol named **bearPaw**. (*Hint*: On the Application bar, click Insert, and then click New Symbol.) In symbol-editing mode, on the center of the Stage, draw a small circle about 40 pixels wide and 40 pixels high. Use brown (#663300) for the fill color, black (#000000) for the stroke color, solid for the stroke style, and 1 for the stroke height.
8. Zoom in to the circle and use the Selection tool to move the top part of the circle's stroke down to give the circle a slightly flattened appearance. Using the same stroke and fill colors as the circle, draw four small ovals equally spaced above the flattened part of the circle, as shown in Figure 2-53, and then exit symbol-editing mode.
9. Drag four instances of the bearPaw symbol from the Library panel to the Stage. Place two instances below the top text block, place one instance to the left of the bottom text block, and place one instance to the right of the bottom text block.
10. Use the Free Transform tool to resize two of the bearPaw instances to make them slightly smaller. Also, rotate the lower-left instance on the Stage slightly to the left, and then rotate the lower-right instance on the Stage slightly to the right.
11. Apply a bevel effect to one of the bearPaw instances on the Stage. Change the filter strength to 80% and change the highlight color to a light peach (#FFCC99). Copy all of the filter's properties, and then apply the copied filter effect to each of the other bearPaw instances on the Stage.

12. Draw a rectangle along the inside edges of the Stage as a border around all of the objects on the Stage. Use a black stroke, a stroke height of 3, the Ragged stroke style, square corners, and no fill color.
13. Export the image to the Tutorial.02\Case2 folder with the name **zooBanner.jpg** and in the JPG file format, using Full Document Size and the rest of the default settings in the Export JPEG dialog box.
14. Submit the finished files to your instructor.

Challenge | Case Problem 3

Extend your skills by using gradients and the Oval Primitive tool as you create a logo for a nursery.

There are no Data Files needed for this Case Problem.

Westcreek Nursery   Alice meets with Amanda, who was contracted to update the company's Westcreek Nursery Web site. Alice requests that a new logo be developed for her business. The logo should contain the business name, phone number, and an appropriate slogan, along with some graphics. You'll create the completed logo shown in Figure 2-54.

Figure 2-54

EXPLORE
1. Create a new document. Change the document properties so that the width is 300 pixels and the height is 150 pixels. Change the background color to light green by typing **#CC99CC** in the color palette's hexadecimal box.
2. Save the document as **wcLogo.fla** in the Tutorial.02\Case3 folder included with your Data Files.
3. Draw a rectangle about 280 pixels wide and 50 pixels high across the top of the Stage. Use the Rectangle tool and the Merge Drawing model with a black stroke, a height of 1, a solid style, no fill color, and a rectangle corner radius of –5 for every corner. Place the rectangle about 10 pixels from the left of the Stage and 10 pixels from the top.
4. Create a single-line text block inside the rectangle. Use Verdana or a similar font family of your choice, a point size of 22, white text, left aligned, and bold style. Type **Westcreek** in the text block, and then position the text block on the left side of the rectangle.
5. Draw a straight vertical line to the right of the text block to split the rectangle into two sections. One end of the line should snap to the top of the rectangle and the other end should snap to the bottom of the rectangle. Use a black (#000000) stroke, a stroke height of 1, and a solid style.

EXPLORE
6. Apply the green radial gradient fill (fourth gradient from the left on the color palette) to the left section of the rectangle.

7. Create a single-line text block on the right side of the rectangle. Use Verdana or a similar font family of your choice, a point size of 22, black text, left aligned, and bold italic style. Type **Nursery** in the text block, and, if necessary, position the text block in the center of the right side of the rectangle.

8. Create a single-line text block below the center of the larger rectangle. Use the same font family as in Step 7, a point size of 14, black text, center aligned, and regular style. Type **We Deliver!** in the text block.

9. Create a single-line text block in the center of the Stage. Use the same font family as Step 7, a point size of 42, reddish brown (#993300) text, left aligned, and bold style. Type **FLOWERS** in the text block. Using the Free Transform tool, skew the text block so that the letters are slanted to the right.

EXPLORE
10. Apply a gradient glow filter effect to the FLOWERS text block. In the Gradient Glow properties, click the Gradient box, click the right gradient marker (small triangle in lower-right corner of gradient), and select an orange tan color (#CC9900) in the color palette.

11. Draw four straight horizontal lines, each about 40 pixels in length, to the left of the letter F in the center text block. Position the lines equally spaced and approximately the same distance from the letter F.

12. Use the Oval Primitive tool to draw a circle with a black fill and no stroke about 30 pixels in diameter on the bottom part of the Stage. If necessary, reset the values for the controls in the Property inspector before drawing the circle.

EXPLORE
13. Change the Inner radius value for the circle to 40 to create the image of a car tire.

14. Convert the circle to a movie clip symbol named **tire**. Add a second instance of the tire symbol from the Library panel to the Stage. Move the two tire instances right below the text block in the center of the Stage. Place one tire right below the L on the FLOWERS text, and place the other tire right below the R.

15. Export the image to the Tutorial.02\Case3 folder with the name **wcLogo.jpg** and in JPG file format, using Full Document Size and the rest of the default settings in the Export JPEG dialog box.

16. Submit the finished files to your instructor.

| Create | **Case Problem 4** |

Use symbols and text blocks to create a banner for an association.

There are no Data Files needed for this Case Problem.

Missions Support Association   Brittany meets with Anissa to discuss improving the Missions Support Association's Web site. They decide to start by developing a new banner for the site's home page, which will include the association's name as well as keywords highlighting the services available to the association's members. You'll create a banner similar of your design to do this. Figure 2-55 shows one possible solution.

Figure 2-55

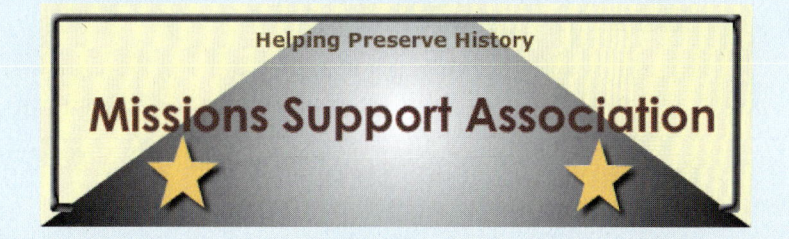

1. Create a new document the dimensions and background color of your choice.
2. Save the document as **msaBanner.fla** in the Tutorial.02\Case4 folder included with your Data Files.
3. Draw two or more shapes using the fill and stroke colors of your choice on the Stage, and then set the X and Y coordinates in the Property inspector as needed to position the shapes.
4. Use guides as needed to modify at least one of the shapes you drew, such as by dragging anchor points to convert the shape to another shape, such as converting a rectangle to a triangle. (*Hint*: You can use the Snap to Objects modifier to make the shape snap to the guides.)
5. Draw a rectangle to frame the banner. Use no fill color but select an appropriate stroke color and stroke height.
6. Modify the frame as needed. For example, you can use the Selection tool to select the bottom frame rectangle that overlaps another shape you drew, and then delete the selected portion.
7. Convert the frame rectangle to a movie clip symbol named **frame**.
8. Apply a filter to the frame instance, change the filter properties appropriately. For example, you can apply a bevel filter, change the quality to high and change shadow color to a lighter gray.
9. Create text block using the font family, style, size, color, and alignment of your choice, and then type **Helping Preserve History** in the text block. Position the text block attractively on the banner.
10. Create another text block, using the font family, style, size, color, and alignment of your choice (for example, you can use a different font family, different style, larger point size, and different color), and then type **Missions Support Association** in the text block. Position the text block attractively on the banner.

EXPLORE

11. Create a new movie clip symbol named **star**. In symbol-editing mode, use the PolyStar tool to draw a star shape on the Stage that is about 50 pixels wide and 50 pixels high. Use a color of your choice for the fill and no stroke. In the Tool Settings, set the style to star, the number of sides to 5, and the star point size to 0.50. Exit symbol-editing mode.
12. Place at least two instances of the star symbol on the banner in attractive positions.
13. Apply a drop shadow effect to each star instance on the Stage, using the settings of your choice for the filter.
14. Export the image to the Tutorial.02\Case4 folder with the name **msaBanner.jpg** and in JPG file format, using Full Document Size and the rest of the default settings in the Export JPEG dialog box.
15. Submit the finished files to your instructor.

| Review | Quick Check Answers |

Session 2.1

1. False; select the Snap to Objects modifier to draw a perfect circle.
2. Click the Set Corner Radius button and enter a point value in the Rectangle Settings dialog box.
3. Oval Primitive
4. Pencil Mode
5. Click an object's stroke with the Eyedropper tool, and then click the other object to apply the stroke's attributes.

6. the Paint Bucket tool
7. the Scale modifier
8. False; the Fill Transform tool is used to modify an object's gradient fill.

Session 2.2

1. A static text block has text that does not change once the document is published. A dynamic text field's content may be changed as it is updated from a Web server.
2. Click and drag on the Stage to set the desired width.
3. the Property inspector
4. Drag the single-line text block's round corner handle.
5. a fixed-width text block
6. to let the user add words not found in the Adobe or language dictionaries but which are spelled correctly, such as a company name
7. steps performed in the current document
8. Drag the slider up to a previous step; steps dimmed in the History panel are undone.

Session 2.3

1. movie clip, graphic, and button
2. to store and organize the symbols contained in a document
3. No matter how many instances of a symbol you create, the symbol is stored only once in the document, which minimizes the document's size.
4. Symbols are reusable elements such as graphics, buttons, and sound files that can be used more than once in a document. An instance is a single use of a symbol.
5. False; modifying a symbol also changes the instances created from that symbol.
6. a special graphic effect, such as a drop shadow, you can apply to movie clips, buttons, and text
7. True

Ending Data Files

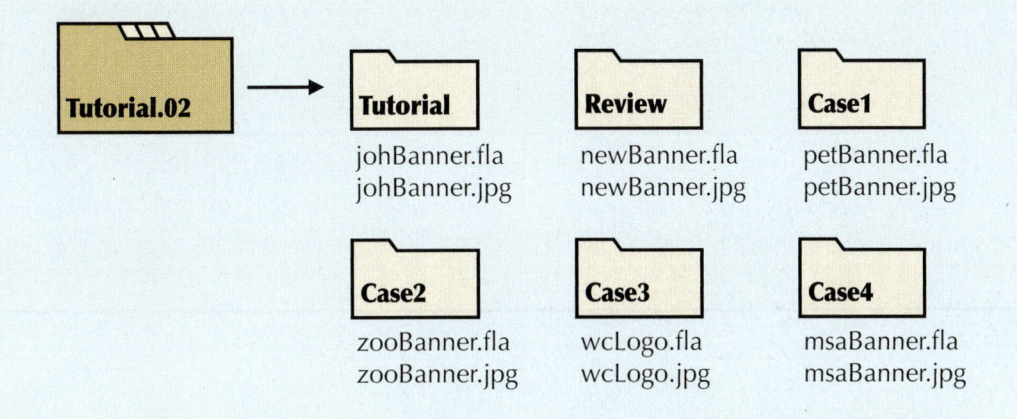

Tutorial.02 →

Tutorial
johBanner.fla
johBanner.jpg

Review
newBanner.fla
newBanner.jpg

Case1
petBanner.fla
petBanner.jpg

Case2
zooBanner.fla
zooBanner.jpg

Case3
wcLogo.fla
wcLogo.jpg

Case4
msaBanner.fla
msaBanner.jpg

Flash | FL 115

Tutorial 3

Objectives

Session 3.1
- Learn the different elements of animation
- Create frames and layers
- Organize frames and layers using the Timeline
- Work with scenes

Session 3.2
- Create animations
- Create and modify motion tweens
- Apply a motion preset animation
- Test animations

Session 3.3
- Create a classic tween animation
- Use graphic symbols in animations
- Create a frame-by-frame animation
- Create shape tween animations

Creating Animations

Developing Tween and Frame-by-Frame Animations

Case | Admiral Web Design

Aly showed Jenny the new Jenny's Oyster Hut banner. Jenny expressed interest in adding animation to the banner to attract more attention to the anniversary specials the banner promotes. Aly then revised the banner you created for Jenny's Oyster Hut to create a partially completed banner, which will be the basis for the new animated banner. The new banner will have an initial animation of a fish pulling a shrimp specials sign while the words "Fried Shrimp" and "Shrimp Scampi" are displayed one after the other. The banner will also include an animated fish swimming as well as a sea plant with moving leaves. Before you complete the animation for the Jenny's Oyster Hut banner, Aly asks you to review and modify a document she recently created for another client, Jackson's Sports.

In this tutorial, you will learn the basics of creating Flash animations and how to coordinate these animations in the Timeline using frames and layers. You will learn how to extend a document using scenes. You will learn how to create motion tweens, classic tweens, frame-by-frame animations, and shape tweens. Finally, you will learn how to create animations using graphic symbols.

Starting Data Files

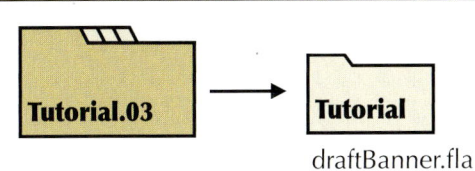

Tutorial.03 →

- **Tutorial**: draftBanner.fla, jacksons.fla
- **Review**: jennysAdDraft.fla
- **Case1**: kprBanner.fla
- **Case2**: aczBanner.fla
- **Case3**: wcLogo.fla
- **Case4**: msaBanner.fla

Session 3.1

Elements of Animation

One of the most powerful features of Flash is its ability to create animation. Animation, which creates the perception of movement, is achieved by changing the location or appearance of an object from one moment in time to the next. Before you create an animation, you will review some basic elements of a Flash document. A document is made up of layers, frames, and the graphic objects such as symbols that are displayed on the Stage. You coordinate these elements from the document's Timeline.

The Timeline

The Timeline, which appears below the Stage, is used to control and coordinate the timing of the animation by determining how and when the frames for each layer are displayed. The Timeline is also a means of creating, modifying, and organizing layers and frames. Figure 3-1 shows the Timeline for an animation Aly created for Jackson's Sports.

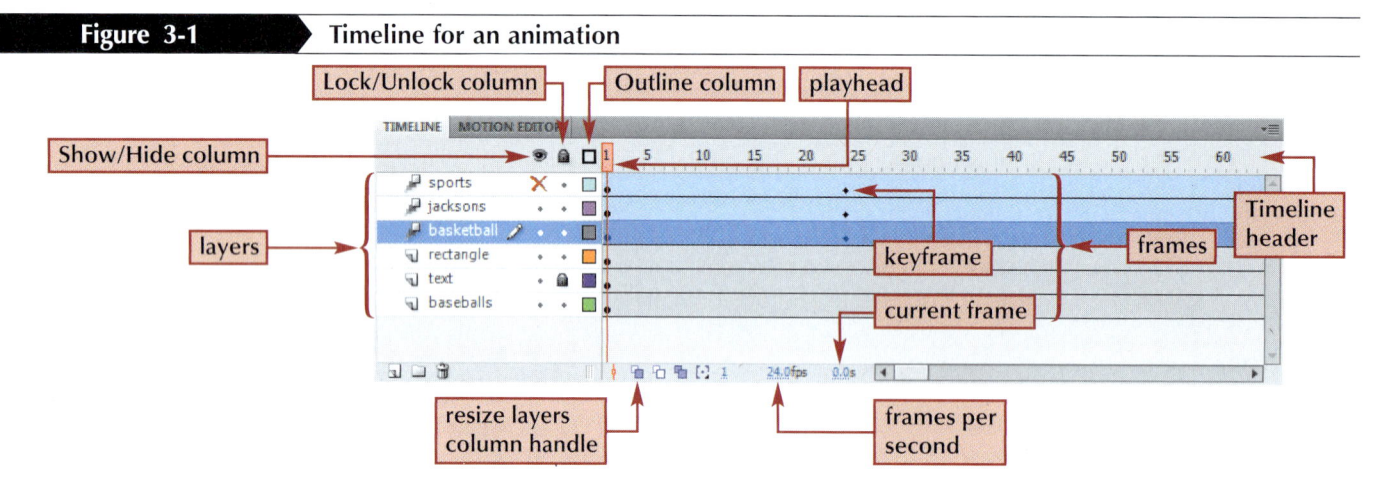

Figure 3-1 Timeline for an animation

Layers

Layers organize the content of a document. A Flash document starts with one layer. You can insert additional layers in a document and then place the graphic objects in the document on different layers. When using the Merge Drawing mode, any object you draw or move on top of other objects splits or merges with those objects. Placing objects on separate layers prevents this and allows you to overlap the objects on the Stage. Objects on different layers can be moved in front of or in back of each other by changing the order in which the layers are organized. Layers are especially useful when you are animating more than one object at the same time. For example, you can have an object on one layer move in one direction at the same time as an object on another layer moves in a different direction. The animations occur simultaneously, but don't impact one another in any way.

Frames

Frames contain the content for an animation and represent a particular instant in time. For example, at the default frame rate of 24 frames per second (fps), each frame appears for 1/24 of a second during the animation. Placing different content on each frame or slightly modifying the content from one frame to the next creates the perception of movement that is animation. Initially, a document contains just one frame, which is a keyframe. A **keyframe** is a frame that contains a new symbol instance or a new graphic object. To create an animation, you need to add more frames to a layer. The frames you add are used to create new content, to keep the content the same, or to change the content from previous frames. If you want the content to remain the same in the new frame, you add a regular frame. If you want to add a new instance of a symbol, you add a keyframe. As you add more frames, the length of the animation increases.

The frames for a layer appear in the Timeline in a row to the right of the layer. Regular frames are white when empty and shaded gray or another color when they have content. Keyframes contain a white dot when they are empty and a black dot when they have content. The layer icon to the left of a layer's name indicates the type of layer it is. For example, regular layers have a page icon.

Working with the Timeline

The layer controls are on the left side of the Timeline. Each row represents one layer. Next to the layer names are three columns: the Show/Hide column, Lock/Unlock column, and Outline column. The Show/Hide column is used to show or hide a layer's content. A dot in this column means the layer's content is shown, whereas a red x means the layer's content is temporarily hidden. The Lock/Unlock column is used to lock or unlock a layer. A dot in this column indicates the layer is unlocked and editable, whereas a lock icon indicates the layer is locked and cannot be edited. The Outline column is used to show the content of a layer in Outline view, which changes the Stage to show an outline of each object in the layer's outline color. You display a layer in Outline view by clicking its colored square. Outline view is useful when you are working with a complex animation and you want to see how the objects from the various layers overlap each other. You can control the column settings for all layers at one time by clicking the column's corresponding icon above the list of layers.

| InSight | **Locking Completed Layers** |

If you have multiple objects in different layers, it might become difficult to select an object on one layer without accidentally selecting another object on a different layer. A good practice when working with objects on multiple layers is to lock a layer after you finish editing its contents. Objects in a locked layer are not selectable.

You will explore the Timeline of the Jackson's Sports banner that Aly has been developing. The banner's Timeline contains several layers. The layers include animations of a baseball, a basketball, and text. Each layer has a name descriptive of its contents and contains 75 frames. You'll play the animation and watch the Timeline as it displays the elements of the document.

To explore the Timeline of the Jackson's Sports banner:

▶ 1. Open the **jacksons.fla** file located in the Tutorial.03\Tutorial folder included with your Data Files, and then save the document as **jacksonsRev** in the same folder.

▶ 2. On the Application bar, click the **Workspace Switcher** button, and then click **Reset 'Essentials'**. The workspace returns to the default Essentials layout. See Figure 3-2.

FL 118 Flash | Tutorial 3 Creating Animations

Figure 3-2   Jackson's Sports banner

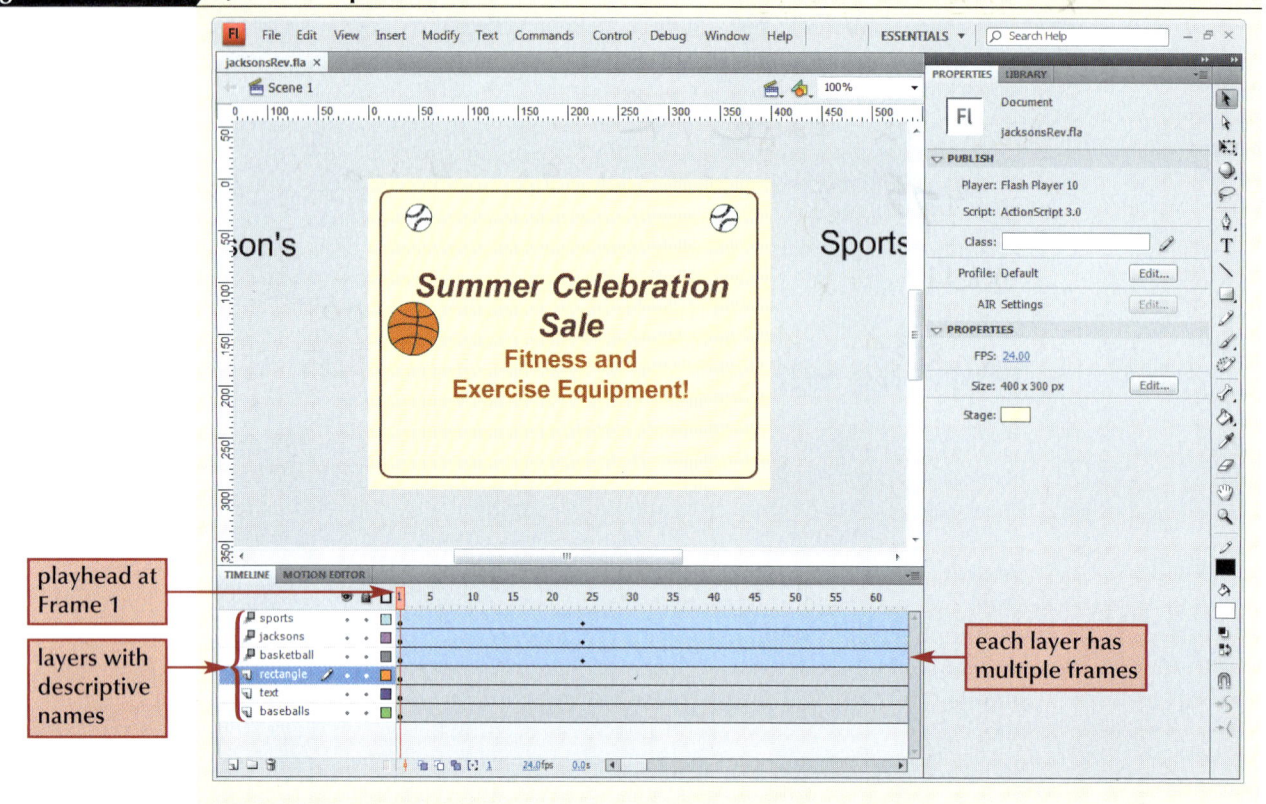

playhead at Frame 1

layers with descriptive names

each layer has multiple frames

Tip

You can also press the Enter key to play the Timeline.

3. On the Application bar, click **Control**, and then click **Play**. As the playhead moves from Frame 1 to Frame 24 in the Timeline, the basketball moves across the Stage and the text moves in from the sides of the Stage. After Frame 24, the contents on the Stage remain stationary through Frame 75.

4. Locate the playhead, and then review the current frame (75), frame rate (24.0 fps), and elapsed time (3.1 s) at the bottom of the Timeline. See Figure 3-3.

Tutorial 3 Creating Animations | Flash | FL 119

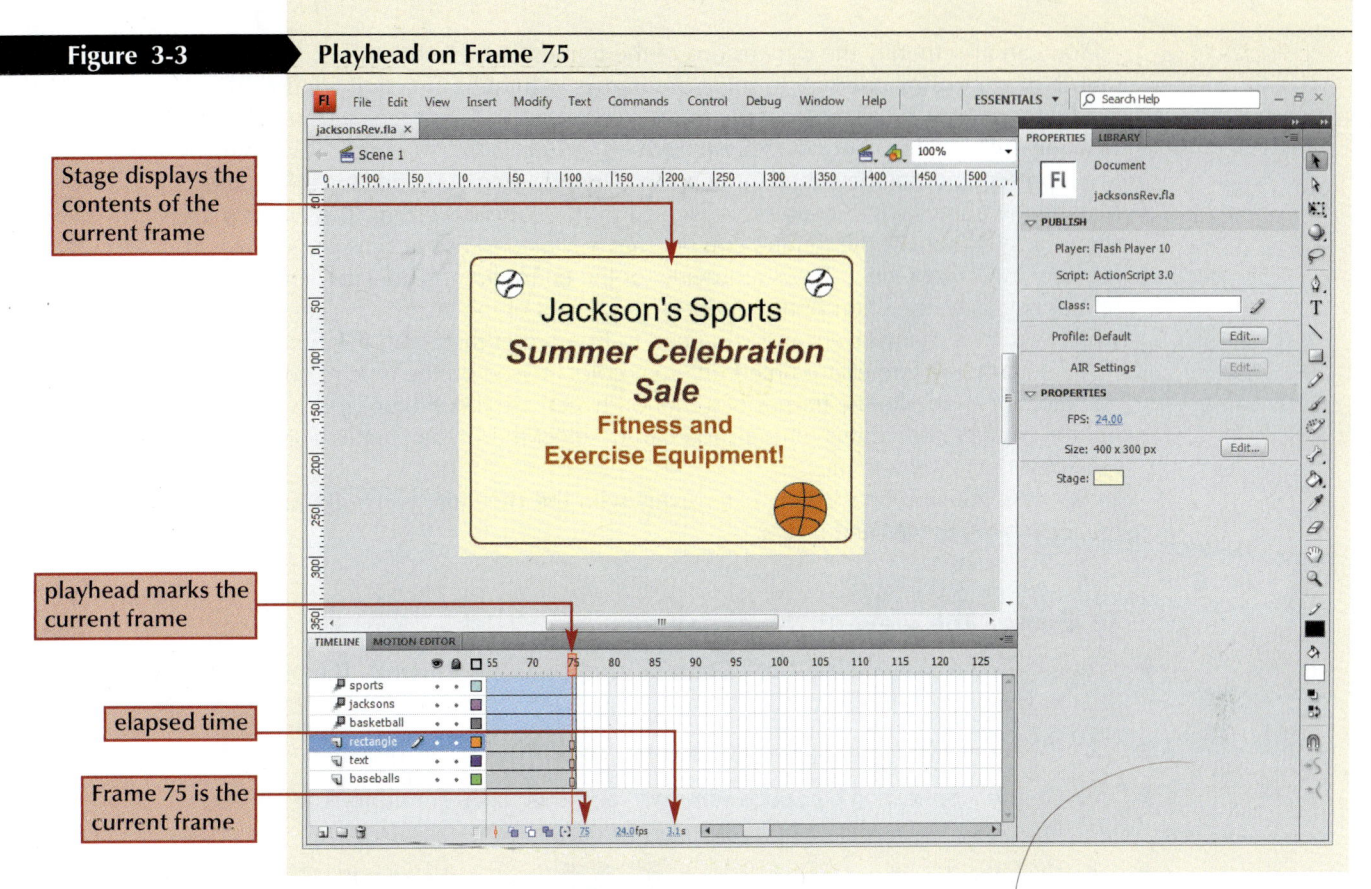

Figure 3-3 | **Playhead on Frame 75**

- Stage displays the contents of the current frame
- playhead marks the current frame
- elapsed time
- Frame 75 is the current frame

The Timeline displays useful information that you might review as you test an animation. The Elapsed Time control displays the time that has elapsed from Frame 1 to the frame that the playhead is currently on. The elapsed time depends on the frame rate, which is also shown at the bottom of the Timeline. By default, the frame rate is 24 frames per second, which means that an animation that spans 24 frames takes one second to play. The length of the Jackson's Sports banner animation you just viewed can be determined by looking at the elapsed time when the playhead is in the last frame. In this case, the length of the animation is 3.1 seconds.

| InSight | **Checking the Frame Number Before Modifying Content** |

A document can have a large number of frames, and the contents of the frames often look very similar from one frame to the next. As you work with content on the Stage, be aware of which frame is displayed because that is the frame whose content you are working with. Be careful that you do not change or create the content for the wrong frame. To determine which frame you are working with, check the location of the playhead in the Timeline header.

Changing the View of the Timeline

As you develop an animation, the number of frames can grow very rapidly, as can the number of layers. At some point, you might need to change the view of the Timeline to work more efficiently with the elements in the animation. The Timeline can be modified in several ways. You can extend the Timeline to show more frames by closing the panels in the Flash program window. You can place the Timeline above, below, to the left, or to the right of the document window. Or, you can undock the Timeline and display it as a floating panel.

You can also modify the dimensions of the frames. You change the width of the frames from Normal to Tiny or Small to see more frames within the Timeline window or to Medium or Large to see more of the frame's contents. The change is visible when you are working with sounds. (Sounds will be covered in Tutorial 5.) A sound's waveform, which is a representation of the sound, appears in a frame when you add it to a document. Making the frames wider enables you to see more of the waveform. The Preview view shows a thumbnail of the frame's content that is scaled to fit the Timeline's frame. The Preview in Context view shows a preview of the entire frame's contents, including white or empty space. The Short option reduces the height of the layers. This can be useful when you have many layers and you need to fit more of them into the Timeline window.

By default, the frames are tinted different colors based on the type of content they contain. For example, the frames of a motion tween are tinted blue. You will learn about motion tweens later in this tutorial. You can deselect the Tinted Frames option to remove the color tints on the frames.

Because you will be working extensively with the Timeline, you will practice changing the view of its frames and layers.

To change the view of the Timeline:

▶ 1. On the Application bar, click **Control**, and then click **Rewind**. The playhead moves to Frame 1.

▶ 2. Press the **F4** key. The panels disappear. You'll display the Timeline next.

▶ 3. On the Application bar, click **Window**, and then click **Timeline**. The Timeline appears.

▶ 4. Click the Timeline's **panel menu** button to open the panel's menu, and then click **Preview**. The frames increase in size and the content in Frame 1 is displayed. See Figure 3-4.

Figure 3-4 **Frames in Preview view**

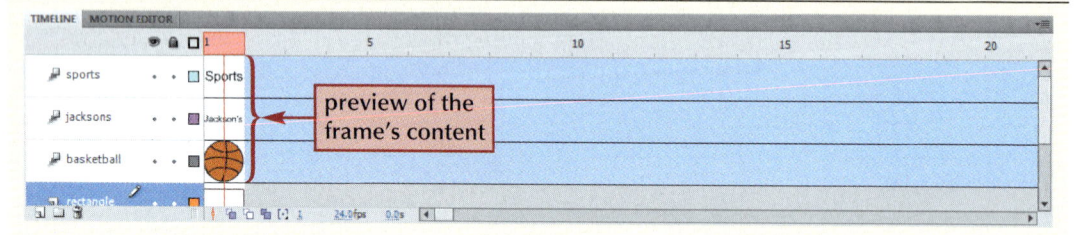

▶ 5. Click the Timeline's **panel menu** button, and then click **Small**. The frames decrease in size.

▶ 6. Click the Timeline's **panel menu** button, and then click **Short**. The height of the layers decreases. See Figure 3-5.

Figure 3-5 **Frames in Short view**

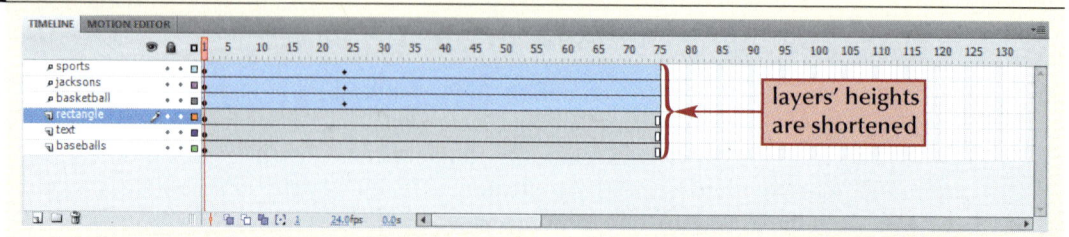

7. Click the Timeline's **panel menu** button, and then click **Short** to turn off Short view.

8. Click the Timeline's **panel menu** button, and then click **Normal**. The frames return to their default, or Normal, view.

9. On the Application bar, click the **Workspace Switcher** button, and then click **Reset 'Essentials'**. The workspace returns to the default Essentials layout.

Organizing Layers Using the Timeline

A new document in Flash contains one layer and one frame within that layer. As you create an animation, you add more layers to the document. A lengthy or complex animation could have a large number of layers, which can become difficult to manage. The Timeline is a useful tool for working with the different layers and frames in your document most efficiently.

You select a layer to edit its content. The selected layer is highlighted and a pencil icon appears to the right of the layer's name. You can also delete layers and add new layers as needed. As you add more layers to the Timeline, it's a good idea to name each one according to the content it contains. This helps keep the content organized as the complexity of the animation increases. Layers can also be renamed as needed.

Tip

To see all of a layer's selected properties, double-click its layer icon in the Timeline to open the Layer Properties dialog box.

InSight | Organizing Content in Layers

The number of layers in a document can quickly increase as you add more content or animation to the document. In fact, it is best to insert new layers as you add new content to a document. This helps you work with and organize the document's contents more easily. For complex documents with many layers, you can temporarily hide some layers as you work with the content of other layers. Additional layers don't add to the overall size of the finished file. Keep in mind that you want to keep the size of the final published SWF file as small as possible so it downloads quickly from the Web server to the viewer's computer.

You should assign layers meaningful names that correspond to their content. Then you or someone else who needs to edit the document can easily locate a layer based on its name. Although layer names can include spaces and punctuation marks, they are often omitted for simplicity.

Adding Layer Folders

When you have multiple layers in the document's Timeline, you can create layer folders to help you work more efficiently. A **layer folder** is a container in the Timeline in which you can place layers. The names of layers in a layer folder are indented under the layer folder in the Timeline, as shown in Figure 3-6.

Figure 3-6 Layer folder

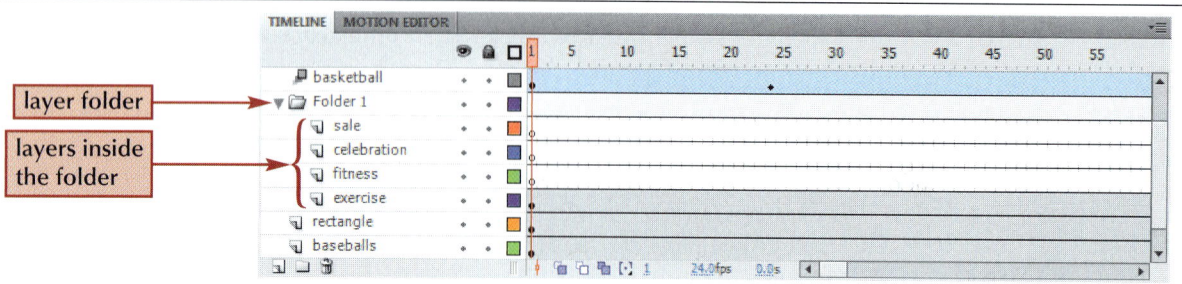

- layer folder
- layers inside the folder

Using a layer folder is similar to how you use a folder on your computer's hard drive—you place related files into the folder to make the files easier to find and manage. You can use a layer folder to keep related layers together. For example, you can create a folder in which to place all of the layers that contain text. Then you can quickly find the text layers when you need to edit them. You can name a layer folder with a descriptive name the same way you name a layer, making it easier to know what each folder contains. You can collapse the layer folders so that the layers in the folders are not visible. This makes the Timeline less cluttered and makes it easier to work with the other layers in the document. Collapsing the folder's layers does not affect the view of the layers' content on the Stage.

You'll add a layer folder in the Jackson's Sports document, and then move the related layers into it.

To insert a layer folder in the Jackson's Sports banner:

1. In the Timeline, click the **sports** layer. The layer is selected.

2. In the Timeline, click the **New Folder** button. A layer folder named Folder 1 is inserted above the sports layer.

3. Double-click **Folder 1** to select the folder name, type **text layers** as the new name, and then press the **Enter** key. The name of the folder changes.

4. Drag the **sports** layer to the text layers folder, releasing the mouse when a dark line appears below the text layers folder. The sports layer is indented underneath the text layers folder, as shown in Figure 3-7.

Figure 3-7 Sports layer inside the text layers folder

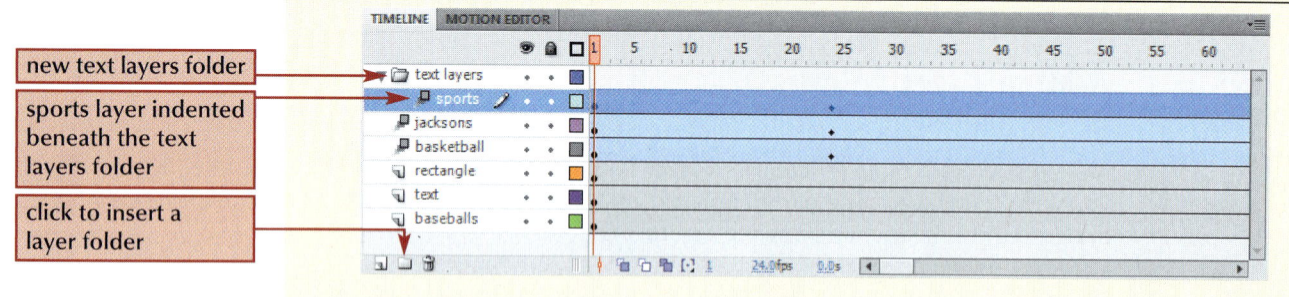

- new text layers folder
- sports layer indented beneath the text layers folder
- click to insert a layer folder

5. Drag the **jacksons** and **text** layers into the text layers folder. Each of the layers containing text appears indented underneath the text layers folder. The order of the text layers is not important because the text blocks do not overlap one another.

Tutorial 3 Creating Animations | Flash | FL 123

Tip
To expand the folder's contents and display the layers, click the folder's Expand arrow.

▶ 6. Click the text layers folder's **Collapse arrow** ▼. The folder's icon changes to a closed folder and the text layers are no longer visible.

Selecting, Copying, and Moving Frames

A document's frames can be copied or moved within the same layer or from one layer to another. To copy or move frames, you must first select them. You can select individual or multiple frames in the Timeline. You can select frames within one layer or across multiple layers.

You'll select and copy frames in the Jackson's Sports banner.

To select, copy, and paste frames:

▶ 1. In the Timeline, click the **baseballs** layer. The layer is selected.

▶ 2. In the Timeline, click the **New Layer** button. A new layer is inserted above the baseballs layer.

▶ 3. Double-click the new layer's name, type **new baseballs**, and then press the **Enter** key. The layer is renamed.

▶ 4. Click the name of the **baseballs** layer. All of the frames for the baseballs layer are selected.

You'll copy the selected frames to the new baseballs layer.

▶ 5. Right-click the selected frames to open the context menu, and then click **Copy Frames**.

▶ 6. Click the name of the **new baseballs** layer to select all of its frames.

▶ 7. Right-click the selected frames to open the context menu, and then click **Paste Frames**. The layer's frames are replaced with the copied frames from the baseballs layer.

▶ 8. In the Tools panel, click the **Selection** tool, if necessary. The two copied baseball instances remain selected.

▶ 9. Drag the left baseball instance to the lower-left corner of the Stage. Both instances move at the same time. See Figure 3-8.

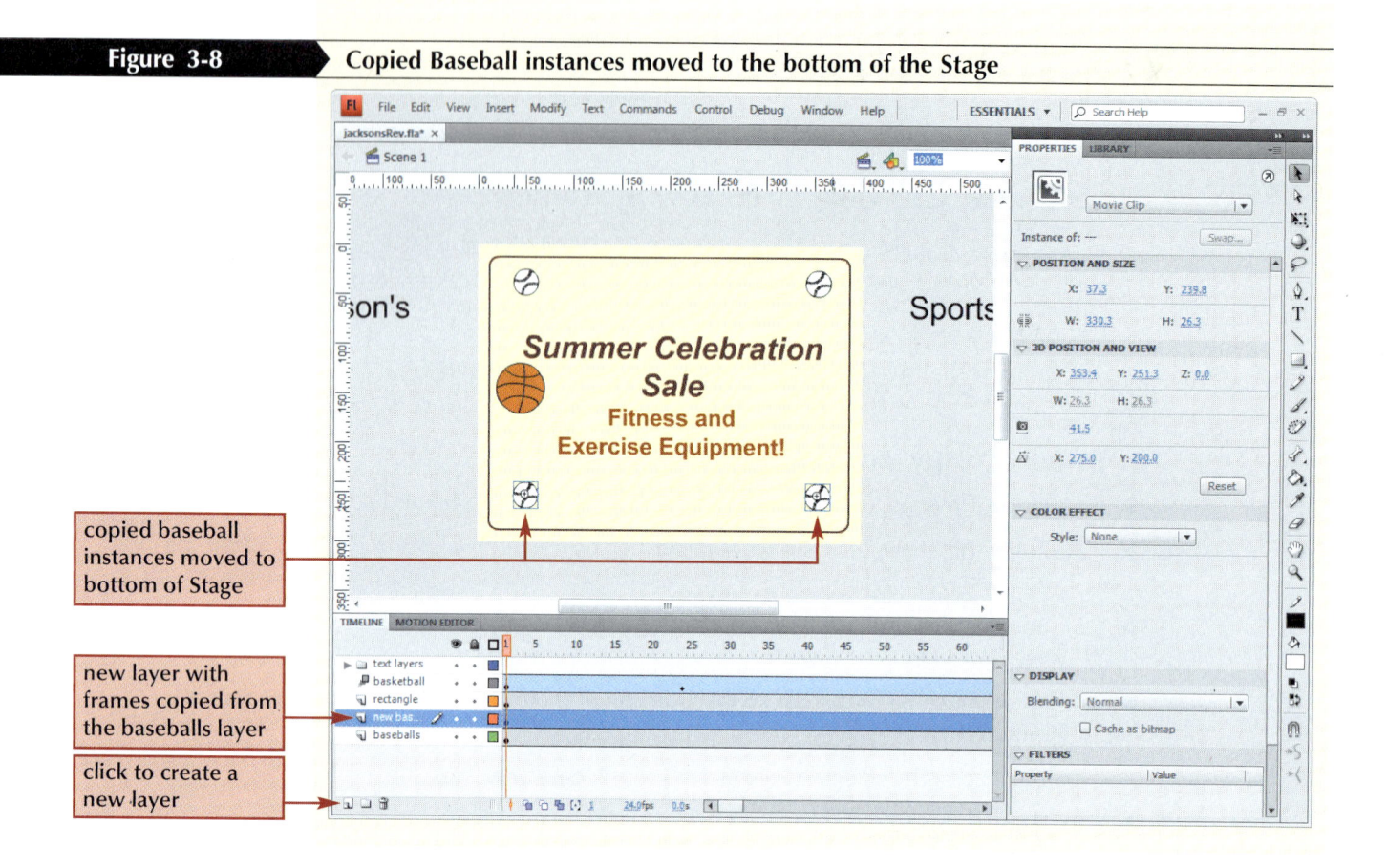

Figure 3-8 Copied Baseball instances moved to the bottom of the Stage

copied baseball instances moved to bottom of Stage

new layer with frames copied from the baseballs layer

click to create a new layer

Using Scenes and Multiple Timelines

Scenes provide a way to break up a long or complex document into smaller sections that are more manageable. Every Flash document starts with one scene that contains a Timeline. For more complex animations, a document can have more than one scene, and each scene has its own Timeline, as shown in Figure 3-9. A document's scenes are similar to those of a motion picture. In the same way that the scenes in a motion picture are played in order, the scenes in a document are played one after the other. The content of all layers is displayed one frame at a time within a scene's Timeline. When you add new scenes to a document, you are essentially adding new Timelines that contain their own frames with new content.

| Figure 3-9 | Multiple scenes in one document |

contents of Scene 1 → (timeline showing sports, jacksons, basketball, rectangle, text, baseballs layers)

contents of Scene 2 → (timeline showing sports, jacksons, basketball, rectangle, text, baseball1, baseball2 layers)

After a document with multiple scenes is published, the SWF file plays in a Web page using the Flash Player. The player treats all the scenes in an SWF file as one long Timeline. So, for example, if a Flash document has two scenes and each scene has 30 frames, the Flash Player treats this as one long Timeline with 60 consecutive frames and plays them according to the order of the scenes in the Scene panel.

Using the Scene Panel

The Scene panel lists the scenes in the current document in the order in which they will play. From the Scene panel, you can change the order the scenes will play as well as duplicate, add, and delete scenes. A duplicate scene has the same name as the original with the word "copy" added to its name and it has the same contents as the original. Any new scene you add has the name Scene followed by a number that is one higher than the previous scene.

InSight | Naming Scenes

When a document has only a few scenes, using the default scene names such as Scene 1, Scene 2, and Scene 3 might be okay. When a document has many scenes, it is better to assign more meaningful names to each scene to make it simpler to manage the document. If you have 10 scenes, for example, you might not remember the content of each of the 10 scenes. You would then have to search through several scenes to find the one containing the content you want to work with. By giving each scene a meaningful name, you can more easily remember what each scene contains. Scene names can include spaces, symbols, and punctuation marks.

When you add a new scene or create a duplicate of a scene, the Stage automatically displays the new scene. You can tell which scene is currently displayed by the scene number in the upper-left corner of the Stage window or by looking at the Scene panel to see which scene is currently selected. You can switch between scenes at any time.

Aly wants you to rename and reorder the scenes in the Jackson's Sports document.

Tip

You can also press the Shift+F2 keys to open and close the Scene panel.

To work with scenes in the Jackson's Sports banner:

1. On the Application bar, click **Window**, point to **Other Panels**, and then click **Scene**. The Scene panel opens, showing two scenes named Scene 1 and Scene 2. You will rename these scenes with more meaningful names. See Figure 3-10.

Figure 3-10 Scenes displayed in the Scene panel

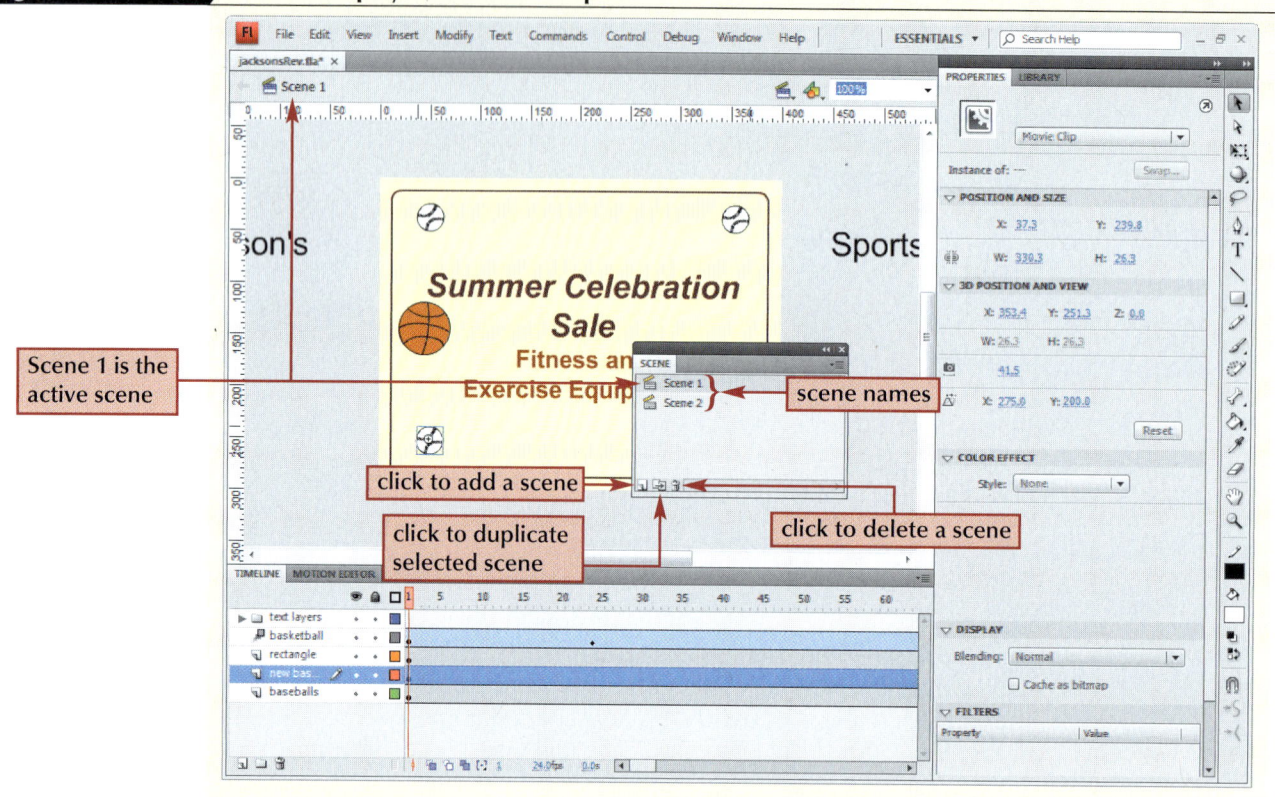

2. In the Scene panel, double-click **Scene 1** to select the name, type **Fitness and Exercise** as the new name, and then press the **Enter** key to rename the scene.

3. In the Scene panel, click **Scene 2**. The Scene 2 scene name appears on the Edit bar, the contents of the Timeline change to that scene, and the view of the Stage switches to the first frame of that scene.

4. In the Scene panel, double-click **Scene 2**, type **Celebration**, and then press the **Enter** key. The scene is renamed and the Celebration scene name appears on the Edit bar. See Figure 3-11.

Figure 3-11 **Renamed scenes**

Celebration scene is currently displayed

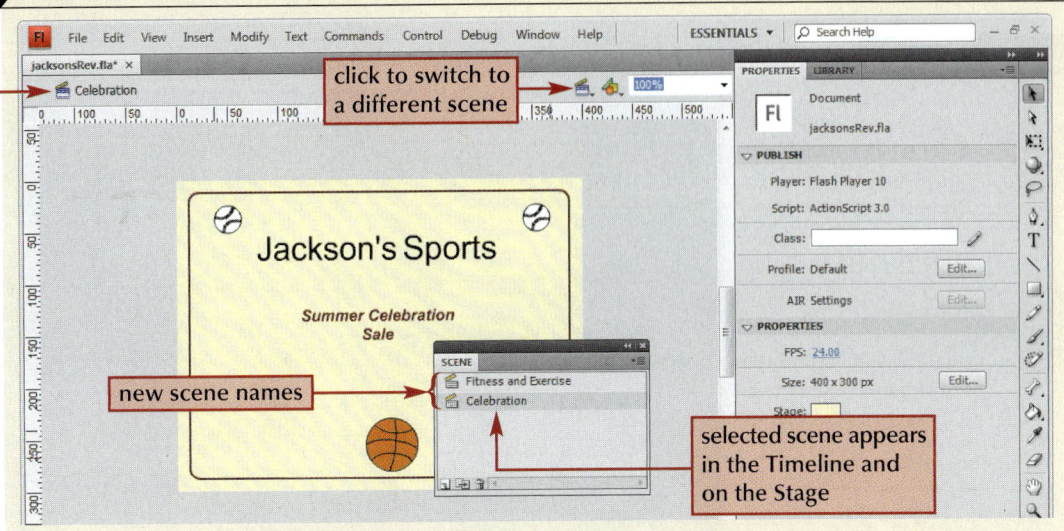

click to switch to a different scene

new scene names

selected scene appears in the Timeline and on the Stage

▸ 5. Drag the Scene panel to the right of the Stage, and then, on the Application bar, click **Control** and click **Play**. The animation for the Celebration scene plays, showing the center text block increasing in size and the baseballs moving.

You'll test the animation to see how both scenes play one after the other.

▸ 6. On the Application bar, click **Control**, and then click **Test Movie**. A new window opens, showing the SWF file as it plays the animation of the Fitness and Exercise scene followed by the animation of the Celebration scene.

▸ 7. On the Flash Player Application bar, click **File**, and then click **Close**. The Flash Player window closes and you return to the document.

You can use the Scene panel to reorder the scenes in a document.

▸ 8. In the Scene panel, click and drag the **Celebration** scene so that it is before the Fitness and Exercise scene.

▸ 9. On the Application bar, click **Control**, and then click **Test Movie**. The movie plays, but the sequence of the animations changes based on the order of the scenes in the Scene panel. The Celebration scene's increasing text and baseballs animation play first, followed by the animation in the Fitness and Exercise scene.

▸ 10. On the Flash Player Application bar, click **File**, and then click **Close** to return to the document.

▸ 11. On the Edit bar, click the **Edit Scene** button to open a menu that lists all the scenes in the document, and then click **Fitness and Exercise**. The Timeline and Stage for the Fitness and Exercise scene appear.

▸ 12. On the Edit bar, click the **Edit Scene** button, and then click **Celebration** to return to the Celebration scene.

▸ 13. Save and close the jacksonsRev.fla document.

Adding a Duplicate Scene

Based on the planning instructions and Aly's sketch shown in Figure 3-12, the new animated banner for Jenny's Oyster Hut will have two different animation sequences. The first sequence will show a fish swimming across the Stage with a sign advertising shrimp specials along with an animation of phrases being displayed being one after the other. The second animation sequence will show a fish swimming back and forth in the ocean and plant leaves moving.

Figure 3-12 Jenny's Oyster Hut partially completed banner

add initial animation of a fish pulling a sign and the phrases "Fried Shrimp" and "Shrimp Scampi" displayed one after the other

animate fish to swim from one side of the Stage to the other

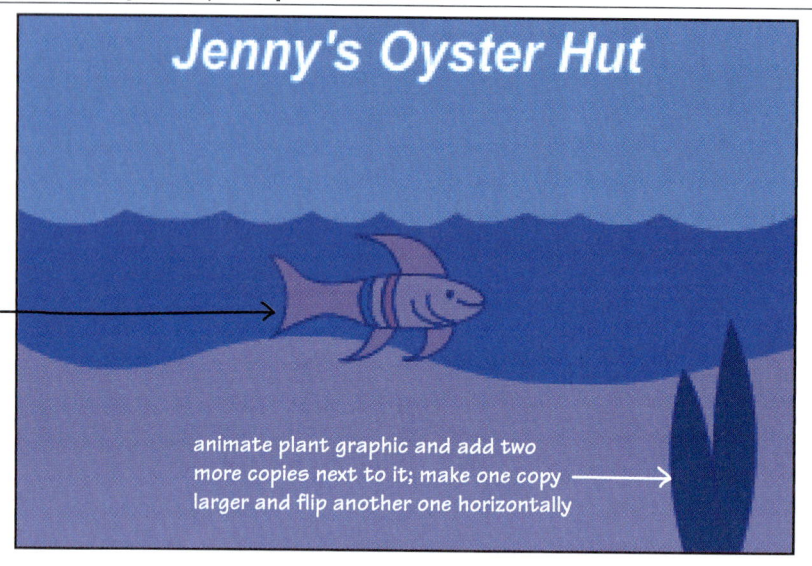

animate plant graphic and add two more copies next to it; make one copy larger and flip another one horizontally

To make it easier to manage the two animation sequences, you will create each in a separate scene. You'll add a new scene to the banner Aly has started by duplicating the initial scene, and then renaming both scenes with more meaningful names.

To duplicate and rename scenes in the Jenny's Oyster Hut banner:

1. Open the **draftBanner.fla** file located in the Tutorial.03\Tutorial folder included with your Data Files, and then Save the document as **jennysBanner** in the same folder. The Scene panel shows one scene named Scene 1.

2. In the Scene panel, click the **Duplicate Scene** button. The duplicate scene appears in the Scene panel with the name Scene 1 copy.

3. In the Scene panel, double-click **Scene 1**, type **Shrimp Specials** as the new name, and then press the **Enter** key to rename the scene. The scene is more descriptively labeled.

4. In the Scene panel, double-click **Scene 1 copy**, type **Fish and Plant**, and then press the **Enter** key. The new scene name appears in the Scene panel, making it simple to distinguish the contents of the scenes.

5. Close the Scene panel, and then save the document.

Now that you have added a new scene to the Jenny's Oyster Hut banner document, you are ready to create the animations. In this session, you learned about the basic elements of Flash that are used in creating animations—layers and frames. You worked with these elements using the Timeline. You also learned how scenes can help you manage a longer or more complex document. In the next session, you will create animations.

Review | Session 3.1 Quick Check

1. What is the purpose of the Timeline?
2. How can you tell which is the current frame in the Timeline?
3. What is the default frame rate for a Flash document?
4. What is the difference between frames and layers?
5. What is a layer folder and what is its purpose?
6. What is a scene?
7. When you have more than one scene, how can you tell in what order the scenes will play?
8. Why would you rename a scene from its default name?

Session 3.2

Creating Animation

Animation is accomplished by displaying the content of different frames one after another. Each frame contains some graphic element that is displayed for a short instant in time. As the content of each frame is displayed in succession, the graphic elements appear to be moving. You can create several types of animations in Flash: motion tweens, classic tweens, shape tweens, and frame-by-frame animations. A **tween** is an animation where you create the beginning content and the ending content, and Flash creates the in-between frames, varying the content evenly in each frame to achieve the animation. The word tween comes from the words in-between. In a frame-by-frame animation, you create or modify the content in each frame of the animation.

The animations of the fish in the new animated banner for Jenny's Oyster Hut will be created with motion tweens. In the second scene, the plant leaves will be animated so that the leaves' tips appear to be moving. This movement will be created with a frame-by-frame animation because you need to specify the positions of the leaves at different moments in time.

Creating a Motion Tween

Tip

If a frame is part of a motion tween, it is called a **tweened frame**; otherwise, it is called a **static frame**.

A **motion tween** is an animation where an object changes its position, rotates, scales in size, or even changes in color. It can also make an object fade in or out. Motion tweens can only be applied to instances of symbols and to text blocks. Motion tweens in Flash are called **object-based animations** because after you create a motion tween, you can easily modify the tween as one entity as you would any other object. You can change the duration of a motion tween, change the direction of the object being animated, or move the motion tween within the Timeline. When you make changes to the motion tween, Flash automatically adjusts the contents of all the frames in the tween. The frames that make up a motion tween are called the **tween span** and are tinted blue in the Timeline. A layer with a motion tween is called a **tween layer** and can contain only one symbol instance known as the **target object**. A target object in a tween can be replaced by a different instance without having to re-create the tween. Any frame where you change the properties of the target object is called a **property keyframe**. Property keyframes contain a black diamond in the Timeline. See Figure 3-13.

Figure 3-13 Motion tween in the Timeline

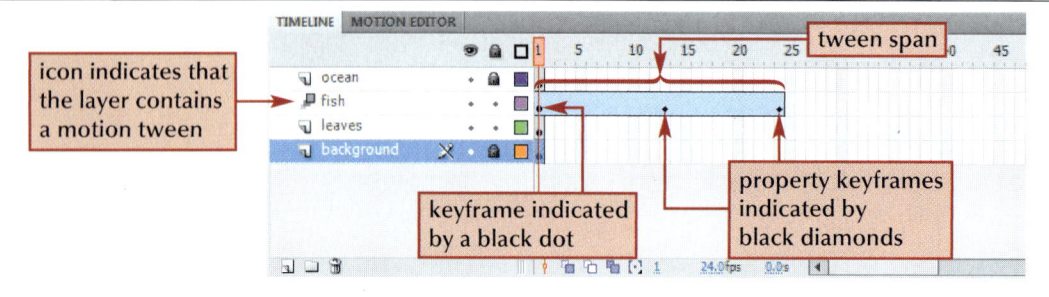

- icon indicates that the layer contains a motion tween
- tween span
- keyframe indicated by a black dot
- property keyframes indicated by black diamonds

The process for creating a motion tween animation is relatively simple. You add an instance of a symbol or a text block in one frame at the start of the animation and then apply a motion tween to the object. Flash creates a tween span in the Timeline that extends for one second or 24 frames when the frame rate is set to its default value. You can only have one object in the layer in which you create the motion tween. If you have more than one object, Flash places the other objects into separate layers. At any point in the tween span, you can modify the object by moving the object to a different position or changing its properties, such as its size, color tint, or color brightness. At each point where you modify the object's properties, a property keyframe is created and Flash varies the content in each intermediate frame to change the object's position or properties slightly from one frame to the next.

After you create a motion tween, the Property inspector provides additional settings, as shown in Figure 3-14. The Ease value makes an object accelerate or decelerate to create a more natural appearance of movement. The Rotate value allows you to specify whether the object should also rotate in the direction you specify during the motion tween. CW causes the object to rotate in a clockwise direction. CCW rotates the object in a counterclockwise direction. You specify how many times to rotate the object throughout the motion tween in the Rotation count box.

Figure 3-14 Motion tween properties

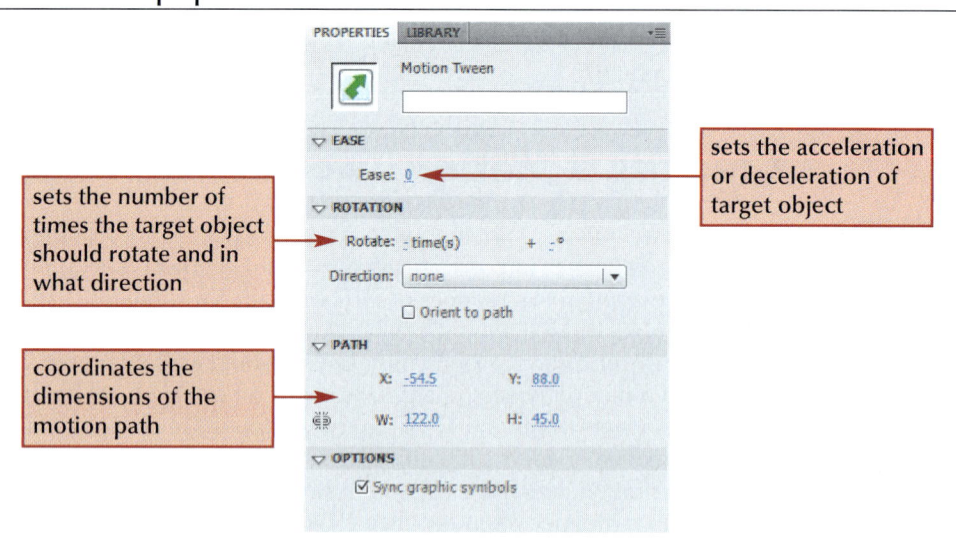

- sets the acceleration or deceleration of target object
- sets the number of times the target object should rotate and in what direction
- coordinates the dimensions of the motion path

In the Fish and Plant scene, you will use two motion tweens to create an animation of a fish swimming from one side of the banner to the other. One motion tween will move the fish across the Stage from left to right and the other motion tween will move the fish from right to left.

Tutorial 3 Creating Animations | Flash | FL 131

To create a motion tween with an instance of the fish symbol:

1. If you took a break after the previous session, make sure the jennysBanner.fla file is open, the workspace is reset to the default Essentials layout, and the Fish and Plant scene is displayed.

2. In the Timeline, in the Show/Hide column of the ocean layer, click the **dot** to hide its contents.

3. In the Timeline, click the **fish** layer to select it, and then convert the fish graphic to a movie clip symbol with the name **fish**. The fish symbol is created.

> **Tip**
> You can press the F8 key on the keyboard to open the Convert to Symbol dialog box.

4. On the Stage, drag the **fish** instance to the pasteboard to the left of the Stage, keeping the instance in the same relative vertical position. The fish will swim in from the left of the Stage.

5. Right-click the **fish** instance, and then click **Create Motion Tween**. A tween span is created from Frame 1 through Frame 24 in the Timeline and the playhead moves to Frame 24. See Figure 3-15.

Figure 3-15   Motion tween created

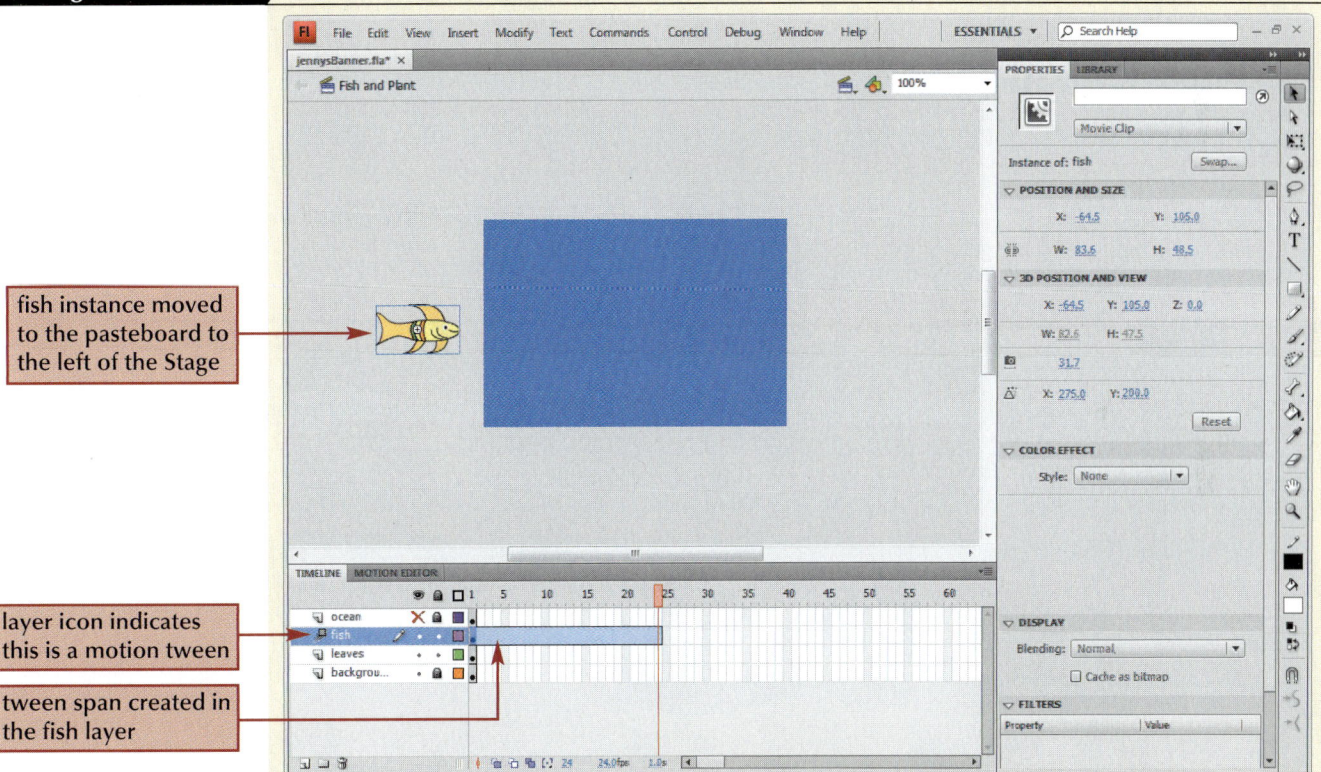

- fish instance moved to the pasteboard to the left of the Stage
- layer icon indicates this is a motion tween
- tween span created in the fish layer

You will extend the tween span before adding frames to the other layers.

6. In the Timeline, drag the right side of the tween span in the fish layer to the right, and then release the mouse button at Frame 50. The motion tween extends through Frame 50. See Figure 3-16.

Figure 3-16 | Tween span extended in the Timeline

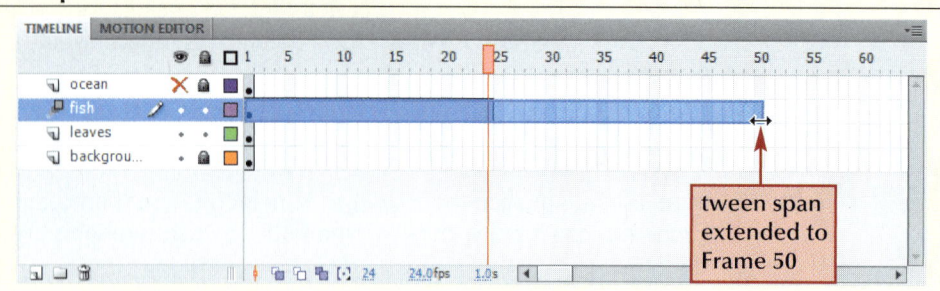

screenshot showing Timeline with tween span extended to Frame 50

The plant and background graphics disappeared when you added the motion tween because these graphics exist only in Frame 1. For these graphics to exist through Frame 50, you need to add frames to their respective layers. You'll extend these layers next.

▸ 7. In the Timeline, click **Frame 50** of the ocean layer, and then, on the Application bar, click **Insert**, point to **Timeline**, and click **Frame**. A regular frame is added at Frame 50. Regular frames are also automatically added between Frames 1 and 50 to fill the empty intervening frames.

▸ 8. Repeat Step 7 for the leaves and background layers to insert a regular frame to extend each layer to Frame 50.

You'll create a motion path for the motion tween next.

▸ 9. Drag the **fish** instance from the left side of the Stage to the right side of the Stage, placing it in the pasteboard in the same relative vertical position. A motion path is created and displayed on the Stage. See Figure 3-17.

Figure 3-17 | Motion path displayed on the Stage

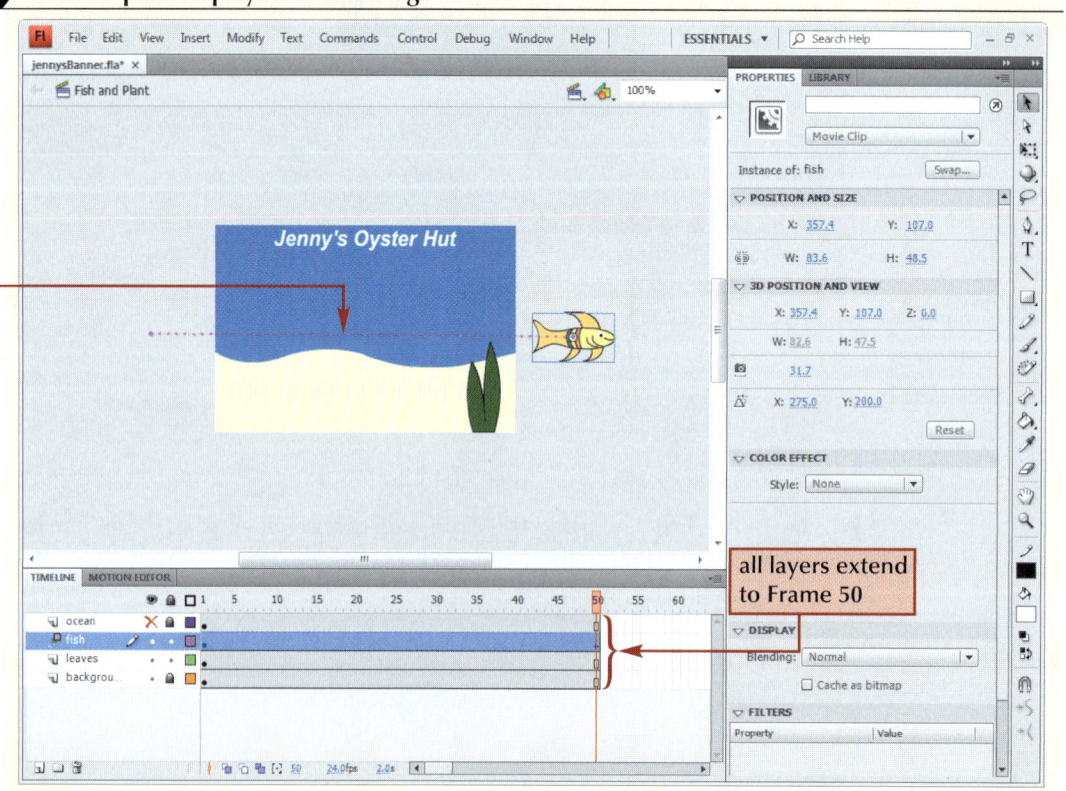

> 10. Press the **Enter** key to play the motion tween. The fish moves across the Stage from left to right following the motion path.

The fish is animated to move across the Stage. Recall from Aly's instructions that the fish will also move from the right side of the banner to the left. To create this part of the animation, you will create another motion tween in a new layer of a fish moving from right to left. You will use another instance of the same fish symbol and will flip the instance so that it faces to the left.

To create a motion tween for a second fish instance:

> 1. In the Timeline, in the Eye column of the fish layer, click the **dot** to hide its contents temporarily.
> 2. In the Timeline, click the **New Layer** button. A new layer is inserted in the Timeline above the fish layer.
> 3. Double-click the name of the new layer to select it, type **second fish**, and then press the **Enter** key to rename the layer.
> 4. Click the **LIBRARY** tab to display the Library panel, and then drag an instance of the **fish** symbol from the Library panel to the pasteboard on the right side of the Stage at the same relative location as the fish instance in the fish layer.
> 5. On the Application bar, click **Modify**, point to **Transform**, and then click **Flip Horizontal**. The fish flips so that it faces to the left.
> 6. Right-click the **fish** instance, and then click **Create Motion Tween**. A tween span is created from Frame 1 through Frame 50 in the Timeline.
> 7. Drag the **fish** instance from the right side of the Stage to the left side of the Stage, placing it in the pasteboard in the same relative vertical position. A motion path is created. See Figure 3-18.

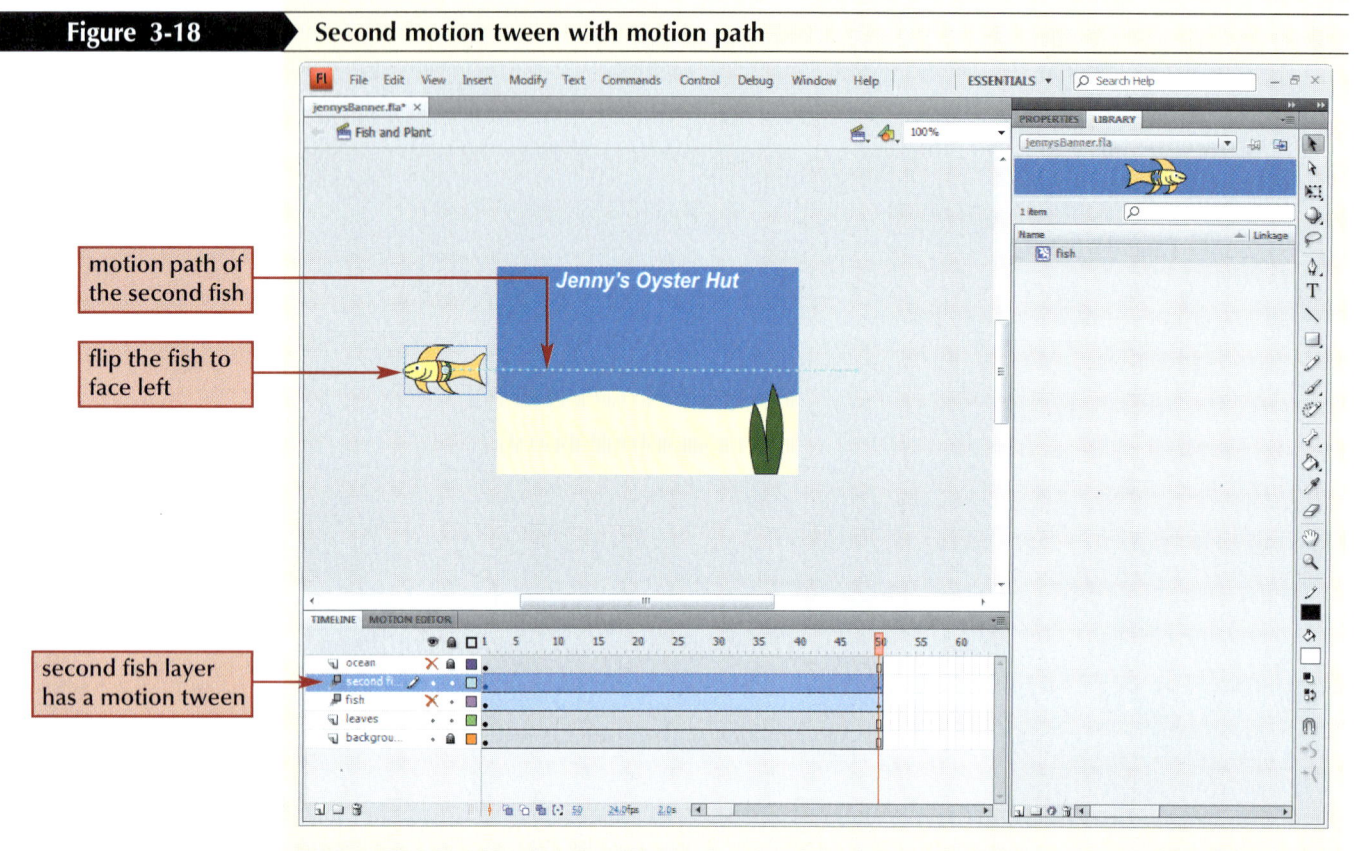

Figure 3-18 Second motion tween with motion path

- motion path of the second fish
- flip the fish to face left
- second fish layer has a motion tween

▶ 8. In the Timeline, in the Show/Hide column for the ocean layer, click the **Hidden layer** icon ✗ to unhide it. Also in the Show/Hide column for the fish layer, click the **Hidden layer** icon ✗ to unhide it.

▶ 9. On the Application bar, click **Control**, and then click **Play**. The first fish instance moves across the Stage from left to right while the second fish instance moves from right to left.

Modifying a Motion Tween

You can modify a motion tween by changing the properties of the target object anywhere within the tween span or by changing the curve of the motion path. When you make changes to the target object or to the motion path, Flash automatically adjusts the rest of the motion tween. If the target object's properties change, Flash adds property keyframes where the change is made.

Tutorial 3 Creating Animations | Flash | FL 135

> **InSight** | **Controlling an Object's Speed in an Animation**
>
> Objects don't usually move at a constant rate of speed. They might start slowly and then accelerate, or they might start quickly and then decelerate. For example, a kicked ball starts moving quickly but then slows toward the end of its movement. To simulate this natural movement, you can adjust a motion tween's Ease value in the Property inspector. A negative value causes the object to begin slowly and accelerate toward the end of the animation. A positive value causes the object to begin rapidly and decelerate toward the end of the animation. For more control over a motion tween, you can use the Custom Ease In/Ease Out dialog box, which displays an adjustable graph representing an object's degree of motion over time.

You'll modify the properties of the motion tweens.

To modify the properties of the motion tweens:

▶ 1. In the Timeline, hide the second fish layer, and then click the **fish** layer to select it. The tween span is selected.

▶ 2. Click the **PROPERTIES** tab to display the Property inspector. You will change the motion tween's properties.

▶ 3. In the Property inspector, drag the Ease value to the right to change the value to **50**. The fish instance will slow down toward the end of the motion tween.

▶ 4. In the Tools panel, click the **Selection** tool, if necessary.

▶ 5. On the Stage, point to the center of the motion path to change the pointer to, and then drag the pointer up slightly to curve the motion path, as shown in Figure 3-19. The fish instance will follow a curved path.

| Figure 3-19 | Motion path being changed |

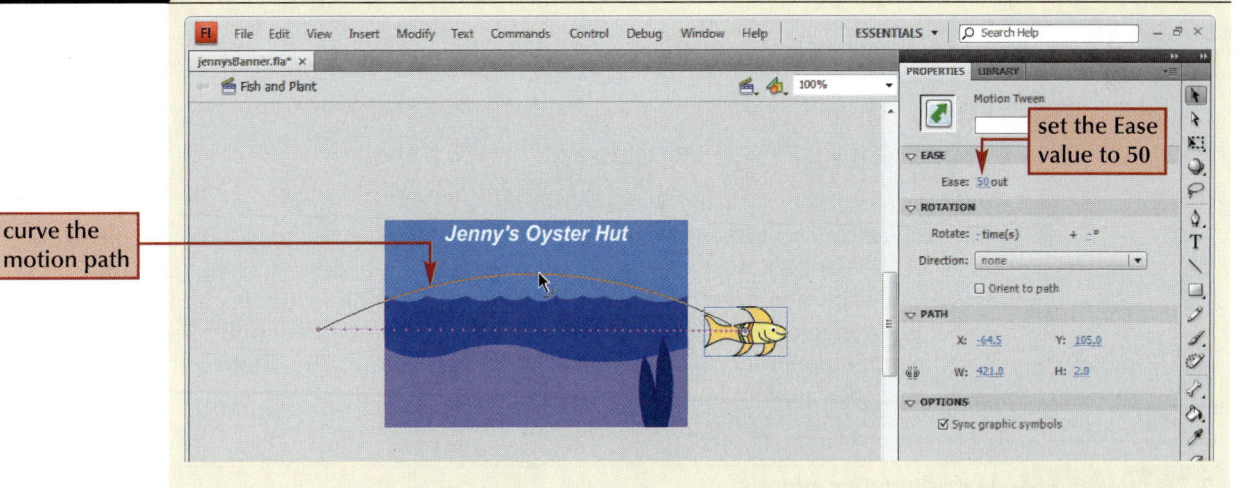

▶ 6. In the Timeline, hide the contents of the fish layer, display the contents of the second fish layer, and then click the second fish layer's name to select it.

▶ 7. In the Property inspector, drag the Ease value to the left to change it to **−50**. The fish instance will move faster toward the end of the motion tween.

▶ 8. Point to the center of the motion path on the Stage and drag it up slightly to curve it. The fish instance will follow a curved path.

Because you don't want both fish animations to occur at the same time, you'll move the tween span for the second fish so that its animation occurs after the first fish animation.

To move the tween span for the second fish:

▶ 1. In the Timeline, point to a frame within the first part of the tween span in the second fish layer, and then drag the span to the right so that its first frame starts on Frame 51. See Figure 3-20.

Figure 3-20	Tween span moved

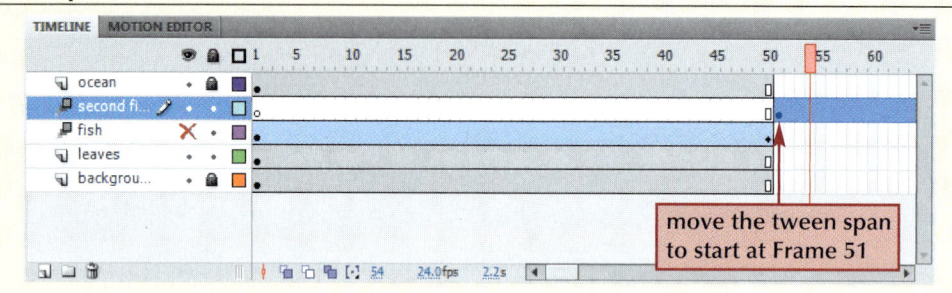

move the tween span to start at Frame 51

▶ 2. In the Timeline, move the playhead to the right to Frame 100.

▶ 3. In the Timeline, add regular frames at Frame 100 to the ocean, leaves, and background layers. The entire movie now occupies 100 frames.

▶ 4. In the Timeline, in the Show/Hide column for the fish layer, click the **Hidden layer** icon ✗ to display the contents of the fish layer.

▶ 5. On the Application bar, click **Control**, and then click **Play**. The first fish moves across the Stage from left to right moving slightly above the water at the center of its path, and then the second fish moves across the Stage from right to left. It also moves slightly above the water at the center of its path.

▶ 6. Save the banner.

Using Motion Presets

The simplest and quickest way to create a motion tween is to apply a motion preset to an object selected on the Stage and let Flash create the necessary elements for the animation. A **motion preset** is a prebuilt motion tween animation. Each motion preset you apply is created on its own layer and the new frames added to the Timeline are based on that motion preset. Figure 3-21 describes some of the 30 default motion preset animations available in the Motion Presets panel.

Figure 3-21	Default motion presets

Motion Preset	Description
bounce-smoosh	Simulates an object bouncing on a surface
fly-in-blur-bottom	Animates an object to fly in from the bottom up; a blurring effect is applied to the object to simulate a rate of speed
fly-in-left	Animates an object to fade in and move from the left to the right
med-bounce	Animates an object to bounce across the Stage
pulse	Animates an object to create a pulsating effect

After you select a motion preset, the preview window in the Motion Presets panel displays a preview of the effect. Figure 3-22 shows an example of the flyin-pause-flyout motion preset.

Figure 3-22 | Example of motion preset

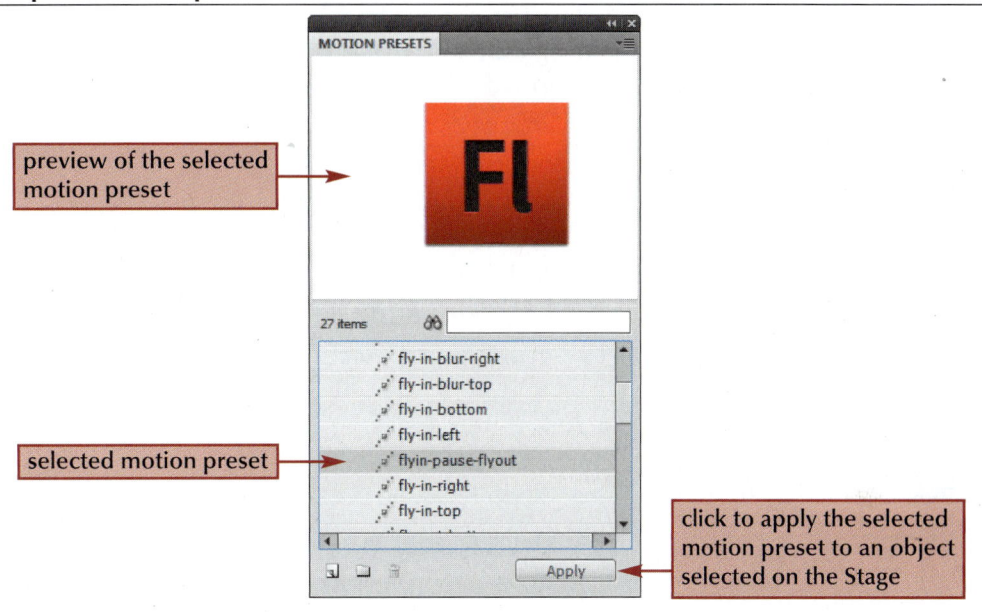

- preview of the selected motion preset
- selected motion preset
- click to apply the selected motion preset to an object selected on the Stage

When you apply a motion preset to an object, Flash converts the layer in which the object resides into a motion tween layer and creates frames with the appropriate content for the animation. If the selected object is not a symbol, Flash prompts you to create a new symbol before applying the motion preset animation.

Applying a Motion Preset Animation

One of the animation sequences for the Jenny's Oyster Hut banner is of a fish moving across the Stage pulling a shrimp specials sign. You will create this animation in the Shrimps special scene using the fly-in-left motion preset. Before you apply the motion preset, you'll draw the sign graphic.

To draw the sign graphic for the animation:

1. On the Edit bar, click the **Edit Scene** button, and then click **Shrimp Specials** to make it the current scene. The plant leaves will not be used in this scene, so you'll delete the leaves layer.

2. In the Timeline, click the **leaves** layer to select it, and then click the **Delete** button. The leaves layer is deleted.

3. In the Timeline, in the Show/Hide column for the ocean layer, click the **dot** to hide the layer temporarily. With the ocean layer hidden, it will be easier to focus on the sign.

4. On the Edit bar, click the **Zoom control arrow**, and then click **200%**. The contents of the Stage are magnified, making it easier to draw the sign.

5. Display the rulers, and then create horizontal guides approximately **140 pixels** and **180 pixels** from the top of the Stage and create vertical guides approximately **100 pixels** and **170 pixels** from the left of the Stage.

FL 138   Flash | Tutorial 3 Creating Animations

▶ 6. In the Tools panel, click the **Rectangle** tool, click the **Black and white** button to change the stroke color to black and the fill color to white, and then, if necessary, click the **Object Drawing** button to deselect it.

▶ 7. In the Property inspector, if necessary, set the Rectangle corner radius to **0**, the stroke height to **1**, and the stroke style to **Solid**.

▶ 8. In the Timeline, select the **fish** layer, and then, on the Stage, draw a rectangle that is approximately **70 pixels** wide and **40 pixels** high below the fish inside the rectangular area formed by the guides. The rectangle will be the sign the fish pulls across the banner. You'll add the words to the sign next.

▶ 9. In the Tools panel, click the **Text** tool, and then, in the Property inspector, if necessary, change the font family to **Arial**, the font style to **Bold**, the point size to **14**, the text (fill) color to **black** (#000000), and the format to **Align center**.

▶ 10. Create a text block inside the rectangle you drew in Step 8, type **Shrimp** in the text block, press the **Enter** key, and then type **Specials!**.

▶ 11. In the Tools panel, click the **Selection** tool, reposition the text block on the Stage so that it is centered within the rectangle, and then click an empty area of the Stage to deselect the text block. See Figure 3-23.

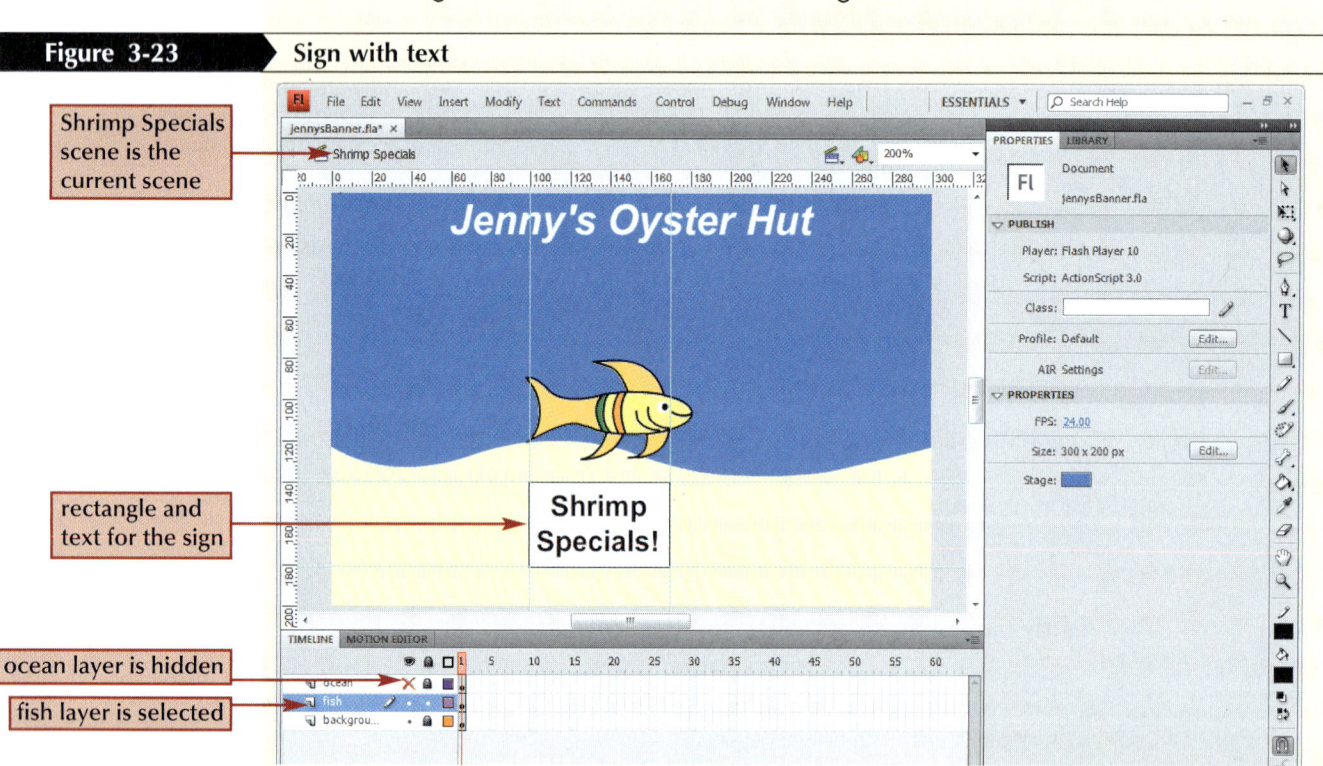

Figure 3-23   Sign with text

- Shrimp Specials scene is the current scene
- rectangle and text for the sign
- ocean layer is hidden
- fish layer is selected

▶ 12. On the Application bar, click **View**, point to **Guides**, and then click **Clear Guides**. The guides are cleared from the Stage.

Tip
You can also press the Q key to select the Free Transform tool.

▶ 13. In the Tools panel, click the **Free Transform** tool, and then draw a marquee around the rectangle. Both the rectangle and the text block are selected. You'll skew the selected rectangle.

Trouble? If the fish is selected, the marquee you drew probably encompassed the fish. Click the pasteboard, and then draw the marquee again, being sure to select only the rectangle and the text block.

▶ 14. In the Tools panel, click the **Rotate and Skew** button, move the pointer over the bottom side of the rectangle until it changes to ⇆, and then drag the bottom side of the rectangle slightly to the left to skew it.

Tutorial 3 Creating Animations | Flash | FL 139

▶ 15. In the Tools panel, click the **Line** tool, and then, if necessary, click the **Snap to Objects** button to select it.

▶ 16. In the Property inspector, set the stroke color to **black** (#000000), the stroke height to **1**, and the stroke style to **Solid**.

▶ 17. On the Stage, draw a line from the fish's lower-left fin to the top of the rectangle, and then draw a line from the fish's lower-right fin to the top of the rectangle. The two lines connect the sign to the fish. See Figure 3-24.

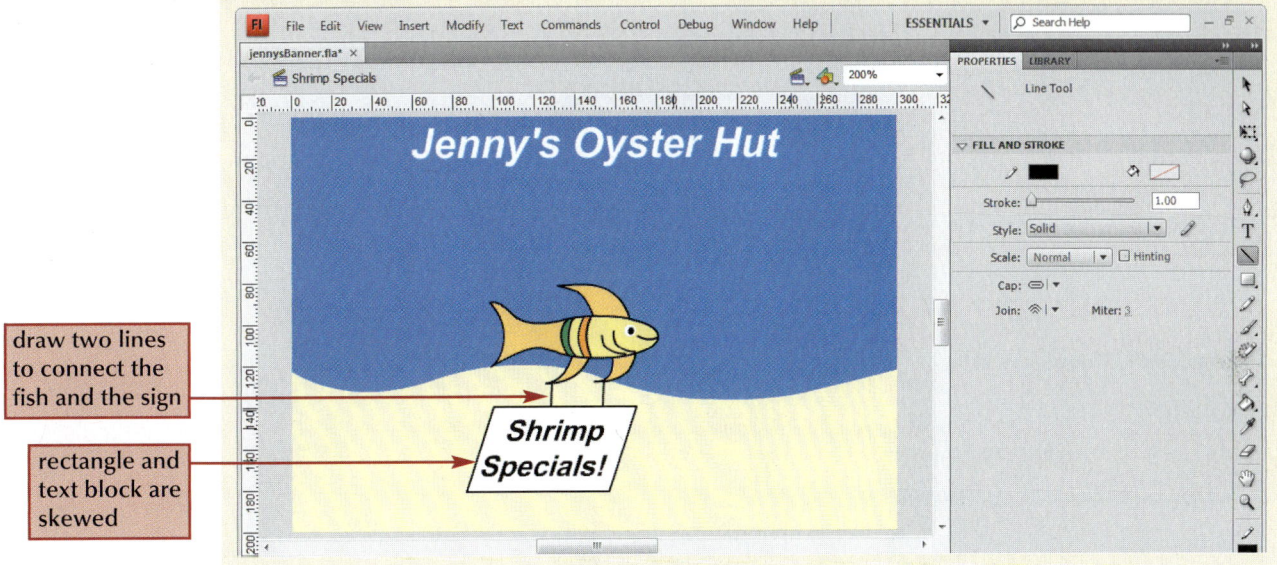

Figure 3-24 Sign attached to the fish

draw two lines to connect the fish and the sign

rectangle and text block are skewed

The graphic of the fish pulling the sign is complete. You are ready to animate the graphic using the fly-in-left motion preset. The animation of the fish and sign will start in the pasteboard to the left of the Stage, move across the Stage, and end near the center of the Stage. Before you can apply the motion preset, you must convert the sign, lines, and fish to a symbol.

To add the fly-in-left motion preset to the Jenny's Oyster Hut banner:

▶ 1. In the Tools panel, click the **Selection** tool, and then draw a marquee around the sign, lines, and fish graphic to select all the objects.

▶ 2. Convert the selected object to a movie clip symbol with the name **fish sign**.

▶ 3. On the Edit bar, click the **Zoom control arrow**, and then click **100%**. The magnification level of the Stage is reduced.

▶ 4. Using the Selection pointer, move the fish instance to the left of the Stage and place it on the pasteboard. The fish will start off the Stage and then will move in to the center of the Stage.

▶ 5. On the Application bar, click **Window**, and then click **Motion Presets**. The Motion Presets panel opens.

▶ 6. If necessary, drag the Motion Presets panel to the right of the Stage.

▶ 7. Double-click the **Default Presets** folder icon, if necessary, to expand the list of motion presets, scroll down, and then click **fly-in-left**. The fly-in-left motion preset is selected and a preview of the animation is displayed in the preview pane of the Motion Presets panel.

8. In the Motion Presets panel, click the **Apply** button. The motion preset is applied to the selected fish sign instance on the Stage. The fish layer's icon in the Timeline changes to indicate that a motion tween has been created, new frames are added to the layer, and the fish sign instance becomes transparent. See Figure 3-25.

Figure 3-25 Motion tween created from a motion preset

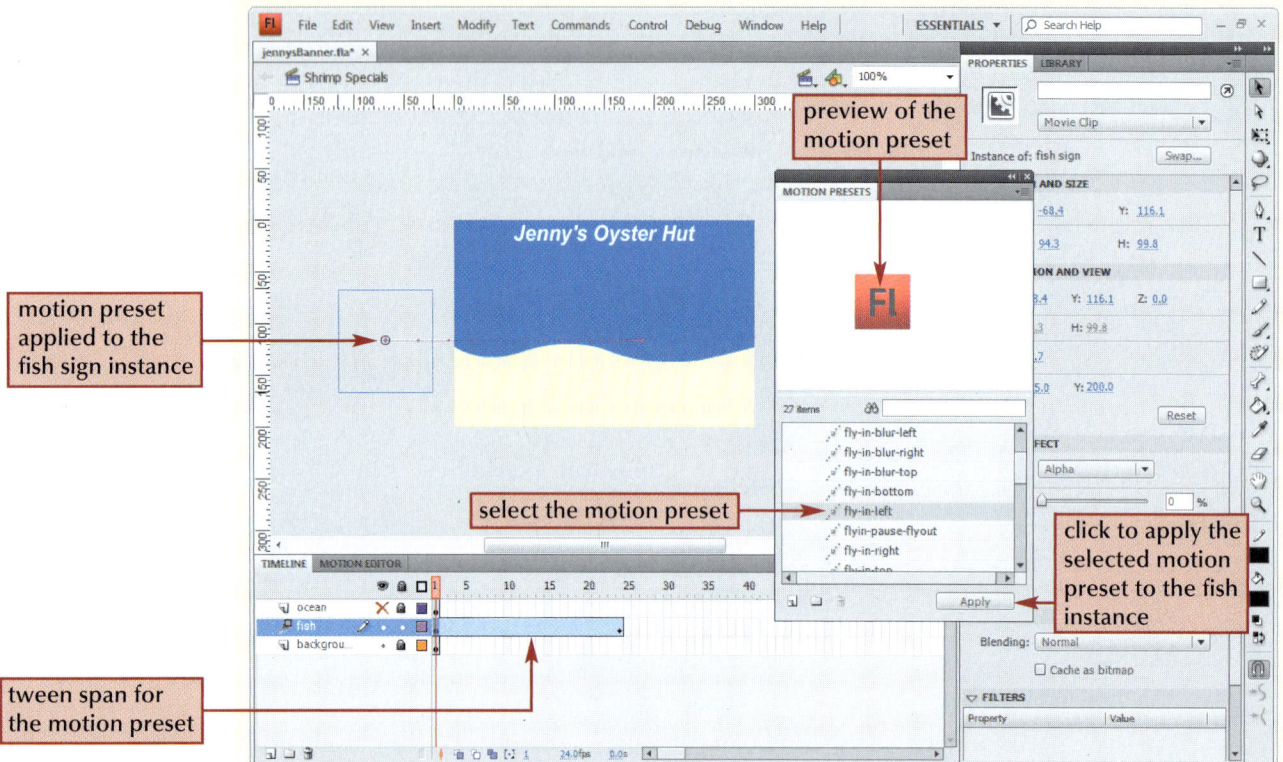

9. Close the Motion Presets panel. You'll complete the animation.

10. In the Timeline, point to the end of the tween span and drag it to the right to extend the tween span to Frame 40.

Tip

You can also press the F5 key to insert a regular frame in the selected location.

11. In the Timeline, in the Show/Hide column for the ocean layer, click the **Hidden layer** icon. The contents of the ocean layer are visible again.

12. In the Timeline, click **Frame 60** of the ocean layer to select it, click **Insert** on the Application bar, point to **Timeline**, and then click **Frame** to insert a regular frame. The graphics in the ocean layer are displayed through Frame 60.

13. Repeat Step 12 for the fish and background layers to display their graphics through Frame 60. All the layers exist for 60 frames, and the contents of all the layers will display 20 frames after the end of the tween span.

14. On the Application bar, click **Control**, and then click **Play**. The fish and sign move across the Stage from the left to the right, starting quickly and slowing down slightly when they reach the end of the animation.

15. Save the banner.

Testing an Animation

After you create a document with animation, you need to test it to make sure it works correctly. To test the document's animation, you have several options. You can play the full animation on the Stage. You can test some or all of the animation by scrubbing the playhead back and forth through the frames, which is useful for testing a short animation sequence. Another way to test a document's animation is to create an SWF file from the document, and then play the file using the Flash Player plug-in. Finally, you can test an animation in a Web page. Flash publishes the document as an SWF file and also creates a Web page. The Web page with the SWF file is displayed in your computer's default browser. The SWF files created when testing the animation are saved in the same folder as the FLA file.

Reference Window | Testing a Document's Animation

- To test an animation on the Stage, on the Application bar, click Control, and then click Play (or press the Enter key).
- To test a few frames of animation, scrub the playhead along the Timeline header.
- To test the animation in a Flash Player window, on the Application bar, click Control, and then click Test Movie.
- To test the animation in a Web page, on the Application bar, click File, point to Publish Preview, and click Default - (HTML).

You will test the banner to see how its various animations work. When you test a document's animation on the Stage, Flash plays only the current scene. To see how all of the scenes work together, you need to test the movie in the Flash Player window. Each scene then plays in sequence with the animation repeating until you close the Flash Player window. You will test the banner document in a Flash Player window so you can see the animations in both scenes.

To test the document's animation in a Flash Player window:

Tip
You can also press the Ctrl+Enter keys to test the movie.

1. On the Application bar, click **Control**, and then click **Test Movie**. The movie plays in a Flash Player window starting with the Shrimp specials scene. You can control how the animation plays.

2. On the Flash Player Application bar, click **Control**, and then click **Loop** to turn off the loop feature and stop the animation from repeating. The animation stops at the current scene.

3. On the Flash Player Application bar, click **File** on the Flash Player, and then click **Close**. The Flash Player window closes.

The fish animations for both scenes of the banner are complete. In the next session, you will add animation to the plant leaves using a frame-by-frame animation. You will also animate text blocks using classic tween animations.

Review | Session 3.2 Quick Check

1. What is a motion preset?
2. True or False? Each motion preset is created in its own layer.
3. After you create a motion tween in your document, how can you change its properties?

4. Briefly describe the difference between a frame-by-frame animation and a motion tween.
5. How many objects can you have on a layer with a motion tween?
6. What type of tweened animation would you create to have an object move from one side of the Stage to the other?
7. Why is it important to test an animation after you create it?

Session 3.3

Creating a Classic Tween

A **classic tween** is another type of tween for creating motion in a document. In a classic tween, you define changes in the content using keyframes. The frames in a classic tween are tinted blue in the Timeline and a black arrow appears between the keyframes. If the final keyframe is missing, a dashed line appears in the layer.

Creating a Classic Tween Animation

You create a classic tween by inserting a symbol instance in one keyframe at the beginning of the tween, creating another keyframe at the end of the tween, and then changing the instance's properties in the ending keyframe. Flash modifies the frames between the keyframes, gradually changing the instance's properties from the beginning keyframe to the ending keyframe. You can only modify the instance in the keyframes and not in the intermediate frames. With a classic tween, there can only be one symbol instance in a layer.

Reference Window | Creating a Classic Tween Animation

- In the Timeline, select a frame, and then, on the Application bar, click Insert, point to Timeline, and then click Keyframe.
- Insert an instance of a symbol in the keyframe.
- In the same layer, select another frame, and then, on the Application bar, click Insert, point to Timeline, and click Keyframe.
- In the second keyframe, modify the instance's properties.
- Select the first keyframe, and then, on the Application bar, click Insert, and click Classic Tween.

or

- Right-click a frame between the keyframes, and then click Create Classic Tween.

The Jenny's Oyster Hut Web site banner should contain an animation that displays the phrases "Fried Shrimp" and "Shrimp Scampi" on the Stage. These phrases will appear one at a time and continuously change from one phrase to another. The animation will be placed in several places in the document. Aly suggests that you create the animation only once, as a symbol, and then create several instances of this symbol in the Shrimp Specials scene.

The registration point of a symbol is usually at the center of the symbol, and it can be used to control how the symbol is animated. To align several symbols in an animation, make each symbol's registration point the same. You can set the registration point when you create the symbol in symbol-editing mode by setting the symbol's X and Y coordinates. You can set the symbol's coordinates in the Info panel, which displays the registration point coordinates when the Registration/Transformation button displays a small circle in its lower-right corner. When the X and Y coordinates are set to 0, the symbol appears on the center of the Stage.

To create the symbol for a classic tween animation:

1. If you took a break after the previous session, make sure that the jennysBanner.fla file is open, the workspace is reset to the default Essentials layout, the Stage magnification is set to 100%, and the Shrimp Specials scene is displayed on the Stage.

2. Create a new movie clip symbol named **Phrases**. The Phrases symbol appears in symbol-editing mode.

3. In the Tools panel, click the **Text** tool T, and then, in the Property inspector, set the font family to **Monotype Corsiva**, the point size to **24**, the text (fill) color to **white (#FFFFFF)**, and the format to **Align center**.

4. On the center of the Stage, create a single-line text block, and then type **Fried Shrimp**.

5. In the Tools panel, click the **Selection** tool to select the text block.

6. On the Application bar, click **Window**, and then click **Info** to open the Info panel.

7. In the Info panel, click the **Registration/Transformation point** button so that it displays a small circle in its lower-right corner, if necessary. You can now set the X and Y coordinates for the symbol.

8. In the X box, type **0**, and then, in the Y box, type **0**, and press the **Enter** key. The text block is centered on the Stage. See Figure 3-26.

> **Tip**
> After you click the Font arrow in the Property inspector, you can type the first letter of the font name to scroll the list to that name.

Figure 3-26 — Settings in the Info panel

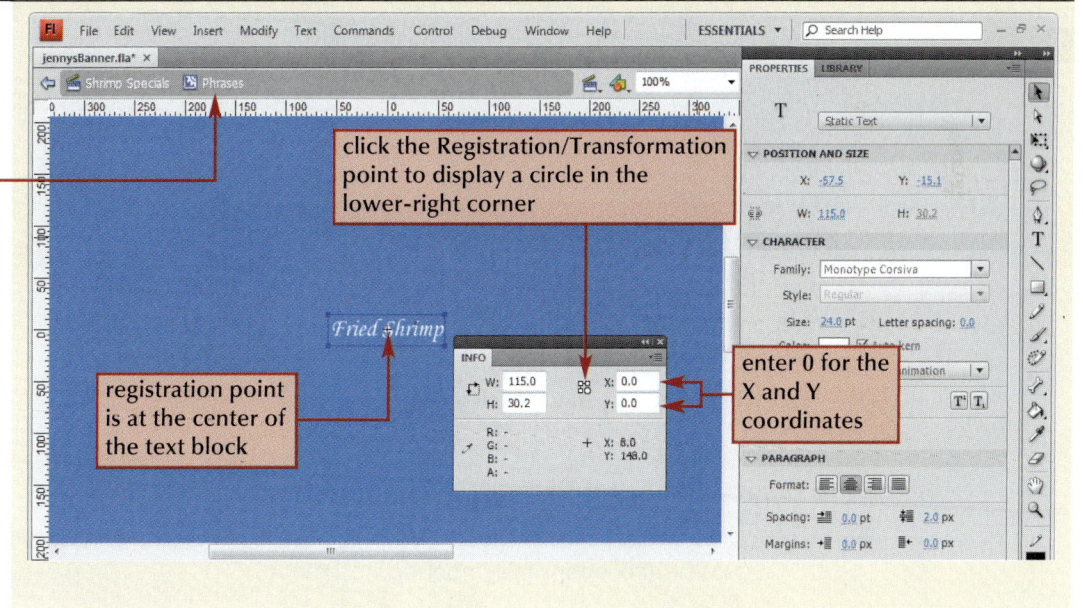

- Phrases symbol is in symbol-editing mode
- click the Registration/Transformation point to display a circle in the lower-right corner
- registration point is at the center of the text block
- enter 0 for the X and Y coordinates

Next, you will convert the text block to a movie clip and duplicate it. To animate the text block using a classic tween, the text block must be a symbol.

To convert the text block to a movie clip and duplicate it:

1. With the text block still selected, convert the text block to a movie clip symbol named **Fried Shrimp text** in the Name box, clicking the **center** registration point in the Convert to Symbol dialog box. The movie clip symbol is created inside the Phrases symbol.

2. Open the Library panel, and then duplicate the Fried Shrimp text symbol, creating a movie clip symbol with the name **Shrimp Scampi text**.

   You will change the text in the duplicate symbol.

3. On the Edit bar, click the **Edit Symbols** button, and then click **Shrimp Scampi text**. The symbol opens in symbol-editing mode.

4. In the Tools panel, if necessary, click the **Selection** tool, double-click the text block, change the text to **Shrimp Scampi**, and then click the **Selection** tool again.

5. In the Info panel, set the X and Y values to **0**, if necessary. See Figure 3-27.

Figure 3-27   Edited Shrimp Scampi text symbol

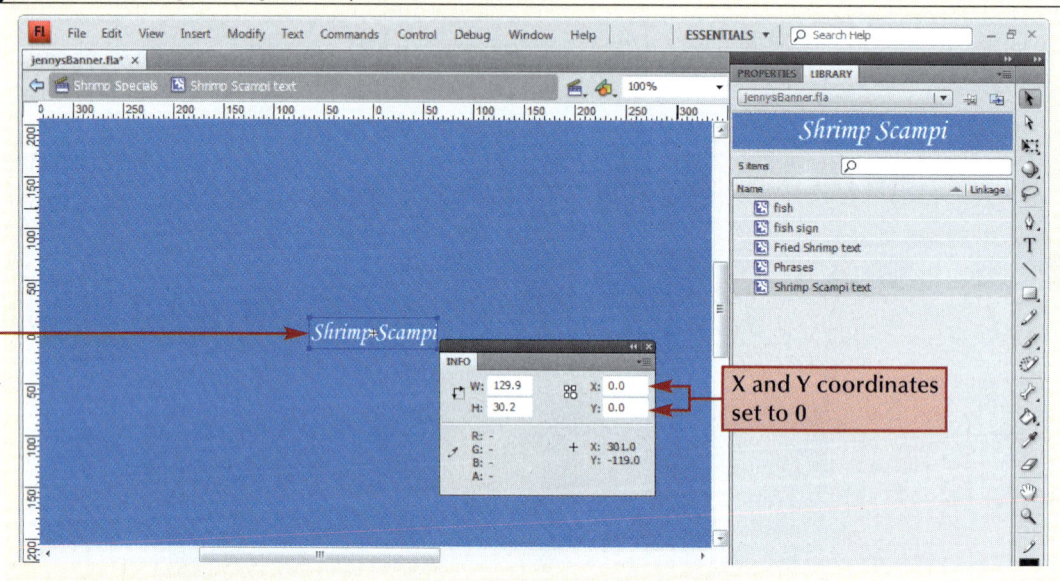

6. Close the Info panel.

You will create the Fried Shrimp text animation.

To create the Fried Shrimp text animation:

1. On the Edit bar, click the **Edit Symbols** button, and then click **Phrases**. The Phrases symbol opens in symbol-editing mode.

2. In the Timeline, rename Layer 1 to **Fried Shrimp**, and then click **Frame 25**.

3. On the Application bar, click **Insert**, point to **Timeline**, and then click **Keyframe**. A keyframe is inserted in Frame 25 and regular frames are added in Frames 2 through 24.

4. In the Tools panel, click the **Selection** tool, if necessary, and then select the **Fried Shrimp text** instance.

5. In the Color Effect section of the Property inspector, click the **Color styles** button, click **Alpha**, type **0** in the Alpha amount box, and then press the **Enter** key. The Fried Shrimp text disappears because an alpha amount of 0% makes an object completely transparent.

6. In the Timeline, right-click **Frame 1** to open the context menu, and then click **Create Classic Tween**. The classic tween is created between Frames 1 and 25. See Figure 3-28.

Figure 3-28 Classic tween created

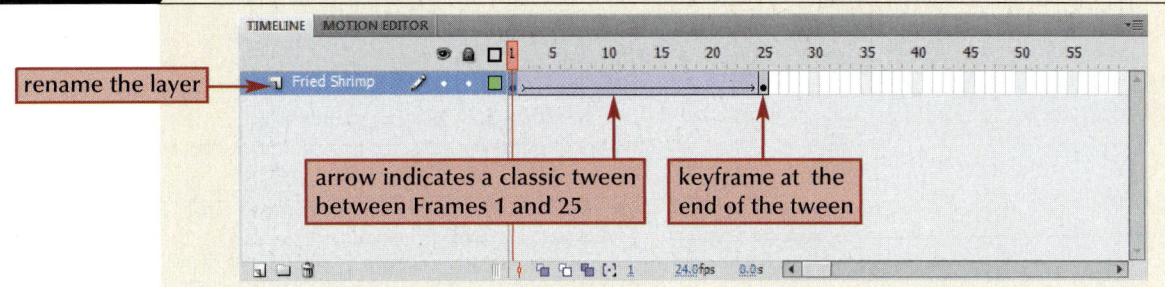

rename the layer
arrow indicates a classic tween between Frames 1 and 25
keyframe at the end of the tween

7. Press the **Enter** key to test the animation. The Fried Shrimp text instance fades out throughout the animation.

You need to create a similar animation for the next phrase. Instead of repeating all of these steps in a new layer, you can copy the frames in the Fried Shrimp layer and paste them into a new layer. Then, you can swap the instances of the Fried Shrimp text symbol with instances of the Shrimp Scampi text symbol. Recall that a classic tween has a beginning keyframe and an ending keyframe and that each keyframe has an instance of a symbol. When swapping instances of a symbol in a classic tween, you need to swap the instances in both the beginning and ending keyframes. Finally, you will reposition the frames that contain the classic tween so that the animation for the second phrase starts later than the animation for the first phrase.

To create a classic tween animation for the Shrimp Scampi text symbol:

1. In the Timeline, click the **Fried Shrimp** layer name to select all of its frames.

2. Right-click the selected frames, and then click **Copy Frames**. The frames are copied to the Windows Clipboard.

3. On the Application bar, click **Insert**, point to **Timeline**, and then click **Layer** to insert a new layer.

4. In the Timeline, rename Layer 2 to **Shrimp Scampi**, and then click the **Shrimp Scampi** layer name to select all of its frames.

5. Right-click the selected frames, and then click **Paste Frames**. The frames containing the Fried Shrimp text animation are pasted into the Shrimp Scampi layer.

You need to swap the Fried Shrimp text symbol with the Shrimp Scampi text symbol.

6. In the Timeline, click **Frame 1** of the Shrimp Scampi layer, and then click the instance of the Fried Shrimp text symbol at the center of the Stage. You can tell the instance is selected because the Property inspector shows "Instance of: Fried Shrimp text."

7. In the Property inspector, click the **Swap** button to open the Swap Symbol dialog box, and then click **Shrimp Scampi text**. See Figure 3-29.

Tip

You can use the Duplicate Symbol button in the Swap Symbol dialog box to make a copy of a symbol that is stored in the document's library.

Figure 3-29   Swap Symbol dialog box

preview of the selected symbol

select the Shrimp Scampi text symbol

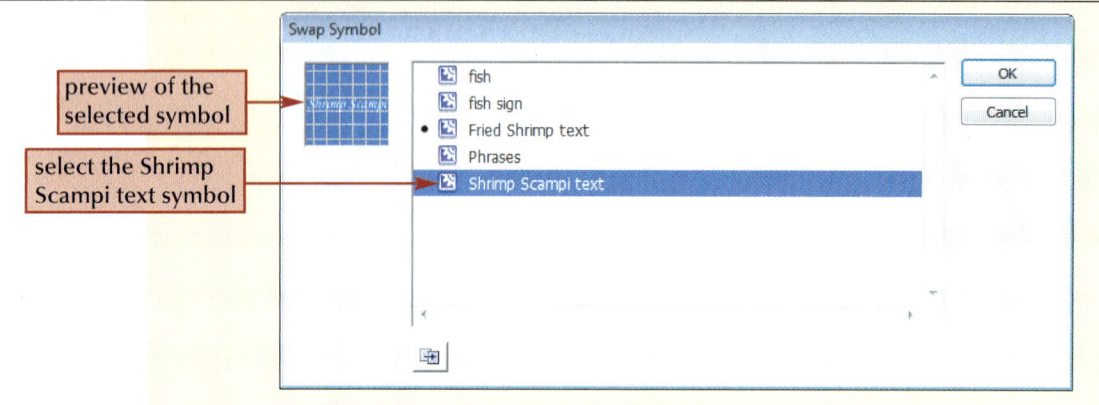

▶ 8. Click the **OK** button. The Fried Shrimp text instance is replaced with the Shrimp Scampi text instance. The text blocks for the two layers overlap on the Stage, so one word appears on top of the other. You will fix this in the next set of steps.

Next, you'll swap the instance in the second keyframe.

▶ 9. In the Timeline, click **Frame 25** of the Shrimp Scampi layer, and then click the blue outline of the **Fried Shrimp text** instance at the center of the Stage. The words are not visible because you set the alpha amount to 0% at this keyframe.

▶ 10. In the Property inspector, click the **Swap** button to open the Swap Symbol dialog box, click **Shrimp Scampi text**, and then click the **OK** button. The Fried Shrimp text instance is replaced with the Shrimp Scampi text instance.

The animation in the Shrimp Scampi layer works the same as the one in the Fried Shrimp layer, except that the symbol being animated is the Shrimp Scampi text symbol and not the Fried Shrimp text symbol. Instead of having to repeat the steps to create an animation in the new layer, you copied an existing animation and swapped the instances in the keyframes.

Now that both animations are complete, you need to reposition the Shrimp Scampi text animation so that the two animations do not occur at the same time. You want the Fried Shrimp text animation to start first, followed by the Shrimp Scampi text animation. This means that the Shrimp Scampi text animation will begin at Frame 26 after the Fried Shrimp text animation ends. The Shrimp Scampi text animation's 25 frames will end at Frame 50. You can easily change the location of frames within a layer.

To reposition the frames within the Shrimp Scampi layer:

▶ 1. In the Timeline, click the **Shrimp Scampi** layer name to select all the frames that make up the Shrimp Scampi text animation.

▶ 2. Drag the selected frames to the right so that the first keyframe starts on **Frame 26** of the Shrimp Scampi layer, as shown in Figure 3-30.

Tutorial 3 Creating Animations | Flash **FL 147**

Figure 3-30 | Selected frames being moved

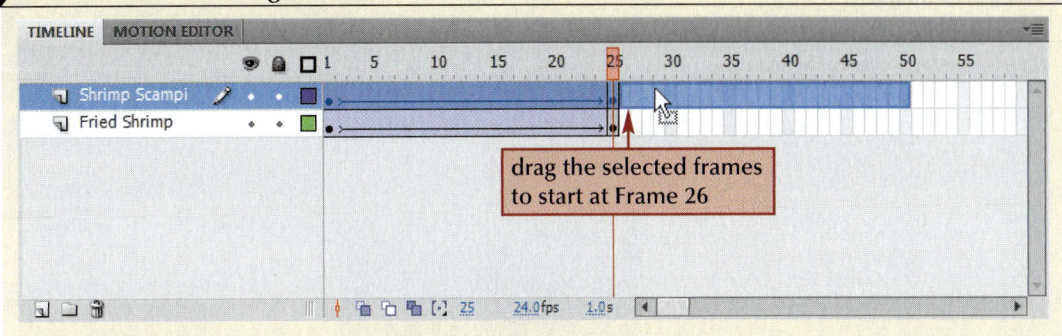

drag the selected frames to start at Frame 26

> 3. Release the mouse button. The selected frames start on Frame 26 and end on Frame 50.
>
> 4. On the Application bar, click **Control**, and then click **Rewind** to move the playhead to Frame 1.
>
> 5. Press the **Enter** key. The phrases appear and fade out in turn as the animation plays.
>
> 6. On the Edit bar, click the **Shrimp Specials** scene to exit symbol-editing mode and return to the Shrimp Specials scene.

Tip

You can also press the Shift+, keys to rewind the movie to Frame 1.

The Phrases symbol is complete. You will insert two instances of the Phrases symbol onto the Stage for the Shrimp Specials scene.

To insert instances of the Phrases symbol and test the Shrimp Specials scene:

> 1. In the Timeline of the Shrimp Specials scene, insert a new layer above the ocean layer, name the layer **Phrases**, and then click **Frame 1** of the Phrases layer.
>
> 2. Drag two instances of the **Phrases** symbol from the Library panel to the bottom part of the Stage. See Figure 3-31.

FL 148 Flash | Tutorial 3 Creating Animations

Figure 3-31 | Phrases graphic symbol instances

instances of the Phrases symbol

instances added to the Phrases layer

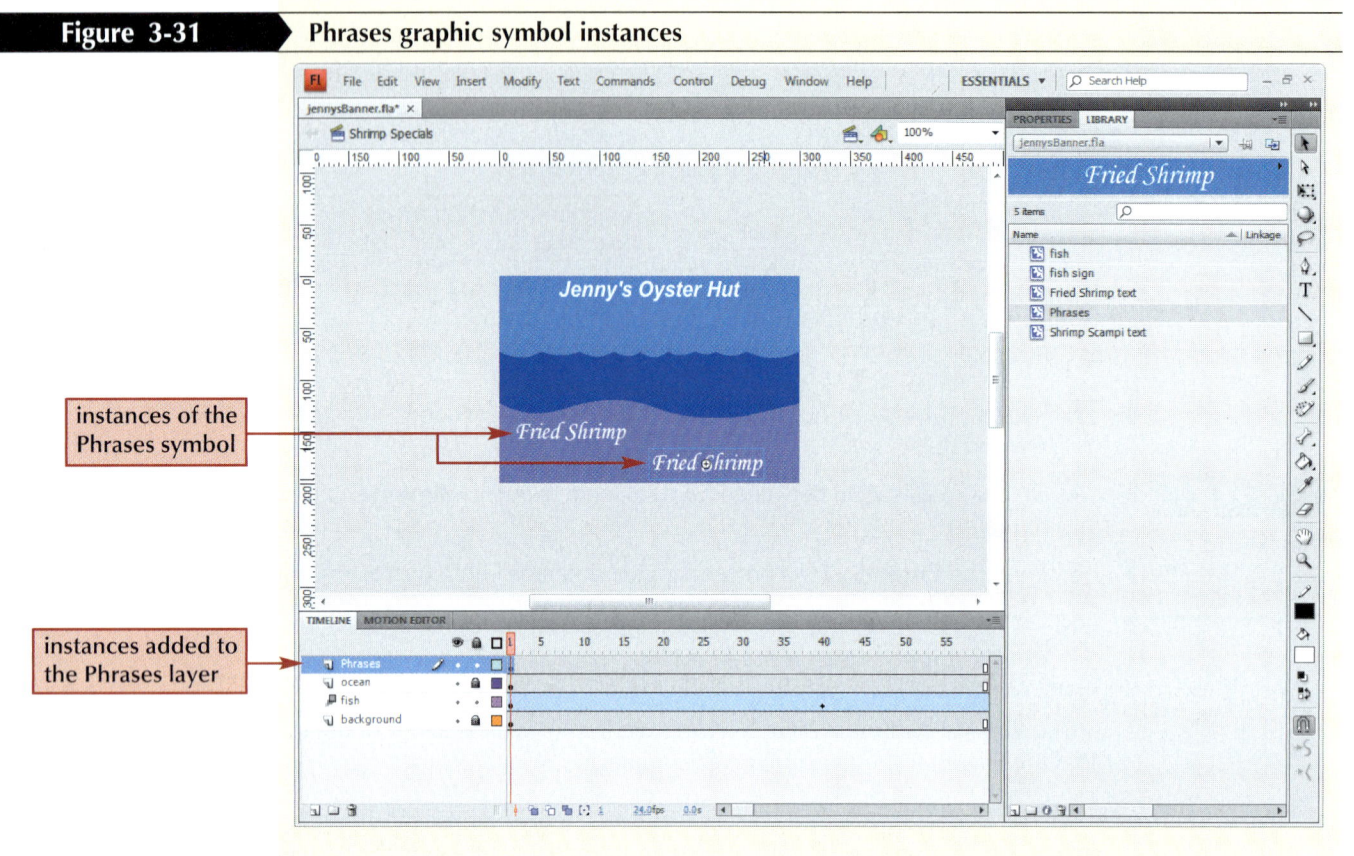

▶ 3. On the Application bar, click **Control**, and then click **Play**. The Phrases instances do not display their animations on the Stage. You will test the scene's animation in a Flash Player window.

▶ 4. On the Application bar, click **Control**, and then click **Test Scene**. The scene opens in a Flash Player window and the fish move across the Stage as the Phrases instances display the two text blocks in turn.

▶ 5. On the Flash Player Application bar, click **File**, and then click **Close**. The Flash Player window closes.

The two instances of the Phrases symbol display their respective text blocks at the same time. Aly wants you to change one of the instances so that its animation starts at a different frame and is not in sync with the other instance. You cannot change the starting frame of a movie clip instance so you will need to convert it to a graphic instance.

Using Graphic Symbols in Animations

Movie clip instances always start playing from their first frame. With a graphic instance, however, you can specify which of its frames to play first. As a result, if you create an animation with a graphic symbol and then create several instances of the symbol, each instance can have a different starting frame. For example, one instance can start playing at Frame 1 of its Timeline while another instance can start playing at Frame 20. Using this technique, you can create multiple instances of one graphic symbol in the same scene and have each instance exhibit a different behavior.

Both movie clip and graphic symbols have their own Timelines. With a movie clip symbol, the frames in its Timeline play independently of the document's main Timeline. However, with a graphic symbol, the frames in its Timeline are synchronized with the document's main Timeline. For example, suppose you insert a movie clip instance that contains an animation with 10 frames into a document whose main Timeline has only one frame. Even though the main Timeline contains only one frame, the movie clip's 10 frames still play in their entirety. But, if you insert a graphic instance that contains an animation with 10 frames into a document whose main Timeline has only one frame, then only one frame of the graphic instance will play. If you want all 10 frames of the graphic instance to play, you must extend the length of the document's main Timeline to at least 10 frames. Graphic symbols are useful when you want to synchronize the animations in the symbol to that of the main Timeline.

Unlike movie clip symbol instances, graphic symbol instances display their animation when you scrub the playhead in the document's main Timeline or play the main Timeline's animation on the Stage. You don't need to test the document in the Flash Player to see the animations contained in instances of graphic symbols as you do with animations contained in instances of movie clips, which appear as static objects when played on the Stage. This occurs because the frames of graphic symbols are synchronized with the document's main Timeline, while the frames of a movie clip symbol are independent of the document's main Timeline.

When you select a symbol instance on the Stage, you can use the Property inspector to change the instance's type without changing the symbol's type in the document's library. For example, a movie clip symbol instance on the Stage can be changed to a graphic instance. The instance will then exhibit all the properties of a graphic symbol instance even though the original symbol is still a movie clip.

When you select a graphic instance, you can indicate in which frame you want the instance's animation to begin by entering a value in the First frame box in the Property inspector.

You can also specify how you want the instance's animation to play in the Options drop-down list. The Loop option plays the animation continuously. The Play Once option plays the animation only one time starting with the frame specified in the First frame box. The Single Frame option plays only the frame specified in the First frame box.

You will change one of the Phrases movie clip instances on the Stage to a graphic instance and then change its starting frame.

To change a Phrases symbol instance to a graphic instance:

▶ 1. On the right side of the Stage, select the **Phrases** symbol instance, if necessary.

▶ 2. In the Property inspector, click the **Instance behavior** button, and then point to **Graphic**. See Figure 3-32. You want to change the Phrases instance behavior to the graphic type.

| Figure 3-32 | Instance behavior being changed |

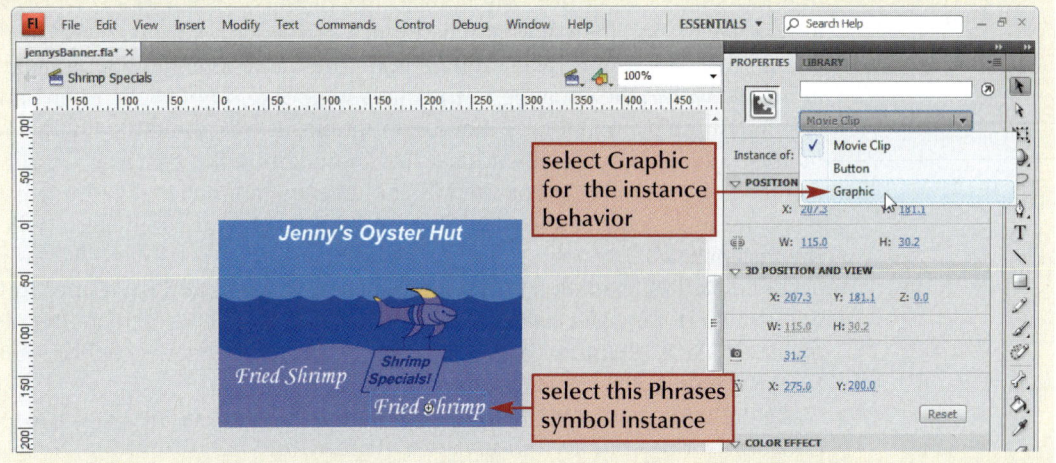

▶ 3. Click **Graphic**. The Phrases instance behavior changes to graphic.

▶ 4. In the Looping section of the Property inspector, type **20** in the First frame box. This instance will start after the first classic tween begins, but before the second classic tween begins in the Phrases animation.

▶ 5. In the Property inspector, make sure the instance's option is set to **Loop**. The animation will play continuously. The Fried Shrimp text is displayed slightly faded.

▶ 6. On the Application bar, click **Control**, and click **Test Scene**. The scene opens in a Flash Player window and the Phrases instances each start at a different frame as they fade in and out.

▶ 7. On the Flash Player Application bar, click **File**, and then click **Close**. The Flash Player window closes.

▶ 8. Save the banner.

Creating Frame-by-Frame Animations

To create a **frame-by-frame animation**, you need to create the graphic elements of the animation for each of its individual frames. If, for example, the animation will have 15 frames, you need to create the content for each of the 15 frames. Some of the content can be the same from one frame to the next, but other content can be slightly modified. As the frames are displayed one after another, the perception of movement is achieved. To create a frame-by-frame animation, you start with a graphic object in the initial frame. Then, for each place in the animation where you need the object to change, you add a keyframe. Depending on the animation, every frame can be a keyframe or you can have intervening frames where the graphic objects do not change. As you add keyframes, you change the position of the graphic object. After you have created all of the keyframes, you test the animation.

| InSight | Choosing When to Create Frame-by-Frame Animations |

Avoid creating frame-by-frame animations when possible because frame-by-frame animations produce larger file sizes. A frame-by-frame animation usually has multiple keyframes and Flash stores the contents of every keyframe. In a motion tween animation, Flash only stores the contents of the target object and the property keyframes.

The Fish and Plant scene of the Jenny's Oyster Hut banner contains a graphic element that looks like a plant. You will convert this plant graphic into a symbol with a movie clip behavior, and then animate the plant's leaves so that they appear to be moving in the ocean. You will do this by creating a frame-by-frame animation. The plant's leaves will be animated within the Timeline of the plant symbol and not in the main Timeline of the document. Recall that a movie clip symbol has its own Timeline that is independent of the document's Timeline. By adding the animation in the symbol's Timeline, every instance of the symbol automatically includes the animation. This means that each plant instance you create on the Stage will have the same animation built in as part of the instance.

To create the animation of the plant leaves, you will add keyframes to Frames 5, 10, 15, and 20 of the plant leaves layer. This will be sufficient to create the movement of the leaves. In each keyframe, you will move the tips of the leaves slightly, first in one direction and then in the opposite direction.

Before you can create the frame-by-frame animation of the plant leaves, you need to convert the object to a symbol.

Tutorial 3 Creating Animations | Flash **FL 151**

To convert the leave shapes in the Fish and Plant scene to a symbol:

1. On the Edit bar, click the **Edit Scene** button, and the click **Fish and Plant** scene to make it the current scene. You will create a symbol of the leaves graphic.
2. In the Timeline, in the Show/Hide column for the ocean layer, click the **dot** to hide the layer temporarily.
3. In the Tools panel, click the **Selection** tool, if necessary, and then, on the Stage, select the leaves graphic, including both its stroke and its fill.
4. Convert the leaves graphic to a movie clip symbol named **leaves**.

You are ready to animate the leaves symbol. You first need to select the symbol from the Library panel so you can edit it to create an animation within its Timeline.

To create a frame-by-frame animation of the leaves symbol:

1. In the Library panel, double-click the **leaves** symbol icon. The symbol opens in symbol-editing mode.
2. In the symbol's Timeline, click **Frame 5**. This is the frame where you want to change the animation. See Figure 3-33.

| Figure 3-33 | Leaves symbol in symbol-editing mode |

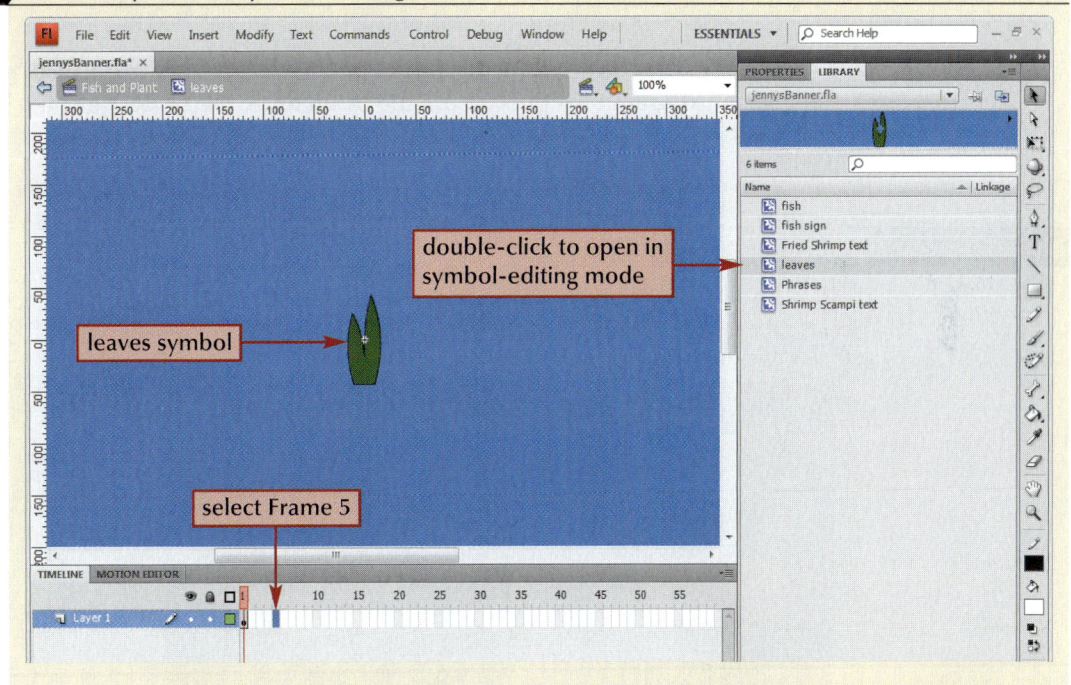

3. Click **Insert** on the Application bar, point to **Timeline**, and then click **Keyframe**. A keyframe is inserted in Frame 5 and regular frames are added to Frames 2, 3, and 4 to fill the empty intervening frames. The leaves graphic is automatically copied to all the new frames. See Figure 3-34.

> **Tip**
> You can also press the F6 key on the keyboard to insert a keyframe at the selected location.

Figure 3-34 Keyframe added to the leaves symbol in the Timeline

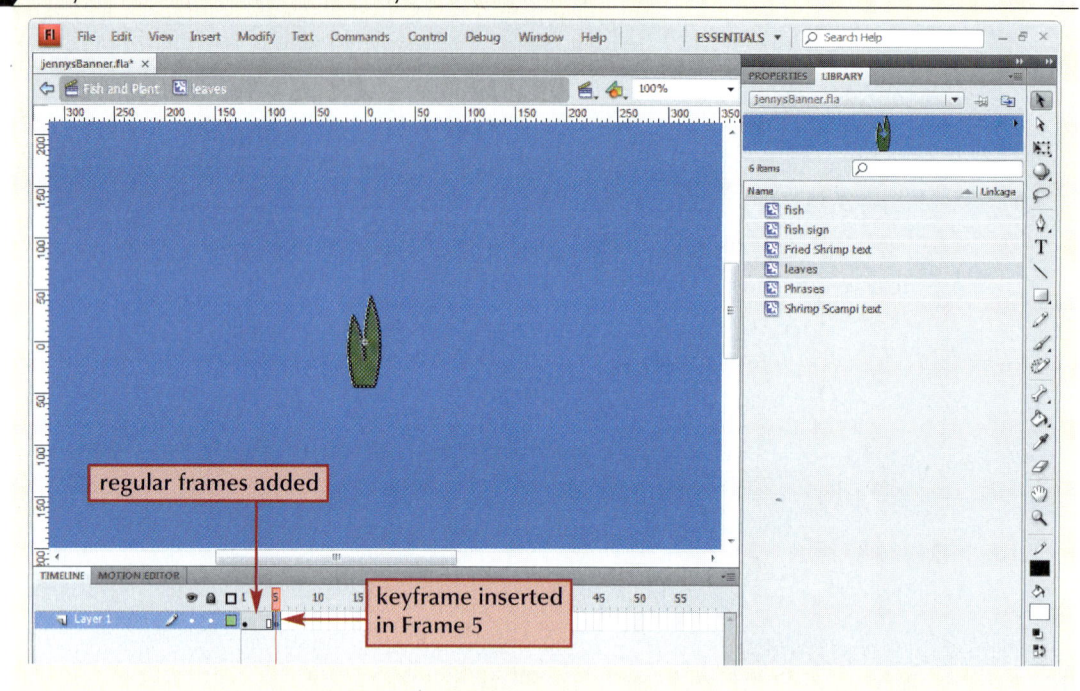

regular frames added

keyframe inserted in Frame 5

In Frame 5, you'll move the tips of the leaves slightly to the right.

▸ 4. In the Tools panel, click the **Selection** tool if necessary, click another area of the Stage to deselect the plant, move the pointer over the tip of one of the leaves until it changes to , and then click and drag the tip of the leaf slightly to the right.

▸ 5. Repeat Step 4 to reposition the other leaf's tip slightly to the right. See Figure 3-35.

Figure 3-35 Tips of plant leaves modified

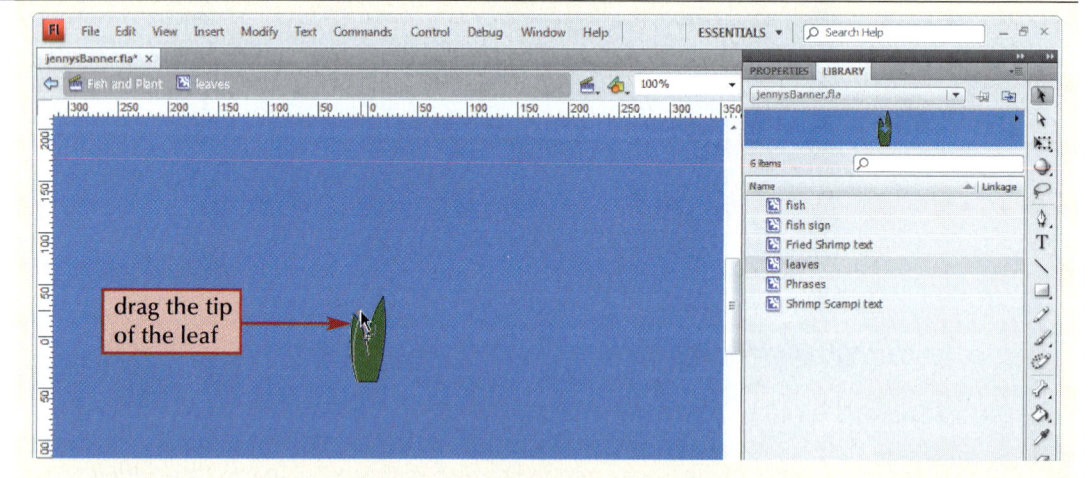

drag the tip of the leaf

You will repeat this process to add a keyframe every fifth frame and reposition the leaves' tips farther right, then back left, and finally back to their starting positions.

▸ 6. Click **Frame 10**, insert a keyframe, and then repeat Steps 4 and 5 to reposition both of the leaves' tips slightly more to the right.

▸ 7. Click **Frame 15**, insert a keyframe, and then repeat Steps 4 and 5 to reposition the leaves' tips back slightly to the left.

Tutorial 3 Creating Animations | Flash | FL 153

▸ 8. Click **Frame 20**, insert a keyframe, and then repeat Steps 4 and 5 to move the leaves' tips slightly more to the left to almost the same positions where they started in Frame 1.

▸ 9. Scrub the playhead through these frames to get a sense of what the animation looks like. This frame-by-frame animation is complete.

▸ 10. On the Edit bar, click the **Fish and Plant** link to exit symbol-editing mode.

You have created a frame-by-frame animation within the leaves symbol. Because the animation was created within the symbol's Timeline, each instance of the symbol has the same animation. You can, therefore, place several instances of the leaves symbol in the document and all the instances will be animated.

Recall from Aly's instructions that the banner should have three animated plants in the lower-right corner of the Stage. Because one instance of the animated plant leaves is already on the Stage, you need to add two more instances. The second instance needs to be modified to make it larger than the first, and the third instance needs to be modified so its leaves point to the right.

To create and modify two instances of the animated leaves symbol:

▸ 1. On the Edit bar, click the **Zoom control arrow**, and then click **Show All**. All the contents on the Stage and pasteboard are displayed.

▸ 2. In the Timeline, select the **leaves** layer, if necessary, and then drag an instance of the **leaves** symbol from the Library panel to the Stage and place it to the left of the existing instance.

▸ 3. In the Tools panel, click the **Free Transform** tool, and then click the **Scale** button.

▸ 4. On the Stage, drag one corner of the bounding box around the plant to make this leaves instance slightly larger than the other instance. See Figure 3-36.

Figure 3-36 | Enlarged leaves instance

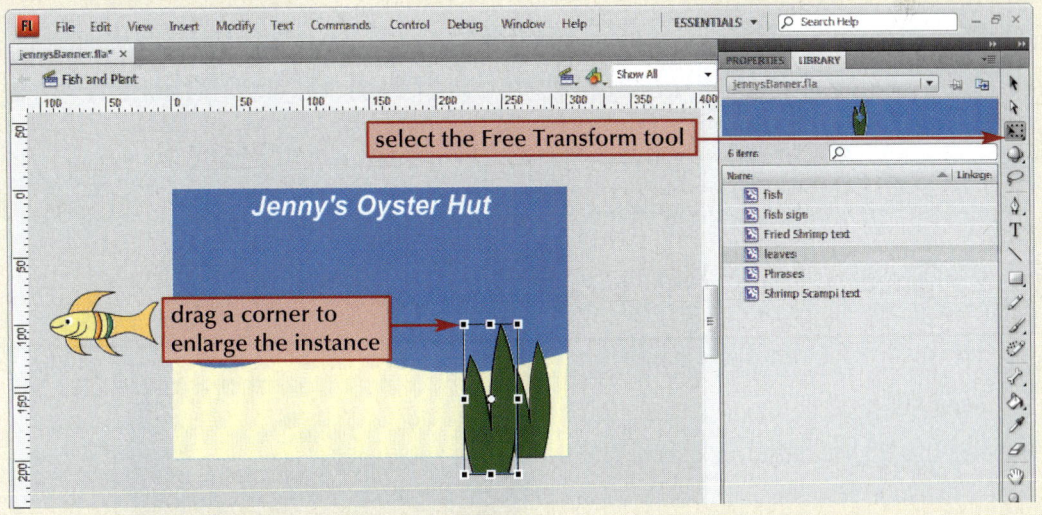

▸ 5. In the Tools panel, click the **Selection** tool to select it, and then reposition this instance as needed to align it with the bottom edge of the other leaves instance.

▸ 6. Drag another instance of the **leaves** symbol from the Library panel to the Stage and place it to the left of the larger leaves instance.

▶ 7. With the third leaves instance still selected on the Stage, on the Application bar, click **Modify**, point to **Transform**, and then click **Flip Horizontal**. The leaves of the instance now face to the right.

▶ 8. If necessary, line up the bottoms of the leaves with the bottom part of the Stage. See Figure 3-37.

Figure 3-37   Three leaves instances arranged on the Stage

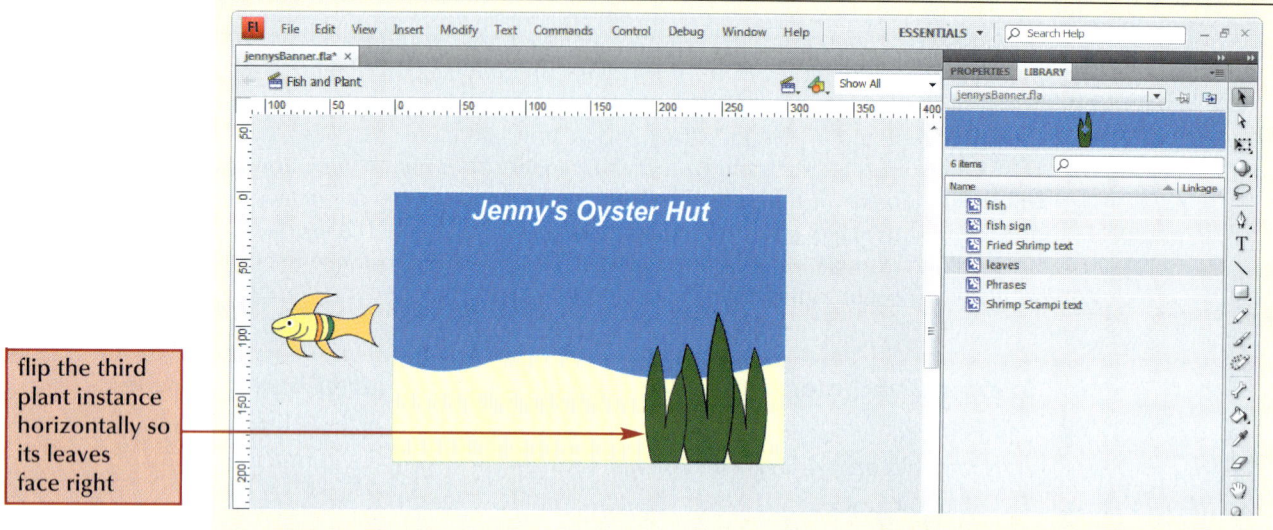

flip the third plant instance horizontally so its leaves face right

▶ 9. In the Timeline, in the Show/Hide column of the ocean layer, click the **Hidden layer** button ✗. The contents of the ocean layer reappear on the Stage.

▶ 10. Save the banner.

Because the leaves symbol's animation is within its own Timeline, you need to test the animation as an SWF file. The movie will appear in a Flash Player window. If you test the animation on the Stage, the leaves symbol's animation will not play. You can also test the animation in a Web page.

To test the document's animation in a Flash Player window and a Web page:

▶ 1. On the Application bar, click **Control**, and then click **Test Movie**. The movie plays in a Flash Player window starting with the Shrimp specials scene. The leaves display their animation, as shown in Figure 3-38.

Figure 3-38   Flash Player window with the leaves animation

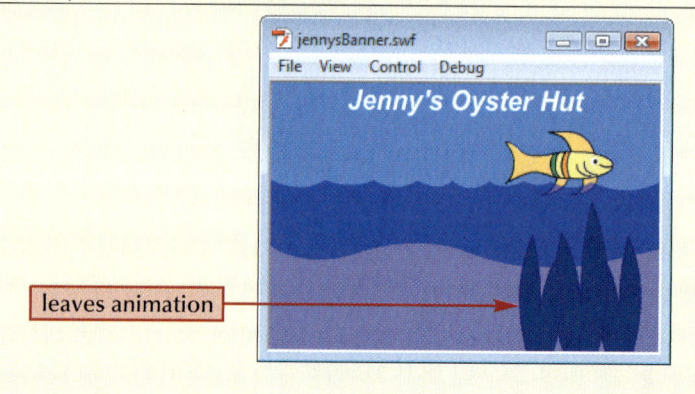

leaves animation

> **Tip**
> You can also press the F12 key to preview the animation in a Web page in your computer's default browser.

  2. On the Flash Player Application bar, click **File**, and then click **Close**. The Flash Player window closes.
  3. On the Application bar, click **File**, point to **Publish Preview**, and then click **Default - (HTML)**. Your computer's default browser opens and the animation plays in a Web page.
  4. Close the browser window when you are finished viewing the animation.
  5. Save and close the banner.

Creating a Shape Tween

Shape tweens are created similarly to motion tween animations. A **shape tween** is an animation that takes one shape and transforms it into another shape. To create a shape tween, you create the graphic content in the beginning and ending frames of the animation and Flash creates the tweened frames to complete the animation. The object in a shape tween must *not* be a symbol or a grouped object. This is different from a motion or classic tween where the object must be a symbol. A shape tween is indicated in the Timeline by a black arrow and a light green color for the frames. You can also control the shape tween's acceleration and deceleration by changing the Ease value in the Property inspector. The Jenny's Oyster Hut banner does not require a shape tween.

In this session, you created animations using frame-by-frame and classic tween animations and you learned how to create shape tweens. You also learned how to create animations using graphic symbols. Aly is pleased with the completed banner for Jenny's Oyster Hut Web site and is looking forward to showing it to Jenny.

Review | Session 3.3 Quick Check

1. How can you animate a movie clip symbol so that each of its instances automatically contains the animation?
2. List two differences between a movie clip symbol and a graphic symbol.
3. Why do animations within graphic symbols play in a document's main Timeline without the document having to be tested in the Flash Player?
4. In a frame-by-frame animation, what kind of frame do you need to have in the Timeline when the content changes on the Stage?
5. True or False? To create a frame-by-frame animation, the object being animated must first be converted to a symbol.
6. Can you include regular frames in a frame-by-frame animation? Why or why not?
7. True or False? To create a shape tween, the object being animated must first be converted to a symbol.

Review | Tutorial Summary

In this tutorial, you learned about the different elements that make up a Flash animation. You explored the Timeline and worked with layers and frames with multiple scenes. You created animations in Flash using motion tweens, classic tweens, motion presets, frame-by-frame animations, and animations using graphic symbol instances and you learned how to create shape tween animations. You also learned the different ways to test an animation.

Key Terms

classic tween	motion preset	static frame
frame	motion tween	target object
frame-by-frame animation	object-based animation	tween
keyframe	property keyframe	tween layer
layer	scene	tween span
layer folder	shape tween	tweened frame

Tutorial 3 Creating Animations | Flash **FL 157**

Practice | Review Assignments

Practice the skills you learned in the tutorial.

Data File needed for the Review Assignments: jennysAdDraft.fla

After reviewing an animated ad banner, Aly asks you to modify the banner so that a text animation in the first scene include the words "Lunch," "Dinner," and "Anytime!" displayed one after the other. She also wants you to animate the fish and sign so that they move across the Stage and for the title text block in the first scene to fade in as the fish pulls the sign. Finally, she asks you to add two instances of an animated fish in the second scene that swim in opposite directions.

1. Open the **jennysAdDraft.fla** file located in the Tutorial.03\Review folder included with your Data Files, save the file in the same folder as **jennysAd.fla**, and then reset the workspace to its default Essentials layout.
2. In the Daily specials scene, select the fish and sign graphics on the Stage, and then convert them to a movie clip symbol named **fish with sign**.
3. Move the fish with sign instance to the pasteboard in the lower-left corner of the Stage. Create a motion tween so that the fish with sign instance moves into the lower-left corner of the Stage, moves diagonally upward across the Stage, and stops in the middle-right part of the Stage. Extend the motion tween so that it spans 70 frames. Insert a regular frame in Frame 70 of the background layer to extend it.
4. In the Library panel, make two duplicates of the lunch text symbol, and name one duplicate **dinner text** and the other **anytime text**. Edit the dinner text symbol by changing the Lunch text to **Dinner**. Edit the anytime text symbol by changing the Lunch text to **Anytime**.
5. Create a new graphic symbol named **text animation**. In symbol-editing mode, change the Layer 1 name to **lunch**. Drag an instance of the lunch text symbol from the Library panel to the center of the Stage and in the Property inspector, change its X and Y coordinates to 0.
6. Right-click the lunch text instance and create a motion tween. With the playhead on Frame 24 and the lunch text instance selected on the Stage, set the alpha amount to 0% in the Color Effect section of the Property inspector to make the instance transparent. Hide the contents of the lunch layer.
7. In the Timeline, insert a new layer and name it **dinner**, and then drag an instance of the dinner text symbol from the Library panel to the center of the Stage. In the Property inspector, change its X and Y coordinates to 0.
8. Right-click the dinner text instance and create a motion tween. Move the playhead to Frame 24, if necessary, and then select the dinner text instance on the Stage and set its alpha amount to 0% to make it transparent. Hide the contents of the dinner layer.
9. In the Timeline, insert a new layer and name it **anytime**, and then drag an instance of the anytime text symbol from the Library panel to the center of the Stage. In the Property inspector, change its X and Y coordinates to 0.
10. Right-click the anytime text instance and create a motion tween. Move the playhead to Frame 24, if necessary, and then select the anytime text instance on the Stage and set its alpha amount to 0% to make it transparent.
11. Drag the tween span in the dinner layer so that it starts in Frame 24 of the same layer. Drag the tween span in the anytime layer so that it starts in Frame 47 of the same layer. Unhide the lunch and dinner layers and test the text animation. The words appear and fade out in turn. Exit symbol-editing mode.

12. In the Daily specials scene, insert a new layer and name it **text**, and then add two instances of the text animation symbol to the Stage. Place one on the lower-left side of the Stage. Place the other on the lower-right side of the Stage and start its animation in Frame 35.
13. In the Library panel, make a duplicate of the small fish symbol and name it **second small fish**, and then edit the second small fish symbol by changing the color of each of its fins to pink (#FF00FF) and the color of its body to yellow (#FFFF00). Do not change the color of the green and blue bands on the fish body. Exit symbol-editing mode.
14. In the fish layer of the Swimming fish scene, drag an instance of the small fish symbol to the pasteboard next to the lower-left corner of the Stage. Insert a keyframe in Frame 40 and then create a classic tween between Frames 1 and 40. At Frame 40, move the small fish instance to the pasteboard next to the lower-right corner of the Stage. The small fish will move across the Stage from left to right.
15. Insert a keyframe at Frame 41 of the fish layer, change the small fish instance so that it faces to the left, and then insert another keyframe at Frame 80. Create a classic tween between Frames 41 and 80 to have the small fish instance move right to left across the Stage.
16. In the Swimming fish scene, insert a new layer above the fish layer and name it **second fish**. In this layer, drag an instance of the second small fish symbol to the pasteboard next to the center-right side of the Stage. Create two classic tweens for this second fish instance similar to the classic tweens in the fish layer. You want the second small fish instance to start from the pasteboard on the right side of the Stage, swim left across the Stage to the pasteboard, and then turn around and swim back to its starting point.
17. Insert a regular frame at Frame 80 of the background layer to extend it.
18. Submit the finished file to your instructor.

Apply | **Case Problem 1**

Modify an existing Flash document by adding motion tweens, a motion preset, and a frame-by-frame animation using a graphic symbol.

Data File needed for this Case Problem: kprBanner.fla

Katie's Pet Resort Planning is well underway at Katie's Pet Resort for the grand opening celebration. Katie is expecting a good turnout for the celebration. Katie meets with John to discuss the development of the banner for the new Web site. Katie asks John to make the banner more festive by adding animation to it. John has started developing the revised banner shown in Figure 3-39 and wants you to help him complete the task by adding animations for block graphics and balloon graphics. The balloons will float up as the block graphics rotate. You will also add a fly-in animation to the Grand Opening text.

Tutorial 3 Creating Animations | Flash | FL 159

Figure 3-39

Katie's Pet Resort

Grand Opening!

- create different colored copies of the balloon and animate them to float up
- add a drop in animation to the text block
- animate block graphics to rotate

1. Open the **kprBanner.fla** file located in the Tutorial.03\Case1 folder included with your Data Files, and then save the banner in the same folder as **petBanner.fla**. The document contains some of the graphic elements that will be used to create the animated banner.
2. Select the grouped object in the lower-right corner of the Stage with the green square and the word "Katie's." Convert the object to a graphic symbol named **square**. Delete the square instance from the Stage.
3. Convert the balloon into a movie clip symbol named **balloon1**. Be sure to include both the balloon and the string.
4. Create a duplicate of the balloon1 symbol and name it **balloon2**. Edit the balloon2 symbol to change the color of the balloon to blue (#0000FF). Create another duplicate of the balloon1 symbol and name it **balloon3**. Edit the balloon3 symbol to change its color to pink (#FF00FF).
5. Create a motion tween with the balloon1 instance on the Stage. Extend the tween span to Frame 60. At Frame 60 move the balloon1 instance to the pasteboard above the Stage. The balloon1 instance will move from the bottom of the Stage to the pasteboard right above the Stage.
6. Rename the graphics layer to **balloon1** and then insert a new layer above the balloon1 layer and name it **balloon2**. On this layer, select Frame 1, and then drag an instance of the balloon2 symbol to the lower-middle part of the Stage. Create a motion tween so that the balloon moves up to the pasteboard above the Stage. Make sure the tween span extends through Frame 60.
7. Insert a new layer above the balloon2 layer and name it **balloon3**. On this layer, select Frame 1, and then drag an instance of the balloon3 symbol to the lower-right corner of the Stage. Create a motion tween so that the balloon moves up to the pasteboard above the Stage. Make sure the tween span extends through Frame 60.
8. Add a regular frame to Frame 60 of the background layer.
9. Select Frame 1 of the grand opening layer, convert the Grand Opening text on the Stage to a movie clip symbol named **grand opening**, and then move the instance to the pasteboard above the Stage.
10. From the Motion Presets panel, apply the fly-in-top motion preset found in the Default Presets folder to the grand opening instance so that the Grand Opening text drops in from above the Stage to the center of the Stage. Extend the tween span to Frame 40 of the grand opening layer. Add a regular frame to Frame 60 of the same layer.

11. Double-click the square symbol in the Library panel to open it in symbol-editing mode. In the square's Timeline, insert a keyframe in Frame 10. Use the Transform tool with the Rotate and Skew modifier to rotate the square and text graphic to the right so that the Katie's text is horizontal.
12. Insert a keyframe at Frame 20 and rotate the square and text graphic to the left to its original position. Insert a keyframe at Frame 30 and rotate the square and text graphic to the right so that the text is horizontal. Insert a regular frame at Frame 40. Return to Scene 1.
13. Insert a new layer and name it **squares**. Insert an instance of the square symbol and place it in the lower-left corner of the Stage. Insert another instance of the square symbol and place it in the lower-right corner of the Stage. Have the second instance start its animation in Frame 10 of its Timeline.
14. Test the animation. The Grand Opening! text drops in as the balloons float up and out of sight and the squares at the bottom shift back and forth.
15. Submit the finished files to your instructor.

Apply | Case Problem 2

Create a banner containing a frame-by-frame animation in a movie clip symbol, motion tweens with text, and a motion preset animation.

Data File needed for this Case Problem: aczBanner.fla

Alamo City Zoo Janet meets with Alex to review the banner that Alex has developed promoting the new bear exhibit. They agree to make the banner more interesting by adding animation to it. Alex has started developing a revised banner, and he wants you to help him complete the task by adding two text blocks that will be animated and by animating the bear paw graphic. Figure 3-40 shows the initial version of the Alamo City Zoo banner.

Figure 3-40

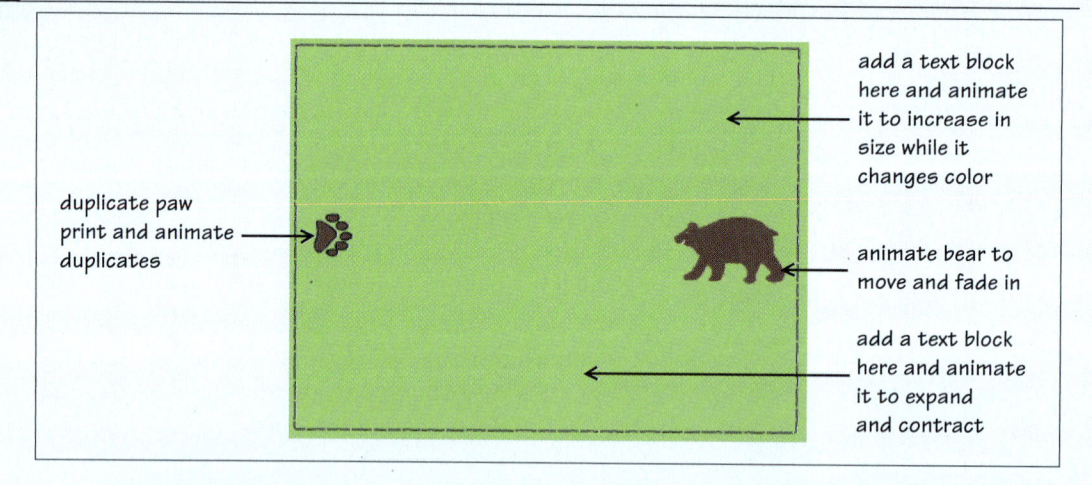

- add a text block here and animate it to increase in size while it changes color
- duplicate paw print and animate duplicates
- animate bear to move and fade in
- add a text block here and animate it to expand and contract

1. Open the **aczBanner.fla** file located in the Tutorial.03\Case2 folder included with your Data Files, and then save the banner in the same folder as **bearBanner.fla**. The document contains some of the graphic elements that will be used to create the animated banner.
2. Delete the bear and bear paw instances from the Stage, rename Layer 1 as **background**, and then lock the layer.
3. Create a new movie clip symbol named **bear tracks**. In symbol-editing mode, add a horizontal guide at the center of the Stage that aligns with the 0 mark on the left vertical ruler. Add another horizontal guide approximately 40 pixels above the first guide.

4. Drag an instance of the bear paw symbol from the Library panel to the center of the Stage. If necessary, select the instance and set both the X and Y values in the Position and Size section of the Property inspector to 0 so that the center of the instance is exactly centered on the Stage.

5. Insert a keyframe at Frame 10, and then drag another instance of the bear paw symbol so that its center is on the top guide and approximately 30 pixels to the right of the first instance. Insert a keyframe at Frame 20, and then drag an instance of the bear paw symbol so that its center is on the bottom guide and approximately 30 pixels to the right of the second bear paw instance.

6. Insert a keyframe at Frame 30, and then drag an instance of the bear paw symbol so that its center is on the top guide and approximately 30 pixels to the right of the third instance. Insert a keyframe at Frame 40, and then drag an instance of the bear paw symbol so that its center is on the bottom guide and approximately 30 pixels to the right of the fourth bear paw instance. Insert a keyframe at Frame 50, and then drag an instance of the bear paw symbol so that it is positioned on the top guide approximately 30 pixels from the fifth bear paw.

7. Insert a regular frame at Frame 70 of Layer 1 in the Timeline to extend the end of the animation, and then test the animation. The bear paws should be displayed one at a time.

8. In the main Timeline, insert a new layer and name it **tracks**. Drag an instance of the bear tracks symbol from the Library panel to the Stage. Position the instance so that it is on the left side of the Stage in the bear paw instance's original position.

9. Insert regular frames at Frame 70 of the tracks layer and background layer.

10. Insert a new layer above the tracks layer and name it **bear**. Drag an instance of the bear symbol to the lower-right corner of the Stage. In the Motions Preset panel, select the fly-in-bottom preset from the Default Presets, and then apply the preset to the bear instance. Extend the tween span in the bear layer to Frame 40 and then add a regular frame at Frame 70.

11. Select Frame 40 of the bear layer and then move the bear instance down slightly so that it aligns with the bear tracks instance at the end of the motion tween.

12. Insert a new layer above the bear layer and name it **title**. In Frame 1 of this layer, create a text block with the text **Alamo City Zoo**. Use a fancy font such as Monotype Corsiva and use a point size such as 24. Select maroon (#660000) for the font color and select Align center for the paragraph format. Center the text block on the banner above the bear tracks and bear.

13. Select the text block and convert it to a movie clip symbol named **title text**. Right-click the title text instance and create a motion tween. Select Frame 30 of the title layer, and then select the title text instance on the Stage. In the Position and Size section of the Property inspector, change the width of the instance to 250. Make sure the height value changes proportionally.

14. Insert a new layer and name it **exhibit**. Create a text block in Frame 1 of the exhibit layer with the text **Visit the Bear Exhibit!** using the same font family and size as the title text. Use white for the font color. Center the text block below the bear tracks and bear.

15. Select this text block and convert it to a movie clip symbol named **exhibit text**. Right-click the text instance and create a motion tween. Select Frame 1 of the exhibit layer, and then select the exhibit text instance on the Stage. In the Color Effect section of the Property inspector, select the Alpha color style and change the alpha amount to 0%.

16. Select Frame 35 of the exhibit layer, and then select the exhibit text instance. In the Color Effect section of the Property inspector, change the alpha amount to 100%.
17. Test the animation. The title text expands, the bear tracks are displayed one after the other, the bear moves and fades in from the bottom of the banner, and the exhibit text fades in.
18. Submit the finished files to your instructor.

Challenge | Case Problem 3

Create a logo with shape tweens, motion tweens, and a frame-by-frame animation using a graphic symbol.

Data File needed for this Case Problem: wcLogo.fla

Westcreek Nursery   Amanda shows Alice the logo she developed for the Westcreek Nursery Web site, and they both agree that the logo could be enhanced by adding some animation. Amanda decides to revise the logo by adding shape tweens to the Westcreek Nursery company name and applying a motion tween to the word Flowers. The banner will look similar to the one shown in Figure 3-41.

Figure 3-41

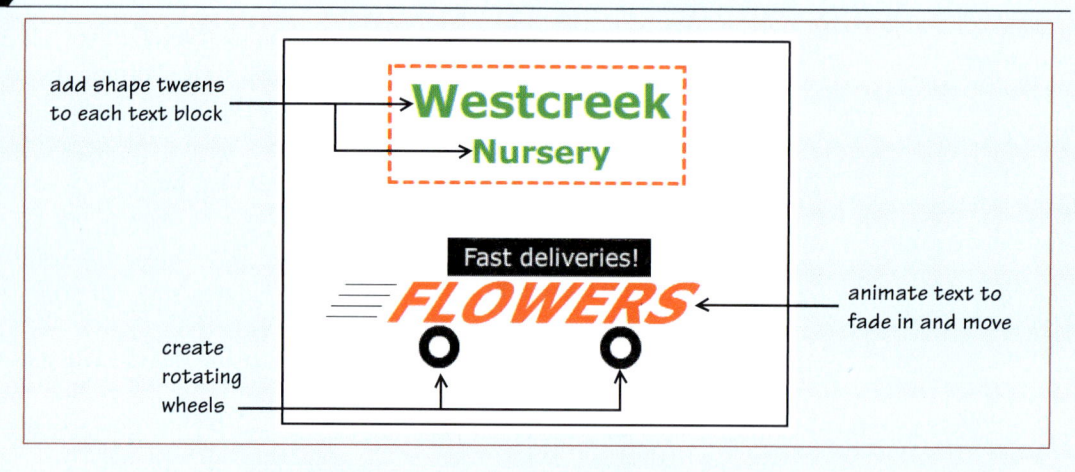

[Banner showing: "Westcreek Nursery" (add shape tweens to each text block), "Fast deliveries! FLOWERS" (animate text to fade in and move), with wheels below (create rotating wheels)]

1. Open the **wcLogo.fla** file located in the Tutorial.03\Case3 folder included with your Data Files, and then save the file in the same folder as **nurseryLogo.fla**.
2. Rename Layer 1 to **background**, and then insert regular frames so that the layer extends to Frame 60.
3. Insert a layer and name it **westcreek**. Insert another layer and name it **nursery**. Insert a third layer and name it **flowers**.
4. Select the Westcreek text block. Use the Cut command on the Edit menu to cut the text block. Then, on Frame 1 of the westcreek layer, use the Paste in Place command on the Edit menu to place the text in the same relative position as it was in the background layer.
5. Select the Nursery text block. Use the Cut command to cut the text. Insert a keyframe on Frame 30 of the nursery layer. In this frame, use the Paste in Place command to place the text in the same relative position as it was in the background layer.
6. Select the FLOWERS text block in the center of the Stage. Make sure you don't select any other graphics besides the text. Use the Cut command to cut the text block. Then, on Frame 1 of the flowers layer, use the Paste in Place command to place the text in the same relative position as it was on the background layer.

7. Use the Scene panel to create a duplicate of Scene 1. Rename Scene 1 copy to **wheel animation** and rename Scene 1 to **flowers animation**.

EXPLORE 8. In the flowers animation scene, select the Westcreek text and use the Break Apart command to break the text apart into individual letters. Use the command a second time to break the letters into filled shapes.

EXPLORE 9. Insert a keyframe in Frame 30 of the westcreek layer. In Frame 1, draw a rectangle over the Westcreek text block. Use green (#009900) for the rectangle's fill and do not include a stroke. If necessary, turn off Snap to Objects to make it easier to draw the rectangle. The size of the rectangle should be just slightly larger than the text block itself. Insert a shape tween between Frames 1 and 30. Test the animation. The rectangle should transform into the text Westcreek.

10. In Frame 30 of the nursery layer, select the Nursery text and apply the Break Apart command twice to break the text into filled shapes. Insert a keyframe in Frame 50 of the nursery layer.

11. In Frame 30 of the nursery layer, draw a rectangle with a green (#009900) fill and no stroke over the Nursery text block. The rectangle should be slightly larger than the text block. Insert a shape tween between Frames 30 and 50. Test the animation. The rectangle should transform into the text Nursery.

12. In the same scene, select the FLOWERS text in Frame 1 of the flowers layer and convert the text block into a movie clip symbol named **flowers text**. Right-click the symbol instance and create a motion tween. Select Frame 1 of the flowers layer, and then, if necessary, select the flowers text instance on the Stage. In the Property inspector, select Alpha for the Color style and change the alpha amount to 0%.

13. Select Frame 30 of the flowers layer, and then, if necessary, select the flowers text instance. Change the alpha amount to 100%.

EXPLORE 14. Select Frame 45 of the flowers layer, and then, if necessary, select the flowers text instance. Press the Right arrow key eight times to move the instance eight pixels to the right.

15. Preview the motion tween to see the text block move slightly to the right and fade in gradually.

16. Switch to the wheel animation scene. Select the left oval representing a wheel below the FLOWERS text and convert it to a graphic symbol named **wheel**. Open the wheel symbol in symbol-editing mode.

17. Zoom in on the wheel graphic, and then draw a short horizontal line across the middle of the white area of the wheel graphic to represent a wheel spoke. Use black as the color and 2 for the stroke height. Draw a short vertical line across the middle of the white area of the wheel graphic to represent another wheel spoke.

EXPLORE 18. Create a frame-by-frame animation to rotate the wheel, as follows: Open the Transform panel. Insert a keyframe in Frame 3. Select the wheel graphic, if necessary, and in the Transform panel enter a value of 30 for the number of degrees to rotate the wheel. (Be sure to press the Enter key to apply the Rotate value.) Insert another keyframe at Frame 5 and enter 30 for the rotate value in the Transform panel to rotate the wheel again. Insert one more keyframe at Frame 7 and enter 30 for the rotate value in the Transform panel to rotate the wheel again. Exit symbol-editing mode and return to the wheel animation scene.

19. Delete the original wheel under the R of FLOWERS on the Stage and add an instance of the wheel graphic symbol in the same position. In the Looping section of the Property inspector, change the First frame of the instance to 3.

EXPLORE

20. Switch to the flowers animation scene and replace the two wheel graphics with instances of the wheel symbol. In the Looping section of the Property inspector, set the Looping for each instance to Single Frame and make sure the First frame of each instance is set to 1.

21. Test the animation. Two rectangles transform into the Westcreek Nursery company name, the Flowers text shifts right, and then the wheels rotate.

22. Submit the finished files to your instructor.

Create	Case Problem 4

Create tween animations, shape animations, and a frame-by-frame animation.

Data File needed for this Case Problem: msaBanner.fla

Missions Support Association Brittany meets with Anissa to discuss the progress in the development of a new banner for the Missions Support Association's Web site. They decide that adding animation to the banner will enhance its appearance. Anissa has started to develop the banner shown in Figure 3-42 and instructs you to complete it by adding animation using the shapes she has created. You will also create an animation of the key phrases Volunteer Opportunities, Special Events, School Tours, and Join Now! on the banner.

Figure 3-42

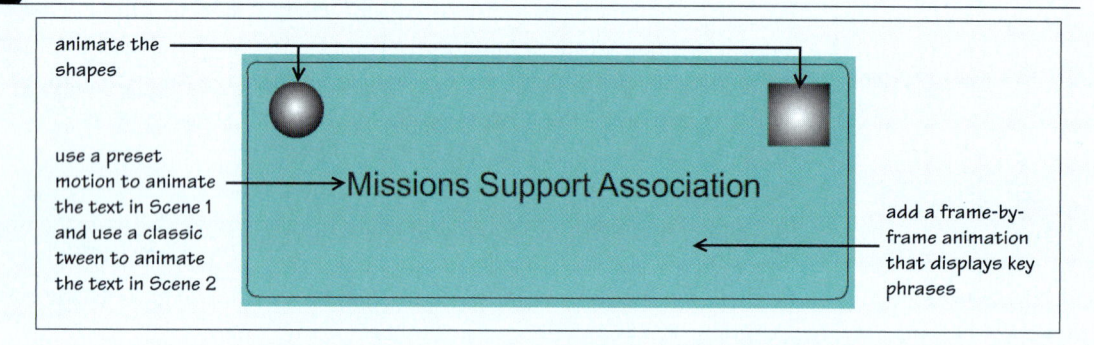

animate the shapes

use a preset motion to animate the text in Scene 1 and use a classic tween to animate the text in Scene 2

Missions Support Association

add a frame-by-frame animation that displays key phrases

1. Open the **msaBanner.fla** file located in the Tutorial.03\Case4 folder included with your Data Files, and then save the file in the same folder as **missionsBanner.fla**. The document contains some of the graphic elements that will be used to create the animated banner.

2. Animate the circle and shapes on the Stage using motion or shape tweens to provide interest. For example, the shapes could move from corner to corner around the banner, or the circle and square could change into triangles. The Timeline should extend to at least 45 frames. (*Hint*: You'll need to create each animation in its own layer.)

3. Use a preset motion to animate the Missions Support Association text.

4. Create a duplicate of Scene 1 in which to create animation for the key phrases. Delete the circle and square layers from Scene 2, and then rename both scenes appropriately.

5. In the second scene, use a classic tween to animate the Missions Support Association text block to move near the top of the Stage.

6. Insert a new layer in which to create a frame-by-frame animation that changes the text block to a different phrase periodically, and then rename the layer with a descriptive name.

7. In Frame 6, create a text block with the words **Preserve History** on the center of the Stage, using the font family, color, and size of your choice. Convert the text block to a graphic symbol.

8. Edit the graphic symbol to create a frame-by-frame animation that changes the text block to a different phrase periodically between Frames 1 and 45. Use the Info panel to set X and Y coordinates to 0. (For example, in symbol-editing mode, you can insert a keyframe every tenth frame, edit the text block at each keyframe to change the key phrase, and then insert a regular frame at Frame 45 to extend the symbol's timeline.) Exit symbol-editing mode.
9. Test the animation.
10. Submit the finished files to your instructor.

Review | Quick Check Answers

Session 3.1

1. to coordinate and control the frames that make up an animation and to organize the layers that contain the different elements of a document
2. by looking at the location of the playhead on the Timeline header or the current frame number displayed at the bottom of the Timeline
3. 24 fps
4. Frames contain content that is displayed for an instant in time and frames are displayed one after another to create the perception of movement. Layers are made up of one or more frames and are used to organize the graphic elements of a document.
5. a container in the Timeline in which you can place layers; allows you to work more efficiently when you have a lot of layers
6. a way to break up a Flash document into separate mini-movies, each with its own Timeline
7. by the order they are listed in the Scene panel or by the order they appear in the Edit Scene button on the Edit bar
8. to make it easier to know what a scene contains, especially when you have multiple scenes in a document

Session 3.2

1. a prebuilt motion tween that you can apply to an object on the Stage to create an animation
2. True
3. Select the target object and modify its properties or modify the motion path on the Stage.
4. A frame-by-frame animation requires that you create the content for each of the frames. With a tweened animation, Flash creates the frames between the beginning and ending keyframes.
5. only one object
6. a motion tween or a classic tween
7. to ensure the animation works the way you intended and meets the project's requirements

Session 3.3

1. Create the animation in the symbol's Timeline instead of in the document's Timeline. Each instance of the movie clip symbol then automatically contains the animation.
2. A movie clip symbol's Timeline is independent from the document's main Timeline, whereas a graphic symbol's Timeline is synchronized with the main document's Timeline. Also, when you test the document's animation within Flash, movie clip animations do not play, while graphic symbol animations do play. And you can also specify from which frame a graphic instance's animation should start. A movie clip animation always starts from the first frame of its Timeline.
3. The frames of a graphic symbol are synchronized with the document's main Timeline.
4. a keyframe
5. False; the object being animated in a frame-by-frame animation does not need to be a symbol.
6. Yes, you include regular frames in a frame-by-frame animation to indicate that the content has not changed from the previous keyframe.
7. False; an object used in a shape tween must *not* be converted to a symbol.

Ending Data Files

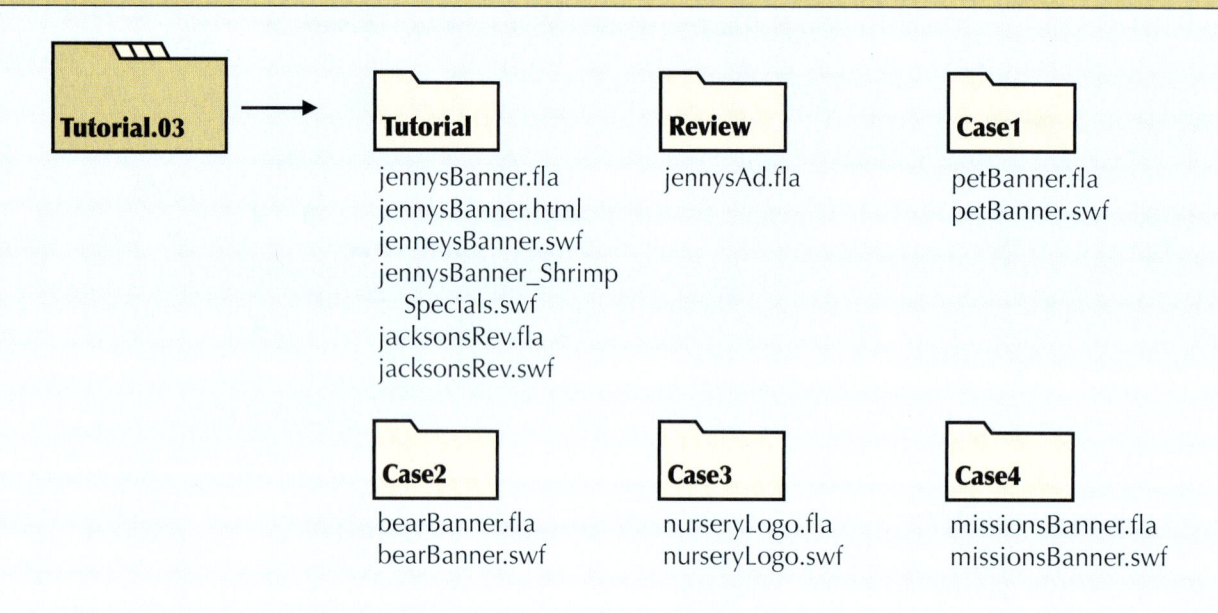

Tutorial.03 →

Tutorial
jennysBanner.fla
jennysBanner.html
jenneysBanner.swf
jennysBanner_Shrimp
  Specials.swf
jacksonsRev.fla
jacksonsRev.swf

Review
jennysAd.fla

Case1
petBanner.fla
petBanner.swf

Case2
bearBanner.fla
bearBanner.swf

Case3
nurseryLogo.fla
nurseryLogo.swf

Case4
missionsBanner.fla
missionsBanner.swf

Flash | FL 167

Tutorial 4

Objectives

Session 4.1
- Modify an animation's motion path
- Modify motion tweens using the Motion Editor
- Create an animation using a mask layer

Session 4.2
- Animate text blocks
- Animate individual letters within a text block
- Apply 3D rotation effects to movie clips

Session 4.3
- Test animations using onion skinning
- Create nested movie clips
- Create an inverse kinematic animation
- Learn how to use the Movie Explorer

Creating Complex Animations

Animating with Masks, Text Blocks, Onion Skinning, 3D Rotations, and Inverse Kinematics

Case | Admiral Web Design

Aly wants to develop a second banner for the Jenny's Oyster Hut Web site so that Jenny can have more than one to choose from. The second banner will consist of two scenes. The first scene will have a fish swimming across the banner. Aly started the first scene, but you need to change it so that the fish swims along a curved path rather than in a straight line. You will also create a second animated fish that exhibits more natural movements of its fins and tail as well as an animation showing a spotlight effect on the Jenny's Oyster Hut name. The second scene will include an animation of the company name. This will be a complex animation where the individual letters of the Jenny's name rotate in three-dimensional (3D) space one after another on the screen. As each letter rotates, it will increase and decrease in size. The scene will also contain several text blocks promoting the restaurant's anniversary.

In this tutorial, you will create an animation using a mask layer and you will modify motion paths using the Selection tool and the Motion Editor. You will create complex animations using text blocks, individual letters, and nested movie clips. You will apply a 3D animation to text and you will create an animation using inverse kinematics with the Bone tool. You will also test an animation using onion skinning. Finally, you will use the Movie Explorer to review all of the document's elements.

Starting Data Files

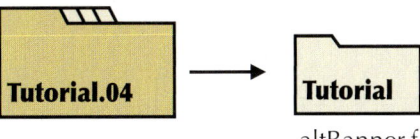

Tutorial.04

- **Tutorial**
  - altBanner.fla
  - sportsLetters.fla
  - sportsMask.fla
  - sportsSample.fla
- **Review**
  - johDraft.fla
- **Case1**
  - kprDraft.fla
- **Case2**
  - aczAdDraft.fla
- **Case3**
  - wcDraft.fla
- **Case4**
  - msaDraft.fla

Session 4.1

Modifying Motion Tweens

Aly started the scene of the banner that includes motion tweens of fish swimming across the Stage. This scene requires a curved path for the fish to follow, so you need to modify the motion paths. Also, the fish need to move more slowly during the middle part of the animation.

Modifying a Motion Path

When you create a motion tween in which an object moves from one part of the Stage to another, Flash creates a motion path. The **motion path** guides the object throughout the animation. Initially, the motion path is created as a straight line, but you can modify the path the same way you modify a stroke by curving the path, extending its length, deleting the path, or even replacing the path with a custom stroke. Modifying the motion path enables you to animate objects to move in a more natural way instead of having objects move only in straight lines. For example, you can make a ball appear to be bouncing up and down while gradually coming to a stop, you can have a car move along a curved road, or you can have a bird fly in a circular pattern.

You can quickly modify a motion path with the Selection tool by dragging any segment of the path using the Selection tool pointer the same way you modify a stroke. You can also extend a motion path's length by dragging either of its endpoints. You can move a selected motion path to a different location on the Stage. As you adjust the motion path, the target object stays attached to the path and the motion tween automatically changes based on your adjustments.

You can also modify the motion path with the Subselection tool. You click the motion path with the Subselection tool pointer to display the path's control points, which are indicated by small squares on the motion path. A **control point** indicates a place on a path where a change was made to the path or to the target object. You can drag a control point to reposition it or you can click a control point to display its Bezier handles. **Bezier handles** are used to modify the curve of the path around the control point by dragging or extending the endpoints of the handles, as shown in Figure 4-1.

Figure 4-1 Bezier handles on a curve

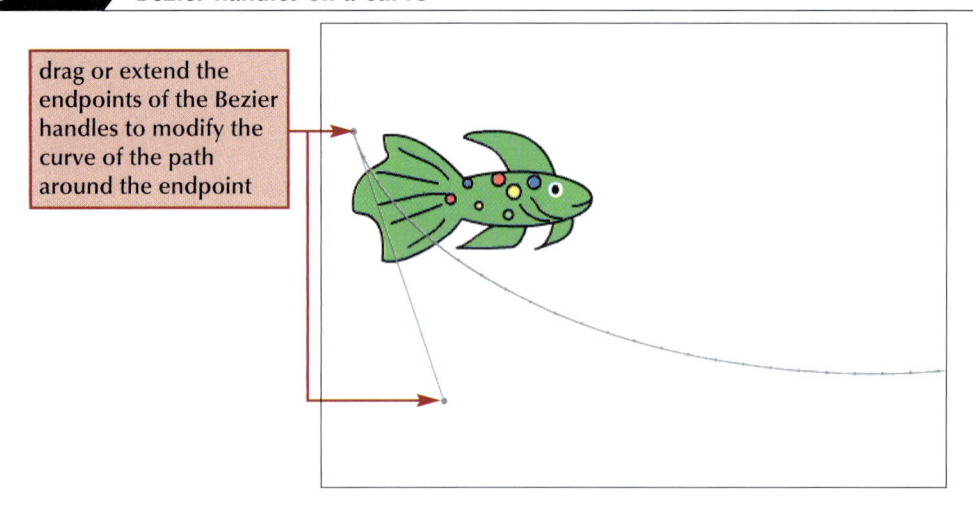

drag or extend the endpoints of the Bezier handles to modify the curve of the path around the endpoint

Another way you can modify a motion path is by using the Free Transform tool to rotate, skew, or scale the path, as shown in Figure 4-2.

Figure 4-2 — Motion path modified with the Free Transform tool

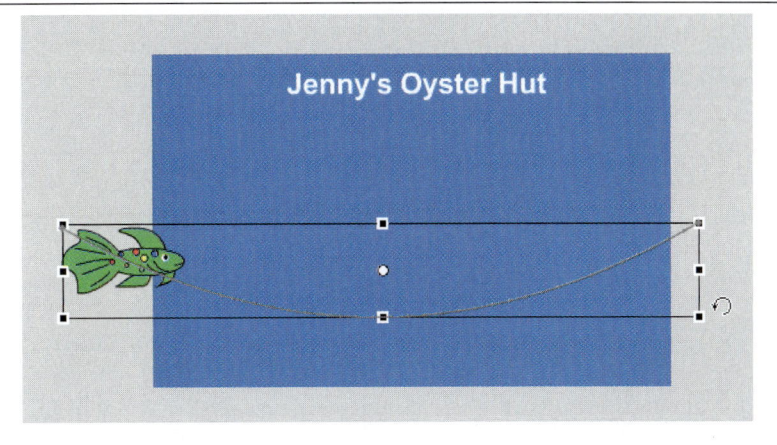

Finally, you can modify a motion path by selecting it and then making changes to its properties in the Property inspector or in the Transform panel.

Modifying a Tween's Motion Path

The alternate banner for Jenny's Oyster Hut that Aly started includes a fish swimming across the banner in a straight line. Aly's notes, shown in Figure 4-3, indicate that the fish needs to swim along a curved path. You will change the existing motion tweens by modifying the motion paths the fish follows. The motion paths will guide the fish along a curved path from the left side of the banner, down toward the bottom of the banner, up to the right side of the banner, and then back to the left side of the banner.

Figure 4-3 — Animation plan for the fish swimming across the banner

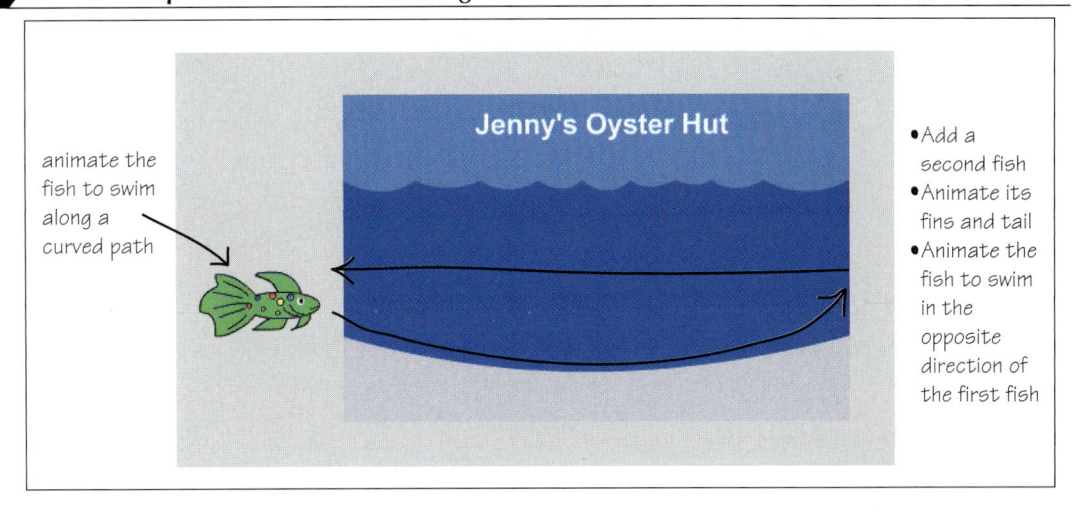

| Reference Window | **Modifying a Tween's Motion Path**

- In the Tools panel, click the Selection tool, and then drag a segment of the motion path to curve it or drag one of its endpoints to extend the path.

or

- In the Tools panel, click the Subselection tool, click the motion path to select it, and then drag one of its control points to reposition it or click a control point and then drag a Bezier handle to adjust the path's curve around the control point.

or

- In the Tools panel, click the Free Transform tool, click the motion path to select it, click the Rotate and Skew modifier or the Scale modifier, and then drag the handles on the path to adjust it.

or

- Select the motion path on the Stage, and then, in the Property inspector, change its X and Y coordinates or its width and height values.

or

- Select the motion path on the Stage, and then, in the Transform panel, change the path's dimensions, rotate properties, or skew properties.

You will modify two existing motion paths in the banner created by Aly. Each motion path guides the fish across the Stage.

To modify motion paths to make the fish swim along a curved path:

1. Open the **altBanner.fla** file located in the Tutorial.04\Tutorial folder included with your Data Files, save the file as **hutBanner.fla** in the same folder, and then reset the workspace to the Essentials layout.

2. In the Timeline, hide the ocean layer temporarily, and then select the **fish1** layer. The motion path followed by the fish is displayed on the Stage.

3. In the Tools panel, click the **Selection** tool to select it, if necessary, and then, on the Stage, drag the center of the motion path downward to curve it. See Figure 4-4.

Figure 4-4 | Motion path modified

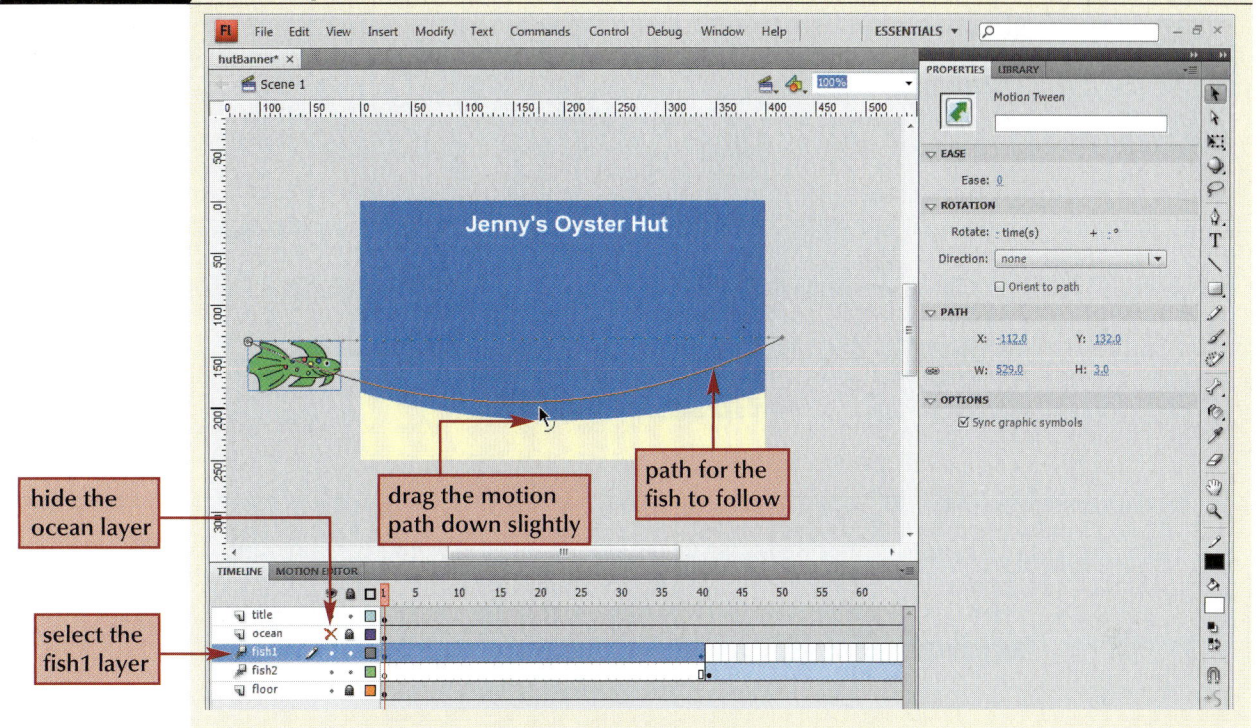

hide the ocean layer
drag the motion path down slightly
path for the fish to follow
select the fish1 layer

▸ **4.** Release the mouse button. The motion path is curved.

▸ **5.** In the Timeline, select the **fish2** layer, and then drag the playhead to **Frame 41**. The motion path for the tween is displayed on the Stage.

▸ **6.** On the Stage, drag the center of the tween span's motion path downward to curve it similarly to the first tween span's motion path.

▸ **7.** In the Timeline, drag the playhead to **Frame 1**, and then press the **Enter** key to play the animation. The fish follows the curved motion paths.

When you animate an object to follow a curved path, the object stays in a horizontal position as it moves along the path. You'll usually want the object to move in a more natural way. The Orient to path option in the Property inspector causes the object to align itself with the direction of the path, making the movement appear more natural. This works best with curves that have gentle slopes.

You'll orient the fish to follow the slope of the path by selecting the Orient to path option in a frame within each motion tween.

To orient the fish to the curved paths:

▸ **1.** In the Timeline, click **Frame 1** of the fish1 layer.

▸ **2.** In the Rotation section of the Property inspector, click the **Orient to path** check box to check it. Property keyframes are added in Frames 2 through 40, representing how the fish is slightly rotated in each frame of the tween span. The fish will have a more natural movement during the animation. See Figure 4-5.

Figure 4-5 — Orient to path applied to motion tween

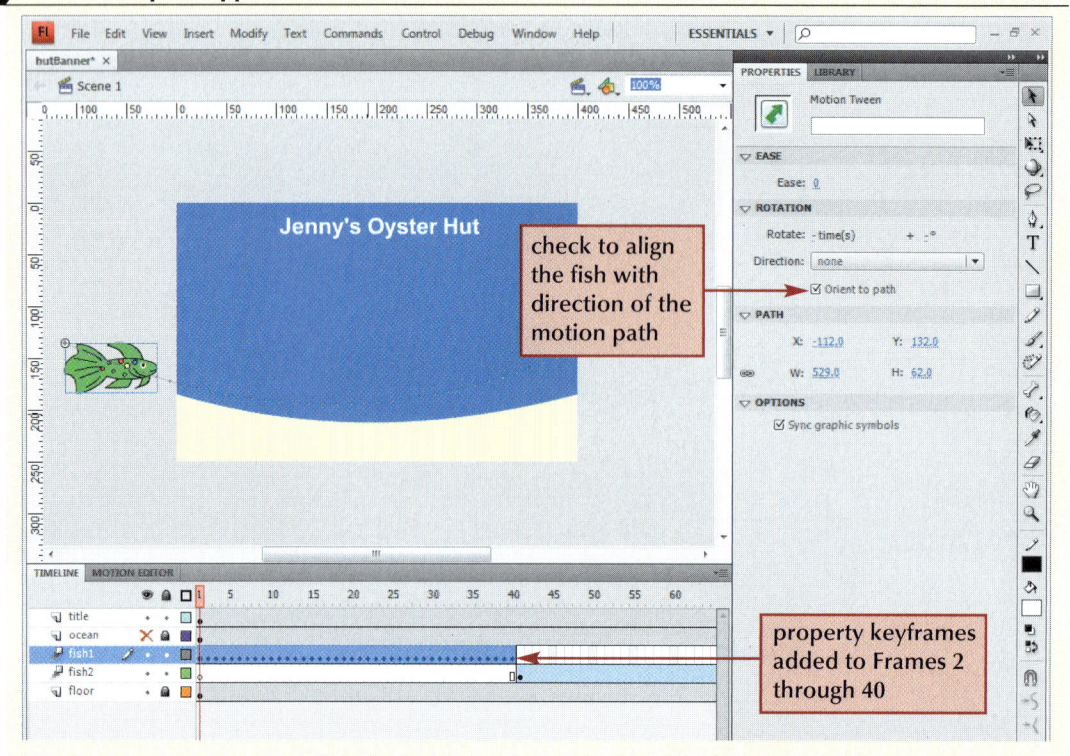

[Screenshot of Flash interface showing the hutBanner scene with "Jenny's Oyster Hut" banner, a fish graphic on a motion path, and the Properties panel showing Motion Tween settings.]

- check to align the fish with direction of the motion path
- property keyframes added to Frames 2 through 40

▸ 3. In the Timeline, click **Frame 41** of the fish2 layer, and then, in the Property inspector, click the **Orient to path** check box to check it. Property keyframes are added to the tween span.

▸ 4. In the Timeline, move the playhead to **Frame 1**, and then press the **Enter** key to play the animation again. The fish orients itself to the slope of the motion paths.

▸ 5. Save the banner.

Using the Motion Editor

The **Motion Editor** displays all properties and property keyframes for the selected motion tween and enables you to control the target object's coordinates, rotation, and transformation properties at each property keyframe. Using the Motion Editor, you can modify a motion tween more precisely by setting the values of individual property keyframes, adding or removing property keyframes, and adding or removing filters or color effects. The Motion Editor displays the values of a motion tween's properties both as numbers and as curves to make it simpler to change the properties and create complex animations.

You'll use the Motion Editor to explore and modify a sample animation that Aly created for another client, Jackson's Sports.

To view a motion tween's properties using the Motion Editor:

▸ 1. Open the **sportsSample.fla** file located in the Tutorial.04\Tutorial folder included with your Data Files, and then save it as **sportsModified.fla** in the same folder.

▸ 2. Press the **Enter** key to play the animation. The Jackson's text block moves into the Stage and the Annual Sale text fades in.

▸ 3. In the Timeline, move the playhead to **Frame 1**, and then select the **jacksons** layer.

Tutorial 4 Creating Complex Animations | Flash **FL 173**

▶ 4. Click the **MOTION EDITOR** tab to open the panel. You want to resize the Motion Editor to see more of the panel.

▶ 5. Point to the top edge of the Timeline and Motion Editor panel group until the pointer changes to ⭥, and then drag up to increase the size of the panel group. See Figure 4-6.

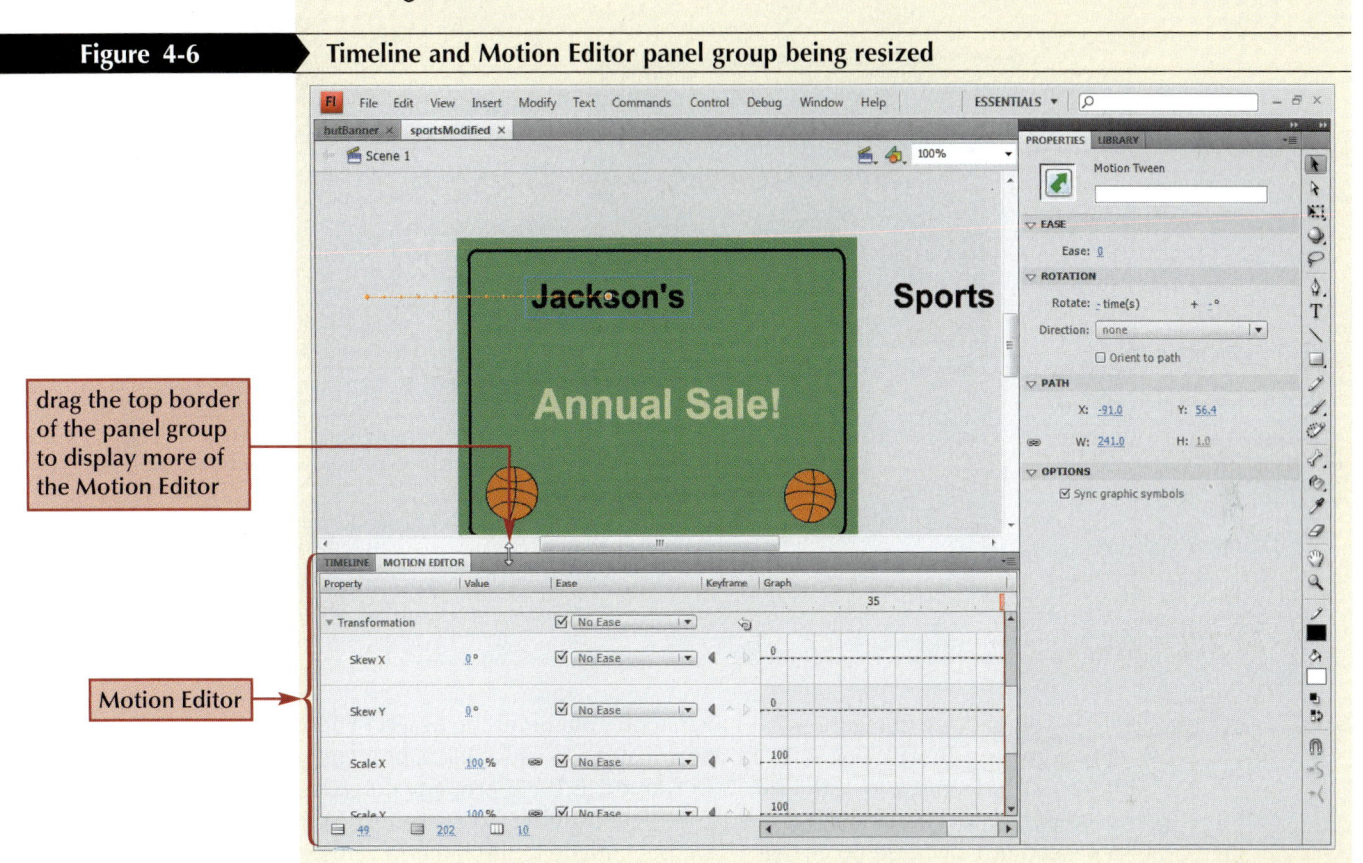

Figure 4-6 **Timeline and Motion Editor panel group being resized**

drag the top border of the panel group to display more of the Motion Editor

Motion Editor

▶ 6. In the Motion Editor, scroll up, if necessary, and then in the Property column, click the small triangle to the left of the Basic motion category to expand the category, if necessary. The Motion Editor displays the X, Y, and Rotation Z properties for the motion tween along with their associated values in the Value column. At Frame 1, the X property value is −91 px, which places the Jackson's text block to the left of the Stage.

▶ 7. In the Motion Editor, move the playhead to **Frame 15**. The Jackson's text block moves to the center of the Stage and the X property value in the Motion Editor changes to 150.3 px. See Figure 4-7.

Figure 4-7 X property value in the Motion Editor

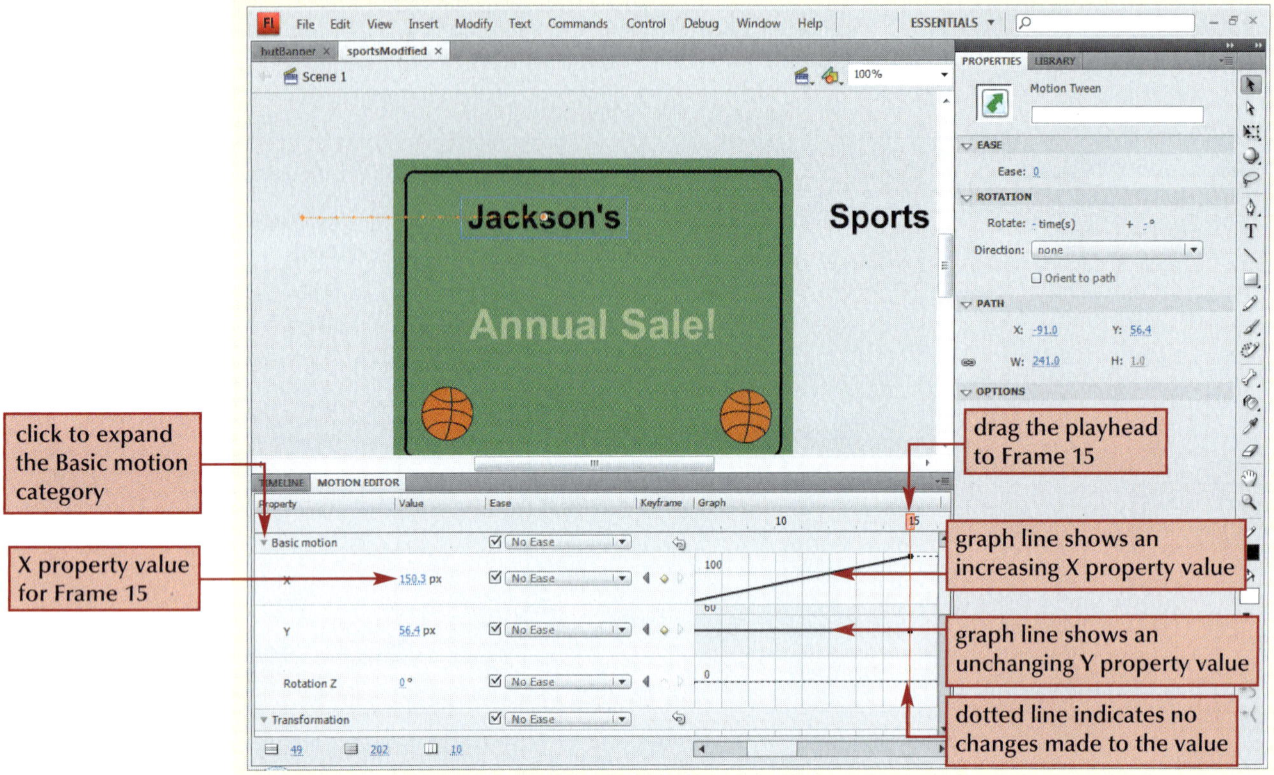

- click to expand the Basic motion category
- X property value for Frame 15
- drag the playhead to Frame 15
- graph line shows an increasing X property value
- graph line shows an unchanging Y property value
- dotted line indicates no changes made to the value

As you can see in Figure 4-7, in the Graph column of the Motion Editor, the X property curve is a straight line with an upward slope because the X property value increases from –91 in Frame 1 to 150.3 pixels in Frame 15. The Y property curve is a flat line because the text block doesn't change vertical position. The Rotation Z property contains a dashed line because no changes have been made to the rotation value.

You'll create a new motion tween and modify it using the Motion Editor.

To create a motion tween and modify it:

1. On the Stage, right-click the **Sports** text block, and then click **Create Motion Tween** on the context menu. The Graph column of the Motion Editor displays dashed lines because no motion paths have been created yet.

2. Make sure the playhead is on **Frame 15**, and then, in the Keyframe column of the X property in the Motion Editor, click the **Add or Remove keyframe** icon to add a property keyframe. Flat lines are added in the Graph column for the X and Y property curves. See Figure 4-8.

Tutorial 4 Creating Complex Animations | Flash | FL 175

Figure 4-8 — Property curves added in the Graph column

Tip

You can change the Expanded Graph Size value at the bottom of the Motion Editor to reduce or increase the area in the Graph column.

[Screenshot annotations: "click to add a property keyframe at the current frame"; "playhead at Frame 15"; "flat lines added for the X and Y property curves"]

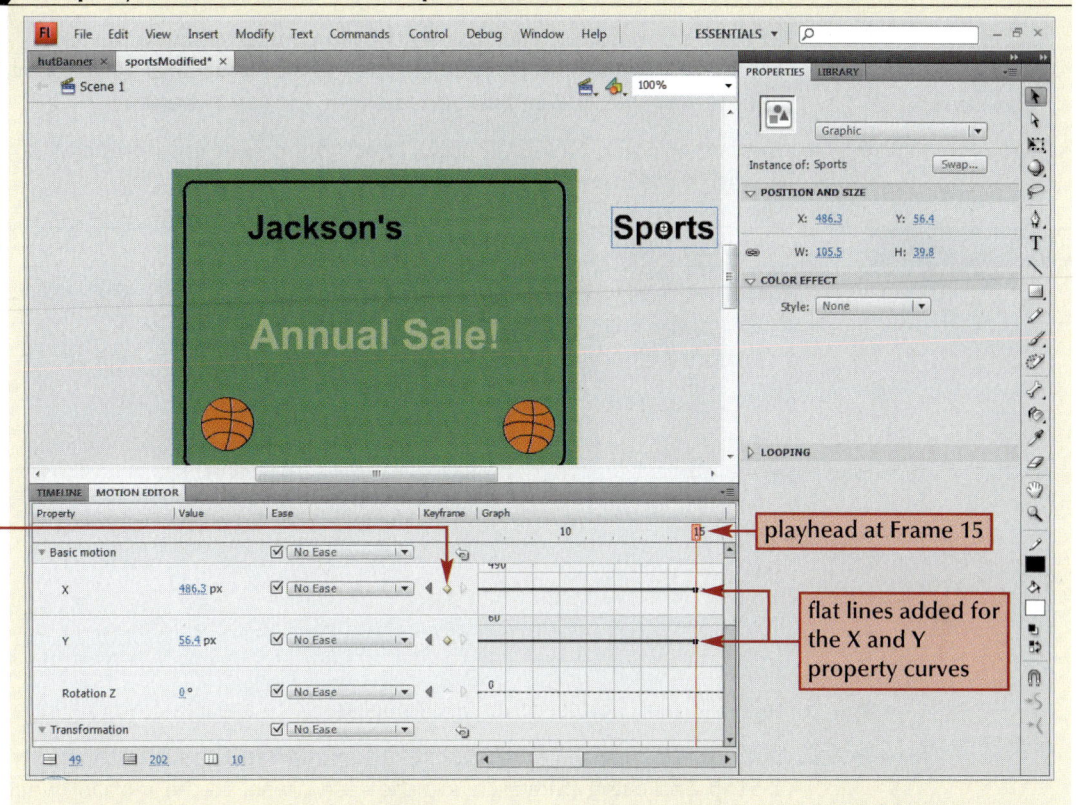

▶ 3. In the Value column of the Motion Editor, drag the value for the X position to the left to change the value to **285**. A downward slope is added to the property curve in the Graph column to reflect the new X property value. The Sports text block moves to the center of the Stage.

   Trouble? If you reach the left side of the screen before reaching 285, release the mouse button, and then repeat Step 3 to continue to reduce the X position value.

▶ 4. Move the playhead to **Frame 1**, and then press the **Enter** key to play the animation. The Sports text block moves from the right of the Stage as the Jackson's text block moves in from the left of the Stage.

▶ 5. Save and close the sportsModified.fla file.

Next, you will use the Motion Editor to modify the motion tweens for the fish in the banner for Jenny's Oyster Hut. Aly wants you to add easing to the motion tweens to make the fish slow down in the middle of the animation. **Easing** controls how fast or slow an object moves throughout an animation, which can make the animation appear more natural.

In addition to controlling an object's position and rotation throughout a motion tween, you can use the Motion Editor to add different preset eases to a motion tween and to modify its properties. You'll add a preset ease to the motion tweens for both fish instances.

To add an easing effect to a motion tween:

▶ 1. In the hutBanner.fla document, click the **TIMELINE** tab to display the Timeline, and then click **Frame 1** of the fish1 layer to select its motion tween.

▸ 2. Click the **MOTION EDITOR** tab to display the Motion Editor, and then scroll down, if necessary, to see the Eases category.

▸ 3. In the Motion Editor, click the **Add Color, Filter or Ease** button for the Eases category, and then, in the pop-up menu, click **Stop and Start (Slow)**. The preset ease is available and can be added to the motion tween.

▸ 4. In the Motion Editor, scroll down to see the preset ease property and curve displayed in the Eases category. See Figure 4-9.

Figure 4-9   Stop and Start (Slow) ease available in the Eases category

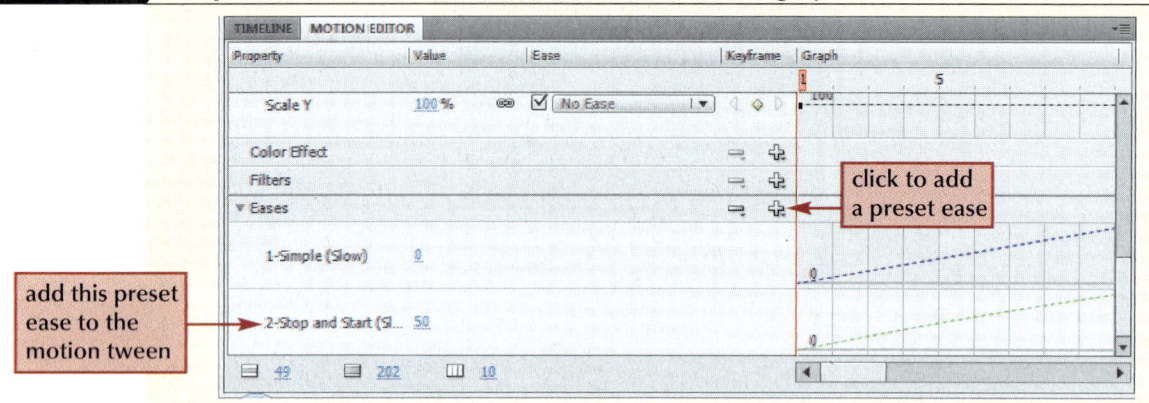

▸ 5. In the Motion Editor, scroll up, if necessary, to the Basic motion category.

▸ 6. In the Basic motion category, click the **Selected Ease** button, and then click **2-Stop and Start (Slow)** to add the ease preset to the motion tween's X and Y properties. The ease is displayed as a green dashed curve next to the X and Y property curves in the Graph column. See Figure 4-10.

Figure 4-10   Ease curves in the Graph column

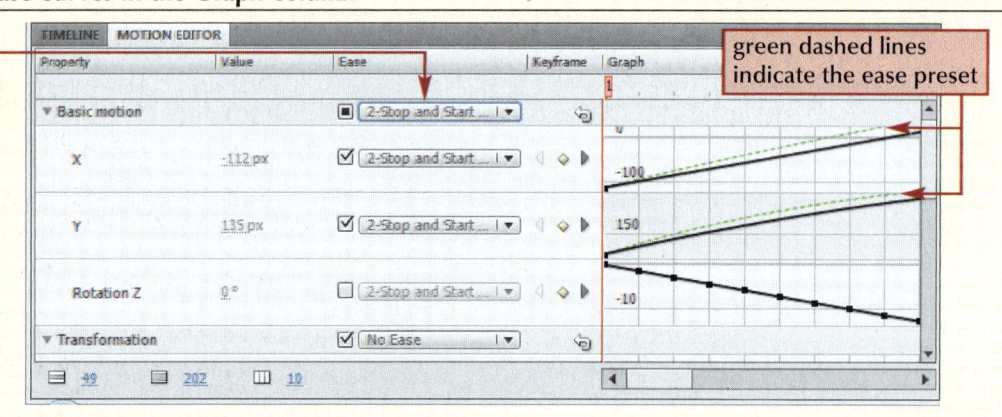

▸ 7. Click the **TIMELINE** tab to display the Timeline, and then click **Frame 41** of the fish2 layer to select its motion tween.

▸ 8. Click the **MOTION EDITOR** tab to display the Motion Editor, and then scroll down, if necessary, to the Eases category.

▸ 9. In the Motion Editor, click the **Add Color, Filter or Ease** button for the Eases category, and then click **Stop and Start (Slow)**. The preset ease is now available.

▸ 10. In the Motion Editor, scroll up, if necessary, to the Basic motion category.

▶ **11.** In the Basic motion category, click the **Selected Ease** button, and then click **2-Stop and Start (Slow)** to add the ease preset to the motion tween's X and Y properties. The Stop and Start (Slow) ease has been added to both motion tweens.

▶ **12.** Click the **TIMELINE** tab to display the Timeline, move the playhead to **Frame 1**, and then press the **Enter** key to play the animation. The fish swims across the Stage as before, but now it slows down in the middle of the motion tweens.

▶ **13.** Save the banner.

Using a Mask Layer in an Animation

You can also create animations that incorporate a mask layer to create special effects. A **mask layer** contains a graphic element that hides the contents of the layer below it, which is called the **masked layer**. A mask layer can also be used with motion tweens and frame-by-frame animations. For example, you can create an animation in a mask layer to show different areas of a masked layer throughout the animation.

To create an animation using a mask layer, you create the object to be masked on one layer and add a new layer above it that will contain the mask. When you change the top layer to a mask layer, the bottom layer becomes the masked layer. The masked layer is indented below the mask layer in the Timeline.

Reference Window	**Creating a Mask Layer Animation**

- Select the layer whose content will be masked.
- In the Timeline, click the Insert Layer button.
- Add content to the new layer that will be used as the mask.
- Right-click the new layer's name, and then click Mask.
- Unlock the layers and create an animation in either the mask layer or the masked layer.
- Lock the layers, and then test the animation.

The object on the mask layer can be a filled shape, such as an oval or a rectangle. It can also be text or an instance of a symbol. The fill of the shape on the mask layer will reveal the content in the underlying masked layer. This shape determines what part of the masked layer's content is visible. The color of the shape is irrelevant because its color is not displayed. You can animate either the object on the mask layer or the object on the masked layer. For example, you can animate an oval shape on the mask layer so that it moves over some stationary text on the masked layer. This technique creates a spotlight effect, as shown in Figure 4-11.

Figure 4-11 Masked layer example

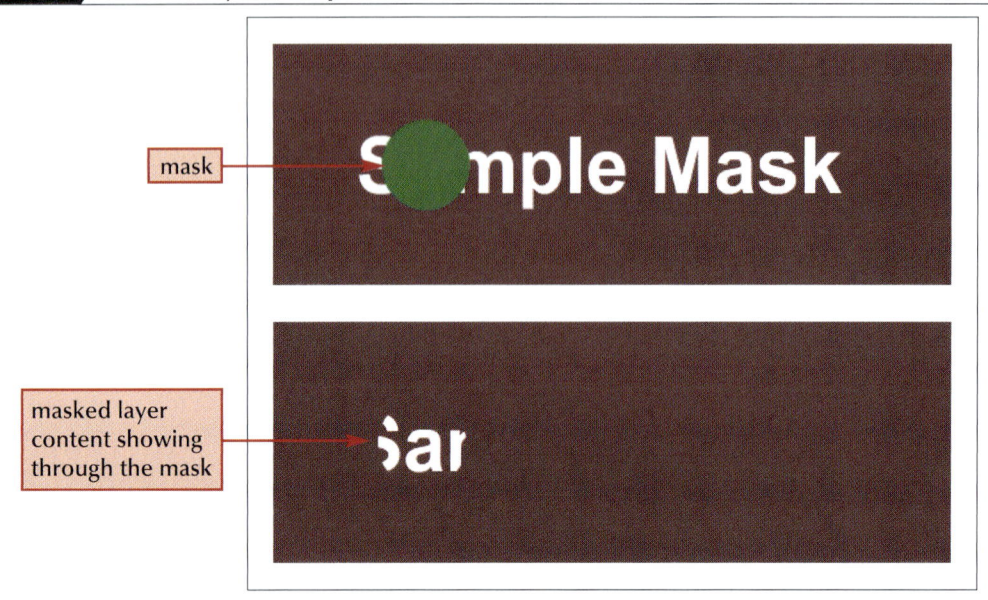

mask

masked layer content showing through the mask

If you animate the object on the masked layer while the object on the mask layer remains stationary, you can create a different type of effect. For example, you can create a scrolling text effect by drawing a rectangle on the mask layer and then animating a block of text on the masked layer. As the text block moves across the mask, only the portion of the text behind the rectangle is visible, as shown in Figure 4-12.

Figure 4-12 Masked layer with scrolling text effect

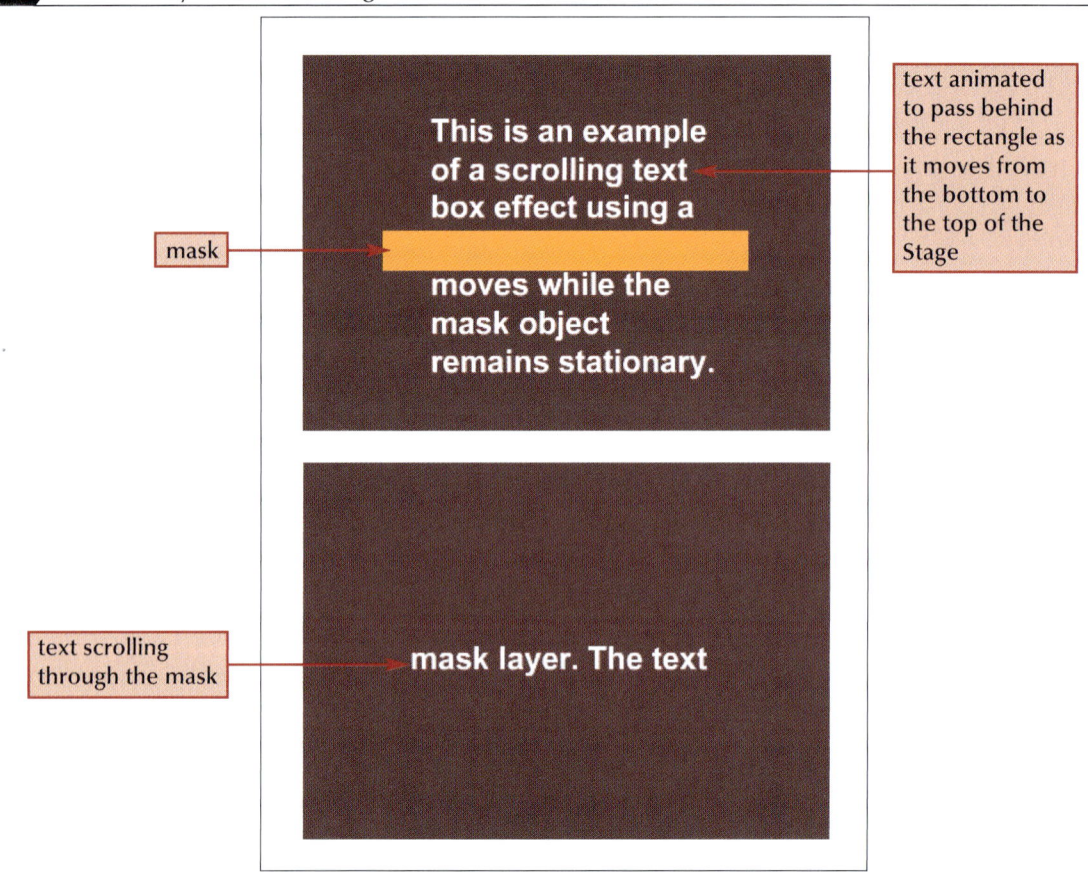

mask

text animated to pass behind the rectangle as it moves from the bottom to the top of the Stage

text scrolling through the mask

Tutorial 4 Creating Complex Animations | Flash | FL 179

| InSight | **Creating an Animated Picture Masked with Text** |

An interesting effect you can create with mask layers is to use text for the mask object and have another object such as a picture show through the text. With this technique, the text acts like a window for the content behind it. For example, if you animate a picture on the masked layer, as the picture moves, only the parts of the picture that are behind the text will be visible.

When you first create a mask layer, Flash locks both the mask and the masked layers. These layers must be locked to preview the effects of the mask on the Stage. When the layers are locked, the mask layer object is not visible, and only the content in the masked layer that is behind the mask layer object becomes visible. You need to unlock the layers to work with the objects on both layers, and then lock the layers again to test the animation.

You'll explore a mask layer animation Aly created for Jackson's Sports.

To explore the mask layer animation in the Jackson's Sports banner:

1. Open the **sportsMask.fla** file located in the Tutorial.04\Tutorial folder included with your Data Files, and then reset the workspace to the Essentials layout. The sportsMask.fla document opens, but the mask layer content is not visible because the layer is locked.

2. In the Timeline, in the Lock/Unlock column of the mask layer, click the **lock** icon 🔒. The layer is unlocked, and you can see the contents of the mask layer.

3. In the Timeline, in the Show/Hide column of the light text layer, click the dot to hide the layer temporarily. See Figure 4-13.

Figure 4-13 **Mask layer animation**

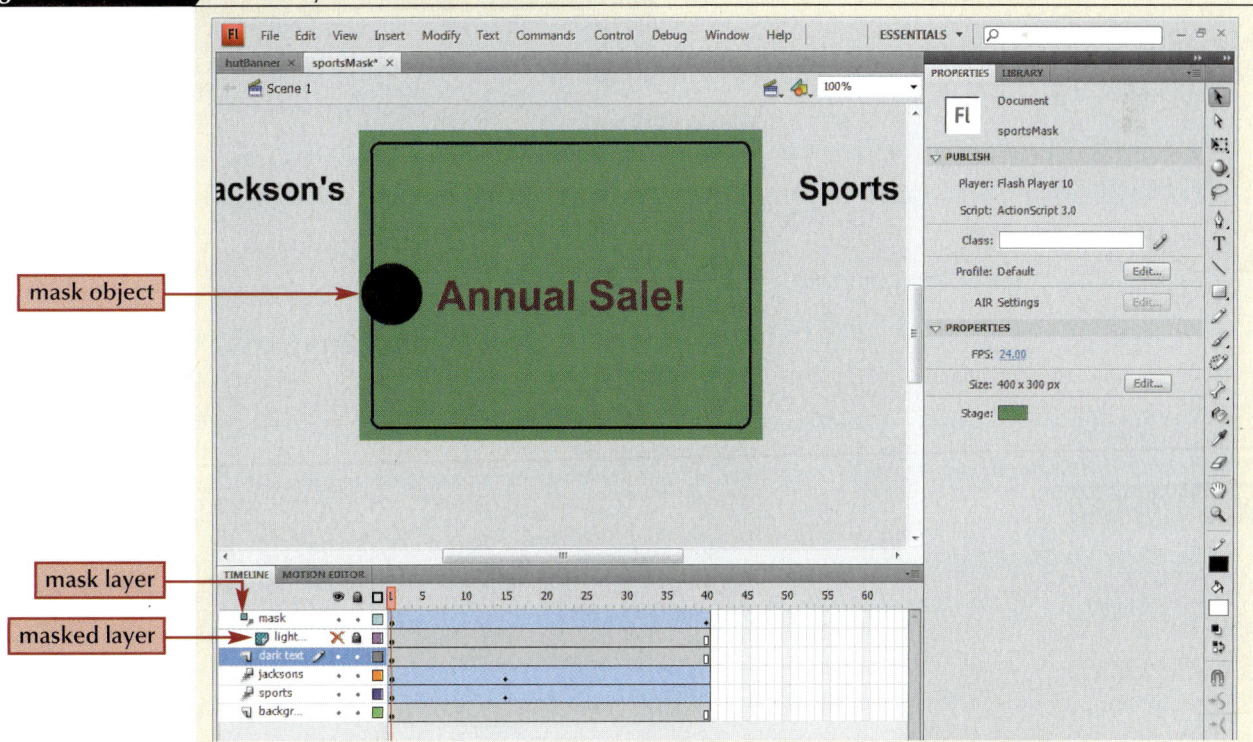

The content of the mask layer is just a motion tween animation of a circle shape. As the circle moves from left to right, different parts of the underlying light-colored Annual Sale text become visible. You'll lock the mask layer again and unhide the light text layer so that you can test the animation. When a mask layer is locked, the masking effect is visible on the Stage.

▶ 4. In the Timeline, in the Lock/Unlock column of the mask layer, click the dot to lock the layer, and then, in the Show/Hide column of the light text layer, click the red x to unhide the layer. The mask layer is locked, as indicated by the padlock icon and the light text layer is no longer hidden.

▶ 5. Press the **Enter** key to play the animation. The part of the light text layer under the circle becomes visible as the circle moves across the Stage.

▶ 6. Close the sportsMask.fla document without saving any changes.

Creating an Animation Using a Mask Layer

As shown in Figure 4-14, Aly's notes for the Jenny's Oyster Hut banner indicate that the Jenny's Oyster Hut text block should have a spotlight effect. You will create a spotlight effect where the spotlight moves across the Jenny's Oyster Hut text block.

Figure 4-14   Animation plan for spotlight effect

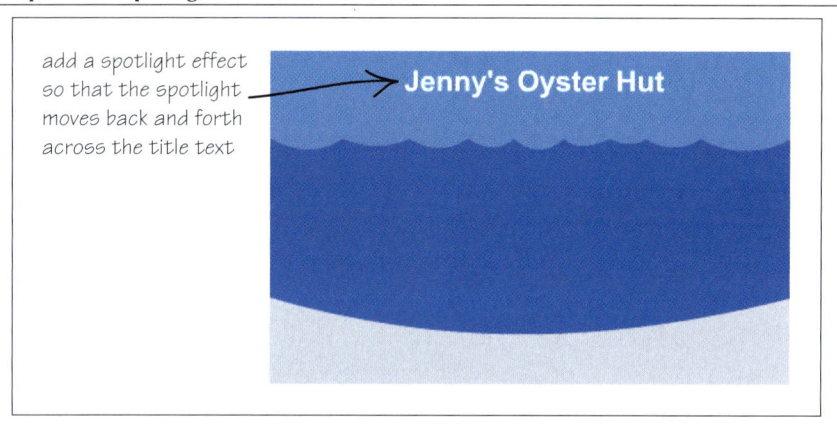

add a spotlight effect so that the spotlight moves back and forth across the title text → **Jenny's Oyster Hut**

You'll create the mask layer animation next. You will start by creating a duplicate of the title text block.

To add layers for the mask animation:

▶ 1. On the Stage, click the **Jenny's Oyster Hut** text block to select it. You need to create a duplicate of this text block.

▶ 2. On the Application bar, click **Edit**, and then click **Copy**. The text is copied to the Clipboard.

▶ 3. In the Timeline, select the **ocean** layer, click the **New Layer** button to insert a new layer above the ocean layer, and then rename the new layer as **gray text**.

▶ 4. On the Application bar, click **Edit**, and then click **Paste in Place** to paste the text block in the new gray text layer in the same relative position as it is in the title layer.

▶ 5. In the Timeline, in the Show/Hide column of the title layer, click the dot to hide the layer's content.

Tip

You can also press the Ctrl+C keys to copy the selected object and press the Ctrl+Shift+V keys to paste it in place.

▶ 6. On the Stage, click the text block to select it, and then, in the Property inspector, change the text (fill) color of the text block to **dark gray** (#333333).

▶ 7. In the Timeline, lock the gray text layer, and then show the title layer. The text in the title layer will provide the white text in the spotlight effect.

▶ 8. In the Timeline, select the **title** layer, click the **New Layer** button to insert a new layer above the title layer, and then rename the new layer as **title mask**. The title mask layer will be the mask layer and contain a motion tween of a circle.

▶ 9. In the Timeline, right-click the **title mask** layer name, and then click **Mask** on the context menu. The layer changes to a mask layer and the title layer changes to a masked layer indented below the title mask layer. Both layers are locked. See Figure 4-15.

Figure 4-15 Locked mask and masked layers

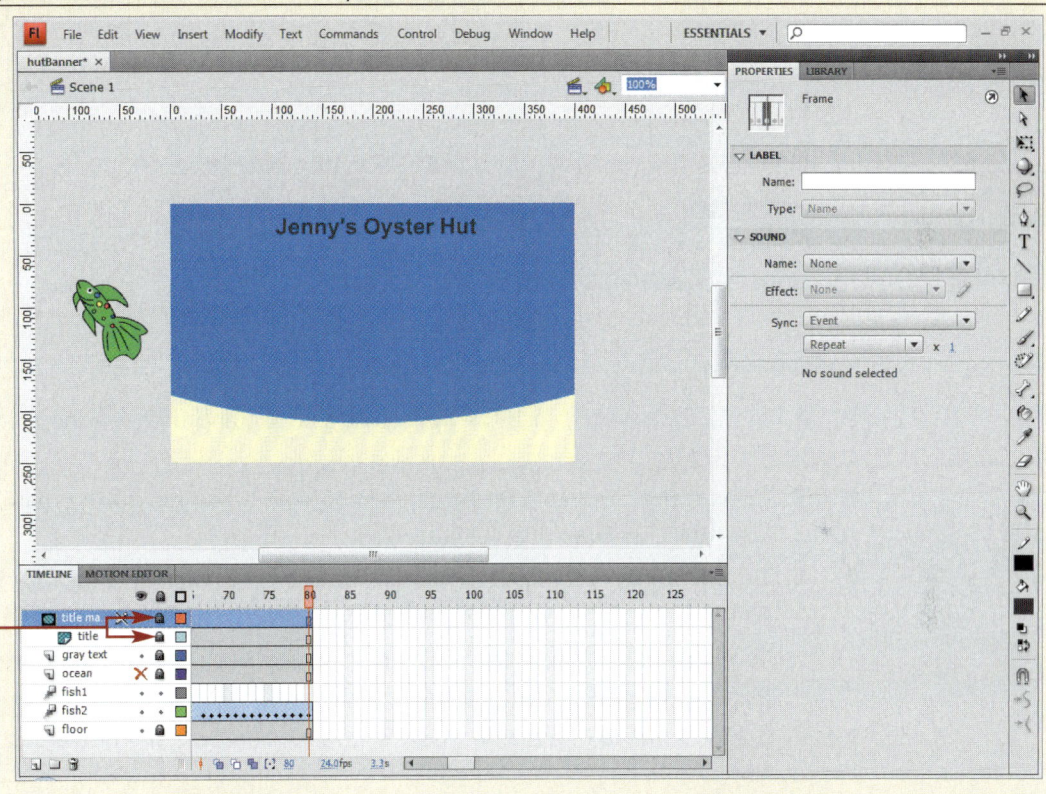

mask and masked layers are locked

Now you need to create a motion tween of a circle and have it move across the text. You will draw the circle shape, convert it to a symbol, and then create a motion tween.

To create the mask layer animation:

▶ 1. In the Timeline, unlock the title mask layer, and then click **Frame 1** of the title mask layer. You will draw a circle on the title mask layer to represent the spotlight.

▶ 2. In the Tools panel, click the **Oval** tool, and then set the fill color to **white** (#FFFFFF) and the stroke color to **no color**.

▶ 3. On the Stage, draw a small circle to the left of the letter J in the Jenny's Oyster Hut text block. See Figure 4-16.

FL 182 Flash | Tutorial 4 Creating Complex Animations

Figure 4-16 — Circle drawn in the title mask layer

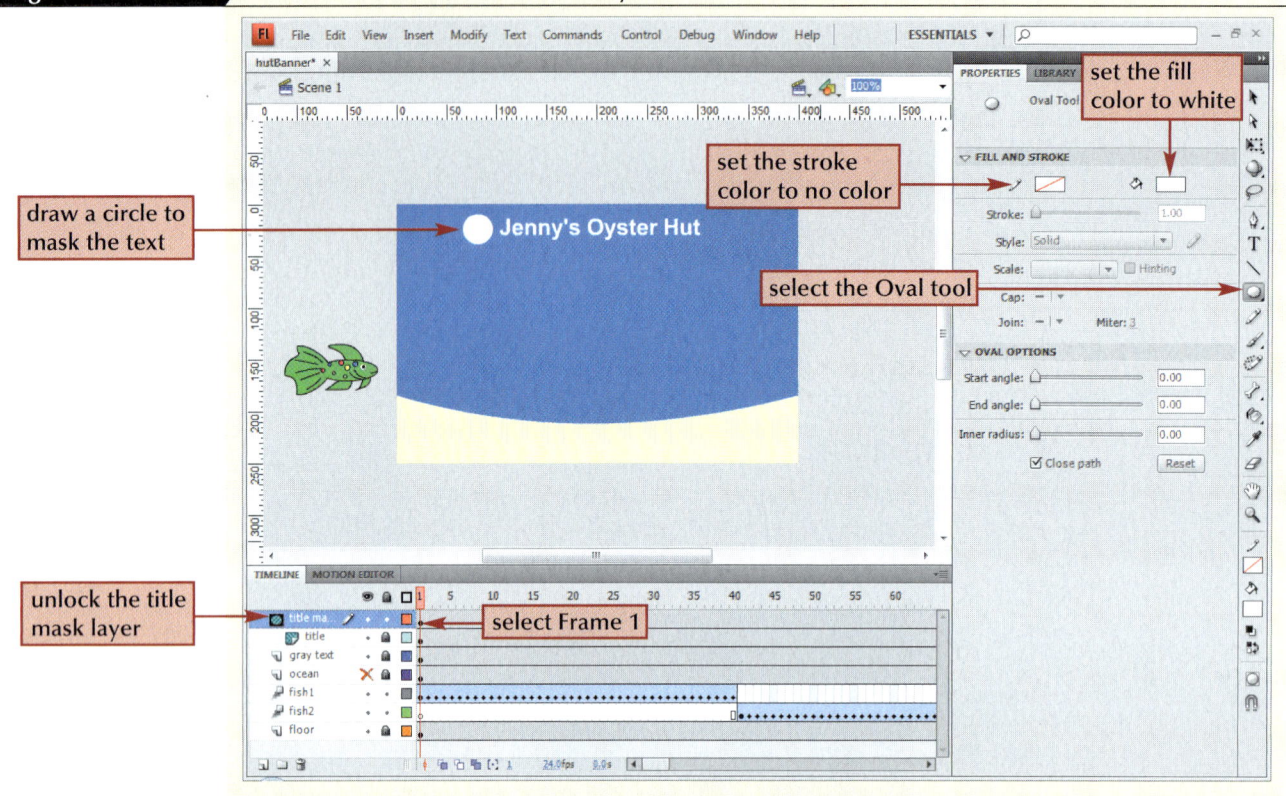

Callouts on figure:
- draw a circle to mask the text
- set the stroke color to no color
- set the fill color to white
- select the Oval tool
- unlock the title mask layer
- select Frame 1

---

4. In the Tools panel, click the **Selection** tool, and then, on the Stage, select the circle.

5. Convert the circle to a movie clip symbol named **circle**. You'll create a motion tween for the circle instance.

6. On the Stage, right-click the **circle** instance, and then click **Create Motion Tween** on the context menu. A motion tween is created in the title mask layer.

    You'll create a highlight effect by moving the circle to the right of the title text block and then back to its starting point.

7. Click **Frame 40** of the title mask layer, and then drag the **circle** instance to the right of the last letter of the text block.

8. Select **Frame 80** of the title mask layer, and then drag the **circle** instance back to the left of the first letter of the text block. Frame 80 represents the end of the motion tween where the circle moves back to its starting point.

9. In the Timeline, lock the title mask layer so that you can play the animation.

10. Move the playhead to **Frame 1**, and then press the **Enter** key to play the animation. The circle creates a spotlight effect as it moves across and back over the title text.

11. Save the document.

> **Tip**
> When testing an animation, you can move the playhead forward or back one frame at a time by pressing the period or comma key, respectively.

In this session, you modified a motion path to make the fish instance swim along a curved path. You also created a mask layer animation to create a spotlight effect. In the next session, you will create text animations on the banner.

Review | Session 4.1 Quick Check

1. List two ways you can modify a motion path.
2. What are Bezier handles and how can you use them to modify a motion path?
3. What is the purpose of the Orient to path option in the Property inspector?
4. Name two motion tween properties you can modify in the Motion Editor.
5. How can you see the effect that a mask layer has on a masked layer when testing an animation within the Flash workspace?
6. True or False? Text cannot be used as a mask in a mask layer.
7. True or False? In a mask layer animation, the contents of the mask layer are revealed when the object in the masked layer moves over it.

Session 4.2

Animating Text Blocks

You can animate text to create special effects. For example, you can have text move onto the Stage in a fly-in effect. Or, in a more complex animation, you can make the individual letters of a text block rotate and fade in as they appear one at a time on the Stage to form a word or phrase. You can also animate text so that it increases and decreases in size to create a pulsating effect.

You can animate text blocks using motion tweens or frame-by-frame animations. For example, you can have a text block move from one side of the Stage to the other using a frame-by-frame animation by changing the location of the text in each keyframe. Using a motion tween, you can animate a text block so that it rotates or changes in size as the animation is played. If you convert the text block to a symbol and then apply a motion tween, you can have the text block exhibit other changes throughout an animation such as fading in or changing color.

You can also apply a shape tween to text. However, you must first convert the text to fills by using the Break Apart command. When you apply the Break Apart command to a text block, each character in the text block becomes an individual text block. You can apply the command again to the individual letters to convert them to fills. After the text blocks are converted to fills, you can apply a shape tween to them. For example, you can make the letters change into an rectangle shape, as shown in Figure 4-17. Be aware that after you convert the text to fills, you can no longer edit the fills as text.

Figure 4-17   Sample shape tween

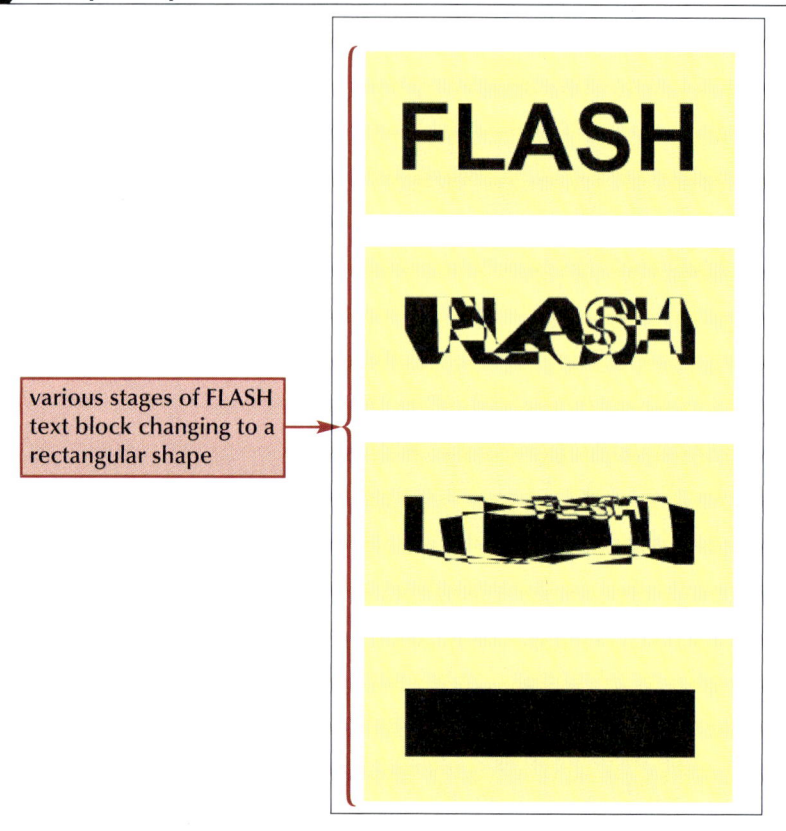

various stages of FLASH text block changing to a rectangular shape

Reference Window | Creating Text Animations

- For a shape tween, select the text block in the first frame of the animation.
- On the Application bar, click Modify, and then click Break Apart to break the text into individual letters.
- On the Application bar, click Modify, and then click Break Apart a second time to convert the text to fills.
- Create a keyframe in the last frame of the animation and change the shape of the text fills.
- Right-click between the first and last keyframe, and then click Create Shape Tween on the context menu.

or

- For a motion tween, select the text block in the first frame of the animation, and then, optionally, convert the text block into a symbol.
- Right-click the text block, and then click Create Motion Tween on the context menu.
- On the last frame of the animation, change the text block's position, size, or orientation or change the symbol instance's tint or transparency.

Adding Animated Text

Based on Aly's notes for completing the banner, shown in Figure 4-18, you need to add three text blocks to the banner for the second scene. The Celebrating text block will rotate once as it moves in from the pasteboard to the center of the Stage. The our text block will appear below the Celebrating text block. The 10th Anniversary! text block will fade in after the first two text blocks and will increase in size. Each text block will be on its own layer so you can animate it individually.

Tutorial 4 Creating Complex Animations | Flash | FL 185

| Figure 4-18 | Animation plan for text blocks |

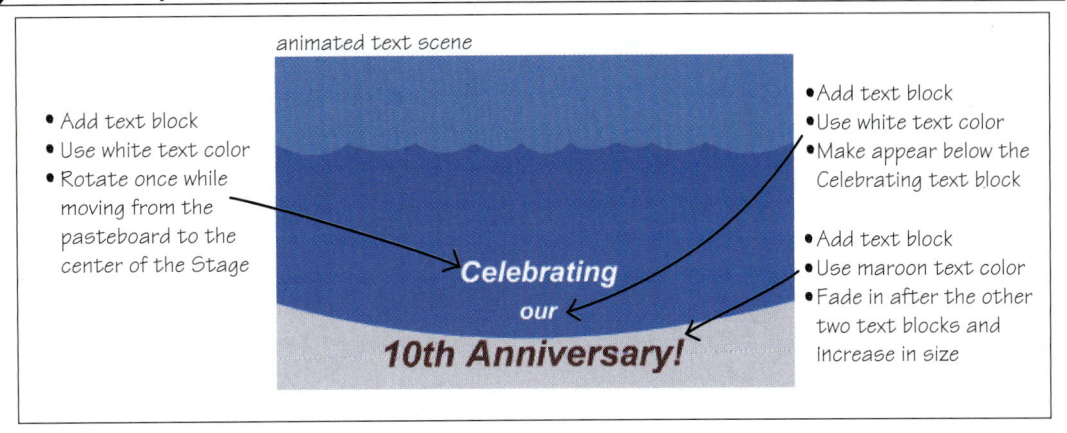

- Add text block
- Use white text color
- Rotate once while moving from the pasteboard to the center of the Stage

animated text scene

Celebrating
our
10th Anniversary!

- Add text block
- Use white text color
- Make appear below the Celebrating text block

- Add text block
- Use maroon text color
- Fade in after the other two text blocks and increase in size

You will start by adding a new scene named animated text that will contain the text animations. In this scene you will add three new layers, one for each text block.

To add a new scene and the layers for the text animations:

1. If you took a break after the previous session, make sure the hutBanner.fla file is open and the workspace is reset to the Essentials layout.

2. Open the Scene panel.

Tip

You can press the Shift+F2 keys to open and close the Scene panel.

3. In the Scene panel, click the **Duplicate Scene** button. A copy of Scene 1 is added to the document. You'll rename both scenes.

4. In the Scene panel, double-click **Scene 1**, type **fish swimming**, and then press the **Enter** key to rename the scene.

5. In the Scene panel, double-click **Scene 1 copy**, type **animated text**, and then press the **Enter** key to rename the scene. The animated text scene is the current scene.

6. Close the Scene panel.

7. In the Timeline, click **Frame 1** of the fish1 layer, and then click the **Delete** button. The fish1 layer is deleted.

8. Repeat Step 7 to delete the fish2, title mask, title, and the gray text layers. The unneeded layers in the animated text scene are deleted.

9. In the Timeline, select the **ocean** layer of the animated text scene, if necessary, and then insert three new layers and name them **celebrating**, **our**, and **anniversary**, respectively. The new layers appear above the ocean layer. See Figure 4-19.

| Figure 4-19 | New layers added to Timeline |

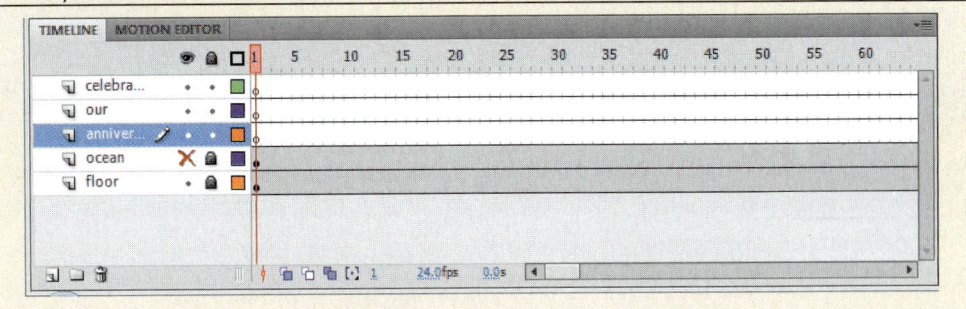

Next, you will add a new text block with the word "Celebrating." Then, you will animate the text block so that it moves from the left of the Stage to the center of the Stage and rotates once throughout the animation.

To create and animate the Celebrating text block:

1. If necessary, display the rulers, and then drag a horizontal guide to approximately **170 pixels** from the top of the Stage and drag a vertical guide to approximately **200 pixels** from the left of the Stage. The guides will help you align the text.

2. In the Tools panel, click the **Text** tool, and then, in the Property inspector, set the font family to **Arial**, the font style to **Bold Italic**, the point size to **22**, the text fill color to **white** (#FFFFFF), and the paragraph format to **Align center**. You will use these text properties for the text block you will create in Frame 1 of the celebrating layer.

3. In the Timeline, click **Frame 1** of the celebrating layer, and then, on the Stage, click the intersection of the two guides to create a text block and type **Celebrating**. The formatted text is entered in the text block.

4. In the Tools panel, click the **Selection** tool, and then reposition the text block on the horizontal guide. This is the final position for the text block. See Figure 4-20.

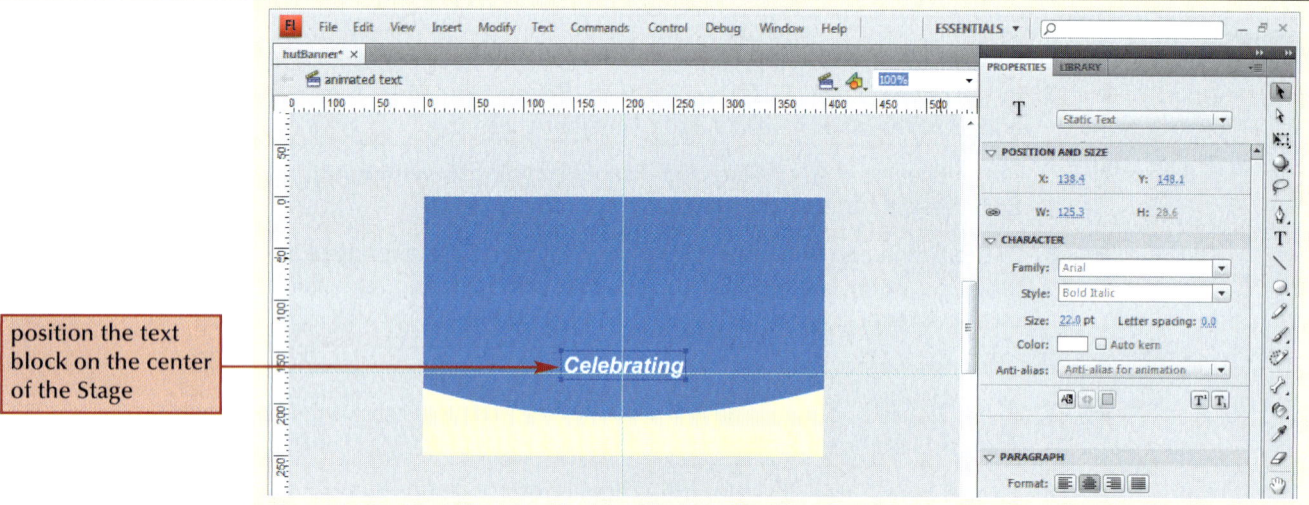

Figure 4-20 | Ending position for the Celebrating text block

position the text block on the center of the Stage

You'll create a motion tween next from Frame 1 through Frame 24 so that the text rotates and moves in from the left of the Stage to its current position. First, you'll insert a keyframe at Frame 25 so that the text block is in the current position after the motion tween.

5. In the Timeline, click **Frame 25** of the celebrating layer, and then insert a keyframe. This indicates the final frame of the motion tween.

6. In the Timeline, click **Frame 1** of the celebrating layer, and then, on the Stage, right-click the **Celebrating** text block and click **Create Motion Tween** on the context menu. A tween span is created from Frame 1 through Frame 24.

7. On the Stage, drag the **Celebrating** text block to the pasteboard to the left of the Stage, keeping the text aligned with the horizontal guide. This is the text block's starting position. See Figure 4-21.

Tutorial 4 Creating Complex Animations | Flash   FL 187

Figure 4-21   **Starting position for the Celebrating text block**

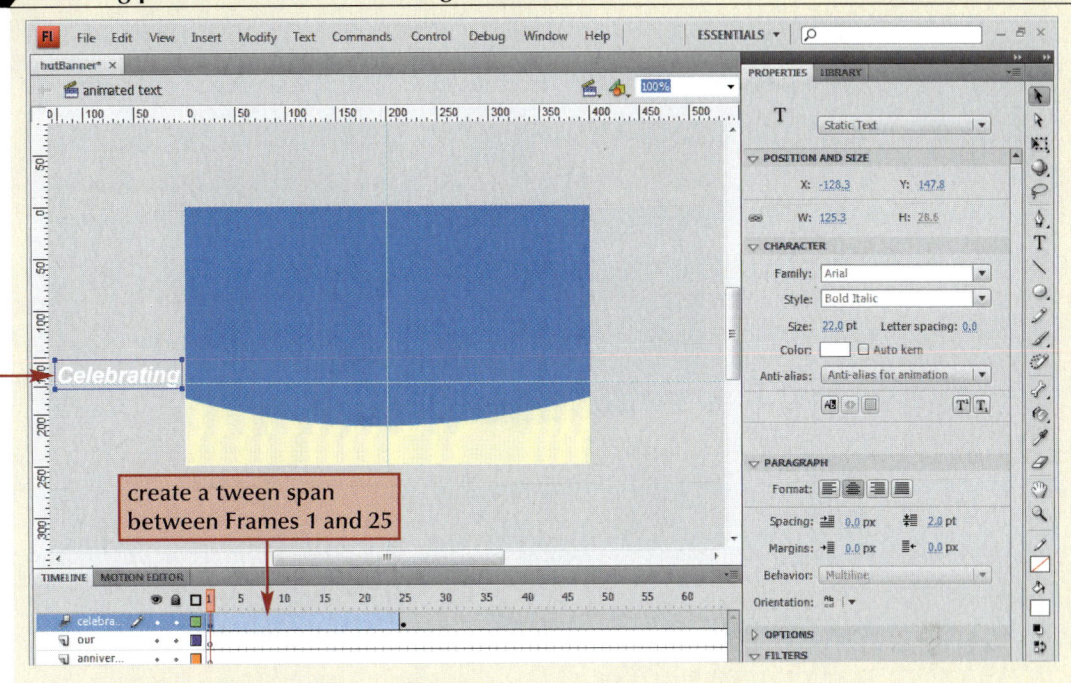

position of the text block in Frame 1

create a tween span between Frames 1 and 25

▶ 8. In the Timeline, select **Frame 24** of the celebrating layer, and then move the text block back to the center of the Stage. This is the text block's position at the end of the motion tween. You will set the motion tween's rotation value next.

▶ 9. On the Stage, click the tween's motion path to select it, and then, in the Rotation section of the Property inspector, set the rotate value to **1** and make sure the rotation direction is **CW** (clockwise).

▶ 10. Scrub the playhead from Frame 1 through Frame 24. The text block moves from the left of the Stage to the center of the Stage, rotating once. The motion tween for the Celebrating text block is complete.

The text block for the our layer will not have a motion tween because it won't be animated. Instead, the our text will only appear starting with Frame 30. This means that the our text is not displayed from Frame 1 through Frame 29, but is displayed from Frame 30 through Frame 80.

To add the our text block:

▶ 1. In the Timeline, click **Frame 30** of the our layer, and then insert a keyframe. The our text block will appear in Frame 30.

▶ 2. In the Tools panel, click the **Text** tool T, and then, in the Property inspector, change the point size to **18**. The other properties of the our text block are the same as the Celebrating text block.

▶ 3. On the Stage, create a text block on the vertical guide below the Celebrating text block, and then type **our**. The formatted text is entered in the text block.

▶ 4. In the Tools panel, click the **Selection** tool, and then drag the text block so that it is centered on the Stage. See Figure 4-22.

Tip

You can press the T key to select the Text tool.

Figure 4-22   The our text block centered on the Stage

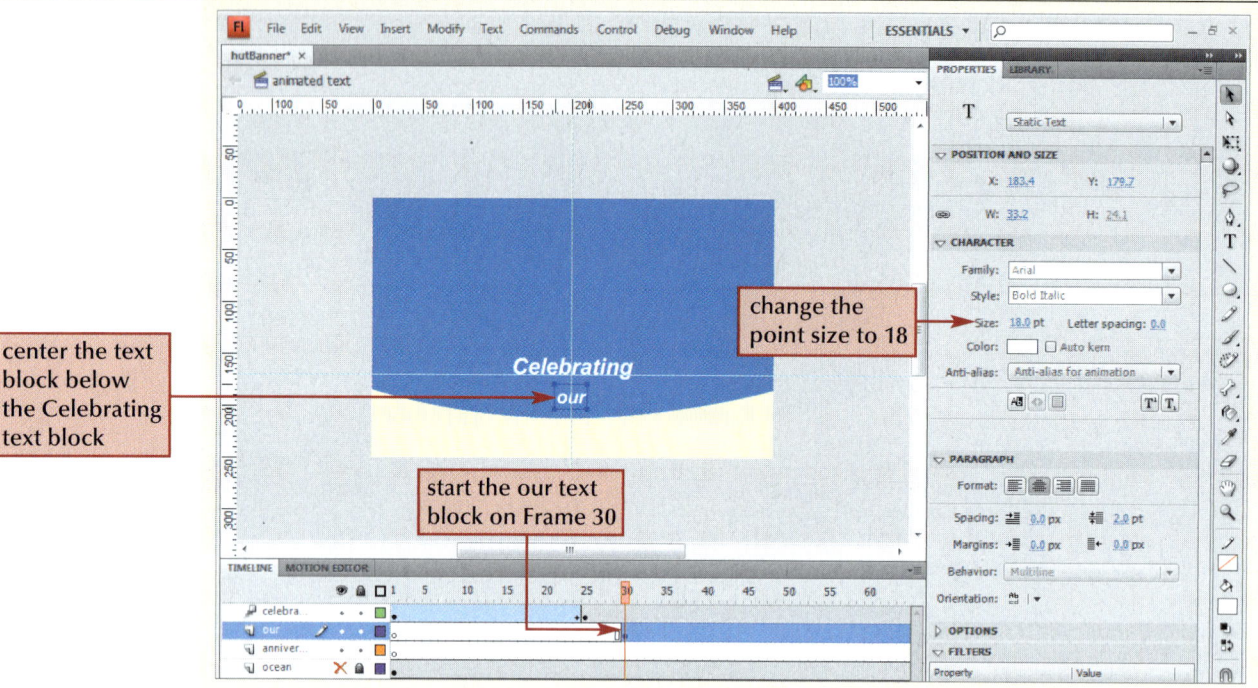

Callouts on figure:
- center the text block below the Celebrating text block
- change the point size to 18
- start the our text block on Frame 30

The 10th Anniversary! text block will be animated with a motion tween. Although the text block will not move, it will change in size and fade in throughout the animation. Recall that to change a text block's transparency or color, it must first be converted to a symbol. To create the fade-in effect, you need to convert the 10th Anniversary! text block to a movie clip symbol. The text block will not be visible until Frame 30, at which point the motion tween will start.

To create and animate the 10th Anniversary! text block:

1. In the Timeline, click **Frame 30** of the anniversary layer, and then insert a keyframe. The motion tween for the 10th Anniversary! text will begin at Frame 30.

2. In the Tools panel, click the **Text** tool T, and then, in the Property inspector, change the point size to **12** and change the font color to **maroon** (#660000).

3. On the Stage, click the vertical guide below the our text block, and then type **10th Anniversary!**. The formatted text is entered in the text block.

4. In the Tools panel, click the **Selection** tool, and then, on the Stage, drag the **10th Anniversary!** text block so that it is centered about 230 pixels from the top of the Stage. See Figure 4-23.

Figure 4-23 | The 10th Anniversary! text centered on the Stage

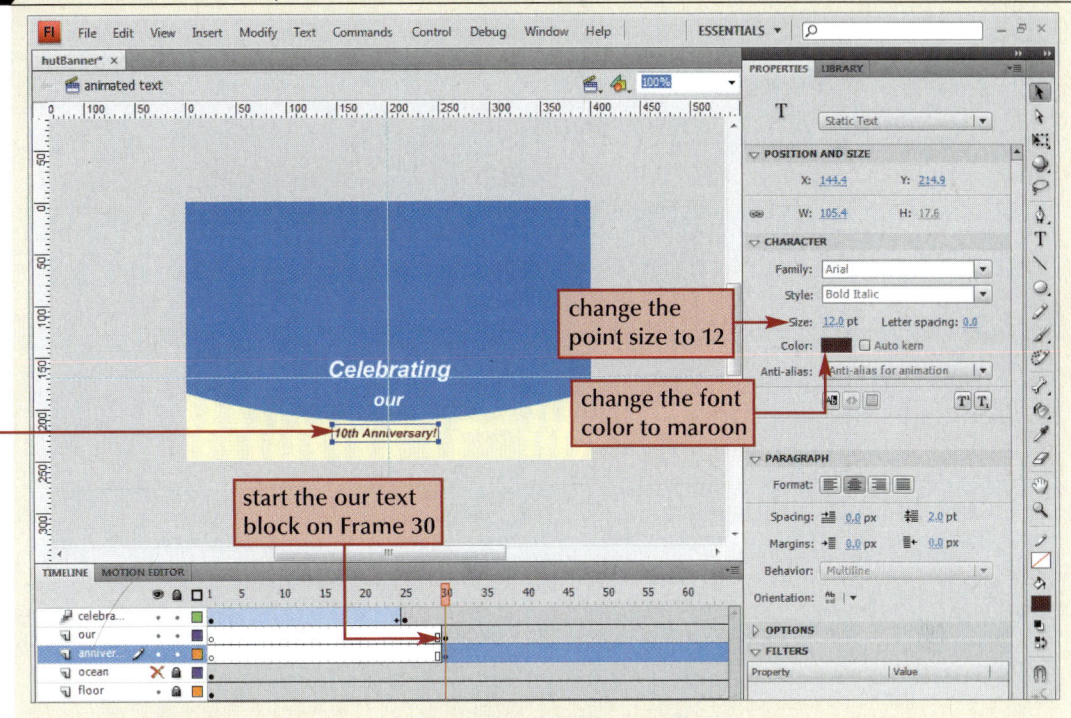

- center the text block 230 pixels from the top of the Stage
- change the point size to 12
- change the font color to maroon
- start the our text block on Frame 30

5. Convert the text block to a movie clip symbol named **anniversary text**.

6. On the Stage, right-click the anniversary text instance, and then click **Create Motion Tween** on the context menu. A tween span is added between Frame 30 and Frame 80.

7. In the Timeline, click **Frame 45** of the anniversary layer. The text block will fade in and reach its maximum size at this frame.

8. On the Application bar, click **Window**, and then click **Transform** to open the Transform panel.

Tip

You can also press the Ctrl+T keys to open and close the Transform panel.

9. On the Stage, make sure that the **10th Anniversary!** text block is still selected.

10. In the Transform panel, click the **Constrain** button, if necessary, to change it to .

11. In the Transform panel, click the Scale Width value, type **230%** in the Scale Width box, and then press the **Enter** key. The size of the text in the 10th Anniversary! text block increases. See Figure 4-24.

Figure 4-24   Size of the 10th Anniversary! text scaled

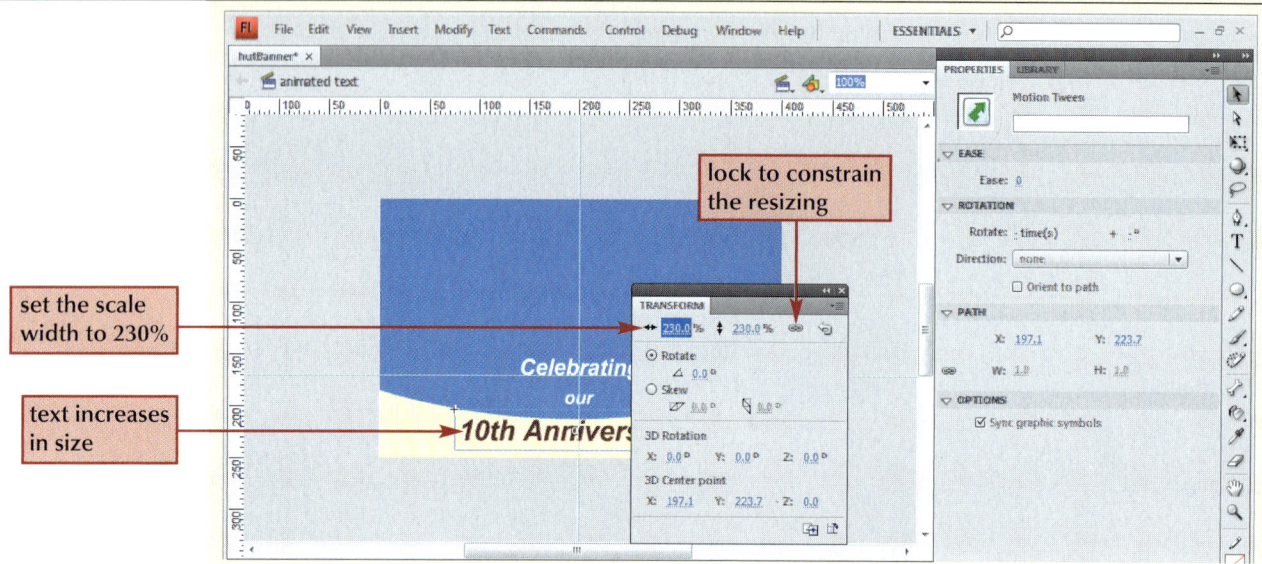

set the scale width to 230%

lock to constrain the resizing

text increases in size

▶ **12.** Close the Transform panel, and then scrub the playhead between Frames 30 and 45 to see the text block increase in size throughout the motion tween animation.

Aly's notes indicate that in addition to increasing in size, the 10th Anniversary! text block should fade in throughout the animation. You will change the alpha amount of the text block at the beginning and end of the motion tween to create the fade-in effect.

To apply a fade-in effect to the 10th Anniversary! text block:

▶ **1.** In the Timeline, click **Frame 30** of the anniversary layer.

▶ **2.** On the Stage, select the **10th Anniversary!** text block.

▶ **3.** In the Color Effect section of the Property inspector, click the **Color styles** button, and then click **Alpha**. The Alpha amount slider and box appear.

▶ **4.** Drag the **Alpha** slider to the left to set the alpha amount to **0**. The text block becomes transparent.

▶ **5.** In the Timeline, click **Frame 45** of the anniversary layer, and then, on the Stage, select the **10th Anniversary!** text block.

▶ **6.** In the Property inspector, drag the **Alpha** slider to the right to set the alpha amount to **100**. The text block becomes opaque at Frame 45.

▶ **7.** Scrub the playhead between Frames 30 and 45 to see the 10th Anniversary! text block increase in size and fade in throughout the animation.

▶ **8.** In the Timeline, drag the playhead to **Frame 1**, and then press the **Enter** key to play the animation. The Celebrating text block moves in from the side of the Stage to the middle of the Stage, the our text block appears, and then the 10th Anniversary! text block fades in below the our text block and increases in size.

▶ **9.** On the Application bar, click **View**, point to **Guides**, and then click **Clear Guides**. The guides are cleared.

▶ **10.** Save the document.

Animating Individual Letters

You can animate individual letters in a word or phrase to create interesting text effects. For example, you can animate the letters of a word to fall into place on the Stage one at a time. Or, you can have a word explode with the individual letters flying off the Stage in different directions. Another example is to have the individual letters of a word increase and decrease in size to create a pulsating effect. To create most of these text effects, you first need to break a word into its individual letters and then animate each letter separately. The simplest way to animate each letter is to create motion tweens. This means that each letter must reside on its own layer.

| InSight | Creating Symbols when Animating Text Blocks |

When animating text blocks, it's a good idea to create a symbol for each text block even though converting text to symbols is not required in certain types of animations. Converting text blocks to symbols enables you to use the text block instances more than once in a document without increasing the file size. You can also add color or transparency changes as part of an existing animation without having to create new duplicate text blocks. And, with text blocks as symbols, advanced users of Flash can manipulate the text block instances through programming code to create more complex animations.

Aly has been working on a banner for Jackson's Sports that includes individual letter text animation. In this banner, each letter has the same motion tween applied to it to create a pulsating effect. The text blocks in this animation did not have to be converted to symbols because the motion tweens only include changes to the text blocks' dimensions.

To explore the Jackson's Sports banner with individual letters text effect:

▶ 1. Open the **sportsLetters.fla** file located in the Tutorial.04\Tutorial folder included with your Data Files.

▶ 2. Press the **Enter** key to play the animation. Each letter increases and decreases in size one after the other. Notice that each letter resides on its own layer.

▶ 3. In the Timeline, click **Frame 1** of the J layer, and then look at the size of the letter J on the Stage.

▶ 4. In the Timeline, click **Frame 5** of the J layer, and then look at how the letter J increases in size on the Stage. The property keyframe in this frame represents the change in the text block's dimensions.

▶ 5. In the Timeline, click **Frame 10** of the J layer, and then look at the letters J and A on the Stage. In this frame, the letter J returns to its original size. At the same time, the next letter, A, increases in size. A property keyframe in this frame represents the change in dimensions for the J text block. See Figure 4-25.

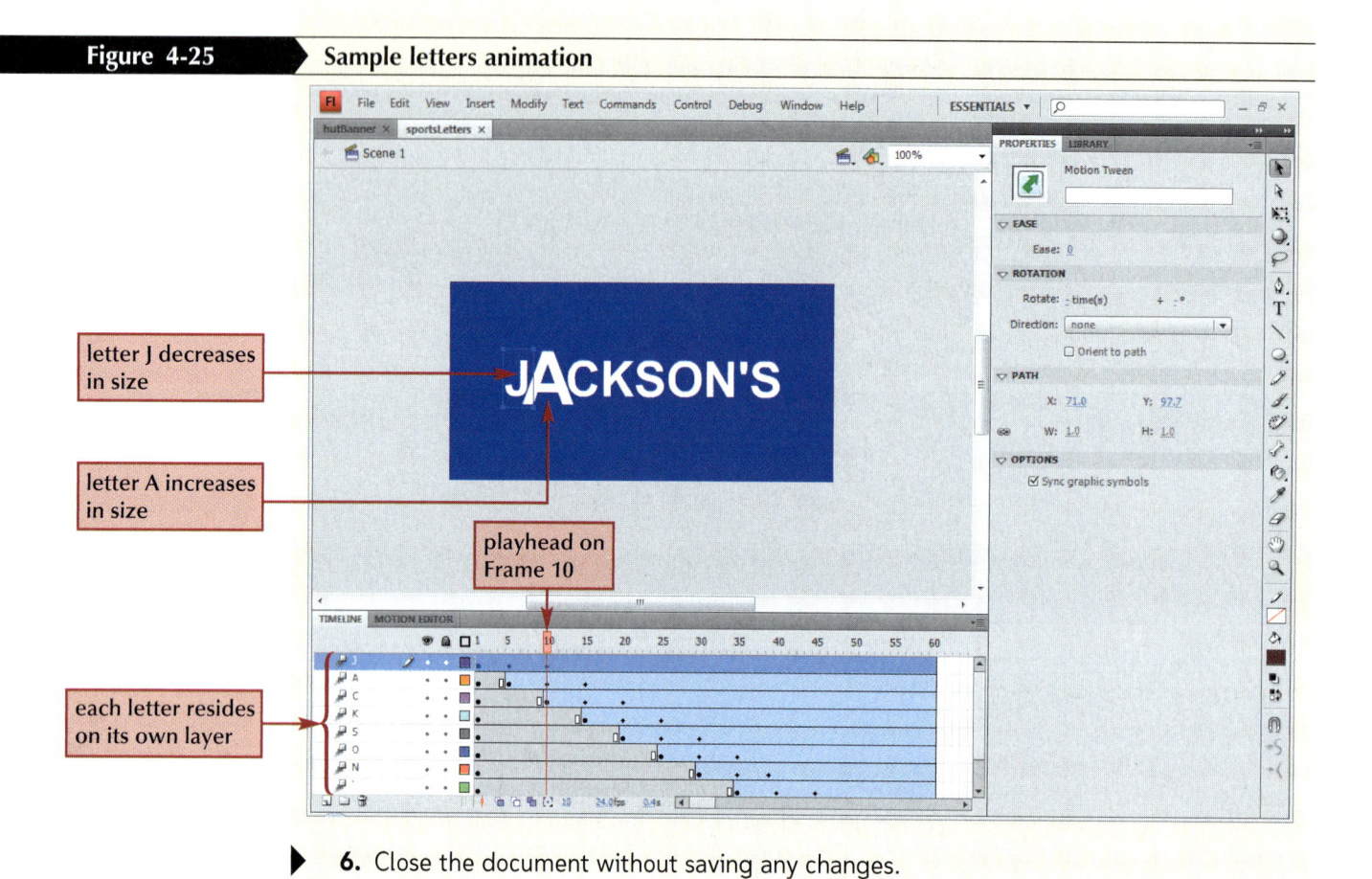

Figure 4-25 Sample letters animation

- letter J decreases in size
- letter A increases in size
- playhead on Frame 10
- each letter resides on its own layer

▶ **6.** Close the document without saving any changes.

Creating a Complex Text Animation

The next animation you will create for the Jenny's Oyster Hut banner consists of individual letters rotating one after the other, as described in Aly's notes shown in Figure 4-26. Each letter will rotate around an imaginary axis in three-dimensional space. Three-dimensional graphics are discussed later in this session. Each letter will also increase and decrease in size as it rotates. This effect involves animating the individual letters of the word in a similar way to the animated text in the banner Aly created for Jackson's Sports. To create the animations for the individual letters, you will first create the Jenny's text block, convert each letter in that text block into its own individual text block, and then distribute these individual letter text blocks onto their own layers.

Figure 4-26 — Animation plan for Jenny's text

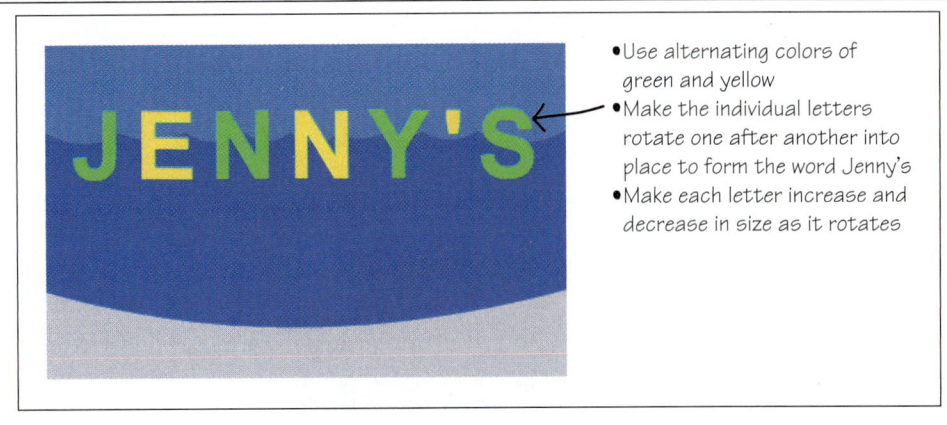

- Use alternating colors of green and yellow
- Make the individual letters rotate one after another into place to form the word Jenny's
- Make each letter increase and decrease in size as it rotates

---

Reference Window | Animating Individual Letters

- On the Stage, select the text block containing the letters to be animated.
- On the Application bar, click Modify, and then click Break Apart.
- On the Application bar, click Modify, point to Timeline, and then click Distribute to Layers.
- Delete the original layer, which is now empty.
- If necessary, convert each letter that will be animated to a symbol with an appropriate name.
- Create a motion tween for each letter.

Before animating the letters, you will change the colors of the letters in the Jenny's text block to alternate between yellow and green to enhance the special effect. You will initially create the Jenny's text block in a new layer folder. Then, when you distribute the letters to individual layers, all of the new layers will be inside the folder. This new animation will reside in the animated text scene, which will play after the fish swimming scene in the document. You'll create a new layer folder for the new text block.

To create the JENNY'S text block in the animated text scene:

1. In the Timeline, click **Frame 1** of the celebrating layer, click the **New Layer** button to insert a new layer, and then name the new layer **title**. The title layer is created above the celebrating layer.

2. In the Timeline, click the **New Folder** button to create a new layer folder, insert a new layer folder, and then rename the new layer folder **letters**. The letters layer folder is created above the title layer.

3. In the Timeline, drag the **title** layer into the letters folder, and then click **Frame 1** of the title layer.

4. In the Tools panel, click the **Text** tool, and then, in the Property inspector, set the font family to **Arial**, the font style to **Bold**, the point size to **70**, the letter spacing to **10**, the text fill color to **yellow** (#FFFF00), and the paragraph format to **Align center**.

5. On the Stage, create a text block, and then type **JENNY'S**.

6. In the Tools panel, click the **Selection** tool, and then, on the Stage, drag the **JENNY'S** text block to center it about 100 pixels from the top of the Stage. See Figure 4-27.

Figure 4-27   **JENNY'S text block**

text block centered 100 pixels from the top of the Stage

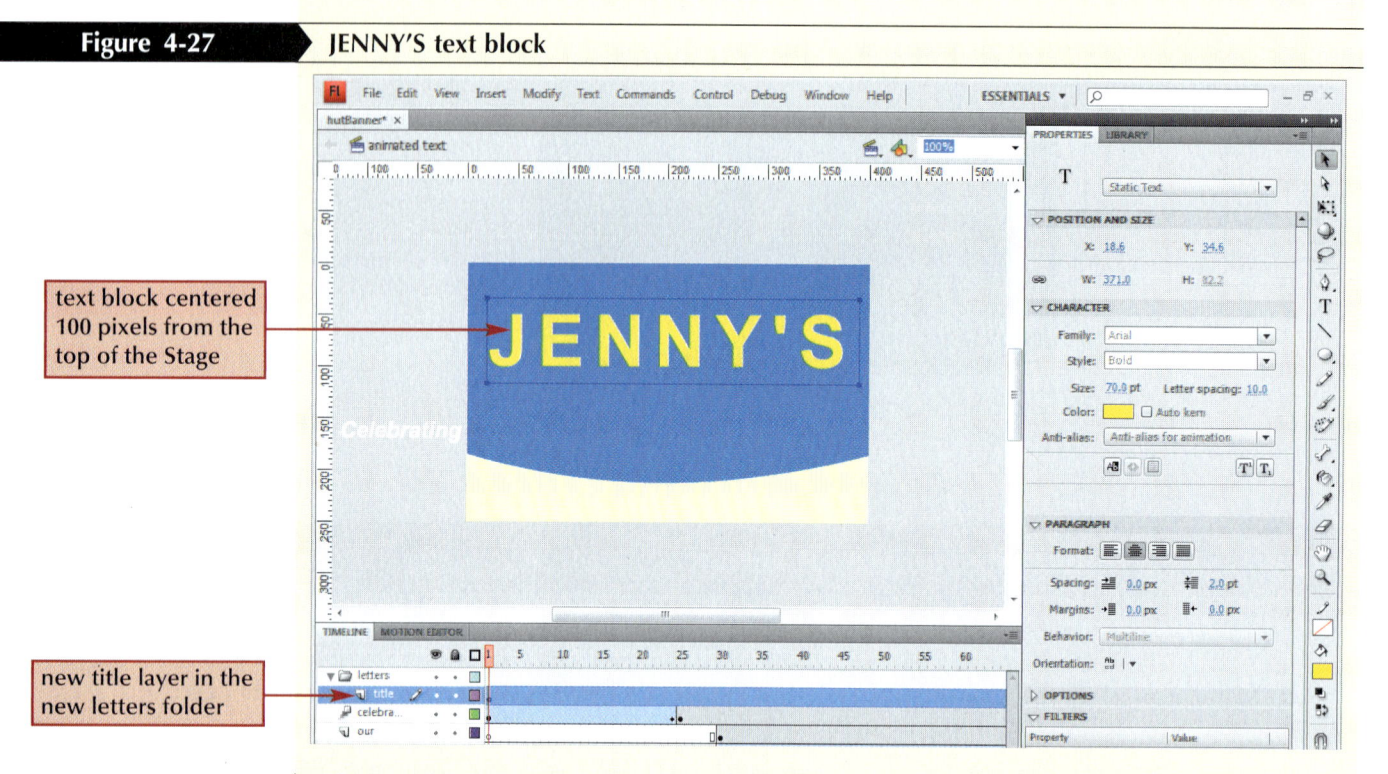

new title layer in the new letters folder

▸ 7. On the Stage, double-click the **JENNY'S** text block, click and drag in the text block to select the letter **J**, and then change the letter's text fill color to **green** (#00FF00).

▸ 8. Repeat Step 7 to change the color of the first letter **N**, the letter **Y**, and the letter **S** to the same color green. The letters in the word JENNY'S alternate between green and yellow.

▸ 9. In the Tools panel, click the **Selection** tool . The Jenny's text block remains selected.

Distributing Objects to Individual Layers

Animating a word's individual letters as in the Jackson's Sports banner requires each letter to be placed on its own layer. A quick way to place each letter into its own layer is to use the Distribute to Layers command. This command takes a group of selected objects and places each individual object onto its own layer. Each new layer is named based on its content. For example, if the objects distributed are text blocks, the names of the new layers are the same as the text in the text blocks. If the objects are symbols, the names of the new layers are the same as the names of the symbols. Other layers are named "Layer" followed by a number. This helps you to identify which layers the selected objects have been distributed to. The layer that originally contained the grouped objects will be empty after you apply the Distribute to Layers command and can be deleted. Before you apply the Distribute to Layers command, be sure to select all of the objects you want distributed.

Tutorial 4 Creating Complex Animations | Flash | FL 195

InSight | Organizing Distributed Layers in a Layer Folder

Before distributing a group of objects to layers, create a new layer folder and move the layer containing the objects into the layer folder. After the objects are distributed to layers, all of the new layers will reside inside the layer folder. You can then collapse the layer folder to hide the individual layers when you aren't working with them. This makes it easier to work with the document's Timeline and any other layers in your document.

To convert the Jenny's text block into individual letters so they can be distributed to individual layers, you need to break the text block into separate text blocks, one for each letter, using the Break Apart command. When you apply the Distribute to Layers command to the selected text blocks, each letter is placed on its own layer. You then can create the necessary motion tween animations for each of the letters.

You will start by separating the letters into individual text blocks and distributing the text blocks into individual layers.

To create the individual letters from the word JENNY'S:

1. On the Application bar, click **Modify**, and then click **Break Apart**. Each letter is placed in its own text block and all the text blocks are selected. See Figure 4-28.

Figure 4-28 | **Individual letter text blocks**

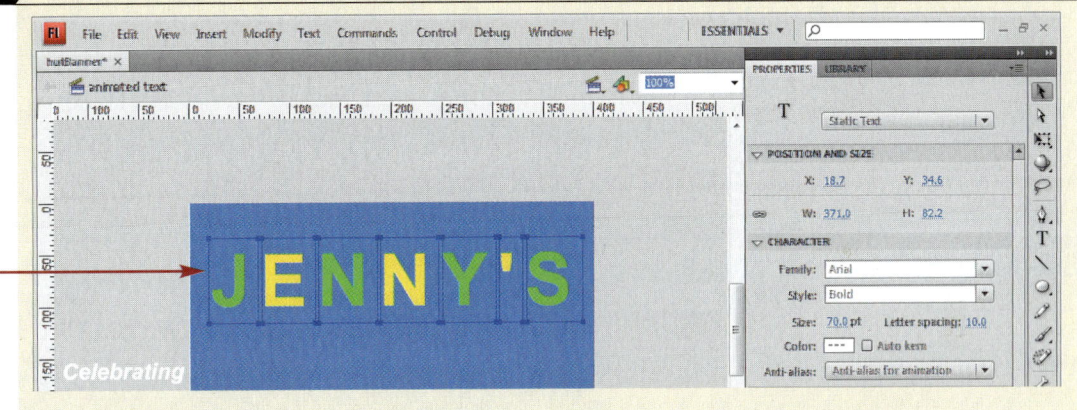

each letter in the title layer is a text block

Tip
You can press the Ctrl+B keys to break apart letters into individual text blocks; you can press the Ctrl+ Shift+D keys to distribute selected objects to individual layers.

2. With all of the letters still selected, on the Application bar, click **Modify**, point to **Timeline**, and then click **Distribute to Layers**. Each letter is placed on its own layer that is named with the letter it contains. The title layer is empty and is no longer needed.

3. In the Timeline, delete the **title** layer. The empty title layer is deleted from the Timeline.

Now that the letters in the JENNY'S text have been split into individual text blocks and onto separate layers, you can animate each letter to create the animation. You will convert each letter into a movie clip symbol and then create a motion tween for each letter instance. The motion tween for letter J, the first letter, will start in Frame 1. The other motion tweens will start every fifth frame.

To convert each letter to a symbol and create motion tweens:

1. On the Stage, select the letter **J**, and then convert the letter to a movie clip symbol named **J**. The symbol is added to the document's library.

▸ 2. Repeat Step 1 for each of the remaining letters, naming each symbol for the letter it represents, using **N1** as the symbol name for the first letter N, **N2** as the symbol name for the second letter N, and **Apostrophe** as the symbol name for the apostrophe. All the letters are converted to symbols.

▸ 3. In the Timeline, insert a keyframe at **Frame 5** of the E layer. The animation for the letter E will start in the fifth frame of the layer. You didn't insert a keyframe for the letter J because it will start in the first frame of the layer.

▸ 4. Repeat Step 3 to insert a keyframe in the first layer N at **Frame 10**, in the second layer N at **Frame 15**, in layer Y at **Frame 20**, in layer ' (apostrophe) at **Frame 25**, and in layer S at **Frame 30**. See Figure 4-29.

Figure 4-29 ▸ Keyframes inserted in each layer

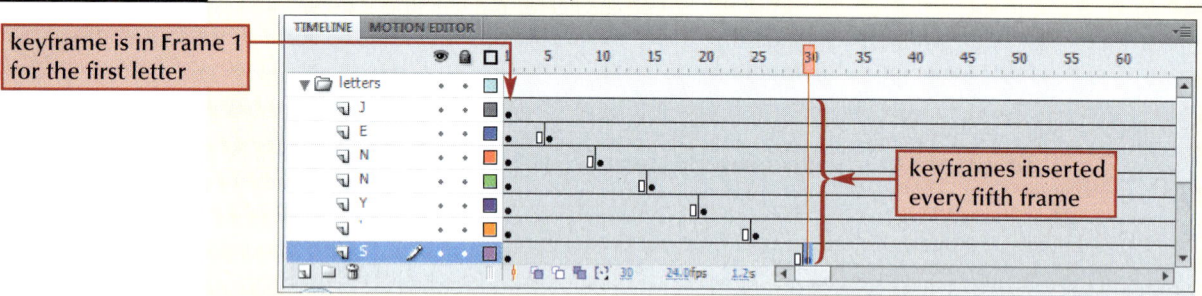

keyframe is in Frame 1 for the first letter

keyframes inserted every fifth frame

▸ 5. In the Timeline, right-click **Frame 1** of layer J, and then click **Create Motion Tween** on the context menu. The motion tween is created for the letter J.

▸ 6. Repeat Step 5 for each of the other letter layers to create motion tweens at **Frame 5** in layer E, at **Frame 10** in the first layer N, at **Frame 15** in the second layer N, at **Frame 20** in layer Y, at **Frame 25** in layer ' (apostrophe), and at **Frame 30** in layer S. See Figure 4-30.

Figure 4-30 ▸ Motion tweens created for each layer

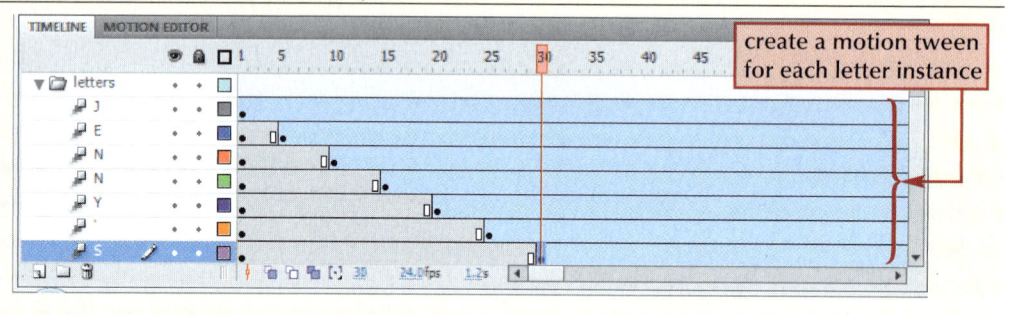

create a motion tween for each letter instance

Now that each layer has a motion tween, you need to change the properties of each instance at the starting frame for its tween span.

Creating 3D Graphic Effects

Every object in Flash has x and y properties, which represent the object's coordinates relative to the Stage. By adding a third property, the z property, you can create an illusion of depth where an object appears to be closer or farther away than other objects and you can manipulate an object in three dimensions along its x-, y-, or z-axis. To create this illusion in Flash, you create three-dimensional (3D) effects by moving and rotating movie clips in 3D space. A **3D space** is created by including the z-axis as a property of a movie clip instance. You can only apply 3D properties to movie clip instances. These

Tutorial 4 Creating Complex Animations | Flash | FL 197

instances can be moved along their z-axis using the 3D Translation tool or rotated along their x- or y-axis with the 3D Rotation tool.

You will use the 3D Rotation tool to rotate each letter along its y-axis.

To rotate each letter instance in 3D space:

1. In the Timeline, click **Frame 1** of the J layer.
2. In the Tools panel, click the **3D Rotation** tool to select it. The J instance is overlaid with 3D axes. You change the 3D properties of an instance by dragging one of its axes. See Figure 4-31.

Figure 4-31 | **J instance selected with 3D Rotation tool**

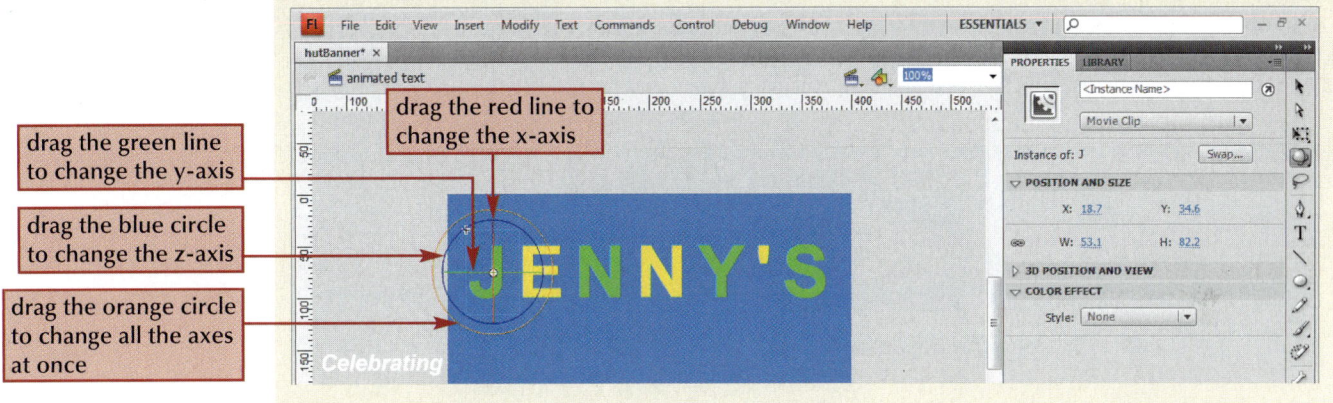

- drag the green line to change the y-axis
- drag the red line to change the x-axis
- drag the blue circle to change the z-axis
- drag the orange circle to change all the axes at once

3. On the Stage, drag the green line on the right of the J movie clip instance to its left to rotate the letter so that it faces to its left. The J movie clip instance rotates along its y-axis in 3D space. See Figure 4-32.

Figure 4-32 | **J instance being rotated**

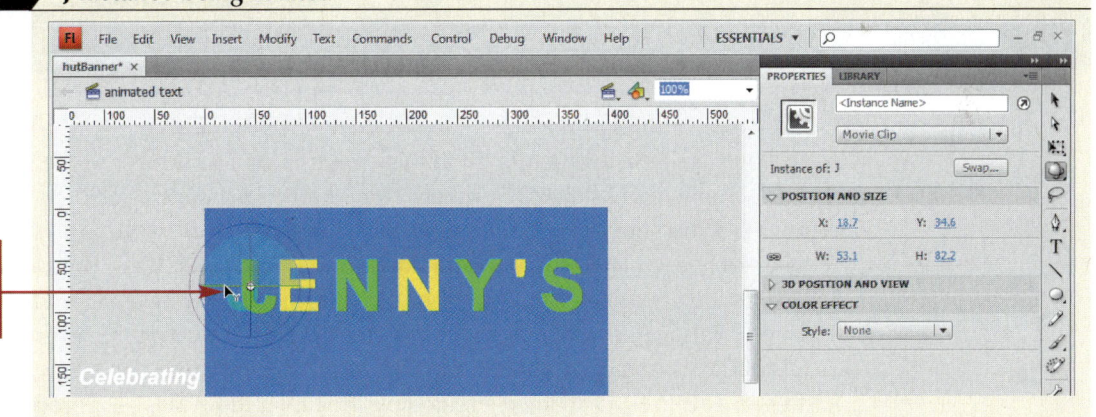

- drag the green line left to rotate the letter along its y-axis

4. In the Timeline, click **Frame 10** of the J layer.
5. On the Stage, drag the green line on the left of the J movie clip instance to its right to rotate the letter so that it faces to its right. The J instance rotates back to its original orientation in Frame 10.

Tip

To prevent selecting more than one letter at one time, lock layers you aren't working with and then unlock the layers as needed to modify them.

6. Scrub the playhead through Frames 1 through 10 to see the 3D rotation effect on the letter J. Because the letter instance was rotated with the 3D Rotation tool, Flash converts the movie clip into a 3D movie clip.

7. Repeat Steps 3 through 5 for each letter instance to rotate each letter left in the starting keyframe of its tween span and rotate the letter back to its original orientation 10 frames later.

8. Drag the playhead to **Frame 1**, and then press the **Enter** key to play the animation. Each letter in JENNY'S rotates in 3D space one after the other. See Figure 4-33.

Figure 4-33 | Completed JENNY'S text animation

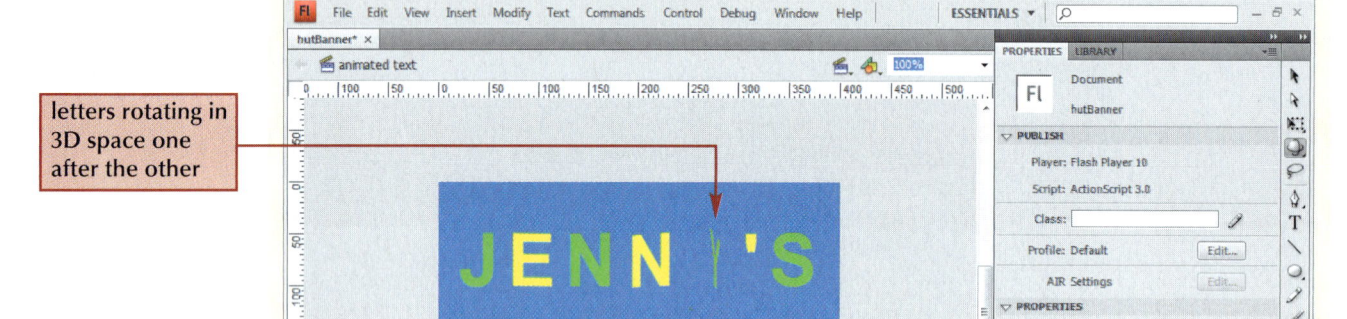

letters rotating in 3D space one after the other

9. Save the document.

In this session, you animated text blocks in the second scene of the banner. You also created an animation of the individual letters of the Jenny's name and applied a 3D rotation effect to each letter. In the next session, you will complete the banner by adding a complex animation to the first scene.

Review | **Session 4.2 Quick Check**

1. List two examples of how text can be animated.
2. To apply a shape tween to a text block, what must you do first to the text?
3. If you apply the Distribute to Layers command to a group of selected text blocks, how will the new layers be named in the Timeline?
4. Why must each letter to be animated be on its own layer?
5. Why is it a good idea to place all of the individual letter layers in a layer folder?
6. True or False? A layer whose contents are distributed to separate layers with the Distribute to Layers command retains a copy of its original contents.
7. True or False? A 3D space is created by including the z-axis as a property of a movie clip instance.

Session 4.3

Creating Complex Animation with Nested Symbols

As you have seen, complex animations can be created by animating objects on separate layers. For example, you can animate one object to move across the Stage on one layer while at the same time another object on another layer rotates and increases in size. So, by adding more layers to the document's main Timeline, you can create complex animation effects. Sometimes, however, you cannot achieve the desired special effect by just adding layers with more animations. For example, the Jenny's banner has a fish swimming across the Stage, but the fish's fins and tail remain stationary in relation to the fish. A better design creates animations for the fins and the tail so that the fish moves more realistically. You could separate the fins and the tail from the body of the fish, convert them to movie clip symbols, and then create animations for each one on separate layers. Then, you could animate the fish body, fins, and tail to move across the Stage at the same time as one object to achieve a more natural look. This is difficult to do, however, because it requires that you synchronize all the animations to work together. A simpler way to do this is to create a nested symbol.

A **nested symbol** is a symbol that contains instances of other symbols within its Timeline. Recall that each symbol has its own Timeline. In the case of movie clip symbols, their Timelines are independent of the document's main Timeline. Within the Timeline of a movie clip symbol, you can insert instances of other symbols that in turn can contain their own animations within their own Timelines. The nested movie clip instances are referred to as the **child movie clips** and the movie clip they are nested within is referred to as the **parent movie clip**. Instances of the parent movie clip can be inserted into the document's main Timeline, and then modified and animated just like any other symbol instance. When you modify or animate the parent movie clip, the child movie clips are also affected. In the case of the fish, the parent movie clip can consist of the fish body plus nested instances of the fins and the tail, as shown in Figure 4-34.

Figure 4-34 Example of a nested movie clip

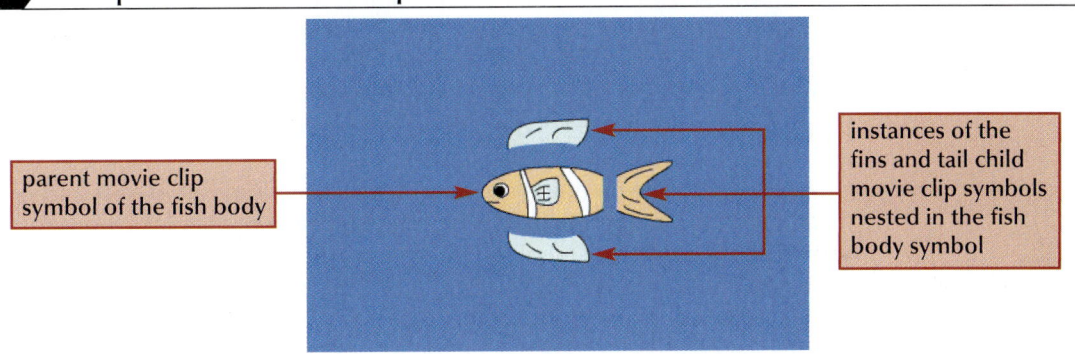

parent movie clip symbol of the fish body

instances of the fins and tail child movie clip symbols nested in the fish body symbol

The fins and tail movie clip instances can contain their own animations to make them change slightly to simulate the movement of a real fish. These animations are independent of the fish body. The whole fish, which is the parent movie clip, can then be inserted in the document's main Timeline and animated to move across the Stage. When you apply a motion tween to the whole fish to make it move across the Stage, the motion tween is also applied to its nested instances. As a result, the fish body, fins, and tail all move across the Stage as one object while the fins and tail exhibit their own animations.

Creating a Nested Movie Clip

Because the first scene of the banner requires a fish that has its fins and tail animated to appear more natural, Aly wants you to create a fish using separate fin and tail symbols that contain their own animations. You will create a nested movie clip symbol using symbols she has already created for the fish body, fin, and tail. You will create frame-by-frame animations for the fin and the tail. Then, you will add two instances of the fin movie clip and one instance of the tail movie clip to the fish body. The resulting nested movie clip symbol will then be inserted into the fish swimming scene of the restaurant's banner and will be animated to move across the Stage.

You will start by creating a frame-by-frame animation for the fin. To create the animation for the fin, you'll add keyframes at every other frame of the fin Timeline starting at

Frame 3. You will then change the shape of the fin slightly at each keyframe for a total of nine frames.

To insert frames for the fin frame-by-frame animation:

1. If you took a break after the previous session, make sure the hutBanner.fla file is open and the workspace is reset to the Essentials layout.

2. On the Edit bar, click the **Edit Symbols** button, and then click **Fin**. The Fin symbol opens in symbol-editing mode.

3. On the Edit bar, click the **Zoom control arrow**, and then click **200%**. The magnification of the Stage increases, making it easier to see the Fin symbol on the Stage.

4. In the Timeline, insert keyframes in the Layer 1 layer at **Frame 3**, **Frame 5**, **Frame 7**, and **Frame 9**. The fin is copied to each of the new frames.

Creating and Testing Animations Using Onion Skinning

When working with complex animations, it is often helpful to use onion skinning. **Onion skinning** displays more than one frame at a time on the Stage. This can be especially helpful when creating a frame-by-frame animation where you need to compare the current frame's contents to the previous frame's contents. Usually, you see only the current frame's contents on the Stage. With onion skinning, the current frame plus two or more frames appear on the Stage at once. The content of the current frame, indicated by the position of the playhead, appears in full color as usual. The contents of the frames before and after the current frame appear dimmed.

When you toggle on onion skinning, the Start Onion Skin marker and End Onion Skin marker appear on the Timeline header on either side of the playhead. The content displayed on the Stage is determined by the frames that are within the onion skin markers. You can also choose to display only the outlines of the content on the Stage, which can be helpful when working with complex animations, by clicking the Onion Skin Outlines button. The Edit Multiple Frames button makes the content of all the frames in a frame-by-frame animation that are within the onion skin markers available for editing.

| InSight | **Locking Layers While Onion Skinning** |

When using onion skinning with a complex document, a confusing array of images might be displayed on the Stage. Because the content of locked layers is not affected when onion skinning is turned on, lock any layers you are not editing. You can then focus on the content of the layers you are editing. Remember to toggle off onion skinning when you are finished using it so as not to display multiple frames at one time.

You will toggle on onion skinning to help you as you create the fin frame-by-frame animation.

To create the fin frame-by-frame animation:

1. In the Timeline, click the **Onion Skin** button. The onion skin markers appear in the Timeline header.

Tutorial 4 Creating Complex Animations | Flash | FL 201

Tip

You can also drag the onion skin markers on the Timeline header to increase or decrease the number of frames displayed on the Stage.

2. In the Timeline, click the **Modify Onion Markers** button, and then click **Onion 2**. The two frames before and after the current frame appear on the Stage.

3. In the Timeline, click **Frame 3** of the Layer 1 layer. This is the frame where you will first modify the fin.

4. In the Tools panel, click the **Selection** tool if necessary, click an empty area of the Stage to deselect the fin, and then drag the right side of the fin slightly to the left. The onion skinned frames provide a reference of the changed fin. See Figure 4-35.

Figure 4-35 Frame 3 of the Fin movie clip modified

move the side of the fin left

onion skin markers indicate how many frames appear on the Stage

click to toggle onion skinning on and off

click to modify the onion skin markers

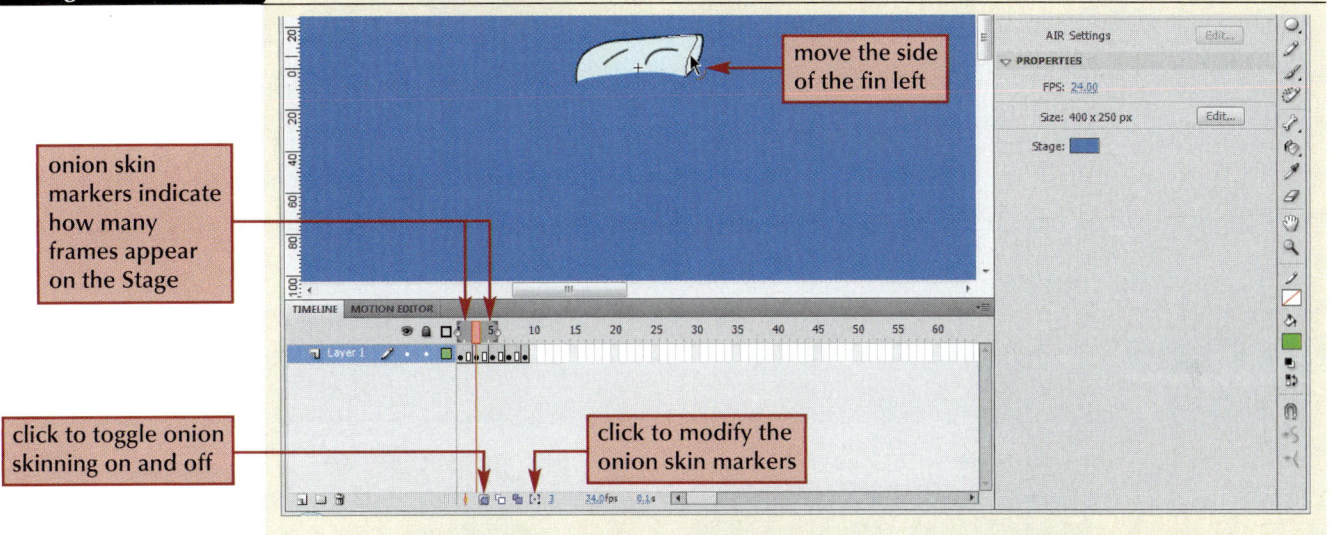

You'll repeat this process to modify other parts of the fin in Frames 5 and 7. In Frame 9, the fin returns to its original state, so you will not make any changes in this frame.

5. In the Timeline, click **Frame 5**, deselect the fin on the Stage, and then drag the top edge of the fin slightly up. See Figure 4-36.

Figure 4-36 Frame 5 of the Fin movie clip modified

move the top edge of the fin

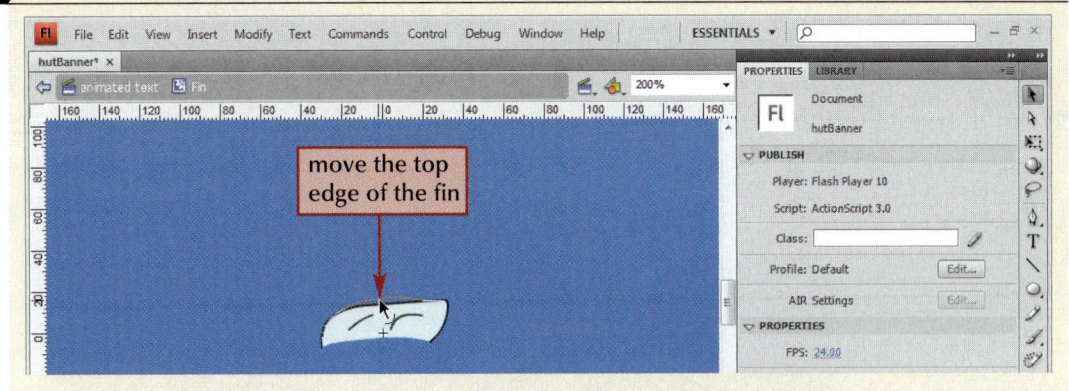

6. In the Timeline, click **Frame 7**, deselect the fin on the Stage, and then drag the upper-right tip of the fin slightly to the right. The fin animation is complete.

7. Drag the playhead to **Frame 1**, and then press the **Enter** key to play the frame-by-frame animation. The fin changes slightly at each keyframe throughout the animation.

The frame-by-frame animation for the fin is complete. You will create a similar frame-by-frame animation for the Tail symbol. You'll use the same number of keyframes for the Tail symbol as you did for the Fin symbol and change the shape of the tail slightly at each keyframe.

To create the tail frame-by-frame animation:

1. On the Edit bar, click the **Edit Symbols** button, and then click **Tail**. The Tail symbol opens in symbol-editing mode.

2. In the Timeline, insert keyframes in the Layer 1 layer at **Frame 3**, **Frame 5**, **Frame 7**, and **Frame 9**. The tail is copied to each of the new frames. Onion skinning is still on and stays on until you click the Onion Skin button.

3. In the Timeline, click **Frame 3** of the Layer 1 layer, and then click an empty area of the Stage to deselect the tail.

4. On the Stage, drag the two tips on the right side of the tail slightly inward. The dimmed tail from the previous frame provides a reference as you change the shape of the tail. See in Figure 4-37.

Figure 4-37 — Frame 3 of the Tail movie clip symbol modified

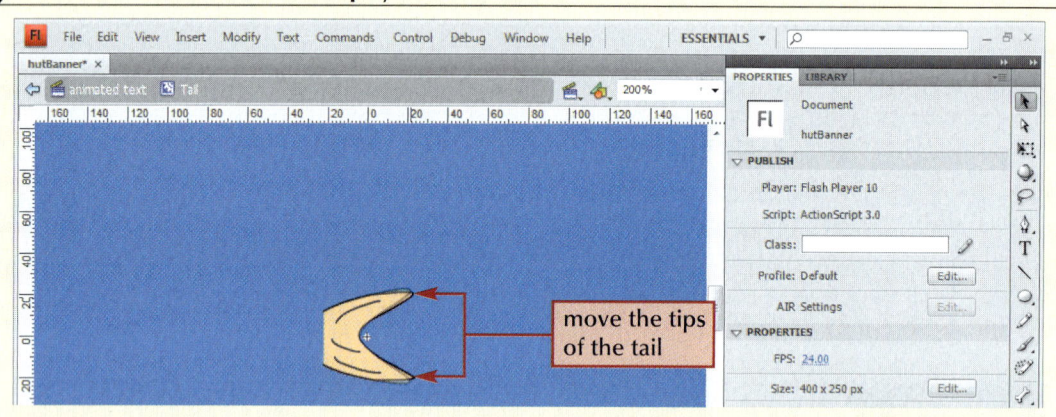

5. In the Timeline, click **Frame 5**, deselect the tail on the Stage, and then drag the tail's top edge near the left side of the tail slightly down. See Figure 4-38.

Figure 4-38 — Frame 5 of the Tail movie clip symbol modified

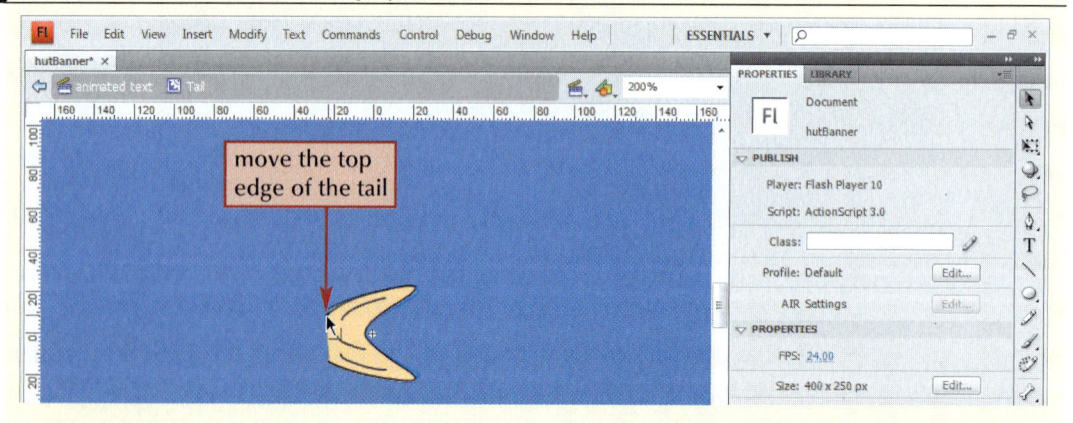

6. In Frame 5, drag the tail's bottom edge near the left side of the tail slightly up. The midsection of the tail is narrower.

7. In the Timeline, click **Frame 7**, deselect the tail on the Stage, and then drag the two tips on the right side of the tail slightly inward as you did in Step 4. The tail returns to its original state in Frame 9, so no changes are needed in this frame.

8. In the Timeline, click the **Onion Skin** button. Onion skinning toggles off.

9. In the Timeline, click **Frame 1**, and then press the **Enter** key to play the frame-by-frame animation. The tail changes slightly at each keyframe throughout the animation.

Now that you have created the animations for the Fin movie clip symbol and the Tail movie clip symbol, you are ready to insert instances of these symbols in the Fish2 symbol, which contain the fish body. The instances will be nested inside the Fish2 symbol.

To create the Fish2 nested movie clip symbol:

1. On the Edit bar, click the **Edit Symbols** button, and then click **Fish2**. The Fish2 symbol opens in symbol-editing mode.

2. Click the **LIBRARY** tab, and then drag an instance of the **Fin symbol** from the Library panel and place it directly above the fish body on the Stage. See Figure 4-39.

Figure 4-39 — Fin instance placed on top of the fish

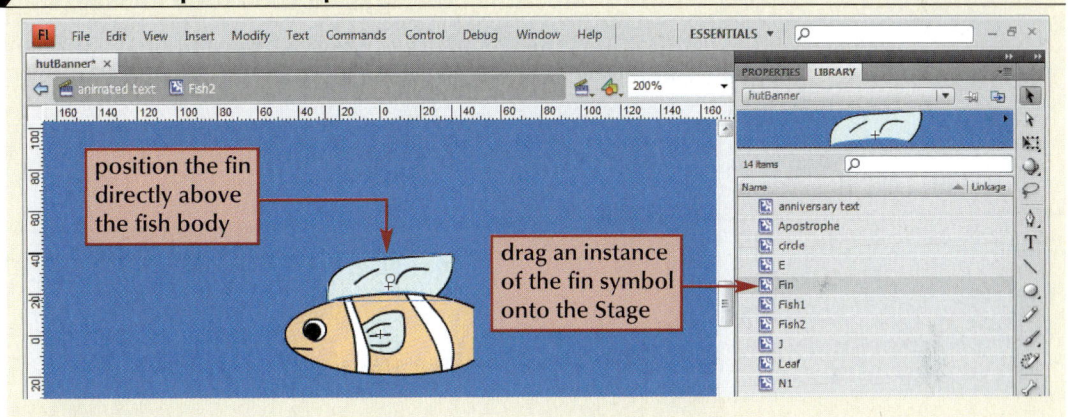

3. If necessary, press the arrow keys to nudge the fin into place.

4. Drag another instance of the **Fin symbol** from the Library panel and place it below the fish body.

5. On the Application bar, click **Modify**, point to **Transform**, and then click **Flip Vertical**. The fin will now fit below the fish body.

6. Position the **Fin** instance right below the fish body, pressing the arrow keys as needed to nudge the fin into place.

7. Drag an instance of the **Tail symbol** from the Library panel and place it to the right side of the fish, positioning the tail precisely against the fish body. The fish is now complete. See Figure 4-40.

Figure 4-40   The completed nested symbol

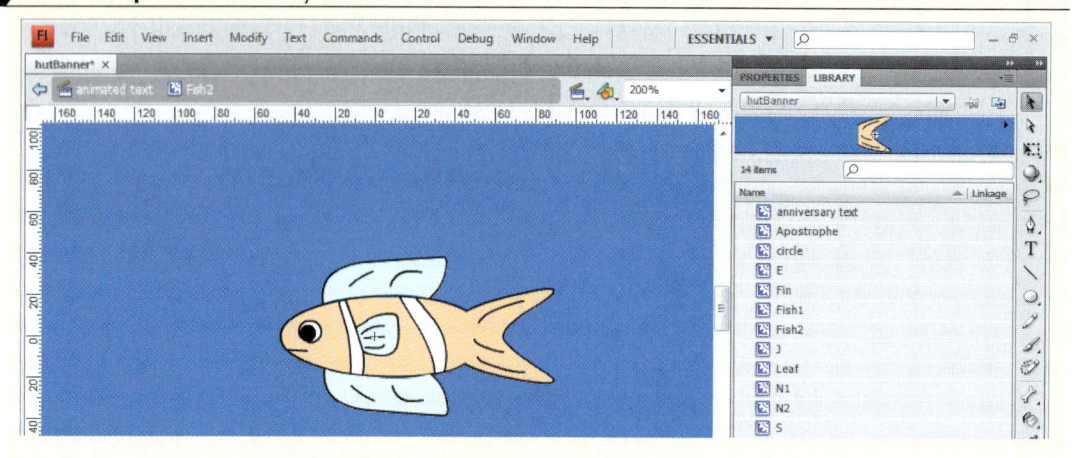

The Fish2 symbol is complete with its nested movie clip symbols. You will place the complete fish in the fish swimming scene and apply a motion tween to make the fish swim across the Stage. The fins and tail will move together with the fish.

To insert and animate the Fish2 symbol in the fish swimming scene:

1. On the Edit bar, click the **Edit Scene** button, and then click **fish swimming**. The fish swimming scene appears.

2. Change the zoom magnification to **100%**.

3. In the Timeline, select the **title mask** layer, and then insert a new layer above the title mask layer named **nested fish**. The nested fish layer is selected in the Timeline.

4. Drag an instance of the **Fish2** symbol from the Library panel and place it on the pasteboard to the right of the Stage about 130 pixels from the top of the Stage.

5. In the Tools panel, click the **Free Transform** tool, and then click the **Scale** button.

6. On the Stage, drag a corner handle of the Fish2 symbol to reduce the size of the instance so that it is about the same size as the Fish1 instance on the Stage. See Figure 4-41.

Figure 4-41   Nested movie clip instance added to the fish swimming scene

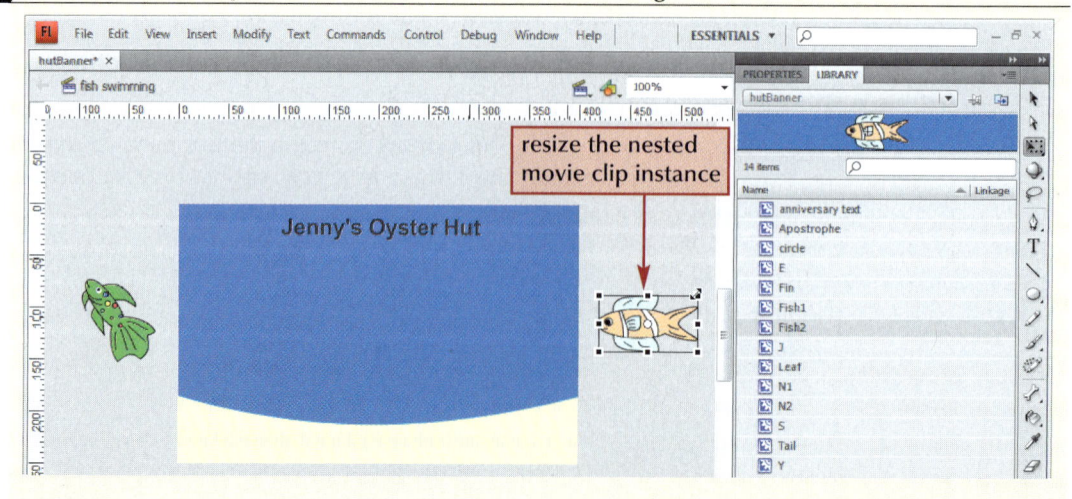

resize the nested movie clip instance

▶ 7. In the Tools panel, click the **Selection** tool.

▶ 8. On the Stage, right-click the **Fish2** instance, and then click **Create Motion Tween**. A tween span is added to the nested fish layer.

▶ 9. In the Timeline, click **Frame 50** of the nested fish layer, and then move the **Fish2** instance to the pasteboard on the left side of the Stage. The fish will move across the Stage as the frames play.

The motion tween animation is complete for the Fish2 instance. You'll test the animation next. Because the Fin and Tail symbols are movie clip symbols and their Timelines are independent of the main document's Timeline, their animations will not play when you test the animation of the fish within the Document window. To see their animations, you will play the current scene as an SWF file in the Flash Player.

To test the nested movie clip animation:

▶ 1. In the Timeline, click **Frame 1** of the nested fish layer, and then press the **Enter** key to play the motion tween animation. The Fish2 instance moves across the Stage, but the nested fin and tail animations do not play.

▶ 2. On the Application bar, click **Control**, and then click **Test Scene**. The fish swimming scene plays in a Flash Player window. As the Fish2 instance moves across the Stage as before, its fins and tail now exhibit their animations.

> **Tip**
> You can also press the Ctrl+Alt+Enter keys to test the current scene in the Flash Player.

You will stop the main document's Timeline from playing to see only the animations for the Fin and Tail instances.

▶ 3. When the Fish2 instance moves across the Stage, press the **Enter** key. The fish stops swimming. The fins and tail of the Fish2 instance continue their animations because they are on independent Timelines.

▶ 4. Press the **Enter** key. The fish starts swimming again.

▶ 5. Close the Flash Player window.

▶ 6. Save the banner.

Using Inverse Kinematics

In Flash, you can use inverse kinematics to animate one or more objects in relation to each other. **Inverse kinematics** is an animation method used to create bone structures. A **bone** is a link from one symbol instance to another or from one interior part of a shape to another. When one bone moves, the other bones move in relation to it.

With inverse kinematics, you can easily create complex animations and natural movement. For example, you can create character animation in which the arms and legs of a body are connected to each other with bones. When a bone in one part of the character moves, the other bones move accordingly without you defining every single movement. You specify only the start and end positions of an object by positioning its bones. A chain of bones is called an **armature**. Bones can be added to connect one symbol instance to another or they can be added to the interior of a shape object so you can move or animate parts of the shape without having to draw the shape multiple times. When you add bones to a symbol instance or to a shape, the instance or shape and its armature are moved to a new layer called a **pose layer**.

Aly's notes indicate that you need to create a plant leaf animation. You will use the Bone tool to add bones to a leaf shape that Aly created. You will then move the bones slightly at different frames in the pose layer to create the animation.

To create a plant leaf animation using inverse kinematics:

▸ 1. On the Edit bar, click the **Edit Symbols** button and then click **Leaf**. The Leaf symbol opens in symbol-editing mode.

▸ 2. Increase the zoom magnification to **200%**.

▸ 3. In the Tools panel, click the **Bone** tool to select it. You use the Bone tool to add bones to an instance or to a shape. Each time you click and drag with the Bone tool, a new bone is created.

▸ 4. On the Stage, click the base of the plant leaf and drag the pointer up to about one-third of the length of the leaf shape. A bone is added to the shape and a new Armature layer is created. See Figure 4-42.

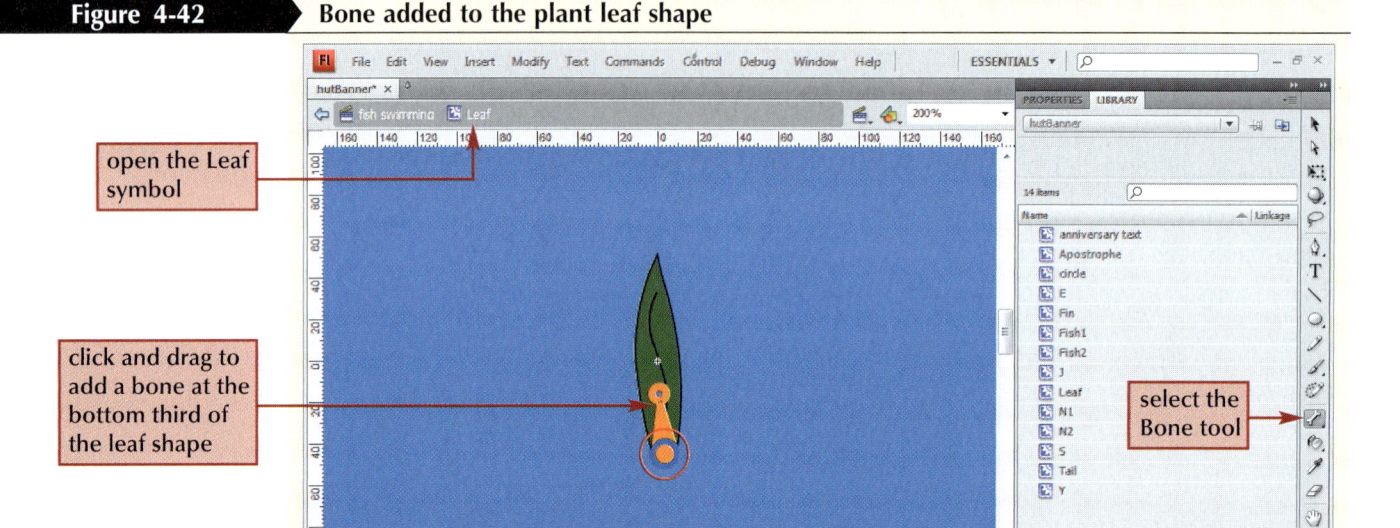

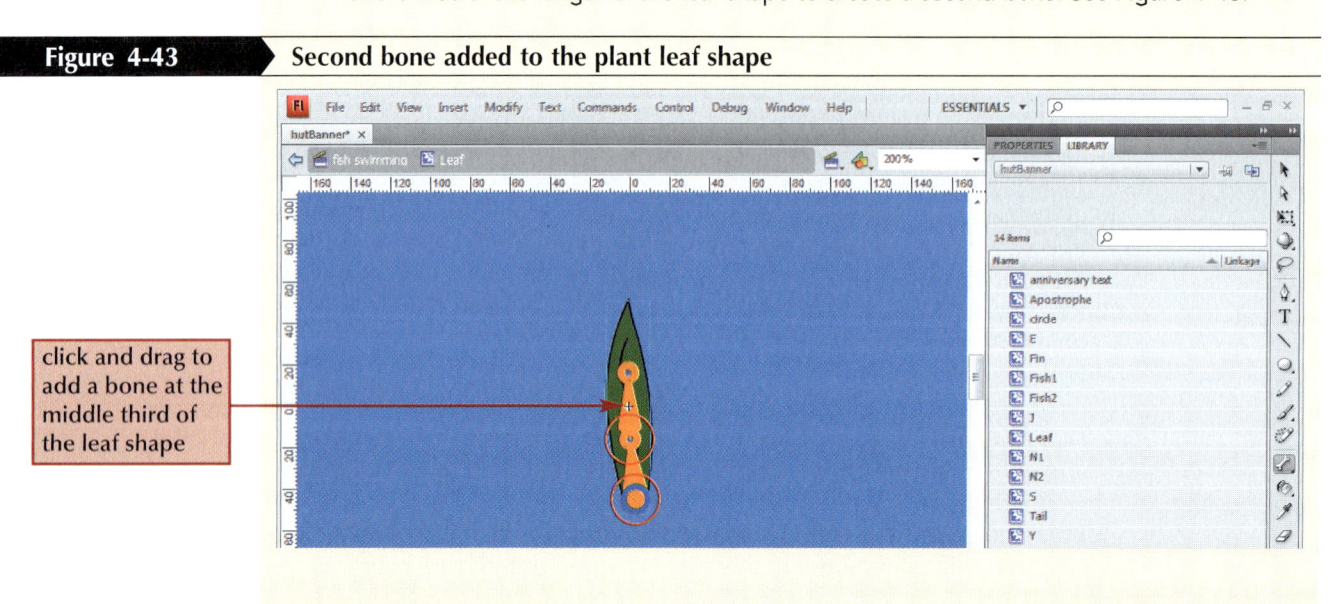

Figure 4-42 — Bone added to the plant leaf shape

- open the Leaf symbol
- click and drag to add a bone at the bottom third of the leaf shape
- select the Bone tool
- new layer added to the Timeline

▸ 5. On the Stage, click the end point of the first bone and drag the pointer up to about two-thirds of the length of the leaf shape to create a second bone. See Figure 4-43.

Figure 4-43 — Second bone added to the plant leaf shape

- click and drag to add a bone at the middle third of the leaf shape

Tutorial 4 Creating Complex Animations | Flash | FL 207

▶ 6. On the Stage, click the end point of the second bone and drag the pointer up to right below the tip of the leaf shape to create a third bone. You will move the bones to create an inverse kinematic animation.

▶ 7. In the Tools panel, click the **Selection** tool to select it, and then, in the Timeline, click **Frame 1** of the Armature layer, if necessary.

▶ 8. On the Stage, drag the top bone slightly to the left. See Figure 4-44.

Figure 4-44	Plant leaf starting position

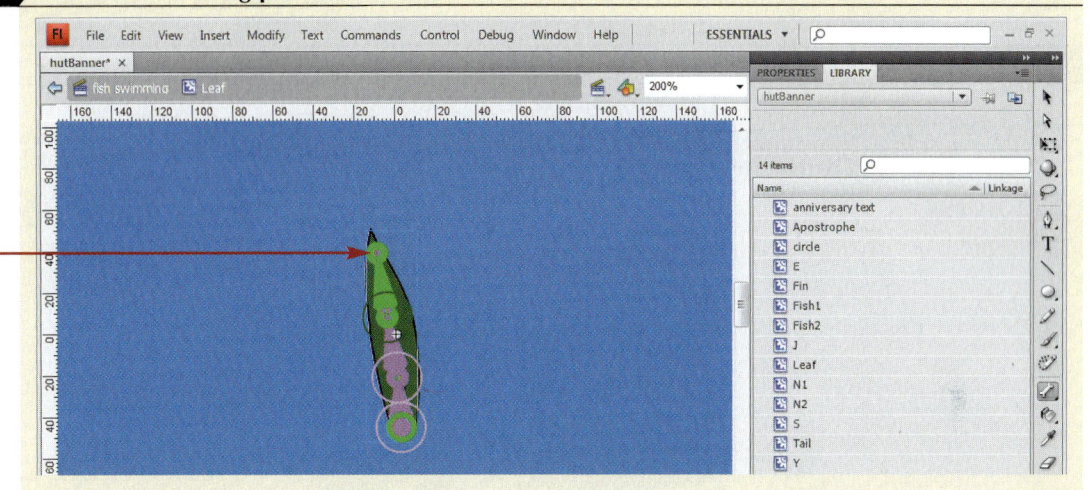

drag the top bone to the left

▶ 9. In the Timeline, click **Frame 20** of the Armature layer, and then, on the Stage, drag the top bone slightly to the right of the leaf's original position. A new pose is created at Frame 20. See Figure 4-45.

Figure 4-45	New pose created in plant leaf symbol

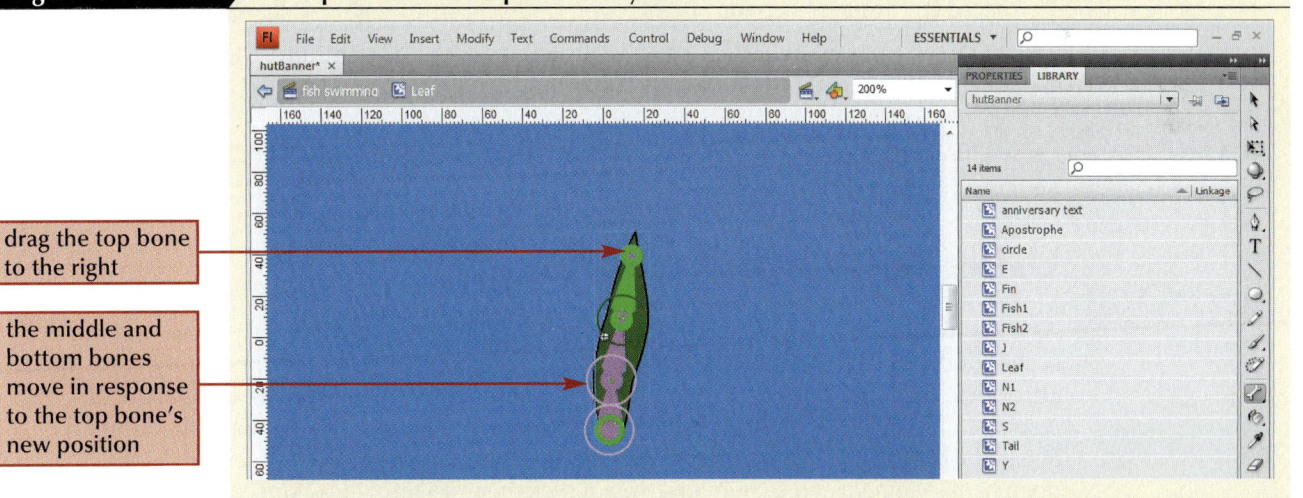

drag the top bone to the right

the middle and bottom bones move in response to the top bone's new position

▶ 10. In the Timeline, click **Frame 40** of the Armature layer, and then, on the Stage, drag the top bone slightly to the left to approximately the leaf's original position. A new pose is created at Frame 40.

▶ 11. Scrub the playhead between Frames 1 and 40 to see the inverse kinematic animation.

The plant leaf animation is complete. Several instances of the plant leaf symbol will be added to the fish swimming scene. One instance will be flipped horizontally so that its animation moves in the opposite direction of the other two instances.

To add the plant leaf animation to the fish swimming scene:

▶ 1. On the Edit bar, click the **Edit Scene** button, and then click **fish swimming**. The fish swimming scene is the current scene.

▶ 2. In the Timeline, move the playhead to **Frame 1**, insert a new layer above the nested fish layer, and then name the new layer **plant leaves**.

▶ 3. Drag an instance of the **Leaf** symbol from the Library panel and place it in the lower-right corner of the Stage, and then drag two more instances of the **Leaf** symbol and place them next to the first instance. See Figure 4-46.

Figure 4-46   Leaf instances arranged on the Stage

make fish swimming the current scene

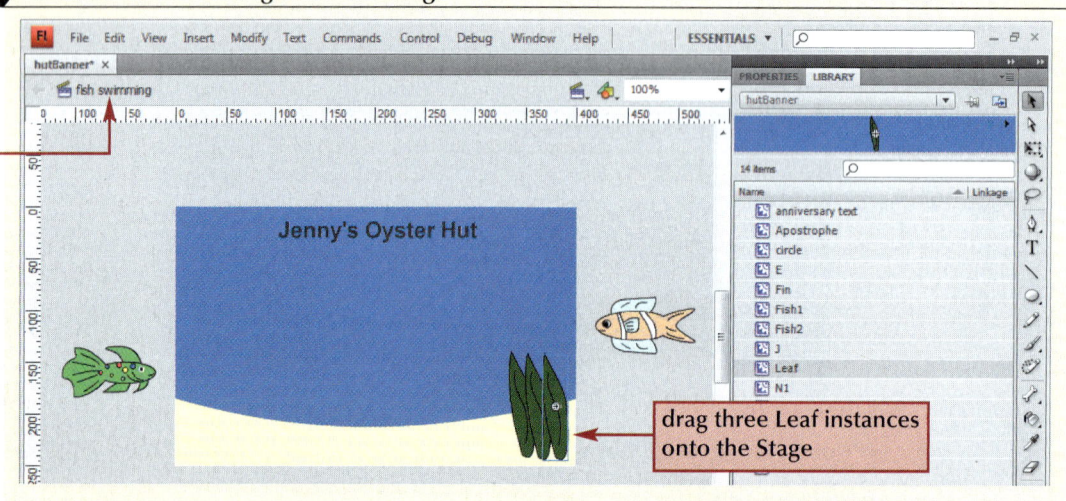

drag three Leaf instances onto the Stage

▶ 4. Click the middle **Leaf** instance to select it, and then, on the Application bar, click **Modify**, point to **Transform**, and click **Flip Horizontal**. The middle leaf instance faces the other direction.

▶ 5. On the Application bar, click **Control**, and then click **Test Movie**. The movie plays in a Flash Player window. The Leaf instances exhibit their animation.

▶ 6. Close the Flash Player window, and then save the banner.

Using the Movie Explorer

As a Flash document gets more complex with many symbols, text blocks, layers, and scenes, it can become difficult to manage all the elements or to find a specific element. The Movie Explorer, shown in Figure 4-47, can help. The **Movie Explorer** is a panel that displays a hierarchical view of all the elements in a document, making it simpler to manage and locate individual elements. You can use the Movie Explorer to view each of the document's elements, to search for a specific element, to find all instances of a particular symbol, or even to print a list of the document's elements as listed in the Movie Explorer.

Figure 4-47   Movie Explorer

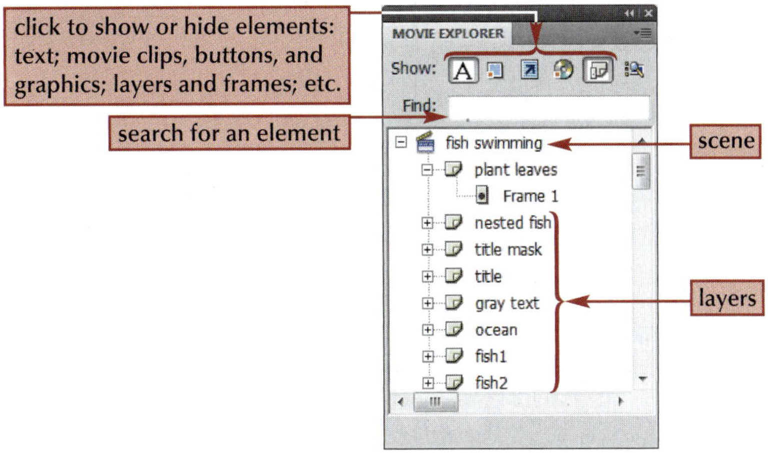

click to show or hide elements: text; movie clips, buttons, and graphics; layers and frames; etc.

search for an element

scene

layers

The display options in the Movie Explorer enable you to select which elements to display in the Movie Explorer panel. For example, if you want to see only the text blocks used in the document, you can click the Show text button but not the other buttons in the Movie Explorer. The panel displays each text block with information about the font and point size used in the text block. If you want to see each instance of the symbols used in the document, click the Show movie clips, buttons, and graphics button. If you select an instance in the Movie Explorer, information about where the instance is located in the document appears at the bottom of the panel.

You can select additional options from the Movie Explorer's panel menu button. For example, you can specify whether to show the document's elements or the symbol definitions or both. The document's elements include the layers, frames, and instances used in the document. The symbol definitions are displayed below the document's elements along with each symbol and its elements. Other options available on the Movie Explorer's panel menu include the following:

- Go to Symbol Definition, which selects the symbol definition for the symbol selected in the Movie Explorer.
- Show in Library, which displays the selected symbol in the Library panel.
- Show Movie Elements, which displays the document's elements such as its layers, frames, and symbol instances.
- Show Symbol Definitions, which displays all elements associated with a symbol.
- Show All Scenes, which displays the elements and symbols for all scenes in the document, not just the current scene.

InSight | Using the Movie Explorer to Troubleshoot Problems

If you are working with a Flash document developed by someone else, use the Movie Explorer to become familiar with the way the scenes, symbols, and other elements are organized. You can explore how and where each of the document's symbols is used as well as how the symbol is constructed. You can then more easily modify the document. Also, when working with a complex animation, you can use the Movie Explorer to troubleshoot problems. For example, if an animation is not working correctly, you can check the symbol instances that are part of the animation and determine whether they are in the correct scene, layer, and frame.

Because the banner you created for the Jenny's Oyster Hut Web site has multiple scenes, layers, and symbols, you can use the Movie Explorer to review all of its elements and view how all the various symbol instances throughout the document are organized.

To use the Movie Explorer to examine the banner's elements:

▸ 1. On the Application bar, click **Window**, and then click **Movie Explorer**. The Movie Explorer opens.

▸ 2. If necessary, click the **Show text** button [A] to select it and click the other Show buttons to deselect them.

▸ 3. Click the **Movie Explorer panel menu** button, and then click **Show Movie Elements** to select it, if necessary.

▸ 4. Repeat Step 3 to select **Show Symbol Definitions** and **Show All Scenes**. The panel displays the scenes that contain text blocks as well as the symbols that contain text. This display can make it easier to locate text blocks within the document.

▸ 5. Drag the bottom edge of the Movie Explorer window down to increase its size so you can see more of the elements in the window.

▸ 6. If necessary, click the **plus sign** next to the animated text scene name to expand its contents. The Movie Explorer displays all of the text blocks for the scene, including the text properties. You can compare the text properties of all the text blocks in the scene. This information can be useful if you need to maintain consistency across all of the text blocks within a scene. See Figure 4-48.

> **Tip**
>
> If a text block does not reside in a locked layer, you can double-click the text block in the Movie Explorer to change its contents.

Figure 4-48 Movie Explorer displaying text blocks

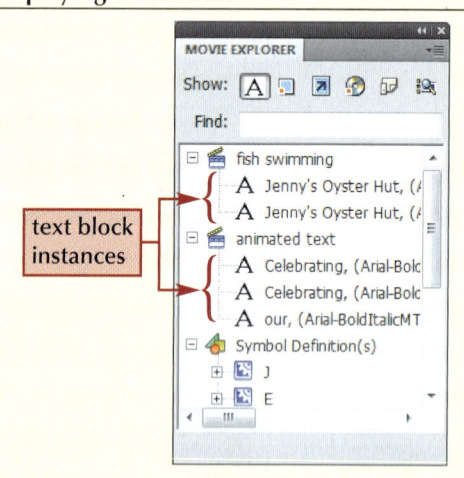

▸ 7. In the Movie Explorer, click the **Show frames and layers** button to select it, and then click the **plus sign** next to the fish swimming scene to expand its display, if necessary. Each layer of the fish swimming scene is displayed in the panel. Selecting a layer name in the panel also selects the layer in the document, enabling you to find specific layers in a complex document.

▸ 8. In the Movie Explorer, scroll down the panel, click the **fish2** layer name under the fish swimming scene, and then, if necessary, click the **plus sign** next to it. Each keyframe within the fish2 layer is displayed. See Figure 4-49.

Tutorial 4 Creating Complex Animations | Flash | **FL 211**

| Figure 4-49 | Movie Explorer displaying the fish2 layer and its keyframes |

Tip

Selecting a keyframe in the Movie Explorer also selects that keyframe in the Timeline.

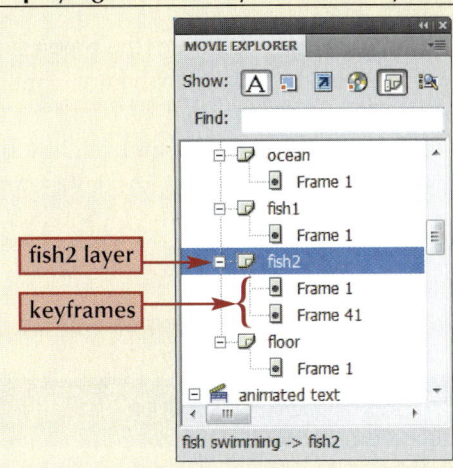

▶ **9.** In the Movie Explorer, click the **Show movie clips, buttons, and graphics** button to select it, and then click the **Fish1** instance in Frame 41 of the fish2 layer. The path of the instance at the bottom of the panel indicates where the instance is located within the document. See Figure 4-50.

| Figure 4-50 | Fish1 instance in Frame 41 of the fish2 layer |

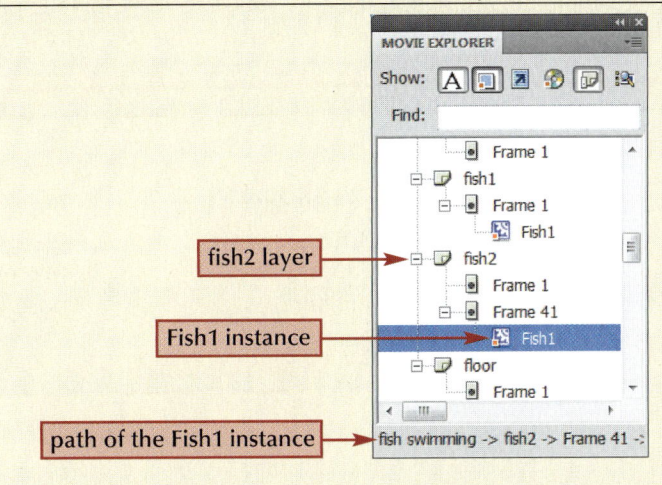

▶ **10.** In the Movie Explorer, click the **Movie Explorer panel menu** button, and then click **Go to Symbol Definition**. The Movie Explorer shows the Fish1 symbol under the Symbol Definitions area. The Symbol Definitions area shows all the elements associated with the selected symbol.

▶ **11.** Close the Movie Explorer, and then close the hutBanner.fla file.

Tip

You can also press the Alt+F3 keys to open and close the Movie Explorer.

Aly is pleased with the document elements and is ready to show the banner to Jenny. In this session, you used onion skinning to display the contents of multiple frames on the Stage. You also created nested movie clips, which contain instances of other movie clips within their Timelines. You also created an inverse kinematic animation using bones. Finally, you used the Movie Explorer to review the elements of a complex document.

Review | Session 4.3 Quick Check

1. How can you change the position of the onion skin markers in the Timeline header?
2. How can onion skinning help you when working with a complex animation?
3. What is a nested movie clip?
4. What is a movie clip that has other movie clips nested within it called?
5. Why will the animations of movie clips embedded in a nested movie clip not play when you test them within the Flash Player window?
6. True or False? Inverse kinematics uses bones to create complex animations and natural movement.
7. How can you use the Movie Explorer to find the definition of a particular symbol?

Review | Tutorial Summary

In this tutorial, you modified a motion tweens path and you created animations using mask layers. You used these techniques to modify an animation, and create a spotlight effect animation with text. You also created various types of text animations, including an animation of the individual letters of a word and applied a 3D rotation effect to the letters. You created a complex movie clip animation with symbols nested inside another movie clip symbol. You also used onion skinning to create and test complex animations and you created an inverse kinematic animation. Finally, you used the Movie Explorer to examine all the elements of a Flash document.

Key Terms

3D space	easing	Movie Explorer
armature	inverse kinematics	nested symbol
Bezier handles	mask layer	onion skinning
bone	masked layer	parent movie clip
child movie clip	Motion Editor	pose layer
control point	motion path	

Practice

Practice the skills you learned in the tutorial.

Review Assignments

Data File needed for the Review Assignments: johDraft.fla

Based on Jenny's feedback of the banners you created for the restaurant's Web site, Aly wants you to create a third banner. You will have two fish swimming along curved paths. In the same scene, you will add a mask effect to the Jenny's Oyster Hut title that makes the text block appear gradually from left to right. You will also create a new animation of a small circular sign that contains rotating text inside. Two instances of the sign will be animated to move in the scene.

1. Open the **johDraft.fla** document located in the Tutorial.04\Review folder included with your Data Files, and then save the file as **johBanner.fla** in the same folder.
2. In Frame 1 of the Fish1 layer, add an instance of the Fish1 symbol to the pasteboard on the left side of the Stage so that its center is about 170 pixels from the top of the Stage.
3. Insert a keyframe at Frame 36 of the Fish1 layer, and then create a motion tween at Frame 1 of the Fish1 layer.
4. At Frame 35, move the Fish1 instance to the pasteboard on the right side of the Stage. Curve the center of the motion path up. Orient the fish to the path.
5. At Frame 36 of the Fish1 layer, move the Fish1 instance to the right side of the pasteboard, and then flip the Fish1 instance to face to the left. Create a motion tween at Frame 36 of the Fish1 layer.
6. At Frame 70, move the Fish1 instance to the pasteboard on the left side of the Stage. Curve the center of the motion path up. Orient the fish to the path.
7. Insert a new layer above the Fish1 layer and name it **Fish2**. Add an instance of the Fish2 symbol to the right side of the Stage slightly below the top edge of the ocean.
8. Insert a keyframe at Frame 36 of the Fish2 layer, and then create a motion tween at Frame 1 of the Fish2 layer.
9. At Frame 35, move the Fish2 instance to the pasteboard on the left side of the Stage. Curve the center of the motion path down. Orient the fish to the path.
10. At Frame 36 of the Fish2 layer, move the Fish2 instance to the pasteboard on the left side of the Stage, and then flip the Fish2 instance to face to the right. Create a motion tween at Frame 36 of the Fish2 layer.
11. At Frame 70, move the Fish2 instance to the pasteboard on the right side of the Stage. Curve the center of the motion path down. Orient the fish to the path.
12. Insert a new layer above the Title layer, name it **Mask**, and then change its type to Mask. Make sure the Title layer's type is changed to Masked and that it is indented below the Mask layer.
13. Unlock the Mask layer, and then draw a rectangle with no stroke and a fill color of your choice that covers the entire Jenny's Oyster Hut text block. The rectangle's width should be the same width as the text block and its height should be only as high as the text block. Convert this rectangle to a movie clip symbol named **Rectangle**.
14. Insert a keyframe at Frame 35 of the Mask layer. At Frame 1, move the rectangle to the left of the text block to reveal the entire text block. Create a motion tween from Frame 1 to Frame 34 so that the rectangle moves from left to right to gradually cover the text block. Lock the Mask layer and test the mask animation effect. The text block should appear gradually from left to right.

15. Create a new movie clip symbol named **Rotating text**. In symbol-editing mode, add a text block to the center of the symbol's Stage. Use Arial for the font family, bold italic for the font style, 12 for the point size, 0 for the letter spacing, white for the text color, and align center for the paragraph format. Type **Shrimp** in the text block. In the Property inspector, set the text block's X and Y coordinates to 0.
16. Insert a keyframe at Frame 15, create a motion tween between Frames 1 and 15, and then, in the Property inspector, set the text to rotate clockwise one time.
17. Insert a keyframe at Frame 20 and replace the Shrimp text with the word **Catfish**. Insert another keyframe at Frame 35 and create a motion tween between Frames 20 and 35. Set the Catfish text block to rotate counterclockwise one time.
18. Insert a keyframe at Frame 40 and replace the Catfish text with the word **Oysters**. Insert another keyframe at Frame 55 and create a motion tween between Frames 40 and 55. Set the Oysters text block to rotate clockwise one time. Insert a regular frame at Frame 60. Exit symbol-editing mode.
19. Create a new movie clip symbol named **Rotating sign**. In symbol-editing mode, add a small circle with a dark blue (#003366) fill color and no stroke to the center of the symbol's Stage. Use the Property inspector to make the circle 60 pixels wide and 60 pixels high. Also, set its X and Y coordinates to 0. Drag an instance of the Rotating text symbol to the center of the circle. Exit symbol-editing mode.
20. Insert a new layer above the Mask layer and name it **Rotating sign**. On this layer, drag an instance of the Rotating sign symbol to the lower-left side of the pasteboard just to the left of the Stage. Create a motion tween between Frames 1 and 35 so that the Rotating sign instance moves from the pasteboard to the center of the beach graphic at the bottom of the Stage.
21. Test the new animations for the document using the Test Movie command.
22. Submit the finished files to your instructor.

Apply	**Case Problem 1**

Animate the letters in a text block, add motion tweens for text, and create motion guide layers to set a path for animated graphics.

Data File needed for this Case Problem: kprDraft.fla

Katie's Pet Resort Katie asks John about creating a new Flash document that will serve as an advertisement on the Katie's Pet Resort Web site. In particular, she would like text information promoting the resort's services. You will create the advertisement based on a document John has developed. You'll add new text messages promoting the grand opening sale and the services provided by the resort. The resort's name will be animated so that it is displayed one letter at a time. After the resort's name appears, the next text message will fade in. Another text message will appear and will increase in size and change in color. Also, you'll add several instances of the balloon symbol. The finished advertisement is shown in Figure 4-51.

Figure 4-51

Katie's Pet Resort

Grand Opening Sale all Week!

Grooming, Training, Boarding and More!

1. Open the **kprDraft.fla** file located in the Tutorial.04\Case1 folder included with your Data Files, and then save the document as **kprBanner.fla** in the same folder.

2. Create a new layer folder named **letters** above the resort layer and move the resort layer inside the folder. Convert the text block in the resort layer to individual text blocks, one for each character. Distribute the characters to individual layers inside the letters layer folder and delete the empty resort layer.

3. Move the keyframes in Frame 1 of each letter layer so that each starts one frame after the previous character. The first letter, K, starts in Frame 1. The second letter, a, starts in Frame 2. The third letter, n, starts in Frame 3, and so on. The characters will appear one at a time to form the complete resort name. Collapse the letters layer folder.

4. Insert a new layer above the background layer and name it **sale**. At Frame 25 of the sale layer, insert a keyframe, and then drag an instance of the Sale symbol from the Library panel to the center of the Stage. Animate the text block instance to fade in over the next 15 frames. (*Hint*: Insert a keyframe at Frame 40 on the sale layer. At Frame 25, create a motion tween and change the alpha amount of the Sale instance to 0%. At Frame 39, change the alpha amount to 100%.)

5. Animate the text of the Sale text block instance to change from red to blue. At Frame 55, insert a keyframe. At Frame 40, create a motion tween. At Frame 54, change the tint of the Sale text instance to 100% blue (#0000FF). At Frame 55, change the tint to 100% blue (#0000FF) to match the text block's tint at the end of the motion tween.

6. Change the tint of the Sale text block back to red. At Frame 55, create a motion tween. At Frame 70, change the text block's tint to 100% red (#FF0000). Lock the sale layer.

7. Insert a new layer above the sale layer and name it **services**. At Frame 40, insert a keyframe, drag an instance of the Services symbol to the lower part of the Stage, and then create a motion tween.

8. At Frame 40, use the Transform panel to reduce the size of the Services instance to 50% of its original size and change the alpha amount to 0%. At Frame 55, change the size of the instance back to 100% and change its alpha amount to 100%. The text block will fade in as it increases in size from Frame 40 to 55.

9. At Frame 60 of the services layer, reduce the size of the Services instance in this frame to 80% of its original size. At Frame 65, increase the size of the text block back to 100%. The text block will decrease in size slightly and increase back to its original size. Lock the services layer.

10. Insert a new layer above the background layer and name it **balloon1**. Drag an instance of the Balloon symbol to the lower-left side of the Stage. At Frame 1 of the balloon1 layer, create a motion tween. At Frame 50, move the Balloon instance to the upper-right corner of the Stage. Use the Selection tool to curve the motion path down slightly.
11. Insert a new layer above the balloon1 layer and name it **balloon2**. At Frame 20, insert a keyframe, drag an instance of the Balloon symbol to the lower-right side of the Stage, and then create a motion tween. At Frame 70, move the Balloon instance to the upper-left corner of the Stage. Use the Selection tool to curve the motion path down slightly.
12. Test the animation in Flash and in the Flash Player.
13. Submit the finished files to your instructor.

Apply | Case Problem 2

Add a mask layer effect, animations of individual letters, and text block animations to an advertising banner.

Data File needed for this Case Problem: aczAdDraft.fla

Alamo City Zoo Janet asks Alex to develop a new advertising banner for the Alamo City Zoo Web site. She wants to see new animations that highlight the Alamo City Zoo name. She also wants several text messages displayed on the banner promoting the zoo's attractions, including the new bear exhibit. You will create the new advertisement based on a banner that Alex started. You'll add a spotlight effect where the spotlight starts small at the center of the banner and increases to reveal the banner. You'll also develop a special text effect for the zoo's name where the letters increase in size one after the other to give it a pulsating effect. Finally, you will add the text messages promoting the zoo. The finished banner is shown in Figure 4-52.

Figure 4-52

1. Open the **aczAdDraft.fla** file located in the Tutorial.04\Case2 folder included with your Data Files, and then save the document as **aczAd.fla** in the same folder.
2. Create a new movie clip symbol named **circle**. In symbol-editing mode, draw a circle with a white fill and no stroke at the center of the Stage. In the Info panel, set its dimensions to 40 pixels wide and 40 pixels high, and set the X and Y registration point coordinates to 0. Exit symbol-editing mode.
3. Insert a regular frame at Frame 20 of the Alamo City Zoo layer. Insert a new layer above this layer and name it **mask**. At Frame 1 of the mask layer, drag an instance of the circle symbol from the Library panel to the center of the Stage. In the Property inspector, set the instance's X and Y coordinates to 150 each to center it on the Stage.

4. Select the circle instance and create a motion tween. At Frame 20 of the mask layer, change the size of the circle instance to 300 pixels wide by 300 pixels high.
5. Copy all the frames on the mask layer to the Clipboard. Insert a new layer above the mask layer, select all of its frames, and then paste the copied frames to the new layer. Rename the layer to **circle**.
6. Temporarily hide the contents of the mask layer to work with the contents of the circle layer. At Frame 1 of the circle layer, change the alpha amount of the circle instance on the Stage to 40%. Move the circle layer below the Alamo City Zoo layer.
7. Show the mask layer, right-click the layer, and then change its type to Mask. Make sure the Alamo City Zoo layer is masked. Test the animation. The mask gradually reveals the company name. The motion tween on the circle layer displays the dimmed circle to coincide with the circle on the mask layer to create the special effect.
8. Hide the mask layer temporarily, unlock the Alamo City Zoo layer, and then copy the text block on the Stage. Insert a new layer above the mask layer and name it **name**. Use the Paste in Place command to paste the text block in the name layer in the same relative position as in the Alamo City Zoo layer.
9. Insert a layer folder above the name layer, name it **letters**, and then move the name layer inside the letters folder.
10. Select the text block in the name layer, convert the text to individual letters, and then distribute the letters to individual layers. Delete the empty name layer. Move all the letter keyframes to Frame 20 by selecting all the Frame 1s of the individual letter layers and dragging them all to start in Frame 20. This is where the individual letters' animation will begin.
11. Extend all of the layers except the mask and Alamo City Zoo layers by inserting regular frames at Frame 100 of each layer.
12. To make each letter change in size for a moment, insert two keyframes in each layer where the size of the letter is increased slightly in the first of the two new keyframes. So for the A layer, add keyframes at Frames 22 and 24, and then use the Transform panel to change the size of the instance in Frame 22 to 130% larger. For the next letter in layer l, insert keyframes at Frames 26 and 28, and then increase the size of the instance in Frame 26 to 130%. For the letter a in layer a, insert keyframes at Frames 30 and 32, and then increase the size of the letter in Frame 30 to 130%.
13. Repeat Step 12 for each letter, starting two frames after the previous letter. The last layer (for the second o in Zoo) will have keyframes at Frames 66 and 68. Show the mask layer, lock the Alamo City Zoo layer, and then test the animation. The individual letters should increase in size one at a time after the mask effect. Collapse the letters folder.
14. Place horizontal guides about 50 pixels, 100 pixels, and 200 pixels from the top of the Stage.
15. Insert three new layers above the letters folder and name them **text1**, **text2**, and **text3**. At Frame 20 of the text1 layer, insert a keyframe, and then create a text block centered just below the guide 50 pixels from the top of the Stage. Use the Monotype Corsiva font family, a 20 point size, and black text fill color. Type **Monkeys and Gorillas!** in the text block.
16. Create a motion tween in Frame 20 of the text1 layer. At Frame 20, use the Transform panel to reduce the size of the text block to 50% of its original size. At Frame 25, increase the size of the text back to 100%. The text will increase in size throughout the motion tween.

17. Insert a keyframe of Frame 25 of the text2 layer. Create a new text block in the pasteboard to the left of the Stage just below the guide 100 pixels from the top. Use the same text settings as in Step 15 and type **Elephants and Tigers!** in this text block.
18. Create a motion tween in Frame 25 of the text2 layer. At Frame 30, move the text instance to the Stage about 100 pixels from the top and centered on the banner. The text will fly in from the left of the Stage throughout the motion tween.
19. Create another text motion tween in the text3 layer between Frames 30 and 35. Create a text block with the words **New Bear Exhibit!** in the pasteboard to the right of the Stage just below the guide 200 pixels from the top of the Stage. This text block should fly in from the right of the Stage to the center of the banner about 200 pixels from the top. Clear the guides.
20. Insert a new layer above the text1 layer and name it **paw1**. Insert a keyframe at Frame 35. Drag an instance of the bear paw symbol to the upper-left corner of the banner, staying within the large circle. Insert a keyframe at Frame 45 and move the bear paw instance toward the bottom so that it is below the letters "Ne" in the New Bear Exhibit! text. Create a motion tween at Frame 35 of the paw1 layer and have the bear paw instance rotate clockwise twice. At Frame 44, move the bear paw instance to the same position as it is in Frame 45.

EXPLORE
21. Use the Motion Editor to apply the Spring ease to the motion tween in the paw1 layer. The paw instance will exhibit a spring effect at the end of its motion tween.
22. Insert a new layer above the paw1 layer and name it **bear**. Insert a keyframe at Frame 45. Drag an instance of the bear symbol to the right of the bear paw instance below the New Bear Exhibit! text. Create a motion tween at Frame 45 and change the bear instance's alpha amount to 0%. At Frame 55, change the alpha amount to 100% so that the bear instance fades in throughout the tween.
23. Insert a new layer above the bear layer and name it **paw2**. Insert a keyframe at Frame 55. Drag an instance of the bear paw symbol to the upper-right side of the banner, staying within the large circle. Insert another keyframe at Frame 65 and move the bear paw instance toward the bottom so that it is below the New Bear Exhibit! text and to the right of the bear instance. Create a motion tween at Frame 55 and have the bear paw instance rotate counterclockwise twice. At Frame 64, move the bear paw instance to the same position as it is in Frame 65.

EXPLORE
24. Use the Motion Editor to apply the Spring ease to the motion tween in the paw2 layer. The paw instance will exhibit a spring effect at the end of its motion tween.
25. Test the banner's animation in Flash and the Flash Player to view all the animations.
26. Submit the finished files to your instructor.

Challenge | Case Problem 3

Create an ad with 3D animations of individual letters, text block animations, a nested movie clip, and an animation along a curved motion path.

Data File needed for this Case Problem: wcDraft.fla

Westcreek Nursery Westcreek Nursery is expanding and opening a store at a new location. To advertise the new location and promote her business, Alice started a new marketing campaign. As part of this campaign, she asks Amanda to develop an ad to place on the local newspaper's Web site. To help Amanda, you will create several animations, including one where the letters in the word "Westcreek" fall into place followed by an animation of the word "Nursery" to create the title for the ad. Then several animated text blocks will move into place on the ad, followed by a graphic of the word "Flowers" that will move across the ad banner simulating a truck. The graphic will have animated tires. Figure 4-53 shows the completed advertisement.

Figure 4-53

1. Open the **wcDraft.fla** file located in the Tutorial.04\Case3 folder included with your Data Files, and then save the document as **westcreekAd.fla** in the same folder.
2. Create horizontal guides at 50 pixels and at 150 pixels from the top of the Stage.
3. Insert a new layer and name it **title1**, and then create a text block with the word **Westcreek**. Use white for the text color, Arial for the font family, Bold Italic for the font style, and 40 for the point size. Center the word on the guide 150 pixels from the top of the Stage.
4. Insert a layer folder above the title1 layer and name it **westcreek text**. Move the title1 layer to the new layer folder. Then select the title1 text block, break it apart, and distribute the individual letters to separate layers. The new layers for the letters should be inside the layer folder. Delete the title1 layer.

EXPLORE

5. Convert each of the letters into symbols with movie clip behavior. Use the following names for the symbols to match the letters they represent: **W**, **E1**, **S**, **T**, **C**, **R**, **E2**, **E3**, and **K**. Create a new folder in the Library, name it **Westcreek**, and then move all the letter symbols inside the folder.
6. Each letter will be animated to drop in from the top part of the Stage to its current location 150 pixels from the top. The letters will move one at a time, rotating in 3D space, and fading in as they move to form the word Westcreek. The first letter will start in Frame 1 and every other letter will start every 10 frames. Move each of the letters' keyframes that are in Frame 1 of their respective layers to start every 10 frames. The keyframes should be moved to the following frames: W – Frame 1; e – Frame 10; s – Frame 20; t – Frame 30; c – Frame 40; r – Frame 50; e – Frame 60; e – Frame 70; k – Frame 80. Be sure to keep each letter in its own layer.
7. Create a motion tween for each letter in its own layer.

EXPLORE

8. Select Frame 10 of the W layer, open the Motion Editor, and insert a property keyframe for the X property under the Basic Motion category. A property keyframe is automatically added for the Y property. Select Frame 1 and use the 3D Translation tool to move the W instance up so that its center is on the guide 50 pixels from the top of the Stage. Move the instance slightly to its left. In the Motion Editor, at Frame 1, set the Rotation X and the Rotation Y properties to 90 degrees. At Frame 10, insert a property keyframe for the Rotation X and the Rotation Y properties, and then set their values to 0 degrees. At Frame 10, select the Alpha property under the Color Effects category and add a property keyframe. Set the alpha amount in Frame 1 to 0% and in Frame 10 to 100%. The W instance will rotate, fade in, and move into place from Frame 1 to 10.

9. Repeat Step 8 for each letter instance so that it rotates, fades in, and falls into place using the following starting and ending frames: – e layer – Frames 10–20; s layer – Frames 20–30; t layer – Frames 30–40; c layer – Frames 40–50; r layer – Frames 50–60; e layer – Frames 60–70; e layer – Frames 70–80; k layer – Frames 80–90. Test the letter animations. The letters for the word Westcreek drop into place one at a time. They fade in and rotate as they fall. Collapse the Westcreek text folder and lock it to make it easier to work with the other layers in the Timeline.

10. Insert a layer above the Westcreek text layer folder and name it **nursery**. Insert a keyframe at Frame 91. Create a text block using the same type settings as in Step 3. Type **Nursery** in the text block. Center this text block on the guide 50 pixels from the top of the Stage.

11. Convert the Nursery text block to a movie clip symbol named **Nursery text**. Create a motion tween for the Nursery text instance. At Frame 91, change the alpha amount of the instance to 0%. At Frame 100, move the instance so that it is centered below the Westcreek text and change its alpha amount to 100%. The Nursery text should move from its initial position to below the Westcreek text and should fade in as it moves into position.

12. Insert a new layer and name it **text1**. Insert a keyframe at Frame 100 of this layer and then create a text block in this frame. The text should be white, use Arial for the font, use 26 for the point size, and use Bold for the font style. Place the text block on the pasteboard to the left of the Stage about 50 pixels from the top. Type **Always Fresh!** in this text block. Create a motion tween on the this text block, and at Frame 105, move the text block to the center of the Stage, keeping it about 50 pixels from the top. The text block moves in from the left of the Stage.

13. Insert a new layer and name it **text2**. Insert a keyframe at Frame 105 and create a text block using the same settings used in Step 12, but change the font size to 20. Place the text block in the pasteboard to the right of the Stage about 350 pixels from the top. Type **Delivered on Time!** in this text block. Create a motion tween on this text block, and at Frame 110, move the text block to the center of the Stage, keeping it about 350 pixels from the top. The text block moves in from the right of the Stage.

14. To create a graphic that will simulate a truck moving across the Stage, start by creating a rotating wheel symbol that will be embedded in the truck graphic. Create a new movie clip symbol named **Rotating wheel**. In symbol-editing mode, insert an instance of the Wheel symbol from the library to the center of the Stage. In the Property inspector, if necessary, set the X and Y coordinates to 0. Create a motion tween on the Wheel instance and in the Property inspector, set the Wheel instance to rotate clockwise one time. The Rotating Wheel symbol is complete. Exit symbol-editing mode.

15. Create a new movie clip symbol named **Truck**. In symbol-editing mode, create a text block at the center of the Stage using Arial for the font, 36 for the point size, and green (#65FF98) for the font color. Make the text bold and italic. Type the word **FLOWERs** in all uppercase, except for the letter s. Reduce the font size of the letter s to 30. Use the Info panel to set the X and Y registration point coordinates to 0 to center the text on the Stage.

16. Use the Line tool to draw a short horizontal line about 30 pixels wide using a stroke color of yellow (#FFFF00) and a stroke height of 1. Draw the line about 5 pixels to the left of the letter F. Create two copies of this line and place the lines to the left of the letter F. Each line should be about the same distance from the letter F and they should be equally spaced from each other. The lines will add to the effect of the FLOWERs text moving.

17. Drag an instance of the Rotating Wheel symbol to the Stage and place it right below the letter L in FLOWERs. Drag another instance and place it below the letter R. These instances will be the wheels for the truck. The Truck symbol is complete. Exit symbol-editing mode.

18. Insert a new layer above the text2 layer and name it **truck**. Insert a keyframe at Frame 70 and drag an instance of the Truck symbol in the pasteboard to the upper-left side of the Stage. Create a motion tween at Frame 70 for the Truck instance. At Frame 100, move the Truck instance to the center of the Stage below the Nursery text block.

◆ EXPLORE 19. Use the Selection tool to drag the center of the motion path for the Truck instance down slightly to curve it. Use the Subselection tool to click an endpoint on the motion path to reveal the curve's Bezier handles. Drag the top endpoint Bezier handle to the left to further curve the top part of the motion path. Drag the bottom endpoint Bezier handle up and to the right to create an upward curve on the bottom part of the motion path.

20. Test the animation in Flash and the Flash Player.
21. Submit the finished files to your instructor.

| Create | **Case Problem 4** |

Create an ad banner with a mask animation, motion tween animations, and individual letters.

Data File needed for this Case Problem: msaDraft.fla

Missions Support Association Brittany meets with Anissa to discuss the development of a new advertisement banner that the Missions Support Association can use to promote the association in various Web sites. The ad will contain the association's name, an animation of a star moving across the banner, and several graphics containing text messages. You'll create the new ad, which will be similar to the one shown in Figure 4-54.

Figure 4-54

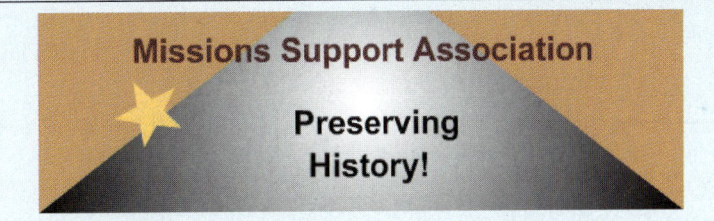

1. Open the **msaDraft.fla** file located in the Tutorial.04\Case4 folder included with your Data Files, and then save the document as **msaAd.fla** in the same folder.

2. In a new layer, create a text block with the text **Missions Support Association** at an appropriate location on the Stage, using the text properties of your choice.
3. Create a spotlight effect for the text using a mask animation.
4. In a new layer, create an animation of an instance of the star symbol that rotates as it moves. For example, the Star instance could move from the lower-left corner of the Stage in a curved path up toward the center of the Stage, move back down to the lower-right corner of the Stage, and then move in a curved path back toward the lower-left corner.
5. At the frame(s) of your choice, in separate layers, create a text block for each word of the text **Preserving History**. The words should appear on the Stage in an appropriate location. Use the text properties of your choice.
6. Create a pulsating effect on the individual letters of the word "History."
7. Make any other changes you feel enhance the advertisement.
8. Test the document's animation in Flash and the Flash Player.
9. Submit the finished files to your instructor.

Review | Quick Check Answers

Session 4.1

1. use the Selection tool to curve a motion path; use the Subselection tool to modify a control point on the motion path; and change the dimensions of a selected motion path in the Property inspector
2. handles used to modify the curve of a the path around a control point by dragging or extending the endpoints of the handles with the Subselection tool
3. to make a motion tweened object orient itself to the slope of the path it is following
4. basic motion properties, rotation properties, transformation properties
5. Lock both layers.
6. False; text can be used as a mask in a mask layer.
7. False; the contents of the masked layer are revealed when the object in the mask layer moves over it.

Session 4.2

1. Text can be animated to move from one part of the Stage to another. Text can be animated to rotate, fade in or fade out, and increase or decrease in size. Individual letters of a text block can be animated to create special effects.
2. break it apart twice
3. according to the text in each text block
4. because you cannot have more than one object or symbol on a layer with a motion tween
5. to make the letter layers easier to work with and organize in the Timeline, for example, a layer folder can be collapsed to hide its layers to make it easier to work with the other layers
6. False; the original layer content is moved to the new, separate layers.
7. True

Session 4.3

1. Drag the onion skin markers left or right or use the Modify Onion Markers button to change how many frames are onion skinned.
2. You can see the contents of the frames before and after the current frame, which helps you compare what the current frame contents should be in comparison to the other frames.
3. a movie clip that contains other movie clips in its Timeline, which can have animations in their respective Timelines
4. parent movie clip
5. because each nested movie clip has its own Timeline that is independent of the document's main Timeline
6. True
7. In the Movie Explorer, select an instance of a symbol, click the panel menu button, and then click Go to Symbol Definition.

Ending Data Files

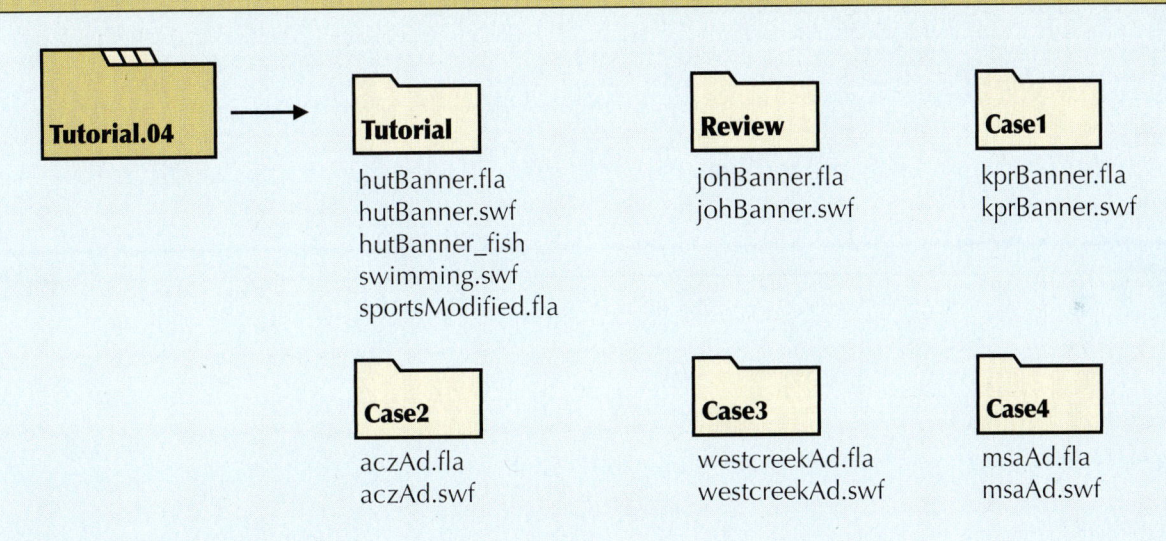

Tutorial.04 →

Tutorial
hutBanner.fla
hutBanner.swf
hutBanner_fish
swimming.swf
sportsModified.fla

Review
johBanner.fla
johBanner.swf

Case1
kprBanner.fla
kprBanner.swf

Case2
aczAd.fla
aczAd.swf

Case3
westcreekAd.fla
westcreekAd.swf

Case4
msaAd.fla
msaAd.swf

Flash | FL 225

Tutorial 5

Objectives

Session 5.1
- Explore the different button states
- Add a button from the Buttons library
- Edit a button instance
- Create a custom button
- Align objects on the Stage

Session 5.2
- Learn about actions
- Use the Actions panel
- Add actions to buttons
- Add actions to frames

Session 5.3
- Compare different types of sound effects
- Learn how to acquire sounds
- Import sounds from a file or the Sounds library
- Add sound to buttons
- Add a background sound to a document
- Change sound settings and add sound effects

Making a Document Interactive

Adding Buttons, Actions, and Sounds

Case | Admiral Web Design

Admiral Web Design is designing a lunch specials page for the Jenny's Oyster Hut Web site. Jenny Emerson wants the new banner design for the lunch specials page to be similar to the site's other banners and to include a background sound as well as animation. Aly suggests that visitors have the option to turn off the animation and the background sound, which some visitors might find distracting while they view the page. She suggests adding several buttons to the banner to control the animation and to mute the sound. She also suggests that the buttons include their own sound effects to help the visitor know when the button has been clicked. Jenny agrees to Aly's suggestions and approves the development of the new banner.

In this tutorial, you will create buttons, including buttons that change in response to the pointer. You will add buttons to a document and then add actions to the buttons so they can be used to control the animation. You will also learn how to change the way the animation plays by using frame actions. Finally, you will add sound effects to the buttons and a background sound to the animation.

Starting Data Files

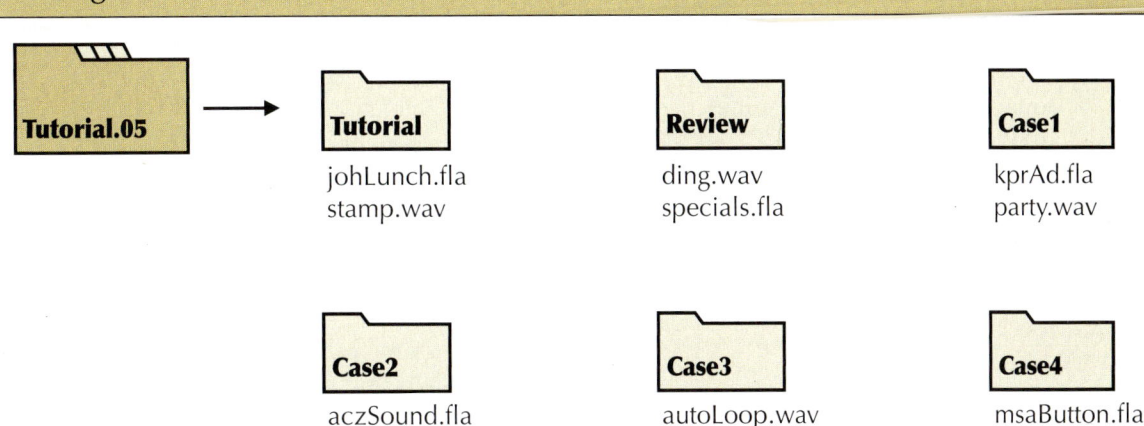

Tutorial.05 →

Tutorial
johLunch.fla
stamp.wav

Review
ding.wav
specials.fla

Case1
kprAd.fla
party.wav

Case2
aczSound.fla
pianoLoop.wav

Case3
autoLoop.wav
wnLogo.fla

Case4
msaButton.fla

Session 5.1

Exploring the Different Button States

Published Flash SWF files, also called movies, can include interactive elements. **Interactive** means that the user has some control over the movie, such as being able to stop or play its animation. Adding interaction to a movie draws the viewer in because the viewer is able to do more than passively watch the animation. One of the simplest ways to include interactivity is to add buttons that perform an action. Recall that a button is a symbol that contains a Timeline with only four frames. A button can take many forms, can include sound effects, and can even change appearance or behavior when the user places the pointer over it or clicks it. The first three frames represent different states of the button and can contain different content, as shown in Figure 5-1.

Figure 5-1 Sample button states

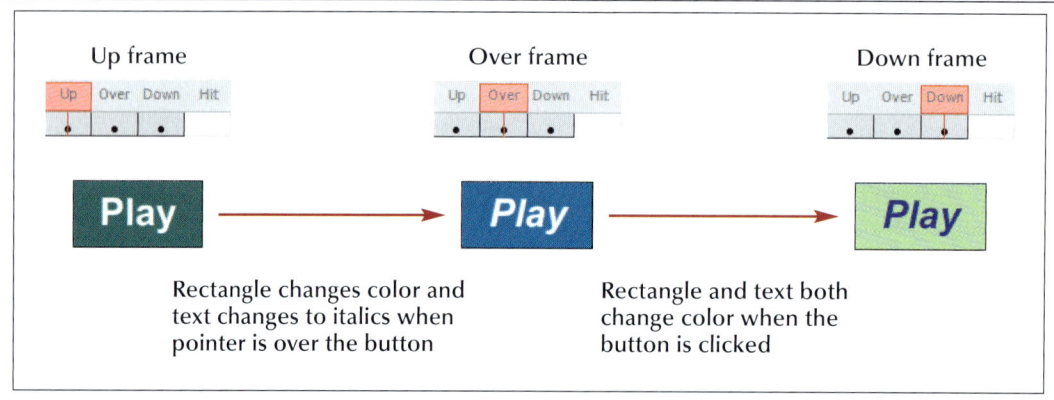

Up frame — Over frame — Down frame

Rectangle changes color and text changes to italics when pointer is over the button

Rectangle and text both change color when the button is clicked

The content of each frame appears in response to the pointer's action. The **Up frame** contains the button's default state, which is the button's appearance when the user is not pointing to or clicking the button. When the pointer is over the button, the **Over frame** is displayed. If the Over frame content is different from the Up frame content, it creates a **rollover effect**—that is, when the user moves the pointer over the button, the button changes to show what is in the Over frame. The **Down frame** shows what the button looks like as the user clicks it. You can make the Down frame different from the other frames to give the user a visual clue that the button has been clicked. The **Hit frame** does not change the appearance of the button, but, instead, represents the clickable or active area of the button. This is the area of the button that responds to a mouse click and displays the hand pointer when the pointer is over it. In Figure 5-1, the rectangle is green in the Up frame, the rectangle changes color and the text becomes italic in the Over frame, and then the rectangle changes color and the text changes color but remains italic in the Down frame. The Hit frame is empty because the rectangle provides an easy-to-click area. You will make the banner for Jenny's Oyster Hut lunch specials page interactive by adding buttons with these different states to control the animation and mute the background sound.

Tutorial 5 Making a Document Interactive | Flash | FL 227

| InSight | Choosing When to Include a Button's Hit Frame |

The Hit frame is the area of the button the user can roll over or click to perform an action. When a button is a solid shape, such as a rectangle or oval, the button area is easy to click and you can leave the Hit frame empty. When a button consists of text, the user must click the letters in the text to activate the button. This can be difficult, especially if the text is small. To make it easier to click the button, draw a filled shape such as a rectangle to cover the text in the Hit frame. The shape is not visible in the published movie, but it represents the area the user can click to activate the button.

Adding a Button from the Buttons Library

A quick way to add a button to a document is by using one of the predesigned buttons in the Buttons library. The Buttons library is one of the Common Libraries, which store symbols that install with Flash and can be copied to your documents. The library's button symbols can be copied to a document's library and used within that document. Recall that symbols are stored in a document's library, and that you add copies of the symbol, called instances, to the Stage.

Aly included a background sound in the new banner design, which is shown in Figure 5-2. You will add a button from the Buttons library that allows the user to mute the background sound that you will add later. This way, users can decide whether they want to listen to background sounds when visiting the Web site.

Figure 5-2 | Initial banner design

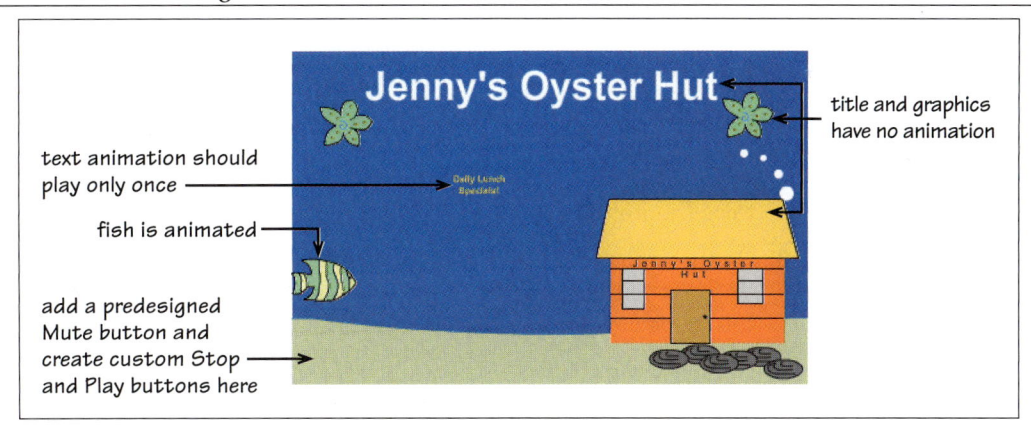

Jenny's Oyster Hut

- title and graphics have no animation
- text animation should play only once
- fish is animated
- add a predesigned Mute button and create custom Stop and Play buttons here

You will add the Mute button to the banner design that Aly started.

To add the flat blue stop button from the Buttons library:

1. Open the **johLunch.fla** file located in the Tutorial.05\Tutorial folder included with your Data Files, and then save the file as **johLunchSpecials.fla** in the same folder.

2. Reset the workspace to the Essentials layout, move the playhead to **Frame 1**, and then display the rulers, if necessary. All of the banner contents are visible.

3. In the Timeline, add a new layer above the title layer, and then rename the new layer **buttons**. You will place all the buttons for the banner on the buttons layer.

▶ 4. On the Application bar, click **Window**, point to **Common Libraries**, and then click **Buttons**. The Buttons Library panel opens in the middle of the program window. The library contains 277 items organized into folders by categories such as Buttons Oval and Classic Buttons.

▶ 5. In the Buttons Library panel, scroll down and then double-click the **playback flat** folder icon. The folder expands, displaying a list of buttons.

▶ 6. In the Buttons Library panel, scroll down and then click the **flat blue stop** button to select it. A preview of the button appears at the top of the panel. See Figure 5-3. You want to copy the flat blue stop button into the buttons layer of the document.

Figure 5-3   Buttons Library panel

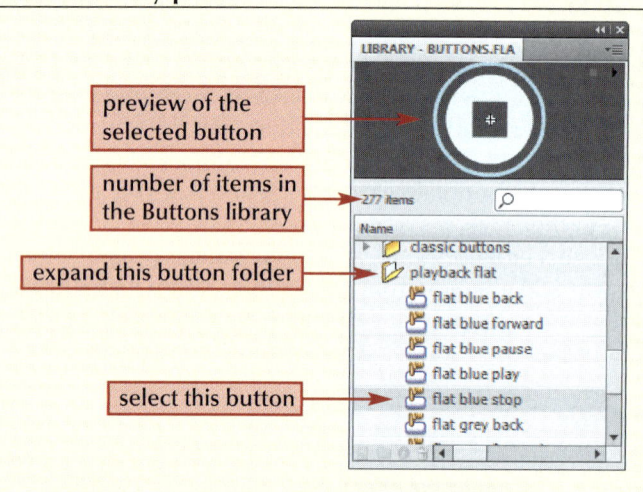

▶ 7. In the Timeline, make sure that the buttons layer is still selected, and then drag the **flat blue stop** button from the Buttons Library panel to the lower-left corner of the Stage to create an instance of the button. The flat blue stop button is added as a symbol with a button behavior to the document's library. The library now contains five items.

▶ 8. On the Stage, drag the **flat blue stop** button instance approximately **10** pixels from the left edge of the Stage and approximately **210** pixels from the top of the Stage.

▶ 9. On the Buttons Library panel tab, click the **Close** button. The Buttons library closes. See Figure 5-4.

Tutorial 5 Making a Document Interactive | Flash **FL 229**

Figure 5-4   Button symbol added to the banner

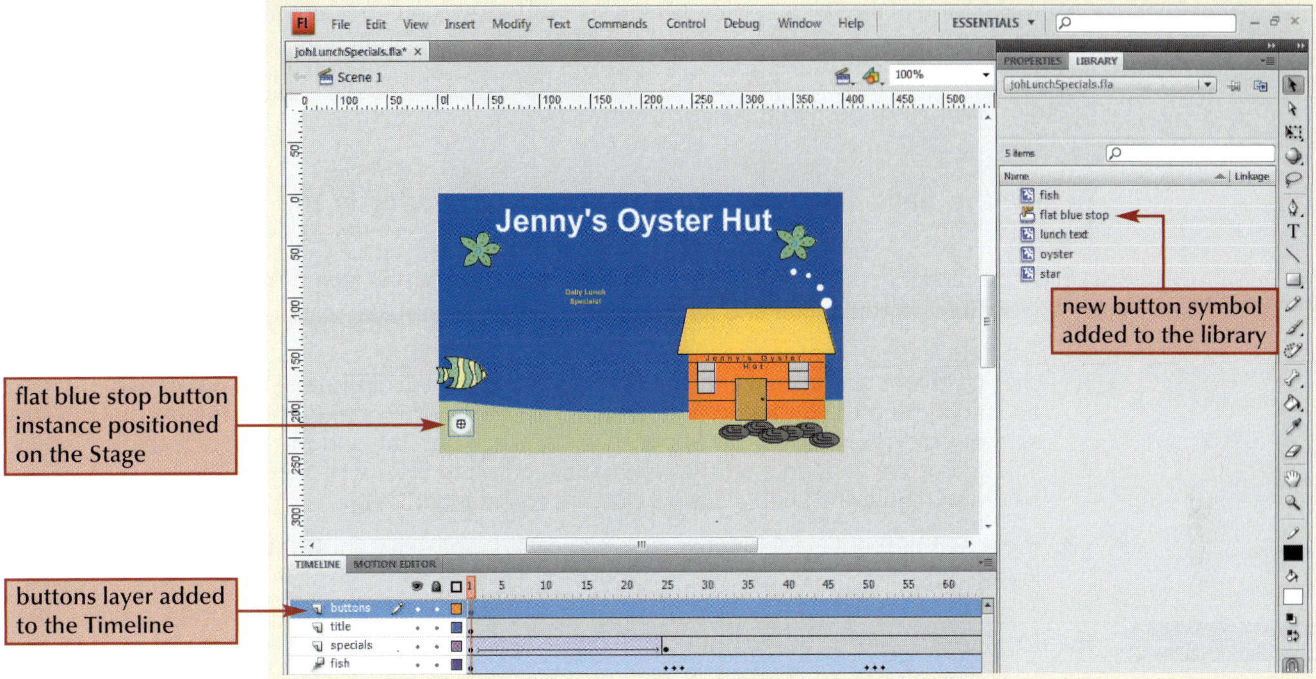

flat blue stop button instance positioned on the Stage

new button symbol added to the library

buttons layer added to the Timeline

After you add a button instance to a document, you should test it to be sure that it works as expected. You can do this within the Flash program window by turning on the Enable Simple Buttons command. When you turn this command on, the button exhibits its behavior on the Stage. When you move the pointer over the button, the pointer changes to a hand pointer and the button displays any rollover effects that are part of the button. After you review the button's behavior, you must turn off the Enable Simple Buttons command to select the button instance on the Stage and continue to modify it. You cannot select a button with the hand pointer.

You'll use the Enable Simple Buttons command to test the new button instance.

To view the flat blue stop button's behaviors:

▶ 1. On the Application bar, click **Control**, and then click **Enable Simple Buttons**. The command is toggled on so you can test the button.

▶ 2. On the Stage, click an empty area away from the button to deselect the button.

▶ 3. On the Stage, position the pointer over the flat blue stop button instance. The pointer changes to 👆, indicating that an action will occur after the button is clicked.

▶ 4. Click the **flat blue stop** button. The button changes color to indicate that it was clicked.

Editing a Button Instance

You can edit any button you add from the Buttons library. For example, you can change the contents of the Over frame to change the button's rollover effect or you can change the contents of the Down frame to change the effect that occurs when the button is clicked. You can also change the colors or graphics in a predesigned button to match the design of the document and to make it look less like a predesigned button. You can even delete the contents in one of the button's frames if you don't want the button to exhibit a certain behavior such as a rollover effect.

You will modify the flat blue stop button so that it uses a different color for its Down frame. This frame is displayed when the button is clicked, giving the user visual feedback that the button has been clicked. Because the button is a symbol, you must be in symbol-editing mode to modify it.

To edit the flat blue stop button to change the color in the Down frame:

▶ 1. In the Library panel, double-click the **flat blue stop** button icon. The button opens in symbol-editing mode and its four-frame Timeline appears.

Trouble? If you cannot open the button in symbol-editing mode, you might be clicking the button instance on the Stage and not the button icon in the library. Try double-clicking the button icon in the library. If the button still doesn't open in symbol-editing mode, on the Application bar, click Control, and then click Enable Simple Buttons to toggle off the command, complete this set of Steps 1 through 6, and then toggle the Enable Simple Buttons command back on.

▶ 2. Increase the zoom magnification to **400%** to get a better view of the button. See Figure 5-5.

Figure 5-5 The flat blue stop button in symbol-editing mode

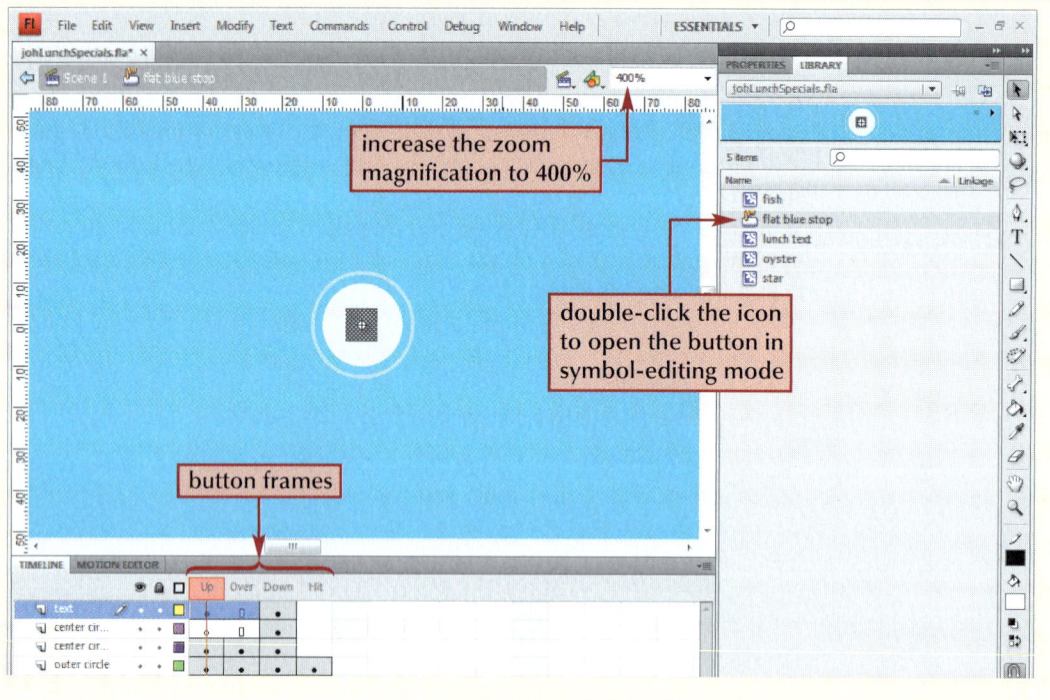

Tip

You can also press the comma or period key to move the playhead backward or forward, respectively, one frame at a time.

▶ 3. In the Timeline, drag the playhead back and forth between the Up frame and the Down frame to see how the button changes.

▶ 4. In the Timeline, click the **Down** frame of the text layer. The small white square in the center of the button is selected, which is indicated by the fine dot pattern.

▶ 5. In the Tools panel, change the fill color of the square to **green** (#00FF00). See Figure 5-6.

Tutorial 5 Making a Document Interactive | Flash **FL 231**

| Figure 5-6 | **Color changed in the button's Down frame** |

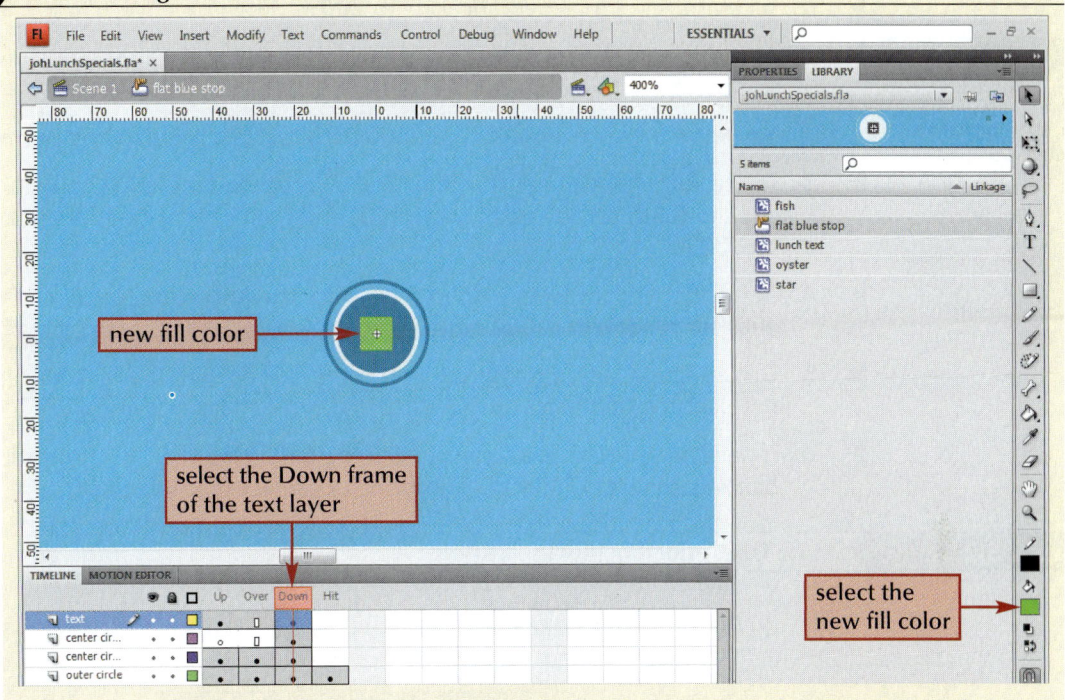

[Screenshot of Flash interface showing the button editing mode with callouts: "new fill color", "select the Down frame of the text layer", and "select the new fill color"]

▶ 6. On the Edit bar, click the **Scene 1** link to exit symbol-editing mode and return to the document.

▶ 7. On the Stage, click the **flat blue stop** button instance. The small gray square in the center of the button turns green when you click the button instance.

▶ 8. On the Application bar, click **Control**, and then click **Enable Simple Buttons**. The Enable Simple Buttons command is toggled off, so you can select the button instance on the Stage.

InSight | **Anti-aliasing Text**

To improve readability, Flash uses a rendering engine that provides high-quality, clear text in Flash documents. Anti-aliasing, which is part of the rendering process, smoothes the edges of text displayed on the computer screen. Anti-aliasing is especially effective when using small font sizes. When text is selected on the Stage, you can choose a font-rendering method in the Property inspector. Two of the methods available are Anti-alias for animation and Anti-alias for readability. Select Anti-alias for animation when the text will be animated such as when you apply a motion tween to a text object. This results in a smoother animation. If the text will not be animated, select Anti-alias for readability. This improves the legibility of the text.

Labels often identify the purpose of each button so that it is clear to the user what will happen when a button is clicked. You should add a label either within the button's frames or to an instance of a button on the Stage. You will add text below the flat blue stop button instance on the Stage to label it as the Mute button. This tells the user what happens when the button is clicked. Otherwise, the user may not know what purpose the button serves.

Tip

You can also hold down the Spacebar to change the pointer to a hand pointer, drag the document on the Stage, and then release the Spacebar to return to the previous pointer.

To add text to identify the Mute button instance:

▶ 1. Increase the Stage magnification to **200%**.

▶ 2. In the Tools panel, click the **Hand** tool, and then drag the document to center the button instance on the Stage.

   You will set the text properties and add a text block below the button.

▶ 3. In the Tools panel, click the **Text** tool, set the font family to **Arial**, set the font style to **Bold**, set the point size to **10**, and then set the text fill color to **black** (#000000).

▶ 4. In the Property inspector, if necessary, click the **Anti-alias** button, and then click **Anti-alias for readability**. This anti-aliasing option improves the legibility of the text.

▶ 5. On the Stage, add a text block below the button with the text **Mute**, and then deselect the text block.

▶ 6. If necessary, in the Tools panel, click the **Selection** tool, reposition the text block as shown in Figure 5-7, and then deselect the text block.

Figure 5-7   Mute label added below the button

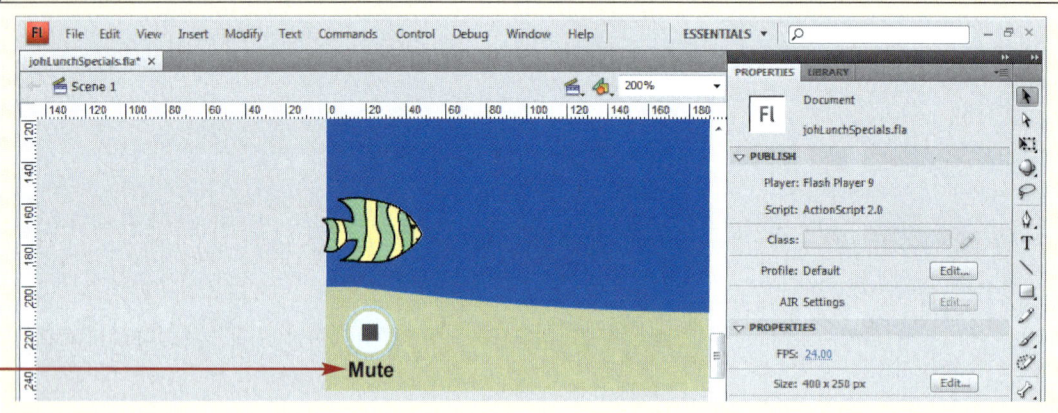

add the text block below the button

▶ 7. Save the document.

Creating a Custom Button

The buttons in the Common Buttons Library provide many choices to use in documents. For a more professional look, you will often want to create unique buttons that match your project's design. Flash has the tools to create almost any kind of button you need. Buttons can be any shape, such as rectangles and ovals or even text.

    You can convert an existing object on the Stage, such as a rectangle, into a button symbol and then edit the button in symbol-editing mode, creating or modifying the contents for each of the button's four frames as needed. The object on the Stage becomes an instance of the button symbol and the symbol is added to the library. You can also create a new symbol with a button behavior and then draw the button shape in symbol-editing mode as well as create or modify the contents for each of the button's four frames. The button you created is stored in the document's library, available for you to create instances of the button on the Stage.

Tutorial 5 Making a Document Interactive | Flash | FL 233

| Reference Window | **Creating a Custom Button** |

- On the Stage, create the button's shape, and then select the shape.
- On the Application bar, click Modify, and then click Convert to Symbol.
- Type a name in the Name box, click the Type button, click Button, and then click the OK button.
- Switch to symbol-editing mode, and then modify the contents for each of the button's four frames as needed.

or

- On the Application bar, click Insert, and then click New Symbol.
- Type a name in the Name box, click the Type button, click Button, and then click the OK button.
- Create the button's shape on the Stage.
- Switch to symbol-editing mode, and then modify the contents for each of the button's four frames as needed.

Based on Aly's instructions, you need to create two buttons for the banner. Both buttons are rectangles with rounded corners. However, one button is a Stop button, which the user clicks to stop the animation while it is playing. The second button is a Play button, which the user clicks to start the animation playing at any time. Because the buttons have a similar appearance, you can create the Stop button, and then modify a copy of the Stop button to create the Play button.

To create the Stop button:

Tip

In the Property inspector, click the Reset button to set the corner radius values to zero and lock the values.

1. In the Tools panel, click the **Rectangle** tool, and then, in the Property inspector, lock the corner radius controls and enter **10** as the Rectangle corner radius. Each corner radius is set to 10.

2. In the Property inspector, set the stroke color to **black** (#000000), set the fill color to **red** (#FF0000), set the stroke height to **2**, and then set the stroke style to **Solid**.

3. In the Timeline, select the **buttons** layer, if necessary.

4. On the Stage to the right of the Mute button, draw a rectangle that is approximately 60 pixels wide and 20 pixels high. See Figure 5-8.

FL 234 Flash | Tutorial 5 Making a Document Interactive

Figure 5-8 | **Rectangle button shape**

draw the rectangle next to the Mute button

make sure the buttons layer is selected

select a red fill, and solid, 2pt, black stroke

set the corner radius values to 10

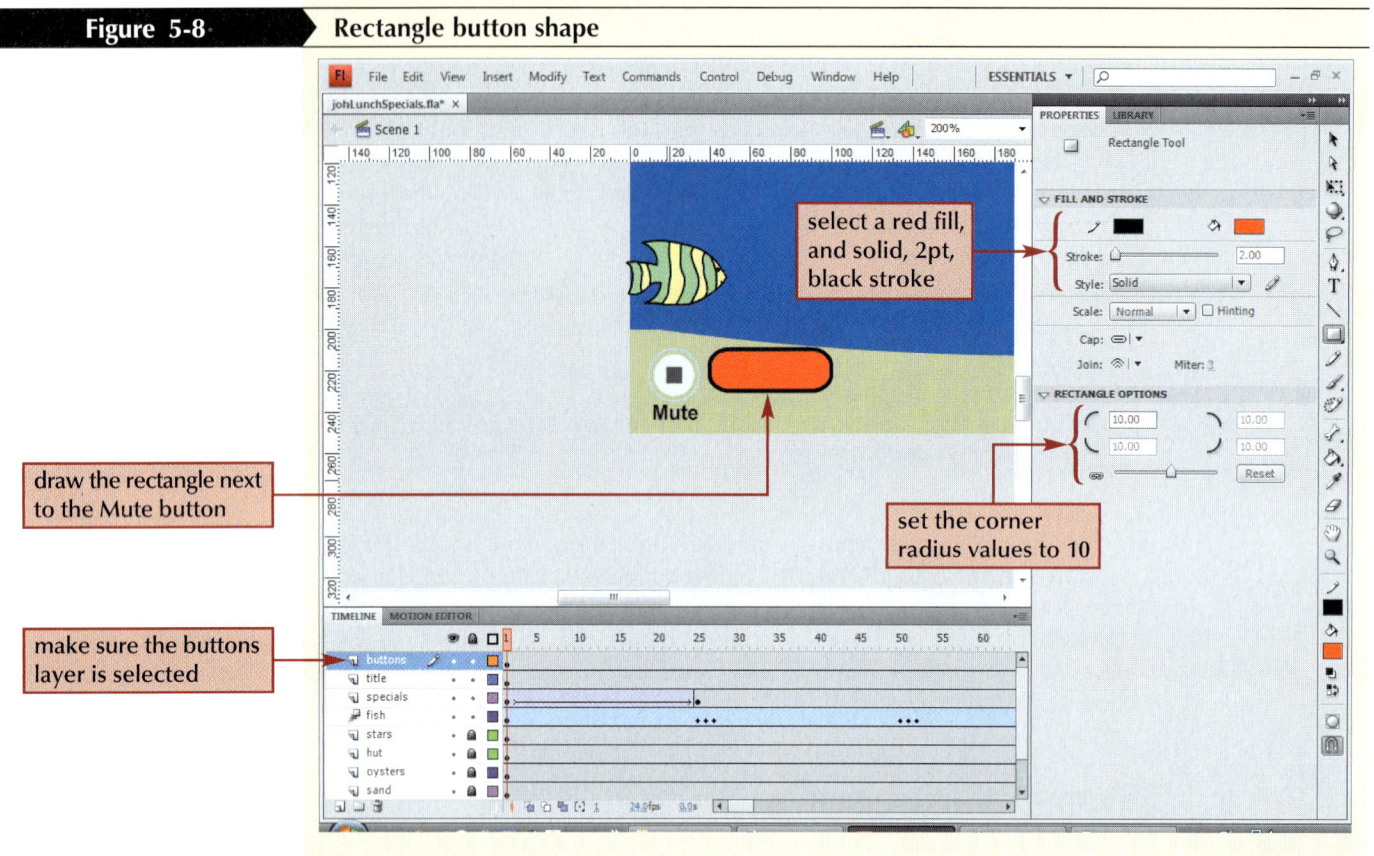

▶ 5. In the Tools panel, click the **Selection** tool, and then, on the Stage, double-click the **rectangle** to select both its fill and its stroke. You'll convert the selected button shape to a symbol.

▶ 6. Convert the selected rectangle to a button symbol named **Stop button**. The new button is added to the document's library, and the selected button instance remains on the Stage.

You will edit this button to add a text label and to create the different states of the button. The Stop button will have a rollover effect so that when the pointer moves over the button, the button's fill color changes from red to a red radial gradient. This provides a visual clue to the user that something will happen if the button is clicked. The button will also move when it is clicked, providing visual feedback that reinforces the user's action. The button's Timeline contains the four frames. The Up frame has a keyframe and contains the rectangle you created for the default state of the button. You will add text to the Up frame and then add keyframes to the Over and Down frames to create the different states of the button. You don't need to add anything to the Hit frame because the rectangle shape provides the clickable or active area for the button.

To add text to the Stop button and create the different states of the button:

▶ 1. In the Library panel, double-click the **Stop button** icon to open the button in symbol-editing mode, and then increase the zoom magnification to **200%**. See Figure 5-9.

Tutorial 5 Making a Document Interactive | Flash **FL 235**

Figure 5-9   **Stop button in symbol-editing mode**

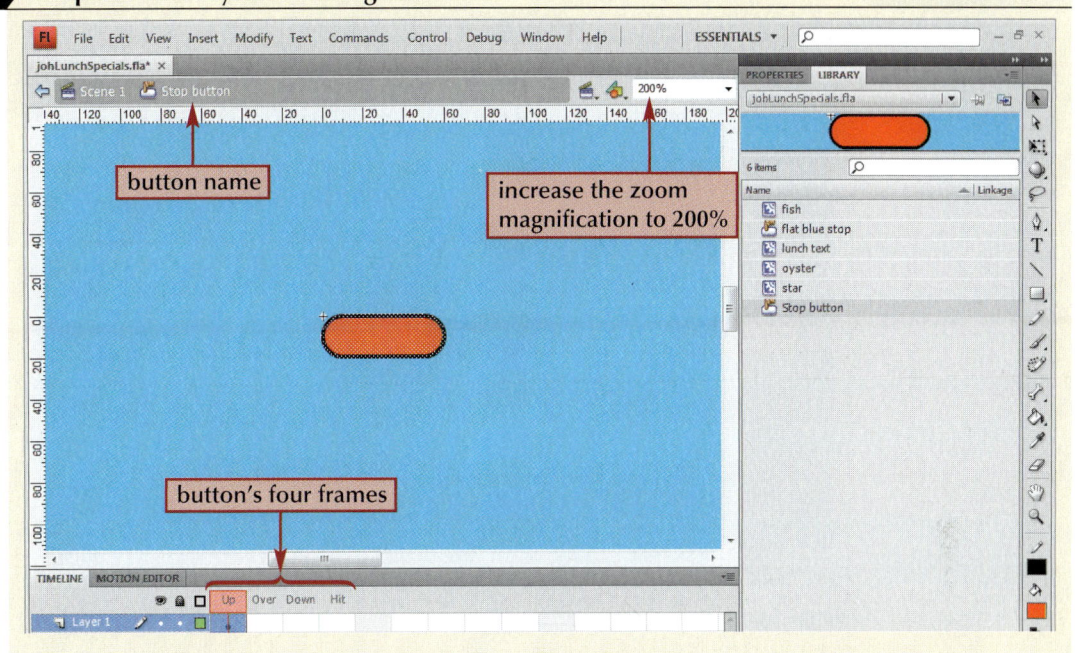

[Screenshot of Flash interface in symbol-editing mode showing the Stop button. Annotations point to: "button name", "increase the zoom magnification to 200%", and "button's four frames".]

▸ **2.** In the Tools panel, click the **Text** tool T to select it, and then, in the Property inspector, if necessary, set the font family to **Arial**, set the font style to **bold**, set the point size to **10**, and set the text fill color to **white** (#FFFFFF).

▸ **3.** Inside the rectangle, create a text block, and then type **Stop**. You want the text block to be centered inside the rectangle.

▸ **4.** In the Tools panel, click the **Selection** tool ▸ to select it, and then click the **Snap to Objects** button to deselect it.

▸ **5.** On the Stage, drag the text block so that it is centered inside the rectangle. See Figure 5-10.

Figure 5-10   **Label added to the Stop button**

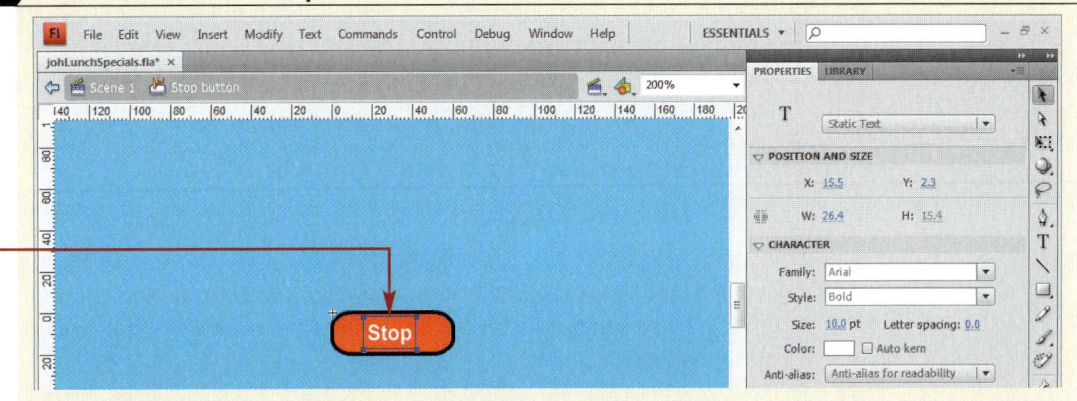

[Screenshot of Flash interface showing the Stop button with "Stop" text label centered inside the rectangle. Annotation: "center the text block within the rectangle". Property inspector shows Static Text, Position and Size (X: 15.5, Y: 2.3, W: 26.4, H: 15.4), Character settings with Family: Arial, Style: Bold, Size: 10.0 pt.]

▸ **6.** In the Timeline, click the **Over** frame to select it, and then insert a keyframe. The contents of the Up frame are automatically copied to the Over frame. You will change the button's fill color in the Over frame so that the button's color changes when the user moves the pointer over the Stop button.

▸ **7.** In the Tools panel, change the fill color to the **red radial gradient**, which is the third swatch in the bottom row of the color palette. The red radial gradient replaces the rectangle's red fill. See Figure 5-11.

Figure 5-11   Rectangle's fill changed in the Over frame

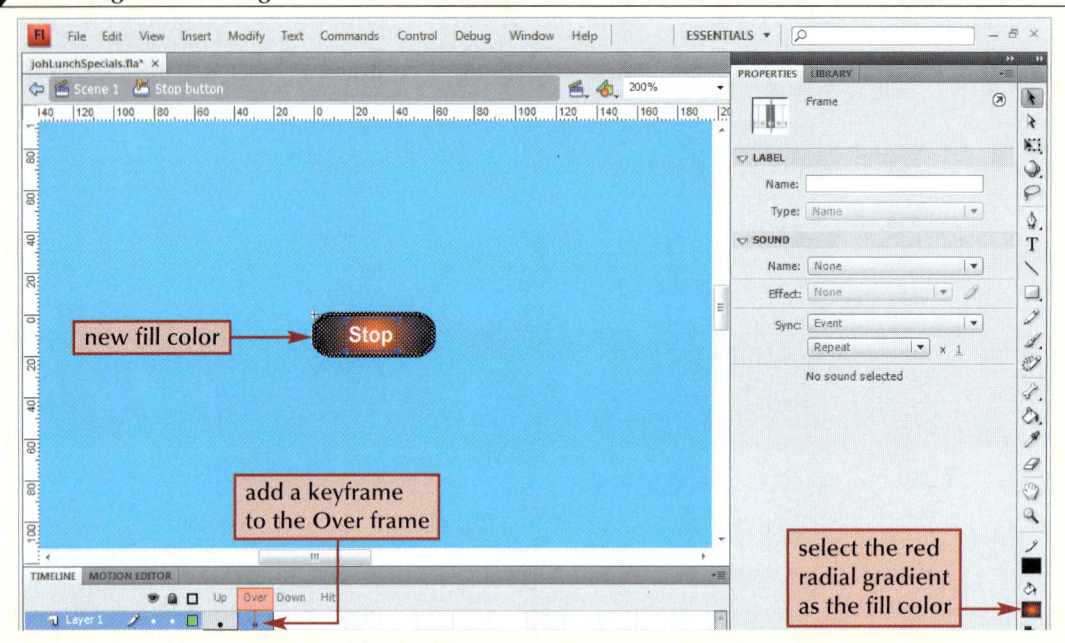

(Screenshot callouts: "new fill color", "add a keyframe to the Over frame", "select the red radial gradient as the fill color")

▶ 8. In the Timeline, click the **Down** frame, and then insert a keyframe. The contents of the Over frame are copied to the Down frame. You need to change the button's position in the Down frame so that when the user clicks the Stop button, the button appears as if it has been pressed and released.

▶ 9. With the rectangle and text box still selected, press the **Down** arrow key three times, and then press the **Right** arrow key three times. The rectangle moves three pixels down and three pixels to the right, which makes the button appear to shift when the user clicks it.

▶ 10. On the Edit bar, click the **Scene 1** link to exit symbol-editing mode and return to the document.

The button and its different states are complete. You'll preview the button instance's behavior on the Stage to make sure the different effects you created appear correctly. You use the Enable Simple Buttons command to preview the effects.

To test the Stop button instance's rollover effects:

▶ 1. On the Application bar, click **Control**, and then click **Enable Simple Buttons**. The command is on and you can test the button.

▶ 2. On the Stage, click a blank area to deselect the button, and then move the pointer over the **Stop button** instance. Because of the rollover effect, the button changes color. See Figure 5-12.

Tutorial 5 Making a Document Interactive | Flash | FL 237

| Figure 5-12 | Stop button's rollover effect |

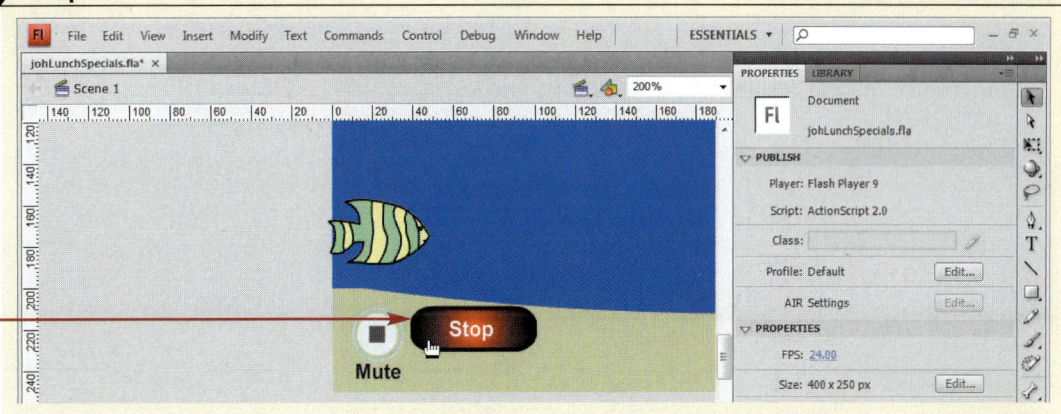

rollover effect changes the button's color

3. Click the **Stop** button instance. The button shifts down and right, providing a visual cue that the button was clicked. You are done testing the visual effects of the Stop button.

4. On the Application bar, click **Control**, and then click **Enable Simple Buttons**. The command is off and you can again select the button instances on the Stage.

Copying and Editing a Custom Button

Many times, a Flash document requires two or more buttons that are similar. Rather than creating each button individually, you can create the first button and then copy and modify the button for each of the remaining buttons. This method is faster and helps to ensure consistency in the design of the buttons.

The lunch specials banner requires a Play button, which looks very similar to the Stop button. Instead of creating a new button, you will make a copy of the Stop button, and then modify it to create the Play button.

To create a copy of the Stop button:

1. In the Library panel, right-click the **Stop button**, and then click **Duplicate** on the context menu. The Duplicate Symbol dialog box opens with the duplicate button's name, Stop button copy, selected. You will rename the button.

2. In the Name box, type **Play button**. The symbol type remains set to Button and the folder in which the Play button symbol is stored remains the root folder of the library.

3. Click the **OK** button. The Duplicate Symbol dialog box closes, and the Play button symbol is added to the document's library. See Figure 5-13.

Figure 5-13   Play button symbol in the library

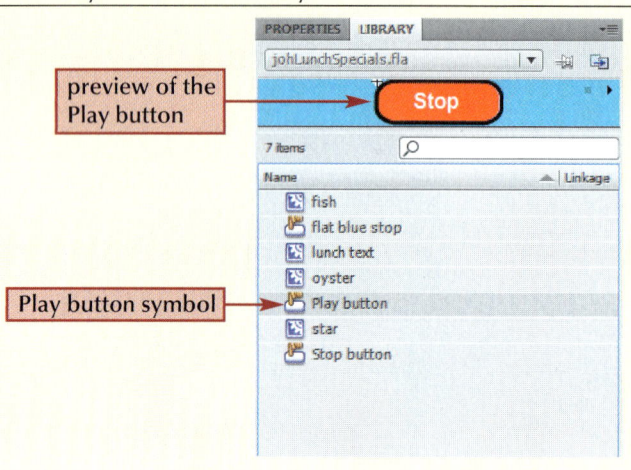

You need to modify the Play button so it is not an exact copy of the Stop button. The Play button will be green in its default state and change to a green radial gradient color when the user positions the pointer over the button. As you change the button's colors, check that you have selected the appropriate frame. Also, make sure that you don't change the text block. For example, in the Up frame, you want to change only the color of the rectangle's fill to green. So the Up frame must be selected and the text block must be deselected. After you modify the Play button in the document's library, you need to create an instance of the button symbol in the document.

To edit the Play button and add an instance of the button to the Stage:

▶ 1. In the Library panel, double-click the **Play button** icon. The button opens in symbol-editing mode.

▶ 2. Increase the zoom magnification to **200%**. The close-up view of the button makes the button easier to edit.

For the Up frame you only want to change the color of the rectangle's fill to green, so you need to make sure the Up frame is selected and the text block is deselected.

▶ 3. In the Timeline, click the **Up** frame, click a blank area of the Stage to deselect the rectangle and the text block, and then click the rectangle's fill to select it. Only the rectangle's fill in the Up frame is selected. You will apply a different color to the button.

▶ 4. In the Tools panel, set the fill color to **dark green** (#006600). The Play button's fill color changes to green, replacing the red color. See Figure 5-14.

Tutorial 5 Making a Document Interactive | Flash | FL 239

Figure 5-14   **Play button's fill changed**

change the rectangle's fill color to green

select the Up frame

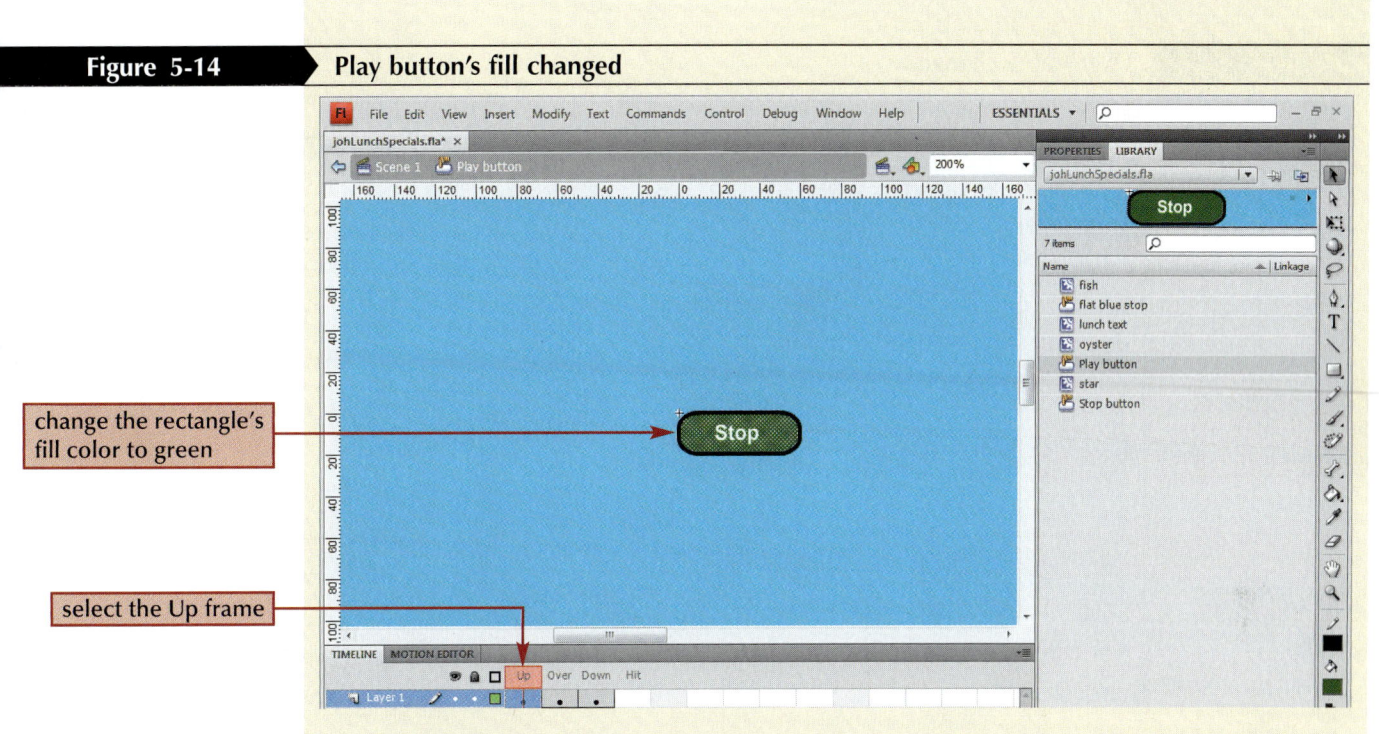

▶   **5.** In the Tools panel, click the **Text** tool [T], and then make sure the font family is **Arial**, the font style is **bold**, the point size is **10**, and the text fill color is **white** (#FFFFFF).

▶   **6.** On the Stage, click the **Stop** text block, and then change the text to **Play**. The button text reflects the button's purpose.

So far, you changed the color and text of the Up frame. The Over and Down frames still contain the red fill and the Stop text. You will modify those frames next.

▶   **7.** In the Timeline, click the **Over** frame to select the button.

▶   **8.** On the Stage, deselect the button and select the rectangle's fill, and then, in the Tools panel, set the fill color to the **green radial gradient**, the fourth gradient swatch in the bottom row of the color palette. The button's fill color changes color. You will change the button's text next.

▶   **9.** In the Tools panel, click the **Text** tool [T], and then, on the Stage, click the **Stop** text block and change the text to **Play**. The Over frame is edited for the Play button. See Figure 5-15.

FL 240 Flash | Tutorial 5 Making a Document Interactive

| Figure 5-15 | Over frame changed |

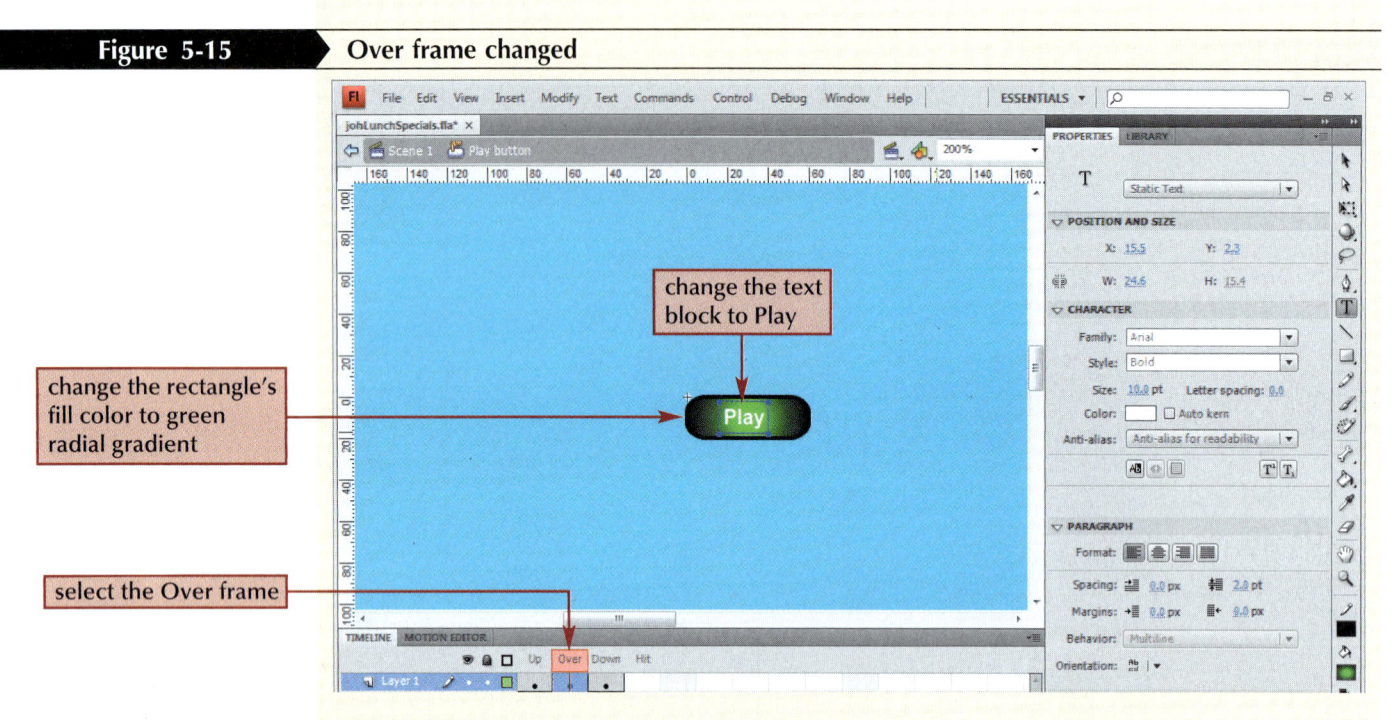

change the rectangle's fill color to green radial gradient

change the text block to Play

select the Over frame

▸ 10. In the Timeline, click the **Down** frame, and then repeat Steps 8 and 9. The button changes in the Down frame to the green radial gradient fill and the button text is updated to Play.

▸ 11. On the Edit bar, click the **Scene 1** link to exit symbol-editing mode. The Play button is complete.

▸ 12. Drag the **Play** button from the Library panel to the Stage, placing the instance to the right of the Stop button instance. See Figure 5-16.

| Figure 5-16 | Play button instance added to the document |

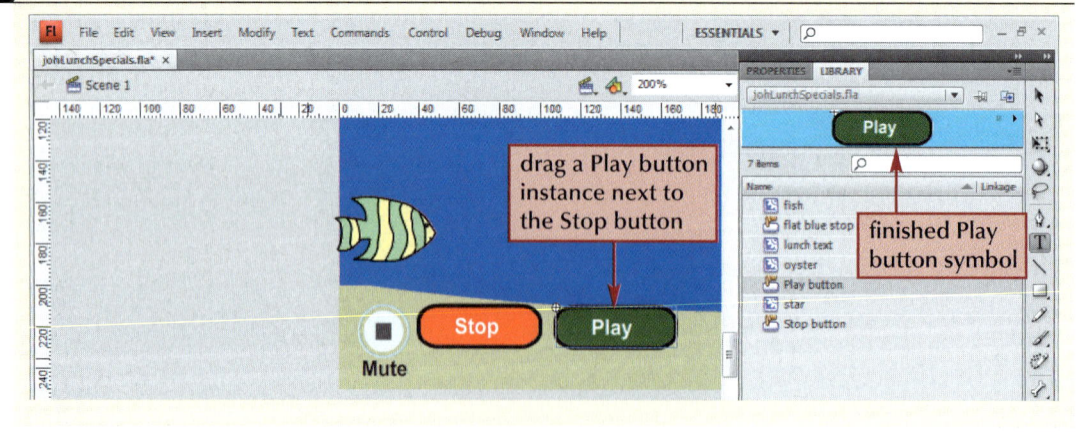

drag a Play button instance next to the Stop button

finished Play button symbol

Aligning Objects on the Stage

When a document includes multiple objects similar in design, you should align them with each other. If several objects are placed vertically, align them by their left or right sides. If the objects are placed horizontally, align them by their top or bottom sides. Also, make the space between the objects the same. Taking the time to align and space the objects evenly gives a document a more polished and professional appearance. The Align panel includes different options to arrange a group of selected objects on the Stage. You

Tutorial 5 Making a Document Interactive | Flash **FL 241**

can line up selected objects by their edges or centers and you can also distribute them so that they are evenly spaced. Objects will align with the leftmost or rightmost selected object when aligned by their left edges or right edges, respectively. They will align with the topmost or bottommost selected object when aligned by their top edges or bottom edges, respectively.

The Mute, Stop, and Play buttons should be aligned by their bottom edges. You also need to make sure that they are positioned with an equal amount of space between them.

To align the Mute, Stop, and Play buttons using the Align panel:

▶ 1. On the Application bar, click **Window**, and then click **Align**. The Align panel opens. See Figure 5-17.

Figure 5-17 Align panel

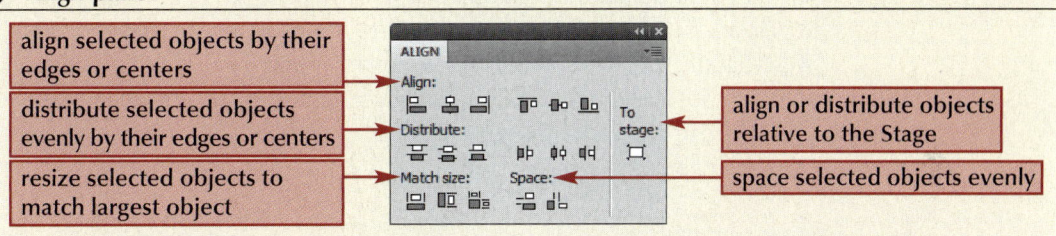

Tip
You can also press the Ctrl+K keys to open and close the Align panel.

- align selected objects by their edges or centers
- distribute selected objects evenly by their edges or centers
- resize selected objects to match largest object
- align or distribute objects relative to the Stage
- space selected objects evenly

▶ 2. In the Tools panel, click the **Selection** tool to select it.

▶ 3. On the Stage, click the **Mute** button instance, press and hold the **Shift** key, click the **Stop** button instance, click the **Play** button instance, and then release the Shift key. All three buttons instances are selected on the Stage.

▶ 4. In the Align panel, click the **Align/Distribute to stage** button to deselect it, if necessary. The selected objects will align relative to each other and not relative to the Stage.

▶ 5. In the Align group of the Align panel, click the **Align bottom edge** button. The three button instances align along their bottom edges.

▶ 6. In the Space group of the Align panel, click the **Space evenly horizontally** button. The button instances now have an equal amount of space between them. See Figure 5-18.

Figure 5-18 Three buttons aligned and evenly spaced

- click to align the buttons' bottom edges
- deselect to align the buttons relative to each other
- click to evenly space the buttons
- buttons aligned and evenly spaced

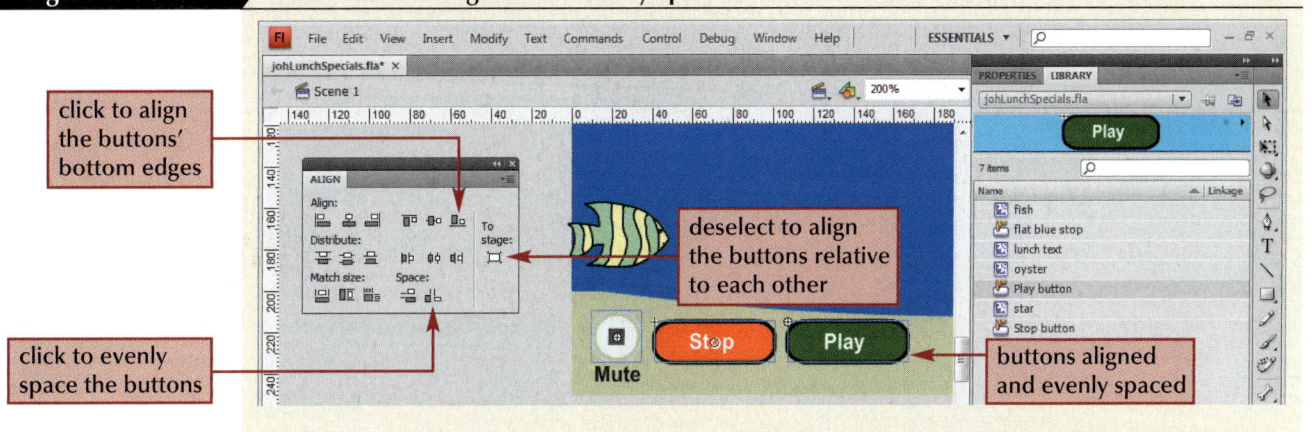

▶ 7. Close the Align panel, click a blank area of the Stage to deselect the buttons, and then save the document.

In this session, you created buttons to mute, stop, and play animation. You added a button from the Buttons library to the banner, and then modified it to create a Mute button. You also created custom buttons for the Stop and Play buttons. You then aligned the buttons along their bottom edges and spaced the buttons evenly. The buttons, though attractive and professional looking, do not control anything yet. You will modify them in the next session to control the banner's animation.

Review | Session 5.1 Quick Check

1. What is a button?
2. Why would you add buttons to a document?
3. How can you add a button from the Buttons library to your document's library?
4. What are the four frames in a button's Timeline?
5. How do you create a rollover effect for a button?
6. How can you test a button in Flash?
7. How can you align several objects on the Stage?

Session 5.2

Understanding Actions

The buttons you added to the banner do not yet allow the user to control the document's animation. When the button is clicked, the animation does not change. The document still plays sequentially one frame after another until it reaches the end of the animation. According to Aly's instructions, the buttons should allow the user to stop and play the animation. To make a button fully functional and interactive, you need to add an **action**, which is an instruction that is used to control a document while its animation is playing. Actions are part of the programming language used in Flash called **ActionScript**. The ActionScript language is very similar to the Web language **JavaScript**, which is used to add interactive elements to Web pages. Many of the actions in ActionScript are simple and can be used to create basic navigation controls to manage a document's animation. For example, you can add actions that stop or play an animation. You use ActionScript to create scripts that tell Flash what action to take when a certain event occurs. A **script** is a set of one or more actions that perform some function. An **event** is a situation where the user is interacting with a button, such as clicking a button with the mouse and then releasing it. The Flash Player listens for these events, which can be used to trigger or start the actions in a script.

The sample script shown in Figure 5-19 contains three lines of code. The first line has the mouse event handler on, followed by the event release in parentheses. Release is an event that occurs when the user clicks and then releases the mouse button. An **event handler** tells Flash how to respond to an event. The second line has the action. In this script, the event handler is triggered when the user clicks and then releases the button, causing the stop action to execute. The movie then stops playing. You will add this script to the Stop button instance in the banner.

Figure 5-19 | Sample script

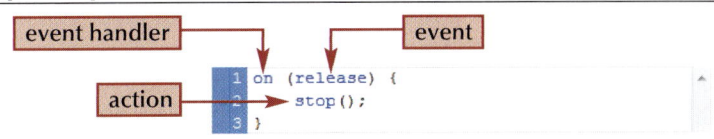

```
1  on (release) {
2      stop();
3  }
```
- event handler → `on (release)`
- event → `release`
- action → `stop();`

Adding Actions Using the Actions Panel

You do not need to fully understand ActionScript to use its basic actions. Also, you don't need to write the scripts yourself. Instead, Flash can create the scripts for you when you select actions in the Actions panel, which is shown in Figure 5-20. Flash creates the scripts needed for these actions to work in your document.

Figure 5-20 | Actions panel

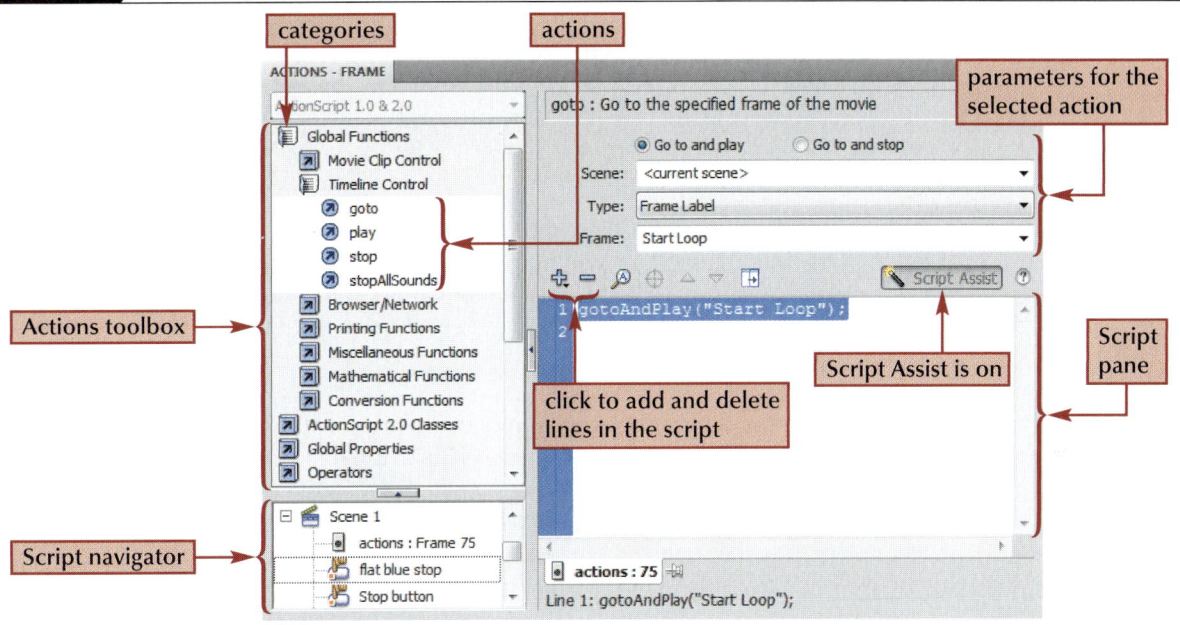

Labels in figure:
- categories
- actions
- parameters for the selected action
- Actions toolbox
- Script Assist is on
- Script pane
- click to add and delete lines in the script
- Script navigator

ActionScript 3.0 is the default version for Flash CS4 Professional. ActionScript 3.0 is conceptually different from ActionScript 1.0 and 2.0 and supports more complex programming structures. You will work with ActionScript 3.0 in Tutorial 8. In Tutorials 5 through 7, you will use ActionScript 2.0, which is simpler to use when adding basic navigation actions to buttons.

InSight | ActionScript Versions

ActionScript 3.0, the latest version of the Flash programming language, is compliant with industry standards and is based on an international standardized programming language known as ECMAScript. Programs written in ActionScript 3.0 can run up to 10 times faster than those written in previous versions and require Flash Player version 9 or higher to run. Using ActionScript 3.0 also makes developing highly complex applications easier. For a novice, learning ActionScript 3.0 can be a challenging task. However, if you only need to add simple actions to a document, you can still use previous versions of the language such as ActionScript 2.0.

In ActionScript 2.0, you can use the Actions panel in normal mode or Script Assist mode. In normal mode, you write the scripts yourself. This requires a more in-depth understanding of the ActionScript language. In Script Assist mode, Flash provides actions you select from the Actions toolbox, located on the left side of the Actions panel. The Actions toolbox organizes the available actions into categories. For example, the Global Functions category contains the Timeline Control category, which contains a list of actions that control the timeline. The Script pane, located on the right side of the Actions panel, is where the script is created. When you select an action, Flash automatically adds the appropriate statements to the script, depending on the action and the object to which the action is applied. Some actions require additional settings called **parameters**, which can be selected or entered in the parameters area of the Actions panel.

| Reference Window | **Using the Actions panel** |

- In the Actions panel, click the Script Assist button to turn on Script Assist mode.
- If necessary, click the Show/Hide Toolbox button to show the Actions toolbox.
- Click a category in the Actions toolbox to display additional categories or actions.
- Double-click or drag an action to add it to the Script pane.
- To delete an action from the Script pane, select it and then click the Delete (–) button.
- Select or enter values in the parameters section.

When you plan how and where the user needs to interact with a document, you also need to plan what interactions will be part of the document and where these interactions will be placed. You can add actions to buttons or to frames in the Timeline.

Adding Actions to Buttons

Buttons are one way to give the user control over the animation. If you want to use buttons, you need to plan what actions are required to make the buttons functional. You then add the appropriate actions to the button instances on the Stage, and not to the button symbol in the library. A button symbol cannot have actions applied to it, only instances of the button. Different instances of the same button symbol can have different actions.

You will add the stop action to the Stop button and the play action to the Play button.

To add actions to the Stop and Play buttons:

▶ 1. If you took a break after the previous session, make sure the johLunchSpecials.fla file is open, the workspace is reset to the Essentials layout, the Stage magnification is 200%, and no elements are selected on the banner.

▶ 2. On the Stage, click the **Stop** button instance to select it. You will add the stop action to this button instance.

▶ 3. On the Application bar, click **Window**, and then click **Actions**. The Actions panel opens.

▶ 4. In the Actions panel, click the **filter** button, and then click **ActionScript 1.0 & 2.0**, if necessary.

▶ 5. In the Actions panel, click the **Script Assist** button to select it, if necessary. The parameters area appears in the upper-right corner of the Actions panel and the Action toolbox displays a list of action categories. The stop action is located in the Global Functions category.

▶ 6. In the Actions toolbox, click **Global Functions** to display its subcategories. The stop action controls the Timeline, so it is located in the Timeline Control category.

▶ 7. In the Actions toolbox, click **Timeline Control** to display its actions. A list of the available Timeline Control actions appears.

▶ 8. Double-click **stop**. The stop action is added to the Stop button instance, and the action and its script are visible in the Script pane. See Figure 5-21.

Figure 5-21	Stop script

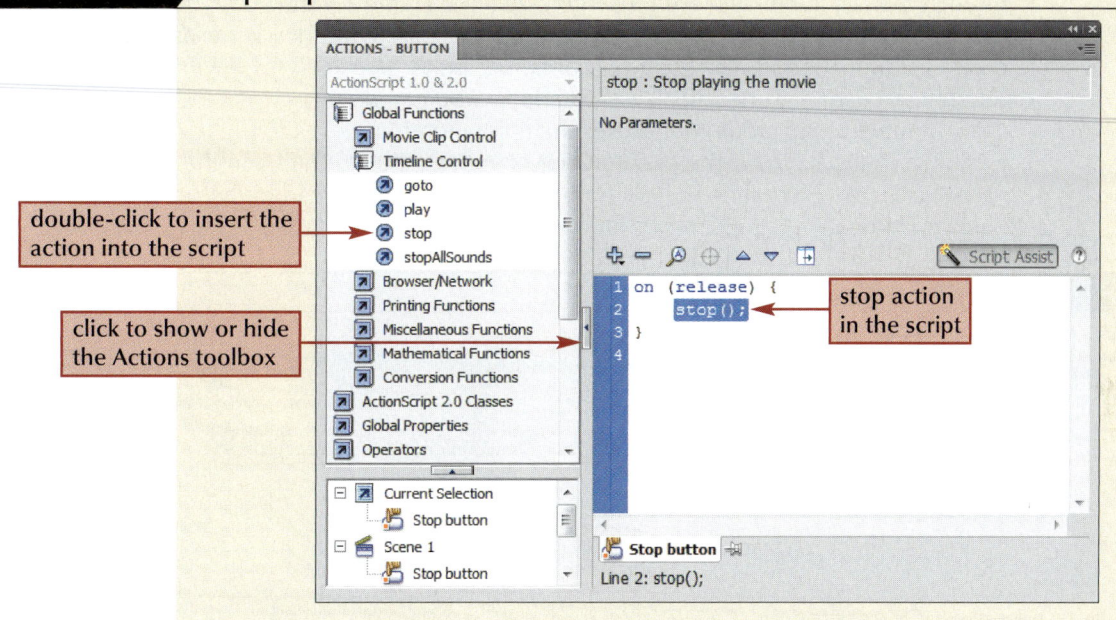

double-click to insert the action into the script

click to show or hide the Actions toolbox

stop action in the script

Tip
To delete an action from the script, select the action and then click the Delete the selected action(s) button above the Script pane.

Now you can add the play action to the Play button. To do so, you first need to select the button instance.

▶ 9. Click the **Actions panel title bar** to collapse the panel so that you can see the Stage, click the **Play** button instance on the Stage to select it, and then click the **Actions panel title bar** to expand the Actions panel.

▶ 10. In the Timeline Control category of the Actions toolbox, double-click **play**. The play action and its script are added to the Play button instance.

▶ 11. Click the **Actions panel title bar** to collapse the Actions panel.

Now that you have added the appropriate actions to the Stop and Play buttons, you will test them to make sure they work correctly.

To test the Stop and Play button actions:

▶ 1. On the Application bar, click **Control**, and then click **Test Movie**. The animation plays in the Flash Player, and the fish swims across the banner.

▶ 2. In the Flash Player, click the **Stop** button to stop the animation.

▶ 3. Click the **Play** button to restart the animation. The buttons work in Flash Player.

▶ 4. Close the Flash Player, and then save the document.

Adding Actions to Frames

Actions that have been added to buttons are executed when certain events occur, such as when the user clicks the button. Another place where you can add actions is in individual frames. Actions in a frame execute when that particular frame is played. Scripts created for frame actions do not require an event handler, unlike those created for buttons. For example, if you add a stop action to a frame, the script contains only one line with stop();. Frame actions do not depend on an event to occur. Instead, they execute as soon as the frame they are in is played.

Frame actions can be used to change the sequence in which the frames are played in the Timeline. A movie usually plays sequentially, starting with Frame 1, continuing through the last frame, and then repeating again at Frame 1. However, you can create a special animation effect by playing the frames in a different order. For example, you can create an animation in which a group of frames plays repeatedly by having the playhead return to an earlier frame. This is called a **loop**. You can do this by placing an action in the last frame of the group that causes the animation to go back to the frame you specify, as shown in Figure 5-22. The frame action is indicated by a small a in the frame—in this case, Frame 50. Every time the last frame is played, the playhead in the Timeline jumps back to Frame 25.

Figure 5-22   Loop created with frame action

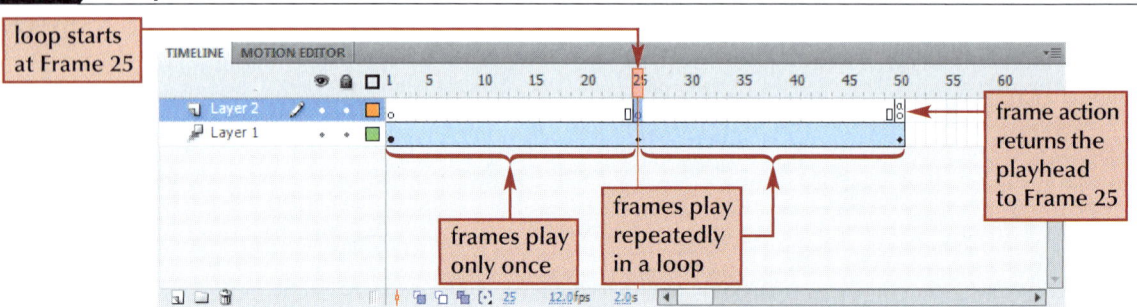

When you need to refer to specific frames in an action, you should use frame labels instead of the frame numbers. A **frame label** is a name you assign to a keyframe that appears in the Timeline, as shown in Figure 5-23. Remember, anytime a change occurs in a frame, including adding a label, a keyframe must be inserted at that frame. You refer to the frame label in an action the same way you refer to a frame number. If you use frame numbers in an action and then later add or delete frames from the Timeline, the action might reference the wrong frames. This is because adding or deleting frames causes the subsequent frames to be renumbered. You would then have to update each action that refers to the renumbered frame. However, if you use frame labels, adding or deleting frames does not affect the labels. For example, if you add a frame label to Frame 25 and then delete Frame 14, the label stills exists but in Frame 24. The renumbered frames still have the appropriate labels attached to them. Any actions that refer to the frames by their labels work correctly and, therefore, do not have to be changed.

Figure 5-23   Frame label

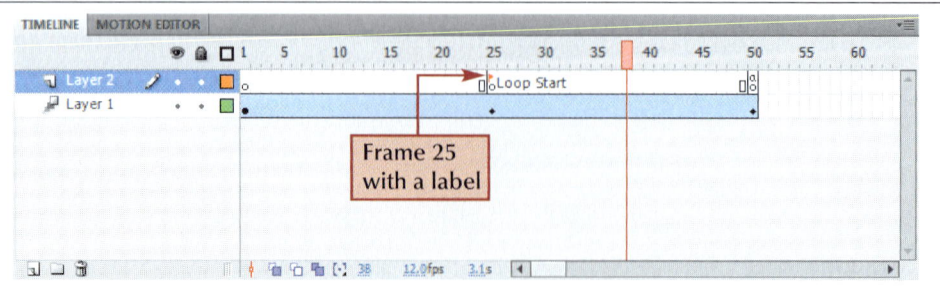

InSight | Organizing Documents Using Layers

To keep documents you create in Flash organized, place frame actions and frame labels on separate layers. Although not required, the separate layers make it easier to keep track of the actions and frames, especially when a document contains more than one. If you later need to modify other parts of the document, the actions and frame labels are not affected. As a Flash document gets more complex, placing the different elements on separate layers makes it easier to keep track of them.

The lunch specials banner contains three motion tweens to make the fish swim back and forth. It also contains a motion tween that animates the Daily Lunch Specials text block. When the banner is published, the text and fish motion tweens repeat continuously because the movie plays from Frame 1 to Frame 75 and then restarts again at Frame 1. Aly wants you to change the animation sequence so that the text animation plays only once and then remains stationary as the fish continues to swim. This means that the text motion tween should not be repeated. To accomplish this, you need to change the animation sequence so that the animation returns to Frame 25 where the text animation ends instead of Frame 1 and then continues to loop from Frame 25 to Frame 75. You will add a frame action to the last frame in the document that moves the playhead to Frame 25. The playhead then continues from Frame 25 to Frame 75 again. As a result, the playhead does not replay the text block's animation, but instead continues with the last two fish motion tweens. Because frames might be added or deleted from the banner at a later date, the frame action in the last frame should refer to a frame label and not to a frame number. You'll add a frame label at Frame 25 that can be referred to by the frame action in Frame 75.

To add a frame label and an action to the banner:

1. In the Timeline, insert a new layer above the buttons layer and name it **actions**, and then insert a new layer above the actions layer and name it **labels**. The labels layer is the current layer.

   Before adding a label at Frame 25, you need to make Frame 25 a keyframe. Without a keyframe at Frame 25, the label would be added to Frame 1.

2. In the Timeline, insert a keyframe in Frame 25 of the labels layer. The keyframe in Frame 25 of the labels layer is selected.

3. In the Label section of the Property inspector, type **Start Loop** in the Name box, and then press the **Enter** key. The frame label is added to Frame 25 of the labels layer. See Figure 5-24.

FL 248 Flash | Tutorial 5 Making a Document Interactive

Figure 5-24 | **Frame label added**

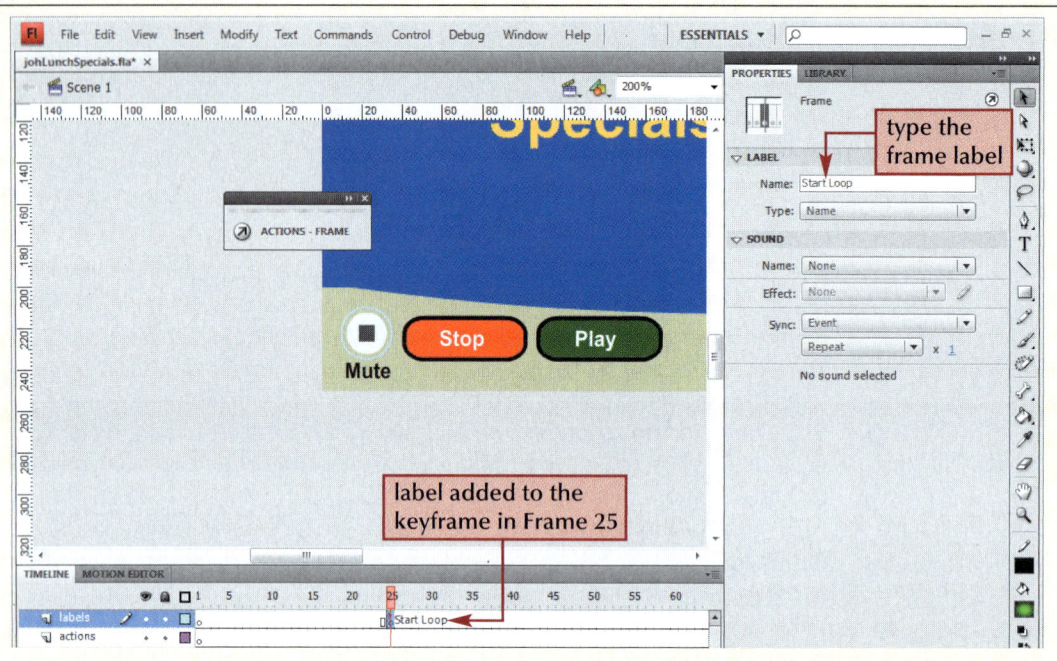

[Screenshot of Flash interface showing: "type the frame label" annotation pointing to Name: Start Loop in the LABEL section of Properties panel; "label added to the keyframe in Frame 25" annotation pointing to Start Loop label in the Timeline at frame 25]

You will add a frame action to the last frame of the actions layer. This frame action directs the animation to go back to the Start Loop frame. This last frame also needs to be a keyframe.

▶ 4. In the Timeline, insert a keyframe in Frame 75 of the actions layer. You'll add the frame action to this frame.

▶ 5. Click the **Actions panel title bar** to expand the Actions panel.

▶ 6. In the Actions toolbox, under the Global Functions category and Timeline Control subcategory, double-click the **goto** action. The action is added to the Script pane.

The script in the Script pane reads gotoAndPlay(1);. This means that the action causes the playhead to go back to Frame 1. You want to change the action so that the playhead goes back to Frame 25 instead of Frame 1, which is where the text block motion tween ends. Rather than referring to a frame number in the script, you will refer to the frame label you added to Frame 25.

▶ 7. In the parameters area of the Actions panel, click the **Type** button to display the available types, and then click **Frame Label**.

▶ 8. Click the **Frame** arrow to display the available labels, and then click **Start Loop** to insert it into the script. The Script pane displays gotoAndPlay("Start Loop");. The frame action is indicated by a small a in Frame 75 of the actions layer in the Timeline. See Figure 5-25.

> **Tip**
>
> You can also click the Add a new item to the script button above the Script pane, point to an action category, and then click an action to add it to the Script pane.

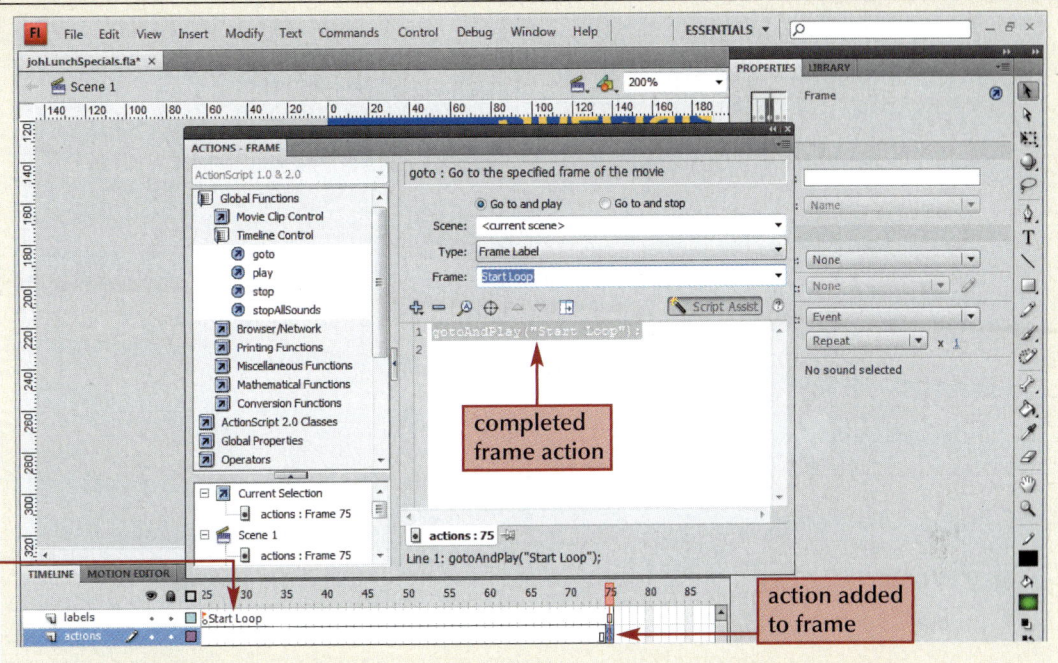

Tutorial 5 Making a Document Interactive | Flash | FL 249

Figure 5-25   Frame action

[Screenshot of Flash Actions panel showing:
- frame label referenced in the action (pointing to "Start Loop" label on timeline)
- completed frame action (pointing to gotoAndPlay("Start Loop"); script)
- action added to frame (pointing to frame 75 on actions layer)]

▸ 9. Close the Actions panel.

You should test the frame action you added to make sure the animation plays properly. You can do this within the Flash program window by turning on the Enable Simple Frame Actions command. When you turn this command on, frame actions will play when you press the Enter key or use the Play command to test the movie. Testing the frame actions within the Flash program window is another way to test the movie in the Flash Player.

To test the frame action:

▸ 1. On the Application bar, click **Control**, and then click **Enable Simple Frame Actions**. The command is turned on and the frame action will play.

▸ 2. On the Application bar, click **Control**, and then click **Play**. The animation plays on the Stage. When the playhead reaches Frame 75, it goes back and starts again at the frame labeled Start Loop, which is Frame 25. This makes the fish swim back and forth continuously while the text remains stationary.

▸ 3. On the Application bar, click **Control**, and then click **Stop**. The animation stops.

▸ 4. On the Application bar, click **Control**, and then click **Enable Simple Frame Actions**. The command is turned off.

▸ 5. Save the document.

In this session, you added actions—which are part of ActionScript language—to button instances and to frames on the banner to control the animation. Then, you tested the actions. In the next session, you'll add sounds to the banner.

Review | Session 5.2 Quick Check

1. What is ActionScript?
2. True or False? To use ActionScript, you must know JavaScript.
3. What are actions?
4. Why do scripts created for frame actions not require an event handler?
5. True or False? Actions are added to a button symbol and not to an instance of the symbol.
6. What is an example of an event that triggers an action on a button to execute?
7. Why is it better to refer to a frame label in an action instead of a frame number?
8. What is the difference between a frame action and a button action?

Session 5.3

Using Sounds in a Flash Animation

Flash offers several ways to use sounds. You can add sounds to a document that play continuously and that are independent of the Timeline, such as a background sound. You can add sound effects to instances of buttons to make them more interactive. For example, you can add a sound that plays when a user clicks a button. You can add sounds that are synchronized with the animation, such as a sound simulating a clap of thunder that coincides with an animation of a lightning bolt. You can also add sounds in the form of a voice narration to supplement the information being displayed in the Web page as text or graphics.

Finding Sounds for Animations

Adding sound to an animation can have a very powerful effect, bringing another level of excitement to a well-designed document. The sound you use can be subtle or loud. You can create sounds with a separate sound-editing program and then import the sounds or you can acquire prerecorded sounds from other sources. Most vendors offer a wide variety of sound effects and music that can be purchased on CDs or DVDs. Sounds are also available for purchase on the Web. You can even download sounds for free from Web sites such as Flash Kit (*www.flashkit.com*). Flash Kit provides a wealth of resources for Flash developers. At its site, shown in Figure 5-26, you can find sounds under Sound FX and under Sound Loops. You can search for sounds using keywords or browse for sounds by category. Sounds listed at the site can also be previewed before being downloaded. Note that the Flash Kit Web site may have been updated or modified since this tutorial was published.

> **Tip**
>
> Sound files you download may be in a compressed format; decompress the file with a utility program such as WinZip before using the sounds.

Figure 5-26 Flash Kit Web site

Other Web sites offer sounds for purchase. These Web sites have preproduced sounds from which you can select. They will even create customized sounds for a fee. Two examples of such sites are RoyaltyFreeMusic (*www.royaltyfreemusic.com*) and SoundShopper (*www.soundshopper.com*). These sites also have a few sounds that you can download for free to use in personal projects such as a family or hobby Web site.

InSight	**Licensing Issues When Using Sounds**

When acquiring sound files, carefully examine the license agreement that determines how you can use the sounds. Even though a sound file can be downloaded for free, restrictions may apply on how you can use it, especially if you plan to distribute the sound with a document. Look for sounds that are **royalty-free**, which means that no additional usage fees apply when you distribute the sounds with your projects. An alternative to downloading free sounds or purchasing sounds is to record your own. This is not always possible, but if you record a sound file yourself, you don't have to worry about licensing issues.

Adding Sounds to a Document

Because you cannot create sounds in Flash, the sound files you use in documents must first be imported into Flash. The sounds you import must be in a file format that is compatible with Flash, which include Windows Waveform (WAV), Audio Interchange File Format (AIFF) used with Macintosh computers, MPEG-3 (MP3) used with both Windows and Macintosh operating systems, and Adobe Soundbooth (ASND) used with both Windows and Macintosh operating systems. The WAV and AIFF formats are not compressed and tend to be larger than MP3 files, which are compressed. Compressed files are smaller because the parts of the sound data that listeners are not likely to notice have been removed. Compressing a sound

FL 252 Flash | Tutorial 5 Making a Document Interactive

> **Tip**
>
> Use MP3 sound files in Flash movies; this format produces small sound files, retains very good sound quality, and is compatible with Windows and Macintosh computers.

file basically means that its size has been reduced without sacrificing too much of the sound quality. You need to pay attention to the size of sound files you add to a Flash document, because they can significantly increase the overall size of the published file, affecting its download time. You can import a WAV file into a document and then compress it to MP3 format within Flash.

Sound files you import are placed in the document's library along with any symbols and buttons already in the library. In the library, a sound is preceded by a sound icon. Also, when you select a sound in the library, its waveform appears in the Library panel's preview box. A **waveform** is a graphical representation of a sound. After you have a sound file in the document's library, you can use it as many times as you need in the document. The additional uses do not further increase the document's file size, because only one copy of the sound is stored in the file.

Before you add a sound to a document, you should create a separate layer for each sound and name the layer for the sound it contains. This makes it easier to identify the sound in the Timeline. Also, sounds can be added only to keyframes in the main Timeline or a button's Timeline. After you add a sound to a keyframe, it plays when the playhead reaches the keyframe.

To import the stamp.wav sound to the library:

▶ 1. If you took a break after the previous session, make sure the johLunchSpecials.fla file is open, the workspace is set to the Essentials layout, and the Stage magnification is 200%.

▶ 2. On the Application bar, click **File**, point to **Import**, and then click **Import to Library**. The Import to Library dialog box opens.

▶ 3. Navigate to the **Tutorial.05\Tutorial** folder included with your Data Files, click the **stamp.wav** sound file, and then click the **Open** button. The stamp.wav file is added to the document's library.

▶ 4. In the Library panel, click the **stamp.wav** sound. The preview box shows the sound's waveform. See Figure 5-27.

Figure 5-27 | The stamp.wav sound in the Library panel

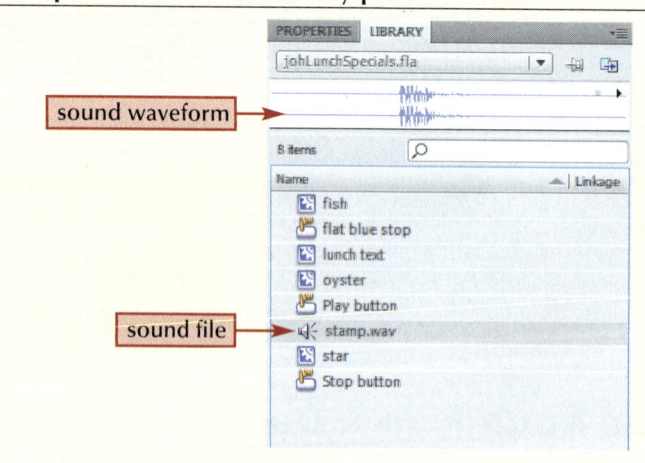

Adding Sound to a Button

You can add sounds to buttons to make a button more interactive, such as a sound that plays when the user clicks the button or even when the user moves the pointer over the button. You add a sound to a button's Over frame or to its Down frame. A sound added to the Over frame plays when the pointer is moved over the button. A sound placed in the Down frame plays when the button is clicked.

Reference Window | Adding a Sound to a Button

- Open the button in symbol-editing mode.
- In the button's Timeline, create a new layer for the sound.
- In the frame where the sound will be placed, create a keyframe and then select it.
- In the Sound section of the Property inspector, click the Name button, and then click the sound (or drag the sound from the Library panel to the Stage).

Based on the banner plan, Aly wants you to add a sound effect to the Stop and Play buttons. You'll add a stamp sound to the Down frame, so that it plays when the user clicks the button, providing an audio cue that the button was clicked.

To add the stamp.wav sound effect to the Stop button:

1. On the Stage, double-click the **Stop button** instance. The Stop button opens in symbol-editing mode.

2. In the Timeline, insert a new layer and name the layer **sound**. You will add the stamp.wav sound to the sound layer.

3. On the sound layer in the Timeline, click the **Down** frame to select it, and then insert a keyframe. You will add the stamp.wav sound to this keyframe.

4. In the Sound section of the Property inspector, click the **Name** button to display the available sounds, and then click **stamp.wav**. The sound is added to the Down frame. See Figure 5-28.

Figure 5-28   Sound added to the Down frame

Tip

You can also add a sound to a document by selecting the keyframe where the sound starts and dragging the sound from the Library panel to the Stage.

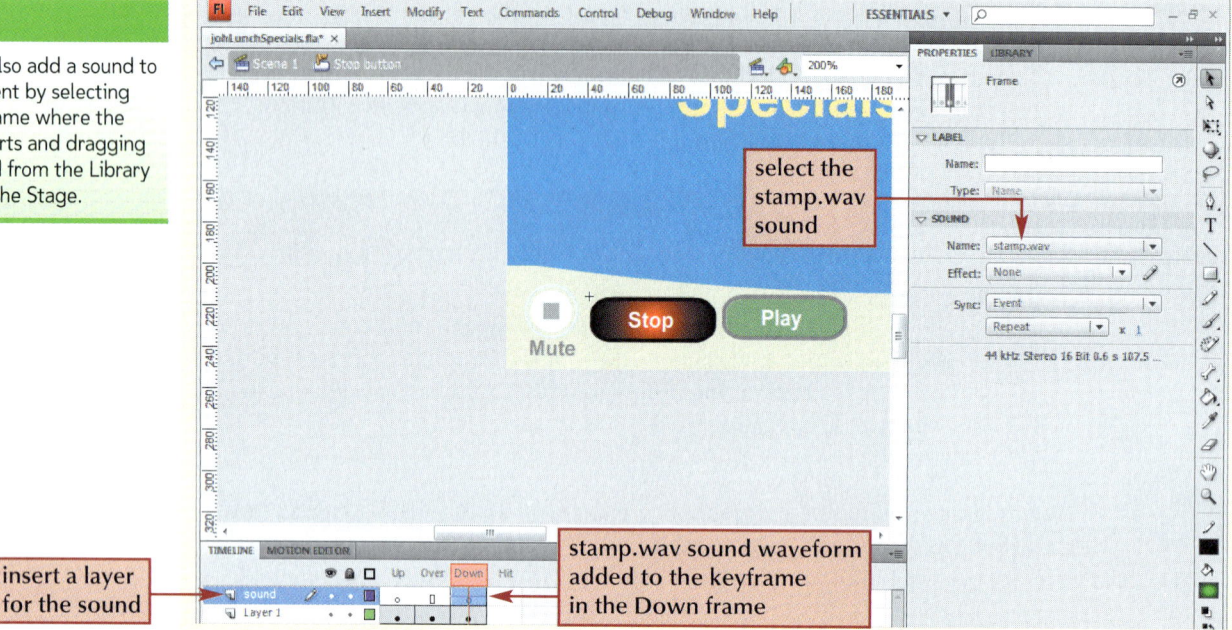

[Screenshot of Flash interface showing:]
- select the stamp.wav sound
- stamp.wav sound waveform added to the keyframe in the Down frame
- insert a layer for the sound

▶ **5.** On the Edit bar, click the **Scene 1** link to return to the document and exit symbol-editing mode.

You should test sounds you add to make sure they work correctly. You can test sounds within the Flash program window after you turn on the Enable Simple Buttons command. In this case, when clicked, the Stop button should exhibit its rollover effect and play the stamp.wav sound.

To test the sound effect added to the Stop button:

▶ **1.** On the Application bar, click **Control**, and then click **Enable Simple Buttons**. The command is selected, so clicking the Stop button tests the button rather than selects it.

▶ **2.** On the Stage, click the **Stop** button. The stamp.wav sound plays.

Trouble? If you don't hear a sound when you click the Stop button, your computer's speakers might be off or at a soft volume. Make sure that the speakers are turned on and the volume control is turned up.

▶ **3.** On the Application bar, click **Control**, and then click **Enable Simple Buttons**. The command is turned off.

The Play button uses the same stamp.wav sound effect. Because the stamp.wav sound file is already part of the document's library, you don't need to import another copy to the library. You'll use another method to add the sound to the Play button.

To add the stamp.wav sound effect to the Play button:

▶ **1.** In the Library panel, double-click the **Play button** icon. The button opens in symbol-editing mode.

▶ **2.** In the Timeline, insert a new layer and name it **sound**. You will add the sound to this new layer.

3. On the sound layer in the Timeline, click the **Down** frame, and then insert a keyframe.

4. Drag the **stamp.wav** sound from the Library panel onto the Stage. The sound is added to the Down frame.

5. On the Edit bar, click the **Scene 1** link to return to the document.

6. On the Application bar, click **Control**, and then click **Enable Simple Buttons**. You can now test the button by clicking it.

7. Click the **Play** button on the Stage to hear the sound.

8. On the Application bar, click **Control**, and then click **Enable Simple Buttons**. The command is off, and you can again select the button on the Stage.

Adding a Background Sound

The user's experience with a Flash movie can be enhanced by playing a background sound. You add a background sound in a separate layer and in the keyframe where you want the sound to start playing. As before, you can import a sound you have purchased or recorded yourself into Flash. Another option is to use a sound from the Sounds library that comes with Flash. The Sounds library includes 186 MP3 sounds from a wide range of categories, such as animal sounds, cartoon sounds, household sounds, sports sounds, technology sounds, transportation sounds, weather sounds, and more.

Aly wants you to use a bubbling sound as the background sound for the banner. You will import a sound from the Sounds library into your document's library, and then add it as a background sound.

To import a bubbling background sound to the banner:

1. On the Application bar, click **Window**, point to **Common Libraries**, and then click **Sounds**. The Sounds library panel opens.

2. In the Sounds library panel, scroll about halfway down the alphabetical listing of sounds, click the **Liquid Water Bubble Surfacing And Popping Multiple 02.mp3** sound, and then click the **Play** button ▶ in the upper-right corner of the panel to play the sound.

3. In the Sounds library panel, scroll down the alphabetical list of sounds, click the **Underwater Water Ambience Fish Aquarium Filter Bubbles 01.mp3** sound, and then click the **Play** button ▶ to play the sound. The bubbling sound continues for 90 seconds.

4. In the Sounds library panel, click the **Stop** button ■ to end the sound. You'll use this bubbling sound in the animation.

5. In the Sounds library panel, drag the **Underwater Water Ambience Fish Aquarium Filter Bubbles 01.mp3** sound to the document's library. The sound file is added to the document's library.

6. Close the Sounds library panel.

7. In the Timeline, insert a new layer above the labels layer, and then name the new layer **sound**. You will add the sound to this layer.

8. In the Timeline, click **Frame 1** of the sound layer.

9. In the Property inspector, click the **Name** button to view the available sounds, and then click **Underwater Water Ambience Fish Aquarium Filter Bubbles 01.mp3**. The sound is added to the sound layer. See Figure 5-29.

> **Tip**
>
> If you cannot see the entire name of a sound file in the Sounds library or the document's library, drag the right border of the Name heading to the right to expand the column size.

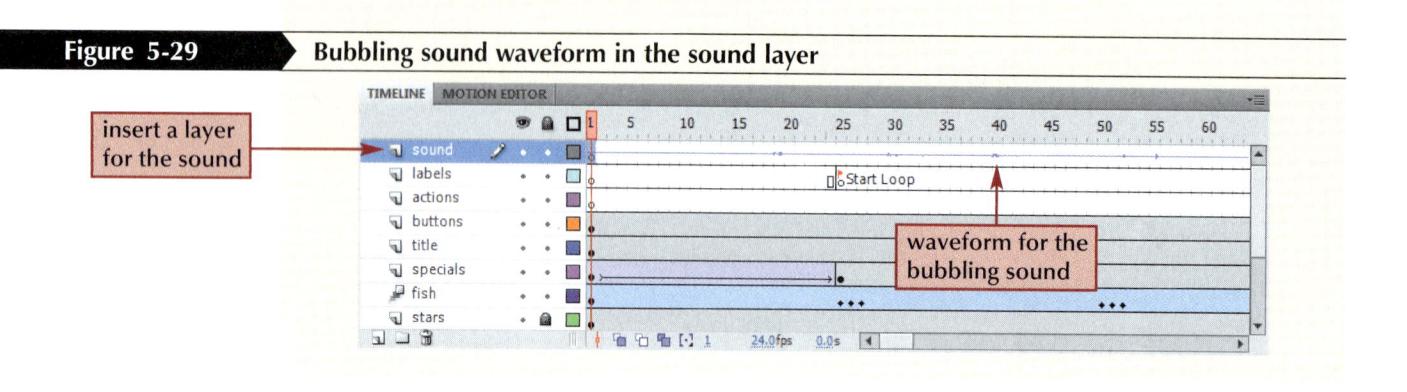

Figure 5-29 | Bubbling sound waveform in the sound layer

insert a layer for the sound

waveform for the bubbling sound

Changing the Sound Sync Settings

After you have added a sound to a document, you can control the way the sound plays by using the sound settings in the Property inspector. The Sync setting lets you set the sound as an event sound or as a stream sound, the two main types of sounds used in Flash. An **event sound** does not play until the entire sound has downloaded completely. Event sounds are not synchronized with the Timeline, which means that after an event sound is started, it continues to play regardless of the Timeline until the entire sound is played or the user takes an action to stop it. A **stream sound** is synchronized with the Timeline and begins playing as soon as enough data has downloaded. Stream sounds are useful when you want the animation in a movie to coincide with the sound.

InSight | Using Stream Sounds

Before adding a stream sound to a Flash document, consider your target audience. When a movie has a stream sound, Flash forces the animation to keep pace with the sound. If a user has a slow computer, the Flash Player might skip frames to play the sound. This can result in a less than ideal viewing experience for the user. Unless there is a need to synchronize a sound to the Timeline, use the event sound setting.

After an event sound starts, the sound continues to play until it is stopped by the user or finishes. As a result, several instances of the same sound might play at one time. Because event sounds play independently of the Timeline, an event sound starts to play when the playhead reaches the sound's keyframe and continues to play until it is completely finished. If the playhead returns to the keyframe with the sound before the sound has finished playing, another instance of the sound starts playing at the same time. This means that one sound instance overlaps the other. To prevent this, you can change the Sync setting of the sound to Start instead of Event. With the Start Sync setting, a new instance of the sound does not start if the first instance of the sound is still playing, preventing the overlap of multiple instances of the same sound. Finally, the Stop Sync setting ends a sound that is playing. For example, you might want a sound that starts playing in Frame 1 to stop playing in Frame 10. You add the same sound in Frame 1 to Frame 10 but use the Stop Sync setting. When the playhead reaches Frame 10, the sound stops playing.

The Loop and Repeat sound settings let you set how many times a sound replays. If you want a sound to play continuously for a period of time, select Repeat and then specify how many times the sound should play. For example, if you want a sound to play for 2 minutes and the sound is 10 seconds long, enter 12 as the number of times to repeat; the sound will play 12 times for a total of 120 seconds or 2 minutes. If you want the sound to repeat continuously, select Loop.

The banner's background sound should be an event sound. You'll make this change now.

Tutorial 5 Making a Document Interactive | Flash | FL

To change the Sync setting for the background sound, and then test it:

1. In the Property inspector, click the **Sync** button, and then click **Event**, if necessary. Event is the default setting and is used when you don't need the sound synchronized with the Timeline.

2. In the Property inspector, click the **Sound loop** button, and then click **Repeat**, if necessary. You will set how many times the sound should repeat.

3. In the Property inspector, set the number of times to loop to **2**. The information below the Sync box indicates that the sound is 90.2 seconds long. If the Repeat setting is 0, the sound ends if the user views the animation for more than 90.2 seconds. By changing the Repeat setting to 2, the sound continues playing for 180.4 seconds—approximately 3 minutes. See Figure 5-30.

Figure 5-30   Sound settings in the Property inspector

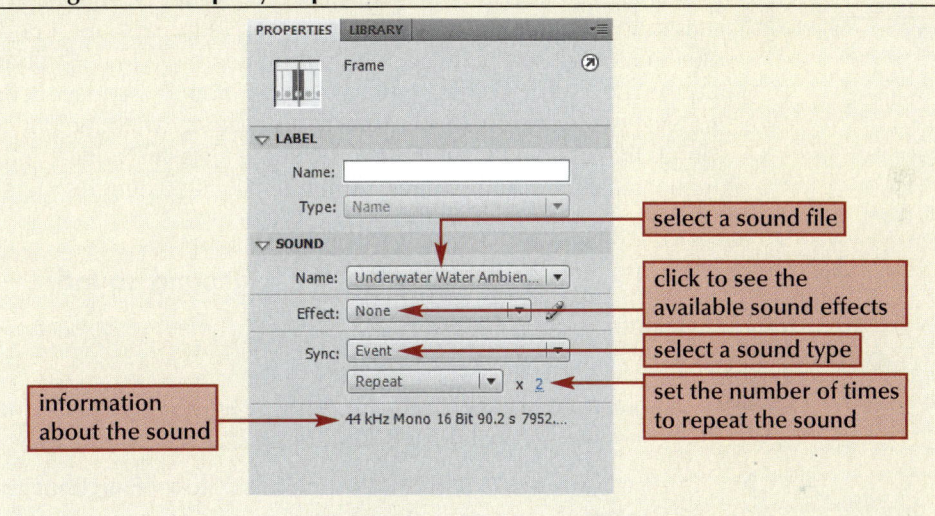

information about the sound

select a sound file

click to see the available sound effects

select a sound type

set the number of times to repeat the sound

Tip

You can test a sound by playing the movie in a Flash Player window or in a Web page.

4. On the Application bar, click **Control**, and then click **Test Movie**. The movie opens in a Flash Player window. The bubbling background sound plays.

5. Close the Flash Player window to return to the document.

Adding Sound Effects

The sound effect setting changes the way a sound plays. The Left channel effect plays the sound only in the left speaker, whereas the Right channel effect plays the sound only in the right speaker. The Fade to right effect starts the sound in the left speaker and gradually moves the sound to the right speaker. The Fade to left effect starts the sound in the right speaker and gradually moves the sound to the left speaker. The Fade in effect gradually increases the sound, whereas the Fade out effect gradually decreases the sound. Finally, the Custom setting allows you to create your own sound effects by adjusting the sound's starting point and controlling its volume.

Aly wants you to explore the sound effect settings to see how they impact the banner's background sound.

To explore the sound effect settings with the background sound:

1. In the Timeline, click **Frame 1** of the sound layer to select it, if necessary. You will try different sound effects for the sound in this layer.

▶ 2. In the Property inspector, click the **Effect** button to display the list of effects, and then click **Fade to right**. The effect is applied to the bubbling background sound.

▶ 3. On the Application bar, click **Control**, click **Test Movie** to play the movie and hear the background sound, and then close the Flash Player window to return to the document.

▶ 4. Repeat Steps 2 and 3 to apply and test at least three other sound effect settings.

▶ 5. In the Property inspector, click the **Effect** button, and then click **Fade in**. The effect is applied to the background sound and fits well with the overall design and purpose of the banner. Even though the background sound is set to repeat twice, the fade-in effect will not be repeated. The sound effect is applied only when the sound first starts playing.

Although some users may enjoy the background sound, other users may not want to hear it. You want to give the user the option to turn off the sound. You already added a Mute button for this purpose, but you still need to add an action to the button instance to turn off the sound. Using the Actions panel, you will add an action to the Mute button instance that will stop all sounds that are playing when the button is clicked. Subsequent sounds that are played, such as the sound effects you added to the Stop and Play buttons, are not affected because they will not be playing when the Mute button is clicked.

To add an action to mute the background sound:

▶ 1. On the Stage, click the **Mute** button to select it. Be sure to select the button and not the Mute text block.

▶ 2. Right-click the selected **Mute** button, and then click **Actions** on the context menu. The Actions panel opens. You'll display the basic Timeline control actions.

▶ 3. If necessary, in the Actions toolbox, click **Global Functions**, and then click **Timeline Control**. The action to stop the background sound is in this list.

▶ 4. Double-click **stopAllSounds**. The action is selected and its script is added to the button instance and appears in the Script pane. See Figure 5-31.

Figure 5-31 | Stop all sounds script

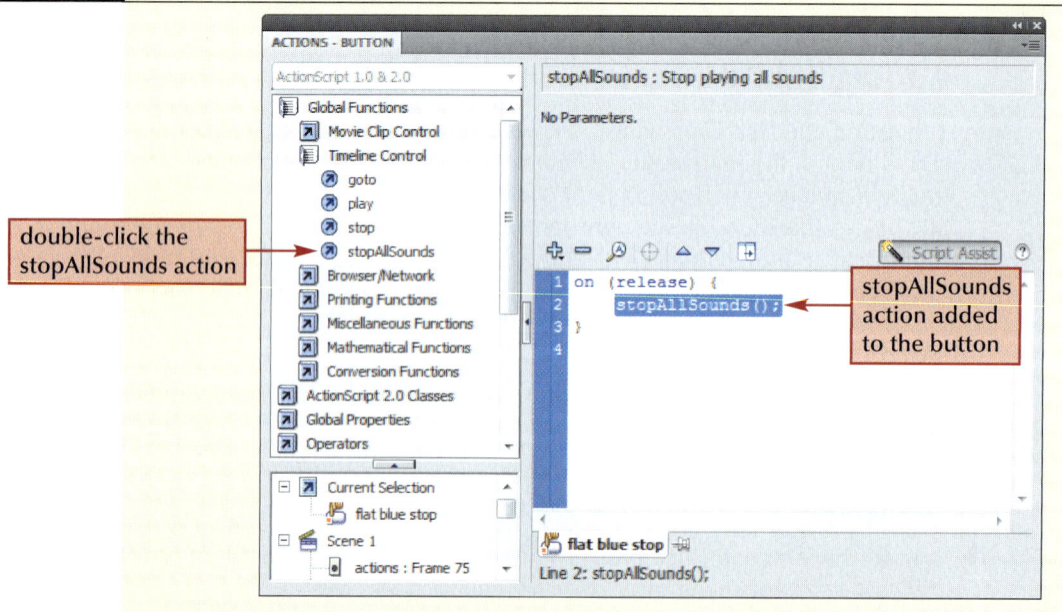

> 5. Close the Actions panel, and then save the document.
>
> 6. On the Application bar, click **Control**, and then click **Test Movie**. The animation and the background sound play in the Flash Player.
>
> 7. In the Flash Player window, click the **Mute** button. The sound stops, but the animation continues to play.
>
> 8. Close the Flash Player window, and then close the document.

You have completed the banner by adding buttons, actions, and sounds. Jenny is pleased with the progress you made on the banner. In this session, you learned how to acquire sounds, what types of sounds that Flash uses, and the different sound file formats that can be imported into documents. You imported sounds to the document's library, and then added the sounds to buttons and as a background sound to the document. You also changed the sound effect settings. Finally, you added an action to a button to stop all sounds from playing.

Review | Session 5.3 Quick Check

1. List two Web sites from which you can download sounds to use with your documents.
2. What are three sound file formats that can be imported into Flash?
3. Where is sound that you import into a document stored?
4. True or False? Sounds can only be added to keyframes.
5. Describe the two main types of sounds used in a Flash document.
6. List three simple effects you can add to a sound in a document.
7. Why would you assign the Start Sync setting to a sound?

Review | Tutorial Summary

In this tutorial, you added a button from a library of existing buttons that are included with Flash and created a custom button with a rollover effect. You aligned the buttons using the Align panel. You used the Actions panel to add actions to the buttons you created. You also added an action to a frame, and then you tested these actions in your browser. You learned about the different sound file formats and how to adjust the various sounds you added to the document. You added sound effects to the buttons you created, and you added a background sound to the document. You also changed the sound settings, making the sound repeat and adding a sound effect.

Key Terms

action	Hit frame	rollover effect
ActionScript	interactive	royalty-free
Down frame	JavaScript	script
event	loop	stream sound
event handler	Over frame	Up frame
event sound	parameter	waveform
frame label		

Practice | Review Assignments

Practice the skills you learned in the tutorial.

Data Files needed for the Review Assignments: specials.fla, ding.wav

Aly asks you to make some changes to another interactive banner she has started for a fish and shrimp specials page. You will modify the Mute button and add an action to stop all sounds when the button is clicked. You will add actions to the Play and Stop buttons to control the animation of the fish and to change the animation for the Fish and Shrimp Specials text block to only play one time. Finally, you will select a different sound effect for the Stop and Play buttons and to change the text on the Play button to Start.

1. Open the **specials.fla** file located in the Tutorial.05\Review folder included with your Data Files, save the document as **fishSpecials.fla** in the same folder, and then reset the workspace to the Essentials layout.
2. Open the Mute button symbol in symbol-editing mode, select the Down frame in Layer 2, change the color of the small black square in the middle of the button to green (#00FF00), and then exit symbol-editing mode.
3. Use the Actions panel in Script Assist mode to add a stopAllSounds action to the Mute button instance.
4. Use the Actions panel in Script Assist mode to add an action to the Play button instance to play the animation when the button is clicked, and then add an action to the Stop button instance to stop the animation when the button is clicked.
5. In the Timeline, insert a new layer above the buttons layer and name it **actions**, and then insert a new layer above the actions layer and name it **labels**.
6. Create a frame label in Frame 20 of the labels layer with the name **Loop**.
7. Use the Actions panel in Script Assist mode to add a gotoAndPlay action to Frame 60 of the actions layer. In the parameters area, set the type to Frame Label and select Loop as the frame.
8. Import the **ding.wav** file located in the Tutorial.05\Review folder to the document's library.
9. Open the Stop button symbol in symbol-editing mode, insert a new layer and name it **sound**, and then add the ding.wav sound to the Down frame so that the sound plays when the button is clicked.
10. Open the Play button symbol in symbol-editing mode, insert a new layer and name it **sound**, and then add the ding.wav sound to the Down frame.
11. Change the text block in the Play button to from Play to **Start**. (*Hint*: Be sure to change the text in each of the button's frames.)
12. Test the banner in the Flash Player to make sure each of the buttons works properly and that the Fish and Shrimp text block animation plays only one time.
13. Submit the finished files to your instructor.

Apply | Case Problem 1

Create an interactive banner with sounds for a store's Web site.

Data Files needed for this Case Problem: kprAd.fla, party.wav

Katie's Pet Resort Katie asks John to create a variation of the advertisement you created for the Katie's Pet Resort Web site. The banner contains text animations that display text blocks with the resort's name and a grand opening sale announcement and that list the services provided by the resort. John wants you to add sound and two buttons from the Buttons library to the advertisement. The Repeat and Play Song buttons should be similar in design, appear after the first set of animations is finished, and have a short sound effect that plays when the buttons are clicked. Then, you'll add an action to the Repeat button so that it plays the first set of animations, and add an action to the Play Song button so that it plays the second set of animations plus a background sound. Finally, you will add a frame action to the last frame that moves the playhead to the start of the second set of animations. The finished advertisement is shown in Figure 5-32.

Figure 5-32

1. Open the **kprAd.fla** file located in the Tutorial.05\Case1 folder included with your Data Files, and then save the document as **kprAdWithSound.fla** in the same folder.
2. Insert a new layer above the letters layer folder, name it **buttons**, and then insert a keyframe at Frame 40 of the buttons layer.
3. In the Buttons library, expand the classic buttons folder, and then expand the Circle Buttons folder. Make sure the buttons layer is selected, and then drag the circle button – previous button to the lower-left corner of the Stage and drag the circle button – next button to the right of the first button.
4. Open the circle button – previous button in symbol-editing mode, insert a new layer and name it **sound**, import the **Impact Wood Drop 04.mp3** sound from the Sounds library to the document's library, and then add the sound to the Down frame of the sound layer.
5. Open the circle button – next button in symbol-editing mode, insert a new layer and name it **sound**, add the Impact Wood Drop 04.mp3 sound to this button in its Down frame of the sound layer, and then exit symbol-editing mode.
6. Insert a new layer and name it **labels**, add a frame label in Frame 1 with the text **Start**, and then add a frame label in Frame 40 with the text **Part2**.
7. Insert a new layer and name it **actions**, and then add a stop action at Frame 40 of the actions layer.
8. Add the gotoAndPlay action to the circle button – previous button instance and set the parameters so that the playhead moves to the Start frame, repeating the first set of animations.
9. Add the play action to the circle button – next button instance. This causes the second set of animations to play.

EXPLORE

10. Add a gotoAndStop action at Frame 100 of the actions layer and then set the parameters so that the playhead moves to the Part2 frame. (*Hint*: Double-click the goto action in the Timeline Control category within the Global Functions category in the Actions panel, and then click the Go to and stop option button in the parameters.)
11. Insert a new layer and name it **background sound**.
12. Import the **party.wav** sound file located in the Tutorial.05\Case1 folder included with your Data Files to the document's library, add the party.wav sound to start at Frame 41 of the background sound layer, make its Sync setting Start, and then set the number of times to repeat to 1.

13. Test the revisions to the advertisement. Make sure the buttons work properly and that the sounds play.
14. Submit the finished files to your instructor.

Challenge | Case Problem 2

Add sound and interactivity to an animated banner for a zoo.

Data Files needed for this Case Problem: aczSound.fla, pianoLoop.wav

Alamo City Zoo Janet asks Alex to develop a new banner with some enhancements for the Alamo City Zoo Web site. In particular, she wants sound added to the banner to make it interesting. Alex also suggests adding some interactivity to the banner. You will complete the banner Alex created by adding an action that repeats the movement of the bear and bear paws without repeating the text animations. You will add a button that resembles a bear paw that users can click to start the animation from the beginning. You will also add a background sound to the banner and a sound effect to the button. The finished banner is shown in Figure 5-33.

Figure 5-33

[Banner image: Orange background with text "Monkeys and Gorillas!", "Elephants and Tigers!", "Alamo City Zoo", "New Bear Exhibit!" with a bear silhouette and paw prints, and a "Replay" button with a paw icon.]

1. Open the **aczSound.fla** file located in the Tutorial.05\Case2 folder included with your Data Files, and then save the document as **aczSoundButtons.fla** in the same folder.
2. In the Timeline, insert a new layer above the paw2 layer and name it **labels**, and then insert a new layer above the labels layer and name it **actions**.
3. In Frame 1 of the labels layer, add the label name **Start**, and then, in Frame 16, add the label name **Loop**. The motion tweens for the bear paws begin in Frame 16.
4. In Frame 60 of the actions layer, add a gotoAndPlay action and set the parameters to make the playhead go to the Loop frame to repeat the last group of frames that keep the animated bear and bear paws moving.
5. In the Timeline, insert a new layer and name it **music**, and then import the **pianoLoop.wav** sound located in the Tutorial.05\Case2 folder included with your Data Files into the document's library.
6. Add the pianoLoop.wav sound to Frame 10 of the music layer, and then change its Sync setting to Start and have it play one time.

EXPLORE
7. Create a duplicate of the bear paw symbol in the library, name the copy **bear paw button**, and set its type to Button.
8. Open the bear paw button in symbol-editing mode, and then use the Transform panel to set the bear paw's Rotate value to –90 and its width and height to 60%.

9. Add a keyframe in the Over frame, and then change the color of the bear paw's fill to the green color of your choice.
10. Add a keyframe in the Down frame, and then use the arrow keys to move the bear paw three pixels up and three pixels to the right.

EXPLORE 11. Add a keyframe in the Hit frame, and then draw a rectangle that covers the bear paw for the clickable area of the button. (*Hint*: The stroke and fill colors of the rectangle do not show in the animation.)

EXPLORE 12. Insert a new layer into the button's Timeline and name it **sound**, import a sound of your choice from the Sounds library, add the sound to the Down frame of the sound layer, and then exit symbol-editing mode. (*Hint*: Play the sound in the Sounds library before importing it to be sure the sound is short and complements the banner.)
13. In the Timeline, insert a new layer and name it **button**. Add an instance of the bear paw button symbol to the banner in the button layer, and then place the instance in an appropriate location on the banner.
14. On the Stage, select the bear paw button instance, if necessary, and then, in the Actions panel, add the gotoAndPlay action and set the parameters so that the action refers to the Start frame. When the button is clicked, the playhead goes to the Start frame and repeats all of the animation.
15. Add a text block above the bear paw button with the text **Replay**. Use a small font size and black text.
16. Test the animation to make sure the background music plays and that the button works.
17. Submit the finished files to your instructor.

| Apply | **Case Problem 3** |

Add sounds and interactive components to an animated logo for a nursery.

Data Files needed for this Case Problem: wnLogo.fla, autoLoop.wav

Westcreek Nursery Alice and her employees have several suggestions for a new animated logo for the Westcreek Nursery Web site, including adding sound and some interactive components to the logo. Amanda asks you to complete the revisions by adding a background sound to the logo as well as adding a Stop button and a Go button, each with a sound effect. You also will add a frame action to control how the animation plays. The wheels should continue to rotate after the Westcreek text shape animation has finished. The Stop button will stop the wheel animations, and the Go button will start the wheel animations. The finished logo is shown in Figure 5-34.

Figure 5-34

1. Open the **wnLogo.fla** file located in the Tutorial.05\Case3 folder included with your Data Files, and then save the file as **wnLogoAnimated.fla** in the same folder.
2. Insert three layers above the flowers layer, and then name the layers **action**, **stopLabel**, and **loopLabel**, respectively.

3. In Frame 19 of the stopLabel layer, add the frame label **Stop**, and then, in Frame 20 of the loopLabel layer, add the frame label **Loop**.
4. In the last frame of the action layer, add an action that makes the playhead go to the frame with the Loop label and continues playing the animation from that frame. The shape tween animation plays one time and the tire animations play repeatedly.
5. Import the **autoLoop.wav** sound located in the Tutorial.05\Case3 folder included with your Data Files to the document's library, insert a new layer and name it **sound**, add the autoLoop.wav sound to Frame 20 of the sound layer, and set it to play three times without overlapping itself.

EXPLORE

6. In Frame 55 of the sound layer, add a keyframe, and then add the autoLoop.wav sound, and change the Sync sound setting to Stop.
7. Insert a new button symbol named **Stop button**, and then make the button shape a circle about 20 pixels in diameter with a red fill and black stroke to represent a red stop light.
8. Import a car horn sound of your choice from the Sounds library, and then add the sound to the Stop button's Down frame. (*Hint*: Look in the Transportation sounds, and play the sound before importing it.)
9. Duplicate the Stop button, name the duplicate **Go button**, and then change its fill to green.
10. Insert a new layer in Scene 1 and name it **buttons**.
11. In Frame 19 of the buttons layer, add an instance of the Go button in the lower-right corner of the Stage, and then add an instance of the Stop button above the Go button instance. Align the buttons as needed.
12. Add an action to the Stop button instance that causes the playhead to go to the frame with the Stop label at which point the animation should stop.
13. Add an action to the Go button instance that causes the playhead to go to the frame with the Loop label and continue to play the animation.
14. Test the logo animation, making sure the sounds play and that the buttons work properly.
15. Submit the finished files to your instructor.

| Create | **Case Problem 4** |

Download sounds, add actions to control an animation, and create a button to replay the animation.

Data File needed for this Case Problem: msaButton.fla

Missions Support Association   Brittany wants Anissa to add some interaction with appropriate sounds to enhance the impact of the advertisement banner that Missions Support Association will use to promote the association. You will modify the advertisement banner so that the animation stops when it reaches the last frame. You will also add a button that complements the design to repeat the animation. You will search the Web to find a background sound for the advertisement banner and a sound effect to add to the button. The starting banner is shown in Figure 5-35.

Tutorial 5 Making a Document Interactive | Flash | FL 265

Figure 5-35

Missions Support Association

Preserving History!

EXPLORE

1. Open the **msaButton.fla** file located in the Tutorial.05\Case4 folder included with your Data Files, and then save the document as **msaButtonSounds.fla** in the same folder.
2. Go to the Flash Kit Web site (*www.flashkit.com*) or another site of your choice that has sound files you can download and use for free. Find two sound files appropriate for the advertisement. One sound should be short to use as a sound effect on a button. The other should be a sound loop to use as a background sound. Download the sounds to the Tutorial.05\Case4 folder.
3. Import the sound loop you downloaded into the document's library, and then add the sound to the first frame of a sounds layer that you create above the letters layer folder. Add appropriate sound effect, sync, and loop settings.
4. In the last frame of a new actions layer, add a stop action that stops the animation and keeps it from repeating.
5. Duplicate a symbol in the library or create a new symbol using the Button behavior type and the name **repeat button**. (*Hint*: If you duplicate the star shape, you can create an interesting effect by placing the button instance over the star symbol in the last frame of the animation. The button instance will look the same as the start symbol until the pointer is moved over it and the rollover effect changes the way it looks.)
6. In the Over frame of the button, change the button in some way to provide a visual clue that the pointer is over the button.
7. In the Down frame, shift the button so that it is offset by a few pixels, and then add the sound effect you imported.
8. In the last frame of a new buttons layer that you insert in Scene 1, add a repeat button instance in an attractive place on the advertisement banner.
9. Add a play action to the button instance so that the animation will start to play.
10. Test the banner animation, making sure the sounds play and that the button works properly.
11. Submit the finished files to your instructor.

Review | Quick Check Answers

Session 5.1

1. a special symbol that contains its own four-frame Timeline
2. to provide an interactive element to a Flash document so users can control how they watch the published movie
3. Open the Buttons library, drag a button from the Buttons library to the Stage, which automatically adds the button to the document's library, or drag a button from the Buttons library to the document's library.
4. Up, Over, Down, and Hit frames
5. Make the Over frame's contents different from the Up frame's contents. When the pointer is over the button, the contents in the Over frame are displayed in place of the contents in the Up frame.

6. Turn on the Enable Simple Buttons command on the Control menu
7. Select the objects to align, and then click the appropriate buttons in the Align panel.

Session 5.2

1. the scripting language used in Flash to create scripts to control how a movie plays
2. False; you do not need to know JavaScript or any other scripting language.
3. instructions that are used to control how a movie plays
4. Scripts created for frame actions are executed when the frame is played and do not depend on an event to occur.
5. False; actions are added to a button instance and not to the symbol.
6. The user clicks and releases a button.
7. If you later add or delete frames, the scripts do not have to be changed.
8. You add a frame action to a keyframe, whereas you add a button action to a button's instance.

Session 5.3

1. *www.flashkit.com, www.royaltyfreemusic.com,* or *www.soundshopper.com*
2. WAV, AIFF, MP3, and ASND
3. the document's library
4. True
5. An event sound does not play until the entire sound has downloaded completely and is not synchronized with the Timeline. A stream sound is synchronized with the Timeline and begins playing as soon as enough data has downloaded.
6. three of the following: Left channel, Right channel, Fade to right, Fade to left, Fade in, and Fade out.
7. to prevent several instances of the sound from playing at the same time

Ending Data Files

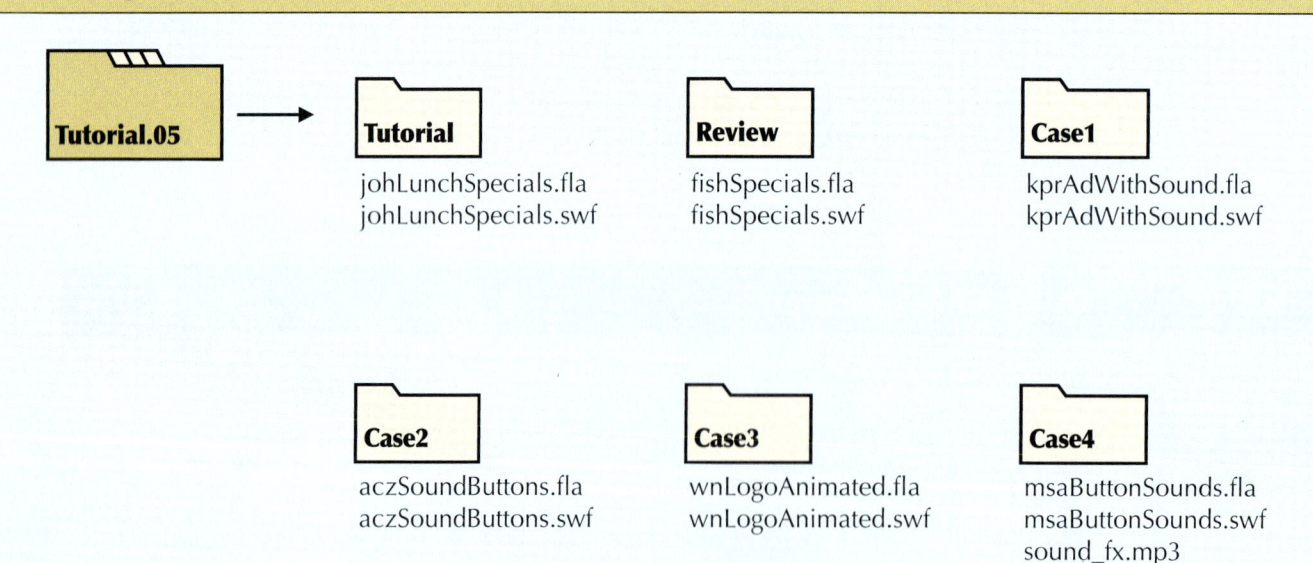

Tutorial.05 → **Tutorial**
johLunchSpecials.fla
johLunchSpecials.swf

Review
fishSpecials.fla
fishSpecials.swf

Case1
kprAdWithSound.fla
kprAdWithSound.swf

Case2
aczSoundButtons.fla
aczSoundButtons.swf

Case3
wnLogoAnimated.fla
wnLogoAnimated.swf

Case4
msaButtonSounds.fla
msaButtonSounds.swf
sound_fx.mp3
sound_loop.mp3

Flash | FL 267

Tutorial 6

Objectives

Session 6.1
- Import bitmap graphics into a document
- Change a bitmap graphic's properties
- Convert a bitmap graphic to a vector graphic
- Create a fade effect animation using bitmaps

Session 6.2
- Learn about gradients
- Create and save a new gradient
- Use and transform a gradient

Session 6.3
- Explore the Flash publish settings
- Publish a Flash movie
- Create a publish profile
- Export a Flash graphic
- Insert a Flash movie into an existing Web page

Creating Special Effects with Graphics and Gradients

Working with Bitmaps and Gradients, and Publishing Flash Files

Case | Admiral Web Design

Jenny wants to update the Jenny's Oyster Hut Web site with a new banner for the home page and a new logo throughout the Web site. During the planning meeting, Aly suggests using photos of sample seafood items as part of an animation. Chris suggests using a gradient for the banner's background to create a professional-looking design. As you complete the banner and create the logo, you will be adding bitmaps, creating gradients, and preparing the final movies for use on the restaurant's Web site.

The banner will include an animation where two photos of seafood dishes are displayed in turn within a mask, fading in and then fading out. For the banner's background, you will create a radial gradient that will be a blend of a light blue color that transitions into a dark gray color. The gradient's light blue center will be positioned behind the seafood animation, giving the photos a highlighted effect. The logo will have the restaurant name over a picture of a lobster in the background.

In this tutorial, you will import bitmap graphics into a Flash document, change the bitmaps' properties, convert a bitmap into a vector graphic, and create animations using bitmaps. You will also create, modify, and use gradients to add a special effect to the banner. Finally, you will explore the various export and publish options available with Flash, and then incorporate the banner and logo into an existing Web page.

Starting Data Files

Tutorial.06

Tutorial
crab.jpg
jennys.fla
jennysbanner.jpg
lobster.jpg
logo.jpg
sample.htm
tuna.jpg

Review
hutBanner.jpg
jennysAlt.fla
salmon.jpg
sampleAlt.htm

Case1
kprLogo.fla
pet1.jpg
pet2.jpg

Case2
aczLogo.fla
giraffe.jpg

Case3
flower1.jpg
flower2.jpg
flower3.jpg
wcnLogo.fla

Case4
mission.jpg

Session 6.1

Working with Bitmaps

The banner and logo you will create for Jenny's Oyster Hut use photographs. A photograph is a bitmap graphic. Recall that a bitmap graphic is stored as a row-by-row list of every pixel in the graphic, along with each pixel's color. The most common bitmap file formats for Web graphics are JPEG and GIF. Bitmap graphics are different from vector graphics, which are stored as mathematical instructions that describe the color, outline, and position of all the shapes in the graphic. Bitmap graphics do not resize well and their file sizes tend to be larger than the vector graphics created in Flash. As a result, using bitmaps in a Flash movie increases the movie's download time. However, file size and download time alone should not keep you from using bitmap graphics in Flash documents. Just make sure that the graphic is really needed in the document's design.

> **InSight** | **Using Bitmaps in Flash**
>
> You cannot easily edit bitmap graphics within Flash, so you should use an image-editing program such as Adobe Photoshop or Adobe Fireworks to edit and resize the bitmaps before importing them into a Flash document. Before using a bitmap graphic in Flash, optimize it by reducing its size while maintaining its quality. Reducing the file size of the bitmap minimizes its impact on the download time of the Flash document. If possible, also consider the target audience and the types of Internet connections they have. Flash documents targeted at users with slower connections should include few, if any, bitmap graphics even if the bitmap graphics can greatly enhance a document's design.

Importing Bitmaps

You cannot create bitmap graphics in Flash, so you need to import them into the Flash documents. After you have imported a bitmap into Flash, you can change properties such as compression settings, use it in animations, and even change it into a vector graphic. Importing a bitmap into a Flash document places the bitmap in the document's library. After the bitmap is in the document's library, you can create multiple instances of it on the Stage. No matter how many instances you create, only one copy of the bitmap is stored with the file. A bitmap in the document's library is not a symbol, although the copies you drag onto the Stage are called instances. An instance of a bitmap on the Stage can be converted into a symbol that can be used in a motion tween animation. This symbol is stored in the document's library separately from the original bitmap.

> **Reference Window** | **Importing a Bitmap**
>
> - On the Application bar, click File, point to Import, and then click Import to Stage or Import to Library.
> - In the Import or Import to Library dialog box, navigate to the location of the bitmap file, and then select the bitmap file in the file list.
> - Click the Open button.

The new Jenny's Oyster Hut banner, shown in the sketch provided by Aly in Figure 6-1, uses an animation that includes two photos of seafood. You need to import these photos into the library of the partially completed banner that Aly has created.

Tutorial 6 Creating Special Effects with Graphics and Gradients | Flash | FL 269

Figure 6-1   Sketch for the new Jenny's Oyster Hut banner

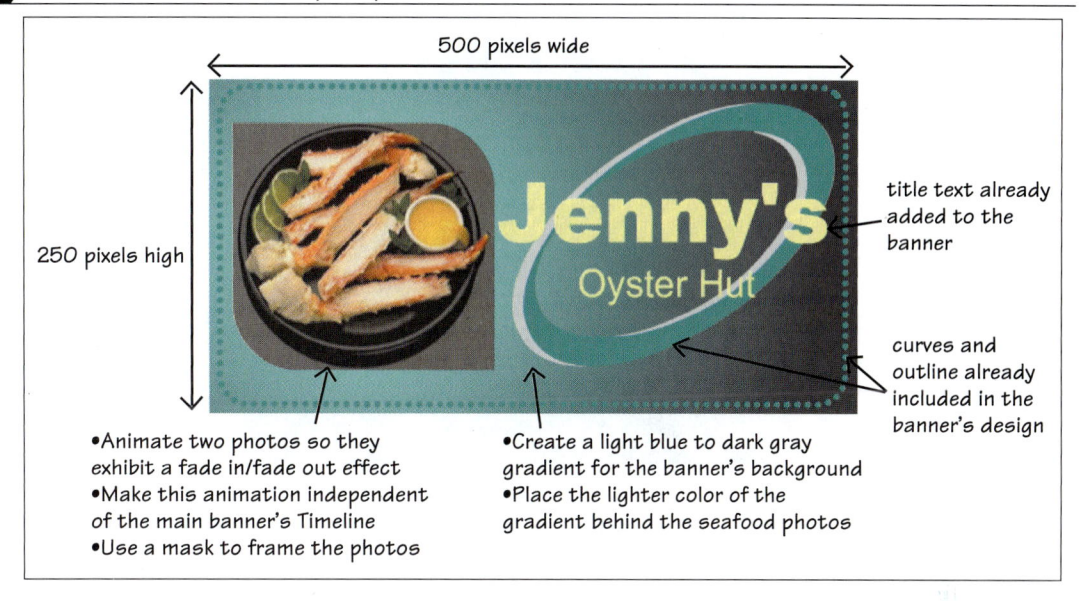

- 500 pixels wide
- 250 pixels high
- title text already added to the banner
- curves and outline already included in the banner's design
- Animate two photos so they exhibit a fade in/fade out effect
- Make this animation independent of the main banner's Timeline
- Use a mask to frame the photos
- Create a light blue to dark gray gradient for the banner's background
- Place the lighter color of the gradient behind the seafood photos

You'll import the photos into the banner's library.

To import the seafood bitmap images into the banner document:

1. Open the **jennys.fla** file located in the Tutorial.06\Tutorial folder included with your Data Files, save the file as **photosBanner.fla** in the same folder, and then reset the workspace to the **Essentials** layout. Next, you will import a bitmap into the document's library.

2. On the Application bar, click **File**, point to **Import**, and then click **Import to Library**. The Import to Library dialog box opens.

3. Click the **All Formats** button, and then click **All Image Formats**.

4. Navigate to the **Tutorial.06\Tutorial** folder included with your Data Files, click the **crab.jpg** file, press and hold the **Ctrl** key, click the **tuna.jpg** file, and then release the Ctrl key. The two files are selected.

5. Click the **Open** button. The two bitmap files are imported into the document's library and appear in the Library panel.

6. In the Library panel, click the **crab.jpg** bitmap. The crab.jpg picture appears in the preview area. See Figure 6-2.

> **Tip**
>
> You can use the Import to Stage command to simultaneously place a bitmap in the document's library and create an instance on the Stage.

Figure 6-2 | Bitmaps in the Library panel

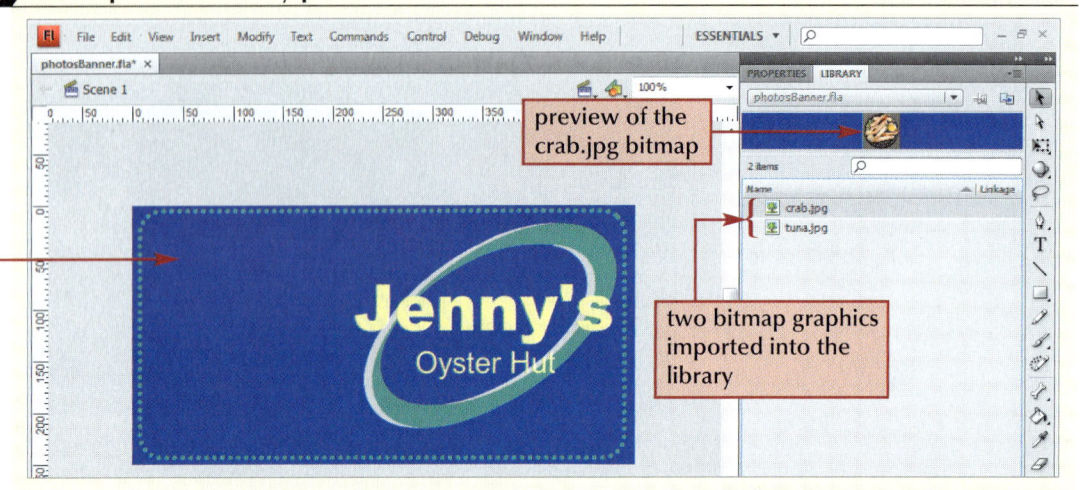

- partially complete banner
- preview of the crab.jpg bitmap
- two bitmap graphics imported into the library

▶ 7. In the Library panel, click the **tuna.jpg** bitmap. The tuna.jpg picture appears in the preview area.

Setting a Bitmap's Properties

You can modify a bitmap's properties by changing the bitmap's name, updating the bitmap if the original file has been modified, and even changing its compression settings. **Compression** takes away some of a file's data to reduce its size. You can compress a bitmap yet maintain its quality. **Lossy compression** removes some of the original data in the image to achieve a smaller file size. **Lossless compression** retains all the original data in the image, but is limited to 256 colors. JPEG is a lossy compression method designed for compressing full-color images such as photographs. Although JPEG removes some of the image data, it stores full-color information, resulting in very good image quality. The GIF and PNG formats are better for images with solid areas of color such as logos and drawn shapes. The PNG format is not as widely used as the GIF format, but is supported by most current Web browsers.

InSight | Finding the Right Compression for a Bitmap

A bitmap file in the JPEG file format is already compressed. Compressing it further in Flash can degrade the quality of the picture, so you need to balance how much compression to apply to a bitmap with the picture's quality. Keep in mind that pictures in a Flash movie don't always have to be of the highest quality, especially if they are small and are used as part of a larger graphic. Applying additional compression to bitmaps in Flash reduces the overall size of the final movie.

Experiment with several quality values to compare how the quality of the picture is affected. Select the value that maintains the quality of the picture needed for the particular design while still compressing the bitmap as much as possible.

The bitmap properties available depend on the bitmap's file type. Figure 6-3 describes the different properties, which are available in the Bitmap Properties dialog box.

Figure 6-3 Bitmap properties

Property	Description
Name	The name of the bitmap in the document's library.
Smoothing	The option to smooth the edges of the bitmap so they do not appear jagged.
Compression	The type of compression. Lossless (PNG/GIF) is for bitmaps in the PNG or GIF file format or that have large areas of single colors. Photo (JPEG) is for bitmaps with many colors or many color transitions such as photographs.
Quality	The amount of compression to apply to the bitmap, ranging from 0 (most compression) to 100 (least compression). The more compression that is applied, the more data that is lost. You can also keep the quality setting of the original bitmap for JPEGs or use the quality value set for the whole document for PNGs or GIFs.

Before placing the bitmaps in the banner, Aly wants you to minimize the size of the final movie by changing the compression settings for each bitmap. You will reduce the JPEG quality to decrease the overall size of the final movie, and then check what effect the new JPEG quality value will have on the pictures.

To change the crab.jpg and tuna.jpg bitmap properties:

1. In the Library panel, click the **crab.jpg** bitmap, and then click the **Properties** button at the bottom of the panel. The Bitmap Properties dialog box opens.

2. Right-click the **bitmap preview** in the upper-left corner, and then click **Zoom In** on the context menu. The preview image is larger so you can more easily see the effects of changes to the bitmap's properties.

3. Click the **Custom** option button. You want to adjust the bitmap's compression rather than use its imported compression data. The Quality box shows the default value of 50.

4. In the Quality box, double-click **50**, type **20**, and then click the **Test** button. The preview shows the bitmap with the new compression settings. With the lower quality value, the picture quality is poor. Some colors have changed significantly and the picture has less detail as evidenced by the small blocks that appear throughout the picture. See Figure 6-4.

Tip: You can drag the preview image in the Bitmap Properties dialog box to see other areas of the bitmap.

Figure 6-4 Bitmap with a lower compression value

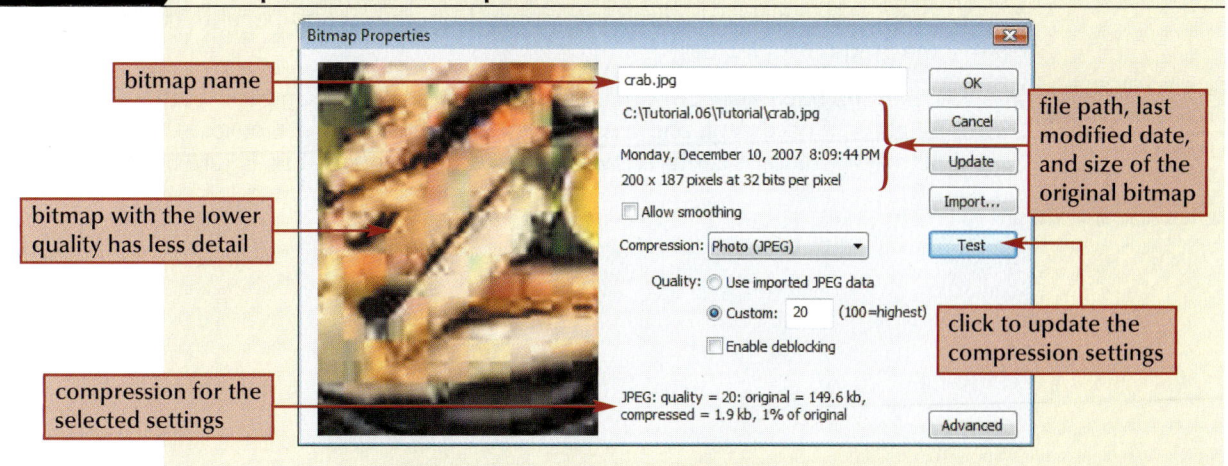

You want to find a quality value that maintains the photo's quality while reducing its file size.

5. In the Quality box, type **80** and then click the **Test** button. The compressed bitmap is smaller than the original file and the picture quality is not adversely affected.

6. Click the **OK** button to accept the compression value. You need to adjust the quality for the other bitmap.

7. In the Library panel, click the **tuna.jpg** bitmap, and then click the **Properties** button. The Bitmap Properties dialog box opens.

8. Click the **Custom** option button, type **80** in the Quality box, and then click the **Test** button. The preview of the tuna.jpg picture looks fine with this setting.

9. Click the **OK** button to accept the compression value.

Animating Bitmaps

You animate an imported bitmap the same way you animate any other object. For instance, you can create a motion tween that causes the bitmap to move, rotate, change in size (scale), or fade in or out. To animate a bitmap in a motion tween, you first need to convert the bitmap instance on the Stage to a symbol.

Aly's instructions for the banner indicate that the crab.jpg and tuna.jpg bitmaps are part of an animation where one bitmap appears and then fades away while the second bitmap fades in over the first. To accomplish the fade effect, you change the alpha amount for each instance. The **alpha amount** controls the transparency of an image. The alpha amount is a percentage from 0 to 100. An alpha amount of 0% makes the object completely transparent. An alpha amount of 100% makes the object completely opaque, which means it has no transparency. A motion tween that starts the object at an alpha amount of 100% and changes it at the end of the tween to 0% makes the object appear to fade out of view. You reverse the amounts to make the object appear to fade into view. Because this animation should be independent of any other animation that may be added to the banner, you will create a movie clip symbol that contains the seafood pictures animation within its own Timeline, independent of the main document's Timeline.

To create a new movie clip symbol and convert the crablegs bitmap into a symbol:

1. Create a new movie clip symbol named **seafood animation**. The new movie clip symbol opens in symbol-editing mode.

2. Drag an instance of the **crab.jpg** bitmap from the Library panel to the center of the Stage.

3. Open the Info panel, click the Registration/Transformation point button to select it, if necessary, and then enter **0** in both the X and Y boxes. The selected bitmap instance is centered within the editing window. See Figure 6-5.

> **Tip**
> You can press the Ctrl+I keys to open or close the Info panel.

Tutorial 6 Creating Special Effects with Graphics and Gradients | Flash | FL 273

| Figure 6-5 | The crab.jpg bitmap instance centered |

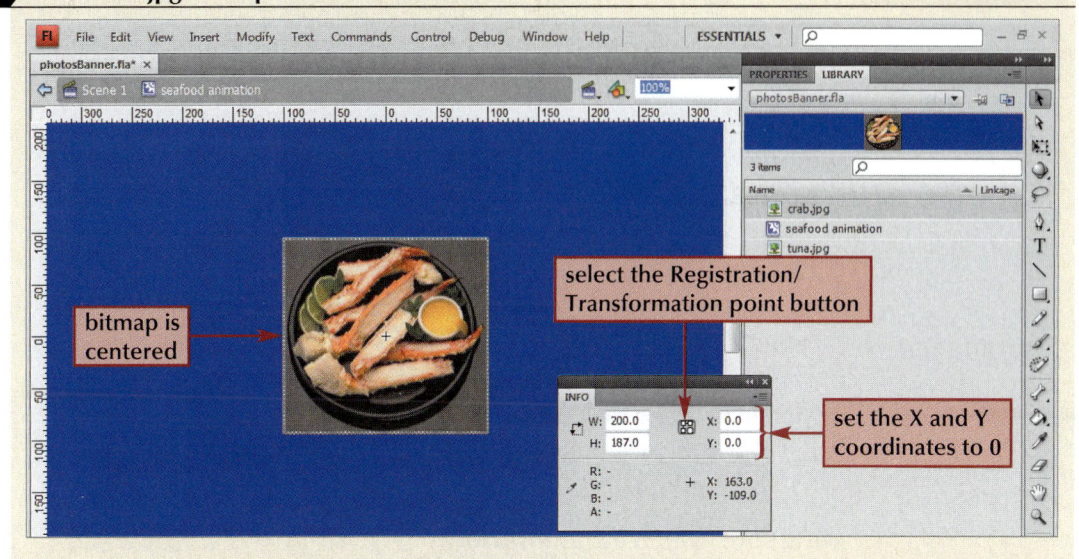

bitmap is centered

select the Registration/Transformation point button

set the X and Y coordinates to 0

▶ 4. Convert the **crab.jpg** bitmap instance on the Stage into a movie clip symbol named **crab symbol**, and then click the center registration point in the Registration icon. The registration point specifies what part of the symbol is used for alignment. Because the crab.jpg and the tuna.jpg images need to be in the same position on the Stage, you specified a point in the crab image to use for alignment when you position the tuna image. See Figure 6-6.

| Figure 6-6 | Convert to Symbol dialog box |

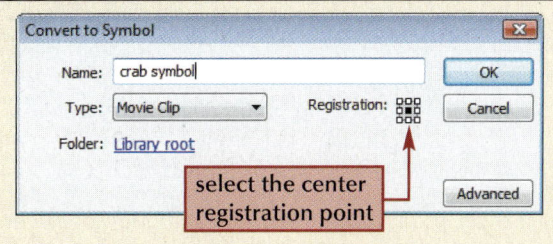

select the center registration point

▶ 5. Click the **OK** button. The crab symbol is created, and you can use it in a motion tween animation.

▶ 6. Close the Info panel.

In the animation, the crab.jpg bitmap fades out of view after a period of time and then the tuna.jpg bitmap fades in. Aly provides the sketch shown in Figure 6-7 that outlines how the animation occurs. Based on the sketch, the animation of the pictures takes place over six seconds. During the first two seconds, the crab.jpg picture is displayed. During the third second, the crab.jpg picture fades out as the tuna.jpg picture fades in. Then, during the next two seconds, the tuna.jpg picture is displayed. Finally, during the last second, the tuna.jpg picture fades out and the crab.jpg picture fades back in. Because the frame rate is 24 frames per second, each second requires 24 frames. Converting these time specifications to frame numbers means that you need keyframes at Frames 1, 48, 72, 120, and 144. These are the frames where a change occurs from the previous frames.

Figure 6-7 — Fade animation plan

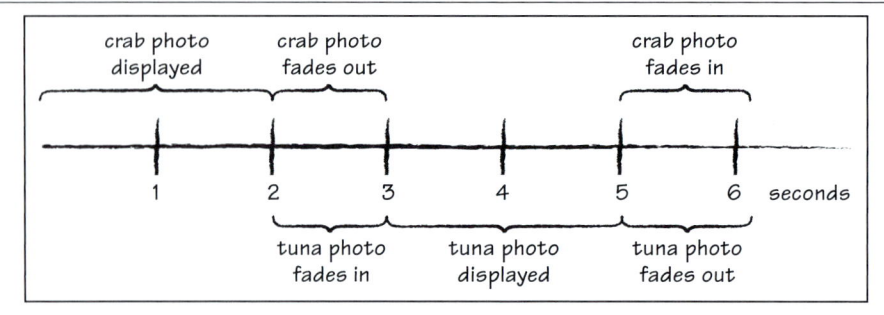

crab photo displayed | crab photo fades out | | crab photo fades in

1 2 3 4 5 6 seconds

tuna photo fades in | tuna photo displayed | tuna photo fades out

You'll create the crab animation. You'll insert keyframes for the animation, create a motion tween, and then set the alpha amounts for the crab instance to control the transparency, which creates the fade-in and fade-out effect.

To create the crab animation:

1. In the Timeline, rename Layer 1 as **crab**, select **Frame 1** of the crab layer, and then select the **crab symbol** instance on the Stage.

2. In the Color Effect section of the Property inspector, click the **Style** button, and then click **Alpha**. The Alpha setting appears in the Property inspector.

3. If necessary, drag the **Alpha** slider to the right until **100** appears in the % box. The crab symbol instance is fully visible with the alpha amount set to 100%.

4. In the crab layer, insert a keyframe at **Frame 48**, select the **crab symbol** instance on the Stage, and then, in the Color Effect section of the Property inspector, make sure the alpha amount remains set to **100%**.

5. In the Timeline, insert a keyframe at **Frame 72**, select the **crab symbol** instance on the Stage, and then, in the Color Effect section of the Property inspector, drag the Alpha slider to the left until **0** appears in the % box.

6. In the Timeline, create a motion tween between Frame 48 and Frame 72.

7. In the Timeline, right-click **Frame 71**, point to **Insert Keyframe**, and then click **Color**. A property keyframe is added to the motion tween, so you can set the ending alpha amount for the motion tween.

8. Select the **crab symbol** instance on the Stage, and then, in the Color Effect section of the Property inspector, set the alpha amount to **0%**. The crab symbol instance becomes transparent. See Figure 6-8.

Tutorial 6 Creating Special Effects with Graphics and Gradients | Flash **FL 275**

| Figure 6-8 | Transparent crab symbol instance |

- bitmap becomes transparent
- select Alpha
- set the alpha amount to 0%
- insert keyframes at Frames 48 and 72
- insert a property keyframe at Frame 71
- rename the layer

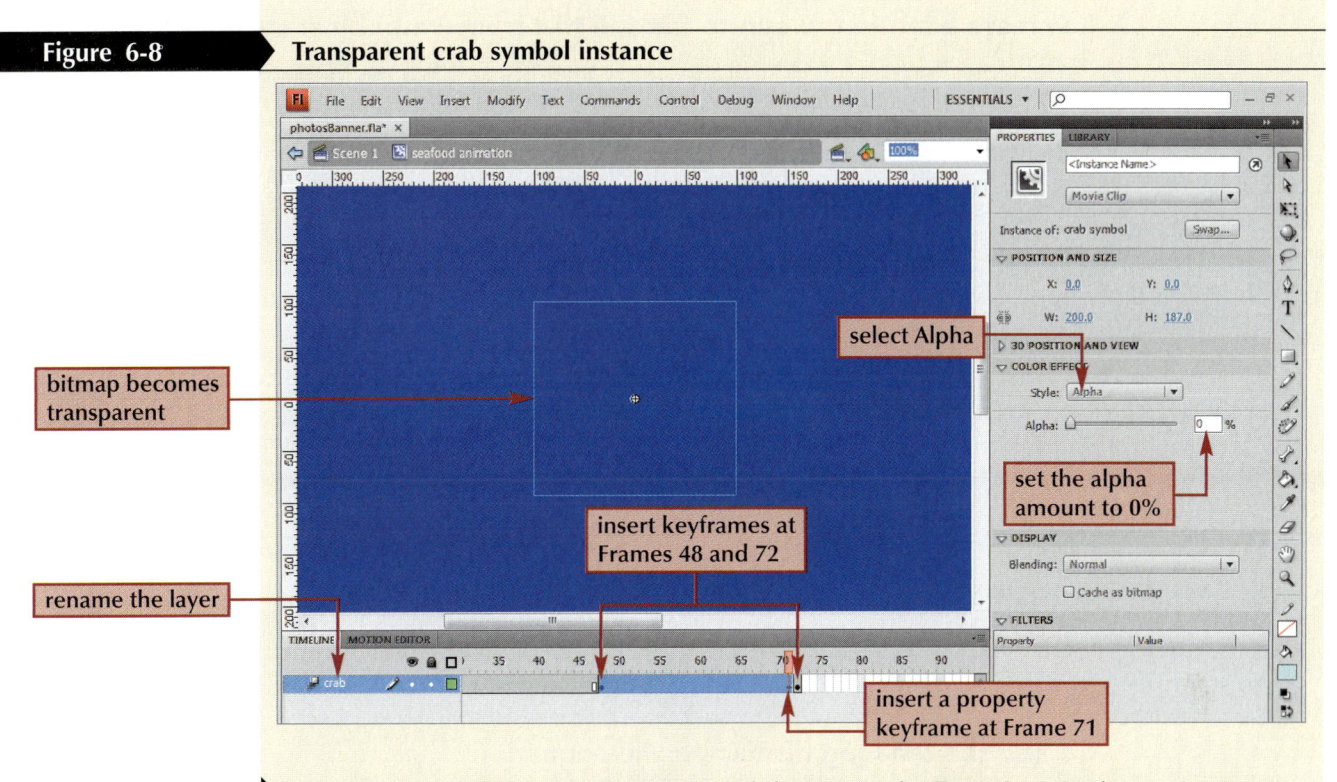

▶ 9. Move the playhead to **Frame 1**, and then press the **Enter** key. As the motion tween plays, the crab symbol instance is displayed and then fades out. See Figure 6-9.

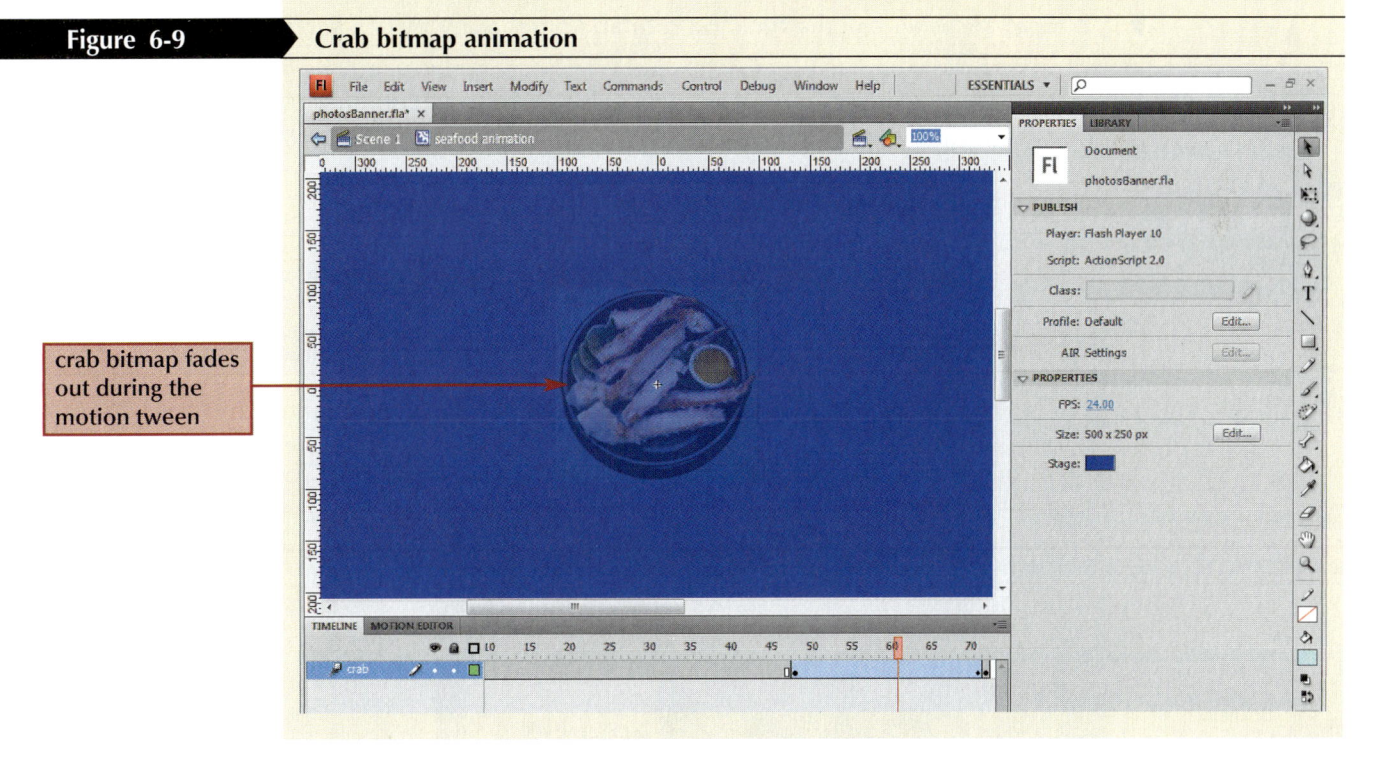

| Figure 6-9 | Crab bitmap animation |

- crab bitmap fades out during the motion tween

The crab photo is supposed to fade out and then fade back into view at the end of the animation. You will create another motion tween to fade in the crab.

To create a motion tween to fade in the crab symbol instance:

1. In the Timeline, insert keyframes at **Frame 120** and **Frame 144**, and then create a motion tween at Frame 120.

2. In the Timeline, right-click **Frame 143**, point to **Insert Keyframe**, and then click **Color**. A property keyframe is added to the motion tween, so you can set the ending alpha amount for the motion tween.

3. Select the **crab symbol** instance on the Stage, and then, in the Property inspector, set the alpha amount to **100%**. The motion tween is created to fade in the crab symbol instance.

4. In the Timeline, click **Frame 144**, select the **crab symbol** instance on the Stage, and then, in the Property inspector, set the alpha amount to **100%**. The crab symbol instance becomes fully visible for the last frame of the animation.

5. Move the playhead to **Frame 1**, and then press the **Enter** key. The crab symbol instance is displayed, fades out, and then fades back in at the end of the animation.

You will follow a similar process to make the tuna.jpg bitmap fade in as the crab.jpg bitmap fades out. The tuna.jpg bitmap will then fade out as the crab.jpg bitmap fades back in. You'll place the tuna animation on a separate layer.

To add the tuna.jpg bitmap to the animation:

1. In the Timeline, insert a new layer, name the layer **tuna**, and then insert a keyframe at **Frame 48**.

2. Drag an instance of the **tuna.jpg bitmap** from the Library panel to the center of the Stage.

3. Open the Info panel, enter **0** in the X and Y boxes, and then close the Info panel. The tuna.jpg bitmap instance is centered on the Stage. See Figure 6-10.

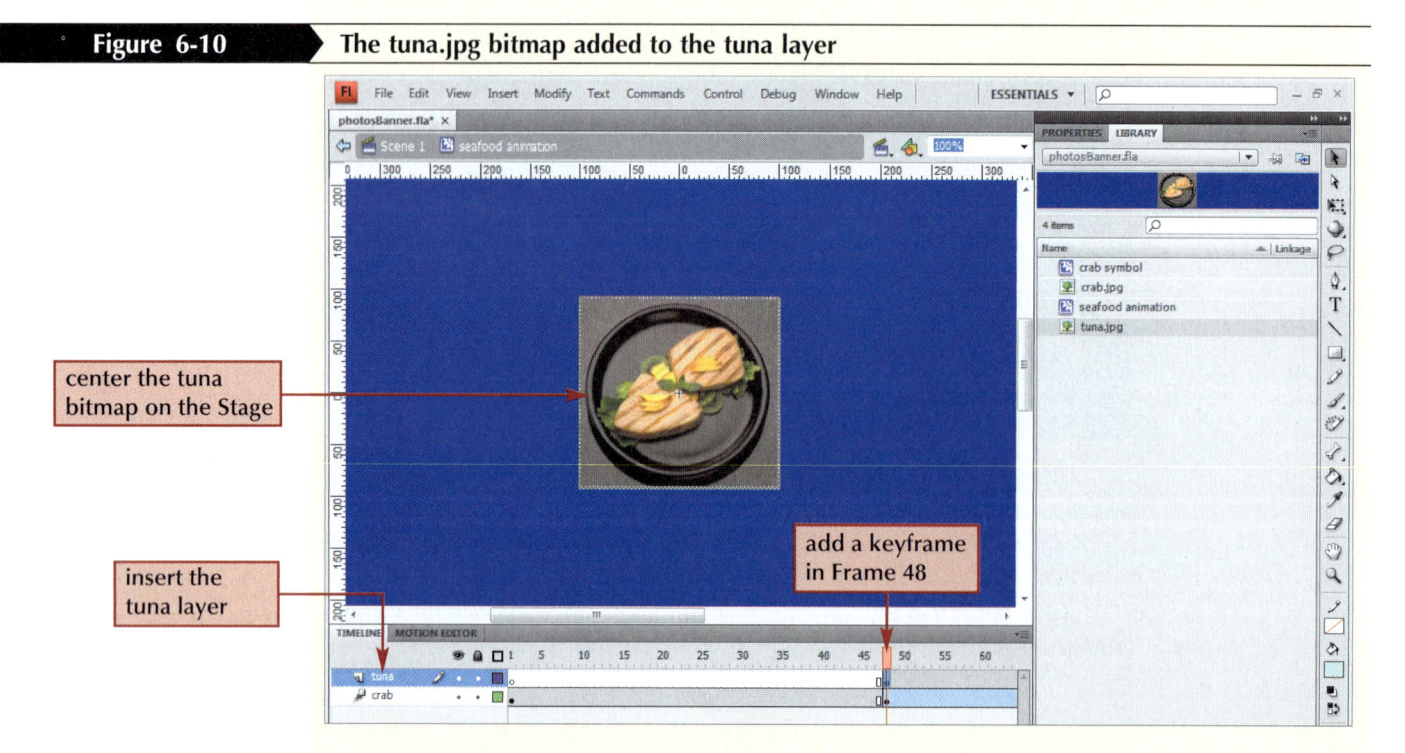

Figure 6-10   The tuna.jpg bitmap added to the tuna layer

center the tuna bitmap on the Stage

insert the tuna layer

add a keyframe in Frame 48

Tutorial 6 Creating Special Effects with Graphics and Gradients | Flash | FL 277

▶ 4. Convert the tuna.jpg bitmap on the Stage to a movie clip symbol named **tuna symbol** with the center registration point selected in the Registration icon.

▶ 5. In the Timeline, insert a keyframe at **Frame 72** of the tuna layer, select the **tuna symbol** instance on the Stage, and then, in the Color Effect section of the Property inspector, click the **Style** button, click **Alpha**, type **100** in the % box, and press the **Enter** key. The tuna symbol instance becomes fully visible in this frame.

▶ 6. In the Timeline, click **Frame 48** of the tuna layer, select the **tuna symbol** instance on the Stage, and then, in the Color Effect section of the Property inspector, click the **Style** button, click **Alpha**, type **0** in the % box, and press the **Enter** key. The tuna symbol instance becomes transparent, allowing the crab symbol instance to show through.

▶ 7. In the Timeline, create a motion tween at **Frame 48** of the tuna layer.

▶ 8. In the Timeline, right-click **Frame 71** of the tuna layer, point to **Insert Keyframe**, and then click **Color**. A property keyframe is added to the motion tween, so you can set the ending alpha amount for the motion tween.

▶ 9. Select the **tuna symbol** instance on the Stage, and then, in the Property inspector, set the alpha amount to **100%**. The motion tween is created to fade in the tuna symbol instance.

▶ 10. In the Timeline, drag the playhead between Frame 48 and Frame 72 to preview how the tuna picture fades in while the crab picture fades out. See Figure 6-11.

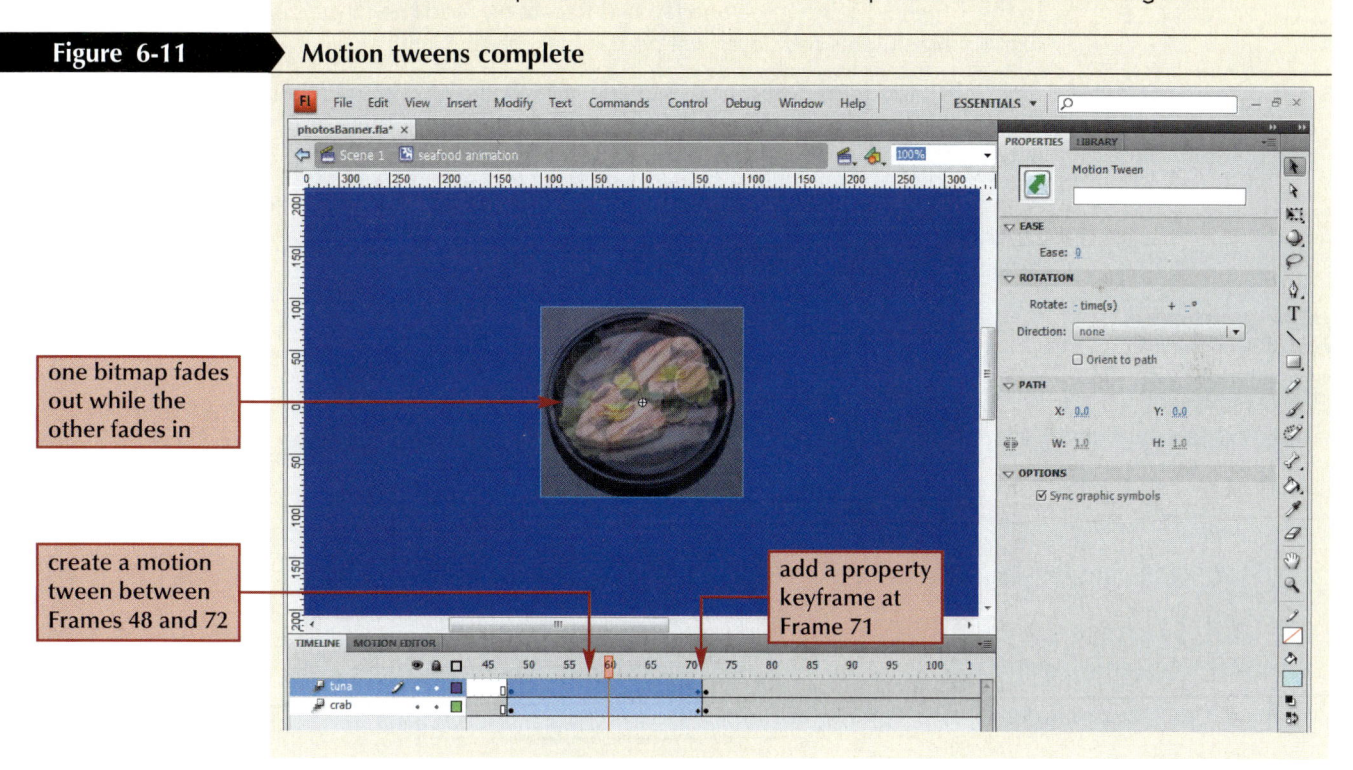

| Figure 6-11 | Motion tweens complete |

one bitmap fades out while the other fades in

create a motion tween between Frames 48 and 72

add a property keyframe at Frame 71

You'll create the motion tween for the tuna symbol instance to fade out of view and the crab symbol instance to fade back into view.

To create the motion tween to fade out the tuna symbol instance:

▶ 1. In the Timeline, insert keyframes at **Frame 120** and **Frame 144** of the tuna layer, and then create a motion tween.

▶ 2. In the Timeline, click **Frame 144** of the tuna layer. You will set the alpha amount for the tuna symbol instance to 0% in this frame.

▶ 3. On the stage, click the **tuna symbol** instance to select it, and then, in the Property inspector, set the alpha amount to **0%**.

▶ 4. In the Timeline, insert a property keyframe at **Frame 143** of the tuna layer, select the **tuna symbol** instance on the Stage, and then, in the Property inspector, set the alpha amount to **0%**. The motion tween fades out the tuna symbol instance.

▶ 5. In the Timeline, move the playhead to **Frame 1**, and then press the **Enter** key to play the animation. The crab picture is displayed and then fades out when the tuna picture fades in. Then the crab picture fades back in while the tuna picture fades out. The seafood animation is complete.

Based on Aly's instructions, you need to add a mask. Recall that a mask is created on a separate mask layer. The layer below the mask layer becomes the masked layer. The contents of the masked layer that are covered by the filled shape in the mask layer appear when the movie is played. In this case, you need to create a mask layer, draw a filled shape that covers the seafood animation, and then make both the crab layer and the tuna layer masked layers. The filled shape determines how much of the seafood animation shows through.

To create the mask layer for the seafood animation:

▶ 1. In the Timeline, select the **tuna** layer, if necessary, and then insert a new layer and name it **mask**. This new layer will be the mask layer.

▶ 2. Right-click the **mask** layer, and then click **Mask** on the context menu. The mask layer's icon changes to represent the layer's property. The tuna layer is indented, and its icon changes to indicate it is a masked layer.

▶ 3. Right-click the **crab** layer, and then click **Properties** on the context menu. The Layer Properties dialog box opens so you can change the crab layer's properties to Masked. See Figure 6-12.

Figure 6-12 Layer Properties dialog box

Tip
You can also double-click a layer's icon to open its Properties dialog box.

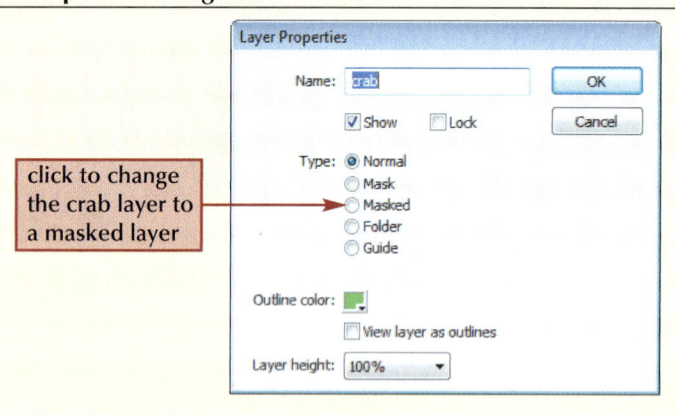

click to change the crab layer to a masked layer

▶ 4. Click the **Masked** option button, and then click the **OK** button. The dialog box closes. The crab layer in the Timeline is indented and its icon changes to indicate that it is a masked layer. The mask layer starts out locked to display its effect. See Figure 6-13.

Tutorial 6 Creating Special Effects with Graphics and Gradients | Flash **FL 279**

| Figure 6-13 | Layers converted to masked layers |

- mask layer
- masked layers are indented

▶ 5. In the Timeline, click the **mask** layer, and then click the **lock** icon to unlock the layer. With the layer unlocked, you can draw the shape for the mask, which can be any shape that contains a fill. The area covered by the shape's fill determines which part of the masked layer's contents is displayed.

▶ 6. In the Tools panel, click and hold the **Rectangle** tool, click the **Rectangle Primitive** tool, and then set the fill color to **yellow** (#FFFF00). Although you set the shape's fill to yellow, the shape's fill can be any color because it is not displayed.

▶ 7. On the Stage, drag the crosshair pointer from the upper-left corner of the crab symbol instance to its lower-right corner. The yellow rectangle covers the entire picture.

▶ 8. Open the Info panel, set the rectangle's width to **200**, its height to **185**, and its X and Y coordinates to **0**, and then close the Info panel. The rectangle frames the seafood animation.

▶ 9. In the Property inspector, click the **lock** icon for the corner radius boxes to unlock the values, enter **50** in the lower-left corner radius value box, and then enter **50** in the upper-right corner radius value. The rectangle shape has two rounded corners. See Figure 6-14.

| Figure 6-14 | Mask covers the bitmaps |

- set the fill to yellow
- use the Primitive Rectangle tool to draw the shape
- yellow shape is the mask
- set the lower-left and upper-right corner radiuses

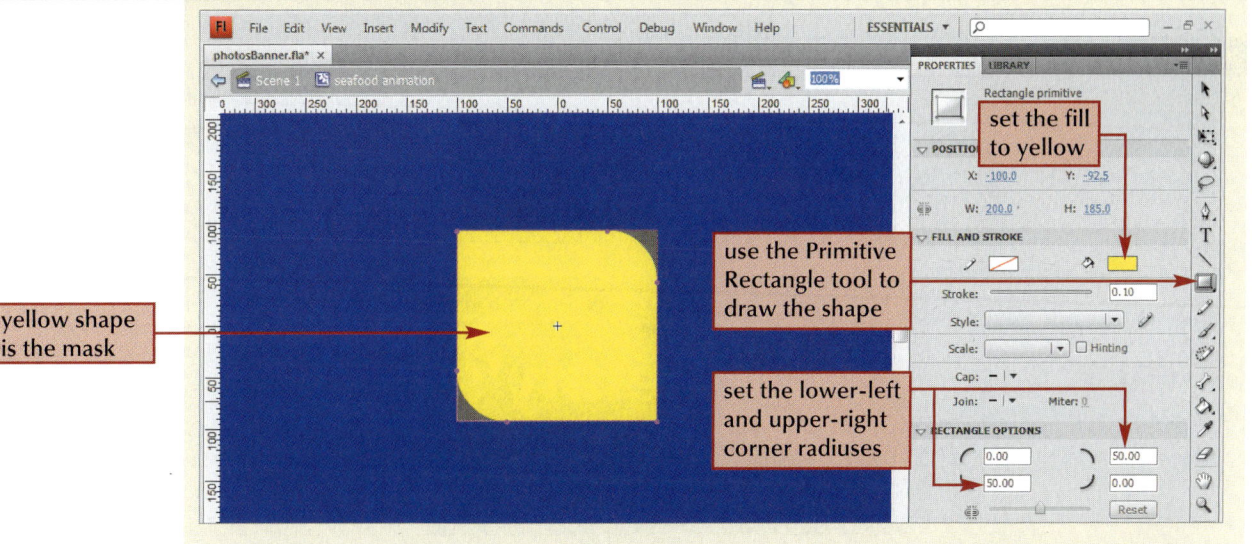

▶ 10. In the Timeline, click the **Lock/Unlock All Layers** icon to lock all of the layers and display the result of the mask. The crab picture shows through the mask. The mask for the seafood animation is complete. See Figure 6-15.

FL 280 Flash | Tutorial 6 Creating Special Effects with Graphics and Gradients

Figure 6-15 | **Bitmaps show through the mask**

bitmaps are visible through the mask

▶ 11. Click the **Scene 1** link on the Edit bar to exit symbol-editing mode and return to the document's main Timeline.

You need to add the completed seafood animation movie clip to the banner. Based on the specifications that Aly provided for this banner, the seafood animation is to be placed on the left side of the banner.

To add the seafood animation to the banner and preview it:

▶ 1. In the Timeline, insert a new layer above the text layer and name it **bitmaps**. You'll add the seafood animation to the banner in this layer.

▶ 2. Drag the **seafood animation** symbol from the Library panel to the left side of the Stage. The animation is added to the banner.

▶ 3. In the Position and Size section of the Property inspector, enter **118** for the X coordinate and **125** for the Y coordinate. The animation is positioned attractively in the banner. See Figure 6-16.

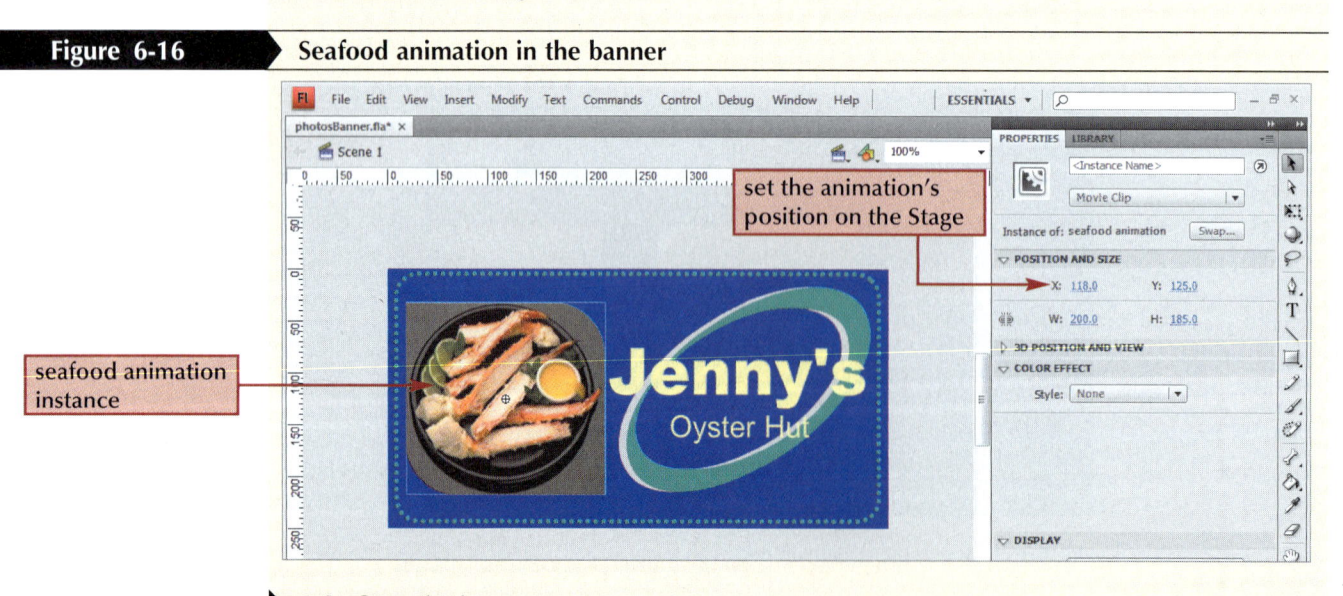

Figure 6-16 | **Seafood animation in the banner**

set the animation's position on the Stage

seafood animation instance

▶ 4. Save the banner.

> Because the animation was created inside the movie clip's Timeline, you cannot preview it within the main document's Timeline. To preview the seafood animation with the banner, you need to create an SWF file and play it in a separate window or in a Web page.
>
> ▶ 5. On the Application bar, click **Control**, and then click **Test Movie**. A Flash Player window opens with the banner and the seafood animation.
>
> ▶ 6. View the animation in the banner, and then close the Flash Player window.

Converting a Bitmap to a Vector Graphic

A bitmap instance on the Stage can also be converted to a vector graphic. You can modify the converted graphic just like any other vector graphic created in Flash. The converted graphic is no longer linked to the imported bitmap in the document's library. So, any changes you make to the vector graphic do not affect the original bitmap in the library, which can still be used to create instances of the bitmap on the Stage.

Converting a bitmap to a vector graphic has several benefits. If the imported bitmap is geometric, converting it to a vector graphic enables you to use the Flash editing tools to edit the graphic. You might also want to convert a bitmap to a vector graphic so you can create a visual effect with the image. Finally, converting a bitmap instance to a vector graphic can reduce the file size of the final movie.

The Trace Bitmap command converts a bitmap instance on the Stage into a vector graphic by comparing each pixel in the graphic and assigning each a specific color. Pixels with similar colors are converted into areas of one color, essentially reducing the number of colors in the picture. Also, areas of contrasting color are converted to lines and curves. You specify how Flash should do this conversion through the settings in the Trace Bitmap dialog box, which are described in Figure 6-17.

Figure 6-17   Trace Bitmap dialog box settings

Setting	Description
Color threshold	Determines how pixels are compared to assign colors to them. The value ranges from 1 to 500. Higher values create fewer distinct colors because adjacent pixels must vary more before they are considered a different color. Smaller values result in more distinct colors.
Minimum area	Specifies the number of surrounding pixels to average when assigning a color to each pixel. The value ranges from 1 to 1000. A smaller minimum area compares fewer surrounding pixels, creating more colors. A larger area compares more surrounding pixels, creating fewer colors.
Curve fit	Specifies how smoothly the outlines are drawn. The value ranges from Pixels, which results in more detail, to Very Smooth, which results in less detail.
Corner threshold	Specifies whether sharp edges are retained or smoothed out. The Many Corners setting results in more detail, whereas the Few Corners setting results in less detail.

Selecting different values for the settings in the Trace Bitmap dialog box creates different effects in the converted graphic. For example, a bitmap that is converted to a vector graphic using a color threshold of 50, a minimum area of 50, a normal curve fit, and a normal corner threshold creates the special effect shown in Figure 6-18.

Figure 6-18 — Bitmap converted to a vector

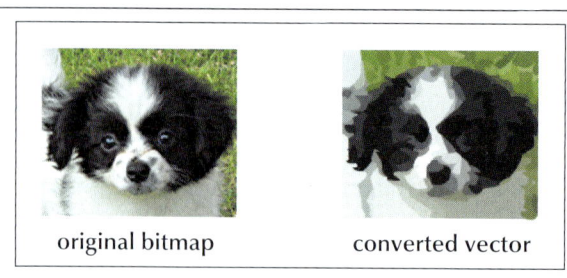

original bitmap   converted vector

Jenny wants the new company logo to include a photo of a lobster, as shown in the sketch of the logo in Figure 6-19. Aly provides a lobster photo to use as the logo's background. You will convert the bitmap to a vector graphic to create a special effect using the Trace Bitmap command.

Figure 6-19 — Sketch for the new Jenny's Oyster Hut logo

- Use lobster photo for the background
- Apply a specal effect

- Add text blocks with the restaurant name
- Use a gradient for the Jenny's text block

136 pixels high

200 pixels wide

You'll convert the bitmap to a vector graphic.

To convert the lobster bitmap to a vector graphic:

1. Create a new **Flash File (ActionScript 3.0)** document, and then set the document properties so that the width is **200** pixels and the height is **136** pixels. The document's dimensions are set to match the logo dimensions provided by Aly.

2. Save the file as **jennysLogo.fla** in the Tutorial.06\Tutorial folder included with your Data Files, reset the workspace to the **Essentials** layout, and then set the Stage magnification to **200%**.

3. Import the **lobster.jpg** bitmap file located in the Tutorial.06\Tutorial folder included with your Data Files to the document's library.

4. Drag a copy of the **lobster.jpg** bitmap from the Library panel to the Stage, and then, in the Position and Size section of the Property inspector, set the X and Y coordinates to **0**. The lobster bitmap instance is centered on the Stage and remains selected.

5. On the Application bar, click **Modify**, point to **Bitmap**, and then click **Trace Bitmap**. The Trace Bitmap dialog box opens. See Figure 6-20.

Tutorial 6 Creating Special Effects with Graphics and Gradients | Flash | **FL 283**

| Figure 6-20 | Trace Bitmap dialog box |

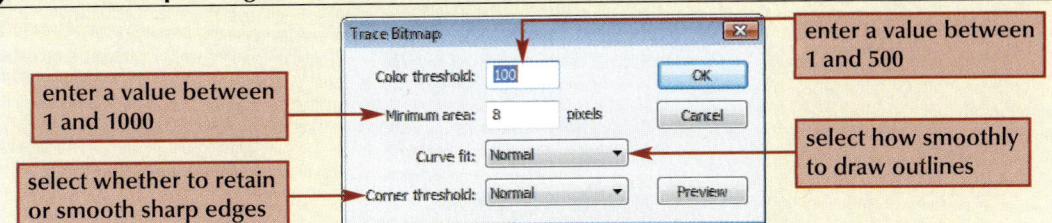

Trace Bitmap dialog box annotations:
- enter a value between 1 and 1000 → Minimum area
- select whether to retain or smooth sharp edges → Corner threshold
- enter a value between 1 and 500 → Color threshold
- select how smoothly to draw outlines → Curve fit

▸ 6. Type **60** in the Color threshold box. The color threshold setting determines how pixels are compared to assign colors to them.

▸ 7. Type **10** in the Minimum area box. The minimum area setting specifies how many surrounding pixels to average when assigning a color to each pixel.

▸ 8. Click the **Curve fit** button, and then click **Very Smooth**. This setting affects how the outlines are drawn. Very Smooth results in less detail.

▸ 9. Click the **Corner threshold** button, and then click **Many corners**. This setting determines whether sharp edges are retained or smoothed out. Many corners results in more detail.

▸ 10. Click the **OK** button. The lobster bitmap converts to a vector graphic based on the settings you entered in the Trace Bitmap dialog box. The lobster vector graphic contains less detail, larger areas of solid color, and smoother outlines than the original bitmap.

▸ 11. In the Tools panel, click the **Selection** tool, and then click the pasteboard to deselect the graphic. The changes to the graphic are visible.

▸ 12. In the Timeline, rename Layer 1 as **graphic**, and then lock Layer 1 to prevent accidentally changing its contents. See Figure 6-21.

FL 284 Flash | Tutorial 6 Creating Special Effects with Graphics and Gradients

Figure 6-21   **The lobster picture converted to a vector graphic**

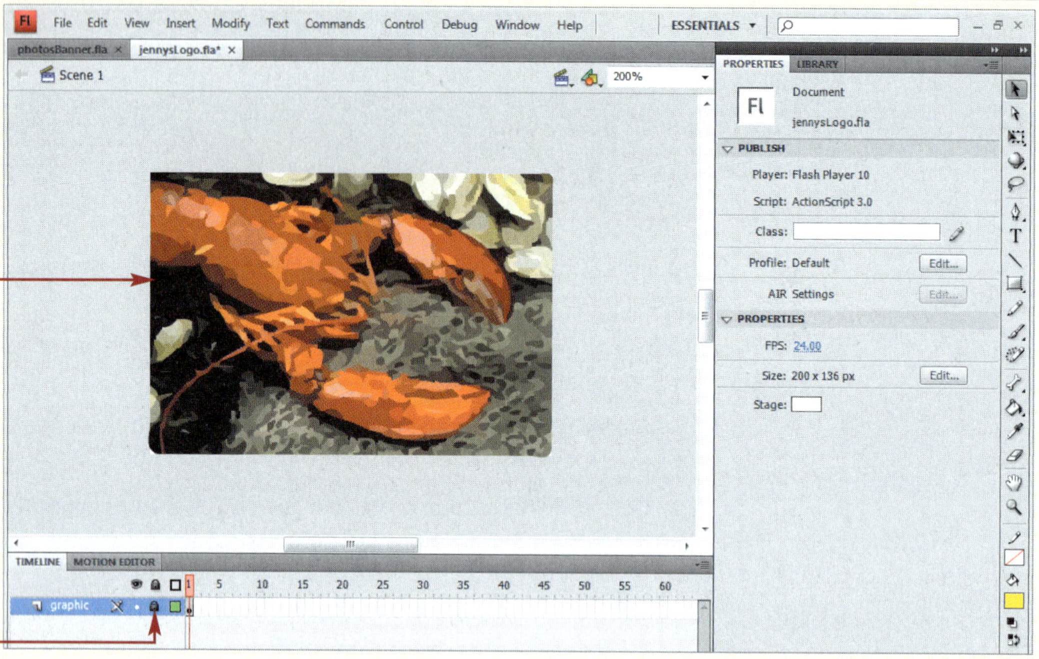

vector graphic

lock the background layer

You will complete the logo by adding text on top of the graphic, as shown in Aly's planning sketch. The graphic is the background for the logo. You will add the text on a separate layer.

To complete the logo by adding text:

1. In the Timeline, insert a new layer and name it **jennys**. You will create the text for the logo in this layer.

2. In the Tools panel, click the **Text** tool, and then, in the Property inspector, change the font family to **Arial**, change the font style to **Black**, change the point size to **38**, change the text color to **green** (#00FF00), and change the paragraph format to **Align Left**.

3. Click the left-center area of the lobster, type **Jenny's**, select the letter **J**, and then, in the Property inspector, change the point size to **58**. The first letter is larger than the rest of the name.

4. In the Tools panel, click the **Free Transform** tool, and then click the **Rotate and Skew** button. A bounding box appears around the text block.

5. Drag a corner handle on the bounding box around the text to rotate the text block counterclockwise, and then reposition the text block as needed to center it on the picture. See Figure 6-22.

Tutorial 6 Creating Special Effects with Graphics and Gradients | Flash **FL 285**

| Figure 6-22 | Rotated and centered text block |

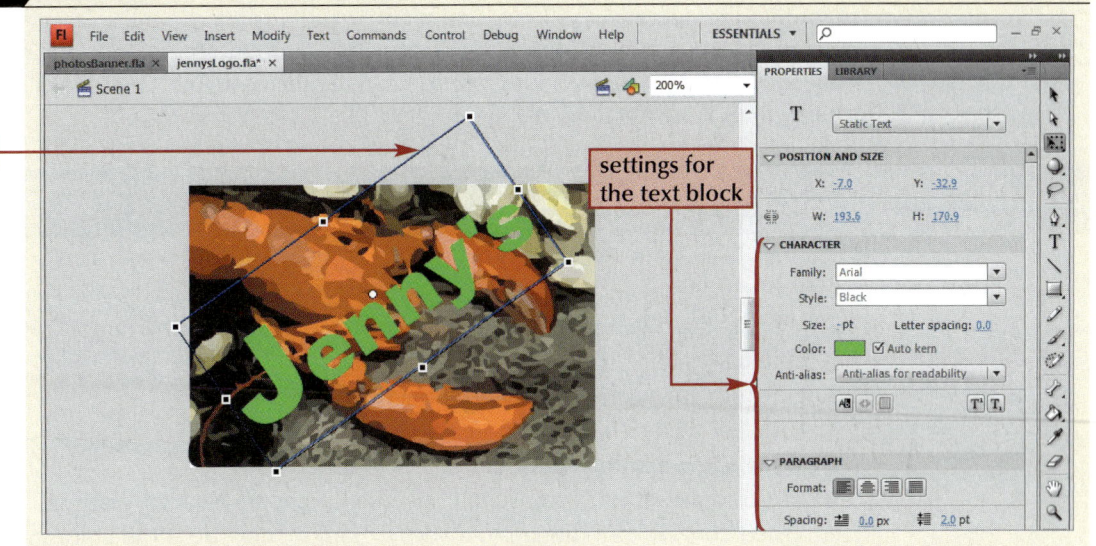

bounding box — *settings for the text block*

▶ 6. Click the pasteboard to deselect the Jenny's text block. You need to create two more text blocks for the other words in the restaurant name. Each word will have a slightly different color.

▶ 7. In the Tools panel, click the **Text** tool T, and then, in the Property inspector, change the point size to **24** and change the text color to **light yellow** (#FFFF99).

▶ 8. On the lower-right corner of the Stage, create a text block, type **Oyster**, and then click the pasteboard to deselect the text block.

▶ 9. In the Property inspector, change the text color to a **lighter yellow** (#FFFFCC), and then, on the Stage, create another text block below the Oyster text and type **Hut**.

Trouble? If the lighter yellow (#FFFFCC) is not available on the color palette, then you need to enter the code manually. Point to the hexadecimal code in the color palette, click the code, type the new code, and then press the Enter key.

▶ 10. In the Tools panel, click the **Selection** tool, and then reposition the two text blocks so that they are in the lower-right corner of the Stage and their right edges are aligned. See Figure 6-23.

| Figure 6-23 | Logo with text |

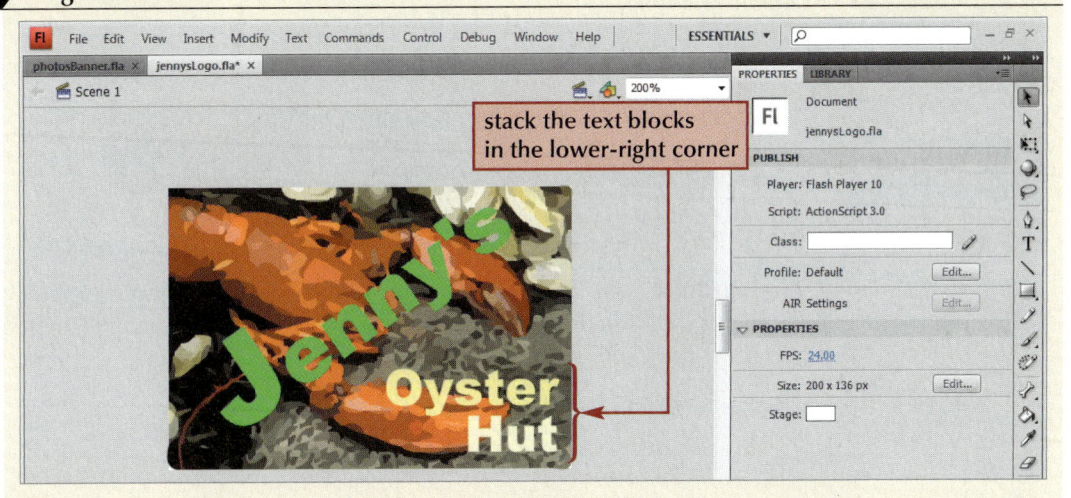

stack the text blocks in the lower-right corner

▶ 11. Save the logo.

In this session, you added bitmaps to the lunch specials banner. You imported the bitmaps into the document's library and then created instances on the Stage. You created an animation with two bitmaps, changing the alpha amount to create a fade effect. You also converted a bitmap to a vector graphic to create the new logo. In the next session, you'll modify the logo with gradients.

Review | Session 6.1 Quick Check

1. What is a bitmap?
2. What is the difference between the Import to Stage and the Import to Library commands?
3. How do you access a bitmap's properties within Flash?
4. For what type of bitmaps should you use the Photo (JPEG) compression setting?
5. What alpha amount makes an object transparent?
6. What command do you use to convert a bitmap to a vector graphic?
7. When converting a bitmap to a vector graphic, how does the color threshold value affect the resulting graphic?

Session 6.2

Using Gradients

A **gradient** is a gradual blend or transition from one color to another. Gradients can create special effects and add a professional touch to documents. For example, you can use a gradient for a banner's background, create a gradient to simulate a sunset or a rainbow, or use a gradient as part of an animation. Gradients can be added as fills to any object the same way you add solid color fills.

The two types of gradients you can create in Flash are linear and radial. A **linear gradient** blends the colors from one point to another in a straight line. A **radial gradient** blends the colors from one point outward in a circular pattern. Figure 6-24 shows examples of linear and radial gradients.

Figure 6-24 | **Gradient examples**

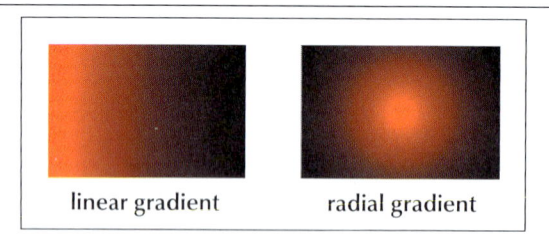

linear gradient   radial gradient

Flash includes several preset gradients in the color palette and in the Swatches panel. You can use these gradients as fills for any closed shape. You can also create custom gradients using the Color panel.

> **InSight** | **Gradients Impact Performance**
>
> Although gradients are easy to create and add to a Flash document, they increase the processing requirements of the computer displaying the SWF movie. Because of the greater number of colors in a gradient, a computer's processor might have to work harder to display a gradient compared to displaying solid colors. If you have concerns about a movie's performance when displayed on a user's computer, you can reduce the number of gradients used in the movie or omit them altogether if the SWF movie contains complex graphics or animations. You should always test the movie to ensure its quality is acceptable.

Creating and Saving a Custom Gradient

You create a new gradient in the Color panel. First you specify whether to use a linear or radial gradient as the fill style, and then you add a **color pointer** to the gradient definition bar at each spot you want to change the color in the gradient. A gradient can have anywhere from two to fifteen color pointers. Each color pointer creates a **fall-off point**, which is the spot where the gradient shifts or transitions from one color to another. A gradient's colors are displayed in the color space at the bottom of the Color panel. You can add a new gradient to the document's color swatches that appear in the color palette and in the Swatches panel. The gradient is stored only with the current document.

> **Reference Window** | **Creating, Editing, and Saving a Gradient**
>
> - To create a gradient, open the Color panel, click the Type button, and then click Linear or Radial (or click a preset gradient in the color palette or the Swatches panel).
> - To edit a gradient, add or delete a color pointer.
> - To specify a color for a color pointer, select the color pointer, and then enter the color's RGB values, hexadecimal value, or click the color picker in the Color panel.
> - To add a color pointer, click a spot on the gradient definition bar.
> - To remove a color pointer, drag it down, away from the gradient definition bar.
> - To reposition a color pointer, drag it to the left or right on the gradient definition bar.
> - To save a gradient with the current document, click the Color panel options menu, and then click Add Swatch.

The background of the new banner for the Jenny's Oyster Hut should be a radial gradient using a blend of a light blue color that transitions into a dark gray color. You will create the radial gradient to use as the fill for the banner's background.

To create a custom radial gradient for the banner:

1. If you took a break after the previous session, make sure the photosBanner.fla and the jennysLogo.fla files are open and the workspace is reset to the Essentials layout.

2. Click the **photosBanner.fla** tab to make the document active, and then open the **Swatches** panel. The preset gradients appear at the bottom of the Swatches panel.

3. In the Swatches panel, click the **gray radial gradient** (the second gradient from the left) with the eyedropper pointer. You'll modify this gradient to create the custom gradient. See Figure 6-25.

> **Tip**
>
> You can press the Ctrl+F9 keys to open and close the Swatches panel, and press the Shift+F9 keys to open and close the Color panel.

Figure 6-25 Swatches panel

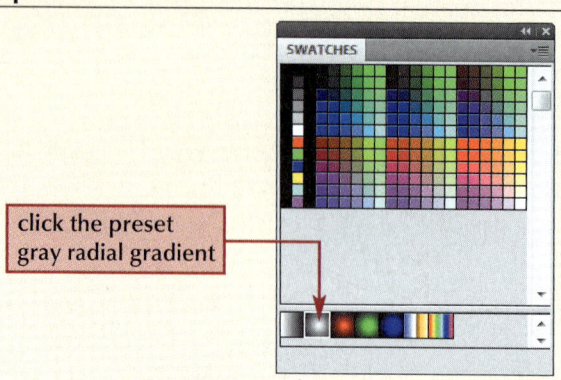

click the preset gray radial gradient

4. Open the **Color** panel, and then drag the Colors panel into the same dock as the Swatches panel. The Color panel displays the preset gray radial gradient and its two color pointers. You'll change these color pointers to create the new gradient based on the colors specified in the planning sketch.

5. In the Color panel, click the **left color pointer** below the gradient definition bar to select it. The small triangle for the color pointer changes to black to indicate it is selected.

6. Type **#99FFFF** in the Hex box, and then press the **Enter** key. The left color point for the gradient changes to a light blue color.

7. Click the **right color pointer** below the gradient definition bar, type **#333333** in the Hex value box, and then press the **Enter** key. The right color pointer is set to a dark gray color, and the color preview shows the new gradient. See Figure 6-26.

Figure 6-26 Color panel with the custom gradient

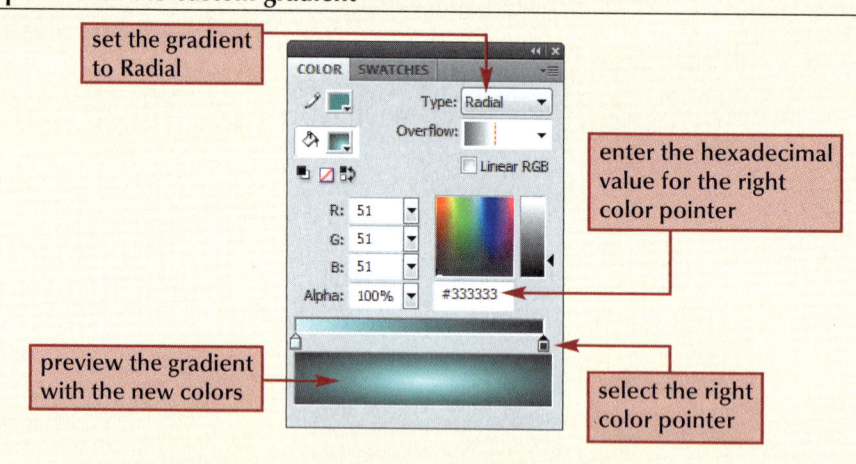

set the gradient to Radial

enter the hexadecimal value for the right color pointer

preview the gradient with the new colors

select the right color pointer

You'll save this gradient as a swatch in the Swatches panel for the document. If you don't save the gradient, it is discarded when you close the document.

8. In the Color panel, click the **panel menu** button, and then click **Add Swatch**. The gradient is saved with the document and the custom gradient appears at the end of the preset gradients in the Swatches panel.

9. Click the **SWATCHES** tab to display the Swatches panel. See Figure 6-27.

Tip

To delete a swatch, click the Swatches panel menu button, and then click Delete Swatch.

Figure 6-27 | **New gradient in the Swatches panel**

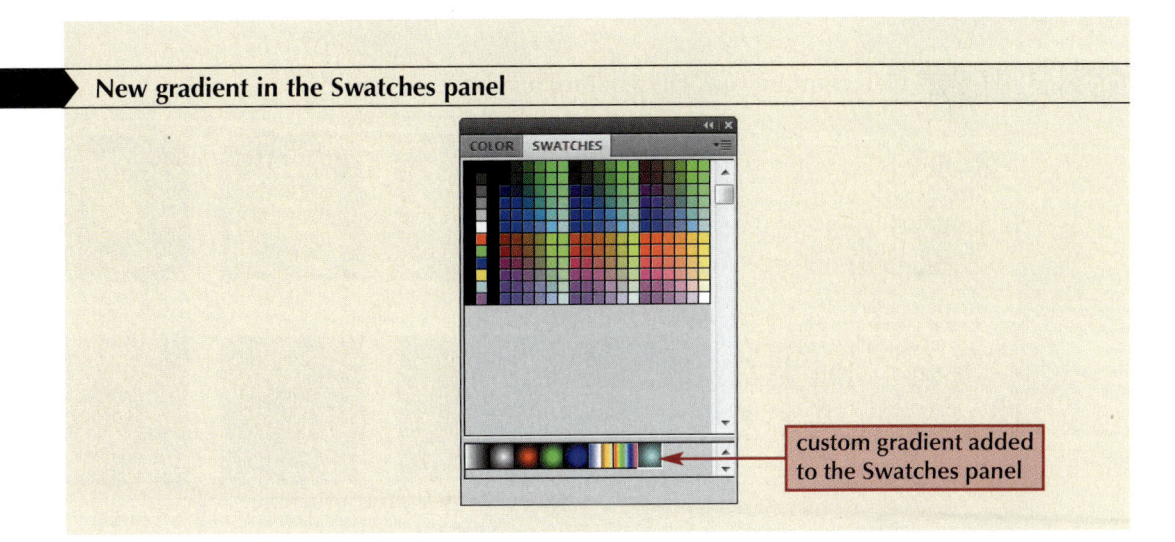

custom gradient added to the Swatches panel

Applying a Gradient Fill

Gradient fills can be applied to shapes such as circles, rectangles, and triangles as well as to text. You apply a gradient fill to an object the same way you apply a solid fill. You can select the gradient fill color before you draw a shape such as a rectangle, or you can use the Paint Bucket tool to apply a gradient to an existing shape. When using the Paint Bucket tool to apply a radial gradient, you specify the gradient's center point, which is where the first color begins. The point you click becomes the gradient's center point, as shown in Figure 6-28. When using the Paint Bucket tool to apply a linear gradient, you draw a straight line with the Paint Bucket pointer. The line you draw determines the direction of the gradient.

Figure 6-28 | **Radial gradient being applied with the Paint Bucket tool**

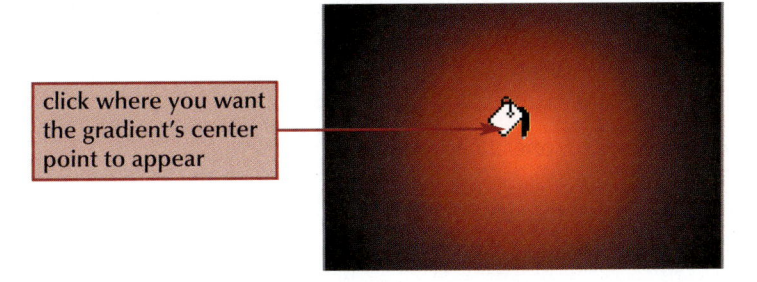

click where you want the gradient's center point to appear

You can also use the Paint Bucket tool's Lock Fill modifier when applying gradients. With the Lock Fill modifier selected, the Paint Bucket tool paints one gradient across several objects on the Stage rather than one gradient for each object, as shown in Figure 6-29.

FL 290 Flash | Tutorial 6 Creating Special Effects with Graphics and Gradients

| Figure 6-29 | Effect of the Lock Fill modifier on gradients |

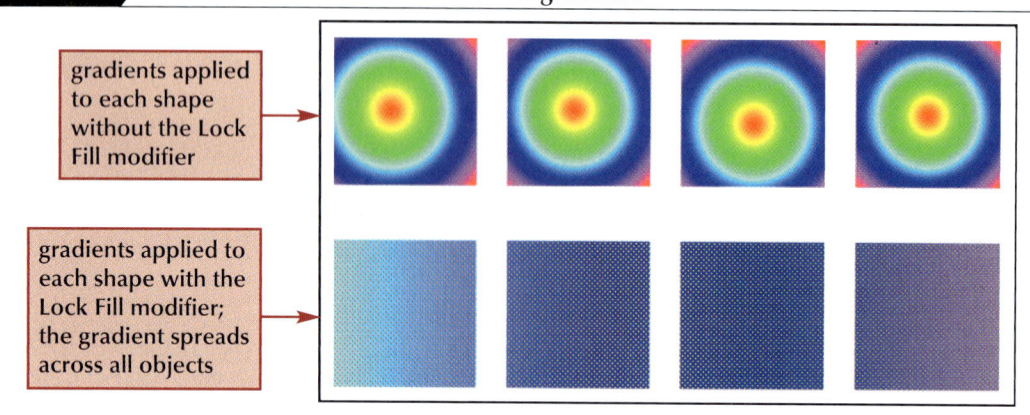

gradients applied to each shape without the Lock Fill modifier

gradients applied to each shape with the Lock Fill modifier; the gradient spreads across all objects

You will use the custom gradient as the fill for a rectangle that will be the banner's background.

To add a rectangle with the custom gradient to the background layer:

1. In the Timeline, select the **background** layer. You'll draw the rectangle for the banner's background in this layer.

2. In the Tools panel, click and hold the **Rectangle Primitive** tool, and then click the **Rectangle** tool to select it.

3. In the Tools panel, set the fill color to the gradient you created, which appears in the bottom row of the color palette. The rectangle will use the gradient you created as its fill.

4. In the Tools panel, set the stroke color to **no color**. The rectangle you draw will not have a visible stroke.

5. On the Stage, draw a large rectangle the size of the Stage. The rectangle covers the entire Stage but does not obscure the text and images because the rectangle is in the bottommost layer. See Figure 6-30.

6. Save the photosBanner.fla banner.

Tip

You can also toggle between the Rectangle Primitive tool and the Rectangle tool in the Tools panel by pressing the R key once to select the tool and again to switch the tool.

| Figure 6-30 | Gradient background added to the banner |

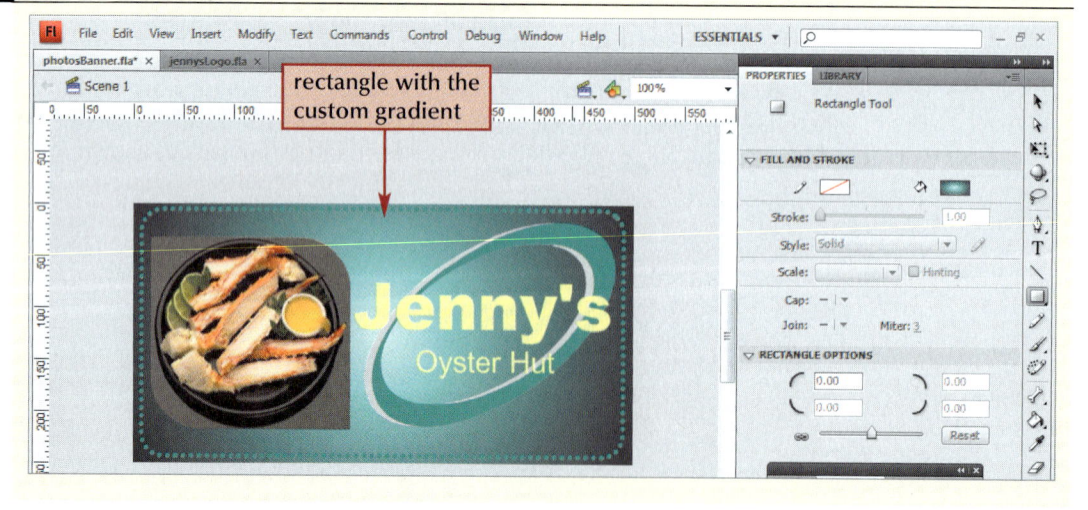

rectangle with the custom gradient

Tutorial 6 Creating Special Effects with Graphics and Gradients | Flash | FL 291

Filling Text with a Gradient

You can also apply a gradient fill to text. Before you can apply a gradient to text, you must first convert the text to a fill with the Break Apart command. If the text block has multiple letters, the first time you apply the Break Apart command to a text block, the text block is broken into smaller text blocks consisting of the individual letters. When you apply the Break Apart command a second time, the letter text blocks are converted into fills. Then, you can apply a gradient to the individual letters the same way you do any other shape. If the text block only has one letter, the Break Apart command needs to be applied only once to convert the letter into a fill.

The Jenny's text block in the logo should have a gradient fill applied to it. You will convert the text block to fills, apply a preset gradient, and then modify the colors to create a custom gradient.

To apply a gradient fill to the Jenny's text block:

1. Click the **jennyslogo.fla** tab to make the logo document active.

2. In the Tools panel, click the **Selection** tool, and then select the **Jenny's** text block on the Stage. You'll break apart the text block so you can apply a gradient fill.

3. On the Application bar, click **Modify**, and then click **Break Apart**. The text block breaks into individual blocks for each letter. See Figure 6-31.

Figure 6-31 | Jenny's text block broken apart

individual text blocks created for each letter

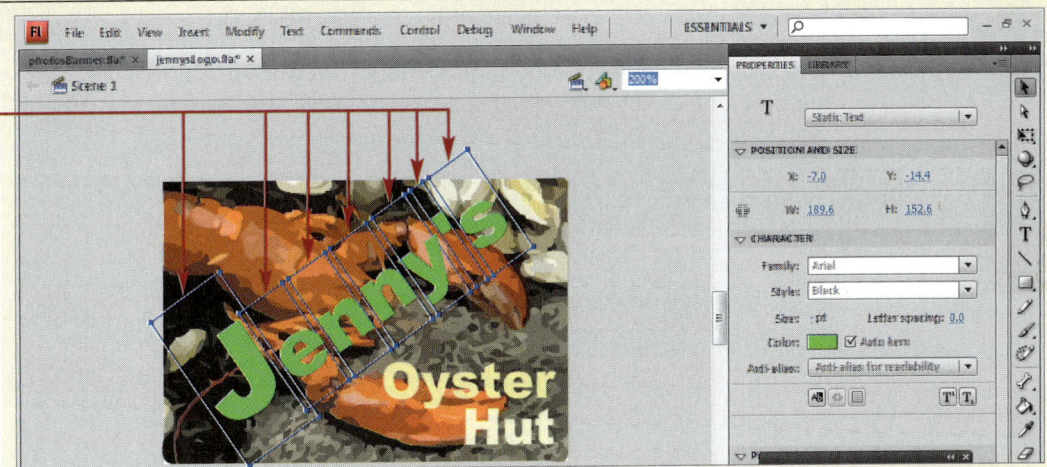

4. On the Application bar, click **Modify**, and then click **Break Apart**. The individual text blocks are converted to fills. The text fills are selected and ready for you to apply a gradient fill.

5. In the Color panel, click the **Type** button, and then click **Linear**. A linear gradient is applied to the text fills.

   You will modify the gradient used in the selected text fills.

6. In the Color panel, click the **left color pointer** below the gradient definition bar to select it, type **#FFFFFF** in the Hex box, and then press the **Enter** key. The starting color for the linear gradient is set.

7. In the Color panel, click the **right color pointer** to select it, type **#FFFF00** in the Hex box, and then press the **Enter** key. The ending color for the linear gradient is set, and the text gradient fill color changes.

8. Click the pasteboard to deselect the text. See Figure 6-32.

Figure 6-32   Gradient applied to text fills

Jenny's text with modified linear gradient fill

▶ 9. Close the Color and Swatches panels, and then save the jennysLogo.fla banner.

Transforming Gradient Fills

A gradient fill in an object can be modified by using the Gradient Transform tool. You can move a gradient's center, change its size, or change its direction. When you select a linear gradient with the Gradient Transform tool, a bounding box surrounds it. When you select a radial gradient, a bounding circle surrounds it. The gradient's center point also appears along with editing handles, as shown in Figure 6-33. You drag these handles to transform the gradient.

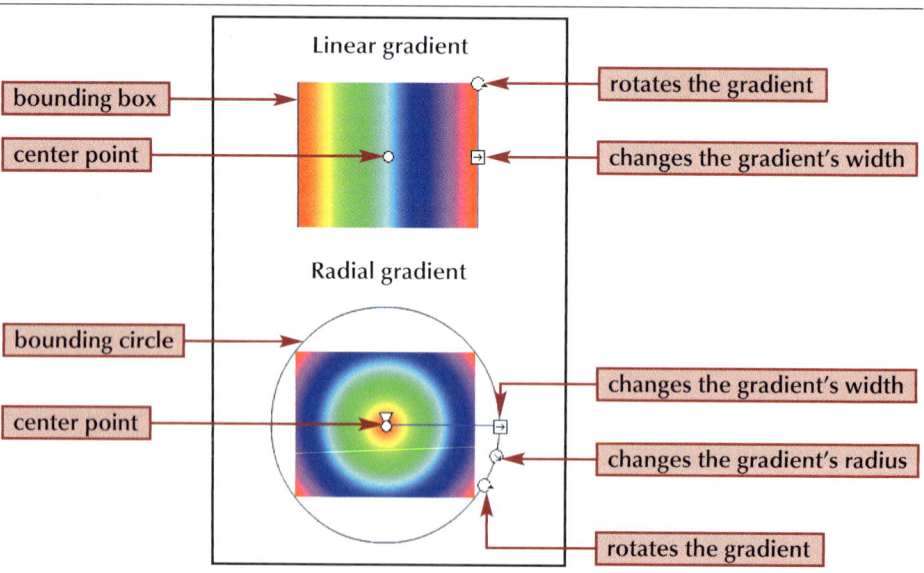

Figure 6-33   Editing handles

Linear gradient
- bounding box
- center point
- rotates the gradient
- changes the gradient's width

Radial gradient
- bounding circle
- center point
- changes the gradient's width
- changes the gradient's radius
- rotates the gradient

You drag a gradient's center point to reposition it. The linear gradient has a circular handle to rotate the gradient and a square handle to change the gradient's width. The radial gradient has two circular handles. The middle circular handle changes the gradient's radius and the bottom circular handle rotates the gradient. It also has a square

Tutorial 6 Creating Special Effects with Graphics and Gradients | Flash | **FL 293**

handle, which changes the gradient's width. A radial gradient also has a focal point, indicated by a small triangle, which is initially in the same position as the center point. You can drag the small triangle to change the gradient's focal point.

Aly wants you to modify the gradient in the banner background so that the lighter color of the gradient is behind the animation of the seafood pictures. To do this, you will move the gradient's center point to the left side of the banner over the seafood animation and increase its radius slightly to spread more of the lighter color to the rest of the banner.

To modify the gradient in the banner background:

▶ 1. Click the **photosBanner.fla** tab to make the document active. The banner appears on the Stage.

▶ 2. In the Tools panel, click and hold the **Free Transform** tool, and then click the **Gradient Transform** tool. The Gradient Transform tool is selected.

▶ 3. Click the rectangle with the gradient fill. The gradient's bounding circle and editing handles appear.

▶ 4. Set the Stage magnification to **50%**. The entire bounding circle is visible, making the rectangle easier to work with. See Figure 6-34.

| Figure 6-34 | Gradient selected for transformation |

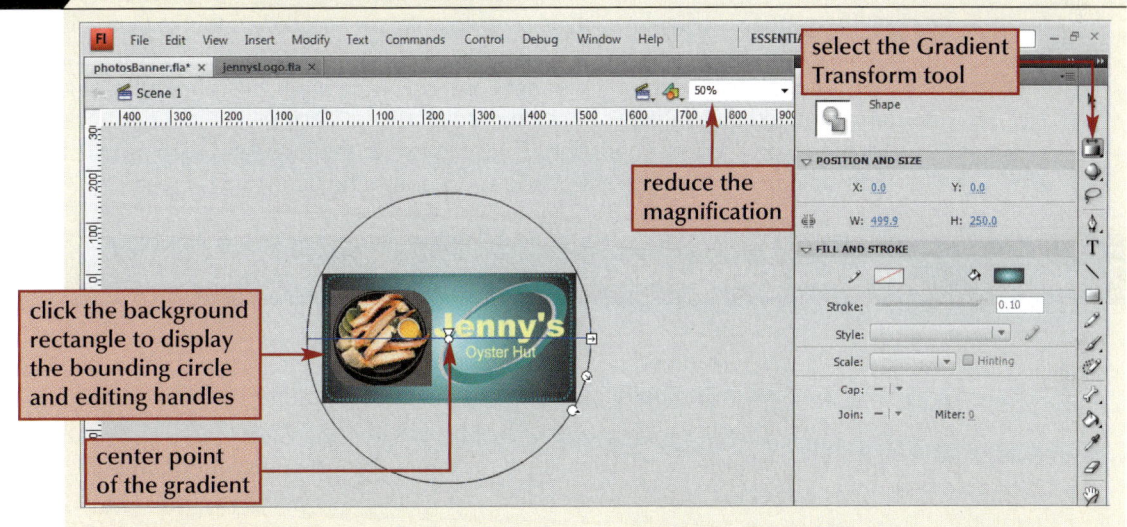

Screenshot callouts:
- select the Gradient Transform tool
- reduce the magnification
- click the background rectangle to display the bounding circle and editing handles
- center point of the gradient

▶ 5. Move the pointer over the center point of the gradient until the pointer changes to ✥ to indicate it is over the center point, and then drag the center point of the gradient to the left until it is positioned over the center of the seafood animation instance. The entire bounding circle moves as you reposition the center point of the gradient.

▶ 6. Drag the **radius handle** outward until the right side of the bounding circle touches the right of the letter "s" in the Jenny's text. See Figure 6-35. The gradient's radius increases so that the light blue color extends more than halfway across the banner.

Figure 6-35   Gradient's radius increased

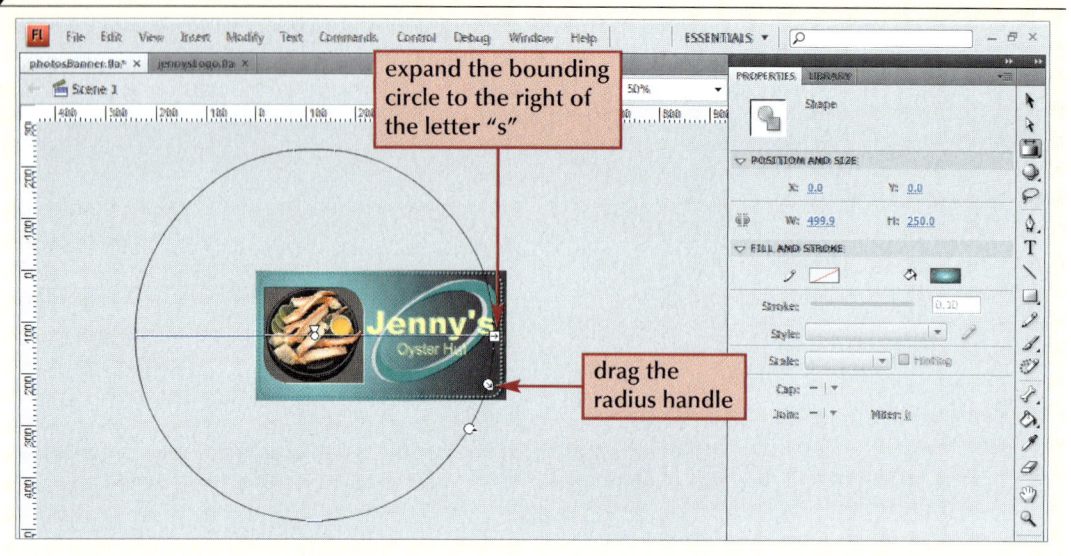

(screenshot showing Flash workspace with expanded bounding circle to the right of the letter "s" and drag the radius handle annotations)

> 7. Save the photosBanner.fla banner.

The banner is complete. Aly is pleased with your work and thinks the banner will look great on the Jenny's Oyster Hut Web site. In this session, you worked with gradients. You created a custom gradient for the banner and used it in the background rectangle you drew. You also modified the gradient's position, size, and width using the Gradient Transform tool. In addition, you applied a gradient to existing text in the logo, and then modified the colors in the gradient. In the next session, you will publish the banner you created.

Review | Session 6.2 Quick Check

1. What is a gradient?
2. Describe two different kinds of gradients available in Flash.
3. How do you save a gradient?
4. True or False? A gradient is saved only within the current document.
5. How do you add another color to a gradient with two colors?
6. True or False? You can apply a gradient to an existing object using the Gradient Transform tool.
7. When using the Paint Bucket tool to apply a linear gradient, how do you specify the direction of the gradient?
8. What are two changes you can make to a radial gradient with the Gradient Transform tool?

Session 6.3

Comparing Publishing Options

FLA documents created in Flash are usually made available for use on the Web. To do so, the document must be published or exported into a format readable by a Web browser. You have done this when you published FLA documents as SWF movie files in previous tutorials to test or preview the movie. You have used the Test Movie command, which creates an SWF file that plays in a separate Flash Player window. You have also used the Default – (HTML) command, which creates both an SWF file and an HTML file to play the movie. The browser uses the Flash Player plug-in to play the movie. In most cases, when you create movies for the Web, you want to publish an SWF file. However, sometimes you need to publish or export the document in a different file format. Flash allows you to publish Flash documents in such file formats as JPEG, GIF, and PNG.

You can also save the publishing settings as a profile that you can use with other documents.

| InSight | **Creating a Projector File** |

A Flash file can be published as a projector file, which is a stand-alone application with the .exe extension. A projector file has the Flash Player incorporated into it and plays the movie in its own window rather than in a Web browser. This is a useful option if you want to distribute a Flash movie on a platform other than the Web. The advantage to distributing a Flash projector file is that it can be viewed on a computer that does not have the Flash Player plug-in installed. The disadvantage is that its file size will be larger than the corresponding SWF file because the Flash Player is embedded in the projector file.

Selecting a Document's Publish Settings

You specify how you want an FLA document published in the Publish Settings dialog box. The Formats tab lists the file formats in which you can publish a Flash document. Most of the time, you will use only the Flash (.swf) and HTML (.html) file types because the documents you create are meant to be played in a Web page. However, you can choose to publish a document in a different format such as the JPEG Image (.jpg) file format. Each file format selected on the Formats tab has a corresponding tab in the Publish Settings dialog box with additional options and settings for that file type.

| InSight | **Choosing a Flash Player Version** |

When publishing Flash movies, you can specify that they run on the latest version of the Flash Player. If you are certain that everyone in the target audience has the latest player installed on their computers, then publishing to the latest format is not a problem. Publishing to the latest format ensures that all features of the Flash CS4 program work in the Flash Player. If you are unsure which version of Flash Player the audience has, it's a good idea to publish to a player that is two or three versions earlier. For example, if the current version of the Flash Player is version 10, you can set the version in the Publish Settings dialog box to version 7 or 8 to ensure that most of your target audience can see the Flash movies. If you publish to version 7 of the Flash Player, for example, then anyone with Flash Player 7 or later can see the Flash movie. Publishing the Flash movie to the latest version might limit the number of people who can see the movie.

The banner you just completed will be added to the home page of the Jenny's Oyster Hut Web site. Because the Web page already exists, you need to publish the banner only as an SWF file. When publishing in the Flash (.swf) format, the Flash tab in the Publish Settings dialog box contains options to specify the player and the script versions as well as other settings. Player specifies the oldest version of the Flash Player in which the published movie will play. The published banner SWF file should be compatible with all Flash Player plug-ins starting with version 7. Script specifies which version of ActionScipt (the Flash programming language) the published movie will use. In this case, the banner does not use ActionScript, so you don't need to change the default setting. The JPEG quality and audio settings can also be changed in this dialog box. However, the bitmap

Tip

A file published with the compressed movie option only plays in Flash Player 6 or later. Compression is especially useful for a text-intensive Flash document.

properties you set as you worked with the photos override these JPEG settings. This movie includes no sounds, so the audio settings are not used. Aly wants you to generate a size report, which shows the size of the different parts of the movie. The report is created as a text file using the FLA file's name plus the word Report followed by the extension .txt. The report also appears in the Output panel after the file is published.

To publish the photosBanner.fla file in the SWF file format:

▶ 1. If you took a break after the previous session, make sure the photosBanner.fla and jennysLogo.fla files are open, the workspace is reset to the Essentials layout, and the photosBanner.fla document is active.

▶ 2. On the Application bar, click **File**, and then click **Publish Settings**. The Publish Settings dialog box opens to the Formats tab. See Figure 6-36.

Figure 6-36   Formats tab in the Publish Settings dialog box

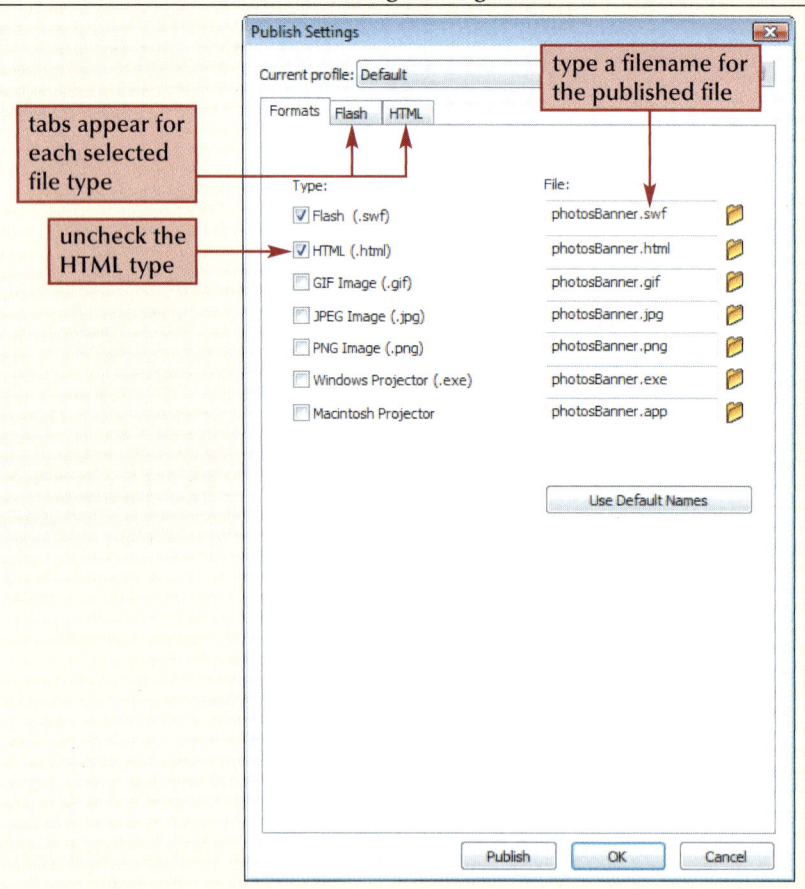

▶ 3. On the Formats tab, click the **HTML (.html)** check box to remove the check mark and its corresponding tab, and then make sure that the **Flash (.swf)** check box is checked. You want to publish the banner only in the Flash format.

▶ 4. In the File box to the right of Flash (.swf), type **banner.swf** to specify the name for the published SWF file.

▶ 5. To the right of the Flash (.swf) File box, click the **Select Publish Destination** button. The Select Publish Destination dialog box opens.

▶ 6. Navigate to the **Tutorial.06\Tutorial** folder included with your Data Files, if necessary, and then click the **Save** button to specify the folder in which to save the published SWF file.

▶ 7. In the Publish Settings dialog box, click the **Flash** tab to display the settings for this format. You will set the publishing options for the published movie on this tab.

▶ 8. Click the **Player** button, and then click **Flash Player 7**. You selected the earlier version so that the movie can be played on all computers with Flash Player 7 or later. You'll leave ActionScript 2.0 as the script version because the banner does not use ActionScript.

▶ 9. In the SWF Settings section, click the **Compress movie** check box to remove the check mark. You don't need to compress the movie because it is not a large file.

▶ 10. In the SWF Settings section, click the **Include hidden layers** check box to remove the check mark. The movie doesn't have any hidden layers, so you don't need this option.

▶ 11. In the SWF Settings section, click the **Include XMP metadata** check box to remove the check mark.

▶ 12. In the Advanced section, click the **Generate size report** check box to insert a check mark. The report will specify how big each part of the movie is. See Figure 6-37.

Figure 6-37   Flash publish settings

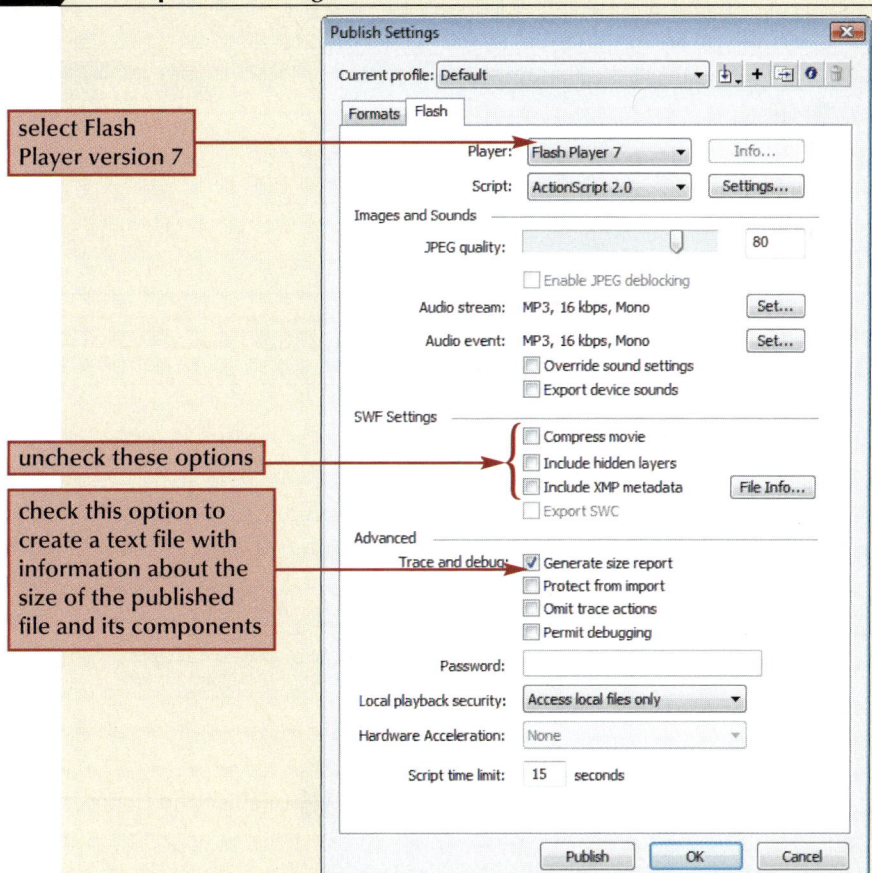

▶ 13. Click the **Publish** button. The Publish Settings dialog box remains open, and the SWF file and the size report file are created in the same folder as the FLA file. The report also appears in the Output panel.

▶ 14. Click the **OK** button to close the Publish Settings dialog box.

You'll review the size report text file generated by Flash when you published the banner. The file opens in the Output panel, but you can also open it in Notepad, which is part of Windows. The report file shows information about the movie, including its number of frames, the total size of the movie in bytes, a list of the symbols in the movie, and a list of the bitmaps. This information can be useful when optimizing a larger, more complex movie to find ways to reduce its size. You will view the report in the Output panel.

To view the size report file in the Output panel:

▶ 1. Drag the Output panel to the center of the Stage.

   Trouble? If the Output panel is not open, you need to open it manually. On the Application bar, click Window, and then click Output.

▶ 2. Drag the lower edge of the Output panel to enlarge the panel as needed, and then scroll to the top of the panel to view the report. The report shows that the movie is 31260 bytes in size, has three symbols with a total size of 61 bytes, and has two bitmaps, each of which is compressed. See Figure 6-38.

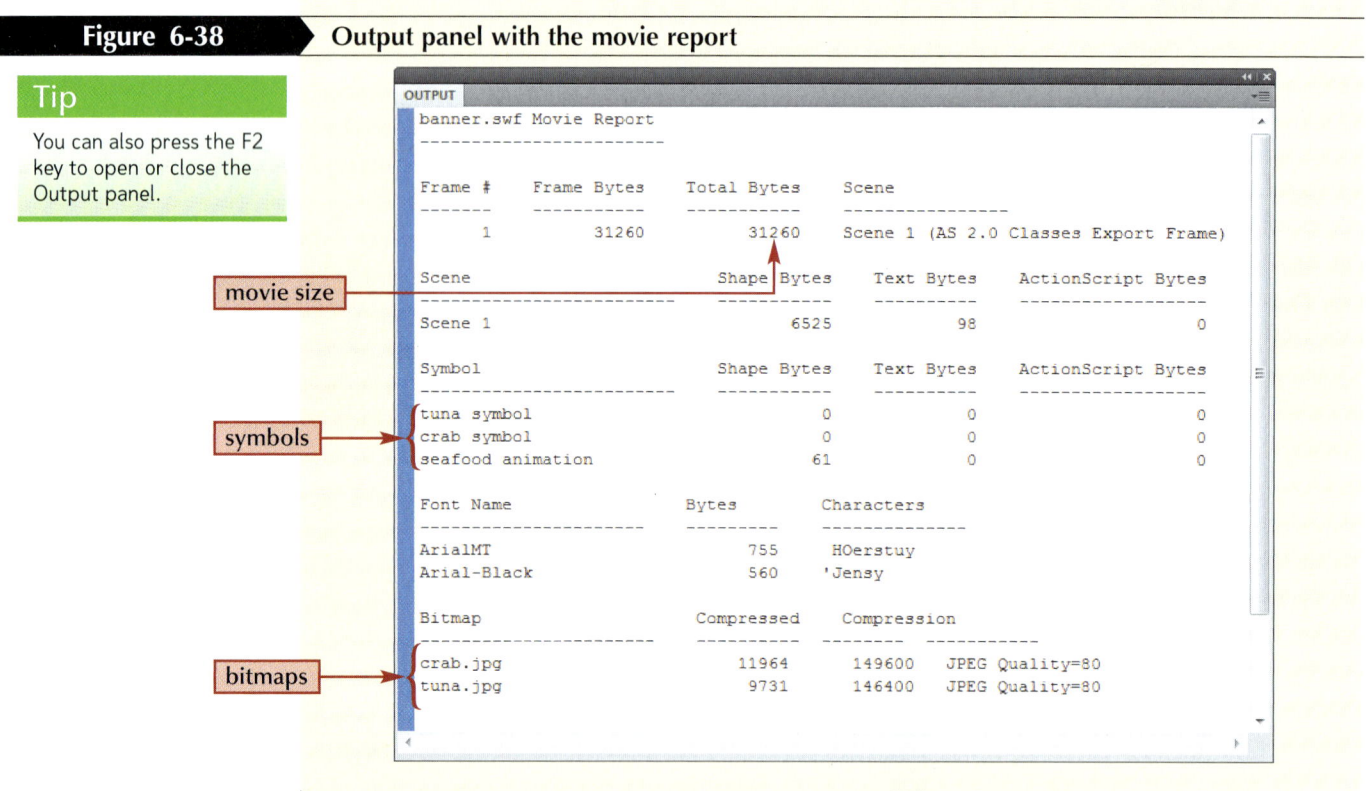

Figure 6-38 | Output panel with the movie report

Tip
You can also press the F2 key to open or close the Output panel.

```
OUTPUT
banner.swf Movie Report
------------------------

Frame #      Frame Bytes    Total Bytes    Scene
-------      -----------    -----------    -----
    1            31260          31260      Scene 1 (AS 2.0 Classes Export Frame)

Scene                       Shape Bytes    Text Bytes     ActionScript Bytes
-----                       -----------    ----------     ------------------
Scene 1                         6525           98                  0

Symbol                      Shape Bytes    Text Bytes     ActionScript Bytes
------                      -----------    ----------     ------------------
tuna symbol                      0             0                   0
crab symbol                      0             0                   0
seafood animation               61             0                   0

Font Name                   Bytes          Characters
---------                   -----          ----------
ArialMT                      755           HOerstuy
Arial-Black                  560           'Jensy

Bitmap                      Compressed     Compression
------                      ----------     -----------
crab.jpg                     11964          149600         JPEG Quality=80
tuna.jpg                      9731          146400         JPEG Quality=80
```

movie size → (points to 31260)
symbols → (points to tuna symbol, crab symbol, seafood animation)
bitmaps → (points to crab.jpg, tuna.jpg)

▶ 3. On the Output panel, click the **Close** button ✕ to close the panel.

You can save your preferred publish settings for a document, including the Flash and HTML settings, as a **publish profile**. The settings in the publish profile are available to any document you create in Flash on the same computer. After you save a publish profile, the Publish command publishes the files according to the settings saved in the profile. A profile can be deleted in the Publish Settings dialog box. Also, if you remove HTML (.html) as a format for a file, the Publish Preview command will default to the first format selected in the Formats tab of the Publish Settings dialog box. You'll create a publish profile for all the Jenny's Oyster Hut documents.

To create a publish profile for the Jenny's Oyster Hut documents:

▶ 1. On the Application bar, click **File**, and then click **Publish Settings**. The Publish Settings dialog box opens.

▶ 2. Click the **Create new profile** button [+]. The Create New Profile dialog box opens.

▶ 3. Type **Oyster Hut** in the Profile name box, and then click the **OK** button. The Oyster Hut profile is created and appears as the current profile in the Publish Settings dialog box. All the settings revert to the defaults. See Figure 6-39.

Figure 6-39 | Publish Settings dialog box with a publish profile

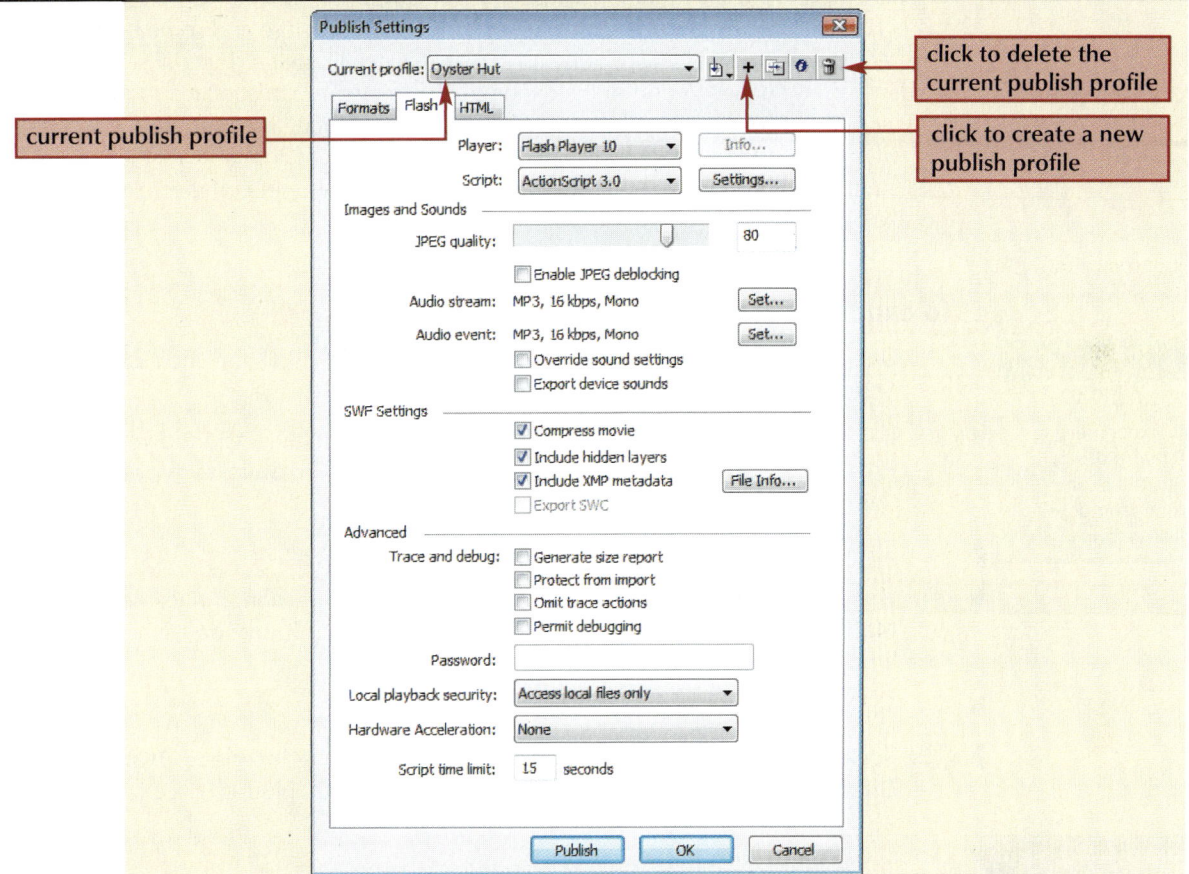

▶ 4. Click the **Player** button, and then click **Flash Player 9** to select this version.

▶ 5. In the SWF Settings section, click the **Compress movie** check box to remove the check mark.

▶ 6. Click the **Publish** button to publish the SWF and HTML files.

Aly wants to check some statistics about the target users and the version of Flash they might have on their computers. So you will delete this publish profile.

▶ 7. In the Publish Settings dialog box, click the **Delete profile** button, and then click the **OK** button in the dialog box that opens to confirm the deletion. The Oyster Hut profile is not saved, but you can easily create a new publish profile at any time.

▶ 8. Click the **OK** button to close the Publish Settings dialog box.

▶ 9. Save and close the photosBanner.fla document.

Exporting a Flash Document as an Image

The JPEG and GIF file formats are the most common file formats used for images in Web pages. JPEG format is best for images that include many colors, such as the original photograph of the lobster. GIF format is best for images with fewer colors, such as the lobster bitmap you converted to a vector for the logo. You can use the Publish Settings dialog box to select JPEG or GIF as the format in which to publish. You can also use the Export Image command, which allows you to specify the type of format you want to export to and then displays settings you can change based on the selected file format. Some of the formats you can export to include JPEG Image (*.jpg), GIF Image (*.gif), and PNG (*.png).

Because the logo you created is static, includes only a picture and some text, and contains mostly solid areas of color, you can export it as a GIF image. The GIF settings include the dimensions and resolution of the exported GIF image, the image area to export, and the number of colors to export. If the document has empty space, the Minimum Image Area setting will not export the empty space. The standard number of colors in a GIF image is 256, but if an image uses fewer colors, you can reduce the number of colors to export, shrinking the size of the file.

To export the logo as a GIF image:

Tip

The Publish command saves the export settings you select with the document; the Export Image command does not store these settings.

1. On the Application bar, click **File**, point to **Export**, and then click **Export Image**. The Export Image dialog box opens.

2. If necessary, navigate to the **Tutorial.06\Tutorial** folder included with your Data Files, type **jennysLogo** in the File name box, click the **Save as type** button, and then click **GIF Image (*.gif)**.

3. Click the **Save** button. The Export GIF dialog box opens.

4. Make sure Include is set to **Full Document Size**, and then, if necessary, click the **Match Screen** button to change the dimensions to 200 by 136 pixels and the resolution to 72 dpi.

5. Make sure Colors is set to **Standard colors**.

6. Make sure the **Smooth** check box is checked and the **Interlace**, **Transparent**, and **Dither solid colors** check boxes are unchecked. See Figure 6-40.

Figure 6-40 Export GIF dialog box

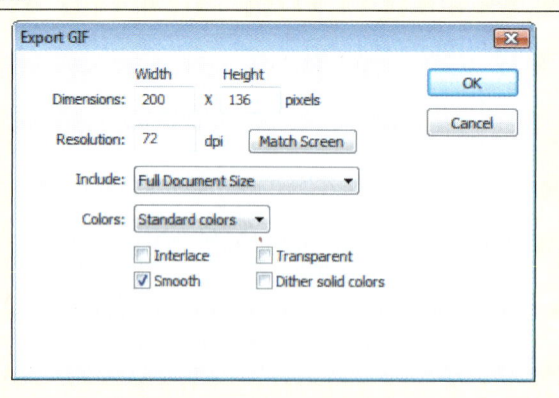

7. Click the **OK** button. The dialog box closes, and the logo is saved as a GIF image.

8. Close the jennysLogo.fla document.

Adding Flash Graphics to a Web Page

The final output of creating movies with Flash is a Web page that displays the movies along with text, hyperlinks, and other graphics. After you complete a Flash graphic, such as a banner or a logo, you need to incorporate its file information into the Web page's HTML. When you publish a movie with the HTML format option, Flash creates a simple Web page to display the movie. More often, you'll want to add the SWF file to an existing Web page, which requires you to edit the actual Web page. You can do this with a Web page editing program such as Adobe Dreamweaver. You can also edit the HTML in a text editor such as Notepad.

The published banner and exported logo are ready to be placed in a Web page that Chris created. The Web page has a simple banner and logo that you will replace. You will edit the Web page using Notepad.

To add the banner and logo to a sample Web page:

1. Click the **Start** button on the taskbar, click **All Programs**, click **Accessories**, and then click **Notepad**. The Notepad program starts.

2. On the Notepad menu bar, click **File**, and then click **Open**. The Open File dialog box opens.

3. Navigate to the **Tutorial.06\Tutorial** folder included with your Data Files, set the file type to **All Files**, click **sample.htm** in the file list, and then click the **Open** button. The HTML for the sample Web page opens in the Notepad window.

4. Click the **Maximize** button on the title bar to maximize the program window. See Figure 6-41.

Figure 6-41   Sample Web page HTML

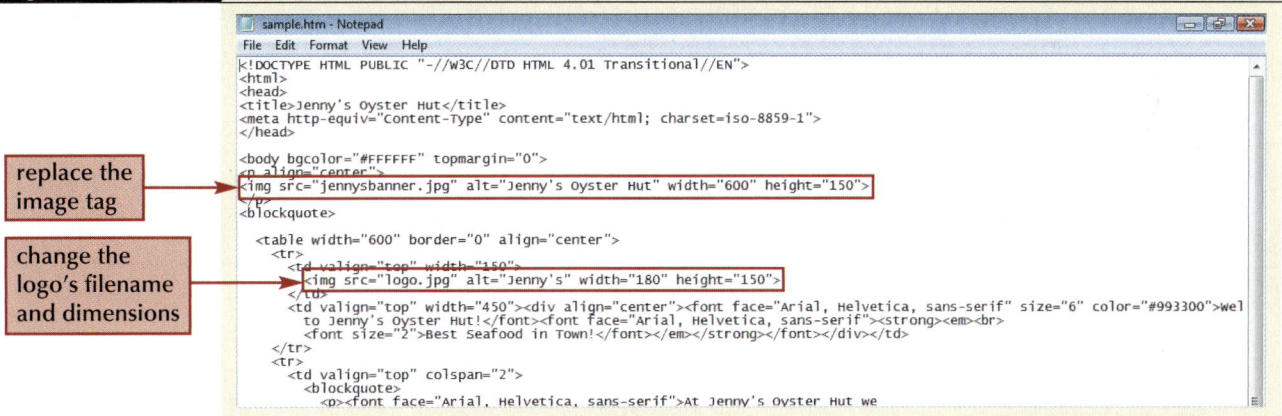

The tenth line contains the image tag `<img src= "jennysbanner.jpg" alt="Jenny's Oyster Hut" width="600" height="150" >` that places the current banner at the top of the Web page. You need to replace this tag with a special EMBED tag for the SWF file. EMBED is not a standard HTML tag, but is used to load external media such as an SWF movie that requires the use of a plug-in.

> **Tip**
>
> When possible, use an HTML editor such as Adobe Dreamweaver to insert Flash graphics into a Web page. Dreamweaver inserts code in addition to the embed tag so that Flash movies are displayed properly in most browsers.

▶ 5. In line 10, replace the image tag, including the two angle brackets, with the following code: `<embed src="banner.swf" width="500" height="250">`

You need to replace the reference for the current logo with a reference for the new logo file, jennysLogo.gif, and then update the logo's dimensions.

▶ 6. On line 17, replace `logo.jpg` with `jennysLogo.gif`. The code references the logo you created.

▶ 7. On line 17, replace `width="180" height="150"` with `width="200" height="136"`. The code includes the correct dimensions for the logo.

▶ 8. Save and close the file, and then exit Notepad. The Web page is updated with the new banner and logo.

You changed the HTML of the sample Web page so that the page will display the animated banner and logo that you created for Jenny's Oyster Hut. You will test the Web page by opening the page in your browser.

To preview the sample.htm Web page:

▶ 1. Start your Web browser, and then, if necessary, click the **Tools** button and click **Menu Bar** to display the menu bar.

▶ 2. On the menu bar, click **File**, and then click **Open**. The Open dialog box opens.

▶ 3. Click the **Browse** button, navigate to the **Tutorial.06\Tutorial** folder included with your Data Files, click **sample.htm** in the file list, and then click the **Open** button. The file path to the sample Web page appears in the Open box.

▶ 4. Click the **OK** button, and then click the **Tools** button and click **Menu Bar** to hide the menu bar. The sample Web page opens in the browser window. The banner at the top of the page plays the animation and the logo appears below the banner. See Figure 6-42.

Tutorial 6 Creating Special Effects with Graphics and Gradients | Flash | FL 303

Figure 6-42 | Sample Web page with Flash graphics

new banner

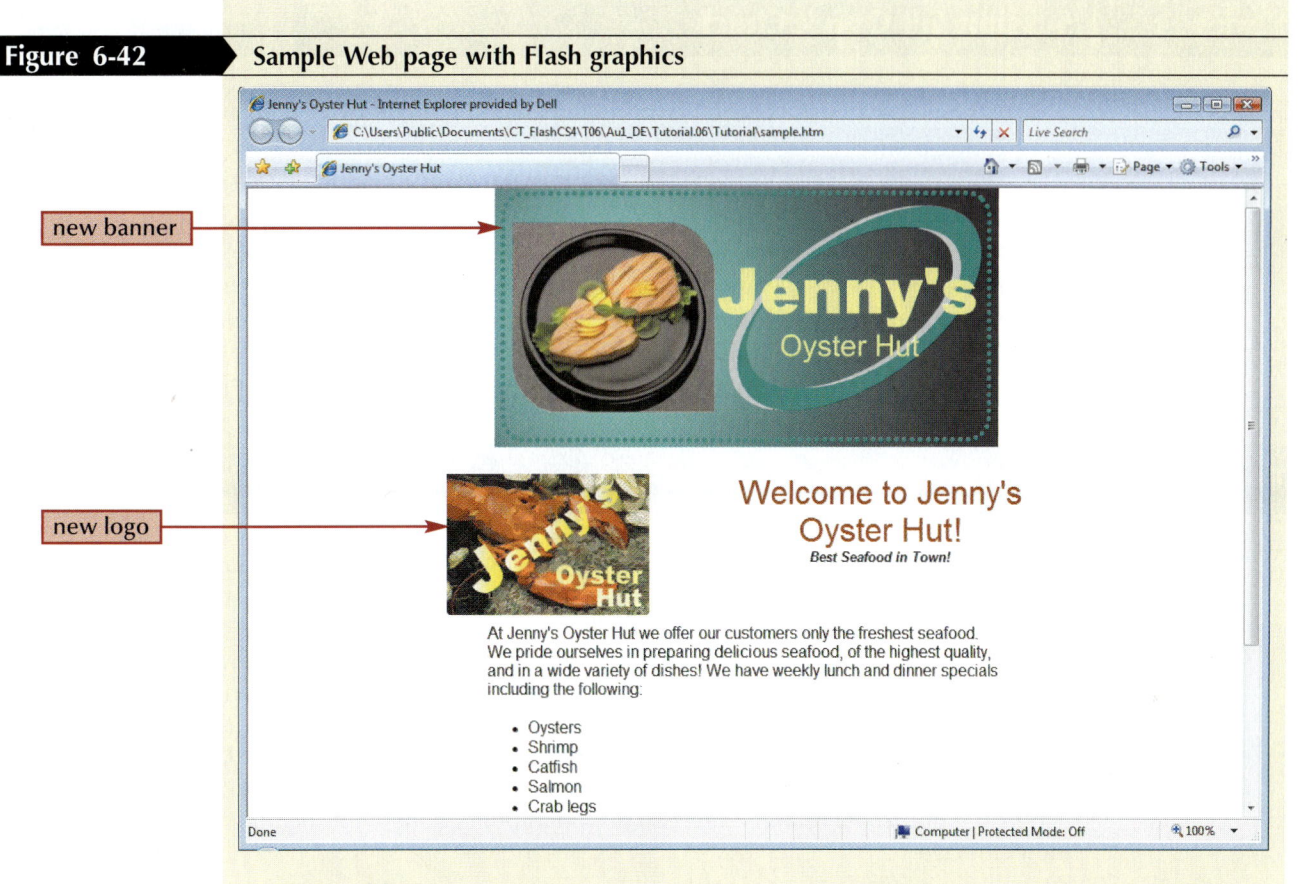

new logo

Trouble? If a dialog box opens, indicating that Internet Explorer needs to open a new window to display the Web page, click the OK button. The page opens a new window.

Trouble? If a security warning appears in the Information Bar, you need to allow blocked content to view the page. Click the Information Bar, click Allow Blocked Content, and then click the Yes button in the Security Warning dialog box.

5. Close the browser window when you are done previewing the Web page.

Aly likes the look of the new banner and logo in the Web page and will present the finished pieces to Jenny at their next meeting. In this session, you published the Jenny's Oyster Hut banner and you exported a logo for the restaurant's Web site. You also edited a sample Web page to incorporate references for the new banner and logo.

Review | Session 6.3 Quick Check

1. What is the purpose of the Player setting in the Flash tab of the Publish Settings dialog box?
2. What is the purpose of the Script setting in the Flash tab of the Publish Settings dialog box?
3. How do you display the GIF tab in the Publish Settings dialog box?
4. How can you use the information generated by a size report when publishing a file?
5. Why would you save a document's publish settings in a publish profile?
6. What is the purpose of the EMBED tag?
7. True or False? To add an SWF file to an existing Web page, you must use Notepad.

Review | Tutorial Summary

In this tutorial, you worked with bitmaps. You imported bitmap graphics into a Flash document, changed the bitmap properties, and then created a movie clip animation using the bitmaps. You also converted a bitmap graphic to a vector graphic and used the resulting graphic to create a logo. Next, you used preset gradients. You created a new gradient using the Color panel, saved the new gradient within a document, and then applied the gradient to an object on the Stage. You also applied a gradient to text and then modified the applied gradient. Finally, you learned about the publishing options in Flash. You explored the publishing settings, and then you published a document as an SWF file and exported a document as a GIF file. You also incorporated the published files into an existing Web page.

Key Terms

alpha amount	gradient	lossy compression
color pointer	linear gradient	publish profile
compression	lossless compression	radial gradient
fall-off point		

Tutorial 6 Creating Special Effects with Graphics and Gradients | Flash | FL 305

Practice | Review Assignments

Practice the skills you learned in the tutorial.

Data Files needed for the Review Assignments: jennysAlt.fla, salmon.jpg, sampleAlt.htm, hutBanner.jpg

Aly wants you to make some changes to an alternate version of the Jenny's Oyster Hut banner before she shows it to Jenny. She wants you to add a salmon bitmap in the seafood animation. The salmon bitmap will appear after the fish bitmap, be displayed for two seconds, and then fade out while the salmon bitmap fades in. This will extend the animation by three seconds. She also asks you to change the letters in the Jenny's text block to a gradient fill.

1. Open the **jennysAlt.fla** file located in the Tutorial.06\Review folder included with your Data Files, and then save the banner as **jennysAlternate.fla** in the same folder.
2. Import the **salmon.jpg** bitmap located in the Tutorial.06\Review folder included with your Data Files into the document's library. Modify the salmon bitmap's properties so that the quality value is 80.
3. Open the seafood animation movie clip in symbol-editing mode, add a new layer above the shrimp layer and name it **salmon**. Make sure the salmon layer is indented under the mask layer. Temporarily hide the contents of the fish layer, the shrimp layer, and the mask layer while you work with the salmon layer.
4. At Frame 120 of the salmon layer, insert a keyframe, and then drag a copy of the salmon bitmap to the Stage. In the Info panel, set the X and Y values to 0 and make sure the center registration point is selected. Convert the salmon.jpg bitmap into a movie clip symbol named **salmon symbol** with the center registration point selected.
5. At Frame 144 of the salmon layer, insert a keyframe. At Frame 120, change the alpha amount of the salmon symbol to 0%. At Frame 144, make sure the alpha amount is 100%. Create a motion tween at Frame 120. Insert a color property keyframe at Frame 143 and set the alpha amount to 100%.
6. At Frame 216 of all the layers, add regular frames to extend the layers.
7. In the salmon layer, insert a keyframe at Frame 192 and at Frame 216. At Frame 216, change the alpha amount of the salmon symbol to 0%. Create a motion tween at Frame 192. Insert a color property keyframe at Frame 215 and set the alpha amount to 0%.
8. Temporarily hide the contents of the salmon layer and show the contents of the fish layer. Select Frames 120 through 144 of the fish layer, and then drag the selected frames to the right, placing them in Frames 192 through 216 of the fish layer.
9. Show all the layers, lock all the layers, test the animation, and then exit symbol-editing mode.
10. On the Stage, select the Jenny's text block, and then apply the Break Apart command twice to convert the text to fills.
11. With the text still selected, use the Color panel to select the white-to-black linear gradient, change the color of the left color pointer to #FF6600, and leave the right color pointer at #000000.
12. Publish the banner as an SWF file with the name **altBanner.swf**, and then change the Flash publish settings to uncheck the SWF Settings options and do not generate a size report.
13. In your text editor, open the **sampleAlt.htm** Web page located in the Tutorial.06\Review folder included with your Data Files, replace the image tag that has the hutBanner.jpg reference to an EMBED tag with the altBanner.swf reference using the statement **<embed src="altBanner.swf" width="500" height="250">** so that the Web page will display the new banner.

14. Save and close the sampleAlt.htm file, and then preview sampleAlt.htm in a Web browser.
15. Submit the finished files to your instructor.

| Apply | Case Problem 1 |

Create and then export a logo with a bitmap fade animation and a gradient fill for the letter.

Data Files needed for this Case Problem: kprLogo.fla, pet1.jpg, pet2.jpg

Katie's Pet Resort Katie asks John to develop a new logo for the resort's Web site. She wants the logo to include two pictures that each are displayed for a few seconds at a time. John asks you to create an animation of the pictures where one fades out while the other fades in to use as the background for the logo. He also wants you to create a gradient to use as the fill for the letters in the logo. Figure 6-43 shows the completed logo.

Figure 6-43

1. Open the **kprLogo.fla** file located in the Tutorial.06\Case1 folder included with your Data Files, and then save the document as **katieLogo.fla** in the same folder.
2. Import the **pet1.jpg** and **pet2.jpg** bitmaps located in the Tutorial.06\Case1 folder included with your Data Files directly into the document's library. Modify each bitmap's properties by changing the compression quality to 80%.
3. Create a new movie clip symbol named **resort animation**. In symbol-editing mode, drag an instance of the pet1.jpg bitmap to the center of the Stage, and then, in the Info panel, set its X and Y coordinates to 0, and, if necessary, select the center registration point. Convert the bitmap instance to a movie clip symbol named **pet1 symbol**. Rename Layer 1 to **pet1**.
4. In the pet1 layer, insert keyframes at Frames 36 and 48. At Frame 36, set the alpha amount for the pet1 symbol instance to 100%. At Frame 48, change the alpha amount for the pet1 symbol instance to 0%. Create a motion tween at Frame 36, and then add a color property keyframe at Frame 47 and set the alpha amount for the pet1 symbol instance to 0% so that the pet1 symbol instance fades out between Frames 36 and 48.

5. In the pet1 layer, insert a keyframe at Frame 84, create a motion tween at Frame 84, extend the motion tween to Frame 96, add a color property keyframe at Frame 96, and then set the alpha amount for the pet1 symbol instance to 100% so that the pet1 symbol instance fades in between Frames 84 and 96.
6. In the Timeline, add a new layer and name it **pet2**. In Frame 36, insert a keyframe, and then add an instance of the pet2.jpg bitmap to the Stage. In the Info panel, center the bitmap on the Stage and select its center registration point. Convert the pet2.jpg bitmap instance to a movie clip symbol named **pet2 symbol**.
7. In the pet2 layer, insert a keyframe at Frame 48. In Frame 36, change the alpha amount of the pet2 symbol to 0%. Create a motion tween at Frame 36, and then add a color property keyframe at Frame 47 and set the alpha amount for the pet2 symbol instance to 100% so that the pet2 symbol instance fades in between Frames 36 and 48.
8. In the pet2 layer, insert a keyframe at Frame 84, set the alpha amount for the pet2 symbol instance to 100%, create a motion tween, and then insert a color property keyframe at Frame 96 and set the alpha amount to 0% so that the pet2 symbol instance fades out between Frames 84 and 96. Exit symbol-editing mode.
9. In the Timeline, select the background layer, and then drag a copy of the resort animation from the library to the center of the Stage. In the Align panel, align the bitmap to the left edge and the top edge of the Stage. Lock the background layer.
10. In the pet resort layer, change the text to fills by applying the Break Apart command twice.
11. In the Swatches panel, select the gray radial gradient. In the Color panel, change the color of the right color pointer to #CC0000. The text now has a white to red gradient. Deselect the text, and then lock the pet resort layer.
12. Publish the logo in the SWF, HTML, and JPEG file formats. Use the default names and settings for the published files.
13. Preview the logo in a Web browser using the HTML file created by Flash.
14. Submit the finished files to your instructor.

Apply	Case Problem 2

Create and then publish a logo with a background that includes an imported bitmap and a custom gradient with transparency.

Data Files needed for this Case Problem: aczLogo.fla, giraffe.jpg

Alamo City Zoo Janet asks Alex to create a new logo that can be used as an advertisement on other Web sites to promote the Alamo City Zoo's new giraffe exhibit. Alex suggests that the logo include a picture of a giraffe and use a gradient in the background. To complete the logo, you need to import a bitmap of a giraffe and then add the bitmap as a background for the logo. You will also add a rectangle with a radial gradient that is partially transparent over the bitmap to enhance the logo. Figure 6-44 shows the completed logo.

Figure 6-44

[Figure shows Alamo City Zoo logo with giraffe and "New Giraffe Exhibit Now Open!" text]

1. Open the **aczLogo.fla** file located in the Tutorial.06\Case2 folder included with your Data Files, and then save the document as **zooLogo.fla** in the same folder.
2. Import the **giraffe.jpg** bitmap located in the Tutorial.06\Case2 folder included with your Data Files to the document's library, and then change the bitmap's compression quality to 80%.
3. In the background layer, drag a copy of the giraffe bitmap from the library to the center of the Stage. In the Position and Size section of the Property inspector, set the X and Y coordinates to 0. Lock the background layer.
4. In the Timeline, insert a new layer above the background layer and name it **gradient**. In the Swatches panel, select the gray radial gradient. In the Color panel, change the Hex value of the right color pointer to #FFFF99.

EXPLORE

5. In the Color panel, set the alpha amount to 10% to make the gradient partially transparent.
6. In the gradient layer, draw a rectangle with no stroke and the new gradient as its fill that covers the entire Stage. If necessary, in the Property inspector, set the X and Y coordinates to 0, set the width to 300, and set the height to 225.
7. With the rectangle still selected, use the Gradient Transform tool to display the gradient's bounding circle. Drag the middle editing handle on the lower-right side of the bounding circle to reduce the gradient's radius to about half its original size.
8. Drag the gradient's center point to the upper-left corner of the Stage between the letters A and l in the Alamo text.
9. In the Publish Settings dialog box, create a new profile and name it **zooProfile**. Set the zooProfile to publish a Flash file, an HTML file, and a JPEG image file using the default names.
10. In the Flash publish settings, change the player version to Flash Player 8 and do not export hidden layers. In the HTML publish settings, in the Playback section, do not display the menu and do not loop. In the JPEG publish settings, change the quality value to 90. Publish the files.
11. Preview the logo in a browser using the HTML file created by Flash.
12. Submit the finished files to your instructor.

Tutorial 6 Creating Special Effects with Graphics and Gradients | Flash | FL 309

| Challenge | Case Problem 3 |

Create and publish an animated logo that includes imported bitmaps in an animation with a mask and an animated gradient that highlights the title text.

Data Files needed for this Case Problem: wcnLogo.fla, flower1.jpg, flower2.jpg, flower3.jpg

Westcreek Nursery   Alice and her staff like the interactive logo developed for the Westcreek Nursery Web site, but think that pictures of flowers in an animation could enhance the logo even more. Amanda agrees and wants you to add some sample pictures of flowers to the logo. Amanda also suggests changing the logo's title to make it more dynamic. You'll help Amanda revise the logo by creating an animation with the flower bitmaps and adding a new, more dynamic title. Figure 6-45 shows the completed logo.

Figure 6-45

1. Open the **wcnLogo.fla** file located in the Tutorial.06\Case3 folder included with your Data Files, and then save the document as **flowerLogo.fla** in the same folder.
2. Import the **flower1.jpg**, **flower2.jpg**, and **flower3.jpg** bitmaps located in the Tutorial.06\Case3 folder included with your Data Files to the document's library. Modify the properties of each bitmap to have a compression quality of 80%.
3. Create a new movie clip symbol named **flower animation**. In symbol-editing mode, extend Layer 1 to Frame 90, rename Layer 1 to **flower1**, drag an instance of the flower1 bitmap to the center of the Stage, and then use the Info panel to center it on the Stage.
4. Convert the flower1 bitmap instance to a movie clip symbol named **flower1 symbol**. Create a motion tween between Frames 10 and 20 to fade out the flower1 symbol instance (the alpha amount should be 100% at Frame 10 and 0% at Frame 20). Create a motion tween between Frames 80 and 90 to fade in the flower1 symbol (the alpha amount should be 0% at Frame 80 and 100% at Frame 90).
5. Insert a new layer and name it **flower2**. In Frame 20, insert a keyframe and then drag an instance of the flower2 bitmap to the center of the Stage, using the Info panel to center it.
6. Convert the flower2 bitmap instance to a movie clip symbol named **flower2 symbol**. Create a motion tween between Frames 20 and 30 to fade in the flower2 symbol. Create a motion tween between Frames 40 and 50 to fade out the flower2 symbol.

7. Insert a new layer and name it **flower3**. In Frame 50, insert a keyframe, and then drag an instance of the flower3 bitmap to the center of the Stage, using the Info panel to center it on the Stage.
8. Convert the flower3 bitmap instance to a movie clip symbol named **flower3 symbol**. Create a motion tween between Frames 50 and 60 to fade in the flower3 symbol. Create a motion tween between Frames 70 and 80 to fade out the flower3 symbol.
9. Insert a new layer above the flower3 layer and name it **mask**. Change it to a mask layer, and then change all of the flower layers into masked layers. The flower layers should all be indented under the mask layer.

EXPLORE

10. In the mask layer, draw a five-sided star shape with a point size of 0.50, no stroke, and a fill color of your choice. In the Info panel, set the star shape's width to 200, its height to 195, and its X and Y coordinates to 0. Lock all of the layers. Exit symbol-editing mode. (*Hint*: To draw a star shape, select the PolyStar tool in the Tools panel, click the Options button in the Tools Settings section of the Property inspector, and then set the appropriate options in the Tool Settings dialog box.)
11. Insert a new layer and name it **star**. Move the star layer below the content layer. In the star layer, add an instance of the flower animation symbol to the center of the Stage.
12. Open the title symbol in symbol-editing mode. Copy the text block in the title text layer. Add a new layer and name it **title mask**. In this layer, use the Paste in Place command to paste a copy of the text in the same relative position as in the title text layer. If necessary, deselect the text.

EXPLORE

13. Create a new linear gradient. Select the gray linear gradient from the Swatches panel as a starting point. In the Color panel, add two more color pointers close together in the center of the gradient definition bar. Make these two new gradient colors white (#FFFFFF). Make the far left gradient color black (#000000). The middle of the gradient has a narrow white band. (*Hint*: Click the color definition bar to place a new color pointer.)
14. Insert a new layer above the title text layer and name it **gradient**. In the gradient layer, draw a rectangle with the gradient you created as the fill and with no stroke that covers "West" in Westcreek and is 150 pixels wide and 55 pixels high.
15. Convert the rectangle to a movie clip symbol name **gradient symbol**. Extend all the layers to Frame 20. Insert keyframes in the gradient layer at Frames 10 and 20. In Frame 10 of the gradient layer, move the gradient instance to the right so that it covers the last four letters ("reek") of Westcreek. Create motion tweens at Frames 1 and 10.
16. Change the title mask layer to a mask layer, and make sure the gradient layer becomes the masked layer. The letters mask the gradient, giving the text a moving highlight effect. Exit symbol-editing mode.
17. In the Publish Settings dialog box, create a new profile and name it **wcnProfile**. Set the profile to publish a Flash file, an HTML file, a GIF file, and a PNG file using the default filenames.
18. In the Flash publish settings, change the Player to Flash Player 9, and then check the Compress movie, Include hidden layers, Include XMP metadata, and Protect from import options. In the HTML publish settings, use the default settings. In the GIF publish settings, check the Optimize colors, Interlace, Smooth, and Dither solids options. In the PNG publish settings, set the Bit depth to 24-bit. Publish the files.

EXPLORE

19. Export the new profile and save it with its default name in the Tutorial.06\Case3 folder included with your Data Files. (*Hint*: Click the Import/export profile button in the Publish Settings dialog box, and then click Export.)

Tutorial 6 Creating Special Effects with Graphics and Gradients | Flash | FL 311

20. Preview the logo in a browser using the HTML file created by Flash. Make sure the flowers within the star fade in and out and the Westcreek text has the gradient moving through its letters.
21. Submit the finished files to your instructor.

Create | Case Problem 4

Create and publish a banner that uses a bitmap background and custom gradients applied to graphics.

Data File needed for this Case Problem: mission.jpg

Missions Support Association   Brittany asks Anissa to create a new banner that can be used on the Missions Support Association Web site to promote the association to its members. The banner should include the mission.jpg bitmap (which has the dimensions of 300 pixels x 300 pixels), motion tweens that create a fade effect for a symbol instance, and gradients. You will design and create the new banner. Figure 6-46 shows one possible banner.

Figure 6-46

1. Create a new document, and then save it as **msaPromotion.fla** in the Tutorial.06\Case4 folder included with your Data Files. Edit the document properties to set the dimensions and Stage color appropriately.
2. Import the **mission.jpg** bitmap located in the Tutorial.06\Case4 folder included with your Data Files to the document's library. Modify the properties of the bitmap to allow smoothing and to have a quality setting of 80%.
3. Create a fade effect using the mission.jpg bitmap somewhere in the banner design. For example, you could create a movie clip symbol of the bitmap and have the image fade in as the banner's background.
4. Add the association's name, **Missions Support Association**, to the banner, using the properties of your choice. For example, you can create a movie clip symbol that includes the text block on a background shape with a custom gradient that fades in or moves onto the banner.
5. Add the key points about the association to the banner, using the text properties of your choice. You can use the text **Special events**, **Volunteer opportunities**, and **Educational tours**, or make up your own. For example, you could make the text fade in and then fade out of the banner.

6. Use at least one gradient fill color in the banner. Customize the fill color to match your banner design. Transform the gradient appropriately.
7. Publish the banner as a Flash file and an HTML file using the default filenames. In the Flash publish settings, check the Protect from import, Compress movie, Export hidden layers, and Include XMP metadata options. In the HTML publish settings, use the default options.
8. Preview the logo in a browser using the HTML file created by Flash.
9. Submit the finished files to your instructor.

Review | Quick Check Answers

Session 6.1

1. a graphic that is stored as a row-by-row list of pixels, along with each pixel's color information
2. Both commands place the imported bitmap into the library. The Import to Stage command also places an instance of the bitmap on the Stage.
3. Select the bitmap in the library and then double-click the bitmap icon in the Library panel, or click the Properties button.
4. for bitmaps with many colors or many color transitions, such as photographs
5. 0%
6. the Trace Bitmap command
7. The color threshold value determines how many colors are used. A smaller value results in more colors.

Session 6.2

1. a gradual blend or transition from one color to another
2. A linear gradient blends the colors from one point to another in a straight line. A radial gradient blends the colors from one point outward in a circular pattern.
3. In the Color panel, click the panel menu button, and then click Add Swatch.
4. True
5. Add another color pointer by clicking on or below the gradient definition bar.
6. False. The Gradient Transform tool is used to modify an existing gradient.
7. Draw a straight line with the Paint Bucket pointer. The line you draw determines the direction of the gradient.
8. Change the gradient's radius and rotate the gradient.

Session 6.3

1. to specify the oldest version of the Flash Player in which the published movie will play
2. to specify which version of ActionScript the published movie will use
3. Click the GIF Image (.gif) check box.
4. The size report includes the total size of the movie and the size of the movie's elements, such as its symbols and bitmaps, which can be used to reduce the size of the movie.
5. so that you can apply the same settings to another document created on the same computer
6. to load external media such as an SWF movie that requires the use of a plug-in
7. False. You can also add an SWF file to an existing Web page using Adobe Dreamweaver or other Web-page editing tools.

Ending Data Files

Tutorial.06 →

Tutorial
banner.swf
banner Report.txt
jennysLogo.fla
jennysLogo.gif
photosBanner.fla
photosBanner.html
photosBanner.swf
sample.htm

Review
altBanner.swf
jennysAlternate.fla
sampleAlt.htm

Case1
katieLogo.fla
katieLogo.html
katieLogo.jpg
katieLogo.swf

Case2
zooLogo.fla
zooLogo.html
zooLogo.jpg
zooLogo.swf

Case3
flowerLogo.fla
flowerLogo.gif
flowerLogo.html
flowerLogo.png
flowerLogo.swf
wcnProfile.xml

Case4
msaPromotion.fla
msaPromotion.html
msaPromotion.swf

Flash | FL 315

Tutorial 7

Objectives

Session 7.1
- Review the structure of a Flash Web site
- Plan and create a Flash Web site
- Review Web site accessibility

Session 7.2
- Create a Flash template and use the template to create Flash documents
- Make a Flash Web site accessible
- Work with external libraries
- Create a navigation bar with complex buttons

Session 7.3
- Load external SWF files into the Flash Player using levels
- Learn basic ActionScript 2.0 commands
- Use the Actions panel
- Load external image files into the Flash Player using a movie clip
- Use the Behaviors panel

Planning and Creating a Flash Web Site

Building a Site with a Template, a Navigation Bar, and ActionScript

Case | Admiral Web Design

Jackson's Sports, a local sports equipment and supply company, provides discounted equipment, team uniforms, and player trophies to youth basketball, baseball, softball, volleyball, and soccer teams. Dan Jackson, owner of the company, wants Admiral Web Design to develop a new Jackson's Youth Sports Web site that is accessible through links provided on the existing site and that focuses on services the company provides to local youth sports. The Web site will have a home page with appropriate graphic elements and a navigation scheme that will lead to the other key areas of the site. Chris, as site developer, suggests using Flash to develop the entire site—not just the graphic elements of the site. With Flash, the site can be more visually interesting and include multimedia elements such as team photos that change regularly to showcase different teams and players. You will work with Chris and Aly to plan and create the Web site.

In this tutorial, you will plan and create a Flash Web site based on the client's requirements. The Web site will include a navigation bar. You will use levels to load one SWF file on top of another in the Flash Player and use ActionScript commands to control how an SWF file is loaded. You will create a Flash template to create additional documents. You will also load external image files into a movie clip.

Starting Data Files

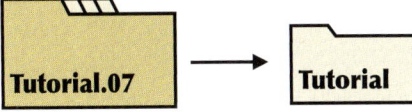

Tutorial.07

Tutorial
jSports.fla
leslies.fla
leslies.swf
lesliesHome.fla
lesliesHome.swf
lesliesLocation.fla
lesliesLocation.swf
lesliesSpecialties.fla
lesliesSpecialties.swf
photo1.jpg
photo2.jpg
soccer.jpg

Review
home.fla
home.swf
mainDraft.fla
photosDraft.fla
picture1.jpg
picture2.jpg
services.fla
services.swf
specialsDraft.fla
teams.fla
teams.swf

Case1
katies.fla
main.fla
welcome.fla

Case2
zooGraphics.fla

Case3
flower1.jpg
flower2.jpg
flower3.jpg
wcDraft.fla

Case4
mission.jpg

Session 7.1

Understanding the Structure of a Flash Web Site

Many of the Web sites you see on the Internet consist mainly of HTML or XHTML documents. XHTML is the latest version of HTML. These documents, often called **Web pages**, can contain text, graphics, hyperlinks, and multimedia elements such as those created with Flash. The animations and graphic elements you have created so far with Flash are all meant to be part of an HTML document. However, Flash can also be used to create a complete Web site that consists primarily of Flash SWF files and not HTML documents.

A Flash Web site includes a navigation system that allows users to move between the various SWF files. In some cases, a Web site is built in two versions, one using mostly HTML and one using mostly Flash. An organization might build an HTML version of the Web site in addition to the Flash version to accommodate users who don't have a fast Internet connection or users who don't have the latest version of the Flash Player installed on their computers. An example of a Flash Web site is shown in Figure 7-1.

Figure 7-1   Ford F-Series Truck Flash Web site

The SWF files that make up the Web site are referenced from an HTML document. The HTML document is usually created by the site developer using a program such as Adobe Dreamweaver. It can also be created in Flash by selecting the HTML format in the publish settings for the document. Notice that the URL of the Flash site shown does not reference an SWF file. Instead, the URL shows the path that leads to the site's default home page, which is an HTML document. The HTML document appears in the Web browser and then calls or references the SWF file that activates the Flash Player plug-in, which, in turn, enables the Web browser to play SWF files. Within the HTML document, the Flash Player plays the SWF file and initially displays the home or main page of the Web site. In the Web site shown in

Figure 7-1, when the user clicks the Dual-Stage Turbos button on the Ford F-Series page, another SWF file containing the dual-stage turbochargers information page loads into the Flash Player using the same HTML document, as shown in Figure 7-2.

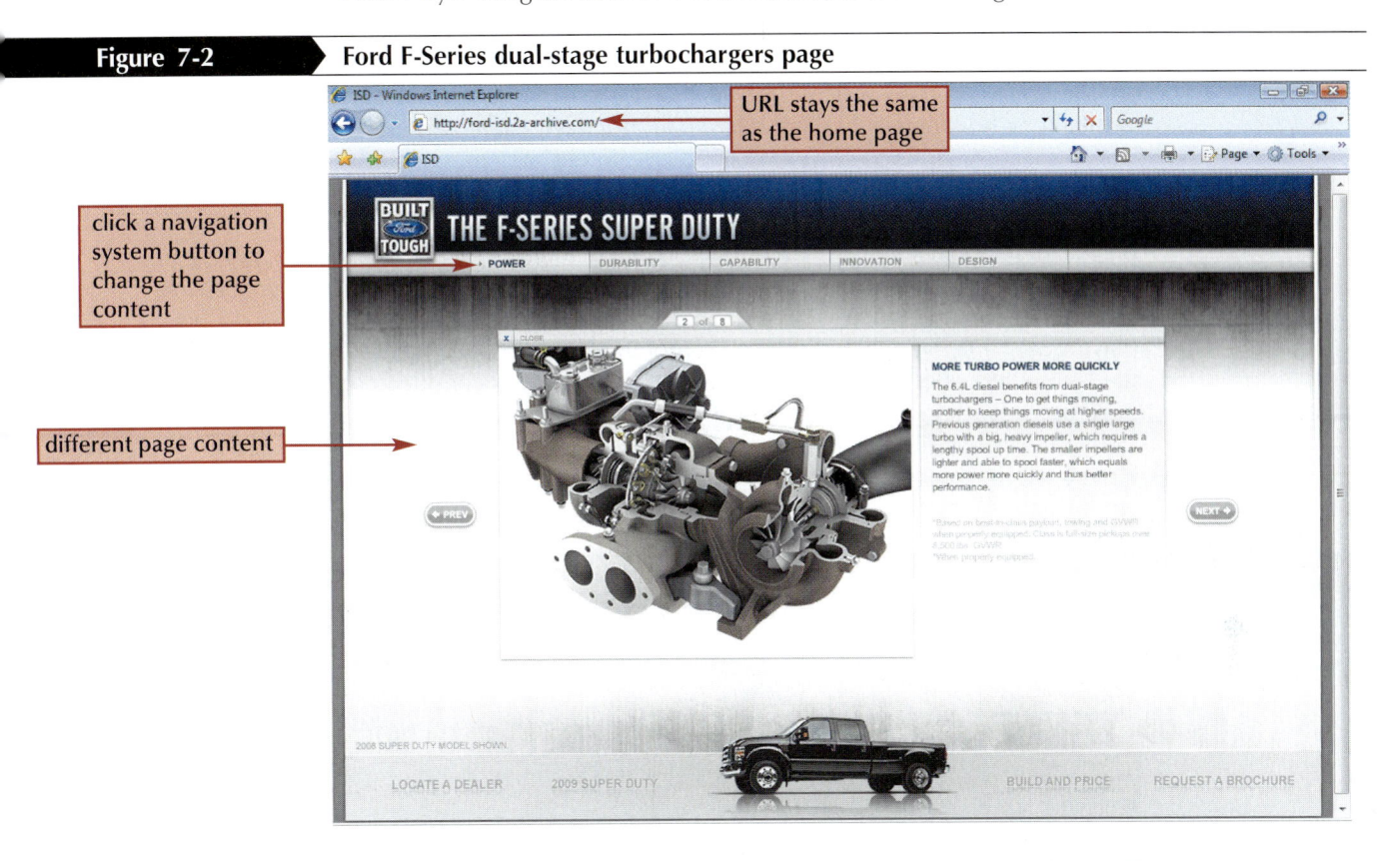

Figure 7-2 | Ford F-Series dual-stage turbochargers page

URL stays the same as the home page

click a navigation system button to change the page content

different page content

InSight | Comparing Navigation Systems for Flash and HTML Web Sites

Because a Flash Web site uses only one HTML document rather than of a series of HTML documents, the Back and Forward buttons on the Web browser toolbar do not provide the same functionality as they do for an HTML Web site. With a traditional HTML Web site, each time you navigate to a different Web page within the Web site, the browser tracks a history of which Web pages you visited and the URL in the Address bar changes based on the filename of the current Web page. In a Flash Web site, however, only one HTML document might be displayed, so the URL does not change even though the frames or SWF files being displayed in the Flash Player within the HTML document change. The HTML document displayed in the Web browser acts only as a container for the Flash content. After a user has navigated to several parts of the Flash Web site, the browser's Back button does not display the most recently visited SWF file. Instead, it returns to the most recently visited URL. As a result, it is vitally important to provide a clear and intuitive navigational system within the Flash Web site so that users can easily understand how to navigate within the site without using the browser navigation buttons.

Creating a Navigation System

The **navigation system** for a Flash Web site is a set of buttons or other graphic elements that users click to navigate to the various parts of one or more SWF files. When the navigation system is simply a set of buttons that the user clicks, the buttons can be arranged vertically or horizontally and are referred to as a **navigation bar**.

A navigation system can work in two ways. In one system, the buttons cause the playhead to go to different frames in the same Timeline. The content for each part of the Web site is placed in separate frames and actions are added to the frames to control the playhead. In another system, the buttons load a different SWF file using levels. **Levels** are like different planes in which the Flash Player can load SWF files or other content such as images. You can load an SWF file into the Flash Player so that it replaces the currently playing SWF file or so that it loads on top of the currently playing SWF file. The first SWF file is usually loaded into the Flash Player at level 0 and is considered the home or main page of the Flash Web site. Other SWF files can then be loaded at higher levels. For example, an SWF file specified to load at level 1 plays on top of the SWF file that is already playing at level 0, and the content of the SWF file at level 0 shows through any empty areas of the SWF file at level 1, as shown in Figure 7-3.

Figure 7-3 ▸ **SWF files loaded at different levels**

If an SWF file loads at a level already occupied by another SWF file, the newly loaded SWF file replaces the file currently playing. The properties of the SWF file at level 0 take precedence over those of the SWF files loaded at higher levels. For example, if the SWF file at level 0 has a green background and an SWF file with a blue background is loaded at level 1,

Tutorial 7 Planning and Creating a Flash Web Site | Flash **FL 319**

then the level 1 SWF file also has a green background. The same applies to the Stage dimensions. The dimensions of the SWF file at level 0 take precedence over the dimensions of the SWF files that load at higher levels. It is important, therefore, to make certain that the contents of the loaded SWF files do not interfere with those of the SWF file loaded at level 0.

Exploring a Sample Flash Web Site

The Jackson's Youth Sports Web site will use levels in its navigation system. To get a better idea of how a Flash Web site that uses levels works, you will explore a sample site that Aly and Chris have been working on for another client, Leslie's Fruit Shop. The site is organized with a home page, a location page, and a specialties page. The SWF file that contains the title, background picture, large rectangle, and buttons is loaded at level 0 of the Flash Player. Each button, when clicked, will load a different SWF file at level 1 to replace the content within the rectangle.

To explore the Leslie's Fruit Shop Flash Web site:

1. Open the **leslies.fla** file located in the Tutorial.07\Tutorial folder included with your Data Files, and then reset the workspace to the Essentials layout.

2. On the Application bar, click **File**, point to **Publish Preview**, and then click **Default – (HTML)**. Your browser opens and displays the leslies.html file with the leslies.swf file playing in the Flash Player plug-in.

3. Click the **Location** button. The location information appears in the Flash Player window, although the URL in the Address bar still shows leslies.html as the last part of the URL. See Figure 7-4.

Figure 7-4   Leslie's Fruit Shop Flash Web site

4. Click the **Specialties** button. The specialties information appears, although, again, the URL does not change.

5. Click the **Home** button to return to the home page. The home page appears, although the URL remains unchanged.

6. Close the browser to return to Flash.

You will view another of the documents used in this Web site.

Tip

You can also press the Ctrl+Alt+W keys to close all documents at once.

7. Open the **lesliesSpecialties.fla** file located in the Tutorial.07\Tutorial folder included with your Data Files. This document contains only the information about the specialty items. It does not contain the navigation buttons or any of the graphic elements of the Web site such as the background and title banner. Those elements are contained only in the leslies.fla file.

8. On the Application bar, click **File**, and then click **Close All** to close the leslies.fla and lesliesSpecialties.fla files without saving any changes.

Planning a Flash Web Site

The first and most crucial task in creating a Flash Web site is to plan the content and structure for the site. As discussed, a Flash Web site might consist of a series of Flash SWF files that work together to present the desired information. The basic process for developing a Web site requires the following steps. First, identify the goals and objectives for the Web site based on the needs of the client. Based on the goals and objectives, develop the content of the site. The content then leads to the design of the Web pages including the navigation system. Finally, build the site and test it to make sure all parts of the site work as designed.

Reference Window | Developing a Flash Web Site

- Identify the site goals and objectives.
- Determine the target audience.
- Develop the site content.
- Create a storyboard, and design the navigation system and the site pages.
- Build the site and test it.

Identifying the Site Goals and Objectives

The first step in the development process is to identify the goals of the site. **Site goals** represent what the Web site is intended to accomplish. A Web site can have one goal or many goals, but initially you should define only three to five goals to ensure that the developed site can effectively accomplish these goals. It is essential that the goals be clearly defined; otherwise, the developed site might not meet the needs of the client. You start defining the goals of the site by meeting with the client and discussing what he or she wants the site to accomplish.

Consider these examples. The client might want the site to help the company sell a product or to provide information about the services offered by the company. The client might want the site to increase brand awareness for the company's products or to provide information for the company's employees, such as company policies and procedures. Or, the client might want to disseminate information to customers about how to use certain products. Each of these goals requires a different approach and results in a different type of Web site. The success of the site depends on how well it meets the goals that have been developed and agreed to by the client. The goals identified for a Web site impact the overall design of the Web site and determine how the site is developed.

To develop goals for the Jackson's Youth Sports Flash Web site:

1. Write down three goals for the Jackson's Youth Sports Web site.

2. Review the list of goals to make sure they are clearly defined.

3. Compare your goals to those identified by Aly and Chris after their meeting with Dan Jackson. See Figure 7-5.

Figure 7-5 | **Jackson's Youth Sports Web site goals**

> **Goals for Jackson's Youth Sports Web Site**
>
> - Promote the Jackson's Sports name.
> - Increase sales to local youth sports teams.
> - Provide a site dedicated to serving local youth sports.

Based on the site goals, develop a list of objectives. The **site objectives** more clearly define the information the Web site will contain, the types of media that are required, and the number of Web pages necessary to provide the information and fulfill the needs of the client. The objectives also help determine how the Web site pages are organized and what types of pages to develop. For example, one type of site might require pages with many pictures and little text, whereas another type of site might require pages with a lot of text and only a few pictures. Other sites might require pages that display animations or even videos.

The objectives must be clear and measurable so that after the site is complete, you can determine whether each objective has been met. For example, if one site goal is to enhance a company's brand awareness, then one objective might be to include a list of the benefits of using the company's products and another objective might be to highlight the company logo that appears on all of its products. These objectives are focused and quantifiable. You can easily develop a page that has a list of the benefits of using the company's products. You can also include the company logo on all the pages of the Web site, increasing the company's brand awareness.

To develop objectives for the Jackson's Youth Sports Flash Web site:

1. Review the Jackson's Youth Sports Web site goals.
2. Determine four objectives based on the site's goals.
3. Compare your objectives to those developed by Aly. See Figure 7-6.

Figure 7-6 | **Jackson's Youth Sports Web site objectives**

> **Objectives for Jackson's Youth Sports Web Site**
>
> - Include the message that Jackson's Sports supports local youth sports.
> - Provide a list of products and services offered by Jackson's Sports.
> - Provide the names of local teams doing business with Jackson's Sports.
> - Include pictures of the teams; these pictures will change every few weeks.

Determining the Target Audience

As part of the planning process, you must consider the **target audience**, which is the group of people intended to use the site. The characteristics of the people who will be using the site impact how the information is presented on the Web site. The characteristics could be based on demographic information such as the age group, education level, or economic level of the audience. A young audience might indicate that more engaging animations need to be included, whereas a more mature audience might indicate that the site include less animation and perhaps a more conservative color scheme. You can also try to determine the expectations of the target audience. Do they expect to be entertained or do they expect to obtain detailed information about a product? This determines whether to include interactive games and graphics or detailed information in the form of text. The target audience for the Jackson's Youth Sports Web site consists of team coaches, players, and players' parents. The site, therefore, should appeal to both young sports participants and the adults involved with the teams.

Making a Web Site Accessible

The **World Wide Web Consortium (W3C)** is an international consortium whose mission is to develop Web standards. The W3C has established the **Web Content Accessibility Guidelines (WCAG) 2.0**, which is a standard to help Web designers and developers create Web sites with the needs of users with disabilities in mind. The guidelines cover a wide range of recommendations for making Web content more accessible to users with disabilities such as impaired vision, blindness, hearing loss, or deafness.

One method used to apply these recommendations is to make Web content accessible to a **screen reader**, which is software that visually impaired users run to read a Web site's text content aloud. A screen reader can read descriptions you provide for the SWF file or for the movie clips, images, or other graphical content within the file. You make an object accessible to a screen reader by assigning a name and description to the object. You can also specify whether to make a movie clip's child objects accessible. A **child object** is an object inside the movie clip. In addition to making objects accessible to a screen reader, you can also make objects that present no inaccessible content so as not to confuse the user.

If you know that part of your audience might include people with disabilities, consider making your Web site content accessible. The target audience for the Jackson's Youth Sports Web site might include users with impaired vision. The site, therefore, should be made accessible to screen readers.

The rest of the Web site planning process is guided by the site's goals, objectives, target audience, and accessibility needs. They determine which Flash documents need to be developed, what information each document should contain, and how the documents should be organized.

Developing the Web Site Content

The next step is to determine what content the site's pages will contain. The content is determined in large part by what the client wants the site to accomplish and partly by the target audience. The site goals and objectives identified in the first step help determine the pages and media that the Web site must include. Each objective for the Jackson's Youth Sport site will result in one or more separate Web pages designed to meet that specific objective. For example, one page will display pictures that need to change regularly, so that capability has to be designed as part of the page.

One way to determine the site's content is to develop an outline with categories and subcategories. Each category might correspond to one objective or a stated objective may have more than one category. The categories in the outline can correspond to the pages that will be developed for the site and also help determine the navigation system for the site.

You'll develop an outline for the Jackson's Youth Sports Web site.

To develop an outline for the Jackson's Youth Sports Web site content:

▶ 1. Review the Jackson's Youth Sports Web site objectives.

▶ 2. Develop an outline with categories that correspond to the objectives.

3. Compare your outline with the one developed by Aly and Chris, which has one page for each objective. See Figure 7-7.

Figure 7-7 Jackson's Youth Sports Web site outline

> Outline for Jackson's Youth Sports Web Site
>
> 1. Home page
>   a. Banner
>   b. Message about Jackson's Sports' support of local youth sports
>   c. Navigation bar with buttons exhibiting rollover effects and animation
> 2. Services
>   a. List products and services
> 3. Teams
>   a. Names of local teams
> 4. Photos
>   a. Pictures of local teams

After the outline is complete, you can start to gather and organize the required information, bitmaps, videos, and other graphics to include on the site. The client usually provides much of the information for a site, such as the products and services available. Graphic elements, such as bitmap files of pictures or video files, often need to be prepared by the site developer or the graphic designer.

Developing a Storyboard and Designing the Navigation System and Site Pages

After the Web site's main areas of content are outlined, you create a **storyboard**, which is a diagram that shows how all of the site's pages are organized. The storyboard shows a sketch of each page with lines indicating how the page links to the other pages. The way the pages link to each other determines the navigation system for the site. As you develop the navigation system, you should keep in mind the characteristics of the target audience. For example, if a large segment of the target audience has limited Internet skills, you should keep the navigation simple and easy to understand.

Based on the content outline for the Jackson's Youth Sports Web site, Aly and Chris have developed a storyboard for the site, as shown in Figure 7-8. The storyboard shows the site's main page as well as the other pages that will be developed and the basic design of each page. The main page will be loaded at level 0 in the Flash Player. The other pages, which will be loaded at level 1, include the Teams page, the Services page, and the Photos page. In addition, the Welcome page will appear when the main page is first displayed. The Welcome page will be replaced when another page is loaded at level 1. When the site visitor clicks the Home button, the Welcome page will load again, replacing the page currently at level 1.

Figure 7-8 Storyboard for Jackson's Youth Sports Web site

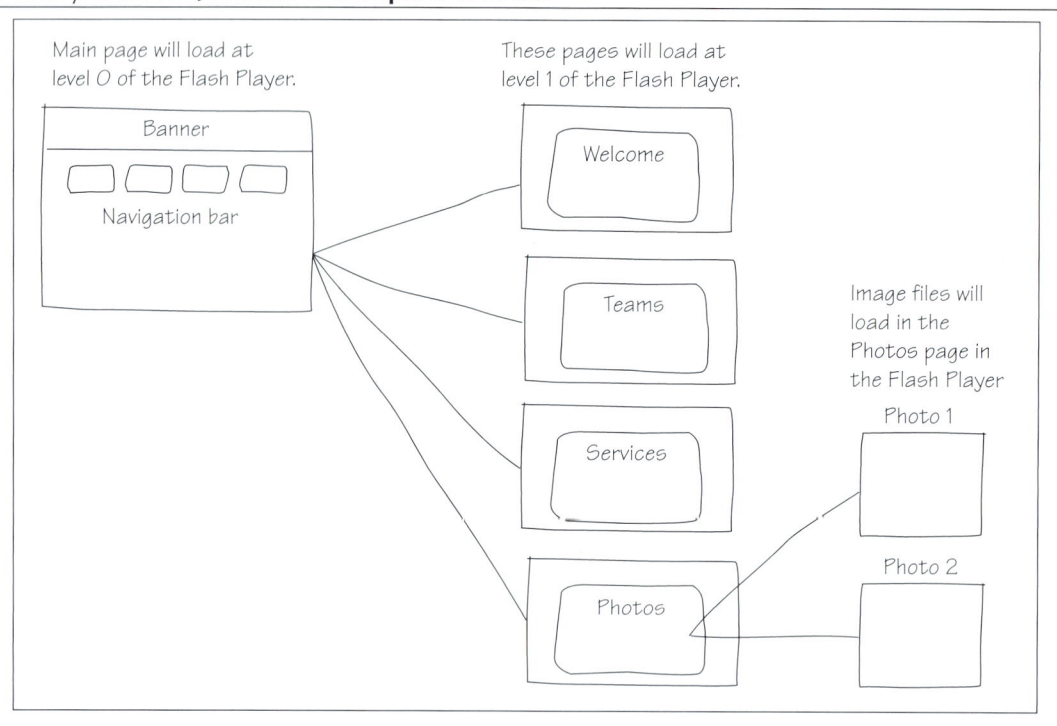

Main page will load at level 0 of the Flash Player.

These pages will load at level 1 of the Flash Player.

Banner
Navigation bar

Welcome
Teams
Services
Photos

Image files will load in the Photos page in the Flash Player

Photo 1
Photo 2

| InSight | Documenting Web Site Specifications |

After you develop the goals, objectives, outline, and storyboard for a Web site, you should compile all of this information in a written report. Then, you should meet with the client and have the client review and sign the report to indicate that he or she is in agreement. It's very important to have the client sign off on the Web site specifications before you start creating the Flash files for the Web site. Otherwise, the client might request changes to the Web site specifications during the development of the Flash files, forcing you to revise or re-create files you have already completed. After you start creating the Web site files, any changes requested by the client should also be in writing. When the Web site is complete, the documentation is proof that the site you developed meets the agreed-upon specifications.

So far, you have reviewed the process for developing a Flash Web site. During the planning of the Jackson's Youth Sports Web site, you determined the site's goals and objectives, you developed an outline of the site's contents, you determined the accessibility needs, and you created a storyboard to show the site's pages and navigation system. The planning for the Jackson's Youth Sports Web site is complete. In the next session, you will create the pages for the Jackson's Youth Sports Web site and the navigation bar.

| Review | Session 7.1 Quick Check |

1. The SWF files that make up a Flash Web site are referenced from a(n) _____ document.
2. True or False? The first SWF file in a Flash Web site is usually loaded into the Flash Player at level 1 and is considered the home or main page.
3. The Flash Player uses _____ to load more than one SWF file at one time.

4. True or False? When an SWF file is loaded at the same level already occupied by another SWF file, the new SWF file is automatically loaded at a higher level.
5. List the steps in the planning process for developing a Web site.
6. How can you start to define the goals of the site?
7. What is a screen reader?
8. What is a storyboard?

Session 7.2

Creating a Web Site's Contents

To create a site's contents, you start by creating a Flash document that will be the main page that is displayed when the user first enters the Web site. You create this document in the same way you have created other Flash documents, but you also include a navigation system that works with other Flash documents. Because you want the site's documents to work together and to provide a consistent viewing experience, all the documents should be the same size and have the same background.

As in the Leslie's Fruit Shop Web site, the main document of the Jackson's Youth Sports Web site will contain the background, banner, and navigation system. The other documents in the Web site will contain only the elements specific to a particular component of the Web site. These documents can have any number of graphic elements, including animations. Because these documents will play on top of the main document, you need to make certain that the elements on one document do not hide or overlap the elements of the main document.

Creating the Main Document

Based on Aly's instructions, the main page of the Jackson's Youth Sports Web site will have a banner with an animation of the store's name and a background picture. It will also contain a navigation bar consisting of a set of buttons. The page needs to be accessible to screen readers. You will start to create the Web site's main document by creating the banner. Because you will use ActionScript 2.0 for the actions in this document, you'll create a new Flash file with the ActionScript 2.0 profile.

To create the Jackson's Youth Sports Web site's main page:

Tip
You can also create the new document by clicking Flash File (ActionScript 2.0) in the Create New section of the Welcome screen.

1. On the Application bar, click **File**, click **New** to open the New Document dialog box, and then click the **General** tab, if necessary.

2. In the Type box, click **Flash File (ActionScript 2.0)**, and then click the **OK** button. The new document opens in the Document window.

3. Save the document as **main.fla** in the Tutorial.07\Tutorial folder included with your Data Files.

4. In the Properties section of the Property inspector, click the **Edit** button. The Document Properties dialog box opens.

5. Set the dimensions to **700 px** width and **500 px** height, set the background color to **gray** (#666666), and then click the **OK** button. The document's properties are set.

6. Reset the workspace to the Essentials layout, and then change the Stage magnification to **Show Frame**. The Stage resizes to fill the Document window.

You can make a Flash document or an individual object accessible to a screen reader from the Accessibility panel by assigning a name and description to it and specifying whether to make child objects accessible. If you select an object on the Stage, such as a movie clip, you can make that object accessible. If no objects are selected on the Stage, you can use the Accessibility panel to make the entire Flash document accessible. The panel also has options to make a document's child objects accessible or to have labels automatically assigned to objects. An individual object must have an instance name assigned to it in the Property inspector to have accessibility options applied to it. Note that Flash movies made accessible to screen readers must be viewed in Internet Explorer on Windows.

To make the Jackson's Youth Sports main page accessible to screen readers, you will use the Accessibility panel to assign a name and description.

To make the Jackson's Youth Sports Web site accessible:

1. On the Application bar, click **Window**, point to **Other Panels**, and then click **Accessibility**. The Accessibility panel opens.

2. In the Name box, type **Jackson's Youth Sports**. This is the instance name.

3. In the Description box, type **Jackson's Sports Web site promoting youth sports services and local teams**. This description will be read by the screen reader.

4. Make sure the **Make movie accessible**, **Make child objects accessible**, and **Auto label** check boxes are checked. See Figure 7-9.

Figure 7-9 | Accessibility panel

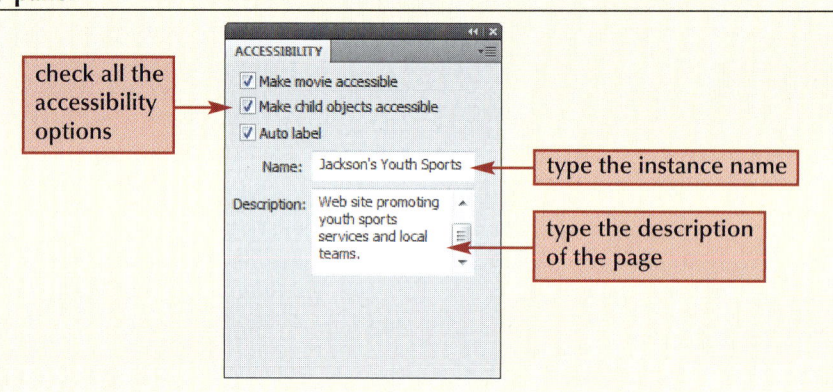

5. Close the Accessibility panel.

The banner in the main document will include a text animation. You'll create the banner as a symbol.

To create the Jackson's Youth Sports Web site's main page:

1. Create a new movie clip symbol named **jsBanner**. The banner will be a movie clip symbol.

2. In the Tools panel, click the **Rectangle** tool to select it, set the rectangle corner radius to **0**, set the fill color to **light blue** (#6699CC), set the stroke color to **no color**, and then draw a rectangle on the center of the Stage.

3. In the Tools panel, click the **Selection** tool to select it, and then select the rectangle on the Stage.

Tutorial 7 Planning and Creating a Flash Web Site | Flash **FL 327**

> 4. Open the Info panel, select the center registration point if necessary, set the width to **700 pixels**, set the height to **80 pixels**, set the X and Y coordinates to **0**, and then close the Info panel. The rectangle is resized and centered on the Stage.

> 5. Import the **soccer.jpg** bitmap located in the Tutorial.07\Tutorial folder included with your Data Files to the library. The soccer photo is added to the document's library.

> 6. Drag an instance of the **soccer.jpg** bitmap from the Library panel to the left edge of the rectangle on the Stage. The bitmap picture is included as part of the banner.

Tip
You can also press the Ctrl+Alt+1 keys to align the left edges of the selected objects and you can press the Ctrl+Alt+4 keys to align the top edges of the selected objects.

> 7. On the Application bar, click **Edit**, and then click **Select All**. Both the bitmap and the rectangle are selected.

> 8. Open the Align panel, click the **To stage** button to deselect it if necessary, click the **Align left edge** button, click the **Align top edge** button, click an empty area of the Stage to deselect the objects, and then close the Align panel. The left and top sides of the two objects on the Stage are aligned. See Figure 7-10.

Figure 7-10 Bitmap and rectangle aligned

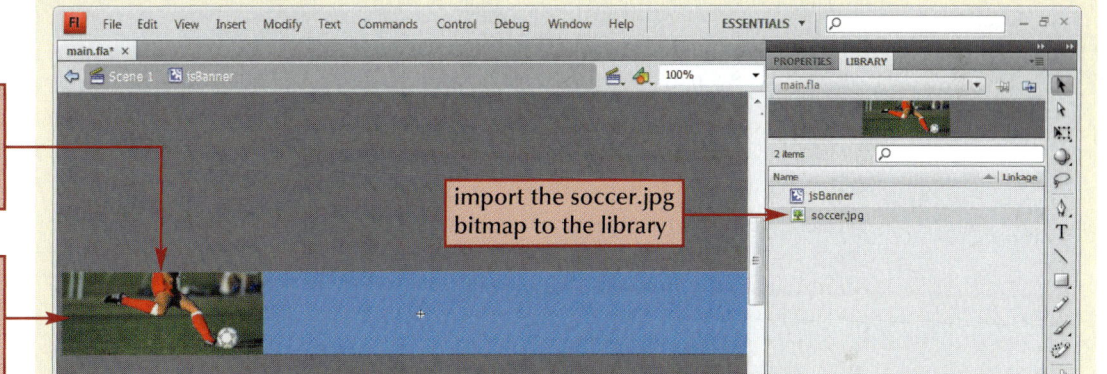

drag an instance of the Soccer bitmap to the left side of the rectangle

import the soccer.jpg bitmap to the library

align the bitmap and rectangle along their left and top edges

> 9. In the Timeline, rename Layer 1 as **background**, insert a regular frame at **Frame 30** to extend the content through Frame 30, and then lock the layer to prevent its objects from being moved accidentally.

> 10. In the Timeline, insert a new layer and name it **Jackson's**. You'll add text to the banner in this layer.

> 11. In the Tools panel, select the **Text** tool, and then, in the Property inspector, set the font family to **Verdana**, set the font style to **Bold Italic**, set the point size to **26**, set the text color to **white** (#FFFFFF), set the font rendering method to **Anti-alias for animation**, and then set the paragraph format to **Align left**.

> 12. On the Stage, click the left side of the picture to create a text block, type **Jackson's**, and then change the point size of the letter J to **35**.

> 13. Create a text block below the Jackson's text using the same attributes you set in Step 11, type **Sports**, and then change the point size of the letter S to **35**.

> 14. In the Tools panel, select the **Selection** tool, position the two text blocks over the picture as shown in Figure 7-11, and then deselect the text blocks.

Figure 7-11   Text blocks added to the banner

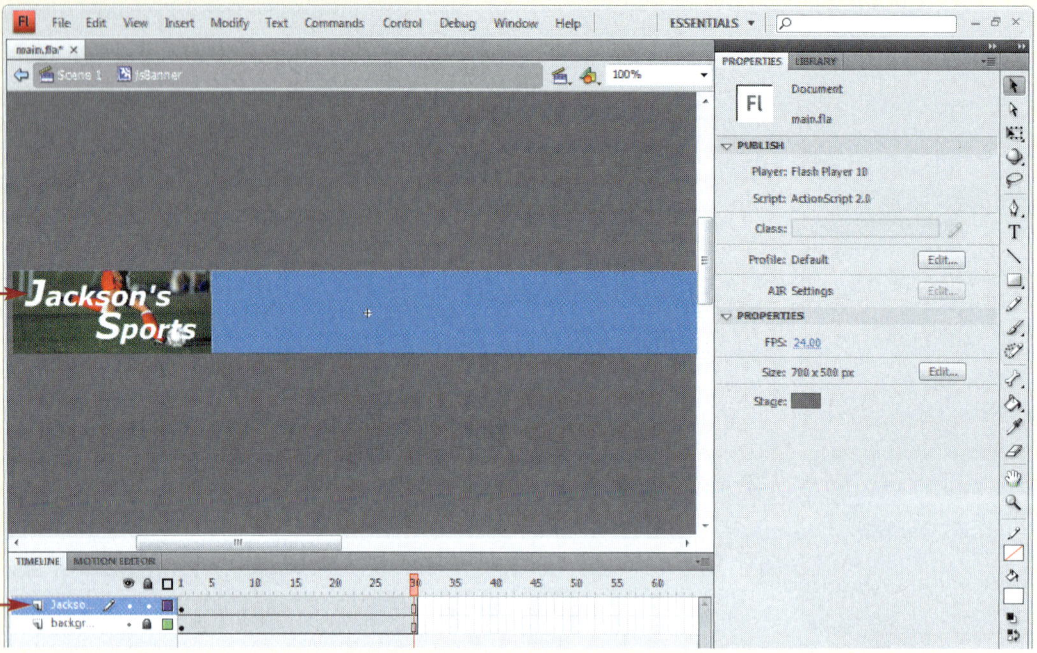

position the text blocks over the picture

insert the Jackson's layer for the text blocks with the store's name

The site plan calls for creating an animation using the text over the picture. The text will be animated to increase in size over a short period of time and then decrease. Aly wants the animation to span 30 frames. You will create a motion tween in which the text starts out 50% smaller than its original size and then increases to its original size. After a short pause, the text will decrease back to 50% of its original size.

To animate the Jackson's Sports text:

1. On the Stage, select the **Jackson's** text block, press and hold the **Shift** key, select the **Sports** text block, and then release the **Shift** key. Both text blocks are selected.

2. Convert the selected text blocks to a movie clip symbol named **jsTitle**. You will create an animation of the jsTitle instance where the text will start small at Frame 1, be full size at Frame 15, and decrease again at Frame 30.

3. On the Stage, right-click the **jsTitle** instance, and then click **Create Motion Tween** on the context menu. A motion tween is created in the Jackson's layer.

   You'll change the size of the symbol next.

4. In the Timeline, select **Frame 1** of the Jackson's layer, open the Transform panel, click the **Constrain** button to lock it if necessary, and then set the width to **50%**. The jsTitle instance decreases to half its size in Frame 1.

5. In the Timeline, select **Frame 15** of the Jackson's layer, and then, in the Transform panel, set the width to **100%**. The jsTitle instance increases to its original size at Frame 15.

6. In the Timeline, select **Frame 30** of the Jackson's layer, and then, in the Transform panel, set the width to **50%**. The jsTitle instance decreases at Frame 30 to the same size as it is in Frame 1.

Tutorial 7 Planning and Creating a Flash Web Site | Flash | FL 329

7. In the Timeline, drag the playhead to **Frame 1**, and then press the **Enter** key to play the animation. The jsTitle instance starts small, increases in size, and then decreases to its original size. The text animation is complete.

8. Close the Transform panel.

The final part of the banner is a text block over the rectangle with a message about Jackson's Sports' support of youth sports. This text block uses a smaller font than the title text. The banner will also be aligned along the left and top edges of the Stage.

To create another text block for the banner:

1. In the Timeline, insert a new layer above the Jackson's layer and name it **Youth Sports**.

2. On the Youth Sports layer, create a text block on the rectangle to the right of the picture, using **Verdana** for the font family, **Bold Italic** for the font style, **32** for the point size, **white** (#FFFFFF) for the text color, and **Align left** for the paragraph format, and then type **Supporting Youth Sports!** in the text block.

3. In the Tools panel, click the **Selection** tool, and then center the text block over the blue area of the rectangle. See Figure 7-12.

Figure 7-12 | **Title text block added to the banner**

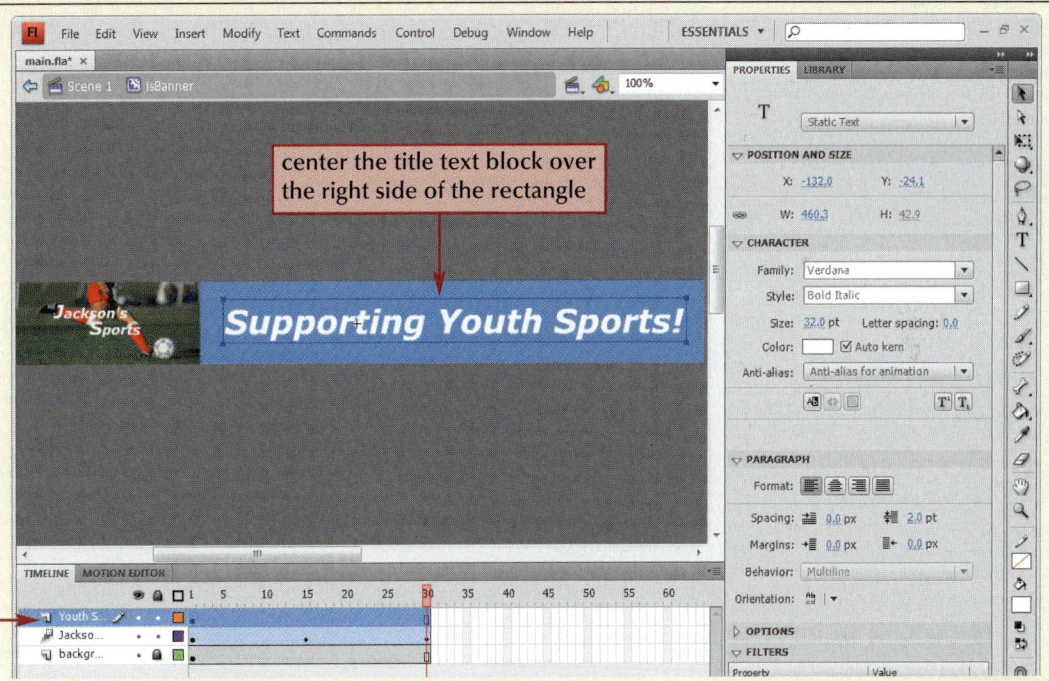

[Screenshot showing the Flash workspace with the "Supporting Youth Sports!" text block centered over the blue rectangle area of the banner. Callout: "center the title text block over the right side of the rectangle". Callout: "insert the Youth Sports layer for the title text".]

4. On the Edit bar, click the **Scene 1** link to exit symbol-editing mode and return to the main document.

5. In the Timeline, rename Layer 1 to **banner**.

6. Drag an instance of the **jsBanner** symbol from the Library panel to the top of the Stage.

▶ 7. Open the Align panel, click the **To stage** button to select it, click the **Align left edge** button, click the **Align top edge** button, click an empty area of the Stage to deselect the objects, and then close the Align panel. The banner aligns with the left and top sides of the Stage.

▶ 8. Lock the banner layer. The banner instance now cannot be repositioned.

The main page uses a background to enhance the appearance of the content that will appear for each document in the Web site. Aly wants you create a rectangle with a gradient fill that covers the Stage area below the banner. Because the Stage is 700 pixels wide, the rectangle should also be 700 pixels wide. Because the Stage is 500 pixels high and the banner covers the top 80 pixels, the rectangle should be 420 pixels high. You'll also align the rectangle to the bottom-left edge of the Stage.

To add a background rectangle to the main page:

▶ 1. In the Timeline, insert a new layer and name it **background**. You will add the rectangle to this layer.

▶ 2. In the Tools panel, select the **Rectangle** tool, set the fill color to the **gray radial gradient**, and change the stroke color to **no color**.

▶ 3. On the Stage, draw a rectangle on the Background layer that covers all of the Stage below the banner.

▶ 4. In the Tools panel, click the **Selection** tool, and then, on the Stage, select the rectangle.

▶ 5. In the Property inspector, click the **Lock width and height values together** button to unlock it, if necessary, and then set the rectangle size to **700 pixels** wide by **420 pixels** high.

▶ 6. Open the Align panel, click the **Align left edge** button, click the **Align bottom edge** button, click an area of the pasteboard to deselect the rectangle, and then close the Align panel. The rectangle is aligned with the left and bottom sides of the Stage. See Figure 7-13.

| Figure 7-13 | Rectangle aligned with the Stage |

align the rectangle with the left and bottom edges of the Stage

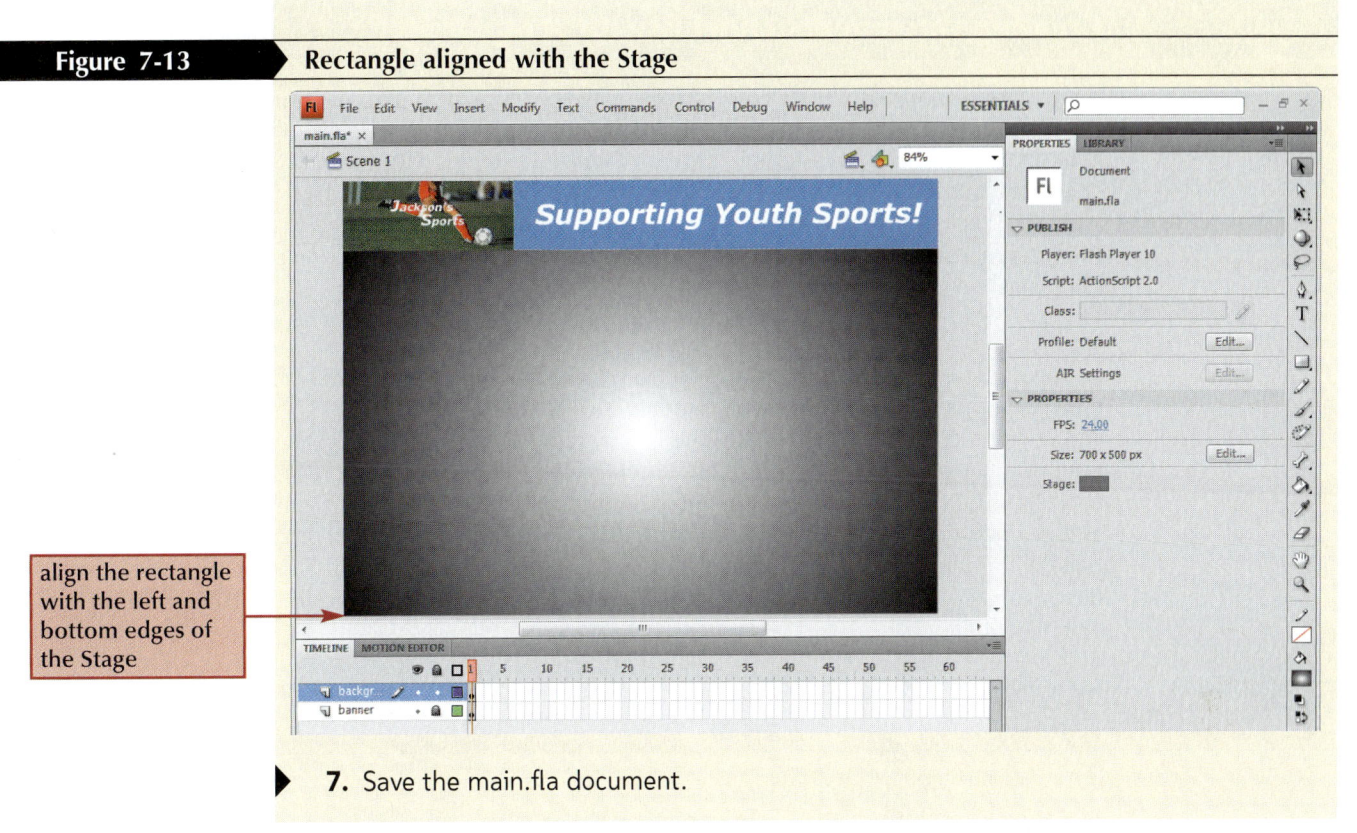

7. Save the main.fla document.

The graphics for the main page are complete. The only item missing is the navigation bar with the buttons to control how the Web site pages are loaded. Before creating the navigation bar, you will create the additional pages for the Web site using a Flash template.

Using a Flash Template to Create Additional Web Pages

The additional documents for the Web site will load on top of the main document. The main document will be at level 0 and its contents will remain visible on the Stage as other documents are loaded at higher levels. These additional documents, therefore, don't need to include the banner or background rectangle contained in the main document. They should include only the content to be displayed. These documents will have the same dimensions as the main page to ensure that the additional text appears consistently in the correct location. The background color of the loaded documents does not matter because the documents automatically default to the gray background of the main document. To ensure that all the additional documents have the same dimensions as the main document and to make it simpler to create new documents for this Web site, you can create a Flash template. A **template** is a prebuilt document that can be used as a starting point for a Flash project. Flash installs with several templates, and you can also create your own Flash templates.

| InSight | **Creating Documents Quickly with Templates** |

The preinstalled templates available in Flash enable you to quickly create professional documents such as advertisements, photo slideshows, or documents that play on mobile devices. You can then customize the templates to produce a document with the look and feel you want. Additional templates are available through the Flash Exchange, which is accessible from the Help menu or the Welcome screen. The **Flash Exchange** is an Adobe Web site with many templates created by the Flash developer community. If the preinstalled templates don't meet your needs, explore the ones available on the Flash Exchange.

You can create custom templates based on existing documents. From the custom template, you can then create new documents, saving development time. For example, you can create a template that contains the basic graphic elements, background, and animations you want to include in other documents. Then, each time you create a new document based on the template, the graphic elements, background, and animations are already included with the new document. You can save any Flash document as a template within an existing template category or a new category. You can also include a description of the template that appears when the template is selected in the New from Template dialog box.

| Reference Window | **Creating a Flash Template** |

- Create a Flash document.
- On the Application bar, click File, and then click Save as Template.
- Type a name for the template.
- Select an existing template category or create a new category.
- Type a description for the template.
- Click the Save button.

Because you need to create several documents for the Jackson's Youth Sports Web site and because each document will have the same dimensions as well as other similar elements, Aly wants you to create a template. First, you will create the document with the basic graphic elements. Then you will save the document as a template, which you will use to create the other documents.

The banner occupies the top 80 pixels of the main document. The navigation bar, consisting of buttons arranged horizontally, will be placed right below the banner. Therefore, the content of the new documents must be placed below the navigation bar so it will not interfere with the content on the main document. You will place a horizontal guide 150 pixels from the top edge of the Stage, and then add the new content below the horizontal guide.

To create a Flash template for the Jackson's Youth Sports Web pages:

▶ 1. Create a new **Flash File (ActionScript 2.0)** document, click the **Edit** button in the Properties section of the Property inspector to open the Document Properties dialog box, set the dimensions to **700 px × 500 px**, and then click the **OK** button.

▶ 2. Change the Stage magnification to **Show Frame** to display the entire Stage in the Document window.

▶ 3. Show the rulers, and then drag a horizontal guide to **150** pixels from the top edge of the Stage. The content for each document based on this template will be added below the horizontal guide.

▶ 4. In the Tools panel, click the **Rectangle** tool, and then, if necessary, click the **Object Drawing** button to deselect it.

Tutorial 7 Planning and Creating a Flash Web Site | Flash | **FL 333**

▶ 5. In the Property inspector, set the fill color to **light blue** (#6699CC), set the stroke color to **no color**, and then set the rectangle corner radius to **10**. The rectangle you draw will be light blue with rounded corners.

▶ 6. On the Stage, draw a rectangle with its top edge aligned with the horizontal guide.

▶ 7. In the Tools panel, click the **Selection** tool , and then select the rectangle on the Stage.

▶ 8. In the Property inspector, set the rectangle's width to **600** pixels, set its height to **320** pixels, and then center the rectangle horizontally on the Stage. See Figure 7-14.

Figure 7-14 | **Rectangle aligned with the horizontal guide**

set the rectangle's dimensions

center the rectangle horizontally below the guide

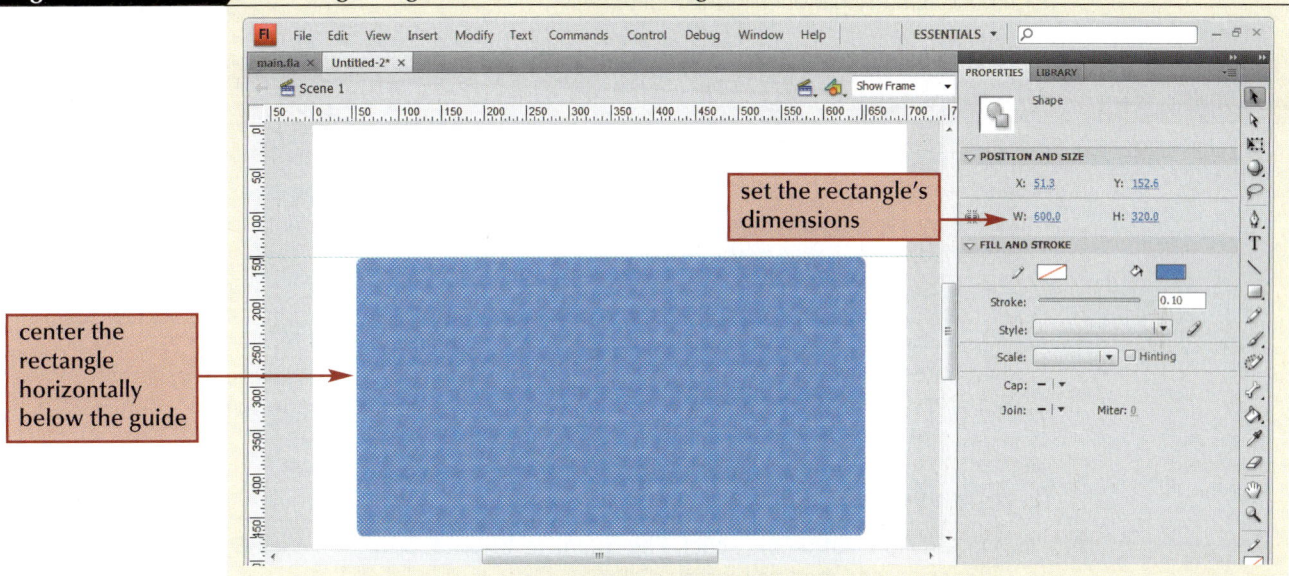

▶ 9. In the Timeline, change the name of Layer 1 to **rectangle**, insert a regular frame at **Frame 60**, and then insert a new layer and name it **contents**. The contents layer will remain empty in the template, but will be used to create the content of each new Web site document.

▶ 10. On the Application bar, click **File**, and then click **Save as Template**. The Save as Template dialog box opens.

▶ 11. Type **jsDocument** in the Name box, type **Jackson's Sports** in the Category box, and then type **Use this template to create the Jackson's Youth Sports Web site pages.** in the Description box. See Figure 7-15.

Figure 7-15 | **Save as Template dialog box**

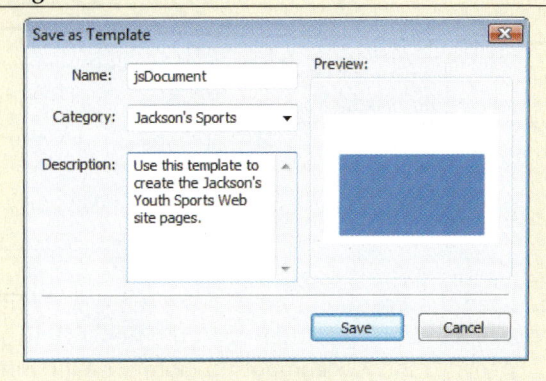

▶ 12. Click the **Save** button to save the template.

Using External Libraries

The template will contain animations of a baseball and of a basketball. Rather than creating a new graphic object of each ball, you can copy them from existing symbols in another Flash document to the template document. Both symbols will then be available to every document created from the template. To copy symbols from an existing document, you open the document's library as an external library. An **external library** contains the symbols for a stored document and makes these symbols available to the currently active document. An external library opens in a Library panel separate from the current document's Library panel. You can drag instances of the symbols from the external library's Library panel to the current document's Library panel or to the Stage.

| Reference Window | Copying Symbols from an External Library |

- On the Application bar, click File, point to Import, and then click Open External Library.
- Select the file with the symbols you want to copy, and then click the Open button.
- Drag an instance of a symbol from the external library's Library panel to the current document's Library panel or to the Stage.
- Close the external library.

Aly created a sample document for Jackson's Youth Sports that contains a basketball symbol and a baseball symbol. You will copy these symbols to the template document.

To copy symbols from an external library:

▶ 1. On the Application bar, click **File**, point to **Import**, and then click **Open External Library**. The Open as Library dialog box opens.

▶ 2. Click the **jSports.fla** document located in the Tutorial.07\Tutorial folder included with your Data Files, and then click the **Open** button. The jSports.fla Library panel opens as an external library. See Figure 7-16.

Figure 7-16 | jSports.fla external library

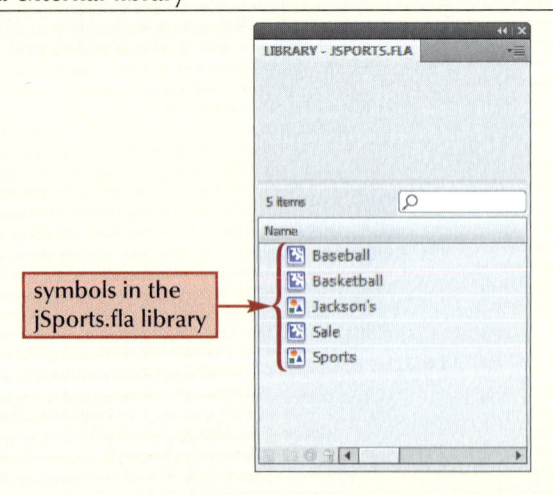

▶ 3. Drag the **Baseball** symbol from the jSports.fla Library panel to the jsDocument.fla Library panel, and then drag the **Basketball** symbol from the jSports.fla Library panel to the jsDocument.fla Library panel. Both symbols are copied to the current document's library.

Tutorial 7 Planning and Creating a Flash Web Site | Flash | FL 335

Trouble? If the symbols do not copy to the jsDocument.fla Library panel, you are probably dragging the symbol to the preview area. Drag the symbol from the jSports.fla Library panel to the lower pane of the jsDocument.fla Library panel.

4. Close the jSports.fla Library panel. The external library closes.

Both the basketball and the baseball symbols are stored in the current document's library. You will use the baseball in an animation that you will create next as part of the jsDocument template. You will use the basketball symbol in an animation you create later in this tutorial.

To create an animation with the baseball symbol:

1. In the Timeline, insert a new layer above the contents layer and name it **animation**.

2. Drag an instance of the **Baseball** symbol from the Library panel to the lower-left corner of the blue rectangle on the Stage.

3. On the animation layer, insert a keyframe at **Frame 30**, and then create a motion tween on **Frame 1** and create a second motion tween at **Frame 30**.

4. In the Timeline, select **Frame 29** of the animation layer and move the Baseball instance horizontally to the lower-right corner of the blue rectangle. The baseball will move from the left to the right in the tween span.

5. In the Timeline, select **Frame 30** of the animation layer and move the Baseball instance horizontally to the lower-right corner of the blue rectangle, and then select **Frame 60** and move the instance back to the lower-left corner of the blue rectangle. The baseball will move from the right to the left in the second tween span.

Next, you will add a rotation effect.

6. In the Timeline, select **Frame 1** of the animation layer, and then, in the Property inspector, set the rotation count to **2** and set the direction to **CW**. The baseball will rotate clockwise two times.

7. In the Timeline, select **Frame 30** of the animation layer, and then, in the Property inspector, set the rotation count to **2** and set the direction to **CCW**. The baseball will rotate counterclockwise two times.

8. Move the playhead to **Frame 1** and press the **Enter** key. As the animation plays, the baseball moves left to right and rotates clockwise twice, and then it moves from right to left and rotates counterclockwise twice. The animation is complete.

9. Save and close the jsDocument.fla file. The main.fla document remains open.

> **Tip**
> You can move an object in a straight horizontal, vertical, or diagonal line by holding down the Shift key as you drag the object with the Selection tool.

The template for the Jackson's Youth Sports Web site is complete. You are ready to create the additional pages according to Aly's instructions. The first page you will create will load initially with the main document. This page's content will be displayed the first time the Web site is visited and each time the Home button is clicked. You will create the Home button later in this session.

To create the home page from the jsDocument.fla template:

1. On the Application bar, click **File**, click **New** to open the New Document dialog box, and then click the **Templates** tab. The template you created is added to the category you specified—Jackson's Sports.

2. Click **Jackson's Sports** in the Category box, and then, if necessary, click **jsDocument** in the Templates box. The template is selected. See Figure 7-17.

FL 336 Flash | Tutorial 7 Planning and Creating a Flash Web Site

Figure 7-17   New from Template dialog box

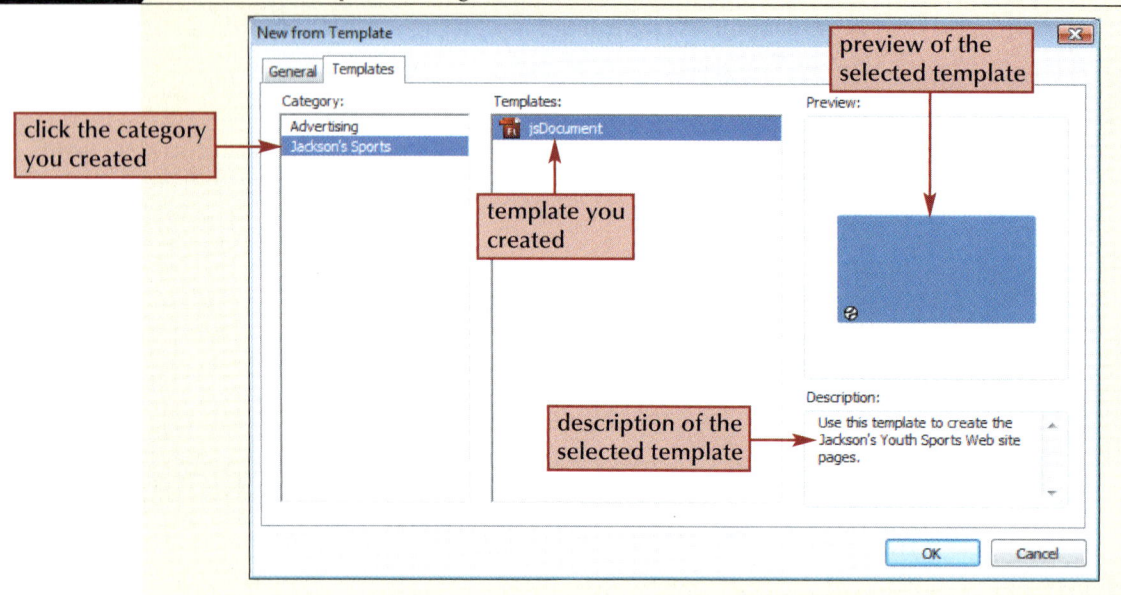

click the category you created

template you created

preview of the selected template

description of the selected template

▸ 3. Click the **OK** button. A new untitled document based on the jsDocument template opens.

▸ 4. Save the document as **home.fla** in the Tutorial.07\Tutorial folder included with your Data Files.

▸ 5. Change the Stage magnification to **Show All** to display all the contents on the Stage.

The home page includes all of the contents contained in the jsDocument template. You'll add the specific content needed for the home page.

To add content to the home page:

▸ 1. In the Timeline, select the **contents** layer.

▸ 2. In the Tools panel, click the **Text** tool ⊤ , and then, in the Property inspector, set the font family to **Arial**, set the font style to **Bold**, set the point size to **24**, set the text color to **black** (#000000), and set the paragraph format to **Align left**.

▸ 3. On the Stage, create a text block at the top of the blue rectangle approximately **150 pixels** from the left edge of the Stage and **175 pixels** from the top of the Stage, type **Welcome to Jackson's Youth Sports!** as the page title, and then deselect the title text block.

▸ 4. In the Property inspector, set the point size to **14**, and then set the font style to **Regular**.

▸ 5. On the Stage, create a text block approximately **150 pixels** from the left edge of the Stage and **230 pixels** from the top of the Stage, and then drag to the right to approximately **550 pixels** from the left edge of the Stage. A fixed-width text block with an approximate width of 400 pixels appears on the Stage. The text you type will wrap onto separate lines within the text block as opposed to appearing on one long line.

Tutorial 7 Planning and Creating a Flash Web Site | Flash | FL 337

▶ 6. In the text block, type the following paragraphs of text, allowing the text to wrap around to the next line when it reaches then right side of the text block, and pressing the **Enter** key twice after the first paragraph:

At Jackson's Sports, we value your business and we'll do our best to provide you the best sports equipment and supplies at the best prices.

We are proud to support our local youth sports teams. We have been supplying equipment and sports supplies to many of the local teams for over 15 years.

▶ 7. Check the spelling in the document, making any corrections needed. See Figure 7-18.

Figure 7-18	Text for the home page

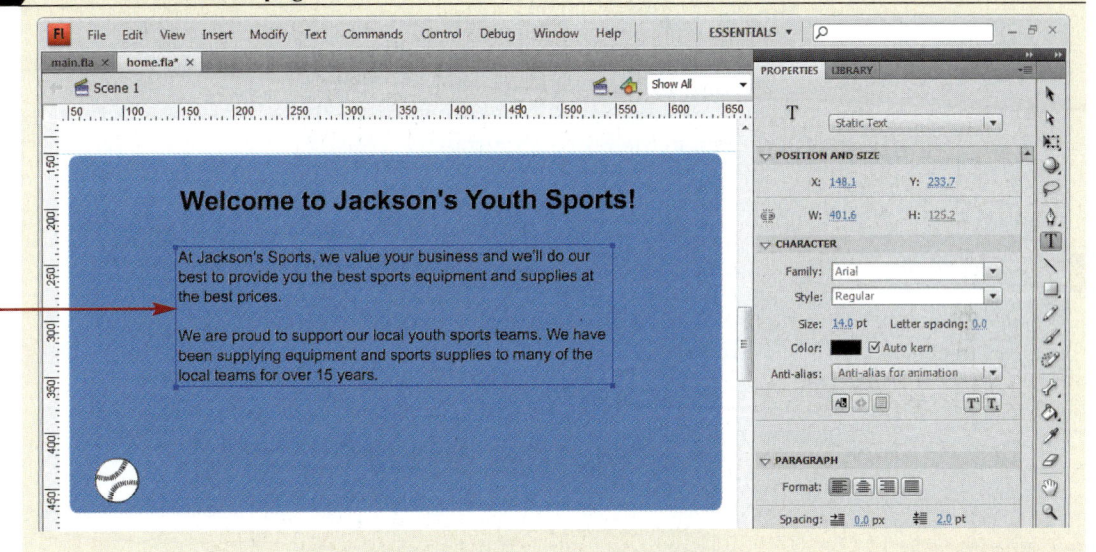

paragraphs typed in a fixed-width text block

Trouble? If a dialog box opens indicating that, based on your settings, there is nothing to check, you need to set up the spelling options. On the Application bar, click Text, click Spelling Setup to open the Spelling Setup dialog box, select the Check Text Fields Content check box under Document Options, select the Suggest typographical matches check box under Checking options, click the OK button, and then repeat Step 7.

Tip

You can also press the Ctrl+S keys to save the active document.

▶ 8. Save the document.

The home page that appears on top of the main document when the main document is first displayed is complete. You need to create three other pages. One contains the names of local sports teams that have done business with Jackson's Sports. The second is a list of services offered by the store. The third contains pictures of local teams and players. You will create each of these pages using the jsDocument template as a starting point.

To create the Teams page:

▶ 1. Create a new document based on the **jsDocument** template, save the document as **teams.fla** in the Tutorial.07\Tutorial folder included with your Data Files, and then change the Stage magnification to **Show All**. The entire contents of the Stage appear.

▶ 2. In the Timeline, if necessary, select the **contents** layer.

▶ 3. On the Stage, create a text block centered at the top of the blue rectangle approximately **240 pixels** from the left edge of the Stage and **175 pixels** from the top of the Stage, set the font family to **Arial**, set the font style to **Bold**, set the point size to **24**, set the text color to **black** (#000000), set the paragraph format to **Align left**, and then type **Local Sports Teams** in the text block. The title text block is complete.

▶ 4. Deselect the title text block, set the point size to **14**, set the font style to **Regular**, and then create a fixed-width text block approximately **150 pixels** from the left edge of the Stage, **230 pixels** from the top of the Stage, and **400 pixels** wide.

▶ 5. Type the following paragraphs of text in the text block, pressing the **Enter** key twice after the first paragraph and once between the other paragraphs:

Jackson's Sports is proud to support the following youth sports teams. For more information about these teams, contact our staff.

The Stars Basketball Team
The Sting Volleyball Team
The Tigers Softball Team
The Angels Baseball Team

▶ 6. Check the spelling of the document, correcting any misspelled words.

▶ 7. In the Tools panel, click the **Selection** tool, select the **rectangle** on the Stage, and then, in the Property inspector, change the rectangle's fill color to **peach** (#FFCC99). The changed color of the background rectangle will provide a visual cue to the user that a different page has loaded. See Figure 7-19.

Figure 7-19   Text for the Teams page

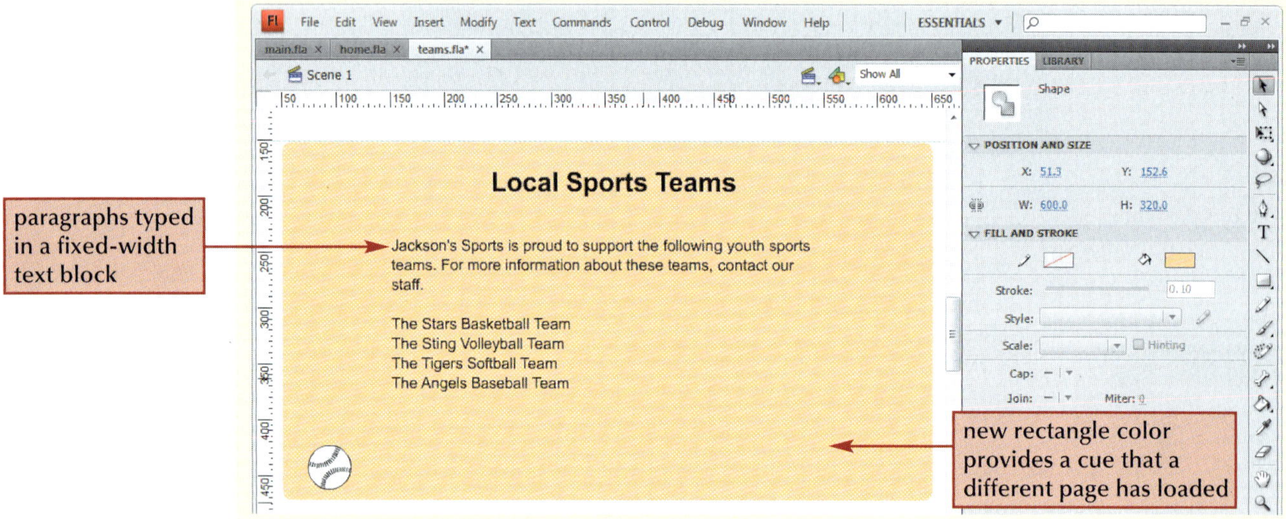

▶ 8. Save the document.

The Services page contains a list of the main services offered by Jackson's Sports. The document has a format similar to the Home and Teams documents, but will use the basketball graphic in the animation instead of the baseball.

To create the Services page:

▶ 1. Create a new document based on the **jsDocument** template, save the file as **services.fla** in the Tutorial.07\Tutorial folder included with your Data Files, and change the zoom to **Show All**. The entire contents on the Stage appear.

▶ 2. In the **contents** layer, create a text block centered at the top of the blue rectangle approximately **160 pixels** from the left edge of the Stage and **175 pixels** from the top of the Stage, set the font family to **Arial**, set the font style to **Bold**, set the point size to **24**, set the text color to **black** (#000000), set the paragraph format to **Align left**, and then type **Jackson's Youth Sports Services** in the text block.

3. Deselect the title text block, set the point size to **14**, set the font style to **Regular**, and then create a fixed-width text block approximately **150 pixels** from the left edge of the Stage, **230 pixels** from the top of the Stage, and **400 pixels** wide.

4. Type the following paragraphs of text in the text block, pressing the **Enter** key twice between paragraphs, and then check the spelling, correcting any misspelled words.

   - Sale of equipment and supplies at a discount

   - Team and individual trophies, including engraving of players' names

   - Sponsorship of tournaments

   - Team and player pictures

5. In the Tools panel, click the **Selection** tool, select the **rectangle** on the Stage, and then, in the Property inspector, change the rectangle's fill color to **light green** (#99FFCC), and then deselect the rectangle. The color of the rectangle provides a visual cue that a different page is loaded. See Figure 7-20.

Figure 7-20   **Text for the Services page**

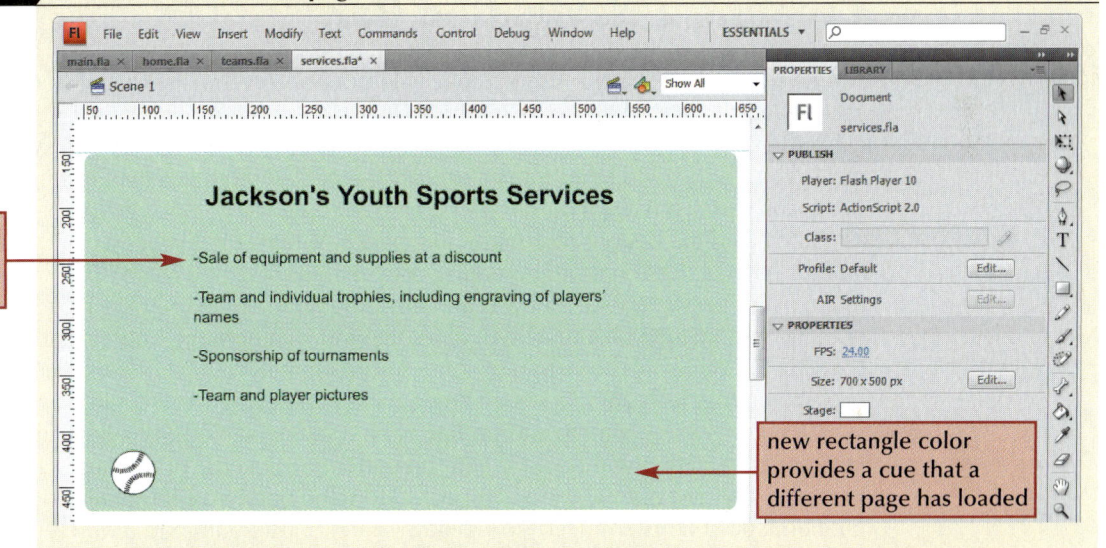

paragraphs typed in a fixed-width text block

new rectangle color provides a cue that a different page has loaded

Next, you will change the animated graphic to the basketball symbol you copied from the external library earlier.

6. In the Timeline, select **Frame 1** of the animation layer, click the **Baseball** instance on the Stage, and then in the Property inspector, click the **Swap** button. The Swap Symbol dialog box opens.

7. Click the **Basketball** symbol, and then click the **OK** button. The Baseball instance changes to a Basketball instance on the Stage.

8. Repeat Steps 6 and 7 for **Frame 30** of the animation layer to swap the other Baseball instances in the keyframe of the second motion tween.

9. Save the document, and then play the animation. The basketball moves from left to right and rotates twice clockwise and then it moves from right to left and rotates twice counterclockwise.

The Photos page contains buttons that load pictures of local teams or players. This document will be similar in format to the previous documents, but it will not include the animation.

To create the Photos page:

1. Create a new document based on the **jsDocument** template, save the file as **photos.fla** in the Tutorial.07\Tutorial folder included with your Data Files, and then change the zoom to **Show All**. The entire contents of the Stage are visible.

2. In the **contents** layer, create a text block centered at the top of the blue rectangle approximately **230 pixels** from the left edge of the Stage and **175 pixels** from the top of the Stage, set the font family to **Arial**, set the font style to **Bold**, set the point size to **24**, set the text color to **black** (#000000), set the paragraph format to **Align left**, type **Team and Player Photos** in the text block, and then deselect the text block.

3. In the Timeline, select the **animation** layer, and then click the **Delete** button. The layer is deleted, removing the animation from the page because it is not used with this page.

4. Save the document. You will complete the Photos page later in this tutorial.

> **Tip**
> To delete a layer, you can also right-click the layer's name in the Timeline, and then click Delete Layer on the context menu.

Creating a Navigation Bar

A Web site needs a way for users to navigate from one Web page to another. In an HTML-based Web site, hyperlinks load another HTML document into the Web browser when clicked. In a Flash Web site, the hyperlinks are replaced with a navigation system that moves the playhead to other frames or loads other SWF files into the Flash Player. In most Web sites, this is a navigation bar. You create the buttons for a navigation bar the same way as you created the buttons to control animations. When using levels to load SWF files, the buttons have ActionScript programming code that instructs the Flash Player which SWF file to load and how to load it. You will add this programming code in the next session. The buttons must include obvious visual clues that indicate how the buttons can be used to navigate the site. It is also helpful if some sort of animated effect occurs when the pointer is over the button, indicating that something will happen when you click the button.

The buttons used in a **navigation bar** often look the same but have different text to indicate what action will occur when the button is clicked. For the Jackson's Youth Sports Web site, the navigation bar will appear below the banner of the main document and include four buttons arranged horizontally. Each button will load a different SWF file when clicked. To make it easier to create and place on the Stage, you will create the navigation bar as a symbol and add an instance of it to the main document. The navigation bar will always appear as long as the main document is played in the Flash Player.

To create the Home button for the navigation bar:

1. Click the **main.fla** page tab to make the main document active.

2. Create a new button symbol named **Home button**. The Home button symbol opens in symbol-editing mode.

3. In the Tools panel, click the **Rectangle** tool, and then, in the Property inspector, set the stroke color to **white** (#FFFFFF), set the fill color to **light blue** (#0098FF), and set the rectangle corner radius value to **0**.

4. Draw a small rectangle centered in the editing window.

5. In the Tools panel, click the **Selection** tool, select both the stroke and the fill of the rectangle, and then, in the Property inspector, set the rectangle's width to **125 pixels**, set its height to **25 pixels**, and then set the X and Y coordinates to **0**.

You will add a rollover effect to the button.

6. In the Timeline, insert a keyframe in the Over frame of Layer 1, select all of the rectangle if necessary, and then, in the Property inspector, change the fill color to **dark green** (#009900) and change the stroke color to **black** (#000000).

7. In the Timeline, rename Layer 1 to **background**, lock the background layer, insert a new layer, and then name it **text**. You will add text to the button on the new text layer.

8. In the Tools panel, select the **Text** tool T, and then, in the Property inspector, set the font family to **Verdana**, set the font style to **Regular**, set the point size to **16**, set the text color to **white** (#FFFFFF), and set the paragraph format to **Align center**.

9. In the Timeline, click the **Up** frame of the text layer, and then type **Home** in the center of the button.

10. In the Tools panel, click the **Selection** tool, and then position the text block at the center of the rectangle. The rollover effect is complete. See Figure 7-21.

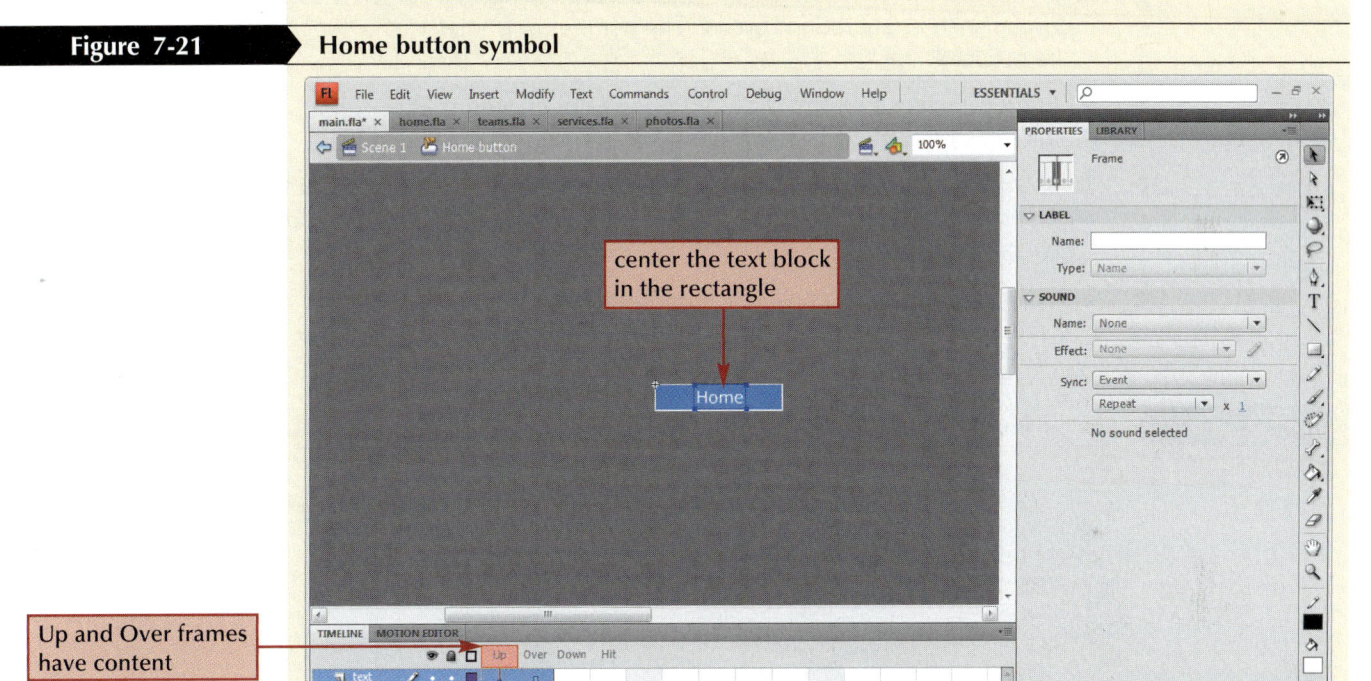

Figure 7-21   Home button symbol

Adding an Animation to a Button Frame

A simple rollover effect reinforces the fact that clicking the button causes something to happen. You can also add animations to any of the Up, Over, or Down frames of the button's Timeline to provide visual cues. One common effect is an animation in the Over frame of the button that appears only when the pointer is over the button. When the pointer is not over the button, the animation does not appear. To create this effect, you need to create a separate movie clip symbol with an animation in its Timeline and then place an instance of the symbol in the Over frame of the button symbol. The animation of the movie clip appears only when the Over frame is active, which is when the pointer is over the button. This effect is similar to the nested movie clip animations you created that included an instance of a movie clip inside the Timeline of another symbol. In the case of buttons, you will place an instance of another symbol inside the button's Timeline.

Aly wants you to add an animation to the Home button that appears only when the pointer is over the button. You will create the animation in a movie clip symbol. This animation will be a simple motion tween of a small circle with a pulsating effect.

To create the small circle animation:

1. Create a new movie clip symbol named **Button animation**. The Button animation symbol opens in symbol-editing mode. You will create a small circle.

2. In the Tools panel, click the **Oval** tool, set the fill color to the **gray linear gradient**, set the stroke color to **no color**, and then draw a small circle in the center of the editing window.

3. In the Tools panel, click the **Selection** tool, select the circle, and then, in the Property inspector, set the circle's width and height to **16 pixels** and set the X and Y coordinates to **0**. The circle is positioned and resized.

4. With the circle still selected, convert the circle to a movie clip symbol named **Circle**. The circle is a symbol that you can animate with a motion tween.

5. Right-click the circle, and then click **Create Motion Tween** on the context menu. A tween span is created in Layer 1. The number of frames in the tween span needs to be reduced.

6. In the Timeline, point to the right edge of the tween span and drag the edge to the left to reduce the tween span to 10 frames.

7. In the Timeline, click **Frame 5** of Layer 1 to select it, and then, click the circle, if necessary, to select it. You'll increase the size of the circle in the middle of the tween span.

8. Open the Transform panel, click the **Constrain** button to lock it if necessary, type **120** in the width box, and then press the **Enter** key. The circle increases in size. See Figure 7-22.

Figure 7-22   Size of small circle increased in Frame 5

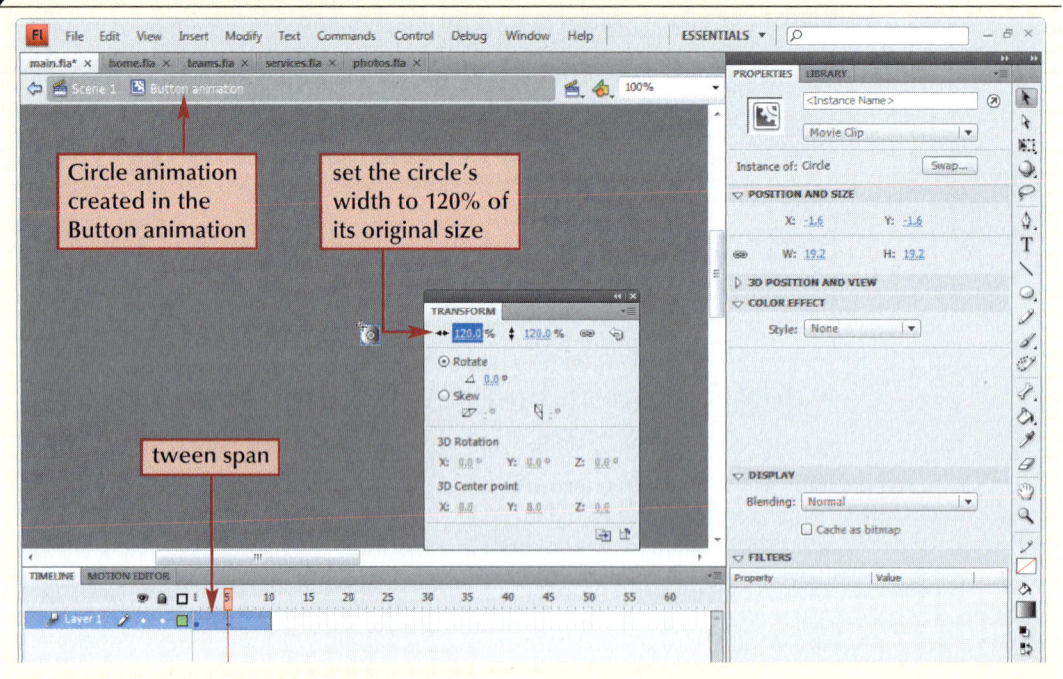

Tutorial 7 Planning and Creating a Flash Web Site | Flash | FL 343

▶ 9. In the Timeline, click **Frame 10** of Layer 1 to select it, and then, in the Transform panel, type **100** in the width box and press the **Enter** key. The circle decreases in size.

▶ 10. Close the Transform panel, move the playhead to **Frame 1**, and then press the **Enter** key. As the animation plays, the circle increases in size and returns to its original size in a pulsating effect.

The Circle animation is complete. Next, you'll add the animation to the Over frame of the button symbol so that the animation plays only when the pointer is over the button.

To add the Circle animation to the Over frame:

▶ 1. On the Edit bar, click the **Edit Symbols** button, and then click **Home button**. and then The Home button opens in symbol-editing mode.

▶ 2. In the Timeline, insert a new layer above the text layer and name it **animation**. You'll create a movie clip animation on this layer.

▶ 3. Insert a keyframe in the Over frame of the animation layer. You'll add the movie clip animation to this frame.

▶ 4. Drag an instance of the **Button animation** symbol from the Library panel to the left side of the button in the editing window. See Figure 7-23.

Figure 7-23   Button animation instance added to the button's Over frame

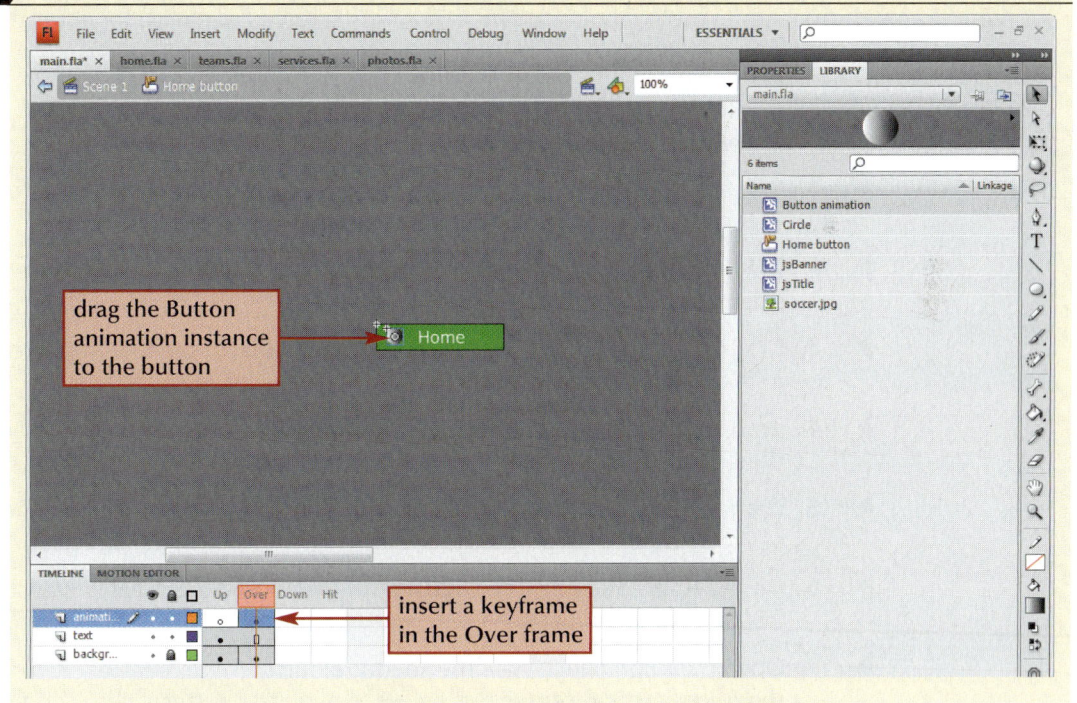

drag the Button animation instance to the button

insert a keyframe in the Over frame

The Home button symbol is complete. The other three buttons for the navigation bar are similar to this button. The only difference will be the text that appears on the buttons. Rather than creating the other buttons from scratch, you will make duplicates of the Home button symbol and then change the text for the other buttons.

To create three additional buttons for the navigation bar:

1. In the Library panel, right-click the **Home button**, and then click **Duplicate** on the context menu. The Duplicate Symbol dialog box opens.

2. Type **Teams button** in the Name box, and then click the **OK** button. The Teams button is added to the library.

3. Repeat Steps 1 and 2 to create a duplicate of the Home button named **Services button** and a duplicate of the Home button named **Photos button**. The four buttons are exactly the same. You'll change the text of the buttons next.

4. On the Edit bar, click the **Edit Symbols** button, and then click **Teams button**. The Teams button symbol opens in symbol-editing mode.

5. In the Timeline, select the **Up frame** of the text layer, click the **Text** tool T in the Tools panel, click the **Home** text block, select **Home**, and then type **Teams**.

6. Repeat Steps 4 and 5 to open the **Services button** in symbol-editing mode and change the Home text to **Services**.

7. Repeat Steps 4 and 5 to open the **Photos button** in symbol-editing mode and change the Home text to **Photos**.

> **Tip**
> When the Selection tool is selected, you can double-click the text to switch to the Text tool and make the text box active.

The additional buttons are complete. You will combine button instances in a movie clip symbol to create the navigation bar. The navigation bar will contain the Home, Teams, Services, and Photos buttons arranged horizontally. After you place the button instances in the symbol, you will add an instance of the navigation bar to the Stage of the main document.

To create the navigation bar:

1. Create a new movie clip symbol named **Navbar** in the Name box. You will add instances of the buttons in symbol-editing mode.

2. Drag an instance of the **Home button** symbol from the Library panel to the left side of the editing window.

3. Drag an instance of the **Teams button** symbol from the Library panel to the right of the Home button instance.

4. Drag an instance of the **Services button** symbol from the Library panel to the right of the Teams button instance.

5. Drag an instance of the **Photos button** symbol from the Library panel to the right of the Services button instance.

6. On the Application bar, click **Edit**, and then click **Select All** to select all the button instances at one time.

7. Open the Align panel, click the **To stage** button to deselect it if necessary, click the **Align vertical center** button to align the buttons, click the **Space evenly horizontally** button to space the buttons evenly, and then close the Align panel.

8. If necessary, in the Tools panel, click the **Selection** tool, and then center all the button instances in the editing window. See Figure 7-24.

Tutorial 7 Planning and Creating a Flash Web Site | Flash | **FL 345**

| Figure 7-24 | Completed navigation bar |

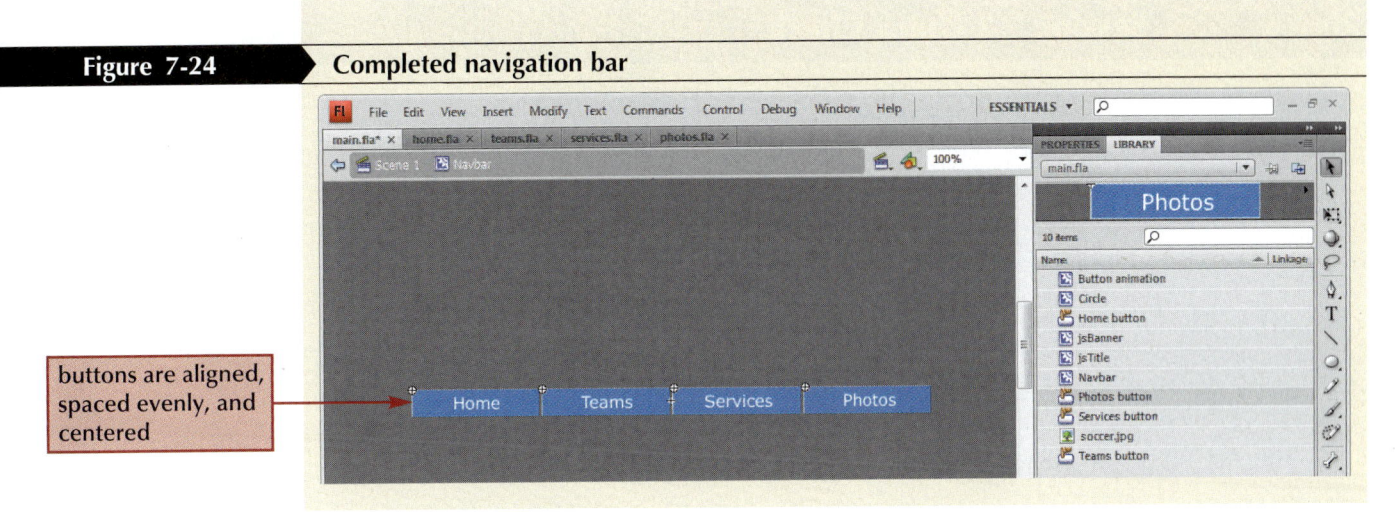

buttons are aligned, spaced evenly, and centered

The navigation bar is complete. You will add an instance of the navigation bar below the banner in the main document.

To add the navigation bar to the main document:

▸ 1. On the Edit bar, click the **Scene 1** link to return to the main document's Timeline, and then set the zoom to **Show All** to display all the contents on the Stage.

▸ 2. In the Timeline, insert a new layer above the background layer and name it **navbar**.

▸ 3. Drag an instance of the **Navbar** symbol from the library to the Stage below the banner, and then center the navigation bar horizontally. See Figure 7-25.

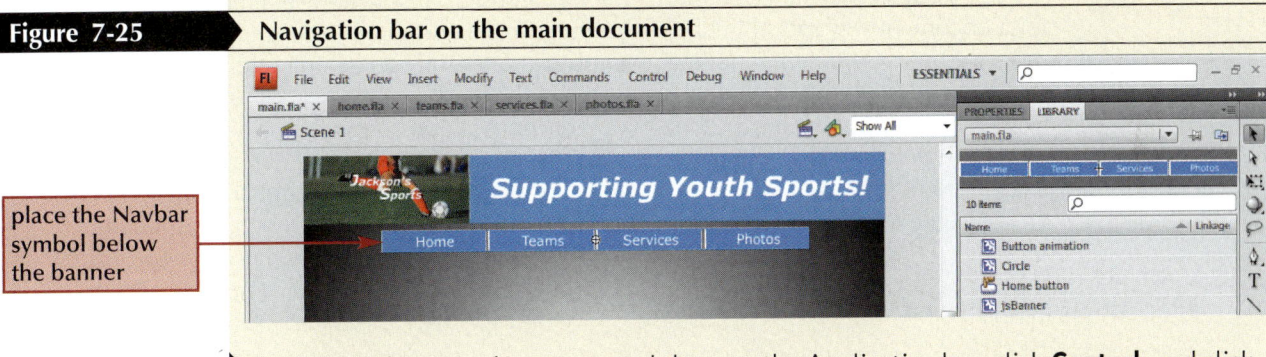

| Figure 7-25 | Navigation bar on the main document |

place the Navbar symbol below the banner

▸ 4. Save the main document, and then, on the Application bar, click **Control**, and click **Test Movie**. The SWF file opens in a separate window.

▸ 5. Move the pointer over each of the four buttons to test how the button changes color and plays the circle animation while the pointer is over it.

▸ 6. Close the Flash Player to return to the main document.

In this session, you created the documents that make up the Jackson's Youth Sports Web site. You created the site's main document, and then created a Flash template that you used to create the additional documents for the site. You also created the navigation bar with a set of buttons to navigate from one document to another in the Web site. The buttons include a movie clip animation that is displayed when the pointer is over the buttons. Although the navigation bar and its buttons are complete, they do not yet control anything. In the next session, you will add the ActionScript code to these buttons.

Review | Session 7.2 Quick Check

1. What is a Flash template?
2. What is the purpose of opening a document's library as an external library in another document?
3. A(n) _____ effect reinforces the fact that clicking a button causes something to happen.
4. True or False? An external library opens in a Library panel separate from the Library panel for the current document.
5. In a Flash Web site, _____ are replaced with buttons that move the playhead to other frames or load other SWF files into the Flash Player when clicked.
6. Briefly explain how you add an animation to a button that is displayed when the pointer is over the button.

Session 7.3

Using ActionScript

A Flash Web site's navigation system consists of a set of buttons. When you click a button, the Flash Player loads a different SWF file at the specified level. The navigation bar you created for the Jackson's Youth Sports Web site has buttons that don't yet control anything. To make the buttons operational, you need to add ActionScript instructions to them. ActionScript, the programming language used within Flash, allows you to add actions to objects or frames in a document. Actions are instructions that are used to control a document while its animation is playing. You have added actions to buttons to make the buttons control an animation. You can also add actions to buttons to control how a movie loads into the Flash Player. You will use the Actions panel to add actions in the form of scripts, which can contain one or more actions as well as other programming code to control how the actions are executed. The actions will be added to the button instances on the Navbar symbol. The two latest versions of ActionScript are versions 2.0 and 3.0, and you can use either version, depending on the complexity of the animation. Because you need to add only simple scripts to the buttons to control how the Web site's pages are loaded, you will use ActionScript 2.0. You will work with ActionScript 3.0 in Tutorial 8.

Using the loadMovieNum Action

In a Flash Web site, the main document loads into the Flash Player at level 0 and other SWF files can then be loaded at different levels. An SWF file loaded at a higher level will be on top of the SWF file at level 0. Using this method, you can load the Web site's main document with the banner, background, and navigation bar at level 0, and then load the other pages of the Web site at level 1 or higher. For example, you will load the Services page at level 1 so it will be displayed on top of the main document loaded at level 0.

To load an SWF file into the Flash Player at a specific level, you need to create an ActionScript script with the `loadMovieNum` action. This action has the following format:

```
loadMovieNum("filename.swf", level)
```

Within the parentheses, you specify the parameters of the action. The parameters give the action the information it needs to execute properly. In the case of the `loadMovieNum` action, the two parameters are the name of the SWF file to be loaded and the level number at which the file will be loaded. The name of the SWF file must be enclosed in quotation marks and a comma must separate the filename and the level number. For example, the following action loads the Services page at level 1:

```
loadMovieNum("services.swf", 1)
```

The `loadMovieNum` action is executed only when the button instance to which it is attached is clicked and released. For the action to work with the button, you must add an event handler that determines when to execute the action. Flash uses event handlers to check for events, such as when a button is clicked or when it is released. The event handler determines the action to take when a specific event occurs. Buttons use the on event handler, which has the following format:

```
on (mouseEvent)
```

The `mouseEvent` can be press or release. Press refers to a button being clicked. The event handler is followed by a pair of curly braces within which you place statements such as the `loadMovieNum` action. When the button is clicked with the mouse, the press event occurs. When the mouse button is released, the release event occurs. So, the following on event handler executes an action after the button is released:

```
on (release)
```

The event handler is then followed by the statement to be executed within curly braces. The complete script to load the Services page is as follows:

```
on (release)  {
      loadMovieNum("services.swf", 1);
}
```

Tip
In the Script pane, you can format the code automatically by pressing the Ctrl+Shift+F keys.

The curly braces can be placed on the same lines as other statements or on separate lines. The preceding format is recommended to make the script easier to read. It is also recommended practice to end ActionScript statements with a semicolon.

Using the Actions Panel

You can use the Actions panel in either Script Assist mode or normal mode. In Script Assist mode, Flash helps you create the scripts when you select actions from the Actions toolbox. In normal mode, you write all or part of the scripts yourself. You will use normal mode to write the scripts so you gain a better understanding of ActionScript.

Reference Window | Adding ActionScript Code to a Button

- Select the button instance on the Stage.
- In the Actions panel, select a category from the Actions toolbox, and then double-click an action to add its code to the Script pane.
- If necessary, type required code such as parameters that reference filenames.
- Click the Check syntax button to check the script for errors.

Because the navigation bar for the Jackson's Youth Sports Web site has buttons that are designed to load an SWF file when clicked, you will add the on event handler with the release parameter. So, when the button is clicked and then released, the event handler executes the `loadMovieNum` action to load the specified movie at a particular level. This script will be added to each button instance with the corresponding name of the SWF file.

To add ActionScript to the Home button:

1. If you took a break after the previous session, make sure the main.fla, home.fla, teams.fla, services.fla, and photos.fla documents are open, the main.fla document is active, and the workspace is reset to the Essentials layout.

2. On the Edit bar, click the **Edit Symbols** button, click **Navbar** to open the symbol in symbol-editing mode, deselect the button instances, and then select only the **Home button** instance. This is the first button to which you will add ActionScript.

3. Open the Actions panel, and then click the **Script Assist** button to deselect it, if necessary.

> **Tip**
> You can press the F9 key to open and close the Actions panel.

4. If necessary, click the **ActionScript version** control located below the Actions – Button tab, and then click **ActionScript 1.0 & 2.0**. The Actions panel is set to write code for ActionScript 1.0 and 2.0.

5. In the Actions toolbox, click **Global Functions** to expand the category, click **Movie Clip Control** to expand the category, and then double-click the **on** event handler. The on event handler is added to the Script pane along with parentheses and curly braces. Also, a code hints list of events opens so that you can quickly add the appropriate event to the script. See Figure 7-26.

Figure 7-26   Script pane with the event handler

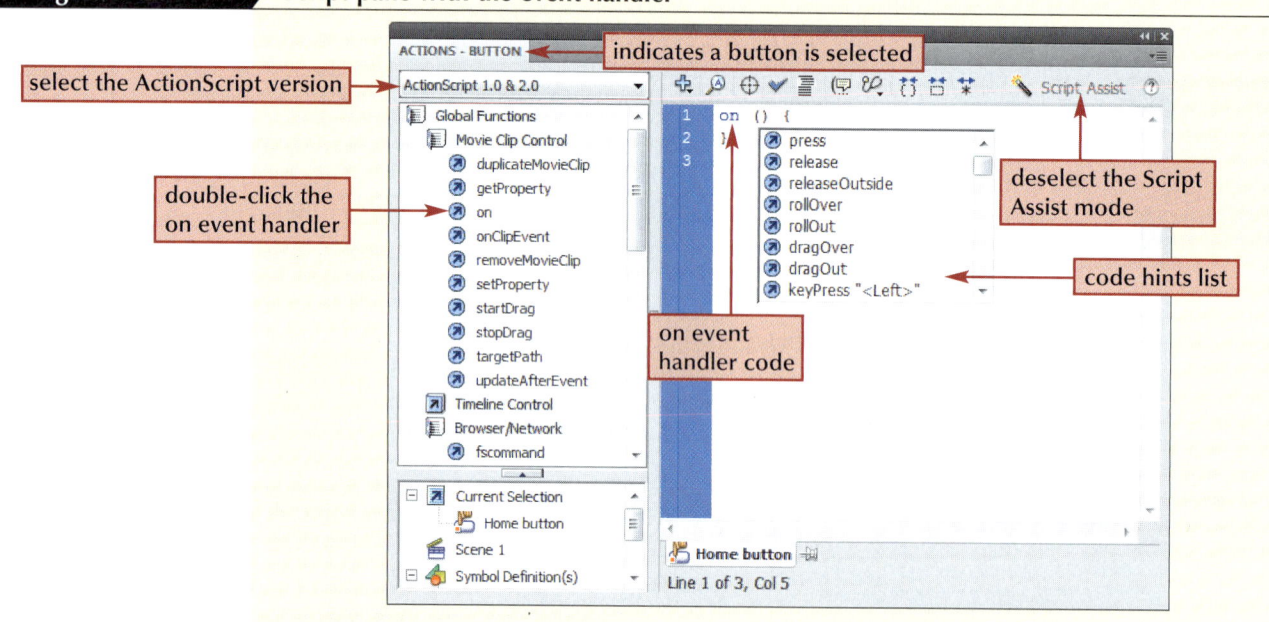

- select the ActionScript version
- double-click the on event handler
- indicates a button is selected
- deselect the Script Assist mode
- code hints list
- on event handler code

6. Double-click the **release** event. The word "release" is added between the parentheses. The `loadMovieNum action` must now be added between the two curly braces.

   Trouble? If the list of events does not open, type **release** within the parentheses.

7. Press the **Right** arrow key until the insertion point is at the end of the first line after the opening curly brace in the Script pane, and then press the **Enter** key to add a new line between the curly braces.

8. In the Actions toolbox, scroll down as needed, and then click **Browser/Network** to expand this category. A list of actions opens.

9. Scroll down as needed, and then double-click the `loadMovieNum` action to add it to the script. A tooltip appears, prompting you to type the parameters for the filename and the level number within the parentheses.

10. In the Script pane, within the parentheses of the `loadMovieNum` action, type **"home.swf", 1** to complete the script. See Figure 7-27.

Figure 7-27   Completed script for the Home button

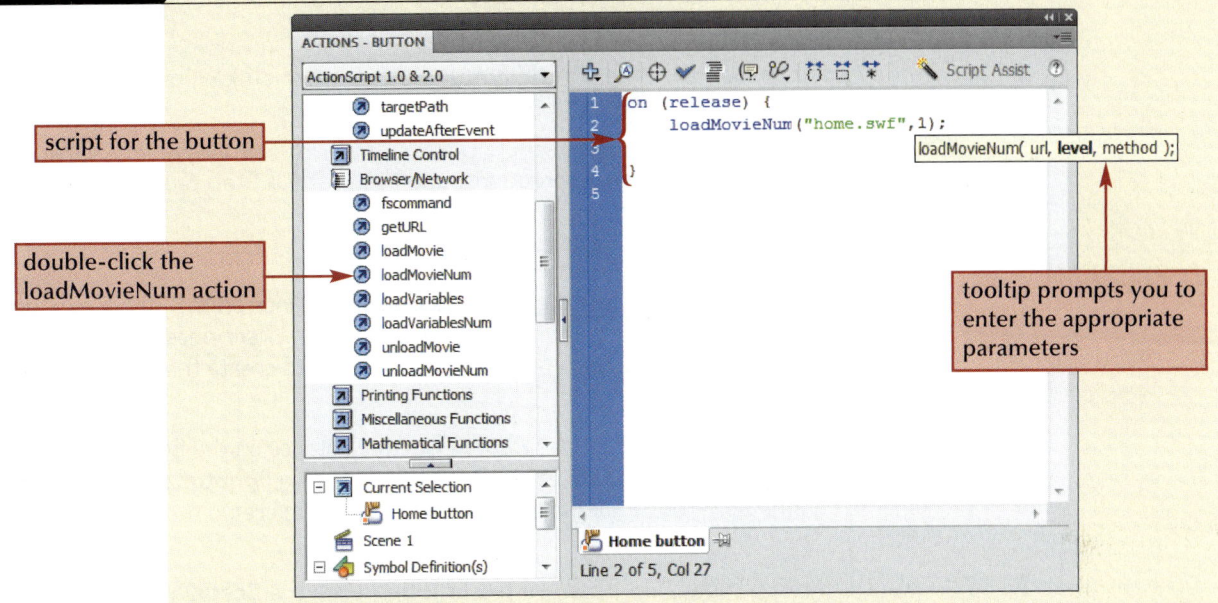

script for the button

double-click the loadMovieNum action

tooltip prompts you to enter the appropriate parameters

The Actions panel includes an option to check the script for errors. You will use this option to ensure the script does not contain errors.

11. In the Actions panel, click the **Check syntax** button. A dialog box opens stating "This script contains no errors."

Trouble? If a dialog box opens stating "This script contains errors. The errors encountered are listed in the Compiler Errors Panel.", your script contains errors. The Compiler Errors panel opens at the bottom of the screen with a list of the errors. Close the Compiler Error panel, compare your script to the script shown in Figure 7-27, make any necessary corrections, and then repeat Step 11 until no errors are encountered.

12. Click the **OK** button to close the dialog box.

The Home button is operational. When clicked, the button loads the home.swf file into the Flash Player at level 1. The same script must be added to the rest of the buttons. The only difference is the name of the SWF file within the parentheses of the `loadMovieNum` action. You will add the scripts to the remaining buttons.

To add ActionScript to the remaining buttons:

1. Click the **Collapse to Icons** button at the top of the Actions panel to collapse it, select the **Teams button** instance on the Stage, and then click the **Expand Panels** button to expand the Actions panel.

2. In the Actions toolbox, double-click the **on** event handler in the Movie Clip Control category to add it to the Script pane, and then double-click the **release** event from the list of events. The event handler and event are added to the Script pane.

3. Press the **Right** arrow key until the insertion point in the Script pane is at the end of the first line after the opening curly brace, and then press the **Enter** key to add a new line.

▶ 4. In the Actions toolbox, double-click the `loadMovieNum` action in the Browser/Network category to add it to the script.

▶ 5. In the Script pane, within the parentheses of the `loadMovieNum` action, type **"teams.swf", 1** to add the parameters for the filename and the level number, completing the script.

▶ 6. In the Actions panel, click the **Check syntax** button ✓ to check the script for errors, and then click the **OK** button to close the dialog box.

Trouble? If the Compiler Errors panel opens, your script contains errors. Close the panel, make the necessary corrections, and then repeat Step 6 until no errors are encountered.

Next, you'll create the script for the Services and Photos button.

▶ 7. Collapse the Actions panel, select the **Services button** instance on the Stage, expand the Actions panel, and then repeat Steps 2 through 6, typing **"services.swf"** for the filename parameter in the `loadMovieNum` action in Step 5 to create the script for this button.

▶ 8. Collapse the Actions panel, select the **Photos button** instance on the Stage, expand the Actions panel, and then repeat Steps 2 through 6, typing **"photos.swf"** for the filename parameter in the `loadMovieNum` action in Step 5 to create the script for this button.

▶ 9. Close the Actions panel, and then, on the Edit bar, click the **Scene 1** link to return to the main document.

The scripts for the buttons are complete. You want to ensure that the buttons work as expected. To test the buttons, you must first publish each of the site's documents as SWF files. Remember, the `loadMovieNum` action will load the SWF files named in the parameter portion of the ActionScript code. You will publish the Flash documents you created and saved as FLA files using the Publish Settings command. After the documents have been published, you will use the Test Movie command for the main document to test the buttons in the navigation bar.

To test the buttons in the navigation bar:

▶ 1. Click the **home.fla** page tab to make the home document active.

▶ 2. On the Application bar, click **File**, and then click **Publish Settings**. The Publish Settings dialog box opens. This file needs to be published only as an SWF file.

▶ 3. Deselect the **HTML (.html)** check box so that only the **Flash (.swf)** check box is selected, and then click the **Publish** button to publish the SWF file. The home.swf file is created and saved to the same folder as the home.fla file.

▶ 4. Click the **OK** button to close the Publish Settings dialog box.

▶ 5. Switch to the **teams.fla** document, and then repeat Steps 2 through 4 to publish the teams.swf file.

▶ 6. Switch to the **services.fla** document, and then repeat Steps 2 through 4 to publish the services.swf file.

▶ 7. Switch to the **photos.fla** document, and then repeat Steps 2 through 4 to publish the photos.swf file.

▶ 8. Switch to the **main.fla** document, and then, on the Application bar, click **Control**, and click **Test Movie**. Flash creates the SWF file for the main.fla document and displays the main.swf file in a separate window.

Tutorial 7 Planning and Creating a Flash Web Site | Flash | **FL 351**

▶ 9. Click the **Home** button on the navigation bar to display the home.swf file. See Figure 7-28.

Figure 7-28   Home page of the Jackson's Youth Sports Web site

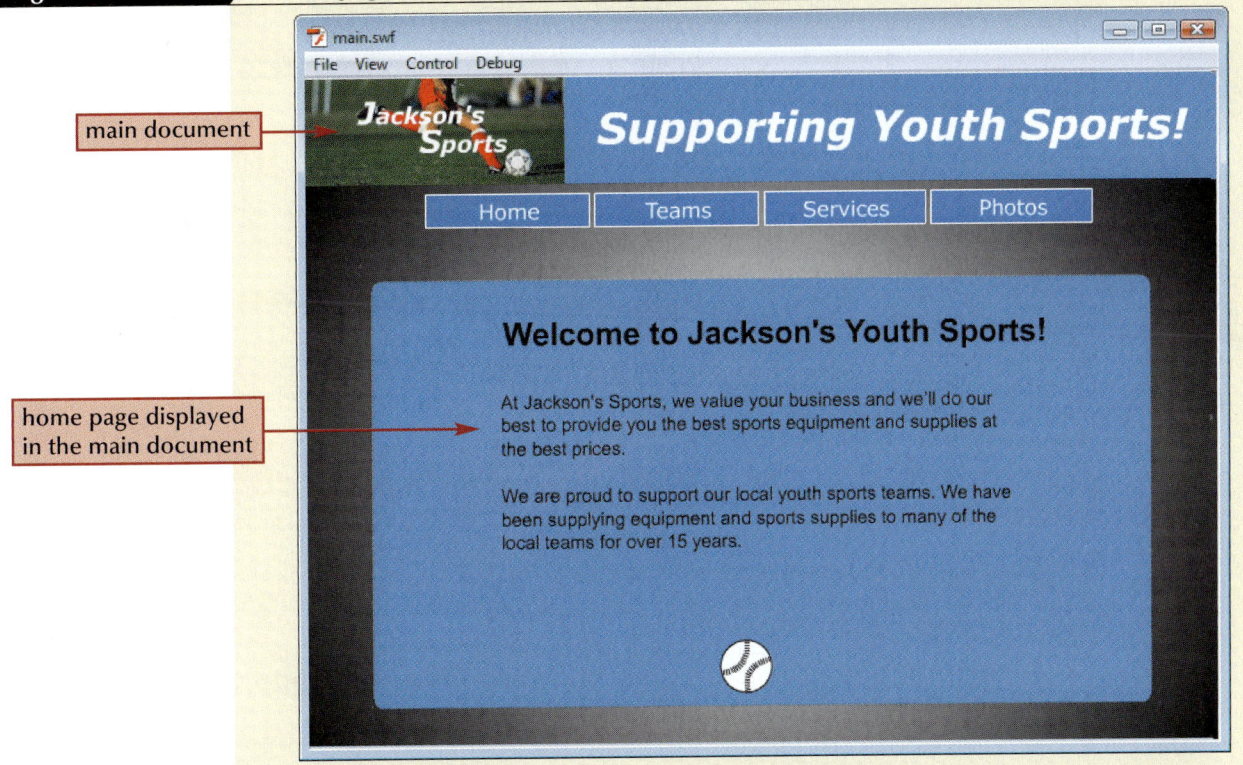

main document

home page displayed in the main document

▶ 10. Click the **Teams**, **Services**, and **Photos** buttons to display their respective SWF files. The corresponding SWF file appears when each button is clicked.

▶ 11. Close the Flash Player.

When the main.swf file was first displayed, the contents of the home.swf file did not appear until you clicked the Home button. When someone visits the Jackson's Youth Sports Web site, you want the home.swf file to load right away without requiring the site visitor to click the Home button. This requires another `loadMovieNum` action to tell the Flash Player to load the home.swf file as soon as the main.swf file is loaded. Because this action is not part of a button, it is not enclosed within an event handler. Instead, the action is added to Frame 1 of the main.fla document's Timeline. Then, when the main.swf file is loaded into the Flash Player and Frame 1 plays, the `loadMovieNum` action causes the home.swf file to load right away. You will add this action next.

To add the loadMovieNum action to Frame 1 of the main document:

▶ 1. In the Timeline of the main document, insert a new layer, name it **action**, and then select **Frame 1** of the action layer. You'll add the action to this frame.

▶ 2. Open the Actions panel, and then, in the Actions toolbox, double-click the `loadMovieNum` action in the Browser/Network category to add it to the Script pane.

▶ 3. In the Script pane, within the parentheses of the `loadMovieNum` action, type **"home.swf", 1** to enter the parameters for the filename and the level number and complete the action. See Figure 7-29.

Figure 7-29   Script in Frame 1

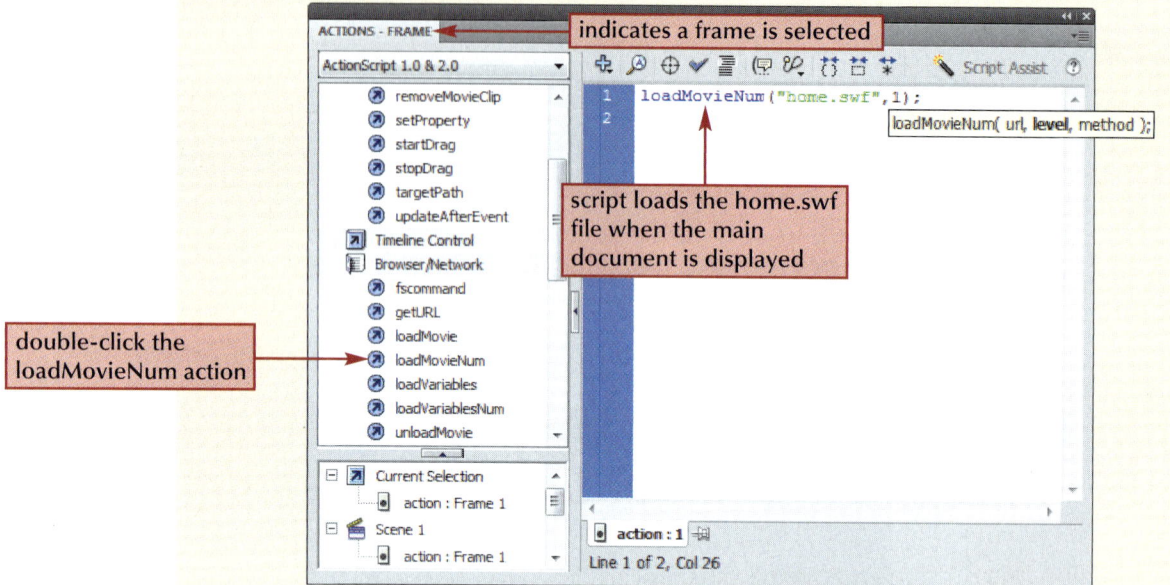

(Screenshot of the Actions panel showing:)
- ACTIONS - FRAME — indicates a frame is selected
- ActionScript 1.0 & 2.0
- double-click the loadMovieNum action
- Script: `loadMovieNum("home.swf",1);`
- Tooltip: `loadMovieNum( url, level, method );`
- script loads the home.swf file when the main document is displayed

---

4. In the Actions panel, click the **Check syntax** button ✓ to check the script for errors, and then click the **OK** button to close the dialog box.

   Trouble? If the Compiler Errors panel opens, there are errors in your script. Close the panel, make the necessary corrections, and then repeat Step 4 until no errors are encountered.

5. Close the Actions panel.

6. On the Application bar, click **Control**, and then click **Test Movie**. The main.swf file opens in a separate window with the contents of the home.swf also displayed.

7. Close the Flash Player, and then save the main.fla document.

The ActionScript scripts you added make the navigation bar buttons operational and load the home.swf file when the main.swf file is first loaded into the Flash Player. The site is almost complete. You only need to complete the Photos page so that it displays several pictures of local youth sports teams and events.

Loading External Image Files

The Photos page will display bitmap pictures of sports teams and individual players. The pictures will change as different teams submit pictures to Jackson's Sports. Usually, a picture displayed in a Flash document is imported and becomes part of the document. However, because the pictures on the Photos page will change regularly, you would need to modify the document each time a different set of pictures is to be displayed. A better option is to leave the pictures as separate files and bring them into the Flash Player only when they are to be displayed. These external image files should reside in the same folder as the photos.swf file, which will make it easier to reference the files from within the Photos page. All the pictures will be displayed in the same area of the page, so they should be no larger than the display area. The images should be assigned nonspecific filenames such as photo1.jpg so that the replacement picture can be assigned the same name of photo1.jpg and saved to the same folder. When the photos.swf file loads the photo1.jpg file, the new picture appears. The Flash document doesn't have to be modified each time the pictures are replaced.

> **InSight** | **Preparing Pictures for Flash Documents**
>
> When using pictures in a Flash document, determine the dimensions of the area in the Flash document where the pictures will be displayed. Then size the pictures in an image-editing program such as Adobe Photoshop so that the pictures fit within the specified dimensions. You should also optimize each picture by reducing its file size while maintaining its quality. This will help minimize the download time.

Using the loadMovie Action

Loading external image files into an SWF file in the Flash Player can be accomplished by using the `loadMovie` action. The `loadMovie` action is similar to the `loadMovieNum` action but can be used to load image files into a movie clip instance instead of a level. You create an empty movie clip symbol in a document, add an instance of the symbol to the Stage, and then use the `loadMovie` action to load a picture into the movie clip instance. The format of the `loadMovie` action is:

`movieclip.loadMovie("filename")`

In this action, `movieclip` represents the name of the movie clip instance. To use this action, you must assign a name to the movie clip instance on the Stage in addition to the name of the symbol in the library. If you have a movie clip instance named picture_mc, the following action loads the picture file photo1.jpg into the instance:

`picture_mc.loadMovie("photo1.jpg")`

You can create this `loadMovie` action along with the event handler code using the Actions panel similarly to how you created the `loadMovieNum` action. However, you can also add this action to a button using the Behaviors panel, which is simpler than using the Actions panel.

When using the `loadMovie` action, the image files for the pictures need to be in the standard JPEG file format and not in the progressive JPEG format. The **progressive JPEG** format causes a picture that is downloading to a Web browser to appear to fade in by gradually downloading the data that makes up the picture.

Aly has prepared two pictures for the Jackson's Youth Sports Web site. You will use the Behaviors panel to add the `loadMovie` action to a new set of buttons you will create on the Photos page. You will add the movie clip, buttons, and behaviors to complete the Photos page. There will be two buttons, one for each picture. The buttons will be created as part of a navigation bar that will be placed at the bottom of the rectangle in the photos page.

To create the buttons for the navigation bar in the Photos page:

▶ 1. Click the **photos.fla** page tab to make the document active.

▶ 2. Create a new button symbol named **Photo1 button**. The symbol opens in symbol-editing mode.

▶ 3. In the Tools panel, click the **Rectangle Primitive** tool, and then, in the Property inspector, set the stroke color to **black** (#FFFFFF), set the stroke height to **1**, set the stroke style to **Solid**, and then set the fill color to **cyan** (#66CCCC).

▶ 4. Click the **Lock corner radius controls to one control** button to unlock it, set the upper-left rectangle corner radius to **10**, and then set the lower-right rectangle corner radius to **10**.

▶ 5. Draw a small rectangle at the center of the editing window.

▶ 6. In the Tools panel, click the **Selection** tool, and then select the rectangle (both the stroke and the fill) in the editing window.

▶ 7. In the Property inspector, click the **Lock width and height values together** button to unlock it, set the width to **60**, set the height to **26**, and then center the rectangle in the editing window.

▶ 8. In the Timeline, insert a keyframe in the Over frame, select the rectangle in the editing window, and then, in the Tools panel, change the rectangle's fill color to **light yellow** (#FFFF99). The rectangle's color is different in the Over frame of the button.

▶ 9. In the Timeline, rename Layer 1 to **rectangle**, insert a new layer and name it **text**, and then click the **Up** frame of the text layer.

▶ 10. In the Tools panel, click the **Text** tool, set the font family to **Verdana**, set the font style to **Regular**, set the point size to **12**, set the text color to **black** (#000000), set the paragraph format to **Align left**, and then type **Photo 1** inside the rectangle. The button is labeled.

▶ 11. In the Tools panel, click the **Selection** tool, and then drag the text block to center the text over the rectangle. See Figure 7-30.

Figure 7-30   Photo1 button symbol

text block centered over the oval button

create the text block in the Up frame of the text layer

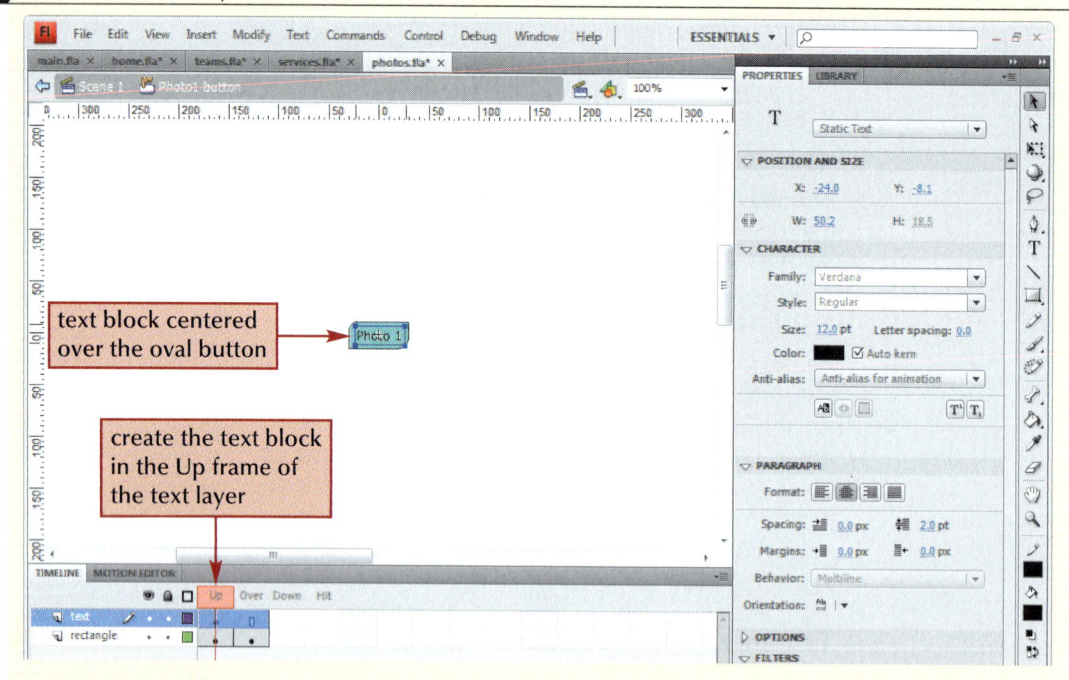

▶ 12. In the Library panel, create a duplicate of the Photo1 button symbol named **Photo2 button**. The new symbol is an exact copy of the Photo1 button symbol. You will use the Photo2 button to create the second button for the photos navigation bar.

▶ 13. On the Edit bar, click the **Edit Symbols** button, click **Photo2 button** to open the button in symbol-editing mode, double-click the text block, and then change the text to **Photo 2**. The button label is changed.

You have created the two buttons for the navigation bar. Next, you will create the navigation bar as a movie clip symbol and add instances of the buttons.

To create the navigation bar for the Photos page:

1. Create a new movie clip symbol named **Photos Navbar**. The symbol opens in symbol-editing mode.

2. Drag an instance of the **Photo1 button** symbol from the library to the center of the editing window, and then drag an instance of the **Photo2 button** symbol and place it below the Photo1 button instance.

3. On the Application bar, click **Edit**, and then click **Select All** to select both button instances at the same time.

4. On the Application bar, click **Modify**, point to **Align**, and then click **Horizontal Center** to align the buttons to each other.

5. On the Edit bar, click the **Scene 1** link to return to the document's main Timeline.

6. In the Timeline, click the **contents** layer to select it, and then drag an instance of the **Photos Navbar** from the Library panel to the left side of the rectangle on the Stage, as shown in Figure 7-31.

Figure 7-31   Navigation bar added to the Photos page

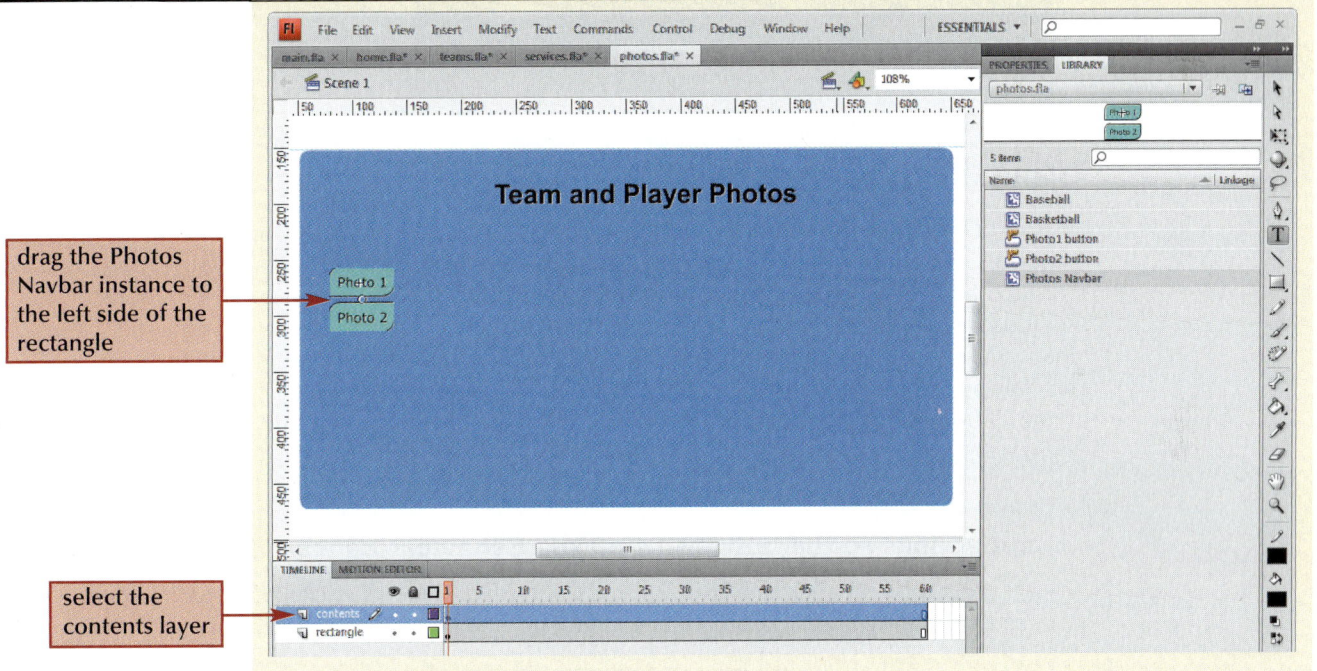

drag the Photos Navbar instance to the left side of the rectangle

select the contents layer

The buttons for the Photos page's navigation bar are complete. To make them operational, however, you need to add the `loadMovie` action to each button instance. Before you add the action, you will create an empty movie clip symbol and place an instance of it on the Stage. The instance will be indicated by a small circle on the Stage, which is the symbol's registration point. When a picture is loaded into the movie clip instance, the upper-left corner of the picture will be aligned with the registration point of the instance. Also, the instance must be named so that the `loadMovie` action can refer to it when it loads the pictures to the instance on the Stage.

To create the Picture holder movie clip:

1. Create a new movie clip symbol named **Picture holder**. The Picture holder symbol opens in symbol-editing mode. Because the movie clip will be empty, you will exit symbol-editing mode.

▶ 2. On the Edit bar, click the **Scene 1** link to return to the document's main Timeline.

▶ 3. Drag an instance of the **Picture holder** symbol from the Library panel to the Stage below the title, and then place the instance approximately **220 pixels** from the top of the Stage and **300 pixels** from the left of the Stage. The instance is indicated by a small circle.

▶ 4. In the Property inspector, type **picture_mc** in the Instance name box, and then press the **Enter** key. The instance is named. See Figure 7-32.

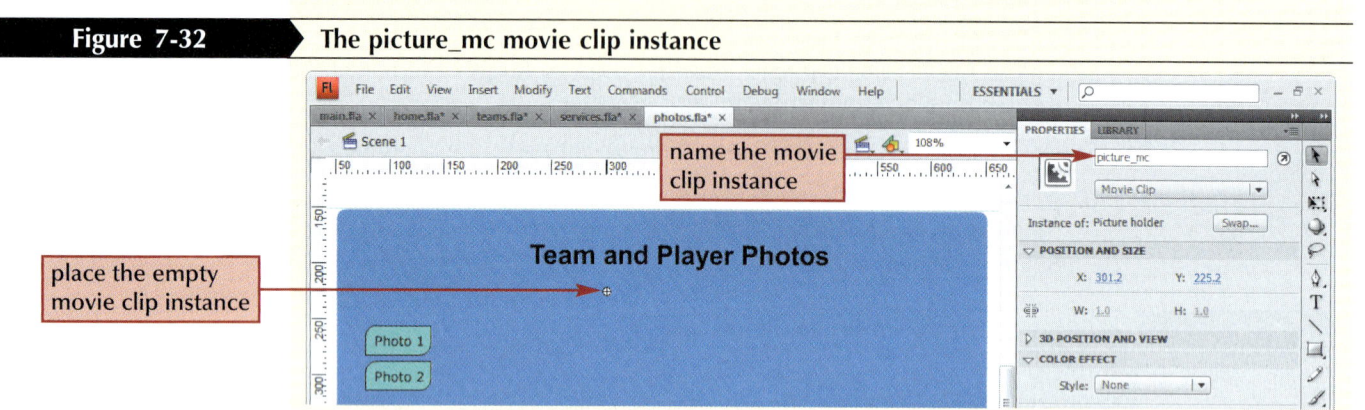

Figure 7-32 | The picture_mc movie clip instance

Using the Behaviors Panel

Instead of writing actions with the Actions panel, you can use precoded actions called behaviors. A **behavior** is an action with a prewritten ActionScript script that assigns controls and transitions to an object on the Stage. You can use behaviors to control an object in a document without writing any ActionScript coding yourself. A variety of behaviors are available for Flash objects, including movie clips, video, and sound files. Behaviors are only available with ActionScript 1.0 and 2.0.

You'll use the Behaviors panel to add actions to the Photo1 button and the Photo2 button.

To add actions to the buttons using the Behaviors panel:

▶ 1. On the Edit bar, click the **Edit Symbols** button, and then click **Photos Navbar** to open the symbol in symbol-editing mode.

▶ 2. Select the **Photo1 button** instance by itself in the editing window.

▶ 3. On the Application bar, click **Window**, and then click **Behaviors**. The Behaviors panel opens.

Tip

You can also press the Shift+F3 keys to open and close the Behaviors panel.

▶ 4. In the Behaviors panel, click the **Add Behavior** button, point to **Movieclip**, and then click **Load Graphic**. The Load Graphic dialog box opens.

▶ 5. Type **photo1.jpg** in the Enter the URL to the .JPG to load box, click **picture_mc** in the list of movie clips at the center of the dialog box, and then click the **Relative** option button if necessary. See Figure 7-33.

Figure 7-33   Load Graphic dialog box

enter the bitmap filename → photo1.jpg

select the name of the movie clip instance → picture_mc

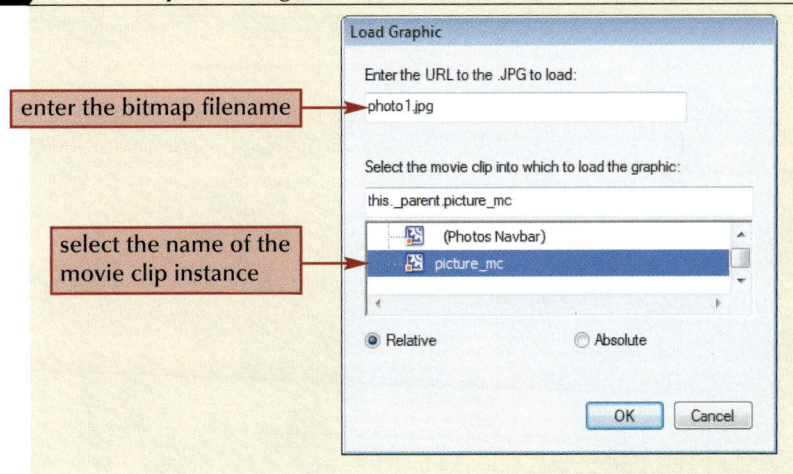

▸ 6. Click the **OK** button to create the behavior and close the Load Graphic dialog box.

▸ 7. Select the **Photo2 button** instance on the Stage, and repeat Steps 4 through 6, typing **photo2.jpg** in the Enter the URL to the .JPG to load box in Step 5 to add the behavior to the other button.

▸ 8. Close the Behaviors panel, and then, on the Edit bar, click the **Scene 1** link to return to the photos.fla document's main Timeline.

The photos.fla document needs to be saved and published as an SWF file so that it will work with the main document.

> **Tip**
> You can also press the Shift+F12 keys to publish a document.

▸ 9. Save the photos.fla document, click **File** on the Application bar, and then click **Publish** to create the photos.swf file.

The photo buttons and the Photos page are complete. When the Photos page is loaded into the Flash Player, the buttons appear. The site visitor can click one of the photo buttons to load a picture into the Flash Player. You will test the completed Web site in a browser.

To save and publish the main page:

▸ 1. Click the **main.fla** page tab to make that document active. You need to set the publish settings.

▸ 2. On the Application bar, click **File**, and then click **Publish Settings**. The Publish Settings dialog box opens.

▸ 3. Make sure that the **Flash (.swf)** and the **HTML (.html)** check boxes are checked, and then click the **OK** button to close the dialog box.

▸ 4. On the Application bar, click **File**, point to **Publish Preview**, and then click **Default - (HTML)**. The Jackson's Youth Sports Web site opens in your Web browser.

▸ 5. Click the **Photos** button to display the Photos page, and then click the **Photo 1** button to display the first picture. See Figure 7-34.

Figure 7-34 | **Photos page previewed in a Web browser**

[Screenshot of main.html in Internet Explorer showing the Jackson's Sports "Supporting Youth Sports!" page with Home, Teams, Services, Photos navigation buttons, a "Team and Player Photos" panel with Photo 1 and Photo 2 buttons, and a photo of a baseball player batting.]

▶ 6. Click the **Photo 2** button to display the second picture.

▶ 7. Close the browser, and then save and close all the documents.

In this session, you used the Actions panel to add ActionScript scripts to the buttons in the navigation bar to make them operational. You also used the Behaviors panel to add actions to buttons on the photos page to load external image files into the Flash Player. The site is ready to show to Dan and Gloria.

Review | Session 7.3 Quick Check

1. What is ActionScript?
2. Write the ActionScript statement to load the staff.swf file to level 1 of the Flash Player.
3. What is the purpose of the on event handler?
4. What option in the Actions panel can be used to check for errors in your script?
5. What action can be used to load external image files into a movie clip instance?
6. When you use the Load Graphic behavior, you must assign a(n) _____ to the movie clip instance where the picture will be loaded.

Review | Tutorial Summary

In this tutorial, you reviewed the process for developing a new Flash Web site and learned how a Flash Web site differs from a non-Flash Web site. In the process of planning a Flash Web site, you identified the site's purpose and objectives, and developed a storyboard showing the major parts of the site and its navigation system. You then built a Flash Web site by creating the home page, creating a template that you used for additional pages, and creating a navigation bar for the site. You used the Actions panel to add ActionScript instructions to the navigation bar buttons you created. Finally, you created a page for the Web site with buttons to display pictures and appropriate ActionScript instructions to control how the pictures are loaded into a movie clip in the Flash Player.

Key Terms

behavior
child object
external library
Flash Exchange
levels
navigation bar
navigation system
progressive JPEG
screen reader
site goal
site objective
storyboard
target audience
template
Web Content Accessibility Guidelines (WCAG) 2.0
Web page
World Wide Web Consortium (W3C)

Practice | Review Assignments

Practice the skills you learned in the tutorial.

Data Files needed for the Review Assignments: specialsDraft.fla, mainDraft.fla, photosDraft.fla, picture1.jpg, picture2.jpg, home.fla, home.swf, services.fla, services.swf, teams.fla, teams.swf

Aly developed an alternative Web site for Jackson's Sports. She wants you to add a new Specials page that includes information about the weekly sales promotion offered by Jackson's Sports and to complete the main document's navigation bar by adding buttons to load the Web site's pages. You also will complete the Player photos page to display two photos.

1. Open the **specialsDraft.fla** file located in the Tutorial.07\Review folder included with your Data Files, and then save the file as **specials.fla** in the same folder.
2. Select the contents layer, and then add a text block near the top of the rectangle with the text **Specials of the Week!**, using Times New Roman for the font family, 24 for the point size, black for the text color, bold for the font style, and align center for the paragraph format. Position the text block on the rectangle approximately 170 pixels from the top and 310 pixels from the left.
3. Add another text block in the center of the rectangle (approximately 270 pixels from the top and 280 pixels from the left), using Times New Roman for the font family, 16 for the point size, black for the text color, regular for the font style, and align center for the paragraph format, and then enter the following text:

   The following items are on sale this week:
   Softball bats—as low as $89
   Softballs—$3.99 each
   Batting gloves—$12.99

4. Save and publish the document to create the specials.swf file.
5. Open the **mainDraft.fla** file located in the Tutorial.07\Review folder included with your Data Files, and then save the file as **main.fla** in the same folder.
6. In the Library panel, make a duplicate of the Home button symbol named **Teams**, and then edit the Teams button symbol by changing the text in the Up and Over frames of the text layer to **Teams**.
7. Repeat Step 6 to create three more duplicates of the Home button symbol named **Services**, **Photos**, and **Specials**, and then edit each symbol to change the text in the Up and Over frames of the text layer to **Services**, **Photos**, and **Specials**, respectively.
8. Edit the JSNavbar symbol and add instances of the Teams, Services, Photos, and Specials symbols below the Home button instance and within the blue rectangle. Select all of the buttons on the Stage simultaneously, and then use the Left command in the Align submenu of the Modify menu to align the buttons by their left edges and use the Distribute Heights command in the Align submenu of the Modify menu to distribute the buttons evenly.
9. Add the `loadMovieNum` action to the Teams, Services, Photos, and Specials button instances, using the on event handler so that the action executes when the button is released after being clicked. The `loadMovieNum` action should load the respective SWF file (teams.swf, services.swf, photos.swf, specials.swf) into level 1 of the Flash Player.
10. Save and publish the main.fla file to create the main.swf file.
11. Open the **photosDraft.fla** file located in the Tutorial.07\Review folder included with your Data Files, and then save the file as **photos.fla** in the same folder.
12. Make a duplicate of the Pic_button1 symbol named **Pic_button2**, and then edit the Pic_button2 symbol by changing the text to **Picture 2**.

13. Add an instance of the Pic_button2 symbol to the Stage below the Pic_button1 instance in the content layer, and then align the two instances vertically.
14. Create a new movie clip symbol named **Picture holder**. The symbol should be empty and will be used to load the pictures onto the Stage.
15. Add an instance of the Picture holder symbol to the Stage, place it 200 pixels from the top of the Stage and 350 pixels from the left of the Stage, and then assign the name **picture_mc** to the instance.
16. Add the Load Graphic behavior to the Pic_button1 instance so that it loads the **picture1.jpg** file located in the Tutorial.07\Review folder included with your Data Files. The picture should be loaded to the picture_mc movie clip instance.
17. Repeat Step 16 to add the Load Graphic behavior to the Pic_button2 instance so that it loads the **picture2.jpg** file into the picture_mc movie clip instance.
18. Save and publish the photos.fla file to create the photos.swf file.
19. Test the Web site to make sure the Teams, Services, Photos, and Specials buttons load the respective pages and the Photos page displays photos using the buttons.
20. Submit the finished files to your instructor.

Apply | Case Problem 1

Create a new Flash Web site based on a template with a navigation bar and custom graphics.

Data Files needed for this Case Problem: katies.fla, main.fla, welcome.fla

Katie's Pet Resort   Katie asks John to create a new Web site for Katie's Pet Resort that will include information to promote some of the resort's special services. She wants the site to be visually appealing and easy to use for anyone who owns pets. Based on John's meeting with Katie, John develops the following list of goals for the Web site:
- Promote the Katie's Pet Resort name.
- Increase awareness of its services.

Based on these goals, John puts together the following list of objectives:
- Provide a list of services.
- Highlight the pet training classes available.
- Highlight the monthly pet adoption service.

John then prepares the outline for the site, which includes a home page with a banner at the top with the name of the store and a navigation bar on the left side. The navigation bar will have buttons in rectangular shapes that link to a Services page, a Training page, and an Adoption page.

John asks you to create the Web site that will include the Main, Welcome, Services, Training, and Adoption pages. You will create the Services, Training, and Adoption pages based on the Welcome page that John has prepared. The banner and the navigation for the site will be in the site's main page. John also created a document with several symbols that you will use in the site, including a rectangular symbol for the buttons in the navigation bar, a picture and various graphics for the banner, and an animation for some of the pages. Figure 7-35 shows the completed home page.

Figure 7-35

[Screenshot of Katie's Pet Resort website showing a banner with a dog photo and "Katie's Pet Resort" title, a left navigation bar with Home, Services, Training, and Adoptions buttons, and a welcome message area.]

Welcome to Katie's Pet Resort!

At Katie's Pet Resort our goal is to offer you the best pet boarding, grooming, and training services with an emphasis on meeting your pet's needs as conveniently and affordably as possible. We have the staff and resources to make your pet's visit here an exciting and fun experience.

Give us a call at 1-800-22-KATIE!

1. Create a new document 600 pixels wide by 400 pixels high based on ActionScript 2.0. Use a light yellow (#FFFFCC) for the background color. In the Accessibility panel, enter **Katie's Pet Resort** as the name, and enter **Special Services Web Site** for the description. Save the document as **kprMain.fla** in the Tutorial.07\Case1 folder included with your Data Files.

2. Create a new movie clip symbol named **petBanner**. In the petBanner symbol, create a rectangle 600 pixels wide by 100 pixels high. Use a light green color (#CCCC99) for the fill and do not include a stroke. Center the rectangle on the Stage. Rename Layer 1 as **background**.

3. Insert a new layer and name it **graphics**. Open the **katies.fla** file located in the Tutorial.07\Case1 folder included with your Data Files as an external library. On the graphics layer, add an instance of the masked dog symbol from the external library to the left side of the banner. Also, add two instances of the triangle symbol, placing one instance to the right of the masked dog instance and the other instance on the upper-right side of the rectangle.

4. Insert a new layer above the graphics layer and name it **text**. On the text layer, add a text block in the center of the rectangle. Use Comic Sans MS for the font family, bold for the font style, 40 for the point size, and maroon (#660000) for the text color. Type **Katie's Pet Resort** in the text block. If necessary, center the text block within the banner. The banner is complete.

5. In Scene 1, insert an instance of the petBanner symbol at the top of the Stage. Align the petBanner instance with the top and left sides of the Stage. Rename Layer 1 as **background**.

6. Create a new movie clip symbol named **petNavbar**. In the petNavbar symbol, create a rectangle 100 pixels wide by 300 pixels high. Use a light orange color (#FFCB65) for the fill and do not include a stroke. Center the rectangle on the Stage. Rename Layer 1 as **background** and lock it.

7. Insert a new layer and name it **buttons**. On the buttons layer, drag an instance of the square button symbol from the external library to the upper-left side of the rectangle. Rename the square symbol to **Home button**.

8. Edit the Home button symbol. Click the center of the Home button graphic to select the inside square area, and then change the fill color to light green (#66CC66). In the button's Timeline, insert a keyframe in the Over frame. In the Over frame, select the inside square area of the Home button graphic, and then change the fill color to light yellow (#FFFF99).
9. Insert a new layer and name it **text**. On the text layer, add a text block with the word **Home**. Use Comic Sans MS for the font family, bold for the font style, 12 for the point size, black for the text color, and align center for the paragraph format. Place the text block at the center of the square.
10. Make three duplicates of the Home button, and then rename the duplicate buttons as **Services button**, **Training button**, and **Adoptions button**, respectively. Change the text in the Services button to **Services**. Change the text in the Training button to **Training**. Change the text in the Adoptions button to **Adoptions**.
11. Edit the petNavbar symbol. Add an instance of the Services button below and to the right of the Home button instance, placing it close to the right edge of the rectangle. Add an instance of the Training button, placing it below and to the left of the Services button instance, near the left edge of the rectangle. Add an instance of the Adoptions button, placing it toward the lower-right side of the rectangle.
12. Select the Home button in the petNavbar symbol, open the Actions panel, and add a `loadMovieNum` action so that when the button is clicked and then released, the welcome.swf file loads at level 1 of the Flash Player. Add `loadMovieNum` actions to the other button instances to load SWF files at level 1. The Services button should load the services.swf file. The Training button should load the training.swf file. The Adoptions button should load the adoptions.swf file.
13. Return to Scene 1, insert a new layer, and name it **navbar**. On the navbar layer, add an instance of the petNavbar symbol to the left side of the Stage below the banner. Align the petNavbar instance with the left and bottom edges of the Stage.
14. Insert a new layer and name it **action**. In Frame 1 of the action layer, add a `loadMovieNum` action that loads the welcome.swf file at level 1 as soon as Frame 1 is played. This displays the welcome.swf file as soon as the main.swf page plays in the Flash Player. Save the kprMain.fla file.
15. Open the **welcome.fla** file located in the Tutorial.07\Case1 folder included with your Data Files. Rename Layer 1 to **content** and then insert a new layer and name it **animation**. In the animation layer, add an instance of the animated dog symbol from the external library so that it is in the lower-right corner of the Stage.
16. Save the welcome.fla file as a template named **kprTemplate** in a new template category called **Pet Resort** with **Template for the Katie's Pet Resort Web site pages** as the description. Close the kprTemplate.fla file. The welcome.fla document remains unchanged.
17. Create a new document based on the kprTemplate, and then save this document as **services.fla** in the Tutorial.07\Case1 folder included with your Data Files. Change the top text block to **Katie's Pet Resort Services!**, and then center the text block above the second text block. Change the second text block to the following text, and then spell check the text and make the necessary corrections:
Katie's offers many of the services you need to keep your pet happy, including boarding, grooming, and training. We also have a variety of pet supplies including pet food, pet toys, and pet accessories to keep your pet safe and healthy. Check back regularly for sales and special promotions.

18. Create a new document based on the kprTemplate, and then save this document as **training.fla** in the Tutorial.07\Case1 folder included with your Data Files. Change the top text block to **Pet Training Classes are Fun!**, center it above the second text block, and then change the text color to blue (#0000FF). Change the second text block to the following text, spell check the text and make the necessary corrections, and then change the text color to red (#FF0000):

    Here at Katie's, we can teach your pet new tricks. We can train your dog how to use the pet door, come when you call him, or even to give you a high-five! We can even train your cat to stay off your kitchen counters. Training classes are scheduled each month and are affordably priced. Make your reservations early as our classes fill up fast.

19. Create a new document based on the kprTemplate, and then save this document as **adoptions.fla** in the Tutorial.07\Case1 folder included with your Data Files. Change the top text block to **Katie's Adoption Events!**, center the text block above the second text block, and change the text color to dark green (#006600). Change the second text block to the following text, and then spell check the text and make the necessary corrections:

    Ask about our regular adoption events. Every third Saturday of each month, we hold an adoption event at Katie's Pet Resort in conjunction with the local pet shelter. During each adoption event, you'll have an opportunity to see a variety of pets ready for adoption. Light snacks are served. Ask one of our staff members for more details.

20. Save and publish each of the documents to create the services.swf, training.swf, and adoptions.swf files. Open the **welcome.fla** file located in the Tutorial.07\Case1 folder included with your Data Files, and then publish it to create the welcome.swf file. Return to the kprMain.fla document and test the Web site by using the Test Movie command. Test each of the buttons and make certain the individual pages are loaded. Make any necessary corrections.

21. Submit the finished files to your instructor.

| Apply | **Case Problem 2** |

Create a new Flash Web site based on a custom template with a navigation bar and custom graphics for a zoo.

Data File needed for this Case Problem: zooGraphics.fla

Alamo City Zoo Janet meets with Alex to discuss the development of a new Web site to showcase some special exhibits at the Alamo City Zoo. They agree on the following goal for the Web site: Promote some of the unique exhibits available at Alamo City Zoo.

Based on this goal, Alex puts together the following list of objectives:
- Highlight the zoo's special animal exhibits.
- Highlight the zoo's educational resources.
- Promote the kids' summer camps.

You will help Alex create the new Web site based on these goals and objectives. Alex designed a background picture for the Web site as well as some of the graphics you will use. He provided these graphics in a Flash document. You'll develop the main page, shown in Figure 7-36, and then create a template for the remaining pages. The navigation system will use a bear paw graphic for the buttons that appears when the user moves the pointer over the buttons.

Tutorial 7 Planning and Creating a Flash Web Site | Flash | FL 365

Figure 7-36

[Figure showing Alamo City Zoo web page mockup with banner, navigation menu (Home, Exhibits, Education, Summer Camps), and welcome text block over a giraffe background image]

1. Create a new document that is 600 pixels wide by 400 pixels high based on ActionScript 2.0 with white for the background color, and then save the document as **aczMain.fla** in the Tutorial.07\Case2 folder included with your Data Files.
2. Open the **zooGraphics.fla** document located in the Tutorial.07\Case2 folder included with your Data Files as an external library, drag an instance of the zooBack.jpg bitmap onto the Stage, align the picture with the left and bottom edges of the Stage, and then rename Layer 1 as **background**.
3. Create a new movie clip symbol named **zooBanner**. In the zooBanner symbol, create a rectangle 600 pixels wide by 70 pixels high with a brown color (#996633) for the fill, a black color (#FFFFFF) for the stroke, and a stroke height of 2. Center the rectangle on the editing window, and then rename Layer 1 as **background**.
4. Drag an instance of the bear symbol from the external library to the right side of the rectangle.
5. Insert a new layer and name it **text**. Add a text block in the center of the rectangle. Use Times New Roman for the font family, bold italic for the font style, 58 for the point size, black for the text color, and align center for the paragraph format. Type **Alamo City Zoo** in the text block, and then center the text inside the rectangle. If necessary, set the Font rendering method to Anti-alias for readability. The banner is complete.
6. Return to Scene 1, add an instance of the zooBanner symbol to the top of the Stage, and then align the instance with the top and left edges of the Stage.
7. Create a new button symbol named **Home button**. In symbol-editing mode, rename Layer 1 to **text**. Add a text block at the center of the editing window. Use Times New Roman for the font family, bold for the font style, 20 for the point size, black for the text color, and align left for the paragraph format. Type **Home** in the text block. Insert a regular frame in the Over frame to have the text be displayed when the pointer is over the button.
8. Insert a new layer and name it **graphic**. In the graphic layer, insert a keyframe in the Over frame and then drag an instance of the bear paw symbol from the external library to the left of the Home text. The bear paw instance will be present only in the Over frame of the button's Timeline.

9. Insert a blank keyframe in the Hit frame of the text layer. Turn on onion skinning and extend the onion skin markers to cover all four frames of the Timeline. In the Hit frame of the text layer, draw a small rectangle to cover the area for both the bear paw and the text. The Home button is complete.
10. Make three duplicates of the Home button, and then name the duplicate buttons **Exhibits button**, **Education button**, and **Camps button**, respectively.
11. Change the text in the Up frame of the Exhibits button to **Exhibits**, and then resize the rectangle in the Hit frame of the text layer to cover all the text. Change the text in the Up frame of the Education button to **Education**, and then resize the rectangle in the Hit frame to cover all the text. Change the text in the Up frame of the Camps button to **Summer Camps**, and then resize the rectangle in the Hit frame to cover all the text.
12. Create a new movie clip symbol named **Navbar**. In the Navbar symbol, drag an instance of the Home button to the center of the editing window, and then drag an instance of the Exhibits button, the Education button, and the Camps button below the previous button instance. Align the instances vertically and space them evenly using the Align panel.
13. Select the Home button in the Navbar, open the Actions panel, and add a `loadMovieNum` action so that when the button is clicked and then released, the home.swf file loads at level 1 of the Flash Player. Add `loadMovieNum` actions to the other button instances to load SWF files at level 1. The Exhibits button should load the exhibits.swf file. The Education button should load the education.swf file. The Camps button should load the camps.swf file. The Navbar is complete.
14. Return to Scene 1, insert a new layer and name it **navbar**, and then drag an instance of the Navbar symbol to the left side of the Stage. Place the instance below the banner approximately 50 pixels from the left side of the Stage.
15. Insert a new layer and name it **action**. In Frame 1 of the action layer, add a `loadMovieNum` action that loads the home.swf file at level 1 as soon as Frame 1 is played. This displays the home.swf file as soon as the aczMain.swf page plays in the Flash Player.
16. Create a new document to save as the Home page and as a template that is 600 pixels wide by 400 pixels high. Drag a horizontal guide to 100 pixels from the top edge of the Stage and drag a vertical guide to 200 pixels from the left of the Stage.
17. Draw a rectangle below and to the right of the guides to frame the contents of each page. Use a maroon color (#660000) for the stroke, a stroke height of 2, and no fill color. Make the rectangle 350 pixels wide by 270 pixels high. Align the upper-left corner of the rectangle with the intersection of the guides. Rename Layer 1 as **rectangle**.
18. Insert a new layer and name it **text**. Add a text block inside the rectangle. Place it close to the top of the rectangle. Use Times New Roman for the font family, 22 for the point size, black for the text color, bold for the font style, and align left for the paragraph format. Type **Welcome to the Alamo City Zoo** in the text block. Center the text block within the rectangle.
19. Add a fixed-width text block below the first text block. Use Times New Roman for the font family, regular for the font style, 14 for the point size, black for the text color, and align left for the paragraph format. Type the following in this text block: **The Alamo City Zoo has an extensive collection of the world's most exotic animals. Come visit our world-famous exhibits and see animals in their native habitats. The zoo also offers group tours, special classes, and summer camps for kids.**

20. Center the two text blocks within the rectangle. Insert a new layer and name it **graphics**. Save this page as **home.fla** in the Tutorial.07\Case2 folder included with your Data Files, and then save this same document as a template named **aczTemplate** in a new template category called **Alamo** with the description **Template for the Alamo City Zoo Web site pages**. Close the azcTemplate.fla file.

21. Create a new document based on the azcTemplate, and save the document as **exhibits.fla** in the Tutorial.07\Cases2folder included with your Data Files. Change the top text block to **Alamo City Zoo Exhibits**, and then center the text block within the rectangle. Change the second text block to the following text:

    Alamo City Zoo has one of the largest collections of exotic animals from all over the world. We have bears, elephants, giraffes, and rhinoceros to name a few. Come visit our zoo and plan to spend the day enjoying the many animal exhibits with the animals shown in their natural habitats.

22. Select the graphics layer, and then drag an instance of the elephant.jpg bitmap from the external library to the lower-left corner of the Stage. Flip the bitmap horizontally so that the elephant faces to the right.

23. Create a new document based on the aczTemplate, and then save the document as **education.fla** in the Tutorial.07\Case2 folder included with your Data Files. Change the top text block to **Zoo Educational Classes**, and then center the text block within the rectangle and change the text color to dark orange (#CC3300). Change the second text block to the following text:

    Alamo City Zoo has an exciting schedule of educational and fun classes. These classes are available for the general public, with some special classes available to zoo members only. Local schoolteachers can bring their students to visit the zoo and get special discounts on educational tours.

24. Select the graphics layer, and then drag an instance of the rhino.jpg bitmap from the external library to the lower-left corner of the Stage.

25. Create a new document based on the aczTemplate, and then save the document as **camps.fla** in the Tutorial.07\Case2 folder included with your Data Files. Change the top text block to **Summer Camps**, center the text block within the rectangle, and change the text color to dark green (#006600). Change the second text block to the following text:

    Alamo City Zoo offers a full schedule of summer camps for kids 8–14. Kids get to visit up close with many of the zoo animals and will learn more about how zoo staff feed and care for the animals. Be sure to ask about our overnight camps.

26. Select the graphics layer and drag an instance of the bear.jpg bitmap from the external library to the lower-left corner of the Stage.

27. Save and publish each of the documents to create the exhibits.swf, education.swf, and camps.swf files. Open the **home.fla** file and publish it to create the home.swf file. Return to the azcMain.fla document, and then test the Web site. Test each of the buttons and make certain the individual pages are loaded. Make any necessary corrections.

28. Submit the finished files to your instructor.

FL 368 Flash | Tutorial 7 Planning and Creating a Flash Web Site

| Challenge | **Case Problem 3** |

Create a new Flash Web site based on a template with a navigation bar and custom graphics for a nursery.

Data Files needed for this Case Problem: flower1.jpg, flower2.jpg, flower3.jpg, wcDraft.fla

Westcreek Nursery Alice asks Amanda about creating a new Web site to showcase Westcreek Nursery's weekly specials. This Web site will be separate from the current Web site. After meeting with Alice, Amanda develops the following goals for the new Web site:
- Promote the Westcreek Nursery name.
- Showcase weekly specials available for delivery.

Based on these goals, Amanda develops the following objectives:
- Provide a welcome message with contact information.
- Showcase flowers and plants available for delivery.
- Display photos of flowers and plants.

You will help Amanda create the Web site. The outline Amanda prepared for the site includes a home page with a banner at the top consisting of the Westcreek Nursery name with an animation. The navigation bar will have buttons in the shape of a car wheel, which rotate when the pointer is over them. She wants a link to the Photos page, with buttons to display each of three pictures. You will start with a document Amanda has created and use the graphics and photos she has provided. Figure 7-37 shows the completed home page.

Figure 7-37

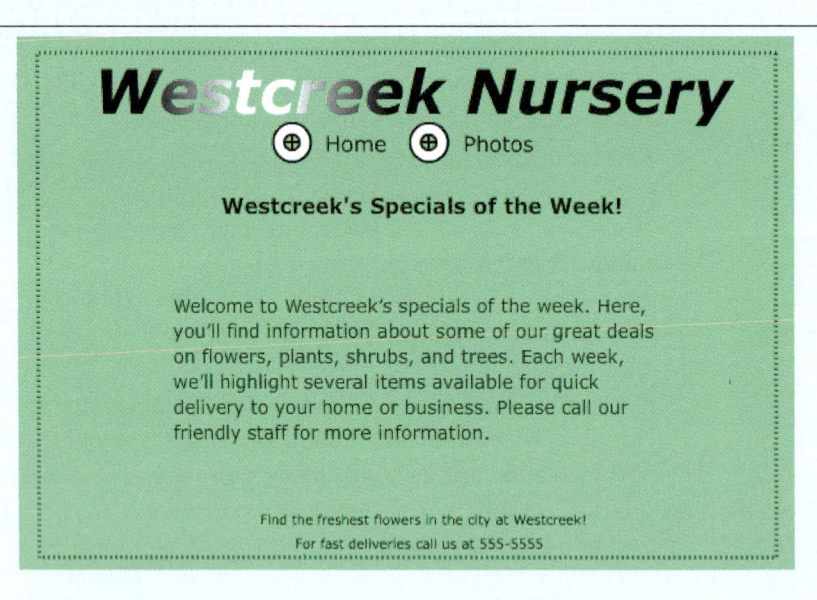

1. Open the **wcDraft.fla** file located in the Tutorial.07\Case3 folder included with your Data Files and then save the document as **wcMain.fla** in the same folder.
2. Create a new movie clip symbol named **wcBanner**. In the wcBanner symbol, create a text block in the center of the editing window. Use Verdana for the font family, bold italic for the font style, 46 for the point size, black for the text color, and align center for the paragraph format. Type **Westcreek Nursery** in the text block. Center the text block and then change the name of Layer 1 to **text1**.

⊕ EXPLORE

3. Insert a new layer and name it **text2**. Copy the text block on the text1 layer, and then use the Paste in Place command to paste the copy on the text2 layer in the same position as the original text block.

4. Insert a new layer between the text1 and text2 layers and name it **gradient**. Drag an instance of the Gradient symbol to Frame 1 of the gradient layer, placing the instance on the right side of the text block so that the rectangle's left side covers the letter y. Create a motion tween in Frame 1 of the gradient layer. Insert regular frames at Frame 24 of both the text1 and text2 layers to extend them.
5. At Frame 24 of the gradient layer, move the Gradient instance to the left side of the text block so that the rectangle's right side covers only the letter W. The Gradient instance will move across the text from the right to the left side.
6. Change the text2 layer to a mask layer and make certain that the gradient layer becomes a masked layer. The banner is complete.
7. Return to Scene 1, insert a new layer and name it **banner**. On the banner layer, add an instance of the wcBanner symbol to the top of the Stage. Center the instance right below the top edge of the box created by the rectangle on the Stage.
8. Create a new button symbol named **Home button**. Drag an instance of the Wheel symbol from the library to the center of the editing window. Add a text block to the right of the Wheel instance in the editing window. Use Verdana for the font family, regular for the font style, 16 for the point size, and black for the text color. Type **Home** in the text block.
9. Insert a keyframe in the Over frame, swap the Wheel instance with an instance of the Rotating Wheel symbol, and then change the text color to red (#FF0000).

EXPLORE

10. Add a blank keyframe in the Hit frame of Layer 1. Turn on onion skinning and extend the onion skin markers to cover all four frames of the Timeline. In the Hit frame of Layer 1, draw a small rectangle to cover the area for both the wheel and the text. The Home button is complete.
11. Make a duplicate of the Home button named **Photos button**. Change the text in both the Up and Over frames of the Photos button to **Photos**, and then resize the rectangle in the Hit frame of the Photos button to cover all of the text.
12. Create a new movie clip symbol named **Navbar**. In the Navbar symbol, drag an instance of the Home button to the left side of the crosshair on the editing window. Drag an instance of the Photos button to the right of the Home button. Align both symbol instances along their top edges.
13. Select the Home button in the Navbar, open the Actions panel, and add a `loadMovieNum` action so that when the button is clicked and then released, the nursery.swf file loads at level 1 of the Flash Player. Add a `loadMovieNum` action to the Photos button instance to load the photos.swf file at level 1. The Navbar is complete.
14. Return to Scene 1, insert a new layer, and name it **navigation**. Drag a horizontal guide to 100 pixels from the top edge of the Stage. On the navigation layer, drag an instance of the Navbar symbol to the Stage and center it below the banner and above the horizontal guide.
15. Insert a new layer and name it **action**. Add a `loadMovieNum` action at Frame 1 of the Action layer that loads the nursery.swf file at level 1 as soon as Frame 1 is played. This file is displayed as soon as the wcMain.swf page plays in the Flash Player.
16. Create a new document 600 pixels wide by 400 pixels high. Drag a horizontal guide to 100 pixels from the top edge of the Stage. The content for the page will be below this guide.

17. Add a text block below the guide, 150 pixels from the top edge of the Stage. Use Verdana for the font family, bold for the font style, 16 for the point size, black for the text color, and align left for the paragraph format. Type **Westcreek's Specials of the Week!** in the text block. Add a fixed-width text block below the first text block. Change the font style to regular and change the point size to 14. Type the following in this text block:

    Welcome to Westcreek's specials of the week. Here, you'll find information about some of our great deals on flowers, plants, shrubs, and trees. Each week, we'll highlight several items available for quick delivery to your home or business. Please call our friendly staff for more information.

18. Center the two text blocks on the Stage, and then save the page as **nursery.fla** in the Tutorial.07\Case3 folder included with your Data Files.

19. Create a new document 600 pixels wide by 400 pixels high. Drag a horizontal guide to 100 pixels from the top edge of the Stage. The content for the page will be below this guide.

20. Create a new movie clip symbol named **Photo holder**. Exit the movie clip's symbol-editing mode and return to Scene 1. Drag an instance of the Photo holder symbol to the Stage. Use the Property inspector to place the movie clip instance at the X coordinate of 200 and the Y coordinate of 100. Also, assign the name **photo_mc** to the movie clip instance.

21. Create a new movie clip symbol named **Photos navbar**. In symbol editing mode, draw a star shape with a dark green (#006600) fill and a black stroke. Set the star's width and height to 45 pixels each. Convert the star shape to a button symbol named **Photo button**. Edit the Photo button symbol, add a keyframe in the Over frame, and then, in the Over frame, change the color of the star's fill to light peach (#FFCC99).

EXPLORE

22. Return to the Photos navbar symbol, add two more instances of the Photo button to the Stage, and then arrange the instances vertically below the first instance. Add a text block above the buttons. Use Verdana as the font family, regular for the font style, 12 for the point size, and black for the text color. Type **Click stars to see pictures:** in the text block.

23. Select the top button instance, open the Behaviors panel, and add a Load Graphic behavior to the button instance. The behavior should load the flower1.jpg file into the photo_mc movie clip instance. The Behavior text box should display this._parent.photo_mc, indicating the graphic will load into the photo_mc instance on the Scene 1 Timeline. Also, add the Load Graphic behavior to the other two button instances on the Stage. One should load the flower2.jpg file and the other should load the flower3.jpg file. Both photos should load in the photo_mc movie clip instance.

24. Return to Scene 1, and then drag an instance of the Photos navbar symbol to the left side of the Stage right below the guide and 20 pixels from the left of the Stage. Save the page as **photos.fla** in the Tutorial.07\Case3 folder included with your Data Files.

25. Publish each of the documents to create the **nursery.swf** and **photos.swf** files. Return to the wcMain.fla document and test the Web site in the Flash Player. Test each of the buttons and verify that the individual pages and photos are loaded. Make any necessary corrections.

26. Submit the finished files to your instructor.

Tutorial 7 Planning and Creating a Flash Web Site | Flash | FL 371

| Create | **Case Problem 4** |

Create a Flash Web site based on a template with a navigation bar and custom graphics for an association.

Data File needed for this Case Problem: mission.jpg

Missions Support Association Anissa is developing a preliminary version of a new Web site for Missions Support Association that will highlight special services available to the association's members. Based on discussions with Brittany, president of the association, the following goals are developed:

- Promote the association's main services.
- Promote the association's name.

Based on these goals, Anissa and Brittany develop the following objectives for the Web site:

- Provide information about special events.
- Provide information about volunteer opportunities.
- Provide information about tours available for schools.
- Use a picture for the background of the content and allow for the picture to be changed periodically.

You will develop the Web site for Anissa. The Web site will be a preliminary version and the content for each page is under development. Figure 7-38 shows one possible design for the Web site.

Figure 7-38

1. Plan the Flash Web site, including a main page with the organization's name, navigation bar, and a content area for the level 1 pages, as well as the level 1 pages for the different informational areas. Also, plan how you will use the **mission.jpg** file included in the Tutorial.07\Case4 folder with your Data Files in the Web site.
2. Create a new document for the main page, save it as **msaMain.fla** in the Tutorial.07\Case4 folder included with your Data Files, and use the dimensions and background color of your choice.
3. In a new layer, create a text block, using the text properties and location of your choice, with the organization's name, **Missions Support Association**.
4. Create the buttons for the navigation bar to load the different level 1 pages in the main page. Be sure to include some distinguishing characteristic in each frame to provide visual cues for the user. Include an animation in one frame (for example, you can create motion tweens to increase the width of the button's shape to 120% between Frames 1 and 5, and then decrease to its original size in Frame 10). Label each button appropriately. Add a clickable shape in the Hit frame, if necessary. You can use onion skinning to see all the contents of the frames as you draw a rectangle that covers any shapes and text in the button. (*Hint*: You can create one button, and then edit duplicates of the button to create the other buttons you need.)
5. Create a navigation bar for the main page that includes each button you created. Add a `loadMovieNum` action to each button so that when the button is clicked and then released, the corresponding file loads at level 1 of the Flash Player. Place the navigation bar on the main page.
6. Add an action to Frame 1 of the main page that loads one of the files at level 1 as soon as Frame 1 is played.
7. Create a new document with the same document dimensions and background color as the main page, and then save it as a template named **msaTemplate** in a new template category using an appropriate description. You will use this template to create the level 1 pages. Follow your design plan to complete the template, adding images, shapes, text, actions, and guides as needed.
8. Create a new document based on the template for each level 1 page you need to create for the site, saving each document with an appropriate filename (such as **main.fla**, **events.fla**, **tours.fla**, **volunteer.fla**, and so on) in the Tutorial.07\Case4 folder included with your Data Files. Add appropriate content to the page in the location specified by the guides.
9. Save and publish each of the documents to create the SWF files.
10. Return to the main document, and then test the movie, verifying that when you click each button, the corresponding page loads. Make any necessary corrections.
11. Submit the finished files to your instructor.

Review | Quick Check Answers

Session 7.1

1. XHTML or HTML
2. False; the first SWF file in a Flash Web site is usually loaded into the Flash Player at level 0.
3. levels
4. False; when an SWF file is loaded at the same level that already has an SWF file playing, the new SWF file replaces the file that is currently playing.

5. Identify the goals and objectives for the Web site based on the needs of the client. Based on the goals and objectives, consider accessibility needs and develop the content of the site. The content leads to the design of the Web pages, including the navigation system. Finally, build the site and test it to make sure all parts of the site work as designed.
6. by meeting with the clients and discussing what they want the site to accomplish
7. software that visually impaired users run to read a Web site's text content aloud
8. a diagram showing a sketch of how all of the site's pages are organized with lines indicating how each page links to the other pages

Session 7.2

1. a prebuilt document that installs with Flash and provides a way to quickly develop a new Flash document
2. to add instances from the external library to the library of the current document
3. rollover
4. True
5. hyperlinks
6. Create a separate movie clip with an animation, and then place an instance of the movie clip in the Over frame of the button's Timeline.

Session 7.3

1. a programming language within Flash you use to add actions to objects or frames in a document
2. `loadMovieNum("staff.swf", 1);`
3. determines what action to take when a specific button event occurs
4. the Check Syntax button
5. the `loadMovie` action
6. name

Ending Data Files

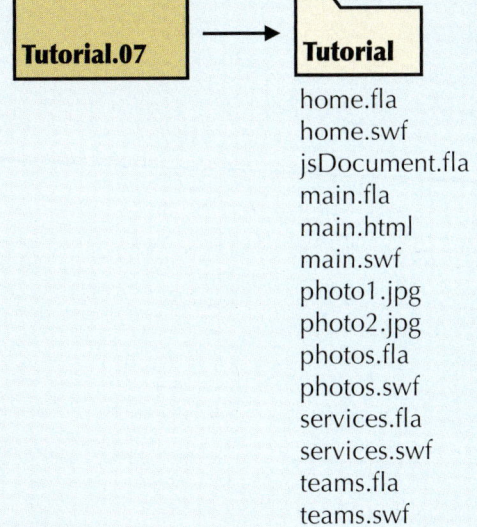

Tutorial.07

Tutorial
home.fla
home.swf
jsDocument.fla
main.fla
main.html
main.swf
photo1.jpg
photo2.jpg
photos.fla
photos.swf
services.fla
services.swf
teams.fla
teams.swf

Review
home.swf
main.fla
main.swf
photos.fla
photos.swf
picture1.jpg
picture2.jpg
services.swf
specials.fla
specials.swf
teams.swf

Case1
adoptions.fla
adoptions.swf
kprMain.fla
kprMain.swf
kprTemplate.fla
services.fla
services.swf
training.fla
training.swf
welcome.swf

Case2
aczMain.fla
aczMain.swf
aczTemplate.fla
camps.fla
camps.swf
education.fla
education.swf
exhibits.fla
exhibits.swf
home.fla
home.swf

Case3
nursery.fla
nursery.swf
photos.fla
photos.swf
wcMain.fla
wcMain.swf

Case4
events.fla
events.swf
main.fla
main.swf
msaMain.fla
msaMain.swf
msaTemplate.fla
tours.fla
tours.swf
volunteer.fla
volunteer.swf

Flash | FL 375

Tutorial 8

Objectives

Session 8.1
- Review the basics of ActionScript programming
- Compare ActionScript 2.0 and ActionScript 3.0
- Learn ActionScript 3.0 syntax
- Write ActionScript 3.0 code to create functions and handle events

Session 8.2
- Create links to external Web sites
- Create and test a Flash preloader

Session 8.3
- Create input and dynamic text fields
- Create an input form

Programming with ActionScript 3.0

Adding Interactive Elements to a Flash Web Site

Case | Admiral Web Design

Dan Jackson, owner of Jackson's Sports, meets with Aly and Chris and requests additional pages for the Jackson's Sports Web site. He wants a Resources page, which will contain hyperlinks to other sports-related Web sites. He also wants a page that team coaches can use to calculate the cost of team jerseys by entering the number of jerseys needed and choosing from various options to calculate and display the total cost. Aly and Chris revise the design of the Jackson's Sports Web site. You will add the requested pages as well as a simple animation that will provide visual feedback while the site contents load into the Flash Player.

In this tutorial, you will learn how to use ActionScript 3.0 to add interactive elements to Flash documents. You will learn about the structure and syntax of the ActionScript programming language. You will write ActionScript code to control the navigation for the Web site, to create links to other Web sites, to input values, and to perform calculations.

Starting Data Files

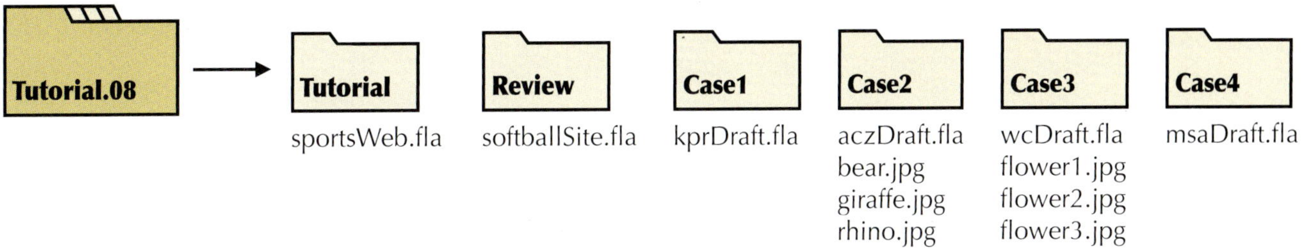

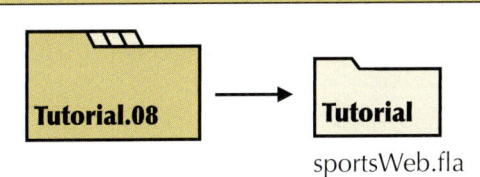

Tutorial.08

- **Tutorial**
  sportsWeb.fla

- **Review**
  softballSite.fla

- **Case1**
  kprDraft.fla

- **Case2**
  aczDraft.fla
  bear.jpg
  giraffe.jpg
  rhino.jpg

- **Case3**
  wcDraft.fla
  flower1.jpg
  flower2.jpg
  flower3.jpg

- **Case4**
  msaDraft.fla

Session 8.1

Programming with ActionScript 3.0

ActionScript is a robust programming language that gives Flash developers a virtually unlimited number of ways to make a Flash document interactive. ActionScript can be used to create actions that control multimedia elements such as buttons, and to control the way the different parts of a movie are played. ActionScript programming requires writing scripts that consist of actions, event handlers, and other programming statements to control how the actions are executed. In previous tutorials, you added actions to buttons that controlled animations in movies and controlled when and how SWF files were loaded into the Flash Player.

In addition to controlling the order in which frames play in a document's Timeline or making buttons operational, ActionScript can be used to enable the viewer to input data and have the Flash Player process that data to return a result. ActionScript can also be used to change the properties of movie clips while they play in the Flash Player. For example, you can have a movie clip with a graphic of a car that changes color when a button is clicked. With ActionScript, you can also test a condition and then execute different actions based on the test results. For example, you can create a script that compares an input value with a set value to determine what actions to execute.

In this tutorial, you will write ActionScript code to control multimedia elements, access external Web pages, and provide the user a means of entering and processing information in the Jackson's Sports Web site.

Comparing ActionScript 3.0 and ActionScript 2.0

ActionScript 3.0 is the latest version of the ActionScript programming language and is conceptually different from the previous version, ActionScript 2.0, which you used in earlier tutorials. ActionScript 3.0 has many more capabilities than ActionScript 2.0 and is designed to enable Flash developers to create highly complex applications. The Flash Player plug-in (versions 9 and later) uses the **ActionScript Virtual Machine 2 (AVM2)**, which is the Flash Player built-in code that plays Flash movies. Previous versions of the Flash Player use the original ActionScript Virtual Machine (AVM1). Improvements in the AVM2 enable current versions of the Flash Player to run faster and more efficiently than previous versions. ActionScript 3.0 code does not run on the AVM1, so Flash movies using ActionScript 3.0 run only on Flash Player 9 or later.

In a previous tutorial, you used ActionScript 2.0 to create an event handler assigned to a button instance. The event handler carried out an action such as stopping or playing a movie when the button was clicked and then released. In ActionScript 3.0, you cannot add actions to a button instance or to a movie clip instance. Instead, you add the actions to frames in the Timeline.

Working with Objects and Properties

ActionScript is used to control and modify objects. An **object** is an element in Flash that has **properties**, or characteristics, that can be examined or changed with ActionScript. The multimedia elements you work with in Flash, such as buttons, movie clips, and text

> **Tip**
> You can run SWF files that contain ActionScript 2.0 or earlier in current versions of the Flash Player.

blocks, are considered objects. For example, a button has properties such as width, height, and location on the Stage. An instance of a movie clip symbol has similar properties. ActionScript code can be written to read or change these properties in response to certain events, such as a mouse click, a key press, or a certain frame in the Timeline being played. The properties for an object include alpha (which controls the movie clip's transparency), rotation (which controls the movie clip's orientation), and visible (which controls the movie clip's visibility). These properties can be examined and modified using ActionScript.

Any object you want to reference in ActionScript requires a name. Recall that you can have multiple instances of one movie clip symbol, which means that multiple objects are based on the same symbol. When using ActionScript to refer to a specific instance, you must refer to its instance name.

After you assign a name to an instance, you can refer to it in the action using dot notation. **Dot notation** links an object to its properties and methods. (Methods are discussed later in this session.) For example, if a movie clip instance is named circle_mc, the following code changes the alpha property of the instance to 30%:

```
circle_mc.alpha = .30
```

The values for an object's alpha property range from 0 to 1, where 1 represents 100%. The dot (.) links the property to the particular instance or object.

InSight | Naming Objects Effectively

When naming an instance of an object, include a suffix that identifies the object's type. Flash recognizes the following suffixes:

- _mc for movie clip instances
- _btn for button instances
- _txt for text field instances

Although not required, using these suffixes takes advantage of code hints in the Actions panel. When you enter ActionScript code, Flash displays code hints based on what is typed. For example, if you assign the name circle_mc to a movie clip instance on the Stage, and then use the name in the Actions panel, Flash displays code hints specific to movie clips. As you type the first few letters after the dot, the matching code is highlighted in the code hints list. The highlighted code is added to the script when you press the Enter key. This makes it easier to enter the correct code and avoid typing mistakes.

Aly and Chris sketched the storyboard with the design of the Jackson's Sports Web site, as shown in Figure 8-1. The sketch shows the new pages to be completed as well as the site navigation.

Figure 8-1 | Jackson's Sports Web site storyboard

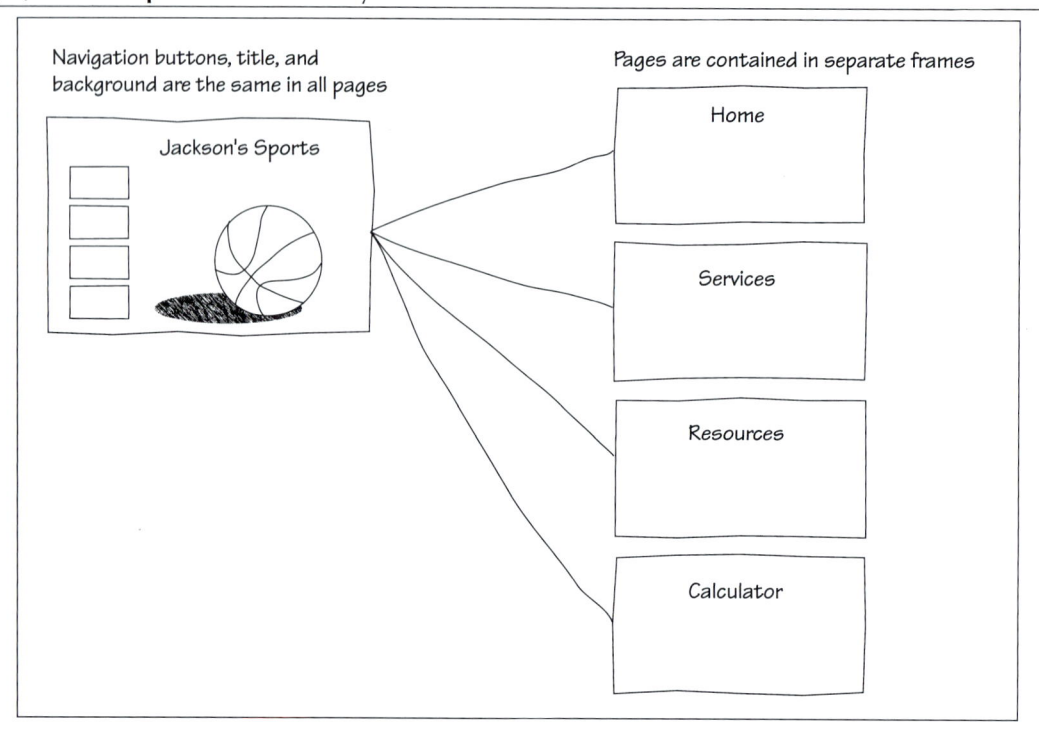

Navigation buttons, title, and background are the same in all pages

Jackson's Sports

Pages are contained in separate frames

- Home
- Services
- Resources
- Calculator

You will review the new Jackson's Sports Web site that Aly and Chris created, assign names to the objects representing the buttons for the site's navigation, and then extend the Timeline of the document to add the Resources and Calculator pages.

To name button objects and extend the Timeline in the Jackson's Sports Web site:

1. Open the **sportsWeb.fla** file located in the Tutorial.08\Tutorial folder included with your Data Files, save the file as **jsWebSite.fla** in the same folder, reset the workspace to the **Essentials** layout, and then change the Stage magnification to **Show Frame**.

2. In the Timeline, move the playhead to **Frame 10**, if necessary, to display the Home page for the Web site on the Stage, and then move the playhead to **Frame 20** to display the Services page. Each Web page in the site will be in a separate frame.

3. In the Tools panel, click the **Selection** tool, and then, on the Stage, click the **Home** button to select it. The name of the Home button instance, home_btn, appears in the Instance name box in the Property inspector. See Figure 8-2.

Tutorial 8 Programming with ActionScript 3.0 | Flash | FL 379

Figure 8-2 | Home button instance name

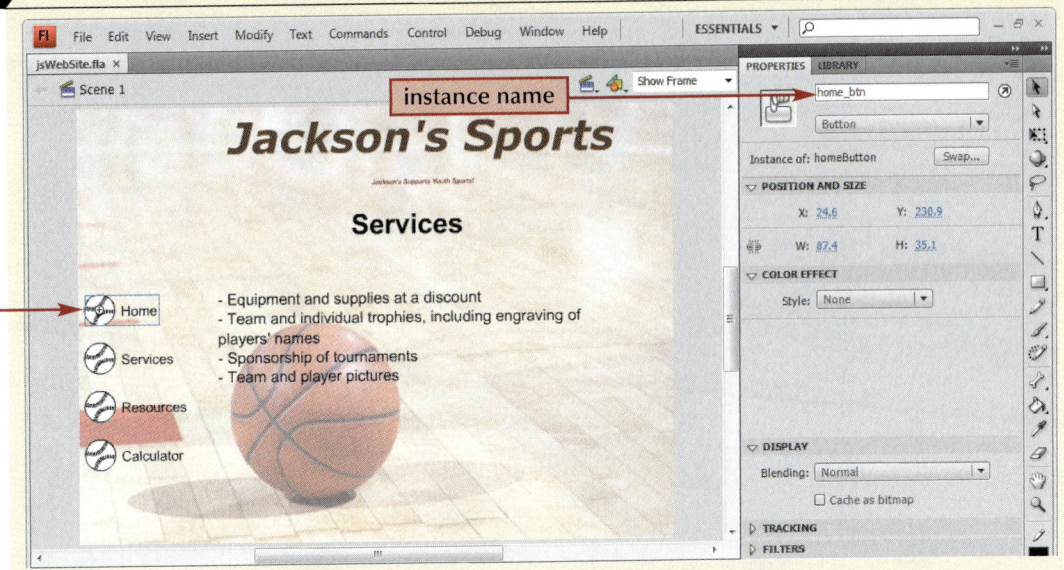

select the Home button

4. On the Stage, click the **Services** button to select it, and then, in the Property inspector, type **services_btn** in the Instance name box and press the **Enter** key. The name services_btn is assigned to the Services button instance.

5. Repeat Step 4 to assign the instance name **resources_btn** to the Resources button instance and the instance name **calculator_btn** to the Calculator button instance.

6. In the Timeline, insert regular frames at **Frame 50** of all the layers, and then, in the labels layer, insert keyframes at **Frame 30** and **Frame 40**.

7. In the labels layer, select **Frame 30**, and then, in the Label section of the Property inspector, type **Resources** in the Name box and press the **Enter** key. The Resources frame label appears in the Timeline next to Frame 30 of the labels layer.

8. Repeat Step 7 to select **Frame 40** and enter the frame label **Calculator**. The Calculator frame label appears in the Timeline next to Frame 40 of the labels layer. Each frame that will contain content for the site's pages is labeled. See Figure 8-3.

Figure 8-3 | Timeline with labels for the pages

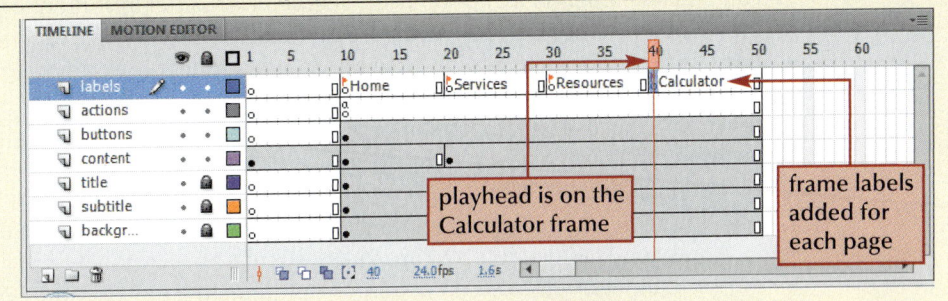

9. In the content layer, insert a keyframe at **Frame 30**, and then, on the Stage, replace the Services text with **Sports Web Site Resources** and delete the large text block in the center of the Stage. You will add the page content later in this tutorial.

10. In the content layer, insert a keyframe at **Frame 40**, and then, in this frame, replace the Sports Web Site Resources text with **Team Jersey Calculator**. See Figure 8-4.

Figure 8-4   **Content for the Calculator page**

Calculator page content added in Frame 40

select Frame 40 of the content layer

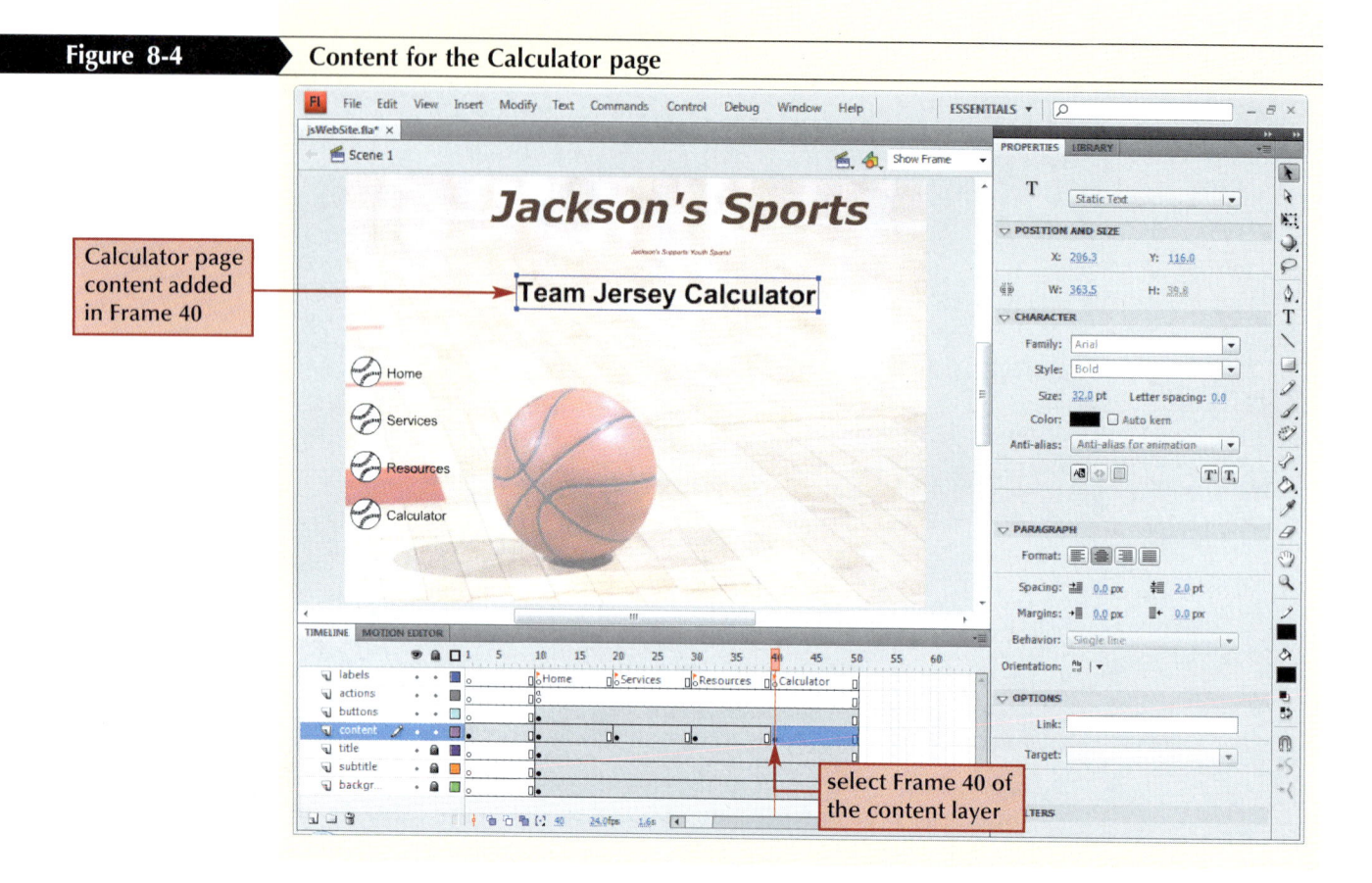

Using Actions, Methods, and Functions

An action is a statement, such as `gotoAndStop()`, that instructs the SWF file to do something. The terms *action* and *statement* are often interchangeable.

    A **function** is a block of statements that processes information and returns a value or performs some action. Flash includes a number of prebuilt functions, such as the `trace()` function, which displays values in the Output panel, and the `math.Random()` function, which returns a random number. You can also create your own functions. For example, you can create a function that accepts the temperature value in Fahrenheit degrees and returns the value in Celsius degrees. Then you can **call**, or execute, the function from different parts of the script in which it is defined. To use a function, you need to know what value or values to send to it and what value or values to expect in return. The values you send to a function are called **parameters**, or arguments, and are enclosed in parentheses. For example, the text "You are here" in the action `trace ("You are here")` is a parameter of the function. Not all functions require parameters. For example, the `math.Random()` function requires no parameters, so nothing is enclosed in the parentheses.

    A **method** is a function specific to a particular object. It is a built-in capability of the object that performs a certain action or responds to a certain event. Methods are similar to other functions and actions, but they are part of an object and can be used to control the object. For example, if you have a movie clip instance named circle_mc in the document's main Timeline that has 20 frames in its own Timeline, you can control which of the 20 frames will play. You do this with the `gotoAndPlay()` method for the movie clip. Using dot notation, you code the object name followed by a dot followed by the method's name. The following code sets the movie clip instance to start playing at Frame 10 of its Timeline:

```
circle_mc.gotoAndPlay(10)
```

The parameter value of 10 in the parentheses specifies to which frame the playhead will go. Because `gotoAndPlay()` is a method of the movie clip object, the movie clip knows how to respond when the method is executed. The `gotoAndPlay()` method is also considered an action in the main Timeline because the main document is considered an object. When using the `gotoAndPlay()` method for the document's main Timeline, it is not necessary to specify an object name.

The Jackson's Sports Web site will use functions to move the playhead to specific frames in the Timeline by referring to frame labels. For example, the `gotoAndStop("Home")` action will move the playhead to the frame labeled Home, Frame 10 of the labels layer, which contains the home page for the site. The content of each page of the Jackson's Sports Web site is in a separate frame that will be referred to by its label.

Writing ActionScript Code

When writing ActionScript code, you must follow certain rules, which are known as the **syntax** of the language. As shown in previous examples, actions and functions are often written in mixed uppercase and lowercase letters. For example, the `gotoAndPlay()` function uses the uppercase letters A and P, but lowercase for the remainder of the letters. Because ActionScript is case sensitive, writing this function as `gotoandplay()`, with all lowercase letters, will generate an error message. Also, even though most statements work without an ending semicolon, it is good programming practice to include it. Ending the statements with a semicolon follows the format of other programming languages. Other required syntactical elements are parentheses, which are used to group arguments in methods and functions, and curly braces, which group a block of related statements. Figure 8-5 shows a sample ActionScript syntax.

Figure 8-5 Sample ActionScript syntax

```
1  function preloader(progressEvt:ProgressEvent):void {
2
3      if (loadedBytes==totalBytes) {
4          gotoAndPlay("Home");
5      } else {
6          gotoAndPlay("Preload");
7      }
8  }
9
```

- parentheses enclose parameters
- semicolons end statements
- curly braces group statements

You'll review the actions in Frame 10 of the actions layer of the Jackson's Sports Web site.

To review the actions in Frame 10 of the actions layer:

1. In the Timeline, click **Frame 10** of the actions layer. The a at the top of the frame indicates that the frame contains an action.

2. On the Application bar, click **Window**, and then click **Actions**. The Actions panel opens and displays a script.

3. If necessary, click the **collapse** button in the vertical bar between the Actions toolbox and the Script pane. The Actions toolbox collapses and the Script pane expands. See Figure 8-6.

Figure 8-6 — Script for Frame 10 of the actions layer

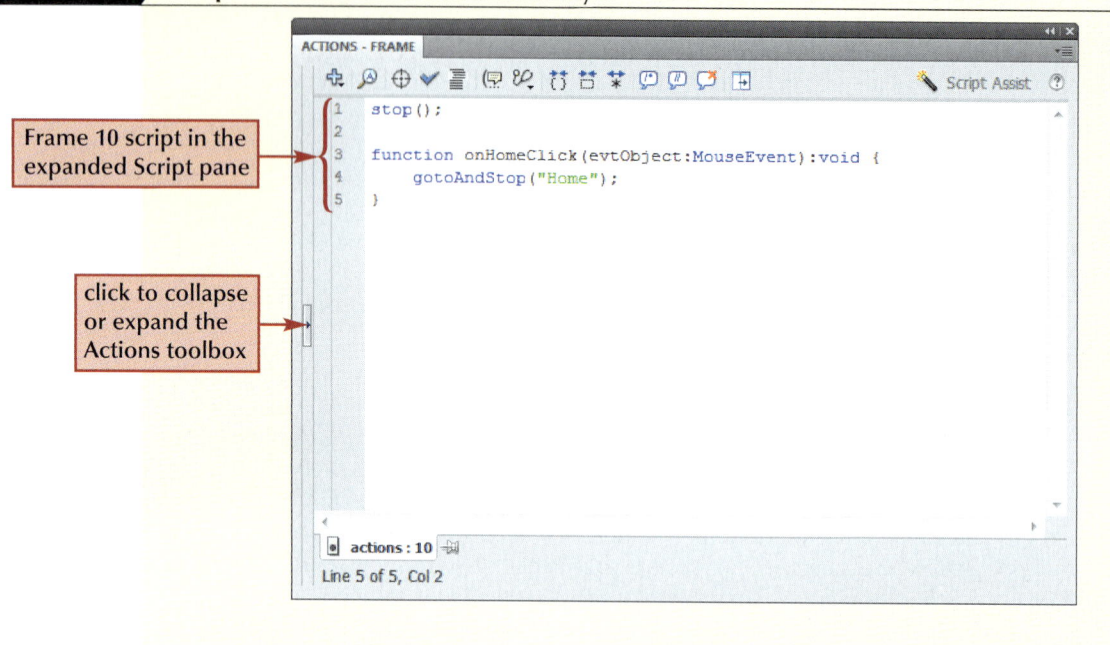

```
stop();

function onHomeClick(evtObject:MouseEvent):void {
    gotoAndStop("Home");
}
```

Frame 10 script in the expanded Script pane

click to collapse or expand the Actions toolbox

Tip
You can also double-click the vertical bar between the Actions toolbox and the Script pane to collapse or expand the Actions toolbox.

The first line of the Actions panel contains `stop();`, which will stop the playhead on Frame 10 and prevent the movie from playing continuously. The third line contains `function onHomeClick(evtObject:MouseEvent):void {`, which defines the onHomeClick function.

To define a function, you use the function keyword followed by the function name. A **keyword**, also called a reserved word, is a word that has a specified use or meaning in ActionScript and cannot be used in another context in a statement. The function name is a user-defined name and should be unique. The name should not start with a number, but it can include letters, numbers, the underscore character, and the dollar sign character. Within the parentheses following the function name, you specify the parameter of the function, which in this case is an event object with the user-defined name of evtObject. An **event object** represents an actual event such as the clicking of the mouse button and contains information about the event such as its properties. The event object must be assigned an event type—in this case, MouseEvent. Object types are coded with a colon followed by the type identifier. The event type, MouseEvent, distinguishes evtObject from other types of events.

InSight | Using a Standard Naming Convention

When assigning names to objects such as functions, variables, movie clips, and buttons, use a mixed case format where the first letter of the name is lowercase and the first letter of each word that is part of the name is capitalized. This naming convention makes it easier to read names within the ActionScript code and is consistent with other programming languages.

A function can return a value, such as the result of a calculation, based on the actions in the function. The results of the function, such as a return value, must also be assigned a data type. If the function does not return a value, you include the void keyword after the colon to indicate no value is returned. The statements in a function must be enclosed in curly braces. In this case, the curly braces enclose the statement `gotoAndStop("Home");`, which is the action to be performed when the function is called. Although this function requires only one statement, functions can include multiple statements. When the onHomeClick function is called, the playhead will move to the frame labeled Home and the movie will stop playing. The function structure is shown in Figure 8-7.

Figure 8-7 Structure of the onHomeClick function

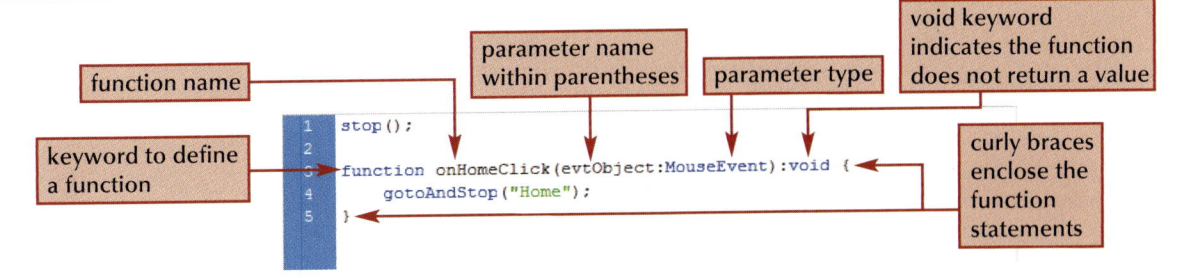

```
1  stop();
2
3  function onHomeClick(evtObject:MouseEvent):void {
4      gotoAndStop("Home");
5  }
```

- function name
- keyword to define a function
- parameter name within parentheses
- parameter type
- void keyword indicates the function does not return a value
- curly braces enclose the function statements

You will write similar functions to move the playhead to each frame representing a Web page.

To add new functions for the Jackson's Sports Web site:

1. In the Actions panel, click at the end of line 5 after the closing curly brace, and then press the **Enter** key to insert a new line.

2. Type the following lines of code to create a function that moves the playhead to the Services page.

   ```
   function onServicesClick(evtObject:MouseEvent):void {
       gotoAndStop("Services");
   }
   ```

3. Press the **Enter** key after the closing curly brace to move the insertion point to a new line, and then type the following lines of code to create functions that move the playhead to the Resources page and the Calculator page.

   ```
   function onResourcesClick(evtObject:MouseEvent):void {
       gotoAndStop("Resources");
   }
   function onCalculatorClick(evtObject:MouseEvent):void {
       gotoAndStop("Calculator");
   }
   ```

4. In the Actions panel, click the **Check syntax** button to check for syntax errors in the code you entered. A dialog box opens, indicating whether the script contains errors.

5. Click the **OK** button. The dialog box closes. The error-free functions appear in the Script pane. See Figure 8-8.

Tip

You can also copy and paste the code and then edit the pasted code to add the additional functions.

Figure 8-8 — Functions in the Script pane

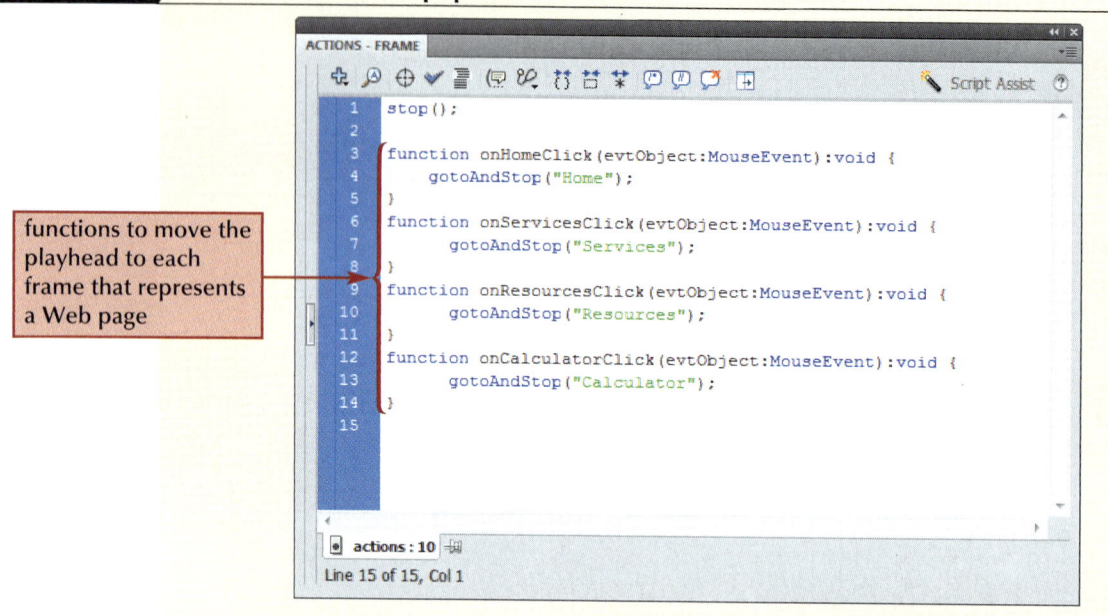

```
ACTIONS - FRAME
1  stop();
2
3  function onHomeClick(evtObject:MouseEvent):void {
4      gotoAndStop("Home");
5  }
6  function onServicesClick(evtObject:MouseEvent):void {
7      gotoAndStop("Services");
8  }
9  function onResourcesClick(evtObject:MouseEvent):void {
10     gotoAndStop("Resources");
11 }
12 function onCalculatorClick(evtObject:MouseEvent):void {
13     gotoAndStop("Calculator");
14 }
15
```

functions to move the playhead to each frame that represents a Web page

Trouble? If the script contains errors, the functions probably contain typing errors. If the Compiler Errors panel is hidden behind the Actions panel, click the Actions panel title bar to collapse the panel. In the Compiler Errors panel, review the error message(s), and then close the panel. Click the Actions panel title bar to expand the Actions panel, compare the code in the Actions panel with the code shown in Figure 8-8, and then correct your code as needed until it matches the code in the figure. Repeat Steps 4 and 5 until your code is error-free.

Adding Events and Event Handling

Events are things that happen when a movie is playing, such as when the user clicks a button or presses a key. ActionScript can respond to or handle an event by carrying out instructions based on the event. The code to respond to or handle events consists of three elements: the event source, the event, and the response. The **event source**, also known as the event target, is the object to which the event will happen, such as a button instance. The event is the thing that will happen to the object, such as a button click or a key press. The **response** is the steps that are performed when the event occurs. The ActionScript code you write to handle events must include these three elements.

Creating an Event Listener

In the Jackson's Sports Web site, clicking a button with the mouse is the event that will control which function is called. If the Home button is clicked, for example, then the onHomeClick function should be called to move the playhead to the Home frame. To call a function when a button is clicked, you need to create an event listener. An **event listener** is a method that the Flash Player executes in response to specific events. Every object that has an event has an event listener.

To create an event listener, you first create a function to be called in response to an event, as you did in the previous steps. Then you use the object's `addEventListener()` method to establish a connection between the function, such as onHomeClick, and the event source, such as the home_btn instance. The `addEventListener()` method registers the function to be called with the event source to listen for a specified event. When

Tutorial 8 Programming with ActionScript 3.0 | Flash | FL 385

the event occurs, the Flash Player can respond by calling the associated function. The `addEventListener()` method has two parameters: the event to listen for and the function to call when the event happens. The code for the event listener for the home_btn is:

`home_btn.addEventListener(MouseEvent.CLICK, onHomeClick);`

This code contains the three elements required to respond to an event. The event source is the home_btn, which is the instance name of the Home button, the event is CLICK, which is a property of the MouseEvent object and represents the clicking of the mouse, and the response is the call to the onHomeClick function. The `addEventListener()` method is called to register the onHomeClick function with the button instance. The code structure is shown in Figure 8-9.

Figure 8-9 — Format of an event listener

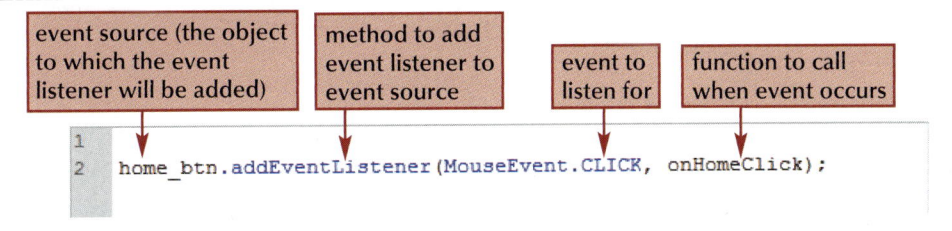

- event source (the object to which the event listener will be added)
- method to add event listener to event source
- event to listen for
- function to call when event occurs

```
1
2  home_btn.addEventListener(MouseEvent.CLICK, onHomeClick);
```

You will add the event listener code to register the functions with the mouse click event for the button instances.

To add the event listener code to the script:

1. In the Actions panel, place the insertion point after the closing curly brace at the end of the script, and then press the **Enter** key to move the insertion point to line 15. You'll enter the event listener code, starting on line 15.

2. Type the following line of code for the first part of the event listener for the Home button, as shown in Figure 8-10.

   `home_btn.addE`

Figure 8-10 — The `addEventListener` method selected in the code hints list

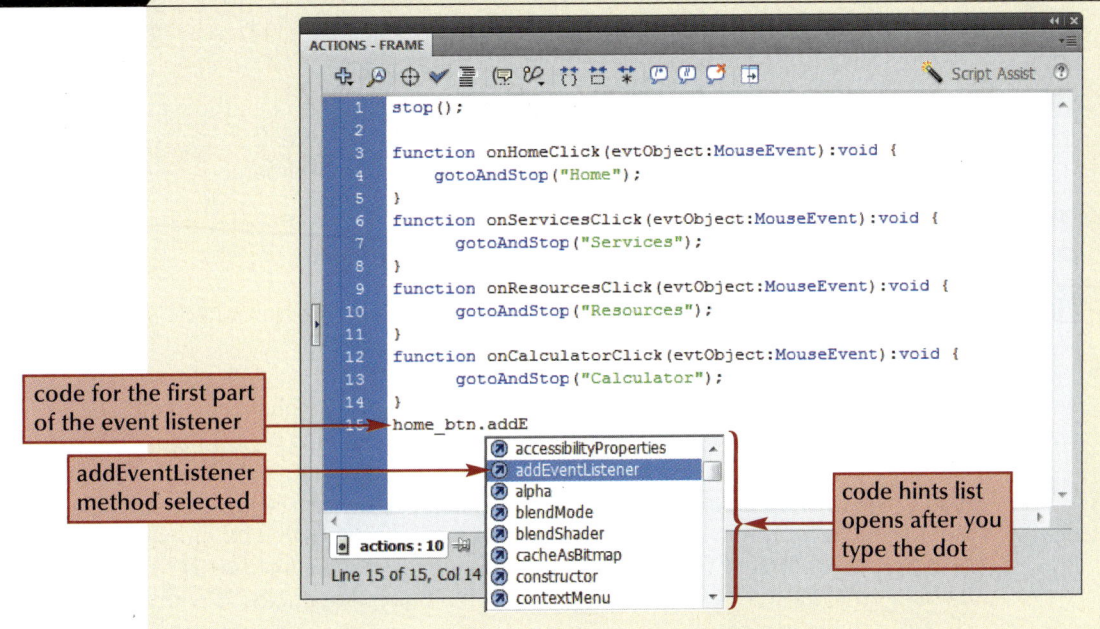

```
1  stop();
2
3  function onHomeClick(evtObject:MouseEvent):void {
4      gotoAndStop("Home");
5  }
6  function onServicesClick(evtObject:MouseEvent):void {
7      gotoAndStop("Services");
8  }
9  function onResourcesClick(evtObject:MouseEvent):void {
10     gotoAndStop("Resources");
11 }
12 function onCalculatorClick(evtObject:MouseEvent):void {
13     gotoAndStop("Calculator");
14 }
15 home_btn.addE
```

- code for the first part of the event listener
- addEventListener method selected
- code hints list opens after you type the dot

accessibilityProperties
addEventListener
alpha
blendMode
blendShader
cacheAsBitmap
constructor
contextMenu

actions : 10
Line 15 of 15, Col 14

Tip

You can also double-click the desired code in the code hints list to add the code to the script.

After you type the dot, the list of code hints opens, and scrolls to the first method that begins with the next letters you typed. In this case, the `addEventListener` method is selected in the code hints list.

3. Press the **Enter** key. The rest of the `addEventListener` method name is added to the script.

4. Type the rest of the code for the event listener as shown below, and then press the **Enter** key to insert a new line.

   ```
   MouseEvent.CLICK, onHomeClick);
   ```

   The complete code for the Home button event listener is `home_btn.addEventListener(MouseEvent.CLICK, onHomeClick);`. Parentheses are not included for the onHomeClick function when it is used as a parameter in the `addEventListener` method.

5. Type the following lines of code to create the event listeners for the other buttons, pressing the **Enter** key after each.

   ```
   services_btn.addEventListener(MouseEvent.CLICK, onServicesClick);
   resources_btn.addEventListener(MouseEvent.CLICK, onResourcesClick);
   calculator_btn.addEventListener(MouseEvent.CLICK, onCalculatorClick);
   ```

6. In the Actions panel, click the **Check syntax** button to check for syntax errors in the code you entered. A dialog box opens, indicating whether the script contains errors.

7. Click the **OK** button to close the dialog box. The error-free functions appear in the Script pane.

   Trouble? If the script contains errors, the code probably contains typing errors. If the Compiler Errors panel is hidden behind the Actions panel, collapse the Actions panel, review the error message(s) in the Compiler Errors panel, close the Compiler Errors panel, expand the Actions panel, compare the code in the Actions panel with the code shown in Steps 2 through 5, and then make the necessary corrections so that your code matches the code. Repeat Steps 6 and 7 until your code is error-free.

8. Save the document. You will test the Jackson's Sports Web site.

9. On the Application bar, click **Control**, and then click **Test Movie**. The movie opens in the Flash Player window. The Loading text appears briefly, and then the Home page opens.

10. Click the **Services** button to display the Services page, click the **Resources** button to display the Resources page, click the **Calculator** button to display the Calculator page, and then click the **Home** button to display the Home page.

11. Close the Flash Player window and return to the document.

Adding Comments

As scripts get longer and more complex, comments become increasingly helpful. A **comment** is a note within the ActionScript code that explains what is happening, but does not cause any action to be performed. A comment is not necessary for the action to work. However, comments are very useful to the programmer writing the code and to other programmers who might later modify the code. Single-line comments are indicated by two forward slashes (//). Any text after the slashes in the same line is not interpreted by the Flash Player. Comments that span multiple lines are enclosed with the /* and */ characters.

You will add comments to the script in the Jackson's Sports Web site document.

To add comments to the Jackson's Sports Web site script:

1. In the Actions panel, place the insertion point to the left of `stop()`; on the first line, and then type the following code, pressing the **Enter** key after each line to create a multiple-line comment.

   ```
   /* ActionScript code to make the buttons in the
   Jackson's Sports Web site functional.
   The first action will stop the playhead to
   keep it from advancing automatically. */
   ```

2. Press the **Enter** key to add a blank line between the comment and the first line of code.

3. In the Actions panel, place the insertion point to the left of the word function on line 8 (which contains the onHomeClick function), type the following code, and then press the **Enter** key to create a single-line comment.

   ```
   // These functions control the site's navigation.
   ```

4. In the Actions panel, place the insertion point to the left of home_btn on line 21 (which defines the first event listener), type the following code, and then press the **Enter** key to create a single-line comment.

   ```
   // This code creates the event listeners.
   ```

5. Save the document. See Figure 8-11.

Figure 8-11 | Comments added to the script

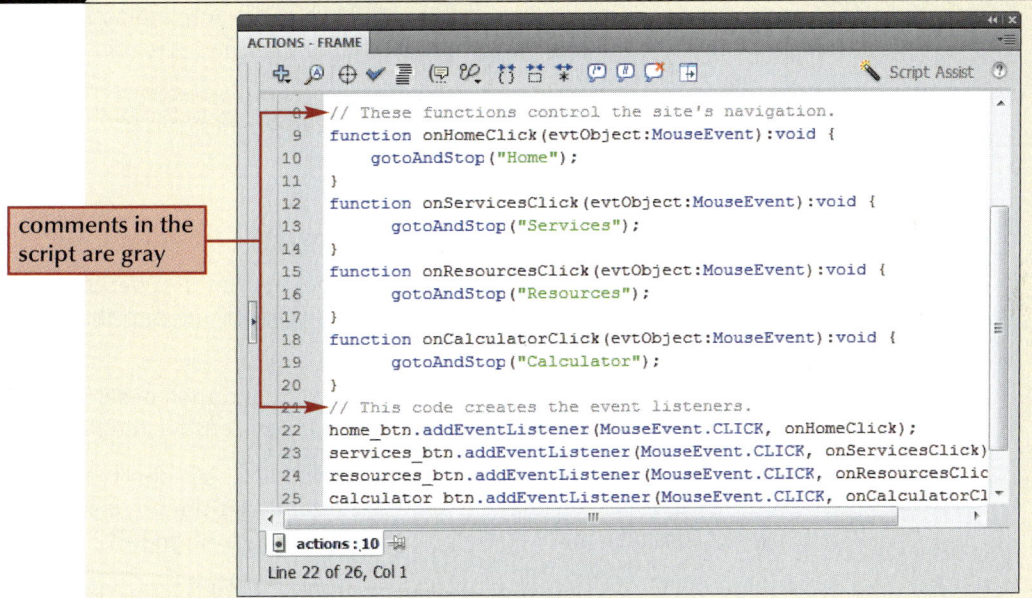

```
// These functions control the site's navigation.
function onHomeClick(evtObject:MouseEvent):void {
    gotoAndStop("Home");
}
function onServicesClick(evtObject:MouseEvent):void {
    gotoAndStop("Services");
}
function onResourcesClick(evtObject:MouseEvent):void {
    gotoAndStop("Resources");
}
function onCalculatorClick(evtObject:MouseEvent):void {
    gotoAndStop("Calculator");
}
// This code creates the event listeners.
home_btn.addEventListener(MouseEvent.CLICK, onHomeClick);
services_btn.addEventListener(MouseEvent.CLICK, onServicesClick);
resources_btn.addEventListener(MouseEvent.CLICK, onResourcesClic
calculator_btn.addEventListener(MouseEvent.CLICK, onCalculatorCl
```

comments in the script are gray

6. Close the Actions panel.

In this session, you learned the basic components and rules for the ActionScript programming language. You learned about actions, functions, methods, and event listeners. You entered code to make the Jackson's Sports Web site's navigation operational. In the next session, you will write ActionScript code for the two new pages that will be added to the Jackson's Sports Web site.

| Review | **Session 8.1 Quick Check**

1. What is ActionScript?
2. True or False? In ActionScript 3.0, you can add code to a button instance to handle mouse events.
3. A(n) _____ is an element in Flash that has properties or characteristics that can be examined or changed with ActionScript.
4. What is the advantage of adding suffixes to movie clip and button instance names?
5. Write the expression to change the alpha property of the car_mc instance to 50.
6. What three programming elements are needed to respond to or handle events?
7. Why should you add comments to ActionScript code?

Session 8.2

Creating Links to Web Sites

Dan wants the Resources page of the Jackson's Sports Web site to include three links to Web sites on the Internet that might be of interest to his clients. A Flash document can include links in the form of buttons or movie clips that use ActionScript to direct the Flash Player to open the specified Web site. You will complete the Resources page by creating buttons that represent links to the external Web sites and adding the corresponding ActionScript code. When the viewer clicks a button, a browser window will open, displaying an external Web site.

You will start by creating three buttons and assigning names to the button instances on the Stage.

To add button instances to the Resources page:

▶ 1. If you took a break after the previous session, make sure the jsWebSite.fla document is open, the workspace is reset to the Essentials layout, and the Stage magnification is set to Show Frame.

▶ 2. In the Timeline, click **Frame 30** of the content layer, and then deselect the title text. The content layer is where you will create the buttons for the Resources page.

▶ 3. In the Tools panel, click the **Text** tool T, and then, in the Property inspector, set the font family to **Arial**, set the font style to **Regular**, set the point size to **20**, set the text color to **black**, and set the paragraph format to **Align left**.

▶ 4. Create a text block at the center of the Stage below the title, typing **US Youth Soccer Online** in the text block.

▶ 5. In the Tools panel, click the **Selection** tool . The text block remains selected.

▶ 6. Convert the text block to a button symbol named **soccerButton**.

▶ 7. On the Edit bar, click the **Edit Symbols** button , and then click **soccerButton**. The symbol opens in symbol-editing mode.

▶ 8. In the Timeline, insert a keyframe in the Over frame, select the **US Youth Soccer Online** text on the Stage, and then, in the Property inspector, change the font style to **Bold**. The text is bolded, providing visual feedback when the user moves the pointer over the button.

Tutorial 8 Programming with ActionScript 3.0 | Flash FL 389

▶ 9. In the Timeline, insert a keyframe in the Hit frame, click the **Rectangle** tool in the Tools panel, and then draw a rectangle with a **black** fill that is about **250** pixels wide by **25** pixels high to cover the text block. The rectangle you drew over the text block in the Hit frame makes it easier for the viewer to click the button. Without it, the viewer must move the pointer directly over a letter to activate the button. See Figure 8-12.

Figure 8-12 Rectangle in the button's Hit frame

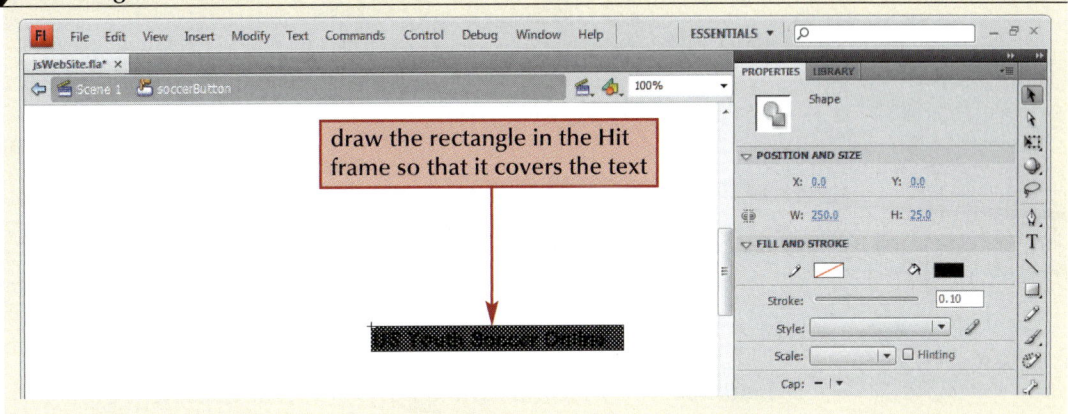

draw the rectangle in the Hit frame so that it covers the text

▶ 10. On the Edit bar, click the **Scene 1** link to return to the document's main Timeline.

You'll create duplicates of the soccerButton symbol, and then modify the text in the Up and Over frames of each of the duplicate button symbols to create the other two buttons for the Resources page.

To create the other button instances for the Resources page:

▶ 1. In the Library panel, duplicate the **soccerButton** symbol twice to create a button symbol named **asaButton** and a button symbol named **naysButton**. Copies of the soccerButton symbol named asaButton and naysButton appear in the library.

▶ 2. On the Edit bar, click the **Edit Symbols** button, and then click **asaButton** to open the button in symbol-editing mode.

▶ 3. In the Tools panel, click the **Text** tool to select it, and then change the button text to **American Softball Association** in both the Up frame and the Over frame.

▶ 4. On the Edit bar, click the **Scene 1** link to exit symbol-editing mode. The button text is updated.

▶ 5. Repeat Steps 2 through 4 to open the **naysButton** symbol in symbol-editing mode, change the button text to **National Alliance of Youth Sports** in both the Up and Over frames, and then exit symbol-editing mode.

▶ 6. From the Library panel, drag an instance of the **asaButton** symbol to below the soccerButton instance on the Stage, and then drag an instance of the **naysButton** to below the asaButton instance on the Stage.

> **Tip**
> You can also use the Selection tool to draw a marquee around the buttons on the Stage to select them simultaneously.

▶ 7. In the Tools panel, click the **Selection** tool to select it, press and hold the **Shift** key, click each of the three button instances on the Stage, and then release the Shift key. All three button instances on the Stage are selected.

▶ 8. On the Application bar, click **Modify**, point to **Align**, and then click **To Stage**, if necessary, to deselect it. The buttons on the Stage will align relative to each other.

▶ 9. On the Application bar, click **Modify**, point to **Align**, and then click **Left** to align the buttons along their left edges.

FL 390 Flash | Tutorial 8 Programming with ActionScript 3.0

▶ **10.** On the Application bar, click **Modify**, point to **Align**, click **Distribute Heights** to space the buttons evenly, and then deselect the button instances. See Figure 8-13.

Figure 8-13 | Text buttons on the Resources page

vertically align and evenly distribute the text buttons for Web links

Trouble? If the location of the buttons in your document differs from Figure 8-13, you need to reposition the buttons. With the Selection tool, select all three buttons, and then drag them to the location shown in the figure.

Aly wants you to add a message for site visitors explaining that a browser window will open when one of the buttons is clicked. Also, the three button instances must be assigned names before you can add ActionScript code that references them.

To add instructions and name the button instances to the Resources page:

▶ **1.** In the Tools panel, click the **Text** tool [T] to select it, and then set the font family to **Arial**, set the font style to **Italic**, set the point size to **12**, set the text color to **black**, and set the paragraph format to **Align left**.

▶ **2.** On the Stage, add a text block above the soccerButton instance, type **Clicking a button below will open the Web site in a new window** in the text block, and then deselect the text. See Figure 8-14.

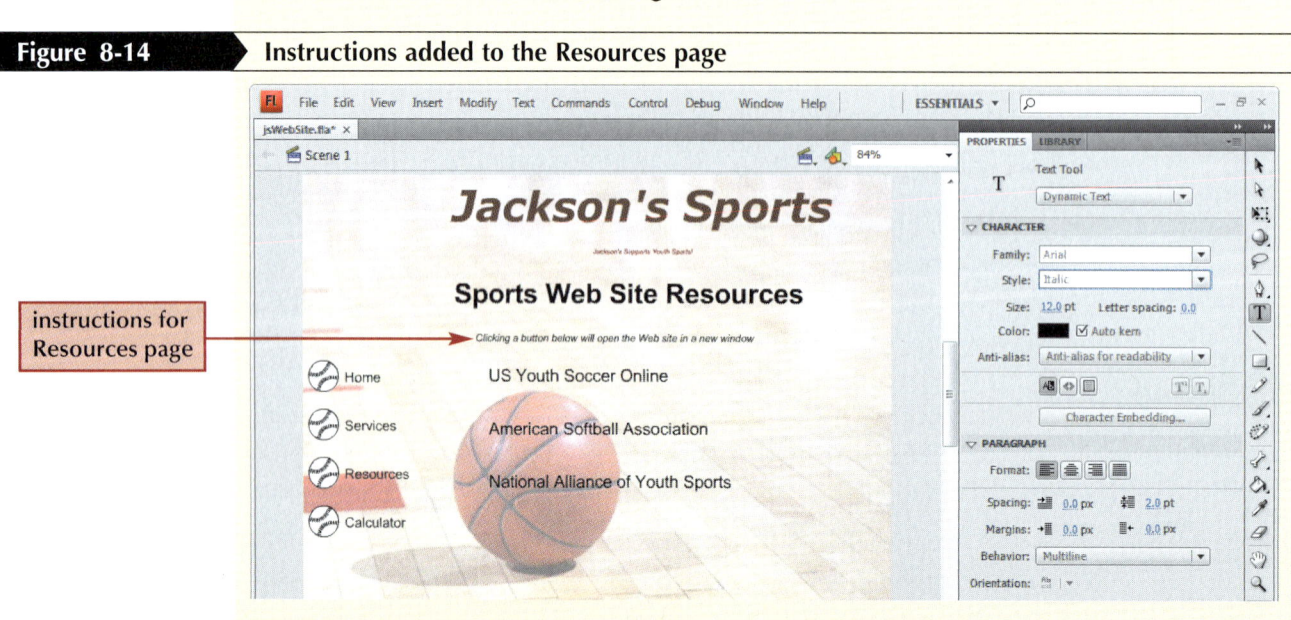

Figure 8-14 | Instructions added to the Resources page

instructions for Resources page

▶ 3. In the Tools panel, click the **Selection** tool, and then select the **soccerButton** instance on the Stage. You will assign the button instance a name.

▶ 4. In the Property inspector, type **soccer_btn** in the Instance name box, and then press the **Enter** key. The _btn suffix indicates that this is a named instance of a button.

▶ 5. Repeat Steps 3 and 4 to name the **asaButton** instance as **softball_btn** and name the naysButton instance as **alliance_btn**.

Using the URLRequest Class

To create a link to an external Web site, you need to create a function as you did in the previous session. The function will use the URLRequest() class to define an object with the value of the Web address of the site to which you want to link. A **class** is a blueprint for an object that describes the properties, methods, and events for the object. All objects in ActionScript are defined by classes. The ActionScript code for the function to link to a Web site is as follows:

```
function gotoSoccerSite(eventobj:MouseEvent):void {
   var soccerURL:URLRequest = new
URLRequest("http://www.usyouthsoccer.org/");
   navigateToURL(soccerURL);
}
```

The first line in the code defines the function by listing the function's name and parameter. This is the same way you defined the functions in the previous session. The second line of the code creates a variable named soccerURL as an object that represents a Web address. A **variable** is a user-defined object that holds data and whose value can change while the SWF movie plays. You define a variable using the var keyword followed by the variable's name, which must be one word that includes only alphanumeric, the underscore, and dollar sign characters. A variable must be **typed**, which means you need to specify what type of data it can contain. The data type of the variable is listed after a colon character. In this case, the data type is URLRequest, which means that the variable can only hold data representing a Web address.

The equal sign in the statement is an assignment operator and is used to assign a value to the soccerURL variable. **Operators** are used in ActionScript statements to tell the Flash Player how to manipulate values. On the right side of the assignment operator, the new operator is used to create an instance of an object based on the URLRequest class. Creating an instance using the new operator is known as calling the constructor method for the class. The **constructor** is a special method used to create instances of objects based on a class. The Web address to be assigned to the soccerURL variable is specified in the parameter of the URLRequest class.

The next line of the code is the navigateToURL() function, which will open a Web site in the computer's default browser using the value in its parameter for the Web address. In this case, the function's parameter is soccerURL, which contains the Web address specified in the previous line of the script.

You will add the code to create the functions for the Web site links in the Resources page.

To create a script with functions to control the Resources page buttons:

▶ 1. In the Timeline, insert a keyframe in **Frame 30** of the actions layer, and then open the Actions panel. The Script pane is empty. You will add the code for the first function.

▶ 2. In the Actions panel, type the following lines of code to create a function to open the US Youth Soccer Web site.

```
function gotoSoccerSite(evtObject:MouseEvent):void {
     var soccerURL:URLRequest = new URLRequest("http://www.usyouthsoccer.org/");
     navigateToURL(soccerURL);
}
```

▶ 3. Press the **Enter** key twice after the closing curly brace to insert a blank line, and then type the following lines of code to create two more functions that open the American Softball Association site and the National Alliance of Youth Sports site, pressing the **Enter** key twice between the functions and once after the third function.

```
function gotoSoftballSite(evtObject:MouseEvent):void {
     var softballURL:URLRequest = new URLRequest("http://www.softball.org/");
     navigateToURL(softballURL);
}

function gotoAllianceSite(evtObject:MouseEvent):void {
     var allianceURL:URLRequest = new URLRequest("http://www.nays.org/");
     navigateToURL(allianceURL);
}
```

▶ 4. In the Actions panel, click the **Check syntax** button to check the ActionScript code for syntax errors. A dialog box opens, indicating whether the script contains errors.

▶ 5. Click the **OK** button. The dialog box closes. The error-free functions appear in the Script pane. See Figure 8-15.

Figure 8-15 — Functions added to the Resources script

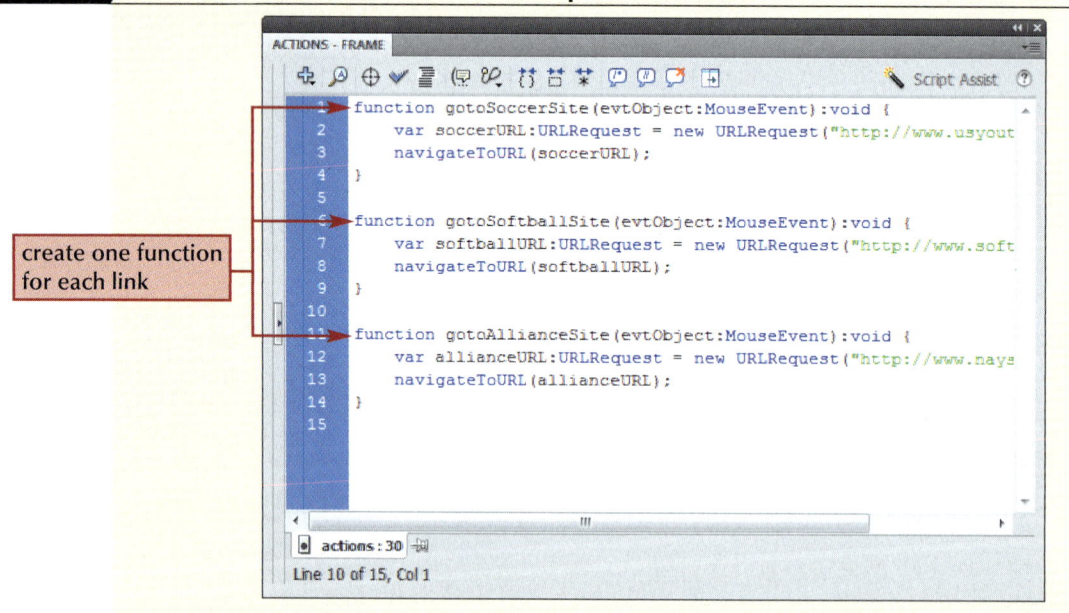

create one function for each link

Trouble? If the script contains errors, the functions probably contain typing errors. If the Compiler Errors panel is hidden behind the Actions panel, collapse the Actions panel, review the error message(s) in the Compiler Errors panel, close the Compiler Errors panel, expand the Actions panel, compare the code in the Actions panel with the code shown in Figure 8-15, and then make the necessary corrections so that your code matches the code in the figure. Repeat Steps 4 and 5 until your code is error-free.

Tutorial 8 Programming with ActionScript 3.0 | Flash | FL 393

Just as you had to add event listeners to the code in Frame 10 of the actions layer to make the navigation buttons operational, you need to add similar event listeners to make the buttons on the Resources page operational. The event listeners for the Resources page have the same format as the ones for the navigational buttons. You use the `addEventListener()` method for each button instance to register a button's CLICK event with the associated function. You will type the event listener code next.

To add the event listener code for the Resources page:

1. In the Actions panel, place the insertion point after the closing curly brace ending the last function, press the **Enter** key to add a blank line, and then type the following line of code to create the event listener for the US Youth Soccer button.

   ```
   soccer_btn.addEventListener(MouseEvent.CLICK, gotoSoccerSite);
   ```

2. Press the **Enter** key after the closing semicolon to insert a new line, and then type the following lines of code to create the event listeners for the other buttons, pressing the **Enter** key after each line.

   ```
   softball_btn.addEventListener(MouseEvent.CLICK, gotoSoftballSite);
   alliance_btn.addEventListener(MouseEvent.CLICK, gotoAllianceSite);
   ```

3. In the Actions panel, click the **Check syntax** button ✓ to check the ActionScript code for syntax errors. A dialog box opens, indicating whether the script contains errors.

4. Click the **OK** button. The dialog box closes. The error-free functions appear in the Script pane.

   Trouble? If the script contains errors, the functions probably contain typing errors. If the Compiler Errors panel is hidden behind the Actions panel, collapse the Actions panel, review the error message(s) in the Compiler Errors panel, close the Compiler Errors panel, expand the Actions panel, compare the code in the Actions panel with the code in Steps 1 and 2, and then make the necessary corrections so that your code matches the code in the steps. Repeat Steps 3 and 4 until your code is error-free.

5. Save the jsWebSite.fla document.

The code for the functions and event listeners, necessary to make the buttons operational, is complete. You will test the links in the Resources page.

To test the buttons in the Resources page:

1. On the Application bar, click **File**, point to **Publish Preview**, and then click **Default - (HTML)**. The Jackson's Sports Web site opens in the default browser.

   Trouble? If the Web page does not open and the Information Bar appears, indicating that Internet Explorer has restricted this Web page from running scripts, you need to allow the blocked content. Click the Information Bar, click Allow Blocked Content, and then click the Yes button in the dialog box that opens to confirm that you want to allow the blocked content.

2. In the browser window, click the **Resources** button to display the Resources page, and then click the **US Youth Soccer Online** button to open the Web site in a separate window. If necessary, switch to the window displaying the US Youth Soccer Web site.

   Trouble? If an error message appears stating the page cannot be displayed, your computer might not be connected to the Internet. If necessary, connect to the Internet and repeat Step 2. If your computer is connected to the Internet, check the URL in the `URLRequest()` parameter to make certain it is correct. If you cannot connect to the Internet, then read the remainder of the steps in this section.

Trouble? If an Adobe Flash Player window opens, stating that an ActionScript error has occurred, click the Continue button.

Trouble? If an Adobe Flash Player Security dialog box opens, stating that the Flash Player stopped a potentially unsafe operation, click the Settings button. A Web page displays the Adobe Flash Player Settings Manager. In the Settings Manager, click the Edit locations button and then click Add location. In the Trust this location box, click the Browse for files button, navigate to the folder containing the jsWebSite.swf file, select the file, and then click the Open button. Close the Web browser, and then repeat Steps 1 and 2.

▶ 3. Switch to the browser window displaying the Jackson's Sports Web site, and then click the **American Softball Association** button to test that it opens the appropriate Web site.

▶ 4. Repeat Step 3 to test the **National Alliance of Youth Sports** button.

▶ 5. Close the browser windows to return to the jsWebSite.fla document. The Resources page is complete. You have added the buttons and ActionScript code to open external Web sites in a browser.

Using a Flash Preloader

SWF files, like HTML files, are downloaded over the Internet from a Web server to the user's computer, known as the **client computer**, where the files will reside. A major factor that affects the amount of time a file takes to download is the size of the file, measured in kilobytes. A **kilobyte** is approximately 1000 bytes, and a **byte** is equivalent to one character of information. Flash Web sites typically contain various multimedia elements, such as graphics, animations, pictures, audio, and video. Each of these elements adds to the overall size of the published file. Even though the SWF files are compressed and contain vector graphics that tend to be small, they might still take some time to download.

Another factor that affects download time is the type of Internet connection used by the client computer. The type of Internet connection can be a broadband connection using a cable or DSL modem, which provides high-speed download capability, or it could be a much slower dial-up connection using a telephone modem, as is the case with many personal computers. When the SWF file starts to download from a Web server to a client computer, it is loaded into the Flash Player one frame at a time. The first frames start playing in the Flash Player as soon as they load, even though other frames of the file are still downloading. This is because of the streaming capability of Flash files. **Streaming** means that as the file is downloading, the initial content can start playing while the rest of the content continues to be downloaded, which reduces the wait time for the user. A problem occurs, however, when the client computer plays all of the loaded frames and then has to wait for additional frames to load. This can happen if a particular frame has a large amount of content such as bitmap images. The wait causes the Flash Player to pause the playing of the SWF file while additional frames load. This delay affects the way the SWF file plays and might confuse or frustrate the user. Also, if the wait is more than a few seconds and no visual indication appears that something is still loading, the user may think the Web site is not working and decide to go to another site.

To avoid losing site visitors, Flash developers usually add a **preloader**, which is a short animation or message located in the first few frames of the Flash file. The preloader typically contains a short animation and the word "Loading" to indicate that the Web site is still loading. This visual feedback helps assure the site visitor that the Web site is loading while the frames of the SWF file continue to download. After all the content has downloaded, the preloader stops and the rest of the SWF file plays. Several examples of preloaders are shown in Figure 8-16.

Figure 8-16   Examples of preloaders

Creating the Preloader

Adding a preloader to a Flash file requires ActionScript code along with a loading message and/or an animation placed in the first frame of the Timeline. The preloader message and animation are displayed only while the file is being loaded. A script can be added to a later frame in the Timeline to control the preloader and to check if all of the content has downloaded. The basic logic involves knowing how much of the SWF file has loaded and comparing that with the total size of the file. The amount of content that has loaded and the total size of the file can be measured in either number of frames or number of bytes, both of which can be examined using ActionScript. By checking how much content has been loaded and comparing it to the total size of the file, different actions can be performed. For example, if the number of bytes that have loaded into the Flash Player is equal to the total number of bytes for the file, the entire SWF file has loaded. At that point, the SWF file can play as designed. Otherwise, the preloader animation continues to play.

If the SWF file contains a large number of frames, you can create a preloader that checks the number of frames loaded. In the case of the Jackson's Sports Web site, the number of frames is small, so it is best to check the number of bytes loaded. To create the preloader code, the script will need to get the total number of bytes to be loaded and the number of bytes loaded. The number of bytes loaded will increase as more of the file is loaded into the Flash Player. As long as these two values are not the same, the preloader animation will continue to play. When the two values are the same, the SWF has finished loading. At that point, the preloader animation will stop and the rest of the frames in the movie will be played. The steps for the preloader code are as follows:

    Get the total number of bytes
    Get the number of bytes loaded
    Update the preloader animation
    If the number of bytes loaded equals the total number of bytes
        play the rest of the SWF file
    Otherwise
        continue playing the preloader animation

These steps will be followed to create the code for the preloader for the Jackson's Sports Web site.

To get the total number of bytes, you will create a function with an instance of the ProgressEvent class as its parameter. The ProgressEvent class has the event type PROGRESS, which includes the properties bytesTotal and bytesLoaded. The bytesTotal property contains the total number of bytes in the SWF file. The bytesLoaded property contains the number of bytes loaded. These numbers will be compared to each other to determine if the SWF file has completed loading into the Flash Player. The numbers can also be used to calculate what percentage of the file has loaded.

You will start creating the script for the preloader in the first frame of the actions layer by creating a function and defining two variables.

To create the first part of the preloader script:

1. Collapse the Actions panel, and then, in the Timeline, click **Frame 1** of the labels layer. You will add the preloader script in this frame.

2. In the Label section of the Property inspector, type **Preload** in the Name box, and then press the **Enter** key. This label will be referred to in the script for the preloader.

3. In the Timeline, click **Frame 1** of the actions layer, expand the Actions panel, and then, in the Script pane of the Actions panel, type the following line of code and press the **Enter** key.

   ```
   function preloader(progressEvt:ProgressEvent):void {
   ```

   This code creates a function named preloader with the object progressEvt as its parameter. The progressEvt object is set as a ProgressEvent data type.

4. In the Script pane of the Actions panel, type the following lines of code, pressing the **Enter** key after each line.

   ```
   var totalBytes:Number = progressEvt.bytesTotal;
   var loadedBytes:Number = progressEvt.bytesLoaded;
   ```

   The first var line creates a new variable named totalBytes whose data type is Number. The value of the bytesTotal property of the progressEvt object is assigned to the variable. The second var line creates a variable named loadedBytes with a data type of Number. The value of the bytesLoaded property of the progressEvt object is assigned to the variable.

Creating the Preloader Animation

The totalBytes and loadedBytes variables can also be used to control the animation used in the preloader. Recall from the previous session that the properties of a movie clip instance can be modified using ActionScript. You can create a movie clip in the shape of a rectangle and then gradually increase the horizontal size of the rectangle to match how much of the file has been loaded. Because the rectangle instance is an object, you can modify the object's scaleX and scaleY properties, which represent the relative size of the object compared to its original size. The scaleX property can be used to scale the object horizontally. The property uses a fractional value such as 0.5 to represent a percentage of the object's original size. For example, a scaleX value of 0.5 changes the object to display 50% of its original size. So by changing the scaleX property of the rectangle from 0 to 1, the rectangle appears to grow horizontally from 0% to 100% of its original size.

You will create an instance of a movie clip in the shape of a rectangle with a registration point on its upper-left corner. The rectangle will grow horizontally, starting from the left side and growing to the right side. When the rectangle is back to its original size, the SWF file has finished loading.

> **InSight** | **Calculating the scaleX Property**
>
> To determine the value to assign to the scaleX property of the rectangle, divide the loadedBytes value by the totalBytes value, resulting in fractional values ranging from 0 to 1. The result, which represents the percentage of how much of the file has loaded, can be assigned to the scaleX property of the rectangle. It increases gradually until the two values are equal, resulting in a value of 1, which means all of the file's content has loaded and the scaleX property of the rectangle is 100%.

You'll add a preloader animation to the content layer.

To add the graphic and code for the preloader animation:

1. Close the Actions panel to see the Stage, and then, in the Timeline, click **Frame 1** of the content layer.

2. Below the Loading text block on the Stage, draw a rectangle with a **dark green** (#009900) fill and no stroke that is **300** pixels wide and **20** pixels high. See Figure 8-17.

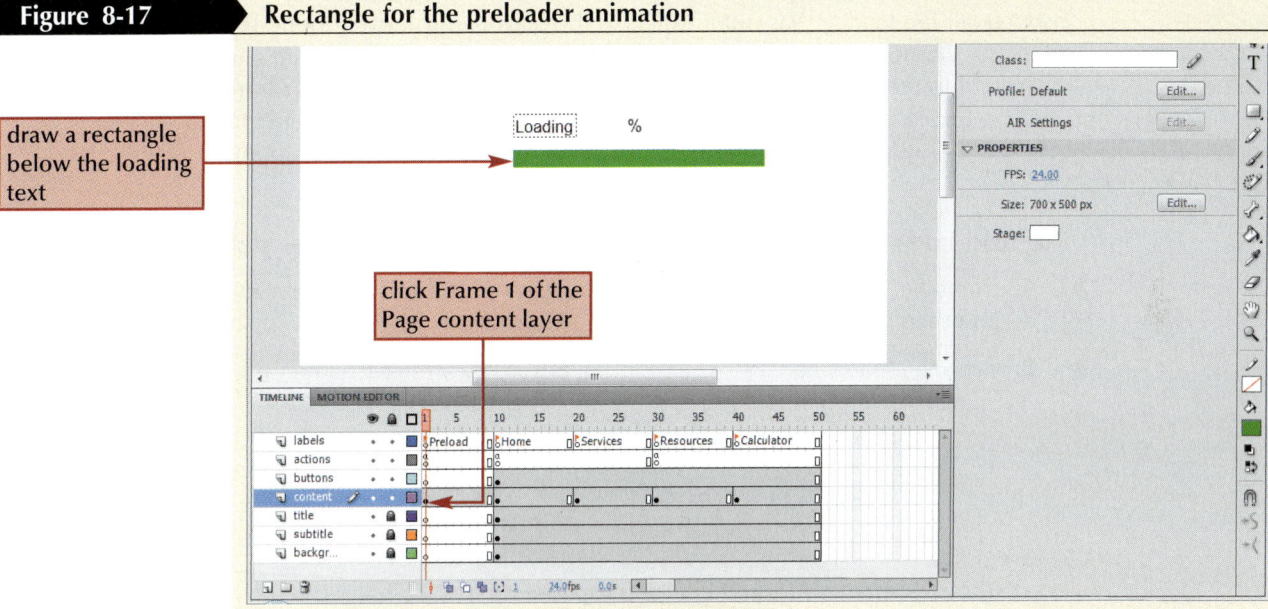

Figure 8-17 | Rectangle for the preloader animation

draw a rectangle below the loading text

click Frame 1 of the Page content layer

3. Convert the rectangle to a movie clip symbol named **rectangle** with the upper-left registration point selected.

4. In the Property inspector, type **loadBar_mc** in the Instance name box, and then press the **Enter** key to name the movie clip instance. The preloader movie clip instance is complete.

   You will add the code to change the loadBar_mc's scaleX property.

5. In the Timeline, click **Frame 1** of the actions layer, open the Actions panel, and then, in the Script pane at the end of the script type the following code, pressing the **Enter** key after each line.

   ```
   var amtLoaded:Number = loadedBytes/totalBytes;
   loadBar_mc.scaleX = amtLoaded;
   ```

The amtLoaded variable will hold the result of dividing loadedBytes by totalBytes. This resulting number is a fractional value that represents the percentage of how much of the SWF file has been loaded. This value is assigned to the scaleX property of the Rectangle movie clip, loadBar_mc, causing it to increase horizontally each time the loadedBytes value changes.

In addition to the loadBar_mc animation, you will add a special type of text box that will display a changing value, from 0% to 100%, indicating how much of the SWF file has loaded. You will add this text box and its associated ActionScript code in Session 8.3.

Completing the Preloader Code

The next part of the function is a comparison using a conditional statement. A **conditional statement** compares one value to another. Based on the result of the comparison, certain actions are performed. Conditional statements use **comparison operators**, such as ==, which is used to test for equality. This is different from the assignment operator =, which is used to assign a value to a variable. Other comparison operators include >, <, and !=, which are used to test for greater than, less than, and not equal to, respectively. You create a conditional statement using the `if` keyword, which tests a condition. If the condition is true, the Flash Player performs actions within the curly braces that follow it. You can also include the `else` keyword, which contains the actions to perform when the condition is false.

The if statement compares the values of loadedBytes and totalBytes. If the values are not equal, the loading has not finished so the playhead is moved to the Preload frame, which is Frame 1. If the values are equal, then the loading has finished and the playhead is moved to the first part of the Web site, which is the frame with the Home label. You use the `gotoAndPlay()` function to direct the playhead to a specific frame, referring to a frame by its label. You will add the if conditional statement to the script next.

To add code to compare the loadedBytes and totalBytes values:

▶ 1. In the Script pane of the Actions panel, click at the end of the script, if necessary, and then press the **Enter** key to add a blank line.

▶ 2. Type the following code, pressing the **Enter** key after each line.

```
if (loadedBytes == totalBytes) {
    gotoAndPlay("Home");
} else {
    gotoAndPlay("Preload");
}
}
```

The condition, enclosed in parentheses, compares the values in the loadedBytes and totalBytes variables. If the values are equal, the `gotoAndPlay("Home");` statement is executed, causing the playhead to move to the first page of the Web site. If the values are not equal, the `gotoAndPlay("Preload");` statement is executed, causing the playhead to move to the frame labeled Preload. This causes the script to run again. The closing curly brace on the last line closes the preloader function.

The function for the preloader script is complete. However, it will not work until an event listener is added to the script. Recall that event listeners were added to previous scripts to register button instances with functions to be performed when a button was clicked. The CLICK property of the MouseEvent event object was used as a parameter in the `addEventListener()` method. In the preloader script, you need to add an event listener to call the preloader function when a specific event occurs. In this case, the event is not when a button is clicked. Instead, the event is when a part of the SWF file has loaded into the Flash Player. The progressEvent.PROGRESS event will indicate when a new part of the SWF file has loaded. Because the event is dispatched or generated by a LoaderInfo object of the main Timeline, you need to register the event listener with the object. You can do this using the `addEventListener()` method of the loaderInfo object.

You will add the event listener to the script.

To add the event listener code to the preloader script, check for errors, and test the script:

1. In the Script pane of the Actions panel, at the end of the script, press the **Enter** key to add a blank line, and then type the following code.

   `loaderInfo.addEventListener(ProgressEvent.PROGRESS, preloader);`

   When content is loaded into the Flash Player, the PROGRESS event occurs and the addEventListener() method calls the preloader function. You will check for syntax errors before testing the script.

2. In the Actions panel, click the **Check syntax** button to check for syntax errors. A dialog box opens, indicating whether the script contains errors.

3. Click the **OK** button. The dialog box closes. The error-free code appears in the Script pane. See Figure 8-18.

Figure 8-18 — Preloader script

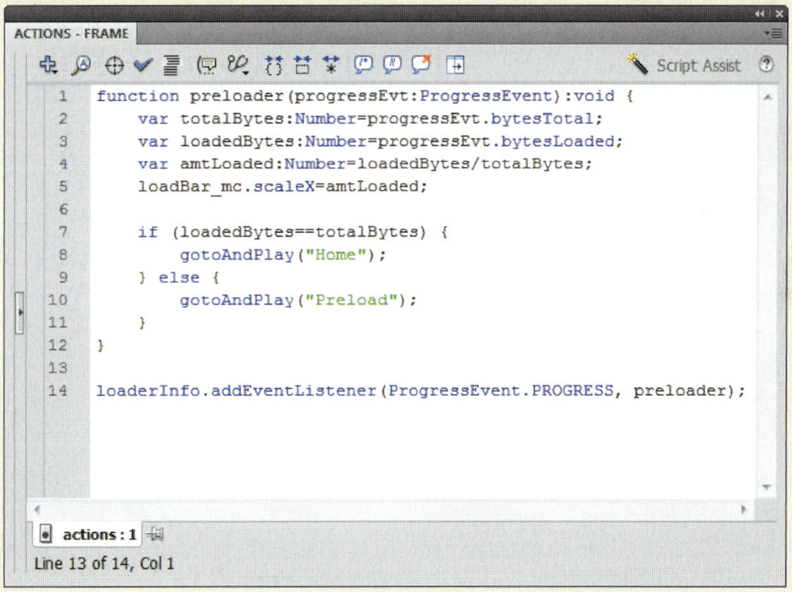

```
function preloader(progressEvt:ProgressEvent):void {
    var totalBytes:Number=progressEvt.bytesTotal;
    var loadedBytes:Number=progressEvt.bytesLoaded;
    var amtLoaded:Number=loadedBytes/totalBytes;
    loadBar_mc.scaleX=amtLoaded;

    if (loadedBytes==totalBytes) {
        gotoAndPlay("Home");
    } else {
        gotoAndPlay("Preload");
    }
}

loaderInfo.addEventListener(ProgressEvent.PROGRESS, preloader);
```

Trouble? If the script contains errors, the functions probably contain typing errors. If the Compiler Errors panel is hidden behind the Actions panel, collapse the Actions panel, review the error message(s) in the Compiler Errors panel, close the Compiler Errors panel, expand the Actions panel, compare the code in the Actions panel with the code in Figure 8-18, and then make the necessary corrections so that your code matches the code in the figure. Repeat Steps 2 and 3 until your code is error-free.

4. Save the jsWebSite.fla document, and then close the Actions panel.

▶ **5.** On the Application bar, click **Control**, and then click **Test Movie**. The SWF file plays in the Flash Player; however, the preloader appears for only a fraction of a second.

Because the SWF file is loading from your computer's drive, the file's content loads instantly. As a result, the preloader animation is only visible for a very short time. This will not be the case when the SWF file is downloaded from the Internet. To test the preloader, you can use the Simulate Download command. This command simulates the time it takes to download the SWF file based on the type of Internet connection you select.

▶ **6.** On the Flash Player Application bar, click **View**, point to **Download Settings**, and then click **56K (4.7 KB/s)** to select it, if necessary.

▶ **7.** On the Flash Player Application bar, click **View**, and then click **Simulate Download**. After a few seconds, the preloader animation plays. See Figure 8-19.

Figure 8-19 Simulated download process

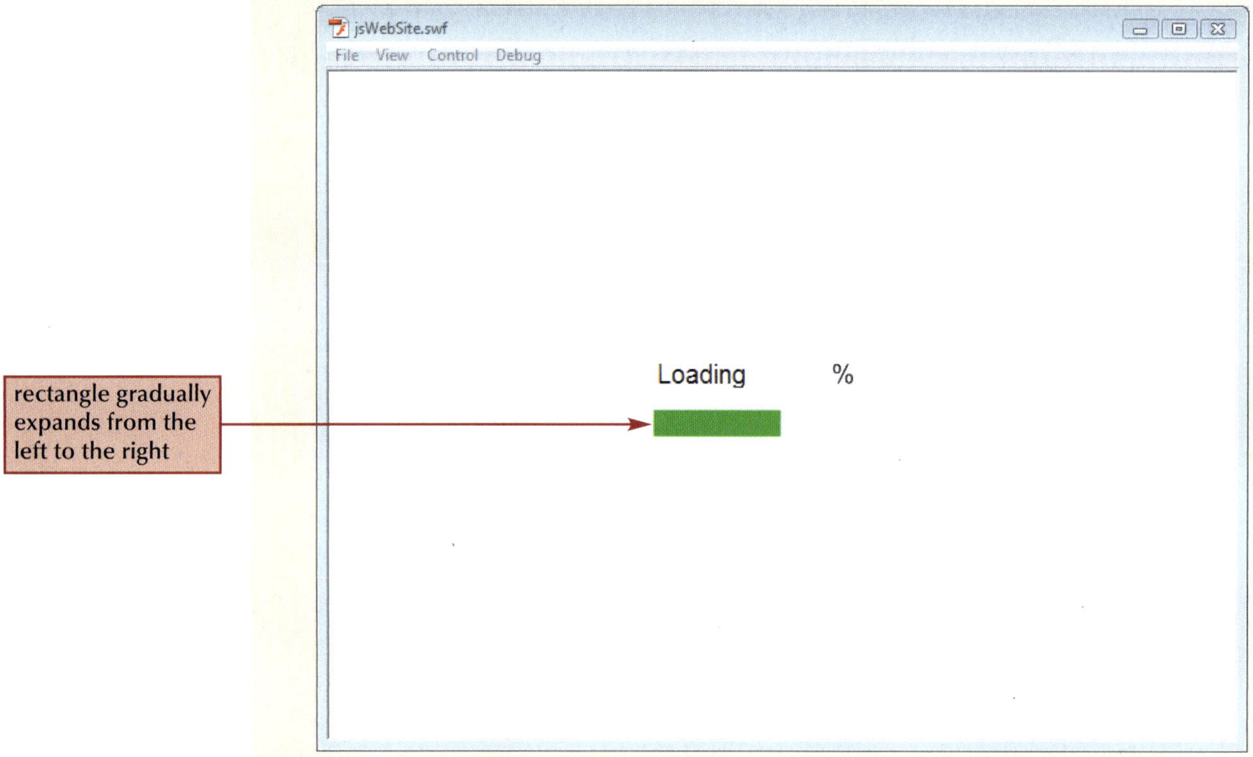

rectangle gradually expands from the left to the right

After the green rectangle is scaled to its original size, the home page of the Jackson's Sports Web site appears.

▶ **8.** Close the Flash Player window to return to the jsWebSite.fla document.

The preloader for the Jackson's Sports Web site is complete. In this session, you used the `URLRequest()` function to create buttons with URL links to Web sites on the Internet. You also created a preloader using ActionScript and tested the preloader by simulating the download speed of a 56K modem Internet connection.

Review | Session 8.2 Quick Check

1. Write the ActionScript code to create a function named `gotoCourseSite()` that will use the `URLRequest()` class to open the Web site *http://www.course.com*.
2. What does it mean that a variable has to be typed?
3. What is a constructor method?
4. What is the purpose of a preloader?
5. An object's scaleX and scaleY properties represent the relative size of the object compared to its _____ size.
6. Explain how you can simulate the downloading of an SWF file within Flash.

Session 8.3

Creating an Input Form

An input form is a common element found on many Web sites. An **input form** allows the user to enter data into text boxes. The data can then be submitted for storage and processing on a Web server. The server software sends results of the processing back to the user's computer to be displayed on the same form or on another Web page. A page developed with Flash can also allow the user to enter data, have the data processed, and return a result directly from the Flash Player on the user's computer. The page developer uses ActionScript to write the underlying functions required to create a form with several input fields coded to accept data from the site visitor, such as the number and type of items to be purchased. Other fields on the form display results based on the site visitor's input, such as a total price. Creating an input form requires the use of dynamic and input text.

Using Dynamic and Input Text

Text is an important element of a Flash document. All of the text you have created so far has been static text. Static text cannot be changed after the document plays in the Flash Player. Recall, however, that there are two other types of text in Flash: dynamic text and input text. Although static text cannot change, dynamic text can. Dynamic text can receive text in the form of characters or numbers from a Web server or from an expression in ActionScript and display the text on a Web page in the Flash Player. Dynamic text is defined to display the contents of a variable. The variable can be used in ActionScript to change the value displayed. For example, if a dynamic text block is assigned the variable Amount, you can code an expression in ActionScript that assigns the result of a calculation to the variable. The value stored in the variable Amount will then appear in the text block on the Web page. Input text is used to allow the user to enter text into the text block. This text can then be stored in a variable and used in an ActionScript script.

Based on Dan's request, you will create a form for the Calculator page for the Jackson's Sports Web site. This page will allow a user such as a team manager to enter several values for the type and number of team jerseys the team needs to buy. The page will contain a button that when clicked will use the entered values to calculate a total cost and display the result. One of the values that the user will enter is which type of jersey is desired. One option is a team jersey for $10 with the team name only. The other option is a team jersey for $12 with both the team name and a player number. Then, the user will enter whether the jersey will contain the name of the player for an additional $1.50 per jersey. Finally, the user will enter the number of players and number of coaches to determine the number of jerseys needed.

You will complete the Calculator page by creating the input and dynamic text blocks. You will also add a Calculate button and write the ActionScript code to make the button operational so that it calculates the total cost. You will start by adding the static text blocks for the page.

To create the static text boxes for the Calculator page:

1. If you took a break after the previous session, make sure the jsWebSite.fla document is open, the workspace is reset to the Essentials layout, and the Stage magnification is set to 100%.

2. In the Timeline, click **Frame 40** of the content layer. The Calculator page appears on the Stage.

3. Display the rulers, and then create a horizontal guide **200** pixels from the top edge of the Stage and a vertical guide **500** pixels from the left edge of the Stage. The guides will be used to place the text blocks.

4. Deselect the title text block, click the **Text** tool [T] in the Tools panel, and then, in the Property inspector, set the font family to **Arial**, the font style to **Regular**, the point size to **22**, the text color to **black**, and the paragraph format to **Align right**.

5. On the Stage, click the vertical guide below the horizontal guide to create a text block, type **Type of Jersey**, press the **Enter** key to create a new line, type **Enter 1 for team name only - $10.00 each**, press the **Enter** key to create a new line, and then type **Enter 2 for team name & player number - $12.00 each**.

6. Select the last two lines of the text block, and then, in the Property inspector, change the point size to **14**. See Figure 8-20.

Figure 8-20	Type of Jersey text block

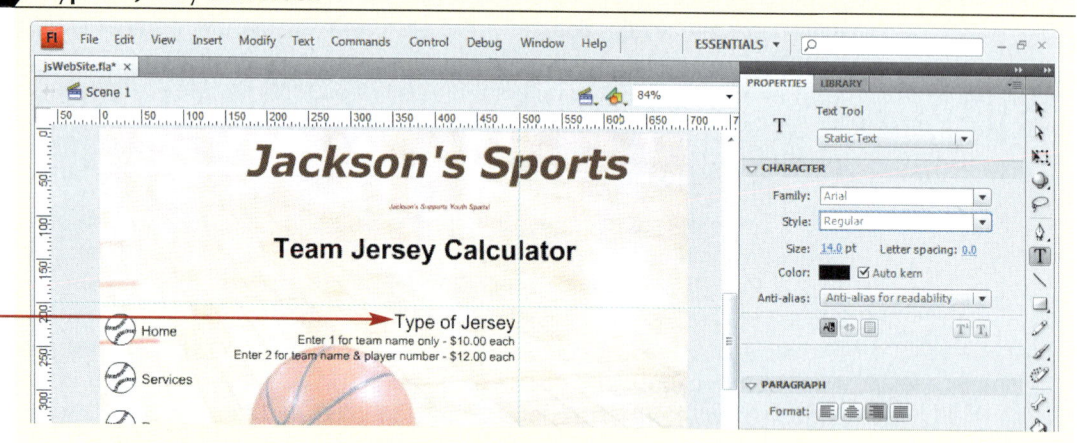

text block added to the Stage

7. Create another text block below the Type of Jersey text block, use the same text attributes as the first text block but change the point size to **22**, type **Include player names (Enter Y or N)**, press the **Enter** key, and then type **$1.50 per player**.

8. Select the second line in the text block, and then, in the Property inspector, change the point size to **18**.

9. Create a text block below the previous text block, use the same text attributes as the previous text block but change the point size to **22**, and then type **Number of players**.

10. Create a text block below the previous text block, use the same text attributes, and then type **Number of coaches**.

11. Create a text block below the previous text block, use the same text attributes, and then type **Total cost (w/o tax) =**.

▶ 12. In the Tools panel, click the **Selection** tool, reposition the text blocks on the Stage as needed so that their right edges are aligned, and then deselect the text blocks. See Figure 8-21.

Figure 8-21 | **Static text blocks**

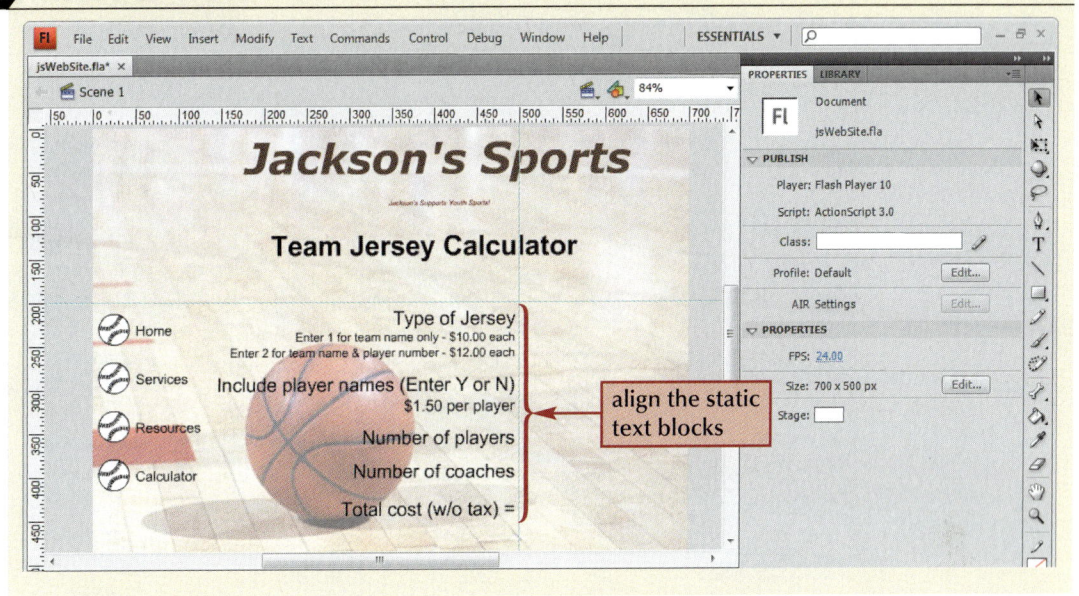

The static text blocks are complete. Each text block provides instructions to the user about the values that can be entered into the input text boxes. You will create the input text boxes next. You will also assign instance names to each input text box so that it can be referenced in the ActionScript code.

To create the input text boxes for the Calculator page:

▶ 1. In the Tools panel, click the **Text** tool, and then, in the Property inspector, click the **Text type** button and click **Input Text**. The next text block you create will be for input text.

▶ 2. In the Property inspector, set the font family to **Arial**, set the font style to **Regular**, set the point size to **20**, set the text color to **black**, and then set the paragraph format to **Align right**.

▶ 3. On the Stage, click to the right of the Type of Jersey text block to create an input text block, and then, in the Tools panel, click the **Selection** tool. The input text block remains selected on the Stage.

▶ 4. In Property inspector, enter **jerseyType** as the Instance name, and then, in the Position and Size section, set the dimensions to **70** pixels wide and **30** pixels high.

▶ 5. In the Character section of the Property inspector, click the **Show border around text** button to select it.

▶ 6. In the Paragraph section of the Property inspector, click the **Behavior** button, and then click **Single line** to set the line type.

▶ 7. In the Options section of the Property inspector, set the Max chars to **1** to allow only one character in the input box. See Figure 8-22.

FL 404 Flash | Tutorial 8 Programming with ActionScript 3.0

Figure 8-22   **Input text block properties**

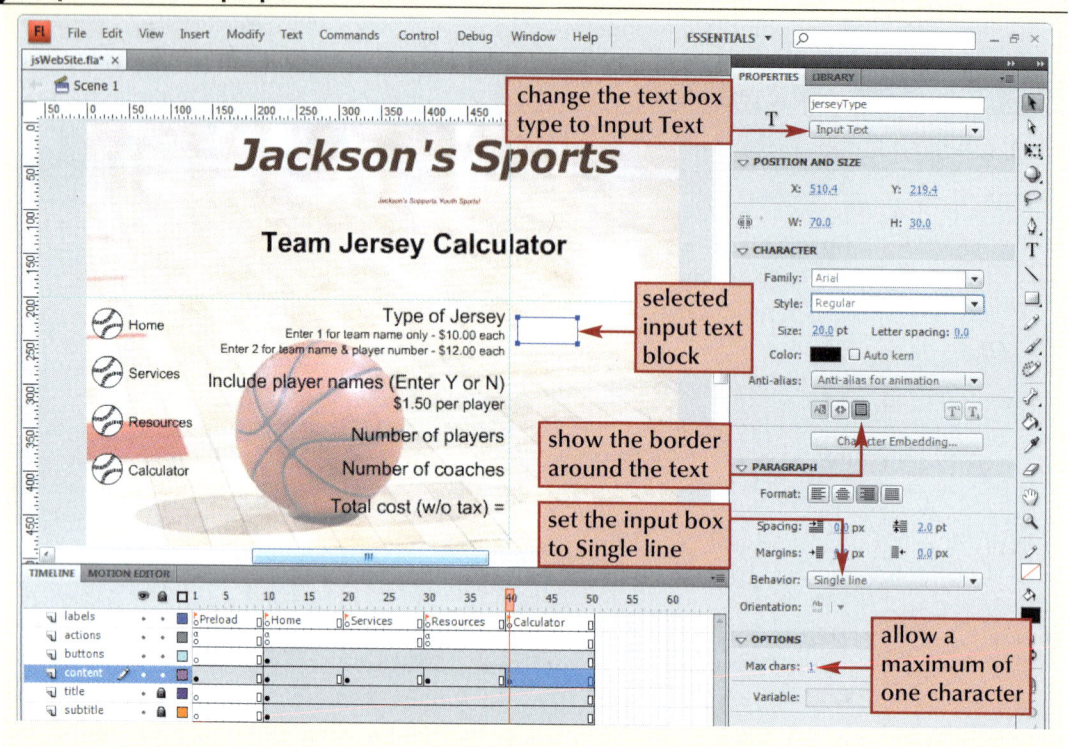

[Screenshot of Flash interface showing the Team Jersey Calculator with an input text block selected. Annotations point to: "change the text box type to Input Text", "selected input text block", "show the border around the text", "set the input box to Single line", and "allow a maximum of one character".]

You'll create additional input text blocks.

▶ 8. Repeat Steps 1 through 7 to create an input text block to the right of the Include player names (Enter Y or N) line, entering **playerNames** as the instance name.

▶ 9. Repeat Steps 1 through 7 to create an input text block to the right of the Number of players line, entering **numberOfPlayers** as the instance name and setting the maximum characters to **0**.

▶ 10. Repeat Steps 1 through 7 to create an input text block to the right of the Number of coaches line, entering **numberOfCoaches** as the instance name and setting the maximum characters to **0**.

▶ 11. In the Tools panel, click the **Selection** tool, reposition the input text boxes as needed so that they are vertically aligned, and then deselect the text boxes. See Figure 8-23.

> **Tip**
>
> Setting the maximum characters to 0 allows the input box to accept an unlimited number of characters, and not zero characters.

Figure 8-23   Completed input text boxes

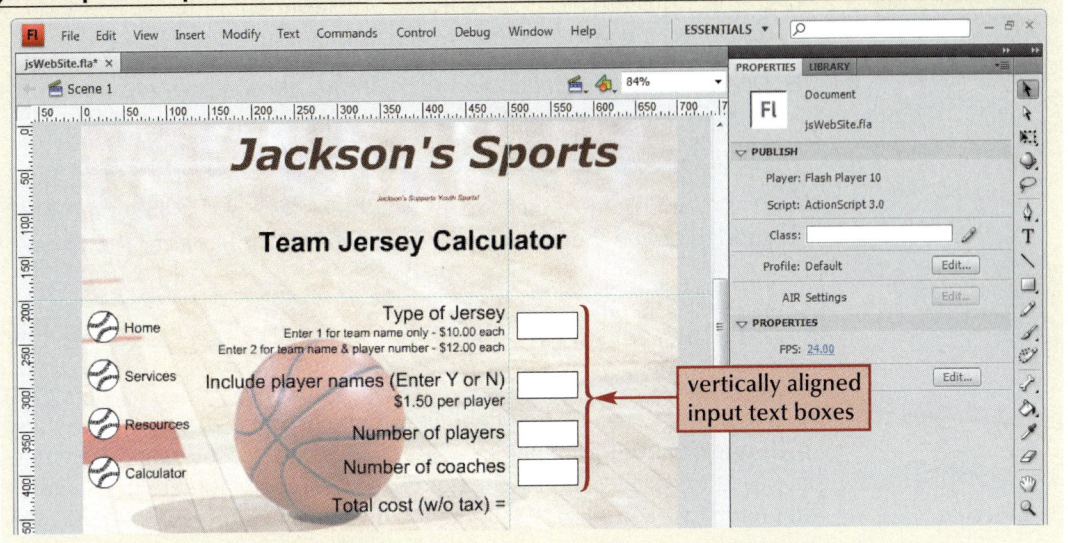

[Screenshot of Flash workspace showing the Jackson's Sports Team Jersey Calculator page with vertically aligned input text boxes for Type of Jersey, Include player names, Number of players, and Number of coaches.]

The input text boxes the visitor will use to enter data are complete. You will add a dynamic text block next. This text block instance must also be assigned a name. You will also create an instance of a Calculate button that Aly created.

To add the dynamic text box and button to the Calculator page:

1. In the Tools panel, click the **Text** tool, and then create a text block to the right of the Total cost (w/o tax) = line.

2. In the Property inspector, set the text type to **Dynamic Text**, set the font family to **Arial**, set the font style to **Regular**, set the point size to **20**, set the text color to **black**, and then set the paragraph format to **Align right**.

3. In the Tools panel, click the **Selection** tool, and then, in the Property inspector, enter **total** as the instance name, set the text block dimensions to **70** pixels wide and **30** pixels high, and click the **Selectable** button to deselect it, if necessary. The properties for the dynamic text block are set.

4. Drag an instance of the **calcTotalButton** symbol from the Library panel to the right side of the dynamic text block, and then, in the Property inspector, enter **calc_btn** as the instance name. The button instance is placed on the Stage and assigned a name.

Writing ActionScript Code to Do a Calculation

The calcTotalButton instance requires ActionScript code to make it operational. The user will enter values in the input text boxes you created, and then click the calcTotalButton instance to compute the total cost for the jerseys. As you have done with previous scripts, you need to define a function. The function will process the values entered in the input text boxes and calculate a total cost that will be displayed in the dynamic text box. The first line of the script will create a function called `calculateTotal`. After defining the function, you will add several statements to define variables that will be used within the script. These variables do not represent objects on the Stage, but instead hold intermediate values used as part of the calculations. Each variable is defined with the `var` keyword, a name, and the Number data type. The Number data type specifies that the variables will contain numbers.

To define the function and the initial variables for the script:

1. In the Timeline, insert a keyframe at **Frame 40** of the actions layer. Actions for the Calculator page will be created in Frame 40.

2. Open the Actions panel, and then, in the Script pane, type the following line of code to define the function.

   ```
   function calculateTotal(evtObject:MouseEvent):void {
   ```

3. Press the **Enter** key twice to insert a blank line, and then type the following lines of code to define the variables, pressing the **Enter** key after each line.

   ```
   var price:Number;
   var totalCost:Number;
   var numberOfJerseys:Number;
   ```

> **Tip**
>
> You can also right-click the frame, and then click Insert Keyframe to add a keyframe.

The first input text block will contain either a 1 or a 2 for the type of jersey. To determine which price to use for the jersey, you must use an if conditional statement. The condition that needs to be checked is whether the jerseyType value the user entered is 1 or 2. You will create two conditional statements; one to check for the value of 1 and one to check for the value of 2. Based on the results of the conditions, the price variable will be assigned a value of 10 or 12, corresponding to the cost of the selected jersey.

Using Expressions and Operators

An **expression** is a statement that is used to assign a value to a variable. For example, the expression UserName = "Tom" assigns the text "Tom" to the variable UserName. When referring to text in an expression, it is enclosed in quotation marks. The characters within the quotation marks are considered string data, which is handled differently than numeric data. **String data** is a series of characters—such as letters, numbers, and punctuation—and is always enclosed in quotation marks. **Numeric data** is a number or numbers that are not enclosed in quotation marks. So, to assign a numeric value to a variable, you do not enclose the value in quotation marks. For example, the expression Amount = 20 assigns the numeric value 20 to the variable named Amount.

The equal sign in the expression is an example of an operator. Operators are used in expressions to tell Flash how to manipulate the values in the expression. There are several types of operators. For example, the equal sign is an example of an **assignment operator** because it assigns a value to a variable. ActionScript also has **arithmetic operators** such as +, –, *, and / that are used to indicate addition, subtraction, multiplication, and division, respectively. Another type of operator is a comparison operator, which is an operator used in conditional statements, as you learned earlier.

The script to calculate the results will use expressions and operators.

To code the statements to determine the price of the jerseys:

1. In the Script pane of the Actions panel, type the following lines of code at the end of the script, pressing the **Enter** key after each line.

   ```
   if (jerseyType.text == "1") {
       price = 10;
   }
   ```

In this code, jerseyType is the name assigned to the first input text block and it contains the value entered by the user. The text property of the jerseyType object represents the value contained in the input box. The conditional operator == compares the input box value to the text value of "1". If the values are equal, the next line assigns a value of 10 to the price variable. You'll code a second conditional statement to check for a jerseyType value of "2".

▶ 2. Type the following lines of code, pressing the **Enter** key after each line.

```
if (jerseyType.text == "2") {
    price = 12;
}
```

If the text value of the jerseyType object is "2", a value of 12 is assigned to the Price variable.

After the second if statement is performed, the price variable will contain either a value of 10 or 12 depending on the jerseyType value entered by the user.

The next action to perform is another if statement to determine whether the user entered Y or N. This determines if the player names will be included on the jerseys. If the user entered Y, you will add 1.50 to the price of the jerseys. Because ActionScript is case sensitive, you need to check for both a lowercase y and an uppercase Y. This will ensure that the correct value is calculated, regardless of how the user entered the letter.

There is no need to check for the letter N because if the user entered N, the price will not change. To check for two conditions within the same if statement, you use the logical operator ||, which represents the Or comparison. You will add the ActionScript code for the if statement next.

> **Tip**
>
> You can use shortcuts to combine assignment and arithmetic operators, such as Amount += 5 instead of Amount = Amount + 5 to increment the value in the variable Amount by 5.

To code the statement to check if player names will be included:

▶ 1. In the Script pane of the Actions panel, type the following lines of code at the end of the script, pressing the **Enter** key after each line.

```
if (playerNames.text =="Y" || playerNames.text == "y") {
    price += 1.50;
}
```

In this code, playerNames is the name of the input text box that contains the value the user enters to specify whether the names of the players will be included on the jerseys. The text property represents the value entered by the user. The || operator causes the condition to be true if either one of the comparisons is true. If the condition is true, the variable price is increased by 1.50.

The next two input text blocks contain values that represent how many players and coaches are on the team. These two values will be added together to get the total number of jerseys to be purchased. Before the values can be added, they need to be converted to numbers. Because the number of players and number of coaches are whole numbers, you will use the int() function.

> **InSight** | **Converting Values to Numeric Data**
>
> Values entered into an input text block are considered string data and not numeric data. That is, the values are not treated as numbers, but instead are treated as text characters. Using the + operator to add the two values will not yield the correct result if the values are not first converted to numeric data. The `int()` function can be applied to the values to convert them to integer numbers, which are whole numbers that do not include decimals.

After you have calculated the number of jerseys, you can multiply the number by the price of each jersey to get a total cost. You will add the statements to determine the total cost next.

To code the statements to determine the total cost of the jerseys:

▶ 1. In the Script pane of the Actions panel, at the end of the script, type the following line of code.

```
numberOfJerseys = int(numberOfPlayers.text) +int(numberOfCoaches.text);
```

The numberOfPlayers and numberOfCoaches variables were defined in the input text blocks. The text property is used to get the value entered by the user for each text box. These values are converted to integers and then added together. The result is then assigned to the variable numberOfJerseys.

▶ 2. Press the **Enter** key twice to insert a blank line, and then type the following line of code.

```
totalCost = numberOfJerseys*price;
```

The value in the numberOfJerseys is multiplied by the value in price and the result is assigned to the totalCost variable.

The final step is to assign the value in totalCost to the dynamic text block so that it will be displayed for the user. The dynamic text block can contain only string data. Because the totalCost value is a number, it must first be converted to string data before it can be assigned to the dynamic text box named total. To convert the number to a string, you apply the `String()` function to the totalCost value. The results of the `String()` function can then be assigned to the total dynamic text box. You will add this code next.

To code the statement to display the final result:

▶ 1. In the Script pane of the Actions panel, at the end of the script, type the following line of code.

```
total.text = String(totalCost);
```

The totalCost value is converted to a string and assigned to the text property of the total dynamic text box. The value will then be displayed to the user.

▶ 2. Press the **Enter** key, and then type **}** (a closing curly brace) to complete the script. See Figure 8-24.

Figure 8-24 — Script for calculation

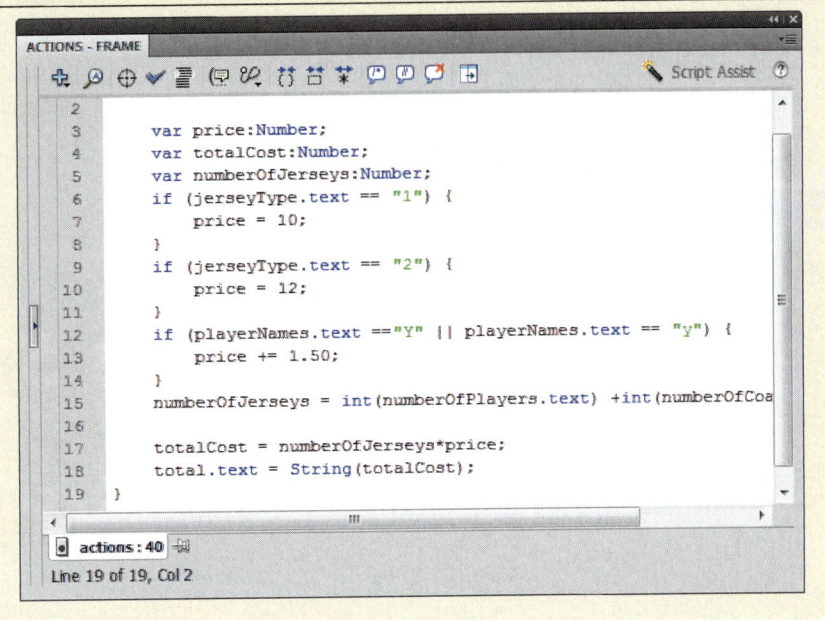

```
ACTIONS - FRAME
                                                            Script Assist
 2
 3      var price:Number;
 4      var totalCost:Number;
 5      var numberOfJerseys:Number;
 6      if (jerseyType.text == "1") {
 7          price = 10;
 8      }
 9      if (jerseyType.text == "2") {
10          price = 12;
11      }
12      if (playerNames.text =="Y" || playerNames.text == "y") {
13          price += 1.50;
14      }
15      numberOfJerseys = int(numberOfPlayers.text) +int(numberOfCoa
16
17      totalCost = numberOfJerseys*price;
18      total.text = String(totalCost);
19  }

actions : 40
Line 19 of 19, Col 2
```

To make the Calculate button operational, you need to add an event listener. The event listener for the Calculate button has the same format as the ones used for the other site buttons. You will use the `addEventListener()` method for the calc_btn button instance to register the button's CLICK event with the calculateTotal function. You will type the event listener code next.

To add the event listener code, check for errors, and test the script:

▶ 1. In the Actions panel, place the insertion after the closing curly brace ending the Calculate function, and then press the **Enter** key to add a blank line.

▶ 2. Type the following line of code to create the event listener for the Calculate button.

   `calc_btn.addEventListener(MouseEvent.CLICK, calculateTotal);`

   Before testing the script, you should check for syntax errors and make corrections as needed.

▶ 3. In the Actions panel, click the **Check syntax** button ✓ to check for syntax errors. A dialog box opens, indicating whether the script contains errors.

▶ 4. Click the **OK** button. The dialog box closes. The error-free code appears in the Script pane.

   Trouble? If the script contains errors, the code probably contains typing errors. If the Compiler Errors panel is hidden behind the Actions panel, collapse the Actions panel, review the error message(s) in the Compiler Errors panel, close the Compiler Errors panel, expand the Actions panel, compare the code in the Actions panel with the code in previous sets of steps, and then make the necessary corrections so that your code matches the code in the steps. Make certain that the variable names and ActionScript keywords have the correct case and that the parentheses and curly braces are organized and paired correctly. Repeat Steps 3 and 4 until your code is error-free.

▶ 5. Save the jsWebSite.fla document.

▶ 6. On the Application bar, click **Control**, and then click **Test Movie** to open the document in the Flash Player.

▶ 7. Click the **Calculator** button to advance to the Team Jersey Calculator page, and then enter **1** in the Type of Jersey box, **Y** in the Include player names box, **10** in the Number of players box, and **2** in the Number of coaches box.

▶ 8. Click the **Calculate** button. The Total cost field displays 138. See Figure 8-25.

Figure 8-25   Results of the calculation

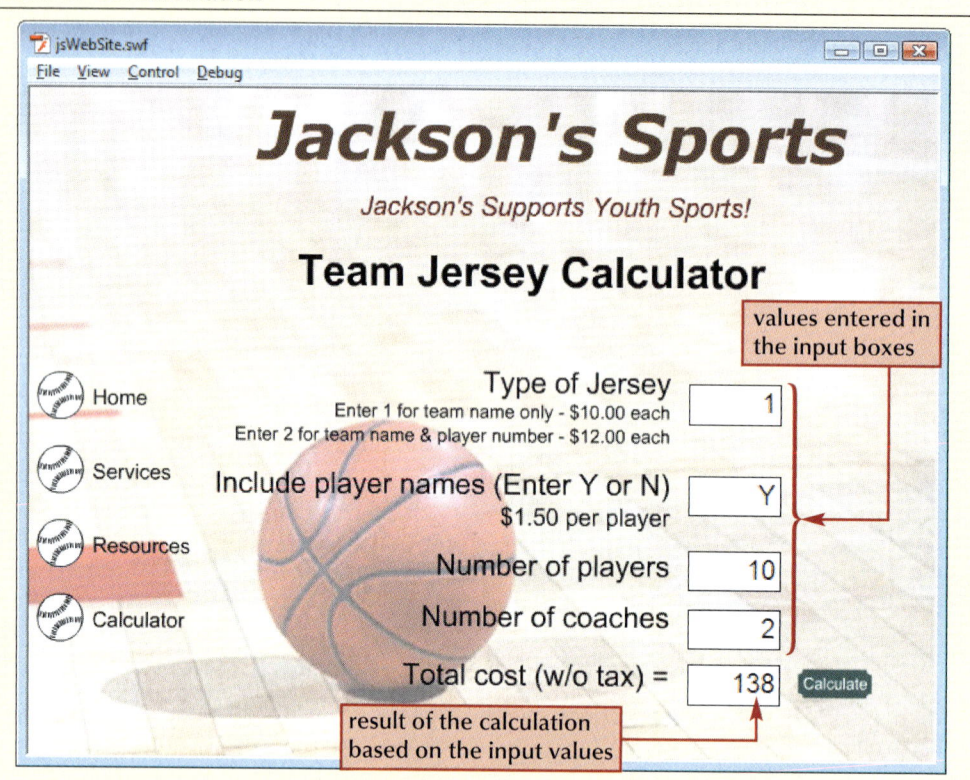

Trouble? If you don't get the correct results, make sure you entered the correct input values and also check the variable names of your input and dynamic text boxes. Remember that ActionScript is case sensitive. If the case of the variable names assigned to the text boxes differs from that used in the code, the result will be incorrect.

▶ 9. Enter a set of input values of your choice, click the **Calculate** button to see the total cost, and then repeat with another set of input values.

▶ 10. Close the Flash Player window to return to the jsWebSite.fla document.

Adding Numeric Feedback to the Preloader

In the previous session, you created an animation for the preloader to provide visual feedback to the user. In the animation, the scaleX property of a rectangle was changed based on how much of the SWF file had loaded into the Flash Player. In addition to the visual feedback, Flash developers often include numeric feedback showing what percentage of the file has been loaded. The same value used to change the scaleX property of the rectangle can be displayed as a percentage. To display the number, you need to create a dynamic text block similar to the one you created to display the results of the calculation in the Calculator page. You will add a dynamic text block for the preloader and then you will add the code to calculate and display the percentage of the file loaded.

To add a dynamic text block to the preloader:

1. Close the Actions panel to view the Stage, clear the guides, and then in the Timeline, click **Frame 1** of the content layer.

2. On the Stage, create a dynamic text block between the Loading text block and the % text block, set the font family to **Arial**, set the font style to **Regular**, set the point size to **18**, set the text color to **black**, set the paragraph format to **Align right**, and then deselect the **Show border around text** button.

3. In the Property inspector, set the text block's dimensions to **30** pixels wide and **26** pixels high, and then enter **percent_txt** as the instance name of the text block instance. See Figure 8-26.

Figure 8-26   Dynamic text block

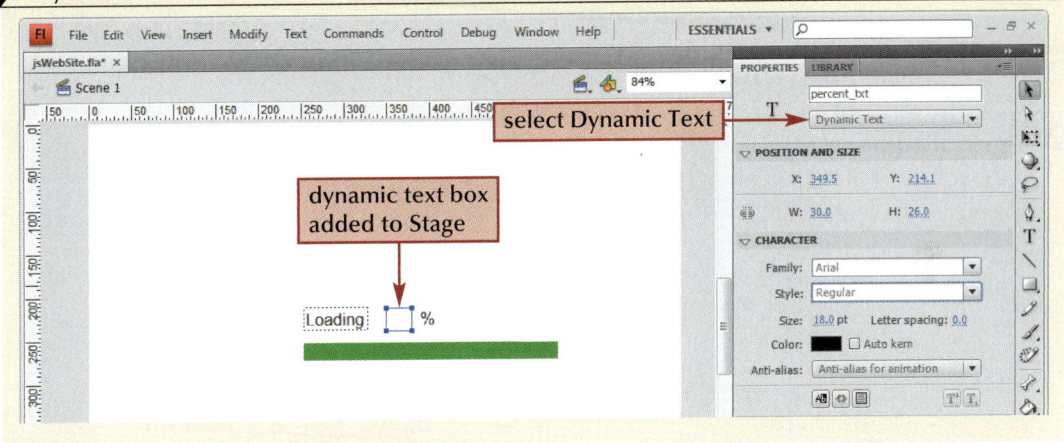

Next, you will add the code to the preloader function to calculate and display the percentage of the file loaded.

To add numeric feedback code, check for errors, and test the script:

1. In the Timeline, click **Frame 1** of the actions layer, and then open the Actions panel.

2. In the Script pane of the Actions panel, place the insertion point in front of the line with the if conditional statement, press the **Enter** key to add a blank line, and then in the blank line, type the following line of code.

   ```
   var percent:int = amtLoaded*100;
   ```

   This line creates a new variable named percent with integer as its data type. The value in amtLoaded is multiplied by 100 to change the amtLoaded value to a percentage. This percentage is assigned to the percent variable.

3. Press the **Enter** key to add a new line, and then type the following line of code.

   ```
   percent_txt.text = String(percent);
   ```

   The value in the percent variable is converted to a string using the `String()` function and the result is then assigned to the text property of the percent_txt object, which is the dynamic text block instance on the Stage. The result is that the percent value is displayed in the dynamic text box instance.

4. In the Actions panel, click the **Check syntax** button to check for syntax errors. A dialog box opens, indicating whether the script contains errors.

▶ 5. Click the **OK** button. The dialog box closes. The error-free functions appear in the Script pane.

   Trouble? If the script contains errors, the code probably contains typing errors. If the Compiler Errors panel is hidden behind the Actions panel, collapse the Actions panel, review the error message(s) in the Compiler Errors panel, close the Compiler Errors panel, expand the Actions panel, compare the code in the Actions panel with the code in Steps 2 and 3, and then make the necessary corrections so that your code matches the code in the steps. Repeat Steps 4 and 5 until your code is error-free.

▶ 6. Save the jsWebSite.fla document.

▶ 7. On the Application bar, click **Control**, and then click **Test Movie**. The SWF file plays in the Flash Player.

▶ 8. On the Flash Player Application bar, click **View**, and then click **Simulate Download**. After a few seconds, the preloader animation plays and the percent loaded value is displayed. See Figure 8-27.

Figure 8-27   Simulated download process

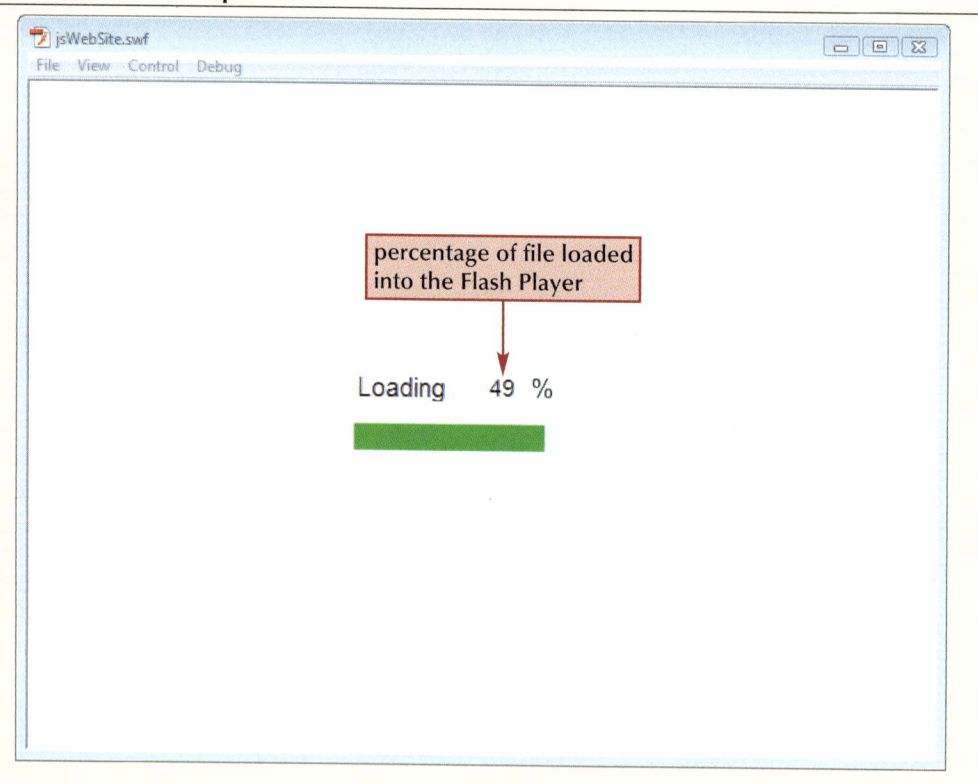

After the percent loaded value reaches 100%, the home page of the Jackson's Sports Web site appears.

▶ 9. Close the Flash Player window, and then close the jsWebSite.fla document.

You have completed and tested the input form page that allows the user to enter values in input text blocks, calculates the total cost of the jerseys based on the values entered, and displays the result in a dynamic text block. You also added a dynamic text block to display the percent loaded value with the preloader animation.

Review | Session 8.3 Quick Check

1. What is the purpose of input text?
2. How can you limit the number of characters that can be entered in an input text block?
3. Write a statement to multiply the value in the numeric variable subTotal by 15 and assign the result to the dynamic text block with the instance name of subtotal_txt.
4. Explain the purpose of the || operator in the following conditional statement:
   if (Code == "1" || Code == "2").
5. What is the purpose of the int() function?

Review | Tutorial Summary

In this tutorial, you learned the basic elements of ActionScript programming, how to create scripts to control objects in a Flash document, and the structure and syntax of a script written in ActionScript. You also learned about the differences between ActionScript 2.0 and ActionScript 3.0. You used ActionScript to make navigational buttons operational for a Flash Web site and to create links to other Web sites. You then created an input form using input and dynamic text blocks that enable the user to enter data and receive the result of a calculation. Finally, you created a preloader function to display an animation and numeric feedback while a SWF file loads in the Flash Player.

Key Terms

ActionScript Virtual Machine 2 (AVM2)
arithmetic operator
assignment operator
byte
call
class
client computer
comment
comparison operator
conditional statement
constructor
dot notation
event listener
event object
event source
expression
function
input form
keyword
kilobyte
method
numeric data
object
operator
parameter
preloader
property
response
streaming
string data
syntax
typed
variable

FL 414 Flash | Tutorial 8 Programming with ActionScript 3.0

Practice | Review Assignments

Practice the skills you learned in the tutorial.

Data File needed for the Review Assignments: softballSite.fla

Aly developed a different version of the Jackson's Youth Sports Web site with an emphasis on softball teams. She asks you to complete the Web site by adding links to the Web Links page, adding input and dynamic text boxes to the Player Trophy Cost page, and adding the ActionScript code to make the navigational buttons, the Web Links, and the Trophy cost calculate button operational. You also need to complete the preloader animation and code.

1. Open the **softballSite.fla** file located in the Tutorial.08\Review folder included with your Data Files, and then save the file as **jsSoftball.fla** in the same folder.
2. In the labels layer, insert keyframes at Frame 20, Frame 30, and Frame 40, and then add the label **Preload** at Frame 1, the label **Services** at Frame 20, the label **Weblinks** at Frame 30, and the label **Trophies** at Frame 40.
3. On the Stage, select the Home button instance, and then, in the Property inspector, name the instance **home_btn**. Name the Services button instance as **services_btn**, name the Web Links button instance as **weblinks_btn**, and then name the Trophies button instance as **trophies_btn**.
4. In the Timeline, select Frame 10 of the actions layer, and then, in the Actions panel, insert the following comment before the first line.

    ```
    //Keep the playhead from advancing automatically
    ```
5. In the Actions panel, insert the following comment on the line before the function statement.

    ```
    //Button functions
    ```
6. In the Actions panel, on the line after the closing curly brace, type the following code.

    ```
    function onServicesClick(evt:MouseEvent):void {
         gotoAndStop("Services");
    }
    function onWeblinksClick(evt:MouseEvent):void {
         gotoAndStop("Weblinks");
    }
    function onTrophiesClick(evt:MouseEvent):void {
         gotoAndStop("Trophies");
    }
    ```
7. In the Actions panel, on the line after the last closing curly brace, type the following code.

    ```
    // Event listeners
    home_btn.addEventListener(MouseEvent.CLICK, onHomeClick);
    services_btn.addEventListener(MouseEvent.CLICK, onServicesClick);
    weblinks_btn.addEventListener(MouseEvent.CLICK, onWeblinksClick);
    trophies_btn.addEventListener(MouseEvent.CLICK, onTrophiesClick);
    ```
8. Check the code for syntax errors, make any necessary corrections, and then collapse the Actions panel.
9. In the Library panel, make a duplicate of the asaYouth button symbol named **youthSoftball**, and then edit the youthSoftball button by changing the text in both its Up frame and Over frame to **Youth Softball**. In the button's Timeline, insert a keyframe in the Hit frame, and then draw a rectangle with a black fill and no stroke to cover the text block.

10. In the Library panel, make a duplicate of the asaYouth button symbol, name the duplicate **myTeamZone**, and then edit the myTeamZone button by changing the text in both its Up frame and Over frame to **My Team Zone**. In the button's Timeline, insert a keyframe in the Hit frame, and then draw a rectangle with a black fill and no stroke to cover the text block.

11. Edit the asaYouth button by inserting a keyframe in its Hit frame, and then draw a rectangle with a black fill and no stroke to cover the text block.

12. In the Timeline, select Frame 30 of the content layer, add an instance of the youthSoftball button below the asaYouth button instance, and then add an instance of the myTeamZone button below the youthSoftball button instance. Select all three button instances on the center of the Stage, and then, in the Align panel, deselect the To stage button, click the Align left edge button, and click the Space evenly vertically button to align the instances and distribute them evenly.

13. On the Stage, select the asaYouth button instance and name the instance **asaYouth_btn**, select the youthSoftball button instance and name the instance **youthSoftball _btn**, and then select the myTeamZone button instance and name the instance **myTeamZone_btn**.

14. In the Timeline, select Frame 30 of the actions layer, and then, in the Actions panel, type the following code above the //Event listeners comment line.

    ```
    function gotoYouthSoftballSite(eventobj:MouseEvent):void
    {
        var youthSoftballURL:URLRequest = new URLRequest("http://www.infosports.com/softball/");
        navigateToURL(youthSoftballURL);
    }
    function gotoMyTeamZoneSite(eventobj:MouseEvent):void
    {
        var myTeamZoneURL:URLRequest = new URLRequest("http://www.myteamzone.com/teamwebsites/SoftBall.aspx");
        navigateToURL(myTeamZoneURL);
    }
    ```

15. In the Actions panel, type the following code after the last line, and then check the code for syntax errors, making any necessary corrections.

    ```
    youthSoftball_btn.addEventListener(MouseEvent.CLICK, gotoYouthSoftballSite);
    myTeamZone_btn.addEventListener(MouseEvent.CLICK, gotoMyTeamZoneSite);
    ```

16. Collapse the Actions panel, select Frame 40 of the content layer, create an input text block to the right of the Add individual names (Enter Y or N) text block, select Arial for the font family, black for the text color, 20 for the point size, and right align for the paragraph format, make the text block 70 pixels wide and 30 pixels high, set the line type to Single line, show the border around text, set the maximum characters to 1, and then name the input text box instance as **playerNames**.

17. Create an input text block to the right of the Number of players text block using the same dimensions and properties as the playerNames text box, except set the maximum characters to 0, and name the input text box instance as **numberOfPlayers**.

18. Create a dynamic text block to the right of the Total cost (w/o tax) = text block using the same dimensions and properties as the playerNames text box, except name the dynamic text block instance **total**.

19. In the Timeline, select Frame 40 of the actions layer, and then, in the Actions panel, type the following code above the //Event listener comment line, check the code for syntax errors, and make any necessary corrections.

    ```
    if (trophyType.text == "1") {
        price = 5.95;
    }
    if (trophyType.text == "2") {
        price = 8.95;
    }

    if (playerNames.text =="Y" || playerNames.text == "y") {
        price += .50;
    }

    totalCost = int(numberOfPlayers.text)*price;
    total.text = String(totalCost);
    }
    ```

20. Collapse the Actions panel, select Frame 1 of the content layer, deselect all the contents on the Stage, and select the rectangle's green fill but not its stroke. Convert the rectangle's fill to a movie clip symbol named **Rectangle** with the upper-left registration point selected. In the Property inspector, name the Rectangle instance **loadBar_mc**.

21. On the Stage, create a dynamic text block to the left of the % text block, set the font family to Arial, set the font style to regular, set the point size to 20, set the text color to black, set the paragraph format to align right, deselect the Show border around text button, make the dimensions of the text block 70 pixels wide and 40 pixels high, and then name the text block instance **percent_txt**.

22. In the Timeline, select Frame 1 of the actions layer, and then, in the Actions panel, type the following code before the //Event listener line, check the code for syntax errors, and make any necessary corrections.

    ```
    loadBar_mc.scaleX = amtLoaded;

    var percent:int = amtLoaded*100;
    percent_txt.text = String(percent);

    if (loadedBytes == totalBytes) {
        gotoAndPlay("Home");
    } else {
        gotoAndPlay("Preload");
    }
    }
    ```

23. Save the jsSoftball.fla document, and then test it. In the Flash Player, use the Simulate Download command to test the preloader. Click the Web Links button to go to the Web Links page. On the Web Links page, click each link button to open its linked Web site in a browser window. (If an error message appears indicating an error opening the Web pages, the URLs for these Web sites might have changed since the printing of this tutorial. See your instructor or technical support person for assistance.)

24. Click the Trophies button to go to the Player Trophy Cost page. In the Type of Trophy text box, type **1**. In the Add individual names (Enter Y or N) text box, type **Y**. In the Number of players text box, type **11**. Click the Calculate button to display 70.95 for the total cost.

25. Submit the finished files to your instructor.

| Apply | **Case Problem 1** |

Add Web links, an input form, and ActionScript code in a Flash Web site for a pet boarding store.

Data File needed for this Case Problem: kprDraft.fla

Katie's Pet Resort Katie meets with John to discuss adding two new elements to the Web site, including a new page with hyperlinks to Web sites with additional pet adoption information. She also wants a page for customers to select from several options for pet boarding. These options include the type of boarding (day or overnight), the number of days if overnight boarding, and whether grooming is included. The page will then display the cost of the boarding based on the selections. You will make the changes to the Web site, including the Boarding page, which is shown Figure 8-28.

Figure 8-28

1. Open the **kprDraft.fla** document located in the Tutorial.08\Case1 folder included with your Data Files, and then save the file as **resortWeb.fla** in the same folder.
2. In the Timeline, insert a new layer above the buttons layer and name it **actions**. In the actions layer, insert keyframes at Frame 10 and Frame 20. Insert a layer above the actions layer and name it **labels**. In the labels layer, insert keyframes at Frame 10 and Frame 20, and then add the label **Home** in Frame 1, add the label **Resources** in Frame 10, and add the label **Boarding** in Frame 20.
3. On the Stage, select the Home button instance, and then, in the Property inspector, name the instance as **home_btn**. Name the Resources button instance as **resources_btn**, and name the Boarding button instance as **boarding_btn**.
4. In the Timeline, select Frame 1 of the actions layer, and then in the Actions panel, insert the following code and check the code for syntax errors, making any necessary corrections.

```
//Keep the playhead from advancing
stop();
//Button functions
function onHomeClick(evt:MouseEvent):void {
    gotoAndStop("Home");
}
function onResourcesClick(evt:MouseEvent):void {
    gotoAndStop("Resources");
}
function onBoardingClick(evt:MouseEvent):void {
```

```
            gotoAndStop("Boarding");
}
// Event listeners
home_btn.addEventListener(MouseEvent.CLICK, onHomeClick);
resources_btn.addEventListener(MouseEvent.CLICK, onResourcesClick);
boarding_btn.addEventListener(MouseEvent.CLICK, onBoardingClick);
```

5. In the Timeline, select Frame 10 of the content layer, and then, on the Stage, create a static text block within the yellow rectangle at about 200 pixels from the left edge of the Stage and 270 pixels from the top edge of the Stage. Use Arial for the font family, regular for the font style, 16 for the point size, black for the text color, and align left for the paragraph format. Type **Adopt a Pet** in the text block.

6. Create another static text block below the first one with the same text properties, and then type **Best Friend Pet Adoption** in the text block. Create another static text block below the second one with the same text properties, and then type **SPCA of Texas** in the text block. Select the three text blocks, and then align them by their left edges and distribute them evenly vertically.

7. Convert each of the three text blocks into a button symbol named **adopt button**, **bestFriend button**, and **spca button**, respectively.

8. Edit the adopt button symbol, insert a keyframe in its Over frame and make the text italic, and then insert a keyframe in the Hit frame and draw a rectangle to make it easier to click the button. Edit the bestFriend button symbol and the spca button symbol in the same way. Exit symbol-editing mode.

9. On the Stage, select the adopt button instance, and then, in the Property inspector, name the instance **adopt_btn**. Name the bestFriend button instance **bestFriend_btn**, and then name the spca button instance as **spca_btn**.

10. In the Timeline, insert a keyframe at Frame 10 of the actions layer, and then, in the Actions panel, type the following code to make the buttons operational and check the code for syntax errors, making any necessary corrections.

```
//Button functions
function gotoAdoptSite(eventobj:MouseEvent):void {
    var adoptURL:URLRequest = new URLRequest
    ("http://www.adoptapet.com/");
    navigateToURL(adoptURL);
}

function gotoBestFriendSite(eventobj:MouseEvent):void {
    var bestURL:URLRequest = new URLRequest
    ("http://www.bfpa.org/");
    navigateToURL(bestURL);
}

function gotospcaSite(eventobj:MouseEvent):void {
    var spcaURL:URLRequest = new URLRequest
    ("http://www.spca.org/");
    navigateToURL(spcaURL);
}
//Event listeners
adopt_btn.addEventListener(MouseEvent.CLICK, gotoAdoptSite);
bestFriend_btn.addEventListener(MouseEvent.CLICK,
gotoBestFriendSite);
spca_btn.addEventListener(MouseEvent.CLICK, gotospcaSite);
```

11. Create a new static text block below the third button. Use Arial for the font family, italic for the font style, 10 for the point size, black for the text color, and align left for the paragraph format. Type **Clicking the buttons above will open a browser window.** in the text block.
12. In the Timeline, select Frame 20 of the content layer, and create an input text block to the right of the Enter letter for the desired boarding option line. Make the text block 40 pixels wide by 20 pixels high. Use Arial for the font family, 12 for the point size, regular for the font style, black for the text color, and align right for the paragraph format. If necessary, select single line as the line type behavior, show the border around the text, and enter **1** as the maximum characters. Name the text block instance as **boardingType_txt**.
13. Create a second input text block with the same dimensions and properties as the boardingType_txt text block. Place this text block to the right of the How many days? line. Set the maximum characters to 0 and name the text block instance as **days_txt**.
14. Create another input text block with the same dimensions and properties as the boardingType_txt text block, and place it to the right of the Bath and grooming for $24.95 (Y- yes or N- no) line. Set the maximum characters to 1 and name the text block instance as **grooming_txt**.
15. Create a dynamic text block to the right of the Total cost (w/o taxes) line. Use the same dimensions and text properties as the input text blocks. Name the text block instance as **total_txt**.
16. Drag an instance of the calc button from the Library panel to the left side of the Total cost (w/o taxes) line, and then name the text block instance as **calc_btn**.
17. In the Timeline, select Frame 20 of the actions layer, and then, in the Actions panel, type the following code, check the code for syntax errors, and make any necessary corrections.

```
//Calculate cost of retreat
function Calculate(evt:MouseEvent):void {

var price:Number;
var totalCost:Number;

if (boardingType_txt.text == "D" || boardingType_txt.text == "d") {
          price = 14.95;
          } else {
          price = 19.95;
          }


totalCost = int(days_txt.text)*price;

if (grooming_txt.text =="Y" || grooming_txt.text == "y") {
          totalCost += 24.95;
}

total_txt.text = String(totalCost);
}
//Event listener
calc_btn.addEventListener(MouseEvent.CLICK, Calculate);
```

FL 420 Flash | Tutorial 8 Programming with ActionScript 3.0

18. Save the resortWeb.fla document, and then test it. Click the Resources button to display the Resources page. Click each link to open its Web site in a browser window. (If an error message appears indicating an error opening the Web pages, the URLs for these Web sites might have changed since the printing of this tutorial. See your instructor or technical support person for assistance.)
19. Click the Boarding button to display the Boarding page. Enter **O** for the type of boarding, **2** for the number of days, and **Y** for bath and grooming. Click the Calculate Total button to display 64.85 for the total cost.
20. Submit the finished files to your instructor.

Apply | Case 2

Create a Flash Web site with buttons that when clicked display the contents of previous and next frames for a zoo exhibit.

Data Files needed for this Case Problem: aczDraft.fla, bear.jpg, giraffe.jpg, rhino.jpg

Alamo City Zoo Web Site Janet meets with Alex to request a new Web site that will display zoo animals. Several pages will display special exhibits and the user will be able to change the display from one exhibit to another. Alex asks you to help him modify a draft page by adding buttons to control the display of each exhibit and by adding each exhibit on a separate frame. Each exhibit will display a picture of a zoo animal and a short message about the exhibit. Alamo City Zoo currently has three special exhibits. Figure 8-29 shows the contents of Frame 1.

Figure 8-29

Alamo City Zoo

Wild Animal Exhibits

The Alamo City Zoo has an extensive collection of the world's most exotic animals. Come visit our world-famous exhibits and see animals in their native habitats. The zoo also offers group tours, special classes, and summer camps for kids.

Click the buttons below to see some of our animals.

1. Open the **aczDraft.fla** document located in the Tutorial.08\Case2 folder included with your Data Files, and then save the file as **exhibits.fla** in the same folder.
2. In the Timeline, insert three new layers above the contents layer, and then name the layers **buttons**, **actions**, and **labels**.
3. In the Timeline, select the buttons layer, open the Buttons Common Library, drag an instance of the flat blue back symbol from the playback flat folder to the Stage, place the instance below the text block and rectangle at the center of the Stage, and then name the instance **prev_btn**. Drag an instance of the flat blue forward symbol, place the instance just to the right of the flat blue back instance, and then name the instance **next_btn**. Close the Buttons library panel.
4. Select both of the button instances, top align the buttons relative to each other, and then lock the buttons layer to prevent accidentally changing its contents.

5. In the Timeline, insert regular frames at Frame 10 of all the layers. Insert a keyframe in Frame 2 of the contents layer, and then delete the bottom and middle text blocks.
6. Import the **bear.jpg**, **giraffe.jpg**, and **rhino.jpg** files located in the Tutorial.08\Case2 folder included with your Data Files to the document's library. Drag an instance of the rhino.jpg bitmap from the document's Library panel to the center of the rectangle and place it below the title text block.
7. In Frame 2 of the contents layer, add a fixed-width static text block to the left of the rhino picture. Make the text block's width about 140 pixels and place it about 180 pixels from the top of the Stage and about 100 pixels from the left of the Stage. Use Arial for the font family, regular for the font style, 14 for the point size, maroon (#660000) for the text color, and align left for the paragraph format. Type **The rhinoceros stands about 60 inches at the shoulder and weighs between 1 to 1½ tons. Rhinos are vegetarians and live up to 40 years.** in the text block.
8. In the Timeline, insert a keyframe at Frame 3 of the contents layer. On the Stage, swap the instance of the rhino.jpg bitmap with an instance of the giraffe.jpg bitmap. Change the text in the text block to the left of the picture to **The giraffe stands at a height of 14 to 18 feet and weighs up to 2 tons. Giraffes are vegetarians and are able to grasp leaves with their tongue.**
9. In the Timeline, insert a keyframe at Frame 4 of the contents layer. On the Stage, swap the instance of the giraffe.jpg bitmap with an instance of the bear.jpg bitmap. Change the text in the text block to the left of the picture to **Bears, such as the grizzly bear, grow from 5 to 7 feet in length and weigh up to 900 pounds. Bears eat plants, insects, fish, and meat and have a lifespan of about 25 years.**
10. In the Timeline, select Frame 1 of the labels layer. In the Property inspector, assign the label **Begin** to this frame. Insert a keyframe at Frame 4 of the labels layer, and assign the label **End** to the frame.
11. In the Timeline, select Frame 1 of the actions layer. In the Actions panel, type the following code (this code stops the playhead at Frame 1; the function will move the playhead to the next frame unless the playhead is on Frame 4, in which case the playhead will move to the frame labeled Begin).

```
//Keep the playhead from advancing
stop();

//Advance the playhead to the next frame
function onNextClick(evt:MouseEvent):void {
    if (currentFrame!=4) {
        nextFrame();
    } else {
        gotoAndStop("Begin");
    }
}
```

12. In the Actions panel, type the following code after the last line (the function will move the playhead to the previous frame unless the playhead is on Frame 1, in which case the playhead will move to the frame labeled End).

```
//Advance the playhead to the previous frame
function onPrevClick(evt:MouseEvent):void {
    if (currentFrame!=1) {
        prevFrame();
    } else {
        gotoAndStop("End");
    }
}
```

13. In the Actions panel, type the following code after the last line (this code creates the event listeners for the buttons).

    ```
    // Event listeners
    prev_btn.addEventListener(MouseEvent.CLICK, onPrevClick);
    next_btn.addEventListener(MouseEvent.CLICK, onNextClick);
    ```
14. Check the code for syntax errors, and make any necessary corrections.
15. Save the exhibits.fla file, and then test it. Click the buttons to display each exhibit in the frames.
16. Submit the finished files to your instructor.

Challenge | Case 3

Add ActionScript code to advance the playhead from one frame to another and add a preloader to a Flash Web site for a nursery.

Data Files needed for this Case Problem: wcDraft.fla, flower1.jpg, flower2.jpg, flower3.jpg

Westcreek Nursery Web Site   Alice requests a different version of the photos page to display pictures of flowers and plants for sale. Because the number of pictures varies each week, only one button will be used. Each time the button is clicked, a different picture will appear. This will allow more pictures to be added without adding more buttons. You will modify a revised photos page by adding one picture with text per frame and adding a button to advance from one frame to the next. You will also add a preloader, which will display a message and an animation indicating the progress of the loading. Figure 8-30 shows the photos page with the first picture.

Figure 8-30

1. Open the **wcDraft.fla** file located in the Tutorial.08\Case3 folder included with your Data Files, and then save the file as **wcPhotos.fla** in the same folder.
2. In the Timeline, insert a new layer above the background layer and name it **pictures**. Insert two layers above the preloader layer, and name them **actions** and **labels**.
3. In the pictures layer, insert a keyframe at Frame 10. Use the Import to Stage command to import the **flower1.jpg** file located in the Tutorial.08\Case3 folder included with your Data Files. Click the Yes button to import all of the images in the sequence, which places each of the three pictures in separate frames.
4. In the Timeline, insert regular frames at Frame 12 of all the layers except the pictures layer.

5. Select Frame 10 of the pictures layer, and then create a static text block in the lower-center of the picture. Use Arial for the font family, regular for the font style, 24 for the point size, and white for the text color. Type **$9.95–$29.95** in the text block.
6. Select Frame 11 of the pictures layer, create a static text block in the lower-center of the picture using the same properties as in Step 5, and then type **$4.95–$16.95** in the text block.
7. Select Frame 12 of the pictures layer, create a static text block in the lower-center of the picture using the same properties as in Step 5, and then type to **$8.95–$25.95** in the text block.
8. Insert a keyframe at Frame 10 of the labels layer, and then add the label **preload** in Frame 1 and the label **begin** in Frame 10.
9. On the Stage, name the nextPicture button instance as **next_btn**.
10. Select Frame 1 of the preloader layer, and then, on the Stage, draw a rectangle above the Loading text block. Use orange (#FF9900) for the fill, do not include a stroke, and use 15 for the rectangle corner radius. Set the rectangle's dimensions to 300 pixels wide and 20 pixels high. Convert the rectangle to a movie clip symbol named **loadBar** with the upper-left registration point selected. In the Property inspector, name the instance as **loadBar_mc**.
11. Select Frame 1 of the actions layer, type the following code in the Actions panel, and then check the code for syntax errors, making any necessary corrections. The code will check and compare the bytes loaded with the total bytes and increase the scale of the rectangle as the document is loaded. After the document is loaded, the playhead is moved to the frame labeled begin.

```
//Keep the playhead from advancing
stop();

//Preloader function
function preloader(progressEvt:ProgressEvent):void {
       var totalBytes:Number = progressEvt.bytesTotal;
       var loadedBytes:Number = progressEvt.bytesLoaded;
       var amtLoaded:Number = loadedBytes/totalBytes;
       loadBar_mc.scaleX = amtLoaded;

       if (loadedBytes == totalBytes) {
              gotoAndPlay("begin");
       } else {
              gotoAndPlay("preload");
       }
}
//Event listener
loaderInfo.addEventListener(ProgressEvent.PROGRESS, preloader);
```

EXPLORE

12. In the actions layer, insert a keyframe at Frame 10, type the following code in the Actions panel, and then check the code for syntax errors, making any necessary corrections. The code will advance the playhead to the next frame each time the button is clicked.

    ```
    //Keep the playhead from advancing
    stop();
    //Advance the playhead
    function onNextClick(evt:MouseEvent):void {

        if (currentFrame == 12) {
            gotoAndStop("begin");
        }else {
            nextFrame();
        }
    }

    //Event listener
    next_btn.addEventListener(MouseEvent.CLICK, onNextClick);
    ```

13. Save the wcPhotos.fla file, and then test it. Use the Simulate Download command to test the preloader. After the document loads, the first picture is displayed. Click the Next picture button to display the next picture.
14. Submit the finished files to your instructor.

Create | Case 4

Complete a Flash Web site by adding ActionScript code to compare user input against possible values and calculate a result.

Data File needed for this Case Problem: msaDraft.fla

Missions Support Association While reviewing the Web site with the association's president, Brittany suggests adding a page that enables the visitor to calculate the cost of a group tour. The group tour calculator will enable the user to enter a type of tour and the number of people in the group. The calculator will determine and display the cost of the tour based on the values entered. The formula to determine the cost of the tour is as follows:

group tour cost = base cost of tour × cost per person × number of people

The base cost of tour is a cost assigned to each type of tour. A guided 30-minute tour of one mission has a base cost of $20. A guided one-hour tour of three missions has a base cost of $30. A two-hour bus tour of all the missions has a base cost of $40. The cost per person depends on the number of people in the group. For a group of fewer than 8 people, the cost is $10 per person. For groups of 8 to 15 people, the cost is $8 per person. For groups with more than 15 people, the cost is $5 per person.

You will develop the new page for the Web site, similar to the one shown in Figure 8-31, based on a document that Anissa has developed from the information Brittany provided.

Tutorial 8 Programming with ActionScript 3.0 | Flash | **FL 425**

Figure 8-31

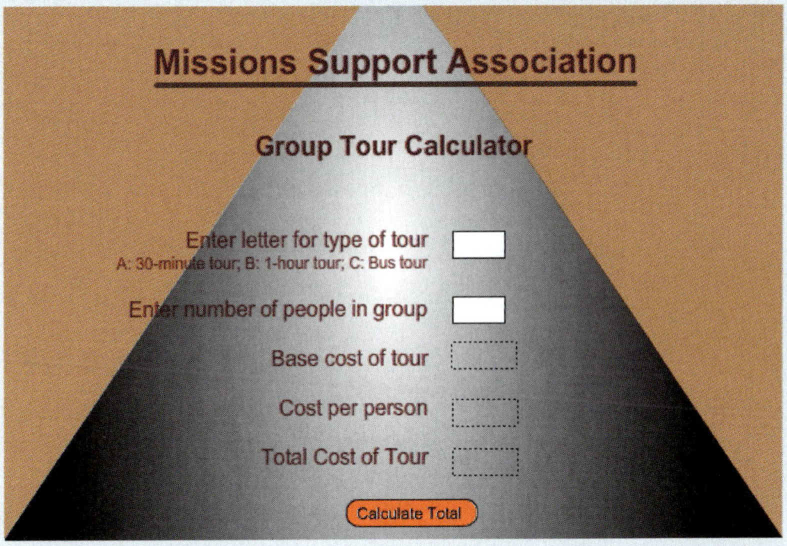

Missions Support Association

Group Tour Calculator

Enter letter for type of tour
A: 30-minute tour; B: 1-hour tour; C: Bus tour
Enter number of people in group
Base cost of tour
Cost per person
Total Cost of Tour

Calculate Total

1. Open the **msaDraft.fla** document located in the Tutorial.08\Case4 folder included with your Data Files, and then save the file as **tourCalc.fla** in the same folder.
2. In the Timeline, insert four new layers above the background layer and name them **contents**, **text fields**, **button**, and **actions**, respectively.
3. In the Timeline, select the contents layer and create a text block below the title text block. Use a smaller font size than the title text and type **Group Tour Calculator**. Create another text block below the Group Tour Calculator text, with a smaller font size and type **Enter letter for type of tour**, press the Enter key and type **A: 30-minute tour; B: 1-hour tour; C: Bus tour**. Reduce the font size for the second line.
4. In the contents layer, create another text block below the previous text block using the same font size as the Enter letter for type of tour text block and type **Enter number of people in group**. Create three more text blocks arranged vertically below the previous one with the following contents: **Base cost of tour, Cost per person, Total Cost of Tour**.
5. In the text fields layer, create an input text block to the right of the Enter letter for type of tour text. Create another input text block to the right of the Enter number of people in group text block. Assign instance names to each input text block.
6. In the text fields layer, create a dynamic text block to the right of the Base cost of tour text block. Create another dynamic text block to the right of the Cost per person text block. Create one more dynamic text block to the right of the Total Cost of Tour text block. Assign instance names to each dynamic text block.
7. Create a new button symbol that will be used to calculate the results. In the Timeline, add an instance of the button symbol in the button layer. Assign an instance name to the button.
8. Select Frame 1 of the actions layer, and then, in the Actions panel, type the following code to create a function that will calculate the cost of the tour.

```
// Function to calculate total tour cost
function tourBaseCost(evt:MouseEvent):void {
```

EXPLORE 9. In the Actions panel, use a switch statement to determine the base cost of the tour, which is different for each type of tour a user can select. The user will enter a letter into an input text box that represents the type of tour. The switch statement will check the value in the input text block and then compare the value to the values in the case statements. If the value entered matches a value in the case statement, the statement following the case statement is executed. For example, if the value entered into the input text box is either A or a, the value 20 should be assigned to the base cost. A break statement is used to exit each case statement. The first part of the switch statement code is as follows. The var statement defines a variable used to store the base cost assigned.

```
var base_cost:Number;
switch (tourType_txt.text) {
    case "A" :
    case "a" :
        base_cost=20;
        break;
```

EXPLORE 10. Type additional case statements to check for B or b and for C or c and to assign the appropriate value to the base_cost.

EXPLORE 11. End the switch statement with a default statement as follows. If the letter entered does not match any of the case statements, the base cost will be 40.

```
default :
    base_cost=40;
}
```

12. Type an if else statement to determine the cost per person. The cost per person is determined by the value entered into the input text block for the number of people. Remember to convert the value entered in the input text block into an Integer number first as shown below.

```
// Convert input value into Integer number
    var people:Number=int(numberOfPeople_txt.text);
```

13. Type a line of code to calculate the total cost. The total cost is based on the base cost plus the number of people times the cost per person. Include a comment that identifies the code you entered.

14. Type lines of code to display the base cost, cost per person and total cost in the corresponding dynamic text blocks. End the function. Remember to convert the values into strings before assigning them to the dynamic text blocks. Also, include a comment that identifies the code you entered.

15. Type a line of code to create an event listener to execute the function. Include a comment that identifies the code you entered.

16. Check for syntax errors and make any necessary corrections.

17. Save the file and test it. Enter **B** for the type of tour and **11** for the number of people. Click the Calculate Total button. The base cost is 30, the cost per person is 8, and the total cost of the tour is 118.

18. Submit the finished files to your instructor.

Review | Quick Check Answers

Session 8.1

1. a programming language that allows you to make Flash documents interactive by manipulating objects
2. False
3. object
4. Flash will display code hints in the Actions panel when the names with suffixes are used.
5. `car_mc.alpha = 50;`
6. the event source, also known as the event target, the event, and the response
7. Comments enable the programmer writing the code to document the purpose of each section of the code and are beneficial to other programmers who might have to modify the code at a later date.

Session 8.2

1. ```
   function gotoCourseSite(eventobj:MouseEvent):void
   {
   var courseURL:URLRequest = new URLRequest("http://www.course.com");
   navigateToURL(courseURL);
   }
   ```
2. Variables should be typed to specify what type of data they can contain.
3. a special method used to create instances of objects based on a class
4. to provide visual feedback to the site visitor such as a short animation or message while the rest of the file's contents load into the Flash Player.
5. original
6. Use the Simulate Download command in the Flash Player to simulate the time it takes to download an SWF file based on the type of Internet connection you select.

Session 8.3

1. to enable the user to enter data into a text block
2. In the Property inspector, enter a number in the Maximum characters box to specify the limit for the number of characters that may be entered in the input box.
3. `subtotal_txt.text = String(subTotal * 15);`
4. The || operator causes the condition to be true if the value in Code is either 1 or 2.
5. to convert values to integer numbers, which are whole numbers that do not include decimals
   ```

Ending Data Files

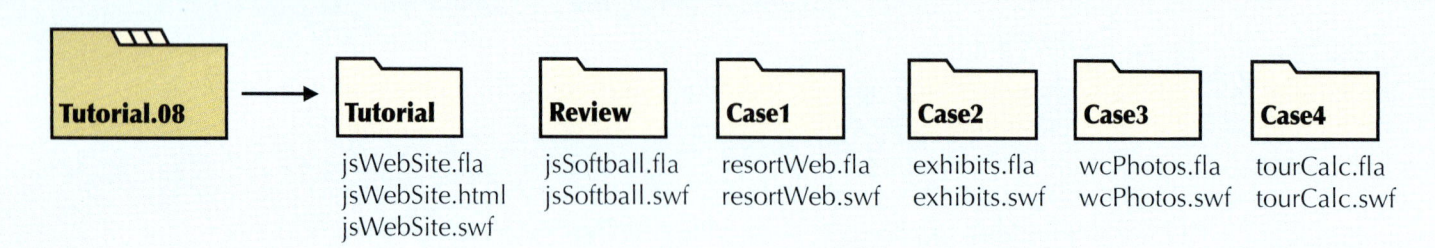

Tutorial.08 →

Tutorial
jsWebSite.fla
jsWebSite.html
jsWebSite.swf

Review
jsSoftball.fla
jsSoftball.swf

Case1
resortWeb.fla
resortWeb.swf

Case2
exhibits.fla
exhibits.swf

Case3
wcPhotos.fla
wcPhotos.swf

Case4
tourCalc.fla
tourCalc.swf

Flash | FL 429

Tutorial 9

Objectives

Session 9.1
- Add Web links using the ComboBox component
- Add photos using the UILoader and Button components
- Add a ProgressBar component
- Add ActionScript to control components

Session 9.2
- Learn the basics of using digital video
- Format video with Adobe Media Encoder
- Import video
- Modify the FLVPlayback component
- Add button components to control video

Session 9.3
- Prepare Flash content for printing
- Control printing with ActionScript
- Create Flash content for mobile devices

Using Components and Video, and Creating Content for Printing and Mobile Devices

Adding Web Links, Photos, and Video to a Flash Web Site and Creating Mobile Content

Case | Admiral Web Design

Dan Jackson wants changes made to the Jackson's Youth Sports Web site. Aly and Chris ask you to incorporate the changes. You will add Web links to the home page and complete the Photos and Videos pages. The Videos page, which will display short video segments of youth sports games, will contain buttons to select from two video clips and include controls to play and pause the videos and mute the audio. You will also create a page that displays a coupon the user can print to redeem at the store. You will use components to create these interactive elements in Flash. Finally, you will create a sample ad that can be sent to customers' mobile phones.

Starting Data Files

Tutorial.09 →

Tutorial
basketballBlue.avi
basketballRed.avi
jSports.fla
photo1.jpg
photo2.jpg

Review
clip.mpg
sbDraft.fla
sbPhoto1.jpg
sbPhoto2.jpg

Case1
kprDraftWeb.fla

Case2
aczDraft.fla
zooClip1.avi
zooClip2.avi

Case3
flower1.jpg
flower1_sm.jpg
flower2.jpg
flower2_sm.jpg
flower3.jpg
flower3_sm.jpg
wcDraft.fla
wcLandscape.avi

Case4
mission1.jpg
mission2.jpg
msaDraft.fla

Session 9.1

Using Flash Components

A **component** is a prebuilt movie clip installed with Flash that includes a set of user interface and video components. The component is actually a movie clip that has been exported with the .swc extension. Some components installed with Flash can be used to create user interface elements in documents. For example, you can use the CheckBox component to create check boxes with options that a user can select on a form. When the user clicks a check box, a check mark appears in the check box. This information can then be processed using ActionScript. Using a component such as the CheckBox component means you don't have to create the necessary graphics and functionality because they are already built into the component. Other components include the ComboBox, which displays a drop-down list from which the user can make a selection, and the ProgressBar, which displays the loading progress of content loading into the Flash Player.

InSight | **Downloading Additional Components**

You can add more components by downloading them from Web resources such as the Flash Exchange, which is an Adobe Web site with resources for Flash developers. You can also purchase components from other sources such as *www.flashloaded.com*. Downloaded components are installed using the Adobe Extension Manager. You can also create your own components by exporting a movie clip symbol from the document's Library panel. The Flash Exchange and the Adobe Extension Manager are both accessible from the Help menu.

The Flash components are located in the Components panel. The first time you add a component to a document, simply drag an instance of the component from the Components panel to the Stage. The component's movie clip and other elements are added to the document's library. Then, you can add more instances of the same component by dragging them from the Library panel to the Stage. You can assign each instance a name and view or change its parameters using the Parameters tab in the Component inspector panel. The Parameters tab contains the most commonly used parameters based on the selected component.

Reference Window | **Adding a Flash Component**

- On the Application bar, click Window, and then click Components.
- In the Components panel, double-click the components list to expand it, if necessary.
- Drag an instance of the component from the Components panel to the Stage.
- Reposition and align the component instance on the Stage as needed.
- In the Property inspector, name the instance and enter width and height values.
- In the Parameters tab of the Component inspector, enter the appropriate values.

Using the ComboBox Component

Based on Aly's instructions, in place of the Resources page you created previously for the Jackson's Youth Sports Web site, you will add a drop-down list of Web links to the home page, as shown in Figure 9-1. The user can then click an item on the list to navigate to another Web site.

Tutorial 9 Using Components and Video, and Creating Content for Printing and Mobile Devices | Flash | **FL 431**

Figure 9-1   Home page with Web links

Jackson's Sports home page screenshot showing Welcome message and Web Links combo box with Soccer, Softball, Youth Sports items; annotation: "add list of Web links to the home page"

You will create the Web links by adding a ComboBox component to the Jackson's Youth Sports Web site home page, setting its parameters, and adding ActionScript code to make the items in the ComboBox functional.

To add a ComboBox instance to the home page:

▶ 1. Open the **jSports.fla** file located in the Tutorial.09\Tutorial folder included with your Data Files, save the file as **jsWebSite.fla** in the same folder, reset the workspace to the **Essentials** layout, and then change the zoom to **Fit in Window**.

▶ 2. In the Timeline, select **Frame 10** of the content layer, if necessary. The Home page content appears on the Stage.

▶ 3. On the Application bar, click **Window**, and then click **Components**. The Components panel opens.

▶ 4. In the Components panel, if necessary, double-click **User Interface** to expand its list of components. See Figure 9-2.

Tip

You can also press the Ctrl+F7 keys to open the Components panel.

Figure 9-2 Components panel

ComboBox component → shown in Components panel

double-click to display the User Interface components

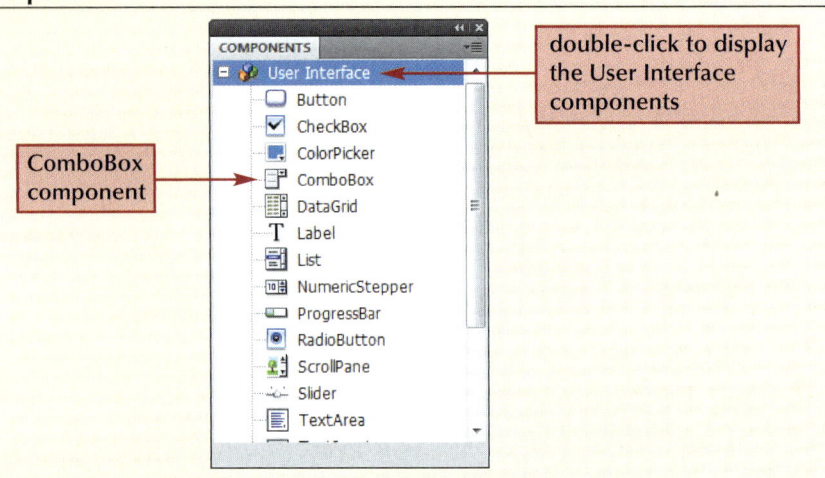

Components listed: Button, CheckBox, ColorPicker, ComboBox, DataGrid, Label, List, NumericStepper, ProgressBar, RadioButton, ScrollPane, Slider, TextArea

▶ 5. Drag an instance of the **ComboBox** component from the Components panel to the Stage, and then close the Components panel.

▶ 6. On the Stage, if necessary, reposition the ComboBox instance below the text block containing the welcoming paragraphs, aligning its left edge with the left margin of the text block.

▶ 7. In the Property inspector, name the instance **webLinks_mc**, change the width of the instance to **120** pixels, and make sure the height is **22** pixels. The ComboBox instance is positioned and sized for the Home page.

The ComboBox component instance has properties, called parameters, which can be modified in the Parameter tab of the Component inspector. The dataProvider parameter defines the labels that appear on the drop-down list and the values that are associated with each item. The editable parameter, when set to true, enables the user to edit the items in the list. The contents of the prompt parameter appear on the ComboBox instance on the Stage. The rowCount parameter determines how many rows to allocate to the drop-down list.

You will enter values for the prompt and dataProvider parameters.

To set parameter values for the ComboBox instance:

▶ 1. On the Application bar, click **Window**, and then click **Component Inspector**. The Component inspector opens.

▶ 2. In the Component inspector, click the **Parameters** tab, if necessary. The Parameters tab displays the parameters for the selected ComboBox instance.

▶ 3. On the Parameters tab, click in the **Value** box for the prompt parameter, type **Web Links**, and then press the **Enter** key. The Web Links text appears in the ComboBox instance on the Stage.

▶ 4. In the Parameters tab, double-click the **Value** box for the dataProvider parameter. The Values dialog box opens.

▶ 5. Click the **Add value** button ➕. A label and data without values are inserted.

▶ 6. In the label Value column, click **label0**, and then type **Soccer**. The label value is added.

> **Tip**
> You can also click the magnifying glass button in the Value column of the dataProvider parameter to open the Values dialog box.

Tutorial 9 Using Components and Video, and Creating Content for Printing and Mobile Devices | Flash | FL 433

▸ 7. Press the **Tab** key to move the insertion point to the data Value box, and then type **1** to add the data value. The first value is added to the dataProvider parameter.

▸ 8. Repeat Steps 5 through 7 to add two more values to the dataProvider parameter, using **Softball** and **2** for the second label and value and **Youth Sports** and **3** for the third label and value. See Figure 9-3.

Figure 9-3 — Values dialog box

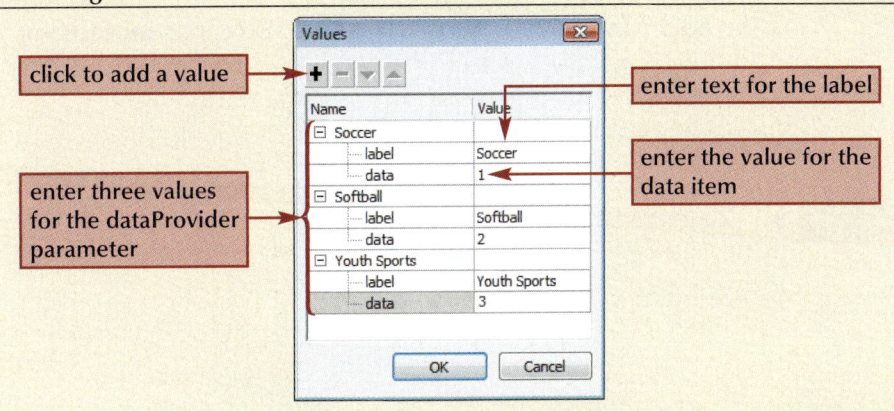

click to add a value

enter three values for the dataProvider parameter

enter text for the label

enter the value for the data item

Name	Value
⊟ Soccer	
label	Soccer
data	1
⊟ Softball	
label	Softball
data	2
⊟ Youth Sports	
label	Youth Sports
data	3

▸ 9. Click the **OK** button. The Values dialog box closes, and the three dataProvider values appear in the Parameters tab.

▸ 10. Close the Component inspector.

With the ComboBox component instance added to the Stage and its parameters set, you need to add ActionScript code to make the ComboBox instance operational. When the user clicks an item in the drop-down list, the value associated with the item can be checked using ActionScript code. For example, if a user clicks the Soccer item, the value of the ComboBox instance is 1 because that value is associated with Soccer. ActionScript uses the ComboBox value to determine which URL to use to navigate to a Web site.

To check which of the three URLs will be used, you can use a switch statement, which is helpful when you need to execute one of several statements or blocks of statements based on the value of the same expression. Each block of statements that may be executed is enclosed between a case statement and a break statement. Each case statement has a value associated with it, as shown in Figure 9-4.

Figure 9-4 — Sample switch statement

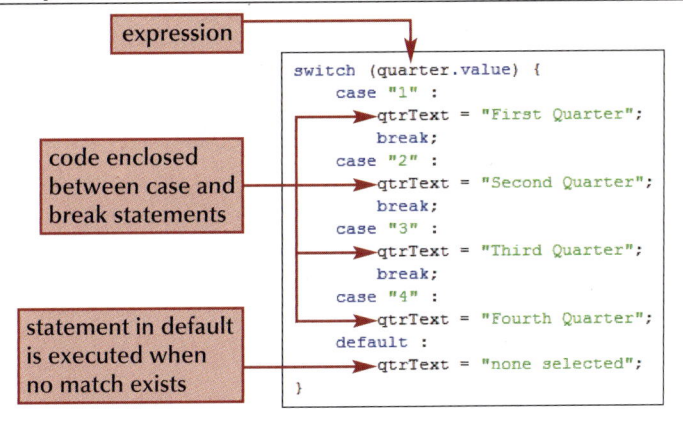

expression

code enclosed between case and break statements

statement in default is executed when no match exists

```
switch (quarter.value) {
    case "1" :
        qtrText = "First Quarter";
        break;
    case "2" :
        qtrText = "Second Quarter";
        break;
    case "3" :
        qtrText = "Third Quarter";
        break;
    case "4" :
        qtrText = "Fourth Quarter";
    default :
        qtrText = "none selected";
}
```

The expression is evaluated and its value is compared with the values in each case statement. If a match exists, the statements following the case statement are executed.

The break statement is used to exit the switch statement. The default statement executes when there is no match.

You will add a switch statement to check the value of the selected ComboBox item, which can be 1, 2, or 3. When a match is found, the associated code within the case statement assigns a Web site URL to a string variable. No default value is needed because a user can select only three possible values. After the switch statement, the value in the string variable is used to navigate to the corresponding Web site.

To add functionality to the ComboBox instance using ActionScript:

▶ 1. In the Timeline, select **Frame 10** of the actions layer, open the Actions panel, and then, if necessary, click the **collapse** button in the vertical bar between the Actions toolbox and the Script pane. The Actions toolbox collapses and the Script pane, which contains the code for the Web site's navigational buttons, expands.

> **Tip**
> You can click the Auto format button in the Actions panel to align and apply indentation to the code to improve readability.

▶ 2. In the Script pane, place the insertion point at the end of the last line, and then press the **Enter** key to insert a blank line.

▶ 3. Starting in the blank line, type the following lines of code, pressing the **Enter** key after each line, to create the function that determines which URL will be used.

```
// Function to check which site was selected
function gotoSite(eventObj:Event):void {
    // Variable that will hold the URL
    var linkText:String;
    // Switch statement determines which URL to assign
    switch (webLinks_mc.value) {
    case "1" :
        linkText = "http://www.usyouthsoccer.org/";
        break;
    case "2" :
        linkText = "http://www.softball.org/";
        break;
    case "3" :
        linkText = "http://www.nays.org/";
        break;
    }
```

▶ 4. In the Script pane, type the following lines of code after the last line to create the URLRequest object that is used in the navigateToURL function. The URLRequest uses the URL assigned to the linkText variable in the switch statement.

```
//Open Web site using the selected URL
var siteURL:URLRequest = new URLRequest(linkText);
navigateToURL(siteURL);
```

▶ 5. In the Script pane, type the following lines of code after the last line to change the value displayed in the ComboBox instance after the Web site is opened. Without this statement, the ComboBox instance will display the label of the item selected by the user.

```
//Set ComboBox to display the prompt, Web Links
webLinks_mc.selectedIndex = -1;
}
```

▶ 6. In the Script pane, type the following lines of code after the last line to create an event listener. When a change occurs in the ComboBox instance, webLinks_mc, the gotoSite function is called.

```
// Event listener
webLinks_mc.addEventListener(Event.CHANGE, gotoSite);
```

▶ 7. In the Actions panel, click the **Check syntax** button to check for syntax errors in the ActionScript code. A dialog box opens, indicating whether the script contains errors.

Tutorial 9 Using Components and Video, and Creating Content for Printing and Mobile Devices | Flash | FL 435

▶ 8. Click the **OK** button. The dialog box closes. The error-free functions appear in the Script pane.

Trouble? If the script contains errors, the functions probably contain typing errors. Collapse the Actions panel, review the error message(s) in the Compiler Errors panel, close the Compiler Errors panel, expand the Actions panel, and then compare the code in the Actions panel with the code shown in Steps 3 through 6, making any necessary corrections. Repeat Steps 7 and 8 until your code is error-free.

▶ 9. Close the Actions panel, and then save the jsWebSite.fla document.

You will test the links you added to the ComboBox on the Home page by opening the movie in the Flash Player and clicking each link in the ComboBox.

To test the ComboBox instance on the Home page:

▶ 1. On the Application bar, click **Control**, and then click **Test Movie**. The Home page appears in the Flash Player window.

▶ 2. On the Home page, click the **Web Links** button to display the link selections, and then point to **Softball**. See Figure 9-5.

Figure 9-5 | Web links on the Home page

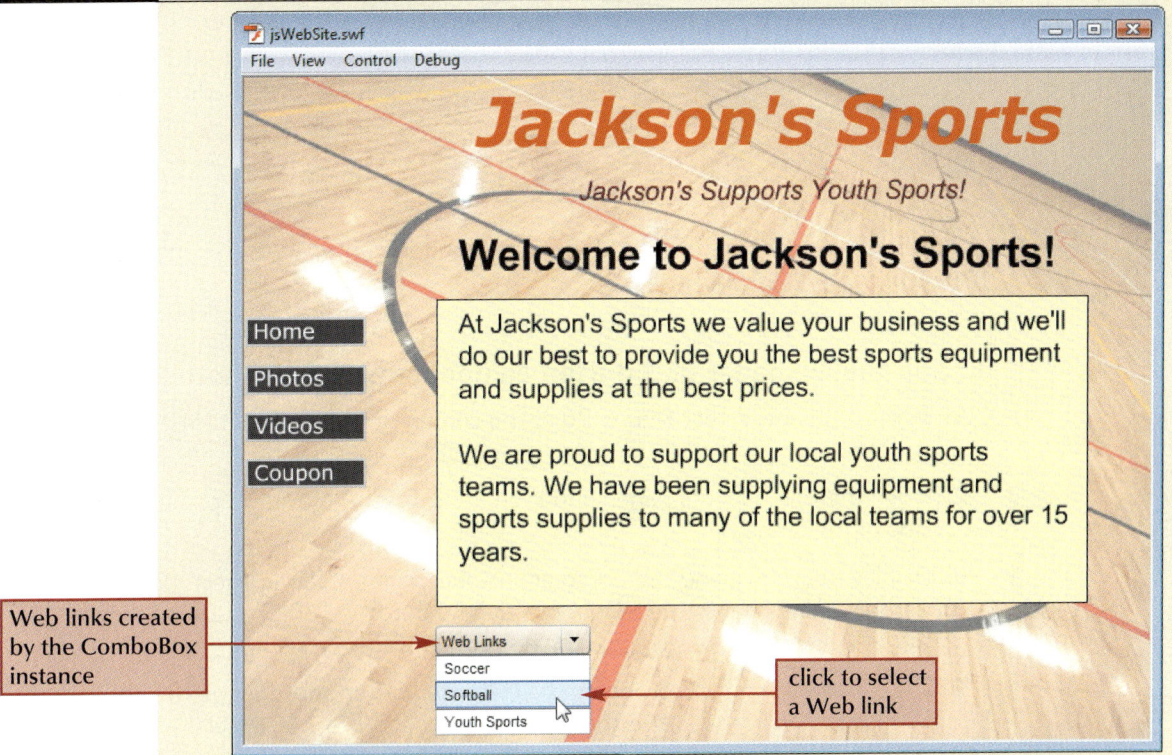

Web links created by the ComboBox instance

click to select a Web link

▶ 3. Click **Softball**. The Web site that corresponds to the selected item opens in a browser window.

▶ 4. On the Home page, click the **Web Links** button, and then click **Soccer** to open the Web site that corresponds to the selected item in a browser window.

▶ 5. On the Home page, click the **Web Links** button, and then click **Youth Sports** to open the Web site that corresponds to the selected item in a browser window.

▶ 6. Close the Flash Player window and the browser windows.

Using the UILoader Component to Display Photos

The revised Web site created by Aly and Chris contains a Photos page to display youth sports team photos, as shown in Figure 9-6. You will add an instance of the UILoader component, which can be used to load content such as images and SWF files, to the page. The youth sports photos can be loaded into an instance of the UILoader component. You will then use the Button component to add buttons that control which pictures are loaded into the UILoader instance.

Figure 9-6   Photos page

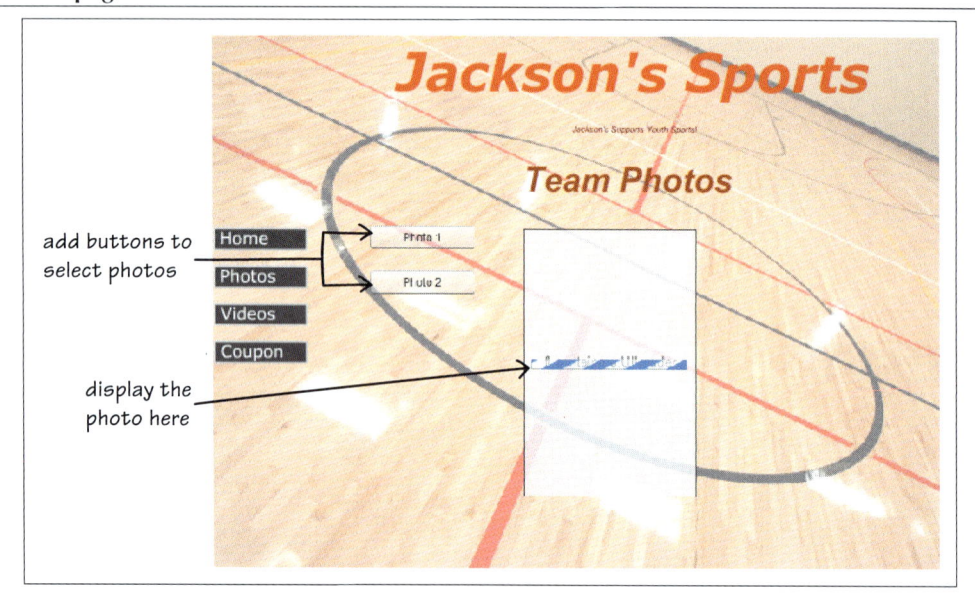

You will add instances of the UILoader and Button components to complete the Photos page.

To add the UILoader and Button components to the Photos page:

1. In the Timeline, select **Frame 20** of the content layer. The Photos page appears on the Stage.

2. Open the Components panel, and then, if necessary, move the panel to the right side of the Stage.

3. Display the rulers, and then drag an instance of the **UILoader** component from the Components panel to the Stage, positioning it about **180** pixels from the top of the Stage and **300** pixels from the left of the Stage.

4. In the Property inspector, name the instance **loader_mc**, change the width of the instance to **165** pixels, and then change the height to **250** pixels.

5. Drag an instance of the **Button** component from the Components panel to the Stage, positioning it about **180** pixels from the top of the Stage and **150** pixels from the left of the Stage.

6. Drag another instance of the **Button** component to the Stage, positioning it about **220** pixels from the top of the Stage and **150** pixels from the left of the Stage, and then close the Components panel.

Tutorial 9 Using Components and Video, and Creating Content for Printing and Mobile Devices | Flash | **FL 437**

▶ 7. Select the first Button instance on the Stage and, in the Property inspector, name the instance **photo1_btn**, and then repeat to name the second Button instance on the Stage **photo2_btn**.

▶ 8. On the Edit bar, change the zoom magnification to **100%** to magnify the view of the buttons, and then open the Component inspector.

▶ 9. On the Stage, select the **photo1_btn** instance, and then, in the Parameters tab, click the **Value** box for the label parameter to select the text Label, type **Photo 1**, and press the **Enter** key. The Button instance on the Stage changes to reflect the new label.

▶ 10. Repeat Step 9 to select the **photo2_btn** instance and change its label to **Photo 2**. The second Button instance on the Stage changes to reflect its new label.

▶ 11. Close the Component inspector. See Figure 9-7.

Figure 9-7 | UILoader and Button instances

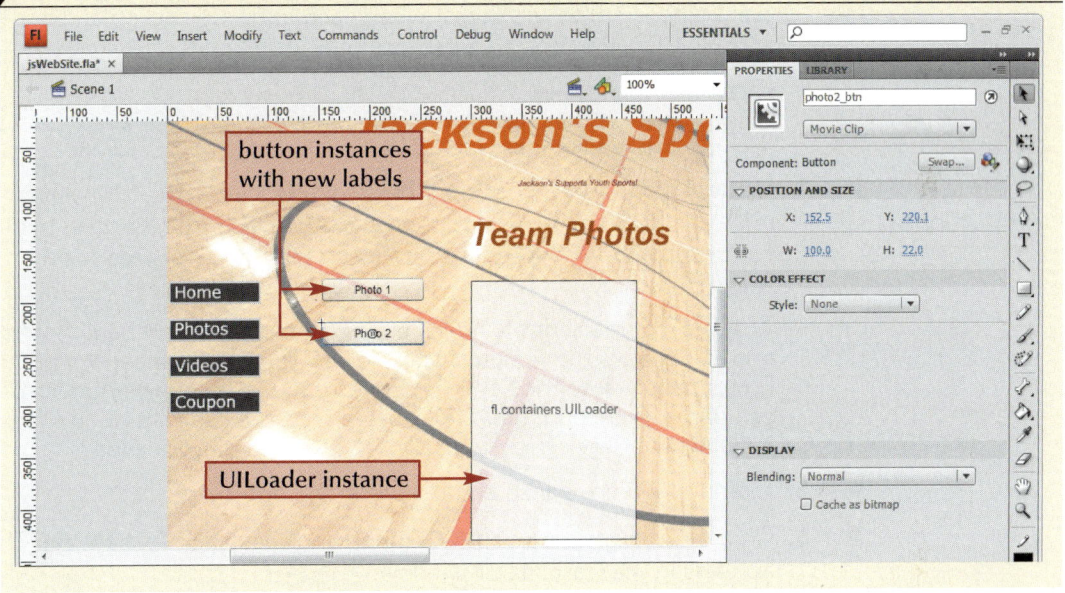

The UILoader and Button components are added to the document. To make the component instances operational, you need to add ActionScript code similar to the code you used for the Web links on the Home page. You create a function with the URLRequest object that contains the name of the photo file to be loaded. Then, instead of using the navigateToURL function, you use the load function of the UILoader instance. You then add an event listener to the button instance to listen for the CLICK event and to run the function that will load the photo.

To make the UILoader and Button instances operational:

▶ 1. In the Timeline, select **Frame 20** of the actions layer, and then open the Actions panel.

2. In the Script pane, type the following lines of code to create the functions that will create the URLRequest object with the photo's filename. The load method of the loader_mc movie clip instance will be used to load the photo into the UILoader instance.

```
// Function to load the first photo
function loadPhoto1(eventObj:MouseEvent):void
{
     var photoURLReq:URLRequest = new URLRequest("photo1.jpg");
     loader_mc.load(photoURLReq);
}
// Function to load the second photo
function loadPhoto2(eventObj:MouseEvent):void
{
     var photoURLReq:URLRequest = new URLRequest("photo2.jpg");
     loader_mc.load(photoURLReq);
}
```

3. In the Script pane, type the following lines of code after the last line to create the event listeners that will detect when each button is clicked and run the corresponding function to load a photo.

```
// Event listeners
photo1_btn.addEventListener(MouseEvent.CLICK, loadPhoto1);
photo2_btn.addEventListener(MouseEvent.CLICK, loadPhoto2);
```

4. In the Actions panel, click the **Check syntax** button to check for syntax errors in the ActionScript code, and then click the **OK** button to close the dialog box that indicates whether the script contains errors. The error-free functions appear in the Script pane.

   Trouble? If the script contains errors, the functions probably contain typing errors. Collapse the Actions panel, review the error message(s) in the Compiler Errors panel, close the Compiler Errors panel, expand the Actions panel, and then compare the code in the Actions panel with the code shown in Steps 2 and 3, making any necessary corrections. Repeat Step 4 until your code is error-free.

5. Close the Actions panel, and then save the document.

6. On the Application bar, click **Control**, and then click **Test Movie**. The Home page appears in the Flash Player window.

7. On the Home page, click the **Photos** navigation button to display the Photos page.

8. On the Photos page, click the **Photo 1** button to load the first photo, and then click the **Photo 2** button to load the second photo. Each photo, in turn, is loaded into the UILoader instance and appears on the Stage. See Figure 9-8.

Tutorial 9 Using Components and Video, and Creating Content for Printing and Mobile Devices | Flash | FL 439

Figure 9-8 UILoader instance operational

click a button to load a photo into the UILoader instance

photo loaded into the UILoader instance

▶ 9. Close the Flash Player window.

Using the ProgressBar Component

The Photos page now displays photos in the UILoader instance each time a photo button is clicked. To improve the user experience with the Photos page, you will add a pre-loader that provides visual feedback when the photos are loading. This is helpful to someone using a slow Internet connection. To create a preloader that requires only a minimal amount of ActionScript and that shows the progress of the photos loading into the Flash Player, use the ProgressBar component.

The ProgressBar component can work together with the UILoader component to display the progress of loading content, such as a photo file, into the UILoader instance. As the photo file loads into the UILoader instance, the ProgressBar instance displays an animation that depicts the loading progress. For the ProgressBar to detect the loading of the content, you enter the name of the UILoader instance into the source parameter of the ProgressBar instance. This establishes a connection between the two component instances.

You will add a ProgressBar component to display a preloader animation for the Photos page.

To add an instance of the ProgressBar component to the Stage:

▶ 1. Set the zoom magnification to **Fit in Window**, open the Components panel, and then, in the Timeline, select **Frame 20** of the content layer.

▶ 2. Drag an instance of the **ProgressBar** component from the Components panel to the center of the UILoader instance on the Stage, and then close the Components panel.

FL 440 Flash | Tutorial 9 Using Components and Video, and Creating Content for Printing and Mobile Devices

▸ 3. In the Property inspector, name the instance **pbar_mc** and change the height to **10** pixels.

▸ 4. Open the Component inspector panel, and then, on the Parameters tab, click in the **Value** box for the source parameter, type **loader_mc**, and press the **Enter** key. The ProgressBar instance will use the contents of the UILoader instance as the source of the content whose progress will be tracked. As the content loads into the loader_mc movie clip, the pbar_mc instance will display a preloader animation.

▸ 5. Close the Component inspector, save the document, and then test the movie. The Home page appears in the Flash Player window.

▸ 6. On the Flash Player Application bar, click **View**, point to **Download Settings**, and then click **DSL (32.6 KB/s)** to select the download speed for the simulation.

> **Tip**
> In the Flash Player window, you can also click the Ctrl+Enter keys to run the Simulate Download command.

▸ 7. On the Flash Player Application bar, click **View**, and then click **Simulate Download**. The Home page appears after a few moments.

▸ 8. On the Home page, click the **Photos** navigational button to display the Photos page. The ProgressBar instance appears on the Photos page.

▸ 9. On the Photos page, click the **Photo 1** button to load the first photo. The ProgressBar instance displays an animation indicating the content is being loaded. When the photo appears, the ProgressBar animation stops, but remains visible. See Figure 9-9.

Figure 9-9 ProgressBar instance on the photo

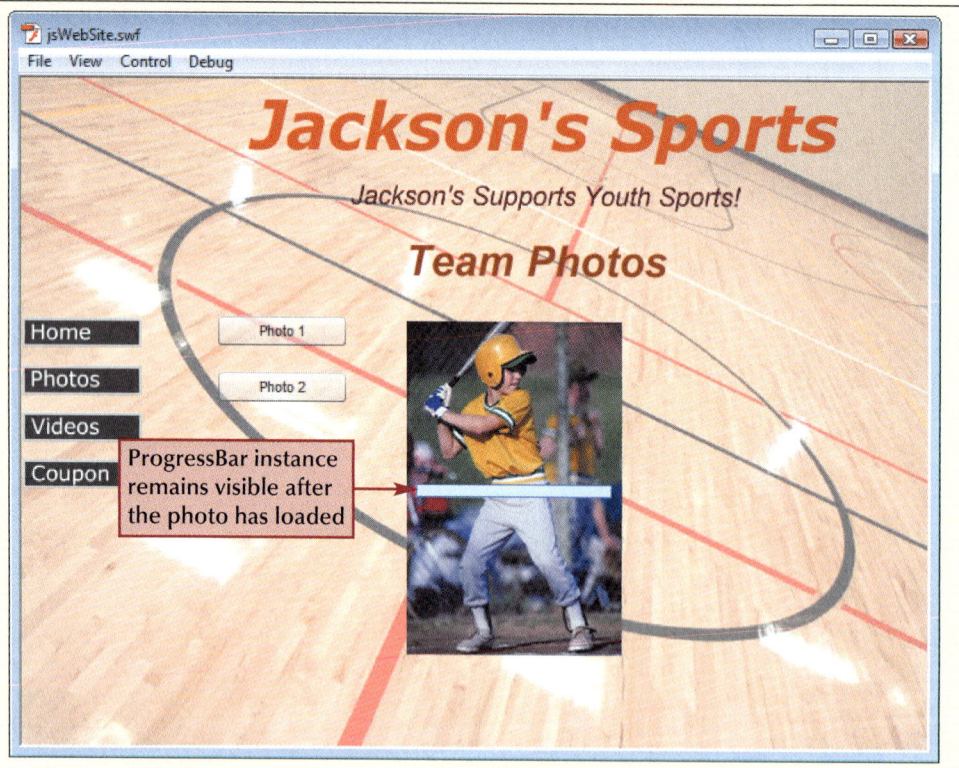

▸ 10. Close the Flash Player window.

The ProgressBar instance works as expected; however, it appears before and after a photo is loaded. To hide the ProgressBar instance before a photo is being loaded, you need to change its visible property to false. When a photo is about to be loaded into the UILoader instance, you change the visible property of the ProgressBar instance to true so that it appears. After the photo loading is complete, you change the visible property back to false. You also need to add an event listener that will check for the COMPLETE event

Tutorial 9 Using Components and Video, and Creating Content for Printing and Mobile Devices | Flash | **FL 441**

of the UILoader instance, which indicates that the loading of the content into the UILoader is complete. When the COMPLETE event is detected, the event listener will run a function to set the visible property of the ProgressBar instance to false so the instance disappears from the Stage.

To add ActionScript code to control the ProgressBar instance:

1. In the Timeline, select **Frame 20** of the actions layer, and then open the Actions panel.

2. In the Script pane, place the insertion point at the beginning of the first line, press the **Enter** key to add a blank line, and then, starting in the blank line, type the following lines of code to hide the pbar_mc instance when the Photos page is displayed.

   ```
   // Hide the ProgressBar instance
   pbar_mc.visible = false;
   ```

3. In the Script pane, place the insertion point after the opening curly brace within the loadPhoto1 function, press the **Enter** key to add a blank line, and then, in this blank line, type the following line of code to display the pbar_mc instance before the first photo is loaded.

   ```
   pbar_mc.visible = true;
   ```

4. In the Script pane, place the insertion point after the opening curly brace within the loadPhoto2 function, press the **Enter** key to add a blank line, and then, in this blank line, type the following line of code to display the pbar_mc instance before the second photo is loaded. See Figure 9-10.

   ```
   pbar_mc.visible = true;
   ```

Figure 9-10 Visibility set for the ProgressBar instance

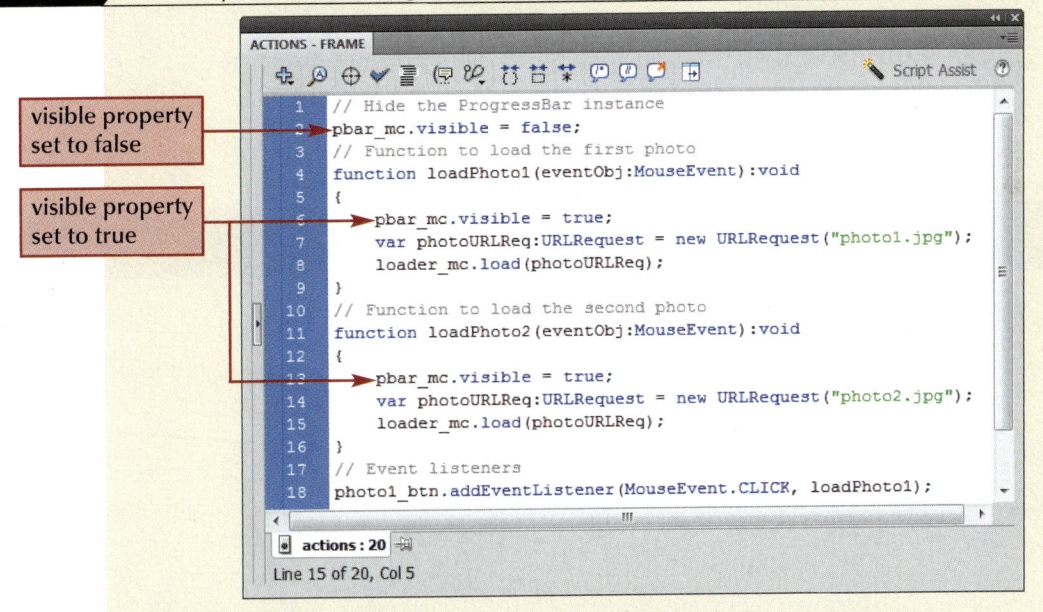

```
ACTIONS - FRAME                                           Script Assist
1    // Hide the ProgressBar instance
2    pbar_mc.visible = false;          ← visible property set to false
3    // Function to load the first photo
4    function loadPhoto1(eventObj:MouseEvent):void
5    {
6        pbar_mc.visible = true;        ← visible property set to true
7        var photoURLReq:URLRequest = new URLRequest("photo1.jpg");
8        loader_mc.load(photoURLReq);
9    }
10   // Function to load the second photo
11   function loadPhoto2(eventObj:MouseEvent):void
12   {
13       pbar_mc.visible = true;
14       var photoURLReq:URLRequest = new URLRequest("photo2.jpg");
15       loader_mc.load(photoURLReq);
16   }
17   // Event listeners
18   photo1_btn.addEventListener(MouseEvent.CLICK, loadPhoto1);

actions : 20
Line 15 of 20, Col 5
```

5. In the Script pane, place the insertion point after the closing curly brace of the loadPhoto2 function, press the **Enter** key to add a blank line, and then, starting in this blank line, type the following lines of code to create a function that will hide the pbar_mc instance when the loading of a photo is completed.

   ```
   // When the loading is complete, hide the ProgressBar instance
   function hideBar(eventObj:Event) {
        pbar_mc.visible = false;
   }
   ```

6. In the Script pane, type the following line of code after the last line to create an event listener that runs the hideBar function when the COMPLETE event occurs for the loader_mc instance.

   ```
   loader_mc.addEventListener(Event.COMPLETE, hideBar);
   ```

7. In the Actions panel, click the **Check syntax** button to check for syntax errors in the ActionScript code, and then click the **OK** button in the dialog box that indicates whether the script contains errors. The error-free functions appear in the Script pane.

   Trouble? If the script contains errors, the functions probably contain typing errors. Collapse the Actions panel, review the error message(s) in the Compiler Errors panel, close the Compiler Errors panel, expand the Actions panel, and then compare the code in the Actions panel with the code shown in Steps 2 through 6, making any necessary corrections. Repeat Step 7 until your code is error-free.

8. Close the Actions panel, save the document, and then test the movie.

9. On the Flash Player Application bar, click **View**, and then click **Simulate Download**. The Home page appears after a few moments.

10. On the Home page, click the **Photos** navigational button to display the Photos page, and then click the **Photo 1** button to load the first photo. The ProgressBar animation appears, followed by the photo. The ProgressBar instance disappears after the photo is loaded.

11. Click the **Photo 2** button to load the second photo. The ProgressBar animation appears, followed by the photo. The ProgressBar instance disappears after the photo is loaded.

12. Close the Flash Player window. The Photos page is complete.

In this session, you learned about components and how to use them in your Flash documents. You used the ComboBox, Button, UILoader, and ProgressBar components along with ActionScript to add Web links to the Home page and buttons to load player photos on the Photos page.

Review | Session 9.1 Quick Check

1. What is a Flash component?
2. What is the purpose of the dataProvider parameter of the ComboBox component?
3. In the ComboBox component, the contents of the _____ parameter appear on the ComboBox instance on the Stage.
4. Which statement is used to exit a block of code in a switch statement?
5. Write the ActionScript code to hide a ProgressBar component instance named progress_mc.
6. For a ProgressBar instance to detect the loading of content into a UILoader instance, you enter the name of the UILoader instance into the _____ parameter of the ProgressBar instance.

Session 9.2

Adding Video to a Flash Document

So far, the Flash documents you have created include a variety of multimedia elements, such as graphics, bitmaps, and sounds. You can also add video to Flash documents. Video can make a Web site more visually appealing and exciting. Before you work with video in Flash, you should understand some basic terminology and concepts about how video is prepared and in what format video can be imported into Flash. You need to consider the frame size, frame rate, and file size of video files. You also need to understand that using video on your Flash Web site can significantly increase a site's overall download time.

Selecting the Frame Rate and Frame Size

A video's **frame rate**, which is similar to the frame rate of a document in Flash, represents how many frames play each second. Video frame rates vary, depending on where the video is played. For example, video played on television plays at 29.97 frames per second whereas video on film plays at 24 frames per second. Video played on the Web, however, should play at lower frame rates, such as 12 to 18 frames per second. Frame rate also affects the size of the file. The higher the frame rate, the larger the file size of the video. For example, a 10-second video clip formatted at 30 frames per second contains 300 frames. The same 10-second video clip formatted at 12 frames per second contains 120 frames. Of course, the higher the frame rate, the better the quality of the video.

Deciding on the frame rate to use is a balance between the quality of the video and the size of the file. Lowering the frame rate lowers the quality of the video but decreases the video's file size. Keep in mind the following factors when deciding the appropriate frame rate to select for a video:

- **Content.** Video with a minimal movement, such as someone talking in front of the camera, can be played on the Web at rates of 10 or fewer frames per second. Video with more movement, such as children playing a sport, is best played at a higher frame rate, such as 15 frames per second.
- **Internet connection of target users.** High frame rates do not play well with a dial-up connection because the connection speed cannot download the frames fast enough to play smoothly on the client computer. A faster broadband connection can better handle higher frame rates.
- **Client computer.** A slow computer with minimal capabilities might not be able to support videos with high frame rates.

When editing video clips and preparing them for use in Flash, you should also determine what frame size to use. The **frame size** refers to a video's width and height dimensions. You can decide the frame size by considering the type of Internet access that target users will have and the length of the video. If you are targeting users with dial-up connections, limit the frame size of videos to something like 164 pixels wide by 120 pixels high. If the majority of the target users have faster connections, you can set the video's frame size to higher dimensions, such as 360 pixels wide by 264 pixels high or even 640 pixels wide by 480 pixels high.

| InSight | **Using a High-Quality Video Source File** |

The quality of the source, or original, file is critical to consider when using video in Flash. The better the quality of the source file, the better the result when the video is imported into Flash. You should start with a high-quality video file before importing the video into Flash.

You can use a digital camcorder to record video and then transfer the video from the camcorder's media to the computer. You can also connect the camcorder to a computer and record video directly to the computer. Another method is to convert video from an analog format such as a VCR tape into a digital format that you can store on a computer. However, whenever possible, it is best to use a digital source file. Converting from analog to digital can produce lower-quality video compared to video that is captured in a digital format.

Regardless of the video source, you should edit the video using a video-editing program such as Adobe Premiere after it is transferred to the computer but before it is imported into Flash. Although Flash provides some editing options when video is imported, the options are limited. A video-editing program allows you to trim unwanted parts of the video or select part of the video, depending on how you plan to use it. You can also change other attributes of the video, such as its frame rate and frame size.

Using Compression and Decompression

Another factor affecting the use of video over the Web is the size of the video file. The amount of data required to represent a few seconds of video can make downloading the video over the Internet a slow process. As a result, compression, which removes redundant data, is used to reduce the size of the video file. The process of compressing the video is called **encoding**. You can specify how much to compress a video when you edit it using a video-editing program or by using an encoder program, also known as a **compressor**. Before the compressed video can be played, it needs to be decompressed with a decoder program, also known as a **decompressor**.

A video compressor/decompressor program is called a **codec**. Various codecs are available to work with video. The codecs used by Flash are On2 VP6, Sorenson Spark, and H.264. These codecs compress the video, and the Flash Player contains the corresponding decompressor to decompress the video for playback. By default, Flash uses the On2 VP6 codec when you publish video content to Flash Player 8 or higher. The H.264 codec, introduced with Flash Player 9, produces higher-quality video with smaller file sizes but requires that you publish the video to Flash Player 9 or higher. If you publish video content to Flash Player 6 or 7, Flash uses the Sorenson Spark codec. Videos published for older versions of the Flash Player will also run on more recent versions of the plug-in, but those published for Flash Player 8 or higher will not work on earlier versions. Because Flash uses codecs to compress video, it is best to avoid compressing the video before bringing it into Flash.

Using Adobe Media Encoder

After video is captured and prepared using a video-editing program, preparing the video for Flash requires two basic steps. First, convert the video to one of the Flash video file formats: FLV or F4V for videos encoded using the H.264 codec. Second, import the video file into a Flash document. To convert the video into a Flash video file format, you can use **Adobe Media Encoder**, an encoder program installed with Flash. Adobe Media Encoder is a separate program that accepts several video file formats, including .mpg, .avi, and .dv. Other formats such as .mov can also be used if your computer has the QuickTime plug-in installed. When you bring a video file into Adobe Media Encoder, you select options for how you want the video to be encoded, and then you encode the video to produce a file in the FLV or F4V format.

Tutorial 9 Using Components and Video, and Creating Content for Printing and Mobile Devices | Flash | **FL 445**

Aly prepared two short video clips of local youth sports to add to the Video page, as requested by Dan. You will use the Adobe Media Encoder to encode and convert the videos into the FLV format.

To encode the sports video clips using the Adobe Media Encoder:

1. If you took a break after the previous session, make sure the jsWebSite.fla document is open, the workspace is reset to the Essentials layout, and the Stage magnification is set to Fit in Window.

2. Click the **Start** button on the taskbar, click **All Programs**, click the **Adobe Flash CS4 Professional** folder, and then click **Adobe Media Encoder CS4**. The Adobe Media Encoder program window opens.

3. Click the **Add** button, navigate to the **Tutorial.09\Tutorial** folder included with your Data Files, click **basketballBlue.avi**, and then click the **Open** button. The selected video file is added to the queue.

Tip
You can also drag files from the storage location and drop them into the queue.

4. Repeat Step 3 to add the **basketballRed.avi** file to the queue.

5. In the Preset column for the basketballBlue.avi file, click the **Preset arrow** button to open a list of presets, and then click **FLV - Web Medium (Flash 8 and Higher)**. The selected preset is listed in the Preset column.

6. Repeat Step 5 to select the **FLV - Web Medium (Flash 8 and Higher)** preset for the basketballRed.avi video file. See Figure 9-11.

Figure 9-11 | Presets selected for video files in the queue

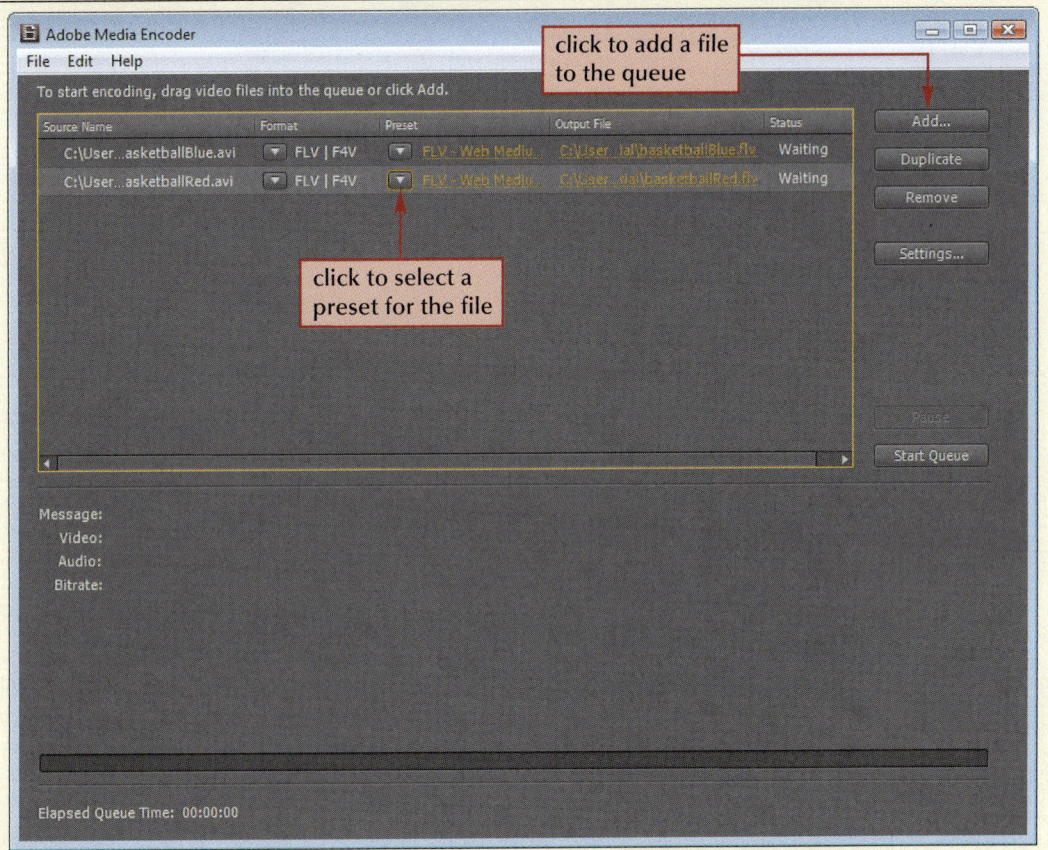

7. In the Preset column of the basketballBlue.avi file, click the **FLV - Web Medium (Flash 8 and Higher)** link. The Export Settings dialog box opens.

▶ 8. Click the **Advanced Mode** button, if necessary, to display additional options. See Figure 9-12.

Figure 9-12   Export Settings dialog box

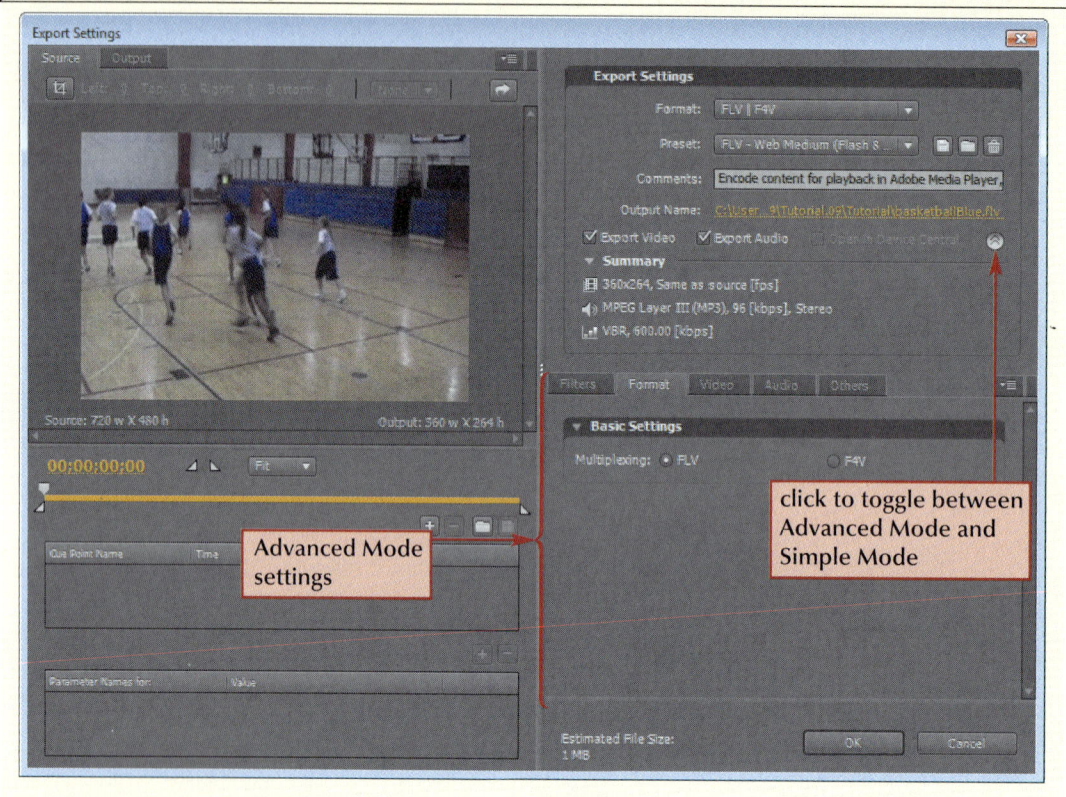

[Screenshot of Export Settings dialog box with callouts: "Advanced Mode settings" and "click to toggle between Advanced Mode and Simple Mode"]

Advanced Mode settings can be used to modify the way the video will be encoded. You can change the format of the output video to FLV or F4V, change the video's frame rate, change the way the audio is formatted, and also crop and resize the video clip as well as add cue points. **Cue points** are markers you set in the video to synchronize the video with animation, graphics, or text in the Flash document.

To select the Advanced Mode settings in the Adobe Media Encoder:

▶ 1. In the Advanced Mode settings, click the **Video** tab, click the **Frame Rate [fps]** button, and then click **15**. The output video file's frame rate is reduced to 15 frames per second.

▶ 2. In the Advanced Mode settings, click the **Audio** tab, and then click the **Mono** option button in the Output Channels section. Mono creates a smaller output file than Stereo.

▶ 3. Click the **OK** button to close the Export Settings dialog box.

▶ 4. In the Preset column of the basketballRed.avi file, click the **FLV - Web Medium (Flash 8 and Higher)** link to open the Export Settings dialog box, and then repeat Steps 1 through 3 for the basketballRed.avi video file using the same settings as you did for the basketballBlue.avi file.

▶ 5. Click the **Start Queue** button to start the encoding process for both video files. The encoding process starts for the first file. The encoding progress is displayed at the bottom of the program window. See Figure 9-13.

Tutorial 9 Using Components and Video, and Creating Content for Printing and Mobile Devices | Flash | FL 447

| Figure 9-13 | Video files being encoded |

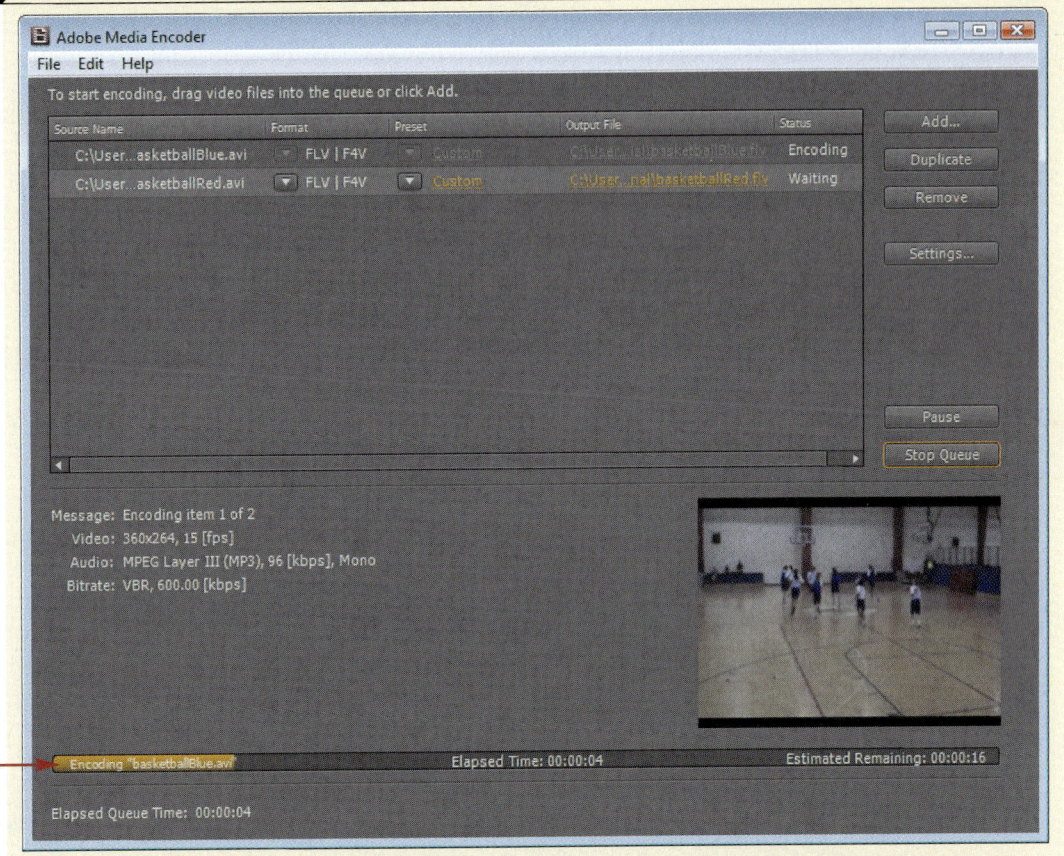

progress of the encoding

Tip

You can press the Ctrl+Q keys to exit Adobe Media Encoder.

6. After both files have finished encoding, close Adobe Media Encoder. The basketballBlue.flv and basketballRed.flv files are stored in the Tutorial.09\Tutorial folder included with your Data Files, ready to be imported into your Flash document.

Each converted file is placed in the same location as the original file unless you specify a different location by clicking the file's path link in the Output File column. The encoding process can be time consuming, depending on the size of the video files and the capabilities of the computer. If you have multiple files to encode, you can encode all the files in a batch mode by adding them to the queue, setting the export settings for each file, and then starting the encode process. Adobe Media Encoder encodes each file in turn until all the files in the queue are converted.

Delivering Video

For video to be available as part of a Web site, it must be uploaded to a Web server, just like the site's Web pages and SWF files. When you import video into Flash, you need to know the type of Web server to which the video will be uploaded and how the video will be delivered to a client computer. You can deliver video using Flash in three ways: stream the video using Adobe Flash Media Server, progressively download the video from a Web server, or embed the video in a Flash document.

Video streaming requires that the video file be uploaded to a Web server running **Adobe Flash Media Server**, the server software that provides Web developers features to add interactive audio and video to Web sites. With video streaming, only the part of the video file to be viewed is downloaded on the user's computer, not the entire video file.

This also enables the user to select any part of the video to view without having to wait for the entire video to be downloaded.

Progressive downloading downloads the entire video file, which is stored on a Web server, to the user's computer for viewing. This method is best for shorter videos that are accessed infrequently or by only a few users at the same time. With video streaming and progressive downloading, the video file is saved separately from the Flash SWF file you create to play the video. This makes it easier to change video content without having to change or republish the SWF file.

Embedded video places the entire video in the Flash document, similar to the way that bitmaps are imported and become part of the document. When you publish the Flash file, the video is published as part of the SWF file and can significantly increase the size of the published file. Embedding video is recommended only when you are targeting site visitors with slow Internet connections or visitors using older versions of the Flash Player, or when the video clip is fewer than 10 seconds in length. Embedded video must be in the FLV format, not in the F4V format.

Using the Import Video Wizard

After you convert videos into the FLV or F4V format using Adobe Media Encoder, you can use the Import Video wizard in Flash to embed or link the video in the Flash document. The Import Video wizard presents a series of dialog boxes that guide you through the import process. You first select the video file, and then you choose if the video is to be loaded externally during playback, or if it will be embedded in the Flash document. If the video is to be loaded externally during playback using video streaming or progressive downloading, Flash creates an instance of the FLVPlayback component on the Stage that serves as the video player. If you are using embedding, the video can be embedded directly on the Stage or within a movie clip symbol. By default, the Timeline expands to match the number of frames in the video.

If the video is to be played using the FLVPlayback component, you also select the playback controls such as play, pause, and mute to add to the Flash document. These playback controls are referred to as a **skin** and consist of an SWF file, which is stored separately from the document, and FLV files. The wizard makes it easy to add playback controls by providing many preconfigured skins in the Skin list. You can also create a custom skin.

You will use the Import Video wizard to create an instance of the FLVPlayback component, which will serve as the video player for the sports video clips in the Jackson's Youth Sports Web site. You will then modify the FLVPlayback parameters and add two Button components to enable playing the two video clips in the same player, as shown in Figure 9-14. Finally, you will add the necessary ActionScript code to make the buttons operational.

Figure 9-14   Videos page

add buttons to select the video clips

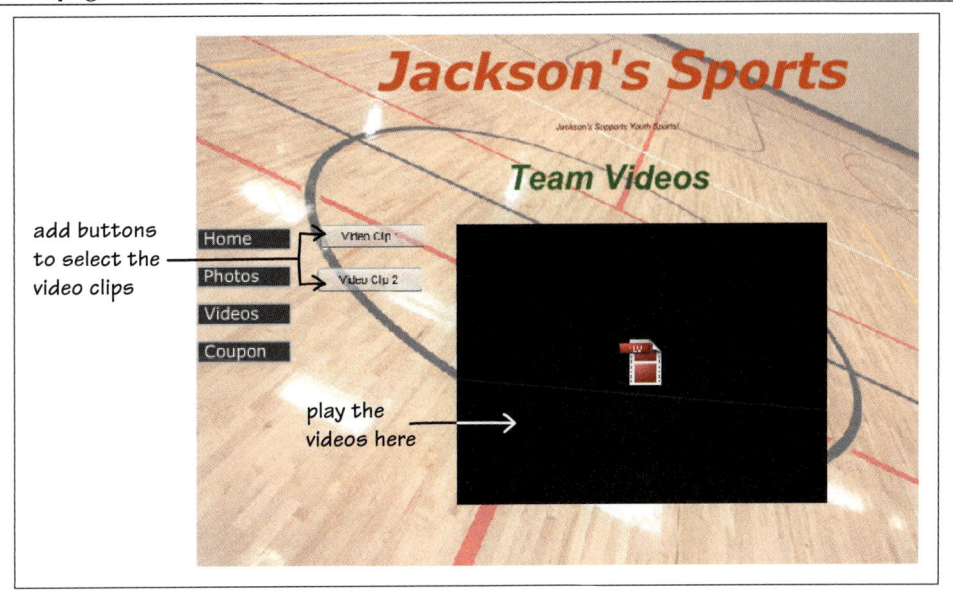

play the videos here

You'll start by adding the basketballBlue.flv video to the Videos page.

To import the basketballBlue.flv video clip using the Import Video wizard:

1. In the Timeline, select **Frame 30** of the content layer. The Videos page content starts in this frame.

2. On the Application bar, click **File**, point to **Import**, and then click **Import Video** to start the Import Video wizard. The Select Video dialog box opens, prompting you to specify the location of the video file to be imported, which is on your computer or on a Web server. In this case, the video file is located on your computer.

3. Click the **Browse** button, navigate to the **Tutorial.09\Tutorial** folder included with your Data Files, and then double-click **basketballBlue.flv**. The video file is selected.

4. Click the **Load external video with playback component** option button, if necessary, to select it.

5. Click the **Next** button. The Skinning dialog box opens, so you can select the type of playback controls to add to the Flash file.

6. Click the **Skin** button, and then click **SkinUnderPlaySeekMute.swf**. The skin is applied to the video component in the preview area. See Figure 9-15.

Figure 9-15 — Skinning dialog box in the Import Video wizard

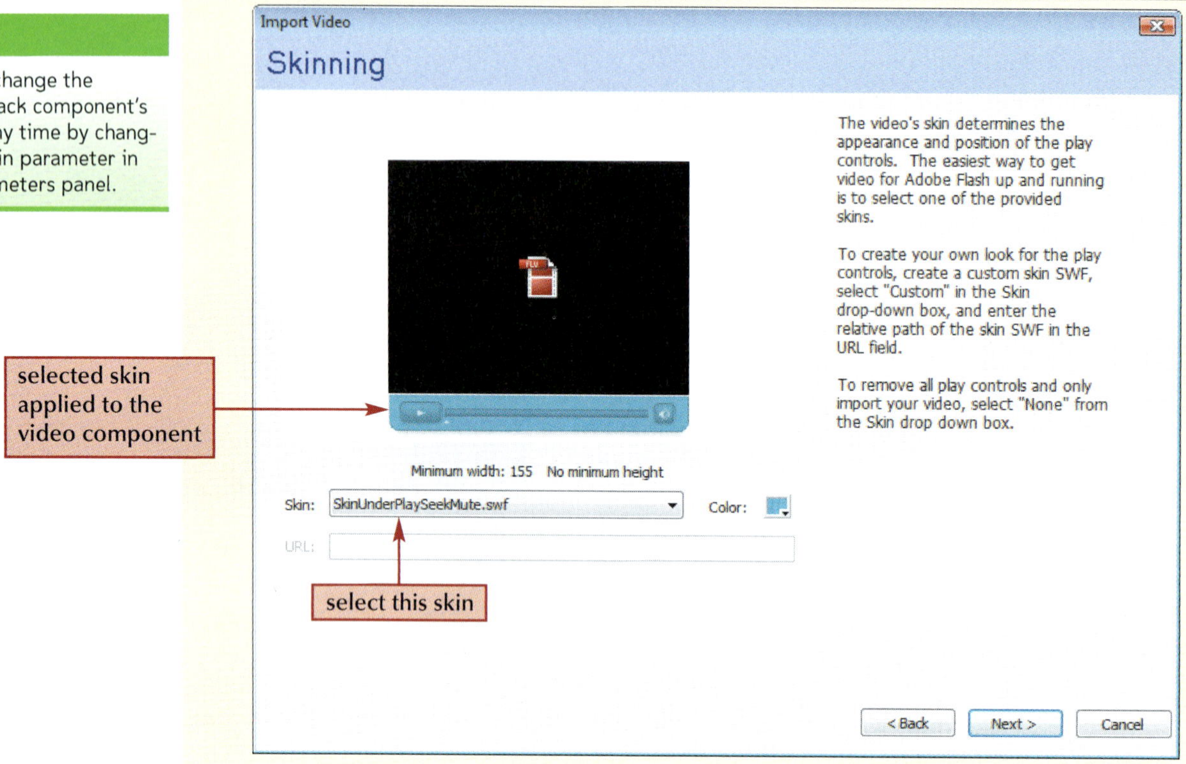

Tip

You can change the FLVPlayback component's skin at any time by changing its skin parameter in the Parameters panel.

selected skin applied to the video component

select this skin

After you select a skin, the final dialog box in the wizard shows a summary of your selections and indicates what will be done when you click the Finish button. When you use progressive download or video streaming, an FLV file is created and an instance of the FLVPlayback component with the selected playback controls is added to the Stage. The FLVPlayback component provides the display area in which the video is viewed.

To complete the import process for the basketballBlue.flv video clip:

1. Click the **Next** button. The Finish Video Import dialog box displays a summary of the import process, including the location of the basketballBlue.flv file.

2. Click the **After importing video, view video topics in Flash Help** check box, if necessary, to remove the check mark.

3. Click the **Finish** button. A Getting metadata dialog box opens, showing the importing progress of the video. When the process is complete, an instance of the FLVPlayback component is placed on the Stage.

4. Reposition the FLVPlayback instance to **180** pixels from the top of the Stage and **250** pixels from the left of the Stage. See Figure 9-16.

Figure 9-16 | **FLVPlayback instance added to the Stage**

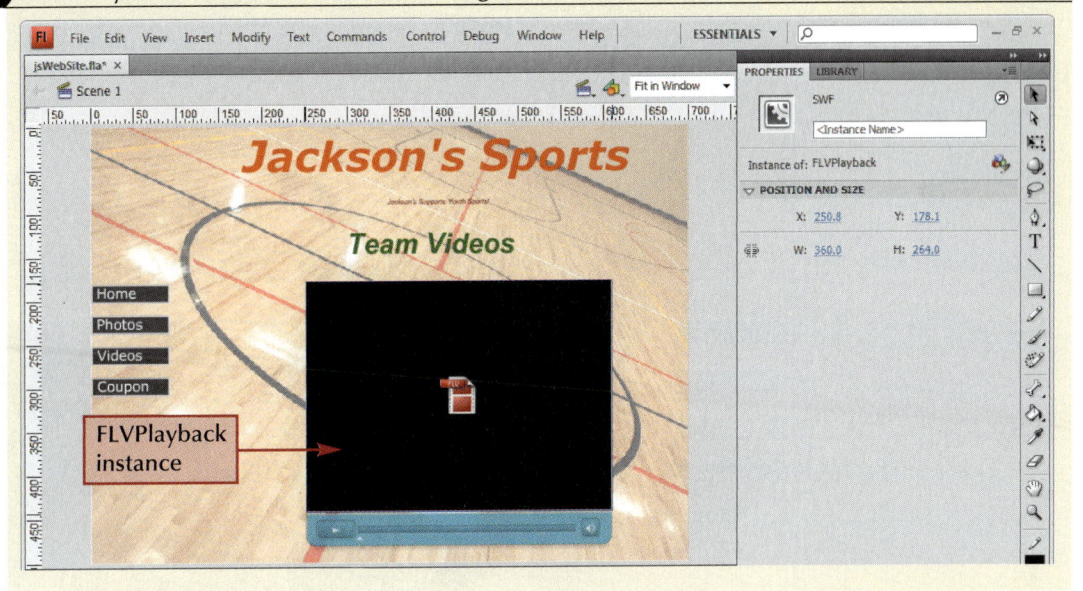

You will save and test the FLVPlayback component instance you added to the Videos page.

To test the FLVPlayback component instance on the Videos page:

1. Save the jsWebSite.fla document, and then test the movie. The Home page opens in the Flash Player window.

2. In the Flash Player window, click the **Videos** button to advance to the Videos page. The Videos page appears and the video clip starts to play.

3. After the video stops playing, on the video controls, click the **Play/Pause** button to play the video again, and then click the **Play/Pause** button to pause the video. As the video plays, the small triangle under the seek bar moves to indicate the progress of the video. See Figure 9-17.

| Figure 9-17 | Video playing on the Videos page |

[Screenshot of jsWebSite.swf showing Jackson's Sports Team Videos page with a basketball video playing; annotation: "seek bar shows the video's progress as it plays"]

▶ 4. Close the Flash Player window to return to the Flash document.

The Videos page displays the basketballBlue.flv video clip and includes controls to play, pause, and mute the video. To enable the FLVPlayback component to also play the basketballRed.flv video, you will add two buttons and ActionScript code so that when each button is clicked, a different video plays, enabling users to choose between the two videos. Because the video you added to the page uses the FLVPlayback component, you can modify the component's parameters so that the video played is determined by ActionScript.

To modify the FLVPlayback's parameters:

▶ 1. Open the Component inspector, and then click the **Parameters** tab, if necessary. The Parameters tab of the Component inspector displays the properties of the FLVPlayback instance.

▶ 2. On the Stage, select the **FLVPlayback** instance, if necessary, and then, on the Parameters tab, double-click the **Value** box for the skin parameter. The Select Skin dialog box opens.

▶ 3. Click the **Skin** button, and then click **None** to remove the skin from the FLVPlayback instance.

▶ 4. Click the **OK** button. The dialog box closes, and the skin with the player controls is removed from the Stage.

▶ 5. In the Parameters tab of the Component inspector, double-click the **Value** box for the source parameter. The Content Path dialog box opens and the basketballBlue.flv filename is selected. See Figure 9-18.

Figure 9-18 Content Path dialog box

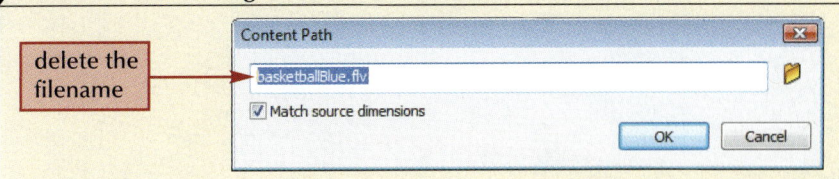

delete the filename — basketballBlue.flv
☑ Match source dimensions

▸ 6. Press the **Delete** key to delete the filename, and then click the **OK** button. The source file is removed.

▸ 7. In the Property inspector, name the FLVPlayback instance **videoPlayer**. The name assigned to the FLVPlayback instance can be referenced with ActionScript.

Because you previously added an instance of the Button component to the document, the Button component is already in the document's library. You can add instances of the same Button component by dragging them from the Library panel.

To add Button instances to the Videos page:

▸ 1. In the Timeline, insert a keyframe at **Frame 30** of the buttons layer. You will add Button instances in this frame.

▸ 2. Drag an instance of the **Button** component from the Library panel to the Stage, and then place the instance approximately **180** pixels from the top of the Stage and **120** pixels from the left of the Stage.

▸ 3. On the Stage, select the **Button** instance, if necessary, and then, in the Property inspector, name the instance **videoButton1_btn**.

▸ 4. In the Parameters tab of the Component inspector, click the **Value** box for the label parameter, type **Video Clip 1**, and then press the **Enter** key. The videoButton1_btn instance on the Stage is relabeled as Video Clip 1.

▸ 5. Repeat Steps 2 through 4 to create a second Button instance approximately **220** pixels from the top of the Stage and **120** pixels from the left of the Stage with the instance name **videoButton2_btn** and the label **Video Clip 2**. The videoButton2_btn instance on the Stage is relabeled as Video Clip 2. See Figure 9-19.

Figure 9-19 Buttons added to the Videos page

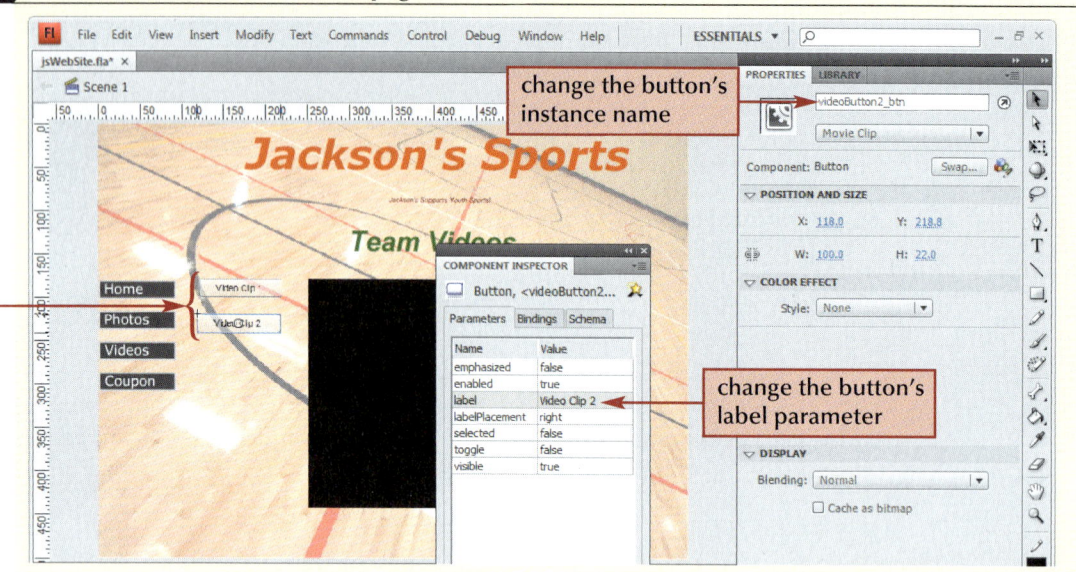

change the button's instance name

place two button instances to the right of the navigation buttons

change the button's label parameter

▸ 6. Close the Component inspector.

Next, you will add the ActionScript code that controls the loading of the video clips into the FLVPlayback component. The code will include two functions, one for each video. Each function will assign the name of the video clip to the source parameter of the FLVPlayback instance and it will assign SkinUnderPlaySeekMute.swf to the skin parameter. Event listeners will be added so that when a button is clicked, the associated function will run.

You will add ActionScript code to make the video clip buttons operational on the Videos page.

To add ActionScript code to play the two videos on the Videos page:

▸ 1. In the Timeline, select **Frame 30** of the actions layer, and then open the Actions panel.

▸ 2. In the Script pane, type the following lines of code to define the functions that load a video clip file and a skin into the FLVPlayback instance.

```
// Functions to add video clips and skin to FLVPlayback component
function playVideo1(eventObj:MouseEvent):void {
    videoPlayer.source = "basketballBlue.flv" ;
    videoPlayer.skin = "SkinUnderPlaySeekMute.swf";
}
function playVideo2(eventObj:MouseEvent):void {
    videoPlayer.source = "basketballRed.flv" ;
    videoPlayer.skin = "SkinUnderPlaySeekMute.swf";
}
```

▸ 3. In the Script pane, type the following code after the last line to add the event listeners so that when a button is clicked, its associated function is run.

```
// Event listeners
videoButton1_btn.addEventListener(MouseEvent.CLICK, playVideo1);
videoButton2_btn.addEventListener(MouseEvent.CLICK, playVideo2);
```

Tutorial 9 Using Components and Video, and Creating Content for Printing and Mobile Devices | Flash | FL 455

▶ 4. In the Actions panel, click the **Check syntax** button ✓ to check for syntax errors in the ActionScript code, and then click the **OK** button in the dialog box that indicates whether the script contains errors. The error-free functions appear in the Script pane.

Trouble? If the script contains errors, the functions probably contain typing errors. Collapse the Actions panel, review the error message(s) in the Compiler Errors panel, close the Compiler Errors panel, expand the Actions panel, and then compare the code in the Actions panel with the code shown in Steps 2 and 3, making any necessary corrections. Repeat Step 4 until your code is error-free.

▶ 5. Close the Actions panel, save the document, and then test the movie. The Home page opens in the Flash Player.

▶ 6. On the Home page, click the **Videos** button to advance to the Videos page, and then, on the Videos page, click the **Video Clip 1** button to play the first video clip. The video plays in the FLVPlayback instance and the video controls appear under the video. See Figure 9-20.

| Figure 9-20 | Buttons and video player in the Flash Player |

click a button to play a video

video plays in the FLVPlayback instance

video controls appear under the video

▶ 7. Click the **Video Clip 2** button to play the second video.

▶ 8. Close the Flash Player window to return to the Flash document. The Videos page is complete, and the Web site can showcase video clips of youth sports teams.

In this session, you learned basic concepts involved in using video and importing it into Flash. You reviewed the video formats you can use with Flash and different types of compression techniques. You encoded videos using the Adobe Media Encoder and then you imported a video file using the Video Import wizard in Flash. Finally, you modified the parameters of the FLVPlayback component and added ActionScript code to play two videos. In the next session, you will prepare content for printing and for displaying on mobile devices.

Review | Session 9.2 Quick Check

1. List three video formats that can be imported into a Flash document.
2. Why is it important to compress video files?
3. _____ video places the video in the Flash document, similar to the way that bitmaps are imported and become part of the document.
4. What is a codec?
5. Which codecs are used by Flash?
6. _____ are markers you can set in the video to synchronize the video with animation, graphics, or text in the document.
7. Which option in the Import Video wizard creates an instance of the FLVPlayback component on the Stage?

Session 9.3

Creating Printable Content

The graphics and animations created with Flash are meant to be displayed on computer screens and are usually not designed to be printed on paper. However, users can print the content of a Flash Web site using the Print command in the Web browser or the Flash Player. The Print command in the Flash Player can be disabled when the document is published.

The Web browser's Print command sends the content currently displayed in the Web page to the printer. However, if the content of the SWF file is designed to occupy most of the width of the computer screen, part of the content might be truncated, or cut off. This is because the layout of the computer screen is in **landscape orientation**, which means it is wider than it is tall. The printed page, however, is usually in **portrait orientation**, which means it is taller than it is wide and is meant to fit on a standard $8^{1/2} \times$ by 11-inch sheet of paper.

The Flash Player's Print command, which is available on the context menu that opens when the user right-clicks SWF file content in the Flash Player, provides several printing options. From the context menu, the user can choose to print the current selection so that only the currently displayed frame of the SWF file is printed. If the user chooses to print all contents, then all the frames of the SWF file are printed. This might not produce the desired result because the SWF file can contain a long animation with many frames.

Tutorial 9 Using Components and Video, and Creating Content for Printing and Mobile Devices | Flash **FL 457**

| InSight | **Designing Printing Capabilities for Flash Documents** |

A Flash document should include options to print specific frames rather than relying on the Web browser or the Flash Player to control the printing of the SWF file. Provide buttons that the user can click to print specific elements of the Web site. This helps to prevent the user from becoming frustrated with undesirable print results. Depending on the site requirements, design certain parts of the Web site specifically for printing. For example, a store might want to place a map of the store's location on the Web site. The map can be designed to print on a standard sheet of paper. Or, a restaurant might want to include a coupon on its Web site that the user can print and redeem at the restaurant. Also, you can link to documents that are saved as Adobe Acrobat PDF files, which are already formatted for printing. In any case, if a Flash document contains elements that a user might want to print, be sure to design the printing capabilities into the document.

Creating Content for Printing

Dan requested that a coupon be added to the Jackson's Youth Sports Web site that a user can print and redeem at the store, as shown in Figure 9-21. The coupon will be for 10% off any item in the store. You will modify the printable coupon and then create a button to control the printing of the coupon.

Figure 9-21   Coupon page

add a button to print the coupon

coupon that users might want to print

Aly has created the coupon as a movie clip with content and a yellow background. However, when the user prints the coupon, you don't want the background to print. You will modify the coupon by adding a second frame to the coupon movie clip that will contain the contents of the coupon but not the background rectangle. The second frame will contain the content to print.

To modify the Coupon movie clip:

▶ **1.** If you took a break after the previous session, make sure the jsWebSite.fla document is open, the workspace is reset to the Essentials layout, and the Stage magnification is set to Fit in Window.

▶ **2.** Open the **Coupon** symbol in symbol-editing mode.

3. In the Timeline, select **Frame 2** of the content layer, and then insert a regular frame. The text and graphics appear in Frame 2, but the background rectangle does not.

4. In the Timeline, insert a new layer, name it **action**, and then, in the action layer, select **Frame 1**.

5. Open the Actions panel, and then type the following line in the Script pane to add a `stop()` action to the first frame that keeps the playhead from advancing to the second frame.

   `stop();`

6. Close the Actions panel, and then exit symbol-editing mode.

The coupon is complete. You are ready to add an instance of the coupon to the Coupon page. You will also add an instance of the Button component that will be used to control the printing of the coupon.

To create instances of the Coupon and Button symbols:

1. In the Timeline, insert a keyframe at **Frame 40** on the buttons layer. The navigation and video buttons are copied to this frame.

2. Delete the Video Clip 2 button instance. You will change the properties of the first video button in a later step.

3. In the Timeline, select **Frame 40** of the content layer, and then drag an instance of the **Coupon** symbol from the Library panel to the Stage.

4. Reposition the instance about **250** pixels from the left of the Stage and **180** pixels from the top of the Stage. The Coupon instance is in the correct position on the Coupon page.

5. In the Property inspector, name the Coupon instance **coupon_mc**. The Coupon instance is named.

6. On the Stage, select the Video Clip 1 button, and then, in the Property inspector, change the name of the instance to **printCoupon_btn**. The video button on the Videos page has a different instance name than the button on the Coupon page.

7. Open the Component inspector, and on the Parameters tab, click the **Value** box for the label parameter, and then type **Print Coupon**. The Button instance is named and labeled. See Figure 9-22.

Tutorial 9 Using Components and Video, and Creating Content for Printing and Mobile Devices | Flash | FL 459

Figure 9-22 Coupon and button in Coupon page

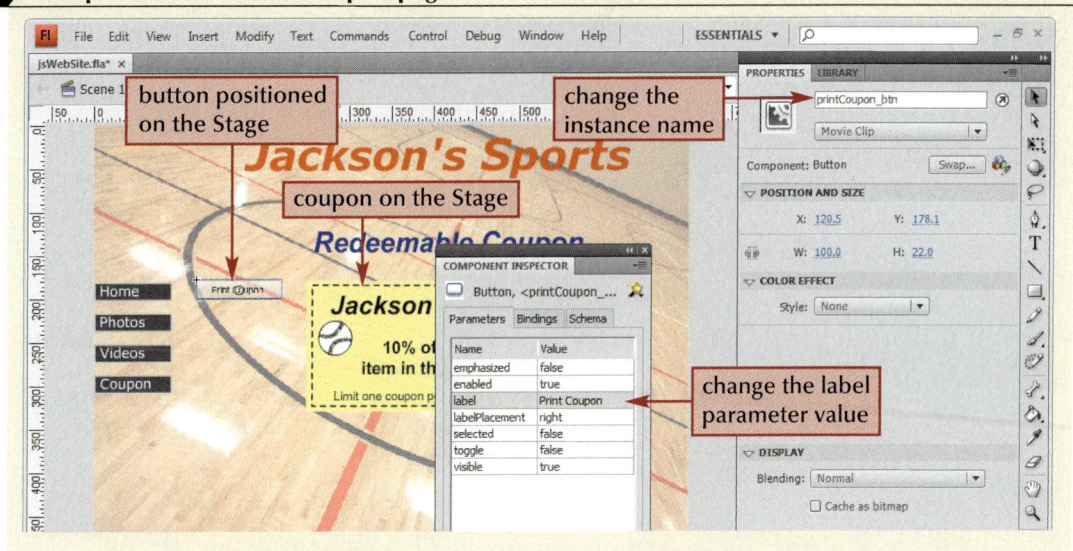

[Screenshot of Flash IDE showing: button positioned on the Stage, coupon on the Stage, change the instance name (printCoupon_btn), change the label parameter value]

▸ **8.** Close the Component inspector.

Using the PrintJob Class to Control Printing

The Coupon page contains the coupon and button. Next, you need to add the ActionScript so that when the print coupon button is clicked, the coupon prints. The Flash Player can communicate with a computer's operating system's printing interface so that pages can be passed to the print spooler. The **print spooler** manages the print jobs that are sent to the printer by the various programs running on the computer. To control printing within the Flash Player, you use the ActionScript printJob class and follow these steps in sequence:

1. Create an instance of the PrintJob class.
2. Initiate the printing process.
3. Add pages to the print job.
4. Send the pages to the operating system's printer.

You will create a function for the coupon that will create an instance of the PrintJob class using the new operator, start the print process using the `start()` method, add a page to the print job using the `addPage()` method, and then send the print job to the computer's operating system using the `send()` method. You should also include code to prevent an error being generated by the Flash Player if the user cancels the printing process. You can use an `if()` statement that checks if the printing process has been initiated. If the printing process has been initiated, the steps to print the coupon run. Otherwise, the steps do not run.

To add ActionScript code to print the coupon:

▸ **1.** In the Timeline, select **Frame 40** of the actions layer, and then open the Actions panel.

> **Tip**
>
> You can click the Apply line comment button in the Actions panel to add the // comment characters to the Script pane.

2. In the Script pane, type the following lines of code to define the function that will print a coupon. The third line defines a variable named myPrintJob of type PrintJob and assigns the variable an instance of the PrintJob class using the new operator. The `start()` method is then called for the myPrintJob instance. If the `start()` method is successful, the `addPage()` method adds the movie clip contents to the print job and the `send()` method sends the print job to the operating system.

   ```
   // Function to print the coupon
   function printCoupon(eventObj:MouseEvent):void {
       var myPrintJob:PrintJob = new PrintJob();
       if (myPrintJob.start()) {
           myPrintJob.addPage(coupon_mc);
           myPrintJob.send();
       }
   }
   ```

3. In the Script pane, type the following lines of code after the last line to add the event listener so that when the button is clicked, its corresponding function is run.

   ```
   // Event listeners
   printCoupon_btn.addEventListener(MouseEvent.CLICK, printCoupon);
   ```

4. In the Actions panel, click the **Check syntax** button to check for syntax errors in the ActionScript code, and then click the **OK** button in the dialog box that indicates whether the script contains errors. The error-free functions appear in the Script pane.

   Trouble? If the script contains errors, the functions probably contain typing errors. Collapse the Actions panel, review the error message(s) in the Compiler Errors panel, close the Compiler Errors panel, expand the Actions panel, and then compare the code in the Actions panel with the code shown in Steps 2 and 3, making any necessary corrections. Repeat Step 4 until your code is error-free.

5. Close the Actions panel, save the jsWebSite.fla document, and then test the movie. The Home page appears in the Flash Player.

6. On the Home page, click the **Coupon** button to advance to the Coupon page, and then on the Coupon page, click the **Print Coupon** button to print the coupon. The operating system's print dialog box opens.

7. Select the appropriate printer, and then click the **Print** button. The coupon prints.

8. Close the Flash Player window to return to the Flash document.

The first frame of the coupon movie clip printed. You want only the second frame to print because it contains the coupon without the filled rectangle as a background. To print the second frame of the movie clip, you need to specify the frame number as a parameter in the `addPage()` method. You can include three optional parameters in the `addPage()` method in addition to the name of the movie clip to print. The first optional parameter specifies the area to print, which can be defined by specifying rectangular coordinates. The second optional parameter specifies whether the content prints as a vector or a bitmap. By default, the content is printed as a vector. If the content to print includes a bitmap, you can set this parameter to `{printAsBitmap:true}`. The third optional parameter is a number that specifies which frame to print. If you want to use this optional parameter without specifying the two other optional parameters, you need to use `null` as the middle parameters. The method to print the second frame of the coupon_mc movie clip is:

```
myPrintJob.addPage(coupon_mc, null, null, 2);
```

You will add the parameters to the `addPage()` method for the coupon.

To add the parameters to the addPage() method:

1. Open the Actions panel, and then, in the Script pane, revise the `addPage()` method on line 5 for the function to include the additional parameters.

   `myPrintJob.addPage(coupon_mc, null, null, 2);`

2. In the Actions panel, click the **Check syntax** button to check for syntax errors in the ActionScript code, and then click the **OK** button to close the dialog box that indicates whether the script contains errors. The error-free functions appear in the Script pane.

   Trouble? If the script contains errors, the functions probably contain typing errors. Collapse the Actions panel, review the error message(s) in the Compiler Errors panel, close the Compiler Errors panel, expand the Actions panel, and then compare the code in the Actions panel with the code shown in Step 1, making any necessary corrections. Repeat Step 2 until your code is error-free.

3. Close the Actions panel, save the document, and then test the movie. The Home page opens in the Flash Player window.

4. On the Home page, click the **Coupon** button to display the Coupon page.

5. On the Coupon page, click the **Print Coupon** button to print the coupon, select a printer in the operating system's print dialog box, and then click the **Print** button. The second frame of the coupon movie clip prints.

6. Close the Flash Player window to return to the Flash document.

Aly wants you to modify the ActionScript code so that the size of the printed coupon is larger than the coupon's original size. To print a coupon in a larger format, you need to temporarily scale the movie clip to a larger size, print the coupon, and then scale it back to the size originally set on the Stage.

You use the scaleX and scaleY properties to scale a movie clip. The scaleX property is the scale factor of the width of the movie clip and the scaleY property is the scale factor of the height of the movie clip. A scale factor of 1 represents 100%. To enlarge the size of the coupon movie clip to twice its original size requires a scale factor of 2 for both the scaleX and scaleY properties, which represents 200%. After the coupon is printed, you need to return the coupon to its original size of 100% as it was originally set on the Stageby setting the scale factor back to 1, which represents 100%. The statement to change a movie clip's scaleX property to 200% is:

`coupon_mc.scaleX = 2;`

You will add the ActionScript code to the print functions so that the coupon prints at twice its original size.

To scale the coupon movie clip for printing:

1. Open the Actions panel, and then, in the Script pane, place the insertion point after the opening curly brace for the `if` statement in the printCoupon function, press the **Enter** key to add a blank line, and, starting in the blank line, type the following lines of code to increase the size of the coupon.

   ```
   // Increase the size of the coupon to 200%
   coupon_mc.scaleX = 2;
   coupon_mc.scaleY = 2;
   ```

▶ 2. In the Script pane, place the insertion point at the end of the `addPage()` statement in the printCoupon function, press the **Enter** key to add a blank line, and then, starting in the blank line, type the following lines of code to reduce the size of the coupon. See Figure 9-23.

```
// Reduce the size of the coupon to 100%
coupon_mc.scaleX = 1;
coupon_mc.scaleY = 1;
```

Figure 9-23 ActionScript code to scale the Coupon movie clip

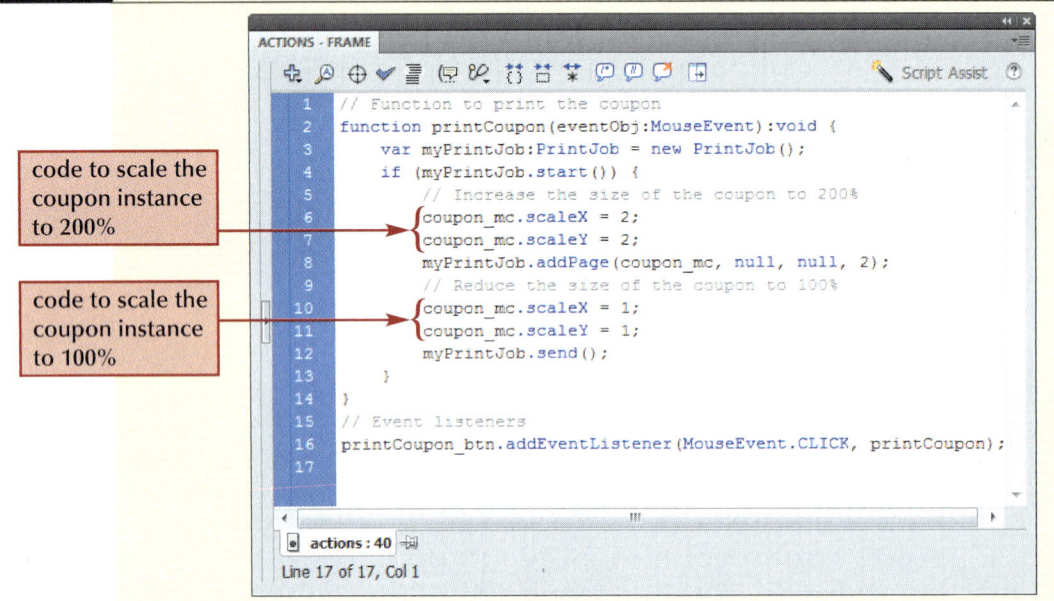

```
 1  // Function to print the coupon
 2  function printCoupon(eventObj:MouseEvent):void {
 3      var myPrintJob:PrintJob = new PrintJob();
 4      if (myPrintJob.start()) {
 5          // Increase the size of the coupon to 200%
 6          coupon_mc.scaleX = 2;
 7          coupon_mc.scaleY = 2;
 8          myPrintJob.addPage(coupon_mc, null, null, 2);
 9          // Reduce the size of the coupon to 100%
10          coupon_mc.scaleX = 1;
11          coupon_mc.scaleY = 1;
12          myPrintJob.send();
13      }
14  }
15  // Event listeners
16  printCoupon_btn.addEventListener(MouseEvent.CLICK, printCoupon);
17
```

code to scale the coupon instance to 200% → (lines 6-7)

code to scale the coupon instance to 100% → (lines 10-11)

▶ 3. In the Actions panel, click the **Check syntax** button ✓ to check for syntax errors in the ActionScript code, and then click the **OK** button in the dialog box that indicates whether the script contains errors. The error-free functions appear in the Script pane.

Trouble? If the script contains errors, the functions probably contain typing errors. Collapse the Actions panel, review the error message(s) in the Compiler Errors panel, close the Compiler Errors panel, expand the Actions panel, and then compare the code in the Actions panel with the code shown in Steps 1 and 2, making any necessary corrections. Repeat Step 3 until your code is error-free.

▶ 4. Close the Actions panel, save the document, and then test the movie. The Home page opens in the Flash Player window.

▶ 5. On the Home page, click the **Coupon** button to display the Coupon page, click the **Print Coupon** button to print the coupon, select the appropriate printer in the operating system's print dialog box, and then click the **Print** button. The coupon prints in a larger size.

▶ 6. Close the Flash Player window to return to the Flash document.

The Coupon page for the Jackson's Youth Sports Web site is complete and site visitors can print the coupon. Aly will show the completed Web site to Dan Jackson at their next meeting. She is confident he will be pleased with the finished site.

Creating Mobile Content

Flash content can be played on a wide variety of mobile devices using **Flash Lite**, which is a smaller version of the Flash Player. Flash Lite comes in various versions, including Flash Lite 2.0 and 2.1, which are based on Flash Player 7. These versions support many of the features in Flash Player 7 and include features specific to mobile development. Flash Lite 3.0 and Flash Lite 3.1 are also based on Flash Player 7, but have support for Flash video and provide improved Web browsing on mobile devices.

Developing content to play on a mobile device using Flash Lite is similar to developing content for a Web site. However, several factors need to be considered. The main factor is screen size. Content developed for a mobile device must fit on a much smaller screen than content developed for a Web site. Mobile devices also don't have the same processing power or memory as computers, so complex animations using bitmaps and videos may not work as well on a mobile device as they do on a Web site viewed on a computer.

Another factor to consider is that mobile devices come in many varieties and with varying capabilities. Testing content to make sure it works properly on all mobile devices can be a daunting and time-consuming task. Because there are many different mobile devices from many manufacturers and each device has different characteristics, you need to target a specific device or group of devices for which you will create Flash content.

Adobe Device Central, a stand-alone program installed with Flash, lets you create and test content on a wide variety of mobile devices without having to load the content on all the actual devices. Device Central provides an online library of mobile devices from which to choose. Each device has a profile that contains information about the device, including the type of media and content it supports such as wallpaper and screensavers. You can view one or more device profiles at one time and you can compare several targeted devices to help you determine the best screen size to use for the content. Device Central emulates what each device looks like and how the Flash content will appear on the device. It also provides information on how content on a device will affect the device's performance levels, memory, battery power, or even how the content is affected by different types of lighting.

InSight | **Designing Content for Mobile Devices**

When designing Flash content for mobile devices, keep in mind that the processors in mobile devices are not as powerful as those on desktop or laptop computers. SWF movies that play smoothly on computers may not play as well on mobile devices. You should avoid creating Flash content that uses complex graphics, has many motion tweens, or uses transparency because these elements place a greater burden on a mobile device processor and negatively impact its performance. You should limit the number of simultaneous tweens and sequence animations so that they don't overlap. You should also avoid certain visual effects, such as masks or extensive gradients, to reduce the demands on the processor.

Creating Content for the Flash Lite Player

To create a Flash document for a mobile device, you select Flash File (Mobile) as the document type when you create a new document in Flash. Adobe Device Central opens so you can choose which devices to target. You can also create a new Flash document from within Adobe Device Central. In Device Central you select the devices on which you want to test your content and then you create a new document. Flash opens with the Stage size matching the screen size of the mobile device you selected.

> **Reference Window | Creating Flash Documents for Mobile Devices**
>
> - In Flash, create a new document, selecting Flash File (Mobile) as the document type.
> - In Adobe Device Central CS4, on the New Document tab, select the player version, the ActionScript version, and the content type.
> - In the Online Library of Adobe Device Central, expand the manufacturer, and then double-click each device to target.
> - In the Local Library, expand the manufacturer category, and then double-click a device to make it active and view its profile (or click a category to view multiple devices in a table).
> - Click the Create Document button.
> - In Flash, create content as usual.

Dan wants advertisements that his customers can view on their mobile devices. Aly asks you to create a sample ad for an upcoming baseball tournament that is targeted for several mobile devices. This ad will give Dan an idea of the type of marketing he can explore to expand his business.

You'll start by creating a new document targeted for mobile devices and specify the devices on which the ad will be tested.

To create a new mobile Flash file:

1. On the Application bar, click **File**, click **New** to open the New Document dialog box, and then click the **General** tab, if necessary.

2. In the Type box, click **Flash File (Mobile)**, and then click the **OK** button. Adobe Device Central CS4 opens.

3. On the New Document tab, change the Player Version to **Flash Lite 2.0**, change the ActionScript Version to **ActionScript 2.0**, and change the Content Type to **Screen Saver**. The Online Library panel shows all the devices that are available to download to the Local Library. These devices are arranged by manufacturer and their profiles are updated regularly.

4. In the Online Library panel, scroll down to **Nokia**, and then click the expand arrow. Devices that are compatible with the criteria you set appear in black type. Mobile devices that do not meet these criteria are dimmed. See Figure 9-24.

Tutorial 9 Using Components and Video, and Creating Content for Printing and Mobile Devices | Flash | FL 465

Figure 9-24 | **Mobile devices in the Online Library**

- set the criteria for the mobile content
- your list may differ
- Nokia mobile devices that don't meet the criteria are dimmed

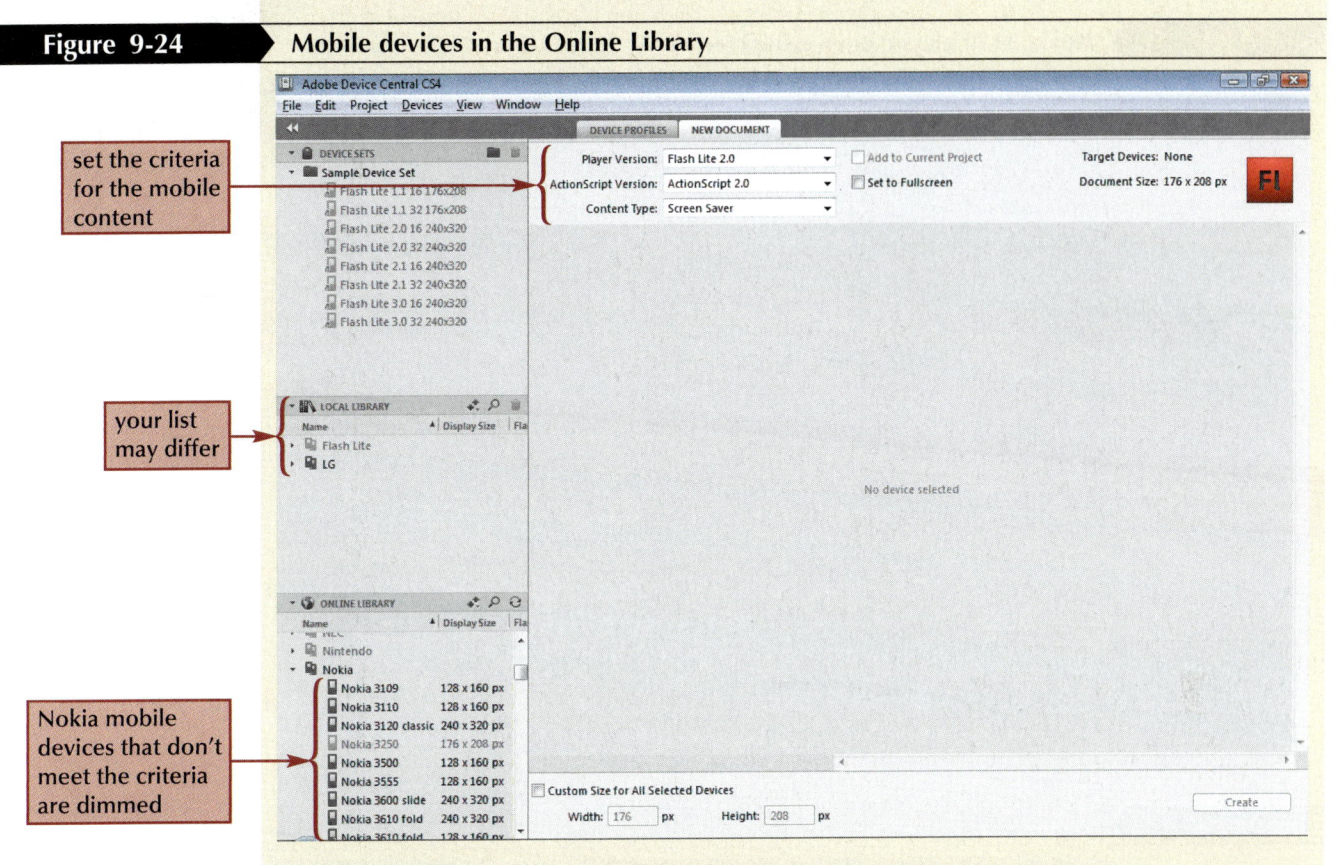

Trouble? If your list of mobile devices differs from that shown in Figure 9-24 and subsequent figures of Adobe Device Central, then Adobe has updated the online profiles since this tutorial was written. Select the closest available device in Steps 5 through 7.

5. In the Online Library, double-click **Nokia 3120 classic** to add the profile for this mobile phone to the Local Library.

6. In the Local Library, expand the **Nokia** category, and then click **Nokia 3120 classic** in the list. The mobile device is displayed in the New Document tab. See Figure 9-25.

Tip

You can also drag a device profile from the Online Library panel to the Local Library panel to add it to the Local Library.

Figure 9-25 Nokia 3120 classic device selected in the Local Library

select the device in the Local Library

pictures of the selected mobile device

▶ 7. In the Online Library, double-click **Nokia 3600 slide**, and then double-click **Nokia 5300**. The Nokia 3600 slide and Nokia 5300 profiles are added to the Local Library so you can create content targeted for all three devices.

▶ 8. Click the **Device Profiles** tab, and in the Local Library, click the **Nokia** category name. The profiles of the three Nokia devices in the Local Library appear in a table. See Figure 9-26.

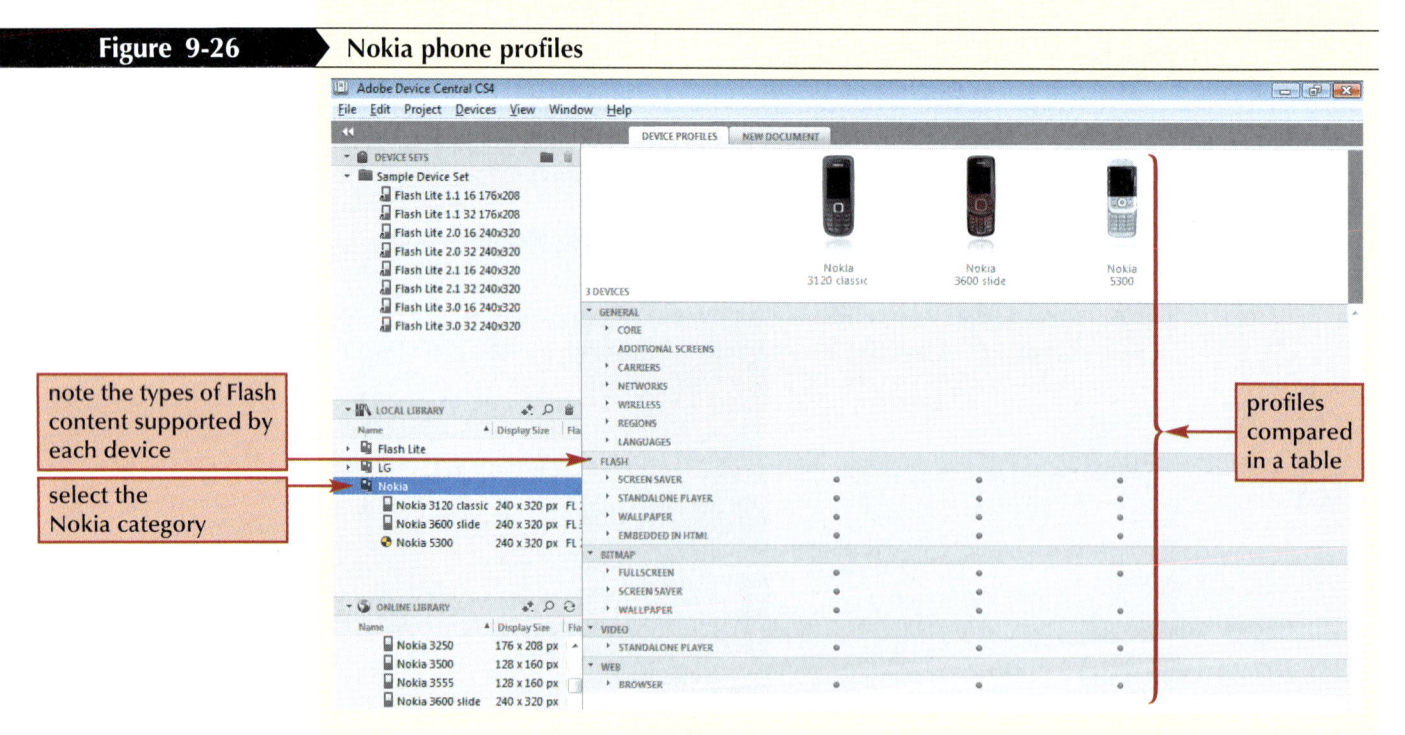

Figure 9-26 Nokia phone profiles

note the types of Flash content supported by each device

select the Nokia category

profiles compared in a table

▶ 9. In the Local Library, double-click the **Nokia 3120 classic** profile to select it. Its icon changes to a light orange and black Active Device icon.

▶ 10. On the Device Profiles tab, click **Flash**, and then click **Screen Saver**. The profile details for the selected mobile phone are displayed. See Figure 9-27.

Tutorial 9 Using Components and Video, and Creating Content for Printing and Mobile Devices | Flash | FL 467

Figure 9-27   Nokia 3120 classic phone details

[Screenshot of Adobe Device Central CS4 showing Nokia 3120 classic phone details, with callouts:]
- click Screen Saver
- note the version of Flash Player supported by the device
- click Flash
- available screen size affects the content you create for device
- double-click to display the Active Device icon

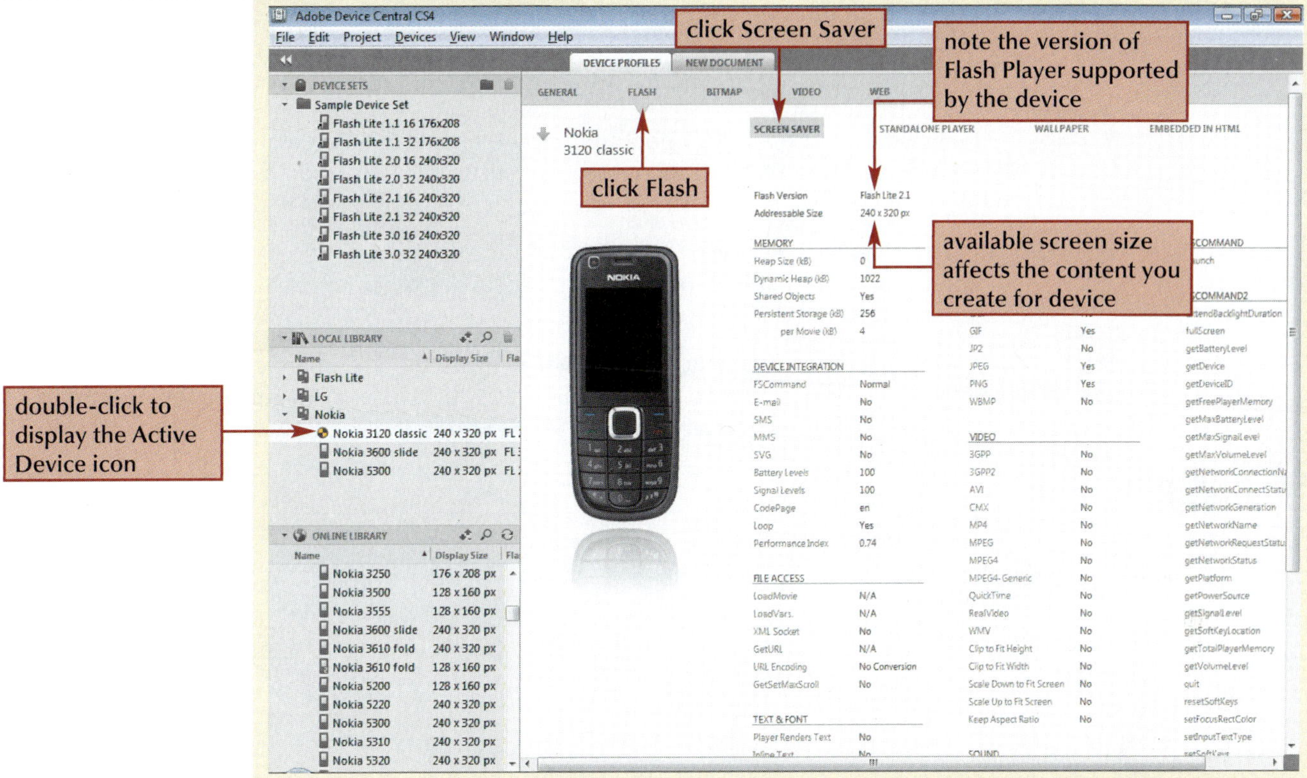

▶ 11. Click the **New Document** tab, and then click the **Create** button. A document is created in Flash with the same dimensions as the screen area of the mobile device selected in Adobe Device Central—in this case, the three Nokia phones in the Local Library.

After you select the mobile device profile in which you will test the mobile content, you are ready to create the content in Flash. You create the content for a mobile device in the same way you create other Flash documents. You'll create the content for the Jackson's Sports Store ad in a new document targeted for the Nokia 3120 classic phone.

To create the Jackson's Sports ad for mobile devices:

▶ 1. Save the new document as **jsMobileAd.fla** in the Tutorial.09\Tutorial folder included with your Data Files.

▶ 2. In the Tools panel, select the **Text** tool T, and then, in the Property inspector, set the font family to **Arial**, set the font style to **Regular**, set the point size to **20**, set the text color to **black** (#FFFFFF), and set the paragraph format to **Align center**.

▶ 3. Create a text block at the top of the Stage and type **Citywide Baseball**, press the **Enter** key to start a new line, type **Tournament**, press the **Enter** key to start a new line, and then type **This Weekend!**.

▶ 4. Reposition the text block centered at the top of the Stage, if necessary.

▶ 5. Create a new movie clip symbol and name it **text**. In symbol-editing mode, create a text block at the center of the editing window and type **Sponsored by**, press the **Enter** key to start a new line, and then type **Jackson's Sports!**.

▶ 6. In the Tools panel, click the **Selection** tool, and then, in the Property inspector, change the text block's font style to **Italic**, its point size to **24**, and its text color to **maroon** (#660000). Exit symbol-editing mode.

▶ 7. In the Timeline, rename Layer 1 to **title text**, and then insert a new layer above the title text layer and name it **animated text**.

▶ 8. Drag an instance of the text symbol to the center of the Stage below the title text block, right-click the text instance, and then click **Create Motion Tween** on the context menu. A tween span is created.

▶ 9. In the Timeline, click **Frame 1** of the animated text layer to select it, and then, on the Stage, click the text instance, if necessary, to select it. You'll decrease the size of the text in the start of the tween span.

▶ 10. Open the Transform panel, click the **Constrain** button to change it to the locked icon, if necessary, type **20** in the Scale Width box, and then press the **Enter** key. The text instance decreases in size. See Figure 9-28.

Figure 9-28 Text block size decreased

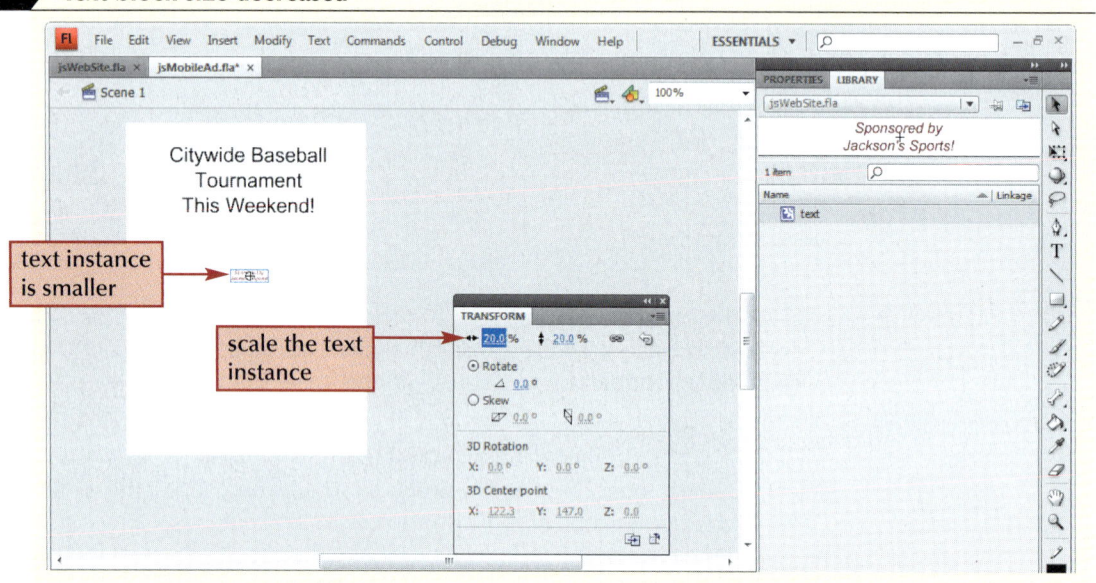

▶ 11. In the Timeline, click **Frame 15** of the animated text layer, and then, in the Transform panel, type **100** in the Scale Width box and press the **Enter** key. The text instance increases to its original size. The motion tween is complete.

▶ 12. Close the Transform panel, and then, in the Timeline, add regular frames at **Frame 60** of both layers.

The last part of the ad is an animation of a baseball graphic. You will copy the Baseball symbol from the jsWebSite.fla library to the current document and then create a new animated baseball symbol.

To add a graphic animation to the Jackson's Sports ad:

▶ 1. In the Timeline, insert a new layer above the animated text layer, name it **graphic**, and then select **Frame 1** of the graphic layer.

▶ 2. In the Library panel, click the button with the **jsMobileAd.fla** name at the top of the panel to display a list of active documents, and then click the **jsWebSite.fla** name. The contents of the jsWebSite.fla library appear in the panel.

Tutorial 9 Using Components and Video, and Creating Content for Printing and Mobile Devices | Flash   FL 469

▶ 3. Drag an instance of the **Baseball** symbol from the Library panel to the Stage and center it at the bottom of the Stage below the animated text instance. A copy of the symbol is also placed in the jsMobileAd.fla document's library.

▶ 4. Convert the Baseball symbol to a movie clip symbol named **animated baseball**.

▶ 5. Open the animated baseball symbol in symbol-editing mode, right-click the **baseball** instance on the editing window, and click **Create Motion Tween**.

▶ 6. In the Timeline, select **Frame 1** of Layer 1, and then, in the Property inspector, enter **1** in the Rotate text box to rotate the baseball graphic once clockwise.

▶ 7. Exit symbol-editing mode, click an empty area of the Stage to deselect the symbol, and then, in the Property inspector, change the Stage color to **light yellow** (#FFFF99). The ad is complete. See Figure 9-29.

Figure 9-29 Mobile ad completed

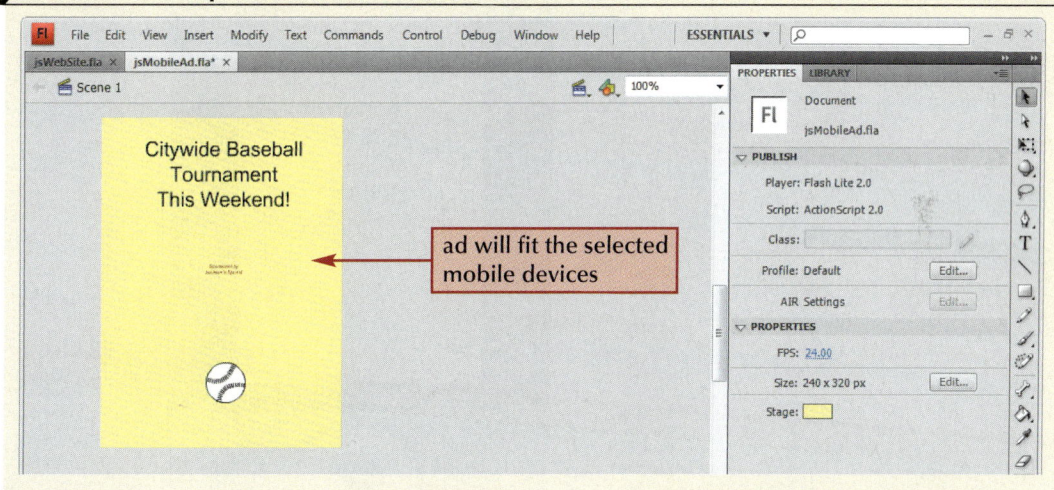

▶ 8. Save the document, and then test the movie. Adobe Device Central opens with the Flash ad displayed in the Nokia 3120 classic mobile device.

When you test a Flash document published for the Flash Lite Player, Adobe Device Central opens to the Emulator tab and the Flash document is displayed on the screen of the selected mobile device. You can use any of the devices listed in the Local Library panel to test how the Flash content appears on different screens. You can then use the testing panels to see how the Flash movie impacts the mobile device's performance or how the content is affected by different types of lighting.

InSight | Testing Flash Content on Targeted Devices

Whenever possible, test the Flash content on the targeted devices. Adobe Device Central emulates a mobile device, but it doesn't truly emulate all aspects of the device such as its processor speed or the color depth of its screen. For example, a color gradient that appears smooth in the emulator within Device Central may be displayed differently when viewed on the actual device. After you test the Flash content on a device, you might need to modify the document's design in Flash and then retest it.

You will test the Flash ad in several mobile devices and under different lighting conditions.

FL 470 Flash | Tutorial 9 Using Components and Video, and Creating Content for Printing and Mobile Devices

To test the Jackson's Sports mobile ad in Adobe Device Central:

▶ 1. In the Local Library panel of Adobe Device Central, double-click **Nokia 5300** in the Nokia category to make it the active device. The device in the Emulator tab changes to reflect the new selection.

▶ 2. Click the **Content Type**, **File Info**, and **Display** panel title bars to expand the testing panels, if necessary. See Figure 9-30.

Figure 9-30   Jackson's Sports ad displayed on the Nokia 5300 device

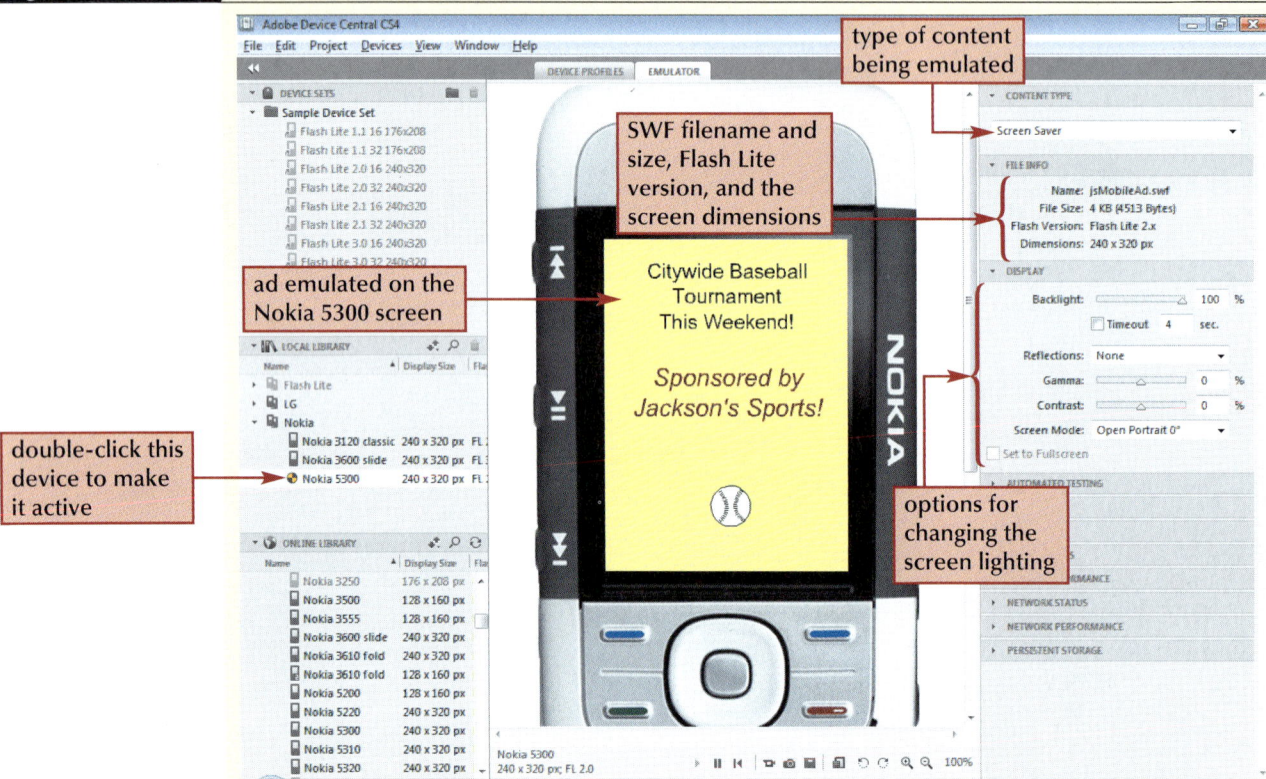

▶ 3. In the Display panel, click the **Reflections** arrow, and then click **Indoor**. The display changes to simulate how the content will appear if indoor lighting is reflected on the device. See Figure 9-31.

Tutorial 9 Using Components and Video, and Creating Content for Printing and Mobile Devices | Flash | FL 471

Figure 9-31 | Content on screen with indoor reflection

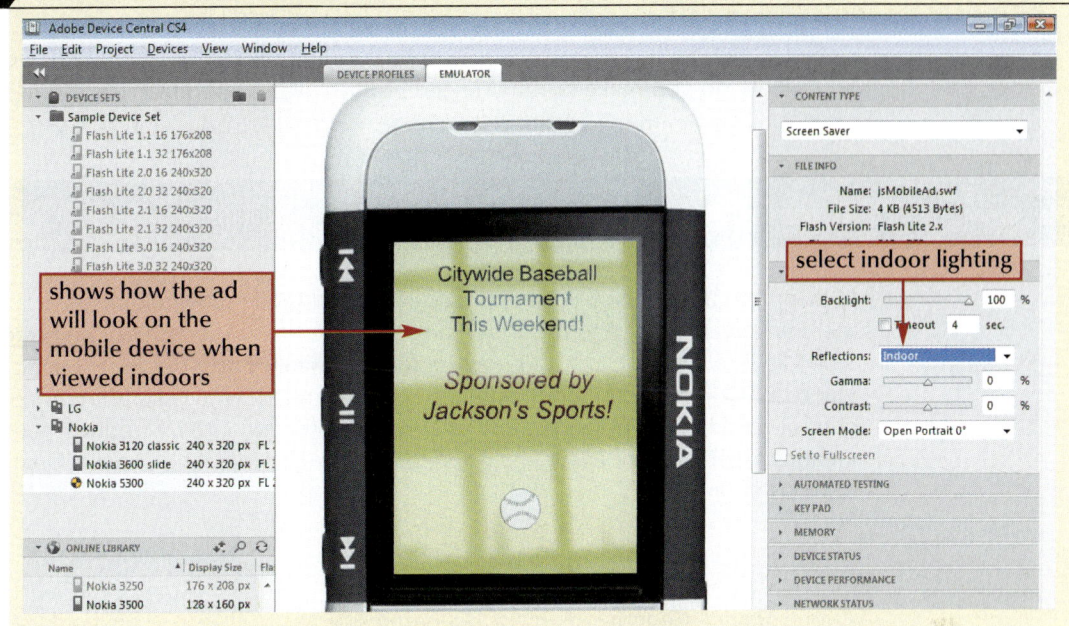

shows how the ad will look on the mobile device when viewed indoors

select indoor lighting

▶ 4. In the Display panel, click the **Reflections** arrow, and then click **Outdoor**. The display changes to simulate how the content will appear if outdoor lighting is reflected on the device.

You will test the Flash ad on a different device.

▶ 5. In the Local Library panel, double-click the **Nokia 3600 slide** device profile to make it the active device. The device in the Emulator tab changes to reflect the new selection.

▶ 6. In the Display panel, click the **Reflections** arrow, and then click **None** to see how the content appears on the device without any reflections. The testing is complete.

▶ 7. On the Application bar, click **File**, and then click **Return to Flash**.

Tip

You can also press the Shift+Ctrl+O keys to return to Flash.

▶ 8. In Flash, close the jsMobileAd.fla and jsWebSite.fla files.

The mobile ad for the Jackson's Youth Web site is complete. Aly will show the completed ad to Dan Jackson at their next meeting. In this session, you created Flash content for printing. You used the PrintJob class to enable printing from within the Flash Player. You also specified which frames in the document to print and how to scale the content to print. Finally, you created and tested content to play on mobile devices using the Flash Lite Player.

Review | Session 9.3 Quick Check

1. What two methods can be used to print Flash content?
2. Write an `addPage()` statement that adds the third frame of the map_mc movie clip to the print job.
3. Write the ActionScript statements to scale both the width and the height of the map_mc movie clip so that it is 150% of its original size.
4. True or False? If the Flash Player's Print command is used, only the current frame of the SWF file can be printed.

5. The print _____ manages the print jobs that are sent to the printer by the various programs running on the computer.
6. List two factors to consider when developing content for mobile devices.
7. How do you make mobile device profiles available to test Flash content in Adobe Device Central?

Review | Tutorial Summary

In this tutorial, you used Flash components to add interactive elements to a document, including Web links, photos, a preloader, and buttons. You learned the basics of digital video as it relates to Flash and how to add video to a Flash document using the Flash video component. You made content in Flash printable and entered ActionScript code to control the Flash components and the printing process. Finally, you learned the basics of creating Flash content to play on mobile devices and you used Adobe Device Central to test Flash content.

Key Terms

Adobe Device Central	decompressor	landscape orientation
Adobe Flash Media Server	embedded video	portrait orientation
Adobe Media Encoder	encoding	print spooler
codec	Flash Lite	progressive downloading
component	frame rate	skin
compressor	frame size	video streaming
cue point		

Tutorial 9 Using Components and Video, and Creating Content for Printing and Mobile Devices | Flash | FL 473

Practice | Review Assignments

Practice the skills you learned in the tutorial.

Data Files needed for the Review Assignments: sbDraft.fla, clip.mpg, sbPhoto1.jpg, sbPhoto2.jpg

Aly wants you to complete a new version of the Softball site she started for Jackson's Sports. You need to add Web links to the site's Home page in the form of a drop-down list. You will also add a Photos page with softball team photos, a Videos page to showcase team videos, and a Coupons page with printable coupons for softball equipment.

1. Open the **sbDraft.fla** file located in the Tutorial.09\Review folder included with your Data Files, and then save the file as **jSoftball.fla** in the same folder.
2. In the Timeline, select Frame 10 of the content layer, drag an instance of the ComboBox component from the Components panel to the Stage, position the ComboBox instance 320 pixels from the left of the Stage and 350 pixels from the top of the Stage, name the instance **softballLinks_mc**, and then change the width of the instance to 150 pixels. Do not change its height.
3. With the ComboBox instance selected, in the Parameters tab of the Component Inspector, enter **Softball Links** for the prompt parameter, and then enter the following label/data value pairs in the dataProvider parameter: **ASA Youth Softball**, **1**; **International Softball**, **2**; and **Sports Teams Web Sites**, **3**.
4. In the Timeline, select Frame 10 of the actions layer, place the insertion point after the last line of the existing code in the Actions panel, and then type the following lines of code to make the Web links operational.

```
// Function to check which site was selected
function gotoWebsite(eventObj:Event):void {
      // Variable that will hold the URL
      var weblinkText:String;
      // Switch statement determines which URL to assign
      switch (softballLinks_mc.value) {
      case "1" :
        weblinkText = "http://www.softball.org/youth/";
          break;
      case "2" :
        weblinkText = "http://www.internationalsoftball.com/index.asp";
          break;
      case "3" :
        weblinkText = "http://www.myteamzone.com/teamwebsites/SoftBall.aspx";
          break;
      }
//Open Web site using the selected URL
var siteURL:URLRequest = new URLRequest(weblinkText);
navigateToURL(siteURL);
//Set ComboBox to display the prompt, Web Links
softballLinks_mc.selectedIndex = -1;
}
// Event listener
softballLinks_mc.addEventListener(Event.CHANGE, gotoWebsite);
```

5. In the Timeline, select Frame 20 of the content layer, and then drag one instance of the UILoader component and two instances of the Button component from the Components panel to the Stage. Position the UILoader instance 300 pixels from the left of the Stage and 180 pixels from the top of the Stage. Position the first Button instance 160 pixels from the left of the Stage and 180 pixels from the top of the Stage and the second Button instance 160 pixels from the left of the Stage and 220 pixels from the top of the Stage.

6. Name the first Button instance **softballPhoto1_btn**, name the second Button instance **softballPhoto2_btn**, name the UILoader instance **photoLoader_mc**, and then change the dimensions of the UILoader instance to 165 pixels wide by 250 pixels high.

7. On the Parameters tab of the Component inspector, change the label parameter of the first Button instance to **Photo 1** and the second Button instance to **Photo 2**.

8. In the Timeline, select Frame 20 of the actions layer, and then, in the Actions panel, type the following lines of code so that when a button is clicked, the corresponding softball photo will load into the UILoader instance.

```
// Functions to load photos
function loadPhoto1(eventObj:MouseEvent):void
{
    var photoURLReq:URLRequest = new URLRequest("sbPhoto1.jpg");
    photoLoader_mc.load(photoURLReq);
}
function loadPhoto2(eventObj:MouseEvent):void
{
    var photoURLReq:URLRequest = new URLRequest("sbPhoto2.jpg");
    photoLoader_mc.load(photoURLReq);
}
// Event listeners
softballPhoto1_btn.addEventListener(MouseEvent.CLICK, loadPhoto1);
softballPhoto2_btn.addEventListener(MouseEvent.CLICK, loadPhoto2);
```

9. In Adobe Media Encoder, add the **clip.mpg** file located in the Tutorial.09\Review folder included with your Data Files to the queue.

10. Select the FLV – Web Medium (Flash 8 and Higher) preset for the file, change the audio output channel to Mono and the frame rate to 15 and then encode the file.

11. In Flash, select Frame 30 of the content layer, and use the Import Video wizard to import the **clip.flv** video file. For the delivery option, select Load external video with playback component. In the Skinning dialog box, select SkinUnderPlayMute.swf for the skin.

12. On the Stage, position the FLVPlayback instance about 250 pixels from the left of the Stage and 170 pixels from the top of the Stage. In the Parameters tab of the Component inspector, change the autoPlay value to false.

13. In the Timeline, insert a keyframe at Frame 40 of the labels layer, and then, in the Property inspector, assign the label name **Coupons**. Select Frame 40 of the content layer, drag an instance of the coupon1 movie clip from the Library panel to the Stage, reduce the size of the instance by 50%, and name the instance **coupon1_mc**. Drag an instance of the coupon2 movie clip from the Library panel to the Stage, reduce the size of the instance by 50%, and name the instance **coupon2_mc**.

14. Position the coupon1_mc instance 220 pixels from the left of the Stage and 180 pixels from the top of the Stage. Position the coupon2_mc instance 420 pixels from the left of the Stage and 180 pixels from the top of the Stage.

15. Drag two instances of the Button component movie clip from the Library panel to the Stage. Place one button below the coupon1_mc instance and place the second button below the coupon2_mc instance. Name the first Button instance **printCoupon1_btn** and change its label parameter to **Print Coupon**. Name the second Button instance **printCoupon2_btn** and change its label parameter to **Print Coupon**.
16. In the Timeline, insert a keyframe at Frame 40 of the actions layer. In the Script pane of the Actions panel, type the following lines of code so that clicking the buttons will print the corresponding coupon. Frame 2 of each coupon is printed at 200% of its original size.

```
// Function to print the first coupon
function printCoupon1(eventObj:MouseEvent):void {
    var myPrintJob1:PrintJob = new PrintJob();
    if (myPrintJob1.start()) {
        // Increase the size of the coupon to 200%
        coupon1_mc.scaleX = 2;
        coupon1_mc.scaleY = 2;
    myPrintJob1.addPage(coupon1_mc, null, null, 2);
        // Reduce the size of the coupon to 50%
        coupon1_mc.scaleX = .5;
        coupon1_mc.scaleY = .5;
    myPrintJob1.send();
    }
}
// Function to print the second coupon
function printCoupon2(eventObj:MouseEvent):void {
    var myPrintJob2:PrintJob = new PrintJob();
    if (myPrintJob2.start()) {
        // Increase the size of the coupon to 200%
        coupon2_mc.scaleX = 2;
        coupon2_mc.scaleY = 2;
    myPrintJob2.addPage(coupon2_mc, null, null, 2);
        // Reduce the size of the coupon to 50%
        coupon2_mc.scaleX = .5;
        coupon2_mc.scaleY = .5;
    myPrintJob2.send();
    }
}
// Event listeners
printCoupon1_btn.addEventListener(MouseEvent.CLICK, printCoupon1);
printCoupon2_btn.addEventListener(MouseEvent.CLICK, printCoupon2);
```

17. Save the jSoftball.fla file and test the Web site to make sure the Web links work, the photos load, the video plays, and the coupons print. (*Hint:* If the Web site links do not work, the URLs for the sites might have changed since the printing of this book.)
18. Submit the finished files to your instructor.

Flash | Tutorial 9 Using Components and Video, and Creating Content for Printing and Mobile Devices

Apply | Case Problem 1

Add Web links with a ComboBox component and a printable coupon with a Button component to a Flash Web site.

Data File needed for this Case Problem: kprDraftWeb.fla

Katie's Pet Resort Katie wants to add links to the Resources page of the resort's Web site without cluttering the page with individual buttons. She also wants a coupon added to the Boarding page for 20% off the cost of one night of boarding. You will add these new elements to the Resources and Boarding pages of the Web site, which are shown in Figure 9-32.

Figure 9-32

1. Open the **kprDraftWeb.fla** file located in the Tutorial.09\Case1 folder included with your Data Files, and then save the file as **katiesWeb.fla** in the same folder.

2. In the Timeline, insert two layers above the buttons layer and name them **actions** and **labels**, respectively. In the labels layer, insert keyframes at Frame 10 and Frame 20, and then add the label **Home** to Frame 1, the label **Resources** to Frame 10, and the label **Boarding** to Frame 20. In the actions layer, insert keyframes at Frame 10 and Frame 20.

3. On the Stage, select the Home button and name the instance **home_btn**. Repeat to name the Resources button instance **resources_btn** and the Boarding button instance **boarding_btn**.

4. Select Frame 1 of the actions layer, and then, in the Script pane of the Actions panel, type the following lines of code so that clicking the navigational buttons advances the playhead to the corresponding label.

```
//Keep the playhead from advancing
stop();
//Button functions
function onHomeClick(evt:MouseEvent):void {
     gotoAndStop("Home");
}
function onResourcesClick(evt:MouseEvent):void {
     gotoAndStop("Resources");
}
function onBoardingClick(evt:MouseEvent):void {
     gotoAndStop("Boarding");
}
// Event listeners
home_btn.addEventListener(MouseEvent.CLICK, onHomeClick);
resources_btn.addEventListener(MouseEvent.CLICK, onResourcesClick);
boarding_btn.addEventListener(MouseEvent.CLICK, onBoardingClick);
```

5. Select Frame 10 of the content layer, drag an instance of the ComboBox component from the Components panel to the Stage, place the instance 240 pixels from the left of the Stage and 270 pixels from the top of the Stage, name the instance **resourceLinks**, and then change the width of the instance to 170 pixels. Do not change its height.
6. With the ComboBox instance selected, open the Parameters tab in the Component inspector, enter **Pet Adoption Links** for the prompt parameter and enter the following label/data value pairs in the dataProvider parameter: **Adopt a Pet**, **1**; **Best Friends, 2**; and **SPCA**, **3**.
7. Select Frame 10 of the actions layer, and then, in the Script pane of the Actions panel, type the following lines of code to make the ComboBox operational.

```
// Function to check which site was selected
function gotoWebsite(eventObj:Event):void {
     // Variable that will hold the URL
     var reslinkText:String;
     // Switch statement determines which URL to assign
     switch (resourceLinks.value) {
     case "1" :
          reslinkText = "http://www.adoptapet.com/";
          break;
     case "2" :
          reslinkText = "http://www.bfpa.org/";
          break;
     case "3" :
          reslinkText = "http://www.spca.org/";
          break;
     }
//Open Web site using the selected URL
var siteURL:URLRequest = new URLRequest(reslinkText);
navigateToURL(siteURL);
//Set ComboBox to display the intial prompt
resourceLinks.selectedIndex = -1;
}
// Event listener
resourceLinks.addEventListener(Event.CHANGE, gotoWebsite);
```

8. Create a new movie clip symbol named **Coupon**. In symbol-editing mode, draw a rectangle at the center of the Stage using light orange (#FFCC00) for the fill color and black for the stroke color. Select a dotted line for the stroke style, and use a stroke height of 2. Change the rectangle's width to 300 pixels and its height to 150 pixels. If necessary, change its X and Y coordinates to 0. Rename Layer 1 to **background** and lock the layer.
9. Insert a new layer and name it **graphics**. Add four instances of the triangle symbol. Place each instance in a separate corner of the rectangle. Use the Free Transform tool to rotate the instances so that the long side of each triangle faces the center of the rectangle.
10. Insert a new layer and name it **text**. Create a static text block at the top part of the rectangle. Use Comic Sans MS for the font family, Regular for the font style, 22 for the point size, maroon (#660000) for the text color, and Align center for the paragraph format. Type **Katie's Pet Resort** in the text block. If necessary, center the text block in the top part of the rectangle.

11. Create a text block in the center of the rectangle. Change the point size to 16, the font style to Bold, and the text color to black. Type **Take 20% off**, press the Enter key, and then type **One Night of Boarding!**. If necessary, center the text block within the rectangle.
12. Create a text block at the bottom of the rectangle. Change the point size to 8 and the font style to Regular. Type **Must be redeemed by March 31**, press the Enter key, and then type **Call to make a reservation!**. If necessary, center the text block in the bottom part of the rectangle.
13. In the Timeline, insert keyframes at Frame 5 of the text layer and graphics layer and insert a regular frame in Frame 5 of the background layer. In Frame 5 of the text layer, add a text block below the rectangle. Change the point size to 16. Type **Clip this coupon for great savings!** in this text block. In Frame 5 of the graphics layer, add an instance of the scissors symbol, and place it on the lower-left corner of the rectangle so that its midpoint is over the rectangle's stroke.
14. In the Timeline, insert a new layer above the text layer and name it **action**. Select Frame 1 of the action layer, open the Actions panel, and then enter the following line so the playhead will stop at Frame 1. Exit symbol-editing mode.

    `stop();`
15. In the main document Timeline, select Frame 20 of the content layer, add an instance of the coupon symbol to the center of the Stage, use the Transform panel to reduce the size of the instance by 50%, and then assign the instance the name **coupon_mc**.
16. In Frame 20 of the content layer, drag an instance of the Button component from the Components panel to below the coupon instance on the Stage. Name the Button instance **print_btn**, and then, on the Parameters tab of the Component inspector, change its label parameter to **Print Coupon**.
17. Select Frame 20 of the actions layer, and then, in the Script pane of the Actions panel, type the following lines of code so that when the button is clicked, the size of the coupon instance is increased to 100%, the fifth frame of the coupon instance is printed, and then the size of the coupon instance is reduced to 50%.

    ```
    // Function to print the coupon
    function printCoupon(eventObj:MouseEvent):void {
        var myPrintJob:PrintJob = new PrintJob();
        if (myPrintJob.start()) {
            // Increase the size of the coupon to 100%
            coupon_mc.scaleX = 1;
            coupon_mc.scaleY = 1;
          myPrintJob.addPage(coupon_mc, null, null, 5);
            // Reduce the size of the coupon to 50%
            coupon_mc.scaleX = .5;
            coupon_mc.scaleY = .5;
          myPrintJob.send();
        }
    }
    // Event listeners
    print_btn.addEventListener(MouseEvent.CLICK, printCoupon);
    ```
18. Save the katiesWeb.fla file, and test it to make sure the navigational buttons work, the resource links work, and the coupon prints. (*Hint*: If the Web site links do not work, the URLs for the sites might have changed since the printing of this book.)
19. Submit the finished files to your instructor.

Tutorial 9 Using Components and Video, and Creating Content for Printing and Mobile Devices | Flash | FL 479

| Apply | Case Problem 2

Add a video clip with the FLVPlayback component and a printable schedule with a Button component in a Flash Web site, and create an ad for a mobile device.

Data Files needed for this Case Problem: aczDraft.fla, zooClip1.avi, zooClip2.avi

Alamo City Zoo Janet requests that video clips be incorporated into the Exhibits page of the zoo's Web site to show examples of animals on exhibit. She also wants a schedule of tours added to the site that can be printed so visitors can plan tours ahead of time. In addition, she wants an ad to send to the mobile devices of registered zoo members. Alex instructs you to add two video clips to the Exhibits page, add the printable schedule to the Education page, and create an ad targeted to a mobile device. You will encode the video clips and then import them into the document so they load as external FLV files and are displayed on the Exhibits page. You will add buttons to control the playing of the videos. Then you will create the printable schedule and add a button to the Education page to control printing of the schedule. Finally, you will create an ad with animation that can be displayed on a mobile device. Figure 9-33 shows the completed Exhibits and Education pages and the mobile ad.

Figure 9-33

1. Open the **aczDraft.fla** file located in the Tutorial.09\Case2 folder included with your Data Files, and then save the file as **aczWeb.fla** in the same folder.
2. In the Timeline, insert two layers above the content layer and name them **actions** and **labels**, respectively. In the labels layer, insert keyframes at Frame 10 and Frame 20, and then add the label **Home** to Frame 1, the label **Exhibits** to Frame 10, and the label **Education** to Frame 20. In the actions layer, insert keyframes at Frame 10 and Frame 20.
3. On the Stage, name the Home button instance **home_btn**, name the Exhibits button instance **exhibits_btn**, and then name the Education button instance **education_btn**.

4. In the Timeline, select Frame 1 of the actions layer, and then, in the Script pane of the Actions panel, type the following lines of code so that clicking the navigational buttons advances the playhead to the corresponding label.

```
//Keep the playhead from advancing
stop();
//Button functions
function onHomeClick(evt:MouseEvent):void {
    gotoAndStop("Home");
}
function onExhibitsClick(evt:MouseEvent):void {
    gotoAndStop("Exhibits");
}
function onEducationClick(evt:MouseEvent):void {
    gotoAndStop("Education");
}

// Event listeners
home_btn.addEventListener(MouseEvent.CLICK, onHomeClick);
exhibits_btn.addEventListener(MouseEvent.CLICK, onExhibitsClick);
education_btn.addEventListener(MouseEvent.CLICK, onEducationClick);
```

5. In Adobe Media Encoder, add the **zooClip1.avi** and **zooClip2.avi** files located in the Tutorial.09\Case2 folder included with your Data Files to the queue.

6. Select the FLV – Web Medium (Flash 8 and Higher) preset for both files. For each file, change the audio output channel to Mono and the frame rate to 15 and then encode both files.

7. In Flash, select Frame 10 of the content layer. Use the Import Video wizard to import the **zooClip1.flv** video file. For the delivery option, select Load external video with playback component.

EXPLORE

8. In the Skinning dialog box, select SkinUnderPlayMute.swf for the skin, and then change the skin color to gray (#999999) with an alpha amount of 50%.

9. After you import the video, open the Transform panel, select the constrain button, and change the width of the FLVPlayback component instance to 70%. Reposition the FLVPlayback instance below the Alamo City Zoo Exhibits inside the rectangle on the Stage. In the Parameters tab of the Component Inspector, set the autoPlay value to false. In the Property inspector, name the FLVPlayback instance **videoPlayer**.

10. Drag two instances of the Button component from the Component panel to the Stage. Place the instances below the rectangle containing the FLVPlayback instance. Align the two Button instances horizontally. In the Component Inspector, change the label of the first Button instance to **Video Clip 1** and change the label of the second Button instance to **Video Clip 2**. In the Property inspector, assign the first button instance the name **clip1_btn** and the second Button instance the name **clip2_btn**.

11. In the Timeline, select Frame 10 of the actions layer, and then, in the Script pane of the Actions panel, type the following lines of code so that clicking the video clip buttons plays the corresponding videos.

```
// Functions to add video clips to FLVPlayback component
function playVideo1(eventObj:MouseEvent):void {
    videoPlayer.source = "zooClip1.flv" ;
}
function playVideo2(eventObj:MouseEvent):void {
    videoPlayer.source = "zooClip2.flv" ;
```

Tutorial 9 Using Components and Video, and Creating Content for Printing and Mobile Devices | Flash **FL 481**

```
}
// Event listeners
clip1_btn.addEventListener(MouseEvent.CLICK, playVideo1);
clip2_btn.addEventListener(MouseEvent.CLICK, playVideo2);
```

12. In the Timeline, select Frame 20 of the content layer. Add an instance of the Button component from the Library to the Stage. Place the button below the text block on the center of the Stage. Name the instance **print_btn**. In the Parameters tab of the Component inspector, change the button's label to **Print Tour Schedule**. In the Property inspector, change the width of the button to 120 pixels. Keep its height at 22 pixels.

13. Create a new movie clip symbol named **Tour Schedule**. In the symbol's Timeline, rename Layer 1 **schedule**, and then add a new layer and name it **action**. In the Actions panel, add the following line to stop the playhead at Frame 1 of the action layer.

    ```
    stop();
    ```

14. In the schedule layer, draw a rectangle at the center of the Stage with an orange (#FF9900) fill and a black stroke. Make the rectangle 90 pixels wide and 40 pixels high and set its X and Y coordinates to 0. Add a text block at the center of the rectangle. Use Arial for the font family, 12 for the point size, bold for the font style, black for the text color, and align center for the paragraph format. Type **Tour**, press the Enter key, and then type **Schedule**. If necessary, realign the text block over the rectangle.

15. In the schedule layer, insert a blank keyframe at Frame 2, and then change the zoom level of the Stage to 50%. In Frame 2, draw a rectangle with no fill, a black stroke, a stroke height of 2, and a solid stroke style. Make the rectangle 550 pixels wide and 600 pixels high. Set the rectangle's X and Y coordinates to 0.

16. In Frame 2, add a text block inside the top of the rectangle. Use Monotype Corsiva for the font family (the font is listed with the C fonts), 54 for the point size, black for the text color, align center for the paragraph format, and then type **Alamo City Zoo**. Add another text block below the first text block. Use Arial for the font family, 24 for the point size, black for the text color, Align center for the paragraph format, and then type **Educational Tour Schedule**. Center both text blocks within the top part of the rectangle.

17. Create a new text block using Arial for the font family, 18 for the point size, black for the text color, and align center for the paragraph format. Place the text block inside the rectangle below the first two text blocks, and then type the following, pressing the Enter key twice after each line to double space the text:

    Group Tours
    Mondays and Wednesdays – 12:00 noon, 4:00 pm
    Tuesdays and Thursdays – 10:00 am, 2:00 pm, 6:00 pm
    Fridays – 11:00 am, 1:00 pm, 3:00 pm, 6:00 pm
    Saturdays – 9:00 am, 11:00 am, 3:00 pm, 6:00 pm
    Book your tour ahead of time by calling 444-TOUR
    (Tours fill up fast!)
    ***Schedule is subject to change.**

18. Drag an instance of the bear.jpg bitmap from the library to the lower-left corner of the rectangle. Drag an instance of the rhino.jpg bitmap from the library to the lower-right corner of the rectangle. Exit symbol-editing mode.

19. In Frame 20 of the content layer, add an instance of the Tour Schedule symbol to the Stage. Place it below the Print Tour Schedule button instance. Name the instance **tour_mc**.

20. In the Timeline, select Frame 20 of the actions layer, and then, in the Script pane of the Actions panel, type the following lines of code so that when the button is clicked, the second frame of the Tour Schedule movie clip prints.

    ```
    // Function to print the schedule
    function printSchedule(eventObj:MouseEvent):void {
        var myPrintJob:PrintJob = new PrintJob();
        if (myPrintJob.start()) {
            myPrintJob.addPage(tour_mc, null, null, 2);
            myPrintJob.send();
        }
    }
    // Event listeners
    print_btn.addEventListener(MouseEvent.CLICK, printSchedule);
    ```

21. Save the aczWeb.fla file, and then test it to make sure the video clips play and the tour schedule prints.
22. Create a new **Flash File (Mobile)** document. In Adobe Device Central, on the New Document tab, change the Player Version to **Flash Lite 2.0**, change the ActionScript Version to **ActionScript 2.0**, and change the Content Type to **Screen Saver**.
23. Add the profile for the Sony Ericsson C702 mobile phone located in the Ericsson category in the Online Library panel to the Local Library, and then create a new document in Flash.
24. In Flash, change the Stage color to light orange (#FFCC99). Draw a rectangle with a maroon (#660000) stroke color, a stroke height of 2, a ragged stroke style, rounded corners, and no fill. The rectangle should form a frame around the inside of the Stage. Rename Layer 1 to **background** and lock the layer.
25. Insert a new layer and name it **title**. In this layer, create a text block at the top of the Stage and inside the rectangle. Use Times New Roman for the font, bold italic for the font style, 28 for the point size, and black for the font color. Type **Alamo City Zoo** in the text block.
26. Insert a new layer and name it **animation**. In this layer, create a second text block below the title text. Use Times New Roman for the font, regular for the font style, 16 for the point size, and black for the font color. Type **Dine with the Animals!**, in the text block, press the Enter key, type **April 3rd!**, press the Enter key, and then type **6:00 pm**.
27. Create a motion tween on the text block. In Frame 24 of the animation layer, move the text block to the bottom of the Stage to create an animation where the text block moves from the top of the Stage to the bottom. In Frame 1 of the animation layer, change the size of the text block to 50% of its original size. In Frame 24 of the animation layer, change the size back to 100%. The text block will increase in size as it moves to the bottom of the Stage.
28. Add a regular frame at Frame 60 of each layer to expand all the layers.
29. Save the file as **aczMobileAd.fla** in the Tutorial.09\Case2 folder included with your Data Files, and then test the file in Adobe Device Central to see it in the Sony Ericsson phone.
30. Submit the finished files to your instructor.

Tutorial 9 Using Components and Video, and Creating Content for Printing and Mobile Devices | Flash | FL 483

Challenge | Case Problem 3

Add photos and buttons using ProgressBar and UILoader components and import a video to complete a nursery Web site.

Data Files needed for this Case Problem: wcDraft.fla, flower1_sm.jpg, flower2_sm.jpg, flower3_sm.jpg, flower1.jpg, flower2.jpg, flower3.jpg, wcLandscape.avi

Westcreek Nursery Alice tells Amanda that she wants a short video clip of a sample landscape added to the Weekly Specials page of the Web site to give potential customers an idea of the nursery's landscaping work. She also wants the Photos page to display thumbnails of the flower pictures to make it easier for potential customers to know what is on sale. Amanda asks you to import the short video and to complete a new Photos page. She has prepared the small versions of the pictures to use as thumbnails. Figure 9-34 shows the completed Weekly Specials and Photos pages.

Figure 9-34

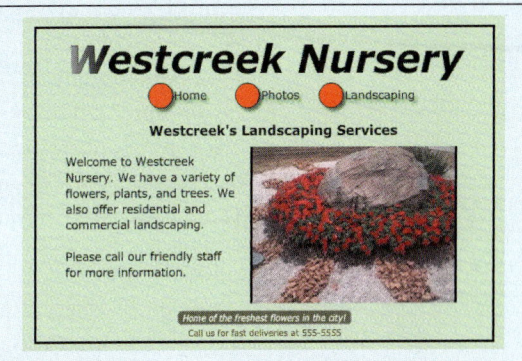

1. Open the **wcDraft.fla** file located in the Tutorial.09\Case3 folder included with your Data Files, and then save the file as **wcWebSite.fla** in the same folder.
2. On the Stage, name the Home button instance **home_btn**, name the Photos button instance **photos_btn**, and then name the Landscaping button instance **landscaping_btn**.
3. In the Timeline, insert two layers above the content layer and name them **actions** and **labels**, respectively. In the labels layer, add the label **Home** to Frame 1, the label **Photos** to Frame 10, and the label **Landscaping** to Frame 20, inserting keyframes as needed. In the actions layer, insert a keyframe at Frame 10.

4. Select Frame 1 of the actions layer, and then type the following lines of code in the Script pane of the Actions panel to keep the playhead from advancing and to make the navigational buttons operational.

```
//Keep the playhead from advancing automatically
stop();
//Button functions
function onHomeClick(evt:MouseEvent):void {
     gotoAndStop("Home");
}
function onPhotosClick(evt:MouseEvent):void {
     gotoAndStop("Photos");
}
function onLandscapingClick(evt:MouseEvent):void {
     gotoAndStop("Landscaping");
}
// Event listeners
home_btn.addEventListener(MouseEvent.CLICK, onHomeClick);
photos_btn.addEventListener(MouseEvent.CLICK, onPhotosClick);
landscaping_btn.addEventListener(MouseEvent.CLICK, onLandscapingClick);
```

5. Select Frame 10 of the content layer, import the **flower1_sm.jpg** picture onto the Stage, and place it 70 pixels from the left of the Stage and 170 pixels from the top of the Stage. Import the **flower2_sm.jpg** picture onto the Stage and place it below the first picture. Import the **flower3_sm.jpg** picture onto the Stage and place it below the second picture. Align the pictures by their left sides and space them evenly.

6. Convert each picture into a button symbol, using the names **flower1 button**, **flower2 button**, and **flower3 button**, respectively. Name the button instances **flower1_btn**, **flower2_btn**, and **flower3_btn**, respectively.

7. For each button symbol, edit the symbol, insert a keyframe in its Over frame, and add a text block on the center of the picture. Use Verdana for the font family, bold italic for the font style, 12 for the point size, yellow (#FFFF00) for the font color, and align center for the paragraph format. Type **Click Me!** in the text block.

8. In the document's main Timeline, select Frame 10 in the content layer, and then drag an instance of the UILoader component from the Components panel to the center of the Stage. Resize the UILoader instance to 250 pixels wide by 187 pixels high. Name the instance **picLoader_mc**. Center the instance below the Westcreek's Photos of the Week text block.

9. Drag an instance of the ProgressBar component from the Components panel to the Stage and place it in the center of the UILoader instance. Name the ProgressBar instance **progressBar_mc**, and change its height to 10. Do not change its width. In the Parameters tab of the Components Inspector, change the source parameter to **picLoader_mc**.

EXPLORE

10. In the Library panel, open the ProgressBar component symbol in symbol-editing mode, double-click the small rectangle to the left of the Bar Skin label to edit the ProgressBar barSkin symbol, and then increase the zoom level to 800%. Double-click the blue stroke of the rectangle to edit it, and then change its color to green (#006600). On the Edit bar, click ProgressBar barSkin, double-click the fill of the rectangle, and then change the fill color to bright green (#00FF00). Exit symbol-editing mode.

11. Select Frame 10 of the actions layer, and in the Script pane of the Actions panel, type the following lines of code to make the picture buttons operational. Clicking a picture button loads the corresponding picture into the picLoader instance. The ProgressBar instance appears temporarily, indicating the picture is loading.

    ```
    // Hide the ProgressBar instance
    progressBar_mc.visible = false;
    // Functions to load photos
    function loadPic1(eventObj:MouseEvent):void
    {
        progressBar_mc.visible = true;
        var picURLReq:URLRequest = new URLRequest("flower1.jpg");
        picLoader_mc.load(picURLReq);
    }
    function loadPic2(eventObj:MouseEvent):void
    {
        progressBar_mc.visible = true;
        var picURLReq:URLRequest = new URLRequest("flower2.jpg");
        picLoader_mc.load(picURLReq);
    }
    function loadPic3(eventObj:MouseEvent):void
    {
        progressBar_mc.visible = true;
        var picURLReq:URLRequest = new URLRequest("flower3.jpg");
        picLoader_mc.load(picURLReq);
    }
    // When the loading is complete, hide the ProgressBar instance
    function hideBar(eventObj:Event) {
        progressBar_mc.visible = false;
    }
    // Event listeners for buttons
    flower1_btn.addEventListener(MouseEvent.CLICK, loadPic1);
    flower2_btn.addEventListener(MouseEvent.CLICK, loadPic2);
    flower3_btn.addEventListener(MouseEvent.CLICK, loadPic3);
    // Event listener: when picture completes loading, hide progress bar
    picLoader_mc.addEventListener(Event.COMPLETE, hideBar);
    ```

12. In Adobe Media Encoder, add the **wcLandscape.avi** file located in the Tutorial.09\Case3 folder included with your Data Files to the queue.

13. Select the FLV – Web Medium (Flash 8 and Higher) preset, change the audio output channel to Mono, change the frame rate to 15, and then encode the file to output the wcLandscape.flv file.

14. Select Frame 20 of the content layer, and then use the Import Video wizard to import the **wcLandscape.flv** video file located in the Tutorial.09/Case3 folder. For the delivery option, select Load external video with playback component.

EXPLORE

15. In the Skinning dialog box, select SkinOverPlaySeekStop.swf for the skin, and then change the skin color to gray (#999999) with an alpha amount of 70%.

16. After you import the video, open the Transform panel, select the constrain button, if necessary, and change the width of the FLVPlayback component instance to 80%. Reposition the FLVPlayback instance below the Westcreek's Landscaping Services text block in the lower-right side of the Stage. In the Parameters tab of the Component inspector, set the skinAutoHide value to true.

EXPLORE

17. Save and test the wcWebSite.fla file. Use the Simulate Download command with a download setting of DSL (32.6 KB/s) to test the photos' ProgressBar. Click each photo thumbnail to display the ProgressBar. After a photo loads, the ProgressBar instance is hidden. Also, make sure the video clip plays in the Landscaping page.

18. Submit the finished files to your instructor.

Create | Case Problem 4

Add photos, Web links, printable content, and the results of a calculation to an association's Web site using components and ActionScript code.

Data Files needed for this Case Problem: msaDraft.fla, mission1.jpg, mission2.jpg

Missions Support Association   Brittany wants a new Web site developed that includes a page with links to sites related to the missions as well as a page that displays photos of some of the missions. She also wants to include a page where visitors can select from a type of tour and enter the number of people in the tour to calculate the cost of a tour. Anissa developed a revised version of the association's Web site that you will complete by adding Web links, a page with photos, and a tour cost calculator page. You will also create an ad for mobile devices that promotes the association's tours. Figure 9-35 shows one possible solution for the photos and tour cost calculator pages and the mobile ad.

Figure 9-35

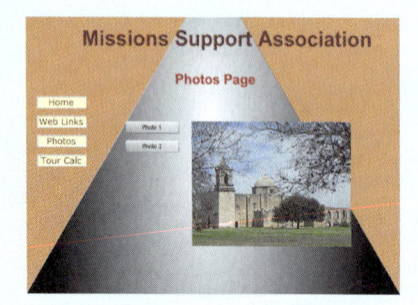

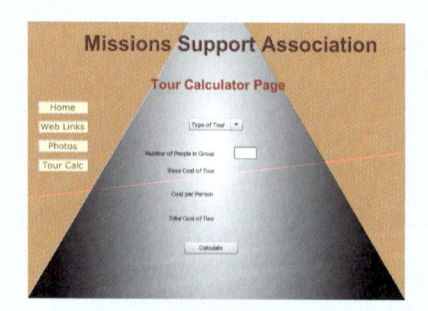

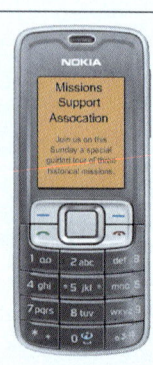

1. Open the **msaDraft.fla** file located in the Tutorial.09\Case4 folder included with your Data Files, and then save the file as **msaWebsite.fla** in the same folder.

2. Use the Home navigational button to create duplicate buttons for the Web Links, Photos, and Tour Calc pages. Add the buttons to the buttons layer and assign instance names to the buttons.

3. In the Timeline, add a layer with descriptive labels in Frames 1, 10, 20, and 30 to correspond to the Web site pages.

4. In the Timeline, add a layer for the actions, and in Frame 1 of this layer add the ActionScript code to make the navigational buttons operational.
5. In the Timeline, select Frame 1 of the content layer, and add a title for the Home page. Repeat to add appropriate titles for each of the other pages in their respective frames in the content layer.
6. In the Timeline, select the frame in the content layer for the Web links page, and then use a ComboBox component to provide a list of three URL links. (*Hint*: You can use the San Antonio Missions Web site, **http://www.nps.gov/saan**, plus two other links from within the same site or other missions-related sites.)
7. In the corresponding frame of the actions layer, add code in the Script pane to make the ComboBox instance operational so that selecting an item in the ComboBox list opens the corresponding Web link.
8. In the Timeline, select the frame in the content layer for the photos page, and then drag two instances of the Button component and one instance of the UILoader component to the Stage. Use the UILoader to display the **mission1.jpg** (300×225) photo when the first Button instance is clicked and the **mission2.jpg** (300×225) photo when the second Button instance is clicked. Add an instance of the ProgressBar component to the UILoader instance so that the progress bar is displayed as the photos are being loaded.
9. In the corresponding frame of the actions layer, add code in the Script pane to make the Button instances operational so that clicking a button displays the corresponding photo in the UILoader instance. The ProgressBar component instance should not be displayed until a photo is loading and it should not be displayed after a photo has completely loaded.
10. In the Timeline, select the frame in the content layer for the tour calculator page, and then use the ComboBox component to list the type of tours (30-Minute Tour, 1-Hour Tour, Bus Tour). Create an input text block for the number of people in the group, create a dynamic text block for the base cost of the tour, a dynamic text block for the cost per person, and another dynamic text block for the total cost of the tour. Add Label component instances to label the input and dynamic text blocks. Add an instance of the Button component to use as a Calculate button. Name all of the instances.
11. In the corresponding frame of the actions layer, add code in the Script pane to make the ComboBox instance and Button instance operational so that when a visitor selects a type of tour, enters the number of people in the group, and clicks the Calculate button, the base cost of the tour, cost per person, and total cost will be displayed.
12. Save and test the msaWebsite.fla file. Make sure the navigational buttons are operational. Also, use the Simulate Download command to test the photos and the ProgressBar. Make sure the Web links work and the tour calculator calculates the correct cost.
13. Create a new mobile Flash file targeted for a mobile device(s) of your choice that uses Flash Lite 2.0 and ActionScript 2.0 for Screen Saver content, and then save the document as **msaMobileAd.fla** in the Tutorial.09\Case4 folder included with your Data Files.
14. Create appropriate content for the mobile ad, and then test the Flash ad in the mobile device(s) you selected and under different lighting conditions.
15. Submit the finished files to your instructor.

Review | Quick Check Answers

Session 9.1

1. a prebuilt movie clip installed with Flash
2. to define the labels that appear on the drop-down list and the values associated with each item
3. prompt
4. break
5. `progress_mc.visible = false;`
6. source

Session 9.2

1. .mpg, .avi, and .dv
2. The amount of data required to represent a few seconds of video can make downloading the video over the Internet a slow process, and compression is used to reduce the size of the video file.
3. Embedded
4. a compressor/decompressor program used to compress video and then decompress it for playback
5. Sorenson Spark, On2 VP6, and H.264 codecs
6. Cue points
7. load external video with playback component

Session 9.3

1. the Flash Player's context menu or the Web browser's Print command
2. `addPage(map_mc, null, null, 3);`
3. map_mc.scaleX = 1.5;
4. map_mc.scaleY = 1.5;
5. False
6. spooler
7. Mobile devices have smaller screen sizes, reduced processor power, and reduced memory; there are a wide variety of devices with different capabilities.
8. Click and drag a device profile from the Online Library to the Local Library or double-click the device profile in the Online Library.

Ending Data Files

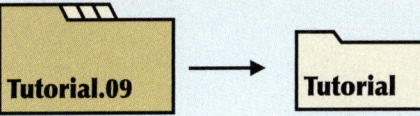

Tutorial.09 →

Tutorial
basketballBlue.flv
basketballRed.flv
jsMobileAd.fla
jsMobileAd.swf
jsWebSite.fla
jsWebSite.swf
SkinUnderPlaySeekMute.swf
photo1.jpg
photo2.jpg

Review
clip.flv
jSoftball.fla
jSoftball.sfw
SkinUnderPlayMute.swf
sbPhoto1.jpg
sbPhoto2.jpg

Case1
katiesWeb.fla
katiesWeb.swf

Case2
aczMobileAd.fla
aczMobileAd.swf
aczWeb.fla
aczWeb.swf
SkinUnderPlayMute.swf
zooClip1.flv
zooClip2.flv

Case3
flower1.jpg
flower2.jpg
flower3.jpg
SkinOverPlaySeekStop.swf
wcLandscape.flv
wcWebSite.fla
wcWebSite.swf

Case4
mission1.jpg
mission2.jpg
msaMobileAd.fla
msaMobileAd.swf
msaWebsite.fla
msaWebsite.swf

Reality Check

Adobe Flash is a professional authoring environment for creating rich, interactive content for the Web, including interactive graphics and advertisements with animation, sound, and video. You can even create entire Web sites using Flash, create online forms to gather data, or display photos in online galleries.

In this exercise, you will use Flash to create a Flash Web site with interactive graphics containing information of your choice, using the Flash skills and tools presented in Tutorials 1 through 9. Use the following steps as a guide to completing your Flash Web site and graphics.

Note: Do *not* include any personal information of a sensitive nature in any graphics or content that you create to be submitted to your instructor for this exercise. Later, you can update the content with such information.

1. Create a list of at least three goals for the Flash Web site.
2. Based on the goals of the Flash Web site, develop a list of objectives. Include the use of audio, video, and bitmaps as part of the objectives for your site.
3. List three characteristics of the site's target audience.
4. Develop an outline with categories and subcategories to correspond to the site's objectives.
5. Develop a storyboard that shows how the site's content and navigation will be organized.
6. Gather relevant graphics for the site's background and banner. Write the headings and content for each of the pages. Gather and prepare the relevant photos, obtain any sound effect clips you plan to use, and obtain and prepare any video clips you plan to show.
7. Sketch the site's design to show how the banner, navigational buttons, page headings, and site graphics will be organized.
8. Create a new document that is at least 600 pixels wide and 400 pixels high. Extend the layer in the document's Timeline to include 10 frames for the site's preloader animation plus an additional 10 frames for each of the site's pages.
9. Make Layer 1 the background layer and insert additional layers, as needed, for content that will be the same on each page of the site, such as the site's navigational buttons.
10. Insert a layer for the content that will be different on each page, insert a layer for the actions, and insert a layer for the labels that identify each page in the site. Rename each layer appropriately.
11. In the labels layer, add labels to identify the preloader section, the home page, and each of the other pages of the site.
12. Based on the site's design, in Frame 10 of the background layer, add a background graphic or image as well as other graphics to the document that will be the same in each page of the site.

13. Create a banner as a movie clip and include the site's title, a bitmap graphic, and a gradient. In Frame 10 of the background layer in the document's main Timeline, add an instance of the banner to the Stage and align it attractively on the banner.
14. Create a movie clip with a motion tween animation of an appropriate graphic and add an instance to the background layer. This animation may be of a rectangle, circle, star, or other shape that appears on all pages of the Web site.
15. Create a Home button symbol. Include a graphic or simple animation in the button's Timeline that is displayed when the pointer is moved over the button. Add a sound effect that plays when the button is clicked.
16. Duplicate and modify the Home button to create buttons for each of the other pages of the site. Add an instance of each button to Frame 10 of the document's main Timeline. Align and space the button instances on the Stage.
17. Assign names to the button instances and then add the ActionScript code to Frame 10 of the actions layer to make the navigational buttons operational.
18. Create a preloader animation in the first frame of the site that includes a graphic and a dynamic text field to display the percentage of the movie's content that has been loaded. Add the ActionScript code to Frame 1 of the actions layer to make the preloader animation work.
19. For each page in your site, create an appropriate page heading and add content and graphics pertinent to that page. Add animated text to one of the pages and a graphic or animation to another page.
20. In one of the site's pages, add a component to display multiple photos saved as JPEG or GIF files. Add buttons that enable the user to choose which photo to display. Include a component to display a progress bar animation as each photo is loaded. Add the ActionScript code to make the buttons and components functional.
21. In one of the site's pages, create a form using input text and dynamic text to enable the user to enter data, click a button, and receive a result based on the data. Add the ActionScript code to process the input values and display the appropriate result.
22. In one of the site's pages, create at least three URL links using a Flash component. The links should be to Web sites related to the site's content based on the objectives you identified for the site. Add the ActionScript code to make the component functional.
23. If you are including video in the site, use Adobe Media Encoder to encode the video clip and to export it in the FLV format. In Flash, import the FLV video, and then add an instance of the video to an appropriate page using the FLVPlayback component and a skin with playback controls.
24. Save the pages, and test them in the Flash Player. Adjust the pages, as needed.
25. Publish the finished document in at least one format other than FLV.
26. Save and close the files, and then submit the completed Web site to your instructor.

Flash ADD 1

Additional Case 1

Creating an Interactive Banner for a Web Site

Case | Metro Children's Museum

The Metro Children's Museum is a nonprofit organization dedicated to providing information and exhibits of special interest to children. The museum has been in operation for more than 15 years and is accredited by the American Museum Association. The museum is open year-round and has recently redesigned its Web site. Cecilia Fuentes, museum director, wants to add a new banner to the Web site to promote an upcoming space shuttle exhibit at the museum. The banner will display several space shuttle pictures and have a link for more information at NASA's Space Shuttle Web site.

Starting Data Files

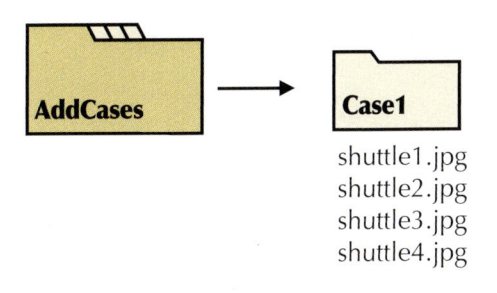

AddCases → Case1
  shuttle1.jpg
  shuttle2.jpg
  shuttle3.jpg
  shuttle4.jpg

ADD 2 Flash | Additional Case 1 Creating an Interactive Banner for a Web Site

1. Create a new document with dimensions of 500 pixels by 300 pixels and a background color of blue (#006699), and then save the file as **shuttlePromo.fla** in the AddCases\Case1 folder included with your Data Files.
2. Insert a regular frame at Frame 40 to extend Layer 1. Create a rectangular border around the inside edges of the Stage, using a stroke color of light yellow (#FFFF99), a stroke style other than Solid, a stroke height of 2, and no fill color.
3. Create a title for the banner by adding a text block at the top of the Stage, using white text and a large font, with the text **Space Shuttle Exhibit**. Center the text block horizontally, and then change the name of Layer 1 to **background**.
4. Import the **shuttle1.jpg**, **shuttle2.jpg**, **shuttle3.jpg**, and **shuttle4.jpg** bitmap files located in the AddCases\Case1 folder included with your Data Files into the document's library.
5. Create a new movie clip symbol named **shuttle1_fade**. In this symbol, insert an instance of the shuttle1.jpg bitmap and use the Info panel to center it in the editing window. Select the shuttle1.jpg bitmap instance and convert it into a movie clip symbol named **shuttle1_mc**.
6. In the shuttle1_fade movie clip Timeline, create a motion tween to fade in the shuttle1_mc instance from a starting alpha amount of 50% to an ending alpha amount of 100%. Set the motion tween span to cover only Frames 1 through 10. Change the name of Layer 1 to **picture**.
7. Insert a new layer and name it **rectangle**. In this layer, draw a filled rectangle with rounded corners over the shuttle1_mc instance. Make the rectangle slightly smaller than the shuttle1_mc instance. Convert the rectangle layer to a mask layer so that the picture layer becomes a masked layer. The picture is displayed through the mask.
8. Insert a new layer and name it **action**, and then add a stop () action to Frame 10 of this layer so that the motion tween is only played once.
9. Repeat Steps 5 through 8 to create a movie clip symbol with a mask and a fade-in effect for each bitmap image that is named based on the bitmap it contains: **shuttle2_fade**, **shuttle3_fade**, and **shuttle4_fade**.
10. In the document's main Timeline, insert a new layer and name it **content**. In Frame 1 of this layer, add an instance of the shuttle1_fade symbol to the left side of the Stage below the title text.
11. Insert a keyframe at Frames 10, 20, and 30. In Frame 10, swap the movie clip instance on the Stage with an instance of the shuttle2_fade movie clip. In Frame 20, swap the instance on the Stage with a shuttle3_fade instance. In Frame 30, swap the instance on the Stage with a shuttle4_fade instance.
12. Insert a new layer and name it **labels**, and then, in the labels layer, add the frame label **shuttle1** at Frame 1, add the frame label **shuttle2** at Frame 10, add the frame label **shuttle3** at Frame 20, and add the frame label **shuttle4** at Frame 30.
13. Create a new button symbol named **picture1 button**. In symbol-editing mode, draw a small triangle (about 36 pixels in width and height) for the button shape using a white fill and black stroke and center the triangle in the editing window. In the button's Over frame, change the color of the triangle's fill and flip the triangle shape vertically to create a rollover effect. Insert a new layer and add a text block with the number 1. The text block should be inside the triangle.

14. Create a duplicate of the picture1 button named **picture2 button**, and then change the text in the symbol to 2. Repeat to create two more duplicates of the button named **picture3 button** and **picture4 button** with the text 3 and 4, respectively.
15. In the document's main Timeline, insert a new layer and name it **buttons**. Insert an instance of each button along the bottom of the Stage, inside the border, and below the picture. Align the button instances horizontally and name the instances **pic1_btn**, **pic2_btn**, **pic3_btn**, and **pic4_btn**.
16. Create a new button symbol named **link button**. In symbol-editing mode, add a text block using a small point size, type **More Info** in the text block, and then center the text. Insert a keyframe in the Over frame and change the font style to Italic. Add a keyframe in the Hit frame and draw a rectangle to cover the text block.
17. In the document's main Timeline, select the buttons layer, and then add an instance of the link button to the right side of the Stage and center it vertically. Assign the name **link_btn** to the instance.
18. Insert a new layer and name it **actions**, and then, in Frame 1, type the following ActionScript code. The stop() action keeps the playhead from advancing. The gotoShuttleSite function is called when the More Info button is clicked.
    ```
    stop();
    function gotoShuttleSite(evtObject:MouseEvent):void {
            var shuttleURL:URLRequest = new URLRequest("http://
    www.nasa.gov/mission_pages/shuttle/main/");
            navigateToURL(shuttleURL);
    }
    link_btn.addEventListener(MouseEvent.CLICK, gotoShuttleSite);
    ```
19. In the Script pane of the Actions panel, type the following ActionScript code after the last line to make the first picture button operational. When the pointer moves over the pic1_btn instance, the onButton1 function is called, which moves the playhead to the frame with the shuttle1 label.
    ```
    function onButton1(evt:MouseEvent):void {
       gotoAndStop("shuttle1");
    }
    pic1_btn.addEventListener(MouseEvent.MOUSE_OVER, onButton1);
    ```
20. Add the appropriate functions and event listeners to the code to make the rest of the picture button instances functional. When the pointer moves over a picture button instance, the playhead should move to the frame with the corresponding label and stop.
21. Save the banner, and then test it in the Flash Player.
22. Submit the finished files to your instructor.

ADD 4 | Flash | Additional Case 1 Creating an Interactive Banner for a Web Site

Ending Data Files

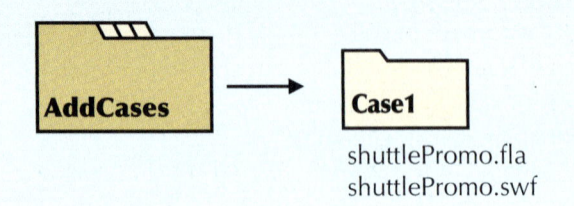

AddCases → **Case1**
shuttlePromo.fla
shuttlePromo.swf

Flash | ADD 5

Additional Case 2

Creating a Web Site with a Banner, a Payment Calculator, a Photos Page, and a Video Page

Case | Discount Autos

Discount Autos of San Antonio has been in business for more than 15 years providing quality used vehicles. Located on the corner of Highway 151 and Alamo Parkway, Discount Autos' sales have been steadily increasing. To continue this trend in sales, owner Allen Bidwell has developed a new marketing campaign. As part of this new campaign, Allen wants to improve the company's Web site by adding a new banner as well as a tool that potential customers can use to calculate their monthly loan payments based on a loan amount, the number of months for the loan, and the interest rate. He also wants the site to include an area to showcase auto specials, using pictures of vehicles and a page to display a video of vehicles for sale.

Starting Data Files

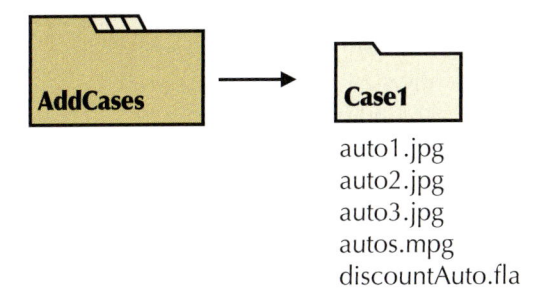

AddCases → **Case1**
auto1.jpg
auto2.jpg
auto3.jpg
autos.mpg
discountAuto.fla

ADD 6 | Flash | Additional Case 2 Creating a Web Site with a Banner, a Payment Calculator, a Photos Page, and a Video Page

1. Open the **discountAuto.fla** file located in the AddCases\Case2 folder included with your Data Files, and save the file as **autoWebsite.fla** in the same folder.
2. In the labels layer, add the label **Video** at Frame 20 and the label **Calculator** at Frame 30.
3. Create two duplicates of the Home button symbol named **Video button** and **Calculator button**. Change the text in the Up and Over frames of the Video button to **Video**. Change the text in the Up and Over frames of the Calculator button to **Calculator**.
4. In the document's main Timeline, select the buttons layer, and then place an instance of the Video button on the Stage to the right of the Photos button and place an instance of the Calculator button to the right of the Video button. Name the Video button instance **video_btn** and name the Calculator button instance **calculator_btn**. Horizontally align and evenly space the four button instances on the Stage.
5. Select Frame 1 of the actions layer, and, then, in the Script pane of the Actions panel, above the Event listeners comment line, type the following lines of code exactly as shown to create the functions for the Video and Calculator buttons.
   ```
   function onVideoClick(evtObject:MouseEvent):void {
           gotoAndStop("Video");
   }
   function onCalcClick(evtObject:MouseEvent):void {
           gotoAndStop("Calculator");
   }
   ```
6. In the Script pane, after the last line of code, type the following lines of code exactly as shown to create the event listeners for the Video and Calculator buttons.
   ```
   video_btn.addEventListener(MouseEvent.CLICK, onVideoClick);
   calculator_btn.addEventListener(MouseEvent.CLICK, onCalcClick);
   ```
7. Test the movie in the Flash Player, clicking each button to make sure it displays its associated page.
8. Create a new movie clip symbol named **autoBanner**. Rename Layer 1 as **background**, and add a regular frame at Frame 120 to extend the layer.
9. Use the Color panel to create a linear gradient. Set the color of the left gradient pointer to light blue (#6188AF) and the right gradient pointer to white. Create a rectangle 604 pixels wide and 100 pixels high using the new gradient as its fill and no stroke. The rectangle will serve as a background for the banner. If necessary, reposition the rectangle so it is centered on the editing window.
10. Create a new layer named **title** for the title text block. Select a font family such as Impact, a text color such as maroon (#660000), and a large point size, and then type **DI$COUNT AUTO$** in the text block. Center the text on the banner. Increase the line spacing slightly for the text, making sure that the text remains centered within the background rectangle.
11. Create a text animation with the dollar sign so that it alternately increases and then decreases in size for a pulsating effect. Start by breaking the title text block into its individual letters and then converting the left $ character into a graphic symbol named **dollar sign**.
12. Edit the dollar sign graphic symbol in symbol-editing mode and create a motion tween. In Frame 5, use the Transform panel to increase the size of the dollar sign to 110% of its original size, being sure to constrain its width and height. In Frame 10, decrease the size of the dollar sign to 100%. In Frame 15, increase its size to 110%. In Frame 20, decrease its size to 100% so that the dollar sign exhibits a pulsating effect throughout the motion tween.

13. In the title layer of the autoBanner Timeline, delete both $ text blocks, and then create a new layer and name it **dollar signs**. In the dollar signs layer, insert an instance of the dollar sign graphic symbol between the letters I and C on the banner, being sure to align the $ with the rest of the letters.
14. In the dollar signs layer, insert another instance of the dollar sign graphic after the letter O in AUTO, being sure to align the $ with the rest of the letters in AUTO. In the Looping section of the Property inspector, change the first frame of the instance to 10.
15. Add a mask effect to the banner using a gradient that moves horizontally across the text. First select all the letters in the title layer (the $ symbols should not be selected) at the same time, and then convert the letters to fills. Copy all the letters at the same time and paste the copies in a new layer above the title layer in the same relative position as the original letters and name the new layer **title2**.
16. Insert a new layer between the title and the title2 layers and name the layer **gradient**. In this layer, draw a rectangle that is about the same size as the Stage. The rectangle should have a linear gradient as its fill and no stroke. The linear gradient should be black on the ends and have a narrow white strip in the middle.
17. Convert the rectangle into a movie clip symbol and then move the rectangle to the left of the letter D. Create a motion tween in Frame 1 of the gradient layer, and in Frame 60, move the rectangle to the right of the $ in AUTO. In Frame 120, move the rectangle back to the left of the letter D. The rectangle should move from the left side of the title text horizontally across to the right side of the title text for 60 frames and then back to the left side of the title text for the next 60 frames.
18. Convert the title2 layer into a mask layer. The gradient layer with the rectangle should be masked. Press the Enter key to test the banner animation. The animation creates a highlight effect on the title text in which the highlight moves across the text and back.
19. Return to the document's main Timeline, and in Frame 1 of the background layer, delete the title text block. Add an instance of the autoBanner to the top of the Stage and align the instance with the left and top sides of the Stage.
20. In the Timeline, select Frame 10 of the content layer and add an instance of the UILoader component to the center of the Stage. Name the instance **photos_mc** and set its width and height at 130 pixels. This is where the auto photos will be loaded.
21. Add a ProgressBar component instance below the UILoader instance. Name the instance **pBar_mc** and in the Component Inspector, type **photos_mc** as its source parameter.
22. Add a Button component instance below the ProgressBar instance. Name the button instance **next_btn** and in the Component Inspector, change its label parameter to **Next**.
23. Insert a keyframe at Frame 10 of the actions layer, and then, in the Script pane of the Actions panel, add the following ActionScript code. When the Next button is clicked, a photo will be loaded into the UILoader instance. The photo filenames

used are auto1.jpg, auto2.jpg, and auto3.jpg. The ActionScript code uses the variable num for the value (1, 2, 3) in the filename. The ProgressBar instance is displayed only while a photo is being loaded.

```
// Code to load photos; set initial value of num to 1
var num:Number = 1;
// Hide the ProgressBar instance
pBar_mc.visible = false;
// Load photos function
function loadPics(eventObj:MouseEvent):void
{

  pBar_mc.visible = true;
  // Create the photo file name using the value in num
  var pic:String = "auto"+num+".jpg";
  // Load the photo into the Loader instance
  var picURLReq:URLRequest = new URLRequest(pic);
  photos_mc.load(picURLReq);
  // Increment the value in num
  num += 1;
  // If num is greater than 3, set it back to 1
  if (num > 3){
     num = 1;


  }


}
// When the loading is complete, hide the ProgressBar instance
function hideBar(eventObj:Event) {
   pBar_mc.visible = false;


}
next_btn.addEventListener(MouseEvent.CLICK, loadPics);
photos_mc.addEventListener(Event.COMPLETE, hideBar);
```

24. Test the movie. In the Photos page, click the Next button three times to display each of the three auto pictures.
25. In Adobe Media Encoder, add the **autos.mpg** file located in the AddCases\Case2 folder included with your Data Files to the queue.
26. Select the FLV – Web Medium (Flash 8 and Higher) preset for the file, change the audio output channel to Mono and the frame rate to 15, and then encode the file.
27. In Flash, in the Timeline, select Frame 20 of the content layer, and use the Import Video wizard to import the **autos.flv** video file. For the delivery option, select Load external video with playback component. In the Skinning dialog box, select SkinUnderPlaySeekMute.swf for the skin.
28. On the Stage, center the FLVPlayback instance on the Stage below the Video text block. In the Parameters tab of the Component Inspector, change the autoPlay value to false.
29. Test the movie. Click the Video button to display the autos.flv video. Click the video's Play button to play the video.
30. In the Timeline, select Frame 30 of the content layer. Create four text blocks using the font family of your choice and a small point size. Type **Loan Amount** for the first text block, **Length of Loan** for the second text block, **Interest Rate** for the third text block, and **Monthly Payment** for the fourth text block. Align the text blocks vertically by their right edges and space them evenly.
31. Create an input text block to the right of the Loan Amount text to be used to enter the amount of the loan. Create another input text block to the right of the Interest Rate text block to be used to enter a rate. Make each input text block 60 pixels wide

and 20 pixels high. In the Property inspector, for each text block, select the Show border around text option, select black (#000000) for the text color, and select Align right for the paragraph format. Name the first input text block instance **loanAmount_txt** and name the second input text block instance **interestRate_txt**.

32. Create a dynamic text block to the right of the Monthly Payment text block. Make the text block 60 pixels wide and 20 pixels high. In the Property inspector, deselect the Show border around text option, select black (#000000) for the text color, and select Align right for the paragraph format. Name the text block instance **monthlyPayment_txt**.

33. Add an instance of the ComboBox component to the right of the Length of Loan text block to be used to select the number of months for the loan. Name the ComboBox instance **lengthOfLoan_mc** and make the instance 65 pixels wide. In the Component Inspector, enter **Months** for the prompt parameter. Add the following labels and data value pairs for the dataProvider parameter: label:**36 mo.**, data:**1**, label:**48 mo.**, data:**2**, label:**60 mo.**, and data:**3**.

34. Add an instance of a Button component to the bottom of the Stage and assign the name **calc_btn** to the instance. In the Component Inspector, type **Estimate** for the label parameter.

35. In the Timeline, insert a keyframe in Frame 30 of the actions layer. In the Script pane of the Actions panel, type the following ActionScript code to calculate the monthly payment and place the result in the Monthly Payment dynamic text block.

```
// Function to determine the monthly payment
function calculatePayment(evt:MouseEvent):void {
   var numberOfMonths:Number;
   switch (lengthOfLoan_mc.value) {
   case "1" :
      numberOfMonths = 36;
      break;
   case "2" :
      numberOfMonths = 48;
      break;
   case "3" :
      numberOfMonths = 60;
      break;
};


   // Convert input values into Integer numbers
   var Loan:Number = int(loanAmount_txt.text);
   var Rate:Number = int(interestRate_txt.text);
   // Determine the monthly interest rate
   var monthlyRate:Number = (Rate/12)/100;
   // Calculate part of the formula using the Math power function
   var factor:Number = 1- Math.pow(1+monthlyRate,-numberOfMonths);
   // Calculate the payment; round to the nearest dollar
   var payment:Number = Math.round((monthlyRate/factor)*Loan);
   // Display the resulting monthly payment
   monthlyPayment_txt.text = String(payment);


}
//Event listener
calc_btn.addEventListener(MouseEvent.CLICK, calculatePayment);
```

36. Save the document, and then test the monthly payment calculator in the Flash Player. Enter **20000** for the loan amount, select **48** mo. for the Months, and enter **5** for the interest rate. Click the Estimate button. The Monthly Payment amount is 461.

37. Submit the finished files to your instructor.

Ending Data Files

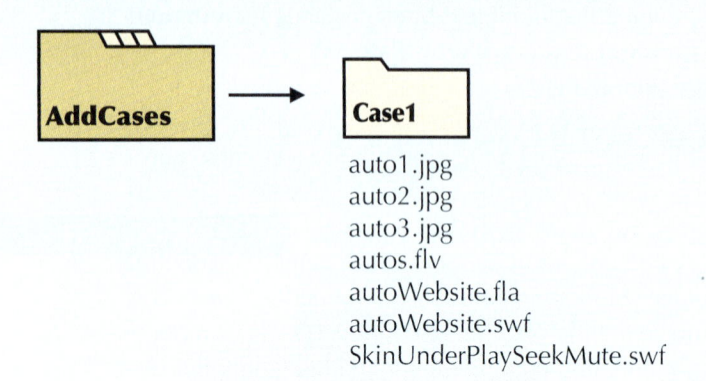

AddCases → **Case1**

auto1.jpg
auto2.jpg
auto3.jpg
autos.flv
autoWebsite.fla
autoWebsite.swf
SkinUnderPlaySeekMute.swf

Appendix A

Flash | FL A1

Becoming an Adobe Certified Associate

Preparing for the Adobe Rich Media Communication Using Adobe Flash CS4 Exam

Adobe Certified Associate

Adobe offers an Adobe Certified Associate (ACA) credential that certifies individuals as having demonstrated the entry-level skills needed to plan, design, build, and maintain effective communications using Flash CS4. The Adobe Certified Associate objectives for Flash CS4 are listed in this appendix. Each objective is followed by a brief discussion of the objective and a reference to the tutorial session in this book where the objective is discussed. For additional training resources, go to *www.adobe.com/education/instruction/ace* and *www.adobe.com/training*.

Starting Data Files

There are no starting Data Files needed for this appendix.

ACA Certification Objectives

Setting Project Requirements

1.1 Identify the purpose, audience, and audience needs for rich media content.

Before adding rich media content such as animations, audio, or video to a project, you should determine the purpose that the content will serve based on the project's goals. Is rich media content necessary to communicate the intended message? Can the message be effectively communicated without rich media content? When starting a new project, develop a plan that includes the goals and objectives of the project to determine whether rich media content is needed and what purpose it will serve.

It is also important to know about the intended audience for the project. You should consider demographic information about the intended audience such as age, gender, education, occupation, and computer literacy, and then use this information in designing the content. The average age of the audience, for example, affects that audience's expectations in terms of rich media content. A younger audience may expect more animations or video than an older, more mature audience.

See Session 7.1 for a discussion of planning a Web site.

1.2 Identify rich media content that is relevant to the purpose of the media in which it will be used (Web sites, mobile devices, and so on).

After outlining the purpose of the project, you can identify appropriate rich media content, such as a Web site or a mobile device. For example, if a Web site's purpose is entertainment, you should identify rich media content such as Flash movies with audio or video to include in the project. An educational Web site, on the other hand, may require interactive rich media content such as Flash movies that present the user with options to choose from based on the information displayed.

See Session 7.1 for a discussion of planning a Web site and developing relevant content. See Session 9.3 for a discussion of creating content for a mobile device.

1.3 Understand options for producing accessible rich media content.

People with disabilities may use assistive technology such as screen readers to read the content on Web pages. A screen reader is a software program that reads the content on the screen so that a visually impaired person can hear it. For Flash media to be interpreted correctly by a screen reader, you should provide accessibility information in Flash using either the Accessibility panel or ActionScript. From the Accessibility panel, you can enter text to describe elements in a Flash movie, which the assistive technology can then read when the movie is played in the Flash Player.

Including accessible rich media content is important to both the client and the target audience. The client, who is providing information, a service, or a product through a Web site, wants the content to be accessible to all members of the target audience. Otherwise, the goals and objectives of the Web site are not met and the needs of members of the target audience with disabilities are not met.

Accessibility elements can be applied to individual objects or to the entire document using the Accessibility panel. Some of the ways to make rich media content accessible include adding keyboard access to all controls such as buttons, adding captions to audio content, or adding alternative text to buttons and images.

See Session 7.1 for a discussion of creating accessible content. For more information, see the Adobe Accessibility Resource Center at *www.adobe.com/accessibility*. You can also find information on Adobe Flash CS4 accessibility at *www.adobe.com/accessibility/products/flash*.

1.4 Demonstrate knowledge of standard copyright rules (related terms, obtaining permission, and citing copyrighted material).

Copyright protects "original works of authorship," including literary, dramatic, musical, artistic, and other intellectual property, or derivative works such as unique compilations or collections of existing content as long as they are fixed in some tangible form, such as on paper or in electronic memory. Since January 1, 1978, copyright in the United States extends for the life of the author plus 70 years. So, works created before January 1, 1923, are now in the public domain, which means they are public property and can be reproduced without permission or charge. Works created after that date may or may not be in the public domain, and should be verified through the Copyright Office. Works created outside the United States are protected in their own countries generally for the life of the author plus 50 or 70 years, depending on the country. A copyright notice includes (1) the symbol © or the word "copyright"; (2) the year of first publication; and (3) the name of the copyright owner.

Elements such as pictures, sound files, and video files are usually copyrighted. To use copyrighted work, whether published or unpublished, you must obtain the copyright owner's permission unless the intended use is a "fair use." Generally, the fair use doctrine allows you to reproduce small amounts of an original work specifically for a review, criticism, or illustration of a point. When creating commercial work, you must be careful to get permission to include anything that is someone else's work. It is a good idea to get permission to reuse anything that you didn't create yourself or that is not owned by the client. Most material on the Internet is copyrighted even if that fact is not explicitly stated.

Whenever you reuse someone else's work—including Web sites, images, sounds, video, and text from the Internet—you should indicate that the content is copyrighted and credit the original source. When you obtain permission, ask the copyright holder for the specific information they want included with the work. If they don't specify the information or the content falls under fair use, include the name of the copyright holder, the copyright year, the work's title, and the source. For works found online, list the URL and the date accessed.

See Session 5.3 for a discussion of acquiring sound files. Also, for more information about copyright issues and laws, visit the U.S. Copyright Office site at *www.copyright.gov*.

1.5 Understand project management tasks and responsibilities.

Large projects often involve a team of designers and developers working together to produce a product. Different team members work on various parts of the project. One person may develop the graphic design of a project, while another person works on the programming requirements of the project. It is important to manage this team to ensure that each member of the team understands his or her role. One way to manage a project and the team is to create a project plan, which outlines the project's scope and goals, lists all the tasks required to complete the project, presents the timeline for completing the tasks, and identifies the resources needed for the project. The project leader assigns tasks to team members along with the timelines or due dates for the tasks. Areas of responsibility must be clearly defined. The plan may be divided into different phases, such as planning, designing, creating, testing, implementing, and launching. The plan should also list what items need to be produced at each phase, such as design specifications, storyboards, flowcharts, Flash files, HTML files, and so on. These items are often referred to as deliverables.

1.6 Communicate with others (such as peers and clients) about design and content plans.

Communication with both the client and team members is essential throughout the life of a project. As you plan a project such as a Web site that incorporates rich media content, you need to meet with the client to establish the project's goals and objectives, including its design and content. Goals that are clearly defined help to ensure that the finished project will meet the client's needs. Also, with open communication during a project, changes can be discussed and implemented as needed. If a team is involved in the project's development, communication among team members is vitally important to ensure that all parts of the project are developed based on the established goals and objectives.

See Session 7.1 for a discussion of working with a client to design a Web site and meeting the client's needs.

Identifying Rich Media Design Elements

2.1 Identify general and Flash-specific best practices for designing rich media content for a Web site.

As you develop Flash content for a Web site, you need to keep in mind how it will be used in the Web site and how the intended user will view the content. Any bitmap images included in the project should be sized and optimized in a program such as Adobe Photoshop before being imported into Flash to ensure that the file size of the bitmap is as small as possible while maintaining the image's desired quality. Sound files and video files embedded in a Flash movie should also be made as small as possible while meeting the goals and objectives of the Web site. When designing rich media content for a Web site, keep in mind the target audience, the type of Internet connection they most likely will have, and their ability to easily interact with rich media (such as audio, video, and so on). The overall goal should be to keep the size of the published SWF files as small as possible to reduce the download time for the user.

Web sites should have consistent elements throughout the site. For example, a consistent navigation system would provide buttons in the same location of each page to make it easy for users to navigate from one part of the Web site to another. You can create consistent buttons by creating a symbol and then duplicating it for the required buttons. Other elements of a Web site that should be uniform are the colors and fonts used throughout the site. You can achieve this consistency in a Web site by using a template. The template created for the Web site, which includes the consistent placement of elements, symbols, fonts, colors, and so on, is then used to create additional pages for the Web site. Using templates reduces the time it takes to develop the pages for a Web site and makes it easier to maintain the Web site. Development of a Web site can be made easier by using motion presets to animate objects. Using motion presets cuts down the time required to achieve certain animation effects.

Before developing content for a Web site, you should determine whether implementing the content by using rich media is appropriate by considering criteria such as the following:

- Will using rich media improve the effectiveness of the message being delivered?
- Will rich media help attract the attention of the user?
- Does the use of rich media improve how information is presented?
- What platforms will the content be delivered to, and how can the rich media be developed so that it is compatible across various platforms?

Using rich media elements such as an interactive menu for selecting multiple levels of information can make it easier for the user to understand how to access the information. Also, if three-dimensional structures are part of the content, using rich media can enhance the user's ability to visualize the structure. Rich media content can also make the user's experience more engaging and improve the likelihood that the content's message will be delivered successfully.

When developing rich media content for other platforms such as Adobe AIR or Adobe Integrated Runtime, you can leverage the skills you learned using Flash. Adobe AIR uses the same technology as used in the Flash Player to play rich media content, except that you can develop content to run on a client computer's desktop rather than a Web browser. When creating video for Adobe AIR applications, you can encode the video files in the FLV format. You can then develop an AIR application using Flash CS4 and with the video files in the FLV format, you can use the same process to import the video into the AIR application as you do to import the video into a Flash movie. As a result, developing video in the FLV format means you can use the same video in both a Flash movie and an Adobe AIR application.

Metadata can be included in a SWF file in the form of Extensible Metadata Platform (XMP) data. The metadata contains information about a file such as its contents, author, title, and copyright status. You can also include metadata specifically for SWFs created for mobile devices. Metadata is entered in the File Info dialog box accessed through the File menu in Flash.

See Session 1.3 for a discussion of colors. See Session 2.3 for a discussion of using library objects and symbols. See Session 3.2 for a discussion of using motion presets to animate objects. See Session 7.2 for a discussion of creating templates for a Web site.

2.2 Demonstrate knowledge of design elements and principles.

Each type of media, such as bitmaps, sound, and video, included in a Flash movie has its own set of characteristics that impact how it is used. As you design a project with rich media content, be aware of these characteristics and design content appropriately. Graphic design principles are important to consider when designing rich media content. These principles guide how you arrange elements on the Stage and help determine the colors you select for the elements. For example, you can use the rule of thirds to arrange graphic elements on the Stage. The rule of thirds method divides the page into three equal sections both vertically and horizontally to form a grid. The lines and intersections of the grid are where you should place the key graphical elements. As you place elements, be aware of how the eye moves along the content, what gets emphasized, how the page is balanced, and what unity and symmetry (horizontal, vertical, diagonal, radial, or asymmetric) is presented. You can improve the legibility of text by using consistent alignment and including margins and white space to delineate different sections of the Web page. Overall, maintain consistency in the design and avoid extraneous elements, overcrowded layout designs, and distracting colors. Also, to avoid having to adapt a design to fit specific content, consider all content that will be included when designing the site to maintain the site's consistency.

2.3 Identify general and Flash-specific techniques to create rich media elements that are accessible and readable.

Many of the elements in a Flash movie can be made accessible and readable by screen readers by setting options in the Accessibility panel. You can select an instance of a movie clip, button, or component on a document's Stage, and then, in the Accessibility panel, specify that the object be made accessible. You can assign a name and a description to the object in the panel. You can also assign a name and description to the entire Flash movie to make it accessible. For keyboard access, you can assign tab order specifying the order in which elements are selected using the Tab key. You can also assign keyboard shortcuts to buttons to provide an option for users to use the keyboard instead of the mouse.

You can improve readability of text by using consistent fonts, avoiding small font sizes, and using proper spacing and appropriate indentation. In the Property inspector, you can specify how anti-aliasing is applied to text depending on whether the text will or will not be animated. For example, for text that will not be animated, select the Anti-alias for readability option.

See Session 7.1 for a discussion of making content accessible using the Accessibility panel.

2.4 Use a storyboard to produce rich media elements.

A storyboard is a diagram that shows a project's major elements and the way these elements are organized. A storyboard may show the state of an animation from one frame to another. A storyboard for a Web site may show a sketch of each page with lines indicating how each page links to other pages in the site. The way the pages link to each other determines the navigation system for the site. You can also include information about specific animations, navigation, images, and text that will be included in the project. Placement of different elements such as buttons and links can also be identified in a storyboard.

See Session 7.1 for an example of using a storyboard during the development of a Web site.

2.5 Organize a Flash document.

A Flash document may consist of many different elements and can easily become complex and unwieldy if you don't organize its contents in a consistent manner. For example, the layers in the Timeline should be named appropriately and similar layers, such as text layers, can be grouped together in layer folders. ActionScript should be placed in one layer at the top of the Timeline and not mixed with other content. Appropriately named labels, such as Start or Loop, should be used when referencing frames rather than using frame numbers. Similar objects in the Library panel should also be arranged in folders to make them easy to find.

See Sessions 1.1, 3.1, and 5.2 for discussions of elements commonly used to organize Flash documents, including folders, scenes, and frame labels.

Understanding the Adobe Flash CS4 Interface

3.1 Identify elements of the Flash interface.

The main elements of the Flash interface include the Stage, pasteboard, Tools panel, Timeline, Property inspector, and panels such as the library. You create the content on the Stage, use the pasteboard as a staging area for content to be animated onto the Stage, use the Timeline to control the frames that make up an animation, and use the Property inspector to set a tool's properties or to change a selected object's attributes. You use the Edit bar to access a document's scenes and symbols as well as to change the magnification of the Stage. You can show and hide panels individually by selecting them in the Windows menu or by pressing the F4 key to hide or show all currently displayed panels at the same time.

See Sessions 1.1 and 1.2 for an overview of the Flash interface including the Stage, pasteboard, Tools panel, Timeline, and Property inspector.

3.2 Use the Property inspector.

The Property inspector provides easy access to the most common attributes of the currently selected tool or object. For example, when you select the Text tool, the Property inspector contains options to select the font, the font style, the text size, text color, and other text attributes. When an object such as text, an image, or a symbol instance is selected, the Property inspector displays properties specific to that object, such as the name of the object, its coordinates, and its dimensions.

See Session 1.2 for an overview of the Property inspector. The Property inspector is used extensively in all tutorials in this book.

3.3 Use the Timeline.

The Timeline contains layers and frames that make up a Flash document. Layers are used to organize the images, animations, and other objects that are part of a document. Frames represent units of time in an animation and may contain different images or different states of the same image. The frame rate determines how many frames are played per a second, creating the illusion of motion, and affects the movie's final file size. The Timeline contains the playhead, a marker that indicates which frame is currently selected in the Timeline.

The Timeline is introduced in Session 1.2 and is used extensively in Tutorial 3 where animation is discussed.

3.4 Use the Motion Editor.

The Motion Editor displays all properties and property keyframes for a selected motion tween and enables you to control the target object's coordinates, rotation, and transformation properties at each property keyframe. You can use the Motion Editor to more precisely modify a motion tween, including changing the timing of the animation and applying easing to create more natural motion. A motion path can be selected on the Stage using the Subselection tool to display its Bezier controls, which you can adjust to modify the path of the object in the motion tween.

See Session 4.1 for a discussion of the Motion Editor and modifying motion paths.

3.5 Understand Flash file types.

A document created in Flash is saved in the FLA format, which contains all of the different elements created in Flash. To revise the document, you edit the FLA file. A published document is saved in the SWF file format and is called a Flash movie. The SWF file requires the Flash Player plug-in to play in a Web browser. Flash files can also be exported in various other file formats, including JPG, GIF, and PNG. You can use the Adobe Media Encoder program to convert video files into the Flash video formats of FLV or F4V files so you can import them into a Flash document.

Other file types in Flash include XMP and XFL files. XMP files contain metadata such as file content information, author, title, and copyright status. XFL files store the same information as an FLA files, but in XML (Extensible Markup Language) format. XFL files can be exported from an application such as InDesign or After Effects and opened in Flash, allowing you to start a project in a separate application and then continue with the project in Flash.

See Session 1.1 for a discussion of bitmap and vector graphic file formats. See Session 2.2 for a discussion of Flash file formats. See Session 5.3 for a discussion of sound file formats that can be used in Flash documents. See Session 6.1 for a discussion of bitmap file formats. See Session 9.2 for a discussion of video file formats that can be imported into Flash.

3.6 Identify best practices for managing the file size of a published Flash document.

It is important to keep the size of a published Flash document as small as possible because the larger the file size, the longer it takes to download to a user's computer. A Flash document's file size increases as you add more graphic elements as well as bitmap, audio, and video elements.

Keep the number of bitmap images in a document to a minimum and optimize bitmap images before importing them into Flash. Also keep the number and size of sound and video files to a minimum and do not embed video files into a Flash document unless it is a very short video. When adding graphics that are similar to each other, convert the graphic to a symbol and then use multiple instances of the symbol. Also, keep shape tweens to a minimum as they can be processor-intensive and can affect the movie's performance.

See Session 6.1 for a discussion of bitmap files. See Session 9.2 for a discussion of video files.

Building Rich Media Elements by Using Flash CS4

4.1 Make rich media content development decisions based on your analysis and interpretation of design specifications.

The rich media elements you create for a project should be based on the design specifications developed as part of the planning process. Otherwise, the resulting project may not meet the needs of the client and may not be accepted by the client. This could lead to having to re-create the rich media elements from scratch and a loss of time and/or money. Consider the technical requirements for the rich media content you create and how it impacts the capability of the user to view the content. Technical factors that impact how the target audience receives the rich media content include download speed, screen resolution, operating system, and type of browser used.

See Session 7.1 for a discussion of the planning process and developing design specifications for a Web site. See Session 9.3 for a discussion of designing and creating content for a mobile device.

4.2 Adjust document properties.

To adjust a document's properties, use the Document Properties dialog box, which is accessible through the Modify command on the Application bar or through the Edit button in the Property inspector. The Document Properties dialog box enables you to set the dimensions, background color, frame rate, and ruler units of a Flash document.

See Session 1.2 for a discussion of changing a document's properties.

4.3 Use Flash guides and rulers.

You can add vertical and horizontal guides on the Stage as you work with a document. Guides are lines that help you to align objects on the Stage. You drag guides from the rulers onto the Stage. You can also change the guide colors and other properties. Rulers display the document's measurement units, such as pixels, and can be used to place objects on the Stage according to specific coordinates.

See Session 1.2 for more information about guides and rulers.

4.4 Use tools on the Tools panel to select, create, and manipulate graphics and text.

The Tools panel, located on the left side of the Flash workspace, contains the tools that you use to draw, paint, select, and modify Flash graphics. The Tools panel also contains tools to change the magnification level of the Stage and to select colors. Tools can be selected in the Tools panel by clicking the tool's button or by pressing the tool's keyboard shortcut. Some tools in the Tools panel are hidden behind other tools and can be accessed by clicking and holding the visible tool button to open a pop-up menu, and then clicking the hidden tool. You can also collapse the display of the Tools panel by clicking the double-arrow icon above the Tools panel.

See Session 1.1 for a discussion of bitmap and vector images. See Session 1.2 for more information about the using the Tools panel and its tools. See Session 1.3 for a discussion of using the selection tools and techniques. See Sessions 2.1, 3.1, and 4.3 for a discussion of using the various drawing tools and tools for working with shapes. See Session 1.3 and Session 6.2 for a discussion of using the Color panel to apply and create colors.

4.5 Import and modify graphics.

Flash CS4 can use graphics created in other applications such as Adobe FreeHand, Adobe Fireworks, Adobe Illustrator, and Adobe Photoshop. Vector graphics and bitmaps can be imported in a variety of file formats such as PNG, JPG, and PSD. When importing files, such as PSD files from Photoshop, the Import dialog box includes options you can select to preserve elements of the imported file such as Photoshop layers. You can import graphics into the Library panel or directly onto the Stage.

See Session 1.1 for a discussion of graphic file types. See Sessions 6.1 and 6.2 for a discussion on importing and working with bitmaps. See Session 3.3 for how to swap a graphic on the Stage with one stored in the library. Also, in the Flash Help system, see the Using imported artwork topics.

4.6 Create text.

In Flash, you can create text blocks in a variety of colors, sizes, and fonts using the Text tool. You can create static text blocks, which contain text that doesn't change after the document is published. You can also create dynamic text blocks or input text blocks. A dynamic text block can be updated while the Flash movie is playing as a result of a calculation or from external data. An input text block allows the user to enter text in forms or surveys. Text can be created in a fixed-width text block that doesn't change as you type, or in a single-line text block that extends as you type. You can check the spelling of text using the Check Spelling command.

See Session 2.2 for a discussion of creating text.

4.7 Adjust text properties.

After you have created a text block, you can change the text properties by selecting the text block and adjusting settings in the Property inspector. You can change the text block's font, size, color, font style, and alignment. You can also select a font-rendering method, which allows you to specify an anti-alias method for text that is to be animated. Text that will not be animated can be rendered differently for improved readability. In addition, text properties such as the text size can be changed using the commands on the Text menu. Also, graphic filters, such as a drop shadow, can be applied to text using the Property inspector.

See Session 2.2 for a discussion of setting text properties. See Session 2.3 for a discussion of adding graphic filters.

4.8 Create objects and convert them to symbols, including graphics, movie clips, and buttons.

Existing graphic objects such as shapes and lines drawn with Flash can be converted to symbols. You can also create new symbols from scratch within the symbol-editing window. Symbols have one of three types of behavior: movie clip, graphic, or button. You can easily change a symbol's behavior type at any time. Movie clips contain their own Timeline and operate independently of the document's main Timeline. A graphic symbol's Timeline operates in sync with the Timeline of the movie in which it appears. A button symbol has its own four-frame Timeline with Up, Over, Down, and Hit frames that can be used to make a symbol into an interactive button. You can also create invisible buttons by creating a new button symbol with content only in its Hit frame. However, you should avoid invisible buttons when creating accessible documents. You can also use symbols from other Flash documents in the current document.

See Session 2.3 for a discussion of creating symbols. See Sessions 5.1 and 7.2 for a discussion of creating button symbols.

4.9 Understand symbols and the library.

Each document has a library whose contents can be viewed and managed using the Library panel. Symbols are stored in the document's library and instances of the symbols are then added to the Stage. Multiple instances of the same symbol can be used in a document, but only one copy of the symbol is stored. This reduces the ultimate file size, ensures consistency of a symbol, and allows editing multiple instances of a symbol at once. In addition, you can incorporate symbols created in one document into other documents. To add an instance of a symbol, you drag it from the Library panel to the Stage. Symbols can also be used with the Spray Brush tool as patterns that can be applied to objects. You can select a symbol to use for the Spray Brush tool from the Property inspector.

See Session 2.3 for a discussion of the Library panel, symbols, and instances of symbols.

4.10 Edit symbols and instances.

Each symbol instance in a document can be edited without changing the symbol in the document's library. For example, you can change the size, orientation, or color tint of one instance without affecting other instances of the same symbol or the symbol. If you modify the symbol, however, all the instances of that symbol also change. You modify a symbol by placing it in symbol-editing mode. A symbol can be edited by itself in symbol-editing mode or it can be edited in place with the rest of the graphics on the Stage dimmed.

See Session 2.3 for a discussion of editing symbols and instances.

4.11 Create masks.

A mask is created using a mask layer, which hides the contents of the layer below it, called the masked layer. The contents of the masked layer are hidden except for the area covered by the object on the mask layer. The object can be a filled shape such as an oval or it can be text. The content of the masked layer shows through only when the object is over it. You can convert any layer into a mask layer. You can also create an animation in a mask layer to show different areas of the masked layer throughout the animation.

See Session 4.1 for a discussion of creating masks.

4.12 Create animations (changes in shape, position, size, color, and transparency).

Objects in a Flash document can be animated by creating different states of an object in different frames and playing the frames over time. An animation can be created by changing the object's shape, size, color, or transparency over time. In Flash, you can create a frame-by-frame animation or a tween animation (which can be a motion tween, a classic motion tween, or a shape tween). In a frame-by-frame animation, you create or modify the objects in each frame. In a motion tween, you change the object's properties in any frame within its tween span. You can also adjust a motion tween's motion path. In a classic tween animation, you change the objects in the starting and ending frames, and then Flash creates the content in the in-between frames. In a shape tween, you create the graphic shape in the starting and ending frames, and Flash creates the tweened frames. Shape tweens should be created with simple shapes and used sparingly.

See Tutorial 3 for a discussion of the elements of an animation; using the Timeline to create frames and layers for an animation; creating Timeline effects, frame-by-frame animations, and tween animations; and using motion presets. See Tutorial 4 for a discussion of motion paths, the Motion Editor, and animating text blocks.

4.13 Add simple controls through ActionScript 3.0.

ActionScript 3.0 is the latest version of the programming language in Flash CS4, which you can use to add interactive elements to a Flash movie. With ActionScript, you can add functionality to buttons as well as control the sequence in which a movie's frames are played. You add ActionScript code through the Script pane in the Actions panel.

See Session 8.1 for an introduction to ActionScript 3.0, using simple actions, object-oriented programming, and event-handling concepts.

4.14 Import and use sound.

Flash offers several ways to use sounds. You can add sounds that play continuously, such as a background sound. You can add sound effects to instances of buttons to make them more interactive. For example, you can add a sound that plays when a user clicks a button. You can add sounds that are synchronized with the animation, such as a sound simulating a clap of thunder that coincides with an animation of a lightning bolt. Because Flash has limited options for editing sounds, you should edit sound files in a sound-editing program before importing them into Flash.

See Session 5.3 for a discussion of importing and using sounds in Flash.

4.15 Add and export video.

Various video formats may be imported into a Flash document. After video is captured and prepared using a video-editing program, it can be encoded using Adobe Media Encoder to create a Flash video file in an FLV or F4V format. The Flash video file can then be imported into a Flash document using the Import Video wizard, which presents a series of dialog boxes in which you select the video file, select playback options, and select a skin or prebuilt playback controls. The Video Import wizard creates an instance of the FLVPlayback component on the Stage.

See Session 9.2 for a discussion of importing and using video in Flash.

4.16 Publish Flash documents.

Documents created in Flash are usually made available for use on the Web and must be published or exported into a format readable by a Web browser. A Flash document is published in the SWF file format and plays in the Flash Player plug-in. You can also publish or export a Flash document in a different file format such as JPEG, GIF, or PNG, depending on where and how the file is to be used. You specify how you want an FLA document published in the Publish Settings dialog box. The Formats tab lists the many file formats in which you can publish a Flash document, such as Flash (.swf), HTML (.html), or JPEG Image (.jpg). Each file format selected on the Formats tab has a corresponding tab in the Publish Settings dialog box with additional options and settings for that file type.

Flash Player detection may be added to a Web page to detect for the installation of the Flash Player plug-in on the user's computer. If the Flash Player is not installed or if the version installed is older than that required to display the SWF file, the user will be prompted to install the plug-in. The detection of Flash Player is important because you want to ensure that the site viewer can view the SWF movie. If the SWF movie does not play, you want to user to know why. You can have Flash create the code needed for Flash Player detection in the Publish Settings dialog box. Select the HTML (.html) tab, and in the HTML publish settings, select Detect Flash Version and then specify the version you want detected. When you publish the document, the code is created in the HTML file.

See Session 6.3 for a discussion of publishing Flash documents.

4.17 Make a document accessible.

A Flash document or an individual object in a document can be made accessible to a screen reader using the Accessibility panel by assigning a name and description to the document or selected object. Select an object on the Stage, such as a movie clip, to make it accessible. Select no objects on the Stage to make the entire Flash document accessible. You can also hide objects from screen readers by selecting the object on the Stage and then deselecting Make object accessible in the Accessibility panel. You hide objects that convey no content or are repetitive, in which case you don't want the screen reader to read the same object's name and description repeatedly.

See Sessions 7.1 and 7.2 for a discussion of accessibility issues and the Accessibility panel.

Evaluating Rich Media Elements

5.1 Conduct basic technical tests.

After you have completed a Flash document, you should test it to ensure that the published movie works as designed and it doesn't cause any errors. You should test it on the most common Web browsers, especially those you expect the target audience to use. You should also test it in both the Windows and Macintosh computer platforms. When conducting a test of the Flash movie, be sure to navigate to all parts of the movie, to play all sounds and videos, and to test all interactive elements of the movie. You can also use the Simulate Download command in the Flash Player to simulate how the movie plays at different download speeds. If part of the movie loads too slowly based on a target download speed, you can make changes to improve performance. The Bandwidth Profiler is another option in the Flash Player you can use to test a movie. The Bandwidth Profiler graphically displays how much data is sent for each frame based on the download speed you select. You can use this information to make changes to the content in frames that are slowing playback of the movie.

When you test a movie using the Test Movie command, a new SWF file is created and played. However, if you preview the movie in HTML, you get to see how the SWF movie is displayed in a Web browser, which better simulates the experience of the user.

Textual content in a Flash document should be checked for correct spelling. This can easily be done using the Check Spelling command on the Text menu, which opens a dialog box with suggestions for potentially misspelled words.

See Session 2.2 for a discussion of checking text for spelling errors. See Sessions 3.2 and 6.3 for a discussion on previewing and testing a movie.

5.2 Identify techniques for basic usability tests.

Usability, as it relates to Flash, means that the user can use the finished Flash movie easily and quickly. The focus of usability testing is on the user experience. You can conduct a usability test by observing a group of users as they perform various tasks with the Flash movie to see how effectively they interact with it. As a result of this observation, as well as interviews with the users, you may determine that certain aspects of the Flash movie need to be changed to improve its usability.

For more information on usability testing, see *www.useit.com*.

Glossary/Index

Note: Boldface entries include definitions.

3D Rotation tool, FL 197

3D space A three-dimensional effect created by including the z axis as a property of a movie clip instance as well as its x and y axes. FL 196–198

3D Translation tool, FL 197

A

ACA (Adobe Certified Associate), preparation for, FL A1–A12

accessibility
    making document, object accessible, FL 326, FL A11
    making rich media accessible, FL A5
    making Web sites accessible, FL 322

action An instruction that is used to control a document's interactive elements. FL 242–243
    adding using Actions panel, FL 243–249
    applying using Behaviors panel, FL 356–357

Actions panel
    adding actions using, FL 243–249
    creating ActionScript, FL 347–352

Actions toolbox, expanding, collapsing, FL 382

ActionScript The programming language used in Flash to add interactive elements such as playback and navigation controls to documents. FL 242
    2.0, FL 325
    2.0 vs. 3.0, FL 376
    3.0, programming with, FL 376–388
    adding controls with, FL A10
    creating input forms, FL 401–412
    creating links to Web sites, FL 388–394
    creating printable content, FL 456–462
    creating using Action panel, FL 347–352
    described, FL 242
    using loadMovieNum action, FL 346–347
    versions of, FL 243

ActionScript Virtual Machine 2 (AVM2) The Flash Player built-in code that plays Flash movies. FL 376

adding
    actions using Actions panel, FL 243–249
    actions using Behaviors panel, FL 356–357
    ActionScript code to buttons, FL 347–350
    animated text, FL 184–190
    animations to button frames, FL 341–343
    background sounds, FL 255–256
    backgrounds to Web pages, FL 330–331
    buttons from Buttons library, FL 227–229
    comments to scripts, FL 386–387
    duplicate scenes, FL 127–129
    easing effects to motion tweens, FL 175–177
    event listeners, FL 384–386, FL 393
    events, event handling, FL 384–388
    Flash components, FL 430
    Flash graphics to Web pages, FL 301–303
    layer folders, FL 121–123
    motion presets, FL 139–140
    numeric feedback to preloaders, FL 410–411
    scenes, FL 185
    sound effects, FL 257–258

    sounds to buttons, FL 253–254
    strokes, fills, FL 32–33
    text to button instances, FL 232
    videos to Flash documents, FL 443–455

addition, arithmetic operators, FL 406–407

additional cases, ADD 1–10

addPage() method, FL 459–462

Adobe Certified Associate (ACA) objectives, FL A1–A12

Adobe Device Central A stand-alone program installed with Flash that is used to create and test content on a wide variety of mobile devices without having to load the content on all the actual devices. FL 463, FL 465, FL 469–471

Adobe Dreamweaver, FL 301, FL 302

Adobe Fireworks, editing bitmaps, FL 268

Adobe Flash Media Server Server software that provides Web developers features to add interactive audio and video to Web sites. FL 447–448

Adobe Media Encoder An encoder program installed with Flash that converts video into a Flash video file format. FL 444–447

Adobe Flash CS4 Professional (Flash) A program that was originally designed to create small, fast-loading animations for use in Web pages that has evolved into an advanced authoring tool for creating interactive media that range from animated logos to Web site navigational controls and entire Web sites to engaging content for mobile devices. FL 1
    authoring panels, FL 46
    developing Web media in, FL 3–6
    documents. See documents
    exiting, FL 47
    getting Help, FL 44–47
    overview of, FL 1
    program window. See workspace
    starting, FL 6–8
    Web sites. See Flash Web sites
    working with objects in, FL 32–44

Adobe Integrated Runtime (AIR), FL A4–A5

Adobe Photoshop, editing bitmaps, FL 268

Adobe Premier, FL 444

AIFF sound files, FL 251

aligning
    objects, FL 327
    objects on the Stage, FL 240–242
    text, FL 84

alpha amount A percentage from 0 to 100 that controls the transparency of an image; 0% makes the object completely transparent; 100% makes the object completely opaque. FL 272

anchor point A point on a stroke or outline of a fill with no stroke that can be dragged with the Subselection tool to modify the stroke or fill. FL 40–41

angle brackets (<>), comparison operators, FL 398

animating
    bitmaps, FL 272–279
    individual letters, FL 191–196
    text blocks, FL 183–190
    text over pictures, FL 328–329

animation A series of images whose content in each image changes and that is displayed in sequence to give the illusion of motion. FL 3
    adding to button frames, FL 341–343
    anti-aliasing for, FL 84
    applying motion preset, FL 137–140
    bitmap and vector, FL 3
    control object's speed in, FL 135
    creating, FL 129–140, FL A10
    creating classic tween, FL 142–148
    creating frame-by-frame, FL 150–155
    creating preloader, FL 396–398
    creating using mask layers. See mask layers
    creating using onion skinning, FL 200–203
    creating with nested symbols, FL 198–200
    elements of, FL 116–117
    fade effects, FL 272–279
    modifying using Motion Editor, FL 172–183
    movie clips. See movie clips
    object-based, FL 129
    synchronizing with videos, FL 446–447
    testing, FL 141, FL 154–155, FL 182
    troubleshooting with Movie Explorer, FL 209–211
    using graphic symbols in, FL 148–150
    using inverse kinetics, FL 205–207
    using sounds in, 250–259
    using Timeline, FL 13–14

anti-aliasing Part of the rendering process that smoothes the edges of text displayed on a computer screen to provide high-quality, clear text in Flash documents. FL 84, FL 231, FL A9

Application bar, FL 7–8

argument See parameter

arithmetic operator An operator such as +, –, *, or / that is used to indicate addition, subtraction, multiplication, or division, respectively. FL 406–407

armature A chain of bones. FL 205–207

assignment operator An operator that assigns a value to a variable such as the equal sign (=). FL 406–407

audience, target for Web sites, FL 321–322, FL A2

authoring panels, FL 46

AVM2 (ActionScript Virtual Machine), FL 376

B

background colors
    changing Stage, FL 31
    specifying, FL 57

background layers, adding, FL 330–331

background sounds
    adding, FL 255–256
    synchronizing, FL 256–257

behavior A predefined ActionScript script that is attached to objects and provides functionality such as loading external bitmap files; only available with ActionScript 2.0 or earlier. FL 356–357
    of symbols, FL A9

Bezier handles Handles used to modify the curve of the path around a control point by dragging or extending the endpoints of the handles. FL 168

bitmap animation Animation created by playing back a sequence of bitmap still images to produce the perception of motion. FL 3

bitmap graphic A graphic that includes a row-by-row list of every pixel in the graphic, along with each pixel's color. FL 2
    animating, FL 272–279
    converting to vector graphics, FL 281–284
    importing, FL 268–269
    loading external image files, FL 352–356
    setting properties, FL 269–272
    working with, FL 268, FL A7

bone A structure used to connect symbol instances or interior parts of a shape so that moving one bone, moves the other bones relative to the bone that initiated the movement; used to more easily create natural motions. FL 205–207

bounding boxes, FL 78–79

Break Apart command, FL 183–184, FL 291

break statements, FL 433–434

browsers
    previewing files in, FL 10–11, FL 89
    viewing SWF files in, FL 5–6

button instances
    changing labels on, FL 437
    creating, FL 388–391

button symbol An interactive button that has its own four-frame Timeline; each frame represents a different state of the button and can contain different content. FL 95

buttons
    adding actions to, FL 244–245
    adding ActionScript code to, FL 347–350
    adding from Buttons library, FL 227–229
    adding sounds to, FL 253–254
    creating custom, FL 232–240
    creating for navigation bar, FL 340–345
    editing instances, FL 229–231
    states of, FL 226–227

byte Equivalent to one character of information. FL 394

C

calcTotalButton, FL 405

Calculator pages, creating, FL 401–412

call To execute a function from within a script in which it is defined. FL 380

case statements, FL 433–434

cases, additional, ADD 1–10

centering text, FL 84

certification, Adobe Certified Associate (ACA), FL A1–A12

changes, undoing, FL 39

changing
    document properties, FL 30–32
    object colors, FL 36–37
    strokes, fills, FL 71–83
    view of Timeline, FL 119–121

Check Spelling command, FL 85–88

child movie clip A nested movie clip instance. FL 199

child object An object inside the movie clip. FL 322

circles, drawing, FL 57

class A blueprint for an object that describes the properties, methods, and events for the object; all objects in ActionScript are defined by classes. FL 391

classic tween A type of tween for creating motion in a document where changes are defined in the content using keyframes; tinted blue in the Timeline and an arrow appears between the keyframes. FL 142–148

client computer A user's computer. FL 394

codec A video compressor/decompressor program. FL 444

Color panel, FL 35–37, FL 287

color pointer The marker in the gradient definition bar in the Color panel that indicates each time the color in a gradient changes. FL 287

colors
    background. *See* background colors
    bitmap-to-vector graphics conversion, FL 281, FL 283
    changing grid, FL 30
    copying using Eyedropper tool, FL 73
    pixel, FL 29
    specifying fill, FL 59–60
    using controls, Color panel, FL 35–37
    using gradients, FL 286–289

combining bitmap and vector graphics, FL 2–3

ComboBox component, using, FL 430–435

commands
    See also specific command
    copying, FL 91

control point A place on a motion path where a change was made to the path or to the target object. FL 168

comment A note within the ActionScript code that explains what is happening but does not cause any action to be performed and is not required for the actions to work. FL 13, FL 386–387

Common Buttons Library, FL 232

comparison operator An operator used in conditional statements; for example, ==, >, <, and !=, which are used to test for equality, greater than, less than, and not equal to, respectively. FL 398, FL 406

component A prebuilt movie clip installed with Flash that includes a set of user interface and video components with parameters that can be changed in the Component inspector panel. FL 430

compression The process of taking away some of a file's data to reduce its size. FL 250–252, FL 269, FL 296, FL 444

compressor An encoder program that compresses video. FL 444

conditional statement A statement in which one value is compared to another and based on the result of the comparison, certain actions are performed. For example, the if action tests a condition; if the condition is true, it performs actions within the curly braces that follow it. FL 398

constructor A special method used to create instances of objects based on a class. FL 391–392

content
    creating mobile, FL 463–471
    creating printable, FL 456–462
    designing rich media, FL A4–A6
    developing Web site, FL 322–323

control point on motion paths, FL 168

controls
    adding, FL A10
    color, FL 35–37

easing, FL 175–177
frame, FL 117
panel, FL 17

converting
    bitmaps to vector graphics, FL 281–284
    graphics to symbols, FL 95–96, FL 131
    objects to symbols, FL A9
    shapes to drawing objects, FL 74
    text blocks to symbols, FL 144
    text to fills, FL 183–184, FL 291
    text to symbols, FL 191

copying
    animated symbols, FL 153–154
    buttons, FL 237–240
    colors with Eyedropper tool, FL 73
    commands, FL 91
    fill or stroke properties, FL 72–73
    frames, FL 123–124
    and repositioning objects, FL 80–82
    symbols, FL 98, FL 145

copyright rules, FL A3

corner radii
    creating specific, FL 57–58
    rounded corners, FL 61

coupons, creating printable, FL 457–459

cue point A marker set in a video to synchronize the video with animation, graphics, or text in the Flash document. FL 446

curly braces ({}) and ActionScript, FL 381, FL 382

curves, drawing curved lines, FL 68–71

customizing
    buttons, FL 232–240
    colors, FL 36
    gradients, FL 287–289

D

Data Files, obtaining, FL 5

debugging using Compiler Errors panel, FL 392, FL 409, FL 438

decompressing files, FL 250–252

decompressor A decoder program that decompresses video before it can be played. FL 444

deleting
    actions from scripts, FL 245
    layers, FL 185

designing rich media content, FL A2–A6

displaying
    document elements with Movie Explorer, FL 209
    grid, rulers, guides, FL 27–30
    guides, FL 63
    layers, FL 14
    Library panel, FL 133
    photos using UILoader component, FL 436–439

Distribute to Layers command, FL 194–196

division, arithmetic operators, FL 406

dock A collection of individual panels or panel groups. FL 17–18

document A Web media created in Flash; includes text, static images, sound, and video as well as animations. FL 3
    See also Web pages

accessibility, FL 326
adding buttons to, FL 227–229
adding navigation bar to, FL 345
adding sounds to, FL 251–259
adding text to, FL 83–85
adding videos to, FL 443–455
animations. *See* animations
changing properties, FL 30–32
closing, FL 47
creating for mobile devices, FL 464
creating new, FL 325
creating printing capabilities for, FL 457
exporting as image, FL 300
layers. *See* layers
multiple scenes in, FL 124–125
organizing, FL A6
organizing using layers, FL 247
previewing, FL 9–10
properties, FL A8
publishing, FL 357–358, FL A11
selecting publish settings, FL 295–299
undoing steps using History panel, FL 90–94
using Movie Explorer with, FL 208–211
Web media, described, FL 3–4

document-level undo The undo mode in which the steps being reversed affect the entire document. FL 93

Document window, FL 8, FL 12

documenting Web site specifications, FL 324

dot notation A dot (.) is used to link an object name to its properties and methods. FL 377

Down frame The frame in a button symbol that shows what the button looks like when the user clicks it. FL 226, FL 341

downloading
    additional components, FL 430
    Flash templates, FL 332
    progressive, FL 448

drawing
    lines and shapes, FL 56–71
    lines with Line tool, FL 76–77
    modes, FL 33–35
    objects, FL 33–35

drop shadow effects, applying, FL 101–104

dynamic, and input text, FL 401–405

dynamic text field A field that contains text that can be updated as a result of actions within the SWF file or with information from a Web server when the document is published and displayed in a Web browser. FL 83

E

Ease value, motion tweens, FL 130

easing How fast or slow an object moves throughout an animation, which can make the animation appear more natural. FL 175–177

ECMAScript, FL 243

Edit bar, FL 7–8

editing
    bitmaps, FL 268
    button instances, FL 229–231
    buttons, FL 234–240
    imported graphics, FL 88

instances, FL 100–101, FL A9
layer content, FL 121
objects within groups, FL 34
personal dictionary, FL 86
symbols, FL 99–101, FL A9
videos, FL 444

editing handles on gradient fills, FL 292

effects
    animating text, FL 183–184
    creating 3-D graphic, FL 196–198
    easing, adding to motion tweens, FL 175–177
    fade-in, FL 190
    rollover, FL 226
    sounds. *See* sounds

embedded video An encoding method that places a video in a Flash document, similar to the way that bitmaps are imported and become part of the document. FL 448

encoding The process of compressing a video. FL 444–447

Enlarge modifier button, FL 66, FL 69

Envelope modifier, FL 79

equal sign (=) comparison operator, FL 398

errors
    ActionScript, FL 384
    debugging using Compiler Errors panel, FL 392, FL 409, FL 438
    syntax, FL 434–435

Essentials layout, panels in, FL 17–18

event A situation that occurs when a movie is playing, such as when the user is interacting with a button, such as clicking a button with the mouse and then releasing it, or pressing a key. FL 242

event handler The part of a script that tells Flash how to handle an event. FL 242, FL 384–388

event listener A method that the Flash Player executes in response to specific events; every object that has an event has an event listener. FL 384–386, FL 393

event object An actual event such as the clicking of the mouse button and contains information about the event such as its properties. FL 382

event sound Sound not synchronized with the Timeline that begins playing only after the entire sound has downloaded completely. FL 256–257

event source The object to which an event will happen, such as a button instance; also known as the event target. FL 384

exiting Flash, FL 47

export To convert a Flash document into another file format such as GIF or JPG, which combines all the individual elements of a document into one graphic. FL 88, FL 300

expression A statement that is used to assign a value to a variable. FL 406–409

Extensible Metadata Platform (XMP), FL A5, FL A7

external library A library that contains the symbols for a stored document and makes these symbols available to the currently active document. FL 334–335

Eyedropper tool The tool used to copy the fill or stroke properties of one object and apply them to another object or to copy the properties of a text block and apply them to another text block. FL 72–73

F

fade effects, animation, FL 272

fade-in effects, adding, FL 190

fall-off point The spot where a gradient shifts or transitions from one color to another. FL 287

field A unit of data such as a person's age or phone number. FL 83

file formats, publishing Flash documents in various, FL 295, FL A7

files
    compressing, decompressing, FL 250–252
    Flash types, FL A7
    loading external image, FL 352–356
    streaming, FL 394

Fill color control, FL 43

filling text with gradients, FL 291–292

fill An area in a Flash graphic that can be painted with color; may or may not be enclosed by strokes. FL 32–33
    applying gradient, FL 289–292
    applying with Paint Bucket tool, FL 72–73
    changing, FL 71–83
    converting text to, FL 183–184
    creating, FL 32–33
    specifying colors, FL 35–36, FL 59–60

filter A special graphic effect, such as a drop shadow, than can be applied to movie clips, buttons, and text. FL 101–104

Fit in Window command, FL 25

fixed-width text block A text block whose width doesn't change as text is typed; text wraps to create new lines as needed. FL 83

FLA file The Flash authoring document being worked with while content is developed using Flash. FL 4

Flash CS4. *See* Adobe Flash CS4 Professional

Flash Exchange An Adobe Web site with resources such as templates created by and for Flash developers. FL 332

Flash Kit, FL 250

Flash Lite A smaller version of the Flash Player that is used to play Flash content on a wide variety of mobile devices. FL 463–469

Flash movie Another name for an SWF file. FL 4, FL A7, FL A12

Flash Player
    choosing version for publication, FL 295
    previewing files in, FL 10–11

Flash Player plug-in Software that allows SWF files in an HTML file to be viewed in a Web browser; also provides controls for magnifying the SWF file's view, changing its quality, printing it, and other functions. FL 4

Flash Web sites
    See also Web sites
    creating contents for, FL 325–331
    creating navigation system, FL 318–319
    example of, FL 319–320
    navigation systems, FL 316–317
    planning, FL 320–325
    structure of, FL 316–320

FLV video format, FL 444, FL 448, FL A4–A5

FLVPlayback component, FL 448–455

folders
  adding layer, FL 121–123
  root, FL 97
fonts, specifying in text blocks, FL 84
forms, creating input, FL 401–412
forward slashes (/) and script comments, FL 386
frame An element that contains the content for an animation and represents a particular instant in time; each frame can contain different images or different states of the same image. FL 116–117
  adding actions to, FL 245–249
  changing dimensions of, FL 120
  checking number before modifying content, FL 119
  described, using, FL 116–117
  repositioning within layer, FL 146–147
  selecting, copying, moving, FL 123–124
  tweened, FL 129
frame-by-frame animation An animation in which the content for each individual frame is created manually. FL 150–155, FL 200–203
frame label A name assigned to a keyframe that appears in the Timeline. FL 246–248
frame rate The number of frames that play each second in a Flash document or in a video. FL 443
frame size The width and height dimensions of a video. FL 443
Free Transform tool The tool used to move, rotate, scale, skew, or distort objects; can transform a particular stroke or fill of an object or can transform the entire object at one time. FL 78
  modifying motion paths using, FL 170
  resizing, rotating, skewing text with, FL 83
  transforming objects using, FL 78–82
function A block of ActionScript statements that processes information and returns a value or performs some action. FL 380, FL 382

G

Gap Size modifier, Paint Bucket tool, FL 71–72
GIF file format, FL 88
  exporting Flash documents in, FL 300
  vs. JPEG, PNG, FL 269
gotoAndPlay() method, FL 380–381
gradient A gradual blend of two or more colors or transition from one color to another.
gradient fills
  applying, FL 289–292
  transforming, FL 292–294
Gradient Transform tool, FL 292
graphic symbol A static or animated image whose Timeline operates in sync with the Timeline of the movie in which it appears. FL 95, FL 148–150
graphics
  See also bitmap graphics, vector graphics
  adding to Web pages, FL 301–303
  converting to symbols, FL 95–96, FL 131
  creating, editing instances of symbols, FL 100–101
  exporting for use on Web, FL 88–90
  importing, modifying, FL A8
  synchronizing with videos, FL 446–447

grid A set of lines behind all objects on the Stage; visible only while editing a document. FL 27–29
group To treat two or more elements as a single object. FL 34
group-editing mode, FL 34
grouping
  objects, FL 33–35
  panels, FL 17–19
  selected elements, FL 71
guide A vertical or horizontal line dragged from the rulers and used to align objects on the Stage. FL 29
  creating, FL 137
  displaying, FL 63
  displaying, using, FL 27–30, FL A8
  hiding, FL 62

H

hand pointer, Property inspector, FL 23
Hand tool
  using, FL 16, FL 41
  viewing objects using, FL 26–27
Help system, using Flash's, FL 44–47
hexadecimal code A value that represents a color (such as #00FF00 for green) based on the three basic colors used on computer monitors—red, green, and blue (RGB). FL 36
hiding
  guides, FL 62
  layers, FL 14, FL 121, FL 151
  rulers, grids, guides, FL 31–32
History panel The panel that shows a record of the steps performed in the current document; used to undo, replay, and save the recorded steps. FL 90–94
Hit frame The frame in a button symbol that represents the clickable or active area of the button; the area of the button that responds to a mouse click and displays the hand pointer when the pointer is over it. FL 226–227
home pages, creating, FL 335–337
HTML documents and Flash Web sites, FL 316–320
HTML editors, FL 302

I

icons
  collapsing panels to, FL 18
  collapsing tools to, FL 16
if keyword, FL 398
if() statements, FL 459
image files
  exporting Flash documents as, FL 300
  loading external, FL 352–356
Import Video Wizard, FL 448–451
importing
  bitmap graphics into Flash, combining with vector graphics, FL 2–3
  bitmaps, FL 268–269
  and modifying graphics, FL A8
  sounds, FL A10
  sounds to library, FL 252, FL 255
  video clips, FL 448–451, FL A10
Info panel, FL 272

Ink Bottle tool The tool to change the attributes or properties of a stroke or to apply a stroke to an object that has no stroke. FL 71
input form A Web page that contains text boxes in which a user can enter data that can then be submitted for storage and processing on a Web server. FL 401–412
input text boxes, creating, FL 403–404
input text field A field that allows the user to enter text in forms or surveys. FL 83
inserting
  keyframes at selected location, FL 151–153
  motion tweens, FL 186
instance A copy of a symbol. FL 100
  bitmap, FL 268
  creating, editing, FL 100–101, FL A9
  editing button, FL 229–231
interactive When a user has some level of control, such as being able to stop or play a movie's animation. FL 226
Internet Explorer, using, FL 5–6
inverse kinematics An animation method where an object or a set of objects is animated in relation to each other using bone structures. FL 205–207

J

JavaScript The Web language used to add interactive elements to Web pages. FL 242
JPEG, progressive, FL 353
JPEG file format
  compression of, FL 269
  exporting Flash documents in, FL 300
JPG file format, converting GIF to, FL 88

K

keyframe A frame that contains a new symbol instance or a new graphic object; in Timeline, has a white dot when empty and a black dot when it has content. FL 117
  inserting, FL 151–153
  property, FL 129
keyword A word that has a specific use or meaning in ActionScript and cannot be used in another context in a statement; also called a reserved word. FL 382
kilobyte Approximately 1000 bytes. FL 394

L

labels, frame, FL 246–248, FL 379
landscape orientation A layout that is wider than it is tall. FL 456
Lasso tool The tool used to select an object, to select several objects at one time, or to select an irregularly shaped area of an object by drawing a free-form marquee. FL 16, FL 42–43
layer An element used to organize the content (images, animations, and other objects) of a Flash document. FL 116
  adding background, FL 330–331
  adding for mask animations, FL 180–181
  adding for text animations, FL 185
  controlling with Timeline, FL 14
  distributing objects to individual, FL 194–196
  in documents, FL 13
  hiding, FL 151

locking, unlocking, FL 91, FL 117
locking while onion skinning, FL 200
mask. *See* mask layers
organizing documents using, FL 247
organizing using Timeline, FL 121
pose, FL 205–207
tween, FL 129

layer folder A container in the Timeline in which to place layers. FL 121–123, FL 195

layouts
resetting workspace, FL 7–8
saving panel, FL 19

letters, animating, FL 191–196

levels Different planes in which the Flash Player can load SWF files or other content such as images. FL 318–319

library The place that stores symbols created for a document; symbols stored in the library can be viewed, organized, and edited from the Library panel. FL 96–98
Buttons, using, FL 227–229
copying symbols from, FL 334–335

Library panel, FL 96–98, FL 133, FL A9

licensing issues for sounds, FL 251

Line tool, using, FL 76–77

linear gradient A gradient that blends the colors from one point to another in a straight line. FL 286, FL 292–293

lines
creating strokes, FL 32–33
drawing, FL 56–71
drawing with Line tool, FL 76–77
drawing with Pencil tool, FL 68–71
grid, displaying, FL 27–29
modifying, FL 77–78

links
testing, FL 435
to Web sites, creating, FL 388–394

loadedBytes variable, FL 396

loading external image files, FL 352–356

loadMovie action, using, FL 353–356

loadMovieNum action, FL 346–347

Lock Fill modifier, Paint Bucket tool, FL 71

locking layers, FL 91, FL 117, FL 179, FL 200, FL 279

loop An animation in which a group of frames is played repeatedly by having the playhead return to an earlier frame. FL 246

Loop and Repeat sound settings, FL 256

lossless compression Compression that retains all the original data in an image, but is limited to 256 colors. FL 269

lossy compression Compression that removes some of the original data in an image to achieve a smaller file size. FL 269

M

Magnification command, FL 25

magnifying and moving the Stage, FL 24–27

marquee An outline that encloses an area to be selected. FL 16, FL 38

mask layer A layer that contains a graphic element that hides the content of the masked layer. FL 177–182, FL A10

masked layer The layer below the mask layer; the contents of the masked layer are hidden except for the area covered by the element on the mask layer. FL 177–182

math.Random() function, FL 380

menus
See also specific menu
panel, FL 17

Merge Drawing mode The default drawing mode in which objects drawn or moved on top of other objects merge with or segment the existing objects on the same layer. FL 64
using, FL 33, FL 59

metadata, including in SWF files, FL A5

method A function specific to a particular object; built-in capabilities of the object that perform certain actions or respond to certain events. FL 380

mobile devices, creating content for, FL 463–471

modifying
See also changing
lines using Selection tool, FL 77–78
motion tweens, FL 134–136, FL 168–172
motions, FL 172–177

Motion Editor A panel that displays all properties and property keyframes for the selected motion tween to provide precise control of the target object's coordinates, rotation, and transformation properties at each property keyframe. FL 172–183, FL A7

motion path A line that guides an object throughout the animation. FL 168–172

motion preset A prebuilt tween animation that is applied to an object selected on Stage and Flash creates the necessary elements for the animation. FL 136–140

motion tween An animation applied to instances of symbols or text blocks where an object changes its position, rotates, scales in size, changes in color, or fades in or out. FL 129
adding easing effects, FL 175–177
animating text, FL 183–184
creating, modifying, FL 174–175
described, creating, FL 129–134
inserting, FL 186
modifying, FL 134–136, FL 168–172

MouseEvent, FL 382

movie clip The default symbol behavior, contains its own Timeline and operates independently of the Timeline of the movie in which it appears. FL 95
See also videos
components, FL 430
converting to graphic instances, FL 148–150
creating, FL 355–356
creating 3-D effects, FL 196–198
nested, FL 198–200
scaling, FL 461–462
usability testing, FL A12

Movie Explorer A panel that displays a hierarchical view of all the elements in a document, making it simpler to manage and locate individual elements; used to view each of the document's elements, search for a specific element, find all instances of a particular symbol, or print a list of the document's elements as listed in the Movie Explorer. FL 208–211

moving
frames, FL 123–124
objects, FL 335
the Stage, FL 24–27
text blocks, FL 84
tween spans, FL 136

MP3 sound files, FL 251–252

multiplication, arithmetic operators, FL 406
muting background sounds, FL 258–259

N

naming
conventions, FL 382
functions, FL 382
layer folders, FL 122
layers, FL 121
objects, FL 377
scenes, FL 125, FL 128
symbols, FL 96–97

navigateToURL() function, FL 391–392

navigating
Flash Help system, FL 44–47
Flash Web sites, FL 317

navigation bar A set of buttons in a navigation system that are arranged horizontally or vertically. FL 318
creating, FL 340–345

navigation system A set of buttons or other graphic elements that users click to navigate to the various parts of one or more SWF files in a Flash Web site. FL 316–317

nested symbol A symbol that contains instances of other symbols within its Timeline. FL 199–200

Nokia 3120 classic, FL 465–466

Notepad text editor, FL 301

numeric data A number or numbers in an expression that are not enclosed in quotation marks. FL 408

O

object An element in Flash that has properties, or characteristics, that can be examined or changed with ActionScript. FL 376–377
accessibility, FL 326
aligning on the Stage, FL 240–242
animating to follow curves, FL 171–172
applying filters to, FL 101–104
changing properties, FL 21–24
child, FL 322
controlling speed of animation, FL 135
converting to symbols, FL 150–151
creating strokes, fills, FL 32–33
distributing to individual layers, FL 194–196
drawing, grouping, FL 33–35
event, FL 382
moving, FL 335
naming, FL 377
resizing, FL 80–82
selecting, FL 37–44
target, FL 129
transforming with Free Transform tool, FL 78–82
working with, FL A9

object-based animation An animation that can be modified as one entity just like any other object; called a motion tween in Flash. FL 129

object-level undo The undo mode in which you steps performed on individual objects are reversed without affecting the steps performed on other objects. FL 93

Object Drawing mode The drawing mode in which drawn shapes are treated as separate objects and do not merge with or alter other objects on the same layer. FL 33, FL 59

onion skinning The display of more than one frame at a time on the Stage; the content of the current frame, indicated by the position of the playhead, appears in full color and the contents of the frames before and after the current frame appear dimmed. FL 200–203

Open dialog box, FL 25

opening
    Movie Explorer, FL 210–211
    new Flash file, FL 7
    Open dialog box, FL 25

operator A character used in expressions to tell Flash how to manipulate the values in the expression. FL 391–392
    comparison, FL 398
    using assignment, arithmetic, FL 406–409

Output panel, FL 296–298

Oval Primitive tool The tool used to create ovals that are treated as separate objects whose characteristics can be modified using the Property inspector without having to redraw the shape from scratch. FL 73–76

Oval tool, FL 57, FL 64, FL 66–67

ovals, creating, FL 73–76

Over frame The frame in a button symbol that contains the content displayed when the pointer is over the button. FL 341

P

Paint Bucket tool The tool used to change the color of an existing fill or add a fill to an enclosed area. FL 71–72
    applying gradient fills, FL 289–292

panel An area that contains controls for viewing and changing the properties of objects, aligning objects, transforming objects, or mixing and selecting colors. FL 8
    See also specific panel
    positioning, docking, collapsing, FL 17–21

panel group Two or more panels displayed together. FL 17–19

parameter An additional setting added to an action; a value sent to a function; also called an argument. FL 244
    ComboBox component, FL 432–433
    function, FL 380

parent movie clip The movie clip in which a child movie clip is nested. FL 199

pasteboard A gray area surrounding the Stage that can be used to place instructions and comments for reference or to store graphic objects until they are added to the Stage; for example, a graphic can be animated to move from the pasteboard onto the Stage. FL 8, FL 12–13

Pencil tool The tool to draw lines and shapes in a freeform manner as using an actual pencil to draw on paper. FL 68–71

pixel The smallest picture element on a monitor screen that can be controlled by a computer; short for picture element. FL 2, FL 29

playhead A marker that indicates which frame is currently selected in the Timeline. FL 13
    moving one frame at a time, FL 230
    and scrubbing, FL 14

PNG format, FL 269

PolyStar tool, FL 57

portrait orientation A layout that is taller than it is wide, such as a standard 8 × by 11 inch sheet of paper. FL 456

pose layer The layer in which a symbol instance or shape and its armature are moved when bones are added to a symbol instance or shape. FL 205–207

positioning
    objects using Free Transform tool, FL 78–82
    objects using Property inspector, FL 21–24
    panels, FL 17–21
    symbols, FL 143

preloader A short animation or a message such as the word "Loading" located in the first few frames of a Flash file to indicate that the Web site is still loading. FL 394
    adding numeric feedback to, FL 410–411
    creating, using, FL 394–401, FL 439–442

Preview in Context view, FL 120

previewing
    documents, FL 9–10
    imported graphics, FL 89–90

primitive tools, FL 73–78

Print command, FL 456

print spooler The software that manages the print jobs that are sent to the printer by the various programs running on a computer. FL 459

printable content, creating, FL 456–462

PrintJob class, using, FL 459–462

problems, troubleshooting, FL 209

profiles
    mobile device, FL 464–467
    publish, FL 298–299

ProgressBar component, using, FL 439–442

progressive downloading An encoding method in which a video file is saved separately from the Flash SWF file to play the video so that the entire video file is downloaded from a Web server to a user's computer for viewing. FL 448

progressive JPEG A file format that causes a picture that is downloading to a Web browser to appear to fade in by gradually downloading the data that makes up the picture. FL 353

project requirements, rich media communication, FL A2–A4

projector files, creating, FL 295

property A characteristic of an object that can be examined or changed. FL 376–377
    changing document, FL 30–32
    motion tweens, FL 130
    setting bitmap, FL 269–272
    viewing layer, FL 121

property keyframe A frame where the properties of the target object in a tween layer are changed; appears as a black diamond in the Timeline. FL 129

Property inspector A panel located at the right of the Flash workspace that provides easy access for reviewing and modifying the most common attributes of the currently selected tool or object. FL 8
    changing instance's type, FL 149–150
    filters, using, FL 101
    getting Help on, FL 45–47
    Oval Options, FL 75–76
    Oval Primitive controls in, FL 74
    selecting colors using, FL 36
    specifying fill and stroke colors, FL 64
    using, FL 21–24, FL A6

Publish command, FL 300

Publish Preview command, FL 298–299

publish profile The saved publish settings for a document that are available to any document created in Flash on the same computer. FL 298–299

Publish Settings dialog box, FL 295–297

publishing
    comparing options, FL 294–299
    Flash documents, FL 4, FL 357–358, FL A11

Q

QuickTime plug-in, FL 444

R

radial gradient A gradient that blends the colors from one point outward in a circular pattern. FL 286–289

Rectangle Primitive tool The tool used to create rectangles that are treated as separate objects whose characteristics can be modified using the Property inspector without having to redraw the shape from scratch. FL 73–74

Rectangle tool, using, FL 57–67

registration point of symbols, FL 142

replaying steps in History panel, FL 91–93

reports, movie size, FL 296–298

repositioning gradient fills, FL 292–293

resetting
    filters, FL 103
    workspace, FL 57

resizing
    See also scaling
    layer name column of Timeline, FL 14
    objects using Free Transform tool, FL 80–82

response The steps that are performed when an event occurs. FL 384

rich media (Adobe Certified Associate)
    building elements, FL A7–A11
    certification objectives, FL A2–A4
    evaluating elements, FL A11–A12
    Flash CS4 interface, FL A6–A7
    identifying design elements, FL A4–A6

rollover effect The effect that occurs when the contents of the Over frame in a button symbol differ from that in the Up frame; when the user moves the pointer over the button, the button changes to show what is in the Over frame. FL 226, FL 234–237

root folder The default folder in the Library panel that contains all the document's symbols; new folders can be created within the root folder to organize the symbols. FL 97

royalty-free Sounds, graphics, and other elements that have no additional usage fees when distributed them with your projects. FL 251

rulers The unit of measurements (such as pixels) displayed on the left and top edges of the Stage window; helpful when placing objects on the Stage according to specific coordinates and used to create vertical and horizontal guides. FL 29–30, FL A8

S

saving
    active document, FL 337, FL 357
    custom gradients, FL 287–289
    graphics in specific format, FL 88–89

scaleX property, FL 396, FL 397, FL 461
scaleY property, FL 396, FL 461
scaling
   See also resizing
   movie clips, FL 461–462
   objects, FL 80–82
   symbols, FL 204
scene A section of an animation that has its own Timeline; used to break up a long or complex document into smaller, more manageable sections. FL 124
   adding, FL 185
   described, using, FL 124–129
   displaying with Movie Explorer, FL 209
   testing, FL 147–148
Scene panel, using, FL 125–128
screen reader Software that visually impaired users run to read a Web site's text content aloud. FL 322, FL 326
script A set of one or more actions that perform some function. FL 242
   See also ActionScript
   adding comments to, FL 386–387
   programming actions using, FL 243–249
   testing, FL 411–412
Script pane, FL 347
scrolling text, FL 178
scrub To drag the playhead back and forth through the frames to play the animation manually; useful for testing an animation during development. FL 14
selecting
   all objects on Stage, FL 99
   frames, FL 123–124
   layers, FL 121
   objects, FL 37–44
   part of fill, stroke, FL 42–43
   tools from Tools panel, FL 15
Selection tool The tool used to select strokes or fills or a group of objects, move selected objects on the Stage or in the pasteboard, and modify objects. FL 85–88
   modifying lines using, FL 77–78
   modifying motion paths using, FL 168–172
   modifying shapes using, FL 65–66
   Property inspector display for, FL 21–22
   using, FL 16, FL 37–40
semicolons (;) and ActionScript, FL 381
send() method, FL 459
shape tween An animation that takes one shape and transforms it into another shape; displayed in the timeline with a black arrow and light green color for the frames. FL 155
   applying to text, FL 183–184
single-line text block A text block that extends as text is typed. FL 83
site goal Something that a Web site is intended to accomplish. FL 320
site objective A description that more clearly defines the information a Web site will contain, the types of media required, and the number of Web pages needed to provide the information and fulfill the needs of the client. Also, helps to determine how the Web site pages are organized and what types of pages to develop. FL 321
size reports, FL 296–298
skewing shapes, FL 138

skin Playback controls added to the FLVPlayback video component. FL 448
slashes (/) and script comments, FL 386
Smooth modifier, FL 38, FL 68
Snap to grid option, FL 27–29
Snap to Objects modifier, FL 38, FL 61, FL 65, FL 67
sounds
   adding actions to mute, FL 258–259
   adding effects, FL 257–258
   adding stream, FL 256
   and changing frame dimensions, FL 120
   changing sync settings, FL 256–257
   importing, FL A10
   using in animations, FL 250–259, FL A10
Sound-Shopper, FL 251
source, event, FL 384
special effects. *See* effects
speed, controlling animation object's, FL 135
spelling, checking, FL 85–88
Spelling Setup dialog box, FL 86
squares, drawing, FL 57
Stage The central area of the Document window where all the graphic objects for a document are created, imported, and assembled. FL 8
   aligning objects on, FL 240–242
   arranging elements on, FL A5
   default size, color, frame rate, FL 31
   importing bitmap instances, FL 269
   magnifying, moving, FL 24–27
   onion skinning and, FL 200–203
   selecting all objects on, FL 99
   using, FL 12
start() method, FL 459
starting Flash, FL 6–8
states, button, FL 226–227
static text block An object that contains text that is entered when the document is created but does not change after the document is published. FL 83
   creating, FL 402–403
static frame A frame that is not part of a motion tween. FL 129
storyboard A diagram that shows a Web site's pages and the way they are organized; the storyboard shows a sketch of each page with lines indicating how each page links to the other pages. FL 323–324
   using to produce rich media elements, FL A5–A6
Straighten modifier, FL 38
stream sounds, adding, FL 256
streaming As a file is downloading from a Web server to a client computer, the initial content can start playing while the rest of the content continues to be downloaded, which reduces the wait time for the user. FL 394
   video, FL 447
stream sound Sound synchronized with the Timeline that begins playing as soon as enough data has downloaded. FL 256
string data A series of characters—such as letters, numbers, and punctuation—and is always enclosed in quotation marks in an ActionScript expression. FL 406

stroke A line that makes up a Flash graphic; may be straight or curved, individual line segments, or connected lines that form shapes. FL 32–33
   changing, FL 71–83
   removing, FL 66
   specifying colors, FL 35–37
Subselection tool The tool used to display and modify anchor points on strokes and on the outlines of fills that have no stroke. FL 16, FL 40–42
   modifying motion paths using, FL 168–169
   subtraction, arithmetic operators, FL 406
swatch A color square in the color palette. FL 36
SWF file The FLA file published to deliver its content for viewing by end users; also called a Flash movie. FL 4
   and Flash file types, FL A7
   and Flash Web sites, FL 316–317
   loading at different levels, FL 318–319
   printing, FL 456
   viewing, FL 5–6
switch statements, FL 433–434
switching between preset workspaces, FL 18–19
symbol An element such as a graphic or a button stored in the document's library and that can be used more than once in a document. FL 94
   behavior of, FL A9
   checking with Movie Explorer, FL 209
   converting graphic to, FL 95–96, FL 131
   converting objects to, FL A9
   converting shape to, FL 150–151
   converting text block to, FL 144
   copying, FL 145
   copying from external libraries, FL 334–335
   creating, organizing, editing, FL 95–101
   creating complex animations with nested, FL 198–200
   creating when animating text blocks, FL 191
   editing, FL A9
   positioning, FL 143
   registration point of, FL 142
   scaling, FL 204
   using graphic, in animations, FL 148–150
synchronizing
   sounds to events, FL 256–257
   videos with animation, graphics, text, FL 446–447
syntax Rules that must be followed when writing code. FL 381–384, FL 434–435

T

tangent handle A handle that appears next to a selected anchor point on a curved line that can be dragged with the Subselection tool to change the curve. FL 79
   adjusting strokes, fills using, FL 40, FL 42
target audience The group of people intended to use a Web site. FL 321–322, FL A2
target object The one symbol instance that a tween span can contain. FL 129
   modifying, FL 134–136
template A prebuilt document that can be used as a starting point for a Flash project. FL 331–333
Test Movie command, FL 127, FL 141, FL 281, FL 294–295
testing
   animations, FL 141, FL 154–155, FL 182

button actions, FL 245
button's rollover effect, FL 236–237
changed bitmap properties, FL 271
ComboBox instance, FL 435
conditions, FL 398
Flash content on mobile devices, FL 469–471
frame actions, FL 248
scenes, FL 147–148
scripts, FL 411–412
sound effects, FL 254–255
Web pages, FL 302–303

text
adding animated, FL 184–190
adding to button instances, FL 232
adding to documents, FL 83–85
adding to layers, FL 284–286
animating, FL 328–329
anti-aliasing, FL 84, FL 231
checking spelling, FL 85–88
converting to fills, FL 183–184, FL 291
creating, FL A8–A9
filling with gradients, FL 291–292
properties, FL A9
synchronizing with videos, FL 446–447
using dynamic and input, FL 401–405

text blocks
animating, FL 183–190
animating letters, FL 191–196
converting to movie clips, FL 144
creating, FL 329–330, FL A8–A9
creating static, FL 402–403

text fields, FL 83

Text tool The tool used to create text blocks for documents in either a fixed-width text block or a single-line text block. FL 83–85

Timeline The panel used to control and coordinate the frames and layers that make up a Flash document. FL 8
changing view of, FL 119–121
and elements of animation, FL 116–117
graphic symbols vs. movie clips, FL 148–150
locking, unlocking layers, FL 91
organizing layers, adding layer folders, FL 121–122
and symbol behaviors, FL 95
using, FL 13–14, FL 117–124, FL A6
using multiple, FL 124–129

tools
See also specific tool
collapsing to icons, FL 16

Tools panel A panel, located on the right side of the Flash workspace, that contains the tools to draw, paint, select, and modify Flash graphics as well as to change the magnification level of the Stage, and to select colors. FL 8, FL 15–16, FL A8

totalBytes variable, FL 396
Trace Bitmap dialog box, FL 281–284
trace() function, FL 380
Transform panel, FL 189
transformation handles on objects, FL 78
transforming
gradient fills, FL 292–294
objects with Free Transform tool, FL 78–82

troubleshooting
color codes, FL 285
Flash documents with Movie Explorer, FL 209

tween An animation in which you create the beginning content and the ending content, and Flash creates the content for the in-between frames, varying the content evenly in each frame to achieve the animation. FL 142

tween layer A layer with a motion tween. FL 129

tween span The frames that make up a motion tween; tinted blue in the Timeline. FL 129, FL 131–132

tweened frame A frame that is part of a motion tween. FL 129

typed The type of data that a variable in ActionScript can contain. FL 391

U

UILoader components, using to display photos, FL 436–439
undoing
changes, FL 39, FL 67
steps using History panel, FL 90–94
unlocking layers, FL 91, FL 117, FL 279

Up frame The frame in a button symbol that contains the button's default state; what the button initially looks like to the user before the user has used the button to take an action. FL 226, FL 341

URL of Flash Web site, FL 316
URLRequest class, using, FL 391–394
usability testing of Flash movies, FL A12

V

values, converting to numeric data, FL 408

variable A user-defined object in ActionScript that holds data and whose value can change while the SWF movie plays. FL 391

vector animation Animation created by playing back a list of shapes or vector graphics and their transformations in sequence to produce the perception of motion. FL 3

vector graphic A graphic that includes a set of mathematical instructions that describe the color, outline, and position of all the shapes of the image. FL 2, FL 281–284

video streaming An encoding method that requires a video file to be uploaded to a Web server running Flash Media Server, which provides Web developers features to add interactive audio and video to Web sites. FL 447

videos
See also movie clips
adding to Flash documents, FL 443–455
embedded, FL 448
importing, adding, FL A10
size of, FL A7

View menu, FL 25
viewing
Flash SWF files, FL 5–6
layer properties, FL 121

views, changing Timeline's, FL 119–121

W

WAV sound files, adding to button instances, FL 251, FL 253–254

waveform A graphical representation of a sound. FL 252

Web Content Accessibility Guidelines (WCAG) 2.0 A standard established by the W3C to help Web designers and developers create Web sites with the needs of users with disabilities in mind. The guidelines cover a wide range of recommendations for making Web content more accessible to users with disabilities such as impaired vision, blindness, hearing loss, or deafness. FL 322

Web links, creating, FL 431–435

Web media The elements of text, graphics, animations, sounds, and videos that make up Web pages. FL 2
developing in Flash, FL 3–6
exporting graphic for use on Web, FL 88–90

Web page An HTML or XHTML document that can contain text, graphics, hyperlinks, and multimedia elements such as those created with Flash. FL 316
See also documents
adding Flash graphics to, FL 301–303
creating using templates, FL 331–333

Web safe colors The 216 colors that display the same on both Internet Explorer and Netscape Navigator browsers, as well as on both Windows and Macintosh operating systems. FL 36

Web servers, FL 447–448
Web sites
See also Flash Web sites
creating interactive banner for, ADD 1–4
creating links to, FL 388–394
creating with banner, payment calculator, photos and video pages, ADD 5–10
designing rich media content for, FL A2–A6
documenting specifications, FL 324
Flash. See Flash Web sites
making accessible, FL 322
printing content, FL 456
site objectives, goals, FL 320–321

Window menu, FL 17
WinZip, FL 250

workspace The Flash program window. FL 6–9
exploring components of, FL 12–24
getting Help on, FL 46
previewing documents in, FL 9–10
resetting, FL 57
setting to default Essential layout, FL 7–8
switching between preset, FL 18–19

Workspace Switcher button, FL 20–21

World Wide Web Consortium (W3C) An international consortium whose mission is to develop Web standards. FL 322

X

XHTML The underlying code used in creating Web pages. FL 2, FL 4, FL 316

XML (Extensible Markup Language) format, FL A7
XMP (Exensible Metadata Platform), FL A5, FL A7

Z

Zoom tool, FL 16
zooming commands, FL 25

Task Reference

TASK	PAGE #	RECOMMENDED METHOD
Action, add to button using Behaviors panel	FL 355	Select button instance, open Behaviors panel, click [+], point to behavior type, click behavior, modify values in dialog box, click OK
Action, add using Actions panel in Script Assist mode	FL 244	Select frame or button instance, expand Actions panel, toggle on Script Assist, click category in Actions toolbox, double-click desired action, set parameters
Actions, check for syntax errors	FL 347	In Actions panel, click [✓], click OK, check errors in Compiler Errors panel
Actions toolbox, collapse or expand	FL 367	In Actions panel, click [icon]
Animation, test	FL 141	See Reference Window: Testing a Document's Animation
Bitmap, change properties	FL 271	In Library panel, select bitmap, click [i]
Bitmap, convert to symbol	FL 272	Select bitmap instance, click Modify, click Convert to Symbol, set options, click OK
Bitmap, convert to vector	FL 282	Select bitmap instance, click Modify, point to Bitmap, click Trace Bitmap, set options, click OK
Bitmap, import to library or Stage	FL 268	Click File, point to Import, click Import to Library or Import to Stage, select bitmap file, click Open
Bone, add to an instance or shape	FL 206	In Tools panel, click [bone icon], click and drag to connect instance or object on Stage
Button, add ActionScript code	FL 346	See Reference Window: Adding ActionScript Code to a Button
Button, add from Buttons library	FL 228	Click Window, point to Common Libraries, click Buttons, expand button category, drag button from Buttons library panel to Stage or library
Button, create	FL 233	See Reference Window: Creating a Custom Button
Button, test within program window	FL 229	Click Control, click Enable Simple Buttons, click button on Stage
Classic tween animation, create	FL 142	See Reference Window: Creating a Classic Tween Animation
Colors, select	FL 37	Click [pencil][color] or [bucket][color] to open color palette, click desired color swatch
Comment, add multiple line to ActionScript code	FL 373	In Actions panel, type /* followed by comment text and then type */
Comment, add single line to ActionScript code	FL 373	In Actions panel, type // followed by comment text
Component, create instance	FL 430	See Reference Window: Adding a Flash Component
Component, set parameters	FL 432	In Component inspector, click Parameters tab, set parameter values
Dynamic text box, create type	FL 391	In Tools panel, click [T]; in Property inspector, click Text type button, click Dynamic Text, create text block on Stage, set properties
External Library, copy symbol	FL 333	Click File, point to Import, click Open External Library, select file with symbols to copy, click Open, drag symbol instance from external library to current document's library or Stage, close external library
Fill, apply with Paint Bucket tool	FL 72	In Tools panel, click [bucket], select fill properties, click [O], click modifier, click object on Stage
Filter, apply to object	FL 101	In Filters section of Property inspector, click [icon], click filter, set properties
Filter, copy and paste	FL 103	In Filters section of Property inspector, click [icon], click Copy All, select object to apply filter to, click [icon], click Paste

REF 9

TASK	PAGE #	RECOMMENDED METHOD
Flash, exit program	FL 47	Click File, click Exit
Flash, start program	FL 7	Click Start button, click All Programs, click Adobe CS4 suite folder, click Adobe Flash CS4 Professional
Flash document, close	FL 47	Click File, click Close
Flash document, create from template	FL 334	Click File, click New, click Templates tab, select category, select template, click OK, add content and save as usual
Flash document, export as image	FL 300	Click File, point to Export, click Export Image, select destination, type filename, select file type, click Save, set options, click OK
Flash document, modify properties	FL 31	Click Modify, click Document
Flash document, open	FL 9	Click File, click Open, select file, click Open
Flash document, preview by scrubbing	FL 14	Drag playhead in Timeline header
Flash document, preview in Flash Player window	FL 10	Click Control, click Test Movie
Flash document, preview in Flash program window	FL 10	Click Control, click Play; or press Enter
Flash document, preview in Web page	FL 11	Click File, point to Publish Preview, click HTML
Flash document, publish	FL 296	Click File, click Publish
Flash document, save with new name	FL 9	Click File, click Save As, select folder, type filename, click Save
Flash document, test download in different settings	FL 386	Click Control, click Test Movie, click View, point to Download Settings, click desired setting, click View, click Simulate Download
Flash Web site, develop	FL 319	See Reference Window: Developing a Flash Web Site
Frame, copy	FL 123	Select frame or frames, right-click selected frames, click Copy Frames
Frame, make Frame 1 current	FL 24	Click Control, click Rewind
Frame, make last current	FL 24	Click Control, click Go To End
Frame, paste	FL 123	Select frame or frames, right-click selected frames, click Paste Frames
Frame-by-frame animation, create	FL 151	Insert graphic object in initial frame, add keyframe and new content or properties at each place the object changes
Frame label, add	FL 247	Select keyframe; in Property inspector, type label in Name box, press Enter
Gradient, create, edit, save	FL 287	See Reference Window: Creating, Editing, and Saving a Gradient
Gradient fill, apply to text	FL 291	Select text block, Click Modify, click Break Apart, click Modify, click Break apart, select gradient for fill color
Gradient fill, transform	FL 293	In Tools panel, click ; click gradient on Stage, adjust gradient
Grid, display	FL 28	Click View, point to Grid, click Show Grid
Grid, modify appearance	FL 28	Click View, point to Grid, click Edit Grid
Grouped object, create	FL 34	Click , draw marquee around objects, click Modify, click Group
Grouped object, edit	FL 37	Double-click grouped object
Grouped object, exit edit mode	FL 37	Click Edit, click Edit All; or on the Edit bar, click Scene 1
Guide, create	FL 29	Display rulers, drag guide from a ruler to Stage
Guides, clear	FL 65	Click View, point to Guides, click Clear Guides

New Perspectives on Adobe Flash CS4 Professional—Comprehensive | REF 11

TASK	PAGE #	RECOMMENDED METHOD
Guides, hide	FL 32	Click View, point to Guides, click Show Guides
Guides, modify appearance	FL 29	Click View, point to Guides, click Edit Guides
Help, display contents	FL 45	See Reference Window: Using the Flash Help System
History panel, open	FL 90	Click Window, point to Other Panels, click History
Image, export	FL 88	Click File, point to Export, click Export Image, select location, enter filename, click Save as type button to select file format, click Save
Input text box, create	FL 389	In Tools panel, click T; in Property inspector, click Text type button, click Input Text, create text block on Stage, set properties
Instance, create	FL 100	Drag copy of symbol from Library panel to Stage
Instance behavior, change	FL 149	Select instance on Stage; in Property inspector, click Instance behavior button, click desired type
Instance name, add	FL 364	Select instance on Stage, enter name in Instance name box in Property inspector
Keyframe, insert	FL 144	Select frame in Timeline, click Insert, point to Timeline, click Keyframe
Layer, insert	FL 123	In Timeline, click
Layer, move into layer folder	FL 122	In Timeline, drag layer over the layer folder
Layer, rename	FL 213	In Timeline, double-click layer name, type new name, press Enter
Layer, select	FL 123	In Timeline, click layer name
Layer folder, insert	FL 122	In Timeline, click
Layer folder, rename	FL 122	In Timeline, double-click folder name, type new name, press Enter
Letter animations, create	FL 193	See Reference Window: Animating Individual Letters
Library panel, open	FL 98	Click Window, click Library or click Library tab
Lines, draw with Line tool	FL 76	In Tools panel, click , set stroke properties, draw on Stage
Lines, draw with Pencil tool	FL 68	In Tools panel, click , click , click modifier, set stroke properties, draw on Stage
Mask layer, create	FL 177	See Reference Window: Creating a Mask Layer Animation
Merge Drawing mode, select or deselect	FL 64	In Tools panel, click
Motion path, add to motion tween	FL 132	Drag instance to new location
Motion path, modify	FL 170	See Reference Window: Modifying a Tween's Motion Path
Motion preset, apply	FL 137	Select symbol instance on Stage; in Motion Presets panel, click desired motion preset in Default Presets folder, click Apply
Motion tween, create	FL 131	Add instance of a symbol or text block in beginning frame, right-click frame, click Create Motion Tween, modify instance in ending frame
Motion tween, modify properties	FL 135	In Property inspector, change settings
Movie Explorer, use	FL 210	Click Window, click Movie Explorer, click Show buttons to select and deselect as needed
Object, change orientation	FL 208	Click Modify, point to Transform, click option
Object, copy and paste	FL 81	Select object, click Edit, click Copy, click Edit, click a paste command
Object, flip horizontally	FL 154	Select object, click Modify, point to Transform, click Flip Horizontal

TASK	PAGE #	RECOMMENDED METHOD
Object, manipulate in 3D	FL 197	Select frame with object, in Tools panel, click, drag red line to rotate x axis, drag green line to rotate y axis, drag blue circle to change z axis, drag orange circle to change all axes
Object, modify anchor points	FL 40	See Reference Window: Using the Subselection Tool
Object, modify with Selection tool	FL 39	In Tools panel, click, drag a line or a corner of the object to change its shape
Object, move	FL 37	In Tools panel, click, click object, drag object
Object, reposition on Stage	FL 16	Drag object with, or change object's X and Y values in Property inspector
Object, scale on Stage	FL 21	Select object with; in Property inspector, change object's W and H values
Object, select with Selection tool	FL 38	In Tools panel, click, click object or draw marquee around object(s)
Object, transform	FL 78	In Tools panel, click, click, , , or, select object on Stage, drag transformation handles and/or tangent handles
Object Drawing mode, select or deselect	FL 64	In Tools panel, click
Objects, align on Stage	FL 241	Select several objects at one time, open Align panel, click align button(s)
Objects, distribute to layers	FL 195	Select objects, click Modify, point to Timeline, click Distribute to Layers
Objects, group	FL 35	Select several objects, click Modify, click Group
Objects, select with Lasso tool	FL 42	In Tools panel, click, click and drag to select objects or click, click points around objects, double-click to complete selection
Onion marker, set number of frames	FL 201	In the Timeline, click, click option
Onion skinning, toggle on or off	FL 200	In the Timeline, click
Oval, draw	FL 63	In Tools panel, click, set stroke and fill properties, click and drag pointer on Stage
Panel, collapse to icons	FL 20	Click Collapse to Icons button
Panel, display	FL 19	Click Window, click panel name
Panels and panel groups, organize	FL 19	See Reference Window: Organizing Panels and Panel Groups
Primitive oval, draw	FL 75	In Tools panel, click, set stroke and fill colors, click and drag pointer on Stage
Publish profile, save	FL 298	In Publish Settings dialog box, click, enter publish profile name, click OK
Publish settings, change	FL 296	Click File, click Publish Settings, select types and enter filenames on Formats tab, select options on file type tabs, click Publish, click OK
Rectangle, draw	FL 59	In Tools panel, click, set stroke and fill properties, click and drag pointer on Stage
Rectangle, set rounded corners	FL 59	In Tools panel, click; in Property inspector, enter Rectangle corner radius value
Regular frame, insert	FL 132	Select frame in Timeline; on Application bar, click Insert, point to Timeline, click Frame
Rulers, display or hide	FL 29	Click View, click Rulers
Scene, duplicate	FL 128	In Scene panel, select scene, click
Scene, rename	FL 126	In Scene panel, double-click scene, type new name, press Enter
Scene, select	FL 127	On Edit bar, click, select scene